STUDIES ON COPYRIGHT

ARTHUR FISHER

MEMORIAL EDITION

STUDIES ON COPYRIGHT

ARTHUR FISHER

MEMORIAL EDITION

Compiled and edited under supervision of

The Copyright Society of the U.S.A.

VOLUME II

PUBLISHERS

FRED B. ROTHMAN & CO.
South Hackensack, New Jersey

THE BOBBS-MERRILL COMPANY, INC.
A Subsidiary of Howard W. Sams & Co., Inc.
Indianapolis—New York

TABLE OF CONTENTS

[The pagination of this publication is indicated by the numbers enclosed in parentheses. Numbers appearing at the top of the pages show paging of the studies as carried in the Congressional Committee prints.]

VOLUME 1

PART I

AN ECONOMIC FOREWORD

PART II

SUBJECT MATTER OF COPYRIGHT

PART III

PUBLICATION AND NOTICE

VOLUME 2

PART VII

RIGHTS

PART VIII

REMEDIES

PART IX

GENERAL REVISION OF THE COPYRIGHT LAW

STUDIES ARRANGED NUMERICALLY

PART VII

RIGHTS

Fair Use, Photoduplication, Performing Rights, Compulsory License and Moral Right

Copyright has often been characterized as a bundle or complex of rights. One will, however, search in vain among the comprehensive studies comprising these volumes for an over-all survey of these rights and an analysis of their scope. This lacuna is of course hardly the result of oversight; it rather reflects the general agreement, except in several specific areas, as to the particular rights presently enjoyed and those which should be accorded by a new statute.

One basis for such agreement is the rule of reason known as "fair use" engrafted by the courts upon the rights of the proprietor to print, copy, make new versions, etc. The taking of a reasonable amount of material under certain circumstances is accordingly permissible. The study on fair use is thus, in an inverted fashion, the only general survey of what constitutes infringement found among the studies. This is perhaps not surprising since the statute does not define infringement, but merely specifies the exclusive rights of the proprietor. The doctrine of fair use is the most general limitation on the seemingly absolute specification of these rights. The most pressing aspect of this problem—photoduplication of copyrighted materials by libraries—has been singled out for specialized treatment.

As indicated above, there are several problem areas relating to rights. These appear to center about the field of music. One such problem, which has generated little litigation but much controversy, is the exemption of performances of music on coin-operated machines, *i.e.,* "juke boxes," from the sweep of the proprietor's exclusive right to perform his work publicly for profit. This problem, like that of designs, has been crystallized into specific legislative proposals on which Congressional hearings have recently been held. Since the Register of Copyrights has viewed these proposals as appropriate for consideration separate from and in advance of general copyright revision, there is no study devoted to the "juke-box" exemption.

It has been noted that rights in music do not extend to all public performances, but only those which are deemed "for profit." Although the "for profit" concept has been continually expanded by the courts, it remains a limitation on performance rights in music, as well as in non-dramatic literary works such as poems, lectures and the like. Dramatic works, on the other hand, are not subject to such a limitation. But

(779)

protected performances of such works must also be "public." The concepts "for profit" and "public performances" are examined in a separate study on limitations on performing rights. This study also reviews the question of performing rights in motion pictures for which the present statute makes no express provision.

Musical copyright is accorded specialized treatment by the statute in another respect. When "mechanical," *i.e.,* recording, rights were extended to music in 1909, they embodied a "compulsory license" provision whereby the recording of music under the authority of the proprietor made the work generally available for recording upon payment of two cents per record. Despite the attention directed to this innovation in the course of the 1909 revision, the provision did not produce much litigation until recently. At least a half dozen cases involving this provision have been decided since publication of the legal study on this subject. Most of these decisions have tended to enhance the proprietor's rights by expansive interpretations of the acts violative of such rights, see *Reeve Music Co. v. Crest Records, Inc.,* 285 F. 2d 546 (2d Cir. 1960); *Famous Music Corp. v. Seeco Records, Inc.,* 201 F. Supp. 560 (S.D.N.Y. 1961), and by the imposition of severe sanctions against infringers, see *Shapiro, Bernstein & Co. v. Remington Records, Inc.,* 265 F. 2d 263 (2d Cir. 1959); *ABC Music Corp. v. Janov,* 186 F. Supp. 443 (S.D. Cal. 1960). *Cf. Norbay Music, Inc. v. King Records, Inc.,* 290 F. 2d 617 (2d Cir. 1961) (proprietor's delay in filing required "notice of use" excuses infringements prior to but not after such filing).

The paucity of earlier litigation involving the compulsory license provision is probably due in part to the gloss imparted to the statutory provisions by rather well-defined commercial folkways. These are examined in the context of economics by a separate factual survey.

The final study on rights deals with the moral right of an author, a right not presently found in the copyright statute. In analyzing the "droit moral" characteristic of a number of foreign systems, this study finds, as did the study on sound recordings, that coverage in the copyright statute is not the only effective means of recognizing literary property or rights akin to such property. Once again, state law is consulted with the finding that injuries to the integrity of a work or the reputation of its author are frequently redressed in the name of unfair competition, breach of contract, defamation or invasion of the right of privacy or of publicity.

STUDY NO. 14

FAIR USE OF COPYRIGHTED WORKS

By Alan Latman

March 1958

FAIR USE OF COPYRIGHTED WORKS

I. INTRODUCTION

Section 1 of the copyright statute accords the proprietor of a copyright a number of exclusive rights. But unlike the patentee, the copyright owner does not enjoy the exclusive right to "use" his copyrighted work.[1] His exclusive rights include, among others, the right to print, publish, copy and vend the work; in other respects, the public may "use" the work. Such use includes not only intellectual and esthetic appreciation, but more concrete utilization as well. For example, there is no impediment to the use of a copyrighted form book in the development of the appropriate forms.[2]

In other areas, particularly where the copyrighted work is used in the production of a new work by the user, a potential conflict arises. The use may be of such a nature and extent as to impinge upon those exclusive rights which the copyright owner does enjoy. Thus, assimilation of the protected material into a new product may conflict with the owner's right to copy or publish. The courts have attempted to resolve this conflict through the introduction of a rule of reason. Where the circumstances render the appropriation a reasonable or "fair" use, the court will refuse to impose liability. Accordingly, one commentator has stated in a frequently-quoted definition that:

> Fair use may be defined as a privilege in others than the owner of the copyright, to use the copyrighted material in a reasonable manner without his consent, notwithstanding the monopoly granted to the owner by the copyright.[3]

The courts have grappled with the problem of fair use without the aid of any specific statutory guide. The language of the statute has always been positive in granting exclusive rights, apparently admitting of no exceptions. In contrast, the statutes of most other countries have attempted to deal with at least some aspects of the problem.[4]

In view of the potential breadth of the problem of fair use, the scope of this study has been consciously limited. In particular, discussion of the peculiar problems facing libraries, chiefly with respect to requests from users for photocopies of copyrighted works,[5] has been minimized. This area is being reserved for specialized treatment. Also, limitations on the right of public performance are the subject of a separate study and will be mentioned only incidentally herein.

---

[1] See Eichel v. Marcin, 241 Fed. 404, 410–411 (S.D.N.Y. 1913); Loew's, Inc. v. Columbia Broadcasting System, Inc., 131 F. Supp. 165, 174 (S.D. Cal. 1955), aff'd, sub nom. Benny v. Loew's, Inc., 239 F. 2d 532 (9th Cir. 1956), aff'd by a 4–4 division of the Supreme Court, 356 U.S. 43 (1958). Cf. 35 U.S.C. § 154 which grants to patent owners "the right to exclude others from * * * using * * * the invention."
[2] American Institute of Architects v. Fenichel, 41 F. Supp. 146 (S.D.N.Y. 1941). Cf. Brightley v. Littleton, 37 Fed. 103 (C.C.E.D. Pa. 1888).
[3] BALL, THE LAW OF COPYRIGHT AND LITERARY PROPERTY 260 (1944).
[4] See IV, infra.
[5] This special problem of libraries is exemplified by the *Report of the Copyright Committee, United Kingdom Board of Trade*, Oct. 1952, pars. 43–53, and § 7 of the United Kingdom Copyright Act, 1956.

II. Present Law

The silence of the 1909 act on the question of fair use is consistent with prior history. There has apparently never been any specific statutory provision dealing with the question in the copyright law of the United States. At least one provision of the 1909 act has, however, had an indirect impact. Section 1(b) extends to the owner of a copyright in a literary work the exclusive right "to make any version thereof." This provision changes the prior case law under which a "bona fide abridgment" was permissible.[6] In general, however, the rationale underlying the fair use doctrine and the criteria for its application are discernible in a body of case law unaffected by legislative developments.

A. THEORETICAL BASES OF THE FAIR USE DOCTRINE

Fair use may be viewed from two standpoints. It may be considered a technical infringement which is nevertheless excused. On the other hand, it may be deemed a use falling outside the orbit of copyright protection and hence never an infringement at all. While this distinction has been said "to have no practical significance,"[7] it may explain different usages of the expression "fair use." For example, the court in *Shipman* v. *R.K.O. Pictures, Inc.*,[8] stated that: "Fair use is defined as copying the theme or ideas rather than their expression." This definition is based on a concept of fair use as an appropriation of unprotected material.[9] Such concept is related to the view that fair use is the negation of infringement, rather than a privileged infringement. This usage is perhaps unorthodox in focusing upon a single inquiry, especially an inquiry which must be made in every infringement action. In other words, there may be no problem of determining the reasonable nature of a taking when nothing legally protectible has been taken.

This inquiry may, however, furnish a useful first step in the laborious weighing of factors characteristic of fair use analysis. Such was the procedure apparently used in a recent case involving the burlesque of a story, where the court stated:

> Burlesque may ordinarily take the locale, the theme, the setting, situation and even bare basic plots without infringement, since such matters are ordinarily not protectible.[10]

Appropriation of even protectible material must always be "substantial" to constitute infringement; thus a minimal amount of copying should perhaps always be considered "fair." It has been suggested that fair use simply represents an attempt by the courts "to bring some order out of the confusion surrounding the question of how much can be copied."[11]

Again, this approach may be directed to the question of infringement in general, rather than fair use in particular.[12] The question of the amount of material copied will be discussed below in conjunction

---

[6] See Folsom v. Marsh, 9 Fed. Cas. 342, 343 No. 4,901. (C.C.D. Mass. 1841); AMDUR, COPYRIGHT LAW AND PRACTICE, 762 (1937).

[7] Cohen, "*Fair Use in the Law of Copyright*" ASCAP, COPYRIGHT LAW SYMPOSIUM, No. 6, 43, 48 (1955).

[8] 100 F. 2d 533, 537 (2d Cir. 1938).

[9] *Cf.* Sheldon v. Metro-Goldwyn Pictures Corp., 81 F. 2d 49 (2d Cir. 1936).

[10] Columbia Pictures Corp. v. NBC, 137 F. Supp. 348, 350 (S.D. Cal. 1955).

[11] Note, 14 NOTRE DAME LAW. 443, 449 (1939).

[12] See Oxford Book Co. v. College Entrance Book Co., 98 F. 2d 688 (2d Cir. 1938). *Cf.* Macmillan Co. v. King, 223 Fed. 862 (D. Mass. 1914).

with the other criteria of fair use.[13] It should be noted, however, that a broad underlying premise for the doctrine of fair use is supplied by the notions that: (1) the user has unlimited use of a great deal of unprotected material embodied in a copyrighted work; and (2) the user may, under any circumstances, copy an insignificant portion of protected material.

The doctrine of fair use goes beyond the boundaries set by these considerations. The amount of protected material freely available may be determined by many factors. One theory behind such permissible copying is the implied consent of the copyright owner. In many cases, duplication of portions of his works should be desired by the author for its beneficial effects.[14] These implications may be supported by express indications of the author's consent.[15] On the other hand, indications of a restrictive intent, such as a statement requiring consent for any quotations, undermine this theory.[16] In its place, there has been offered the theory of a consent enforced by the figurative bargain embodied in the securing of a statutory copyright.[17] In other words, as a condition of obtaining the statutory grant, the author is deemed to consent to certain reasonable uses of his copyrighted work to promote the ends of public welfare for which he was granted copyright. This concept has at least a surface harmony with the general assumption that the fair use doctrine does not apply to common law literary property.[18]

The theory of "enforced consent" suggests another rationale which relies more directly upon the constitutional purpose of copyright. It has often been stated that a certain degree of latitude for the users of copyrighted works is indispensable for the "Progress of Science and useful Arts." [19] Particularly in the case of scholarly works, step-by-step progress depends on a certain amount of borrowing, quotation and comment.[20]

Justification for a reasonable use of a copyrighted work is also said to be based on custom.[21] This would appear to be closely related to the theory of implied consent. It also reflects the relevance of custom to what is reasonable. In any event, it has been stated that fair use is such use as is "reasonable and customary." [22]

B. THE PROBLEM IN CONTEXT

The problem of fair use has so far been discussed in general terms. The defense of fair use has been raised most frequently in certain contexts. The more characteristic situations will be examined. It should be appreciated that the problem arises in other contexts and

---

[13] See II, C, *infra.*

[14] See *e.g.,* Karll v. Curtis Pub. Co., 39 F. Supp. 836 (E.D. Wis. 1941); G. Ricordi & Co. v. Mason, 201 Fed. 182, 183 (C.C.S.D.N.Y. 1911).

[15] See American Institute of Architects v. Fenichel, 41 F. Supp. 146 (S.D.N.Y. 1941).

[16] See Yankwich, *What is Fair Use?* 22 U. of CHI. L. REV. 203, (1954) for the following illustrative legend: "All rights reserved. No part of this book may be used or reproduced in any manner whatsoever without written permission except in the case of brief quotations embodied in critical articles and reviews." Readers are often directed to the party from whom permission or information should be sought.

[17] Note, 15 SO. CALIF. L. REV. 249, 250 (1942).

[18] BALL, *op cit.* note 3 *supra,* at 260 n. 5; Golding v. Radio Pictures Inc., 193 P. 2d 153 (Cal., Dist. Ct. App. 1948). Perhaps the distinction is between published and unpublished works rather than works for which statutory protection has been obtained and those which are protected under the common law. See SHAW, LITERARY PROPERTY IN THE UNITED STATES 67 (1950). The test would be the applicability of the fair use doctrine to unpublished works registered under section 12 of the Federal copyright statute.

[19] See W. H. Anderson Co. v. Baldwin Law Pub. Co., 27 F. 2d 82, 89 (6th Cir. 1928); Chafee, *Reflections on the Law of Copyright,* 45 COLUM. L. REV. 503, 511 (1945).

[20] See Mathews Conveyor Co. v. Palmer-Bee Co. 135 F. 2d 73 (6th Cir. 1943).

[21] Note, 15 SO. CALIF. REV. 249, 250 (1942).

[22] Shapiro, Bernstein & Co. v. P. F. Collier & Son Co., 26 U.S.P.Q. 40, 42 (S.D.N.Y. 1934).

is, in a sense, inherent in much copyright infringement litigation. However, the wide range of situations would seem to be but variations of the basic conflict between the copyright owner anxious for exclusive rights and the user who, for one reason or another, denies that his use of the copyrighted material infringes upon such rights. Examination of the cases will reveal the various criteria of fair use and how they interact.

1. Incidental use

Section 1(b) of the copyright statute grants the exclusive right to make any new version of a literary work and to arrange and adapt a musical work. These rights are sufficiently broad to include a change in the medium of expression of copyrighted material. Thus, it has been held that a television comedy may not copy substantially from a serious motion picture.[23] But a different situation is presented where a reasonable amount of material is used incidentally and as background in an entirely different class of work. Such an appropriation may be considered a fair use. This is best illustrated by the use of excerpts from the lyrics of a copyrighted song in the course of a literary production. The courts have been reluctant to impose liability in such a case.[24] The incidental nature of such use, and its inability to compete with the copyrighted work have produced a finding of fair use.

The absence of music may preclude impairment of the value of the plaintiff's musical composition; it has been so held where portions of the lyrics were used as background for the action in a short story,[25] or in connection with a magazine article about the professional football team on which the song was based.[26] Similarly, a finding of fair use was made even where half of the magazine comment on the death of an actress consisted of extracts from the copyrighted song associated with her.[27] But a contrary result was reached where all the lyrics as well as the melody line of plaintiff's song were included in a narrative history of popular songs in the United States.[28]

Thus, the use of extracts from copyrighted material for illustrative purposes, or merely as a vehicle for an entirely different and noncompeting work, would seem permissible.[29] Reproduction of musical material for the "amateur performer" is not within such immunity.[30]

The fortuitous inclusion of copyrighted material in newsreels or news broadcasts represents an incidental use which has given rise to several legislative proposals. These will be discussed below.

2. Review and criticism

Discussions of fair use often begin with the question of quotation from a work for the purposes of criticism and review. It is universally agreed that "in reviewing a copyrighted work, or in criticising it,

---

[23] Benny v. Loew's Inc., 239 F. 2d 532 (9th Cir. 1956), *cert. granted*, 353 U.S. 946 (1957).
[24] Shapiro, Bernstein & Co. v. P. F. Collier & Son Co., note 22, *supra*; Broadway Music Corp. v. F–R Pub. Corp., 31 F. Supp. 817 (S.D.N.Y. 1940); Karll v. Curtis Pub. Co., 39 F. Supp. 836 (E.D. Wis. 1941).
[25] Shapiro, Bernstein & Co. v. P. F. Collier & Son Co., note 22, *supra*.
[26] Karll v. Curtis Pub. Co., note 24, *supra*.
[27] Broadway Music Corp. v. F–R Pub. Corp., note 24, *supra*.
[28] Sayers v. Spaeth, Copyright Office Bulletin No. 20 at 625 (S.D.N.Y. 1932).
[29] *Cf.* Green v. Minzenheimer, 177 Fed. 286 (C.C.S.D.N.Y. 1909).
[30] Sayers v. Spaeth, note 28, *supra*.

quotations may be taken therefrom." [31]   Thus it has been recently stated:

Criticism is an important and proper exercise of fair use.   Reviews by so-called critics may quote extensively for the purpose of illustration and comment.[32]

It is interesting to note that there is apparently no reported American decision involving alleged infringement in the course of serious criticism. This may be due to the self-restraint on the part of the critics and the desire on the part of authors and publishers to encourage reviews of their works—reasons suggested for the decline in libel litigation involving the cognate doctrine of fair comment.[33]

3. Parody and burlesque

There have been half a dozen American cases dealing with parody, mimicry, and burlesque. These may be considered a humorous type of criticism; but the element of criticism is often absent from burlesque, leaving humor as the only aim.[34] The current importance of the problem of parody as fair use is indicated by the fact that the Supreme Court recently granted certiorari in *Columbia Broadcasting System* v. *Loew's, Inc.*, in which the court, without discussing the issues in its opinion, divided four to four.[35]

The key issue would seem to be the extent, if any, to which the general tests of fair use are to be modified in this area. The early case of *Bloom & Hamlin* v. *Nixon*,[36] indicates that the parody feature is quite significant. The court there stated:

Surely a parody would not infringe the copyright of the work parodied merely because a few lines of the original might be textually reproduced.

While it is not entirely clear that this was held to be so because of the nature of a parody, the court did find that "the good faith of such mimicry is an essential element." Liability was denied on the ground that the use of plaintiff's song was merely incidental to the mimicry of the singer, and not a subterfuge by which to reproduce copyrighted material.

In the well-known *Mutt and Jeff* case,[37] the court apparently assimilated the parody to serious criticism and use of copyrighted material in general. Perhaps because the comic strip was itself humorous, the court found that the defendant's parody constituted a "partial satisfaction of the demand" for the parodied work and accordingly amounted to an infringement.

Recent litigation in the California Federal courts indicates that the interaction between motion pictures and television has heightened the problems posed by parodies and burlesques. In *Loew's Inc.* v. *CBS, Inc.*[38] Jack Benny's television parody of the motion picture "Gaslight" was under attack. It was clear that the taking was substantial. In a comprehensive and analytical opinion, District Judge Carter noted that "parodized or burlesqued taking is treated no dif-

---

[31] AMDUR, *op. cit.* note 5, *supra* at 757.
[32] Loew's, Inc. v. CBS, Inc., 131 F. Supp. at 175.
[33] Ford, *Fair Comment in Literary Criticism*, 14 NOTRE DAME LAW. 270 (1939). For an historical discussion of this area, see Yankwich, *Parody and Burlesque in the Law of Copyright*, 33 CAN. B. REV. 1130 (1955).
[34] See Foley, "*Copyright-Burlesque of Literary Property as Infringement of Copyright*," 31 NOTRE DAME LAW. 46, 48 (1955).
[35] 356 U.S. 43 (1958). Justice Douglas took no part in the decision.
[36] 125 Fed. 977, 978 (C.C.E.D. Pa. 1903).
[37] Hill v. Whalen & Martell, Inc., 220 Fed. 359 (S.D.N.Y. 1914).
[38] 131 F. Supp. 165 (S.D. Cal. 1955), *aff'd sub nom* Benny v. Loew's Inc., 239 F. 2d 532 (9th Cir. 1956), *aff'd* by a 4-4 division of the Supreme Court, 356 U.S. 43 (1958).

ferently from any other appropriation." [39] In finding for the plaintiff, the court held that the change in mode of expression from serious to comic did not preclude infringement. The court also found that the defendent's commercial use of plaintiff's material was directed to a competing entertainment field, although he concluded that reduction in demand for the original, stressed in the *Mutt and Jeff* case, was not essential. This result was affirmed by the Court of Appeals for the Ninth Circuit which emphasized that "wholesale copying" can never be fair use, not even where the treatment of the material is inverted by means of burlesque.[40]

Even more recently, Judge Carter has had before him what he labeled as "the reverse or counterpart" of the *Loew's* case. In *Columbia Pictures Corp.*, v. *NBC*,[41] he found that Sid Ceasar's television burlesque of "From Here to Eternity" did not infringe the copyright of that motion picture. This was so notwithstanding the similarities beyond theme, situation, setting and basic plot. In reaching this result, Judge Carter seems to have modified the *Loew's* approach. He permitted use of an incident, some small part of the development of the story and even "possibly some small amount of dialogue," emphasizing that the burlesquer should be permitted "to bring about this recalling or conjuring up of the original." [42] The court adopted as a conclusion of law the statement that—

the law permits more extensive use of the protectible portion of a copyrighted work in the creation of a burlesque than in the creation of other fictional or dramatic works not intended as a burlesque.[43]

The subsequent 4 to 4 decision of the Supreme Court in the *Loew's* case indicates the uncertainty that exists regarding this problem.

4. *Scholarly works and compilations*

The conflict between the right to "use" and the right to publish or copy is sharply presented in the area of scholarly works; this area includes such fields as science,[44] law,[45] medicine,[46] history [47] and biography.[48] Research is the foundation of such works. And research has flippantly been defined as "plagiarism from two or more sources." [49] One court suggested that—

with reference to works in regard to the arts and sciences, using those words in the broadest sense * * * authors are sometimes entitled, indeed *required* to make use of what precedes them in the precise form in which last exhibited. * * * [50] [Emphasis added.]

The decisions in the field of scholarly works, as well as those concerning compilations, do present special problems by reason of the identity of subject matter covered by groups of works.[51] It may be that the character of a work—as a scientific work, parody, etc.— is an extremely significant factor.[52] In any event, the decisions in

---

[39] 131 F. Supp. 177.
[40] 239 F. 2d 536, 537.
[41] 137 F. Supp. 348 (S.D. Cal. 1955).
[42] *Id*. at 350.
[43] *Id*. at 354.
[44] Simms v. Stanton, 75 Fed. 6 (C.C.N.D. Cal. 1896).
[45] Callaghan v. Myers, 128 U.S. 617 (1888).
[46] Henry Holt & Co. v. Liggett & Myers Tobacco Co., 23 F. Supp. 302 (E.D. Pa. 1938).
[47] Eisenschiml v. Fawcett Publications, Inc., 240 F. 2d 598 (7th Cir. 1957).
[48] Toksvig v. Bruce Pub. Co., 181 F. 2d 664 (7th Cir. 1950).
[49] Pilpel, "But Can You Do That?," Publishers Weekly, Aug. 26, 1957, p. 33.
[50] Sampson & Murdock Co. v. Seaver-Radford Co., 140 Fed. 539, 541 (1st Cir. 1905).
[51] Lipton, *The Extent of Copyright Protection for Law Books*, SECOND COPYRIGHT LAW SYMPOSIUM 11 (1940).
[52] See Thompson v. Gernsback, 94 F. Supp. 453 (S.D.N.Y. 1950).

the lawbook field, for example, have accurately been characterized by a recent court as "somewhat confusing." [53]   Despite this confusion, it may be that the basic issue in each case is whether an earlier work has been collaterally used or substantially copied as well.

A law digester may "use" the citations of cases found in an earlier encyclopedia.[54]   Since use of citations properly consists of reading and independently analyzing the cases, unauthorized copying cannot be said to take place even if the defendant's published list of cases is identical to the plaintiff's.[55]   If the two works are mere compilations of cases, a different rule apparently obtains; even the verification of the original list will not shield the user from liability.[56]

The citations of an earlier work may be used as a check on the later work.   But the copying of such material as headnotes cannot be justified as fair use, even in the case of treatises, encyclopedias, or texts.[57]

The latitude permitted scholars in quoting material from earlier works does not extend to the use of a scholarly work for nonscholarly purposes.   Thus, in *Henry Holt & Co., v. Liggett & Myers Tobacco Co.*,[58] three sentences from the plaintiff's scientific treatise were used in an advertising pamphlet to enhance the sale of the defendant's product.   The court held that defendant's use was not for the scientific purposes for which plaintiff's consent might be implied.   Similarly, the publishers of Sexology magazine met difficulties in attempting to convince the court of the scientific nature of the magazine so as to justify use of "the identical words of earlier books or writings dealing with the same subject matter." [59]

When material from a compilation of facts, names, or other information is used for the purpose of preparing a rival compilation, it is often difficult to avoid mere copying.   The courts have permitted a very limited use of such material as a source [60] or means of verification.[61]   But the use of earlier material as a check upon the completeness or accuracy of the user's work must be followed by a bona fide independent recanvass.[62]   And in any event, independent effort, such as the exercise of judgment in the selection of material, must be expended.[63]   Mere verification of the original material is insufficient.[64]

5. *Personal or private use*

Although the case law is apparently silent on the point, at least one writer has concluded that "anyone may copy copyrighted materials for the purposes of private study and review." [65]   It has, moreover, been vigorously argued that "private use is completely outside

[53] Loew's, Inc. v. Columbia Broadcasting System, Inc., note 38, *supra*, 131 F. Supp. 175.
[54] Edward Thompson Co. v. American Law Book Co., 122 Fed. 922 (2d Cir. 1903).
[55] White v. Bender, 185 Fed. 921 (C.C.N.D.N.Y. 1911).
[56] W. H. Anderson Co. v. Baldwin Law Pub. Co., 27 F. 2d 82 (6th Cir. 1928).
[57] Callaghan v. Myers, 128 U.S. 617 (1888); West Pub. Co. v. Lawyers' Cooperative Pub. Co., 79 Fed. 756 (2d Cir. 1897).
[58] 23 F. Supp. 302 (E.D. Pa. 1938).
[59] Thompson v. Gernsback, 94 F. Supp. 453 (S.D.N.Y. 1950).
[60] See Social Register Ass'n v. Murphy, 128 Fed. 116 (C.C.D.R.I. 1904).   In West Pub. Co. v. Edward Thompson Co., 169 Fed. 833, 853, (C.C.E.D.N.Y. 1909) *mod. and aff'd.*, 176 Fed. 833, (2d Cir. 1910) the court characterized cases involving maps and directories as depending "more upon the idea of unfair use, and the unlawful saving of labor in order to avoid the necessary original research than upon the appropriation of any literary ideas or arrangement, based upon literary ability and studied plan."   *Cf.* Conde Nast Publications, Inc., v. Vogue School of Fashion Modeling, Inc., 105 F. Supp. 325 (S.D.N.Y. 1952).
[61] Dun v. Lumbermen's Credit Ass'n, 144 Fed. 83 (7th Cir. 1906).
[62] Hartford Printing Co. v. Hartford Directory & Publishing Co., 146 Fed. 332 (C.C.D. Conn. 1906).
[63] List Pub. Co. v. Keller, 30 Fed. 772 (C.C.S.D.N.Y. 1887).   *Cf.* Jeweler's Circular Pub. Co. v. Keystone Pub. Co., 281 Fed. 83 (2d Cir. 1922).
[64] Sampson & Murdock Co. v. Seaver-Radford Co., 140 Fed. 539 (1st Cir. 1905).
[65] Cohen, *op cit.*, note 7, *supra* at 58.

the scope and intent of restriction by copyright." [66]   It is difficult to assess the effect of the absence of litigation in this area.   It may reflect acquiescence on the part of copyright owners to copying by scholars for their own use.   That such acquiescence is not complete is indicated by attempts to regulate, by agreement, the role of libraries in supplying copies to scholars.[67]   The increasing use of photoduplication processes will undoubtedly require continuing attention to this area.   For the purposes of the present study, it may be observed that the categorical statements set forth above can neither be supported nor attacked on the basis of authority.   It may well be, however, that the purpose and nature of a private use, and in some cases the small amount taken, might lead a court to apply the general principles of fair use in such a way as to deny liability.

6. News

The strong public policy in favor of the wide dissemination of news might conveniently be furthered by an expanded concept of fair use with respect to news items.   As will be demonstrated below, this approach has been taken by many foreign countries and has been proposed in several attempts at legislative revision in this country. The present U.S. law, however, does not seem to have developed any special rules pertaining to the fair use of news articles.   The incidents and facts embodied in news items cannot, of course, be subject to copyright protection.[68]   News as such is not copyrightable.[69]   But the literary aspect of a news article is entitled to protection and direct quotation or copying of the words or arrangement of the article entails the usual risks, notwithstanding the wider circulation of news achieved by the copying.

The appropriation of a copyrighted news article was directly involved in *Chicago Record-Herald Co.* v. *Tribune Association*.   The court characterized the defendant's article as follows:

It presents the essential facts of that [plaintiff's] article in the very garb wherein the author clothed them, together with some of his deductions and comments thereon in his precise words, and all with the same evident purpose of attractively and effectively serving them to the reading public.[70]

Whether or not such a commercial purpose actuated the defendant in *New York Tribune, Inc.* v. *Otis & Co.*,[71] was one of the inquiries bearing on the defense of fair use which the court there reserved for full trial.   The defendant in *New York Tribune* had photostated an entire editorial dealing with the presidential campaign.   Questions insufficiently illuminated on motion included the number of copies distributed by the defendant, his intent, and the effect of his publication on the distribution of plaintiff's work.

[66] Shaw, *"Publication and Distribution of Scientific Literature,"* 17 College and Research Libraries 294, 301 (1956).
[67] See "Gentlemen's Agreement" between Joint Committee on the Reproduction of Materials for Research and the National Association of Book Publishers, set forth and discussed in 1 Journal of Documentary Reproduction 29 (1939); Smith, "The Copying of Literary Property in Library Collections," 46 Law Lib. Journal 197 (1953); 47 Law Lib. Journal 204 (1954).
   The British have made similar arrangements.   See The Royal Society Information Services Committee, "Fair Copying Declaration and List of Publishing Organizations Subscribing to It".   (June 1950).
[68] *Cf.* Oxford Book Co. v. College Entrance Book Co., 98 F. 2d 688 (2d Cir. 1938).
[69] See Chicago Record-Herald Co. v. Tribune Ass'n, 275 Fed. 797, (7th Cir. 1921).   Relief for unfair competition arising out of the appropriation of news was recognized in the famous case of International News Service v. Associated Press, 248 U.S. 215 (1918).
[70] 275 Fed. 799 (7th Cir. 1921).
[71] 39 F. Supp. 67 (S.D.N.Y. 1941).

7. Use in litigation

No cases have been found involving the permissibility of direct quotation or other use of copyrighted material in judicial or administrative opinions or by lawyers in briefs or otherwise in connection with pending litigation. It would seem that great latitude would be accorded such use. In the absence of reported decisions or records of controversy, the extent of this use cannot be delineated.

8. Use for nonprofit or governmental purposes

In *New York Tribune, Inc.* v. *Otis & Co.*,[72] it was indicated that a commercial motive on the part of the defendant would bear unfavorably upon the defense of fair use. Judge Carter in the *Jack Benny* case [73] analyzed "the impact of commercial gain or profit" even further and concluded that: (1) "in the field of science and the fine arts, we find a broad scope given to fair use"; (2) "As we draw further away from the fields of science or pure or fine arts, and enter the fields where business competition exists we find the scope of *fair use* is narrowed but still exists"; and (3) the writer of a scholarly work "does not invite or consent to its use for commercial gain alone." [74]

It would seem to follow from Judge Carter's analysis that where the commercial element is completely absent, a finding of fair use is strongly indicated. In *Associated Music Publishers, Inc.* v. *Debs Memorial Radio Fund, Inc.*,[75] where the defendant was a nonprofit organization but engaged in commercial activities to raise funds for its expenses, the court rejected the defense of fair use. The infringing use of plaintiff's musical composition consisted of a broadcast of about one-third of the work during the course of a sustaining program of a radio station operated by a nonprofit corporation. The court held that the philanthropic and educational aims of the corporation did not prevent the broadcast from constituting a "public performance for profit" within the meaning of section 1(e) of the act; significant to this holding was the fact that the corporation sought immediate, if not ultimate, commercial gain by allocating one-third of the available time to commercial advertisers. In passing, however, the district court did take note of the fact that the defendants did not contend "that the corporation is a public or charitable institution."[76] The court found the fair use defense to ["require little consideration."[77] In affirming, the Court of Appeals stated:

There can be no doubt that the portion of the plaintiff's composition which was broadcast which amounted to about a quarter of his entire work and was reproduced to aid in building up a listening audience does not come within the definition of "fair use." [78]

The *Associated Music* case may demonstrate the difficulty in establishing the absence of any commercial motive. On the other hand, it may indicate that a finding of fair use will not be compelled by the fact that the defendant seeks no profit from its operation. Undoubtedly, this is but one illustration that generally no single factor will determine whether a use is fair or unfair.

---

[72] 39 F. Supp. 67 (S.D.N.Y. 1941).
[73] Loew's, Inc. v. Columbia Broadcasting System, Inc., 131 F. Supp. 165 (S.D. Cal. 1955), *aff'd sub nom.* Benny v. Loew's, Inc., 239 F. 2d 532 (9th Cir. 1956), *cert. granted*, 353 U.S. 946 (1957).
[74] 131 F. Supp. at 175.
[75] Associated Music Publishers, Inc. v. Debs Memorial Radio Fund, Inc., 46 F. Supp. 829 (S.D.N.Y. 1942), *aff'd*, 141 F. 2d 852 (2d Cir. 1944).
[76] 46 F. Supp. 830.
[77] *Id.* at 831.
[78] 141 F. 2d at 855.

Where the Government is the user of copyrighted material, a different situation is presented. There is considerable doubt whether the Government is liable for copyright infringement.[79] Again, this is, strictly speaking, a situation governed by considerations other than fair use.[80] But immunity of the Government in this area has frequently been associated with the immunity of the members of the public who make a reasonable use of a copyrighted work. For example, a wartime legislative proposal [81] authorized the Librarian of Congress to make copies of copyrighted works for the purpose of furnishing such copies not only to high Government officials, but also:

(3) To any person * * * upon his certification that he cannot otherwise obtain the material and that he desires it for the purpose of private study, research, criticism, review, demonstration, litigation, comment, newspaper summary, or fair use as recognized by the courts * * *.

It should be noted that this proposal (which did not become law) prescribed that the making of copies by the Librarian of Congress shall not constitute infringement. In the absence of such legislation, the Librarian might be personally liable, since the sovereign immunity of the Government in this area has been held not to shield individual Government employees committing the unauthorized copying.[82] It should further be noted that the proposal specifically recognized that subsequent use of the material furnished by the Librarian might constitute infringement. Although not entirely clear, it would seem that such subsequent use might constitute infringement even if within the governmental purposes or the purposes quoted above.

C. ANALYSIS OF THE CRITERIA OF FAIR USE

The cases examined above support the conclusion that fair use is not a predictable area of copyright law. One writer has characterized this situation as follows:

There is one proposition about fair use about which there is widespread agreement: it is not easy to decide what is and what is not a fair use.[83]

The conflicting results possible in this area are graphically illustrated by two cases involving the same plaintiff, court, and year. In *Green* v. *Minzenheimer* [84] and *Green* v. *Luby*,[85] the court found factual differences upon which to distinguish two imitations or parodies of plaintiff's song. These differences do not present any clear guide to the disposition of future litigation. This situation is understandable in any inquiry dependent upon a concept of reasonableness.

The reluctance of courts to rule on the defense of fair use prior to trial has already been illustrated in *New York Tribune Inc.* v. *Otis & Co.*[86] Accordingly, "fair use is to be determined by examination of all the evidence."[87] Once determined, one appellate court treated it as a "question of fact" which the court was reluctant to reexamine.[88]

[79] 101 Cong. Rec. 7894, 84th Cong., 1st Sess. (1955). *Cf.* H.R. 8419, 85th Cong. (1957) which would expressly impose liability on the Government.
[80] One writer points out that the normal rules of fair use should shield many Governmental uses, even without reliance on sovereign immunity. Stiefel, *Piracy in High Places—Government Publications,* ASCAP, *COPYRIGHT LAW SYMPOSIUM, No. 8,* 3 at 9 (1957).
[81] S. 2039, 78th Cong., 2d Sess. (1944).
[82] Towle v. Ross, 32 F. Supp. 125 (D. Ore. 1940) H.R. 8419, 85th Cong. (1957) would make the government liable rather than the individual employee.
[83] Cohen, *op. cit.,* note 7, *supra,* at 52.
[84] 177 Fed. 286 (C.C.S.D.N.Y. 1909).
[85] 177 Fed. 287 (C.C.S.D.N.Y. 1909).
[86] See p. 11, *supra; cf.* Winwar v. Time, Inc., 83 F. Supp. 629 (S.D.N.Y. 1949).
[87] See Mathews Conveyer Co. v. Palmer-Bee Co., 135 F. 2d 73 (6th Cir. 1943).
[88] Eisenschiml v. Fawcett Publications, Inc., 240 F. 2d 598 (7th Cir. 1957). A different view was expressed in 56 COLUM. L. REV. 585 (1956) at 593 n. 37, where it was concluded that: "The question of fair use should be decided by the court, as a *question of law.*" [Emphasis added.]

It has been suggested that:

The cases indicate that there are eight elements which the courts consider; any one of the eight may, in a particular case, be decisive. These factors are: (1) the type of use involved; (2) the intent with which it was made; (3) its effect on the original work; (4) the amount of the user's labor involved; (5) the benefit gained by him; (6) the nature of the works involved; (7) the amount of material used; and (8) its relative value.[89]

Perhaps more basic are the oft-quoted criteria set forth by Mr. Justice Story in *Folsom* v. *Marsh* as:

the objects of the selections made, the quantity and value of the materials used and the degree in which the use may prejudice the sale, or diminish the profits, or supersede the objects, of the original work.[90]

Judge Yankwich found that Story's criteria have been the basis of American case law. He restates the decisive elements as follows:

(1) the quantity and importance of the portion taken; (2) their relation to the work of which they are a part; (3) the result of their use upon the demand for the copyrighted publication.[91]

It has been noted above that the nature of the works involved has been suggested as one factor in determining fair use. This factor might explain what appears to be a stricter rule in the case of compilations than in more scholarly works. Whether special significance attaches to the nature of a work as a parody is involved in the *Loew's* and *Columbia* cases. But Judge Yankwich finds that with respect to the diverse publications which have been the subject of litigation, there has been "uniform application of the principles of 'fair use.' " [92]

Sufficient has been said to emphasize the factual niceties of fair use determinations. Accordingly, it is believed that for purposes of analysis, the criteria of fair use may conveniently be distilled even further, without danger of oversimplification. In fact, the tests may perhaps be summarized by: importance of the material copied or performed from the point of view of the reasonable copyright owner. In other words, would the reasonable copyright owner have consented to the use? At times, custom or public policy defines what is reasonable.

It is well within the bounds of reasonableness for the copyright owner to consider important a use which competes with his own work. A use having such an effect undermines the very basis of his quasi-monopolistic protection. Thus, the court stated in the *Mutt and Jeff* case:

One test which, when applicable, would seem to be ordinarily decisive, is whether or not so much as has been reproduced will materially reduce the demand for the original.[93]

The courts have apparently been prepared to anticipate such a harmful effect; the copyright owner is protected not only against a use having an unfavorable competitive effect,[94] but also a use with a competitive purpose or potential. Thus, in *Shapiro, Bernstein & Co., v. P. F. Collier & Son Co.,*[95] the following tests were set forth:

* * * The extent and relative value of the extracts; *the purpose and whether the quoted portions might be used as a substitute for the original work*; the effect upon the distribution and objects of the original work. [Emphasis added.]

[89] Cohen, *op. cit.*, note 7, *supra*, at 53.
[90] 9 Fed. Cas. 348. See note 6, *supra*.
[91] *Op. cit.*, note 16, *supra*, at 213.
[92] *Id.* at 212.
[93] Hill v. Whalen & Martell, Inc., 220 Fed. 359, 360 (S.D.N.Y. 1914).
[94] Social Register Ass'n v. Murphy, 128 Fed. 116 (C.C.D.R.I. 1904). *Cf.* Hartford Printing Co. v. Hartford Directory & Publishing Co., 146 Fed. 332 (C.C.D. Conn. 1906).
[95] 26 U.S.P.Q. 40, 43 (S.D.N.Y. 1934).

In the *Loew's* case, the competitive element was broadly construed. Judge Carter held that the plaintiff need not establish that the defendant's work reduced the demand for the plaintiff's; yet his emphasis on the commercial nature of the defendant's work has already been noted. In this connection Judge Carter had concluded that "the taking was for commercial gain for use in a competing entertainment field." [96]

A curious commentary on the importance of competition is reflected by *Henry Holt & Co.*, v. *Liggett & Myers Tobacco Co.*, where an extract from the plaintiff's scientific work was used in defendant's advertisement; such use was held to be an infringement. The dissimilarity between the nature of the plaintiff's work and defendant's use appears to have been a crucial consideration.[97] Presumably, had the defendant used plaintiff's work in a competing scientific work, fair use might have been established. It thus appears in the field of scholarly works, the effect of "competition" is mitigated. Scholarly works in any particular field may in a sense compete with one another; but this does not prevent such use of earlier materials as is sanctioned by traditions of research and dictated by the strong policy in favor of encouraging a steady flow of such works.

The importance to the copyright owner of a use made without his express consent also depends on the extent of the material taken and its value,[98] considered in connection with either the copyrighted work or the user's work. Thus, where the material taken constitutes a large part of the plaintiff's work, the use is unreasonable.[99] Of course, in determining the amount of material taken, there is presumably a distinction between the minimal amount which under no circumstances could constitute infringement and the slightly larger quantity which, in conjunction with other factors, amounts to fair use.[100] This distinction is not always clear in the case law.

The significance of material is determined by many factors. In the *Shapiro, Bernstein* case, the court upheld as fair use the reproduction of "some more or less disconnected 'snatches' or quotations from the words of the song." There were apparently three reasons why such material was not considered significant. (1) The amount was small; [101] (2) the quotations were disconnected; and (3) the material consisted of only words and not the music. More recently, qualitative analysis was made of the defendant's use in a 20-second commercial of a melodic obligato from plaintiff's song. The court held that copying of "that portion of plaintiff's song upon which its popular appeal, and hence, its commercial success depended * * *" was not shielded by the doctrine of fair use.[102]

Inquiry into the importance of the material to the defendant's work was made in the *Henry Holt* case discussed above. The material there copied constituted only three sentences from an extensive treatise by the plaintiff, but represented about one-twentieth of the

---

[96] 131 F. Supp. 182–83. See College Entrance Book Co. v. Amsco Book Co., 119 F. 2d 874, 876 (2d Cir. 1941) wherein the Court of Appeals, in reversing the district court, emphasized that both works "met exactly the same demand on the same market."

[97] *Cf.* Sampson & Murdock Co. v. Seaver-Radford Co., 140 Fed. 539 (1st Cir. 1905).

[98] In Folsom v. Marsh, 9 Fed. Cas. 342, 348, No. 4901, Justice Story emphasized the importance of the "value" of an extract rather than its "quantity."

[99] Leon v. Pac. Tel. & Tel. Co., 91 F. 2d 484 (9th Cir. 1938). *Cf.* Benny v. Loew's, 239 F. 2d 532 (9th Cir. 1956), *cert. granted*, 353 U.S. 946 (1957).

[100] See p. 30, *infra*.

[101] *Cf.* Associated Music Publishers, Inc. v. Debs Memorial Radio Fund, Inc., 141 F. 2d 852 (2d Cir. 1944).

[102] Robertson v. Batten, Barton, Durstine & Osborn, Inc., 146 F. Supp. 795 (S.D. Cal. 1956).

defendant's advertising pamphlet. The court found that the matter copied was sufficiently substantial to overcome the threshold argument against a finding of infringement. Presumably, this consideration influenced the court in finding that fair use had not been established.

It might seem that the appropriation of a large amount of material would constitute an unreasonable use, notwithstanding the nature of the material or other circumstances. This view was strongly expressed in *Leon* v. *Pacific Telephone & Telegraph Co.*,[103] where defendant rearranged the order of listings in plaintiff's telephone directory from alphabetical arrangement of names of subscribers to consecutive listings of telephone numbers. The court stated:

Counsel have not disclosed a single authority, nor have we been able to find one, which lends any support to the proposition that wholesale copying and publication of copyrighted material can ever be fair use.

This dictum was relied upon heavily by the court of appeals in the *Loew's* case.[104]

Had the reported progress of *New York Tribune, Inc.* v. *Otis & Co.*, gone further, it might have furnished the "authority" not available at the time of the *Leon* case. The defendant there had photostated an entire editorial. The court, in denying the defendant's motions to dismiss and for summary judgment, apparently considered the issue of fair use an open one to be determined by "consideration of all the evidence in the case." Inasmuch as the court was not considering a motion on the plaintiff's behalf, its failure to rule out the possibility of a fair use defense may not contradict the *Leon* dictum. Yet, some question as to the sweep of the dictum may be raised by *Broadway Music Corp.* v. *F-R Pub. Corp.*,[105] wherein words from the plaintiff's copyrighted song constituted about half of the lines in the defendant's magazine article.

The state of mind of the user, ordinarily immaterial to the determination of infringement,[106] has been considered relevant to the question of fair use.[107] It was stated in the early case of *Lawrence* v. *Dana*,[108] that "evidence of innocent intention may have a bearing upon the question of 'fair use'." "Innocent intention" in this context has been roughly equated with "good faith."[109] The court in the *Broadway Music* case found the absence of an "intent to commit an infringement" to "go to fill out the whole picture."

In the *New York Tribune* case, the intent of the defendant to use the plaintiff's editorial in a noncommercial manner apparently would have been a significant factor. But this suggests that the purpose of a work or the intention to compete may be more crucial than the overall intention of a defendant to infringe or not to infringe. Similarly, the acknowledgment of source would merely reveal an intent to refrain from plagiarism—using another's material *as one's own*—rather than an intent to keep the use within reasonable bounds.

Acknowledgment itself presents an interesting situation. It is ordinarily assumed that credit to the source is a factor which reflects

---

[103] 91 F. 2d 484, 486 (9th Cir. 1938).
[104] See note 40, *supra*. *Cf.* Sayers v. Spaeth, Copyright Office Bulletin, No. 20 at 625 (S.D.N.Y. 1932).
[105] 31 F. Supp. 817 (S.D.N.Y. 1940).
[106] See Buck v. Jewell-La Salle Realty Co., 283 U.S. 191, 198 (1931).
[107] See Peck, *Copyright Infringement of Literary Works*, 38 MARQ. L. REV. 180, 187 (1955).
[108] 15 Fed. Cas. 26, 60 Case No. 8, 136, (C.C.D. Mass. 1869)
[109] Cohen, *op. cit.*, note 7 *supra*, at 60.

favorably upon the user as it helps "to fill out the whole picture." [110] Nevertheless, acknowledgment can have contrary implications. Thus, one court said of crediting the author:

Far from there being any exculpatory virtue in this, it would tend rather to convey to the reading public the false impression that authority to appropriate the extracts from the copyrighted article had been duly secured by the offending publisher.[111]

In any event, it is clear that acknowledgment, in itself, is not sufficient to insure fair use and preclude infringement.[112]

III. Proposals for Legislative Revisions Since 1909

The omission of any mention of fair use in the 1909 act was not inadvertent. At the hearings leading to the act, the Librarian of Congress indicated that the question, "What is fair use?" was not answered by the bill which "leaves to the courts to determine the meaning and extent of terms already construed by the courts." [113] Similarly, the Senate Committee on Patents reported in 1907 that the bill—

is not, however, an attempt to codify the common law. Questions such as that of what is a "fair use" of copyrighted matter, and what is an "infringement," it leaves still to the courts.[114]

This approach was recently suggested by the representative of the book publishers who felt that the judicial doctrine of fair use was preferable to a "for profit" limitation on the performing right of non-dramatic literary works.[115] However, the statutory silence of the 1909 act was not followed in most of the major reform bills since 1909. Rather, there was proposed a wide variety of fair use provisions ranging from a single short sentence in the Sirovich bills to the extensive provisions of the Dallinger and Shotwell bills.

A. DALLINGER BILLS, 1924

The first Dallinger bill [116] proposed immunity for fair use and related situations, section 27 providing for six exemptions from infringement. Most of these were patterned after the British Copyright Act of 1911.[117] (1) The bill broadly exempted "any fair use of any work for the purpose of study, research, criticism, or review." (2) The author of an artistic work retained the right to use models, sketches, etc., even where he did not own the copyright in the work; but such limited right did not authorize him to "repeat or imitate the main design or scope of that work." (3) Permanently exhibited works of art could be freely copied, and sketches or drawings of works of architecture could be made as long as they were not in the nature of architectural plans or drawings. (4) Short passages from published literary works might be included in a collection mainly of noncopyrighted material intended for school use. The educational purpose was to be indicated

---

[110] See Warren v. White & Wyckoff Mfg. Co., 39 F. 2d 922, 923 (S.D.N.Y. 1930).
[111] Chicago Record-Herald Co. v. Tribune Ass'n., 275 Fed. 797, 799 (7th Cir. 1921).
[112] See Henry Holt & Co. v. Liggett & Myers Tobacco Co., 23 F. Supp. 302 (E.D. Pa. 1938); Sayers v Spaeth, Copyright Office Bulletin, No. 20 at 625 (S.D.N.Y. 1932).
[113] *Hearings Before Committee on Patents on S. 6330 and H.R. 19853*, 59th Cong., 1st Sess., at 15 (June 1906).
[114] S. Rep. No. 6187, 59th Cong., 2d Sess (1907).
[115] *Hearings Before Subcommittee No. 3 of the House Committee on the Judiciary on H.R. 3589*, 82d Cong., 1st Sess., 36–37 (1951).
[116] H.R. 8177, 68th Cong., 1st Sess. (1924).
[117] 1 & 2 GEO. 5 c. 46 §2 (1911).

and the source acknowledged. This provision was inapplicable to passages from works which were themselves published for school use, and permitted the use of only two passages from the same author within a 5-year period.   (5) Excluded from infringement was "The reading or recitation in public by one person of any reasonable extract of any published work."   (6) A limited right to reproduce news articles, patterned upon Article 9 of the Berne Convention, was also proposed.   Permitted was the—

reproduction by another newspaper of any newspaper article other than serial or other stories and tales, unless the reproduction thereof is expressly forbidden, provided the source of said article is stated in connection with such reproduction.

In addition, section 28 authorized a newspaper report of a public address.

These provisions seem to embody three general themes. First, scholarly and peculiarly educational use of copyrighted material was accorded special concessions.   Second, reporting and borrowing among newspapers of new items was facilitated.   Third, performing rights and artistic reproduction rights of copyright owners were curtailed.

It will be noted, however, that the proposals failed to resolve many of the questions traditionally left to the courts in this area.   Thus, subsection 1 of section 27 exempted "fair use" for scholarly or critical purposes, but no definition of "fair use" was supplied.   And the educational exemption of subsection (4) was limited to "short passages."   Similarly, the right to public recitation by someone other than the copyright owner was limited to a "reasonable extract" of the copyright work.

The second Dallinger bill [118] limited significantly the public reading exemption of subsection (5).   This use could be made only of nondramatic works and was permitted only where the public reading or recitation was not for profit.

B. VESTAL BILLS, 1931

The Perkins bills [119] apparently contained no provisions concerning fair use.   Neither did the first versions of the Vestal bills, [120] including H.R. 12549 which was passed by the House in the 71st Congress. But in the following session an amended version [121] and its companion bill in the Senate [122] took an interesting approach to the problem of fair use.   They engrafted provisos directly upon the general grant of copyright in section 4, which insured that "nothing in this Act shall prevent the fair use of quotations from copyright matter."   Both bills permitted such fair use only in the absence of an express prohibition by the copyright owner.   And credit was required by the Senate bill where the use was by radio for profit, and by the House bill in every case.

C. SIROVICH AND DILL BILLS, 1932

The provisions of the Sirovich bills probably modified the effect of the silence in the Perkins bills only by an absolute requirement of

---

[118] H.R. 9137, 68th Cong., 1st Sess. (1924).
[119] H.R. 11258 and S. 4355, 68th Cong., 2d Sess. (1925), and H.R. 5841, 69th Cong., 1st Sess. (1925).
[120] H.R. 10434, 69th Cong., 1st Sess. (1926), H.R. 8912, 70th Cong., 1st Sess. (1928), H.R. 6990, 71st Cong., 2d Sess. (1929), and H.R. 12549, 71st Cong., 2d Sess. (1930).
[121] H.R. 139, 72d Cong., 1st Sess. (1931).
[122] Hebert bill, S. 176, 72d Cong., 1st Sess. (1931).

acknowledgement.   Thus, section 11 of the first and second Sirovich bills [123] contained the provision that:

> None of the remedies given to the copyright owner by this Act shall be deemed to apply to—(f) the fair use of quotations from copyright matter provided credit is given to the copyright owner.

The third Sirovich bill [124] introduced the addition of the words "or the work quoted" to the end of subsection, and this modification was retained in all the later versions [125] of the bill.

The Dill bill [126] hedged the privilege of fair use with a further condition and would seem to represent a dilution of the privilege as defined by the courts.   Section 2 provided that:

> Nothing in this Act shall prevent the fair use of quotations from copyright matter, *unless the copyright owner by notice affixed, has expressly prohibited such quotations from the copyrighted work in whole or in part,* but whenever such quotations are printed or reproduced by radio for profit, credit shall be given to the source. [Emphasis added.]

D. THE DUFFY, DALY, AND SIROVICH BILLS, 1935–37

The original Duffy bill,[127] introduced in 1935, incorporated the substance of the provisions of the earlier Sirovich bills by granting immunity to "the fair use of quotations;" and a requirement of "due credit" was imposed.   This provision was deleted in later versions.[128] But the Duffy bills also contained some innovations in U.S. fair-use proposals.   For example, section 17g (4) of S. 3047 [129] exempted from liability the performances of a copyrighted musical work for charitable, religious, or educational purposes as well as:

> The merely incidental and not reasonably avoidable inclusion of a copyrighted work in a motion picture or broadcast depicting or relating current events.

The Daly bill [130] was silent as to fair use, but the Sirovich bill of 1936 [131] maintained the exemption for performances for charitable purposes, as well as the brief statement as to "fair use of quotations" found in the earlier Sirovich bills.   Section 26 also exempted from infringement "the publication of a photograph as an item of public or general interest in the dissemination of news."

Hearings were held on the Duffy, Daly, and Sirovich bills in 1936.[132] The subsection of the Duffy bill quoted above came under attack by the American Society of Composers, Authors & Publishers.   Its extensive brief included the following criticism of the provision:

> There is no reason why exhibitors and distributors of newsreels should be permitted to make a profit from the use of copyrighted material without payment.
> There is nothing to prevent an unscrupulous broadcaster from broadcasting an entire show as a current event.   This could be done by merely coupling the performance with a broadcast of current news events.[133]

On the other hand, the National Association of Broadcasters favored the provision, arguing that the violation of the copyright

---

[123] H.R. 10364 and H.R. 10740, 72d Cong., 1st Sess. (1932).
[124] H.R. 10976, 72d Cong., 1st Sess. (1932).
[125] H.R. 11948, H.R. 12094, and H.R. 12425, 72d Cong., 1st Sess. (1932).
[126] S. 3985, 72d Cong., 1st Sess. (1932).
[127] S. 2465, 74th Cong., 1st Sess. (1935).
[128] S. 3047, H.R. 8557, 74th Cong., 1st Sess. (1935) and S. 7, H.R. 2695 and H.R. 3004, 75th Cong., 1st Sess. (1937).
[129] 74th Cong., 1st Sess. (1935).
[130] H.R. 10632, 74th Cong., 2d Sess. (1936).
[131] H.R. 11420, 74th Cong., 2d Sess. (1936).
[132] *Hearings Before the House Committee on Patents,* 74th Cong., 2d Sess. (1936).
[133] *Id.* at 122.

was merely technical and the damage, minimal. The broadcasters argued further that "important considerations of public policy" dictated unrestricted continuation of—

one of radio's greatest contributions to civilization * * * the instantaneous communication of public events to the public throughout the world.[134]

The representative of the motion picture producers characterized this provision as a very salutary contribution. It was suggested on behalf of the producers that the exemption should not be limited to the depiction of current events, but should extend to all subject matter where the infringement was "incidental and not reasonably avoidable." This extension was deemed necessary by reason of the filming of pictures out of doors and possible inclusion of a work of art in the scene.[135]

The debates on this controversial provision became more extended in the course of the Shotwell meetings.

E. SHOTWELL (THOMAS) BILL, 1940

The Shotwell Committee considered the wide range of problems broadly associated with the question of fair use. These problems occupied a good deal of the time of the Committee. They ranged from the special problems of the scholar to appropriate limitations on performing rights.

In addition to the provisions which ultimately appeared in the Thomas bill to be noted below, three proposals in the preliminary "Ware draft"[136] version of the bill deserve mention. This draft contained a provision[137] which, like subsection 26(6) of the Dallinger bill, was patterned after article 9(2) of the Berne Convention; it granted a qualified right of reproduction in the press with respect to articles of public interest. This provision was short lived as was subsection 18(c) which permitted the nonprofit exhibition of certain motion picture films.

Of longer endurance was a provision protecting "fair dealing" for "the purpose of private study, research, review or newspaper summary."[138] In the course of the discussions on this section, the radio broadcasters sought to delete the word "private" on the ground that "study and research as well as criticism and review are intended for the public and not merely for private edification." It was accordingly urged that "the research should not be limited to private research either as to sponsorship or its dissemination."[139]

The entire section was deleted after the Joint Committee on Materials for Research, apparently considering the position of the scholar more favorable under the case law, convinced all other interested groups except the book publishers that the attempt to codify the doctrine of fair use had been unsuccessful.[140]

---

[134] *Id.* at 478.
[135] *Id.* at 1020.
[136] Ware Preliminary Draft dated April 7–12, 1939, 2 Shotwell Papers 226 (1939). The memoranda, minutes and proposals as collected and paginated in the U.S. Copyright Office are referred to herein as "Shotwell Papers".
[137] *Id.* at 24, 2 Shotwell Papers 248 (1939).
[138] *Id.* at 26, 2 Shotwell Papers 250 (1939).
[139] Memorandum, June 22, 1939, p. 12, 3 Shotwell Papers 289 (1939).
[140] Memorandum, October 16, 1939, p. 9, 4 Shotwell Papers, 11 (1939–1941). The committee reported, "The attempt in Subdivision (f) to codify the doctrine of fair use was not successful and should be abandoned."

Section 12 of the bill as actually introduced by Senator Thomas [141] took several different approaches to the question of fair use and covered a number of controversial situations.　The provisions of subsections (f), (g), and (h) gave permission for translation incident to private study and research as well as for reproduction of single copies by libraries of unpublished or unavailable works needed for study or research.

These subsections were drafted by a subcommittee on scholarship [142] and embodied to some extent the proposals of the Joint Committee on Materials for Research.[143]　The Joint Committee had emphasized the needs of the scholar at the outset of the proceedings.[144]

The general attitude of the Joint Committee is to be contrasted with that of the book publishers who charged that "professors and teachers are the chief pirates of literary matter." [145]　Moreover, the authors had emphasized the question of limiting the scope of the protected class of "scholars," as well as the permissible number of copies; they also stressed the plight of authors whose writings were primarily intended for libraries and scholars.[146]　And Dr. Shotwell acknowledged the possibility of overprotecting the scholar by noting that "the scholar is, in his use of * * * reproductive processes, taking the position of a quasi-publisher." [147]

Subsection (h), which permitted libraries to make single copies of works unavailable to scholars and researchers, was highly controversial.　ASCAP compared it with compulsory licenses for recorded music and questioned its constitutionality.[148]　The Authors League urged greater restrictions to preclude libraries from engaging in the publishing business "under the guise of scholarship." [149]　The motion picture industry feared that the basic concept of this provision might spread to the field of motion pictures.[150]　On the other hand, the Joint Committee apparently felt that the provision did not go far enough since it did not cover privately printed copyrighted books.[151]　It should be noted that subsection (h) provided for the creation of a trust fund in the U.S. Treasury consisting of payments made by libraries for the reproduction of books which were out of print and unavailable.

The incidental infringement provisions consisted of an extension of the Duffy bill approach.　Immunity was granted by subsection (b) to infringement in the course of simultaneous news reporting from the location in question; as in the Duffy bill, the excused infringement had to be "not reasonably avoidable."　In addition, the view of the motion picture industry representative at the Duffy hearings [152] was apparently adopted in subsection (d) which permitted the inclusion of "a work of art visible from a public place" in a photograph, motion picture, or television broadcast.

---

[141] S. 3043, 76th Cong., 3d Sess. (1940).
[142] Ware Preliminary Draft, Note, p. 27, 2 Shotwell Papers 251 (1939).
[143] Minutes of Meeting of Committee for the Study of Copyright (hereinafter, "Minutes") March 2, 1939, p. 12, 2 Shotwell Papers 65 (1939).
[144] Memorandum, July 15, 1938, 1 Shotwell Papers 18-20 (1938-1939).
[145] Minutes, Nov. 3, 1938, p. 42, 1 Shotwell Papers 169 (1938-1939).
[146] Id. at 39, 1 Shotwell Papers 166 (1938-1939).
[147] Id. at 37, 1 Shotwel Papers 164 (1938-1939).
[148] Minutes, Nov. 21, 1938, pp. 16, 17, 1 Shotwell Papers 269-270 (1938-1939).
[149] Id. at 15, 1 Shotwell Papers 268 (1938-1939). See also Comparison of the Drafted Proposals of the Various Interested Groups prepared by Edward Sargoy, dated Nov. 16, 1938, at 17, 18, 1 Shotwell Papers 241 (1938-1939).
[150] Minutes, Mar. 2, 1939, p. 14, 2 Shotwell Papers 67 (1939).
[151] Id. at 13, 2 Shotwell Papers 66 (1939).
[152] See note 135, supra.

Subsection (b) was the subject of considerable discussion, analysis, and controversy. ASCAP originally sought to limit application of the proposal to "events of a patriotic or political nature." [153]   Concern was expressed over the use of the clause under consideration "for the purpose of infringing copyrighted works under the guise of depicting public events." [154]   At a later stage, however, the Society took the position that the entire subsection should be eliminated because there was—

no reason why broadcasters and motion picture producers should be permitted to profit from the use of the property of copyright owners unless the consent of such owners is secured in advance.[155]

ASCAP was prepared to "have the courts pass upon the question as to whether the use is a fair one." [156]

On the other hand, the broadcasters and motion picture producers were proponents of the measure, insisting that they were confronted with the insuperable problem of "clearing" the use of the copyrighted music which might be played at a football game or a parade.[157]   In commenting on the final draft of the bill, the framers explained that the immunity was to be limited to cases in which "permission of the copyright owner could not have been obtained in advance with the use of reasonable diligence." [158]   And the broadcasters agreed to limit the exemption to cases in which the broadcasters received "no direct compensation." [159]

The special immunity granted in subsection (d) with respect to works of art, though supported by music publishers and libraries,[160] was sharply criticized by the songwriters as—

destroying copyright on works of art, since any public exhibition of a work of art would immediately remove copyright protection by permitting photographs to be taken and distributed.[161]

The motion picture industry was willing to qualify the immunity with the requirement that the use be "not for profit." [162]   The book publishers also were of the opinion that the provision was too loosely drawn.[163]

Subsection (c), like subsection (d), was designed to "safeguard the taking of pictures of works of art and architecture when visible from a public place."[164]   Subsection (c) permitted all representations of an architectural work as long as they "are not in the nature of architectural models, designs, or plans." The copyright owner was in any event precluded from enjoining the completion or use of an ininfringing building.

Subsection (a) complemented the limitation of musical performing rights to public performance for profit, found in section 1(e) of the Thomas bill. The remedies of the act were withheld in the case of a performance by a "bona fide charitable, religious, or educational

[153] Minutes, June 13, 1939, p. 17, 3 Shotwell Papers 153 (1939).
[154] Ibid.
[155] Memorandum, June 20, 1939, p. 1, 3 Shotwell Papers 225 (1939).
[156] Ibid.
[157] Id. at 5–7, 3 Shotwell Papers 141–143 (1939).
[158] Notes and comments on the Draft of December, 1939, p. 11, 4 Shotwell Papers 240 (1939–1941).
[159] Outline of changes in the Copyright Law Proposed by Broadcasters and Prepared for the Committee on the Study of Copyright, November 1, 1939, 1 Shotwell Papers 123e–123f (1938–1939).
[160] Collected Comments Upon Sections of Copyright Bill Still on the Agenda, November 10, 1939, p. 6b, 4 Shotwell Papers 99 (1939–1941).
[161] Memorandum, June, 1939, p. 5, 3 Shotwell Papers 265 (1939).
[162] See note 160, supra.
[163] Ibid.
[164] Notes and Comments on the Draft of December, 1939, p. 12, 4 Shotwell Papers 241 (1939–1941).

organization." Two provisos were attached. The entire net proceeds had to be devoted exclusively to charitable, religious, or educational purposes and no part of the proceeds could inure to the private benefit of a promoter. The second proviso was criticized as undermining the entire effect of the immunity;[165] the book publishers, however, insisted on its inclusion.[166]

It might seem that this immunity is narrower than the general concept of a performance "not for profit." On the other hand, the proposal might conceivably excuse certain radio broadcasts which the courts had held were "for profit." In any event, the broadcasters strongly favored this provision, while the authors opposed it.

The Shotwell provisions concerning fair use were elaborate and varied. They may perhaps be grouped under four general headings. (1) The needs of scholarship were recognized in subsections (f), (g), and (h). (2) For somewhat different reasons, broadcasters and televisors were permitted by section (e) to record their programs for private file and reference purposes. (3) Certain incidental infringements were excused by subsections (b) and (d). (4) The rights of the owners of copyrights in musical compositions and architectural works were specifically limited by subsections (a) and (c) so as to sanction certain uses of such works.

IV. Laws of Foreign Countries [167]

Most of the nations having copyright laws have enacted specific provisions concerning fair use. Many of these provisions are extensive and intricate. They often make specific mention of the different classes of copyrighted material open to use. The conditions and qualifications relating to fair use are often specified in some detail. Brief examination will be made of such limiting factors as the purpose or type of the use, the length of quotations and the requirement of acknowledgement, with attention being given to variations among different classes of work. Following this, a more detailed examination of the United Kingdom Act of 1956 will be made in order to afford an integrated picture of a single statute containing relatively extensive fair use provisions. Finally, pertinent provisions of international conventions will be noted.

A. PURPOSE OR TYPE OF USE

The most characteristic fair use provision sanctions limited use of copyrighted material for educational, scientific, or similar purposes including criticism and discussion. The privilege of using extracts for the purposes of criticism and review is frequently permitted by express provision. Representative provisions are found in the statutes of Brazil (art. 666(V)); Denmark (§ 13); France (art. 41); India (§ 52); Italy (art. 70); Lebanon (art. 149); Netherlands (art. 16); Rumania (art. 14); the United Kingdom (§ 6); and other British Commonwealth nations.[168]

---

[165] Memorandum, October 16, 1939, p. 9, 4 Shotwell Papers 22 (1939–1941).
[166] See note 160, *supra*, at 6, 4 Shotwell Papers 97 (1939–1941).
[167] The statutes of foreign countries are translated in COPYRIGHT LAWS AND TREATIES OF THE WORLD (1956) which collection, including its 1957 supplement, is the basis for the discussion of all the foreign laws except the recent statutes of France (Law No. 57-298), India (Law No. 14 of 1957) and the United Kingdom (3 & 4 ELIZ. 2, C. 74).
[168] *E.g.*, Canada § 17.

The particular purposes or types of work entitled to the privilege are not uniform. Article 41 of the French law of 1957 contains fairly broad specifications; permitted are:

Analyses and brief quotations justified by the critical, polemical, pedagogical, scientific, or informational character of the work in which they are incorporated.

Even broader is the provision of the Portuguese law which includes publications for "religious or recreational" purposes as well as the more usual "teaching, scientific, literary, artistic" purposes.[169] The designation of "literary" purpose, repeated in various other statutes,[170] might seem sufficiently broad; the addition of "recreational" renders it difficult to imagine a purpose not covered.

Additional uses and purposes specified in statutes embellish the general theme. For example, the Chinese law includes "reference purposes," [171] while the law of Japan permits quotations "to provide for the aims of a book of ethics." [172] The law of Argentina permits the publication of a photographic portrait for "cultural purposes" generally as well as in connection with events of public interest.[173] And compilations and anthologies are frequently granted certain immunities.[174]

The charitable purpose or nonprofit character of a use are sometimes considered significant, but usually in connection with the privilege of performing a work publicly. Thus, the law of Denmark permits the performance of a musical composition not only in connection with teaching but during "popular meetings and * * * festivals" where there is no admission fee or element of private gain. Public performance is also permitted:

when the proceeds are devoted exclusively to charity or to other purposes of public benefit, provided the performers do not receive any payment.[175]

Private or personal use is sanctioned explicitly by more than 20 countries. Many statutes use the terms "private use" or "personal use." [176] Others take a more indirect or limited approach. Thus the law of Brazil permits "the hand making of a copy of any work, provided that such copy is not intended for sale." [177] These provisions presumably sanction reproduction of the entire work.

B. THE AMOUNT OF MATERIAL

A number of statutes prescribe, to various degrees of specificity, the amount of material which may be used freely by persons other than the copyright owner. Such a restriction is ordinarily imposed in conjunction with other limitations. This is not universally true, however. Under the German law, for example, "single passages or minor portions" of a published literary work may be used in any "independent literary work." [178]

---

[169] Art. 19.
[170] *E.g.*, Panamanian law. Article 1924 of the Administrative Code specifies "a definite literary purpose." The law of Chile permits reproduction of recitations and short extracts in "scientific, *literary* or critical works at public lectures or in educational texts." (Art. 11) [Emphasis added.] But such use must be "solely for the purpose of explaining the text of the work."
[171] Art. 24(1).
[172] Art. 30(3).
[173] Art. 31.
[174] *E.g.*, Guatemala, Art. 17.
[175] § 14(h).
[176] *E.g.*, France (Art. 41, 2); Sweden (§ 10, subdivision 1); Austria (§ 42(1)); Turkey, Art. 38.
[177] Art. 666 (VI).
[178] § 19, 1.

Several statutes set specific quantitative limits on the amount of material which may be taken. Thus, the law of Argentina specifies as a limitation "not more than one thousand words from literary or scientific works, or not more than eight bars from musical works." [179] Such material must, in any case, be "indispensable" for the achievement of the enumerated purpose for which such use may be made. One thousand words and four bars of music are prescribed in the statute of Colombia.[180] The law of Sweden limits certain uses to 1 printed page of a literary work [181] and 30 bars of music which cannot exceed one-twentieth of the new collection.[182] And in the Ukraine, elaborate limitations are imposed, with distinctions in the number of "printed characters" based on the length or nature of the literary work; one-quarter of a page is the limit with respect to a musical score and one reproduction with respect to a work of the fine arts.[183]

More frequent are more general statements of the permissible quantity. For example, the Czechoslovakian law mentions "fragments," and "inclusions * * * within reasonable limits." [184] The law of Denmark speaks of "single published brief poems or musical compositions or single passages extracted from published works." [185] Other limitations include "brief extracts" (Egypt, art. 17,1), "brief sections" (Finland, art. 17), "brief portions" (Norway, sec. 9,1), "isolated portions" (Switzerland, art. 26(c)(2)), and "a few sentences" (Turkey, art. 35,1).

C. OTHER CONDITIONS

In many situations where quotations and other use of copyrighted materials are authorized by statute, a requirement that the source be acknowledged is imposed. This condition is found in the statutes of several dozen countries, at least with respect to certain uses. Some statutes insist upon indication of both the author and the source. Thus, the French law requires mention of both and clearly indicates that this is a condition of quotation, reviews, parodies, or dissemination of public speeches.[186] Other statutes, such as that of Sweden, require only the name of the author.[187] Some statutes provide more generally for a "clear indication of source." [188] Section 6 of the United Kingdom Act of 1956 defines its requirement of "sufficient acknowledgement" to include the title or description of the work and, in most cases, the name of the author.

There are a number of statutes which condition the right to copy material upon the absence of an express reservation of rights by the copyright owner. These apply most frequently to the use of newspaper and periodical articles and are often accompanied by a requirement that the source be acknowledged. Characteristic are the statutes of Belgium (art. 14), Columbia (art. 21), Germany (sec. 18), Mexico (art. 7), and Switzerland (art. 25,4).

The absence of a notice by the copyright owner is also a condition in Finland with respect to architectural drawings; [189] in Iran with

---

[179] Art. 10.
[180] Art. 15.
[181] § 11(3).
[182] § 12(2).
[183] § 9(3).
[184] § 17(c), (d).
[185] § 14(a).
[186] Art. 41, 3.
[187] § 13.
[188] *E.g.*, Chile (Art. 11); Germany (§ 25).
[189] § 17, 8.

respect to the first compilation of the works of a deceased author;[190] in Hungary with respect to photographs of press interest;[191] and in the U.S.S.R. with respect to architectural works, exhibition of any works, and the use of literary matter as a text for a musical work.[192] Another condition imposed in some countries is noninterference with the moral right of the author. In other words, the reproduction must be faithful. Thus, in the Swedish law [193] and the new Mexican statute,[194] the reproduced texts may not be "altered." And the provision of the German law authorizing reproduction of news items in the absence of an express prohibition [195] predicates such authorization on the condition that the reprint "does not distort the sense of the article."

D. THE UNITED KINGDOM ACT OF 1956

Section 6 of the new British copyright statute, sets forth "general exceptions from protection of literary, dramatic, and musical works." This clause is the heart of "fair dealing," an area in which great interest had developed in the preparation of the new law. Section 7 enacts special exceptions respecting libraries and archives. As indicated earlier, this specialized area will not be covered extensively in this study.

Section 6 exempts from infringement "fair dealing" for the purposes of (1) research and private study, (2) criticism or review, and (3) conveying news of current events to the public. The uses described in (2) must be accompanied by "sufficient acknowledgement." Subsection (3) applies to broadcasts and news reels as well as newspapers and magazines; with respect to the latter group, acknowledgement is also required.

Subsection (4) of section 6 permits reproduction "for the purposes of a judicial proceeding or for the purposes of a report of a judicial proceeding." This immunity is apparently absolute and is not by its terms limited to "fair dealing" with the copyrighted material for the purposes enumerated.

Subsection (5) limits performing rights by permitting the public reading or recitation under certain conditions. The permitted reading must be (a) by only one person, (b) of a "reasonable extract," and (c) not for the purposes of broadcasting.

An elaborate provision permitting the inclusion of a short passage from a copyrighted work in a collection of mainly noncopyright material intended for school use is found in subsection (6). This provision does not apply to copyrighted works which themselves were published for school use and does not authorize any publisher to use more than two excerpts from the works of any one author during a 5-year period. In addition, the educational purpose of the work must be clearly indicated by the publisher who must make sufficient acknowledgment in connection with the passage. The similarity between this provision and the section of the Dallinger bills discussed above is not surprising; both were patterned after subsection 2(1)(iv) of the British Act of 1911.

---

[190] Art. 246, 3.
[191] § 71, 9.
[192] § 9.
[193] §§ 11, 12.
[194] Art. 15 (c).
[195] § 18.

Section 6 also grants broadcasters the right to make recordings for their internal use in connection with an authorized broadcast. Restriction upon this right insures that the permission applies only to "ephemeral" recordings.

Section 6 does not contain the only group of provisions covering fair use. Section 9 enacts fair dealing provisions with respect to artistic works. Thus, artistic works are treated in similar fashion to literary, dramatic, and musical works with respect to "fair dealing" for the purposes of private study, research, criticism, and review. In addition, permanent public exhibition of an artistic work entitles the public to paint, draw, photograph, film or televise the work, a right accorded also in connection with architectural works. Artistic works may also be reproduced for the purposes of a judicial proceeding or in its report, and may be included in a motion picture or telecast by way of background or incidental use. In addition, a limited use of studies, sketches, molds, and the like, is reserved to the originator of a work, even if he no longer enjoys its copyright.

Section 41 contains special provisions concerning certain uses in schools. It thus is a counterpart to section 6(6) which permits inclusion of passages from copyrighted works for publications designed for school use. Section 41 deals with uses other than by such publications. In rather complex provisions, the section permits the reproduction of the work "in the course of instruction" and performance for a school audience. The provisions are hedged with limitations and exceptions.

It will be noted that the use of the term "fair dealing" in several different contexts recognizes and perpetuates a good deal of judicial interpretation on the scope of the pertinent privileges. The imprecision of the term was recognized in the parliamentary debates on the bill. The Lord Chancellor observed that:

So far as I know, the term [fair dealing] has never been defined in the courts. Obviously, it is difficult to determine.[196]

It is apparent, however, that the provisions of the new British Act were intended to expand the scope of fair dealing. The report of the Copyright Committee of the Board of Trade indicates several respects in which the wording of the 1911 act was being modified so as to expand the scope of fair dealing. For example, the privilege of the critic was expanded to cover use of a work other than that under review.[197] Similarly, the right of summary enjoyed by newspapers was extended to radio and television broadcasts and motion picture newsreels. And in the House of Lords Committee discussion, it was stated that:

It is obviously desirable that the clause which protects fair dealing with literary and dramatic and musical works, should not be narrowly confined * * *.[198]

The view that authors' rights should not be eroded through expansive fair dealing provisions was voiced by Viscount Hailsham in the parliamentary debates. Against an attempt to add a broad authorization of fair dealing with material in certain publicly supported schools,

---

[196] Hansard, *Parliamentary Debates*, House of Lords, November 29, 1955 at 912.
[197] Paragraph 41.
[198] *Parliamentary Debates*, House of Commons, Standing Committee B, at 160 (June 28, 1956).

he argued that an author ought not be penalized for the adaptability of his work for educational purposes.[199]   He urged that:

As public authorities we should set an example in fair treatment of artists, composers and authors.[200]

Section 41 of the Act apparently represents a compromise on this issue.

Whether or not the British Act achieved fairness and effectiveness cannot yet be determined fully. Nevertheless, it represents an elaborate attempt to deal with the problem of fair use by statute, while permitting a substantial measure of judicial flexibility.

E. INTERNATIONAL CONVENTIONS

It has already been noted that article 9 of the Berne Convention recognizes the right, in the absence of express prohibition, to reproduce certain newspaper articles.   Such articles must be on current economic, political, and religious topics.   Article 10(1) also sanctions short quotations from newspaper articles and periodicals.   Related provisions are found in the Pan-American multilateral conventions. Thus the privilege to reproduce or extract from newspapers, periodical literature or other material of current interest is covered by the Montevideo Convention (art. 7 and 8); the Mexico City Convention (art. 8 and 10); the Buenos Aires Convention (art. 11); and the Washington Convention (art. 62).

The Berne Convention expressly reserves for domestic legislation provision for the right to reproduce speeches, lectures, etc.[201] and make certain uses of extracts of other works for press purposes [202] and for the right to include excerpts of literary works in educational or scientific publications, or in chrestomathies, insofar as this inclusion is justified by its purpose.[203]   The latter right is expressly recognized by the Mexico City [204] and Buenos Aires [205] Conventions.   The latter provides:

The reproduction of extracts from literary or artistic publications for the purpose of instruction or chrestomathy does not confer any right of property, and may, therefore, be freely made in all the signatory countries.

The Washington Convention is slightly broader in this connection; article 12 provides:

The reproduction of brief extracts of literary, scientific, and artistic works in pedagogical or scientific works, in chrestomathies, or for the purposes of literary criticism or of research shall be permitted, provided such extracts are reproduced exactly and that their sources are indicated in unmistakable manner.

V. ANALYSIS: THE ISSUES UNDERLYING FAIR USE AND THEIR POSSIBLE LEGISLATIVE RESOLUTION

The foregoing indicates that the concept of fair use is potentially coextensive with the question of infringement.   Employing "fair use" in its broad connotation—such as signifying an appropriation of

---

[199] Hansard, *op. cit.*, note 196, *supra*, at 909.
[200] *Id.* at 911.
[201] Art. 2 *bis.*
[202] Art. 10 *bis.*
[203] Art. 10, 2
[204] Art. 11.
[205] Art. 12.

unprotected ideas—has been said to add "needless confusion to an already confused area of the law." [206] Whether or not the confusion is needless is not altogether clear. But the variations in usage demand careful scrutiny. Particularly troublesome is the question, in any particular case, whether an insignificant amount of copying constitutes fair use or noninfringement on other grounds.

Even within the narrower meaning of fair use, the cases, foreign statutes and domestic legislative proposals cover a wide variety of situations. The common thread in all these situations is the question whether limitations should be imposed on rights which the copyright owner would otherwise enjoy. The key inquiry for legislative solution of the problem of fair use would then seem to be: Why should such limitations be imposed? [207] Several possible answers suggest themselves.

(1) In certain situations, the copyright owner suffers no substantial harm from the use of his work. This may be due to the small amount of material used. Here, again, is the partial marriage between the doctrine of fair use and the legal maxim *de minimis non curat lex*.

Of course, the view has frequently been expressed to the effect that "if the taking is not sufficient to be substantial the question of fair use does not arise." [208] Yet Judge Carter has stated that although a fair use can never be "substantial," [209] it may be "extensive." [210] These apparent contradictions suggest that there is a borderland between (1) the insignificant amount of appropriation which could never, regardless of purpose, effect, acknowledgment or intent, amount to infringement and (2) the amount of appropriation which, in every case constitutes infringement. Within this borderland, the amount used may, in conjunction with other factors, be insufficient to exceed the bounds of fair use.

A use for a purpose different from that fulfilled by the original work might also be considered harmless.[211] This is graphically illustrated by the cases in which the lyrics of a song were printed in the course of a literary production.[212]

Closely related to difference in purpose is difference in medium. The *Loew's* case and the authorities cited therein indicate that mode of expression will not ordinarily preclude infringement; but such statutory provisions as section 12(c) of the Shotwell bill concerning architecture reach an opposite result, possibly on the ground that certain transpositions are not harmful to the copyright owner.

(2) Practical necessity is at times the rationale of fair use. Thus article 10 of the law of Argentina requires that an excerpt be "indispensable" to the purpose of the later work. The *modus operandi* of certain fields requires that the rights of each author yield to a step-by-

[206] Cohen, *op. cit.*, note 7, *supra*, at 46.
[207] See Recht, *Pseudo-quotation in the Field of the Plastic and Figurative Arts*, 17 REVUE INTERNATIONALE DU DROIT D'AUTEUR 85, 96 (1957). Fair use is viewed in II UNESCO COPYRIGHT BULLETIN 2-3 (1949) at 84 as one of several restrictions on copyright. It was there stated: "The second kind of restriction which one finds in almost all copyright laws or jurisprudence is, in the Anglo-Saxon countries, called 'fair use'. This permits reasonable use of the works of another in the form of quotations, excerpts, or résumés, or for private studies, criticism, reporting, etc."
[208] Note, 56 COLUM. L. REV. 589, 595 (1956).
[209] Columbia Pictures Corp. v. National Broadcasting Co., 137 F. Supp. at 350.
[210] Loew's Inc. v. Columbia Broadcasting System, Inc., 131 F. Supp. 165, 175, (S.D. Cal. 1955) *aff'd sub nom* Benny v. Loew's, Inc., 239 F. 2d 532 (9th Cir. 1956), *cert. granted*, 353 U.S. 946 (1957).
[211] Thus, fair use was summarized as "any reasonable use, noncompetitive," by Arthur Farmer, representative of book publishers, in hearings on the amendment of Section 1(c) of the copyright statute. See *Hearings Before Subcommittee No. 3 of the House Committee on the Judiciary on H.R. 3589*, 82d Cong., 1st Sess. (1951).
[212] See note 24, *supra*.

step progress. This consideration is often linked to the constitutional support for fair use as an indispensable tool in the promotion of "science." Practical necessity and constitutional desirability are strongest in the area of scholarly works.

ᴵ Similarly, in reviews of a work, a certain amount of reconstruction is often necessary; and in burlesque, the user must be permitted to accomplish the "recalling or conjuring up of the original." Of more questionable necessity is the use of an earlier work in the preparation of a compilation. However, extensive use of earlier works as guides and checks appears to be common in this type of work which, although perhaps not achieving the intellectual aims inherent in the constitutional objective of copyright, does produce useful publications.

(3) The rights of the copyright owner may often be limited because of a public policy quite apart from any questions of copyright. Thus, the limitations on performing rights in favor of charitable, educational, or religious organizations seem to reflect a policy of indirect Government support for such organizations. In this sense, they are perhaps more akin to tax exemptions than to problems peculiarly related to copyright. Moreover, the right of the Government to use copyright material springs from the unrelated doctrine of sovereign immunity. An independent public policy would also seem to dictate free use of copyrighted material for the purposes of judicial proceedings or reports of judicial proceedings as insured by the new British statute.

(4) It may well be that the theory of implied consent, frequently is fictitious; it thus fails as an overall basis of fair use. But this theory does have vitality in certain areas. There are situations in which authors generally (not necessarily the plaintiff) permit a particular use. Such can be said for reviews and criticism.[213] Perhaps implied consent can be extended to any use which enhances, rather than impairs, the value of the copyrighted work, but such a rule might require fine-line drawing and difficulties of proof. The creation of a "utilitarian" work such as a form book clearly implies consent to put the work to its intended use. More equivocal is the "dedication" of a musical composition to a professional football team, held in *Karll* v. *Curtis Publishing Co.,* [214] to imply consent to any reasonable use associated with the team.

There are two general approaches to the implementation of the various policy considerations discussed above. One approach is the development of broad ground rules for the determination of fair use. These might include general statements of the permissible purposes for which copyrighted material may be used, conditioned with respect to the amount of such material and the effect of the use on the original work. The other approach is to seek to solve specific problems by specific answers.

By and large, statutory provisions, particularly proposals for legislative revision in the United States, have attempted only the latter course. Thus, the Shotwell bill sought to cover such things as recordings by broadcasters for private file use, and incidental infringement in the course of the depiction of current events. It is true that those provisions of foreign laws which specify maximum amounts of material that may be reproduced cover the area of fair use more generally.

---

[213] See Cane, "Why Ask for Permission?", Saturday Review of Literature, July 1, 1950, p. 20.
[214] 39 F. Supp. 836 (E.D. Wis. 1941).

But even the foreign laws are often limited to particular situations or classes of works.

American case law, on the other hand, rarely involves some of the special situations covered by past legislative proposals. Thus, we find no reported cases directly involving literary criticism or review, use of material for the purposes of litigation, personal or private use, or copying by libraries for scholarly use.[215] Rather, the cases have dealt primarily with fringe uses by competitors, particularly in the compilation and lawbook fields, and more recently with parody and burlesque. Accordingly, they reflect, albeit case by case, an attempt to draw more general guidelines.

The fact that cases and statutes frequently deal with different situations can be quite significant. It may indicate that the statutes attempt in some respects to codify established practices which are so well accepted that they do not produce litigation. Perhaps some of the provisions seek to clarify situations involving technical infringements which are ignored by copyright owners. The statute may attempt either to anticipate problems or to effect workable compromises prior to the development of a practical problem into the litigation stage.

In view of the foregoing, the possibilities for treatment of the problem of fair use in a new statute include the following:

(1) *Follow the approach of the Senate committee in 1907 and maintain the present statutory silence on the question.*—This approach would be based on the premise that the 1909 decision has proved neither ill-advised nor out of date. Arguably, the question of fair use, as merely one dimension of the problem of infringement, is as peculiarly susceptible to case-by-case solution as infringement itself. It could be urged that no statute can effectively cover questions of quantity, shadings of purposes and competitive effect and the like. To select narrow areas for solution might be inequitable unless there are special problems of practical significance to be resolved.

This line of argument was suggested by the approach of ASCAP with respect to the incidental infringement provision of the Shotwell bill. As already noted, ASCAP was quite prepared to leave the question to the courts. The society also argued that "there is no exemption under existing law, and no hardship has resulted."[216]

(2) *Recognize the doctrine and grant it statutory status in broad terms, without clarifying the meaning accorded fair use by the courts.*—This approach was followed in the Sirovich bills of 1932 which did not define or elaborate upon the expression "the fair use of copyrighted matter." The bills did, however, require acknowledgement, a condition which could be attached or ignored in a new proposal.[217] This proposal for statutory recognition in general terms may be subject to criticism on the ground that it is superfluous or may, no matter how well drafted, be read as an inadvertent modification of the case law.[218]

(3) *Specify general criteria.*—This would represent the boldest attempt to treat the problem. It could take the shape of codifying the common law, by merely specifying relevant factors such as the quan-

---

[215] See Smith, *op. cit.*, note 67, *supra*, 46 Law Lib. J. at 205.

[216] Memorandum, June 20, 1939, p. 3, 3 Shotwell Papers 227.

[217] A required acknowledgement does vitiate some of the harmful effects of unauthorized appropriation; it could serve as a safety valve against certain piracies which presently would rely on the fair use doctrine if called to account.

[218] See discussion of the effect of the patent law codification in 1952 in Note, 66 HARV. L. REV. 909 (1953).

tity of the material used, the purposes of the use, the noncompetitive and incidental character of the use, etc.   Or it could provide for controlling effect for certain factors, for example, by making acknowledgement a condition precedent, or by specifying the permissible amounts of material that may be reproduced.   A somewhat greater degree of predictability would be the objective of such an approach.

This approach is beset by the practical obstacles facing any attempt to codify common law or to legislate in an area of subtle factual interaction.   It might be that the established judicial doctrines would survive to fill the gaps which might be left by the new statute.

Of course it is possible to specify general criteria in such a way as to curtail as well as enlarge or recognize the judicial doctrines of fair use.   This was done in the Dill bill which permitted no quotation if permission was expressly denied.

(4) *Cover specific situations.*—Recognizing the difficulties of formulating general effective rules in this area, Congress might follow the general approach of past revision proposals and attempt to cover certain specific situations calling for clarification.

(a) There are certain situations which are presently effective and would require mere recognition by the statute.   These stem either from general acceptance as to what the law is, without any reported cases on the subject, or technical violations of copyright which, for practical and other reasons, are never pressed.   These would include the use for the purposes of criticism or review or litigation.

(b) Other situations have not been completely resolved in actual practice.   One of the more notorious of these presently is burlesque or parody.   Legislative solution of this question might take many forms; in the last analysis it would be directed at the question whether or not the burlesque form of entertainment requires special concessions because of the policy considerations discussed above.   The considerations most directly involved appear to be (*i*) the practical necessity of extensive use of the work being burlesqued in order to create the burlesque, and (*ii*) the benefit, rather than harm, conferred upon the original work.

Judge Carter in the *Sid Caesar* case appeared to have been impressed by the argument of practical necessity.   But this argument presupposes the desirability of supporting burlesques.   One writer has suggested that increased protection of copyright owners at the expense of burlesquers is perhaps "to be welcomed as a spur to more original and ingenious entertainment." [219]   The defendants in the *Loew's* case, on the other hand, warned that the death knell to the art of burlesque, predictable from an adverse decision, "would be a frontal attack on freedom in our democracy."

Judge Carter also emphasized in *Loew's* the importance of the commercial nature of the defendant's work, thereby distinguishing burlesque from a more scholarly endeavor.   But it has been noted that:

The trouble with this commercial-noncommercial distinction is that both commercial and artistic elements are involved in almost every work.[220]

Another area which has become disturbed by recent developments is the field of personal use.   Photoduplication devices may make authors' and publishers' groups apprehensive.   The Copyright Charter recently approved by C.I.S.A.C. emphasizes the concern of

[219] Note, 31 NOTRE DAME LAW. 46, 54 (1955).
[220] Note, 56 COLUM. L. REV. 589, 594 (1956).

authors over "private" uses which, because of technological developments, are said to be competing seriously with the author's economic interests. On the other hand, it has been argued that, at least with respect to books, "none of the photographic processes can compete with the book in print either in price per page or convenience of use."[221]

Perhaps another area for special treatment is that of incidental use in motion pictures and broadcasts of public spectacles, dealt with in the Shotwell bill. Whether this is presently an area of controversy is not known.

In covering specific situations, Congress might choose to affirm or reverse the judicial disposition of a particular issue. An indirect example of the latter approach is found in the reaction to the famous British *Colonel Bogey* case [222] wherein a brief excerpt from plaintiff's musical composition was included in a newsreel and deemed an infringement. This gave rise to the provisions in the Duffy and Shotwell bills excusing such incidental infringements.

VI. Summation of the Issues

1. Should a statutory provision concerning fair use be introduced into the U.S. law?
2. If so:
    (a) Should the statute merely recognize the doctrine in general terms and leave its definition to the courts?
    (b) Should the statute specify the general criteria of fair use? If so, what should be the basic criteria?
3. Should specific situations be covered? If so, what specific situations?

---

[221] Shaw, *op. cit.*, note 66, *supra*, at 302.
[222] Hawkes & Son, Ltd. v. Paramount Film Services, Ltd. [1934] 1 Ch. 593; 50 T.L.R. 363.

STUDY NO. 15

PHOTODUPLICATION OF COPYRIGHTED MATERIAL BY LIBRARIES

By Borge Varmer

May 1959

PHOTODUPLICATION OF COPYRIGHTED MATERIAL BY LIBRARIES

I. Introduction

The various methods of photocopying have become indispensable to persons engaged in research and scholarship, and to libraries that provide research material in their collections to such persons. Effective research requires that the researcher be informed of the findings and opinions of others and have an opportunity to study the materials written by them. These materials are often very extensive and appear in a large number of publications. It is here that the libraries provide an indispensable service to research by furnishing the individual researcher with the materials needed by him for reference and study.

The need of researchers for ready access to a mass of materials is present in every field of scholarly investigation, but the problem is exemplified most clearly in the field of scientific and technical research. The body of scientific and technical literature has grown so rapidly during the last few decades that it would be extremely difficult for the individual scholar or researcher to gain access to the works he may need to consult unless he can obtain copies from a library. This is true especially of periodical literature. It would be virtually impossible for a person engaged in research to subscribe to all the periodicals which from time to time may touch upon his field of interest, and even the libraries where he lives may be unable to furnish the necessary material. Nor can libraries be expected to meet the needs of any number of researchers by loan of the copies in their collections. In response to the needs of researchers, most major libraries are equipped to provide them with photocopies of materials in the library's collections. It is invaluable to a researcher to be able to obtain from a central or specialized library photocopies of the various articles he needs for reference and study.

However, much of the materials needed for scholarship and research is of recent date and is under copyright, and the question arises whether the making and furnishing of photocopies of copyrighted material without the permission of the copyright owner is a violation of his exclusive right to copy secured by section 1(a) of the copyright law.[1] It is the purpose of this study to examine this question and to consider possibilities for its solution.

In general the justification for the photocopying of copyrighted material would seem to be founded on the doctrine of "fair use". In this connection it must be borne in mind that there are two distinct aspects of the "fair use" that researchers might make of a copyrighted work. One aspect concerns the making of copies for the sole purpose of reference and study. The other concerns the reproduction in the researcher's writing, by quotation, etc., of the writings of other

---
[1] 17 U.S.C.

49   (815)

authors.   As already indicated, this study deals only with the former aspect.   The latter has been examined elsewhere in connection with a general analysis of the fair use doctrine.[2]

Aside from the aforementioned practice of furnishing photocopies to researchers for their reference and study, libraries make photocopies for a variety of other purposes.   Rare books and manuscripts are photocopied, usually microfilmed, to secure against their destruction or loss, and to obtain copies which may be made accessible to the public without any risk of harm to the often extremely valuable originals.   Similarly, for the purpose of preservation, photocopies are made of newspapers and other items printed on fast-deteriorating pulp paper.   Other similar purposes could also be mentioned.[3] Common for them all is that they mainly serve intralibrary purposes, namely the maintenance and preservation of the collections.   Photocopying for these purposes may also raise some problem as to copyright infringement.   This problem seems less urgent than that caused by the supplying of photocopies to library patrons, but it will be examined briefly in the following.

II. Present Law and Practice

In relation to copyright protection library collections may be divided into three groups of works: (1) published works protected by statutory copyright; (2) unpublished works protected under the common law; and (3) works in the public domain.

A. PUBLISHED COPYRIGHTED WORKS

For published works under copyright, section 1 of the copyright law provides that the copyright owner shall have the exclusive right:

(a) To print, reprint, publish, copy, and vend the copyrighted work.[4]

The copyright law does not specify any limitations on the exclusive right of the copyright owner to "copy" the copyrighted work.   Nevertheless, this right is limited by the doctrine of "fair use" developed by court decisions.   Unfortunately, there are no decisions dealing specifically with photocopying by libraries, or even with the narrower question of a person making photocopies for his own use.   The courts have dealt with the other aspect of fair use referred to above, namely, that of reproducing in a new work an extract taken from the copyrighted work of another.   However, the criteria of fair use developed by the courts in the latter context might furnish some general indication of the permissible scope of photocopying.

The court decisions indicate that the major criteria as to what constitutes fair use are: (1) the size and importance of the extract taken in relation to the copyrighted work as a whole; (2) the nature of the copyrighted work; (3) the purpose for which the extract is taken; and (4) the effect of the use of the extract upon the demand for the copyrighted work.[5]   It can be argued, though at the risk of oversimplification, that the first three criteria are important chiefly

---

[2] See Latman, *Fair Use of Copyrighted Works*, Copyright Law Revision, Study No. 14, in the present committee print.
[3] See Smith, *The Copying of Liberary Property in Library Collections*, 46 LAW LIB. JOURNAL 197 (1953); 47 LAW LIB. JOURNAL 204 (1954).
[4] Section 1 also specifies other exclusive rights of the copyright owner which are not germane to this study.
[5] Latman, *op cit.*, note 2, *supra*, pp. 14–18.

in their relation to the fourth one, and that the ultimate consideration is the competitive effect of the particular use on the market for the copyrighted work.   And it might be observed that the courts have shown a tendency to apply the doctrine of fair use more liberally to scholarly uses than to commercial uses.[6]

It is, of course, a matter of conjecture as to how the courts would apply the doctrine of fair use to photocopying by libraries.   On the basis of the foregoing summation of the criteria, it seems tenable to argue that the supplying of photocopies to individual researchers for the sole purpose of reference and study might be regarded as fair use in some circumstances; the bounds of fair use may be passed when the supplying of photocopies would operate to diminish the publisher's market.   Whether the publisher's market would be affected materially would seem to depend upon a number of factors such as whether the work is in print, how much of the work is photocopied, how many photocopies of the same work are supplied to various persons, and the relative cost of a photocopy and a publisher's copy.

Text writers on copyright have rarely dealt with this problem.   One text writer goes so far as to say that it would constitute an infringement "in principle, at least, * * * if an individual made copies for personal use, even in his own handwriting." [7]   Another writer has gone to the other extreme in saying that the only copying restrained by copyright is the making of multiple copies for publication, and that anyone is free to make single copies of an entire work for the personal use of himself or of another person.[8]   Both of these views seem dubious, with no clear support in the court decisions.   It may be that copying for one's own private use, at least by hand, is sanctioned by custom; but other factors would seem to be involved in the making of copies by one person for the use of others.

In the absence of any authoritative ruling on the question, libraries have sought to formulate some practical basis for their photocopying policies.

The first attempt to formulate a uniform library policy regarding photoduplication was the informal "Gentlemen's Agreement" issued in May 1937 as a result of discussion between the Joint Committee on Materials for Research of the American Council of Learned Societies and the Social Science Research Council on the one hand, and the National Association of Book Publishers on the other.   Although this "Gentlemen's Agreement" is without legal force,[9] it is not unimportant.   As stated by Miles O. Price, Law Librarian and Professor of Law at Columbia University: "In effect, it gives some status to fair use, though on an informal basis, and prescribes certain minimum conditions to be observed." [10]   Regardless of its informal character, the "Agreement" reflects what its draftsmen considered a fair balance between the interests of researchers and libraries and the rights of copyright owners, and therefore may serve as a convenient starting point for discussion.

---

[6] *Id.* pp. 10, 11.
[7] WEIL, AMERICAN COPYRIGHT LAW, 406 (1917). That Weil may have been thinking of copies made for other persons, rather than for the maker's own use, is indicated by his next sentence: "That the copies are intended for gratuitous distribution is no defense."
[8] SHAW, LITERARY PROPERTY IN THE UNITED STATES, 98, 99 (1950).
[9] One of the parties to the so-called agreement, the National Association of Book Publishers, has since ceased to exist. The book publishers are now organized in the American Book Publishers Council. Furthermore, the periodical publishers, who publish most of the scientific and technical material of interest to researchers, were not generally members of that Association, and even many book publishers were not members.
[10] See Price, *Acquisition and Technical Processing*, 6 LIB. TRENDS 430 (1958).

The "Gentlemen's Agreement" states in part as follows:

A library, archives office, museum, or similar institution owning books or periodical volumes in which copyright still subsists may make and deliver a single photographic reproduction or reduction of a part thereof to a scholar representing in writing that he desires such reproduction in lieu of loan of such publication or in place of manual transcription and solely for the purpose of research; provided—

    (1) That the person receiving it is given due notice in writing that he is not exempt from liability to the copyright proprietor for any infringement of copyright by misuse of the reproduction constituting an infringement under the copyright law:

    (2) That such reproduction is made and furnished without profit to itself by the institution making it.

The "Agreement" contains a paragraph which purports to exonerate the library from liability for possible infringement. This would not seem to absolve the library from liability (if any) to the copyright owner, but it might make it possible for a library to recover from a patron any damages paid as a result of an infringement suit.

The legal basis for permissible photocopying is stated in a subsequent paragraph of the "Agreement" as follows:

The statutes make no specific provision for a right of a research worker to make copies by hand or by typescript for his research notes, but a student has always been free to "copy" by hand; and mechanical reproductions from copyright material are presumably intended to take the place of hand transcriptions, and to be governed by the same principles governing hand transcription.[11]

There may be some question as to the implications of this last assumption that mechanical reproduction is equivalent to hand transcription. It may be that hand transcription created no practical problem because the extent of copying by hand was ordinarily limited by its nature, while mechanical reproduction by modern devices makes it easy to copy extensively and quickly in any number of copies. Moreover, the fact that hand transcription by a scholar himself has long been considered permissible does not necessarily justify the making of photocopies by others for scholars; thus, the supplying of photocopies as a commercial enterprise could hardly be justified on that premise. These factors were apparently recognized by the provisions of the "Gentlemen's Agreement," quoted above, referring to a "single" photocopy of a "part" of a book or periodical to be furnished "without profit."

In 1941, the American Library Association adopted a "Reproduction of Materials Code" formulated as a statement of policy to be observed by the Association members. The "Code" recognizes that "the final determination as to whether any act of copying is a 'fair use' rests with the courts." But it accepts the "Gentlemen's Agreement" as stating "the practical and customary meaning of 'fair use' applicable to reproduction for research purposes." The main portion of the "Code" is a restatement of the rules of the "Gentlemen's Agreement," but additional rules of caution are incorporated. Thus, the "Code" recommends that, "in all cases which do not clearly come within the scope of the agreement, either the scholar requiring the reproduction or the library to which the request is made should seek the permission of the copyright owner before reproducing copyright material." The "Code" further states:

Special care is called for in the case of illustrations or articles that are covered by a special copyright in addition to the general copyright on the whole book or

---

[11] The "Gentlemen's Agreement" is reproduced in full in 2 JOURNAL OF DOCUMENTARY REPRODUCTION 31 (1939).

periodical.   Attention is called to the fact that a publisher's permission is not legal protection to the library unless the publisher is either the copyright owner or an agent of the owner duly authorized to grant such permission.

Finally, the "Code" states:

Legally there is no distinction between in print and out-of-print copyright material.   Reproduction of in print material, however, is more likely to bring financial harm to the owner of the copyright, and it is recommended that libraries be even more careful than in the case of out-of-print material.[12]

There is little available information as to the current practices of libraries generally in making and supplying photocopies.   Perhaps this much can be said: that libraries differ widely in their practices,[13] and that many of them feel that the present uncertainty as to the permissible scope of photocopying hampers their services to researchers and needs to be resolved.

B. UNPUBLISHED WORKS AND MANUSCRIPTS

In the main, the unpublished works involved in the problem of library photocopying consists of the manuscripts that have been deposited in a library.   With some exceptions not pertinent here, such manuscripts are not subject to statutory copyright, but the authors or their successors have literary property rights under the common law which preclude copying without their consent.   Such common law rights are recognized in section 2 of the copyright law.

The A.L.A. "Code" contains the following provision regarding manuscripts:

Manuscript material is protected by common law but the restrictions on its reproduction are probably less rigid than those on copyright material.   Reproduction may probably be made to assist genuine scholarly research if no publication is involved.   Libraries should, however, be careful to observe any restrictions of copying such material that have been stipulated by the donor.

The "Code" further recommends that libraries seek a definite understanding regarding their rights at the time of each donation.

The contention of the "Code" that manuscript material protected by common law is more susceptible to photocopying than published material protected by statutory copyright may be questioned, inasmuch as the "fair use" doctrine is generally thought not to apply to unpublished works.   However, in the absence of any specific restrictions, the donation of manuscripts to a public library may often imply a dedication to the public domain, or at least an authorization to the library to furnish copies of the material to scholars.   In some instances, though, the situation may be complicated by the fact that the donor is not the owner of the common law literary property.[14]

The special questions involved in the photocopying of manuscripts are outside the scope of this study.

C. WORKS IN THE PUBLIC DOMAIN

Works in the public domain present no copyright problems.   But for ethical reasons, the A.L.A. "Code" cautions against unrestricted reproduction of current material in print though not copyrighted. The "Code" states:

---

[12] The "Reproduction of Materials Code" is reproduced in full in 35 A.L.A. Bull. 64 (1941).
[13] See Bray, *Photocopying and Copyright* in the March and Nov. 1957 issues of SPECIAL LIBRARIES.
[14] For example, the manuscripts given to a library may include letters received by the donor or his predecessor.   The literary property is generally in the writers of the letters or their heirs.

In the case of works (in print) which have not been copyrighted in the United States * * * it is evident that it would not be in the best interest of scholarship to engage in widespread reproduction which would deprive the publisher of income to which he appears to be entitled and might result in suspension of the publication. It is recommended, therefore, that before reproducing uncopyrighted material less than 20 years old, either for sale or for use within the library, libraries should ascertain whether or not the publication is still in print and, if it is in print, should refrain from reproducing whole numbers or volumes or series of volumes.

III. LEGISLATIVE PROPOSALS

There seem to be only two bills which have dealt specifically with the problem of photocopying of copyrighted material by libraries. These are: the Thomas (Shotwell) general revision bill of 1940,[15] and a bill introduced by Senator Lucas in 1944.[16]

A. THE THOMAS (SHOTWELL) BILL, 1940

The Thomas bill (§12) provided in effect that the following shall not be an infringement of copyright:

(g) The making of single copies of an unpublished work lawfully acquired by a library if such copies are made and used for study or research only and not for sale or hire.

(h) The making by a library of one copy of a published work for research purposes and not for sale, exchange, or hire: *Provided,* That—

(i) such work has publicly been offered for sale in a published, limited, or general edition by or with the consent of the author or owner of the particular publication right, at a publication price under such circumstances as to pass title in and to the physical copies thereof; and

(ii) the publication and distribution of said edition has been discontinued and the library has offered by registered mail to purchase a copy from, and tendered the retail publication price plus carriage to, the Register of Copyrights on behalf of the owner of said publication right and such owner thereupon failed for a period of thirty days after written notice from the Register of Copyrights addressed to the owner's last-known address either to send a copy of said published edition to such library or to return or direct the Register of Copyrights to return the tendered payment accompanied by a designation of a place where such copy can lawfully be secured at said price; and

(iii) such owner has not filed with the Register of Copyrights a notice of intention to publish a new edition of such work and such edition has not been published within six months from the filing of such notice; and

(iv) the payment tendered by libraries, as hereinabove provided, shall be deposited with the Register of Copyrights, who shall promulgate regulations for the carrying out of this subsection.

(v) There is hereby created in the Treasury of the United States a trust fund to be known as the copyright trust fund. The Register of Copyrights shall deposit in such fund all moneys received by him from libraries as hereinbefore provided in trust for the persons entitled thereto. At least once each year the Register of Copyrights shall certify to the Secretary of the Treasury for payment through the Division of Disbursement from the copyright trust fund to each person entitled thereto all amounts theretofore received in trust for such person and not previously paid to such person * * *.

Under these complicated provisions, a photocopy of a published work was to be authorized only when the work was out of print, and then only after a time-consuming procedure had been followed to make certain that the copyright owner could not supply a copy; and payment of the established price of a publisher's copy was to be made to the copyright owner through the Register of Copyrights.

The above provisions were drafted by the Shotwell Committee after long discussions on the subject of photocopying for scholarly

---

[15] S. 3043, 76th Cong., 3d Sess. (1940).
[16] S. 2039, 78th Cong., 2d Sess. (1944).

purposes. The position of the scholars had been presented to the Shotwell Committee in a memorandum prepared by the Joint Committee on Materials for Research. The memorandum stated:

> The particular problems in which scholars wish to be assured that their activities are within the protection of the law are these:
>
> (1) They need the right to make copies of any material they read in order to form a part of the body of research notes with which they work. This right is probably theirs by custom, since it is not publication but transcription for use that is involved. Copying is here merely an aid to mental reproduction or digestion. Manual transcription, typescript transcription, photostat, and microcopying should be on the same footing for this purpose. The principle is not different regardless of the technique of copying that is used. The cheapness and efficiency of microcopying mean that the amount of this copying in the collection of research notes will probably be much greater in the future than it has been in the past.
>
> The provisions of the copyright law should leave intact a free right to copy as a part of the normal procedure of research. This right to copy should never be confused with the right to publish. The finished product, the book, that results from research is the object to which the copyright law applies, and not the notes and collection of material that enter into the production of the book.
>
> (2) Under some conditions a library may make, without profit to itself, a copy of some work or a part of some work, and the the research man may use the copy instead of borrowing the book from the library.
>
> A person ordering a copy made (whether in manuscript, typing, photographic, or any other form of reproduction) should bear full responsibility. So long as he uses the copy merely as research material, just as he would use a borrowed book, the matter is covered by (1) above. If he goes beyond this, and by publishing it damages the rights of the copyright owner, he and not the library should be held liable.
>
> (3) A special situation arises in connection with learned journals. The number of these journals is so large, and their availability in America so restricted, that articles in many of them are inaccessible to numerous American scholars. We feel that the authors of these articles usually want their writings to reach colleagues in the field and to be used * * *.
>
> (4) Books out-of-print but still under copyright ought not to become inaccessible to scholarship, and it should be lawful to make copies of such books not alone as research notes but as additions to library resources. In some cases, the wear and tear on a library book is so great that the library in order to protect the original, usually out of print, will photostat or microfilm it and have the public use the copy thus made * * *.
>
> An equitable arrangement would be to create a statutory license for the reproduction of out-of-print books * * *.[17]

The Thomas bill apparently attempted to follow the last recommendation of the Joint Committee on Materials for Research by providing a statutory licensing system for photocopying out-of-print works. The procedures required, however, would have been cumbersome and would have imposed a rather long period of delay before a photocopy could have been made. The Thomas bill would have afforded little or no help in solving the problem of photocopying in the more critical area of articles appearing in recent periodicals.

No action was taken on the Thomas bill.

B. THE LUCAS BILL, 1944

Section 1 of the Lucas bill provided that nothing in the copyright law should be construed—

> to prohibit the Librarian of Congress from making, or having made, and furnishing a copy in whole or in part of any published copyright work in the collections of the Library to the following persons.

---

[17] Memorandum on Copyright on Behalf of Scholarship Presented by the Joint Committee on Materials for Research, July 15, 1938, 1 Shotwell Papers 18. (The memoranda, minutes, and proposals of the Shotwell Committee are collected and paginated in the U.S. Copyright Office.)

Among the persons were Members of Congress and judges (subsec. 1), Federal agencies, and authorized Federal officers in certain circumstances (subsec. 2), and other persons (subsec. 3). This last provision stated:

(3) To any person not acting under subsections 1 and 2 of this section, upon his certification that he cannot otherwise obtain the material and that he desires it for the purpose of private study, research, criticism, review, demonstration, litigation, comment, newspaper summary, or fair use as recognized by the courts, and that he assumes all responsibility and liability for any claim of infringement arising from the use, either by himself or another, of the copy furnished by the Librarian of Congress.

The making of copies by the Librarian of Congress as hereinabove provided shall not be deemed to constitute infringement of copyright.

The Lucas bill applied only to the Library of Congress. It would not have solved the problem for the many other libraries in which much material of value to scholars and researchers is found. No action was taken on the Lucas bill.

IV. FOREIGN LAW

Some of the more recent foreign copyright laws have provisions governing various aspects of photocopying. For the purpose of comparison, the laws of Austria, France, Mexico, and the United Kingdom, will be briefly examined. The new draft laws of Germany and the Scandinavian countries will also be mentioned.

A. AUSTRIA

The copyright law of Austria, law of April 9, 1936, as amended, provides:

§ 42. (1) Any person may produce copies of a work of literature, music, or art for his personal use * * *.

*   *   *   *   *   *   *

(3) Single copies may also be made on order for the personal use of another person. However, such a copy of a work of art may only be made without compensation therefor. The copying for compensation of a work of literature or music, for the personal use of another person ordering the copy, may not be made by means other than in longhand or by typewriter except when it concerns minor parts of a work, or an unpublished work, or a work which is out of print.

While a person who makes his own copies or who supplies copies free of charge may avail himself of any copying technique, including photocopying, certain restrictions apply when copies are supplied "for compensation." Whether a charge of the actual cost of making the copy would constitute "compensation" is not clear. Dr. Wilhelm Peter, who has written an extensive commentary on the Austrian copyright law, gives the following interpretation of the above rules as applied to public libraries that make a charge for photocopies. He says:

Photocopies or microfilms of protected works or parts of works kept in public libraries may be made for a charge—without the permission of the author or publisher—when—
(a) there is an order;
(b) the person who has placed the order for a copy does not intend to make the work or the part of the work available to the public (although quotation and other fair use in a published work * * * may be permissbile);

(c) the work is unpublished (manuscripts, dissertations), or the work is out of print, or only a part of a work is wanted.   Articles in periodicals are in this respect to be considered as works and not parts of works.[18]

Under this interpretation by Dr. Peter, it would seem that a library making a charge therefor may supply a photocopy of an article in a periodical only when the periodical is out of print.   The basis for this conclusion is not clear.

The Austrian law does not mention intralibrary photocopying.

B. FRANCE

The French copyright law of March 11, 1957, does not provide rules for library photocopying.   Private copying is permitted under article 41, which excepts from copyright protection:

(2) Copies or reproductions reserved strictly for the private use of the copyist and not intended for collective use, with the exception of copies of works of art * * *.

While this provision permits a person to make copies by any means, including photocopying, for his own private use, nothing is said about having such copies made by libraries or by other persons. The effect of the French law in this latter respect is not clear.

C. GERMAN FEDERAL REPUBLIC

The German copyright law of June 19, 1909, as amended, provides in section 15, second paragraph:

Multiplication for personal use shall be permitted, provided the multiplication does not serve the purpose of obtaining revenue from the work.

The scope of "personal use" was interpreted in a decision handed down on June 24, 1955, by the Supreme Court of the German Federal Republic (1 ZR 88/54).   The case involved a situation in which an industrial corporation had made a number of photocopies of copyrighted articles for the use of its research staff.   Interpreting section 15, second paragraph, the Court first stated in a dictum that it does not follow as a matter of course that photocopying, as opposed to other multiplication methods (especially hand copying or typewriting), is permissible; and the Court held that, whether or not photocopying is permissible in some instances, photocopying by or for an industrial concern is in no case "multiplication for personal use" within the meaning of the law.

To solve the problems posed by this decision, the German Publishing Association and the German Industrial Association in 1958 signed an agreement stipulating the conditions under which periodical articles may be photocopied by or for members of the Industrial Association. For articles in periodicals less than 3 years old the agreement establishes various bases for the payment of fixed royalties.   For articles which are older than 3 years, no royalties are due.   The agreement further states that "only a few photocopies may be made of each work," and that the photocopies may not be commercially distributed. Subscribing publishers obligate themselves to have photomechanical reproduction rights transferred to them.   In cases where authors permit photocopying free of charge, each imprint is to bear a notice to that effect.

---

[18] PETER, DAS OSTERREICHISCHE URHEBERRECHT 123 (Vienna 1954).

The new German draft law on copyright, which has been published with an extensive report by the Federal German Ministry of Justice,[19] contains the following provision:

§47. (1) Any person may make single copies of a work for his personal use, or may have such copies made free of charge by others. Personal use does not include use for professional or trade purposes.

(2) Any person may make or have made single copies of a work, with the exception of a work of art—

    1. when the copying is made by hand or typewriter;

    2. when the work is unpublished or out of print;

    3. when only a small part of a work is involved, or when the work is an article in a newspaper or periodical.

(3) The copies may not be distributed or used at a public reading, performance, or exhibition, or in a broadcast * * *.

According to the official report accompanying the proposal, subsection (2)2 was drafted to meet the needs of libraries and scientific institutions,[20] while subsection (2)3 is intended to serve the purposes of scholarship and research.[21] The report points out that the reproduction of articles in periodicals tends to affect publishers more than authors, since the latter usually receive only nominal fees for the type of articles of interest in this field. Based on findings by the German Research Association (die Deutsche Forschungsgemeinschaft), the report concludes that periodicals in the field of the humanities generally are in a precarious economic situation but that the same is not true of other technical journals. Consequently, since by far most photocopies are made from such technical journals, which can bear the loss, a photocopying privilege for the benefit of scholarship and research must prevail over the interests of the publishers. Conversely, a general prohibition would not aid the journals dealing with the humanities; their troubles have other sources.[22]

D. MEXICO

The Mexican copyright law of December 29, 1956, in article 15 permits:

(d) The copying by manuscript, machine, photography, photostat, painting, drawing, or microfilm of a published work, provided the copy is for the exclusive use of the person making it * * *.

The law does not provide specifically for library photocopying, but it does contain some far-reaching provisions in article 70, which provides:

ART. 70. The publication of literary, scientific, educational, or artistic works necessary or helpful to the advancement, diffusion, or improvement of science or national culture or education is a matter of public interest.

The Federal Executive may, either *ex officio* or upon application, declare a restriction upon copyright in order to permit the publication of the works referred to in the preceding paragraph in the following cases:

    (I) When for a period of 1 year, there are no copies of the work in the capital of the Republic and in three of the chief cities in the country;

    (II) When works are sold at such a price as considerably to impede or restrict their general use, to the detriment of culture and teaching.

Although the law does not expressly say so, it seems obvious that the Federal Executive may use its rather broad regulatory powers in this field to permit photocopying for scholarly purposes in the cases described in subsections (I) and (II).

[19] REFERENTENENTWURFE ZUR URHEBERRECHTSREFORM (Bonn 1954).
[20] *Id.* at 158.
[21] *Id.* at 159.
[22] *Id.* at 170.

E. UNITED KINGDOM

The United Kingdom Copyright Act of 1911 (which has been superseded by the recent Act of 1956) contained the following provision in section 2(1):

* * * Provided that the following acts shall not constitute an infringement of copyright:
(i) Any fair dealing with any work for the purposes of private study, research, criticism, review, or newspaper summary; * * *.

Under this provision students were allowed to copy portions of copyrighted books and other copyrighted items in library collections, but it was considered doubtful whether the "fair dealing" exemption applied to copying by libraries. A report issued in 1952 by the Copyright Committee stated:

What comes within the "fair dealing" exemption if done by the student himself (and in this respect no alteration is proposed) would not necessarily be covered if done by the librarian.[23]

In order to resolve the doubt in one area, the Royal Society representing periodical publishers had issued in 1950 a "Fair Copying Declaration" applicable to copying from certain scientific periodicals. This declaration stated in part:

We will regard it as fair dealing for the purpose of private study or research when a non-profit-making organization, such as a library, archives office, museum, or information service, owning or handling scientific or technical periodicals published by us, makes and delivers a single reproduction of a part of an issue thereof to a person or his agent representing in writing that he desires such reproduction in lieu of a loan or manual transcription and that he requires it solely for the purpose of private study, research, criticism, or review, and that he undertakes not to sell or reproduce for publication the copy supplied provided:
1. The recipient of the copy is given notice that he is liable for infringement of copyright by misuse of the copy and that it is illegal to use the copy for any further reproduction.
2. The organization making and furnishing the copy does so without profit for itself.
3. Proper acknowledgement is given to the publication from which the copy is made.
4. Not more than one copy of any one excerpt shall be furnished to any one person.

The new United Kingdom Copyright Act of 1956 provides in section 6(1):

No fair dealing with a literary, dramatic, or musical work for purposes of research or private study shall constitute an infringement of the copyright in the work.

The new Act also contains very detailed rules governing library photocopying. These rules, which are provided in section 7, cover copying by libraries in regard to (1) articles in periodical publications, (2) parts of other published works, (3) complete published works, and (4) unpublished works.

(1) Under subsection (1), the librarian of a qualified library is entitled to make and supply a copy of an article in a periodical. "Article," as defined in subsection (10), includes an item of any description. The class of libraries qualified to exercise the privilege is to be prescribed by regulations made by the Board of Trade. Subsection (2) provides that the Board of Trade in its regulations "shall

[23] Report of Copyright Committee, Cmd. 8662, para. 43 (1952). See COPINGER AND SKONE JAMES ON COPYRIGHT 229 (9th ed. 1958).

make such provision as the board may consider appropriate for securing" (*a*) that the libraries are not established or conducted for profit; (*b*) that copies are supplied for purposes of research or private study; (*c*) that no person may get more than two copies of the same article; (*d*) that no copies extend to more than one article in any one publication; and (*e*) that the person who gets copies pays for them a sum not less than the cost of their production.

(2) Under subsection (3), qualified libraries may also make and supply copies of parts of published literary, dramatic, or musical works other than periodicals. The privilege extends to illustrations in such works (subsec. 9(c)). The conditions prescribed by the regulations of the Board of Trade under subsection (2), as outlined in the preceding paragraph, must be complied with. In addition, this class of copies may not be made or supplied if the librarian knows the name and address of a person entitled to authorize the making of the copy, or if he could ascertain such information by reasonable inquiry. According to subsection (4), the Board of Trade regulations shall make provision appropriate for securing that no copy extends to more than a reasonable proportion of the work in question.

(3) The rules applicable to complete published works are provided in subsection (5). They are similar to those governing parts of published works, except that complete copies may only be supplied to other libraries.

(4) Under subsection (6), unpublished manuscripts in libraries, museums, and other institutions open to public inspection, may be reproduced for purposes of research or private study, or with a view to publication, if more than 50 years have passed since the author died, and more than 100 years have passed since the work was created. Subsection (7) prescribes the conditions under which manuscripts may be incorporated in "new works" and published. In other words, subsection (6) permits copying of old manuscripts with a view to publication, and subsection (7) prescribes the conditions under which publication may take place. The main condition is that notice of intended publication be given as prescribed in the Board of Trade regulations. Furthermore, the identity of the owner of the copyright in the "old work" must not be known to the publisher of the "new work." If these conditions are met, the "new work" as originally published, or any subsequent edition thereof, shall in this respect not be treated as an infringement of the "old work." If subsequent editions incorporate manuscripts not published in prior editions, a new notice of intended publication is required.

In accordance with the provisions of the Copyright Act, the Board of Trade has issued the Copyright (libraries) Regulations of May 17, 1957. Leaving aside matters of detail, two provisions of the Regulations should be noted. (1) In order to assure that a photocopy is made only for the purposes stated in the Act, the person requesting the copy must declare that he needs it for purposes of research or private study, that he has not previously been supplied with a copy of the item requested, and that he will not use it for purposes other than those stated. (2) One copy only may be supplied to the librarian of any library, unless the librarian of the supplying library is satisfied that a copy previously supplied has been lost, destroyed or damaged.

The detailed provisions of section 7 of the new United Kingdom Act represent an elaborate attempt to arrive at a statutory solution of the problems pertaining to library photocopying. As to single articles in a periodical, subsections (1) and (2) appear to adopt the principles of the earlier "Fair Copying Declaration" of the Royal Society. As to other works, the remaining subsections impose conditions that appear to be quite restrictive. They have been criticized as being too complicated and restrictive; and it has been suggested that libraries, instead of attempting to meet the conditions of section 7, may furnish photocopies to students under the more liberal "fair dealing" provision of section 6.[24]

This last suggestion seems questionable. During the discussion of sections 6 and 7 in the Parliamentary Committee, the Parliamentary Secretary to the Board of Trade (Mr. Derek Walter-Smith) made the following observation:

> Clause 6(1) gives to students the right of copying for research or private study, and, as the Committee will see, that is a very broad right which extends to the work as a whole. It is quite appropriate that the particular fair-dealing provision should be in such wide terms, because there are physical inhibitions upon what the student can do which of themselves operate so as not to require any legal reinforcement. A student copies by hand, and therefore he can be given wide rights because he will not physically be able to do more than provide for his genuine personal needs * * *.
>
> A librarian, of course, will make his copies by these new, or fairly new, mechanical processes. There is no physical limitation upon what he can do, because he has got his photocopying apparatus. The librarian is necessarily in rather a different position from that of the student, both in what should be his legitimate requirements and what is his capacity for making copies of the work. It is not suggested, therefore, that he should have such a wide right as the student. It is in this case not appropriate, I think, that the very wide powers in subsection (1) of clause 6 which apply to students should be given to the librarian for the supplying of copies * * *.[25]

After this statement by the Parliamentary Secretary, an amendment which proposed that librarians should be allowed to do for students what they could do for themselves failed to carry.

The provisions of section 7 of the new United Kingdom Act are discussed in the report issued in 1957 by the Canadian Royal Commission on Patents, Copyright, Trade Marks and Industrial Designs.[26] The Canadian Commission recommended that the United Kingdom provisions be adopted in a new Canadian copyright law, but with several liberalizing modifications. The most important modifications suggested were: (1) that section 7(2)(d) be changed so as to permit the supplying of more than one article in any one periodical publication in cases where more than one article relates to the same subject matter; (2) that section 7(2)(e), which requires a payment for photocopies of not less than the cost of producing them, be omitted in the Canadian law; and, (3) that the provision of section 7(3) requiring permission from the copyright owner, if he can be located by reasonable inquiry, for the photocopying of parts of works other than periodicals, be omitted.

The New Zealand Library Association has recently recommended to a goverment committee, which is working on a new copyright law for New Zealand that rules similar to the United Kingdom rules, but with the modifications suggested by the Canadian Commission, be adopted.[27]

---

[24] See Woledge, *Copyright and Libraries in the United Kingdom*, 14 JOURNAL OF DOCUMENTATION 45 (1958).
[25] Parliamentary Debates, House of Commons, Official Report 192 (3 July 1956).
[26] Report on Copyright 57–60 (1957).
[27] 1959 New Zealand Libraries 12.

F. THE SCANDINAVIAN COUNTRIES

The present Danish, Finnish, Norwegian, and Swedish copyright laws do not expressly provide for any right to make copies of copyrighted material. Provisions to permit the making of copies for personal use are proposed in the new draft laws which have been published recently by the respective Governments. Thus, the Swedish draft contains the following provision:

§ 11. A disseminated work may be reproduced in single copies for private use. Such copies may not be used for other purposes.

It is clear from the official reports issued with the draft laws that this provision is intended to cover the making and supplying of photocopies, etc., by libraries and similar institutions although the privilege is not limited to them. According to the Swedish report, the draftsmen considered limiting the privilege to certain types of works. They found, however, that practical conditions, the price of photocopying, etc., would establish appropriate limitations in this field.[28] The draftsmen also considered a compulsory licensing system, but they abandoned this idea, partly because it would be too complicated to administer, and partly because it might mean that Swedish users would have to pay for the use of foreign periodicals while foreign users of Swedish periodicals might not be subjected to such a burden.[29]

The Swedish draft law (but not the other Scandinavian drafts) also contains the following provision:

§ 12. Upon permission of the King, and according to the conditions he shall stipulate, archives and libraries may make photographic reproductions of a work for the purposes of their activities.

V. SUMMARY AND ANALYSIS OF THE PROBLEM

A. GENERAL OBSERVATIONS

It has long been a matter of common practice for individual scholars to make manual transcriptions of published material, though copyrighted, for their own private use, and this practice has not been challenged. Such transcription imposed its own quantitative limitations; and in the nature of the event, it would not be feasible for copyright owners to control private copying and use. But reproduction for private use takes on different dimensions when made by modern photocopying devices capable of reproducing quickly any volume of material in any number of copies, and when copies are so made to be supplied to other persons. Publisher's copies are bought for the private use of the buyer, and in some circumstances a person supplying copies to others will be competing with the publisher and diminishing his market.

Not only is such competition unfair to the publisher and copyright owner, but it may be injurious to scholarship and research. Thus, it has been pointed out that the widespread photocopying of technical

---

[28] UPPHOVSMANNARATT TILL LITTERARA OCH KONSTNARLIGA VERK 191 (Stockholm 1956).

[29] *Id.* at 190.

journals might so much diminish the volume of subscriptions for the journals as to force the suspension of their publication.[30]

At the same time, the availability of a growing mass of published materials is essential to persons engaged in research, and in many situations they must be able to obtain copies for study from libraries (or similar institutions) where the materials are collected. To fulfill this need, libraries must be able to supply photocopies to the extent that it is not practicable to provide published copies for the use of researchers.

The problem, in essence, may be seen as this: How can researchers be supplied with the materials they need for study, without undercutting the publisher's market? Perhaps various limitations can be placed on photocopying to preclude or minimize the potential injury to publishers or copyright owners, without depriving researchers of the materials they need.

B. PHOTOCOPIES FOR INDIVIDUAL RESEARCH

Some guides to the limitations that might be appropriate for supplying photocopies to individuals might be found in the "Gentlemen's Agreement" of 1937, the "Fair Copying Declaration" of the British Royal Society, the proposals presented to the Shotwell Committee, and the foreign laws and proposed laws, all outlined above.

These sources suggest for consideration limitations such as the following: that photocopying be limited to nonprofit institutions; that only one photocopy be supplied to any one individual or organization; that in the case of periodicals photocopies be limited to one or two articles from any issue; that in the case of other works, photocopies be limited to a reasonable portion of the work (though no mathematical formula would seem to be feasible), except that a photocopy of an entire work might be permitted where it is not available from the publisher.

Other conditions for the photocopying might also be suggested for consideration, for example: that on each photocopy the source should be shown and the copyright notice appearing on the source should be reproduced; that the person requesting the photocopy should be required to state in writing that it is to be used only for his private study; that if he requests a photocopy of an entire work, he be required to state in writing that he has made inquiry and has found that the publisher cannot supply him with a copy.

[30] See, for example, Walter J. Murphy, *Should the Copyright Law Be Abolished?* in CHEMICAL AND ENGINEERING NEWS, Oct. 6, 1958. In regard to scientific journals in particular, it may be the publishers rather than the authors who are concerned about photocopying. In a recent Report by the Subcommittee on Patents, Trademarks, and Copyrights of the Senate Judiciary Committee (S. REP. 97, 86th Cong., 1st Sess. 12 (1959)), appears the following: "Most scientists feel that their work is not published to gain any financial reward for the authors but should provide scientific data which other scientists may freely use and build upon to advance the cause of science. On the other hand, the commercial publishers of scientific articles regard copyright protection as essential to meet their costs of publication. A clash between these authors and publishers occurs when public libraries or private industrial subscribers undertake to circulate numerous copies of scientific articles for the benefit of interested scientific personnel. The authors regard such copying as desirable. The publishers feel that it impairs their circulation and revenue."

C. MULTIPLE PHOTOCOPIES FOR CORPORATE RESEARCH

The limitations mentioned above would seem to preclude the making of multiple photocopies by or for a corporate organization for the use of its staff of research workers. This is a problem of growing importance since scientific research is being conducted increasingly by the staffs of corporate organizations. The materials needed in multiple copies for their research staffs are primarily articles in current technical journals. There is probably not the same need for supplying copies of other kinds of works (such as books or older periodicals) simultaneously to several members of a corporation's research staff. One copy of such other works, to be supplied on the same basis as to an individual researcher, might suffice.

Multiple photocopying for the use of a corporation's research staff seems more difficult to justify than the making of a single photocopy. Publishers of technical journals may well feel that such multiple photocopying of current material would seriously curtail their market, and that corporate organizations, particularly those operated for profit, should be expected to buy the publisher's copies in the number needed for their staff.[31]

As noted above, the Supreme Court of the German Federal Republic in 1955 held that such multiple photocopying by an industrial corporation is an infringement of copyright; and a practical solution to the problem has recently been worked out by an agreement between the German publishing and industrial associations, whereby industrial organizations pay royalties for photocopies they make of articles in periodicals less than 3 years old. Some such royalty arrangement appears to be a reasonable solution for this special problem. In fact, a royalty arrangement might be a solution to the photocopying problem in a broader area, as will be mentioned later.

D. PHOTOCOPYING FOR A LIBRARY'S COLLECTIONS

Mention has been made of the need of libraries to make microfilm or other photocopies of items in their collections for their preservation. Also, libraries have occasion to supply other libraries with photocopies of items not otherwise available. In either case, as long as the copies needed are not available from the publisher, photocopying for a library would not appear to prejudice the interests of the publisher or copyright owner.

VI. APPROACHES TO A SOLUTION

A. GENERAL ALTERNATIVES

Two alternative approaches to a solution of the photocopying problem may be considered: (1) to provide by statute for the making and supplying of photocopies for purposes of research and study, or (2) to leave the matter to the working out of practical arrangements between libraries and research groups on the one hand and publisher and author groups on the other.

1. *Statutory provisions.*—Several kinds of statutory provisions might be suggested for consideration. Possible models are found in

---

[31] See Walter J. Murphy, *op. cit.,* note 30, *supra.*

the laws and proposed laws of other countries outlined in part IV of this study, and perhaps in the two prior bills outlined in part III.

(*a*) The statute might provide in general terms that single photocopies may be made by or for any person for his private use only. Such provisions are found in the Austrian law (with limitations added where copies are supplied "for compensation"), in the present German law and the new draft law for the German Federal Republic (the draft law adding limitations where the copies are not made "free of charge"), and in the new draft laws for the Scandinavian countries (except for certain kinds of works).

Such a general provision would serve to establish the right to make and supply single photocopies for the sole purpose of research and study. It would not limit the persons or institutions by whom photocopies could be made and supplied, or the kinds of works or the quantity of any work that might be photocopied.

The addition of some limitations might be considered; for example, that the photocopies be supplied without profit (which may be the purport of the Austrian law and the new draft law for the German Federal Republic).

A broad provision of this character would have the merit of simplicity, but it might open the door to such extensive photocopying as to present the danger of injury to the interests of publishers and copyright owners, unless further limitations were prescribed.

(*b*) A statutory provision might prescribe precise limitations and conditions under which photocopies may be supplied. Thus, in addition to the general limitations of a single copy for private use only, a number of further limitations and conditions are found in the United Kingdom Act of 1956. It limits the privilege of supplying photocopies to nonprofit libraries. Photocopies of periodicals are limited to one article in any issue (the Canadian Commission has recommended that photocopies of more than one article be authorized where the articles relate to the same subject). Photocopies of other literary, dramatic or musical works are limited to a "reasonable proportion" of the work; and they may be supplied only where the librarian does not know and could not ascertain by reasonable inquiry the name and address of the copyright owner (the Canadian Commission has recommended deletion of this last condition). Under this last condition a photocopy of a complete work may be supplied by one library to another. The recipient must pay for the photocopy not less than the cost of its production (the Canadian Commission has recommended deletion of this requirement).

A detailed statutory prescription of this character would have the apparent advantage of fixing, with some degree of certainty, the permissible scope of photocopying. Thus, the statute could define the institutions authorized to make photocopies, the purposes for which photocopies may be made and supplied to others, the kinds of material and how much of each kind may be photocopied, and the conditions under which photocopies may be made and supplied. Precise limitations and conditions could be imposed in these respects to assure safeguarding the interests of publishers and copyright owners. But any such detailed prescription is likely to prove too complex and too restrictive from the standpoint of libraries and researchers. The new United Kingdom Act has been severely criticized on this score.

Moreover, a considerable degree of flexibility seems desirable. New methods of assembling indexes and collections of the voluminous literature in particular fields of research, new devices for the storage and photoreproduction of such materials, and new methods for providing researchers readily with indexes of the literature in their fields and with photocopies of the materials they want, are developing rapidly. A statutory prescription in precise detail may well become outmoded in a relatively short time.

(c) Another possibility would be to provide generally in the statute that nonprofit institutions may make and supply photocopies for research and study and for other specified purposes (e.g., for maintenance of a library's collections or for another library), with the limitations and conditions left to administrative prescription by rules and regulations. This would permit flexibility to meet changing conditions.

2. *Working arrangement.*—Instead of attempting a statutory solution of the photocopying problem, a working arrangement might be agreed upon between the groups concerned. This would have the advantage of flexibility and the further advantage of reflecting a practical accommodation between the views and interests of the several groups. Those groups might agree on a code of practice with which all concerned would be willing to experiment, and such a code could be changed from time to time as experience and changing conditions show to be necessary.

The "Gentlemen's Agreement" of 1937 and the British "Fair Copying Declaration" illustrate this approach to a solution of the problem. Efforts to work out a code of practice have already begun. It may be desirable to await the outcome of those efforts before seeking to resolve the problem by statutory provisions.

A statutory solution would seem to be particularly difficult in the situation of multiple photocopies for the use of a corporation's research staff, and perhaps in other cases where photocopies are to be made by or for a profitmaking organization. The recent agreement between the German publishing and industrial organizations, mentioned above in part IV c, suggests a possible basis for a working arrangement between the interested groups to solve such special problems. Further, the same principle might have broader application in working arrangements for photocopying generally. Thus, in any situations where publishers are reluctant to have photocopies made without their consent, libraries might establish a sort of clearinghouse through which they would obtain permission from publishers to make photocopies or, if required, would collect and remit royalties to the publishers.

B. RECAPITULATION OF BASIC ISSUES

The following appear to be the primary questions to be considered.

1. Should the copyright statute provide expressly for the photocopying of copyrighted works by libraries? If so:

(a) Should the statute merely provide, in general terms, that a library may supply a single photocopy of any work to any person for his personal use in research and study?

(b) Should the statute specify limitations and conditions with respect to:

(1) the kinds of library institutions that may make and supply photocopies?

(2) the purposes for which they may make and supply photo-copies?

(3) the conditions under which they may make and supply photocopies for such purposes?

(4) the extent to which they may photocopy, under the specified conditions, the contents of (1) periodicals and (2) other publications?

(5) the kinds of published material, if any, which they may not photocopy?

(c) Should the statute provide for photocopying in general terms (as in (a) above) subject to limitations and conditions to be prescribed by administrative regulations?

2. Instead of a statutory prescription, would it be preferable to encourage the libraries, publishers, and other groups concerned to develop a working arrangement, in the nature of a code of practice, to govern photocopying by libraries?

STUDY NO. 16

LIMITATIONS ON PERFORMING RIGHTS

By Borge Varmer

October 1958

LIMITATIONS ON PERFORMING RIGHTS

The "performing rights" to be considered in this study include not only the right to "perform" dramatic or musical works, but also the corresponding rights to "deliver" nondramatic literary works and to "exhibit" motion pictures. All of these are commonly spoken of as the "performing rights." The right to perform literary or musical works (dramatic and nondramatic) is dealt with in Part A of this study. The right to exhibit motion pictures, since it has developed differently and involves somewhat different aspects, is dealt with separately in Part B. The same separation is made in the Analysis of Basic Issues in sections I and II of Part C.

Excluded from this study is the special problem of the exemption in section 1(e) of the present copyright statute for the rendition of music by coin-operated machines (the so-called "jukebox exemption"). That exemption has been the subject of special consideration by Congress over the past several years, most recently in the Senate during the 85th Congress. See S. 1870, 85th Congress; hearings before subcommittee of the Senate Committee on the Judiciary, April 23-25, 1958, on S. 1870; and Senate Report No. 2414, 85th Congress.

A. PERFORMING RIGHTS IN LITERARY AND MUSICAL WORKS

I. LEGISLATIVE HISTORY OF THE PUBLIC PERFORMING RIGHTS AND THE "FOR PROFIT" LIMITATION IN THE PRESENT COPYRIGHT LAW

The author's public performing rights [1] were first included in statutory copyright in respect to dramatic works by the act of August 18, 1856.[2] In the act of January 6, 1897 [3] the public performing rights were extended to musical works. Neither the 1856 nor the 1897 act contained any specific limitations on the new rights, except that they related only to "public" performances.

The 1909 act [4] further extended the public performing rights to works prepared for oral delivery. At the same time, the act imposed the "for profit" limitation on the performing rights in works prepared for oral delivery and musical works but not on the performing rights in dramatic works.

Finally, by the act of July 17, 1952,[5] the author's public performing rights were extended to nondramatic literary works, subject to the "for profit" limitation.

While the public performing rights thus date back to 1856, the history of the "for profit" limitation begins with the copyright reform

---

[1] For the purpose of this paper, the words "performing rights" and "performance" are used in relation to all types of presentations, deliveries and performances, etc., and they include the presentation of live and recorded performances as well as performances given by means of broadcasting and telecasting and by means of radio and television receivers.
[2] 11 STAT. 138 (1859).
[3] 29 STAT. 481 (1897).
[4] 35 STAT. 1075 (1909).
[5] 66 STAT. 752 (1952).

of 1909.   The first of the general revision bills [6] introduced in connection with the 1909 reform imposed the "for profit" limitation only
on the performing rights in lectures, sermons, addresses, and similar
works prepared for oral delivery.   The provision can be traced back
to a memorandum draft bill [7] prepared at a very early stage of the
drafting of the 1909 project.   But the source material does not explain why what "for profit" limitation initially was imposed only on
the performing rights in this specific class of works.

However, during the hearings before the House and Senate Committees on Patents in June 1906,[8] the "for profit" limitation was
discussed in connection with section 1(f) which provided for public
performing rights in music, with no limitation.

Section 1(f) was criticized from various sides by people who feared
that the provision would unduly restrict the free enjoyment of music
and thus interfere with legitimate public interests.   Some felt that
copyright should not extend to performing rights,[9] while others, who
did not consider such rights as outside the proper scope of copyright,
argued that they should be limited to certain performances of vital
interest to the author.[10]   To compromise the various views suggested,
Mr. Arthur Steuart, a representative of the American Bar Association,
proposed to limit the author's public performing rights in musical
works to public performances for profit.[11]   He gave the following
reasons for his proposal:

So far as the introduction of the word "profit" is concerned, in the first line of
that section, there has been a very great protest on the part of many people
against the drastic nature of this bill, proposing to punish the public performance
of copyrighted music.   Now, that is the present law.   The present law is just as
drastic as the present bill in the prohibition of the use of copyrighted music.   I
have conferred with many of the music publishers, and I find that none of them
have any objection to the introduction of the words "for profit" * * * so that
the introduction of the words "for profit" in that clause will, I think, relieve the
clause of all of the objections which have been made against it by those who think
it is too drastic a restraint upon the free enjoyment of music.[12]

While the "for profit" limitation was extended to musical works,
the same was not true of dramatic works.   The final report on the
bill [13] gave the following explanation for the different treatment
accorded to dramatic works:

There has been a good deal of discussion regarding subsection (d) of Section 1.
This section is intended to give adequate protection to the proprietor of a
dramatic work.   It is usual for the author of a dramatic work to refrain from
reproducing copies of the work for sale.   He does not usually publish his work in
the ordinary acceptation of the term, and hence in such cases never receives any
royalty on copies sold. * * * If an author desires to keep his dramatic work in
unpublished form and give public representations thereof only, this right should
be fully secured to him by law.   We have endeavored to so frame this paragraph
as to amply secure him in these rights.[14]

---

[6] S. 6330, 59th Cong., 1st Sess. (1906).
[7] U.S. COPYRIGHT OFFICE BULL. No. 10 (1905).
[8] *Hearings Before the House and Senate Committees on Patents on S. 6330 and H.R. 19853*, 59th Cong., 1st
Sess. (June 1906).
[9] *Id.* at 173, 174.
[10] *Id.* at 200, 201.
[11] *Hearings Before the House and Senate Committees on Patents on S. 6330 and H.R. 19853*, 59th Cong., 1st
Sess., at 161 (Dec. 1906).
[12] *Id.* at 162.
[13] H.R. REPORT No. 2222, 60th Cong., 2d Sess. (1909).
[14] *Id.* at 4.

Stephen P. Ladas in his work on international copyright adds another argument. He says:

> The law considers that persons attending a performance of a dramatic work will not ordinarily attend a second performance of the same work and therefore an unauthorized performance, though gratuitous, will cause the author a monetary loss, by depriving him of a potential audience.[15]

Since 1909, the only change in the copyright law of interest in connection with public performing rights and the "for profit" limitation was brought about by the act of July 17, 1952.[16] This act extended, among other things, the author's public performing rights to nondramatic literary works.

The first bill[17] introduced for this purpose placed the performing rights in nondramatic literary works in section 1(d) concerning dramatic works, thereby giving these new rights the same wide scope as dramatic performing rights. The Copyright Office suggested that the new rights be subjected to the "for profit" limitation. The views of the Office were expressed in a letter of April 26, 1951 from Mr. Arthur Fisher, then Acting Register of Copyrights, to Congressman Bryson. The letter which was offered for the record during the hearings on the bill,[18] contained the following statement:

> H.R. 3589 in its present form extends the coverage of subsection (d) to literary works not enumerated in subsection (c), and thus, if enacted, would grant to such works all public performance rights even if not for profit. This might have the result that a teacher reading excerpts from a copyrighted textbook in a schoolroom, a minister reading from a literary work in a church, a scientist at a convention, or a speaker at a civic meeting would be held to have infringed the copyright. It may be questioned whether such a result would be in the public interest.
>
> With respect to performing rights in literary works other than dramas, this office is therefore of the opinion that the limitation "for profit" should be added.[19]

The "for profit" limitation was discussed at great length during the hearings, both in its general application and its specific application in relation to nondramatic literary works.

Mr. John Schulman, representing the Author's League of America, criticized the "for profit" limitation in the following terms:

> I think that if this exclusive right related to public performances that would be sufficient safeguard and we would not have to have the limitation of a public performance at a profit. Sometimes it is difficult to determine whether a huge performance, which actually is for some money-making purpose, is a performance for profit or not, but, nevertheless, it is a public performance which cuts into the author's utilization of this work.
>
> Now, there is no suggestion that it relates to private performances, for instance, in the schools or any place of that sort. Those would be private performances over which no control could be exercised, and that is why I feel that the public is amply protected when the right relates to public performances. * * * [20]

Mr. Herman Finkelstein, representing ASCAP, suggested that the doctrine of fair use would protect the public interest sufficiently.[21]

[15] 2 LADAS, THE INTERNATIONAL PROTECTION OF LITERARY AND ARTISTIC PROPERTY, 783 (1938).
[16] 66 STAT. 752 (1952).
[17] H.R. 3589, 82d Cong., 1st Sess. (1951).
[18] Hearings Before Subcommittee No. 3 of the Judiciary Committee, House of Representatives, 82d Cong., 1st Sess. (1951).
[19] Id. at 14.
[20] Id. at 12.
[21] Id. at 26, 27.

Mr. Arthur E. Farmer, counsel to the American Book Publishers Council, Inc., also felt that the "for profit" limitation should be omitted. He said:

Now, why not include "for profit"? Well, I should say that you should not include "for profit" for three outstanding reasons.

One, there is no more reason for putting a "for profit" provision with respect to literary works other than dramatic works than there has been for 40 years with respect to dramatic works. It has worked beautifully. There has not been a flood of lawsuits.

Second, any reasonable use, noncompetitive, is simply "fair use" and would not give rise to a cause of action.

Third, and affirmatively, if you put in "for profit" you will repeat the unwitting mistake of the 1909 Act, that is, not taking into account the technological advancement. That is what I have mentioned about broadcasting and television stations operating not for profit. I am not talking about a sustaining program or a station which operated for profit. That would come in even if you did not have "for profit" in it, but you are getting a gradual increase of the nonprofit stations. You are going to have that, and the Army has shown that you are going to have an increase in your recordings rather than your printed word as textual material.[22]

The argument for omitting the "for profit" limitation was criticized from various sides. At the close of the hearings the Committee on Copyright of the Association of the Bar of the City of New York submitted a statement for the record. The statement contained the following recommendation:

The committee on copyright recommends very strongly that the protection accorded to the performance of copyrighted nondramatic literary works should be limited to public performance for profit.

The omission from the bill of the words "for profit" affects adversely only church services, school commencements, Fourth of July ceremonies in public squares, and the like. It will not be possible for a minister to read an inspirational copyrighted poem at a funeral service, for a child to recite such a poem at a school commencement, or for a speaker to recite such a poem at a public ceremony, without a license. Obviously, it may not be practicable for the churches, schools, and public assemblies to make licensing arrangements * * * [23]

The committee report [24] summarized the argument for the "for profit" limitation in words almost identical to those used by the Copyright Office in its letter of April 26, 1951.[25]

Generally, the argument for the "for profit" limitation has centered around the public interest in certain civic, educational, and religious activities. The desire of Congress to protect these activities is indicated also by section 104 of the copyright law, which provides:

That nothing in this title shall be so construed as to prevent the performance of religious or secular works such as oratorios, cantatas, masses, or octavo choruses by public schools, church choirs, or vocal societies, rented, borrowed, or obtained from some public library, public school, church choir, or vocal society, provided the performance is given for charitable or educational purposes and not for profit.

It is not clear why this provision was included in the 1909 act. Inasmuch as it also contains the "for profit" limitation, it would seem that the particular activities mentioned therein are already protected by the general "for profit" limitation in section 1. At most, the provision is evidence to the effect that the activities mentioned therein are those which Congress found most deserving of an exemption from the author's performing rights.

---

[22] Id. at 36, 37.
[23] Id. at 42, 43.
[24] H.R. REP. NO. 1160, 82d Cong., 1st Sess. 1 (1951).
[25] Id. at 2. See also hearings, supra, note 19, at 14 (1951).

II. COURT DECISIONS INTERPRETING "PUBLIC PERFORMANCE" AND THE "FOR PROFIT" LIMITATION

In only a few cases have the courts been presented with the question of what constitutes a "public" performance. These cases will be noted in passing. The more difficult and significant question has been the scope of the "for profit" limitation. Although the words "for profit" as such may seem clear and well defined, the complications of modern economic conditions render them ambiguous in certain situations, and it has taken a number of court decisions to give them a more precise meaning. Specifically, the courts have had to deal with practical situations where the profit element in a public performance was more or less indirect. ,

The first important case to deal with such a situation was *John Church Co.* v. *Hillard Hotel Co.* (221 Fed. 229 (2d Cir. 1915)).[26] The litigation involved a musical composition which had been performed in the dining room of a hotel belonging to the defendant   The case turned upon the meaning of the words "for profit" and the court held that the performances in question were not for profit inasmuch as no admission fee or other direct fee had been charged to the patrons hearing the performances.

It was argued for the plaintiff that the performance of music in the hotel restaurant was a means of attracting paying customers and hence was for profit although no direct fee was charged for the music, but this contention was overruled by the court.

The *Hillard* case was followed shortly by *Herbert* v. *Shanley Co.* (222 Fed. 344 (S.D.N.Y. 1915)), involving somewhat similar facts. The song "Sweethearts" from Victor Herbert's comic opera of the same name had been performed in the defendant's restaurant. Victor Herbert and three other persons who wrote the lyrics to Herbert's music sued for copyright infringement, contending that the performance in question infringed the copyright in the dramatico-musical work. Apparently the plaintiffs did not contend that the performance was for profit but rather relied upon the rule that dramatico-musical works cannot be performed publicly without permission even though the performance is not for profit.

The case was decided against the authors, the decision being based partly on the fact that a separate copyright had been secured in the song "Sweethearts" and partly on the holding in the *Hillard* case that public performance of a work in a restaurant is not a performance for profit.

On appeal, the circuit court upheld in substance the decision of the court below. The opinion of the circuit court (229 F. 340 (C.C.A.N.Y. 1916)) concluded:

> That the copyright of the song "Sweethearts" as a separate musical composition, even if valid, is not infringed by its being rendered in a public restaurant where no admission fee is charged, although the performer is privately paid for rendering it by the proprietor of the resort.

Both the *Hillard* and the *Shanley* cases were appealed to the Supreme Court (242 U.S. 591, (1916)). Deciding the two cases to-

---

[26] Discussed in 81 CENT. L.J. 3.

gether, the Supreme Court reversed the decisions below. Justice Holmes, who delivered the opinion for a unanimous Court, concluded:

If the rights under the copyright are infringed only by a performance where money is taken at the door, they are very imperfectly protected. Performances not different in kind from those of the defendants could be given that might compete with and even destroy the success of the monopoly that the law intends the plaintiffs to have. It is enough to say that there is no need to construe the statute so narrowly. The defendants' performances are not eleemosynary. They are part of a total for which the public pays, and the fact that the price of the whole is attributed to a particular item which those present are expected to order is not important. It is true that the music is not the sole object, but neither is the food, which probably could be got cheaper elsewhere. The object is a repast in surroundings that to people having limited powers of conversation, or disliking the rival noises, give a luxurious pleasure not to be had from eating a silent meal. If music did not pay, it would be given up. If it pays, it pays out of the public's pocket. Whether it pays or not, the purpose of employing it is profit, and that is enough.

The "for profit" limitation was again at issue in *Harms* v. *Cohen* (279 Fed. 276 (D.C. Pa. 1922)), dealing with the public performance of music in a motion picture theater. The case goes back to the era of the silent motion pictures when music was played as a live accompaniment to the silent actions of the screen. The defendant contended that no charge was made for the privilege of listening to the playing of music, and that the music was purely incidental, and not a part of the motion picture exhibited by him in the conduct of his motion picture business. But the court, following the Supreme Court ruling in the *Shanley* case, overruled these contentions, holding that the performances in question were for profit.

The same result was reached in *M. Witmark & Son* v. *Pastime Amusement Co.* (298 F. 470 (E.D.S.C. 1924)).[27] The litigation involved a song, also by Victor Herbert, entitled "Kiss me Again" which had been played by an organist in a film theater. Later, in *Irving Berlin, Inc.* v. *Daigle, Same* v. *Russo* (31 F. 2d 832 (5th Cir. 1929)), the playing of records of copyrighted songs in a film theater was held to infringe the right of public performance for profit.

As already indicated, the above cases are all from the silent film era. The situation is somewhat different in regard to sound films.

In *Famous Music Corp.* v. *Melz* (28 F. Supp. 767 (W.D. La. 1939)), an analogy was drawn with the above-mentioned *Irving Berlin* case. It was held that the playing of the sound track of a film was an infringement of the performing rights. However, it should be noted that the ruling was based upon the fact that the film producer had not been authorized to use the music in his film. In other words, there was infringement "at the source," and the decision did not state what rule should be applied to a sound track recorded with due permission from the authors.

This problem has been settled in regard to ASCAP and ASCAP members by the ASCAP Domestic Consent Decree, Civil Action No. 13–95, amended final judgment, entered March 14, 1950. According to section IV, subsection (E), ASCAP is enjoined and restrained from—

Granting to, enforcing against, collecting any moneys from, or negotiating with any motion picture theater exhibitor concerning any motion picture performance rights;

---

[27] Discussed in 10 ST. LOUIS L. REV. 69.

and according to section XII, subsection (B), the members of ASCAP are prohibited from—

granting a synchronization or recording right for any musical composition to any motion picture producer unless the member or members in interest or ASCAP grants corresponding motion picture performance rights in conformity with the provisions of this judgment.

The BMI Consent Decree, Civil Action No. 459, modified consent decree, entered May 14, 1941, does not contain any similar provisions. However, that is probably due to the fact that BMI does not acquire any film recording rights from its members. In any case, there is little reason to believe that BMI or other performing rights societies would be able to follow another course than that outlined for ASCAP. The same probably applies to individual authors who are not members of any of the societies. In any event, there seem to be no instances of infringement suits against film exhibitors for showing films containing copyrighted music recorded on the sound tracks with the permission of the respective authors. Hence, film music can usually be considered as "cleared at the source." [28]

The above-stated practice, however, does not seem to alter the fact established during the silent film era that performances rendered in connection with the commercial exhibition of silent films are public performances for profit, a fact that is relevant for example in regard to the playing of phonograph records before or after the showing of a film.

As the problem of public performance for profit had come up in regard to hotels, restaurants, dancehalls, film theaters and other public places, it was inevitable that it should arise also in connection with the growing broadcasting industry.

In *M. Whitmark & Sons* v. *L. Bamberger & Co.* (291 F. 776 (D.N.J. 1923)) [29] the defendant had broadcast over its radio station a copyrighted song entitled "Mother Machree." The only point at issue was whether or not the performance thus rendered was "for profit."

The defendant, a large department store in Newark, N.J., operated the radio station, WOR, from which vocal and instrumental concerts and other entertainment and information were broadcast. From time to time the station would also broadcast the following slogan: "L. Bamberger & Co., One of America's Great Stores, Newark, N.J.". Relying on the decisions in *Herbert* v. *Shanley Co.* and *Harms* v. *Cohen*, the Court concluded that the radio station was operated for profit and consequently that the playing of the copyrighted song was for profit.

The following year the District Court of Ohio decided the case of *Jerome H. Remick & Co.* v. *American Automobile Accessories Co.*, 298 F. 628 (S.D. Ohio 1924).[30] The facts of this case were almost identical with those of the *Bamberger* case. The defendant, a manufacturer of radios and radio parts, operated a radio station as a part of its business. During one of its broadcasts the copyrighted song "Dreamy Melody" was played. This time, however, the profit element was not the main issue. The defense mainly relied on the contention that the broadcast in question was not a "public performance." The District Court accepted this view, but the decision

---

[28] *Cf.* ROTHENBERG, COPYRIGHT AND PUBLIC PERFORMANCE OF MUSIC, 33 (1954).
[29] 25 COLUM. L. REV. 90.
[30] 34 YALE L.J. 109, 10 ST. LOUIS L.REV. 69 and 13 GEO. L. J. 426.

in favor of the defendants was reversed by the Circuit Court of Appeals, 5 F. 2d 411 (C.C.A. 6th 1925). Judge Mack stated in his opinion:

A performance, in our judgment, is no less public because the listeners are unable to communicate with one another, or are not assembled within an enclosure, or gathered together in some open stadium or park or other public place. Nor can a performance, in our judgment, be deemed private because each listener may enjoy it alone in the privacy of his home. Radio broadcasting is intended to, and in fact does, reach a much larger number of the public at the moment of the rendition than any other medium of performance. The artist is consciously addressing a great, though unseen and widely scattered audience, and is therefore participating in a public performance.

Ruling also on the applicability of the "for profit" limitation, Judge Mack stated:

That, under the Copyright Act, a public performance may be for profit, though no admission fee is exacted or no profit actually made, is settled by *Herbert* v. *Shanley*, 242 U.S. 591. It suffices, as there held, that the purpose of the performance be for profit, and not eleemosynary.

Thus, the rule established by the *Bamberger* case, that commercial broadcasting is public performance for profit, was followed.

Other important problems came up in connection with the growing broadcasting industry, namely whether or not the broadcasting of a public performance constitutes a new public performance; and similarly, whether or not the playing of radio in public places, whether by means of standard radio receivers or more elaborate receiving installations such as those frequently found in large hotels, constitutes a new public performance aside from the broadcast.

The cases involving instances of "multiple performances" do not deal directly with the question of whether a performance is "public" or with the "for profit" limitation. However, they represent an important chapter in the development of the author's performing right, and contribute to a full understanding of the scope of that right. Unfortunately, the problem of "multiple performance" was somewhat obscured by the fact that the early litigations involved instances in which the initial performances were unauthorized.

The first case to come up was *Jerome H. Remick & Co.* v. *General Electric Co.*, 16 F. 2d 829 (S.D.N.Y. 1926).[31] A copyrighted song had been played by an orchestra at a hotel, and "picked up" by the defendant broadcaster. The court held that the broadcasting of the restaurant music was not a separate performance, but that the broadcast of an unauthorized public performance made the broadcaster a contributory infringer.

Another case, *Buck* v. *Debaum*, 40 F. 2d 734 (S.D. Calif. 1929),[32] concerned a situation involving an authorized initial performance. The defendant, a restaurant owner, had turned on a radio in his restaurant. The station he tuned in brought a musical program which included the copyrighted song "Indian Love Call." The plaintiff, who was president of ASCAP and sued on behalf of his organization, contended that the said acts infringed the author's right of public performance for profit although the broadcast of the song had been duly licensed by ASCAP. The court held that the acts of the defendant did not constitute a new performance and consequently that there was no infringement of the said right.

---

[31] 11 MINN. L.REV. 556.
[32] 10 B.U.L. REV. 536 and 9 TEXAS L. REV. 87.

The opinion cited another case decided a few months previously, namely *Buck* v. *Duncan, Same* v. *Jewell-LaSalle Realty Co.*, 32 F. 2d 366 (W.D. Mo. 1929). In doing so, it distinguished the latter which, like the above mentioned *Remick* case, involved an initial performance not authorized by the copyright owners.

The facts were as follows: The Jewell-LaSalle Realty Co. owned and operated a hotel which had a master radio receiving set by means of which it furnished musical entertainment to the hotel guests through speakers installed both in the various public rooms and in the 200 private rooms. Duncan was a broadcaster who, in one of his programs received in the said hotel, had played copyrighted songs without permission.

The issue of importance in this connection was whether or not the "picking up" of the broadcast constituted a new performance. The court held that it did not.

On appeal of the *Jewell-LaSalle* case, 51 F. 2d 730 (8th Cir. 1931), the Circuit Court of Appeals, before deciding the case, certified the following question to the Supreme Court:

> Do the acts of a hotel proprietor, in making available to his guests, through the instrumentality of a radio receiving set and loud speakers installed in his hotel and under his control and for the entertainment of his guests, the hearing of a copyrighted musical composition which has been broadcast from a radio transmitting station, constitute a performance of such composition within the meaning of 17 U.S.C.A., sec. 1(e)?

The Supreme Court, 283 U.S., 191 (1931),[33] in an opinion delivered by Justice Brandeis held that the said acts did constitute a performance of the music, thus establishing the theory of "multiple performance."

Although the Supreme Court clearly established that the "picking up" of a radio broadcast is a separate performance, it did not decide whether or not such performance infringes the authors' performing rights in cases where the broadcasts are authorized by the authors. Justice Brandeis stated in a footnote to the opinion:

> If the copyrighted composition had been broadcast by Duncan with plaintiff's consent, a license for its commercial reception and distribution by the hotel company might possibly have been implied. Compare *Buck* v. *Debaum* (D.C.) 40 F. (2) 734. But Duncan was not licensed; and the position of the hotel company is not unlike that of one who publicly performs for profit by the use of an unlicensed phonograph record.

Having thus received the answer of the Supreme Court, the Circuit Court of Appeals, 51 F. 2d 726 (8th Cir. 1931), decided the main issue. Judge Booth who delivered the opinion concluded as follows:

> It having been thus determined that the specific acts of the hotel proprietor constituted a performance, we are of the opinion that the record discloses that the performance was a public one and was for profit.

In view of Justice Brandeis' footnote and in order to avoid any risk to member authors, the performing rights societies wrote a limitation into their licenses to broadcasters precluding the latter from granting to others by sublicense, express or implied, the right to perform their music publicly for profit. *Society of European Stage Authors and Composers* v. *New York Hotel Statler Co.*, 19 F. Supp. 1 (S.D.N.Y. 1937),[34] involved a license containing such a limitation. Judge

---

[33] Annotated in numerous Law Reviews.
[34] 22 MINN. L. REV. 437.

Woolsen who delivered the opinion in this case stated in a *dictum* that the limitation was a "redundancy."

Because privity is lacking between the broadcaster and the receiver, it would probably be much more difficult to establish a "clearing at the source" in broadcasting than in the case of film exhibition.[35] But a situation similar to that involving film producers and exhibitors exists between the major networks and their affiliated stations, and between the operators of wired music services and their subscribers. In broadcaster's language, the statement that the "music was cleared at the source" means that the license given to a network or to the operator of a wired music service covers also the affiliated stations or the subscribers. The ASCAP and BMI consent decrees mentioned above both make such "clearance at the source" mandatory for broadcasting; see ASCAP Consent Decree, section V, subsection (A), and BMI Consent Decree, section II, subsection (4).

A more recent case, directly involving the "for profit" limitation is that of *Associated Music Publishers* v. *Debs Memorial Radio Fund*, 141 F. 2d 852 (2d Cir. 1944), in which plaintiff alleged that the defendant's broadcast of a copyrighted musical composition entitled "Petite Suite Espagnole" was an infringement of its performing rights. The case is important because of the following facts: the broadcasting organization was a nonprofit organization; only part of its operating expenses was covered by income from commercially sponsored programs; only part of the radio time, one-third on the average, was set aside for such programs; expenses not covered by the income from commercial broadcasts were covered by substantial private donations; and the remainder of the radio time, about two-thirds, was dedicated to unsponsored, so-called sustaining, programs. The alleged infringement had taken place during one of the sustaining programs, and the defendant argued that the broadcast was not for profit.

However, the Circuit Court of Appeals held otherwise. Judge Augustus Hand who delivered the opinion stated in part as follows:

It seems clear that an important radio station which allots one-third of its time to paying advertisers and thus supports a musical program in which a substantial part of a copyrighted musical work is rendered is engaged in a performance for profit, as to which the copyright owner has an exclusive monopoly.

The fees for advertising are obtained in order to aid the broadcasting station to pay its expenses and repay the advances to it by the Forward Association. The "sustaining" programs are similarly broadcast in order to maintain and further build up the listening audience and thus furnish the field from which the paying advertisers may reap a profit. It can make no difference that the ultimate purposes of the corporate defendant were charitable or educational. Both in the advertising and sustaining programs Debs was engaged in an enterprise which resulted in profit to the advertisers and to an increment to its own treasury whereby it might repay its indebtedness to Forward Association and avoid an annual deficit * * *. It is unimportant whether a profit went to Debs or to its employees or to the advertisers. The performance was for profit and the owner had the statutory right to preclude each and all of them from reaping where they had not sown.

In addition to holding, in line with the *Shanley* and *American Automobile Accessories* decisions, that a public performance which is not in itself a direct source of revenue is still "for profit" where it contributes indirectly to the commercial value of other revenue-producing activities, the decision in the *Debs* case seems to hold that a

---

[35] *Cf.* supra pp. 86, 87 concerning clearing at the source in the case of film exhibition.

public performance given by a nonprofit organization whose primary purposes, as stated by the court are "charitable and educational" is nevertheless "for profit" where the performance is, though indirectly, the source of revenue from which the organization defrays its expenses. Query, whether this implies that a public performance given solely for eleemosynary purposes is "for profit" whenever any revenue is to be used to defray expenses.

Concluding the examination of the court cases dealing with the "for profit" limitation, it is interesting to note that the general trend in the development from the *Hillard* case of 1915 to the *Debs* case of 1944 represents a consistent expansion of the "public" and "for profit" concepts in their practical application to various activities.

All the cases examined have involved the performance of musical works. No decisions have been found concerning works of the categories described in section 1(c) of the copyright law. This is natural inasmuch as musical works so far have been the quantitatively most important group of works to be publicly performed. However, the rules established for musical works undoubtedly apply also to oral and nondramatic literary works, a fact that may prove significant in the future.

III. SIMILAR LIMITATIONS IN FOREIGN COPYRIGHT LAWS AND INTERNATIONAL CONVENTIONS

(a) Foreign Laws

In all foreign copyright laws which grant exclusive performing rights to the author, such rights are limited to public performances. A few countries do not further restrict the author's performing rights, while others have statutory limitations similar in effect to the "for profit" limitation in the U.S. law.[36]

The former group includes Argentina, Belgium, the Netherlands, and Switzerland.

As a matter of principle, France also maintains that the author's performing rights may be exercised in regard to all public performances. However, by an agreement between the French Government and the Société des Auteurs, Compositeurs et Editeurs de Musique, the Society has authorized the public performance of musical works in its repertory by musical societies giving gratuitous public performances and by schools in which students and teachers give such performances, on the payment to the Society of a royalty of 1 franc per year.[37] In this way France has met a practical situation while purporting to maintain its fundamental principles.

The group of countries which have enacted limitations on the author's public performing rights similar in effect to the "for profit" limitation in the U.S. law includes Austria, Bulgaria, Canada, Denmark, Germany, Greece, Italy, Norway, Poland, Spain, Sweden, U.S.S.R. and the United Kingdom. The relevant provisions of the laws of a representative selection of these countries will be summarized in order to arrive at a sound basis for comparison between the U.S. and foreign laws in this respect.

---

[36] By "similar" limitations are meant limitations which involve neither permission from the author nor royalties to him. However, provisions establishing various types of legal or compulsory licenses will also be mentioned.
[37] 1 LADAS, *op. cit. supra*, note 16, at 403, 404.

Austria

The copyright law of Austria, law of April 9, 1936, as amended, lists a number of exceptions to the author's exclusive rights. The exceptions are contained in chapter VII entitled "Limitation on Rights of Exploitation." A number of the provisions permit the free use of small items and brief passages of works in various ways including public performance; and in many respects this right goes further than the American doctrine of fair use. Other provisions specify exceptions in regard to public performances. The following exceptions are listed:

(1) Published literary works may be used, to the extent justified by the purpose, in radio broadcasts designated as school broadcasts when use of the work in the schools has been declared permissible by the Board of Education (sec. 45(2)).

(2) Public delivery of published literary works is permitted when the members of the audience pay no admission or other fee and the delivery is not for profit, or when the receipts are destined exclusively for charitable purposes (sec. 50(1)). The provision applies only when the participants receive no compensation (sec. 50(2)).

(3) Public performance of published musical works is permitted when given by means of hand organs, music boxes and similar instruments not reproducing the work in the form of a personal performance (sec. 53(1)); when the work is performed at an ecclesiastical or civil ceremony or at a military event and the members of the audience are admitted without charge (sec. 53(2)); when the members of the audience pay no admission or other charge and the performance is not for any commercial purpose, or when the receipts are destined exclusively for charitable purposes (sec. 53(3)); and when the performance is given in certain places by nonprofessional musicians who comprise a band certified by the competent State government as serving the development of folklore and who do not participate for profit, and where such performance consists mainly of folk music and other music in the public domain (sec. 53(4)).

Canada

The Canadian copyright law, act of June 4, 1921, as amended, contains a number of specific exemptions. Thus, section 17 (2), (f) and (g), provides:

(2) The following acts do not constitute an infringement of copyright: * * *
(f) the reading or recitation in public by one person of any reasonable extract from any published work;
(g) the performance without motive of gain of any musical work at any agricultural, agricultural-industrial exhibition or fair which receives a grant from or is held under Dominion, provincial or municipal authority, by the directors thereof.

Section 17(3) provides:

(3) No church, college, or school and no religious, charitable, or fraternal organization shall be held liable to pay any compensation to the owner of any musical work or to any person claiming through him by reason of the public performance of any musical work in furtherance of a religious, educational, or charitable object.

In the "Report on Copyright" recently issued by the Royal Commission on Patents, Copyright, Trade Marks, and Industrial Designs

(Ottawa, 1957), the Commission made the following recommendation for section 17(2)(f):

> We think also that the reading or recitation in public by one person of a reasonable extract from a published literary or dramatic work, if accompanied by a sufficient acknowledgment should not constitute an infringement of the copyright in the work.   In other words, we recommend the enactment of a provision to the effect of Section 17(2)(f) of our Copyright Act with the addition of the requirement of acknowledgment (Report, p. 56)

Concerning section 17(2)(g) the Commission stated:

> We recommend that it be amended so as to apply to all agricultural and agricultural-industrial exhibitions and fairs which receive grants from the Government of Canada, a province, or a municipality, and that the exemption apply to every musical work performed at the fair except works which are performed in a place fees for admission to which are charged other than the fee payable for admission to the fair itself, and works which are performed for the purpose of advertising or attracting customers to places fees for admission to which are charged other than the fee payable for admission to the fair itself.   This will have the effect of leaving musical works performed by concession holders and the like (and by the fair authorities themselves if a separate admission fee is charged) subject to performing right fees but exempting the rest (Report, p. 61).

Regarding section 17(3) the Commission observed:

> Section 17(3) is unsatisfactory in certain respects.   It does not provide that the public performance of musical works by a religious, charitable or fraternal organization (if it is in furtherance of a religious, educational or charitable object) is not an infringement.   It merely provides that no compensation is to be paid. It therefore, leaves these organizations liable to injuction proceedings.   Moreover the benefit of the exception does not extend to the performers but only to the organizations.   We recommend that subsection (3) of Section 17 be replaced by a provision to the effect that the public performance of any musical work in furtherance of a religious, educational or charitable object, which is authorized by a church, college, school or religious, charitable or fraternal organization, shall not be an infringement (Report, p. 64).

An additional limitation of the author's public performing rights is found in section 50(7) of the Canadian act.   Section 50(7) provides:

> (7) In respect of public performances by means of any radio receiving set or gramophone in any place other than a theatre that is ordinarily and regularly used for entertainments to which an admission charge is made, no fees, charges or royalties shall be collectable from the owner or user of the radio receiving set or gramophone * * *.

As for public performances by means of radio or television receiving sets, the Commission recommended that they continue to be exempted from any obligation to pay royalties.   The Commission stated:

> The broadcast may at any moment it is broadcast, freely and without infringement of anyone's copyright be caused to be seen or heard in public at the receiving end and with or without profit (Report., p. 29).

As for public performances by means of gramophones, the Commission recommended that, with certain exceptions, they should continue to be exempted (Report., p. 113).   As exceptions, the Commission felt (1) that in principle jukeboxes should not be exempted (but it was a question for Parliament to consider whether jukeboxes should remain exempted as long as they were exempted in the United States), and (2) that since wired music systems paid performance fees, contrivances (such as amplifying loud speaker systems) which competed with wired music systems should not be exempted (Report., pp. 112, 113).

Germany

The German copyright law of June 19, 1901, as amended, is still applicable in the German Federal Republic. The law provides a number of specific exceptions to the author's public performing rights. One exception is contained in section 11 which in regard to the performing rights provides as follows:

Copyright in a dramatic or musical work shall also include the exclusive right publicly to perform a work.

The author of a written work or an address shall have the exclusive right to deliver the work in public as long as it has not been published.

Thus, the exception for oral and nondramatic literary works is rather complete. When such works have been published, the author has no performing rights in them at all, except, of course, in dramatized versions of them.

The exceptions to the author's performing rights in musical works are listed in section 27 which reads:

The consent of the person entitled shall not be required for the public performance of published musical works if such performance has no commercial purpose and the audience is admitted free of charge. Otherwise, such performances shall be permitted without the consent of the person entitled thereto:

    1. Where they take place during folk festivals, with the exception of music festivals;

    2. Where the receipts are intended exclusively for charitable purposes and the performers do not receive any payment for their services;

    3. Where they are given by associations and only members and persons belonging to the household of members are admitted as audience.

These provisions shall not apply to the stage performance of an opera, or of any other musical work which includes a text.

The provisions concerning performing rights in the new German draft law on copyright [38] are somewhat different from those now in force. According to section 46 of the draft, a published work may be publicly performed in the following cases:

    (1) When the performance takes place during folk festivals, with the exception of music festivals;

    (2) When the performance takes place during ecclesiastical or national ceremonies to which the public are admitted free of charge;

    (3) When the performance exclusively serves the education of youth;

    (4) When the net income is intended exclusively for charitable purposes and the performers do not receive any special payment from the promoter for their services;

    (5) When the performance has no commercial purpose for the promoter thereof and the performers do not receive any special remuneration from the promoter for their services, provided the audience is admitted free of charge. In the meaning of this provision a performance given at a staff or employees celebration shall not be considered as serving any commercial purposes.

According to section 46 the above exceptions (1–5) shall not apply to dramatic performances of a work.

---

[38] Published with other drafts in the general field of copyright in: REFERENTENENTWURFE ZUR URHEBERRECHTSREFORM (1954).

Sweden

The copyright law of Sweden, Law No. 381 of May 10, 1919, as amended, provides a number of minutely defined exceptions to author's performing rights. These are as follows:

(1) A published writing may be recited publicly otherwise than by reading, and it may be presented publicly by reading if read by a person who is not a professional performer or, if he is a professional performer, if he is not paid for his performance or his performance is given for the purpose of public education and arranged by a state-subsidized public educational organization (sec. 10(2)).

(2) A published musical work may be performed publicly, if either the audience is admitted free of charge and the performance is not for the purpose of private gain, or if the proceeds of the performance are devoted to charity and the performer does not receive any compensation (sec. 10(3)).

(3) A work may be broadcast for the purpose of religious edification or elementary instruction. Moreover, the public performance of a work may be broadcast, if the audience at the performance has been admitted free of charge and the performance does not serve the purpose of private gain. Finally, a work may be broadcast if the broadcast is in the category of newscasts (sec. 10(4)).

The exceptions in the Swedish law, especially those relating to broadcasting, limit the author's performing rights much more than the corresponding "for profit" limitation in the U.S. law.

United Kingdom

The new British copyright law of November 5, 1956, provides an exception to the author's public performing rights in section 6(5), which provides:

(5) The reading or recitation in public by one person of any reasonable extract from a published literary or dramatic work, if accompanied by a sufficient acknowledgment, shall not constitute an infringement of the copyright in the work:
Provided that this subsection shall not apply to anything done for the purposes of broadcasting.

This provision, which is more in the nature of a fair use exception, resembles section 17(2)(f) of the Canadian law. The other exceptions contained in the Canadian law, however, are not found in the British law.[39]

(b) International Conventions

Some, but not all, of the international copyright conventions expressly provide for the author's exclusive performing rights.

The Berne Convention.—The Berne Convention of 1886 undertook to secure the performing rights, and all the revisions thereof contain similar provisions. [40]

The Berne Convention as revised in Brussels in 1948 contains various provisions for the protection of the author's performing rights.

[39] 1 LADAS, *op. cit. supra*, note 16, at 403, lists Great Britain as one of the countries with no limitations on the author's public performing rights.
[40] *Id.* at 394–401 contains a brief and clear account of the development of the performing rights in the various versions of the Berne Convention up till 1948.

Article 11 deals with the author's rights in regard to live performances of dramatic, dramatico-musical, and musical works. Article 11 *ter* adds (nondramatic) literary works to this enumeration. Article 11 *bis* deals mainly with broadcasting rights but also with the right to use receiving sets, etc., for the purpose of public performance. Finally, Article 13 deals with recording rights and the right to use records for the purpose of public performance.

The exclusive performing rights thus formulated are not counteracted by any express limitations thereon. However, that does not mean that the Berne Convention purports to prevent the enactment of limited restrictions of the performing rights. This is clear from the comments of the Berne Office in the preparatory work of the Brussels Conference. It is stated therein that "it would be chimerical to attach such a meaning" to Article 11. This sentence is followed by the following observation:

> The great majority of Union Countries enumerate certain cases in which the performance of protected works is free. Consequently, the exclusive right of the author is restricted in certain circumstances. The following are examples of performances declared to be free by a number of laws: musical performances for cultural purposes, concerts given by military bands, concerts given for charity or organized for various types of civic festivities. It would not be possible in the Convention to list all the exceptions: they are too varied. Many of them are based upon ancient local traditions with which the interested countries are disinclined to interfere. Hence, it is not to be expected that these exceptions will disappear in the future.[41]

The Washington Convention.—Like the Berne Convention, the Washington Convention of 1946 has provided for the author's performing rights without expressly mentioning that certain limitations may be imposed upon these rights. However, there is no doubt that certain limitations are to be found in the laws of adhering countries.

The Universal Copyright Convention.—The Universal Copyright Convention does not expressly mention the performing rights.

In summary, the above examination of foreign copyright laws reveals a great variety of rules whereby the author's performing rights have been restricted to a smaller or larger extent. In all countries, however, the restrictions are in the nature of exceptions. Basically, the public performing rights are considered as being within the author's exclusive domain, but subject to restrictions to a limited extent. These restrictions most commonly relate to noncommercial performances of music and nondramatic literary works for educational, charitable, or other civic purposes.

IV. LEGISLATIVE PROPOSALS FOR REVISION OF THE PRESENT LAW

Several of the bills introduced in Congress between 1924 and 1940 for general revision of the copyright law proposed to change the law with respect to the "for profit" limitation on public performing rights, particularly for music.

The Perkins bill, 1925

The Perkins bill,[42] introduced in January 1925, was the first general revision bill to propose such a change. The bill omitted the "for

---

[41] DOCUMENTS DE LA CONFERENCE DE BRUXELLES, 5–26 Juin 1948, 255 (1951).
[42] H.R. 11258, 68th Cong., 2d Sess. (1925); see also S. 4355, 68th Cong., 2d Sess. (1925).

profit" limitation, and provided instead the following limitation in section 12(1):

That nothing in this act shall be construed to prohibit the performance of copyright musical works by churches or public schools, provided the performance is given for charitable or educational or religious purposes, unless a fee is charged for admission to the place where the music is so used.

During the hearings on the bill[43] the elimination of the "for profit" limitation and the substitution of a new limitation was discussed at some length by Mr. E. C. Mills, representing ASCAP, and Congressman Reid.[44] Mr. Mills expressed satisfaction with the Perkins provision which he considered more fair to the authors than the "for profit" limitation of the present law.

The Vestal bills, 1926–31

The Vestal bills, introduced in Congress from 1926 through 1931, constituted the next major revision project which dealt with this question. The first of these bills,[45] introduced in March 1926, contained no limitations on the author's public performing rights. Several objections were made to this during the hearings on the bill.[46]

Mr. Solberg, then Register of Copyrights, suggested that the omission was not intended by the drafters of the bill. He said:

The enumeration of the special rights granted in the lettered paragraphs of the Vestal bill, Section 1, is substantially identical in both bills, but in the Vestal bill the clause in the Perkins bill (Section 12) is omitted, perhaps through inadvertence, * * *[47]

While the above testimony indicates that Mr. Solberg favored a reinstatement of the form of the limitation provided in the Perkins bill, a brief filed during the hearings by Mr. Alfred L. Smith, representing the Music Industries Chamber of Commerce, advocated reinstatement of the "for profit" limitation.[48]

In spite of these requests, the next Vestal bill,[49] introduced in January 1928, also failed to impose any limitations on public performing rights. The same is true of the third bill,[50] introduced by Congressman Vestal in December 1929. No action is recorded on the 1928 bill, but hearings were held on the 1929 bill.[51] During these hearings, the request for a limitation similar to the Perkins provision was renewed.[52]

In May 1930 Congressman Vestal introduced a general revision bill[53] containing limitations on the author's public performing rights which appear to be somewhat more extensive than those proposed during the hearings on the previous Vestal bills.

Section 1(d) imposed the "for profit" limitation on performing rights in musical works, and furthermore provided:

That nothing in this Act shall be construed to prohibit the performance of copyright musical works by churches, schools, and/or fraternal organizations, provided the performance is given for charitable or educational or religious purposes, unless a fee is charged for admission to the place where the music is so used.

[43] *Hearings Before House Committee on Patents on H.R. 11258*, 68th Cong., 2d Sess. (1925).
[44] *Id.* at 126–131.
[45] H.R. 10434, 69th Cong., 1st Sess. (1926).
[46] *Hearings Before House Committee on Patents on H.R. 10434*, 69th Cong., 1st Sess. (1926).
[47] *Id.* at 232.
[48] *Id.* at 340.
[49] H.R. 8912, 70th Cong., 1st Sess. (1928).
[50] H.R. 6990, 71st Cong., 2d Sess. (1929).
[51] *Hearings Before House Committee on Patents on H.R. 6990*, 71st Cong., 2d Sess. (1930).
[52] *Id.* at 138 and 250.
[53] H.R. 12549, 71st Cong., 2d Sess. (1930).

Although the exemptions so specified would have been covered in most cases by the "for profit" limitation, that would not be true in all cases. For example, fraternal organizations were here mentioned for the first time among the exempted groups.

The bill was reported out of the House Committee on Patents three times in May and June 1930,[54] but none of the reports submitted mentioned the limitations on public performing rights. The bill was debated on the floor of the House of Representatives on June 28, 1930,[55] and further amendments to the provisions on performing rights were adopted. The "for profit" limitation was extended to the author's broadcasting rights provided in section 1(g),[56] and the following provision was added:

> *Provided*, That the provisions of this Act shall not apply to the reception of such work by the use of a radio-receiving set or other receiving apparatus unless a specific admission or service fee is charged therefor by the owner or operator of such radio-receiving set or other receiving apparatus.[57]

The same provision was added to section 1(h) concerning dramatic and dramatico-musical works.[58]

This new limitation constituted a drastic cut in the author's public performing rights under the existing law. It would have reversed the result of the Supreme Court decision in the *Jewell-LaSalle* case mentioned above.

The various provisions limiting the author's public performing rights were apparently the result of a compromise between the opposing sides. The House passed the bill with amendments on January 13, 1931,[59] and sent it to the Senate.[60] The Senate Committee on Patents held hearings on the bill,[61] but these hearings did not bring out anything new regarding limitations on the performing rights. Amendments further limiting the performing rights were accepted during debates on the Senate floor. One amendment included agricultural fairs among the organizations listed in section 1(d),[62] and another exempted not only coin-operated machines but all mechanical reproduction devices from the author's public performing rights.[63] The latter exemption was considered a necessary correlate to the exemption in favor of radio receiving sets. Another amendment permitting free use of phonograph records for broadcasting did not win approval.[64] The Senate adjourned before reaching a vote on the bill.

The Vestal bill probably came closer to enactment than any of the other general revision bills. Although the Vestal bills as passed by the House would have restricted the author's performing rights more than the present law, the various organizations representing the authors supported it in the Senate because of other features they apparently considered more important. The bill was introduced again in December 1931 in both the House [65] and the Senate,[66] but no action was taken by either.

[54] H.R. REP. No. 1689, 1896 and 2016, 71st Cong., 2d Sess. (1930).
[55] 495 CONG. REC., 11996–12018, (1930).
[56] *Id.* at 12009.
[57] *Id.* at 12012.
[58] *Id.* at 12015.
[59] 499 CONG. REC., 2081 (1931).
[60] H.R. 12549, 71st Cong., 3d Sess. (1931).
[61] *Hearings Before the Senate Committee on Patents on H.R. 12549*, 71st Cong., 3d Sess. (1931).
[62] 504 CONG. REC., 6481 (1931).
[63] *Id.* at 6484.
[64] *Ibid.*
[65] H.R. 139, 72d Cong., 1st Sess. (1931).
S. 176, 72d Cong., 1st Sess. (1931).

The Dill bill, 1932

Shortly after, in March 1932, Senator Dill introduced another general revision bill.[67] The Dill bill was based on the 1909 act but contained substantial changes. Section 1(c) concerning performing rights imposed the "for profit" limitation on performing rights in music, and further provided:

> That nothing in this Act shall be construed to prohibit the performance of any copyright work for public entertainment and not for profit, nor the performance of any work for charitable or educational or religious purposes by churches, schools, and/or fraternal organizations, whether for profit or not: *Provided further*, That the use of a machine, instrument, or instruments serving to reproduce mechanically and/or electrically such work or works, except where such reproduction is by radio or wireless broadcast, shall not be deemed a public performance for profit unless a fee is charged for admission to the place where such reproduction or rendition occurs: *Provided further*, That the provisions of this Act shall not apply to the reception of any work by the use of a radio-receiving set or other receiving apparatus unless a specific admission or operating fee is charged therefor by the owner or operator of such radio-receiving set or other receiving apparatus.

The exemptions contained in this provision were much more extensive than those resulting from the "for profit" limitation of the present law, and also more extensive than any alternative proposed in previous bills. The provision brought all works, including dramatic and dramatico-musical works, under the "for profit" limitation and exempted charitable, educational and religious performances given by churches, schools or fraternal organizations, whether for profit or not. Moreover, the provision exempted all performances rendered by radio receiving sets, phonographs, and similar instruments except in cases where an admission or operating fee is charged. The bill was referred to the Committee on patents, but no hearings were held and no further action taken.

The Sirovich bills, 1932

The next general revision project was sponsored by Congressman Sirovich, who, as chairman of the House Committee on Patents, held extensive hearings [68] before he introduced any bills. During these hearings, which were held in February and March 1932, the subject of the author's musical performing rights was discussed at length, but because of the nature of the hearings it was discussed in general terms, and nothing new was said about the proper scope of the performing rights.

The bills introduced by Congressman Sirovich in March, May, and June 1932 all contained a section providing rather extensive exemptions to the author's public performing rights. In the first Sirovich bill [69] the exemptions were listed in section 11 which read as follows:

> None of the remedies given to the copyright owner by this Act shall be deemed to apply to—
>> (a) any performance or delivery of a copyright work which is neither public nor for profit;
>> (b) the public performance of a copyright musical composition not for profit;
>> (c) the performance of a copyright musical work by a recognized charitable, religious, fraternal, or educational organization for charitable, religious, or educational purposes;

---

[67] S. 3985, 72d Cong., 1st Sess. (1932).
[68] *Hearings Before the House Committee on Patents on General Revision of the Copyright Law*, 72d Cong. 1st Sess. (1932).
[69] H.R. 10364, 72d Cong., 1st Sess. (1932).

(d) the reception of any copyright work by the use of a radio receiving set or other receiving, reproducing, or distributing apparatus, except where admission fees, cover charges, operating charges, or similar charges are made;

(e) the performance (except by broadcasting) of any copyright work by means of a disk, record, perforated roll, or film manufactured by or with the consent of the copyright owner or anyone claiming under him, or of a copyrighted sound disk, sound film record, perforated roll or film, except where admission fees, cover charges, operating charges, or similar charges are made; or

(f) the fair use of quotation from copyright matter provided credit is given to the copyright owner.

This section contained most of the exemptions provided in the last Vestal bill and the subsequent Dill bill. The exemption in favor of agricultural fairs adopted by the Senate during its debates on the last Vestal bill was not included. However, during hearings held on the first Sirovich bill, this exemption was proposed again.[70]

The proposal was accepted in modified form, and section 11(c) of the second Sirovich bill [71] provided:

the performance of a copyright musical work by a recognized charitable, religious, fraternal, agricultural, or educational organization for charitable, religious, or educational purposes;

During the continued hearings, Mr. Nathan Burkan, counsel for ASCAP, criticized section 11 as being too extensive. He especially criticized the limitations on dramatic performances.[72]

The Patents Committee reacted favorably to some of this criticism. Thus, the third Sirovich bill [73] removed dramatic and dramatico-musical works from the operation of the proposed exemptions. Section 12(a) of this bill, which corresponds to section 11(a) of the previous bills, reads as follows:

the performance, delivery, or other presentation of a copyright work which is neither public nor for profit; but this subsection shall not apply to the performance or presentation of a dramatic or dramatico-musical work or any exhibition of a motion picture.

Inasmuch as dramatic performing rights, the so-called grand rights, have never been subjected to any limitations, it may be assumed that a limitation of these rights was not deliberately intended. The Committee on Patents held hearings on this bill,[74] but limitations on the public performing rights were not discussed.

The fourth general revision bill introduced by Congressman Sirovich [75] offered no changes in the list of exemptions, but the exemptions previously adopted in favor of agricultural and fraternal organizations were discussed during the hearings on the bill. Mr. Burkan believed that the provision as adopted would not protect the authors against possible "racketeering" by promoters or others who derive profit from the affairs given by such organizations.[76]

As a result of this and previous testimony by Mr. Burkan, an addition proposed by him was made to section 12(c) of the fifth Sirovich bill.[77] The new subsection read:

the performance of a copyright musical work by a recognized charitable, religious, fraternal, agricultural, or educational organization where the entire proceeds

[70] *Hearings Before House Committee on Patents on H.R. 10740*, 72d Cong., 1st Sess. 33 (1932).
[71] H.R. 10740, 72d Cong., 1st Sess. (1932).
[72] *Hearings, supra* note 70 at 189 (1932).
[73] H.R. 10976, 72d Cong., 1st Sess. (1932).
[74] *Hearings Before House Committee on Patents on H.R. 10976*, 72d Cong., 1st Sess. (1932).
[75] H.R. 11948, 72d Cong., 1st Sess. (1932).
[76] *Hearings Before House Committee on Patents on H.R. 11948*, 72d Cong., 1st Sess. 99 (1932).
[77] H.R. 12094, 72d Cong., 1st Sess. (1932).

thereof, after deducting the reasonable cost of presenting the same, are devoted exclusively to charitable, religious, or educational purposes;

After very brief hearings [78] the bill was reported by the Committee on Patents.[79]   Shortly after, on May 24, 1932, it was debated in the House of Representatives.[80]   Various Representatives were of the opinion that the bill had received too little attention, and after a vote it was sent back to the Committee.

Congressman Sirovich introduced a sixth general revision bill [81] in June 1932.   The provision for exemptions in this bill was identical with the one of the previous bill.   No action was taken on it beyond referring it to the Committee on Patents.

The Duffy, Daly, and Sirovich bills, 1935–37

Further general revision bills were introduced in 1935 and 1936 by Senator Duffy and Congressmen Daly and Sirovich.

The Duffy bill,[82] introduced in May 1935, imposed in section 1 the "for profit" limitation on all performances with the exception of performances of dramatic and dramatico-musical works, including motion pictures, and except performances by means of broadcasting.   Moreover, section 17 of the bill, amending section 25 of the act, provided the following exemptions:

(1) The performance of a copyrighted musical work by a recognized charitable, religious, or educational organization where the entire proceeds thereof, after deducting the reasonable cost of presenting the same, are devoted exclusively to charitable, religious, or educational purposes;

(2) The auditory reception of any copyrighted work by the use of a radio receiving set, wired radio, or other receiving, reproducing, or distributing apparatus, or the performance, other than by broadcasting, of any copyrighted work by a coin-operated machine or machine mechanically or electrically operated or by means of a disk, record, perforated roll, or film, manufactured by or with the consent of the copyright owner or anyone claiming under him, except where admission fees, other than for the ordinary occupation by a guest of a hotel or lodging-house room, are charged to the place of operation or, in the case of restaurants, cover charges distinct from the charges for food, or other minimum charges, are made;

The Duffy bill was passed by the Senate on July 31, 1935, and sent to the House of Representatives but Congress adjourned before any action was taken.   The bill was reintroduced in the following Congress and brought up in hearings before the House Committee on Patents, see below.

The Daly bill,[83] introduced in January 1936, contained limitations on the author's public performing rights which did not deviate essentially from the "for profit" limitation of the present law as interpreted by the courts.

The Sirovich bill,[84] introduced in February 1936, contained an interesting innovation inasmuch as it extended the performing rights in dramatic and dramatico-musical works (as well as in motion pictures) to all performances without the qualification that they be "public."   Moreover, the Sirovich bill imposed the "for profit" limitation only on performances of musical works.

---

[78] *Hearings Before House Committee on Patents on H.R. 12094*, 72d Cong., 1st Sess. (1932).
[79] H.R. Report No. 1361, 72d Cong., 1st Sess. (1932).
[80] 515 CONG. REC. 11059–11072, 72d Cong., 1st Sess. (1932).
[81] H.R. 12425, 72d Cong., 1st Sess. (1932).
[82] S. 3047, 74th Cong., 1st Sess. (1935).
[83] H.R. 10632, 74th Cong., 2d Sess. (1936).
[84] H.R. 11420, 74th Cong., 2d Sess. (1936).

Extensive hearings were held in February, March, and April 1936 on the three bills last mentioned.[85] As in the case of previous committee hearings, the performing rights were discussed at great length. Much of the argument was repetitious, but a few new points were brought out.

It was argued, as previously, that under the "for profit" limitation, any barbershop, tavern or small restaurant could be forced to pay royalties for playing a radio on their premises. To this, Gene Buck, president of ASCAP, had the following to say:

> This society does not charge a hotel in this country for the operation of a broadcasting set either in a public room or a private room, any place in these United States, unless the rooms of that hotel are especially wired and downstairs in the office or in some part of that hotel the proprietor exercises a master control.[86]

In Mr. Buck's opinion the exemption favoring radio receiving sets contained in the Duffy bill was not necessary in order to protect barbershops and small hotels, etc., using only ordinary radio receivers, and would unduly restrict the author's performing rights in instances of large-scale receiving systems.

The Duffy provision was defended by Mr. Wallace McClure of the State Department who was a member of the interdepartmental group which had drafted the bill. Mr. McClure feared that the rulings of the *Shanley* and *LaSalle* cases also would affect operators working on a smaller scale than the operators in these cases.[87]

The Sirovich provision on dramatic works (for performing rights not restricted to "public" performance) was criticized as being too extensive.[88] For example, Congressman Church feared that it would unduly interfere with the private sphere.[89]

While some thought that the exemptions in the Sirovich bill were insufficient, others criticized the Duffy bill as being too restrictive.[90]

After the hearings on these three bills there was no further action. The Duffy and Daly bills were reintroduced in 1937,[91] but no action was taken.

The Thomas (Shotwell) bill, 1940

The Thomas bill,[92] introduced in the Senate in January 1940, represents the last serious attempt at general revision of the copyright law. The bill was drafted by the Shotwell committee after extensive conferences on the revision project.

Section 1 of the bill imposed the "for profit" limitation on the author's public performing rights in all works except dramatic and dramatico-musical works, including motion pictures. In addition, section 12(a) exempted:

> The performance of a copyrighted musical composition, with or without words, by a recognized bona fide charitable, religious, or educational organization; *Provided,* That the entire proceeds thereof, after deducting the actual reasonable

---

[85] *Hearings Before the House Committee on Patents on S. 3047, H.R. 10632 and H.R. 11420,* 74th Cong., 2d Sess. (1936).
[86] *Id.* at 17.
[87] *Id.* at 267.
[88] *Id.* at 449 and 462.
[89] *Id.* at 462.
[90] *Id.* at 558.
[91] The Duffy bill was reintroduced as S. 7, 75th Cong., 1st Sess. (1937). The Daly bill was reintroduced, slightly modified, as H.R. 5275, 75th Cong., 1st Sess. (1937). The Guffey bill, S. 2240, 75th Cong., 1st Sess. (1937), is identical with H.R. 5275.
[92] S. 3043, 76th Cong., 3d Sess. (1940).

cost of presenting the same, are devoted exclusively to charitable, religious, or educational purposes: *And provided further*, That, no part of the proceeds of such performance shall be for the private gain of any promoter or similar participant in the enterprise.

There were several references in the conference documents [93] concerning the scope of the author's public performing rights. A comparative study of the drafted proposals of the various interested groups, prepared by Mr. Edward Sargoy, contains the following observations:

Section 1(c). Delivery in Public for Profit.—All groups suggest the retention of this right with the qualification of "in public for profit". The Book Publishers, ASCAP and Radio extend it, however, to all copyrighted works, whereas the Authors retain the present limitation on this right for lectures, sermons, addresses, and like productions.

Section 1(d). Dramatic Performing Rights.—All groups substantially follow the present law which provides not only a public performing right for dramatic and dramatico-musical works, but also a mechanical instrumentality right. The latter gives the copyright owner of the drama or dramatico-musical composition the exclusive right to control the making, vending and performances or exhibitions of his dramatic manuscript by means of mechanical instrumentalities capable of preserving a particular performance and giving subsequent multiple identical reproductions thereof. This applies, of course, to instrumentalities capable of giving visual performances, such as motion picture films, as well as instrumentalities capable of acoustic performances, or both in synchronization.

Section 1(e) Musical Performing and Mechanical Rights.—All the groups retain in substance the present right publicly to perform for profit in respect of copyrighted music as well as the right to control the making, vending and performing of mechanical instrumentalities capable of reproducing the music. However they have eliminated the present compulsory license feature in respect of the mechanical rights.[94]

During one of the committee meetings an interesting discussion on the subject of classical music took place, interesting because most of the argument concerning the "for profit" limitation has centered around popular music. Some members of the Shotwell Committee felt that the composers of serious music should enjoy the same rights as authors of dramatic and dramatico-musical works. The problem was discussed at some length,[95] and a special provision removing certain works of classical music such as oratorios, concertos, and symphonies from the "for profit" limitation was included in the tentative draft. This provision, however, was later eliminated, probably because of the difficulties arising in connection with a proper distinction between the two classes of musical works involved.

The various attempts heretofore to make a general revision of the copyright law ended with the Thomas (Shotwell) bill on which no action was taken.

Very recently, in January and February 1957, two bills [96] were introduced in Congress which provided that reception of radio or television programs or the playing of phonograph records in hotels shall not constitute a public performance for profit. No action was taken on these bills. In substance they are somewhat similar to provisions in some of the general revision bills referred to above.

[93] The records of the conferences have not been published, but have been collected and are available in the Copyright Office (STUDY OF COPYRIGHT, 4 Volumes).
[94] *Id.* Vol. 1 at 225.
[95] *Id.* Vol. 3 at 62–63.
[96] H.R. 673 and H.R. 4572, 85th Cong., 1st Sess. (1957).

B. Exhibition Rights in Motion Pictures.

I. Development under the Copyright Statute

In the Copyright act of 1909 no mention was made of motion pictures as a specific class of copyrightable works. The Townsend Amendment of 1912 [97] added two new classes of works to those enumerated in section 5: Class L, "Motion picture photoplays", and Class M, "Motion pictures other than photoplays".[98]

Section 1 of the act of 1909 specified (as does sec. 1 of 17 U.S.C. today) the exclusive rights of copyright owners, but neither the Townsend amendment nor any subsequent amendment inserted any reference to motion pictures in section 1, so that the statute now contains no provision as to the rights of copyright owners in motion pictures specifically.

Subsection (a) of the present section 1, specifying the right to "print, reprint, publish, copy, and vend the copyright work," relates by its terms to all classes of copyrighted works and therefore embraces motion pictures. The other subsections of section 1, however, enumerate the particular categories of works to which the rights therein specified pertain. Thus, performing rights are specified as pertaining to nondramatic literary works (sec. 1(c)), dramas (sec. 1(d)), and musical compositions (sec. 1(e)). There is no express provision in the statute for the right to exhibit a motion picture.

Even before the Townsend Amendment of 1912, and in fact before the act of 1909, motion pictures had been considered copyrightable and had regularly been registered in the Copyright Office as photographs.[99] Copyright in a motion picture (as a photograph) had been held in the courts to be infringed by unauthorized copying, in *Edison* v. *Lubin* [100] in 1903 and in *American Mutoscope & Biograph Co.* v. *Edison Mfg. Co.*[101] in 1905.

Mention should also be made of another case decided under the law in effect prior to the act of 1909. In *Kalem Co.* v. *Harper & Bros.*[102] the plaintiff was the copyright owner of the novel "Ben Hur." The defendant made an unauthorized motion picture of the novel and sold films which were publicly exhibited in theaters. The Supreme Court, in an opinion by Justice Holmes, held that the exhibition of the motion picture infringed the right of the copyright owner to dramatize the novel,[103] and that the defendant maker of the films was a contributory infringer by furnishing the films for exhibition.[104] It should be noted that this case did not deal with the right of a copyright owner of a motion picture to exhibit it. This question was considered in later court decisions to which we now turn.

---

[97] Act of Aug. 24, 1912, 37 Stat. 488, c. 356.

[98] The Townsend Amendment also amended § 11 of the 1909 Act (now § 12 of 17 U.S.C.) to provide for the deposit to be made for registration of unpublished motion pictures, and amended § 25(b) of the 1909 Act (now § 101(b) of 17 U.S.C.) to add special provisions regarding damages for infringement of other works by means of motion pictures.

[99] Photographs had been made copyrightable as early as 1865 (13 Stat. 540, c. 126) and were mentioned as a class of copyrightable works in all subsequent revisions of the statute including the Act of 1909, § 5(j).

[100] 122 Fed. 240 (2d Cir. 1903), *app. dismissed* 195 U.S. 624 (1904).

[101] 137 Fed. 262 (C.C.N.J. 1905).

[102] 222 U.S. 55 (1911).

[103] This right—to dramatize a nondramatic work—is now provided for in § 1(b) of 17 U.S.C.

[104] The Circuit Court of Appeals, 169 Fed. 61 (1909), had said that the making of the motion picture was not of itself an infringement of the novel since the motion picture did not reproduce the book, here drawing an analogy to the making of perforated music rolls which had been held in White-Smith Co. v. Apollo Co., 209 U.S. 1 (1908) not to infringe the right to make copies of copyright music. The Supreme Court opinion, though it did not discuss this point, based its decision, as did the Circuit Court, on the exhibition of the motion picture as an infringing dramatization of the novel.

II. COURT DECISIONS REGARDING EXHIBITION RIGHTS [105]

The courts, since 1931, have largely, if not completely, filled the gap in section 1 of the statute with respect to exhibition rights for copyrighted motion pictures. Typical of the judicial process in general, this was done on the basis of the actual facts before the court in a series of decisions. The first reported opinion, *Vitagraph* v. *Grobaski* (46 F. 2d 813 (W.D. Mich. 1931)), simply overruled motions to dismiss, for legal insufficiency, complaints brought by the copyright owners of motion pictures against a licensee for infringement of the copyright in giving unlicensed exhibitions. The court merely stated that no reasons had been urged and none occurred to the court for applying so narrow a construction to the copyright statute as to conclude that it did not apply to exhibitors of motion pictures.

The first opinion to give extended consideration to this question was that in *Tiffany Productions* v. *Dewing* (50 F. 2d 911 (D. Md. 1931)). The copyright owners of motion picture photoplays brought a suit for infringement against a licensee who had shown the photoplays at a theater other than the one for which their exhibition had been licensed. The plaintiffs argued that these copyrighted photoplays were a species of dramatic works and had been publicly performed at the unlicensed theater so as to infringe the right granted under section 1(d) to publicly perform a drama. They also suggested an alternative broader ground, to wit, that the unauthorized exhibitions upon the screen were an unauthorized copying of the motion pictures under section 1(a). Judge Coleman held the unauthorized public exhibitions to be infringement of the copyrights in the photoplays under section 1(d). By way of dictum, he observed that the decision in *White-Smith* v. *Apollo* [106] (holding that the making of pianola music rolls was not an infringing copying of copyrighted sheet music) would appear to preclude exhibition of the motion picture from being deemed an infringing copying of the film.

At about the same time, a contrary opinion was handed down by U.S. District Judge Morton in the first of the three *Metro-Goldwyn-Mayer Dist. Corp.* v. *Bijou Theatre Co.* cases (50 F. 2d 908 (D. Mass. 1931)). This court dismissed, for legal insufficiency, a copyright infringement complaint brought against a licensee who had disregarded license limitations by exhibiting the copyrighted photoplay in the theater licensed on an additional unauthorized day. The court held that, motion pictures being commercially unknown in 1909, Congress never intended, in granting the public performing right to dramatic works under section 1(d), to accord any protection other than to those kinds of dramatic works capable of being performed on a stage by living actors in the presence of an audience. On appeal, this decision was reversed in 59 F. 2d 70 (1st Cir. 1932). However, the Court of Appeals seems to have obtained the impression that this was another *Kalem Co.* v. *Harper & Bros.* situation,[107] and that the copyrights sought to be protected in this case against the unauthorized exhibitions of these films were copyrights in the literary or dramatic materials on which the motion pictures were based. Finding no

---

[105] The author is grateful to Mr. Edward A. Sargoy for the information supplied by him regarding the cases herein reviewed in which he participated, and for his advice on other points as noted.
[106] See note 104, *supra.*
[107] See note 102, *supra* and text thereto.

allegations concerning such copyrights in the restored pleading, the court accordingly directed the plaintiffs to amend their complaints so as to show the copyrighted literary or dramatic works upon which the motion pictures were based. Plaintiffs amended their complaints so as to clarify the situation, by alleging that the copyrights involved were originally secured in the photoplay film prints themselves, and were not based on copyrighted literary or dramatic materials. Defendants thereupon moved to dismiss the amended complaints.

The third opinion in this case (3 F. Supp. 66 (D.C. Mass. 1931)), which gives considerably more clarity to the situation, sustained the amended complaints, and discussed in detail the various applicable theories. Judge McLellan found liability on the theory that the photoplays embodied in the film prints were dramatic works and their public performance was therefore protected under section 1(d). He added alternatively (citing the *Kalem Co.* case) that if they were deemed to be nondramatic rather than dramatic works, their exhibition upon the screen would constitute a dramatization of a nondramatic work under section 1(b). Judge McLellan also discussed at length the "copying" theory under section 1(a), quoting from the plaintiff's arguments in such regard, and indicated that he did not necessarily go along with Judge Coleman's dictum in the *Tiffany* case that *White-Smith* v. *Apollo* precluded the theory that the projection of the film upon the screen could be an infringing copying under section 1(a).

Inasmuch as the courts in the *Tiffany* and *Bijou Theatre* cases held for the plaintiffs on the ground that the public exhibition of a photoplay was a public performance of a drama within section 1(d), it was not necessary for the courts in these cases to consider the argument that the projection of a film on the screen was copying within section 1(a). In dicta, Judge Coleman in the *Tiffany* case rejected this argument, drawing an analogy to *White-Smith* v. *Apollo*, and Judge McLellan in the third *Bijou Theatre* decision questioned that analogy.[108]

Several years later, the theory that the projection of a film is copying within section 1(a) was considered in connection with a motion picture that was not a photoplay, by the Second Circuit Court of Appeals in *Patterson* v. *Century Productions et al.*[109] In this case,

---

[108] Mr. Edward A. Sargoy, who was counsel for the plaintiff copyright owners in these cases and other like cases, as well as in the Patterson v. Century Productions case later discussed, has pointed out some interesting aspects of the above cases: "By agreement of counsel for both sides and the court in the first Metro-Goldwyn-Mayer v. Bijou case, when the motion to dismiss the original complaints was made, it was arranged that the briefs submitted by both sides in the Tiffany cases (50 F. 2d 911), in Maryland, be submitted to the Massachusetts court who then reached an opposite result thereon (50 F. 2d 908). The White-Smith v. Apollo dictum was first raised by Judge Coleman in his opinion, and there was no opportunity to argue it, since judgment was rendered for the copyright owners, and the defendants paid the judgment. An opportunity effectively to indicate that White-Smith v. Apollo (with its holding that an auditory test of identity was insufficient to establish infringing copying, and that the infringing copy must have visual identification with the copyrighted work claimed to have been infringed), was not applicable, arose in the argument before Judge McLellan in the third Metro-Goldwyn-Mayer v. Bijou case. There it was claimed that an enlarged visual copy of each image on the copyrighted film was projected upon the screen and met the visual test called for by the White-Smith case. The purpose in urging the broader ground in these cases, since judgment could simply have been obtained under §1(d), the pictures being copyrighted photoplay films which had been publicly exhibited, was two-fold. In the first place, this theory would be inadequate for exhibition rights for the greater volume of copyrighted motion pictures registered under Class M as nonphotoplays; and secondly, both as to copyrighted photoplays and non-photoplays, the industry strongly felt that they must not be limited in their rights to control licensing to exhibitions given publicly."

[109] 93 F. 2d 489 (2d Cir. 1937), *cert. denied* 303 U.S. 655 (1938). Mr. Sargoy advises: "There were cases in Illinois and West Virginia where the Federal Court overruled motions by exhibitor defendants to dismiss for legal insufficiency under the copyright statute, infringement actions brought against them for unauthorized exhibitions of copyrighted newsreels. Unfortunately, the orders overruling the motions to dismiss such complaints were unaccompanied by any opinion. In the reported opinions of Pathe Exchanges, Inc. v. International Alliance, 3 F. Supp. 63 (S.D.N.Y. 1933), and in the lower court opinion in Patterson v. Century Production, et al., 19 F. Supp. 30 (S.D.N.Y. 1937), the courts in their judgments sustained infringement causes of action against exhibitors for unauthorized exhibition of the copyrighted nonphotoplay films, but discussed other points in their opinions."

the plaintiff, copyright owner of a documentary film (registered under Class M as a motion picture other than a photoplay), brought an infringement action against the producer and printer of another film in which they incorporated some 1,000 to 1,500 feet taken from the plaintiff's film, and also against a theater operator who had exhibited the infringing film. The producer and printer defendants were held to have infringed by making copies of the plaintiff's film in violation of section 1(a) when they made a negative and several positives of the footage taken from the plaintiff's film. As to the defendant theater operator (charged only with having exhibited the infringing film at a theater) the court held that by showing the film, he also violated section 1(a) by making infringing copies when he projected the film on the screen, even though the copies of the images so projected upon the screen were temporary. The Court of Appeals said that this case was not analogous to that of *White-Smith* v. *Apollo* where a pianola roll was held not to be an infringing copy of sheet music. Citing favorably Judge McLellan's dictum in the third *Bijou Theatre* decision, the Court of Appeals pointed out that while a pianola roll did not reproduce the written music itself, the projection of the film on the screen did reproduce the copyrighted motion picture.[110]

The question of exhibition as copying has never apparently been raised again since the *Patterson* case .[111]

While the *Patterson* case involved a public exhibition of a non-dramatic motion picture, the copying theory would seem to apply to any exhibition, public or private, of any motion picture by its projection. This suggests the question of whether the exhibition right for motion pictures should extend to private as well as public exhibitions.

It might be pointed out in this connection that the courts have given a broad scope to the term "public performance" in other contexts. For example, the broadcasting of music has repeatedly been held to be a public performance even though the audience consists of many individuals who hear the performance separately in the privacy of their home.[112] However, in the unreported case of *Metro-Goldwyn-Mayer Distributing Corp.* v. *Wyatt and Maryland Yacht Club*,[113] Judge Coleman, who had previously decided *Tiffany Productions* v. *Dewing*, held that the unlicensed exhibition of copyrighted motion picture photoplays at a yacht club, though given before a substantial audience of people, was not a public performance of the photoplays within the meaning of the applicable section 1(d), since only members of the club and their guests could secure admission to the performance. The test of a public performance as laid down by him was whether the performance was open to members of the general public on the same terms as available to those before whom the performance was actually given. This decision seems questionable but no other case in the United States dealing with a similar situation has been found. Decisions in foreign countries which appear to be to the contrary will be noted below.

---

[110] The question of exhibition as copying under § 1(a) was a major issue raised in the application to the United States Supreme Court for a writ of certiorari in the Patterson case. *Certiorari was denied,* 303 U.S. 655 (1938).

[111] Mr. Sargoy advises: "The motion picture industry has relied upon the application of § 1(a) under the Patterson case, not only to cover exhibition rights for all copyrighted motion pictures whether registered as photoplays or non-photoplays, but as not being called upon to limit its licensing rights under copyright to performances given publicly as in the case of copyrighted dramatic works under § 1(d)."

[112] See Jerome H. Remick & Co. v. American Automobile Accessories Co., 5 F. 2d 411 (6th Cir. 1925) and the other cases discussed *supra*, at pages 87–91.

[113] (D.Md. (1932)); oral opinion set forth in Copyright Office Bulletin No. 21, at 203.

III. EXHIBITION RIGHTS IN FOREIGN COPYRIGHT LAWS AND INTERNA-
TIONAL CONVENTIONS

Under the "copying" theory adopted in the *Patterson* case, the exhibition right in motion pictures would seem to extend to all exhibitions,
whether public or not, except perhaps to such private exhibitions as
might be exempted under the doctrine of fair use. In contrast, all
foreign copyright laws dealing with the matter expressly appear to
limit the exhibition right to public exhibitions.

Thus, in Austria, the author's exclusive right includes the right to
"publicly perform" a work of cinematography (sec. 18(1) of law of
April 9, 1936). In Canada, the author has the exclusive right to
"publicly present a cinematographic production of an original character" (sec. 3(1)(e) of the act of June 4, 1921). In France, the author's
exhibition right is defined as the right of "public projection" (art. 27
of law No. 57–296 of March 11, 1957). In Germany, the author has
the exclusive right to "exhibit" cinematographic works "in public"
(sec. 15(a) of the act of January 9, 1907, as amended). In Sweden,
the author's copyright includes the right to "publicly perform" by
means of cinematography (sec. 3 of law No. 381 of May 30, 1919). In
the United Kingdom, the exhibition right is defined as the right of
"causing the film, insofar as it consists of visual images, to be seen in
public, or, insofar as it consists of sounds, to be heard in public" (sec.
13(5) of the Copyright Act of 1956).[114]

While the Universal Copyright Convention (1952) makes no
mention of performing or exhibition rights, the Berne (Brussels)
Convention (1948) provides that the author's exclusive right in cinematographic adaptations or reproductions shall include the right to
authorize the "public presentation and performance" of such adaptations or reproductions (art. 14). The Washington Convention
(1946) is not entirely clear on the point: "Cinematographic works"
are named in article 3 among the kinds of works protected. Article
2(b) provides for all works the right to "represent, recite, exhibit, or
perform it publicly"; while article 2(c) provides for all works the right
to "reproduce, adapt, or present it by means of cinematography."
Perhaps this latter provision is to be understood as relating to the use
of other works in a motion picture. In the copyright laws of a number
of the countries which have ratified the Washington Convention the
right of exhibition in motion pictures appears to be limited to public
exhibitions.

In comparing the effect of the "copying" theory adopted in the
Patterson case with the law governing in other countries, consideration
should be given to whether the concept of public performance or
exhibition has the same scope in the United States as in other countries.
It would seem that the *Maryland Yacht Club* case was decided on the
basis of a much narrower conception of the term "public" than that
applied in other countries.

For example, in Austria, the Supreme Court has ruled that musical
performances organized by a dancing school for its students, both in
connection with instruction and other activities, were public performances within the meaning of the Austrian copyright law and the

---

[114] All foreign copyright laws examined appear to limit the exhibition right in motion pictures to public
exhibitions. On the other hand, the limitation to "public" exhibitions appears to be the only limitation
imposed.

Berne Convention (decision of March 4, 1953; 3 Ob 9/53).   In reaching its decision, the court referred to a case decided by the Supreme Court of Denmark, in which the playing of radio and records in a factory was held to be "public performance" within the meaning of the Danish copyright laws.   One of the tests applied by the Danish court was whether the members of the audience, in this case the factory workers, were united by a "real, intimate bond."   The same test was applied by the Austrian court to the dancing school performances. The latter court made it clear that it was of the opinion that the concept of "public performance" should be uniform in the Berne countries, and its reliance on a decision from another Berne country was an attempt to reach a common formula.[115]

In the United Kingdom, in the case of *Harms & Chappel* v. *Martan's Club Ltd.* ((1927) 1 Ch. 526), the court held that the performance of music in a social club for the entertainment of its members, who paid membership fees, and their guests was a public performance.   Similarly, in *Jennings* v. *Stephens* ((1936) 1 Ch. 469), a performance of a play given exclusively for the members of a women's club, of which any woman residing in the locality could become a member on payment of a small fee, was held a public performance.

The aforementioned cases obviously gave a broader scope to the term "public performance" than the *Maryland Yacht Club* case.   It is true that Judge Coleman thought the case before him was to be distinguished from the *Harms & Chappel* case.   However, in view of the fact that the motion picture exhibition in *Maryland Yacht Club*, like the musical performances in *Harms & Chappel*, was given for a substantial audience consisting of paying club members and their guests, the distinction seems dubious.   It is, of course, impossible to say whether Judge Coleman's relatively narrow concept would be upheld if the question were again presented to the courts in the United States.   The same question might be posed with respect to performances of literary or musical works.

IV. LEGISLATIVE PROPOSALS FOR REVISION OF THE PRESENT LAW

All of the general revision bills introduced between 1924 and 1940 contained provisions basically similar to those in the existing law for the right to perform dramatic works publicly (as well as the right to copy any work and the right to dramatize nondramatic works).   We shall refer here especially to those bills which mentioned the right to exhibit motion pictures specifically.

The Perkins bill of 1925 [116] was the first of the general revision bills which expressly referred to the exhibition of motion pictures. The bill proposed to secure the exclusive right "to reproduce said work [any copyrighted work] in the form of a motion picture and to exhibit the same" (sec. 12(c)).   But query whether this pertained only to the use of other works in a motion picture.   There was no other provision for the right to exhibit motion pictures specifically.

The Vestal bill as passed by the House of Representatives in 1931 [117]

---

[115] In a subsequent case, a lower Danish court held that musical performances given by a youth club for its members were public performances.   (NIR 1953, page 137)   Similarly, performances for members of a musical association were considered public (NIR 1955, page 46).
[116] H.R. 11258, 68th Cong., 2d Sess. (1925).
[117] H.R. 12549, 71st Cong., 3d Sess. (1931).

made no express provision for the right to exhibit motion pictures. However, in section 1, it first provided, for all works generally, that—

copyright includes the exclusive right—To copy, print, reprint, publish, produce, reproduce, perform, render or *exhibit* the copyright work in any form by any means * * *. [Emphasis added.]

But perhaps this general listing of rights was not meant to be unqualified. Section 1 went on to provide that copyright "shall further include" rights specifically enumerated, some of which were qualified, including public performance of dramatic works, but with no express mention of exhibition of motion pictures.

The Sirovich bills of 1932 [118] provided specifically for an exclusive exhibition right in motion pictures. While the first two bills introduced exempted exhibitions which were neither public nor for profit, subsequent bills did not impose these limitations and provided for the exhibition right without qualification (sec. 12).

The Duffy bill of 1935 [119] and the Daly bill of 1936 [120] both specified the exclusive right "to exhibit the copyrighted work publicly if it be a motion picture" while the Sirovich bill of 1936,[121] like previous bills introduced by Congressman Sirovich, granted the right to exhibit motion pictures without limiting the right to public exhibitions. (See sec. 1(d) of each of the bills.)

During the hearings held on these three bills,[122] the Duffy and Daly provisions were opposed by representatives of the motion picture industry. Thus, Mr. Gabriel L. Hess, appearing in behalf of the National Distributors of Copyrighted Motion Pictures, stated:

The first problem is [that] the unfair competition to licensed theatre users from pirated uses at semipublic establishments will be made possible by the proposed unreasonable limitation of the exclusive exhibit[ion] right to only "public" exhibitions by Section 1(d) of the Duffy and Daly bills.[123]

The distinction made in the copyright law between motion picture photoplays and motion pictures other than photoplays was also criticized in a memorandum submitted by Mr. Hess, as follows:

This distinction is confusing, illogical, and unnecessary. One type of motion picture may be more dramatic than the other type of motion picture and at the same time be an actual recordation of true events as distinguished from a staged or fictional motion picture known as a photoplay. Both have this in common, namely, that primarily the only thing of value is exhibition rights which are licensed by the trade in precisely the same manner. Under the customs of the trade and in principle there is no difference whatsoever between a motion picture which is called "photoplay" and a motion picture which is called "nonphotoplay".[124]

The Duffy bill made no distinction between photoplays and other motion pictures while the Daly and Sirovich bills made such distinction for classification and deposit purposes.

The Thomas (Shotwell) bill of 1940 [125] provided for the exclusive right "to exhibit or perform the work if it be a motion picture" (sec. 4(e)). As in the later Sirovich bills, the exhibition right was not limited to public exhibitions. The Thomas bill made no distinction between photoplays and other motion pictures.

---

[118] H.R. 10364, H.R. 10740, H.R. 10976, H.R. 11948, H.R. 12094, and H.R. 12425, 72d Cong., 1st Sess. (1932).
[119] S. 3047, 74th Cong., 1st Sess. (1935).
[120] H.R. 10632, 74th Cong., 2d Sess. (1936).
[121] H.R. 11420, 74th Cong., 2d Sess. (1936).
[122] *Hearings on Revision of Copyright Laws*, 74th Cong., 2d Sess. (1936).
[123] *Id.* at 1027.
[124] *Id.* at 1346.
[125] S. 3043, 76th Cong., 3d Sess. (1940).

The problem of the scope of the exhibition right in motion pictures had come up before the Shotwell Committee in its proceedings which led up to the drafting of the Thomas bill.   While ASCAP and the book publishers proposed a public exhibition right for copyrighted motion pictures, the motion picture industry opposed any limitation to "public" exhibitions.   In a memorandum comparing the proposals drafted by the various interested groups, Mr. Edward A. Sargoy stated:

> The motion picture industry has consistently maintained that the exhibition right for copyrighted motion pictures is not in the same category as a dramatic performing right, particularly in respect of any such limitation as "public."   The pirating user of a copyrighted stage play takes only the directions in the form of the plot and dialogue, but makes his own production, requiring living actors for each infringing performance.   No two performances are ever exactly identical, and nonpublic performance is not a serious injury.   The unauthorized exhibition of a copyrighted motion picture is a species of "copying" the identical work of the owner (*Patterson* v. *Century Productions, Inc.*, 93 F. 2d 489 (2d Cir. 1937), cert. den. 303 U.S. 655 (1938)).   The pirating user appropriates not merely plot and dialogue, but the best and only production containing the services of artists and actors otherwise unavailable, and can give unlimited identical performances in any place for any gathering, which compete with and destroy the value of the work for the copyright owner and his legitimate exhibition licensees.[126]

The view of the motion picture industry was followed in the Thomas bill, drafted by the Shotwell Committee.   As already mentioned, the bill provided specifically for the exhibition right in motion pictures without limiting it to public exhibitions.

C. Analysis of Basic Issues

I. Performing Rights in Literary and Musical Works

The background material presented in Part A above indicates that there has been no serious contention regarding the propriety of limiting the performing rights in literary and musical works to public performances.[127]   The issues that have been brought into question relate to the "for profit" and other similar limitations on the right of public performance.   Since these limitations have been applied to non-dramatic literary and musical works, but not generally to dramatic works, these two categories will be considered separately.

(a) *Nondramatic works.*—The review in Part A above of the development of the present law, proposed revisions, and foreign laws suggests four alternatives which might be considered in connection with the question of limiting public performing rights in nondramatic literary and musical works: (1) the "for profit" limitation could be maintained in its present form; (2) a provision listing specific exemptions could be substituted for the present "for profit" limitation; (3) a provision listing specific exemptions could be added to the "for profit" limitation; or (4) the "for profit" limitation could be abolished without substituting for it other limitations.   Each of these four alternatives has been proposed in one or more of the past bills for general revision of the U.S. law and is found in the law of some foreign countries.

(1) There are numerous arguments for preserving the "for profit" limitation in its present form.   It has often been emphasized that the

---

[126] See note 94, *supra*.
[127] The Sirovich bill of 1936 would have extended the performing right in dramatic works to all performances, but this was strongly criticized and not defended at the Hearings (see notes 84, 88, 89, *supra* and the text thereto).

author's right to royalties from public performances of nondramatic
works should only extend to the commercial exploitation of his works,
and that a further extension of his rights to noncommercial uses would
unduly interfere with the public interest in fostering the cultural life
of the nation. Moreover, the "for profit" limitation has been in
effect for almost 50 years, during which period the courts have interpreted "for profit" as including all methods of public performance
related directly or indirectly to commercial exploitation. Inquiries
made by the Shotwell Committee in 1938 and 1939 brought out the
fact that most of the interested groups then favored a retention of
this limitation.[128] It is noteworthy, though, that most of the general
revision bills, including the Shotwell bill, contained specific exemptions
in addition to the "for profit" limitation; see below under (3).

(2) One of the general revision bills, the Perkins bill of 1925,
substituted for the "for profit" limitation a provision listing specific
exemptions from the author's public performing rights. The bill
provided:

That nothing in this Act shall be construed to prohibit the performance of copyright musical works by churches or public schools, provided the performance is
given for charitable or educational or religious purposes, unless a fee is charged for
admission to the place where the music is so used.

A number of foreign copyright laws [129] have the same approach,
although the list of exempt activities usually is much more detailed
and extensive than the one proposed in the Perkins bill.

The advantage of this approach is that it would clarify the scope
of the exemptions from the public performing right by specifying in
rather precise detail the performances for which the public interest is
deemed to warrant an exemption. On the other hand, as shown in
previous revision efforts, an attempt at comprehensive specification
raises controversial questions of inclusion or exclusion. Moreover,
such specification would lose the advantage afforded by the general
"for profit" limitation of being flexible and adaptable to changing
conditions in the future.

If a proposal following this pattern were to be drafted, it should
be borne in mind that Congress throughout the years has focused
its attention on musical performances by charitable, educational,
and religious organizations for charitable, educational, or religious
purposes. These are the performances, with some variations, which
were exempted by the Perkins bill and specifically exempted in all
the other bills which added a list of exemptions to the "for profit"
limitation. Although the latter provisions were supplementary to
the "for profit" limitation, they were drafted so that they could
stand alone, and thus may serve as models for a provision intended
to be substituted for the "for profit" limitation.

The aforementioned proposals have limited exempt performances
in two respects. Only certain organizations were exempted, and only
certain performances by such organizations.

The organizations exempted have in some of the revision bills
been limited to churches and schools. In other bills they have been
described as charitable, educational, and religious organizations. In
still other bills agricultural and/or fraternal organizations have been

---

[128] See p. 103, *supra*.
[129] E.g., Austria (p. 92, *supra*), Canada (pp. 92, 93, *supra*), Germany (p. 94, *supra*), Sweden (p. 95, *supra*),
and United Kingdom (p. 95, *supra*).

added; and objections voiced at the hearings were directed principally at the inclusion of these two kinds of organizations.

The performances exempted have in all cases been musical performances for charitable, educational, and religious purposes. During the hearings the fear was expressed that profitmaking performances might be given under the guise of charity or other exempt purposes. In order to prevent abuse, some of the bills further qualified the exempt performances. For example, the Perkins bill exempted such performances only where no admission fee was charged. Other bills, for example the Duffy bill, exempted performances only if the proceeds after deduction of reasonable expenses were devoted exclusively to charitable, educational, or religious purposes. Section 12(a) of the Thomas (Shotwell) bill is another example of a provision containing the latter qualification. It exempted:

> The performance of a copyrighted musical composition, with or without words, by a recognized bona fide charitable, religious, or educational organization: *Provided*, That the entire proceeds thereof, after deducting the actual reasonable cost of presenting the same, are devoted exclusively to charitable, religious, or educational purposes: *And provided further*, That no part of the proceeds of such performance shall be for the private gain of any promoter or similar participant in the enterprise.

A number of the European copyright laws provide that musical performances for the aforementioned or similar purposes are only exempted if participating performers are not paid for their participation.[130]

(3) As already indicated, a number of the general revision bills contained both the "for profit" limitation, applicable to all nondramatic works, and specific exemptions applicable to musical works.[131]

The specific exemptions made the application of the "for profit" limitation more definite in the specified situations. Their practical effect varied: the specific exemptions tended in some cases to extend and in other cases to narrow the scope of the "for profit" limitation. For example, the Vestal bill, in its later versions, exempted musical performances by fraternal organizations for charitable, educational, or religious purposes; this addition might have enlarged the exemptions under the "for profit" limitation insofar as such performances might sometimes involve a profit element. The condition found in this and other bills, "unless a fee is charged for admission," might have enlarged the scope of free performances in some respects (where a profit element is involved but no admission fee is charged), and narrowed it in others (where an admission fee is charged to raise funds for charitable or educational purposes). The condition of an admission fee, where appropriate, has the advantage of establishing an easily recognizable line of demarcation. The condition in the Thomas (Shotwell) and a few other bills, that the proceeds of a performance after certain deductions must be devoted exclusively to charitable, educational, or religious purposes, might be found to be inherent in the "for profit" limitation. Such a condition might have the merit of clarifying a doubtful point, but it would probably be more difficult to administer than the "admission fee" condition.

---

[130] E.g., Austria (p. 92, *supra*), Germany (p. 94, *supra*), and Sweden (p. 95, *supra*).
[131] The bills referred to are: the Vestal bill (note 53, *supra*), the Dill bill (note 67, *supra*), the first Sirovich bill (note 69, *supra*), the Duffy bill (note 82, *supra*), and the Thomas bill (note 92, *supra*).

Mention might be made here of the proviso in section 104 of the present law which exempts performances of certain musical works—

> by public schools, church choirs, or vocal societies, * * * provided the performance is given for charitable or educational purposes and not for profit.

This seems to add nothing to the general "for profit" limitation inasmuch as it exempts the performances listed only if they are "not for profit." Section 104 could well be eliminated.

Two other exemptions from the public performing right for music, unrelated to the "for profit" limitation, were proposed in a few of the previous general revision bills.[132] In broad terms, it was proposed to exempt musical performances (though public and for profit) given by (1) the reception of a broadcast, or by (2) the playing (other than by broadcasting) of a recording, except in either case where admission fees or other charges are made. These exemptions were apparently intended to apply to performances given by means of broadcast receiving sets or by means of records in such places as hotels, taverns, restaurants, etc. Two special bills recently introduced in 1957 proposed to exempt performances given by such means in hotels.[133]

The proponents of such exemptions have argued that such performances should be "cleared at the source" (by the broadcasters or record producers); that the small hotel, restaurant, etc., should not be required to pay performing license fees for such performances; and that with respect to the reception of broadcasts, the receiver has no control over the choice of the works performed. In opposition it has been argued that such performances are given for purposes of commercial gain and those who make commercial use of music should compensate the authors for the use of their property; and it has been said that in practice the small hotel, restaurant, etc., is not called upon to obtain a performing license.

(4) It might be argued that the author's public performing rights should not be limited by any exemptions. That is the rule in some foreign countries, notably in France.[134] Moreover, that was the rule when the performing rights in music were first introduced into the copyright law, and has always been the rule for dramatic works.

Whether or not the "for profit" limitation should be eliminated without any substitute limitation depends upon whether the public interest in fostering the cultural life of the nation in situations where music or literary works are used noncommercially, or the author's right to control the use of his works, is paramount.

It could be argued that although there is a distinct and recognizable public interest in the enjoyment of the works of authors, that interest should in no case deprive the author of a potential source of income. From the author's point of view, it could also be said that he should have the right to determine which activities he desires to support by permitting the free use of his works.

In weighing the arguments for and against unlimited public performing rights, it should be remembered that the words "public performance" constitute a limitation and might be construed so as to protect the public against extreme cases of interference by the authors. If all other limitations were eliminated, the courts might tend to con-

---

[132] The last Vestal bill (note 53, *supra*) as amended on the floor of the House (note 57, *supra*) and on the floor of the Senate (note 63, *supra*); the first Sirovich bill (note 69, *supra*); and the Duffy bill (note 82, *supra*).
[133] See note 96, *supra*.
[134] See page 91, *supra*.

strue the term "public performance" narrowly, or might apply the doctrine of "fair use," so as to exclude from the author's control non-organized, nonprofessional performances which do not in any way compete with the author's economic interests. But there would still be many nonprofit performances that are undoubtedly "public performances."

Only one of the legislative proposals, namely the Vestal bill as first introduced,[135] contained no limitation on the author's public performing rights. This met with violent opposition and both the "for profit" limitation and other exemptions were adopted in later versions.

During the hearings in 1952 on the bill resulting in the amendment of section 1(c) of the present law extending performing rights to non-dramatic literary works, a representative of the authors argued that the rule governing dramatic works has caused almost no difficulties in the past, and that the same rule could be applied to other works without any invasion into legitimate public interests.[136] Congress, after hearing arguments pro and con, chose to maintain the "for profit" limitation.

(b) *Dramatic works.*—The oldest of the performing rights, the right to perform a dramatic work in public, has never been subjected to the "for profit" or other limitations. One of the reasons frequently given for treating dramatic performances differently from performances of nondramatic works is that people who attend a performance of a dramatic work will be less likely to attend a second performance of the same work. Consequently, a free performance will cause the author a serious monetary loss by depriving him of a potential audience. Another reason given is that the dramatic author depends more exclusively upon his public performing rights than other authors who derive substantial parts of their income from publishing, recording, and other rights.[137]

The writer is unaware of any contention that the public performing rights in dramatic works should be limited by the "for profit" or other limitations. The charitable, educational, religious, and other groups that have sought the free use of music have never urged that dramatic works should be freely available for nonprofit performance.

II. EXHIBITION RIGHTS IN MOTION PICTURES

The law regarding performing rights in motion pictures (commonly referred to as "exhibition" rights) has developed differently from performing rights in literary and musical works, and presents somewhat different issues.

There being no specific provision in the statute for exhibition rights in motion pictures, the courts have had to adapt general statutory provisions, designed for other kinds of works, to accord protection to copyright owners of motion pictures against their unauthorized exhibition. The courts found no difficulty in applying to public exhibitions of dramatic motion pictures (photoplays) the statutory right in section 1(d) to perform dramatic works publicly, as was done in the *Tiffany* [138] and third *Bijou Theatre* [139] decisions. In the third

[135] See note 45, *supra.*
[136] See argument pp. 83, 84, *supra.*
[137] See text to notes 14 and 15, *supra.*
[138] Tiffany Productions v. Dewing, 50 F. 2d 911 (D. Md. 1931).
[139] Metro-Goldwyn-Mayer Dist. Corp. v. Bijou Theatre Co., 3 F. Supp. 66 (D.C. Mass. 1931).

Bijou Theatre decision the court also suggested that if a motion picture was deemed to be a nondramatic rather than a dramatic work, its unauthorized exhibition (which was public in that case) would violate the statutory right in section 1(b) to dramatize a nondramatic work. Finally, in the *Patterson* case [140] the Second Circuit Court of Appeals, dealing with an unauthorized public exhibition of a nondramatic motion picture (being unable to apply the statutory right to perform a dramatic work publicly under section 1(d), and apparently overlooking or ignoring the suggestion of the court in the third *Bijou Theatre* decision that exhibition of a nondramatic motion picture is a dramatization under section 1(b)), adopted the theory advanced by the plaintiff copyright owners that the exhibition violated the statutory right in section 1(a) to "copy" a copyrighted work.

This theory of the *Patterson* case—that the temporary reproduction of a work by projecting it on a screen is "copying"—would seem to be a considerable stretch of the traditional concept of the copyright owner's exclusive right to "copy" under section 1(a). If the *Patterson* case, which dealt in fact with the public exhibition, is followed to its logical conclusion, any exhibition of a copyrighted motion picture, whether public or private, would be an infringement if not authorized by the copyright owner. The same result for nondramatic motion pictures might also follow from the theory advanced in the third *Bijou Theatre* decision that exhibition is a dramatization of the motion picture under section 1(b); but to accord more extensive exhibition rights to nondramatic motion pictures than to dramatic motion pictures would seem to be an unreasonable result.

In all of the foregoing decisions the exhibition involved was in fact a public exhibition. Only one decision has been found dealing with an exhibition that the court deemed to be private—the unreported *Maryland Yacht Club* case [141] which was decided before the *Patterson* decision by the same judge who, in the *Tiffany* case, had rejected the "copying" theory. In the *Maryland Yacht Club* case, involving a photoplay, the judge considered that the right of exhibition was limited to public exhibitions (as a species of public performance of a dramatic work under section 1(d)) and was therefore not infringed by a private exhibition.

The *Maryland Yacht Club* case is also the only one found in the United States dealing with the specific question of whether an exhibition given at a club for its members and their guests is public or private. The holding that such an exhibition is private seems questionable, and there are several decisions in foreign countries which hold the contrary in what appear to be similar situations involving musical performances at a dancing school, in a factory, and at a social club.[142] Whether the courts in the United States would now repudiate the *Maryland Yacht Club* case is a matter of conjecture. If the *Patterson* case is followed, the question would not be likely to arise with respect to motion picture exhibitions, but might arise in regard to the performance of musical or literary works.

Also conjectural to some extent is what the courts would now do if presented with a case of a purely private exhibition, as in a private

---

[140] Patterson v. Century Productions, 93 F. 2d 489 (2d Cir. 1937), *cert. denied* 303 U.S. 655 (1938).
[141] Metro-Goldwyn-Mayer Dist. Corp. v. Wyatt and Maryland Yacht Club (D. Md. 1932); unreported opinion set forth in Copyright Office Bulletin No. 21, at 203.
[142] See p. 108, *supra*.

home or in a library for an individual scholar.   While even such an exhibition would seem to be "copying" under section 1(a) if the theory of the *Patterson* decision is carried to its logical conclusion, a court might hesitate to find an infringement in that situation.   It is conceivable that a court might resort to the doctrine of "fair use" to hold such a purely private exhibition not an infringement.

It may be desirable in a general revision of the law, as was done in a number of the previous general revision bills, to make specific provision for the right to exhibit motion pictures.   If that is done, consideration will need to be given to the question of whether this right should extend to all exhibitions or only to public exhibitions.

It might be observed first that insofar as exhibition rights are concerned, no reason is apparent for making any distinction between photoplays and other motion pictures.   For both alike, their chief commercial value lies in their exhibition; and the methods of distribution, licensing, and exhibition are the same.   Both are also alike in regard to the premise that people having seen the motion picture at one exhibition are not likely to pay to see it again.   In all of the previous general revision bills which provided for exhibition rights in motion pictures, the rights pertained to all motion pictures without distinction between photoplays and others.

As to whether the exhibition right should be limited to public exhibitions, such a limitation was imposed in several of the earlier general revision bills,[143] but two of the later bills,[144] provided for an unqualified right of exhibition.   Foreign laws generally limit the right to "public" exhibitions and that term has been given broad scope by the foreign courts.[145]   Representatives of the motion picture industry have argued strongly for an unlimited exhibition right.   Specifically, they have argued that such a right is necessary to assure control of the copyright owner over the exhibition of films in clubs, factories, camps, schools, and other such "semipublic" places to which the general public is not invited, and perhaps even in private homes.[146]   They have pointed out that it is easy for anyone in possession of a film (who leased it for specified exhibitions) to give unauthorized exhibitions of the motion picture in such places, and that those attending such exhibitions are not likely to pay to see the motion picture again.

Because of the special nature of motion pictures, they might require broader protection than stage plays.   Any performance of a stage play requires a good deal of preparation in assembling the cast, scenery, and costumes, in rehearsals, etc., and nonpublic (usually nonprofessional) performances are generally too crude or too fragmentary to compete with a theatrical performance.   But a motion picture is a completed product that can readily be exhibited by anyone having the film and projection equipment, and is the same at every exhibition.

---

[143] The 1932 Sirovich bills (note 118, *supra*), the Duffy bill (note 119, *supra*), and the Daly bill (note 120, *supra*).

[144] The 1936 Sirovich bill (note 121, *supra*) and the Thomas bill (note 125, *supra*).

[145] See Part B III, *supra*.

[146] Mr. Sargoy advises: "It is extremely rare for motion picture prints to be sold to the public like books, newspapers, sheet music and other copyrighted works.   A motion picture is valueless unless it can be exhibited.   Distributors ordinarily license the exhibition right for a specified day or days at a designated place for an agreed upon license fee, and temporarily loan a positive print to the licensee, to be returned immediately after the licensed exhibition.   The motion picture industry serves not only the 17,000 or so theatres which exhibit 35 mm. prints commercially to the public, but a much greater number of nontheatrical outlets with 16 mm. prints.   There are not only hundreds of thousands of homes which have projection equipment, and license 16 mm. prints from time to time from distributors in this field, but there are hundreds of thousands of private or semiprivate establishments such as schools, colleges, clubs, children's camps, factories, and other places to which the general public would be denied access, which are potential exhibition licensees."

As heretofore urged by the motion picture industry, one possible solution to this problem is to provide for an unqualified right of exhibition in motion pictures.

Another approach might be to limit the right to public exhibition with a broad definition of what constitutes public exhibition. There would seem to be good reasons for giving the copyright owner control over the exhibition of motion pictures before a substantial audience at such "semipublic" places as clubs, factories, schools, camps, etc. Whether the copyright owner should have control over strictly private exhibitions, as in private homes or for an individual scholar in a library, may be more questionable. There is some number of 8 and 16 millimeter film prints (largely of motion pictures not produced for theatrical or other public showing) which are being sold for home use, and this practice is likely to increase as home projectors become more common. If it were made clear that exhibitions before a substantial audience in a place other than a private home are to be deemed public exhibitions, a provision giving the copyright owner control over public exhibitions might suffice to serve the needs of the motion picture industry without placing a questionable restraint on strictly private exhibitions.

A word might be added as to the application to motion picture exhibitions of the "for profit" limitation imposed by the present law (sec. 1 (c) and (e)) on public performing rights in nondramatic literary and musical works. No "for profit" limitation is imposed on the public performing right (sec. 1(d)) in dramatic works (stage plays) because the principal commercial value of plays lies in their public performance and the audience at one public performance will be less likely to attend another. These latter considerations would apply also to the exhibition of motion pictures. In fact, they are even stronger in the case of motion pictures, since performances of stage plays (by different producers with different casts, settings, etc.) are not the same, but a motion picture is always the same at every exhibition.

The first Sirovich bill of 1932 [147] suggests the possibility of utilizing the "for profit" concept in a different manner, by granting the exhibition right to all exhibitions which are either public or for profit. Thus, the exhibition right would extend to all public exhibitions, whether or not for profit, and also to any exhibitions deemed not "public" that involved profit. As indicated in Part A of this study, "for profit" has been given broad scope by the courts, and it seems likely that motion picture exhibitions at such "semipublic" places as clubs, camps, factories, etc., would usually involve some element of profit seeking on the part of the exhibitor. In foreign countries the fact that a performance is given for profit has been held to indicate its "public" character.[148] Extending the exhibition right to any nonpublic exhibition for profit might be another approach to giving motion picture copyright owners control over "semipublic" exhibitions without extending their control to strictly private exhibitions, if such a dividing line is deemed desirable.

---

[147] Note 118, *supra.*
[148] See, for example, the United Kingdom case of Harms & Chappel v. Martan's Club Ltd., 136 L. T. Rep. 362 (1927) 1 Ch. 52 (C.A.).

D. Summary of Basic Issues

I. Nondramatic Literary and Musical Works

(*a*) Which of the following four alternatives would be preferable in regard to the public performing rights in nondramatic literary and musical works?

(1) Should the "for profit" limitation be maintained in its present form?

(2) Should a provision listing specific exemptions be substituted for the present "for profit" limitation?

(3) Should the "for profit" limitation be combined with a provision listing specific exemptions?

(4) Should the "for profit" limitation be abolished without substituting for it any other limitations?

(*b*) If alternative (2) or (3) above is preferable, what exemptions should be specified?

(1) Should the kind of organization giving the performance be a criterion for exemption? If so, what kinds of organizations should be specified (*e.g.*, charitable, educational, religious, others)?

(2) Should the purpose of the performance be a criterion for exemption? If so, what purposes should be specified (*e.g.*, charitable, educational, religious, others)?

(3) Should the conditions under which the performance is given be a criterion for exemption? If so, what conditions should be specified (*e.g.*, that no admission fee is charged; or that all the proceeds, or the net proceeds after expenses, be devoted exclusively to an exempt purpose; or other conditions)?

(4) Should the means of giving the performance (*e.g.*, by reception of a broadcast, or by the playing of a recording) be a criterion for exemption? If so, under what conditions?

II. Dramatic Literary and Musical Works

Should any such limitations be imposed on the public performing rights in dramatic works?

III. Motion Pictures

(*a*) Should special provisions be made for exhibition rights in motion pictures? If so:

(*b*) Should such rights be extended to—

(1) All exhibitions without qualification?

(2) Public exhibitions only? If so, should "public exhibitions" be specially defined, and how?

(3) Public exhibitions, and also any nonpublic exhibitions for profit?

(*c*) Should such rights be subject to any other limitations?

STUDY NO. 5

THE COMPULSORY LICENSE PROVISIONS OF THE U.S. COPYRIGHT LAW

By Prof. Harry G. Henn

July 1956

(877)

THE COMPULSORY LICENSE PROVISIONS OF THE U.S. COPYRIGHT LAW

The U.S. Copyright Act of 1909 [1] recognized for the first time recording and mechanical reproduction rights [2] as part of the bundle of exclusive rights secured by statutory [3] copyright in certain classes of works,[4] limiting such mechanical reproduction rights in musical compositions by compulsory license provisions.

Shortly before the passage of the 1909 act, the U.S. Supreme Court, in construing the then-existing copyright statute,[5] in the oft-cited case of *White-Smith Music Publishing Co.* v. *Apollo Co.*,[6] had held that the making and sale of a pianola roll [7] of a copyrighted musical composition did not constitute copying (or publication or, inferentially, vending), and hence was no infringement, of the copyright in such

---

[1] Act of March 4, 1909 (35 Stat. 1075), effective July 1, 1909, 17 United States Code 1 et seq. (1952).

[2] Quaere, whether "recording rights" and "mechanical reproduction rights" are synonymous. If the former are broader than the latter, the compulsory license provision might apply only to the latter. The terminology of the Copyright Act is far from consistent. See pp. 13–14, 54, infra.

[3] Recording has been held violative of common-law rights. *George* v. *Victor Talking Machine Co.*, 38 U.S.P.Q. 222 (D.N.J. 1938), rev'd on other grounds, 105 F. 2d 697 (3d Cir. 1939), cert. denied, 308 U.S. 611, Sup. Ct. 176, 84 L. Ed. 511 (1939). This has long been the assumption of the music publishing and recording industry. See pp. 46–48, infra. Common-law rights are perpetual until publication (see note 71 infra), and are not subject to the compulsory license provision of the U.S. Copyright Act.

[4] Dramatic works (sec. 1(d)) and musical compositions (sec. 1(e)): Prior to the act of July 17, 1952 (66 Stat. 752), effective January 1, 1953, 17 U.S.C. 1(c) (Supp. 1955) no recording rights attached to nondramatic literary works. *Corcoran* v. *Montgomery Ward & Co.*, 121 F. 2d 576 (9th Cir. 1941), cert. denied, 314 U.S. 687, 62 Sup. Ct. 300, 86 L. Ed. 550 (1941) (setting to music and recording poem held not to infringe statutory copyright in poem). See H. Rept. No. 1160, 82d Cong., 2d sess. (1952); Cane, "Belated Justice for Authors," 36 Stat. Rev. 21 (Aug. 22, 1952); Schulman, "Recording Base Widens," 1 American Writer 13–15 (October 1952). Only mechanical reproduction rights in musical compositions are subject to compulsory licensing. (See p. 56, infra.)

[5] Act of Mar. 3, 1891 (26 Stat. 1106), Rev. Stat., sec. 4952 (based on act of July 8, 1870 (16 Stat. 212)), sec. 86, which provided that the author of a copyrighted musical composition should have "the sole liberty of printing, reprinting, publishing, completing, copying, executing, finishing, and vending the same." In 1870, although the mechanical piano (with interchangeable boards or perforated cards) had been previously invented, recording was mainly limited to the single-selection music box, barrel organ, bird organ, chiming clock, or snuff box. Sheet music was the medium through which new songs were enjoyed in the home. By 1900, pianolas, pianophones, aristons, aeolians, aerophones, polyphones, clarophones, phonographs, gramaphones, and graphophones were in widespread use, and a substantial industry had been built up around them and the interchangeable parts they played.

[6] 209 U.S. 1, 28 Sup. Ct. 319, 52 L. Ed. 655 (1908) (Holmes, J., concurring). Lower courts had previously ruled to the same effect. *Stern* v. *Rosey,* 17 App. D.C. 562 (1901); *Kennedy* v. *McTammany,* 33 Fed. 584 (C.C.D. Mass. 1888), appeal dismissed, 145 U.S. 643, 12 Sup. Ct. 983, 36 L. Ed. 853 (1892). Accord: *M. Witmark & Sons* v. *Standard Music Roll Co.,* 213 Fed. 532 (D.N.J. 1914), aff'd, 221 Fed. 376 (3d Cir. 1915) (pre-1909 work).

[7] And, by analogy, disks, bands, and cylinders, which, along with pianola rolls, comprised the interchangeable parts then used in mechanical music-producing machines. (See note 5 supra.) For the problems posed by motion picture sound tracks, long-playing records, wire and tape recordings, electronic devices, etc., see p. 54, infra.

1

musical composition.[8] The result of this case, but not the underlying
rationale, was changed by two provisions of the 1909 act:
  Section 1(e) [9] which, among other things,[10]

> (1) Recognized recording and mechanical reproduction
> rights in musical compositions, except those by foreign
> authors unless their nations granted similar rights to U.S.
> citizens,[11] published and copyrighted [12] after July 1, 1909, the
> effective date of the act; and
>
> (2) Subjected such mechanical reproduction rights to
> compulsory licensing,[13] and

Section 25(e) [14] specifying further remedies for infringement of mechanical reproduction rights.[15]

I. Analysis of Pertinent Provisions of Present Copyright Law

A. LEGISLATIVE HISTORY OF PRESENT COMPULSORY LICENSE PROVISIONS

  As early as 1905,[16] work was commenced on a series of bills looking
toward the codification of the Federal copyright laws.[17] The Librarian of Congress held three conferences with authors, publishers, and

---

  [8] The Court applied a visual test of copying by endorsing the definition of a copy of a
musical composition, within the meaning of the Copyright Act, as "a written or printed
record of it in intelligible notation" (209 U.S. at p. 17, 28 Sup. Ct. at p. 323, 52 L. Ed.
at 662). A copy had to appeal to the eye, not the ear. Cf. 2 Bl. Comm. 405–406. The
Court concluded, after suggesting possible legislative relief, that the copyright statute
as it then stood did not include records such as pianola rolls as copies or publications
of the copyrighted music. Holmes, J., concurred on the basis of the facts and opinions
in the United States and abroad, saying :
  "On principle anything that mechanically reproduces that collocation of sounds ought
to be held a copy, or if the statute is too narrow ought to be made so by a further
act, except so far as some extraneous consideration of policy may oppose."
209 U.S. at p. 20, 28 Sup. Ct. at p. 324, 52 L. Ed. at p. 663. See Universal Copyright
Convention, art. VI, discussed in note 71 infra.
  [9] See p. 12, infra.
  [10] Sec. 1(e), besides recognizing recording and mechanical reproduction rights in musical
compositions, provides for the right of public performance for profit of musical compositions and the right to make any arrangement thereof or the melody thereof in any system
of notation. Public performance rights in musical compositions had been expressly recognized in the act of January 6, 1897 (29 Stat. 481), the limitation "for profit" being added
by the 1909 act. Rights to arrange or adapt musical works are expressly conferred in
sec. 1(b). Besides sec. 1(e) rights of public performance for profit, arrangement, and
recording and mechanical reproduction, musical compositions are presently protected
against printing, reprinting, publishing, copying, and vending (sec. 1(a)), and dramatizing, arranging, or adapting (sec. 1(b)).
  [11] See note 55 infra.
  [12] See note 57 infra.
  [13] The compulsory license provision of sec. 1(e) was the first of two instances (for
second, see note 66 infra) of a compulsory license in Federal copyright and patent enactments, but is not entirely without precedent. Congress, under the Articles of Con-
federation, having no power over copyright, recommended in 1783 that the several States
enact copyright legislation. Of the 12 original States (Delaware being the exception)
which did so between 1783 and 1786, four statutes (Connecticut, Georgia, New York, South
Carolina) contained compulsory license with security provisions applicable when copies
of a copyrighted book were not supplied in reasonable quantity and at reasonable price.
"Copyright Enactments of the United States, 1783–1906," pp. 11–31 (2d ed. 1906) ;
Fenning, "Copyright Before the Constitution," 17 J. Pat. Off. Society 379, 380, 383
(1935). Compulsory patent licensing is one of the most controversial subjects in the
patent field. The Temporary National Economic Committee favored an amendment to
the patent laws which would require licensing of patents at reasonable royalties. Subsequently as an adjunct of enforcement of the antitrust laws in the patent field, a number of antitrust civil decrees required defendants to license patents either at a reasonable
royalty or royalty free. A congressional subcommittee reviewing the American patent
system has undertaken a study of all antitrust decrees requiring compulsory licensing of
patents to determine their effectiveness in promoting competition and the practical problems involved in the administration of compulsory licensing. S. Rept. No. 1464, 84th
Cong., 2d sess., p. 11 (Jan. 16, 1956). Several foreign countries adopted compulsory
license provisions patterned on sec. 1(e) of the U.S. Copyright Act. 1 Ladas, "The International Protection of Literary and Artistic Property," pp. 429–432 (1938). See pp. 36–
41, infra.
  [14] 17 U.S.C. sec. 101(e) (1952) ; see p. 13, infra.
  [15] See pp. 13–21, infra.
  [16] For a summary of developments, see 37 Music Trades 5–6 (Mar. 13, 1909).
  [17] H. Rept. No. 3380, 58th Cong., 3d sess. (1905).

other interested groups in 1905–6 in New York City and Washington, D.C. At the last conference a draft bill, containing the following provision, was discussed: [18]

That the copyright by this Act shall cover and protect the words and music of any song, opera, operetta, oratorio, mass, choral work and cantata, as well as each separate number or part thereof issued in separate form, together with all subsequent translation, arrangement or setting of the original work in any mode of notation, system of signs, figures or devices, or any form of reproduction whatsoever; and the music and words of a mixed composition may be jointly protected under one copyright or may be separately copyrighted.

A series of bills were introduced in Congress, during the 3 years from 1906 to 1909, to recognize recording and mechanical reproduction rights in musical compositions.

1. The 59th Congress

(a) S. 6330 and H.R. 19853

On May 31, 1906, identical bills were introduced by Senator Kittredge (S. 6330) and Representative Currier (H.R. 19853) providing that the copyright should include the sole and exclusive rights [19]—

* * * (g) to make, sell, distribute, or let for hire any device, contrivance, or appliance especially adapted in any manner whatsoever to reproduce to the ear the whole or any material part of any work published and copyrighted after this Act shall have gone into effect, or by means of any such device or appliance publicly to reproduce to the ear the whole or any material part of such work.

The bills were referred to the Committees on Patents of both Houses which held joint hearings on June 6–9, 1906.

John J. O'Connell, as representative of several New York player-piano manufacturers, claimed at the hearings that the above-quoted paragraph (g) would give a monopoly of the music-roll business to one company.[20] He indicated, in response to questions, that the piano manufacturers were not opposed to giving the composer some return provided this was done in such a way that every manufacturer would have the right to use the music upon paying for it. John Philip Sousa and Victor Herbert complained that manufacturers of music rolls and talking-machine records were reproducing part of their brain and genius without paying a cent for such use of their compositions.[21]

No further action was taken at that session. New hearings were commenced at the next session in December 1906. Thereafter, the Senate Committee on Patents, by a divided vote (three members dissenting), reported the original bill, while the House committee, one

---

[18] Sec. 42, Conference, Mar. 13–16, 1906.
[19] S. 6330, H.R. 19853, 59th Cong., 1st sess. (1906).
[20] The Aeolian Co. had received from numerous music publishers exclusive long-term license agreements to manufacture perforated music rolls in consideration for its carrying the *White-Smith Music Publishing Co.* case (see note 6, supra) to 'the U.S. Supreme Court in hope of a decision recognizing mechanical reproduction rights. There was considerable disagreement at the congressional hearings whether such license agreements would survive an adverse Supreme Court holding and apply if mechanical reproduction rights were recognized by legislation. Hearings on S. 6330 and H.R. 19853, 59th Cong., 1st sess., pp. 23–26, 94–97, 139–148, 166, 185–198, 202–206 (June 6–9, 1906). See note 44, infra.
[21] Id., at p. 84.

member dissenting, reported against extending copyright to include recording and mechanical reproduction rights.[22]

(b) S. 1890 and H. R. 25133

Senator Kittredge persisted at this session, introducing on January 29, 1907, a bill (S. 1890) defining the exclusive rights secured by the copyright of a musical composition as including the right [23]—

* * * to make any rearrangement or resetting of it or of the melody of it in any system of notation or any form of record in which the thought of an author may be recorded and from which it may be read or reproduced.

2. The 60th Congress

(a) H.R. 243, S. 2499, S. 2900, and H.R. 11794

At the next Congress, bills were introduced in December 1907, providing that perforated rolls, records, and matrices for the same, did not constitute arrangements or adaptations of a musical work.[24] Shortly thereafter, two bills were introduced providing that the exclusive rights in a musical composition included the right [25]—

* * * to make any arrangement or setting of it or of the melody of it in any system of notation or any form of record in which the thought of an author may be recorded and from which it may be read or reproduced.

At this time, the *White-Smith Music Publishing Co.* case [26] was before the U.S. Supreme Court. The congressional committees decided to postpone action pending the decision of the Supreme Court. The case was argued on January 16 and 17, 1908, and decided on February 24, 1908.

Joint committee hearings were resumed on March 26, 27, and 28, 1908.[27]

(b) H.R. 20388

Antitrust considerations previously raised now began to appear in the drafted bills. On April 6, 1908, Representative Campbell introduced a bill which provided, among other things, that any copyright issued by the United States for a musical composition or a device for reproducing music or musical compositions owned by an individual or firm would cease and terminate upon such individual or firm violating any law of Congress or any State which prohibited, restrained, or regulated trusts and monopolies.[28]

Congressional committee sentiment was largely divided between those who favored recognition of recording and mechanical reproduction rights absolutely and those who wanted such recognition limited by compulsory license provisions. A very small minority opposed recognition of such rights either on constitutional grounds,

---

[22] Hearings on S. 6330 and H.R. 19853, 59th Cong., 2d sess., pp. 156–161, 200–236, 247, 261, 268–298, 342–370 (Dec. 7, 8, 10, 11, 1906) ; S. Rept. No. 6187, 59th Cong., 2d sess., pp. 2–4, pt. 2 (1907) ; H. Rept. No. 7083, 59th Cong., 2d sess., pp. 9–11, pt. 2 (1907). The main objection was that any legislation involving mechanical reproduction rights be postponed pending the decision of the Supreme Court in the *White-Smith Music Publishing Co.* case.
[23] S. 1890, 59th Cong., 2d sess. (1907). A bill introduced by Representative Currier in the House on the same day (H.R. 25133) omitted this provision.
[24] H.R. 243, 60th Cong., 1st sess. (1907) ; S. 2499, 60th Cong., 1st sess. (1907).
[25] S. 2900, 60th Cong., 1st sess. (1907) ; H.R. 11794, 60th Cong., 1st sess. (1908).
[26] See note 6 supra.
[27] Hearings on H.R. 243, S. 2499, S. 2900, and H.R. 11794, 60th Cong., 1st sess., pp. 188–248, 255, 264–281, 293–356 (Mar. 26–28, 1908).
[28] H.R. 20388, 60th Cong., 1st sess. (1908). See note 44 infra.

largely dissipated by the Supreme Court opinions in the *White-Smith Music Publishing Co.* case, or in the feeling that there should be no further burden on the music-loving people of the country.

The issue, in effect, then, was between absolute and qualified recognition of recording and mechanical reproduction rights. Some question was raised as to the constitutionality of a compulsory license provision with an arbitrary royalty rate. Both Mr. O'Connell, counsel for the National Piano Manufacturers' Association, and Arthur Steuart, chairman of the Copyright Committee of the American Bar Association, expressed opinions that Congress in creating new rights had the power to annex conditions thereto since no abridgement of existing rights would be involved.

After the close of the hearings in March 1908, Senator Smoot, chairman of the Senate Committee on Patents, had suggested that the various interested groups attempt to agree on a bill. Accordingly, representatives of the song writers, talking-machine people, and piano manufacturers expressed agreement in favor of the universal royalty idea, and, except for the talking-machine people who thought the 2-cent rate was too high for cheap records, the 2-cent flat rate as proper and reasonable.[29]

(c) *H.R. 21592*

A compulsory licensing provision appears for the first time in a bill introduced on May 4, 1908. To a subsection conferring, among the several rights, the exclusive right to make any arrangement or setting of a musical composition or its melody in any system of notation or any form of record in which the thought of an author may be recorded and from which it may be read or reproduced, was appended the following proviso: [30]

Provided, That the provisions of this Act so far as they secure copyright covering the parts of instruments serving to reproduce mechanically the musical work shall include any compositions published and copyrighted after the passage of this Act: *And provided further*, That whenever the owner of a musical copyright has used or permitted the use of the copyrighted work upon the parts of instruments serving to reproduce mechanically the musical work, any other person may make similar use of the copyrighted work upon the payment to the copyright proprietor of a royalty equal to the royalty agreed to be paid by the licensee paying the lowest rate of royalty for instruments of the same class, and if no license has been granted then per centum of the gross sum received by such person for the manufacture, use, or sale of such parts, and in all cases the highest price in a series of transactions shall be adopted.

A later section of the same bill provided in part:

Whenever the owner of a musical copyright has used or permitted the use of the copyrighted work upon the parts of musical instruments serving to reproduce mechanically the musical work, then in case of infringement of such copyright by the unauthorized manufacture, use, or sale of interchangeable parts, such as disks, rolls, bands, or cylinders for use in mechanical music-producing machines adapted to reproduce the copyright music, no criminal action shall be brought, and in a civil action no injunction shall be granted, but the plaintiff shall be entitled to recover in lieu of profits and damages a royalty as provided in section one, subsection (e) of this Act.

---

[29] 37 Music Trades 5 (Mar. 13, 1909).
[30] H.R. 21592, 60th Cong., 1st sess. (1908).

(d) H.R. 21984

On May 12, 1908, Representative Sulzer introduced a bill combining recognition of recording and mechanical reproduction rights in musical compositions [31] with a compulsory licensing provision, mentioning for the first time the two-cent royalty: [32]

That any person who willfully and for profit shall infringe any copyright secured by this Act, or who shall knowingly and willfully aid or abet such infringement, shall be deemed guilty of a misdemeanor, and upon conviction thereof shall be punished by imprisonment for not exceeding one year, or by a fine not less than one hundred dollars and not exceeding one thousand dollars, or both, in the discretion of the court: *Provided, however,* That no person shall be deemed to infringe the copyright in any musical composition who shall make, vend, sell, or offer for sale any device or contrivance containing any arrangement or setting of the same or of the melody thereof, in which the thought of an author may be recorded and from which it may be read or reproduced, and who shall pay to the copyright proprietor of the same before vending, selling, or offering any such device or contrivance for sale, the sum of two cents in each case where the device or contrivance is a talking-machine record, and a sum equal to one-tenth part of the marked retail price of any other such device or appliance, and shall affix to such devices or appliances before vending, selling, or offering them or any of them for sale a royalty stamp issued to him by the proprietor of the copyright denoting the payment of said sum: *And provided further,* That the proprietor of the copyright shall cause to be prepared, for the payment of the royalty thereof, and shall keep on hand at all times a sufficient supply of stamps, and shall sell the same to any person desiring to purchase the same, in default of which no action shall be maintained nor recovery be had for any infringement by any such device or contrivance. Every manufacturer of any such device or contrivance shall securely affix, by pasting on each such device or contrivance manufactured by him, a label on which shall be printed the name of the manufacturer, his place of residence, the title of the composition which it is adapted to reproduce, the name of the author of such composition, and the retail price of the same, in default of which he shall be liable under the provisions of this Act as an infringer of the copyright: *And provided further,* That the person using or affixing the stamp as herein provided for shall cancel the same by writing thereon the initials of his name and the date on which such stamp is attached or used, so that it may not again be used.

Any person who shall vend, sell, or offer for sale such contrivance or appliance with properly affixing thereon and canceling the stamp denoting the royalty on the same, or affixes a false, fraudulent, or counterfeit stamp, or any dealer who buys, receives, or has in his possession any such device or contrivance on which the royalty has not been paid, or any person who removes or causes to be removed from any such device or contrivance any stamp denoting the royalty on the same, with intent to again use such stamp, or who knowingly uses or permits any other person to use the stamp so removed, or who knowingly receives, buys, sells, gives away, or has in his possession any stamp so removed, or has in his possession any stamp so removed, or who makes any other fraudulent use of any such stamp shall be deemed guilty of a misdemeanor, and shall be fined not less than two hundred and fifty dollars nor more than one thousand dollars and imprisoned for not less than three months nor more than one year.

Nothing in this section declared to be illegal by any court of competent jurisdiction shall in anywise affect or impair any other section or subsection or part thereof in this Act contained, but the same shall remain in full force and effect in the same manner to the same extent as if this section were not embodied in this Act.

(e) H.R. 22071

On May 12 (calendar day May 21), 1908, Representative Sulzer introduced another bill which retained the recording and mechanical reproduction rights and royalty stamp provisions of his earlier bill

---

[31] H.R. 21984, 60th Cong., 1st sess. (1908). Similar to provisions in bills cited in note 25 supra.
[32] H.R. 21592, 60th Cong., 1st sess. (1908).

but limited the compulsory license provision to situations where the proprietor had made or authorized a recording and made the royalty of one-tenth of the marked retail price applicable to all mechanical reproductions, thus supplanting the 2-cent provision for phonograph records.[33]

(f) H.R. 22183

On May 12, 1908, Representative Currier introduced a bill which provided a 2-cent royalty except in the case of disks not exceeding 8 inches in diameter or cylinders not exceeding 4 inches in length, in which case the royalty was to be 1 cent. The provisos read as follows: [34]

* * * *Provided*, That the provisions of this Act, so far as they relate to instruments or machines or parts of instruments or machines which reproduce or serve to reproduce to the ear the musical work, shall include only compositions published and copyrighted after this Act takes effect, and shall not include the works of a foreign author or composer unless the foreign state or nation of which such author or composer is a citizen or subject grants, either by treaty, convention, agreement, or law, to citizens of the United States similar rights: *Provided further*, That any person may make use of the copyrighted work in the manufacture of records or controllers for mechanical music-producing machines, however operated, and may sell or use such records for profit upon payment of a royalty to the copyrighted proprietor by the manufacturer of such record or controller, as hereinafter provided: *And provided further*, That in no event shall the payment of more than one royalty be required on any such record or controller.

In case of the use of such copyrighted composition on such interchangeable records or controllers of such mechanical musical-producing instruments no criminal action shall be brought, and in a civil action no injunction shall be granted, but the plaintiff shall be entitled to recover in lieu of profits and damages a royalty of two cents on each such record or controller, except in the case of disks for talking machines not exceeding eight inches in diameter or cylinders not exceeding four inches in length, in which case the royalty shall be one cent; but in the case of the refusal of such manufacturer to pay to the copyright proprietor within thirty days after demand in writing the full sum of royalties due at the said rate at the date of such demand the court may award taxable costs to the plaintiff and a reasonable counsel fee, and the court may enter judgment therein for any sum above the amount found by the verdict as the actual damages, according to the circumstances of the case, not exceeding three times the amount of such verdict.

Opposition developed on the part of some music publishers with the result that no bill was reported before the end of the session in June 1908.[35]

A special House committee was thereupon appointed to consider the various bills then pending, primarily: H.R. 22183, providing for a 2-cent flat royalty rate; H.R. 21592, permitting the composer to withhold his composition from mechanical reproduction, if he did not permit such use; if he did permit such use, anybody else could make similar use of the composition upon paying a percentage of royalty; and H.R. 21984, providing for a 2-cent royalty on talking-machine records and a 10-percent royalty on music rolls.[36] The special committee met on the reconvening of Congress in December 1908 with a view to framing, on the basis of the various bills, one that would be not only valid but just and reasonable to all interests.[37]

---

[33] H.R. 22071, 60th Cong., 1st sess. (1908).
[34] H.R. 22183, 60th Cong., 1st sess. (1908).
[35] 37 Music Trades 5 (Mar. 13, 1909).
[36] Ibid.   See notes 30, 31, 34, supra.
[37] Ibid.

(g) *H.R. 24782*

Meanwhile, on December 19, 1908, Representative Barchfeld introduced a bill which contained, besides provisions similar to some of the other bills, some new features. The most important of these was that the proprietor of a copyrighted musical work, when he mechanically reproduced it or permitted someone else to do so, should file a written declaration of intention so to use said work with the Register of Copyrights, giving also the nature and extent of such contemplated use; and if such use were permitted to others a duplicate original of the contract under which said use was permitted must also be filed. The Register of Copyrights was required to issue a weekly bulletin or list of the declarations of intention and contracts respecting the use of copyrighted works upon instruments mechanically reproducing the work. The full section read as follows: [38]

That whenever the proprietor of a copyrighted musical work shall use or permit the use of the same for profit upon any instrument serving to reproduce mechanically the musical work, he shall first file with the Register of Copyrights (a) if the use be only by the copyright proprietor, a written declaration of intention so to use said work and the nature and extent of such contemplated use; (b) if such use is permitted to others, a duplicate original of the contract under which said use is permitted, and thereupon any other person subject to the provisions hereof may make similar use of such copyrighted work and to the same extent upon paying to the copyright proprietor of the same before vending, selling, or offering any such instrument for sale, (c) if the said use is to be made by the copyright proprietor, a sum equal to ten per centum of the selling price of any such instrument, but in no event to be less than two cents; (d) or if the use is permitted to others the royalty provided in the contract permitting such use for instruments of the same class. Any person using a copyrighted work under the provision hereof shall affix to such instrument before vending, selling, or offering it for sale a royalty stamp issued to him by the proprietor of the copyright denoting the payment of said royalty, and shall cancel the stamp at the time of affixing the same by writing thereon the initials of his name and the date of cancellation so that it may not again be used.

The proprietor of the copyright shall cause to be prepared and keep on hand for sale proper stamps, bearing his imprint, for the payment of the said royalties, in such denomination as will coincide with the royalty hereinabove specified, in default of which no action shall be maintained nor recovery be had for any infringement by any such instrument.

Any person who shall vend, sell, or offer for sale any such instrument without properly affixing thereon and cancelling the stamp denoting the royalty on the same shall be liable as an infringer of the copyright. Any person who affixes a false or fraudulent stamp or who removes or causes to be removed from any such instrument any stamp denoting the royalty on the same, with intent to again use such stamp, or who knowingly uses or permits any other person to use the stamp so removed, or who knowingly receives, buys, sells, or gives away, or has in his possession any stamp so removed, or who makes any other fraudulent use of any such stamp, shall be deemed guilty of a misdemeanor, and shall be fined not less than two hundred and fifty dollars nor more than one thousand dollars, or imprisoned for not less than three months nor more than one year, or both.

No change shall be made in the contract which has been filed with the register of copyrights in compliance with the requirements of this section except after thirty days' written notice to the register of copyrights, which shall plainly state the change proposed to be made therein. Any copyright proprietor filing a false or fraudulent contract with the register of copyrights, or offering, granting, or giving, or any person soliciting, accepting, or receiving any rebate or refund of any portion of the royalty named in the contract filed by the copyright proprietor with the register of copyrights, shall forfeit to the United States a sum not less than five hundred dollars nor more than five thousand dollars.

---

[38] H.R. 24782, 60th Cong., 2d sess. (1908).

The register of copyrights shall issue a weekly bulletin or list of the declarations of intention and contracts respecting the use of copyrighted works upon instruments hereinbefore provided, specifying the copyrighted work to be used, the name and address of the proprietor, the character and extent of such use, and the terms of royalty and nature of permission, contained in each contract; and it shall be the duty of the register of copyrights to furnish such bulletins to all persons applying for the same at a sum not exceeding five dollars per annum.

Nothing in this section declared to be invalid by any court of competent jurisdiction shall in any wise affect or impair any other section or subsection or part thereof in this Act contained, but the same shall remain in full force and effect in the same manner and to the same extent as if this section were not embodied in this Act.

(h) H.R. 25162

On January 5, 1909, Representative Sulzer again introduced a bill which resembled two of his earlier bills but fixed the royalty at "ten per centum of the selling price of any such instrument, but in no event to be less than two cents * * * or if the use is permitted to others, the royalty provided in the contract * * *":[39]

That whenever the proprietor of a copyrighted musical work shall use or permit the use of the same for profit upon any instrument serving to reproduce mechanically the musical work, he shall first file with the register of copyrights (a) if the use be only by the copyright proprietor, a written declaration of intention so to use said work and the nature and extent of such contemplated use; (b) if such use is permitted to others a duplicate original of the contract under which said use is permitted; and thereupon any other person subject to the provisions hereof may make similar use of such copyrighted work, and to the same extent and upon a similar instrument and not otherwise, upon paying to the copyright proprietor of the same, before vending, selling, or offering any such instrument for sale; (c) if the said use is to be made by the copyright proprietor, a sum equal to ten per centum of the selling price of any such instrument, but in no event to be less than two cents; (d) or if the use is permitted to others, the royalty provided in the contract permitting such use for instruments of the same class. Any person using a copyright work under the provisions hereof shall affix to such instrument, before vending, selling, or offering it for sale, a royalty stamp, to be issued to him by the proprietor of the copyright denoting the payment of said royalty, and shall cancel the stamp at the time of affixing the same by writing thereon the initials of his name and the date of cancellation so that it may not again be used.

The proprietor of the copyright shall cause to be prepared and keep on hand for sale proper stamps, bearing his imprint, for the payment of said royalties, in such denomination as will coincide with the royalty hereinabove specified, in default of which no action shall be maintained nor recovery be had for any infringement by any such instrument.

Any person who shall vend, sell, or offer for sale any such instrument without properly affixing thereon and canceling the stamp denoting the payment of the royalty on the same shall be liable as an infringer of the copyright. Any person who makes, or is knowingly concerned in the making of a counterfeit of any such stamp, or who affixes a false or fraudulent stamp, or who removes or causes to be removed from any such instrument any stamp denoting the payment of the royalty on the same, with intent to again use such stamp, or who knowingly uses or permits any other person to use the stamp so removed, or who knowingly receives, buys, sells, or gives away or has in his posesssion any counterfeit stamp or stamps so removed, or who makes any other fraudulent use of any such stamp shall be deemed guilty of a misdemeanor, and shall be fined not less than two hundred and fifty dollars nor more than one thousand dollars, or imprisioned for not less than three months nor more than one year, or both.

No alteration or modification shall be made in the contract which has been filed with the register of copyrights, in compliance with the requirements of this section, except after thirty days' written notice to the register of copy-

---

[39] H.R. 25162, 60th Cong., 2d sess. (1909).

rights, which shall plainly state the change proposed to be made therein. Any copyright proprietor filing a false or fraudulent contract with the register of copyrights or offering, granting, or giving, or any person soliciting, accepting, or receiving, any rebate or refund of any portion of the royalty named in the contract, or any modification thereof filed by the copyright proprietor with the register of copyrights, shall forfeit to the United States a sum not less than five hundred dollars nor more than five thousand dollars.

The register of copyrights shall issue a weekly bulletin or list of the declarations of intention and contracts respecting the use of copyrighted works upon instruments hereinbefore provided, specifying the copyrighted work to be used, the name and address of the proprietor, the character and extent of such use, and the terms of royalty and nature of permission contained in each contract; and it shall be the duty of the register of copyrights to furnish such bulletins to all persons applying for the same at a sum not exceeding five dollars per annum.

Nothing in this section declared to be invalid by any court of competent jurisdiction shall in any wise affect or impair any other section or subsection or part thereof in this Act contained, but the same shall remain in full force and effect in the same manner and to the same extent as if this section were not embodied in this Act.

(i) H.R. 27310

On January 28, 1909, Representative Washburn introduced a bill, H.R. 27310, combining recognition of mechanical reproduction rights and compulsory licensing provisions, which became operative in the event of the exercise of such rights, and fixing the royalty at "five per centum of the sum derived bona fide by the manufacturer thereof, from the manufacture, use, sale, or lease of such parts." [40]   Two safeguards for the composer were inserted: (1) the requirement that the mechanical reproducer give notice of intention to record under the compulsory license provision to the composer, and (2) the provision for treble royalties in the event of nonpayment of the statutory royalty.

(j) H.R. 28192

On February 15, 1908, Representative Currier introduced a bill similar to immediate forerunners with provisions for reciprocal treatment of the works of foreign authors and composers and for a "royalty of two cents on each such part manufactured." [41]   The 2-cent flat royalty was considered the then equivalent of five percent on the manufacturer's price. The bill, H.R. 28192, was referred to the Committee on Patents which reported it out unanimously without amendment, on February 22, 1909.[42] The bill and report were referred to the Committee of the Whole House on the State of the Union which agreed on amendments on March 2. As amended the bill was passed by the House and rushed through a night session of

---

[40] H.R. 27310, 60th Cong., 2d sess. (1909).
[41] H.R. 28192, 60th Cong., 2d sess. (1909).
[42] H. Rept. No. 2222, 60th Cong., 2d sess. (1909) ; S. Rept. No. 1108, 60th Cong., 2d sess. (1909).

the Senate on March 3, 1909, and approved and signed by the President on March 4, 1909,[43] becoming effective on July 1, 1909.

The congressional reports accompanying the various preliminary bills deal with recording and mechanical reproduction rights of music, but shed little light on the compulsory license provision. The latter was a compromise to placate the expressed fears, particularly among phonograph record and pianola roll manufacturers, that the recognition of mechanical reproduction rights would result in monopolization of the industry by the Aeolian Co.[44]

The report of the House Committee on Patents accompanying the successful bill H.R. 28192 discloses that section 1 (e)[45]—

* * * has been the subject of more discussion and has taken more of the time of the committee than any other provision in the bill.

[43] See note 1 supra, pp. 12–13, infra. The bill which became law, unlike five earlier bills, did not treat each of the rights given the copyright owner as a "separate estate" subject to assignment, lease, license, gift, bequest, inheritance, descent, or devolution. Substantial royalties were expected to be paid composers by player-piano and talking-machine companies.

"In his 'Life of Edison,' Frank L. Dyer, president of the National Phonograph Co., said that in the last 20 years upward of 1,310,000 phonographs have been sold, for which there have been made or sold no less than 97,845,000 records of a musical or other character. Most of these have been musical records. At Orange, N.J., the National Phonograph Co. made 75,000 records a day. The Victor and Columbia companies make thousands of records a day.

"The talking-machine companies have been reticent about making public the figures for individual record sales. The composers, however, believe that as many as 100,000— some say 150,000—records have been sold of such popular songs as 'Love Me and the World Is Mine.' Records of the comic songs, such as 'Waiting at the Church,' have sold into the thousands. The child ballads of Chas. K. Harris have been among the favorites with talking-machine patrons. John Philip Sousa says he has heard records of his marches played by talking-machines in the most remote places.

"Figures of music rolls are also difficult to secure. The Universal music-roll catalogue alone contains 16,500 selections. The Chase & Baker Co., Buffalo; W. W. Kimball Co., Chicago; Connorized Music Co., New York; Autopiano Co., the Q. R. S. Co., and other concerns have very large catalogues. On April 25, 1908, the Aeolian Co. printed a list of the 50 best selling music rolls, no selection in the list being included which had not sold for more than 25,000 rolls. Among the popular numbers in this list were the following: 'Narcissus' 'The Rosary,' 'School Days,' and 'Honey Boy.' "
37 Music Trades 5 (Mar. 13, 1909).

[44] See note 21 supra. Quaere, whether this danger of monopoly was exaggerated.

"The danger of monopoly through the contract between the Aeolian Co. and leading music publishers was greatly exaggerated and distorted by the mechanical instrument people in their powerful opposition to our getting any protection whatever; and was made worse, in my opinion, because the Aeolian Co., in spite of earnest pleading on my part, failed to appear at the hearings before the congressional committee and reply to the absurd, ridiculous and unjust charges brought up against them, they maintaining throughout the controversy an honorable and dignified silence."
Statement by Walter M. Bacon, treasurer, White-Smith Music Publishing Co., 37 Music Trades 6 (Mar. 13, 1909). The congressional committee, however, feared the establishment of a mechanical music trust:

"It appeared that some years ago contracts were made by one of the leading mechanical reproducing establishments of the country with more than 80 of the leading music publishing houses in this country. Some of these contracts were filed with the committee and show that under them the reproducing company acquired the rights for mechanical reproduction in all the copyrighted music which the publishing house controlled or might acquire and that they covered a period of at least 35 years, with the possibility of almost indefinite extension. These contracts were made in anticipation of a decision by the courts that the existing law was broad enough to cover the mechanical reproduction, and one consideration on the part of the reproducing company was an agreement that that company would cause suit to be brought which would secure a decision of the Supreme Court of the United States.

"Later on another set of contracts were prepared, based upon the passage by Congress of a law which would give such rights."
H. Rept. No. 2222, 60th Cong., 2d sess., pp. 7–8 (1909). Provision in the copyright law to promote antitrust policy is not without parallel. The manufacturing clause is primarily grounded on protective tariff considerations. Ashford, "The Compulsory Manufacturing Clause—An Anachronism in the Copyright Act," 49 Mich. L. Rev. 417 (1951). Copyright practices are subject to the antitrust laws. McDonough and Winslow, "The Motion Picture Industry; United States Versus Oligopoly," 1 Stan. L. Rev. 385 (1949); White, L. C., "Musical Copyrights Versus the Antitrust Laws," 30 Nebr. L. Rev. 50 (1950). Comment: "ASCAP Monopoly Violates Sherman Act," 1 Stan. L. Rev. 538 (1949). Notes: 33 Minn. L. Rev. 517 (1949); 33 Minn. L. Rev. 545 (1949); 17 U. of Chi. L. Rev. 183 (1949); 3 Miami L. Rev. 59 (1948); 61 Harv. L. Rev. 539 (1948); 37 Geo. L.J. 542 (1942); 52 Harv. L. Rev. 846 (1939). See also *Watson* v. *Buck*, 313 U.S. 387, 61 Sup. Ct. 962, 85 L. Ed. 1416 (1941). See note 28 supra.
[45] H. Rept. No. 2222, 60th Cong., 2d sess., p. 4 (1909).

Some five and a half pages of the report deal with the recognition of recording and mechanical reproduction rights and the compulsory license provision, emphasizing that the latter was inserted in the public interest to prevent monopolization of mechanical reproduction rights in copyrighted music.[46]

B. THE PRESENT COMPULSORY LICENSE PROVISIONS

Section 1(e) reads in pertinent part as follows:

SEC. 1. EXCLUSIVE RIGHTS AS TO COPYRIGHTED WORKS.—Any person entitled thereto, upon complying with the provisons of this title, shall have the exclusive right—

(e) To perform the copyrighted work publicly for profit if it be a musical composition; [[47]] and for the purpose of public performance for profit, and for the purposes set forth in subsection (a) hereof, to make any arrangement or setting of it or of the melody of it in any system of notation or any form of record in which the thought of an author may be recorded and from which it may be read or reproduced: *Provided*, That the provisions of this title, so far as they secure copyright controlling the parts of instruments serving to reproduce mechanically the musical work, shall include only compositions published and copyrighted after July 1, 1909, and shall not include the works of a foreign author or composer unless the foreign state or nation of which such author or composer is a citizen or subject grants, either by treaty, convention, agreement, or law, to citizens of the United States similar rights. And as a condition of extending the copyright control to such mechanical reproductions, that whenever the owner of a musical copyright has used or permitted or knowingly acquiesced in the use of the copyrighted work upon the parts of instruments serving to reproduce mechanically the musical work, any other person may make similar use of the copyrighted work upon the payment to the copyright proprietor of a royalty of 2 cents on each such part manufactured, to be paid by the manufacturer thereof; and the copyright proprietor may require, and if so the manufacturer shall furnish, a report under oath on the 20th day of each month on the number of parts of instruments manufactured during the previous month serving to reproduce mechanically said musical work, and royalties shall be due on the parts manufactured during any month upon the 20th of the next succeeding month. The payment of the royalty provided for by this section shall free the articles or devices for which such royalty has been paid from further contribution to the copyright except in case of public performance for profit. It shall be the duty of the copyright owner, if he uses the musical composition himself for the manufacture of parts of instruments serving to reproduce mechanically the musical work, or licenses others to do so, to file notice thereof, accompanied by a recording fee, in the copyright office, and any failure to file such notice shall be a complete defense to any suit, action, or proceeding for any infringement of such copyright.

In case of failure of such manufacturer to pay to the copyright proprietor within thirty days after demand in writing the full sum of royalties due at said rate at the date of such demand, the court may award taxable costs to the plaintiff and a reasonable counsel fee, and the court may, in its discretion, enter judgment therein for any sum in addition over the amount found to be due as royalty in accordance with the terms of this title, not exceeding three times such amount.

The reproduction or rendition of a musical composition by or upon coin-operated machines shall not be deemed a public performance for profit unless a fee is charged for admission to the place where such reproduction or rendition occurs.

---

[46] Id., at pp. 4–9, 16.
[47] The act of 1909 contained no punctuation before the phrase "and for the purpose of public performance for profit" and a semicolon instead of a comma after such phrase. In an early case it was contended that a musical composition had to be written for the purpose of public performance for profit to enjoy such performance rights. The court rejected the contention, holding that a semicolon was intended before the above-quoted phrase. *Hubbell* v. *Royal Pastime Amusement Co.*, 242 Fed. 1002 (S.D.N.Y. 1917). The 1947 codification of the copyright law followed this construction by relocating the semicolon. Act of July 30, 1947 (61 Stat. 652). Quaere, why the recognition of recording and mechanical reproduction rights and rights of arrangement is introduced by the phrase: "and for the purpose of public performance for profit, and for the purpose set forth in subsection (a) hereof". See notes 51 and 59 infra.

Section 1(e) is supplemented by section 25(e) (presently sec. 101 (e)), as follows:

§ 101. INFRINGEMENT.—If any person shall infringe the copyright in any work protected under the copyright laws of the United States such person shall be liable:

*   *   *   *   *   *   *

(e) ROYALTIES FOR USE OF MECHANICAL REPRODUCTION OF MUSICAL WORKS.— Whenever the owner of a musical copyright has used or permitted the use of the copyrighted work upon the parts of musical instruments serving to reproduce mechanically the musical work, then in case of infringement of such copyright by the unauthorized manufacture, use, or sale of interchangeable parts, such as disks, rolls, bands, or cylinders for use in mechanical music-producing machines adapted to reproduce the copyrighted music, no criminal action shall be brought, but in a civil action an injunction may be granted upon such terms as the court may impose, and the plaintiff shall be entitled to recover in lieu of profits and damages a royalty as provided in section 1, subsection (e), of this title: *Provided also,* That whenever any person, in the absence of a license agreement, intends to use a copyrighted musical composition upon the parts of instruments serving to reproduce mechanically the musical work, relying upon the compulsory license provision of this title, he shall serve notice of such intention, by registered mail, upon the copyright proprietor at his last address disclosed by the records of the copyright office, sending to the copyright office a duplicate of such notice; and in case of his failure so to do the court may, in its discretion, in addition to sums hereinabove mentioned, award the complainant a further sum, not to exceed three times the amount provided by section 1, subsection (e), of this title, by way of damages, and not as a penalty, and also a temporary injunction until the full award is paid.

The terminology, as well as the substantive provisions, of sections 1(e) and 101(e) is somewhat inconsistent.

Section 1(e), so far as musical compositions protected thereunder are concerned, defines such protection against recording and mechanical reproduction as proscribing:

(1) The making of "any form of record in which the thought of an author may be recorded and from which it may be * * * reproduced";

(2) The making of "parts of instruments serving to reproduce mechanically the musical work";

(3) The making of "mechanical reproductions."

Such protection is qualified by the compulsory license provision stating that whenever the copyright owner has used or "permitted or knowingly acquiesced" in the use of the "parts of instruments serving to reproduce mechanically the musical work," any other person may make similar use thereof upon payment of 2 cents royalty per part manufactured. The owner is required to file a notice of use if he uses the work himself for the manufacture of parts, etc., or "licenses" others to do so. For the failure of the manufacturer to pay the royalty the court can award "any sum in addition over the amount found to be due as royalty * * *, not exceeding three times such amount."

Section 101(e) provides that whenever the owner has used or "permitted" the use of the work upon parts, etc., the specific remedies for infringement by the "unauthorized manufacture, use, or sale of interchangeable parts, such as disks, rolls, bands, or cylinders for use in mechanical music-producing machines" include "a royalty as provided in" section 1(e). In case of a person's failing to send the required notice of intention to use, the award may include, "in addition to sums hereinabove mentioned * * * a further sum, not to exceed three times the amount provided by" section 1(e).

Questions naturally arise whether different meanings were intended by the use of different phraseology. For example, the scope of protection under section 1(e) is defined in three ways: "any form of record in which the thought of an author may be recorded and from which it may be * * * reproduced"; "parts of instruments serving to reproduce mechanically the musical work"; "mechanical reproduction." The last two, unlike the first, contain the qualifying adverb "mechanically" or adjective "mechanical." An additional definition of scope of protection is found in section 101(e): "interchangeable parts, such as disks, rolls, bands, or cylinders for use in mechanical music-producing machines." Here, again, is found the qualifying adjective "mechanical," and, in addition, some elaboration of the term "parts" ("disks, rolls, bands or cylinders") and the additional qualification that such parts be "interchangeable," a requirement lacking from section 1(e). The compulsory license provision uses only the phraseology of the second definition of scope of protection in section 1(e): "parts of instruments serving to reproduce mechanically the musical work." [48]

Different phraseology is used to indicate when the compulsory license, and implementing, provisions come into operation. Thus, under section 1(e), the compulsory license provision becomes operative when the owner has used or "permitted or knowingly acquiesced" in the use of the work upon parts, etc., while the owner must file a notice of use where he uses or "licenses" the manufacture of parts, etc. The specific remedies of section 101(e) are applicable whenever the owner has used or "permitted" the use of the work upon parts, etc.

While the language of section 1(e) seems to be directed against the making of records, the control of parts or reproductions, and the manufacturer of parts, section 101(e) provides specific remedies for the unauthorized "use, manufacture, or sale."

The statutory royalty rate is 2 cents per composition per "part," without any definition of "part." If the same composition is on two sides of a disk, the question naturally arises whether the disk or each side is a "part." In this connection, section 101(e) refers to "parts, such as disks."

Section 1(e) recognizes the right "to make any arrangement" of a musical composition "or of the melody of it in any system of notation" from which it may be read. Since section 1(b) has already recognized the right to arrange or adapt a musical work, it can be contended that the reiteration of the right of arrangement in section 1(e) was intended to permit the reasonable exercise of such right as incident to the making of parts under the compulsory license provision of that subsection.

---

[48] See p. 54, infra. Neither the cases, the congressional report recommending passage of the 1909 act, nor subsequent amendments appear to distinguish between recording rights and mechanical reproduction rights. H. Rept. No. 2222, 60th Cong., 2d sess., pp. 4–9 (1909); 68 Stat. 1030, 17 U.S.C. 9(c)(1) (Supp. 1955).

Under section 1(e) nonpayment of the 2-cent royalty per part manufactured might result in an award for the amount of such royalty and in addition a sum not exceeding three times such amount. Whether this maximum award under section 1(e) is three or four times the amount of the statutory royalty is questionable, presumably the former judging by occasional references to treble recovery and 6 cents.[49] Section 101(e) permits a recovery of the statutory royalty and, where the person has failed to file the required notice of intention to use, in addition thereto, a further sum not to exceed three times the amount provided in section 1(e). Again, there is a problem of construction as to whether this further sum is limited to three times the statutory royalty, or three times the amount of maximum recovery under section 1(e). If the latter, and such maximum recovery under section 1(e) is either three or four times the amount of the statutory royalty, then the overall recovery, under both sections 1(e) and 101(e), could total 12 or 16 times the statutory royalty.

C. JUDICIAL AND ADMINISTRATIVE CONSTRUCTION OF PRESENT PROVISIONS

Except for the relocation of the semicolon in section 1(e) in 1947 [50] to separate the provision relating to public-performance-for-profit rights from the provisions relating to recording and mechanical reproduction rights and the change of numbering of section 25(e) to 101(e),[51] the foregoing statutes have remained the same since 1909.[52]

Section 1(e) is, of course, the fifth and final subsection of section 1 of the copyright law, which enumerates the exclusive rights as to copyrighted works. Section 1(e) consists of three paragraphs, all limited to musical compositions. The first clause confirms public-performance-for-profit rights, which are limited by the so-called "jukebox" exception of the third and final paragraph of section 1(e). The second clause, after a second reference to the right of arrangement,[53] and of the balance of the first and second paragraphs of section 1(e) relate to recording and mechanical reproduction rights.

Under the first paragraph of section 1(e) (subsequent to the first clause), the proprietor of the copyright of a musical composition,[54] written by an American author or a foreign author whose country grants similar rights to U.S. citizens as evidenced by a Presidential

---

[49] See note 65, infra.
[50] See note 47, supra.
[51] Act of July 30, 1947 (61 Stat. 652).
[52] For clause-by-clause analysis of the compulsory license provisions, see Evans, "The Law of Copyright and the Right of Mechanical Reproduction of Musical Compositions" in Third Copyright Law Symposium 113, at pp. 118–131 (1940).
[53] The second clause can be said to embrace two distinct rights: (1) the right to make any arrangement or setting of the musical composition or the melody thereof in any system of notation from which it may be read, and (2) the right to make any form of record from which it may be reproduced. Sec. 1(b) previously recognizes the right to arrange or adapt a musical work. Howell, "Copyright Law," 148 (3d ed. 1952).
[54] The term "musical compositions" is defined by the Regulations of the Copyright Office (37 Code Fed. Regs., sec. 202.6 (1955)) as follows:
"§ 202.6 *Musical compositions (Class E)*. This class includes all musical compositions (other than dramatico-musical compositions), with or without words, as well as new versions of musical compositions, such as adaptations, arrangements and editings, when such editing is the writing of an author."

proclamation,[55] originally [56] copyrighted, either as a published or unpublished work,[57] after July 1, 1909, enjoys, as part of the copyright, the exclusive right to record and make mechanical reproductions thereof.[58] The proprietor need not exercise nor authorize the exercise of such rights. However, if the proprietor does exercise or authorize the exercise of mechanical reproduction rights, any other person may,

---

[55] "Proclamations, Conventions, and Treaties Establishing Copyright Relations Between the United States of America and Other Countries" (Copyright Office, May 1956) ; "International Copyright Relations of the United States of America" (Department of State, revised as of Jan. 20, 1955) ; 29 Ops. Att'y Gen. 64 (1911). The Universal Copyright Convention (see pp. 43–44, infra), and implementing legislation (act of Aug. 31. 1954. **68 Stat. 1030, effective Sept. 16, 1955)**; 17 U.S.C. 9(c) (Supp. 1955) eliminates the sec. **1(e) requirement of reciprocal treatment with respect to mechanical reproduction rights** (since the Convention is based on national treatment) and of special proclamations so far as musical compositions which have qualified for protection under the Convention are concerned. **Sec. 1(e), defining authors whose copyrighted musical compositions are entitled to recording and mechanical reproduction rights, is to be distinguished from the differently worded sec. 9, defining the authors whose works are eligible for statutory copyright.** Compare *G. Ricordi & Co.* v. *Columbia Graphophone Co.*, 258 Fed. 72 (S.D.N.Y. 1919), overruling 256 Fed. 699 (S.D.N.Y. 1919), with *Leibowitz* v. *Columbia Graphophone Co.*, 298 Fed. 342 (S.D.N.Y. 1923). See also H. Rept. No. 2222, 60th Cong., 2d sess., p. 9 (1909).
[56] Sec. 1(e) became effective July 1, 1909, and was not retroactive. *M. Witmark & Sons* v. *Standard Music Roll Co.*, 213 Fed. 532 (D.N.J. 1914), aff'd, 221 Fed. 376 (3d Cir. 1915). The date of original copyrighting controls. Musical compositions originally copyrighted prior to July 1, 1909, are not protected against recording and mechanical reproduction as the result of renewal of copyright subsequent to that date. *E. B. Marks Music Corp.* v. *Continental Record Co.*, 120 F. Supp. 275, on rearg., 100 U.S.P.Q. 446 (S.D.N.Y. 1954), aff'd, 222 F. 2d 488 (2d Cir. 1955), cert. denied, 350 U.S. 861, 76 Sup. Ct. 101, 100 L. Ed. 69 (1955). Rejecting the contention that renewal, since a "new estate," was a "new copyright" for purposes of sec. 1(e), the court stated (222 F. 2d at 491) :
"We think the words above quoted from the proviso to sec. 1(e) are clearly destructive of the plaintiff's contention that Congress intended that the mechanical reproduction of a song, which for years had been in the 'public domain,' may, by renewal, be fenced into a monopolistic field."
See also *Jerome* v. *Twentieth Century Fox-Film Corp.*, 67 F. Supp. 736, 741–742 (S.D.N.Y. 1946), aff'd on other grounds per curiam, 165 F. 2d 784 (2d Cir. 1948) :
"Assuming that plaintiff's copyright does not include the mechanical reproduction rights because the original copyright was obtained in 1896, almost 13 years prior to July 1909, that does not support defendant's argument that the renewal of the copyright in 1923 did not carry with it the motion picture rights."
See also 58 F. Supp. 13, 15 (S.D.N.Y. 1944). Renewal results essentially in a new copyright, distinct from the original copyright. *G. Ricordi & Co.* v. *Paramount Pictures, Inc.*, 189 F. 2d 469 (2d Cir. 1951) ; cf. note 56 supra. The renewal copyright is "free and clear of any rights, interests, or licenses attached to the copyright for the initial term." *Fitch* v. *Schubert*, 20 F. Supp. 314, 315 (S.D.N.Y. 1937) ; *Silverman* v. *Sunrise Pictures Corp.*, 273 Fed. 909 (2d Cir. 1921), cert. denied, 262 U.S. 758, 43 Sup. Ct. 705, 67 L. Ed. 1219 (1923) ; *Southern Music Pub. Co.* v. *Bibo-Lang, Inc.*, 10 F. Supp. 972 (S.D.N.Y. 1935). Quaere, as to the effect of renewal on licenses, negotiated or compulsory, under the original copyright. See note 230 infra.
[57] Musical compositions (music or words and music, but not words alone) (see note 54 supra) may be copyrighted as published works or unpublished works (that is, works not reproduced for sale). See note 235 infra. The word "published," as used in sec. 1(e), has been construed as including unpublished as well as published works. *Shilkret* v. *Musicraft Records*, 131 F. 2d 929 (2d Cir. 1942). Cf. *Marx* v. *United States*, 96 F. 2d 204 (9th Cir. 1938). But see *Leibowitz* v. *Columbia Graphophone Co.*, 298 Fed. 342 (S.D.N.Y. 1923).
[58] This right obviously embraces recording and mechanical reproduction methods known in 1909, e.g., records, disks, and cylinders for phonographs ; rolls for player-pianos. It has never been seriously urged that subsequently developed methods, such as long-playing records, electrical transcriptions, tape and wire recordings, were not covered. Some question, however, has been raised with respect to use in sound motion pictures, so-called "synchronization rights." Early sound films used a record on a turntable synchronized with the film ("Vitaphone"). Today the sound is reproduced by a sound track on the film itself ("Movietone"). See *Jerome* v. *Twentieth Century-Fox Film Corp.*, 67 F. Supp. 736, 741 (S.D.N.Y. 1946) (stating sound track on film is not type of "mechanical reproduction" to which sec. 1(e) applies), aff'd on other grounds per curiam, 165 F. 2d 784 (2d Cir. 1948), criticized in Dubin, "Copyright Aspects of Sound Recordings," 26 So. Calif. L. Rev. 139, at 147–149 (1953). Cf. *Foreign & Domestic Music Corp.* v. *Licht*, 196 F. 2d 627, 629 (2d Cir. 1952) ; *Encore Music Publications, Inc.* v. *London Film Productions, Inc.*, 89 U.S.P.Q. 501 (S.D.N.Y. 1951) ; *Foreign & Domestic Music Corp.* v. *Michael Wyngate, Inc.*, 66 F. Supp. 82 (S.D.N.Y. 1946) ; *Famous Music Corp.* v. *Melz*, 28 F. Supp. 767, 769 (W.D. La. 1939) (dictum). Cf. *L. C. Page & Co.* v. *Fox Film Corp.*, 83 F. 2d 196, 199 (2d Cir. 1936) (copyright of motion picture held to protect music on sound track). Quaere, as to kinescope recordings,. See pp. 13–14, supra, 51–52, infra.

under the compulsory license provision, make "similar use" [59] of the musical composition upon payment by the manufacturer to the proprietor of a royalty of 2 cents "on each such part manufactured," [60] and the proprietor is required to file a notice of use in the Copyright

[59] See 2 Ladas, "The International Protection of Literary and Artistic Property," pp. 790–791 (1938) :
"Thus, not only the same, but a similar use may be made by other persons. This should mean that use by the owner on phonograph records would involve permission for use by others on rolls of piano players."
Textually, sec. 1(e) is capable of the construction that protection to the copyright owner thereunder renders unlawful the making of recordings, whether known in 1909 or subsequently developed, including mechanical reproductions known in 1909 (i.e., disks, rolls, bands, cylinders) ; that the compulsory license provision comes into operation only upon the owner's making or authorizing the making of mechanical reproductions known in 1909 ; and that the "similar use" permitted under compulsory license must, by way of further limitation, be the same type of such mechanical reproduction, thus excluding (by strict construction since the clause is in derogation of the composer's rights) such post-1909 uses as electrical transcriptions and tape and wire recordings for radio broadcasting, kinescope, and television tape recordings for telecasting, and synchronization of sound film by means of disks or sound tracks. Accordingly, even if use on motion picture sound tracks be proscribed by sec. 1(e), it does not necessarily follow that the compulsory license provision would ever apply to permit use on sound tracks, whether the copyright owner permitted use on disks, sound tracks, or otherwise. Cf. Dubin, "Copyright Aspects of Sound Recordings," 26 So. Calif. L. Rev. 139, 147–148 (1953). In connection with the enjoyment of a compulsory license, some latitude is allowed manufacturers to prepare individual instrumental or vocal arrangements of the composition. *Edward B. Marks Music Corp.* v. *Foullon*, 79 F. Supp. 664 (S.D.N.Y. 1948), aff'd, 171 F. 2d 905 (2d Cir. 1949). Furthermore, under a compulsory license, the words of the musical composition may not be used. *F. A. Mills, Inc.* v. *Standard Music Roll Co.*, 223 Fed. 849 (D.N.J. 1915), aff'd, 241 Fed. 360 (3d Cir. 1917). But see *M. Witmark & Sons* v. *Standard Music Roll Co.*, 213 Fed. 532 (D.N.J. 1914), aff'd, 221 Fed. 376 (3d Cir. 1915). Nor may the composition be publicly performed for profit by means of any record made under a compulsory license. *Irving Berlin, Inc.* v. *Daigle*, 31 F. 2d 832 (5th Cir. 1929) ; *Famous Music Corp.* v. *Melz*, 28 F. Supp. 767 (W.D. La. 1939) ; *Associated Music Publishers, Inc.* v. *Debs Memorial Radio Fund, Inc.*, 46 F. Supp. 829 (S.D.N.Y. 1942). Contrariwise, if an exhibitor has a public-performance-for-profit license covering the music composition, a motion picture with a sound track which infringes such composition may be exhibited without making the exhibitor an infringer. *Foreign & Domestic Music Corp.* v. *Licht*, 196 F. 2d 627 (2d Cir. 1952). Persons desirous of making recordings or other uses of the work may always attempt to negotiate a license with the copyright owner in cases where the availability of the compulsory license provision is doubtful. See pp. 51–52, infra.
[60] The term "part" refers to the statutory phrase, "parts of instruments serving to reproduce mechanically the musical work," which codified the ruling of the U.S. Supreme Court in *White-Smith Music Publishing Co.* v. *Apollo Co.*, 209 U.S. 1, 28 Sup. Ct. 319, 52 L. Ed. 655 (1908), that a pianola roll, since incapable of being read, was not a "copy" but a part of a mechanical music-producing machine. Verified reports and royalty payments may be required by the copyright proprietor on the 20th day of each month on the "number of parts" manufactured during the previous month. Two cents per part was thought in 1909 to be equivalent to 5 percent of the manufacturer's selling price, and a "reasonable royalty" and "adequate return" to the composer. H. Rept. No. 2222, 60th Cong., 2d sess., pp. 6, 7 (1909). Quaere, in the case of two or more compositions on the same "part," whether the royalty was intended to be 2 cents per composition, or, if two cents in toto, how it was intended to be allocated ; in the case of disks or tapes, whether each side thereof or the whole is a "part." See p. 14, supra. It has been contended that the royalty should be based on parts sold, not on parts manufactured. 37 Music Trades 6 (Mar. 13, 1909). Although the royalty is at the same rate for all compositions, the statutory royalty provision calls for returns to composers based theoretically on manufacturer's estimates of prospective sales, and hence is automatically geared to public acceptance. Payment of the royalty cannot be avoided by going through the final manufacturing step outside the United States. *G. Ricordi & Co.* v. *Columbia Graphophone Co.*, 258 Fed. 72 (S.D.N.Y. 1919) (disk records made and sold in Canada held subject to statutory royalty as "manufactured" in United States since first eight of nine manufacturing steps occurred in United States. For the Canadian law since 1921, see p. 38, infra. Application of the statutory royalty rate for long-playing records, tape and wire recordings, motion picture sound tracks, etc., obviously creates difficulty, especially in the case of longer musical compositions. If, say, 500 positive prints of a sound motion picture were made to supply exhibition demands, the producer, at the statutory royalty rate, would pay only $10 per musical composition recorded on the sound track. See *Jerome* v. *Twentieth Century-Fox Film Corp.*, 67 F. Supp. 736, 741 (S.D.N.Y. 1946), aff'd on other grounds per curiam, 165 F. 2d 748 (2d Cir. 1948). The payment of the royalty does not compensate for public performance for profit of the recorded musical composition ; permission for such performance must be obtained by actual license.

Office.[61] The proprietor's failure to file such notice of use constitutes a complete defense to any suit, action, or proceeding for an infringement of the recording or mechanical reproduction rights.[62]

Remedies for infringement of recording or mechanical reproduction rights in musical compositions are outlined in various sections of the copyright law. Where the copyright proprietor has not exercised or permitted the exercise of mechanical reproduction rights, and the compulsory license provision, therefore, does not come into operation, the general remedies of sections 101(a)–(d), 104, 106, 108–112, 115–116 of the copyright law, so far as relevant, apply. However, where the mechanical reproduction rights have been duly exercised, thereby activating the compulsory license provision, specific remedies are set forth in sections 1(e) and 101(e). These sections are not consistent in terminology or in substance, as pointed out above.[63]

The second paragraph of section 1(e) provides:

> In case of failure of such manufacturer to pay to the copyright proprietor within thirty days after demand in writing the full sum of royalties due at said rate at the date of such demand, the court may award taxable costs to the plaintiff and a reasonable counsel fee, and the court may, in its discretion, enter judgment therein for any sum in addition over the amount found to be due as royalty in accordance with the terms of this title, not exceeding three times such amount.

These provisions are somewhat restated in the first half of section 101(e):

> SEC. 101. * * * (e) ROYALTIES FOR USE OF MECHANICAL REPRODUCTION OF MUSICAL WORKS.—Whenever the owner of a musical copyright has used or permitted the use of the copyrighted work upon the parts of musical instruments serving to reproduce mechanically the musical work, then in case of infringement of such copyright by the unauthorized manufacture, use, or sale of interchangeable parts, such as disks, rolls, bands, or cylinders for use in mechanical music-producing machines adapted to reproduce the copyrighted music, no criminal action shall be brought, but in a civil action an injunction may be granted upon such terms as the court may impose, and the plaintiff shall be entitled to recover in lieu of profits and damages a royalty as provided in section 1, subsection (e), of this title: *Provided, also* * * *

Then follows the proviso which constitutes the second half of section 101(e) to the effect that whenever any person intends to rely upon the compulsory license provision, he must serve notice of such

---

[61] The notice of use should be filed on Form U, either with or after the application for copyright registration of the composition, and should be accompanied by the $2 recordation fee for a notice containing five titles or less, plus 50 cents for each title over five. The copyright registration numbers, dates of publication or registration, and names of authors should be given as well as the correct titles of the compositions. Copyright Office Circular No. 5 (March 1954). In the fiscal year 1955, almost 8,000 notices of use were filed. Annual Report of the Register of Copyrights for the Fiscal Year Ending June 30, 1955, p. 11. Such notice-of-use requirement, since not a condition of the copyright but a procedural prerequisite to enforcement, is not affected by the Universal Copyright Convention. Cary, "The United States and Universal Copyright: An Analysis of Public Law 743" in "Universal Copyright Convention Analyzed," pp. 100–101 (1955); Sherman, "The Universal Copyright Convention: Its Effect on United States Law," 55 Colum. L. Rev. 1137, 1155 (1955).

[62] Although the statute provides that the proprietor's failure to file the notice of use shall be a complete defense to any suit, action, or proceeding for any infringement of such copyright, the courts have limited the defense to claims of infringement of mechanical reproduction rights, treating the latter as the antecedent of such copyright. *Lutz v. Buck*, 40 F. 2d 501 (5th Cir. 1930); *Irving Berlin, Inc.* v. *Daigle, Irving Berlin, Inc.* v. *Russo*, 31 F. 2d 832 (5th Cir. 1929), rev'g 26 F. 2d 149, 150 (E.D. La. 1928) (public performance for profit); *F. A. Mills, Inc.* v. *Standard Music Roll Co.*, 223 Fed. 849 (D.N.J. 1915), aff'd, 241 Fed. 360 (3d Cir. 1917) (copying of words). The statute failed to incorporate the provisions of some five earlier bills that each of the rights given the copyright proprietor be treated as a "separate estate." See note 43 supra; see also note 56 supra.

[63] See pp. 14–15, supra.

intention, by registered mail, upon the copyright proprietor at his last address disclosed by the records of the Copyright Office, sending to the Copyright Office a duplicate of such notice.[64] If this be not done, the proviso goes on to provide that—

the court may, in its discretion, in addition to sums hereinabove mentioned, award the complainant a further sum, not to exceed three times the amount provided by section 1, subsection (e), of this title, by way of damages, and not as a penalty, and also a temporary injunction until the full award is paid.

These provisions have been rarely invoked, and there are few reported cases attempting to construe them.[65]

Although doubts concerning the constitutionality of the compulsory license provision have been raised from time to time, they apparently have never been seriously urged in any reported litigation.[66]

While the copyright law since 1909 has protected, to the extent indicated above, musical compositions against recording and mechanical reproduction, it has not changed the ruling in *White-Smith Music Publishing Co.* v. *Apollo Co.*[67] that recordings were not "copies" of the musical composition or "writings" of an author within the scope of the existing copyright statute. Accordingly, the copyright statute

---

[64] 17 U.S.C. 101(e) (1952). No special form is required for such notice of intention to use. Copyright Office Circular No. 5 (March 1954).

[65] *Miller* v. *Goody*, 125 F. Supp. 348 (S.D.N.Y. 1954) (award of damages at three times statutory royalty and impounding defendant's filing of notice of intention to use and payment of damages) ; *Edward B. Marks Corp.* v. *Foullon*, 77 U.S.P.Q. 502 (S.D.N.Y. 1948) (award of $333.30 as statutory royalties and damages on 5,555 records, per license agreement, together with costs and attorney's fees), aff'd, 171 F. 2d 905, 907 (2d Cir. 1949) : "Moreover, sec. 1(e) allows the judge to triple the royalties against him if he defaults in his payments ; and sec. 25(e) does the same if he does not serve upon the owner notice of his intention in advance." *Leo Feist, Inc.* v. *American Music Roll Co.*, 253 Fed. 860 (E.D. Pa. 1918) (award of $373.74—equivalent to statutory royalty and $150 counsel fee, and $100 punitive damages for defendant's subsequent failure to report and pay monthly on demand). The only remedies for infringement of recording and mechanical reproduction rights are against the manufacturer under secs. 1(e) and 101(e) ; distributors are accordingly not liable. *Miller* v. *Goody*, 139 F. Supp. 176 (S.D.N.Y. 1956). See also *Foreign & Domestic Music Corp.* v. *Licht*, 196 F. 2d 627 (2d Cir. 1952). (Nonimported motion picture containing sound track infringing musical composition held not subject to seizure in hands of exhibitor licensed to perform composition publicly for profit.)

[66] The constitutional reference to copyright as "the exclusive Right" casts some doubt on the constitutionality of provisions establishing rights lacking in exclusivity, such as compulsory license provisions. Fenning, "Copyright Before the Constitution," 17 J. Pat. Off. Soc'y 379, 385 (1935) ; Fenning, "The Origin of the Patent and Copyright Clause of the Constituiton," 17 Geo. L. J. 109, 116–117 (1929) ; Weil, "American Copyright Law," pp. 62–65 (1917) ; DeWolf, "An Outline of Copyright Law," p. 101 (1925) Of course, the recording and mechanical reproduction rights are exclusive, only becoming nonexclusive by the copyright owner's exercise of mechanical reproduction rights, thereby activating the compulsory license provision. The compulsory license was not introduced to impair existing rights but to define rights then being recognized for the first time in the copyright statute. H. Rept. No. 2222, 60th Cong., 2d sess., p. 9 (1909). But see Evans, "The Law of Copyright and the Right of Mechanical Reproduction of Musical Compositions" in Third Copyright Law Symposium 113, at pp. 148–150 (1940) ; Joiner, "Analysis, Criticism, Comparison and Suggested Corrections of the Copyright Law of the United States Relative to Mechanical Reproduction of Music" in Second Copyright Law Symposium 43, at pp. 66–67 (1940). For one explanation why the constitutionality of the compulsory license provision has not been litigated, at least by copyright owners, see p. 23, infra. Cf. attacks by Representative W. Sterling Cole on the constitutionality of the compulsory license provision of the Atomic Energy Act of 1954 (42 U.S.C., section 2183(e) (Supp. 1955)) on the basis of the constitutional reference to "the exclusive Right" of the inventor ; 2 Hearings on S. 3690 and H.R. 9757, 83d Cong.. 2d sess.. p. 658 (1954) ; 2 U.S. Code Congressional and Administrative News 3487–3491 (1954) ; 100 Congressional Record A5356, A5358, July 23, 1954 ; 102 Congressional Record A1903 (daily ed. Feb. 29, 1956). See also Comment: "The Constitutionality of the Patent Provisions of the 1954 Atomic Energy Act." 22 U. of Chi. L. Rev. 920 (1955).

[67] See note 6 supra ; see also *Miller* v. *Goody*, 139 F. Supp. 176 (S.D.N.Y. 1956).

provides no basis for protecting the recording itself [68] or the rendition recorded.[69]

Whether recordings are "writings" in the constitutional sense and hence constitutionally eligible subject matter for Federal statutory copyright protection, should Congress attempt to extend copyright protection to them; [70] whether the public distribution or sale of a recording constitutes publication of the work and/or rendition so as to terminate any common-law rights therein; [71] and whether a recording is a "copy" which can serve as the medium for securing [72] or perfecting [73] statutory copyright in the recorded work, or which, if published

---

[68] 17 U.S.C. 5 (1952) ; H. Rept. No. 2222, 60th Cong., 2d sess., p. 9 (1909) ; Copyright Office Circular No. 5 (March 1954). But see *Aeolian Co.* v. *Royal Music Roll Co.*, 196 Fed. 926 (W.D.N.Y. 1912), criticized in DeWolf, "An Outline of Copyright Law," pp. 101–102 (1925) ; note, 5 Stan. L. Rev. 433 (1953). Protection may be available on grounds of unfair competition. *Fonotipia Ltd.* v. *Bradley*, 171 Fed. 951 (C.C.E.D.N.Y. 1909). But see *G. Ricordi & Co.* v. *Haendler*, 194 F. 2d 914, 916 (2d Cir. 1952) ; *Hebrew Publishing Co.* v. *Scharfstein*, 288 N.Y. 374, 43 N.E. 2d 449 (1942).

[69] Compare *Capitol Records, Inc.* v. *Mercury Records Corp.*, 221 F. 2d 657 (2d Cir. 1955) with *RCA Mfg. Co.* v. *Whiteman*, 114 F. 2d 86 (2d Cir. 1940). cert. denied, 311 U.S. 712, 61 Sup. Ct. 393, 85 L. Ed. 463 (1940) (sale of records of rendition held divestitive of common-law rights therein). Contra : *Waring* v. *WDAS Broadcasting Station, Inc.*, 327 Pa. 433, 194 Atl. 631 (1937) ; *Waring* v. *Dunlea*, 26 F. Supp. 338 (E.D.N.C. 1939) ; *National Ass'n of Performing Artists* v. *Wm. Penn Broadcasting Co.*, 38 F. Supp. 531 (E.D.Pa. 1941). But see N.C. Gen. Stat.. sec. 66–28 (1950) ; S.C. Code, sec. 66–101 (1952) ; Fla. Stat. secs. 543. 02–03 (1953). For a complete discussion, see Kaplan "Performer's Rights and Copyright : The Capitol Records Case," 69 Harv. L. Rev. 409 (1956) ; Nimmer, "Copyright 1955," 43 Calif. L. Rev. 791, 801–806 (1955) ; note, 31 N.Y.U.L. Rev. 415 (1955).

[70] United States Constitution, art. I, sec. 8, clause 8. The *White-Smith Music Publishing Co.* case involved interpretation of the pre-1909 copyright act and not of the constitutional term "writings." A recent commentator has expressed opinion that constitutionally "writings" include records (and "authors" include performers). Kaplan, "Performer's Rights and Copyright : The Capitol Records Case," 69 Harv. L. Rev. 409, 413–414 (1956).

[71] Until recently it was generally assumed that the sale of records was not publication of the embodied composition. Burton, "Business Practices in the Copyright Field," Seven Copyright Problems Analyzed 80, 102–104 (1952). Recording was neither copying nor publishing. *White-Smith Music Publishing Co.* v. *Apollo Co.*, 209 U.S. 1, 28 Sup. Ct. 319, 52 L. Ed. 655 (1908). Records were likened to a captured performance which was not a publication. *Ferris* v. *Frohman*, 223 U.S. 424, 32 Sup. Ct. 263, 56 L. Ed. 492 (1912). Records have been frequently issued at the outset to test the public reaction, and sheet music might not be issued at all if the record failed to catch on. Sheet music has greatly declined in relative importance as a medium of exploiting popular music. The traditional view was that statutory copyright need not be resorted to unless sheet music be issued. Kaplan, "Publication in Copyright Law : The Question of Phonograph Records," 103 U. of Pa. L. Rev. 469, 472 n. 20 (1955). A growing number of recent cases has held or indicated that the sale of a recording constitutes publication of the recorded composition. *Biltmore Music Corp.* v. *Kittinger*, C.O. Bull. No. 29, p. 32 (S.D. Cal. 1954) ; *Mills Music Co.* v. *Cromwell Music, Inc.*, 126 F. Supp. 54 (S.D.N.Y. 1954) : *Shapiro, Bernstein & Co.* v. *Miracle Record Co.*, 91 F. Supp. 473 (N.D. Ill. 1950) ; *Blanc* v. *Lantz*, 83 U.S.P.Q. 137 (Cal. Super. Ct. 1949) (intentionally making sound track of music public held divestitive of common-law rights in music under then State statute) ; cf. *Capitol Records, Inc.* v. *Mercury Records Corp.*, 221 F. 2d 657 (2d Cir. 1955) ; *Yacoubian* v. *Carroll*, 74 U.S.P.Q. 257 (S.D. Cal. 1947). See Nimmer, "Copyright Publication," 56 Colum. L. Rev. 185, 192–194 (1956). The traditional view was incorporated in the Universal Copyright Convention, art. VI, defining "publication" as meaning the "reproduction in tangible form and the general distribution to the public of copies of a work from which it can be read or otherwise visually perceived." But see *RCA Mfg. Co.* v. *Whiteman*, 114 F. 2d 86 (2d Cir. 1940), cert. denied, 211 U.S. 712, 61 Sup. Ct. 393, 85 L. Ed. 463 (1940).

[72] 17 U.S.C. 10, 12 (1952). "Very doubtful" under the present statute. Kaplan, "Publication in Copyright Law : The Question of Phonograph Records," 103 U. of Pa. L. Rev. 469, 482–484 (1955). Generally, statutory copyright is secured by publication with copyright notice or registration and deposit of a copy of an unpublished work. Logically what amounts to a divestitive publication of a musical composition ought to qualify as an investitive publication thereof, although the converse would not necessarily be so. The location of the copyright notice would present problems. See note 74 infra.

[73] 17 U.S.C. 12, 13 (1952). Phonograph records have not been accepted for registration and deposit by the Copyright Office in recent years, although works in Braille and motion pictures with sound tracks have been accepted. See Kaplan, "Publication in Copyright Law : The Question of Phonograph Records," 103 U. of Pa. L. Rev. 469, 483 n. 65 (1955). The Copyright Office has not refused to accept motion pictures because sound tracks were attached to them, but has made no ruling as to whether the registration does or does not include the sound track. If the sound track were submitted separately, registration would presumably be denied. See also *Yacoubian* v. *Carroll*, 74 U.S.P.Q. 257 (S.D. Cal. 1947) (issuance of records held not reproduction of copies for sale of musical composition previously copyrighted under sec. 12 ; hence deposit of two "copies" not required under secs. 12, 13).

or offered for sale in the United States by authority of the copyright proprietor, must bear the statutory copyright notice,[74] are intriguing questions which are beyond the scope of this study.

II. Legislative History of Compulsory Licensing Provisions In the United States Since 1909

A. PROPOSED BILLS

1. The 68th Congress

The compulsory licensing feature of section 1(e) did not come up for further legislative consideration for 16 years.

(a) H.R. 11258 and S. 4355

On January 2, 1925, Representative Perkins introduced a bill designed to revise the copyright law and permit the entry of the United States into the International (Berne) Copyright Union. H.R. 11258 [75] and its Senate counterpart, S. 4355,[76] had been drafted by the Register of Copyrights, Thorvald Solberg, at the request of the Authors' League, and contained no provision for compulsory licensing of mechanical reproduction rights. Instead, section 12(d) simply granted to authors, their administrators, executors, or assigns the right—

to make, copy, and vend any phonograph record, or any perforated roll or other contrivance by means of which, in whole or in part, the copyright work may be mechanically reproduced * * *.

Hearty support for the complete elimination of the licensing provision was given by Nathan Burkan, of ASCAP, who testified during hearings held from January 22 through February 24, 1925, that compulsory licensing was an arbitrary, discriminatory class legislation which forced authors to do business with persons not of their own choosing at terms contrary to those specified in section 1(e) and without any means of enforcing their claims against unknown record producers.[77] More specifically Mr. Burkan alleged the phonograph industry was reporting on sales of records, rather than the number of records produced; was furnishing uncertified statements of accounts on a quarterly, instead of a monthly, basis; and was charging the author 10 percent for "breakage" as well as costs for "arrangements" and advertising. Mr. Burkan further claimed manufacturers were refusing to pay royalties on records exported abroad or on records produced from matrices shipped abroad. In addition, many record companies produced records without any intention of paying the license fee or delayed payment, sometimes until they became bank-

---

[74] 17 U.S.C. 10 (1952). The statute is silent with respect to the location of copyright notice on records, tape and wire recordings, etc. 17 U.S.C. 19, 20 (1952). Cases in the past have held that a copyright notice was not required on a phonograph record or perforated roll. *Irving Berlin, Inc.* v. *Daigle; Irving Berlin, Inc.* v. *Russo*, 31 F. 2d 832 (5th Cir. 1929) ; *Buck* v. *Heretis*, 24 F. 2d 876 (E.D.S.C. 1928) ; *Buck* v. *Lester*, 24 F. 2d 877 (E.D.S.C. 1928). Quaere, whether a record manufactured under the compulsory license provision (assuming it to be a copy, and its public distribution or sale to be a publication, of the recorded musical composition) can be said to be published or offered for sale by authority of the copyright proprietor.
[75] H.R. 11258, 68th Cong., 2d sess. (1925).
[76] S. 4355, 68th Cong., 2d sess. (1925) (introduced by Senator Ernst, Feb. 17, 1925).
[77] Hearings on H.R. 11258, 68th Cong., 2d sess., pp. 148–168 (1925).

rupt. Thus an author, even after securing judgment, was frequently left without recourse against the manufacturer.[78]

Representatives of the Music Industries Chamber of Commerce and individual record manufacturers replied to these charges by reminding the committee that American business had been passing through an economic recession which had affected other industries as well as phonograph record manufacturers, and that failure to pay royalties had in several of the instant cases been due to the belief that the alien author had not been domiciled in the United States,[79] and therefore not entitled to such payment.

Claiming $2 million in royalties had been paid in 1924 on the basis of a $50 million business to approximately 300 to 400 copyright owners, and that elimination of the compulsory license provision was not necessary for the entry of the United States into the Berne Union, the record manufacturers pleaded for the retention of the compulsory license provision, but with modifications which would (1) change the "unfair method of basing royalty payments upon production"; (2) extend the license to include "word" music rolls;[80] and (3) protect publishers against financially or otherwise irresponsible manufacturers of mechanical devices.[81]

On the last day of the hearings a subcommittee was appointed to consider the bill during recess, and informal hearings were held April 22 and May 8, 1925.

2. The 69th Congress

(a) H.R. 5841

A bill identical to the two bills considered by the 68th Congress was reintroduced by Representative Perkins at the beginning of the 69th Congress, on December 17, 1925,[82] but no further action was taken. For the next 2 years, 1926–27, compulsory licensing continued a controversial subject.

(b) S. 2328 and H.R. 10353

With the rapid development of radio broadcasting in the early 1920's a dispute soon developed between ASCAP and the radio stations over the licensing of the performances of musical compositions. S. 2328[83] and H.R. 10353[84] were introduced on January 26 and March 15, 1926, by Senator Dill and Representative Vestal, respectively, as a possible solution to the controversy between the two interests. By adding a new subsection (f) to section 1, the bills proposed to extend compulsory licensing to musical compositions used for broadcast purposes, with a license fee based on the power of the transmitting station. This license was to be applicable only to sub-

---

[78] Id., at pp. 157–160.
[79] See note 55, supra.
[80] Piano rolls on which the lyrics were printed. Use of the words had been held to infringe under sec. 1(a) of the act. *F. A. Mills, Inc.* v. *Standard Music Roll Co.*, 223 Fed. 849 (D.N.J. 1915), aff'd, 241 Fed. 360 (3d Cir. 1917). Rolls without words were becoming unsalable; 10 cents or more royalty per roll was usually asked. But see *M. Witmark & Sons* v. *Standard Music Roll Co.*, 213 Fed. 532 (D.N.J. 1914), aff'd, 221 Fed. 376 (3d Cir. 1915) (pre-1909 work).
[81] Hearings on H.R. 11258, 68th Cong., 2d sess., pp. 233–275 (1925).
[82] H.R. 5841, 69th Cong., 1st sess. (1925).
[83] S. 2328, 69th Cong., 1st sess. (1926).
[84] H.R. 10353, 69th Cong., 1st sess. (1926).

sequently copyrighted compositions so as not to impair existing contracts.[85]

Joint hearings were held April 5 to 22, 1926, at which a representative of the Music Industries Chamber of Commerce listed the bad features of the existing compulsory license provision as: (1) failure to include the so-called "word" roll; (2) pressure on the part of music publishers to make the record manufacturers take a certain number of compositions each month in order to get the few they actually wanted; and (3) lack of protection for the copyright owner against use of his music by financially irresponsible concerns.[86]

On the other hand, Nathan Burkan questioned the constitutionality of compulsory licensing and explained failure to make an attack in the courts as follows: [87]

Unquestionably this act was so artfully drawn, that if an attack was made upon the compulsory provisions of the act and the court declared them unconstitutional, the whole act would have to fall. That would have left the authors in the same plight they were in from 1888 to July 1909 * * *

Another reason for the failure to make any attack upon the constitutionality of this proposition was the power of boycott that these reproducers of mechanical instruments possessed.

Mr. Burkan also alleged :[88]

The act of 1909, while it provided in case of any infringement of the copyrighted work that the infringer should be liable to very severe penalties, damages, costs, to injunction, seizure, and forfeiture of infringing material, and to criminal punishment, in the case of the illegal mechanical reproduction, the sole remedy * * * is limited to a recovery of three times the royalty fixed by the statute; * * * If the mechanical reproducer made no reports or kept false books as to the number of records or rolls he manufactured then the composers' plight is more desperate * * *

In discussing *Wheaton* v. *Peters*,[89] often cited as a basis for the compulsory licensing provision, Mr. Burkan stated:

This case is no authority for the proposition that Congress can attach to a copyright grant a compulsory license feature.

On the contrary, the holding of the case is that Congress in vesting the exclusive right may impose conditions. A compulsory license is the antithesis of the exclusive right.[90]

In short, Mr. Burkan characterized the two bills as being [91]—

vicious and paternalistic price-fixing measures, lacking in merit and iniquitous because unconstitutional, because depriving a body of useful citizens of their property, without just compensations, for the private benefit of a powerful group * * *

(c) H.R. 10434

In the meantime Representative Vestal had also introduced a general revision bill, H.R. 10434,[92] which was designed to permit the entry of the United States into the Berne Union. Approximately two-thirds of H.R. 10434 contained text identical with the Perkins bill, the remainder constituted compromises worked out by conflict-

---

[85] Hearings on S. 2328 and H.R. 10353, 69th Cong., 1st sess., pp. 31–32 (1926). See note 66 supra.
[86] Id., at p. 87.
[87] Id., at p. 314.   See note 66 supra.
[88] Id., at p. 315.
[89] 8 Pet. 591 (U.S. 1834).
[90] Hearings on S. 2328 and H.R. 10353, 69th Cong., 1st sess., p. 329 (1926). See note 66 supra.
[91] Id., at p. 371.
[92] H.R. 10434, 69th Cong., 1st sess. (1926).

ing interests through a series of meetings held in New York throughout 1925.[93]

Section 1(h) of the bill gave an exclusive right—

to make or to procure the making of any transcription, roll, or record thereof, in whole or in part, or any other contrivance by or from which it may in any manner or by any method or means be communicated, exhibited, performed, represented, produced, or reproduced; and to communicate, exhibit, perform, represent, produce, or reproduce it in any manner or by any means or method whatsoever, * * *

Again, in support of this endeavor to eliminate the compulsory license, ASCAP submitted a brief in which it argued the following points: [94]

1. All that Congress was empowered to grant to an author was the exclusive right as a monopoly for a limited period in the work made the subject of copyright. Congress can give neither more nor less. Freeing the work for use by manufacturers of mechanical records upon the payment of an arbitrary price fixed by Congress is not securing to the author a "monopoly for a limited period" nor the exclusive right in his work.

2. A copyright being private property, Congress had no power to fix the price for which private third parties might use the work. Even if the Government could appropriate or use it itself, it would have to pay just compensation, and the ascertainment of such compensation was a judicial question and not a legislative one, and Congress could not fix the price.

3. Assuming, but not concluding, that Congress could fix the price, the rate fixed in the act was unjust, unreasonable, and confiscatory.

Somewhat similar in tone was the resolution of the American Bar Association: [95]

There should be no compulsory license required of authors, who should be permitted to dispose of and deal in their rights in their absolute discretion. Specifically, we disapprove of the provisions of section 1(e), the act of 1909, for compulsory licenses mechanically to reproduce copyright music. We believe that a composer should have the right to dispose of his music, however it may be produced or reproduced, as he may see fit.

During Mr. Solberg's testimony, a letter from former Representative Washburn, dated April 2, 1926, was read into the record: [96]

That royalty clause was a "makeshift" made necessary to get the bill through. Without it, there would have been no copyright legislation in 1909. The author should have "complete control" of his rights. The constitutional right expressed in the provision that Congress may secure for limited times to authors and inventors the exclusive right to their respective writings and discoveries should, if exercised, not be abridged by legislation—that I believe to be a sound principle.

In reiterating its request for retention, but modification, of the existing compulsory license provision, the phonograph record industry through its representatives claimed success was dependent upon access to all existing musical compositions and pointed out that since 1909 compulsory licensing had been adopted by England, Canada, Australia, New Zealand, India, Newfoundland, Italy, and Germany; and that the industry had flourished under the aegis of the license as compared to the countries having no provision.[97]

What effect these arguments pro and con had on the committee cannot be determined since no report was issued.

---

[93] Hearings on H.R. 10434, 69th Cong., 1st sess., pp. 14–18, 227 (1926).
[94] Id., at p. 261.
[95] Id., at p. 224.
[96] Id., at p. 240.
[97] Id. at pp. 334–335.

(d) H.R. 10987

H.R. 10987,[98] as introduced by Representative Vestal on April 5, 1926, embodied still another attempt to amend section 1(e) by requiring each copyright owner who permitted the use of his work for mechanical reproduction or for radio broadcasting to—

affix in some accessible place on such music and upon the phonograph disk, cylinder, roll, or other contrivance for the mechanical reproduction thereof, a notice of the amount of royalty prescribed for any use of such music for public performance for profit, and thereafter any other person may make similar use of the copyrighted work, and the sale or other distribution of any musical composition, or disk, cylinder, roll, or other contrivance for reproducing said composition which has the rate of royalty for use so affixed, *shall carry with it an implied license * * * to broadcast it, or to use it for the manufacture of mechanical instruments*, as the case may be, from and after payment of the prescribed royalty * * *. [Emphasis supplied.]

This bill, however, saw no legislative action.

(e) H.R. 17276

On February 21, 1927, Representative Vestal introduced still another bill, H.R. 17276,[99] which would have repealed section 25(e) and amended section 1(e) so as to require the recording in the Copyright Office by each copyright owner of his sale, assignment, or license of the right to the mechanical reproduction of his work, and also the recording by every manufacturer of his agreement, under seal, to use the work in full compliance with the terms and conditions of the original grant. Any violation of the license, as recorded, by the manufacturer would be deemed an infringement of copyright, with a possible penalty of his being "forever barred from the benefits and privileges of the compulsory license provisions of this act with respect to any musical work whatsoever, irrespective of the proprietorship thereof." The copyright owner was also to be given the right of discovery, inspection, or examination of books, records, and papers or any manufacturer relative to the production, sale or disposition of mechanical reproductions. No further action on this bill is recorded.

3. *The 70th Congress*

With the beginning of the new Congress, Representative Vestal renewed efforts to amend the compulsory license provisions.

(a) H.R. 8912

H.R. 8912, [100] introduced January 9, 1928, was a general copyright revision bill, similar in text to H.R. 10434 [101] of the previous Congress, but no hearings were held.

(b) H.R. 10655 and S. 3160

Two more bills [102] followed, each proposing amendments similar to H.R. 17276 [103] of the previous Congress, with the exception of the penalty. Instead of barring the infringing manufacturer from fur-

---

[98] H.R. 10987, 69th Cong., 1st sess. (1926).
[99] H.R. 17276, 69th Cong., 2d sess. (1927).
[100] H.R. 8912, 70th Cong., 1st sess. (1928).
[101] See note 92 supra.
[102] H.R. 10655, 70th Cong., 1st sess. (1928) (introduced by Representative Vestal, Feb. 7, 1928) ; S. 3160, 70th Cong., 1st sess. (1928) (introduced by Senator Moses, Feb. 13, 1928).
[103] See note 99 supra.

ther conduct of his business, the bills provided for a fine of not less than $500 nor more than $5,000 for the granting by any copyright owner or the acceptance by any manufacturer of refunds, rebates, discounts or setoffs.

In the hearings on H.R. 10655 are indications that compromise versions of the bills were apparently submitted to the committee both by ASCAP and the phonograph industry.[104] Discussions dealt with the need for accessible music on the part of the phonograph record industry; applicability of the license to foreign authors, and to compositions copyrighted prior to 1909; also an apparent attempt to limit the licensing provision to phonograph records and rolls, to the exclusion of other electronic devices, specifically Vitaphone and Movietone. The 12-cent royalty situation with regard to the "word" rolls was also presented at some length as was the requirement to file notices of use within 10 days by domiciled copyright owners and 20 days by foreign proprietors with failure to do so being a complete defense to any suit or proceeding thereon.[105]

Mr. Solberg appeared as one of the final witnesses and asked to correct the impression that Representative Washburn had been the author of the 2-cent royalty, outlining briefly the legislative history of the compulsory license clause from 1906 to 1909.[106] In conclusion he recommended a short bill be drafted which would merely permit copyright owners to make contracts wherever they desire, but require the contracts be available at some convenient place for examination. Again the committee failed to report the bill out.

(c) H.R. 13452

H.R. 13452,[107] introduced by Representative Vestal on May 1, 1928, had been drafted by a subcommittee of the Committee on Patents.[108] It included some of the language discussed at the hearings on the previous bill, namely, the license was limited to a grant "for the manufacture and sale of *ordinary commercial phonograph records or perforated music rolls.*" [109] Such grant was to be in writing and not effective until recorded in the Copyright Office by the copyright proprietor. Royalties, the amount of which were to be determined by contract, were to be "payable at a specified rate per ordinary commercial phonograph record or perforated music roll * * *" The grants could be altered, modified, extended or canceled by subsequent agreements which would not be effective until 90 days after their recordation in the Copyright Office. Each manufacturer was to be required to file an acknowledged notice under seal of his intention to use. Payment of royalty would free the articles or devices from further contribution except in the case of public performance for profit. It would also be unlawful for any one to change, alter or deviate from the terms of a grant, as recorded, and to give or accept any discriminatory preference under penalty of a $500 to $5,000 fine.

The bill was reported [110] out of committee 4 days after it had been introduced and referred to the House Calendar. In recommending the

---

[104] Hearings on H.R. 10655, 70th Cong., 1st sess., pp. 42–50, 72–94 (1928).
[105] Id., at pp. 193–194.
[106] Id., at pp. 191–192.
[107] H.R. 13452, 70th Cong., 1st sess. (1928).
[108] Hearings on H.R. 13452, 70th Cong., 2d sess, p. 4 (1929).
[109] H.R. 13452, 70th Cong., 1st sess. (1928) (emphasis supplied).
[110] H. Rept. No. 1520, 70th Cong., 1st sess. (1928).

bill favorably, without amendment, Representative Vestal wrote:[111]

Extended hearings were held, and much testimony was taken from representatives of both the copyright owners and manufacturers of devices which serve to mechanically reproduce copyrighted musical works. The matter has been studied for years by the committee, and all interests have generally agreed as to the justice of the principle of free bargaining governing the relationships between the copyright owners and the manufacturers of mechanical devices.

It seemed apparent to your committee that obvious injustice was done to the composers and authors of musical works in depriving them of an opportunity to freely bargain in respect of the terms and conditions under which mechanical reproduction of their works could be licensed to others, and to subject them to a statutory form of compulsory licensing which afforded no adequate protection against dishonest and delinquent manufacturers.

It seemed equally apparent that for the just protection of the manufacturers a musical composition, once released by its copyright owner to any manufacturer for mechanical reproduction, should be available to all manufacturers upon terms equal to those required to be met by the first licensee.

On February 4, 1929, the bill came up on the Consent Calendar of the House. Representative Vestal requested unanimous consent to have the bill passed over in order to iron out differences explaining that an amendment was being prepared by the manufacturers which would be ready later in the day. A comment was made that a number of wires were being received from retailers of phonograph records and piano rolls, and that since they represented the public, perhaps they should be heard. The result was that the bill was unanimously passed over without prejudice or objection.

Hearings were held on H.R. 13452 before the House Committee on Rules on February 13 and 16, 1929. There Representative Chindblom objected to the granting of a rule on the grounds that hearings had not been held before the bill was reported out of committee and he proposed an amendment which would prohibit copyright owners from combining to fix a price or royalty rate for the use of mechanical reproductions.[112] Representative Busby also registered opposition to the bill characterizing it as "half baked", "full of discrepancies", and leaving "the public absolutely at the mercy of a combine [ASCAP]".[113]

Representative Ackerman of New Jersey proposed a number of amendments which, to name a few, would make the license nonretroactive to July 1, 1909; eliminate any reference to the manufacture and sale of ordinary commercial phonograph records or perforated music rolls as being too restrictive; strike out all references to "promptly" as too indefinite and confusing; and eliminate, as being obnoxious, the provision necessitating payment of royalties for the public performance of compositions by mechanical instruments in addition to that paid by the manufacturer.[114]

Representative Wolverton, also from New Jersey, claimed the bill was not framed in the interest of the public and if enacted would do irreparable injury to an industry "that has been built up over a period of 20 years, and that was struggling against the inroads of radio."[115] No further action on the bill and amendments is recorded.

---

[111] Id., at p. 2.
[112] Hearings on H.R. 13452, 70th Cong., 2d sess., p. 19 (1929).
[113] Id., at pp. 25–26.
[114] Id., at pp. 26–30.
[115] Id., at p. 41.

4. The 71st Congress

With the start of another Congress Representative Vestal reintroduced several bills.

(a) H.R. 6989

On December 9, 1929, H.R. 13452 [116] was reintroduced as H.R. 6989,[117] but no action was taken.

(b) H.R. 9639

H.R. 9639 [118] as introduced February 7, 1930, was a somewhat shortened and revised measure designed to repeal outright the compulsory license. At hearings held in March and April 1930, some changes in position were justified by the fact that a number of phonograph record companies had purchased or secured interests in sheet-music publishers, many of whom were copyright owners.[119] It was also pointed out that the only parts of instruments known in 1909 were player-piano rolls and talking-machine records, sold for use in the home; now the number and form of instruments had expanded and, with increasing industrial use, home use was almost insignificant.[120] Furthermore, sale of player-piano rolls was decreasing and since the so-called "word" rolls had not been included in the license, the 12-cent royalty payment on a roll selling for 32 cents was cutting deeply into the manufacturer's profits.[121] In opposition to the complete elimination of the compulsory license provision, the phonograph industry listed as specific objections the following: [122]

(a) The proposed bill constitutes a renunciation of the principle of full accessibility.

(b) If the proposed legislation is enacted into law, it would open wider the door to increased oppression by means of monopoly or combination of publishers, and/or copyright owners.

As a concluding witness, Karl Fenning [123] questioned the constitutionality of the doctrines of accessibility to music and compulsory licensing.[124]

(c) H.R. 12549

Still another revision bill, H.R. 12549,[125] was introduced by Representative Vestal on May 22, 1930, and reported out of the Patent Committee on May 28, with amendments.[126] Relative to compulsory licensing, Representative Vestal stated in his report: [127]

A fair compromise of the matter has been arrived at in drafting the new bill. By section 1, subsection (d), it is provided, in effect, that the 2-cent compulsory license shall continue until January 1, 1932, as to the mechanical-musical provisions of the act of 1909, and the repealer section (sec. 64) of the new bill makes adequate provision by excepting the operation of the repealer to accommodate this purpose. This length of time will give manufacturers time

---

[116] See note 107 supra.
[117] H.R. 6989, 71st Cong., 1st sess. (1929).
[118] H.R. 9639, 71st Cong., 1st sess. (1929).
[119] Hearings on H.R. 9639, 71st Cong., 2d sess., pp. 8–14 (1930).
[120] Id., at p. 13.
[121] Id., at pp. 53–54.
[122] Id., at pp. 74–75.
[123] See Fenning, "Copyright Before the Constitution," 17 J. Pat. Off. Soc'y 379 (1935); "The Origin of the Patent and Copyright Clause of the Constitution," 17 Geo. L.J. 109 (1929).
[124] Hearings on H.R. 9639, 71st Cong., 2d sess., p. 86 (1930).
[125] H.R. 12549, 71st Cong., 1st sess. (1930).
[126] H. Rept. No. 1689, 71st Cong., 2d sess., pts. 1, 2 (1930).
[127] Id., at p. 9.

to adjust themselves, and the new provision still holds open to the compulsory license features of the old act, musical compositions from 1909 to 1932. This does not disturb existing conditions except as to new works after 1932.

It may be said in this connection that within the last few years and, in fact, within the last few months, a great revolution has taken place in the musical world. The advent of radio and of the talking motion picture has resulted in the absorption by radio and motion-picture concerns of most of the business of mechanical-musical reproduction. The provisions of the new bill have been inserted, not only because of the unfairness of the old regime as provided by the 1909 act but also because the practical business situation has undergone significant changes. Regardless of that, however, the compulsory price-fixing principle provided by the 1909 act is one that works obvious injustice, and its effect should be removed as to future works.

The bill was recommitted to the Patent Committee on June 12, 1930.[128] The following day Representative Vestal reported the bill out of the committee, the report being identical with House Report No. 1689, but including the text of the bill with the changes marked.[129] On June 20, the bill was presented for consideration by the whole House with a 2-hour limitation on debate. Once more the bill was recommitted to the Patent Committee and reported out for the third time on June 24,[130] when it was finally referred to the House Calendar. Following a debate on the floor of the House during which several amendments were proposed, the bill was finally passed on January 13, 1931 and sent to the Senate, where it was referred on January 21, 1931 to the Senate Committee on Patents. Although a number of amendments to the bill were presented in the Senate, none pertained to compulsory licensing. Hearings were held January 28 and 29, but the proposed elimination of the licensing feature was overshadowed by discussions concerning the divisibility of copyright, provisions affecting the radio industry and public performance for profit, particularly with relation to coin-operated machines. Senator Hébert filed the committee report on February 23, 1931, in which he refers to the compulsory license as follows: [131]

Under the existing copyright law (act of 1909) it is provided as a condition of extending the copyright control to mechanical reproduction of musical works, where the owner of a musical copyright permits the use of his work upon the parts of instruments serving to reproduce it mechanically, any other person may make similar use of such work upon the payment to the copyright proprietor of a royalty of 2 cents on each part manufactured. This provision applies to the reproduction upon phonograph records, talking machines, player pianos, etc. It is believed this provision for the fixing of a price to be paid to the owner of any property is unique in American legislation. There appears to be no valid reason for any distinction between the author or owner of a musical composition and the author or owner, or producer of any other kind of property or work. As a result of the enactment of the provision in the law of 1909, owners of musical works are at the mercy of those engaged in mechanical reproduction with whom they have no contractual relations and who may be wholly irresponsible. The author is forced to permit the use of his work whether or not he desires to do so and at a price which is fixed by law and over which he has no control.

The provision of the bill under consideration will eliminate the 2-cent compulsory license fee heretofore fixed by law, from and after January 1, 1932, so far as the mechanical reproduction of music is concerned. Thereafter authors and composers, like other American citizens, will be free to make their own contracts upon terms mutually agreed upon. This provision will not disturb existing conditions and will not affect works other than those created subsequent to July 1, 1909, and up to January 1, 1932.

[128] 72 Congressional Record, 10594–10596 (June 12, 1930).
[129] H. Rept. No. 1898, 71st Cong., 2d sess. (1930).
[130] H. Rept. No. 2016, 71st Cong., 2d sess. (1930).
[131] S. Rept. No. 1732, 71st Cong., 3d sess., pp. 26–27 (1931).

The bill, however, failed to receive consideration on the floor of the Senate.

5. The 72d Congress

(a) H.R. 139 and S. 176

H.R. 12549 was reintroduced by Representative Vestal as H.R. 139 [132] on December 8, and by Senator Hébert as S. 176 [133] on December 9, 1931, but no action was taken on either bill.

Commencing February 1, 1932, a series of hearings were had on the general revision of the copyright law. The topic of public performance for profit as presented by the manufacturers of coin-operated phonographs and pianos reflected indirectly on the compulsory license question. The general feeling of members of that industry seemed to be that they did not mind a 2-cent royalty paid at the source, but that they would object, as a form of double taxation, to any provision that required payment of a royalty for each performance of the record on their machines.[134]

At the hearings a brief was submitted in behalf of the phonograph industry by Arthur Garmaize stating in part: [135]

There exists no justification for the agitation to remove the statutory mechanical license now found in our existing copyright law in subdivisions (e) of sections 1 and 25 except the wish to create a mechanical-music monopoly. However, the wish to prevent the creation of a mechanical-musical monopoly is sufficient lawful justification to continue price fixing for the use of music for mechanical reproduction now existing for 23 years through subdivisions (e) of sections 1 and 25 of our copyright law and known as the statutory mechanical license.

Passenger transportation, freight, telephone, telegraph, gas, electricity, streetcar transportation, and subway transportation rates are fixed because it is claimed the purveyors thereof are public utilities. Rents were fixed during the war because of an existing emergency. The price for the mechanical use of music was fixed in 1909 and should be fixed now because of the emergency that then existed and now exists in a threatened mechanical-music monopoly and because the right to control mechanical reproduction is not an inherent right of the common law or of copyright but was created by Congress in 1909 for the first time. This statutory monopoly right created for the first time in 1909 and surrounded by the Congress creating it with the safeguard of the statutory mechanical license should not by the present Congress be utilized as an instrument with which to create a business monopoly on top of the statutory monopoly by repealing subdivisions (e) of sections 1 and 25 of the existing law known as the statutory mechanical license.

Also during the course of the hearings a patent attorney gave still a different interpretation to the problem of compulsory licensing when he testified: [136]

During the hearings the suggestion has been made that the copyright law should provide for compulsory licensing or working of a copyright. Some witnesses have stated that this is entirely unnecessary since the copyright proprietor will for business reasons keep his work in print if there is any demand whatever for it. This statement assumes that all copyright proprietors possess sound business judgment, which unfortunately is not always true * * *. Under the present law there is no way of compelling a temperamental copyright proprietor either to keep a work in print himself or to allow some one else to reprint on a reasonable royalty basis.

---

[132] H.R. 139, 72d Cong., 1st sess. (1931).
[133] S. 176, 72d Cong., 1st sess. (1931).
[134] Hearings on General Revision of the Copyright Law, 72d Cong., 1st sess., pp. 208–217 (1932).
[135] Id., at p. 239.
[136] Id., at p. 480.

The series of Sirovich bills which resulted from these hearings made no provision for compulsory license and no extensive discussion of the subject is to be found in connection with these bills.

6. The 74th Congress

(a) S. 2465 and S. 3047

On March 13, 1935, Senator Duffy introduced the first of his general revision bills, S. 2465.[137]   Two months later, on May 13, 1935, the second, S. 3047,[138] was introduced as a revised version, including a number of committee amendments.   Senator McAdoo reported the bill out of committee on the same day it was introduced.[139]   Amendments by Senators Vandenberg and Trammell were subsequently offered.   The bill, together with the amendments, was debated July 31, 1935 and passed.   During the second session the House Committee on Patents conducted hearings on S. 3047, H.R. 10632 and H.R. 11420, known as the Duffy, Daly, and Sirovich bills, respectively.   With respect to compulsory license, the Duffy bill provided for its retention and in addition would also have given the manufacturer a copyright in his recording; the Daly bill would have eliminated the compulsory license clause.

A brief submitted by Gene Buck of ASCAP claimed that the original license violated the Constitution by denying authors the exclusive right to their writings: [140]

> The Duffy bill not only continues this compulsory license scheme, but provides in addition, that the manufacturer of the record, upon paying the sum of 2 cents, can secure a new copyright in the record or transcription, and can communicate the work to the public by radio facsimile, wired radio, telephone, and television * * *.
> There is no reason why a mechanical-instrument manufacturer who under a compulsory license pays the author only 2 cents per record should have a separate copyright.   For the payment of 2 cents, such manufacturer would be able to license the performance of records in competition with performances by living musicians licensed by the authors.   This would unjustly enrich such manufacturers at the expense of the authors, and would throw a great many musicians out of employment.

Radio and coin-operated machine interests joined in opposing these licensing-plus features, and protested the multiplicity of licensing agencies if the law were enacted.[141]

The president of the Boston Music Publishers' Association, William A. Fisher, testified: [142]

> Under our present law machine and electrical transcription companies manufacture disks and records at a fixed license of 2 cents per record.   This provision not only deprives composers and authors of the right to bargain but at the same time grants the right of manufacture to anybody else at the same ridiculous figure.   Not only does the Duffy bill continue this unjust compulsory license clause with its contemptible 2-cent fee, but, worse still, any purchaser of a record may publicly perform it provided no admission fee is charged.   These disks are increasingly used in restaurants and over the radio, and the bill permits their free communication by wired radio, telephone, and television.   The

---

[137] S. 2465, 74th Cong., 1st sess. (1935).
[138] S. 3047, 74th Cong., 1st sess. (1935).
[139] S. Rept. No. 896, 74th Cong., 1st sess. (1935).
[140] "Hearings on Revision of Copyright Laws," 74th Cong., 2d sess., pp. 112–113 (1936).
[141] Id., at pp. 470, 800.
[142] Id., at p. 558.

old law differentiates between the license to manufacture and sell a record and the right to give such record public performance for profit. The bill in question blurs these rights * * *.

The phonograph industry maintained that if the provision by which all manufacturers were given equal rights were removed, they would be forced to resort to competitive bidding for the right to record, and a temporary, excessive profit would be realized by only a small number of composers. It was contended whereas royalties on records were only one source of revenue for the composer, if too large a percentage of production cost were paid in royalties, the manufacturer would soon go out of business.[143] Miss Isabelle Marks of Decca seconded this reasoning by stating that unless the compulsory license provision remained in the statute—

it would unquestionably create a monopoly in the hands of the one phonograph company in the industry that also happened to have the best financial background * * *.[144]

Upon the conclusion of these hearings, none of the bills was reported out by the House committee.

7. The 75th Congress

(a) S. 7, H.R. 2695, and H.R. 3004

S. 7,[145] introduced by Senator Duffy on January 6, 1937, H.R. 2695 [146] introduced by Representative Moser of Pennsylvania on January 12, and H.R. 3004,[147] introduced by Representative Sol Bloom on January 14, were all identical with S. 3047.[148] No action resulted.

(b) H.R. 5275 and S. 2240

Representative Daly presented H.R. 5275 [149] on March 3, 1937, and Senator Guffey introduced S. 2240 [150] on April 22, 1937, both modified versions of Representative Daly's earlier general revision bill providing for the elimination of the compulsory license and jukebox clauses. No action was taken on them.

(c) H.R. 10633

On May 16, 1938, Representative Moser of Pennsylvania introduced a bill, H.R. 10633,[151] which would have set up a compulsory license for the printing, reprinting, publishing, copying, performing, vending, or exercise of any protected right in respect to any work copyrighted where the person was unable to secure an agreement with the copyright owner, by filing a written application with the Federal Communications Commission for a permit to make the desired use at the rates of royalties or charges therefor as the Commission should determine. No hearings were held on the bill.

---

[143] Id., at pp. 623–624.
[144] Id., at p. 631.
[145] S. 7, 75th Cong., 1st sess. (1937).
[146] H.R. 2695, 75th Cong., 1st sess. (1937).
[147] H.R. 3004, 75th Cong., 1st sess. (1937).
[148] See note 138 supra.
[149] H.R. 5275, 75th Cong., 1st sess. (1937).
[150] S. 2240, 75th Cong., 1st sess. (1937).
[151] H.R. 10633, 75th Cong., 3d sess. (1938).

8. *The 76th Congress*

(a) *H.R. 926, H.R. 4871, H.R. 6160, and H.R. 9703*

Representative Daly reintroduced his general revision bill, formerly H.R. 5275,[152] on January 3, 1939, as H.R. 926,[153] and again in still another revised form on March 8, 1939 as H.R. 4871.[154] The latter version was also introduced by Representative McGranery, as H.R. 6160 [155] and H.R. 9703 [156] in 1939 and 1940. No action, however, was taken on any of these bills.

(b) *H.R. 6243*

Representative Moser also reintroduced his compulsory license bill on May 9, 1939, as H.R. 6243.[157]

(c) *S. 3043*

In the meantime the Shotwell Committee was readying a general revision bill for consideration in this Congress. Apparently the feasibility of continuing the 2-cent compulsory license came up for consideration in March 1939, and several briefs were submitted. The recording interests claimed the compulsory licensing provision had worked well for the past 30 years; the right to use copyrighted music was available to all upon like terms and conditions, and substantial profits had been enjoyed by copyright proprietors. They alleged that no analogy existed to the book-publishing field since no one would claim it desirable for all publishers to issue the same book. In the music industry, however, many orchestras were competing for public favor and performed the same selections for different recording companies and even for the same company in different price classifications.[158]

The Songwriters' Protective Association argued the basic constitutional concept was that copyright protection was for authors and not for commercial exploiters of the authors' creations.[159] The motion picture interests maintained : [160]

In justice to the owners of the paramount rights in musical copyrights it should be noted that, although the recording manufacturers seek to retain the present 2-cent compulsory license fee in respect of the right arbitrarily to manufacture any recorded rendition of a copyrighted musical composition, the record manufacturers are nevertheless not making any proposal to apply the same principle of an arbitrary statutory license, permitting other manufacturers to make physical duplicates of a specially copyrighted recorded rendition. In other words, if a record manufacturer made and copyrighted a Toscanini version of a Beethoven symphony, he would not wish arbitrary statutory licenses to permit other manufacturers to dupe at a 2-cent royalty rate the same Toscanini rendition, although he would say they should be free to make their own renditions of the same public domain symphony or use any copyrighted musical composition for 2 cents per recording.

---

[152] See note 149 supra.
[153] H.R. 926, 75th Cong., 1st sess. (1939).
[154] H.R. 4871, 76th Cong., 1st sess. (1939).
[155] H.R. 6160, 76th Cong., 1st sess. (1939).
[156] H.R. 9703, 76th Cong., 2d sess. (1940).
[157] H.R. 6243, 76th Cong., 1st sess. (1939), formerly H.R. 10633, 75th Cong., 3d sess. (1938).
[158] Memorandum submitted in behalf of the recording interests to Committee for the Study of Copyright in response to memos urging elimination of the compulsory license * * * pp. 1–2 (1939).
[159] Song Writers' Protective Association memorandum in reply to the memorandum submitted in behalf of the recording interests re the compulsory license provision of sec. 1(e) * * *, 1–2 (1939).
[160] Comments of motion picture producers and distributors upon the memorandum submitted in opposition to copyrightability for acoustic recordations by broadcasting interests, the American Society of Composers, Authors and Publishers, and the Song Writers' Protective Association, pp. 5–6 (1939).

The final draft of the Shotwell bill, S. 3043,[161] as introduced by Senator Thomas on January 8, 1940, did not contain a licensing provision. The session ended, before any action was taken on the bill.

9. The 77th Congress

(a) *H.R. 3456*

On February 18, 1941, Representative Martin J. Kennedy introduced a bill, H.R. 3456,[162] which might be considered a variation of the earlier Moser bills.[163] It provided that whenever two or more copyright proprietors of a musical composition refused to enter into an agreement to permit the public use or performance of the composition (especially by radio) upon payment of a reasonable and fair compensation, the Federal Trade Commission could fix a rate of payment and order permission to make use of the composition. Refusal to comply with the Federal Trade Commission's order would result in seizure for confiscation of the copyright. This proposed legislation never reached the hearing stage.

(b) *H.R. 3997 and H.R. 7173*

A general revision bill, based on Representative Daly's earlier bill, but containing a number of changes relative to the rights of performing artists was introduced in this Congress by Representative Sacks as H.R. 3997 [164] but no action was reported.

During the second session, Representative Sacks on June 1, 1942, introduced H.R. 7173 [165] which, among other things, proposed that copyright in an acoustical recording for which the 2-cent royalty had been paid could not be secured without the consent of the paramount copyright owner.

10. The 78th and 79th Congresses

(a) *H.R. 1571, H.R. 3190, and S. 1206*

Three more acoustical recording bills,[166] each identical with H.R. 7173,[167] were introduced in these two Congresses, but without any action thereon.

11. The 80th Congress

(a) *H.R. 1270*

The requirement of securing the copyright owner's consent to the copyrighting of a record upon payment of the 2-cent royalty reappeared in a bill introduced in January 1947, H.R. 1270.[168]

Among the opponents to H.R. 1270 at hearings held between May 23 and June 23, 1947, Don Petty, of the National Association of Broadcasters, declared with respect to the compulsory license provision in section 1(e) : [169]

---

[161] S. 3043, 76th Cong., 2d sess. (1940).
[162] H.R. 3456, 77th Cong., 1st sess. (1941).
[163] See notes 151, 157, supra.
[164] H.R. 3997, 77th Cong., 1st sess. (1941).
[165] H.R. 7173, 77th Cong., 2d sess. (1942).
[166] H.R. 1571, 78th Cong., 1st sess. (1943) ; H.R. 3190, 79th Cong., 1st sess. (1945) : S. 1206, 79th Cong., 1st sess. (1945).
[167] See note 165, supra.
[168] H.R. 1270, 80th Cong., 1st sess. (1947).
[169] Hearings on H.R. 1269, H.R. 1270, and H.R. 2570, 80th Cong., 1st sess., pp. 78–79 (1947).

This provision was designed to enforce the congressional policy against monopoly. While H.R. 1270 purports to leave this policy intact, it nevertheless makes possible the easy circumvention of it. This is so because the amendments proposed to sections 11 and 12 permit works to be copyrighted in the form of acoustic records. At the same time, section 1(f) gives the copyright owner of such works the exclusive right to make or authorize the making of records. This means that the policy of section 1(e) will be defeated if the creator of a musical composition chooses to copyright his work in the first instance as a record.

Miss Isabelle Marks testified as to recording industry practice concerning the royalty fee scale on phonograph records in effect since approximately 1932 as follows: [170]

It is a royalty of 1¼ cents for a 35-cent record, 1½ cents for a 50-cent record, 1¾ cents for a 60-cent record, and 2 cents for 75 cents or more, and that has been universal. Each record that is made is made with a royalty at that price through a definite licensing agreement with the publisher. We either get a license from that publisher to issue the record at that price or we fall back on section 1(e), where we pay 2 cents.

On July 19, 1947, the Subcommittee on Patents, Trademarks, and Copyrights recommended, during an executive session of the Judiciary Committee, that the bill be adversely reported, with the result that the bill was never reported out of the full committee.[171]

No further bills dealing with the compulsory license of copyrighted works have been introduced in the U.S. Congress.[172]

B. SUMMARY

A review of the testimony contained in the hearings and the reports reveals the fact that between the mid-1920's and the late 1930's a number of attempts were made to eliminate or extend the compulsory license provisions. Each attempt, however, provoked considerable controversy. The development of radio and other electronic devices for the recording and reproduction of sound provided the motivation behind many of the proposals, while economic conditions affecting the phonograph industry exerted a counterbalancing influence.

Conflicts arose between the creators and the users. The principle of compulsory license was attacked by the authors because it restricted their bargaining power; the benefits derived from the statutory royalties went to the music publishers as copyright owners, rather than to the authors; and the copyright owners frequently found their works being exploited by unscrupulous, financially irresponsible recording manufacturers. Consistently throughout the period, the manufacturers of piano rolls and phonograph records pleaded the economic necessity of having complete accessibility to all music and of restricting the payment of royalties to a relatively low percentage of the cost of production. When faced with the prospect of being required to pay fees for each performance of recorded music, the radio and jukebox industries threw their support to the recording manufacturers in opposing the introduction of a compulsory license for public performance rights of records and transcriptions.

---

[170] Id., at p. 89.

[171] 93 Congressional Record D-406 (July 19, 1947).

[172] Bills to eliminate the so-called "jukebox exception," strictly speaking, relate to public performance for profit. Public Law 743 (68 Stat. 1030), effective Sept. 16, 1955, eliminated the sec. 1(e) requirement of reciprocal treatment with respect to mechanical reproduction rights for Universal Copyright Convention works but did not affect the compulsory license provision. See note 55 supra.

That the subject of compulsory license is a controversial one may be observed from the number of bills that were introduced in the 68th through the 80th Congresses and the comparatively small number ever reported out of committee or voted upon by either House.

III. Compulsory License Provisions in the Laws of Other Countries and in International Conventions

Various types of compulsory license provisions are found in the copyright laws of certain foreign countries and multilateral copyright conventions.[173]

A. NATIONAL LAWS

1. Great Britain

There are several types of compulsory licenses in the British copyright law.[174]

(a) The proviso of section 3 of the British Copyright Act contains a compulsory license to reproduce a published work after the expiration of 25 years from the death of the author. After that time the copyright is not deemed infringed by reproduction of the work for sale if the person reproducing the work proves that—

    (i) he has given the prescribed notice in writing of his intention to reproduce the work; [175] and

    (ii) the royalties have been paid.[176]

(b) Section 4 of the act contains a compulsory license for republication or performance of a work if after the death of the author of a literary, dramatic or musical work which has been published or publicly performed, a complaint is made to the Judicial Committee of the Privy Council that the owner of the copyright refuses to republish or allow republication or public performance of the work. In that situation the Judicial Committee may order the owner to grant a license for republication or public performance of the work.[177]

The 1952 Report of the Copyright Committee [178] recommended repeal of the proviso in section 3 and of section 4. The British copyright bill of 1955 would repeal the proviso in section 3, and section 4 of the British Copyright Act, 1911.[179]

(c) Section 19(2) of the act contains a compulsory license for mechanical reproduction of a musical work. Contrivances for mechanical performance of a musical work may be made upon proof that—

---

[173] See "Compulsory License" in 2 Pinner, "World Copyright," pp. 124–142 (1954).
[174] Copyright Act, 1911, 1 and 2 Geo. 5, ch. 46. This act, with some slight modifications, has been adopted in Australia, Ceylon, New Zealand, and the Union of South Africa. Except for these self-governing dominions and Canada (see p. 38, infra), it applies throughout the British Commonwealth of Nations. Prior to the 1911 act, reproducing music on interchangeable parts of mechanical instruments was held to be not copying and therefore no infringement of a composition protected under the then-existing copyright statute. *Boosey* v. *Wright* (1899), 1 ch. 836 (1900), 1 ch. 122.
[175] See "Copyright Royalty System (General) Regulations," 1912; Copinger, "Law of Copyright," app. B (8th ed. 1948).
[176] See Copinger, op. cit., supra, note 175, at p. 88.
[177] Id., at p. 86. No such cases are reported.
[178] Report of the Copyright Committee (presented by the President of the Board of Trade to Parliament by Command of Her Majesty, October 1952), par. 23.
[179] Explanatory Memorandum to Copyright Bill, H.L. 1955, fifth schedule 9, and sixth schedule 3, to copyright bill, 1955.

(i) such contrivances have previously been made with the consent or acquiescence of the copyright owner; and

(ii) the prescribed notice of intention to make the contrivances has been given and the royalties paid.

The license includes words and music,[180] but alterations not previously made or necessary for the adaptation are prohibited.[181]

The royalties for records made and sold under the compulsory license were originally set, in the act of 1911, at 5 percent of the ordinary retail selling price of the contrivance, but not less than a halfpenny for each separate musical work reproduced therefor.[182] However, the act of 1911 provided that after a period of 7 years the royalty rate could be changed by an order of the Board of Trade confirmed by Parliament.[183] Accordingly, in 1928, the royalty rate was increased to 6¼ percent, with a minimum of 3 farthings (three-fourths of a penny) for each separate work.[184]

The Copyright Committee recommended that no change be made in regard to the compulsory license provisions of section 19.[185] Section 8 of the copyright bill of 1955 incorporates provisions similar to section 19(2) of the present act. Section 8 of the bill would permit any record manufacturer to make records of a musical work or of an adaptation thereof, under the following conditions:

(*a*) Records of the work, or, as the case may be, of a similar adaptation of the work, have previously been made for the purposes of retail sale, and were so made by, or with the license of, the owner of the copyright in the work;

(*b*) Before making the record, the manufacturer gave to the owner of the copyright the prescribed notice of his intention to make it:

(*c*) The manufacturer intends to sell the record by retail, or to supply it for the purpose of its being sold by retail by another person, or intends to use it for making other records which are to be sold or supplied; and

(*d*) In the case of a record which is sold by retail, the manufacturer pays to the owner of the copyright, in the prescribed manner and at the prescribed time, a royalty of an amount ascertained in accordance with the following provisions of this section.

The bill would fix the royalties at 6¼ percent of the ordinary retail selling price of the record.[186] If, after the end of the period of 1 year after the section becomes effective, the rate ceases to be equitable, the Board of Trade may make an order changing it.[187] In the case of a record which comprises two or more musical works, the minimum royalty is 3 farthings in respect to each work.[188] Under section 8(5) words are included in the compulsory license.

---

[180] Copyright Act, 1911, 1 and 2 Geo. 5, ch. 46, sec. 19(2)(ii). The otherwise similar compulsory license provision in the United States Copyright Act of 1909 is limited to the music. See note 80 supra. The British act, unlike the American act (see note 56 supra), was retroactive. *Monckton* v. *Pathe Freres*, 30 T.L.R. 123 (C.A. 1913).

[181] Id., sec. 19(2)(1).

[182] Id., sec. 19(3)(b). In contrast, the American statutory royalty rate is 2 cents per "part" manufactured. In 1909, 2 cents was considered equivalent to 5 percent of the manufacturer's selling price. See notes 59 supra, 186–188 infra.

[183] Id., sec. 19(3)(b).

[184] Copyright Order Confirmation (mechanical instruments: royalties) Act, 1928, 18 and 19 Geo. 5, ch. 46, confirming an order by the Board of Trade.

[185] Report of the Copyright Committee (op. cit., supra, note 178), par. 81.

[186] Copyright bill, 1955, sec. 8(2).

[187] Id., sec. 8(3).

[188] Id., sec. 8(4)(a).

2. *Canada*

(*a*) Section 7 of the Canadian Copyright Act [189] contains substantially the same compulsory license as the proviso in section 3 of the British act.

(*b*) Section 13 of the act provides that, upon complaint to the Governor in Council, substantially the same compulsory license as in section 4 of the British act may be granted.

(*c*) Section 19 of the act contains substantially the same compulsory license as section 19(2) of the British act. This license applies to motion pictures which are considered "other contrivances, by means of which sounds may be reproduced, and by means of which the work may be mechanically reproduced" as provided in section 19.[190]

(*d*) Section 14 of the act provides that any person may apply to the Minister for a compulsory license for the printing and publishing in Canada of a copyrighted book if the owner of the copyright fails—

  (i) To print the book in Canada; and
  (ii) To supply sufficient copies of such printing to the Canadian market.

This license is granted by the Minister as an exclusive license not to exceed 5 years.[191]

(*e*) Section 15 of the act provides that a compulsory license may be granted for serial publication in Canada if publication of a book in serial form is begun outside the British Dominions or in a foreign country whose nationals are not entitled to the benefits of the Canadian act. This license is also granted by the Minister.

3. *Germany*

Section 22(1) of the German copyright law [192] provides that the author of a musical work, who has authorized another to make mechanical reproductions of the work, must permit any other person domiciled in Germany to make mechanical reproductions of the work. The author is entitled to an equitable remuneration. If the parties cannot agree on an "equitable" remuneration, the courts, with the assistance of experts, may decide.[193] This permission must be given, even if the first person had purportedly been given an exclusive license.

Under section 22(1) the applicant must sue if the license is not forthcoming. To facilitate obtaining a license the German draft law of 1953 proposes that the applicant must inform the copyright

---

[189] Copyright Act, 1921, ch. 32, R.S.C. 1927, as amended by ch. 8, 1931; ch. 18, 1935; ch. 28, 1936; ch. 27, 1938.

[190] Fox, "Canadian Copyright Law," pp. 169, 174, 187 (1944); cf. note 213, infra, and note 59, supra. Under the Canadian act, the royalty is 2 cents for the playing surface of each record (apportioned among different owners of works involved) and 2 cents for each other contrivance. Mechanical reproduction rights apply to literary and dramatic as well as musical works.

[191] Copyright Act (supra, note 189), sec 14(7). No counterparts to this section and sec. 15 are found in the British act. Secs. 14 and 15 apply only if the author is a Canadian or non-Berne Union country national.

[192] Law Concerning Copyright in Works of Literature and Music, June 19, 1901, as amended.

[193] Voigtländer-Elster-Kleine, "Urheberrecht," p. 127 (1952). The mechanical reproduction right remains exclusive even though the author exercises it himself. Only when he licenses its exercise by others does the compulsory license provision become operative. The voluntary license may function as a standard to a court when fixing equitable remuneration.

owner by registered letter of his intention to record; and if 2 weeks have passed without reply the recording may be made.

Section 22(2) provides that this permission extends to the words of the musical work, provided the author of the words has previously permitted their mechanical reproduction. The author of the musical work has the right and the duty to permit mechanical reproduction of the words, and, in that case, must share the royalties with the author of the text.

It should be noted that the compulsory license is not directly given by the law but that the author is compelled by the law to give such license.

4. Italy

Articles 52 to 60 of the Italian copyright law [194] permit broadcasts of copyrighted works by the state broadcasting organizations without the author's consent, except where the work is new or where the broadcast performance is the first of that season.[195] Under article 56 of the law the author of the work broadcast is entitled to a remuneration, the amount of which, in the case of disagreement between the parties, is determined by the judicial authorities.

In view of the fact that broadcasting is a state monopoly in Italy, this limitation might be considered a withholding of an exclusive right rather than a compulsory license given to the state.

Italy has no provision for a compulsory license for recordings.

5. Switzerland

Articles 17 to 21 of the Swiss copyright law [196] provide for a compulsory license in regard to records of musical works. Under article 17, any person having an industrial establishment in Switzerland may require, against payment of an equitable fee, authorization to record a musical work, provided a recording of the work by another has been previously authorized and the records have been placed on the market or the work has been otherwise published. The first license need not have been express, but may have resulted from the circumstances such as complete transfer of the copyright.

Under article 18, the compulsory license extends to the text of a musical work.

Article 19 provides that, after the death of the author, the license must be given even where the author, during his life, would not have given it, even though there was no prior recording.[197]

Article 20 of the law provides that if the parties cannot agree about the authorization to record the work, the courts shall decide the question. Presumably, this includes questions on the amount of the remuneration.

Under article 21, records made under articles 17 to 20 may be publicly performed.

---

[194] Copyright law of April 22, 1941, as amended.
[195] Id., art. 52(3).
[196] Copyright law of Dec. 7, 1922. Sound films are not within the compulsory license provision.
[197] Röthlisberger, "Schutz des Urheberrechtes," p. 238 (1931).

6. Austria

Article 58(1) of the Austrian Copyright Act [198] provides that any record manufacturer domiciled or with his principal place of business in Austria, or in a country which grants reciprocal protection to Austrians, may acquire a license to make and distribute recordings of any published musical work where the composer has permitted similar use. Appropriate royalty would be fixed by the court.

Under article 58(2) the license extends to the text of the musical work.

Article 58(4) provides that the compulsory license does not apply to recordings of both images and sounds. The reason given for thus excluding sound tracks of motion pictures is that a motion picture producer who has acquired the exclusive right to use a musical composition in a motion picture should not be forced to permit the use of the work by other producers.[199]

7. Argentina

Article 6 of the Argentine copyright law [200] provides that the heirs or successors in title of a deceased author may not oppose republication of the work if they have allowed more than 10 years to pass without themselves undertaking a republication. Further, a translation may be made by a third party under the same conditions. If there is no agreement on the conditions of printing or the fee, the question will be decided by arbitration.[201]

Argentina has no compulsory license for recordings.

8. Mexico

Article 30 of the Mexican copyright law [202] provides that publication of literary, scientific, educational, or artistic works useful or necessary to the development of national science, culture, or education shall be considered an act of public use. The Government may permit publication of such works by another than the copyright owner if—

(i) No copies are available in Mexico during the year following publication, or the supply is exhausted; or

(ii) Copies are priced so high as to impede their general use, to the detriment of culture.

The Secretary of Education determines an amount of 15 percent of the retail price of the copies as a deposit in favor of the copyright owner with the Bank of Mexico.[203]

Article 114 of the law provides that no penalties shall accrue under article 113 for unauthorized public performance or broadcast of musical, dramatic, dramatico-musical, choreographic, or pantomimic works, provided the royalties for such performance have been paid. Royalties are fixed by contract with users or groups of users,

---

[198] Federal Act on Copyright in Works of Literature and Art and on Related Rights of Apr. 9, 1936, as amended to July 8, 1953.
[199] Lissbauer, "Urheberrechtsgesetze," p. 282 (1936).
[200] Law No. 11723 of Sept. 28, 1933.
[201] Id., art. 6(3).
[202] Federal copyright law of Jan. 14, 1948, as amended Dec. 31, 1948.
[203] Id., art. 31, V.

or failing this, by means of a royalty schedule issued by the Secretary of Education in accordance with precedents and equity.[204]
Mexico has no compulsory license for recordings.

9. Brazil

Article 660 of the Brazilian Civil Code [205] provides that, if the owner of a published work refuses to authorize the publication of a new edition of the work, the Federal Government or a State Government may expropriate the work on payment of indemnification provided the work is needed for reasons of the public interest.
Brazil has no compulsory license for recordings.

10. France, Belgium, the Netherlands

France has a compulsory license only in regard to toy music boxes, etc.[206] Belgium and the Netherlands have no compulsory license.

B. INTERNATIONAL CONVENTIONS

Broadly speaking, there are three sets of multilateral copyright conventions:
(1) The international copyright conventions (the Berne Convention of 1886 and its successive amendments [207] establishing the International Copyright (Berne) Union) which have been ratified by most of the countries in the Eastern Hemisphere and by Brazil and Canada, but not by the United States, in the Western Hemisphere;
(2) The pan-American copyright conventions,[208] notably the Buenos Aires Convention of 1910 which the United States and most of the Latin American countries, except Cuba, El Salvador,[209] Mexico,[210] and Venezuela have ratified; and

---

[204] Id., art. 81.
[205] Civil Code : Law No. 3071 of Jan. 1, 1916.
[206] Law of Oct. 11, 1917.
[207] Berne Convention of 1886 and annexed acts (hereinafter sometimes called the Berne Convention) ; Additional Act and Declaration signed at Paris, May 4, 1896 (hereinafter sometimes called the Paris Convention) ; Revised Berne Convention for the Protection of Literary and Artistic Works, signed at Berlin, Nov. 13, 1908 (hereinafter sometimes called the Berlin Convention) ; Additional Protocol to the International Copyright Convention of Berlin, signed at Berne, Mar. 20, 1914; Revised Convention for the Protection of Literary and Artistic Works, signed at Rome, June 2, 1928 (hereinafter sometimes called the Rome Convention) ; and Berne Convention for the Protection of Literary and Artistic Works, as revised at Brussels, Belgium, in June 1948 (hereinafter sometimes called the Brussels Convention).
[208] Convention of Montevideo on Literary and Artistic Property, signed Jan. 11, 1889 ; Convention for the Protection of Literary and Artistic Property, signed at Mexico, Jan. 27, 1902 (hereinafter sometimes called the Mexico City Convention) ; Convention for the Protection of Patents of Invention, Drawings and Industrial Models, Trademarks and Literary and Artistic Property, signed at Rio de Janeiro, Aug. 23, 1906 ; Convention Concerning Literary and Artistic Copyright, signed at Buenos Aires, Aug. 11, 1910 (hereinafter sometimes called the Buenos Aires Convention) ; Revision of the Convention of Buenos Aires Regarding Literary and Artistic Copyright, signed at Havana, on Feb. 18, 1928 ; and Inter-American Convention on the Rights of the Author in Literary, Scientific, and Artistic Works, signed at Washington, June 22, 1946 (hereinafter sometimes called the Washington Convention). All are found in Canyes, Colborn, and Piazza, "Copyright Protection in the Americas" (Pan-American Union Law and Treaty Series No. 33) 187–213 (2d ed. 1950).
[209] El Salvador has ratified the Mexico City Convention, which governs its copyright relations with the United States and with the Dominican Republic.
[210] Mexico has ratified the Buenos Aires Convention, but its ratification has not been deposited and hence is not effective.

(3) The Universal Copyright Convention,[211] which became effective September 16, 1955 among certain countries.

1. International Copyright (Berne) Conventions

(a) Brussels Convention, 1948

This Convention, the most recent revision of the International Copyright (Berne) Conventions, itself contains no provision granting a compulsory license. However, there are several provisions permitting a compulsory license applicable to musical works in national laws of member countries. Paragraph (1) of article 11 *bis* of the Convention grants authors the exclusive right of authorizing—

* * * the radio-diffusion of their works or the communication thereof to the public by any other means of wireless diffusion of signs, sounds, or images; 2.° any communication to the public whether over wires or not, of the radio-diffusion of the work, when this communication is made by a body other than the original one; 3.° the communication to the public by loudspeaker or any other similar instrument transmitting, by signs, sounds, or images the radio-diffusion of the work.

Paragraph (2) of article 11 *bis* enables member countries to restrict this exclusive right:

It shall be a matter for legislation in the Countries of the Union to determine the conditions under which the rights mentioned in the preceding paragraph may be exercised * * *

Paragraph (3) of article 11 *bis* provides, in part:

It shall * * * be a matter for legislation in the Countries of the Union to determine the regulations for ephemeral recordings made by a broadcasting body by means of its own facilities and used for its own omissions.

As to recording rights, article 13 of the Convention provides:

(1) Authors of musical works shall have the exclusive right of authorizing 1° the recording of such works by instruments capable of reproducing them mechanically; 2° the public performance of works thus recorded by means of instruments.

Paragraph (2) of article 13 enables member countries to restrict the exclusive right:

Reservations and conditions relating to the application of the rights mentioned in the preceding paragraph may be determined by legislation in each country of the union * * *

However, these restrictions, which may take the form of a compulsory license provision, may not, under article 14(4), be applied to cinematographic adaptations of literary, scientific, or artistic works.[212]

(b) Rome Convention, 1928

Article 11 *bis* of the Rome Convention contained provisions relating to the communication of works "to the public by radio diffusion" which served as the pattern for the expanded, same-numbered article of the Brussels Convention. Article 13 was substantially the same in the Rome and Brussels Conventions, but article 14(4) was sub-

---

[211] Ratified by Andorra, Cambodia, Pakistan, Laos, Haiti, Spain, United States, Costa Rica, Chile, Israel, German Federal Republic, Monaco (effective Sept. 16, 1955). Several additional foreign countries have since ratified or are in the process of ratifying the Convention.
[212] Brussels Convention, art. 14(4).

stantially revised at Brussels to preclude expressly the application of compulsory licensing under article 13(2), to motion pictures.[213]

(c) Berlin Convention, 1908

Article 13 of the Rome and Brussels Conventions found its origin in the same-numbered article of the Berlin Convention.[214]

(d) Paris Convention, 1896

The attempt to insert in the Paris Convention, 1896, a provision protecting musical works against use on disks, rolls, sheets, etc. (as distinguished from use in music boxes and the like) was unsuccessful.[215]

(e) Berne Convention, 1886

The Berne Convention of 1886, the first of the multilateral copyright conventions, contained in its final protocol a provision that the manufacture and sale of instruments for the mechanical reproduction of musical airs was no infringement.[216]

2. Pan-American Copyright Conventions

None of the several pan-American copyright conventions includes any compulsory license provision.[217]

3. Universal Copyright Convention

The Universal Copyright Convention does not specify the particular rights or works subject to protection. These matters, on the principle of national treatment, are left to the domestic law of each country. Recordings are not deemed "published" works for convention purposes.[218]

Article V(1) of the Universal Copyright Convention grants exclusive translation rights, but paragraph 2 of article V provides for restriction of this right by domestic legislation of the contracting countries, subject to the following conditions:

If, after the expiration of a period of seven years from the date of the first publication of a writing, a translation of such writing has not been published in the national language or languages, as the case may be, of the Contracting State, by the owner of the right of translation or with his authorization, any national of such Contracting State may obtain a nonexclusive license from the competent authority thereof to translate the work and publish the work so translated in

---

[213] 1 Ladas, "The International Protection of Literary and Artistic Property," pp. 435–438 (1938). Various proposals for amendment are outlined at 1 id., at pp. 438–440.

[214] 1 Ladas, op. cit. supra note 213, at p. 419 et seq. Art. 13 expressly had no retroactive effect. For a comparative law study of compulsory license systems, and their effects under the Berlin Convention, and subsequent revisions, see 1 id., at pp. 430–435. Foreign courts have refused to apply compulsory license provisions to motion picture sound tracks. 1 id., at pp. 465, 469. See also note 196 supra. But see note 190 supra.

[215] 1 Ladas, op. cit. supra note 213, at pp. 413–414.

[216] See final protocol 3: "It is understood that the manufacture and sale of instruments for the mechanical reproduction of musical airs which are copyrighted, shall not be considered as constituting an infringement of musical copyright." The delegates may have been thinking of music boxes rather than of more modern instruments but the language was broader. 1 Ladas, op. cit. supra note 213, at pp. 412–413, 416.

[217] Nor any express recognition of recording and mechanical reproduction rights, with the exception of the Washington Convention, 1946. *Todamerica Musica Ltda.* v. *Radio Corporation of America,* 171 F. 2d 369 (2d Cir. 1948); *Portuando* v. *Columbia Phonograph Co.,* 81 F. Supp. 355 (S.D.N.Y. 1937); Sherman, "The Universal Copyright Convention: Its Effect on United States Law," 55 Colum. L. Rev. 1137, at pp. 1152–1153 (1955). The Washington Convention included in its scope of protection the exclusive right to "adapt and authorize general or individual adaptations * * * mechanically or electrically * * *" Art. II(d).

[218] Arts. I, II, IV. See note 71 supra.

any of the national languages in which it has not been published; provided that such national, in accordance with the procedure of the State concerned, establishes either that he has requested, and been denied, authorization by the proprietor of the right to make and publish the translation, or that, after due diligence on his part, he was unable to find the owner of the right. A license may also be granted on the same conditions if all previous editions of a translation in such language are out of print.

Article V then prescribes the procedure for obtaining a license if the copyright owner cannot be found, provides for equitable remuneration under the national legislation, for accuracy of the translation, and the scope of the license.

IV. PRESENT MUSIC PUBLISHING-RECORDING INDUSTRY PRACTICES IN THE UNITED STATES

Composers of musical compositions have been primarily interested in the exercise of their rights (1) of publication in the form of sheet music; (2) of public performance for profit; and (3) of use in recorded form.[219]

Publication in the form of sheet music was, prior to the advent of radio, undoubtedly the most important of the foregoing rights. Use in recorded form, once limited to 78 r.p.m. phonograph records and piano-player rolls, has now expanded to extended-play (45 r.p.m.) and long-playing ($33\frac{1}{3}$ r.p.m.) records, motion-picture sound tracks, tape and wire recordings, etc.,[220] and today far exceeds in importance sheet-music use. Piano-player rolls, once of substantial significance, have slight present-day importance.[221] Public-performance-for-profit rights, which are beyond the scope of this study, are now generally licensed through performance societies (ASCAP, BMI, SESAC), which police the exercise of such rights in nondramatic form.[222]

Composers may be individual composers or cocomposers (frequently one of the music and the other of the lyrics),[223] or employees of others. In the latter case, the employers would be deemed the statutory authors of the compositions.[224] Such employer-employee relations are most frequently encountered with respect to arrangements of existing compositions, whether copyrighted or not. To arrange a copyrighted composition requires the consent of the copyright proprietor of such composition, and any derivative copyright in the arrangement is subject to the basic copyrights in such composition.

The Songwriters' Protective Association, organized in 1931, has over 2,000 composer-members. Some 300 to 400 music publishers have signed the SPA basic agreement.

---

[219] See note 5 supra.
[220] See notes 7, 58 supra, pp. 50-52, infra.
[221] Approximately 250,000 rolls were sold last year by the last of the piano-roll makers, Imperial Industries Co. (Max Kortlander), for player piano devotees across the Nation. In 1926, the company produced 10 million rolls. The Wall Street Journal 1 (May 7, 1956).
[222] Rothenberg, "Copyright and Public Performance of Music" (1954); Finkelstein, "Public Performance Rights in Music and Performance Right Societies" in "7 Copyright Problems Analyzed" 69-85 (1952).
[223] Rosengart, "Principles of Co-Authorship in American, Comparative, and International Copyright Law," 25 So. Calif. L. Rev. 247 (1952); Redleaf, "Co-ownership of Copyright," 119 N.Y.L.J. 760, 782, 802, 822 (Mar. 1-4, 1948); Kupferman, "Copyright—Co-owners," 19 St. John's L. Rev. 95 (1945).
[224] 17 U.S.C. 26 (1952).

There are hundreds of music publishers throughout the United States, the vast majority of which are engaged in relatively small-scale operations. A few are music holding companies for stage show or motion picture producers, or subsidiaries or other affiliates of recording companies. Many of the independent music publishers, especially the longer established concerns, are members of the Music Publishers Protective Association.

In 1954, approximately 200 million phonograph records, totaling $185 million, were sold in the United States. Of these roughly 2 percent were imported. The American phonograph record industry earned approximately $24 million (or some 12 percent of its gross receipts) from exports of records and matrices. Most of the $24 million was earned by exporting only the master on which the foreign presser paid royalties proportionate to the number of pressings manufactured.

There is a constantly changing roster of approximately 1,000 music recording companies, societies, and producers in the United States, ranging from large-scale, well-established leaders of the industry, like RCA Victor, Columbia, Capitol, Decca, MGM, Mercury, and London, to relatively insignificant producers. In 1954 these 7 large firms accounted for 85 percent of the dollar volume of business; 25 others for an additional 10 percent; 5 percent of the volume being distributed among the remaining producers. As indicated above, the larger of the recording concerns sometimes have their own publishing affiliates, but these comprise a comparatively minor aspect of their operations.

All the larger concerns are both producers and pressers, i.e., they make both the original recordings (masters or matrices) and the pressings (finished disks as sold to customers). In 1954 the industry produced about 22,000 masters. Some of the smaller companies produce original recordings but have their disks pressed either by their larger competitors or by the so-called contract pressers of which there are between 20 and 30.

The 7 largest firms and many of the medium-size firms are members of the Record Industry Association of America, a trade association of some 50 members.

Among the smaller record producers are record pirates or "disk-leggers" who rerecord or "dub" recordings made by legitimate companies and sell them competitively.[225] Some fly-by-night producers, either in making original recordings or rerecordings, do not bother to seek permission or file notices of intention to use or account for or pay royalties. Copyright proprietors are without apparent remedy against an insolvent manufacturer except, of course, by way of injunction.[226]

---

[225] *Miller* v. *Goody*, 139 F. Supp. 176, at p. 180, note 4 (S.D.N.Y. 1956):
"In this manner, they avoid having to pay the performers for their time, and they have the benefit of the initial recording company's talents in getting the finest rendition possible. Ordinarily, they also omit payment of the copyright, although, as far as the copyright law is concerned, even a pirate has the right to record copyrighted musical compositions provided he files notice of intent and pays the royalties."
[226] Id., at p. 182.

The tape recording industry is in its infancy, there being between 20 or 30 producers of tape recorders, tape phonographs and/or recorded tapes. At first, wire and tape recorded music was developed and used primarily by professionals, such as disk recording studios for the purpose of producing masters, and radio and television stations. Soon it came into use in providing background music services. About the same time, it began to enter the home, where it was taken up by enthusiasts for high fidelity recording and reproduction of music. About a million homes are now supplied with tape phonographs or similar equipment for playing tape recordings. Several firms have issued catalogs of recorded tapes. Some producers of recorded tape make original recordings, and others arrange to have such recordings made for them by recording studios, but probably the bulk of the recorded tapes are made from the master tapes or other matrices of established disk producers. Some 30 members comprise the Magnetic Recording Industry Association.[227]

Musical compositions might be: (1) in the public domain; (2) protected by common-law copyright; or (3) protected by statutory copyright. In each situation, recording industry practices obviously vary.

A. PUBLIC DOMAIN

If in the public domain, the musical composition may be freely used by anyone in any form or medium. Works enter the public domain when they are published without securing statutory copyright; when the statutory copyright is not properly maintained; at the end of 28 years if the original statutory copyright is not duly renewed; or at the end of 56 years, the original and renewal term of statutory copyright. Conceivably the recording and mechanical reproduction rights might be in the public domain while the other rights of statutory copyright are not.[228]

B. COMMON-LAW COPYRIGHT

Common-law copyright, sometimes called the right of first publication, actually includes full control prior to first publication over all uses, including recording.[229] Such common-law recording rights are not only perpetual, short of publication, but are also unqualifiedly exclusive since not subject to the compulsory license provision applicable to statutory copyright.

---

[227] A more recent development is stereophonic tape which has two channels to reproduce the sound through 2 sets of amplifiers and speakers. New York Herald-Tribune Book Review, sec. 11 (June 3, 1956).

[228] See notes 56, 62, supra.

[229] *Harper & Bros.* v. *M. A. Donohue & Co.*, 144 Fed. 491, 492 (N.D. Ill. 1905), aff'd per curiam, 146 Fed. 1023 (7th Cir. 1906); *George* v. *Victor Talking Machine Co.*, 38 U.S.P.Q. 222 (D. N.J. 1938), rev'd on other grounds, 105 F. 2d 697 (3d Cir. 1939), cert. denied, 308 U.S. 611, 60 Sup. Ct. 176, 84 L. Ed. 511 (1939); see also Pickard, "Common Law Rights Before Publication" in "Third Copyright Law Symposium," pp. 298–336 (1940).

Where the musical composition is protected by common-law copyright, the general practice is for the composer to assign his common-law copyright to a music publisher.[230]

Included in the assignment is the right of the music publisher to secure statutory copyright in his own name. Prior to 1932, assignments provided for scant minimum royalties to composers, say, one-half to 1 cent per copy of sheet music or record, without provision for sharing proceeds from synchronization or foreign use.

With the organization of the Songwriters' Protective Association, standard forms of contract containing provisions protective of composers, and limited to the original term of copyright, provided a pattern. Thus, the 1932 form of contract called for the composer to receive one-third of the publisher's receipts from mechanical and synchronization rights, for the composer to share in the exploitation

---

[230] Klein, "Protective Societies for Authors and Creators" in "1953 Copyright Problems Analyzed" 19 at pp. 32–41. At pp. 38–39 are tabulated the relative positions of composers before SPA and under the 1947 SPA contract. For the forms of the 1947 contract and 1950 renewal contract, see id., at pp. 80–93, 94–106.

Before SPA	Under the 1947 SPA contract
Recording, transcription, and motion picture synchronization royalties to the writer were as low as 10 percent and usually not higher than 25 to 33⅓ percent.	Recording, transcription, and motion picture synchronization royalties to the writer are now 50 percent minimum. Par. 4(g) of the 1947 revised contract.
Foreign royalties were often omitted from contracts and even when included seldom exceeded 25 percent of the publisher's income from foreign countries.	Foreign royalties are now a minimum of 50 percent of the publisher's foreign income. Par. 4(c) of the 1947 revised contract.
It was the general practice for publishers to make "bulk" foreign deals for their entire catalogs. This often made it difficult to properly evaluate the earnings of an individual song.	No "bulk" deals are permitted subject to certain limited exceptions. Par. 4(j) of the 1947 revised contract.
Sheet music royalties were as low as 1 cent per copy.	Sheet music royalties are now a minimum of 3 cents per copy, except that when the writer and publisher agree to use the "sliding scale" providing for royalties up to 5 cents per copy, the minimum for the first 100,000 copies is 2½ cents per copy. Par. 4(b) of the 1947 revised contract.
An advance paid by a publisher to a writer for 1 song was usually deductible from the earnings of all that writer's songs in the publisher's catalog.	An advance can be deducted only from the earnings of the song on which it was paid. Par. 4(a) of the 1947 revised contract.
Publishers often required the repayment of an advance as a condition for the return of a song.	The advance remains the property of the writer. Par. 4(a) of the 1947 revised contract.
The publisher was not obliged to print or exploit the song, nor to return the unpublished song to the writer under any circumstances.	The publisher agrees to fulfill the following 2 requirements within 1 year: (1) Publish and place on sale regular piano copies; and (2) publish and place on sale orchestrations or secure the release of a commercial recording or pay an advance of $250. The writer is entitled to the return of the song upon written demand if the publisher does not fulfill the above requirements within 1 year. Par. 6 (a) and (b) of the 1947 revised contract.
Royalty payment periods were not specified in contracts and payments were made at the convenience of the publisher.	Regular royalty payment periods are specified in the contract. Par. 10 of the 1947 revised contract.
Many sources of a publisher's income were not mentioned in old contracts. Therefore, the writer did not share in the income from these sources.	The writer shares to the extent of at least 50 percent in all sources of income not specified in the contract. Par. 4(g) and (n) of the 1947 revised contract.
There was no agreement permitting the writer or his agent to examine the publisher's books.	The writer or his agent may examine the publisher's books. Par. 11 (a), (b), and (c) and 12 (a) and (b) of the 1947 revised contract.
Disputes between writer and publisher could be settled only by expensive actions in courts of law.	The writer has recourse to the simpler, speedier and much less expensive process of "arbitration" under the New York State arbitration law Par. 17 of the 1947 revised contract.

of the composition by subsequently developed methods, for the composition to be published in salable form within a specified period, for periodic royalty statements and payments, etc. This form was revised in 1939 to increase the composer's share of mechanical royalties to 50 percent, to require that the publisher hold these in trust for the composer, and to ban "bulk deals" by publishers. In 1947 the form was substantially revised to limit the assignment of rights in the United States and abroad to the original term of American copyright or 28 years, whichever be shorter; to provide for minimum sheet music royalties either on a straight 3 cents per copy basis or on a sliding scale (2½ to 5 cents per copy); to require publication in sheet music form and the making of phonograph records or $250 payment; to limit reassignment; to require SPA countersignature; etc. Renewal rights [231] are not included in the SPA form of assignment. In 1950, an SPA form of renewal contract was promulgated.

Not all publishers use the SPA forms. One form commonly used by prominent publishers is very short, but includes assignment of the copyright not only for the original term but also for the renewal term, provision for sheet-music royalties of 4 cents per copy of piano or dance orchestration arrangements, of 10 percent of the publisher's proceeds from the sale of copies of other arrangements, and of 50 percent of the publisher's proceeds from recording rights. Absent is any express covenant on the part of the publisher to publish sheet music or make or authorize recordings.

The music publisher might (1) record,[232] license the recording of, or list for licensing, the composition, and/or (2) publish copies of it in the form of sheet music.

If the publisher records, licenses recording, or lists for licensing, without publishing copies, two alternative procedures are possible: (1) continued reliance on common-law copyright; or (2) securing of statutory copyright in the composition as an unpublished work.[233] Since the advantages of the former were once thought to outweigh those of the latter, some publishers preferred to rely, absent publication in sheet music form, on common-law copyright.

A growing number of recent cases, however, has held or intimated that the sale of a recording constitutes a divestitive publication of the recorded composition, resulting in the loss of all common-law rights therein.[234] Unless this present judicial trend be reversed, the more cautious alternative of securing statutory copyright in the composition before selling recordings thereof, should soon replace the older practice completely.

---

[231] Bricker, "Renewal and Extension of Copyright," 29 So. Calif. L. Rev. 23 (1955); Kupferman, "Renewal of Copyright—Section 23 of the Copyright Act of 1909," 44 Colum. L. Rev. 712 (1944); Brown, "Renewal Rights in Copyright," 28 Cornell L.Q. 460 (1943). See note 57 supra.

[232] Through such publisher's recording division.

[243] See note 59, supra, pp. 49–52, infra. Notice of use would be filed. See note 61, supra.

[234] See note 71, supra.

C. STATUTORY COPYRIGHT

Statutory copyright might be secured in the musical composition as (1) an unpublished work, or (2) a published work.[235]

Statutory copyright might be secured in an unpublished work by registration and deposit of a copy.[236] If the work be thereafter published, a second registration and deposit of copies are required as conditions precedent to enforcing such copyright.[237]

Statutory copyright is secured in a published work by publication with proper statutory copyright notice.[238] Registration and deposit of copies are conditions precedent to enforcing such copyright.[239]

Otherwise, statutory copyright in an unpublished work and statutory copyright in a published work are identical. The duration is the same;[240] copies published or offered for sale in the United States by authority of the copyright proprietor must bear the statutory copyright notice;[241] recording and mechanical reproduction rights are protected,[242] subject to the compulsory license provision.

If mechanical reproduction rights are not exercised by the copyright proprietor, anyone interested in recording the work must obviously negotiate a license to make such use. No such negotiated license may, in view of the application of the compulsory license provision, be exclusive. Once mechanical reproduction rights are exercised, anyone, under the compulsory license provision, may make "similar use" of the work at the statutory royalty rate.[243] This consequence, of course, means that the statutory royalty rate operates as a ceiling for any negotiated royalty rate. The first company to record is sometimes charged a lower royalty as a concession for chancing an untested market. If a composition gains public acceptance, competing companies, within a matter of days, can issue their recordings of the composition under the compulsory license provision or under negotiated licenses.[244]

---

[235] Copyright is secured in an unpublished musical composition by registration and deposit, that is, by the deposit in the Copyright Office of one complete copy, an application Form E (regular or "foreign," as the case may be), and the $4 registration fee. If the musical composition is later published, the published copies should contain the proper copyright notice, and the registration and deposit requirements with respect to published works would apply. Copyright is secured in a musical composition in which a claim to copyright was not registered prior to publication, by publication of the composition with proper notice of copyright. Promptly after publication with notice of copyright, two complete copies of the best edition should be deposited in the Copyright Office, along with an application on Form E and the $4 registration fee. If a new version of a musical composition is made, copyright may be secured in any new copyrightable matter contained in such new version, 17 U.S.C. 12, 10, 11, 13, 7 (1952); Copyright Office Circular No. 58 (September 1955). In the fiscal year 1955, 57,527 musical compositions were registered. "Annual Report of the Register of Copyrights for the Fiscal Year Ending June 30, 1955," p. 9. Statutory copyright endures for an original term of 28 years, 17 U.S.C. 24 (1952) ("28 years from the date of first publication"). In the case of works not produced for sale, the 28-year period runs from the date of registration and deposit. *Marx* v. *United States*, 96 F.2d 204 (9th Cir. 1938). Renewal for an additional term of 28 years may be had by timely application. See note 231 supra. Approximately one-third of the 1927 Class E registrations were renewed in 1954. "Annual Report of the Register of Copyrights for the Fiscal Year Ending June 30, 1955," p. 12.

[236] See notes 57, 73, 235, supra.

[237] Ibid.

[238] See notes 57, 72, 73, 74, 235, supra.

[239] See notes 57, 62, 73, 235, supra.

[240] See note 235, supra.

[241] See note 74, supra.

[242] See note 57, supra.

[243] See note 59, supra, pp. 49–52, infra. Notice of use would be filed. See note 61, supra.

[244] According to one observer, the existence of the compulsory license provision has a tendency to smother competition for new and fresh musical material, thus aborting incentive to author and composer and accounting, in part, for the monotony, repetition and impersonal music offered to the American public. Schulman, "Effect of the Copyright Act of 1909 on the Quality of American Music" (address before annual meeting of National Music Council, May 16, 1956).

Practices vary. Music publishers or their trustees [245] or affiliates [246] appointed to hold recording rights file notices of use and list their compositions available for recording. Recording companies, usually attempt to negotiate a license, relying on the compulsory license provision only as a last resort. In the latter event, the recording company would mail a notice of intention to use to the copyright owner and the Copyright Office, and monthly account for and pay to such owner the statutory royalty of 2 cents per composition per side, regardless of the selling price or size or speed of the recording. Where several compositions are to appear on the same side, such as in the case of a medley, the statutory royalty would be 2 cents per composition. For this reason, medleys of several copyrighted compositions are not frequently recorded in the absence of a negotiated license containing concessions by the copyright owner.

Various forms of license are used in licensing the mechanical reproduction of musical compositions.

The Music Publishers Protective Association has two basic forms: (1) a short-form license, where only a one-speed recording is to be released; and (2) a long-form license, where the recording is to be released at more than one speed. Under either form, an MPPA representative serves as publisher's agent-trustee.

The MPPA short-form license follows the compulsory license provisions by prescribing a royalty at the statutory rate on the basis of records manufactured and in other respects [247] except that (1) accounting and payment of royalty shall be quarterly rather than monthly, (2) failure to make such accounting and payment constitutes ground for revocation of the license, and (3) serving and filing of notice of intention to use under section 101(e) of the Copyright Act are waived.[248]

The MPPA long-form license is identical with the short-form license except that the royalty is (1) on the basis of records manufactured *and sold* and (2) at the following schedule of rates (based on manufacturer's suggested retail price):

78 revolutions per minute records:
    35 cents or less_____ 1¼ cents per side.
    36 to 50 cents_____. 1½ cents per side.
    51 to 60 cents_____. 1¾ cents per side.
    More than 60 cents___ Statutory rate.
Extended-play 45 revolutions per minute records:
    $1.40 or less_____ 1½ cents per selection, per side.
    More than $1.40_____ Statutory rate per selection, per side.
Longplaying 33⅓ revolutions per minute records:
    $2.85 or less_____ 1½ cents per selection, per side.
    $2.86 to $3_____ 1¾ cents per selection, per side.
    More than $3_____ Statutory rate per selection, per side.

---

[245] E.g., the Harry Fox Office (Music Publishers Protective Association), which represents a substantial number of music publishers in this respect.

[246] E.g., Music Publishers Holding Corp., a Warner Bros. subsidiary.

[247] Such a license agreement has been held a substitution for, rather than a recognition of, a compulsory license under sec. 1(e), with the statutory royalty rate, provision for triple royalty in event of default in payment, etc., incorporated by reference. *Edward B. Marks Music Corp. v. Foullon*, 171 F. 2d 905, 908 (2d Cir. 1949) ("So far as the parties chose to incorporate into this [Mechanical License Agreement] any of the terms of sec. 1(e), these of course became the measure of their relations like its other terms; but that was only by virtue of the incorporation. Ex proprio vigore the statute fixed nothing between them.")

[248] Such waiver would appear redundant, since sec. 101(e) requires notice of intention to use "in the absence of a license agreement" when reliance is "upon the compulsory license provision." See note 247, supra.

Other prevalent forms of mechanical reproduction license are strikingly similar to the MPPA long-form license, especially so far as the royalty schedule is concerned.   Some forms, instead of merely referring to the "statutory rate" for certain types of records sold, specify 2 cents.   Some forms set forth the royalty rate "for * * * records" of the licensed composition rather than "per selection, per side," but the former is given the same meaning as the latter.   One form covers Canada as well as the United States, setting forth the same royalty schedule for records sold in either nation.   Another form covers the United States and all countries of the Western Hemisphere where such rights are controlled by the licensor but provides that in Argentina, Brazil, Chile, Urguay, and Paraguay the licensee "shall pay the regular current royalty payable for such countries, computed and paid in U.S. currency at the rate of exchange prevailing at the time of payment."   Following the usual royalty schedule, one form has added a provision for a royalty of one-fourth cent per minute of playing time (or fraction thereof) for all extended-play and longplaying records of compositions of an extended nature, with a minimum royalty of 2 cents.   In cases of musical compositions from stage shows or motion pictures, a release date for recordings might be fixed.

Where forms of license are used, the license determines the rights of the parties, and problems of construing the statutory compulsory license provisions, except to the extent that they are incorporated into the license, are avoided.   If the availability of the compulsory license provision is doubtful, the possibility of its being available undoubtedly encourages the negotiation of licenses at royalty rates comparable to the statutory royalty.   Thus the question of the applicability of the compulsory license provision to extended-play and longplaying records, tape and wire recordings, and motion picture sound tracks [249] has apparently never been litigated in this country.[250]

In sound motion picture films, music might serve several functions: (1) as background or thematic music to create audience mood; (2) as song or dance numbers in a musical comedy or revue; (3) as a musical narrative, such as in an operetta; or (4) as a title song (with advantageous promotional tie-ins).   Motion picture producers, when using copyrighted music in sound tracks, negotiate for synchronization rights and do not invoke the compulsory license provision.

Like motion picture producers, the broadcasting industry, in making records, electrical transcriptions,[251] magnetic tape,[252] sound motion

---

[249] Even prior to *Jerome* v. *Twentieth Century-Fox Film Corp.*, 67 F. Supp. 736 (S.D.N.Y., 1946), reviewed on other grounds per curiam, 165 F. 2d 784 (2d Cir. 1948), when it was assumed, at least in certain circles, that a sound track was within sec. 1(e), no one ever attempted to invoke the compulsory license provision. Dubin, "Copyright Aspect of Sound Recordings," 26 So. Calif. L. Rev. 139, 147, note 50 (1953).   See notes 58, 59 supra.

[250] The foreign cases generally have held that sound-track use was not within the respective foreign-law compulsory license provisions invoked. 1 Ladas, op. cit. supra note 213, at 465–469.   But see note 190 supra ; cf. note 213 supra.

[251] Electrical transcriptions, developed over the past 15 years. are essentially 16-inch, 33⅓ revolutions per minute disk recordings, each side of which can contain an entire 15-minute program.   They may be "processed records" or "instantaneous recordings" (taken off the line or off the air and ready for immediate playback).   McDonald, "The Law of Broadcasting" in 7 Copyright Problems Analyzed 31, at p. 36 (1952).

[252] Much of the recorded program material now heard is from tape or from recordings of tape after final editing. Tape may be reclaimed. is easily edited. and has relatively no surface noise. There is also a system of wire recording largely confined in broadcasting to portable equipment used in man-on-the-street interviews and the like. McDonald, op. cit. supra. note 251, at p. 37.

pictures,[253] or kinescope recordings [254] involving copyrighted music for radio and/or television use, negotiates for the necessary recording rights.[255] For example, it has been a longstanding custom to make special payment for recording a copyrighted composition by electrical transcription at the rate of 25 cents for each station expected to broadcast the composition. In the case of production numbers from shows or motion pictures, 50 cents per station has been paid; in the case of record libraries intended for repeated use, an annual fee is usually worked out.[256] Lump-sum payments (e.g., $10) are made for the license to record musical compositions in sound motion pictures or by kinescope or tape recordings for television purposes.

Motion picture films which are sold or leased usually bear the statutory copyright notice on the ground that the film is a copy of at least the visual elements involved and the sale or lease thereof constitutes publication.[257] Such copyright notice functions to secure copyright in all the copyrightable components of the film, and to maintain any subsisting copyrights in the copyrighted components thereof. In the past, copyright notices have generally not been affixed to records, tape, wire or other recordings.[258] In view of the recent trend of cases to the effect that the sale or lease of such recordings constitutes a publication of the recorded composition,[259] the cautious practice now would appear to be to secure statutory copyright in the composition. Whether or not the copyright notice needs to be affixed to all such recordings sold or leased in the United States by authority of the copyright proprietor [260] is a very debatable point. Apart from the legal question there is the serious practical problem of inserting proper copyright notices on already overcrowded labels of phonograph recordings, especially in the case of extended-play and long-playing records containing several compositions of different proprietorships and/or copyright dates. Copyright proprietors when authorizing recordings of musical compositions have rarely requested the insertion of copyright notices.

V. Problems in Evaluating Compulsory License Provisions of Present Copyright Law

The fundamental question in any evaluation of the compulsory license provisions is whether the compulsory license principle should be retained or eliminated.

---

[253] Made with motion picture cameras for general use or primarily for exhibition to paying audience, for television, or for rental for home use, education, promotion material, etc. McDonald, op. cit. supra note 251, at p. 37.

[254] Kinescope recording equipment combines a tiny television receiver and electronically geared motion picture camera. From the negative kinescope recording made off the air or as a "dry run" (either in the "live manner" or by stop-and-start technique), positive prints are made for distribution to television stations for telecasting and file purposes. The use of kinescope recordings permits syndication of a program or transmission on a network basis without the expense involved in coaxial cables and radio circuits. McDonald op. cit. supra note 251, at p. 37. TV tape recordings of visual and audio elements are replacing kinescope recordings.

[255] McDonald, op. cit. supra note 251, at p. 49. Recording may be for purposes of original broadcast, delayed broadcast, rebroadcast and/or file uses.

[256] Ibid.

[257] *Blanc* v. *Lantz*, 83 U.S.P.Q. 137 (Cal. Super. Ct. 1949) ; *White* v. *Kimmell*, 94 F. Supp. 502 (S.D. Cal. 1950). Projection of a motion picture on a screen might constitute copying but not publication. *DeMille Co.* v. *Casey*, 121 Misc. 78, 201 N.Y. Supp. 20 (Sup. Ct. 1923) ; *Patterson* v. *Century Productions, Inc.*, 93 F. 2d 489 (2d Cir. 1937), cert. denied, 303 U.S. 655, 58 Sup. Ct. 759, 82 L. Ed. 1114 (1938).

[258] See note 74, supra.

[259] See note 71, supra.

[260] See note 74, supra.

A. COMPULSORY LICENSE PRINCIPLE

This principle was worked out in 1909 as a compromise between those interests which, fearing monopoly, favored continued non-recognition of recording and mechanical reproduction rights, and those which, stressing the rights of composers and freedom of contract, urged absolute recognition. The resulting qualified recognition, based upon the compulsory license principle, emerged from some 3 years of pre-1909 controversy.[261] The 1909 compromise provided for (1) continued access to compositions by manufacturers of phonograph records and piano rolls, and (2) payment by such manufacturers to composers (or their assigns) of what was then considered a reasonable royalty.

Whether the 1909 compromise was sound in the light of the then-existing situation has been much debated.[262] Be that as it may, the situation today is substantially different.

In 1909, the rights under consideration had been held nonprotectable and hence were available to all. The Aeolian Co. and the then major music publishers had allegedly made exclusive contracts which would become effective upon the recognition of mechanical reproduction rights by court decision or congressional enactment.[263] This potential monopoly, whether real or imagined, was regarded as a serious threat at a time when effective antitrust regulation was still in its infancy.[264]

For almost 50 years now the recording industry has relied on the compulsory license principle. Forms of licensing arrangements, royalty rate schedules, and other industry practices have been predicated upon the compulsory license provision and have become practically standardized. The principal difference between a negotiated license and a compulsory license is that the former usually calls for quarterly rather than monthly royalty reports and payments, dispenses with the notice of intention to use, and prescribes a royalty scale below the statutory royalty of 2 cents per composition per side. Without the compulsory license provision, an exclusive license might be negotiated at substantially higher royalty rates,[265] or even non-exclusive licenses might be negotiated at higher royalty rates in the absence of a statutory ceiling.

Whether the royalty considered reasonable in 1909 is reasonable today is discussed below.[266]

Contentions that the compulsory license principle is unconstitutional obviously would, if sustainable, be sufficient reason for eliminating the principle. However, the principle was not incorporated in the statute to impair existing rights, but was inserted as part of the definition of rights then being recognized for the first time. Hence there would seem to be no deprivation of property without due

---

[261] See pp. 2–12, supra.
[262] See pp. 21–36, supra.
[263] See note 44, supra.
[264] See note 6, supra.
[265] Whether this would result in more or less aggregate recording royalties to composers has yet to be tested. The present arrangements for the exclusive recording services of outstanding artists and performers, being somewhat analogous, might offer helpful information in this respect. Interestingly, the royalty scales have tended to be the same for all compositions whether protected by common law copyright (not subject to compulsory license provision) or by statutory copyright.
[266] See pp. 54–56, infra.

process of law or taking of private property for private use without just compensation. Nor should the constitutional phrase, "the exclusive Right," preclude Congress from subjecting one aspect thereof to compulsory licensing, especially since such right is exclusive until exercised.[267]

To the extent that the present compulsory license provision is of doubtful application with respect to certain uses or operates unfairly under certain circumstances, improvement is possible, as discussed below, without necessarily abandoning the compulsory license principle.

If the compulsory license principle is to be retained, certain subsidiary considerations become relevant.

B. REPRODUCTION PERMITTED UNDER COMPULSORY LICENSE

The framers of the compulsory license provision in 1909 obviously had in mind old-speed phonograph records and player-piano rolls, bands, and cylinders.[268] These were the recording devices then known; they were the ones discussed at the hearings; they are the ones described or named in the statute; they are the ones to which the statutory royalty system was intended to apply. Whether the compulsory license principle applies to extended-play and long-playing records, tape and wire sound recordings, and other types of recordings, such as motion picture sound tracks, kinescope recordings, and television tape recordings, has not been resolved. Obviously the former are more closely analogous to old-speed phonograph records and piano player rolls and cylinders than are the latter. Any revision of section 1(e), then, should clearly differentiate between the various types of recordings, whether by means known in 1909, now or hereafter, and should specify which of such types of recordings, if less than all, are intended to be subject to compulsory licensing. Furthermore, the statutory royalty rates should be adjusted to reflect the different types of recording possible under compulsory licensing.

The "similar use"[269] permitted by compulsory license should also be more clearly defined. Competition in the recording industry, especially as among different types of recordings, would undoubtedly be promoted if the authorization of a recording of one type subject to compulsory licensing, as above discussed, gave rise to a compulsory license with respect not only to that particular type of recording but also to the remaining types subject to compulsory licensing.

Whether or not a compulsory license to record a composition impliedly includes the right to make necessary and proper arrangements of the same, and the limitations on such right of arrangement, require clarification.

C. STATUTORY ROYALTY RATE

Part of the 1909 compromise was the provision for the payment to composers (or their assigns) of what was then considered a reasonable royalty: 2 cents per part manufactured (e.g., per side of old-speed

---

[267] See note 66, supra ; pp. 4–5, 19, supra.
[268] See notes 58, 59, supra.
[269] See note 59, supra.

record, piano roll), 2 cents being the then approximate equivalent of 5 percent of the manufacturer's selling price.[270]

Whether such royalty rate, assuming it was reasonable in 1909, remains reasonable today, would appear worthy of reexamination in view of the decreased purchasing power of money, the subsequently developed types of recordings (assuming the compulsory license provision be applicable to them), and the substantially increased manufacturer's selling prices.

Obviously a royalty fixed by statute may be stated in terms of amount (as in the present statute), or percentage (possible bases: manufacturer's price, retail price), or a combination thereof (e.g., higher or lower of the two), or the rate fixed in the original negotiated license which activates the compulsory license provision. The fixed amount royalty has the advantage of simplicity but obviously should not be the same for longer and shorter recordings. A single flat royalty might have been sufficient for old-speed records and piano rolls (somewhat mollified in the latter case by negotiating royalties for the use of the words of the musical composition).[271] A royalty schedule, with different amounts stated for different uses (per present practice), would appear desirable in the case of extended-play and long-playing records, tape and wire recordings, and other types of recording under compulsory license, or, in the alternative, a percentage-of-price royalty which would, in application, reflect the length of the recording since the length would be reflected presumably in the price. To base the royalty on that fixed in the original negotiated license might have to take into account such variables as the specific provisions of such original lisense and to provide an alternative basis where the proprietor makes his own recording.

The royalty can, of course, be based on records manufactured in the United States, the present statutory method, or on records sold here, the present negotiated method, or both. The sales basis involves such problems as complimentary distributions to disk jockeys and the like and recordings sold and returned, and omits royalties on recordings manufactured in the United States but sold abroad. For the royalty on manufacture, the manufacturer is liable. As between the small record company, society, or other producer, on the one hand, and the contract pressing plant, on the other, the latter is often better established and more financially responsible. While both presumably would be liable for royalties to the copyright proprietor on parts manufactured, the former, as between it and the latter, should be primarily liable. However, because of the secondary liability of the pressing plant, the problem of loss of royalties through insolvency is minimized.

Whether the royalty is per recording, or per side of recording, or allocable if more than one composition is involved, are matters requiring careful definition.[272]

If the royalty is not fixed by the statute, some machinery, either administrative or judicial, would have to be established (and sup-

---

[270] See p. 10, supra.
[271] See note 80, supra.
[272] See note 60, supra.

ported) to fix the royalty either by general regulations or individual action.[273]

Periods and methods of accounting for, and payment of, the royalty should be set forth in the statute in such a way that the composer (or assigns) is assured honest, periodic accounting and prompt payment. Penalties for failure to so account and pay should also be prescribed.[274] Since the copyright owner does not select his licensees, he should have the right of reasonable inspection of the manufacturer's books and records in order to check on the accounting. For the same reason, royalty claims might be collected, in advance, in behalf of the copyright owner, by pressing plants from the licensee under a compulsory license. Perhaps such claims ought to enjoy some preferential status in the event of the insolvency or bankruptcy of a licensee under a compulsory license.

D. PROCEDURAL IMPLEMENTATION

The present section 1(e) requirement [275] that the copyright owner file a notice of use, when recording rights are to be exercised, may be desirable in order to enable interested recording companies to determine which compositions are available for recording under compulsory license. As a practical matter, of course, some recording companies actually commence recording before clearing the rights. Negotiated licenses are attempted before resort to the compulsory license provision. The Copyright Office would seem to be the logical place of filing. Changes in filing procedure would seem to be matters within the discretion of the officials of that office. The filing fee should probably be sufficient to cover the costs involved. The present penalty for failing to file is the barring of an action for infringement of recording rights. This would not appear to be overly burdensome.

The present section 101(e) requirement [276] that the prospective licensee under a compulsory license send to the copyright owner a notice of intention to record the composition would appear to be a slight burden under the circumstances, and should undoubtedly be continued as a means of letting the copyright owner learn of prospective recording of his composition. Appropriate penalties for failure to give such notice should be prescribed.[277] Negotiated licenses usually waive this requirement.

E. EXTENSION OF COMPULSORY LICENSE PRINCIPLE TO NONMUSICAL WORKS

The arguments relating to the retention of the compulsory license principle with respect to musical works do not necessarily apply in the case of nonmusical works. Dramatic works have been protected against recording since 1909, and nondramatic literary works since 1953.[278] When such recording rights were recognized, there was no agitation to subject them to compulsory licensing. There is not and never has been any threat of monopoly; the scale of operations is substantially smaller; there has been no industry reliance on lack of

---

[273] See pp. 34, 38, supra.
[274] See pp. 18–21, supra ; note 65, supra.
[275] See note 61, supra.
[276] See notes 64, 65, supra.
[277] See pp. 18–21, supra ; note 65, supra.
[278] See notes 4, 191, supra.

recognition of such rights or on any compulsory license provision relating to the same. On the other hand, the composer, so far as recording rights are concerned, has a status inferior to that of the creators of other copyrightable works.

F. STATUTORY LANGUAGE

Any revision of the present compulsory license provisions might well eliminate the awkward constructions and inconsistent phraseology of the present provisions.[279]

G. EFFECTIVE DATE OF AMENDMENTS

Any amendments which substantially affect rights in works in which statutory copyright is subsisting should, following the example of the act of 1909, probably not be retroactive. If the revision represents substantial changes, its effective date might well be delayed for a sufficient period to enable the various interests involved to make the necessary adjustments in their trade practices.[280]

VI. RECAPITULATION OF MAJOR ISSUES

A. Should the principle of the compulsory license for the mechanical recording of music be retained or eliminated?

B. If that principle is retained:

(1) What types of recording should be, and what types should not be subject to compulsory license?

(2) If more than one type of recording is subject to compulsory license and the copyright proprietor authorizes the making of one such type, should another person be allowed to make a different such type under compulsory license?

(3) What should be the limitations on the right of arrangement incidental to recording under compulsory license?

(4) Should the royalty rate be a flat sum per composition (or per unit of playing time), a percentage of the retail sales price (or of the manufacturer's price), or something else? What should the flat sum or percentage figure be? Should there be any provision for allocation? How should a composition which is recorded on two sides of a recording be treated?

(5) Should the royalty rate be applied to records manufactured in the United States, to records sold in the United States, or on some other basis? Should only the manufacturer be liable for the same?

(6) Should the present provisions requiring the copyright proprietor to file a notice of use, and making his failure to file such notice a defense to any suit for infringement of recording rights, be retained, modified, or eliminated?

---

[279] See pp. 13–15, supra.
[280] See p. 26, supra. Such matters as the "jukebox exception," protection of musical compositions of foreign authors against mechanical reproduction, and the various matters discussed in notes 68–74, supra, are beyond the scope of this study.

(7) Are the present provisions requiring the manufacturer to give notice of intention to use and to account and pay royalties monthly, adequate to safeguard the copyright proprietor? If not, what other and different safeguards should be provided for?

(8) Should the present penalties for the manufacturer's failure to fulfill the conditions for exercising the compulsory license be retained, modified, or eliminated?

C. Should the compulsory license principle be extended to mechanical recording rights in other classes of works or to other rights in musical compositions and/or other classes of works? If so, what should be the detailed features thereof?

STUDY NO. 6

THE ECONOMIC ASPECTS OF THE COMPULSORY LICENSE

By William M. Blaisdell

October 1958

THE ECONOMIC ASPECTS OF THE COMPULSORY LICENSE

I. The Economic Nature of Compulsory License

Section 1(e) of the Copyright Act of 1909 provides that, once a recording of a musical composition has been agreed to by the owner of the copyright of that composition, then anyone may make a recording of the composition upon the payment of a statutory fee to the copyright holder. This type of provision, known as the compulsory license, is relatively infrequent in American law, except in connection with industries affected by a public interest, and in such cases usually only as a limitation on price; there is no such limitation in other areas of copyright. This specific provision places three limitations on the contractual freedom of the owner of the copyright to a musical composition; it establishes limits on (1) the persons with whom he may refuse to contract; (2) the times at which he may contract; (3) the price at which he may contract. Moreover, the copyright owner may not place any time limitation on the period during which the copyrighted property may be used, provided only that the statutory price is paid. Just as soon as one recording has been agreed to, anyone is free to record the same composition without time limit so long as he makes the required payments, known as "mechanical royalties."

There are several possible variations on each of these three major aspects of the compulsory license provision. For example, the freedom to record might become effective only after a certain time period, or the statutory fee might be varied as a percentage of a price or it might be related to the fee paid by the first recorder. In addition, the compulsory concept itself might be limited to a fixed period after a specified event such as the signature to the first negotiated contract for recording. ' Also, a tribunal might be established to determine a "fair and equitable fee" to be paid by those taking advantage of the provision. Still other variations might be applied, such as a sliding scale of fees increasing as the number of sales of the record increased.

In the present organization of the music business, recordings of various kinds are of increasing significance, and the compulsory license is important, particularly to the producers of popular records, where the large volume of sales creates the chance of large profits. Once a composition has reached the public domain, compulsory license is no longer applicable, of course. However, it is applicable to the copyrighted "standards," i.e., compositions which have been accepted more or less permanently into the musical culture, and to copyrighted classical selections, but since these latter make up a relatively small portion of the total record production, in this study emphasis will be placed on the music business as it treats popular recordings.

91   (939)

II. The Functional Organization of the Music-Recording Business

A. COMPOSERS AND LYRICISTS

The music industry starts with the composition of a tune; it may be designed for a particular purpose such as popular use, television use, or moving picture use. It is hoped, of course, that a specially designed tune will end up in all these uses and perhaps others.

A large number of the composers and lyricists who produce the tunes are organized professionally into the Songwriters Protective Association [1] (SPA). This organization, now some 25 years old, functions primarily to protect the professional status of songwriters through the maintenance of a standard form of contract for use between individual songwriters and the publishers of musical compositions. In its most recent negotiations in 1947-48, it also established a "basic agreement" between the SPA and the Music Publishers Protective Association, which a music publisher must sign before he may purchase the compositions of SPA members under the 1947 Revised Uniform Popular Songwriters Contract. About 2,700 songwriters now belong to the organization and over 900 music publishers have signed the basic agreement. Although the SPA has used the group principle in dealing with music publishers, the standard SPA contract is applied individually by each songwriter to the sale of an individual composition to a publisher.

There is no clear information available as to the extent of the influence of SPA. It seems to be generally agreed that it is composed primarily of writers who are also members of ASCAP. One industry source states that—

The majority of the (popular) hit songs are presently written by nonmembers of SPA and published by firms not having a contract with that organization.

It may be inferred, an inference which is supported by some who are familiar with the industry, that most writers affiliated with BMI are not members of SPA, though some are. Also, there is a belief that regardless of the extent of the use of the SPA contracts (which are copyrighted), the standards established by those contracts are generally effective as a "floor" in the relationships between all songwriters and music publishers.

In contrast to the free-lance concept which dominates the SPA operation, the Composers and Lyricists Guild of America (CLGA) includes in its membership primarily those who write songs for the motion picture producers. The CLGA has about 500 members and there is a large overlap between its membership, on one hand, and that of SPA, the American Federation of Musicians (AFM) and the Writers Guild of America (WGA), on the other. There has been considerable talk about the possible merger of SPA and CLGA,[2] but no merger has taken place. The CLGA has sought to become the bargaining agent for its members in negotiations with the motion picture producers, but the National Labor Relations Board has decided that, for

---

[1] The name of this organization was recently changed to the American Guild of Authors and Composers. For convenience we shall refer to it herein under its former designation.

[2] See, e.g., Billboard, June 23, 1956, and July 7, 1956; also Variety, Feb. 6, 1957.

purposes of the National Labor Relations Act, the members of CLGA are "not employees, but are independent contractors." [3]

Composers and lyricists also appear in other economic guises. As individuals, they may own or participate in music publishing firms, or recording firms, or they may also be recording artists. It is not unusual for a single individual to participate in several aspects of the music business.

The songwriter as such does not ordinarily deal directly with the licensing of his music for recording or for other uses. In practice he assigns his property to a music publisher under an SPA contract. The compulsory license provision affects the songwriter, however, inasmuch as it affects his revenues from the property which he has assigned to the music publisher.

B. MUSIC PUBLISHERS

The major effect of the 1947 Revised Uniform Popular Songwriters Contract (SPA) is to transfer to a music publisher all the rights in a musical composition, including the right to copyright it, under detailed and specific limitations which protect the position of the songwriter. No such contract between a songwriter and a music publisher is valid without the countersignature of the SPA; when a songwriter joins the SPA he transfers to it the recording rights to all his compositions, and it is only through countersignature on his contracts that the SPA releases these rights to a music publisher. In the present state of the music business, no music publisher would purchase a musical composition without obtaining the right to record it.

To the extent that individual songwriters do not belong to SPA, they presumably must protect their rights with respect to recording of their compositions. Within SPA, it may be inferred, the use of the organization countersignature to release recording rights is a method of tightening the organization. Individual songwriters would presumably insert special provisions in their contracts with music publishers in order to cover the potentially very valuable recording right.

Many of the major music publishers are organized into the Music Publishers Protective Association (MPPA). However, some of the very large publishers, notably those controlled by the Warner Bros. motion picture interests, do not belong. Organized in 1918, the MPPA has a membership of about 50 firms.

Although the negotiations with respect to the Minimum Basic Agreement (MBA) and the Uniform Popular Songwriters Contract are carried out by representatives of the MPPA for its members, the MBA itself is a contract between SPA and each individual publisher, and the songwriters contract is between the individual composer and an individual publisher.

The music publishers arrange for the dissemination of musical compositions through various media. With the development of motion pictures, electronic recording, and radio and television broadcasting, the functions of the music publishers have expanded greatly from their earlier activities in the publication and sale of sheet music. These newer developments have shifted the major sources of publishers' and songwriters' income from sales of sheet music and minor amounts of recording and performance royalties, to greatly expanded recording

---

[3] 117 N.L.R.B. No. 4, Jan. 4, 1957.

and performance royalties combined with a relatively small revenue from the sales of sheet music. Between 1951 and 1955, while sheet music royalty payments fell by 44 percent in volume, the volume of mechanical royalty payments by record producers to music publishers increased by 60 percent, the synchronization payments by motion picture producers to music publishers rose by 63 percent, and the performing rights payments by users of copyrighted musical compositions to performing rights organizations increased by 96 percent.[4]

Closely affiliated with the MPPA is the office of Harry Fox, trustee. It is understood that Mr. Fox is the general manager of the MPPA, and also that his office acts independently in a trustee capacity for others than members of the MPPA. The Fox office issues recording licenses and collects recording fees ("mechanicals") for those music publishers he represents as trustee in this connection. The collection function fulfilled by the Fox office is understood to be conducted on a nonprofit basis for the members of the MPPA, and against a percentage fee for other publishers. In these functions of licensing and collecting, the Fox office acts not only for domestic publishers, both members and nonmembers of MPPA, but also for foreign music publishers through contracts with foreign mechanical rights organizations, notably the Bureau International de l'Edition Mechanique (BIEM), the major mechanical rights organization in Europe. In connection with its function as collection agency for the mechanicals due to publishers from recording companies, the Fox office also verifies the accuracy of such payments by examining the books of account of record producers.

In addition to the MPPA, the so-called "standard" music publishers are organized into the Music Publishers Association of the United States, which is the trade association for this group. However, there is no clear line of demarcation between "standard" and "popular" compositions. Some members of MPPA have large catalogs of standard works in addition to their popular catalogs.

The music publishing industry is made up of about a dozen outstanding large firms and several thousand smaller firms, many of which are inactive in that they may merely hold copyrights and collect royalties on them rather than actively engaging in promotional and distributive operations. In 1958 ASCAP had 1,081 publisher members.[5]

Several of the largest music publishers are controlled by motion picture interests: MGM and 20th Century Fox, Paramount Pictures, Warner Bros., and Columbia Pictures.[6] Successful composers and recording artists frequently have their own music publishing firms, and both NBC and CBS own at least one such publisher affiliated with ASCAP and one each affiliated with BMI.[7]

It is primarily upon the music publisher that the direct impact of the compulsory license falls. In practice he is the holder of the copyright to musical compositions, and after his first agreement with a

---

[4] Cf. memorandum prepared by MPPA to the Department of the Treasury dated Feb. 19, 1957, re H.R. 5478, a bill to amend the personal holding company provisions of the Internal Revenue Code.
[5] The Billboard, Mar. 3, 1958.
[6] Cf. hearings, Senate Committee on the Judiciary, 83d Cong., 1st sess., on S. 1106 (jukebox exemption), p. 103.
[7] Cf. House Judiciary Committee hearings, 1956, serial 22, pt. 2, vol. 2, "Television," pp. 4203 and 4205.

record producer for the recording of a tune anyone may record the tune upon payment of the statutory royalty. In the absence of the compulsory license, the music publisher, as owner of the copyright, would be free to negotiate for the recording of the copyrighted material. He could negotiate with whom he chose, offer an exclusive contract if he wished, ask any price he desired, and suggest such time period as he cared to; in general, he could negotiate within the framework usually applicable to business operations having to do with the assignment or licensing of property rights.

In the absence of compulsory license, it may be assumed that the music publisher would recognize his own interest to be in licensing as many recordings and at such royalty rates as would produce the largest net amount of royalties from record sales and public performances—the latter particularly on radio and television—rather than being faced with the necessity of licensing all comers to record a composition at not more than the statutory royalty.

C. RECORD PRODUCERS

When a music publisher has accepted a composition from a songwriter, one of his first moves, frequently even before sheet music publication, is to attempt to have it recorded by a record producer. In recorded form a composition is immediately available for broadcast which is considered to be the major form of "exposure" to the buying public.

Record producers will consider perhaps 50 compositions before they agree to the recording of one. Having accepted a composition, a recording contract is made with the music publisher. The payment to be made for the recording privilege (mechanical royalty) is negotiated on the basis of the statutory provision in section 1(e) of the Copyright Act, that is, the compulsory license provision. In practice the "2-cent per part" limitation in the statute is a ceiling on the payment. When the 78 r.p.m. record was standard in the industry, its playing time was a definition of "part." The industry is now dominated by the EP and LP speeds, and it has developed a new rule of thumb for EP and LP records to the effect that the recording royalty shall be $\frac{1}{4}$ cent per minute of playing time or fraction thereof, but not less than 2 cents per side.[8]

However, in negotiating a recording contract, the bargaining strength of the two parties is important and in general the royalties agreed to in recording contracts are something less than the statutory rate; in fact, it is reported that, on rare ocasions, a music publisher has been willing to waive any mechanical royalty in order to get a new composition recorded by an outstanding artist.[9] The license for use of the tune is usually issued by the Fox office and the mechanical royalty is paid to the Fox office on a quarterly basis.

---

[8] Cf. Henn, Harry G., "The Compulsory License Provisions of the U.S. Copyright Law," p. 50 (study No. 5 in the present committee print) ; and letter from Sydney Kaye, Esq., dated Oct. 2, 1956, in the comments and views appended thereto. A schedule of royalty rates based on the manufacturer's suggested retail price, and included in the MPPA "long form" license is published in Henn. Harry G., op. cit., p. 50 ; and in a letter from Ernest S. Meyers, Esq., dated June 14, 1957, in the comments and views appended thereto. However, it seems that the dominance of the EP and LP speeds is such that the royalty based on the length of play of the record is generally used.
[9] Information from trade sources.

Although there are probably more than 1,000 record producers in existence at any one time,[10] a limited number of them are active at any one time. The record industry trade association, the Record Industry Association of America (RIAA), formed in 1952, reported 53 members as of December 31, 1956.[11] The functions of the RIAA are largely technical research, taxation and legislative activity, and statistical compilation.

Four or five of these producers are usually recognized as "major producers," although there is no recognized definition of a "major". Only four producers have annual gross sales of more than $10 millions,[12] and several others are "semimajors" reaching for an annual gross sales figure of $10 millions.

The relationships between record producers and other parts of the music industry are highly complex and widespread. Both RCA Victor Division and the Columbia Record Co. are closely affiliated, respectively, with the NBC and CBS broadcasting interests, which in turn own music publishers. This gives these two "majors" a distinctive position in the industry in that they can offer special inducements to recording artists in the form of radio and television appearances which are considered to be of major importance both in the sale of records and in the professional advancement of recording artists in the amusement industry.

D. MOTION PICTURE PRODUCERS

Since the advent of sound motion pictures in 1929 the motion picture industry has been a large user of music. The motion picture producer negotiates with the music publisher just as a record producer negotiates, but the use of a copyrighted musical composition in a motion picture is not considered to be subject to the compulsory license provision. Although the law applicable to this situation is not clear,[13] in practice the fees for such use of copyrighted music on a motion picture soundtrack are negotiated freely between the copyright owner (or his agent, the Harry Fox office) and the motion picture producer; and a single payment is usually made for both the right to use the music on the soundtrack (synchronization right) and the right to perform the music in exhibiting the motion pictures (performing right). The increasing use of theatrical motion pictures on television, and particularly the production of motion pictures specially for television use, have greatly enlarged the market for synchronization rights.

Prices paid for synchronization rights (together with the performing rights as to theatrical exhibition) vary widely. In a theatrical motion picture, some of the factors affecting the negotiation are: the total budget of the picture, the importance of the star actors, and the place which any given musical composition will have in the film.

---

[10] "Music Performance Trust Funds, 15th Combined Reports and Statements," p. 5, reports 1,167 phonograph record producers signatory to the 1954 Phonograph Records Trust Agreement as of June 30, 1956. Of the 1,018 signatories at Dec. 31, 1955, 951 reported no sales in the last half of 1955.

[11] Annual Report of the RIAA, Jan. 1, 1956–Dec. 31, 1956, p. 5.

[12] Ibid., p. 5, and bylaws of the RIAA, sec. 2.

[13] See Kupferman, T.R., "Rights in New Media," in Law and Contemporary Problems, vol. 19, No. 2 (1954), pp. 173–174; and Dubin, Joseph S., "Copyright Aspects of Sound Recording," in Southern California Law Review, vol. 26, No. 2 (1953), pp. 139 ff.

Fees may run from as little as $500 to as much as $20,000.   In TV films, the fee for a single use of a song in a syndicated film usually runs from $250 to $500, which includes unlimited runs for several years on a worldwide basis.[14]

Conversely, the motion picture industry is becoming an increasingly important source of musical material for phonograph records.   A good deal of original music is now composed for motion pictures, and this material, first recorded on the soundtrack of a picture, is used for further recording on disks or tapes.   In practice, if original copyrighted musical material is first used on the soundtrack of a motion picture, it is not thereby considered available for recording under the compulsory license provision; the right to first production of such original musical material in the form of recordings is subject to price negotiation, and only after such right has been given to one record producer is it possible for other record producers to invoke the compulsory license provision.

Due to their interest in music the relationships of the motion picture producers ramify throughout the music business: they are major owners of music publishing houses, and are thus influential in MPPA and ASCAP; they own recording companies, and they can direct their original motion picture musical compositions, through their own music publishers, to their own recording companies, if they so desire.[15]

In connection with compulsory license, the motion picture companies are affected as a source of compositions for recording, and hence as composers or copyright owners.   This does not minimize their influence in the music business in other capacities not directly a part of their motion picture activities.

E. RECORDING ARTISTS

A major factor in the salability of a recorded tune is the recording artist or artists.   Artists who perform for recording companies include both the solo artists and "name" groups, and the instrumental accompanists.   Each phonograph record producer has his "stable" of solo artists, usually under exclusive contract; the contracts with these artists are probably his most valuable asset.   In some cases a very well-known artist can maintain a nonexclusive position vis-a-vis phonograph recording but this is unusual.[16]

The contracts between solo artists and phonograph record producers are made under the provisions of a code of fair practice negotiated between the record producers and the American Federation of Television and Radio Artists (AFTRA).   This code is a minimum agreement and individual artists are free to negotiate higher wages and better conditions of employment if they are able to do so.   Well-

---

[14] Information re "sink rights" taken from the Billboard, Feb. 22, 1957.
[15] Such action is not always considered desirable.   In 1957, RKO-Teleradio Pictures owned both RKO Music (a publisher), and RKO-Unique (a record producer), but the picture producer transferred the album recording rights to a specific soundtrack to the subsidiary music publisher (RKO Music) with instructions to negotiate their sale in the open market.   "The (RKO filmusical) soundtrack album rights will be put on the open market by the publishing subsidiary," with the purpose of giving "the RKO publishing subsidiary a better bargaining position with the other disk companies."   Variety, Feb. 20, 1957.
[16] "Bing Crosby is staying with Decca for another 3 years.   However, the new pact gives the crooner the green light to do occasional groovings under other disk banners." Variety, June 6, 1956.

known artists are apparently given annual minimum guarantees with additions dependent upon the success of their records.[17]

Well-known solo recording artists are frequently "names" in the music business for reasons other than their recorded performances. They may own publishing houses and thus be influential in MPPA, ASCAP, or BMI, or they may also be composers or lyricists belonging to SPA. A very well-known performer may have a publishing house which is a member of ASCAP and another affiliated with BMI.

The instrumental musicians who perform for phonograph records, either directly under contract with a phonograph record producer, or indirectly as on a soundtrack under the control of a motion picture producer, are all members of the American Federation of Musicians (AFM), or the Musicians Guild of America (MGA), and are covered by the applicable minimum basic contracts of those unions. Some instrumental groups, such as well-established dance bands or symphony orchestras, are under exclusive recording contract to a particular record producer, but the accompanists for recording artists are frequently freelance musicians employed for the specific recording session.

With the rapid technological developments in recording and the cumulative popularity of recorded music, together with the "exposure" of recorded music by broadcasters, the need for performing instrumentalists has been drastically reduced. This is, of course, the major complaint of AFM. Most of the recording instrumentalists are concentrated in Hollywood and New York where they work on an individual freelance basis for the recording companies. In the calendar year 1955 the total wages received by members of the AFM for recording sessions was $4,171,000.[18]

Neither group of performing artists is directly affected by the compulsory license provision. They are either under contract to a recording company or hired on a freelance basis by those companies. They are not involved directly in the negotiations leading to the recording of a copyrighted musical composition. Only if their contracts contain provisions for compensation related to the number of records sold would they participate directly in the returns from a hit tune. Of course, if a recording artist does have a hit tune his recording company presumably would recognize this attainment in connection with later recordings.

As indicated, a record producer's most valuable asset may well be his "stable" of recording artists. Exclusivity of contract, for recording purposes, between artist and producer is the usual rule. But these contracts are usually for a limited time period, and after a year or two a successful artist will find himself free to renew, or to shift to another producer. The moment an artist shows any promise of popularity, he is signed by some record producer. If he really becomes popular, then the advantages to him of a contract with a producer affiliated with radio or television become apparent; appearances on the air are the best possible exposure for obtaining lucrative personal appearance contracts, which every performer wants.

---

[17] E.g., Jo Stafford's new 5-year contract with Columbia Records "is described as 'one of the costliest' in the business with guarantees well into six figures." Variety, May 5, 1956.

[18] Official Proceedings, 59th Annual Convention, AFM, 1956, p. 131.

F. PERFORMING RIGHTS ORGANIZATIONS

In contrast with, and completely separate from, the so-called "mechanical" royalty, i.e., royalties paid under the compulsory license provision of the Copyright Act, are the royalties paid for the right to perform musical compositions in public. Each public performance for profit of a copyrighted musical composition is subject to a performing license from the copyright proprietor. The several forms and the large number and wide distribution of public performances for profit now existing, as well as the great number of compositions performed, make the issuance of licenses by individual copyright owners a practical impossibility. Therefore, organizations have been formed to license the performing rights in a large catalog of copyrighted musical compositions. These organizations issue blanket licenses to those who wish to perform publicly for profit the compositions controlled by them. The licensing contract provides for payment of performing royalties to the organization which in turn makes payments to composers and publishers in accordance with arrangements established by the organization.

Performing royalties are a legal liability of the organization under whose control the performance is given; e.g., a radio or TV broadcasting station, a restaurant, or a hotel.[19] Payments of such royalties are made directly to the performing rights organization (ASCAP, BMI, or SESAC) under the provisions of a contract which usually licenses the contracting organization to arrange for unlimited performances of copyrighted musical material in the catalogs controlled by the particular performing rights organization.

Performing royalties are to be distinguished from mechanical (recording) royalties, the latter being a legal liability of the record producers who pay the royalties to the music publishers holding the copyright.

Performing rights organizations are not directly affected by the compulsory license provision. However, they are closely allied to both the composers and the music publishers, who receive mechanical royalties from the record producers. Moreover, the use of records in broadcasts is a major source of performing royalties; and the popularity of a recording, particularly as used in broadcasts, will affect the amount of the performing royalties received by the composer and publisher.

G. SUMMARY

How a musical composition becomes a record

Within the framework of the music business, the typical course which a musical composition takes from the composer to the final user can now be followed, particularly in those areas where compulsory license applies; i.e., the recording of a copyrighted musical composition and the distribution of records. The composer of a musical composition (together with one or more colleagues collaborating as composers or lyricists) transfers all his rights in the composition

---

[19] Under the *Alden-Rochelle* decision (56 U.S.P.Q. 28 (S.D.N.Y. 1942); 80 F. Supp. 888 (S.D.N.Y. 1948); 80 F. Supp. 900 (S.D.N.Y. 1948)) motion picture theaters do not pay performing royalties on performances of copyrighted music in the films they exhibit; the payment is made "at the source"; i.e., by the film producer to the copyright owner. However, if a motion picture theater presents live performers who perform copyrighted musical works, the theater is liable for the payment of the performing royalty.

to a music publisher through the negotiation of a contract, frequently on the SPA standard songwriter's form. Presumably the composer is also a member of ASCAP or has contractual arrangements with a music publisher affiliated with BMI or SESAC. Except for the receipt of royalties for the performance, recording, or other use of the composition, all of which are covered in the SPA contract, and presumably in any other similar songwriter-publisher contract, the composer has now lost direct control of his created property.

The music publisher, having secured copyright in the composition, now attempts to license it for recording purposes. When the publisher succeeds in licensing the recording right, he files with the Copyright Office a Notice of Use or loses his defense against any suit for infringement of the recording right. The license for recording of the copyrighted composition is usually issued to the phonograph record producer by the Harry Fox office which sets up an account for the receipt of mechanical royalties from the record producer.[20] The license for such use having been issued, any other person, under the compulsory license provision, may then arrange to have the copyrighted composition recorded upon notifying the copyright owner and agreeing to pay mechanical royalties to him or his agent, the Fox office, and sending a duplicate of the notification to the Copyright Office.[21]

In practice the music publisher (copyright proprietor) is usually prepared to agree to additional recordings of his copyrighted musical compositions at the standard royalty rates without special negotiation; and recording companies generally obtain licenses at those rates. A very popular composition may be issued in as many as 15 or 20 different recordings by different record producers under the compulsory license system, but without ever specifically activating the statutory compulsory licensing provisions as such. Under these conditions payments of mechanical royalties by 15 or 20 producers will be made for the account of the music publisher who is the proprietor of the copyright. On rare occasions a music publisher may not wish a particular record producer to record his composition; under these conditions the record producer may nevertheless proceed, under the compulsory license provisions, to notify the publisher and the Copyright Office, record the composition, and arrange to make payments in accordance with the statute.

The Fox office, after deducting expenses,[22] pays the remainder to the publisher, who, in turn, pays the songwriter(s). The mechanical royalty for the songwriter(s), according to the provisions of the Uniform Popular Songwriters Contract (SPA), is not less than 50 percent of the publisher's receipts on that account.

Recording artists and instrumental musicians are employed by the record producer and are paid by him under provisions of the applicable AFTRA, AFM, and MGA contracts.

---

[20] Standard royalty rates have been established by trade practice, and are generally less than the maximum fixed by the statute.

[21] Sec. 101(e), Copyright Act.

[22] The maximum deduction for expenses is 3½ percent, an increase from a maximum of 2½ percent effective until about 1955. However, since the 1947 Revised Uniform Popular Songwriters Contract provides that no more than 2½ percent may be so used, the additional 1 percent must be borne by the publishers to the extent it is required (sec. 4(h), Songwriters Contract). Cf. Variety, Oct. 31, 1956; increasing volume of sales in the phonograph record business has made it unnecessary for the Fox office to use the entire 1 percent additional fee.

H. THE DISTRIBUTION OF RECORDS

The general pattern of record distribution is for a distributor to cover a certain geographic area for a producer, and for the retail outlets in that area to purchase their supplies from the distributor. Currently the distribution of phonograph records is undergoing rapid metamorphosis. Formerly sold largely through music stores and record shops, phonograph records are now available at retail in drugstores, grocery stores, department stores, bookstores, and in general wherever a rack may be set up, and are distributed through record "clubs." Also records are getting into consumers' hands more and more frequently through advertising "deals." For example, with the purchase of a specific merchandise item a coupon is received by the purchaser which permits him to purchase a record at a reduced price. Also, discounts on records at retail are perhaps the rule rather than the exception, although the volume of retail discount sales is not known.

III. SUPPLY, DEMAND, AND THE COMPULSORY LICENSE

A. THE SUPPLY AND DEMAND PATTERN

The usual industry practice seems to be for a songwriter to contract with a music publisher for the exploitation of a composition, and thus the ownership of most musical copyrights is in the hands of those publishers. Also, both industry information and logic would lead to the conclusion that the Uniform Popular Songwriters Contract of SPA establishes the "floor" for negotiation of such a contract. It would probably not be overstating the case to say that the framework of the music industry places in the hands of music publishers the control over the supply of copyrighted popular musical materials, and that the rights of songwriters are largely protected by the minimums established by SPA.

In negotiating recording licenses, the music publisher is limited under the compulsory license provision by the facts that, (1) he cannot give an exclusive recording license, (2) he cannot limit the time period for the use of the license except as it is limited by the life of the copyright,[23] and (3) he cannot exact a mechanical royalty of more than "2 cents on each such part manufactured."

In this framework, the music publisher has not been able to exact from record producers the full statutory fee for most types of recording, and at times he has been willing to forego the fee entirely in order to get the public "exposure" which a recording by a "big name artist" will give. The most he can hope for is that the composition will prove to be popular, and that a number of recording companies will produce recordings which will result in ample mechanical performing royalties.

A large part of the demand for copyrighted musical material comes from the recording companies. They decide the particular compositions to be recorded. It is the "A. & R. man"—the head of the artists

---

[23] A maximum of 28 years, because, under sec. 1 of the 1947 Revised Uniform Popular Songwriters Contract, the copyright reverts to the composer at the end of the original term.

and repertoire department—who usually makes this decision, and it is his responsibility to match up artists, tunes, accompanists, and musical arrangements to catch the fancy of a very unpredictable public taste. Not only must he make these decisions for compositions for which his company is the first licensee, but also he must be on the lookout for all compositions which other companies have recorded and which may offer an opportunity to catch the public fancy with a new arrangement, new artists, and new accompanists. In negotiating for a license (whether the first or a subsequent license) the recording company knows that it will get the license for the life of the copyright, and that, in all probability, it will need to pay something less than the statutory royalty rate; it also knows that, if the composition promises any public acceptance, the recording will be immediately faced with competition from several (perhaps up to a score) of competing recordings of the composition. Even a single producer may release several different recordings of the same musical material. As a result of his negotiating strength, the record producer may also require that the music publisher agree to contribute a specified amount to the promotional effort to publicize the composition.

The revenue received by the creators and owners of recorded copyrighted musical material is not the retail price of records, but rather the mechanical and performing royalties which are paid for the use of the material. In the present buoyant state of the music business, with worldwide distribution of records, and a seemingly insatiable public appetite for new tunes,[24] there is still such a flood of available compositions[25] that the mechanical royalty feed does not even attain the statutory maximum. It is clear that the competitive possibilities under the compulsory license are so great that no record producer finds it necessary, for most types of recording, to agree to pay even the statutory level of mechanical royalties on a new composition. Although performing and synchronization royalties are increasing at a faster rate than mechanical royalties,[26] and form the bulk of the gross income of the composers, mechanical royalties still loom large in the gross amounts paid to composers and lyricists.[27]

It should be recognized that "music publishers" and "record producers" are not necessarily clear-cut divisions of the industry, but rather functional concepts. In practice, as has been pointed out, music publishers may be owned by artists, composers, motion picture companies, broadcasting companies, performing rights organizations, and even recording companies; the motivation of "music publishers" is not necessarily unitary and unified. Similarly, "record producers" are affected by their relationships with broadcasting companies, performing rights organizations, music publishers, and motion picture companies. One clear fact is that the composers, and lyricists, in this conglomerate of motivation, have not been able to obtain the maximum statutory fee under the compulsory license provision, even though

[24] "* * * about 150 new disks, or 300 tunes, have been hitting the market each week." It is not clear whether these figures include "cover" records, i.e., varying recorded arrangements of the same composition. Variety, Apr. 3, 1957.
[25] In the fiscal year ended June 30, 1956, published and unpublished musical works were registered in the Copyright Office to the number of 58,330.
[26] Cf. pp. 93–94, supra.
[27] Cf. p. 104, infra. Composers and lyricists got an estimated $4.75 million from mechanical royalties and an estimated $12.2 million from performing royalties in 1956.

organization into the SPA and the widespread use of a standard contract has improved their position remarkably in the last 25 years.

It is also clear that this diversification of function in the music business is growing rather than diminishing. In a recent trade magazine article, it is stated, in part: [28]

Diversification is the key word of today's music business, with more and more firms branching out in all directions. Independent radio broadcasters and their staffers are going into record manufacturing, song publishing, TV film syndication, and the talent management game. Publishers are cutting records for their own labels and managing disk talent. TV producers and performers are setting up their own publishing firms, record labels and talent management divisions.

A certain amount of this activity has always existed, but heretofore it has usually been conducted on a relatively minor scale—and in many cases—on [sic] a decidedly hush-hush atmosphere. Today, however, diversification has become an accepted way of doing business not only around the Brill Building, but in all segments of the music business and related industries.

However, in all the confusion and melange of motivation and function, it stands out boldly that three items are required to make records: compositions, artists, and recording equipment and skills. Currently, compositions are controlled by the music publishers; artists, as well as the recording equipment and skills, are controlled by the recording companies.

B. WHO GETS WHAT IN THE MUSIC RECORDING BUSINESS?

In the present organization of the music recording business, the major direct beneficiaries of phonograph record production are the songwriters (composers and lyricists), the music publishers, the recording artists and the record producers. How much does each of these groups receive annually from music recordings?

1. *The songwriters.*—After assigning a composition to a music publisher, the songwriter receives royalties, assuming there are any, from his publisher (mechanical royalties) and from a performing rights organization (performing royalties).

Mechanical recording royalties are received either directly by publishers or from the Fox office, collecting agency for such royalties; at least one-half of all mechanical royalties are probably passed on to the songwriters. Record companies pay an average of 6.5 percent of their revenues to songwriters and publishers.[29] In 1956, the recording industry sold recordings with an approximate retail value of $325 million of which about $150 million went to the record producers.[30] Six and one-half percent of $150 million gives $9.75 million paid for mechanical royalties; of this about one-half,[31] or $4.88 million, was allocated to songwriters. A 2½ percent deduction for collection expenses leaves a total of about $4.75 million paid to songwriters.

2. *Music publishers.*—In the estimate made for the revenues of songwriters, the music publishers received an equal amount. There-

---

[28] The Billboard, July 7, 1956.
[29] Information from trade sources.
[30] Variety, Mar. 13, 1957. In this article, total sales during 1956, computed at retail prices, are estimated by the executive secretary of RIAA at $325 million. This figure is divided by 2.1 to obtain the revenues of the record producers.
[31] 1947 Revised Uniform Popular Songwriters Contract, pars. 4(g) and 4(h). This provides that the songwriter, including both composer(s) and lyricist(s), shall receive not less than 50 percent of all mechanical royalties collected by the publisher, after a maximum deduction of 2½ percent for collection expenses. Most popular songs are probably sold at or above the "floor" established by provisions of this contract.

fore, the estimate of gross revenues for music publishers is the same as that for songwriters, or about $4.75 million.

However, in both cases, the estimate of revenues is gross; i.e., both publishers and songwriters have business expenses to pay before they arrive at a "net income" figure. The gross revenue of an individual received for creative effort is somewhat different from gross revenue received by a business organization in the course of exploiting creative works, and no typical expense pattern is available as a basis for reducing the gross estimates to net figures.

3. *Recording artists.*—According to information from the trade, phonograph record production involves an average cost of 13 percent of gross revenue for the services of recording artists. In 1956, record producers received gross revenues of $150 million; [32] 13 percent of this is $19.5 million.

This includes both instrumental artists and others. AFM reports annually on the revenues of its members from recording and transcription activities; in 1955, they received a total of $4.2 million.[33] This figure seems to be consistent with the estimated total of $19.5 million.

4. *Record producers.*—Of the $150 million gross received by record producers,[34] trade sources indicate that the average net profits are 4 percent of the gross. Thus, in 1956, record producers received an estimated $6 million net.

5. *Summary.*—The estimates of revenue for the four groups follow:

[Millions]

	Gross	Net
Songwriters	$4.75	(?)
Music publishers	4.75	(?)
Recording artists	19.5	(?)
Record producers	150	$6

It must be recognized that the gross revenues of the songwriters, the music publishers, and the recording artists are derived from the $150 million gross of the record producers.

The following table shows the relationships among the various flows of revenue described in the preceding paragraphs.

Estimated gross revenues of phonograph record producers, songwriters, music publishers, and recording artists from the music recording business [1] *(1956)*

Millions

Gross revenues from sales of phonograph records at wholesale___ $150.00
(a) Paid to recording artists as salaries and wages_____ 19.5
(b) Paid as mechanical royalties (Copyright Act, sec. 1e)_____ 9.75
    1. Paid as operating expenses (Fox office)_____ $0.25
    2. Paid to music publishers_____ 9.50

        (a) Paid to composers and lyricists_____ 4.75
        (b) Retained by publishers_____ 4.75

(c) Paid out as other business expenses_____ 114.75
(d) Phonograph record producers' profit_____ 6.0

[1] See accompanying text for explanation of the estimates.

[32] Cf. p. 103, supra.
[33] AFM, Official Proceedings, 1956, p. 131.
[34] Cf. p. 103, supra.

ADDENDUM

REVENUES FROM PERFORMING ROYALTIES

In addition to revenues from mechanical royalties, songwriters and music publishers receive performing royalties from performing rights organizations, primarily ASCAP and BMI; little is publicly known about SESAC, but its gross revenues are presumed to be relatively small. Performing royalties are derived predominantly from the performances of recorded musical works; i.e., radio and television performances of disks or tapes or films.[35] Hence, these performing royalties are closely related to the recording industry, in that they stem from the use of recording techniques.

In 1956 ASCAP received a total revenue of $24.9 million, of which $4.5 million was used for administrative expenses.[36] After reserves of $1.8 million for foreign societies, $9.3 million was paid by ASCAP to songwriters and $9.3 million to music publishers. Also, the songwriters received some part of the ASCAP royalties paid to music publishers through their ownership of ASCAP-member publishing companies, but it is impossible to estimate the amount involved.

BMI collects performing royalties from those who perform its catalog and, after deducting expenses, pays the remainder to its publisher-affiliates who, under the provisions of the standard SPA Songwriters Contract, pay at least one-half of that amount to songwriters. For the fiscal year ended July 31, 1956, BMI received a gross of $9.7 million and paid out as expenses $3.9 million, leaving $5.8 million for payments to publisher-owners and songwriters. A total of $5.7 million was paid, of which the publishers presumably retained about $2.85 million and paid about $2.85 million to composers and lyricists; about $150,000 was retained by BMI as addition to its corporate surplus.[36]

Thus, in summary, the songwriters received estimated mechanical and performing royalties in 1956 as follows:[37]

	Millions
From mechanical royalties	$4.75
From performing royalties:	
From ASCAP	9.30
From BMI	2.85
Total	16.90

A like amount, similarly derived, is estimated to have been received by the music publishers.

Hence, it is estimated that the songwriters as a group, and the music publishers as a group, each received about $17 million from mechanical and performing royalties in 1956. However, of the total of nearly $34 million, a sum of $9.5 million was received from mechanical royalties, and a sum of $24.3 million was from performing royalties, indicating the dominance of performing royalties in the revenues of these two groups from the recording industry, directly or indirectly.

---

[35] In 1957, 88.41 percent of ASCAP's gross receipts from licensees was from radio and television local stations and networks. Hearings before Subcommittee No. 5, House Select Committee on Small Business, 85th Cong., 2d sess., pursuant to H.R. 56, "Policies of ASCAP," p. 542.

[36] Broadcasting, "Telecasting," Sept. 9, 1957, p. 62. Because ASCAP is a membership organization and BMI is a corporation designed not to make profit, it is difficult to cast their financial statements into a uniform mold. However, it is believed that the figures as given are basically comparable as between the two organizations.

[37] Supra p. 104.

The table on the following page shows the relationships among the various flows of revenue described in this addendum. In combination with the table, supra p. 104, the revenue flows from both mechanical and performing royalties may be traced.

Estimated performing royalties received by songwriters and music publishers through ASCAP and BMI (1956)[1]

		Millions
Revenues from performing royalties		$34. 6
(a) Received by ASCAP		24. 9
1. Paid as expenses	$4. 5	
2. Paid to music publishers	9. 3	
3. Paid to composers and lyricists	9. 3	
4. Reserved for payments to foreign organizations	1. 8	
(b) Received by BMI		9. 7
1. Paid as expenses	$3. 9	
2. Paid to music publisher affiliates	5. 7	
(a) Retained by publishers	$2. 85	
(b) Paid to composers and lyricists	2. 85	
3. Retained by BMI as general surplus	.15	

[1] See accompanying text for explanation of estimates.

IV. The Music Recording Business in the Absence of Compulsory License

A. WHAT IS MEANT BY "THE ABSENCE OF COMPULSORY LICENSE"

If the compulsory license were abolished the owner of copyrighted musical material, i.e., usually the music publisher, would be freed from three limitations under which he now labors in negotiating for the licensing of such material.

(1) He could limit the licensing to those individuals he desired to deal with.

(2) He could limit the time period for licensing the material.

(3) He could negotiate freely as to the price to be paid for the use of the material.

On the other hand the recorder of copyrighted musical material would be in a position to negotiate for an exclusive license and if successful in this he would be freed from the competition of multiple versions of the same material which are issued as a result of the compulsory license provision. Thus a new pattern of negotiating strength would be established between the two parts of the music business which control the essentials to that business, namely, copyrighted musical materials on the one hand and recording artists and recording equipment and skills on the other.

It might be possible, of course, to remove only part of the limitations now inherent in the compulsory license, e.g., the limitation on the rate of mechanical royalties. Or the time period alone might be adjusted, i.e., the copyright owner might be completely free for 1 year after the date of copyright registration, at which point compulsory license would become effective.

B. A NEW PATTERN OF NEGOTIATION

Under a "no compulsory license regime", the owner of copyrighted musical material would be in a much stronger negotiating position than he is at present, since he could then grant exclusive or nonexclusive licenses for limited periods of time at royalty rates which he believed to be to his advantage.

It has been suggested that, in the absence of compulsory license, the large and financially powerful recording companies which largely control the leading recording artists would purchase recording options to entire catalogs or entire repertoires of musical publishing firms, with the result that they would assume a strategic control of the entire record business, to the detriment of smaller and less powerful record producers. In the confused organization of the music business it cannot be categorically denied that this possibility might eventuate. However in a consumer market in which a new tune may appear on records and even though successful may disappear within a few weeks or months because it has been exhausted, and in view of the constant stream of new musical compositions that are not recorded, it is at least doubtful whether the owners of new copyrighted musical material would so easily give up the values which they control. Moreover the Uniform Popular Songwriters Contract, which seems to be the "floor" for negotiation between composers and music publishers,[38] prohibits music publishers from including compositions purchased by them under that contract—

In any bulk of block license heretofore or hereafter granted and * * * (the music publisher) will not grant any bulk or block license to include the same, without the written consent of Songwriters Protective Association on behalf of the writer in each instance * * *.[39]

Two exceptions to this general prohibition are (1) for purposes of including a composition in a block license for electrical transcription and (2) for general distribution outside of the United States and Canada.[40] Nevertheless, under this provision, the SPA, or the agents of individual composers, would have to be convinced that the sale of recording options for entire catalogs of repertories would be to the advantage of the composers before they would permit such block sales of recording options to recording companies.[41]

In the present climate of thinking with respect to licensing intellectual property rights such agreement on the part of the composers or publishers would be quite surprising. In every field, copyrighted material is being licensed for use on an increasingly restricted basis, i.e., proprietors are giving up—

only those rights which are necessary for the purposes to which the use is intended and then only so long as those rights are used and paid for.[42]

The numerous current uses to which copyrighted properties can be put have made the owners more and more aware of the potential values which must be protected in any assignment which is made. A careful proprietor of a copyrighted item will assign its use only after assuring himself that all other possible uses are excluded from the assignment and remain in his hands.

---

[38] Cf. supra, p. 92.
[39] Paragraph 4(j).
[40] Ibid.
[41] The use of the 1947 Revised Uniform Popular Songwriters Contract form was due to expire on Dec. 31, 1956. However, both the SPA and many of the music publishers agreed to two 1-year extensions and presumably the negotiations for continuation or revision of the contract will be concluded not later than Dec. 31, 1958.
[42] "1953 Copyright Problems Analyzed," p. 50. "Protective Societies for Authors and Creators," by William Klein II.

Once in a position to limit the utilization of the property, in the absence of compulsory license, it seems more probable that the composers and music publishers would use their position to maximize profits with respect to the recording of each composition rather than optioning the use of large blocks of properties at a bulk price. However, it is conceivable that this situation would turn entirely on the price and other provisions of such an option. Were the price sufficiently high and were the music publishers still free to negotiate a specific price for the actual use of each individual optioned property, i.e., if the original option were only for the right to negotiate for the recording of the compositions in the catalog, the songwriters and publishers might be willing to enter such a contract. However, if a record manufacturer were to purchase an option under such conditions, there is some question as to its profitability for him, and he would undoubtedly not exercise his option on many of the compositions in a particular publisher's catalog. He might try to take what he thinks is the "cream", but the popularity of a particular composition is highly unpredictable. Perhaps the most that can be said is that songwriters and music publishers would not give up their new negotiating strength without getting a quid pro quo which the record producers might not be willing to give.

It is also possible that the reverse result might develop; namely, music publishers might begin to produce records. This would depend of course on the availability of talent but in the rather confused organization of the music business, particularly with music publishers taking on functions of talent agents, it is not improbable that talent "stables" could be slowly built up. The techniques of recordmaking would probably not present a barrier. Thus, within the past few months, announcement has been made of a new record pressing machine priced at only $7,500 which is capable of turning out high-quality disks at a rate of nearly one per second; it is described as being simple to operate and the costs are said to be competitive.[43]

Are the sizes of the firms and the concentration of productive capacity in the phonograph record industry such that it would be easy for the music-publishing industry to control it in the absence of compulsory license? Conversely, are the sizes of firms and the concentration of capacity in the music-publishing business such that it would be easy for the phonograph record industry to control it in the absence of compulsory license? Available figures on these aspects of the industries indicate that the answer to both these questions is in the negative.

The RIAA, with 52 members in 1957, represents a large part of the total record production—perhaps as much as 90 percent. It has four class A members—those with a gross annual sales volume of more than $10 million each; this number has remained unchanged since the founding of the association in 1952. Currently it also has four members in class B—those with a gross annual sales volume of more than $2½ million but less than $10 million each; there were only three such members from 1952 to 1956, the fourth having been added in 1957.[44]

---

[43] Variety, Jan. 23, 1957.
[44] Annual Report of the RIAA, 1955, p. 5, and bylaws of the RIAA, art. 2, sec. 2.

It is generally assumed that the four major record producers are Capitol, Columbia, Decca (New York), and RCA-Victor.[45] Two of these regularly publish their volume of sales: Capitol and Decca; in 1957 Capitol had gross sales of $43.7 million and Decca had gross sales of $31.8 million,[46] a total of $75.5 million for the two. It is probable that the other two major producers are somewhat larger, perhaps accounting for a total gross sales figure of close to $100 million. Total record production for 1957 is estimated at $190 to $200 million, at the producer level,[47] so the four major producers may account for about 80 to 85 percent of the total industry production.

Such a concentration of production may mean a strong monopolistic tendency in the industry.[48] Regardless of monopoly or competition, the structure of the industry does not lend itself to easy acquisition by the music publishers.

As to the structure of the music-publishing industry, not too much is known. However, there are several thousand music publishers in various stages of publishing activity, some of which are large. ASCAP, the major performing rights organization, had three music publisher board members with incomes from performing royalties of $1.8 million, $1.4 million, and $1.3 million, respectively.[49] This does not include music publishers' income from other sources. Most of the 1,000 music publisher members of ASCAP are obviously small, but there are large ones among them. In addition in 1956 about 2,590 music publishers were affiliated with BMI, but the size of these firms is not known, except to the extent that some of them are large.[50] Considering the size and number of music publishers, it is difficult to imagine that there is danger of the recording companies taking control of the music publishers in order that they might control the use of tunes for recording, absent compulsory license.

This indicates clearly that the contending parties in the record production industry currently subject to compulsory license are not of unequal stature. In the absence of a compulsory license, the relatively equal strength of the two groups would tend to assure a fair basis for bargaining while the number of strong companies on each side would tend to maintain competitive conditions within each group.

It is perhaps significant that in the past the record industry has been unable to make up its mind whether, in the absence of compulsory license, the music publishers would take on the aspects of a monopoly. For example in 1929 and 1930 the record industry appears to have feared a combination of publishers and/or copyright

[45] Columbia and RCA-Victor are closely associated, respectively, with CBS and NBC; Decca (New York) owns the largest part of the voting stock of Universal Pictures Co., Inc., a major motion picture producer; and Capitol is owned almost entirely by Electrical and Musical Industries of London (EMI), the major British record and electronics producer.

[46] Billboard, Aug. 18, 1958, and Variety, Mar. 12, 1958.

[47] Billboard, Apr. 14, 1958. The gross retail sales are estimated to have been $400 million to $420 million. This has been divided by 2.1 to get the estimated producers' sales.

[48] In the latter part of 1956 and the early part of 1957 the trade press reported an investigation of the record producing industry by the Department of Justice re possible monopoly in the pricing of LP records. However, there has been no prosecution alleging such monopoly practices.

[49] Hearings before Subcommittee No. 5, House Select Committee on Small Business, 85th Cong., 2d sess., pursuant to H. R. 56, "Policies of ASCAP," p. 531.

[50] Hearings before the Antitrust Subcommittee (Subcommittee No. 5) of the Committee on the Judiciary, House of Representatives, 84th Cong., 2d sess., "Monopoly Problems in Regulated Industries" (1956), p. 4942. Mr. Carl Haverlin, president of BMI, testified that BMI had contracts with "about 2,590 publishers," of which "approximately 2,230" are inactive.

owners.[51]   On the other hand in 1939 the record manufacturers did not refer to this danger but concentrated their arguments on other aspects.[52]

C. THE EFFECTS ON RETAIL PRICES AND VOLUME

On the average, record producers pay 6.5 percent of their gross revenues in the form of mechanical royalties.   If this percentage were doubled in the absence of compulsory license the average wholesale price of records might justifiably increase from about 48 cents to about 52 cents.   It has been indicated that the retail price of records is quite unpredictable ranging all the way from a few cents above wholesale to the suggested retail price which is approximately twice the wholesale price.   It is possible that a doubling of the mechanical royalties would increase the lower ranges of the retail prices by a few cents but it is doubtful whether an increase of such a magnitude would seriously affect the volume of retail purchases, particularly in the buoyant current situation of the music market.

One result of the compulsory license provision has been that the public may be offered a variety of recorded versions of a particular composition.   As already pointed out, under the compulsory license, when one record company issues a recording of a composition that promises to catch the public fancy, other companies are quick to issue recordings by other performers of the same composition.   This might or might not be true if the compulsory license were eliminated, depending upon whether the authors and music publishers found it to their advantage to give exclusive licenses.   If exclusive licenses were granted, the result might well be that instead of several recorded versions of the composition, a larger number compositions would be offered to the public on records issued by the various companies.

V. The Chance of Monopoly

A. THE 1909 COMMITTEE REPORT

The right of the copyright owner to control the mechanical reproduction (recording) of music was first provided for in the Copyright Act of 1909, and this new right was made subject to the compulsory license.   From the 1909 House committee report it is clear that the committee, in its recommendation to include the compulsory license provision, was chiefly concerned with the possibility that one recording company might obtain a monopoly of the recording rights in popular music.   In part the committee said:

This danger (the establishment of a mechanical-music trust) lies in the possibility that some one (recording) company might secure, by purchase or otherwise, a large number of copyrights of the most popular music, and by controlling these copyrights monopolize the business of manufacturing, otherwise free to the world * * *.   The main object * * * has been * * * to so frame an act that it would accomplish the double purpose of securing to the composer an adequate return for all use made of his composition and at the same time prevent the formation of oppressive monopolies, which might be founded on the very rights granted to the composer for the purpose of protecting his interests.

---

[51] Henn, Harry G. "The Compulsory License Provisions of the United States Copyright Law," pp. 27 and 28, Study No. 5 in the present committee print.
[52] Ibid., p. 33.

The report cites the fact that—

contracts were made by one of the leading mechanical reproducing establishments of the country with more than 80 of the leading music publishing houses in this country ;

these contracts provided that—

the reproducing company acquired the rights for mechanical reproduction in all the copyrighted music which the publishing house controlled or might acquire and that they covered a period of at least 35 years, with the possibility of almost indefinite extension.

These contracts never came into effect because they were contingent upon a favorable decision in pending court cases seeking to sustain the right of copyright owners to control the mechanical reproduction of music under the law prior to 1909, and the U.S. Supreme Court ruled adversely in *White-Smith Music Publishing Co.* v. *Apollo Co.* (209 U.S. 1 (1908)). However, to the committee the fact that such contracts had been made meant the strong probability of a monopoly in the music recording business if the mechanical recording right was provided for without some restriction such as the compulsory license.

Since that time, the author and music publisher groups have sought to eliminate the compulsory license provision, while the recording companies have exerted every effort to maintain it.[53]

B. THE PRESENT SITUATION

The retention of the compulsory license provision since 1909 against all adverse attacks has been accompanied by a number of major changes in the music business. The motion pictures have grown to a major industry using music on sound tracks since 1929 as a basic ingredient of their product, and more recently becoming a source of new musical material. They have also adjusted to new competition, as well as a new potential market for motion pictures, in the form of television. The compulsory license has not been applicable to the recording of music in theatrical or television motion pictures, and there has been no sign of a monopoly developing in the use of music in these areas.

It may also be noted that the recording of entire dramatico-musical works (musical plays) is not subject to the compulsory license, and even though the supply is limited there is no indication that any one recording company could acquire a monopoly of such works.

Recording of music for home use has been moved from the era of primitive cylinders, disks, and paper rolls to the era of high fidelity records and tapes at a retail price level which has made the home use of phonographs a commonplace and the distribution of records a $400 million annual retail business. Radio broadcasting has opened up a new market for recorded music and has been a factor in the development of high fidelity recording in that the 3,500 radio stations have demanded more and better records for program purposes. Radio has multiplied the demand for recorded music and the high quality performance of music far beyond anything that was imagined in 1909.

The advent of television has multiplied each of these aspects of the music business still further. Over 400 operating television stations,

---

[53] Cf. Henn, op. cit., ch. II, passim.

and their joint programing through three major networks, have again acted to multiply the demand for recorded music, not only on recordings of sound alone but also through the use of music in both theatrical and television motion pictures used for broadcasts.

The number of recording companies has grown greatly since 1909 with the great increase in the market for records, and there are now some 10 or more companies strongly entrenched in a competitive position.

On the other hand, the creators and publishers of musical materials have organized themselves in order to protect their interests. It has been stated that the MPPA includes the leading music publishers who control approximately 80 percent of the copyrighted popular music in the United States.[54]   Trade sources dispute this figure, pointing out that a large part of the currently popular songs are published by firms which do not belong to MPPA, nor do they subscribe to the SPA Minimum Basic Agreement.   However, regardless of the extent to which the MPPA publishers own the copyrights of currently produced musical materials, it is unquestioned that the existence of MPPA and SPA has done much to regularize the relationships between music publishers and songwriters.

In 1931 the songwriters also organized and through their uniform contract for the sale of musical properties they have obtained a position vis-a-vis the music publishers far different from that of 1909. They now get not less than 50 percent of all royalties collected by the music publishers who own the copyrights on their musical properties and are in a position to prevent a monopoly in the use of their music if it should be detrimental to their interests.

Some analogy may be drawn between the use of music and the use of "talent" (performing artists) in the production of records.   The leading performers are generally signed up to make records exclusively for some one company, but there has been no indication that any one company might develop a monopoly of "talent."   By the same token, the supply of new popular music is so great, and the popularity of any particular composition is so uncertain, that it is difficult to see how any one record company could, in the absence of the compulsory license, secure a monopoly of popular music.

C. THE BALANCE OF FORCES

Although not much is known concerning the details of the organization of the music-recording business in the pre-1909 era, the changes which have taken place since then are clear.   On the demand side, certain large record producers are now closely allied with broadcasting interests which are in turn large users of recorded music. These producers, through their control of artists by exclusive contract, are much stronger than their counterparts in the earlier era because they can now offer radio and television appearances on which the artists depend largely for public "exposure" as a foundation for their lucrative personal appearances in hotels, nightclubs, theaters, auditoriums, etc.

---

[54] Warner, Harry B., "Radio and Television Rights," p. 436 (1953).

On the supply side the industry is also much more highly organized for the licensing of music for recording and the collection of mechanical royalties.   However, the motivating power on the supply side is somewhat attenuated by the invasion of those who use music. The motion picture industry control of some major music publishers has been cited and also the establishment of music publishing companies by the recording interests which are in turn closely allied to broadcasting interests.

It is not implied that there was no organization within the music industry prior to the formation of the groups which have been mentioned.   However, there is no question that the present music industry is much more highly organized than it was 50 years ago.   The present state of the industry indicates that there is a fairly even balance between the two sides in their ability to protect their interests. Currently there is no single producer of recorded music, as there appeared to be in 1909, in a position to monopolize the supply of published music as it emerges from the music publishing houses.   On the contrary, there are a number of large and powerful recording companies competing with one another, plus some hundreds of smaller companies.

The record producers must have a continuous flow of new tunes to prosper.   The music publishers must license a continuous flow of new tunes for recording to reap the benefit of their copyrights.   The two are so interdependent both in relation to their antecedents (e.g., the music publishers' relationship with the songwriters or the relationship between record producers and the broadcasters) and in relation to each other, that powerful as they both are there seems to be little chance that either would be in a position to dominate the other if compulsory license for recorded music were abandoned.

Moreover, the probability of a high degree of centralized control by any one company does not appear to exist either in the ranks of the music publishers or in the ranks of the record producers.

Finally, any monopoly aspects that might develop on either side would be subject to the same limitations as the monopoly aspects of any other business, i.e., the Sherman and Clayton Antitrust Acts.

STUDY NO. 4

THE MORAL RIGHT OF THE AUTHOR

By William Strauss

July 1959

THE MORAL RIGHT OF THE AUTHOR

It is frequently said abroad that the "moral" right of the author, i.e., the right to safeguard his artistic reputation—as distinguished from the property aspects of his copyright—is not sufficiently protected in the law of the United States. Even American lawyers have expressed this opinion.[1] The alleged nonexistence of protection of the author's moral right has been considered one of the principal obstacles to adherence by the United States to the Berne and Washington Copyright Conventions, both of which contain provisions for the protection of the right of the author to claim authorship in his work and to prevent others from interfering with its integrity. In the following pages we shall compare the protection of the author's personality rights under the doctrine of moral right in the European law with the protection given the author's personal rights under our law.

I. THEORY AND APPLICATION OF THE DOCTRINE OF MORAL RIGHT IN THE EUROPEAN COPYRIGHT LAW

A. THE THEORIES OF THE MORAL RIGHT

The theories on the moral right have been developed chiefly by French and German jurists. According to prevalent views, copyright has two facets: the property rights which are objects of commerce and which terminate after the period fixed by law; and the moral right which is inalienably attached to the person of the author and, depending on the particular theory, may or may not survive the property right aspects of the copyright.[2] The French, and to a lesser extent, the German courts have pioneered the application of the doctrine. Therefore, our study will be largely limited to an examination of the doctrine in these countries. There are, however, several important member countries of the Berne Copyright Union which, under their domestic law, provide protection for the author's personal rights without benefit of the moral right doctrine. Their systems will also be discussed briefly.

B. THE CONTENTS OF THE MORAL RIGHT

1. The moral right in the Berne Convention

Under Article 6bis of the Berne Convention in the Rome revision of 1928 the moral right has two components: the author's right of

---

[1] Ladas, The International Protection of Literary and Artistic Property 581 (1938); Roeder, "The Doctrine of Moral Right: A Study in the Law of Artists, Authors and Creators," 53 Harv. L. Rev. (1940) 554; Katz, "The Doctrine of Moral Right and American Copyright Law—a Proposal," 24 So. Calif. L. Rev. (1951) 375; id., Copyright Protection of Architectural Plans, Drawings, and Designs, 19 School of Law, Duke U. (1954) 224.

[2] Under the "German" theory the property rights and the moral right terminate together 50 years after the death of the author; under the "French" theory the moral right lasts forever.

paternity, and his right to the integrity of his work. Article 6*bis* of the Rome text reads as follows:

(1) Independently of the author's copyright, and even after transfer of the said copyright, the author shall have the right to claim authorship of the work, as well as the right to object to any distortion, mutilation, or other modification of the said work which would be prejudicial to his honour or reputation.

(2) The determination of the conditions under which these rights shall be exercised is reserved for the national legislation of the countries of the Union. The means of redress for safeguarding these rights shall be regulated by the legislation of the country where protection is claimed.

At the Brussels conference for the revision of the Berne Convention, held in 1948, the language of paragraph (1) of Article 6*bis* was broadened to prevent "any distortion, mutilation, or other alteration thereof or any other action in relation to the said work, which would be prejudicial to the author's honour or reputation."

Article 6*bis* of the Rome text provided for determination of the conditions and means of safeguarding the moral right by the member countries. Under the Brussels text this determination is left to the member countries only for the time after the author's death.[3] However, this ostensible change seems to be of limited effect, because the means of redress, i.e., the actual enforcement of the right, even during the author's life, is still governed by the laws of the member countries of the Union. As a consequence, protection of the moral right varies considerably from one member country to another.

2. The principal features of the moral right in the Berne countries

General recognition has been accorded in the laws of the Berne countries to the two rights protected under the Berne Convention: (*a*) the paternity right, and (*b*) the right to the integrity of the work.[4]

(*a*) *The paternity right.*—The paternity right is held to consist of the author's right to be made known to the public as the creator of his work, to prevent others from usurping his work by naming another person as the author, and to prevent others from wrongfully attributing to him a work he has not written.[5]

As to the first aspect of this right, it is said that the name of the author must appear on all copies as well as on advertising or other publicity for the work.[6] By virtue of the second aspect the author may prevent plagiarism of his work.[7] The third aspect is said to provide protection against false attribution of authorship, or against being named as the author of a work that has been mutilated.[8]

---

[3] Art. 6*bis* (2). Art. 6*bis* (3), Brussels text, concerns the moral right during the author's lifetime:
"The means of redress for safeguarding the rights granted by this Article shall be governed by the legislation of the Country where protection is claimed."
[4] Application of the terminology of the moral right doctrine in copyright statutes does not much antedate the Rome revision of the Berne Convention. In the copyright laws passed prior to 1928, the moral right is protected as such only in the Portuguese law of 1927. Other laws have dispersed provisions which are applicable to various components of the moral right or, as the Swiss Law (Art. 44), refer protection to general statutes.
[5] Michaelides-Nouaros, Le Droit Moral de L'Auteur (1935) 204, 205; Ulmer, Urheber- und Verlagsrecht (1951) 196; Desbois, Le Droit D'Auteur (1950) No. 591, would not include in the moral right the right to prevent wrongful attribution of authorship. He states that this right is inherent in any person, and has nothing to do with a work or copyright therein.
[6] Pouillet, Propriété Littéraire et Artistique (1908) No. 216, 317*bis*; Michaelides-Nouaros, *op. cit. supra*, at 143; Runge, Urheber- und Verlagsrecht (1948) 219.
[7] Pouillet, *op. cit. supra*, No. 507; Michaelides-Nouaros, *op. cit. supra*, at 212; Runge, *op. cit. supra*, at 59; Ulmer, *op. cit. supra*, at 160.
[8] Michaelides-Nouaros, *op. cit. supra*, at 214; Runge, *op. cit. supra*, at 59; Ulmer, *op. cit. supra*, at 196, 197 discusses only the first and second rights.

The French copyright law of 1957 [9] provides in Article 6 as follows:

The author shall enjoy the right to respect for his name, his authorship, and his work.   This right shall be attached to his person.

It shall be perpetual, inalienable and imprescriptible.

It may be transmitted *mortis causa* to the heirs of the author.

The exercise of this right may be conferred on a third person by testamentary provisions.

Since this law did not become effective until one year after its promulgation, no cases decided under it are available at this time. The cases in which decisions were recently handed down by the French courts were pending when the new law took effect, and the previous French copyright law was applied to them. As far as the moral right is concerned, it may be said that Article 6 of the copyright law of 1957 is a codification of the theories on moral right expressed by the courts, and supplies no substantive changes.   The French courts had extended the scope of the paternity right by holding that an author's name must appear in the work without change even after sale of the work [10] unless the author has consented to such change,[11] and that, in the case of several authors, all names must appear.[12]   A work may not be published anonymously unless the author so stipulates in the contract.[13] False attribution of authorship has been condemned under the general rules of law.[14] An author has also been held entitled to prevent the affixing of his name to a disfigured work.[15]

---

[9] Law No. 57–296 on Literary and Artistic Property ("Journal Official" March 14, 1957, p. 2723 and April 19, 1957, p. 4143) entered into force March 11, 1958 (cf. Art. 79, first par.).   English transl. in CLTW, Suppl. 1958.—Prior to the passing of this law, the French copyright laws dating in substance from 1791 and 1793 had no provision on the moral right except for protection of an author's name under the Law for the Prevention of Frauds of Artistic Works of Feb. 9, 1895.   The false use of an artist's name has recently been protected under this law in a civil action ; *Leroy* v. *Didier, Netter and Ferrand*, Ct. App. Paris, Feb. 25, 1958.   Gazette du Palais [hereinafter Giz. Pal.] May 24–27, 1958.

This provision and related provisions of the new French copyright law are discussed by Desbois, Le Droit Moral, XIX Revue Internationale du Droit d'Auteur (April 1958) 121.

[10] Civil Tribunal Seine [hereinafter Civ. Trib. Seine], March 12, 1836 in Pouillet, *op. cit. supra*, No. 512 ; later cases in Michaelides-Nouaros, *op. cit. supra*, at 143.

[11] Civ. Trib. Seine, August 7, 1868, Le Droit, August 9, 1868 ; Civ. Trib. Seine, December 17, 1838, Gazette des Tribunaux [hereinafter Gaz. Trib.] December 18, 1838 ; Civ. Trib. Seine, December 31, 1845 and December 31, 1868, Huard et Mack, Repertoire No. 1362 ; Civ. Trib. Seine, November 13, 1900, Pouillet, *op. cit. supra*, No. 316*bis* ; Civ. Trib. Seine, December 29, 1896, Pataille [hereinafter Pat.] 1897, 126 ; see also Droit d'Auteur [hereinafter D.A.] 1931, 124.

[12] *Fleg* v. *Gaumont*, Civ. Trib. Seine, Feb. 20, 1922, Gaz. Trib. 1922.2.282 ; *Marquet* v. *Lehmann*, Civ. Trib. Seine, July 12, 1923, Gaz. Trib. 1923.2.271.   In Poulailler called *"Bernard Frank"* v. *Bernhard Frank*, Civ. Trib. Seine, Dec. 7, 1955, Gaz. Pal. March 7, 1956, D.A. 1957, 29, 219, the court held that a writer who had chosen a pseudonym and became well known under that pseudonym, could not prevent a young less well known writer from using his real name as author of his publications.   See also : *Lettre de France*, D.A. 1959, 30.   In *Fernand Léger* v. *Réunion des théatres lyriques nationaux*, Civ. Trib. Seine, Oct. 16, 1954, VI Revue Internationale du Droit d'Auteur (Jan. 1955) 146, a stage designer sued for violation of his moral right because the design of a scene created by him had been omitted since the scene was dropped from the opera. Complainant demanded that all his costumes and stage designs be used in the opera, that defendant pay two million francs in damages and that the judgment be published.   The court held that Léger was not a co-author and had no right to demand changes in the opera.   However, his moral right was held affected by leaving out his designs without his consent and he was awarded 10,000 francs in damages.   The defendants further had to announce in all programs, posters, etc., that Léger was the author of the costumes and stage designs and that the design of the particular scene omitted was not shown because the same had been cut from the opera.

[13] Civ. Trib. Seine, June 2, 1904, Gaz. Trib. Aug. 25, 1904.

[14] Civ. Trib. Montpellier, Dec. 6, 1912 ; Civ. Trib. Seine, June 15, 1883, Michaelides-Nouaros, *op. cit. supra*, at 214 ; Cour de Paris [Court of Appeals, hereinafter Ct. App. Paris], March 20, 1826, Recueil Periodique Sirey [hereinafter S.] 1827.2.155.

[15] *Merson* v. *Banque de France*, Civ. Trib. Seine, May 28, 1930, Ct. App. Paris, March 12, 1936, Recueil hebdomadaire de jurisprudence Dalloz [hereinafter D.H.] 1936.2.246.

The German copyright law grants fairly inclusive statutory protection of the paternity right. The name of an author may not be omitted from his work unless he has consented thereto, or unless he cannot in good faith raise objections to its omission (e.g. in the case of certain contributions to newspapers).[16] An artist's name may be affixed to his work by another person only with the artist's permission. No one may quote from another person's work without indicating the source.[17]

(b) *The right to the integrity of the work.*—The author has the right to have the integrity of his work respected, i.e., he may prevent all deformations of it.[18] By virtue of this right the author is also deemed to be entitled to make changes in the work or to authorize others to do so.[19]

The exercise of the moral right as defined in Article 6 of the French copyright law of 1957 depends, to a large measure, on the method of publication used. Thus, if the work is published by a direct method of reproduction such as printing, the publisher, according to Article 56 of the law, must manufacture the edition in the form agreed to in the contract and may not modify the work in any way without the author's written consent. The same obligation of faithful reproduction presumably applies to a performance of a musical or dramatic work. However, if a work is to be adapted to a different medium, some flexibility must be allowed and, since the new copyright law does not expressly provide otherwise, it would seem that the rationale of the court decisions on this question would continue to be valid, namely, that changes necessitated by the new medium are permissible.[20]

In several instances the law circumscribes the exercise of the moral right in order to prevent abuses by an author. Thus, Article 10 provides that co-authors of a work of collaboration must exercise their rights by common accord and if they cannot agree, the question will be decided by the courts. Even more specifically, Article 16 limits the moral right in a contribution to a motion picture to the completed

---

[16] Copyright Law in Literary and Musical Works of June 19, 1901 [hereinafter LUG] § 9 ; Copyright Law in Works of Art and Photographs of Jan. 9, 1907 [hereinafter KUG]. The Oberlandesgericht [hereinafter Ct. App.] Cologne Oct. 14. 1952, Gewerblicher Rechtsschultz und Urheberrecht [hereinafter GRUR] 1953, 499, held that a newspaper reporter usually has no paternity right in his contributions.
[17] LUG § 18. The Civil Division of the German Supreme Court decided in 110 Entscheidungen des Reichsgerichts in Zivilsachen [hereinafter RGZ] 393, April 8, 1925, that an architect was permitted to affix his name to a restaurant installation which he had created in the employ of another. However, the court was doubtful whether affixing the address of the architect was not misleading to the point of being unfair competition.
[18] Michaelides-Nouaros, *op. cit. supra,* note 5, at 219 ; Ulmer, *op. cit. supra,* note 5, at 197.
[19] Michaelides-Nouaros, *op. cit. supra,* 96. 241 ; Mittelstaedt, "Droit Moral im Deutschen Urheberrecht," GRUR 1913, 87 ; Mueller, Bemerkungen über das Urheberpersönlichkeitsrecht, Archiv für Urheber–Film– und Theaterrecht 1928 (hereinafter UFITA] 366. See *infra* note 34.
The recent case of *Société des Film Roger Richebé* v. *Société Roy Export Films et Charlie Chaplin,* Civ. Trib. Seine, Feb. 15, 1958, Gaz. Pal., June 7–10, 1958, involved protection of the moral right under the French law and under the Universal Copyright Convention. Charlie Chaplin's silent film "The Kid" was shown in France with the addition of a musical accompaniment and of subtitles which had not been approved by the author. Held, that Chaplin as author was entitled to the protection of his moral right (i.e., integrity of the work and respect of his name) under the French law since he enjoyed national treatment in France by virtue of Article 2 of the Universal Copyright Convention.
In *Thiriet, Van Parys and Henri Jeanson* v. *Société "Le Fanal", Jarre and Société "Films Ariane",* Civ. Trib. Seine, Feb. 8, 1957, XV Revue Internationale du Droit d'Auteur (April 1957) 144, phonograph records had been made from the film music without permission from all the authors, and with other unauthorized changes. Held, that there was injury to the moral right of the authors ; defendants had to pay damages and the records had to be destroyed. But see: Roger-Ferdinand, L'affaire Carmen Jones, VIII Revue Internationale du Droit d'Auteur (July 1955) 3, dealing with the film "Carmen Jones" adapted from the opera "Carmen" by Bizet.
[20] See Desbois, *loc. cit. supra* note 9 ; see also note 48.

motion picture unless Article 1382 of the Civil Code is applicable against a person by whose fault the completion of the film was prevented.[21]   As a possible further limitation, Article 15 provides that, if any author refuses or is unable to complete his contribution, he must permit the use of his contribution insofar as it is in existence.

The French courts have held that the user of a work by way of reproduction or performance must adhere strictly to the form and contents given the work by the author.[22]   It is said that the publisher and theatrical producer violate their obligation if they make changes without the author's consent; that they have undertaken to make the work public in the form in which it has been submitted to them and could have refused to do so if they had been of the opinion that the work needed changes.[23]

The German copyright statutes provide, and the courts have held, that the assignee of a copyright usually cannot, without the author's permission, make changes in the work, its title, or in the author statement.[24]

---

[21] Article 1382 of the French Civil Code provides: "Any action that causes damage to another makes the tort feasor liable for damages." Actions for violation of the moral right are more often brought in tort than in contract. However, the author must prove damages to a legitimate interest, violation of a duty and intent. Code Civil (Dalloz ed. 1946) notes to 1382, 1383.

[22] In *Merson* v. *Banque de France*, D.H. 1936.2.246, the Court of Appeals in Paris held that the copyright permits the artist to demand respect for his work even after assignment, and to keep the integrity and every detail of form intact. In *Chaliapine* v. *USSR and Bremer*, Ct. App. Paris, July 28, 1932, Recueil Periodique Mensuel Dalloz [hereinafter D.P.] 1934.2.139 the court said: Every author has a moral right in his work, and this must be recognized by the courts in all countries. The author has the right to prevent his work being altered or mutilated in form or in spirit. *Accord:* Commercial Tribunal [hereinafter Com. Trib.] Seine, Aug. 22, 1845, S. 1845.2.459; Cit. Bordeaux, Aug. 24, 1863, S. 1864.2.194; Com. Trib. Seine, March 11, 1911, D.A. 1912, 141; Civ. Trib. Seine, Dec. 31, 1924, D.H. 1925. 35; Civ. Trib. Seine, Dec. 22, 1926, D.H. 1927. 125; Ct. App. Paris, Feb. 13, 1930, Annales de Droit Commercial [hereinafter ANN.] 1931. 369.
In *James* v. *Bouillet and Hachette Publishers*, Civ. Trib. Seine, December 31, 1924, D.H. 1925.2.54, plaintiff had permitted defendant B. to reproduce, in a school reader, certain extracts from his stories. B. without permission, made considerable changes. Held, that if B. wanted to include plaintiff's stories he should have respected the thoughts of the author and not distorted them.
In *Benoit-Lévy* v. *Soc. de prod. et exploit. du film "La Mort du Cygne" and Cinéma Péreire Palace*, the film "La Mort du Cygne" was presented in a cut version. Held, that, although the author had assigned performance rights, he had retained his moral right. The Paris Court of Appeals, affirming, decided the issue on a breach of contract basis. Civ. Trib. Seine, Oct. 24, 1941, *aff'd.* Ct. App. Paris, May 5, 1942, D.A. 1943, 80. (The lower court did not refer to the contractual clause.)
In *Prévert and Carné* v. *S.N. Pathé Cinéma*, Civ. Trib. Seine, April 7, 1949, Gaz. Pal., May 11, 1949, D.A. 1950, 70, a film was also cut without permission. Held, that the authors were entitled to 100,000 frs. damages each for violation of the moral right, but owed the producer 50,000 francs each in damages for unauthorized seizure of the film. (Copyright having been assigned, there was no infringement, and, therefore, no justification for seizure.)
In *Blanchar, Honegger and Zimmer* v. *Soc. Gaumont*, Gaz. Pal. July 22, 1950, Ct. App., Paris, affirming Civ. Trib. Seine, April 6, 1949, Gaz. Pal. May 21, 1949, the court held that cutting a film without permission by the film authors constituted a breach of contract. The court negatived the presumption of a tacit advance waiver of the moral right.
In *S.A. les Gémeaux* v. *Prévert and Grimault*, Gaz. Pal. May 23, 1953, D.A. 1953, 133. 1954, 39, *modified and aff'd.* Ct. App. Paris, April 18, 1956, D.A. 1957, 30, 31, two of the authors of a motion picture complained that the other authors of the animated design film had violated plaintiff's moral right, and they wanted the film withdrawn from exhibition. Held that the two authors had an inalienable moral right but that this right was limited by the rights of other collaborators; that withdrawing the film would in effect obliterate the moral right which the complainants wished to protect; that the film should be shown, but the receipts impounded until the matter had been decided on the merits.

[23] Desbois, *op. cit. supra*, note 5, No. 594.

[24] Section 9, LUG; § 12, KUG. In 119 RGZ 401, Jan. 14, 1928, the German Supreme Court held that a publisher could not intersperse a contribution to a periodical with criticism of the author's work, and thus distort the sense of the article. Held to be a breach of contract.
The classic German case on this point is the "Rocky Island with Sirens" case, 79 RGZ 397, June 8, 1912. Defendant had commissioned plaintiff to paint a mural in the stairway of his home, but after completion of the work defendant disliked the naked sirens and had them overpainted so that they appeared dressed. Held, that an artist has the right to present his work to the public in its original form. While the vendee has the right to sell or destroy the work, he has no right to change it. In so doing, he invades the artist's copyright which protects the work against unauthorized changes.
Accord: 125 RGZ, 174, July 3, 1929; 1 FR (Fed. Supr. Ct., West Germany) 125/52. Oct. 20, 1953, GRUR, 1954, 80.

3. Other components of the moral right

Some other components have also been claimed as part of the moral right: (a) the right to create a work; (b) the right to publish a work; (c) the right to withdraw a published work from sale; (d) the right to prevent "excessive" criticism of a work; and (e) the right to prevent any other violation of the author's personality.[25]

(a) *The right to create a work.*—The right to create a work is said to become part of the moral right when the author, having contracted with a user to create and deliver a work, is unwilling to do so. The effect of such a contract is said to depend on the moral right because creation is closely related to the personal and moral interests of the author, his honor and his reputation. An author could not be forced to create and publish a work against his will. His refusal to create the promised work, however, makes him liable for damages.[26]

The French courts have frequently refused to decree specific performance (but have awarded damages for breach of contract) where a work has not been delivered to the client; and, according to most text writers, such decisions are based on the author's moral right.[27] In Germany the same result is reached under general contract principles but is not considered to be based on the moral right.[28]

(b) *The right to publish or not to publish a work.*—The right to publish a work or to keep it secret is said to be as natural and incontestable as the right to create. It consists of the right of the creator independently to decide when and how to communicate his work to the public.[29]

Article 19 of the French copyright law of 1957 provides that the author alone has the right to divulge his work, and after his death his executors, if any, and after their death, or if the author willed otherwise, the persons named in Article 19 have such right. Although

---

[25] These are said to be components of the moral right under the dualist or "classical" (French) theory. For other systems see: Smoschewer, UFITA 1930, 349; Mueller, UFITA 1929, 267.

[26] Michaelides-Nouaros, *op. cit. supra,* note 5, at 185, 186.

[27] The standard case cited on this point is *Whistler* v. *Eden,* Civ. Trib. Seine, March 20, 1895, D.H. 1898.2.465; Ct. App., Paris, Dec. 2, 1897, S. 1900.2.201; Supr. Ct. March 14, 1900, S. 1900.1.489, James McNeill Whistler has undertaken to paint Lady Eden's portrait for a fee of 100 to 150 guineas. Lord Eden sent a fee of 100 guineas. Whistler declared the fee insufficient but he cashed the check. The lower court held the contract valid and ordered Whistler—who meanwhile had overpainted Lady Eden's face in the picture—to restore the work to the *status quo ante* and deliver it to Lord Eden, or to pay ten francs penalty for every day of delay and to return the fee plus 5 percent interest and pay 1000 francs damages.
On appeal by Whistler, the Paris Court of Appeals held that this was an executory contract and that Eden, because the painting had never been delivered, had not acquired title to it. Therefore, the artist could not be forced to restore or part with the painting which he had "maliciously changed." However, Whistler was enjoined from otherwise using the painting, had to return the fee plus interest, and was held liable for the damages previously imposed by the lower court. The French Supreme Court affirmed the decision of the Court of Appeals. The case note in Dalloz (1900.1.489 at 490) criticized the decision as against contract rules.
In *Bouillot-Rebet* v. *Davoine,* Civ. Trib. Charolles, March 4, 1949, D.A. 1950, 83, the court held that an artist need not deliver a bust which seemed to him unfinished and unsatisfactory. However, while an artist may justly be jealous of his independence he, like anyone else, must respect contracts.
Plaisant, "Le Propriété Littéraire et Artistique," Extrait du Juris-Classeur Civil Annexes (1954), fasc. 8, No. 35 says: It seems that an author who refuses without justification to transfer title in the work and to deliver it after it has been completed, may be forced to give specific performance. To this statement Professor Escarra remarks in the foreword to Mr. Plaisant's work:
Mr. Plaisant insists that the moral right be subject to the control of the courts in order to prevent abuse of the right. He [Plaisant] also insists that sometimes the author should have to give specific performance. . . . These views which reflect recent tendencies of the courts . . . are open to question. Acceptable *in abstracto* they tend to weaken the basic value of the French doctrine of copyright, namely the preëminence and infrangibility of the moral right, and this at a time where this doctrine is subject to many attacks.

[28] Ulmer, *op. cit. supra,* note 5, at 191.

[29] Michaelides-Nouaros, *op. cit. supra,* note 5, at 187.

there is no provision that the right to divulge a work is a perpetual right, Article 19 further provides that it may be exercised after the expiration of the copyright.[30]

In France, the right to publish has often been tied up with the right to create, and the writers cite the same decisions in support of both rights. German writers generally do not consider the right to publish as part of the moral right.[31] Decisions of the German courts on this point are based on the Law governing publishing contracts and on the general contract provisions of the Civil Code.[32]

(c) *The right to withdraw the work from sale.*—The basis for the right to withdraw a work from the market after it has been published is rather dubious. The usual argument advanced is that, where the

---

[30] Article 29 of the French copyright law of 1957 provides that the copyright is independent of property rights in the material object, but that the author or his successors to the copyright are not entitled to require the proprietor of the material object to place this object at their disposal for the exercise of the copyright. However, if the proprietor of the object manifestly abuses his property rights to prevent publication of the work, the courts may force him to permit publication. The proprietor of the object, on the other hand, has no right of publication. The exploitation right in posthumous works belongs to the successors of the author if disclosed within fifty years from the author's death; and only if the disclosure is made after that time, the exploitation rights belong to the proprietors of the work who effect publication or cause it to be effected (Art. 23).

In *Anatole France* v. *Lemerre*, Civ. Trib. Seine, Dec. 4, 1911, Pat. 1912.1.98, it was held that, as the publisher had not published the manuscript for twenty-five years, the author could not be compelled to damage his reputation by permitting publication of an obsolete work of his. The case turned on the point that the delay was unreasonable. The Com. Trib. Seine, Dec. 8, 1925, in *Wormser* v. *Biardot* (reported in 2 Olagnier, Le Droit d'Auteur 32 (1934)) held that three years' delay was excessive. In *Raynal* v. *Bloch*, Ct. App. Paris, Apr. 26, 1938, S. 1939.2.17, the author had transferred translation and performance rights ; a delay of 4 years, until the last performance took place, was not held excessive.

In *Rouault* v. *Vollard Heirs*, Civ. Trib. Seine, July 10, 1946, D.A. 1946, 107, the heirs of Vollard, Rouault's dealer, had taken possession of a large number of paintings which Rouault claimed were unfinished. Held, that the painter retained all rights in his works and could complete, change, or destroy them.

The decision was adversely commented on by D.A. 1946, 121, 122, as going much too far in upholding the moral right :

"The court was misled into holding that intellectual works are outside the ordinary law and above any contract. There are no two different standards of laws, one for artists, and the other for ordinary human beings. The expression [that] 'despite any contract the right is inalienable,' is outdated and, in any case, too general. The theory of a right in the personality has consequences which appear more and more dangerous. Let us hope that the decision in the Rouault case will not make the moral right the basis of error or whim, and that it will not be invoked in the face of a contract freely entered into."

The Court of Appeals in Paris confirmed the lower court in the *Rouault* case (March 19, 1947, Gaz. Pal. April 26, 1947), but insisted to a greater extent on contract interpretation, and played down the moral right. See comments by Desbois, *op. cit. supra*, note 5, No. 541.

In *Dame Canal* v. *Jamin*, Civ. Trib. Seine, April 1, 1936, D.H. 1936.262, Ct. App. Paris, Feb. 28, 1938, D.A. 1938, 73, *rev'd on other points*, French Supreme Ct., May 1, 1945, D.A. 1946, 10, the court said :

"The concept and execution of literary and musical works are solely a product of the personal intellect ; such works are the expression of the author's genius and part of his personality. The author is sole master of his thought and controls the conditions and the extent to which he wants to disclose them. He is, therefore, sole judge to decide whether or not when, under what condition, his work should be published, and to what extent such publication should take place."

In the case of *Rosa Bonheur*, Ct. App., Paris, July 4, 1865, Pat. 1866.385, the artist's refusal to execute and deliver a painting made her liable to damages for breach of contract. The main difference between the *Bonheur* case and later cases seems to be that at the time of the *Bonheur* case nobody thought of the moral right.

Desbois, *op. cit. supra*, note 5, at 548 ; Michaelides-Nouaros, *op. cit. supra*, note 5, at 188.

In *Consorts Bowers* v. *Consorts Bonnard*, XIV Revue Internationale du Droit d'Auteur (Jan. 1957) 207, the French Supreme Court held that even unfinished artistic works were part of the community property between spouses with the result that the right of the artist to withdraw his work would terminate with partition of the community property. This result has been said to amount to a confirmation of the moral right by the court but at the same time to a withdrawal of all its efficiency. Garson, L'arret Bonnard et la propriété artistique, XV Revue Internationale du Droit d'Auteur (April 1957) 37. See also D.A. 1957, 214. This problem is treated in Article 25 of the copyright law of 1957 which provides that the right to disclose a work, to fix the conditions of the exploitation and to defend its integrity belong to the spouse who is the author or to whom such rights have been transferred. See also : Hauert, Contrôle et limites du droit moral de l'artiste, XXIII Revue Internationale du Droit d'Auteur (April 1959) 51.

[31] Ulmer, *op. cit. supra*, note 5, at 187, 191 ; Runge, *op. cit. supra*, note 5, at 556. The new German draft copyright law (§ 17) considers the right to publish one of the most important ingredients of the moral right (Report, pub. by the Ministry of Justice, Mar. 15, 1954, p. 107).

[32] Thus, 79 RGZ 156 ; 110 RGZ 275, 112 RGZ 173 ; 115 RGZ 858 ; Supr. Ct., Oct. 15, 1930, UFITA 1930, 633.

author has undergone a change of conviction or where, in the light of subsequent developments the work has become obsolete, he cannot be expected to permit further distribution.[33]

Article 32 of the French copyright law of 1957 gives the author the right to correct or retract his work. However, he cannot exercise this right except by indemnifying in advance the transferee of the exploitation rights for the loss that the correction of retraction may cause. If an author were to exercise this right after publication of his work, the cost of this indemnification may well render this right nugatory.[34]

(d) *The right to prevent excessive criticism.*—"Excessive" criticism has been defined as criticism made solely for the purpose of vexation.[35] It is, however, conceded by all writers that reasonable criticism must be free, no matter how severely it may condemn a work.[36]

It has been said that this right represents a new application of the right to the integrity of a work, and that, in France, it may be defended by invoking the law of July 29, 1881, as amended by the law of September 29, 1919.[37] However, under that law anyone, not just an

---

[33] Michaelides-Nouaros, *op. cit. supra,* note 5, at 277 ; Ulmer, *op. cit. supra,* note 5, at 275. Against the right : Plaisant, *supra,* note 27, No. 47.

It seems that the cases brought forward in support of the right of withdrawal after publication in *France* did not support this thesis. They are :

Whistler v. *Eden,* D. H. 1898.2.465, S. 1900.2.201, S–1900.1.489, *supra,* note 27. In that case the work was not published, or even delivered.

Camoin v. *Carco,* D.P. 1928.2.89, Gaz. Pal. 1931.1.678. In that case the painter Camoin had torn up and discarded several of his paintings. Someone found and reassembled the canvasses, and sold them. Held, the painter could prevent such unauthorized publication.

Dame Cinquin v. *Lecocq,* S. 1900.2.122. This case turned on the question whether the property rights inherent in a copyright were community property between spouses. Held in the affirmative, but that the author-spouse retained his right to change the works or even "suppress" them, except where he did so only to annoy his ex-spouse.

Dame Canal v. *Jamin, supra,* note 30. Held, that *prior* to publication the author is the sole judge whether he wants to publish his work.

In *Germany:*

After publication the author has no right of recission, but may buy back at the wholesale price whatever copies the publisher has in stock. The author need have no reason, connected with the moral right or other, to do so.

[34] Desbois, *loc. cit. supra,* note 9, says : This means that in many circumstances the right which he is offered will vanish like a mirage : his means may not allow him to face such payment of damages even on a modest basis. Furthermore, the law is careful to prevent that scruples and remorse serve as a pretext for regrets quite different from a soul searching : the author cannot have recourse to the right of withdrawal in order to make a more advantageous contract than the one he had concluded before, since Article 32, par. 2, provides that if he regrets having exercised the right of withdrawal, he must offer first choice to his contract partner under the previous conditions. Finally, while he may rescind his contract, the injury caused thereby is mitigated since, far from having the right to go back on his word even for the purest of motives, all he has is an option either to overcome his scruples and fulfill his contract or to pay off his previous obligation in money and thereby repurchase his freedom.

Under Article 142 of the Italian copyright law an author may withdraw his work for reasons of the moral right. However, he must notify the Minister of Public Culture who in turn must give public notice of the author's intent. Also, the author must idemnify all persons who have acquired rights in connection with the reproduction, distribution or performance of the work.

Article 33 of the German draft copyright law grants the right of withdrawal if the transferee of the right to use the work does not properly exercise this right. · No moral right seems to be involved here. Apart from various conditions which must be fulfilled before the right may be exercised, the author must pay equitable damages to all concerned.

Under all these laws the "right to withdraw a work is merely the possibility granted by the law, for various reasons, of rescinding a contract and paying damages therefor."

[35] Michaelides-Nouaros, *op. cit. supra,* note 5, at 287, considers the right to prevent such excessive criticism part of the moral right. On the other hand, Ulmer, *op. cit. supra,* note 5, at 188, 189, says : Critique must be free. Even malicious critique, in my opinion, is no violation of the droit moral.

Ulmer criticises the Polish copyright law of 1926 which protects (Art. 58) the author in cases of knowingly false criticism. He says, at 189 : A defense against knowingly false criticism is feasible under the general rules of law. It seems objectionable to relate such a defense to copyright. The theory that the author should have against the critic a right to the respect of his work would lead to the unacceptable result of very extensive control of criticism by the courts.

[36] So held in France : *Borgo* v. *Poneigh,* Civ. Trib. Seine, Jan. 6, 1922, Pat. 1922, 256. *Benoit* v. *Rudler,* Civ. Trib. Seine, July 23, 1921, Pat. 1921.300. The Court of Appeals of Paris held in *Abragam and French Union of Critics* v. *Solane,* D.A. 1954, 37, that criticism of literary, musical or dramatic works is in the public interest and must be free. The writer, musician or actor must accept blame as well as praise, even where the criticism is against him personally as long as it remains within the frame of his work or performance.

[37] Michaelides-Nouaros, *op. cit. supra,* note 5, at 286 *et seq.*

author, has the right to reply in the same medium to any personal attack made upon him in a newspaper or periodical.

In Germany protection is afforded by the law of libel and slander.[38]

(e) *The right to relief from any other violation of the author's personality.*—This right is asserted to provide protection of the author's special personality. Any act is said to be prohibited that hurts the special personality of the author, i.e., his professional standing. Such an act may consist of a violation of an express or implied clause of a publishing contract, or of a tort.[39] This part of the moral right allegedly protects the author against unfair use or misuse of his name, his work, or his personality.[40] Thus, it is not permissible without the author's specific consent to use a work of art for commercial advertising, or to quote the author of a scientific book as endorsing commercial products by virtue of statements made in that book.[41]

4. Inalienability of the moral right

The moral right accrues to the author with the creation of his work and protects his freedom, honor, and reputation. Alienation of the substance of the moral right is considered impossible in view of the nature and the purpose of the right.[42] This approach has led some writers to the conclusion that any contract which permits acts detrimental to the author's honor must be void,[43] because the moral right cannot be an object of commerce.[44, 45] It is sometimes overlooked that this doctrine necessarily is riddled with exceptions and that, even in theory, the possibility of a contractual waiver has been admitted in

---

[38] The provisions on libel and defamation (sec. 193, German Penal Code) or the tort provisions of the German Civil Code (§§ 823(2) and 826). Apparently, there are no decisions on this point involving the rights of authors.

[39] Michaelides-Nouaros, *op cit, supra,* note 5, at 293.

[40] See the *Bernard Frank* case, *supra,* note 12.

[41] *French* cases.
A work of art may not be used for commercial advertising, Civ. Trib. Seine, Apr. 3, 1897, Pouillet, *op. cit. supra,* note 6, No. 204 *bis.* Unreasonable increase in sales price may give rise to the suspicion that the author is mercenary, *Veuve Vaucaire* v. *Vermont,* Gaz. Trib. 1922.2.217. Unjustified interruption of publication of novel in newspaper held to invade moral right, *Viney* v. *Le Matin,* Pat. 1913.2.45.
Reproduction of work of art on cheese label not permitted, *Le Duc* v. *Ponible,* Pat. 1923.359. Text of scientific book may not be used for advertisement, Civ. Trib. Seine, July 22, 1876, March 4, 1880, Pouillet, *op. cit. supra,* No. 510 *bis.* Work of serious music may not be used in film next to Viennese Waltz, *Stravinsky* v. *Soc. Warner Bros.—First National Film,* Civ. Trib. Seine, July 27, 1937, D.A. 1938, 107.
German cases :
Increase in salesprice held *not* a violation of the moral right, 110 RGZ 275. (According to § 21 of the Law on Publishing Contracts a publisher may lower, but *not* increase the salesprice.)
Moving to a new location of, and making changes in a work of art held not violation of moral right, Ct. App. Hamburg, Dec. 23, 1932, GRUR 1933, 327.

[42] Michaelides-Nouaros, *op. cit. supra,* note 5, at 89 ; *accord: Ulmer, op. cit. supra,* note 5, at 60 : Runge, *op. cit. supra,* note 5, at 224 ; Desbois, *op cit. supra,* note 5, No. 569.

[43] Michaelides-Nouaros, *op. cit. supra,* note 5, at 96 ; Mittelstaedt, *supra,* note 19, at 87 ; Mueller, *supra,* note 19, at 388.

[44] As to whether it is not, in fact, an "object of commerce," the opinions seem divided. See the Report of the Internat. Federation of Associations of Film Producers in D.A. 1954, 45 ; Baum, The Brussels Conference for the Revision of the Berne Convention, (English translation) 24 (1949).
Plaisant, *op. cit. supra,* note 27, No. 7 says :
"The inalienability of the moral right is proclaimed by numerous lower court decisions and by certain textwriters [*cit. om.*]. It seems to us, however, that application of this statement, without further qualification, would lead to impossible and inequitable results which, in the last analysis, would be contrary to the interests of the author. . . . It appears that, where the author has made an express contract, he cannot invoke his moral right where it is contrary to such contract."
Michaelides-Nouaros, Revue Hellénique de Droit International, July-Sept. 1953, 239, seems to recede to some extent from his former stand as to the inalienability of the moral right.

[45] Katz, *supra,* note 1, at 407, suggests that the moral right may be destroyed by laches, where the author fails to complain of a violation, but that "A right which is inalienable is not only non-transferable, it is also incapable of being expressly contracted away."

the form of a limited assignment of the exercise of the moral right,[46] or trusteeship.[47]

Article 1 of the French copyright law of 1957 provides that copyright exists by the mere fact of creation of an intellectual work, and Article 6 states that the moral right is inalienable and inprescriptible. Before this law went into effect, the French copyright law specified only that the copyright (i.e., the property rights), may be assigned in whole or in part.[48] Lacking any statutory basis for the claim of the inalienability of the moral right, the justification therefor was sought in the court decisions.

The French courts have consistently ruled out a presumption of a tacit waiver of the moral right,[49] but they permit reasonable changes without the author's consent in the case of a contribution to a collective work[50] or in the case of an adaptation.[51] An express contractual waiver of the moral right by the author is usually held valid.[52]

[46] Michaelides-Nouaros, *op. cit. supra*, note 5, at 93.
[47] Ulmer, *op. cit. supra*, note 5, at 68.
Article 11 of the French copyright law provides that authors of anonymous or pseudonymous work enjoy the moral and pecuniary rights granted in Article 1, but that they are represented in the exercise of these rights by the original publisher until such time as they declare their identity and prove their authorship. Under Article 56 a publisher may make changes in a work with the author's written consent and in the case of an adaptation, necessary changes are always permitted. The provision of Article 31 that "the transfer of authors' rights shall be subject to the condition that each of the rights transferred shall be specifically mentioned in the act of transfer" may well be applied to a contractual clause waiving the moral right, or entrusting its exercise to another person. Since the author, under Article 6, may provide by will for the exercise of the moral right by a third person, it may be that he could also do so by contract *inter vivos*.
[48] The French copyright law of 1957 provides that the exercise of the moral right may be limited by contract; upon written consent by the author, the publisher may make changes in the work (Art. 56, 2).
[49] Thus, *Blanchar, Honegger and Zimmer* v. *Société Gaumont*, note 22, *supra; Metro-Goldwyn-Mayer* v. *Hess*, Gaz. Pal. June 16, 1950; *Prévert and Carné* v. *S.N. Pathé Cinéma*, note 22, *supra; Théatre de l'Opéra Comique* v. *Valdo Barley*, D.H. 1936.2.26.
[50] Author not permitted to object to changes in contributions: Civ. Trib. Marseille, Dec. 19, 1902, Gaz. Trib. 1903.2.393; Civ. Trib. Seine, June 2, 1904, D.A. 1931, 116. If the author refuses to have his name on the changed work he may merely demand that his name be omitted: Ct. of Nancy, May 8, 1863, Pat. 1863. 380.
The right to be named as author of a part of a collective work is denied in Article 9 of the French copyright law of 1957, paragraph 3 of which reads as follows:
"A 'collective work' is a work created by the initiative of a physical person or legal entity who edits it, publishes it and discloses it under his direction and name, and in which the personal contributions of the various authors who participated in its development are merged in the totality of the work for which it was conceived, so that it is impossible to attribute to each author a separate right in the work as realized."
Article 13, par. 2 further provides: "The author's right [in a collective work] shall rest in this person". (i.e., the person in whose name the work was disclosed).
[51] *Bataille* v. *Bernhard*, Ct. App. Paris, Apr. 28, 1910. Ann. 1910.191.
[52] *Bernstein* v. *Matador et Pathé Cinéma*, the so-called "Mélo" case, D.H., 1933.533. D.A. 1933, 104, recently followed in *Barillet and Crédy* v. *Soc. Burgus Films*, Civ. Trib. Bordeaux, Jan. 15, 1951, D.A. 1952, 66.
In *Bernstein* v. *Matador et Pathé Cinéma, supra*, the French landmark case on the question, the playwright, Henri Bernstein, sued the defendant motion picture producers for violation of his moral right because of changes made by the defendants in adapting his work. The defendants admitted the changes, but claimed they were necessary and, furthermore, that they had been agreed to by the plaintiff. The question was whether a covenant which permitted all necessary changes was valid in the face of the author's "inalienable" moral right. The court held that this covenant, though unusual, was binding on the parties. To the plaintiff's allegation that, despite this clause, he retained the right to prevent any change that appeared unacceptable to him, the court replied in part:
"To maintain this theory, [plaintiff] relies on the textwriters and certain court decisions giving to authors of literary and artistic works the continuing right to watch over the integrity of their works that they have assigned, and to prevent mutilation and deformation of such works. These principles have never really come under discussion except in actions on contracts regarding publication and reproduction of a work [as distinguished from adaptation.] In such cases they are explained and justified because any change mutilates and alters the work. The case is different where a dramatic or literary work is adapted for a motion picture. There the original work remains intact, regardless of what is done in the new work which is inspired by, and more or less closely resembles, the original work but which is necessarily different because it is subject to different techniques and serves different ends. Therefore, it is an absolute necessity that such changes be permitted by the author and the author, once he has consented to them, is definitely bound by his consent even if later the changes seem completely to distort his work. The author may also consent to leave the decision concerning the amount of changes to his assignee."
In the *Barillet* case, *supra*, the court held that an author necessarily had to consent to all changes required for adaptation to a different medium, and that the question whether the moral right was violated was for the court to decide.

The German copyright law provides that the assignee of a copyright may not make changes in a work, its title, or the author statement. However, any such changes may be authorized by contract.[53] The law presumes consent where the author could not in good faith object to changes necessitated by the method of reproduction, or adaptation, or by the type of publication in which the work appears.[54] The German decisions are in accordance with these statutory provisions.[55]

The "inalienability" of the moral right may be defined as follows: By its very nature as a personal right, the moral right is not capable of transfer. Where a work is part of a collective work (of the kind in which contributions are commonly anonymous), the right to be named as author is deemed to be waived. Where a work is used by a direct method of reproduction or performance, the courts usually uphold the moral right to prevent changes; but where the work is adapted to a different medium, reasonable changes are permitted even without an express waiver of the moral right. Where the author has expressly waived his moral right he is bound by the contract and his moral right is unenforceable despite its alleged inalienability.

5. Transmission of the moral right to the author's heirs

Rights of personality usually expire with the death of the person under any system of law. But it has been said that the protection of the memory of a deceased author has necessitated an exception to the rule. This exception is alleged to have been generally admitted by the courts, the textwriters, and the laws for the protection of the author's personality.[56] According to most writers, not all components of the moral right pass to the author's heirs: the "positive" components die with the author; only the "negative" ones pass to the heirs. The right to create a work, to publish it, to change it, to withdraw it from circulation, and to destroy it, are said to be innate positive components. On the other hand, the right to prevent others from making changes or from committing acts detrimental to the author's reputation are considered negative components that require no personal act by the author and may, therefore, be transmitted to his heirs.[57]

Articles 19 and 20 of the French copyright law of 1957 carefully regulate the exercise of the right of publication after the death of the author. The group of persons that may exercise the right is quite narrow: first, the executors designated by the author; then, unless the

The Court of Appeals in Paris in *Banque de France* v. *Consorts Luc-Olivier Merson,* March 12, 1936, D.H. 1936.2.246, held that the artistic property right contains a non-pecuniary right which attaches to the person of the owner and which makes it possible, in case of assignment, to enforce the respect due the work regarding its integrity. This right passes to the heirs of the artist. There is no doubt that the artist may forego the exercise of his moral right, but it must be shown that such abandonment clearly results from the documents and circumstances of the case.

[53] LUG, § 9(1) ; KUG, § 12(1).
[54] LUG, § 9(2) ; KUG, § 12(2).
[55] In 119 RGZ 401, Jan. 14, 1928, the German Supr. Ct. held that permission to publish an article in a periodical under the author's name did not carry with it an implied consent to changes completely distorting the sense of the article. Held against tacit waiver of moral right; Supr. Ct., March 28, 1936, GRUR 1936, 827 ; Ct. App. Hamburg, March 20, 1952, GRUR 1952, 588. Held, that contractual waiver of moral right is permissible : Landgericht (Dist. Ct.), Berlin, Nov. 4, 1930, UFITA 1931, 73.
[56] Michaelides-Nouaros, *op. cit. supra,* note 5, at 114, 115. *Accord:* Ulmer, *op. cit. supra,* note 5, at 210. Plaisant, *op. cit. supra,* note 27, No. 66, says :
"The moral right is basically a personal right. . . . After the death of the author the moral right passes to the heirs and legatees. However, the moral right does not keep its strictly personal character when the heirs get it : it becomes somewhat weakened."
[57] Michaelides-Nouaros, *op. cit. supra,* note 5, at 116. It is open to question whether the rights to publish or to destroy a work are, if at all, parts of the moral right, "positive" aspects of this right. Posthumous publication, or destruction of a work by the proprietor is permitted under most laws.

author has made a testamentary provision, the descendants, the spouse if not divorced and remarried, the heirs other than descendants who inherit all or part of the estate, the universal legatees or donees of all the future assets.

If any of the persons abuse the right in the course of its exercise, or if its nonexercise appears to amount to an abuse, the courts will decide on the matter. The same applies when the representatives of the author cannot agree on publication of a work, or when there is no known successor, no heirs and no spouse entitled to the estate. The public interest in the matter is safeguarded by the provision in article 20 that the Minister of Arts and Letters may refer such matters to the court.

Even before the French copyright law of 1957 went into effect, the French courts protected the integrity of a work after the author's death.[58] In one instance, the moral right of the heirs has been recognized after expiration of the copyright,[59] and the integrity of the work has been defended even against the author's heirs.[60]

In Germany, the heirs may enforce all rights inherent in the copyright, including those parts of the moral right recognized in the statute.[61] In view of the German theory of inseparability of the moral right and the property rights, all rights of both categories are held extinguished at the end of the term of copyright protection.[62]

6. Berne countries protecting the author's personal rights outside the copyright law

Some member countries of the Berne Union fulfill the requirements of Article 6bis of the Berne Convention by affording equivalent protection to authors under general laws for the protection of the personal rights of all individuals.[63]

(a) *Great Britain.*—The moral right as such is not part of the domestic British Law.[64] The Report of the Copyright Committee of 1952 preceding the Copyright Act, 1956 stated in part: [65]

219. We have headed this Part of our Report *droit moral* which we believe to be a term unknown to our jurisprudence.

220. We understand that in a number of Continental Countries specific legislation exists extending protection in respect of an author's honour and reputation. In the United Kingdom protection is given by the common law, in addition to various statutory provisions.

---

[58] *Merson* v. *Banque de France, supra,* note 15.

[59] *De Pitray* v. *Schatz,* D.H. 1936.2.548.

[60] *Brugnier Roure* v. *de Corton,* Gaz. Pal. 1906.1.374, D.A. 1907, 137 ; see case of Mr. Taber of New York, in D.A. 1899, 111.

Michaelides-Nouaros suggests, *op. cit. supra,* note 5, at 332, that the exercise of the moral right after the author's death should be, at least in part, the task of professional organizations.

[61] Ulmer, *op. cit. supra,* note 5, at 210. The German Supr. Ct. first denied that the moral right, if it existed at all, passed to the heirs. *Heirs of Richard Wagner* v. *Earl of D.,* 41 RGZ 43 (1898). Later the Court reversed itself : *Heirs of Strindberg, Mueler* v. *Hyperion,* 102 RGZ 134 (1920).

[62] Ulmer, *op. cit. supra,* note 5, at 210.

[63] Fox, The Canadian Law of Copyright (1944) says at 429 : "It must be remembered that the International Conventions have no direct effect either in Canada or in the United Kingdom, as they have not been given any direct statutory effect." See also *id.* at 431, 546.

[64] The British Copyright Act, 1956, 4 and 5 ELIZ. 2, chap. 74, contains no provisions on the moral right.

Hoffmann, Die revidierte Berner Übereinkunft (1935) 108, says that at the Rome Conference for the revision of the Berne Convention, the British and Australian delegates opposed any regulation of the moral right as contrary to British copyright and common law. They acquiesced when it was pointed out that the moral right was the equivalent of protection under the common law by action in tort.

[65] Presented by the President of the Board of Trade to Parliament by Command of Her Majesty, October, 1952.

224. We feel that in general many of the problems involved do not lend themselves to cure by legislative action, but are of a type that can best be regulated by contract between the parties concerned. Authors are already protected at common law against anything amounting to defamation of character.

225. In a field so vague and ill defined it seems to us to be impossible—even if it were considered desirable—to frame legislative proposals to meet all possible problems. In general, the common law of this country provides adequate remedies, and in addition there are certain statutory remedies to meet particular and defined cases. For example, Section 7 of the Fine Arts Copyright Act, 1862, gives artists a measure of protection against the unauthorized alteration of their drawings or the fraudulent affixing of signatures to them. We recommend that this protection should be continued, and that [it] should be extended to apply also in the case of literary and musical works.

(b) *Canada*.—Section 12(5) of the Canadian Copyright Act, 1921,[66] provides:

Independently of the author's copyright, and even after the assignment, either wholly or partially, of the said copyright, the author shall have the right to claim authorship of the work, as well as the right to restrain any distortion, mutilation, or other modification of the said work which would be prejudicial to his honour or reputation. 1931, c. 8, 5.5.

This provision is practically the same as Article 6*bis* (1) of the Rome-Berne Convention.

Mr. Fox, the well-known Canadian copyright expert, has said:[67]

That part of the section [12(5), Copyright Law] is to some extent an illustration of the type of legislation that so often emerges from parliament—conceived in vagueness, poorly drafted, sententious in utterance, and useless in practical application.

. . . Until judicial decision, which is as yet lacking, has considered the section, it will remain the same sort of pious parliamentary hope as S. 11 of the Unfair Competition Act, 1932, . . . which did nothing to the common law.

Presumably in Canada, as in Great Britain, the common law is thought to afford protection to the personal rights of authors.

(c) *Switzerland*. Article 44 of the Swiss Copyright Law of 1922 refers protection of the moral right to the general provisions of the Civil Code and the Code on Obligations.[68]

Thus, the principal basis for protection of an author's personal rights is Article 28 of the Civil Code[69] which states in part: Anyone whose personal rights are violated by an unlawful act, shall have the right to demand that such act be enjoined by the courts. This provision has been said to protect the paternity right, to enable an author to prevent unauthorized changes in, or other acts concerning his work that affect its value,[70] and to defend his right of privacy.[71] In Switzerland, authors as a class enjoy no preferential treatment as regards their personal rights, but the rights are protected in much the same

---

[66] Chap. 32, RSC 1927, as amended by chap. 8, 1931, chap. 18, 1935, chap. 28, 1936, chap. 27, 1938. See also § 26(2) Canad. Copr. Law. Cases on common law protection of authors' personal rights in Canada and Great Britain are to be found in Part II of this study.

[67] U. of Toronto L. J. 1945–46, 126. See also: Fox, The Canadian Law of Copyright (1944) 601, 602.

[68] Art. 27 to 29, Civil Code; Art. 49, Code on Obligations. See Bianco, Revue Suisse de la Propriété Industrielle et du Droit d'Auteur, 1952.2, 150.

[69] Egger, Annotations to the Swiss Civil Code, Art. 28, Note 26.

[70] Buergi, 66 Zeitschrift für Schweizer. Recht 10 (Switzerland 1947).

[71] *Ibid.;* see Tuor, note 72, *infra*.

In *Kasper* v. *Widow Hodler*, BGE (Swiss Fed. Courts) 40.2.127, July 20, 1944, the widow of a painter was held entitled to protection of her husband's memory. Unauthorized exhibit of a painting depicting the well known artist on his deathbed was held an invasion of the widow's right of privacy under Art. 28, Civil Code and Art. 49, Code on Obligations.

In *Mueller* v. *Rossi*, BGE 71.4.225, Dec. 7, 1945, it was held that the Swiss law (§ 173, Penal Code) offered no protection to the *artistic* reputation, but only protected against defamation of an artist's *personal* honor. *Accord:* In re Kupferschmidt, BGE 42.4.172, Oct. 18, 1946.

manner and to the same extent as they are protected in this country by the common law.[72]

II. The Moral Right and the Law of the United States

Only a few writers have discussed the doctrine of moral right in relation to the law of the United States.[73] Their conclusion, that the doctrine of moral right guarantees full protection of personal rights of authors, appears to be based more on the theoretical presentation of the doctrine by its European exponents than on its application by the European courts; conversely, the protection of authors' personal rights in the United States is presented by them in the light of those court decisions most unfavorable to authors.

The doctrine of moral right as such is not recognized in the United States as the basis for protection of personal rights of authors. Nor do our statutes provide for the protection of personal rights of authors as a class. The question is: how does protection given in the United States on other principles compare with that given abroad under the moral right doctrine? In order to find the answer, we shall consider our court decisions under the same headings used above in discussing the contents of the moral right.

1. The paternity right

There is no provision on the right of paternity in the American copyright law. Protection of the right to the proper attribution of authorship is provided under the general principles of law regarding contracts, or torts such as invasion of privacy, libel, or unfair competition.

The omission of an author's name was considered in *Clemens* v. *Press Publishing Co.*[74] An author sold publishing rights to a story and the manuscript contained the author's name, as did the galley proofs. The publisher then refused to publish the story except anonymously. The court held:

Even the matter-of-fact attitude of the law does not require us to consider the sale of the rights to a literary production in the same way that we would consider a barrel of pork. Contracts are to be so construed as to give effect to the intention of the parties . . . . If the intent of the parties was that the defendant should purchase the rights to the literary property and publish it, the author is entitled not only to be paid for his work, but to have it published in the manner in which he wrote it. The purchaser cannot garble it or put it out

---

[72] Tuor, Das schweizerische Zivilgesetzbuch (Swiss Civil Code) 70 (1948) states:
"The main principle on which our whole economic and legal system rests is the principle of personal freedom. This freedom, aside from the fact that its misuse is prohibited, is guaranteed to each person and provides protection against violation by others. This is the case not only where economic interests are violated, but also where there is damage to the personal rights of a person. The term 'personality' includes all rights, which are inseparable from the person."
They are: the right to life, physical and mental peace, freedom, honor, credit, name, and the right to privacy. *Accord:* Troller, Immaterialgüterrechte, vol. 1 (1959), 87.
In contrast thereto, the German Supreme Court, in 58 RGZ 24, Feb. 27, 1904 denied existence of a general right of personality. However, under the post-war Bonn Constitution the Supreme Court of the Federal Republic of Germany seems to have made a beginning toward recognizing a general right of personality. In a decision of May 25, 1954 (Neue Juristische Wochenschrift 54, 1404) the Court held that the Bonn Constitution grants as a constitutional right to each person a general right of personality which is protected as a right to honor and reputation, privacy, freedom of speech, and, generally, to his own personality. See also 15 Entscheidungen des Bundesgerichtshofs (Supreme Ct., Fed. Republic of Germany) 249, and comments by Ulmer in D.A. 1957, 14.
In Italy a general right of personality is not recognized. Sparano, Rassegna di Diritto Cinematographico, III, No. 1, Jan.–Feb. 1954.
[73] *Supra*, note 1. See also Francon, La Propiété Littéraire et Aristique en Grande-Bretagne et aux Etats-Unis (1955) chap. VI.
[74] 67 Misc. 183, 122 N.Y. Supp. 206 (1910).

under another name than the author's; nor can he omit altogether the name of the author, unless his contract with the latter permits him to do so .... As I interpret the contract . . ., their intent was that . . . the defendant should publish [the work] under the author's name. The action of the parties in dicates the interpretation which they placed upon it. When the plaintiff presented his story to the defendant, it contained his name .... The galley proofs . . . had the plaintiff's name printed upon [them]. The plaintiff . . . had the right to insist that the story should not be published except under his name.

Ellis v. *Hurst* [75] involved the unauthorized use of an author's name. Defendants had published under the author's true name the plaintiff's non-copyrighted books which originally had been published under a pseudonym. The court granted the author an injunction for the following reason:

The name of the plaintiff was in no way used in connection with these publications until the defendants assumed to use [it] .... The plaintiff never granted to the defendants the right to use his name .... I think that he has the right to the protection of the statute [76] in order to prevent his own name being used . . . without his consent. [77]

The use of an artist's name in a distorted version of his work was at issue in *Neyland* v. *Home Pattern Co.*[78] An unauthorized crude reproduction of a painting was used as an embroidery pattern and advertised as "straight from the painting" of the artist. The court held that merely to reproduce the painting without changes coupled with the artist's name would not violate his right to the protection of his privacy although it may be an invasion of his copyright. However, to use his painting as a design of a sofa cushion and to employ

---

[75] 66 Misc. 235, 121 N.Y. Supp. 438 (1910); see Wittenberg, The Protection and Marketing of Literary Property (1937) 105.

[76] N.Y. Civil Rights Law, §§ 50, 51. See *Elliot* v. *Jones*, 66 Misc. 95, 120 N.Y. Supp. 898 (1910), aff'd 140 App. Div. 94, 125 N.Y. Supp. 119 (1910).

[77] In the *"Mark Twain"* case, *Clemens* v. *Belford, Clark and Co.*, 14 Fed. 728, (C.C. Ill. 1883), the court sustained a demurrer to complainant's prayer to enjoin defendant from publishing the author's sketches under his pseudonym "Mark Twain." There was no question of copyright as the sketches were in the public domain; they had been previously published without copyright and under the same pseudonym. The court held that defendant would have had the right to publish the works under the author's known real name, and no greater protection was due the author's equally well known pseudonym.
In an interesting dictum on the author's personal rights the court said:
"An author has the right to restrain the publication of any of his literary work which he has never published. . . . [cit. om.]. So, too, an author of acquired reputation and, perhaps, a person who has not obtained any standing before the public as a writer, may restrain another from the publication of literary matter purporting to have been written by him, but which, in fact was never so written. In other words, no person has the right to hold another out to the world as the author of literary matter which he never wrote; and the same would undoubtedly apply in favor of a person known to the public under a *nom de plume,* because no one has the right, either expressly or by implication, falsely or untruly to charge another with the composition or authorship of a literary production which he did not write. Any other rule would permit writers of inferior merit to put their compositions before the public under the name of writers of high standing and authority, thereby perpetrating a fraud not only on the writer, but also on the public."
British law: *Landa* v. *Greenberg*, (1908) 24 T.L.R. 441; *The "Sporting Times" Co.* v. *Pitcher Enterprise Co.*, (1912) Macg. Cop. Cas. 52; *Maitland-Davison* v. *The Sphere and Tatler*, (1919) Macg. Cop. Cas. 1928.

[78] 65 F. 2d 363 (2d Cir. 1933). In this case the painting had been previously published with the artist's permission in an article discussing the painter's work. But the artist had given the defendant no permission to use the painting in any manner. In *Curwood* v. *Affiliated Distributors*, 283 Fed. 219 (D.C.S.D.N.Y. 1922) defendants, without authority, had mutilated plaintiff's story in adapting it for a motion picture, but had given plaintiff as the author. The court granted an injunction against use of author's name and title of the story. Accord: *Packard* v. *Fox Film Corp.*, 207 App. Div. 311, 202 N.Y. Supp. 164 (1923). See also *Metropolitan Opera Association* v. *Wagner-Nichols Recorder Corp.*, 101 N.Y. Supp. 2d 483 (1950), 107 N.Y. Supp. 2d 795 (Sup. Ct. 1951); *Kerby* v. *Hal Roach Studios*, 53 Cal. App. 2d 207, 127 P. 2d 577 (1942). *Harris* v. *Twentieth Century-Fox Film Corp.*, 43 F. Supp., 119 (D.C.S.D.N.Y. 1942); *Lake* v. *Universal Pictures Co.*, 95 F. Supp. 768 (D.C.S.D. Cal. 1950).
Author's right to prevent being given as author of a distorted work upheld; *Drummond* v. *Altemus*, 60 Fed. 338 (C.C. Pa. 1894). Relief granted under theory of unfair competition: *Fisher* v. *Star Co.*, 231 N.Y. 414 (1921): under the theory of libel: *Ben-Oliel* v. *Press Pub. Co.*, 251 N.Y. 250, 167 N.E. 432 (1929); *Gershwin* v. *Ethical Pub. Co.*, 166 Misc. 39, 1 N.Y. Supp. 2d 904 (1937).

his name, without permission, to further the sale of such design was held to be clearly a misuse of the artist's work and name, and a violation of personal rights under section 51 of the New York Civil Rights Law.

The use of a performer's name in a distorted version of his performance was held objectionable in *Granz* v. *Harris*,[79] discussed later in connection with the right to the integrity of the work.

In *De Bekker* v. *Stokes*,[80] where the author was upheld as to his rights to the title and format of his contribution to a musical encyclopedia, the court implied a waiver of the author's right to have his name appear on the work: "The plaintiff was not entitled to have his own name appear in the book. There was no stipulation to expose the authorship. A name was chosen for the work. The parties are limited to it." [81]

False attribution of authorship was involved in *D'Altomonte* v. *New York Herald Co.*[82] An author sued for libel and invasion of privacy as he had falsely been given as the author of a sensational story. It was held that using the plaintiff's name as the author of such a story would expose him to ridicule and contempt and the defendant's demurrer to the libel count was overruled.

The case on the right of authorship cited most prominently by the critics of the United States law is *Vargas* v. *Esquire, Inc.*[83] in which an artist sought to enjoin the reproduction of some of his paintings without authorship credit, and demanded damages for misrepresentation. The complaint was dismissed. The case turned on the court's interpretation of a clause in the contract between the artist and the publisher of Esquire magazine which provided in part that "Vargas agrees . . . [that] the name 'Varga', 'Varga Girl', 'Varga, Esq.', and any and all other names . . . used in connection with [the paintings] shall forever belong exclusively to Esquire, and Esquire shall have all rights with respect thereto." The court found that "there [was] no ambiguity in the granting language, nor [could] there be an implied intention . . . of the parties of any reservation of rights [of authorship] in the grantor . . . , and the fact that no reservation was contained in the contract strongly indicates that it was intentionally omitted.[84]

This decision may well be criticized on the ground that Vargas' consent to the use of his name by Esquire did not necessarily convey the right to omit it altogether. The court could have implied a nega-

---

[79] 198 F. 2d 585 (2d Cir. 1952).
[80] 168 App. Div. 452, 153 N.Y. Supp. 1066 (1916), *aff'd without op*, 219 N.Y. 573, 114 N.E. 1064 (1916). See also: *Jones* v. *American Law Book Co.*, 125 App. Div. 519 (1908); *Locke* v. *Gibbons*, 164 Misc. 877, 299 N.Y. 188, *aff'd without op.* 253 App. Div. 887, 2 N.Y. Supp. 2d 1015 (1938).
[81] *I.e.*, in encyclopedic works authorship need not be attributed. For Canadian (and British) law see Fox, *op. cit. supra*, note 63 at 570:
"The publication of any work under the name of an author, without his consent, which would injure his character or reputation would obviously constitute a libel (*Lee* v. *Gibbins* (1892) 8 T.L.R. 773; *Glyn* v. *Weston Feature Film Co.*, (1916) 1 Ch. 261) . . . , and if the public is induced to purchase such work in the belief that it was the work of the author in question, and such author is damaged by loss of sales of his own work, he has a remedy by way of action for passing off (*Miller* v. *Cecil Film Ltd.*, (1937) 2 All. E.R. 464)."
[82] 208 N.Y. 596, 102 N.E. 1101 (1913), *modifying* 154 App. Div. 453 (1913).
[83] 164 F. 2d 522 (7th Cir. 1947). See also 166 F. 2d 651 (7th Cir. 1948) *cert. denied* 335 U.S. 813 (1948); 81 F. Supp. 306 (D.C. Ill. 1948). *Compare Susy Products, Inc.* v. *Greeman*, 105 USPQ 146 (N.Y. Sup. Ct. 1955).
[84] As to foreign jurisprudence Michaelides-Nouaros, *op. cit. supra*, note 5, says at 208: In the countries . . . where there is no provision regulating this question the solution depends on the interpretation of the contract . . . [which may contain] an express or tacit clause. . . .

tive cove 1ant, i.e., that the right to use the artist's name carried with it the duty not to omit his name.[85]   But since a decision in favor of the artist could have been reached under common law principles, it seems unjustifiable to attack the court, as one writer has done,[86] for its refusal to adopt the moral right doctrine as such.[87]

Some proof for this view may be found in the recent decision in *Susy Products* v. *Greeman*.[88]   An artist, known in his field for his fanciful figures and creations, formed a partnership for the manufacturing and selling of miniature pictures to the gift and novelty trade. He signed these articles with the *nom de plume* "Lowell," which name he had previously used and which was well known.   The artist later withdrew from the firm which claimed that when he sold his stock and interests in the plaintiff corporation (successor to the partnership) he surrendered thereby his right to the use of the name "Lowell."   The corporation brought an action to restrain the artist and others from using this name on products and from marketing products similar to those marketed by the plaintiff.   The court dismissed the complaint and gave judgment to the artist on one of his counterclaims.   The reasoning of the court was in part as follows:

> It is plaintiffs' contention that when defendant . . . sold his stock and interests in the plaintiff corporation he surrendered thereby his right to the use of the name "Lowell."   I do not find this to be the fact, however. . . . [Defendant] never agreed, contracted, sold or assigned his name "Lowell" nor his right to sketch and create his little figures . . .
>
> Upon the proof adduced, plaintiffs' claim to an exclusive right of the use of the name "Lowell" on the future output of the artist . . . is untenable.   The mere fact that during his association with [plaintiffs he] permitted his nom de plume to be used, did not vest in [plaintiffs] the exclusive right to use of the name under which he had been known.
>
> Plaintiffs have failed to establish any proprietary right to the use of the name. There is no proof of a writing or contract which tends to establish that [defendant] transferred or assigned to plaintiffs the exclusive right to the use of the name in question.

In another case [89] a well known pianist sued a record manufacturer on the basis of the New York Civil Rights Law, sections 50 and 51, and alleged that defendant had made inferior reproductions from phonograph records of plaintiff's performances, sold them as plaintiff's performances, and used plaintiff's name in connection with such sales.   The court held that use of plaintiff's name was unauthorized while the plaintiff was under contract with a foreign corporation for reproduction of his performances on records for compensation, and the complaint was held sufficient to allege a cause of action under the Civil Rights Law.   It was further held that the artist had a property right in his performance so that they could not be used for a purpose not intended and particularly in a manner which did not fairly represent his service.

---

[85] Generally, U.S. courts tend to favor implied negative covenants.   Williston, Contracts (1937 ed.) § 1449.   In *Wood* v. *Lady Duff-Gordon*, 222 N.Y. 88, 118 N.E. 214 (1917) Cardozo, J. said: ". . . The law has outgrown its primitive stage of formalism when the precise word was the sovereign talisman, and every slip was fatal.   It takes a broader view today.   A promise may be lacking, and yet the whole writing may be 'instinct with an obligation,' imperfectly expressed [cit. om.]."   See also: *Granz* v. *Harris* note 79, *supra*.
[86] Katz, 24 So. Calif. L. Rev. No. 4, 375, at 412.
[87] There is no doubt that the court considered the allegation of a violation of the moral right in the light of a separate cause of action.   The critics of the Vargas decision also tend to superimpose the moral right on the contractual commitments in the form of an additional abstract right which is inalienable in spite of any waiver in the contract.
[88] 140 N.Y.S. 2d 904 (Sup. Ct. 1955).
[89] *Gieseking* v. *Urania Records*, 155 N.Y.S. 2d 171 (Sup. Ct. 1956).

In *Harms* v. *Tops Music Enterprises* [90] the court summarized the instances in which courts will protect the integrity of a man's intellectual work as follows:

. . . To particularize: Courts will protect against (a) omission of the author's name unless, by contract, the right is given to the publisher to do so [cit. om.], or (b) false attribution of authorship [cit. om.], (c) infringement of originality of arrangement or recording of a song [cit. om.], as well as for (d) distortion or truncation of work as to text or content [cit. om.].

However—

the mere allegation that the lack of control on the part of the plaintiff over the recording [made by the defendant] by resulting in inferior recording, might injure the reputation of the author and the plaintiff, [was] insufficient to bring it within the purview of the rule of unfair competition declared in the cases [cit. om.].

The protection of the paternity right by American courts [91] may be summed up as follows:

The author's right to have his name appear in connection with a contractual use of his work has been upheld in the absence of a waiver of that right. The right may be waived by contract. (The *Vargas* case represented a finding, perhaps erroneous, of such a waiver.) For a contribution to encyclopedic works there is a presumption of waiver if the paternity right is not expressly reserved.

The use of an author's name in a distortion of his work, a false attribution of authorship, and the unauthorized disclosure of an author's name have been held to be torts under the law of libel, unfair competition, or the right to privacy.

2. *The right to the integrity of the work*

The author's right to prohibit changes made by others,[92] to a large extent, is upheld in the United States under the law of libel or unfair competition. Here, as in Europe, the cases usually turn on the question whether or not a contract permits changes.

In *De Bekker* v. *Stokes* [93] the court prevented the defendant from publishing a work in a form other than that agreed upon. It had been stipulated between De Bekker and the Stokes Publishing Company that the plaintiff's book should be published "in such style and manner as [defendant] shall deem expedient." The Stokes Company, concurrently with making sales in the usual trade way, arranged with the defendant University Society to publish the work as two volumes of a ten volume series as a result of which the sales increased. The court said:

It appears . . . that . . . the sales have been accelerated but the tenor of the agreement with plaintiff has not been kept. He has the right to insist that the Stokes Company should publish the book under the name of Stokes Encyclopedia of Music, however advantageous to him some other form of presentation to the public may be. . . . The plaintiff . . . has the right to preserve the identity of his creation.

In *Curwood* v. *Affiliated Distributors* [94] the court said:

While scenery, action and characters may be added to an original story, and even supplant subordinate portions thereof, there is an obligation upon

---

[90] 160 F. Supp. 77 (S.D. Cal. 1958).
[91] It should be noted that protection of the paternity right does not depend on copyright. This right exists as well in works in the public domain.
[92] As to the author's affirmative right to make changes (which does not warrant further discussion here) *supra,* at note 31 ; also: Ulmer, *op. cit. supra,* note 5, at 178.
[93] Note 80, *supra.*
[94] 283 Fed. 219 (D.C.S.D.N.Y. 1922). See also: *Manners* v. *Famous Players Laskq Corp.,* 262 Fed. 811 (D.C.S.D.N.Y. 1919).

the elaborator to retain and give appropriate expression to the theme, thought and main action of that which was originally written. . . . Elaboration of a story means something other than that the same should be discarded, and its title and authorship applied to a wholly dissimilar tale.

In *Granz* v. *Harris* [95] the defendants sold records of abbreviated versions of the plaintiff's musical performance, describing them as presentations of the plaintiff. These unauthorized cuts coupled with the attribution of the abbreviated version to the plaintiff were held to constitute the tort of unfair competition, a breach of contract, and to violate the plaintiff's personal rights in regard to his reputation. The court said in part:

> . . . we think that the purchaser of the master discs could lawfully use them to produce the abbreviated record . . . provided he did not describe it as a recording of music presented by the plaintiff. If he did so describe it, he would commit the tort of unfair competition. But the contract required the defendant to use the legend "Presented by Norman Granz". . . . This contractual duty carries by implication, without the necessity of an express prohibition, the duty not to sell records which make the required legend a false representation. . . . As [specific] damages are difficult to prove, and the harm to the plaintiff's reputation . . . is irreparable, injunctive relief is appropriate.

In a concurring opinion, Judge Jerome Frank stated:

> I agree, of course, that whether by way of contract or tort, plaintiff (absent his consent to the contrary) is entitled to prevention of the publication as his, of a garbled version of his uncopyrighed product. This is not novel doctrine: Byron obtained an injunction from an English court [96] restraining the publication of a book purporting to contain his poems only, but which included some not of his authorship [*cit. om.*] . . . Those courts . . . have granted injunctive relief in these circumstances: an artist sells one of his works to the defendant who substantially changes it and then represents the altered matter to the public as the artist's product. Whether the work is copyrighted or not the established rule is that, even if the contract with the artist expressly authorizes reasonable modifications (e.g., where a novel or stage play is sold for adaptation as a movie), it is an actionable wrong to hold out the artist as author of a version which substantially departs from the original [*cit. om.*].

In *Royle* v. *Dillingham* [97] the court said:

> The plaintiff protests against the production of his play written pursuant to contract for the defendants, on the ground of unauthorized changes and modifications in the text and structural arrangement thereof. The defendant apparently concedes that the changes are of a substantial character, but justifies [his act] on the ground of waiver and consent. I . . . fail to find the claimed waiver or consent. . . . There is nothing . . . that establishes either the proof or the presumption of consent. . . . The defendant by his letter . . . explicitly states that he has accepted plaintiff's play. All subsequent changes are dependent on the will of the plaintiff, whether its exercise be arbitrary or otherwise.

In *Drummond* v. *Altemus* [98] the court stated:

> The complainant did send to a journal . . . and permit its publishers to print . . . reports of eight lectures . . ., but these did not give . . . a full and exact representation of these particular lectures, and of the remaining four lectures. . . . [N]o report . . . was furnished to the press or placed before the public. The defendant's book is founded on the matter which had appeared in the [journal], and if that matter had been literally copied, and so as not to misrepresent its character and extent, the plaintiff would be without remedy; but the fatal weakness in the defendant's position is that, under color of editing the author's work, he has represented a·part of it as the whole, and even, as to the portion published, has materially departed from the reports.

---

[95] 198 F. 2d 585 (2d Cir. 1952).
[96] *Byron* v. *Johnston* (1816), 2 Mer. 29.
[97] 53 Misc. 383 (1907).
[98] 60 Fed. 338, *supra*, note 78.

In *Prouty* v. *National Broadcasting Company* [99] defendant appropriated for broadcasting the title of the plaintiff's novel and used its characters without the plaintiff's consent. The plaintiff alleged that this was done in such a manner as to degrade the artistic quality and harmonious consistency of the novel. The court held:

> If it should appear that in these broadcasts the defendant has appropriated, without plaintiff's consent, plot and principal characters of the novel, and that use being made of her literary production was such as to injure the reputation of the work and [the] author, and to amount to a deception upon the public, it may well be that relief would be afforded by applying well-recognized principles of equity which have been developed in the field known as "unfair competition."

The decision in the equity suit of *Melodion* v. *Philadelphia School District* [100] has been seized upon by the critics of the United States law as an example of the denial of the protection given by the moral right doctrine.[101] The plaintiff, who had entered into a written contract with the School District of Philadelphia to do certain artistic work, averred that his models were so changed by direction of the superintendent of the school board that—

> as a result of the attribution of said [works] . . . to [plaintiff] and the general belief amongst artists and connoisseurs of art that said [works] are actually the creations of [plaintiff], he has been subjected to the ridicule and contempt of all, . . . who are familiar with the [works].

The plaintiff asked for damages and demanded that the school be required to tear down the altered work.

As we interpret the decision, the court declared that the alleged damage to the artist's reputation was a tort which, under a Pennsylvania statute regulating actions concerning public works [102] had to be litigated on the law side of the court. Therefore, the court declined jurisdiction. We are unable to concur in the view that this decision represents a denial of the author's personal rights as such. It was an unfortunate coincidence that, because of the defendant's status as a governmental agency, the plaintiff had no remedy at law.

In *Crimi* v. *Rutgers Presbyterian Church in the City of New York* [103] the plaintiff had painted a mural in the defendants' church. This mural was found objectionable and was obliterated. The artist brought action asking for equitable relief.

The court held for the defendants after an extensive discussion of the artist's moral right [104] and stated that all rights of an artist in

[99] 26 F. Supp. 265 (D.C. Mass. 1939). Criticized by Roeder, *supra*, note 1, because "the doctrine of unfair competition . . . is designed to protect economic rights . . . [and] it seems incongruous to expand it to the protection of purely personal rights."
[100] 328 Pa. 457, 195 Atl. 905 (1938).
[101] Roeder, *supra*, note 1, at 569 says: "At least one court . . . has seen fit to deny altogether the existence of the [moral] right."
[102] Act of April 8, 1846, P.L. 272, 17 P.S. § 299.
[103] 194 Misc. 570, 89 N.Y. Supp. 2d 813 (1949). See notes in 2 Ala. L. Rev. (1949–50) 268; Wash. U.L.Q. (1951), 124.
[104] The court quoted Ladas, Roeder. and other writers on the moral right, and the French decision of the Court of Appeals in Paris in the case of *Lacasse and Welcome* v. *Abbé Quénard*, June 28, 1932, D.H. 1932.487. In that case a parish priest had accepted plaintiff's painting for his church, but the vicar general, on instructions by the bishop, had caused the paintings to be removed. Held, that the church was the property of the local diocese and that the parish priest had no right to accept the paintings on behalf of the bishop, who had not been consulted. Painting the baptismal font was an injury to the property of another. Further, the artist had made no reservation of right, as against the ordinary right of a proprietor to dispose of his property and destroy it.
Michaelides-Nouaros, *op. cit. supra*, note 5, at 231 would permit destruction where it completely obliterates the artist's original work, because in that case the "spiritual link" is broken. Desbois, *op. cit. supra*, note 5 at 607 doubts that the court in the Lacasse case would have sacrificed the artist's right to the respect of his work with the same serenity if the mural had been painted with the consent of the ecclesiastical authorities.

regard to his reputation cease upon sale of his work. This statement seems to go too far, but on all other points in the decision is in line with rulings abroad [105] that after acquiring title and possession the vendee may destroy a work if he is displeased with it.

A curious twist to the assumption that the authors' personal rights find better protection in Europe than in the United States was provided by *Seroff* v. *Simon and Schuster*.[106] In this case the defendants as publishers of the author's book, had sold translation rights in that work to a French publisher who hired a translator and published a French version of the book. The plaintiff, on reading the French version, considered it a complete distortion and a flagrant falsification of the original text. He demanded of the defendants that they insist on recall of the French copies sold and correction of new copies.

The defendants admitted that some of the errors were quite serious and offered a sum to defray a part of plaintiff's expenses in settling the matter with the French publisher. This offer was rejected. When the French publisher denied the existence of any errors and refused to make changes, the defendants offered to the plaintiff an assignment of whatever rights they may have had against the French publisher. Thereupon, plaintiff sued defendants.

The court dismissed the complaint, not because plaintiff had no cause of action, but because he had sued the wrong defendant. The court found that defendants had sold translation rights in the usual manner and were not remiss in their duties in any manner.

As to the substance of the complaint, the court found serious and objectionable errors which—

would warrant the granting of some relief to an author who was entitled to and interested in the preservation and integrity of his work if the parties responsible for the alteration . . . were before the court.

The court further stated that "a right analogous to 'moral right', though not referred to as such, has been recognized in this country and in the common law countries of the British Commonwealth, so that in at least a number of situations the integrity and reputation of an artistic creator have been protected by judicial pronouncements."

To sum up: Under the tort theories of libel or unfair competition the courts have held that in the absence of express contractual consent by the author, no changes in his work may be introduced that are not required by technical necessities of production or adaptation. However, complete destruction of a work which the author has unconditionally sold is not considered an invasion of the author's personal rights.

3. The right to create a work

We have previously pointed out that under the moral right doctrine the right to create a work refers to the author's refusal to perform a contract. Where a personal contract of this nature is in question, American courts commonly refuse to decree specific performance, but will award damages.[107] Negative covenants, on the other hand, may be

---

[105] See the *French Lacasse* case in the preceding note. The German "Rocky Island with Sirens" decision held against mutilation, but *not* against destruction of the mural (see *supra*, note 24).

[106] Misc. 2d 383 (Sup. Ct. 1957).

[107] Corbin, Contracts (1951) § 1184. Contracts to create and deliver a literary or artistic work are personal contracts. Ball, Law of Copyright and Literary Property (1944) 565; Fox, *op. cit. supra*, note 63 at 586. In *Roller* v. *Weigle*, 261 Fed. 250 (D.C. Cir. 1919), the court said that "It would be intolerable if a man could be compelled by a court

enforced whereby an artist will be prevented from performing for another producer,[108] or an author from writing for a different publisher.[109] There are numerous decisions granting injunctions against an artist's or author's serving a competitor where an award of damages for breach of contract was deemed an inadequate remedy.[110]

4. The right to publish or not to publish

The right to publish a work or withhold it from publication is accorded under the copyright statute, [111] by common law copyright,[112] and under the concept of the right of privacy.[113] In the case of letters, the right is enforced even against the recipient.[114]

While in England common law copyright has been abolished,[115] the United States copyright statute provides:

> Nothing in this title shall be construed to annul or limit the right of the author or proprietor of an unpublished work, at common law or in equity, to prevent the copying, publication, or use of such unpublished work without his consent, and to obtain damages therefor.[116]

This common law protection, together with the exclusive statutory right to publish and copy a copyrighted work adequately guarantees the author's excluscive right to publish his work and to prevent others from publishing it without permission.[117]

In *Pushman* v. *New York Graphic Society* [118] the New York Court of Appeals held that a common law copyright does not necessarily pass with the sale of a work of art, but that an artist, if he wishes to retain or protect this right, must reserve it when he sells a painting for pur-

---

of equity to serve another against his will," citing *Boyer* v. *Western Union Tel. Co.*, 124 Fed. 246; *Shubert* v. *Woodward*, 167 Fed. 47; *Gossard* v. *Crosby*, 132 Iowa 155, 109 N.W. 483.

In *Harms and Francis, Day and Hunter* v. *Stern*, 222 Fed. 581, 229 Fed. 42 (2d Cir. 1916) it was held that an agreement to transfer for five years a publishing right in future musical works was a valid and binding contract. "While the agreement could not be specifically enforced, it imposed upon [the composer] an obligation to perform it, and the breach of the agreement could be redressed in an action for damages." See the decision in the French case of *Whistler* v. *Eden supra*, note 27.

[108] *Lumley* v. *Wagner*, 1 De G.M. and G. 604 (Ch. App. 1852); *Duff* v. *Russell*, 133 N.Y. 678, 31 N.E. 622 (1892).

[109] *Tribune Association* v. *Simonds*, 104 A. 386 (Ch. 1918). *Whitwood Chem. Co.* v. *Hardman* (1891) 2 Ch. 416, has somewhat narrowed down the broad decision on enforcing negative covenants in *Lumley* v. *Wagner*, *supra*, note 108. In *Kennerley* v. *Simmonds*, 247 Fed. 822 (D.C. N.Y. 1917) it was held that a negative covenant not to write and publish similar works is not presumed unless indispensable.

[110] *Cincinnati Exhib. Co.* v. *Marsans*, 216 Fed. 269 (D.C. Mo. 1914); *Shubert Theatre Co.* v. *Rath*, 271 Fed. 827 (2d Cir. 1922); *Assoc. Newspapers* v. *Phillips*, 294 Fed. 845 (2d Cir. 1923); *Erikson* v. *Hawley*, 12 F. 2d 491, 56 App. D.C. 268 (1926).

For Great Britain, *accord: Ward, Look and Co.* v. *Long* (1906) 2 Ch. 550; *Macdonald* v. *Eyles*, (1921) 1 Ch. 631.

For Canada, Fox, *op. cit. supra*, note 63, at 582, states that the rule restraining authors from doing anything to render publishers' rights valueless by superseding the first work with another and publishing it through another publisher must be restricted to cases where the author commits actual infringement of the first work.

[111] Title 17, U.S.C. § 1, Act of July 30, 1947 (61 Stat. 652) as amended.

[112] See notes 116 and 117 *infra*.

[113] The right of privacy as a doctrine is not yet universally accepted. 1 Callmann, Unfair Competition and Trademarks (1945) 37.

[114] *Gee* v. *Pritchard* (1818) 2 Swans, 402; *Denis* v. *Leclerc*, Supr. Ct., Territ. Orleans, 1811, 1–3 Mart. 159; *Baker* v. *Libbie*, 210 Mass. 599, 97 N.E. 109 (1912).

[115] British Copyright Act, 1911, 1 and 2 Geo. 5, c. 46. Part III, § 31.

[116] Title 17, U.S.C. § 2. All *commercial* rights in the work after publication depend on statutory protection. *Wheaton* v. *Peters*, 8 Peters 591 (U.S. 1834). The *personal* rights of the author are not affected and are enforceable whether or not the work is published, or under statutory copyright.

[117] In *Millar* v. *Taylor*, 4 Burr. 2303, 98 Engl. Rep. 201 (K.B. 1769) common law copyright was held to be perpetual; the case was overruled in *Donaldson* v. *Becket*, 4 Burr. 2408, 98 Engl. Rep. 257 (1774). In *Wheaton* v. *Peters*, *supra*, note 116, it was also held that common law copyright ends with publication. Until that event takes place the author has a common law action against anyone who publishes his manuscript without authority. *Caliga* v. *Inter Ocean Newspaper*, 215 U.S. 182 (1909).

The right to publish includes, of course, the right to refrain from publishing. *Wallace* v. *Georgia C. and N. Ry. Co.*, 94 Ga. 732, 22 S.E. 579 (1894).

[118] 25 N.Y. Supp. 2d 32 (Sup. Ct. 1914), 39 N.E. 2d 249 (Ct. App. 1942).

poses of publication.   A common law copyright in unpublished works, possession of which is transferred but not for purposes of publication, always remains with the author or his legal successors.   The recipient or possessor may keep or destroy, but may not publish the work.[119]

5. *The right to withdraw the work from circulation*

There is no provision in the United States copyright statute nor has any court decision been found permitting an author to withdraw his work from circulation after it has been published.[120] The author must find relief, if any, either in an action in contract or tort.

6. *The right to prevent excessive criticism*

Not only authors, but any person whose reputation has been unjustifiably injured has an action for libel.   The action, however, dies with the person and, unless the libelous attack reflects on the family, there may be no recovery after the death of the libelled person.[121]

Criticism of literary or artistic works is permitted within the limits of "fair comment." In *Berg* v. *Printers' Ink Pub. Co.*[122] the court said:

Fair and legitimate criticism is always permitted upon any work to which the attention of the public has been invited.   It would not be a libel upon the plaintiff to say that the product of his pen was not good.   Whatever is written cannot be said to be libelous except something which decreases or lowers plaintiff in his professional character [*cit. om.*]. . . . Criticism of another's activities as are matters of public concern is fair, if the criticism, even though defamatory, is based on facts truly stated, . . . is an honest expression of the writer's real opinion or belief, and is not made solely for the purpose of causing hurt to the other.[123, 124]

---

[119] *Baker* v. *Libbie*, 210 Mass. 599, 97 N.E. 109 (1912) ; *Denise* v. *Leclerc, supra,* note 119 ; *Grigsby* v. *Breckinridge*, 65 Ky. 480 (1867) ; *State ex rel. Clemens* v. *Witthaus, Circuit Judge*, 228 S.W. 2d 4 (Missouri 1950).

In *Chamberlain* v. *Feldman*, 84 N.Y. Supp. 2d 713, 89 N.E. 2d 863 (1949) the Appellate Division of the New York Supreme Court held that independently of the sale of the manuscript the common law copyright or control of the right to reproduce belongs to the artist or author until disposed of by him and that, after the author's death, his estate may enjoin publication of an unpublished manuscript.   There was held to be no presumption of transfer of publication rights by virtue of transfer of the manuscript.

[120] Such as Article 32 of the 1957 French copyright law, or section 26, German Law on Publishing Contracts (permitting the author to buy back copies at the lowest trade price), or the Portuguese Copyright Law, Art. 29, under which an author may terminate his contract with the publisher where the latter has so modified the work as to hurt the author's reputation, or Art. 142 of the Italian Copyright Law.   Article V, last paragraph, of the Universal Copyright Convention may possibly be considered as, at least, implied recognition of the right of withdrawal.   It states: "The [translating] license shall not be granted when the author has withdrawn from circulation all copies of the work."

[121] There may be criminal libel of a deceased person.   *State* v. *Haffer*, 94 Wash. 136, 162 Pac. 45 (1917).   The reason is that defamation of a dead person may be resented by relatives and tend to disturb the peace.

[122] 54 F. Supp. 795 (D.C.N.Y., 1943), *aff'd without op.*, 141 F. 2d 1022 (2d Cir. 1944). See also : *Battersby* v. *Collier*, 34 App. Div. 347, 54 N.Y. Supp. 363 (1898) ; *Shapiro, Bernstein and Co.* v. *Collier*, 26 USPQ 40 (D.C.S.D.N.Y. 1934).

[123] The court in the *Berg* case quoted from *Triggs* v. *Sun Printing and Pub. Association*, 179 N.Y. 144, 71 N.E. 739 (1904) :

"The simple purpose of the rule permitting fair and honest criticism is that it promotes the public good, enables the people to discern right from wrong, encourages merit, and firmly condemns and exposes the charlatan and the cheat, and hence is based upon public policy. . . . Criticism never attacks the individual, but only his work."

[124] Roeder, 53 Harv. L. Rev. 554 at 572 objects to the rule that the plaintiff must prove falsity, malice and damages.   This is too harsh a rule," and recommends adoption of the French rule giving the right to a reply in the same medium.   We have numerous provisions of that kind.   "Retraction" statutes have been passed in Alabama, Georgia, Kansas, Michigan, Minnesota, New Jersey, North Carolina, North Dakota, and Ohio, (also Illinois, repealed two years later).   Nevada (Comp. Laws 1929) and Ohio (Gen. Code, 1926, §§ 6319–2 to 6319–9) have penal statutes, making it an offense for a newspaper to refuse to publish an answer.

The right to reply, or to force retraction, may be an alternative to a libel action, but it is no substitute.   Even in France it has not been so considered.   A plaintiff in a tort action for violation of his moral right must also prove malice, injury, and damages.   Dalloz, Code Civil (1946) Art. 1382, 1383, notes.

A public charge that a reporter violated a confidence (*Tryon* v. *Ev. News Assoc.*, 39 Mich. 636 (1878)), or that an author is a museum piece and a literary freak (*Triggs* v. *Sun Printing and Pub. Co., supra*, note 123) is libelous *per se*.   There need be no proof of special damages.

7. The right to relief from any other violation of the author's personal rights

In *Henry Holt and Co.* v. *Ligget and Myers Tobacco Co.*[125] the court said, concerning quotation from a scientific book in a cigarette advertisement, that the "publication was not one in the field in which [plaintiff] wrote nor was it a scientific treatise or a work designed to advance human knowledge. On the contrary, it is clear that the pamphlet intended to advance the sale of [defendant's] product . . . a purely commercial purpose. It cannot be implied that [plaintiff] consented to the use of his work for such a purpose."

In *Kerby* v. *Hal Roach Studios* [126] the supposedly fictitious name as the sender of a letter advertising a motion picture was actually the name of an artist. The court held that—

to suggest that a woman has written such a letter . . . is to impute to her a laxness of character [and] a coarseness of moral fiber . . .; and to spread such imputations abroad, . . . is an invasion of privacy.

In the *Neyland* case [127] the unauthorized commercial use of a work of art was also held objectionable as an invasion of the artist's personal rights.

The case of *Shostakovich et al.* v. *Twentieth-Century Fox Film Corporation* [128] turned on the question whether musical works in the public domain may be reproduced on the sound track of a motion picture, the theme of which was in opposition to the composers' political conviction. Appropriate authorship credit was given to the composers,[129] there was no distortion of the works, and there was nothing in the film to indicate that its theme represented the composers' convictions. The demand for relief was based on Section 51 of the New York civil rights law (invasion of privacy), and on allegations of defamation, the deliberate infliction of an injury without just cause, and violation of the plaintiff's moral right as composers. The court found no invasion of privacy as the works were in the public domain. It found no libel and no injury as the works, being in the public domain, could be reproduced without permission and had, in fact, been faithfully reproduced. Concerning the allegation of a violation of the composers' moral right by the reproduction of their works in an inappropriate manner, the court asked: "Is the standard to be good taste, artistic worth, political beliefs, moral concepts, or what is it to be?"

The *Shostakovich* case has been pointed to by some writers as demonstrating the failure of our courts to protect the personal rights of

---

In *Sullivan* v. *Daily Mirror*, 232 App. Div. 507, 250 N.Y. Supp. 420 (1931) a newspaper article implied that plaintiff sports-writer had been paid to write a favorable critique of a boxer. Held a libel, as plaintiff's honesty and loyalty to his paper and to the public was impugned.

For excessive criticism see further: *Cooper* v. *Stone*, 24 Wend. 434 (N.Y. 1840); *Dowling* v. *Livingstone*, 108 Mich. 321, 66 N.W. 225, (1896); *McQuire* v. *Western Morning News Co.*, (1903), 2K. B. 100; *Spooner* v. *Daniels*, 22 Fed. Cas. 934 (1854); *Potts* v. *Dies*, 132 F. 2d 734 (D.C. App. 1942).

For British and Canadian law, Fox, *op. cit. supra*, note 63 at 594 *et seq.*

[125] 23 F. Supp. 302 (D.C. Pa. 1938).

[126] 53 Cal. App. 2d 207, 127 P. 2d 577 (1942).

[127] *Supra*, note 78.

[128] 196 Misc. 67, 80 N.Y. Supp. 2d 575 (1948), *aff'd by memorandum opinion*, 275 App. Div. 692, 87 N.Y. Supp. 2d 430 (1949).

[129] The credit line read: "music—from the selected works of the *Soviet* Composers—Dmitry Shostakovich, Serge Prokofieff, Aram Khachaturian, Nicholai Miashovsky, conducted by Alfred Newman," (italics added)—making it obvious that the music was *not* composed for the film.

authors.[130] The court has been criticized for not considering the matter from the composers' point of view. In our opinion, the court asked a pertinent question. Even the European exponents of the moral right doctrine disagree as to whether the right should be based on a subjective or objective evaluation of the facts, while the European courts nearly always prefer the latter.[131] Were we to assume—as do the critics—that the circumstances under which the compositions were used were "obviously inappropriate," the answer would be equally obvious. But that is the whole question: *was* the use inappropriate, solely because the theme of the film ran counter to the composers' political beliefs, there being nothing in the film to associate the composers' beliefs with its theme.

Judge Frank said in *Grantz* v. *Harris* [132] in regard to the doctrine of moral right:

> A new name, a novel label expressive of a new generalization, can have immense consequences. . . . But the solution of a problem through the invention of a new generalization is no final solution. The new generalization breeds new problems. Stressing a newly perceived likeness between many particular happenings which had theretofore seemed unlike, it may blind us to continuing unlikenesses. Hypnotized by a label which emphasizes identities, we may be led to ignore differences. . . . For, with its stress on uniformity, an abstraction or generalization tends to become totalitarian in its attitude toward uniqueness.

To arm a composer with the right to suppress the use of his music in a film because he disapproves of the political view expressed in the film, would come close to censorship and would have little, if anything, to do with the protection of his personality.[133]

III. Summary

In the preceding pages three questions have been examined: What is the moral right? What protection is accorded the moral right in the countries which have adopted the doctrine? And what protection,

---

[130] Katz, *supra,* note 1 at 414; Simpson and Schwartz, "Equity" Annual Survey of Am. Law (1948) 642 at 657.

Mr. Katz's hypothetical analogy of including the judge's opinion in a collection of opinions of "radical" judges seems to miss the point: publication of such a work in *this* country may be libel. In *Derounian* v. *Stokes,* 168 F. 2d 305 (10th Cir. 1948), it was held that an imputation of disloyalty to the country in a national crisis is an actionable libel. *Accord: Grant* v. *Reader's Digest Ass'n,* 151 F. 2d 733 (2d Cir. 1945).—But why should the judge care, or what could he do, if the collection were published in Russia?

[131] See the *Barillet* case, *supra,* note 52. Plaisant, *supra,* note 27, No. 15, says: The Supreme Court [of France] has formally held on May 14, 1945, that the exercise of moral right is subject to control and to evaluation by the courts.

[132] *Supra,* note 79.

[133] The *Shostakovich* case was litigated in France in 1953 under the style of *Soc. Le Chant du Monde* v. *Soc. Fox Europe and Soc. Fox Américaine Twentieth Century,* Ct. App. Paris, Jan. 13, 1953, D.A. 1954, 16, 80. The facts were as follows:

On July 7, 1949, plaintiff caused the film "*Le Rideau de Fer*" (Iron Curtain) to be seized. The lower court, on May 31, 1950, ordered the confiscation to be lifted and adjudged the Soc. Le Chant du Monde liable for damages in the amount of $9,000.00.

On appeal, it was held that plaintiff, as assignee of the composers, was entitled to sue for copyright infringement; that Russians enjoyed copyright in France regardless of the lack of reciprocity; and that, under the copyright law of 1793 seizure was in order.

In regard to the moral right the court held that there was "undoubtedly a moral damage." This moral damage, together with the copyright infringement, was thought to be worth $5,000. The film was again seized under Art. 3 of the copyright law of 1793 for infringement.

For British and Canadian law, Fox, *op. cit. supra,* note 63 at 569:

"In a proper case the author has the right to sue for damages to his reputation. *Archhold* v. *Sweet,* (1832), 1 N. and Rob. 162; *Angers* v. *Leprohon,* (1899), 22 Que S.C. 170. . . . Despite the great number of novels and other works which are grossly mutilated in transcribing them into cinematographic productions, no case is on record of this section [12 (5). Can. Copyr. Law] having been invoked."

if any, exists in the United States for the personal rights of authors which, under the doctrine, constitute the components of the moral right?

Article 6*bis* of the revised Berne Convention provides in paragraph (1) that the author shall have the right, during his lifetime, to claim authorship in his work and to object to any violation of the integrity of his work which would be prejudicial to his honor or reputation. This provision contains its own limitation, for a violation is not actionable unless there is a prejudice to the author's professional honor or reputation. Whether or not there is such prejudice is to be determined by the court, and not by the author. At the present time, Article 6*bis* of the Berne Convention seems to represent the limit of agreement among the adherents to the moral right doctrine, because most aspects of the moral right, such as its nature, it components, and its duration are far from crystallized.

Some writers have claimed for the doctrine of the moral right a broad scope which, however, has not yet emerged from the theoretical stage, and which has not found expression in the court decisions of the "moral right countries." The judicial enforcement of the moral right as such, whether based on statutes or, in the absence of any pertinent statutory provision, on court interpretation of the doctrine, rarely goes beyond recognition of the paternity right, and of the right to prevent changes in the work which the court, in its own opinion, considers to be prejudicial to the author's honor or reputation. The European courts, almost without exception, have refused to yield to attempts by authors to invoke the moral right on grounds untenable by objective standards. Manifestly, most courts in the "moral right countries" are not so impressed by the theories of the textwriters as to ignore contractual obligations and the equities on each side of the case.

The other rights claimed by some writers to be components of the moral right are not recognized as such in the Berne Convention. These other rights either have been protected on principles other than the moral right or have not been the subject of litigation. Thus, the right to create a work or to refuse to do so is merely a matter of denying specific performance of a contract to create and deliver a work; and the author is none the less liable for breach of contract. Whether the right to publish a work is considered a property right or a component of the moral right, where the author refuses to fulfill his obligation under a publishing contract, an interpretation of the contract by the court is necessary to settle the question.[134] The right to prevent "excessive" criticism, and the right to prevent any other attack on the author's "special" personality are enforced under the law of defamation, libel or slander, or on some other tort principle unconnected with the copyright law. The right to withdraw a work from circulation apparently has not been litigated in connection with the moral right, and the provisions in several laws granting this right are so restrictive that the right seems hardly more than an illusion.

The question of duration of the moral right is also controversial. Under the German law, present and proposed, the moral right terminates with the copyright, i.e., fifty years after the death of the author.

---

[134] It remains to be seen how the French courts will deal with the provision in Art. 32 of the copyright law of 1957 that "Notwithstanding the transfer of the exploitation rights, the author, . . . shall enjoy, in relation to the transferee, the right to correct or retract."

In French jurisprudence and the French copyright law of 1957, the moral right is independent of the copyright term, and lasts forever. Under the laws of Great Britain and Switzerland personal rights of the author terminate with his death.   The Berne Convention provides for protection of the author's moral right during his lifetime; after his death, according to paragraph (2) of Article 6*bis*, protection of the moral right may exist "insofar as the legislation of the Countries of the Union permits."

Despite strenuous efforts by the proponents of the moral right doctrine during the last thirty years, progress toward a uniform incorporation of the moral right in the copyright laws of the Berne countries has not been impressive.   Some of the member countries of the Berne Union specifically protect the moral right as such (e.g., Austria, France, Italy, Portugal), or recognize it in dispersed provisions concerning one or more of the components of the moral right (e.g., Belgium, Germany, Netherlands), or provide such protection through recognition of the moral right by the courts without benefit of statute (this was the case in France before the copyright law of 1957 was in effect).   Other Berne countries protect the moral right of the author only to the extent that, and in the same manner as, personal rights of all persons are recognized (e.g., Great Britain, Switzerland).

The fact that the French copyright law of 1957 and the German draft copyright law [135] reflect widely divergent theories on the moral right makes it apparent that an agreement on the principles of the doctrine is not to be expected in the foreseeable future.   However, recent writings of European authors on the subject show a tendency to reduce to more acceptable proportions the formerly excessive claims made for the moral right and to consider, to a greater extent, the practical requirements of publishers and users of literary and artistic works.

Much confusion concerning the doctrine has been created by the claim that the moral right is inalienable, whatever may happen to the property aspects of the copyright.   Actually, the moral right is inalienable only in the sense that, like all personal rights, it is not capable of transfer by sale or gift.   But there is no effective rule of law which prevents an author from waiving one or more of the components of the moral right.   While the courts in the "moral right countries" generally do not construe contracts as implying a tacit waiver of the moral right, there seems to be no decision voiding an agreement which expressly and unambiguously waives those personal rights that comprise the moral right.   Moreover, in some situations there is a legal presumption of a waiver of the paternity right or of the right to prevent changes which may prejudice the author's professional standing. Thus, in the case of collective works, such as newspapers or encyclopedias, the paternity right, and sometimes the right to prevent changes, is presumed to be waived.   Further, in the case of an adaptation of a work for a different medium, such changes as are reasonably required by the medium are held to be authorized.

Without using the label "moral right," or designations of the components of the moral right, the courts in the United States arrive at much the same results as do European courts.   Substantially the same personal rights are upheld, although often under different principles.

---

[135] March, 1954.

Also, substantially the same limitations are imposed on these rights, frequently on the same basis.[136]   Thus, both here and abroad:

(1) An author has the right to be given credit in the publication, performance, adaptation or other use of his work; but he may waive this right.   For some types of publications, such as an author's contribution to a collective work, this right is presumed to be waived unless specifically reserved.

Conversely, an author has the right to restrain the use of his name in a work that is not his, or in a distorted version of his work; but he may waive this right.

(2) An author has the right to prevent prejudicial changes in his work; but he may waive this right.   When he authorizes the use of his work in a different medium, he is presumed to have consented to the changes necessary to adapt his work to that medium.

(3) An author cannot be compelled to perform his contract to create a work; but he will be liable in damages for breach of such a contract.

(4) An author has the right to publish his work or to withhold it from publication; but he may assign or license this right.

(5) An author may prevent defamation of character (the "excessive criticism" of the moral right doctrine), and unfair use or misuse of his work by an action in tort, such as defamation, libel, slander, or unfair competition.

Judge Frank concluded in the case of *Granz* v. *Harris* [137] that there were adequate grounds in the common law for enjoining distribution of a distorted version, and hence there was no need to resort to the doctrine of moral right as such.   We believe that this is generally true for all aspects of the personal rights of authors, and that common law principles, if correctly applied, afford an adequate basis for protection of such rights.   In our view, the contention that the author's rights of personality are not sufficiently protected in the United States, and the belief that there is an irreconcilable breach between European and American concepts of protection of authors' personal rights, seem to be dispelled by close scrutiny of the court decisions here and abroad.   While a few American courts may be thought to have been remiss in protecting authors' personal rights (especially in finding implied waivers in ambiguous contracts), such decisions are exceptional and may be considered erroneous under common law principles.   Given the same facts, the large majority of courts in America and abroad employ the same reasonable and equitable standards for the protection of authors' personal rights.   This similarity of protection has been obscured by the differences of approach and terminology. There is a considerable body of precedent in the American decisions to afford to our courts ample foundations in the common law for the protection of the personal rights of authors to the same extent that such protection is given abroad under the doctrine of moral right.

---

[136] We come to the final conclusion that, under different names and by different procedures, the Anglo-Saxon law resembles the French law more than may seem at first blush. To arrive at this conclusion we simply have to forget whether the moral right is or is not subject to alienation. Plaisant, *supra*, note 27, No. 22.
[137] 198 F. 2d 585 (2d Cir. 1952) (*concurring opinion*).

PART VIII

REMEDIES

Damages, Other Remedies, Innocent Infringement

A number of the remedial aspects of copyright infringement follow the rules applicable to analogous torts. At least as many, however, require special study because of the policy or draftsmanship found in particular provisions of the statute. A focal point for such study is the intricate provision for monetary relief. This relief includes recovery for the proprietor's damages "as well as" an accounting of the infringer's profits, with no clear answer as to whether such recovery is cumulative or limited to the larger of damages and profits. In any event, the court may, in its discretion, substitute specified unproven damages in accordance with a set of statutory yardsticks and limits. Moreover, a specific provision authorizes an award of attorney's fees to the prevailing party.

It is perhaps not surprising that the measurement of actual damages in copyright cases, the development of proper accounting rules and the utilization of the statutory damage scheme have been reflected by a considerable amount of litigation. This litigation is analyzed by two separate studies. One is a comprehensive study of the legal dimension of the damage problem; a factual study explores the actual operation of the damage provision in practical terms.

The statute also provides a substantial measure of specific relief. This includes the remedies of injunction and the impounding and destruction of infringing copies, plates, molds, etc. A separate study examines these remedies as well as the criminal sanctions against wilful infringement.

At the opposite end of the spectrum from the wilfulness required for criminal infringement stands infringement committed innocently. A study of the relevance of innocence to the question of infringement indicates that while intent to infringe is not a necessary element of the wrong, innocence may affect the nature and scope of available remedies. Over and above the limited situations in which the statute provides for such mitigation, there appears to be a perhaps increasing judicial tendency to apply the potentially severe sanctions of the statute with varying degrees of rigor, depending on the culpability of the defendant.

STUDY NO. 22

THE DAMAGE PROVISIONS OF THE COPYRIGHT LAW
By William S. Strauss

October 1956

THE DAMAGE PROVISIONS OF THE COPYRIGHT LAW

This study treats two related subjects: First, damages for copyright infringement; and, second, costs and attorney's fees. The first subject includes the questions of compensatory and statutory damages, and profits. The second treats the award of expenses incurred in the prosecution of an infringement action, or in the defense against such action. Despite several legislative efforts at revision, the provisions on damages and costs are still substantially the same as those of the Copyright Act of March 4, 1909.

A. DAMAGES

I. HISTORY OF THE DAMAGE PROVISIONS

1. *Colonial copyright statutes*

On May 2, 1783, the Continental Congress passed a resolution recommending to the several States to secure to the authors or publishers of new books the copyright of such books.[1] All States except Delaware followed this recommendation and passed copyright statutes.

Under the damage provisions of these State statutes an infringer was either liable to pay "just damages," [2] or "double the value of all the copies"; [3] or the statute provided for maximum and minimum damages; [4] or a fixed sum had to be paid for each infringing sheet.[5] In some cases one-half of the payment accrued to the benefit of the injured party, and the other half went to the State.[6] Thus, there were actual damages, statutory damages, forfeitures, and penalties.

2. *The Federal copyright statutes*

Congress exercised the power granted it by article I, section 8, of the Constitution by passing a Federal Copyright Act on May 31, 1790. Section 2 of this act (1 Stat. 124) gave the copyright owner an action against unauthorized publication, the offender to "forfeit and pay the sum of fifty cents for every sheet * * *, the one moiety thereof to and for the use of the United States." Under section 6 an infringer was further "liable to suffer and pay to the * * * author or proprietor all damages occasioned by such injury."

The act of April 29, 1802 (2 Stat. 171) extended copyright protection to designs, engravings, and prints, and provided in section 3 for the forfeiture of $1 for every infringing print, half to accrue to the plaintiff and the other half to the United States.

---

[1] This resolution and the State statutes are collected in "Copyright Laws of the United States of America, 1783–1956," published by the Copyright Office, 1956.
[2] Connecticut, Georgia, and New York.
[3] Connecticut, New Jersey, North Carolina, Pennsylvania, and Virginia.
[4] Massachusetts, New Hampshire, and Rhode Island.
[5] Maryland and South Carolina.
[6] North Carolina and South Carolina.

The act of February 15, 1819 (3 Stat. 481) provided that infringement actions, which previously had to be brought at law, might also be prosecuted in equity. The circuit courts of the United States were given the power to grant injunctions to prevent or stop infringement.

The act of February 3, 1831 (4 Stat. 436) which added musical compositions to the classes of protected works, differentiated between forfeitures in regard to infringement of books on the one hand and of prints, cuts, engravings, maps, charts, and musical works on the other. In the case of infringement of a book the forfeiture amounted to 50 cents per sheet, and in the other cases to $1, half of the proceeds accruing to the use of the United States. Section 9 provided that an infringer was liable for all damages, "to be recovered by a special action on the case founded upon this Act." Section 12 provided "that, in all recoveries under this Act, either for damages, forfeitures, or penalties, full costs shall be allowed thereon."

The act of August 18, 1856 (11 Stat. 138) granted performance and publication rights in dramatic compositions. Unauthorized performance made the infringer—

liable to damages to be sued for and recovered by action on the case or other equivalent remedy with costs of suit * * * , such damages in all cases to be rated and assessed at such sum not less than one hundred dollars for the first and fifty dollars for every subsequent performance.

Section 99 of the Copyright Act of July 8, 1870 (16 Stat. 198) provided that an infringer "forfeit and pay such damages as may be recovered in a civil action." Section 100, in addition to repeating the $1 forfeiture per sheet for infringement of maps, musical compositions, etc., provided that an infringer, in the case of infringement of a painting, statue, or statuary, forfeit $10 for every infringing copy, half of the proceeds to go to the plaintiff and the other half to the United States. Section 101 again provided for damages of $100 for the first, and $50 for all subsequent unauthorized performances of a dramatic work. Section 102 provided for all damages occasioned by an infringement to be recovered in an action on the case. Section 108 allowed full costs in all recoveries under the copyright laws, either for damages, forfeitures, or penalties.[7]

The act of March 2, 1895 (28 Stat. 956) provided that in the case of infringement of a copyrighted photograph made from any object not a work of fine arts, the sum recovered was to be not less than $100 nor more than $5,000, and that in the case of infringement of a copyright in a painting, drawing, engraving, etching, print, or model or design for a work of art, or a photograph of a work of the fine arts, the sum to be recovered was to be not less than $250 nor more than $10,000. One-half of such sum accured to the copyright proprietor and the other half to the United States.

The damage provisions now in effect are the following: Section 101(b) of the copyright law [8] provides for actual damages and profits or, in lieu of actual damages and profits, for statutory damages which "shall not be regarded as a penalty." Section 101(e) in conjunction with section 1(e) provides special remedies for infringement of musical works by means of mechanical reproduction. Section 1(c) prescribes maximum damages for innocent infringement of nondramatic works by broadcast.

---

[7] The act of Mar. 3, 1891, extended protection to foreign authors.
[8] 17 U.S.C., 61 Stat. 652 (1947), as amended. Hereinafter "section" refers to a section of title 17, United States Code, unless otherwise indicated.

3. *Analysis of damage provisions before the act of 1909*

The first provision for minimum damages appeared in the act of 1856, under which any person giving an unauthorized performance of a dramatic work—

shall be liable to damages * * *, such damages in all cases to be rated and assessed at such sum not less than one hundred dollars for the first, and fifty dollars for every subsequent performance, as to the court * * * shall appear to be just.

As to actual damages, the Supreme Court held in *Belford, Clarke and Co. v. Scribner*[9] that the measure of damages was the total profits made by publication of the infringing work. Both the unauthorized printer and the publisher of a copyright book were held liable and required to account for the profits of the unlawful publication. The Court held further that, although the entire work might not have been copied, if the portions copied were so intermingled with the rest of the piratical work that they could not be distinguished, then the entire profits should be given to the plaintiff.[10] In *Callaghan v. Myers*[11] the Court refused to permit the deduction of the cost of stereotyping and of salaries of the defendants.[12] In *Providence Rubber Co. v. Goodyear*[13] the Court stated, in regard to damages, that the elements of price of materials, interest, expenses of manufacture and sale, and other necessary expenditures and bad debts should be taken into account, but in no case should there be a profit to the infringer from his wrongful act. Equity courts permitted recovery of profits (as distinguished from damages) only incidental to awarding an injunction.[14] While there was a statutory provision for the recovery of profits in patent cases,[15] there was none for infringement of copyright.

In all copyright acts before 1909, part of a forfeiture accrued to the United States, and therefore these damage provisions were partly penal and partly remedial.[16] The act of 1909 for the first time provided for the recovery of profits in damage actions,[17] and eliminated the penal aspects from awards of damages.

II. THE PRESENT DAMAGE PROVISIONS

Section 101(b) grants the following types of recovery to the copyright proprietor:

    (a) Such damages as he may have suffered due to the infringement;

    (b) All the profits which the infringer shall have made from the infringement;

    (c) In lieu of actual damages and profits, such damages as to the court shall appear to be just, within the limits specified by the statutes.

---

[9] 144 U.S. 488 (1892).

[10] Citing *Callaghan* v. *Myers*, 128 U.S. 617 (1888) as to the award of the entire profits.

[11] Supra, note 10. The decision was approved in *Westinghouse Co.* v. *Wagner Co.*, 225 U.S. 604 (1912).

[12] The Court distinguished the case from *Providence Rubber Co.* v. *Goodyear*, 76 U.S.788, 9 Wall. 788 (1870), in which salaries of officers of a corporation were held deductible. See also *Whitman Pub. Co.* v. *Writsel*, 83 U.S.P.Q. 535 (S.D. Ohio 1949); *Dam* v. *Kirk La Shelle Co.*, 189 Fed. 842 (S.D.N.Y. 1911).

[13] Note 12, supra.

[14] See *Atlantic Monthly Co.* v. *Post Pub. Co.*, 27 F. 2d 556 (D. Mass. 1928).

[15] Recovery of profits in patent cases was permitted by the act of July 8, 1870, 16 Stat. 198, 35 U.S.C.A. 70. *Stevens* v. *Gladding*, 17 How. 447 (1854); *Callaghan* v. *Myers*, supra, note 11; *Belford, Clarke and Co.* v. *Scribner*, 144 U.S. 488 (1892).

[16] Actions for forfeiture were of a quasi-criminal character. See *Backus* v. *Gould*, 48 U.S. 798 (1849); *Bolles* v. *Outing Co.*, 175 U.S. 262 (1899); *Westermann Co.* v. *Dispatch Printing Co.*, 249 U.S. 100 (1919).

[17] H. Rep. No. 2222, accompanying H.R. 28192, 60th Cong., 2d sess. 15 (1909), states: "The provision that the copyright proprietor may have such damages as well as the profits which the infringer shall have made is substantially the same provision found in sec. 4921 of the Revised Statutes relating to remedies for the infringement of patents."

1. *Actual damages*

In *Hendricks Co.* v. *Thomas Pub. Co.*, [18] "actual damages" were defined as follows:

"Actual" means "real," as opposed to "nominal" [cit. om.]. It means "existent," without precluding the thought of change.

This definition is difficult to apply where no exact determination of the damage suffered is possible. In *Sinclair Refining Co.* v. *Jenkins Petroleum Proc. Co.* [19] the court said that the use made of a patented device is a legitimate aid to the appraisal of the value of the patent at the time of the breach, but that the recovery could not be measured by current prices of a nonexistent market.

In *Straus* v. *Victor Talking Machine Co.*[20] the court said:

The constant tendency of the courts is to find some way in which damages can be awarded * * * . Difficulty of ascertainment is no longer confused with right of recovery.

In *Universal Pictures* v. *Harold Lloyd Corp.*,[21] an action for infringement of copyright in a motion picture, the trial court had awarded plaintiff $40,000 damages and $10,000 for attorneys' fees, finding that 20 percent of the profits in exhibiting the infringing motion picture had been derived from the infringement. The judgment was affirmed on the basis of expert testimony as to the values inherent in the motion picture and plaintiff's own testimony on the value of the misappropriated copyright. The circuit court said that not mathematical exactness but only a reasonable approximation was required, to be arrived at by the court's judgment in consideration of the testimony of expert witnesses.

However, the courts do not seem bound to award actual damages, even when determinable. In *Widenski* v. *Shapiro, Bernstein,*[22] action was brought for a single infringing performance of a musical work. Defendants contended on appeal that the trial court should not have awarded damages under the "in lieu" clause of section 25 of the act. (Sec. 101(b)) because the amount of $10 customarily asked by ASCAP as a license fee for a single performance provided a measure of actual damages. They urged the application of an analogy to the "established royalty" rule [22a] of the patent law. The circuit court held that the "in lieu" clause was, in regard to copyright cases, a substitute for the established or reasonable royalty rule and that damages in a copyright case need not be the price at which the copyright proprietor had indicated his willingness to sell to the infringer.[23]

Because of the difficulty of proving actual damages the courts frequently base their awards on the profits which accrued to the infringer or award statutory damages.[24]

---

[18] 242 Fed. 37 (2d Cir. 1917).
[19] 289 U.S. 689 (1933); see also *Story Parchment Co.* v. *Paterson Parchment Co.*, 282 U.S. 555 (1931) (both patent cases).
[20] 297 Fed. 791 (2d Cir. 1924).
[21] 162 F. 2d 354 (9th Cir. 1947).
[22] 147 F. 2d 909 (1st Cir. 1945). See also *Lundberg* v. *Welles*, 93 F. Supp. 359 (S.D.N.Y. 1950).
[22a] A patentee may show an established royalty as indicative of the value of what was taken, and therefore as affording a basis for measuring the damages. See *Dowagiac Mfg. Co.* v. *Minnesota Plow Co.*, 235 U.S. 641 (1915). This rule applies only after he has failed to prove his loss and the infringer's profit. *Enterprise Mfg. Co.* v. *Shakespeare Co.*, 141 F. 2d 916 (6th Cir. 1944).
[23] As to actual versus statutory damages see infra A, II, 3(a); *Sheldon* v. *Metro-Goldwyn Pict. Corp.*, 309 U.S. 390 (1940); *Woolworth Co.*, v. *Contemporary Arts*, 193 F. 2d 162 (1st Cir. 1951), aff'd 344 U.S. 228 (1952). Also: *Douglas* v. *Cunningham*, 294 U.S. 207 (1935); *Washingtonian Pub. Co.* v. *Pearson*, 140 F. 2d 465 (D C. Cir. 1944); *Toksvig* v. *Bruce Pub. Co.*, 181 F. 2d 664 (7th Cir. 1950); *Advertisers Exchange* v. *Hinkley*, 101 F. Supp. 801 (Mo. 1951), 199 F. 2d 313 (8th Cir. 1952).
[24] *Sammons* v. *Larkin*, 38 F. Supp. 649 (Mass. 1941), see also *Sammons* v. *Colonial Press*, infra. note 62; *Buck* v. *Milam*, 32 F. 2d 622 (Idaho 1929); *Jewell-La Salle Realty Co.* v. *Buck*, 283 U.S. 202 (1931).

2. Profits

Section 101(b) provides that the copyright proprietor is entitled to damages, "as well as all the profits." It would seem clear from this language that both damages and profits may be recovered. It has been so held by at least two courts,[25] and this interpretation has been defended by several textwriters.[26] However, House Report No. 2222 stated that this provision was intended as an analogy to the provision relating to remedies for the infringement of patents.

The courts have usually construed [the patent provision] to mean that the owner of the patent might have one or the other, whichever was the greater.[27]

In patent cases it is the rule that the complainant is entitled to a finding of both damages and profits with the right to choose one or the other.[28] Where the profits alone are an inadequate measure of damages, the court may also allow compensatory damages.[29] Such damages are recoverable if they exceed the profits.[30]

In respect to the question whether in copyright infringement actions profits are to be awarded in addition or as an alternative to damages, the language of the statute does not seem to be in agreement with the legislative intent as stated in House Report No. 2222. Consequently, the rule in copyright cases has not become as well established as it is in patent cases. *This uncertainty should be removed by a revision of the statute.*

As to the amount of profits to be turned over to the plaintiff, the Supreme Court said in *Callaghan* v. *Myers*:[31]

In regard to the general question of the profits to be accounted for by the defendants * * * , the only proper rule to be adopted is to deduct from the selling price the actual and legitimate manufacturing cost.

Under section 101(b), the defendant must prove every element of cost, while the plaintiff must prove sales only.[32] The rule established by the Supreme Court in *Callaghan* v. *Myers*[33] that the infringer is liable for the entire profits made from the infringement on the theory of wrongful confusion of goods,[34] is no longer followed. In *Sheldon* v. *Metro-Goldwyn Corp.*[35] Judge Leibell discussed in detail the unfairness of that rule. He stated that since the greater

---

[25] *Ziegelheim* v. *Flohr*, 119 F. Supp. 324 (E.D.N.Y. 1954); *Sebring Pottery Co.* v. *Steubenville Pottery Co.*, 9 F. Supp. 384 (N.D. Ohio 1934).
[26] Ball, "Law of Copyright and Lit. Prop." 624 (1944); Amdur, "Copyright Law and Practice" 1112 (1936); Weil, "Copyright Law," 467 (1917).
[27] Supra, note 17. The damage provision in the Patent Law (title 35, U.S.C., revised, codified and enacted into law by act of July 19, 1952, ch. 950, 66 Stat. 792) reads as follows:
"§ 284. Damages.
"Upon finding for the claimant the court shall award the claimant damages adequate to compensate for the infringement, but in no event less than a reasonable royalty for the use made of the invention by the infringer, together with interest and costs as fixed by the court.
"When the damages are not found by a jury, the court shall assess them. In either event the court may increase the damages up to three times the amount found or assessed.
"The court may receive expert testimony as an aid to the determination of damages or of what royalty would be reasonable under the circumstances."
[28] *Christensen* v. *Nat. Brake and El. Co.*, 10 F. 2d 856 (Wis. 1926); *Mathey* v. *United Shoe Mach. Corp.*, 54 F. Supp. 694 (Mass. 1944); *Goodyear Tire and Rubber Co.* v. *Overman Cushion Tire Co.*, 95 F. 2d 978 (6th Cir. 1938), cert. dismissed 306 U.S. 665.
[29] *Mathey* v. *United Shoe Mach. Corp.*, supra, note 28.
[30] *Goodyear* v. *Overman*, supra, note 28. In *Lundberg* v. *Welles*, 93 F. Supp. 359 (S.D.N.Y. 1950), Chief Judge Knox pointed out the confusion existing in this regard in copyright actions.
[31] 128 U.S. 617 (1888). See also *Malsed* v. *Marshall Field and Co.*, 96 F. Supp. 372 (W.D. Wash. 1951); *Whitman Pub. Co.* v. *Writsel*, 83 U.S.P.Q. 535 (S.D. Ohio 1949).
[32] As to items which are permissible deductions, see Warner, "Radio and Television Rights," 643 to 645 (1953.)
[33] 128 U.S. 617 (1888).
[34] See also on this point: *Belford, Clarke and Co.* v. *Scribner*, supra, note 15; *Hartford Printing Co.* v. *Hartford Directory and Publ. Co.*, 146 Fed. 332 (C. C.Conn. 1906).
[35] 40 U.S.P.Q. 238 (S.D.N.Y. 1938). See also case cited infra, notes 36 and 37.

part of the motion picture in litigation was defendant's work, an allowance to complainants of 25 percent of the net profits would be appropriate. He considered it:

> * * * primitive and unjust to award all the net profits * * * to the complainants. Yet under the wording of the Copyright Act [sec. 25, act of 1909] as interpreted by the decisions of the appellate courts, I can do nothing less.

On appeal [36] the Second Circuit Court fixed the award to the plaintiffs as a one-fifth share of the net profits. Judge Learned Hand gave the following reason for breaking with the prior rule:

> In cases where plaintiffs fail to prove their damages exactly, we often make the best estimate we can, even though it is really no more than a guess [cit. om.] * * *. However, though we do not press the burden of proof so far, the defendents must be content to accept much of the embarrassment resulting from mingling the plaintiff's property with their own. We will not accept the expert's testimony at its face value; we must make an award which by no possibility shall be too small. It is not our best guess that must prevail, but a figure which will favor the plaintiffs in every reasonable chance of error.

The Supreme Court, upholding Judge Hand, said in part: [37]

> We shall * * * consider the doctrine which has been established upon equitable principles with respect to the apportionment of profits in cases of patent infringement. We now observe that there is nothing in the Copyright Act which precludes the application of a similar doctrine based upon the same equitable principle in cases of copyright infringement.

Distinguishing the *Sheldon* case from *Callaghan* v. *Myers* [38] and *Belford, Clark and Co.* v. *Scribner*,[39] the Court stated that in the *Callaghan* and *Belford* cases it had been impossible to separate the profits in the infringing material from those in the public domain material.

Citing its decision in the patent case of *Dowagiac Mfg. Co.* v. *Minnesota Moline Plow Co.*[40] in which the principle of apportionment of profits was enunciated, and admitting that such apportionment was, to some extent, based on a reasonable approximation, the Court said:

> In the *Dowagiac* case, we again referred to the difficulty of making an exact apportionment and again observed that mathematical exactness was not possible. What was required was only reasonable approximation which usually may be obtained through the testimony of experts and persons informed by observation and experience. Testimony of this character was said to be "generally helpful and at times indispensable" in the solution of such problems. The result to be accomplished "is a rational separation of the net profits so that neither party may have what rightfully belongs to the other * * *." We see no reason why these principles should not be applied in copyright cases.

Although the "20 percent rule" of apportionment, established in the *Sheldon* case, was followed in several other cases,[41] there seems to be no necessity to assume [42] that the Supreme Court intended to fix a rule of rigid apportionment to be used indiscriminately in all cases.[43]

[36] 106 F.2d 45 (2d Cir. 1939).
[37] 309 U.S. 390 (1940).
[38] 128 U.S. 617 (1888).
[39] 144 U.S. 488 (1892).
[40] 235 U.S. 641 (1915).
[41] *Sheldon et al.* v. *Moredall Realty Corp.* 29 F.Supp. 729 (S.D. N.Y. 1939), involving the same plaintiff and the same motion picture; *Stonesifer* v. *Twentieth Century-Fox Film Corp.* 48 F. Supp. 196 (S.D. Cal. 1942); *Universal Pictures* v. *Harold Lloyd Corp.*, 162 F. 2d 354 (9th Cir. 1947).
[42] Accord: Warner, op. cit. supra, note 32 at 641.
[43] In patent cases the apportionment depends on the extent to which the patented feature and the other elements contributed. *Westinghouse Co.* v. *Wagner Mfg. Co.*, 225 U.S. 604 (1912); *Swan Carbureter Co.* v. *Nash Mfg. Co.*, 133 F. 2d 562 (4th Cir. 1943) cert. denied, 320 U.S. 762, rehearing denied 320 U.S. 812 (1943); *Freeman* v. *Premier Mach. Co.*, 25 F. Supp. 927 (Mass. 1938); *Kintner* v. *Atlantic Communication Co.*, 51; 51 F. 2d 109 (S.D. N.Y. 1931); *Baseball Display Co., Inc.* v. *Star Ball Player Co., Inc.*, 35 F. 2d 1 (3d Cir. 1929).

The courts need make no apportionment if the difficulties of separating the infringing from the noninfringing matter are too great, or if there is no evidence permitting a separation of that part of the profits which were due to the infringer's own efforts, from those in the infringing material.[44]

Infringers—

are jointly and severally liable for damages; * * * but an accounting for profits * * * is an equitable remedy and must be according to equitable principles.[45]

Coinfringers are liable only to the extent of the share of profits that each received,[46] since the purpose of recovery of profits is to prevent unjust enrichment.[47]

3. Statutory damages

(a) Actual damages and/or profits versus statutory damages

There are several conflicting decisions on the question whether statutory damages may be awarded when actual damages or profits can be assessed. One of the most recent of these is *Ziegelheim* v. *Flohr*.[48] In this case, statutory damages at $1 per copy would have amounted to $4,100, as the defendant had printed 4,100 copies of the infringing book. Instead the court awarded $1,700, which amount he found a reasonable and just computation of actual damages and profits. The court did not accept the plaintiff's claim of sales lost to him or profits accrued to the defendants, but substituted its own estimate of damages and profits of the infringer, less the cost of printing and binding of the infringing book, which constituted the damages awarded to plaintiff. [49] In *Gordon* v. *Weir* [50] the court said that—

as to infringements as to which neither damage nor profit was proven, the court may assess such damages as it deems just, within the statutory maximum and minimum.

In *Edward B. Marks Music Corp.* v. *Borst Music Pub. Co.* [51] no attempt was made to determine actual damages. The court awarded $250 statutory damages for each infringement.

In *Sheldon* v. *Metro-Goldwyn Pictures Corp.*[52] the Supreme Court interpreted the "in lieu" clause of section 101(b)[53] to the effect that it was not applicable if profits were proved, and that in such cases statutory damages could not be recovered.[54] In *Universal Pictures Co.* v. *Harold Lloyd Corp.*,[55] the defendant contended that the damages were conjectural and speculative, and that the Court should award statutory damages. The Court held that an—

award of statutory damages in the terms of the statute is proper only in the absence of proof of actual damages and profits. The [lower] court having found the extent of both, the point fails.

[44] Patent cases to this effect: *City of Elizabeth* v. *Am. Nicholson Pavement Co.*, 97 U.S. 126 (1878); *Stearns-Roger Mfg. Co.* v. *Ruth*, 87 F. 2d 35 (10th Cir. 1936); *Stromberg Motor Devices Co.* v. *Zenith-Detroit Corp.*, 73 F. 2d 62 (2d Cir. 1934), cert. dismissed 294 U.S. 735 (1935). Copyright cases: *Sammons* v. *Larkin*, 38 F. Supp. 649 (D. Mass. 1941), see also *Sammons* v. *Colonial Press*, infra, note 62; *Alfred Bell and Co.* v. *Catalda Fine Arts*, 86 F. Supp. 399 (S.D.N.Y. 1949).
[45] *Sammons* v. *Larkin*, supra, note 44.
[46] Ibid., citing patent cases.
[47] *Washingtonian Pub. Co.* v. *Pearson*, 140 F. 2d 465 (D.C. Cir. 1944); *Lundberg* v. *Welles*, 93 F. Supp. 359, (S.D.N.Y. 1950).
[48] 119 F. Supp. 324 (E.D.N.Y. 1954). A motion to strike demand for jury trial with respect to damages was denied, even though plaintiffs were willing to waive all claims to damages other than statutory minimum of $250, in *Chappell and Co.* v. *Cavalier Cafe, Inc.*, 13 F.R.D. 321 (Civ. No. 52-821, D.C. Mass., Nov. 7, 1952, as amended Dec. 30, 1952).
[49] See supra at note 25 for theory of damages plus profits.
[50] 111 F. Supp. 117 (E.D. Mich. 1953).
[51] 110 F. Supp. 913 (N.J. 1953).
[52] 309 U.S. 390 (1940). See supra, notes 35–37.
[53] Then sec. 25(b), Copyright Act of 1909, 35 Stat. 1075 (1909).
[54] The question of proving damages did not arise in this case as only profits were claimed.
[55] 162 F. 2d 354 (9th Cir. 1947).

On the other hand, there were no actual damages to the plaintiff in *Toksvig* v. *Bruce Pub. Co.*,[56] but the defendants' profits were ascertained; nevertheless, statutory damages were awarded. In reviewing the decision of the lower court,[57] the Court said that there was no evidence that the defendants had gained anything by their use of the infringing material, and that the plaintiff had suffered no actual damage; that where actual damages may be difficult to establish or where the copyright proprietor has made no proof of actual damages, the trial judge may, in his discretion, allow statutory damages.

Another example of the difficult choice between actual damages and/or profits on the one side, and statutory damages on the other, is presented by *Woolworth Co.* v. *Contemporary Arts.*[58] The Supreme Court[59] affirmed the judgment of the lower court awarding statutory damages in the following language:

> We think that the statute empowers the trial court in its sound exercise of judicial discretion to determine whether on all the facts a recovery upon proven profits and damages or one estimated within the statutory limits is more just.

Under this holding a trial judge would be free to decide whether, as a matter of fairness, he prefers statutory damages to proven damages and/or profits. This seems to contradict *Sheldon* v. *Metro-Goldwyn Pictures.*[60] In both cases profits had been proved. Mr. Justice Jackson, speaking for the majority in the *Woolworth* case, distinguished the *Sheldon* case because in that case the success of the picture had been largely due to factors not contributed by the infringement. The *Woolworth* case was not held to present such a question. Mr. Justice Black, in a dissenting opinion,[61] pointed out that the rule in the *Sheldon* case should be applied, and that the "in lieu" clause should not be invoked where profits had been proved.[62] He said:

> This Court should heed the admonition given in the *Sheldon* case to remember that the object of section 101(b) is not to inflict punishment but to award an injured copyright owner that which in fairness is his "and nothing beyond this."[63]

A commentator on the *Woolworth* decision stated:[64]

> The underlying basis of this decision is very similar to that in the *Toksvig* case[65] * * *, i.e., that in order to prevent injustice and a general emasculation

of the protection against infringement offered by the statute a court, in its discretion, may award such damages as are just in view of the particular circumstances of the case.

The *Woolworth* decision fails to determine under which circumstances a court may award statutory damages in preference to actual damages and profits. *In view of the contradiction between the Sheldon and the Woolworth decisions, the meaning of the words "in lieu" in section 101(b) should be more precisely stated in a revised law.*

(b) Measure of damages

Statutory damages serve a duofold purpose: they prohibit the award of merely nominal damages because of the difficulty in proving actual damages and profits

---

[56] 181 F. 2d 664 (7th Cir. 1950).
[57] E.D. Wis. (not reported).
[58] 193 F.2d 162 (1st Cir. 1951), aff'd 344 U.S. 228 (1952).
[59] By Mr. Justice Jackson.
[60] 309 U.S. 390, supra, note 52. See also *Malsed* v. *Marshall Field and Co.*, 96 F. Supp. 372 (Wash. 1951).
[61] In which Mr. Justice Frankfurter concurred.
[62] Quoting Mr. Chief Justice Hughes in the *Sheldon* case, and citing *Davilla* v. *Brunswick-Balke Collender Co.*, 94 F. 2d 567 (2d Cir. 1938), *Sammons* v. *Colonial Press*, 126 F. 2d 341 (1st Cir. 1942), see also *Sammons* v. *Larkin*, supra, notes 24, 44.
[63] In the *Woolworth* case proven profits were $899.16, the award was for $5,000 statutory damages.
[64] 22 Geo. Wash. L. Rev. 763 (1954).
[65] Supra, note 56.

* * *. Secondly, they furnish the deterrence so necessary for prospective infringers * * *.[66]

Ordinarily, the measure of statutory damages is a minimum of $250, and a maximum of $5,000. In the case of a newspaper reproduction of a photograph the minimum is $50 and the maximum $200;[67] in the case of innocent infringement of a nondramatic work by means of a motion picture the maximum is $100,[68] and in the case of innocent infringement of a nondramatic literary work by broadcast the maximum also is $100.[69]

Within these minimum and maximum limits, section 101(b) specifies the following schedule of statutory damages:

First. In the case of a painting, statue, or sculpture, $10 for every infringing copy made or sold by or found in the possession of the infringer or his agents or employees;

Second. In the case of any work enumerated in section 5 of this title, except a painting, statue, or sculpture, $1 for every infringing copy made or sold by or found in the possession of the infringer or his agents or employees;

Third. In the case of a lecture, sermon, or address, $50 for every infringing delivery;

Fourth. In the case of a dramatic or dramatico-musical or choral or orchestral composition, $100 for the first and $50 for every subquent infringing performance; in the case of other musical compositions $10 for every infringing performance;

The reasons for including a minimum damage provision in the law were stated by the Supreme Court in *Douglas* v. *Cunningham*: [70]

The phraseology of the section [sec. 25, Act of 1909, now sec. 101(b)] was adopted to avoid the strictness of construction incident to a law imposing penalties, and to give the owner of a copyright some recompense for injury done him, in a case where the rules of law render difficult or impossible proof of damages or discovery of profits. In this respect the old law was unsatisfactory. In many cases plaintiffs, though proving infringement, were able to recover only nominal damages, in spite of the fact that preparation and trial of the case imposed substantial expense and inconvenience. The ineffectiveness of the remedy encouraged willful and deliberate infringement.

In *Westermann Co.* v. *Dispatch Printing Co.*,[71] an action for an injunction and damages for infringement of illustrations, the Supreme Court held that, where actual damages could not be determined, the court's conception of what was just, would be the measure of damages, but with the express qualification that the assessment must be within the minimum and maximum limits prescribed by the statute. The Court was confronted with two problems in regard to the total minimum damages: whether there were seven infringements, or only one, and whether the damages should have been assessed at not less than $250 for each. It was held that there had been seven infringements, and that the minimum applied to each infringement.[72]

In *Jewell-LaSalle Realty Co.* v. *Buck* [73] the Supreme Court held that the statutory amount of $10 damages for each performance applied

[66] Warner, op.cit., supra, note 32 at 662.
[67] 17 U.S.C. 101(b).
[68] 17 U.S.C. 101(b) as amended by the act of Aug. 24, 1912, 37 Stat. 489.
[69] 17 U.S.C. 1(c) as amended by the act of July 17, 1952, 66 Stat. 752.
[70] 294 U.S. 207 (1935).
[71] 249 U.S. 100 (1919).
[72] The district court had found seven infringements, but had awarded $10 nominal damages for each. The circuit court, 233 Fed. 609 (6th Cir. 1916) had found only one infringement but had awarded the $250 minimum.   See also: *Toksvig* v. *Bruce Pub. Co.*, 181 F. 2d 664 (7th Cir. 1950); *Amsterdam Syndicate* v. *Fuller*, 154 F. 2d 342 (8th Cir. 1946); *Remick Music Corp.* v. *Interstate Hotel Co.*, 58 F. Supp. 523 (Nebr. 1944), aff'd 157 F. 2d 744 (8th Cir. 1946), cert. den. 329 U.S. 809 (1947); *Widenski* v. *Shapiro, Bernstein*, 147 F. 2d 909 (1st Cir. 1945); *Washingtonian Pub. Co.* v. *Pearson* 140 F. 2d 465 (D.C. Cir.1944); *Dreamland Ballroom* v. *Shapiro, Bernstein*, 36 F. 2d 354 (7th Cir. 1929); *Witmark and Sons* v. *Calloway*, 22 F. 2d 412 (Tenn. 1927).
[73] 283 U.S. 202 (1931).

only where more than 25 infringing performances were proved, and that the schedules in section 101(b) [74] appeared—

> to have been inserted merely as an aid to the Court in awarding such damages as "shall appear to be just" * * * If, as applied to musical compositions, the provisions of the entire section have proved unreasonable, the remedy lies with Congress.

In *Washingtonian Publishing Co.* v. *Pearson* [75] the Court of Appeals for the District of Columbia affirmed the judgment of the lower court [76] in refusing to impose statutory damages against the printer of the infringing work, because it had been shown that there were neither damages to the plaintiffs nor profits to the defendant printer.

The rule established in the *Jewell-LaSalle* case that the award may not be less than $250, and that the schedules in section 101(b) serve only for guidance to compute the damages exceeding this minimum, applies whenever statutory damages are awarded.

As to the maximum of $5,000, the Supreme Court held in the *Westermann* case: [77]

> There is no uncertainty as to what that measure [of statutory damages] is or as to its limitations. The statute says, first, that the damages are to be such as to the court shall appear to be just; * * * that in no case shall they be more than $5,000, except that for a newspaper reproduction of a copyrighted photograph they shall not be more than $200 * * * Within these limitations the court's discretion and sense of justice are controlling, but it has no discretion when proceeding under this provision to go outside of them.

The rationale of the *Westermann* case was also applied in *Douglas* v. *Cunningham*.[78] Thus, the maximum established in section 101(b) seems to be as binding on the courts as is the minimum.

The maximum of $5,000 does not apply to actions for infringement which occur after actual notice has been served on the defendant.[79] In *Shellberg* v. *Empringham*,[80] where defendent had actual notice of the copyright, the plaintiff asked for $50,000 damages—

> one-half of that sum to be for infringement, and the remainder for damages arising through unfair competition, and the violation of defendants of the New York civil rights law.

The court allowed a recovery of $1 for each of the infringing books to the extent of $8,000 in lieu of actual damages and profits.

In *Turner and Dahnken* v. *Crowley* [81] the district court awarded $7,000 statutory damages for distribution of 7,000 infringing copies of a musical composition after notice. The circuit court reduced this amount to $560 to equal the potential profits, because "the duty of the court was to award damages as justified by the nature and circumstances of the case."[82]

In *Sebring Pottery Co.* v. *Steubenville Pottery Co.*[83] the infringement was deliberate and continued after notice. The defendant showed a loss of $923.23. The court found the proof of actual damages and

---

[74] First to fourth.
[75] 140 F. 2d 465 (D.C. Cir. 1944).
[76] 56 U.S.P.Q. 23 (D.C. 1942). Appellants had been awarded profits made by appellee authors. The decision has been criticised in 18 S. Cal. L. Rev. 50 (1944) as contrary to the *Jewell-LaSalle* decision. The *Jewell-LaSalle* case, however, may be distinguished because there were no provable damages or profits. The D.C. Court of Appeals in *Washingtonian* case held that, as there were proven profits in the case of the authors and demonstrably no profits in the case of the printer, to impose statutory damages on the printer would amount to a penalty. Accord: *Gordon* v. *Weir*, 111 F. Supp. 117 (E.D. Mich. 1953).
[77] Supra at note 71.
[78] Supra at note 70. See also *Amsterdam Syndicate* v. *Fuller*, 154 F.2d 342 (8th Cir. 1946).
[79] First paragraph of section 101(b), last sentence.
[80] 36 F. 2d 991 (S.D.N.Y. 1929).
[81] 252 Fed. 749 (9th Cir. 1918), rehearing denied.
[82] Testimony showed that the profit would have been 8 cents per copy, or $560 for 7,000 copies.
[83] 9 F. Supp. 384 (Ohio 1934).

profits unsatisfactory and awarded statutory damages. However, because the plaintiff had offered to settle the case before the defendants' accounting, and that offer of a settlement had been voluntarily placed in the record, the court did not award $1 for every infringing copy, but fixed the award to the plaintiff at $2,500—the amount at which the plaintiff had been willing to settle.

These latter two decisions show that, even if the infringement occurred after notice, where applications of the schedules in section 101(b) would lead to exorbitant statutory damages in comparison with actual damages and would, in fact, amount to a penalty, the courts, as permitted by section 101(b), exercise their discretion in arriving at an equitable result.

(c) Multiple infringements

In the *Westermann* case [84] six of the plaintiff's copyrighted illustrations were published separately by the infringer, five of them once and the sixth one twice. The court held that:

the statute says that the liability * * * is imposed for infringing "the copyright" in any copyright "work". The words are in the singular, not the plural. Each copyright is treated as a distinct entity, and the infringement of it as a distinct wrong * * *. Infringement of several copyrights is not put on the same level with the infringement of one. On the contrary, the plain import of the statute is that this liability attaches in respect of each copyright that is infringed * * *.[85]

In *Burndy Engineering Co.* v. *Sheldon Service Corp.*,[86] a catalog, infringing three copyrights, was published in two separate editions, the second of which had three printings. In addition, there was a separate printing of 500 copies of an infringing page. Statutory damages were allowed as follows: each of the complete printings was treated as a separate infringement, making 12 in all. For each infringement minimum damages were awarded, or a total of $3,000. In addition, $1 per copy was awarded for each of the 500 separate pages. On appeal the judgment was affirmed.[87]

While the awarding of statutory damages in cases of multiple infringement has not created any difficulties if the infringement is by copying in printed publications, there is a problem in cases of infringing performances of musical or dramatic works in network broadcasts. In *Law* v. *National Broadcasting Co.*[88] the plaintiff's composition was performed by NBC on three occasions, with chain hookups of 67, 66 and 85 stations, 218 stations in all. Damages of $2,180 were awarded, on the basis of $10 for each of 218 performances.[89] In *Select Theatres Corp.* v. *The Ronzoni Macaroni Co.*[90] the court held each broadcast performance of a scene from a play a separate infringement.[91] Thus, in the cases involving copying, the statutory damages were computed on the basis of only a single cause

---

[84] Supra at notes 71, 77.
[85] In *Schellberg* v. *Empringham*, 36 F. 2d 991, supra, note 80, three copyrights were infringed. However, the court held that the same matter, in substance, was the subject of three copyrights, and it was difficult to apportion the infringement to the respective copyrights. Therefore, it seemed just not to accumulate liabilities as to the three copyrights. In *Cravens* v. *Retail Credit Men's Ass'n*, 26 F. 2d 833 (Tenn. 1924) replacing an obsolete sheet in an infringing book by another infringing sheet was not held to constitute a separate and distinct infringement. See also *Hillyer* v. *Nash-Kelvinator Corp.*, 79 U.S.P.Q. 50 (N.D. Ill. 1948).
[86] 39 F. Supp. 274 (E.D.N.Y. 1941).
[87] 127 F. 2d 661 (2d Cir. 1942). In *Cory* v. *Physical Culture Hotel, Inc.*, 14 F. Supp. 977 (W.D.N.Y. 1936) the court discussed the question whether seven reproductions of a photograph in seven issues of a magazine constituted seven infringements or one. Without deciding the question, the court awarded $5,000—the maximum for one infringement. The Second Circuit Court affirming, also refused to decide the question, 88 F. 2d 411 (1937).
[88] 51 F. Supp. 798 (S.D.N.Y. 1943).
[89] Relying on *Jewell-LaSalle Realty Co.* v. *Buck*, 283 U.S. 202 (1931).
[90] 59 U.S.P.Q. 288 (S.D.N.Y. 1943).
[91] But see *Cory* v. *Physical Culture Hotel*, supra, note 87.

of action for each infringing publication with due consideration of the size of each edition, while in cases involving infringing performances by radio broadcast, the decision in the *Jewell-LaSalle* case apparently furnished authority for holdings that a performance by each station constituted a separate infringement. Such decisions have sometimes awarded what may be considered disproportionately high damages.[92]

In *Tiffany Productions* v. *Dewing*,[93] a motion picture exhibitor, who was licensed to show the picture at certain times and places, exhibited at other times and places after being notified in writing, not to do so. The court also relied on the *Jewell-LaSalle* decision. As no claim was made for more than the statutory damages of $250 for each infringement, the court so decreed.

Thus, a difficulty in computing statutory damages seems to appear mainly in the case of chain broadcasts, and special consideration may need to be given to this question.[94]

(d) Intent to infringe

In several cases the courts only reluctantly allowed the statutory minimum,[95] because there was no deliberate intent to infringe. In *Dreamland Ball Room* v. *Shapiro, Bernstein and Co.*[96] the owner of a ballroom hired an orchestra, but exercised no control over the selection of musical pieces to be played, and did not know that some of these selections were copyrighted and played without a license. In awarding statutory minimum damages, the court stated its reluctance in the following language:

Appellants' argument in support of their position respecting the amount of damages [i.e., that under the circumstances an award of $250 was excessive], has much appeal. But, unfortunately for them, there are too many judicial precedents which we can neither hurdle nor sidestep, to permit us to adopt their construction of a statute which has been somewhat aptly described as "inartificially drawn".

Minimum damages of $250 may be questionable in instances where the infringer is innocent and makes no profit, and the copyright proprietor suffers no damages.[97] In *Fred Fisher Inc.* v. *Dillingham*[98] an action for infringement of a musical composition for plagiarism of the accompaniment to the introduction, the composer Jerome Kern asserted that copying, if any, had been done unconsciously. Judge Learned Hand expressed his reluctance to award the minimum under such circumstances:

[92] In the *Select Theatres* case (supra, note 90) damages were computed on the basis of $250 per performance as follows: For performing 20 episodes, damages of $750 were awarded against the sponsor, the leading actor and one of the broadcasters, jointly and severally; $750 against another broadcaster; $750 against the leading actor for stage productions; $4,250 against the sponsor, the leading actor and one of the broadcasters, jointly and severally, $4,250 against the second broadcaster, and $750 more against the leading actor—$11,500 in all.
[93] 50 F.2d 911 (Md. 1931). Accord: *Vitaphone Corp. and Vitagraph, Inc.* v. *Hutchinson Amusement Corp.*, 19 F.Supp. 359 (Mass. 1937). See also: *Twentieth Century Fox Film Corp.* v. *Peoples Theatres of Ala.*, 24 F. Supp. 793 (Ala. 1938).
[94] By the consent decree of 1950 (Civ. Action No. 13-95, amended final judgment, S.D.N.Y., Mar 14, 1950, superseding the consent decree of 1941) ASCAP was prevented from requiring separate licenses from network stations (V,(A)) and was ordered to issue motion picture producers a single license for motion picture performances, covering the United States and possessions (V,(C)). The consent decree had far reaching consequences, particularly in regard to possible actions for multiple infringements. The permission of "clearance at the source" applies also to manufacturers and distributors of transcriptions and to advertisers and sponsors thereof, and to producers of television films (V,(B)). See also Hearings on H.R. 12549 (Vestal bill), 71st Cong., 3d sess. (1931), statement by W. S. Hedges for NAB, 42 at 50.
[95] *North and Judd Mfg. Co.* v. *Krischer's Mfg. Co.*, 11 F. Supp. 739 (Conn. 1935); *Witmark and Sons* v. *Calloway*, 22 F. 2d 412 (E.D. Tenn. 1927); *Witmark and Sons* v. *Pastime Amusement Co.*, 298 Fed. 470 (S.C. 1924); *Haas* v. *Leo Feist*, 234 Fed. 105 (S.D.N.Y. 1916).
[96] 36 F. 2d 354 (7th Cir. 1929).
[97] Warner, op. cit., supra, note 32 at 663 said: "The minimum damage clause has been used on more than one occasion by the various performing rights' societies as an effective club to compel consumers to take out music licenses." See also Bouve, "Comments on Suggested Copyright Legislation," III J.D.C. Bar Ass'n, 29 (1936).
[98] 298 Fed. 145 (S.D.N.Y. 1924).

* * * As for damages, it seems to me absurd to suggest that [plaintiff] has suffered any injury. * * * The controversy is a "trivial pother" [cit. om.], a mere point of honor, of scarcely more than irritation, * * *.

However, section 25 * * * [sec. 101(b)] fixes a minimum of $250, which is absolute in all cases. * * * Therefore I must and do award that sum as damages, * * *.

This question will be further discussed in connection with past attempts at revising the law.[99]

(e) Infringement of musical recordings

Subsection (e) of section 101 contains special provisions for infringement by unauthorized manufacture, use,[100] or sale of mechanical recordings of musical works. No actual damages or profits may be recovered, but the plaintiff is—

entitled to recover in lieu of profits and damages a royalty as provided in section 1, subsection (e) of this title.

Section 1(e) provides for a statutory royalty of 2 cents "on each such part manufactured." If, in the absence of a license agreement, a user fails to file a notice of intention to use—

the court may, in its discretion, in addition [to the royalties] award the complainant a further sum, not to exceed three times the amount provided by section 1, subsection (e) * * *, by way of damages, and not as a penalty * * *.

Section 1(e) specifies a 30-day limit after demand for payment of royalties due, in default of which the court may enter judgment awarding up to three times the royalties due, taxable costs and reasonable counsel fee.[101] But there is no time limit for filing a notice of intention to use. This lack of a time limit was exploited in *Ricordi and Co.* v. *Columbia Gramaphone Co.*[102] where the defendant became the plaintiff's licensee pending the appeal by paying royalties.[103]

The special damage provisions for mechanical reproduction of music are treated in a separate study on "The Compulsory License Provisions" and will not be considered further here.

III. PROCEEDINGS FOR INFRINGEMENT IN OTHER COUNTRIES

Copyright laws in other countries generally have provisions for awarding to the injured party damages and/or profits.[104] For purposes of comparison, it will be sufficient to examine some of the representative laws.

Apparently, no other country has an exact equivalent to the "in lieu" provision of section 101(b). Claims for damages in civil actions abroad are limited to actual damages and/or profits. But many laws also provide for punitive damages the amount of which depends largely on the presence or absence of intent to infringe, and lack of good faith may cause an increase in the award of such damages.[105]

---

[99] Infra V, 2.

[100] "The word 'use' in this clause does not refer to the right of publicly performing the copyrighted musical composition for profit, but applies only to such use as would have been authorized had the user been a licensee of the mechanical reproduction right." Ball, op. cit., supra, note 26 at 464. See also *Northern Music Corp.* v. *King Record Distrib. Co.*, 105 F. Supp. 393 (S.D.N.Y. 1952); *Irving Berlin, Inc.* v. *Daigle*, 31 F. 2d 832 (5th Cir. 1929).

[101] 17 U.S.C. 1(e), next to last paragraph.

[102] 258 Fed. 72 (S.D.N.Y. 1919), aff'd 263 Fed. 354 (2d Cir. 1920). Accord: *Miller* v. *Goody*, 125 F. Supp. 348 (S.D.N.Y. 1954), 139 F. Supp. 176 (S.D.N.Y. 1956).

[103] Shafter, "Musical Copyright," 344 (1939), calls this method of shifting from an infringer to a licensee an "ingenious method of evasion."

[104] See UNESCO Copyright Bulletin, II No. 2-3, 118 et. seq. (1949).

[105] Ibid. at 120.

While penal damages may or may not accrue to the copyright proprietor (civil damages always accrue to him), and the foreign methods thus vary from ours, the purpose of such penal damages and of the statutory damages in our law is much the same, namely, to act as a deterrent on willful infringement, and to make infringement expensive.

1. *The British Commonwealth*

(a) *Great Britain* [106]

The Copyright Act, 1911, gives several civil remedies for infringement: Actual damages under section 6(1) of the Act, the measure of which is the depreciation caused by the infringement to the value of the copyright as a chose in action;[107] damages for detinue or conversion under section 7 of the Act, the measure of which is the actual value of the article;[108] an accounting of profits, instead of damages for infringement or conversion, as a remedy incidental to the right to an injunction.[109] Except for the forfeitures under the Fine Arts Act, 1862, fines in criminal actions do not accrue to the injured party. However, the method of their computation is similar to that of the forfeitures under the U.S. copyright acts before 1909, and the amounts of the fines seem of interest for purposes of comparison.

Section 11 of the Copyright Act, 1911 provides remedies against infringement of works other than musical works.[110] Anyone who knowingly makes, sells, distributes, publicly exhibits, or imports any infringing copy of a copyrighted work, is liable to a fine not exceeding 40 shillings for every copy, and not exceeding 50 pounds in respect to the same transaction; anyone who knowingly makes or has in his possession any plate for the purpose of making infringing copies, or knowingly and for his private profit causes any unauthorized public performance of a copyrighted work to be made, is liable to a fine not exceeding 50 pounds.

The Musical Copyright Act, 1906, provides in section 1 that anyone who prints, reproduces, sells, exposes, offers, or has in his possession for sale, any pirated copies of, or plates for printing musical works shall be liable to a fine not exceeding 5 pounds, unless he shows that he acted innocently, and on second or subsequent conviction, to a fine not exceeding 10 pounds.

Under section 7 of the Fine Arts Copyright Act, 1862,[111] the act of fraudulently affixing a signature to, or selling, publishing, exhibiting, or disposing of a work of art or photograph, subjects the offender to a penalty not exceeding 10 pounds, or double the full price of the copies of the infringed work. This sum is forfeited to the person aggrieved. Where double the value of the copies is less than 10 pounds, that amount may still be recovered;[112] where double the value exceeds 10 pounds, then any sum up to such double value may be recovered.[113] This seems to be the only provision in the British law which expressly provides for statutory minimum damages.

---

[106] Copyright Act, 1911, 1 and 2 Geo. 5, c. 46; Fine Arts Copyright Act, 1862, 25 and 26 Vict., ch. 68; Musical Copyright Act, 1906, 6 Edw. 7, ch. 36.

[107] Copinger and Skone James, "Law of Copyright," 164 (hereinafter Copinger) (8th ed. 1948).

[108] Copinger at 164, 166.

[109] Copinger at 169. The copyright bill, 1955 (4 Eliz. 2), would deny damages in cases of innocent infringement, but provides for an accounting of profits (sec. 17(3)). In cases of flagrant infringement the court may increase the damages to the extent he may consider appropriate (sec. 17(4)).

[110] For musical works the Musical Copyright Acts, 1902 and 1906 (see supra, note 106), r main in force: Copyright Act, 1911 (sec. 11(4)).

[111] Supra, note 106.

[112] Copinger at 188.

[113] Ibid.

(b) Canada [114]

Section 25 of the Canadian Copyright Act provides that anyone knowingly making, selling, distributing, exhibiting, or importing copies of a copyrighted work shall be liable to a fine not exceeding $10 for every copy, but not exceeding $200 in respect of the same transaction. Anyone who knowingly makes or has in his possession any plate for the making of infringing copies of a copyrighted work, or who knowingly and for his private profit causes any unauthorized public performance of a copyrighted work to be made is liable to a fine not exceeding $200.

Section 26(1) provides that anyone who, without the written consent of the copyright owner or his legal representative, knowingly performs or causes to be performed publicly and without authority for private profit, the whole or part of a dramatic, operatic or musical work, shall be liable to a fine not exceeding $250.

Section 26(2) provides that anyone who, without authority, makes changes, or causes changes to be made, in the title or the name of the author of a dramatic, operatic, or musical work, or in such a work itself, where such changes are made for the purposes of an unauthorized public performance for profit, shall be liable to a fine not exceeding $500.[115]

In comparing the amounts payable as fines under the laws of the British Commonwealth with the minimum and maximum damages of the U.S. copyright law, it must be remembered that, in cases of intentional infringements, these fines are due in addition to damages or profits and/or other civil remedies.[116]

2. France

The French Criminal Code of 1810[117] provides in part as follows:

Article 427. An infringer or importer [of infringing copies] shall be subject to a fine of not less than 24,000 and not more than 480,000 francs; a seller shall be subject to a fine of not less than 6,000 and not more than 120,000 francs.

A writ of seizure shall issue against the infringer as well as against the importer and the seller. Plates, moulds or matrices for making infringing copies shall be seized.

Article 428. Any director or manager of a theater, or any association of actors who cause to be represented in their theater any dramatic works in violation of the laws and regulations concerning copyright, shall be punishable by a fine of not less than 12,000 and not more than 120,000 francs and by seizure of the receipts.

Article 429. * * * the proceeds from the seizure, or the seized receipts shall be remitted to the copyright proprietor and applied to the damages he has suffered; the remainder of the damages, or if there be no sale of the seized articles or seizure of receipts the entire damages, shall be awarded in the usual mamner.

The law of 1895[118] provides for a fine of not less than 4,000 and not more than 72,000 francs for fraudulently affixing a false name on a work of art or music, or knowingly selling such fraudulent work.

---

[114] Copyright Act, 1921, ch. 32, R.S.C. 1927, as amended by ch. 8, 1931, ch. 18, 1935, ch. 28, 1936, ch. 27, 1938.

[115] Other British Dominions have similar provisions. Australia: Copyright Act, 1912, as modified up to Dec. 16, 1950, sec. 14-21 [secs. 19, 20, repealed]. New Zealand: Copyright Act, 1913, as amended up to Oct. 6, 1924, secs. 14-20. Union of South Africa: the Union of South Africa Act, 1916, as amended up to Apr. 28, 1951, sec. 148.

[116] Copinger at 182; Fox, "Canadian Law of Copyright," 501 (1944).

[117] Code Penal (ed. Petits Codes Dalloz, 1953). Arts. 425 to 429 of the Criminal Code abrogate Art. 3, Law of Jan. 13, 1791, Art. 4, 5, Law of July 19, 1793, Art. 41 et seq., Decree of Feb. 5, 1810 (translation of Art. 427, 428, 429 by W.S.).

The French Draft Law of 1953 would modify Art. 428 of the Penal Code to the effect that an amount equal to the receipts obtained from the infringement would be seized for the benefit of the author or his assignees (Art. 74, 75).

[118] "Loi Sur les Fraudes en Matiere Artistique," Feb. 9, 1895, as amended by Art. 70 of the Finance Act of Apr. 14, 1952. The original amounts were 16 and 3,000 francs, respectively.

These fines are imposed in addition to damages and other remedies to which the copyright proprietor is entitled in a civil action.[119]

3. Germany

The German law [120] provides for a fine up to 3,000 marks for intentional unauthorized reproduction or distribution of a copyrighted work,[121] or for intentional unauthorized performance of a dramatic or musical work.[122] Unauthorized changes in a work, its title or the author statement are punishable by a fine up to 300 marks.[123] Unauthorized reproduction or public performance by mechanical instrument or by motion picture is punishable by a fine up to 1,000 marks.[124] These fines are imposed in addition to the damages and other remedies to which the copyright proprietor is entitled in a civil action.[125] Unauthorized intentional publication of the essential contents of an unpublished work is punishable by a fine up to 1,500 marks.[126] The copyright proprietor may also demand for such unauthorized communication an award of penal damages up to 6,000 marks,[127] and the same amount may be awarded in the case of a work of art or photography.[128] Criminal prosecution in all these cases is initiated by a complaint of the copyright proprietor.[129] The award of penal damages [130] is "in lieu" of actual damages in a civil action, and excludes bringing a civil action for damages.[131] Voigtlaender-Elster [132] says:

Such an award is in the nature of damages, and not a penalty; it is measured not by the degree of fault, but by the extent of the damages suffered * * *. If penal damages are not awarded, civil action may be brought. If insufficient penal damages are awarded, no civil action may be brought for higher damages; an award for actual damages in a civil action does not exclude the award of higher penal damages in a criminal action, but the damages awarded in the civil action must be taken into consideration.

Thus, it appears that, where a civil action precedes the criminal action, the remedies are cumulative. In the reverse sequence, this is not the case.

4. Italy [133]

Article 158 provides that any person injured by an infringing act, may sue for damages or for the destruction of infringing material. Under article 159 such person may ask that the infringing copies or contrivances liable to destruction be delivered to him, and their appraised value applied to the reparation due him.

---

[119] Law of 1895, Art. 1. For comparison, the fines in Art. 427 of the Criminal Code were originally 100 to 2,000 francs (now 24,000 to 480,000 francs).

[120] Law on Copyright, in Literary and Musical Works of June 19, 1901 [hereinafter LUG]; Law on Copyright in Works of Art and Photography of Jan. 9, 1910 [hereinafter KUG]; both as amended up to Dec. 13, 1934 and May 12, 1940, respectively. The draft law of 1954 would eliminate all fixed amounts, and refers simply to "fine."

[121] LUG, sec. 38 (1).

[122] LUG, sec. 38 (2).

[123] LUG, sec. 38, second paragraph.

[124] KUG, sec. 32. There is also a fine up to 1,000 marks for falsely affixing the name of an author to the copy of a work, or publicly exhibiting a person's portrait (KUG, sec. 33), and a fine up to 300 marks for falsely affixing an author's name to an original work (KUG, sec. 34).

[125] Voigtlaender-Elster, "Gesetze Betreffend das Urheberrecht," 160 (4th ed. 1952) (Copyright Laws, Annotations). Under the draft law of 1954, the injured party may demand either damages or profits (sec. 10 (3)).

[126] LUG, sec. 39.

[127] LUG, sec. 40.

[128] KUG, sec. 35.

[129] LUG, sec. 45; KUG sec. 41.

[130] See supra, note 127.

[131] LUG, sec. 40, second paragraph; KUG, sec. 35, second paragraph.

[132] Op. cit., supra, note 125 at 166 (transl.).

[133] Law No. 633 of Apr. 22, 1941, as amended to Aug. 23, 1946.

Article 171 provides for fines of from 500 to 20,000 lire for unlawful reproduction, distribution, performance [134] or recording of a copyrighted work. If the work is not intended for public disclosure, the minimum fine for infringement is 5,000 lire.[135] In cases of infringements committed negligently, the maximum fine is 10,000 lire.[136] In cases where a publisher does not pay the fee due the state for the assistance of the authors' fund,[137] the fine is 2,000 lire.[138] The fines specified above apply where the unlawful act committed does not constitute a more serious offense under the Penal Code or other laws.[139].

5. Netherlands [140]

Article 28 grants the copyright proprietor the right to seize infringing copies or fees paid for admission to an infringing performance. The copyright proprietor also has the right to institute criminal proceedings or civil proceedings for damages.[141] Notwithstanding an assignment of copyright, the author retains the right to bring an action for damages.[142]

Any person who intentionally infringes a copyright is punishable by a fine not to exceed 5,000 guilders. Knowingly distributing or offering for sale an infringing work subjects the infringer to a fine not to exceed 2,000 guilders.[143] Anyone who intentionally and unlawfully makes changes in a copyrighted work, or in the title or the indication of the author of such a work, is punishable by a fine not to exceed 5,000 guilders.[144] Unauthorized public display of a portrait is punishable by a fine not to exceed 200 guilders.[145]

6. Sweden [146]

Unlawful reproduction, distribution, importation or performance [147] of a copyrighted work is punishable by a fine of from 5 to 2,000 kronor.[148] Unlawfully made copies are subject to destruction, or they may be delivered to the injured person and their value deducted from the damages to which he is entitled.[149] Anyone who unlawfully alters a work or the author's name is subject to a fine of from 5 to 200 and 5 to 100 kronor, respectively.[150] Anyone who commits any such infringing act is liable to pay compensation to the injured person for losses and mental distress or other detriment caused by the infringement; and the minimum compensation is 15 kronor.[151] Where the infringer has incurred liability and profited by his unlawful act, compensation not exceeding the profit must be paid.[152]

---

[134] Including broadcasting and motion pictures.
[135] Art. 171(f), second paragraph.
[136] Art. 172,
[137] See Art. 177, 178.
[138] Art. 172, last paragraph.
[139] Art. 173.
[140] Law of 1912 as amended to Feb. 11, 1932.
[141] Art. 28, last paragraph.
[142] Art. 27.
[143] Art. 32.
[144] Art. 34.
[145] Art. 35.
[146] Law No. 381 of 1919 as amended to Apr. 24, 1931.
[147] Including broadcasting and motion pictures.
[148] Sec. 24.
[149] Sec. 25.
[150] Secs. 26, 27.
[151] Sec. 27a, first paragraph.
[152] Sec. 27a, second paragraph.

7. *Guatemala* [153]

The Guatemalan law provides for independent civil and criminal actions.[154] In a civil action the copyright owner, after expert valuation, may request indemnity in respect to damages, including moral damage, if the violation took place willfully or negligently.[155] In the case of an infringement committed in good faith by way of a public performance of a work, the copyright owner may request that the net proceeds be turned over to him.[156] Fines of from 300 to 1,000 quetzales may be imposed if the infringement is fraudulent or caused by gross negligence.[157] Reproduction of a work without mentioning the source may be punished by a fine of from 100 to 500 quetzales.[158]

8. *Bolivia* [159]

Infringers of copyright forfeit the copies illegally published which, together with a sum equal to the value of any copies which may have been sold, are to be delivered to the injured party. If the number of copies illegally published and distributed is not known, the infringer is also liable for a sum equal to the value of 500 copies.[160] Unauthorized public performance of a theatrical work subjects the infringer to a fine of from 5,000 to 50,000 Bolivianos which sum is used for the encouragement of national culture.[161] In criminal proceedings copyright infringement may be punished by a fine equal to four times the amount of the injury caused.[162]

9. *Mexico*

The Mexican Copyright Law [163] provides for fines ranging from 5 to 5,000 pesos, depending on the type and gravity of the infringement. Article 128 of the copyright law provides that the infringing work, or devices for making it, shall be seized as implements of a crime, and, under article 129 such articles may be sold by decree of the court. According to article 132, from the proceeds of such sale shall be paid: first the damages to which the copyright owner is entitled, next the fines imposed.[164]

As for compensatory damages, the Mexican copyright law contains a "minimum damage" provision: [165] Damages shall never be less then 40 percent of the retail sales price of the work, multiplied by the number of copies in the infringing edition. If the exact number of copies cannot be ascertained, it is estimated by judicial decree after hearing the evidence of experts. While this provision contains no fixed amount, it offers a minimum standard for the awarding of damages, regardless of actual damages.

---

[153] Law No. 1037, of Feb. 8–11, 1954.
[154] Art. 29.
[155] Art. 21(4).
[156] Art. 21(5).
[157] Art. 26.
[158] Art. 27.
[159] Law of 1909, as amended to Jan. 15, 1945.
[160] Art. 14.
[161] Art. 21.
[162] Penal Code of Nov. 6, 1834, Art. 658.
[163] Federal Copyright Law of Dec. 31, 1947, as amended to Dec. 31, 1951.
[164] This provision is comparable to Art. 429, French Criminal Code, A, III, 2, supra.
[165] Art. 133.

10. Summary of provisions in foreign laws

The provisions of the foreign laws examined which most closely resemble the minimum and maximum damage provision of the U.S. law, are found in the British Fine Arts Act, 1862, in the "German Copyright Laws in Literary Works," and in "Works of Art," respectively, and in the Mexican copyright law. The British Fine Arts Act contains a minimum damage provision (10 pounds), but no fixed statutory maximum (double the value of the copies).[166] The German laws have a maximum (penal damages of 6,000 marks). The Mexican law has what may be called a minimum damage provision (40 percent of the retail sales price).

Damages are frequently recoverable in criminal proceedings but they accrue to the aggrieved copyright proprietor, not to the State. Under some laws there is neither a minimum nor a maximum amount, but the proceeds from the sale of copies or from gate receipts seized in a criminal action are applied to compensate the copyright proprietor.[167] In many foreign countries, actions for copyright infringement are, at least in part, criminal actions. The damage provisions do not always contain a sharp dividing line between civil and criminal proceedings,[168] and the copyright proprietor does not exclusively depend on a civil action for recovery. The effect of these provisions resembles to some extent that of the "in lieu" clause of section 101(b), title 17, United States Code.

IV. PREVIOUS REVISIONS OF THE DAMAGE PROVISIONS

Since the Copyright Act of 1909 was enacted, two amendments to its damage provisions have been passed: The first introduced a maximum damage provision of $100 in the case of innocent infringement of undramatized or nondramatic works by means of motion pictures [169] and the second limited damages to $100 in cases of innocent infringement of a nondramatic literary work by broadcasting.[170] These two amendments have much in common. Both concern damages for infringement by a medium of mass communication. Both provide for low maximum damages for innocent infringement.[171]

---

[166] Supra, A, III, 1(a).

[167] E.g., French Criminal Code, Art. 429; Art. 54, Swiss Copyright Law.

[168] 17 U.S.C. 104 provides a strict delineation: Willful infringement for profit is deemed a misdemeanor and punishable by fine. There is no possible advantage to the copyright owner in such a criminal proceeding. For a detailed analysis of the distinction between methods of enforcement here and abroad see statement by Gabriel L. Hess, on behalf of motion picture distributors, "Hearings Before Committee on Patents on Revision of Copyright Laws," 74th Cong., 2d sess., 1297 at 1321 (1936).

[169] Amendment to act of Mar. 4, 1909, sec. 25, act of Aug. 24, 1912, 37 Stat. 489 (now 17 U.S.C. 101).

[170] 17 U.S.C. 1(c) as amended by the act of July 17, 1952, 66 Stat. 752.

[171] Concerning the act of July 17, 1952, supra S. Rep. No. 1778, 82d Cong., 2d sess., 3 (1952) states as follows: "The attorney for the broadcasters also testified [Hearings Before Subcommittee No. 3 on the Judiciary on H.R. 3589, 82d Cong. 1st sess., 15 et. seq. (1951)] that his association recommends that the $250 minimum statutory damage clause be replaced by a provision whereby the infringer would be liable for actual damages. It is believed that the subject of damages which affects many of the other provisions of the copyright law requires study as a separate problem or in relation to a complete revision of that law." The statutory damages were assessed at a low figure for innocent infringement by broadcast of non-dramatic literary works, thereby creating a second instance of a distinction between innocent and willful infringement.

V. PREVIOUS PROPOSALS FOR THE REVISION OF THE DAMAGE PROVISIONS

1. *The Vestal bills* [172]

(a) *The damage provisions*

Section 16 of the 1926 and 1930 bills provided in part as follows: If any person shall infringe * * *, such person shall be liable—

*   *   *   *   *   *   *

(b) To pay such damages to the owner of the right infringed as he may have suffered due to the infringement as well as all the profits which the infringer shall have made from such infringement; and in proving profits the plaintiff shall be required to prove only sales, rentals, license fees and/or any other revenue derived from any disposition of an infringing work, and the defendant shall be required to prove every element of cost which he claims;

(c) To pay, at the option of the owner of the right infringed, in lieu of actual damages and profits, such statutory damages as to the court shall appear to be just, and in assessing such damages the court may, in its discretion allow the amounts hereinafter stated; but such statutory damages shall in no case exceed the sum of $5,000, nor be less than $250, and shall not be regarded as a penalty, but this limitation * * * shall not apply to infringements occurring after actual notice * * *.

1. In case of an unauthorized newspaper reproduction of a copyrighted photograph such statutory damages assessed, in lieu of actual damages and profits, shall not exceed the sum of $200 nor be less than the sum of $50; * * *.

Section 14(b) of the 1931 bill was the same as section 16(b) of the previous bills. The provision on statutory damages varied considerably. Section 14(c) reads as follows:

(c) To pay, at the option of the owners of the right infringed, in lieu of actual damages and profits, such statutory damages as to the court shall appear be just: *Provided,* That such statutory damages, in the case of an unauthorized dramatic performance, or of an unauthorized motion picture exhibition with or without sound and/or dialogue, or the unauthorized performance for profit of a musical work, shall not exceed the sum of $10,000 nor be less than $250; and in the case of an unauthorized newspaper or periodical reproduction of a copyrighted photograph, shall not exceed the sum of $200 nor be less than $10, and in any other case shall not exceed the sum of $5,000 nor be less than $100; * * *.

In the case of innocent infringement, section 16 of the 1926 and 1930 bills provided as follows:

(d) For the purpose of avoiding imposition and so-called literary blackmail, in any action for infringement of copyright in any dramatic work (including continuities, motion pictures and motion-picture photoplays), if defendant proves that he was not aware that he was infringing or has been subjected to fraud or substantial imposition by any third person or persons other than one of said defendant's employees and in either case that such defendant has acted in good faith, the plaintiff shall not be entitled to any remedy against such defendant other than an injunction in respect to future infringement: *Provided, however,* That this section shall not apply, in the event of registration of copyright or of an instrument relating to or affecting the same or any right therein, prior to such defendant's entering into or upon the undertaking which results in such infringement, or if the work alleged to have been infringed be a published work, if notice of copyright shall be affixed (on the reverse of the title page, or at the foot of the first page of the text), to each copy published by the copyright owner or under his authority; or if the work alleged to have been infringed be a dramatic work, if such work has had a first class public production in the United States of America.

The 1931 bill did not, like the preceding bills, rule out damages altogether in cases of innocent infringements without constructive

---

[172] H.R. 10434, 69th Cong., 1st sess. (1926); H.R. 6990, 71st Cong., 2d sess. (1930); H.R. 12549, 71st Cong. 3d sess. (1931). The hearings on these bills referred to are: *Hearings* Before the Committee on Patents, House of Representatives.

or actual notice; instead section 14(d) provided for special lower damages as follows:

(d) In any action for infringement of copyright in any work, if defendent proves that he was not aware that he was infringing or has been subjected to fraud or substantial imposition by any third person or persons other than one of said defendant's employees and in either case that such defendant has acted in good faith, the plaintiff shall not be entitled to any remedy against such defendant other than to recover an amount equivalent to the fair and reasonable value of a license, but not less than $50 nor more than $2,500: *Provided, however,* That this subsection shall not apply, in the event of registration of copyright or recordation of an instrument relating to or affecting the same or any right therein, prior to such defendant entering into or upon the undertaking which results in such infringement, or if the work alleged to have been infringed be a published work published with authority from the copyright owner, if notice of copyright be affixed thereto; or if the work alleged to have been infringed be a dramatic work, other than a motion picture, it such work has had a first-class public production in the United States of America of at least one week in a town of not less than one hundred thousand population.

The remedy against innocent secondary infringers, i.e., printers, binders, and manufacturers of copyrighted works (except musical and dramatico-musical works), was limited by all Vestal bills to an injunction against future printing. Section 16(e) of the 1926 and 1930 bills read as follows:

(e) In case of the infringement of any creation of an author (except a dramatico-musical or musical composition) by any person or corporation engaged solely in printing, binding, or manufacturing the same in printed form, where such infringer shall show that he was not aware that he was infringing and that such infringement could not have been reasonably foreseen, the person aggrieved shall be entitled only to an injunction against future printing, binding, and manufacturing the same in printed form, and to the delivery up of all such printed, bound, and manufactured material, and shall not be entitled to any profit made by such infringer from his contract or employment to print, bind, or manufacture in printed form, nor to damages, actual or statutory against such infringer: *Provided,* That in case such printer is also the publisher, distributor, or seller of such creation, or in partnership or regularly engaged in business with such publisher, distributor, or seller, or is in anywise directly or indirectly interested in the publication, distribution, sale, or exploitation of such creation (other than as derived solely from his contract or employment merely to print, bind, or manufacture the same in printed form) or in any profits to be derived from such publication, distribution, sale, or exploitation, then this subsection (e) shall not apply.

Section 14(e) of the 1931 bill changed the proviso to read as follows:

* * * *Provided,* That any injunction against the continuation or repetition of such infringement in future issues of such newspaper, but not against the completion of the publication and distribution of any issue of such newspaper where actual printing of such issue has commenced; nor, where such actual printing has commenced, shall any order be granted to sequester, impound, or destroy the issue containing such infringing matter.

The 1931 bill contained an additional provision limiting liability of publishers of newspapers and periodicals in regard to advertisements. The following limitation seems to have been inserted on the insistence of magazine publishers:[173]

Sec. 14. * * * (f) In the event that any advertising matter of any kind carried by a newspaper or periodical shall infringe any copyright work, where the publisher of the newspaper or periodical shall show that he was not aware that he was infringing and that such infringement could not reasonably have been foreseen, the person aggrieved shall be entitled to an injunction only before work of manufacture of the issue has commenced and only against the continuation or repetition of such infringement in future issues of such newspaper or periodical,

---

[173] See Hearings on H.R. 10434 (1926), statement by George C. Lucas, executive secretary, National Publishers' Association, 161 at 169.

but shall not be entitled to any profit made by such publisher from his contract or employment to carry such advertising matter, nor to damages, actual or statutory against him: *Provided, however,* That no injunction shall lie against the completion of the publication and distribution of any issue of such newspaper or periodical containing alleged infringing matter where work of manufacture of such issue has commenced: *Provided further,* That this clause shall in no wise limit the remedies of the person aggrieved against the advertiser, advertising agency, or the person or corporation responsible for the infringement: *Provided further,* That if the publisher of the newspaper or periodical is in anywise interested in the commodity or subject matter advertised, or is the advertiser or advertising agency, or engaged in business with the advertiser or advertising agency, in such wise that the publisher is entitled to any profits or benefit from the sale of the subject matter advertised, or from the handling or placing of such advertising matter (other than profits derived by the publisher merely from his contract or employment to run such advertising matter in his newspaper or periodical), then the immunity granted by this subsection (f) shall not apply.

(b) The hearings [174]

Mr. Solberg, then Register of Copyrights, strongly opposed the provisions of the 1926 bill to safeguard innocent infringers.[175] He said in part:

All these proposals are virtually inroads upon the author's right to the protection of his exclusive privileges, and they have the regrettable effect of cutting down the powers of the courts to properly adjudicate the trespass committed.

If such provisions are enacted into law there seems to be no logical bar to the extent to which special classes of infringers may continue to claim special exemption until at length the sound legal maxim that "ignorance excuses no one" will, so far as copyright is concerned, be legislated out of existence.

And further: [176]

* * * the deliberate statement in the bill that the profits, which in the very language of the bill it is admitted have been made by the innocent infringer, shall not be divided with the author is the subject of criticism.

Mr. Weil criticized Mr. Solberg's view which he considered based upon practical misconceptions or * * * on a failure * * * to see what was really intended, and I think that was due to the fact that after all all legislation is made for practical men, and however accurate theory may be theory when carried to its ultimate extreme is not fitted for the ordinary realities of life.[177]

In the 1931 hearings, the National Association of Broadcasters submitted a report [178] in which it was stated:

To be satisfactory a copyright law must provide maximum and minimum statutory damages which are reasonable and not excessive in amount. This applies to the case of both willful and innocent infringement. In fact a great deal is to be said for eliminating any mention of minimum damages so that in proper cases the damages may be purely nominal.

Mr. Caldwell, counsel for the NAB, objected to the minimum amounts of damages for both willful and innocent infringement:[179]

* * * look at the amount of the statutory damages which are the sort which will usually be sought against broadcasters and practically all others except cases where there is an easily provable profit. A single performance for profit * * * entails damages from $250 to $10,000 * * *. The cost of a license of such work based on annual licenses * * * would be a few cents or less. Two hundred and fifty dollars is high as a maximum for such a case. Instead the maximum under the present law of $5,000 has been increased to $10,000. Yet the newspaper reproduction of a copyrighted photograph is to be subject to

---

[174] Supra, note 172.
[175] Hearings on H.R. 10434 (1926), statement by Thorvald Solberg, 226 at 237.
[176] Ibid.
[177] Hearings on H.R. 10434 (1926), statement by Arthur W. Weil, Counsel for MPPA, 248 at 249. See also, Hearings, statement of W. H. Osborne, chairman of the Copyright Committee of the Author's League of America, 290 at 293.
[178] Through Mr. Hedges, supra, note 94.
[179] Hearings on H.R. 12549 (1931) 52 at 78.

damages from $10 to $200. These are penalties and not damages in spite of the provisions to the contrary.

Mr. Caldwell proposed a minimum of $100.[180] For innocent infringement his amendment to section 14(d) provided for recovery of an amount equivalent to the fair and reasonable value of a license fee for the specific infringement, but not less than $10 or more than $1,000.[181] The words "for the specific infringement or infringements complained of" were added in order to bring these statutory damages into relationship with the amount of ASCAP license fee for the performance of the work.[182]

Mr. Weil, for the Motion Picture Producers and Distributors, opposed the maximum of $10,000 statutory damages in view of the possibility that multiple performances in theaters would lead to an unjustified multiplication of that sum.[183] He proposed to to limit the total responsibility for infringement in cases where no damage and no profits were shown, to $10,000.[184] Mr. Weil approved the provision for reduced liability in the case of an innocent infringer, but considered that "he should pay something for the benefit that he has had.[185]

Mr. Burkan submitted a brief on behalf of ASCAP [186] in which he stated that the proposed section 14(c) regarding innocent infringement made piracy "cheaper than a license", and was "without the slightest justification * * * except to encourage wholesale piracy." [187]

2. The Sirovich and Duffy bills [188]

(a) The damage provisions

Section 24 of the Sirovich bill provided in part as follows:

Subject to the limitations provided in sections 25 and 26, the author or other owner of any right secured by this Act is entitled to the following remedies against any infringer of such right: * * *.

(b) The recovery of (1) such damages as the owner of the right infringed has suffered from the infringement * * *; and (2) the part of the profits of the defendant to which such owner may be justly entitled; * * *; but where the defendant establishes that he was an innocent infringer, recovery under this subdivision (b) shall be limited to an amount which shall justly compensate the owner of the right infringed for the use made of the copyright or any right therein * * *.

(c) In lieu of the remedies provided under subsection (b) the plaintiff may at any stage of the trial claim the statutory damages which he shall be awarded in an amount not in excess of $20,000 nor less than $250, except that in the case of an infringement of a musical composition which is not a component part of a copyrighted motion picture or dramatico-musical composition, the minimum statutory damages shall be $125, and such statutory damages shall not be regarded as a penalty, provided the limitation as to the maximum amount of recovery as statutory damages shall not apply to a willful infringement.

---

[180] Id. at 90.
[181] Id. at 91.
[182] Id. at 92.
[183] Id., 207 at 213.
[184] Ibid.
[185] Id. at 214.
[186] Id. at 299.
[187] Reports on the Vestal bills (all on H.R. 12549), 71st Cong., 2d sess.: No. 1689, May 28, 1930 (majority); No. 1689, pt. 2, June 3, 1930 (minority); No. 1898, June 13, 1930; No. 2016, June 24, 1930. 71st Cong., 3d sess.: No. 1732, Feb. 17, 1931.
These reports stressed, as the main feature of a revised damage provision, the distinction between willful and innocent infringement. The innocent infringer was said to be someone who violated a property right and had to suffer some consequences, but not the same consequences as a willful infringer or an infringer with notice. Still less liability was to be imposed on a printer who printed or bound an infringing work while acting in good faith.
[188] Sirovich bill, H.R. 11420, 74th Cong. 2d sess. (1936); Duffy bill, S. 3047, 74th Cong., 1st sess. (1935); Daly bill, H.R. 10632, 74th Cong., 2d sess. (1936); the hearings on these bills referred to are: Hearings Before the Committee on Patents, House of Representatives, February, March, April, 1936.

Section 25 provided that a secondary innocent infringer such as a printer would be subject only to an injunction against future printing.

The damage provisions of the Duffy bill [189] read in part as follows:

SEC. 25. (a) That if any person shall infringe the copyright * * * , such person shall * * * be liable: * * *.

(2) To pay such damages to the owner of the right infringed as he may have suffered due to the infringement, as well as all or such parts of the profits which the infringer shall have made from such infringement as the court may decree to be just and proper; * * *.

(3) To pay in lieu of the proved damages and profits * * *, such damages, not exceeding $20,000 for all infringements by any one infringer up to the day of suit, as shall in the opinion of the court be sufficient to prevent their operation as a license to infringe, and as shall be just, proper, and adequate, in view of the circumstances of the case * * * : *Provided* * * *, That an unauthorized performance by radio broadcasting transmitted simultaneously by two or more connected stations shall be regarded as the act of one infringer.

The exceptions from liability for secondary innocent infringers were similar to, but more elaborate than, those in the Sirovich bill.

Both the Sirovich and Duffy bills contained provisions for reduced liability in cases of innocent infringement.

(i) *The Sirovich bill.*—Under this bill, the court had discretion to hear expert testimony as to current prices and other pertinent matters, to determine actual damages. The amount of damages was not necessarily based on market value, but was to be sufficient to prevent their operation as a license.[190] In the case of innocent infringement recovery was to be limited to just compensation for the use made of the infringed right, and the compensation was to be determined with the aid of expert testimony as to current rates.[191]

The minimum damages were to be reduced to $125 in the case of musical compositions not a part of a motion picture or dramatico-musical composition. The maximum damages were to be raised to $20,000 which could be exceeded in the case of willful infringement.[192]

An infringer who printed a work for others and established that he was an innocent infringer, was to be subject only to an injunction against future printing.[193]

Infringement by printing advertising matter in a periodical was to entitle the owner to an injunction and/or damages only against the advertiser and advertising agency; in the case of any innocent infringer who participated in publishing such advertising matter, the sole remedy was an injunction against future publication,[194] and such injunction was not to be available in respect to an issue of a periodical in process of publication or to previous issues.[195]

(ii) *The Duffy bill.*—The bill entitled the owner of a copyright to actual damages and profits made from the infringement, to be determined by the court as it thought just and proper.[196] In lieu of proved damages and profits the court could award statutory damages not exceeding $20,000 for infringements committed up to the date of suit. The exact amount was to be determined by the court so as to be sufficiently high not to operate as a license to infringe and to be just, proper, and adequate. In the case of a newspaper reproduction

---

[189] This bill passed the Senate on Aug. 7, 1935.
[190] Sec. 24(b)(1).
[191] Sec. 24(b)(2).
[192] Sec. 24(c).
[193] Sec. 25(a).
[194] Sec. 25(b).
[195] Sec. 25(c).
[196] Sec. 25(a)(2).

of a photograph, maximum damages were to be $200, and an unauthorized performance by radio broadcasting over a network was to be considered a single infringement.[197]   In the case of architectural works statutory damages could not be assessed unless the infringer was "possessed of actual knowledge thereof".[198]   There was no statutory minimum.

In any action for infringement the plaintiff had to prove registration and, in the case of published works, notice of copyright, or he was limited to an injunction, or the fair and reasonable value of a license in a sum not more than $1,000 or both, as determined by the court.[199]

For innocent secondary infringers the Duffy bill made far-reaching exceptions from liability.[200]   Printers, binders or manufacturers of infringing works were to be subject only to an injunction against future infringement—

where such infringer shall show that he was not aware that he was infringing and that he was acting in good faith, and that such infringement could not have been reasonably foreseen.[201]

The person aggrieved was not entitled to any profit made from the printing, or to damages, actual or statutory.[202]

There was no right to enjoin publication of an infringing periodical manufacture of which was commenced prior to the time when action was brought except upon proof to the satisfaction of the court that the manufacture was commenced with actual knowledge that copyright existed in the work alleged to have been infringed.[203]

Seizure of infringing articles was not permitted in cases of infringement by a publisher or distributor of a newspaper, magazine, or periodical, a broadcaster, or a motion picture producer or distributor, who acted innocently and in good faith.[204]

(b) *The hearings*[205]

(i) *In favor of the Duffy bill.*—The Copyright Office did not express ts preference for any of the bills.[206]   However, Mr. Wallace McClure, Assistant Chief of the Treaty Division, Department of State, and and chairman of the Interdepartmental Committee on Copyright, supported the Duffy bill.[207]

Mr. McClure was opposed to minimum damages in the copyright law because, in his opinion, they were penalties imposed without the safeguards of the criminal law and did not require affirmative proof of intent.[208]   Even constructive intent need not, and often could not, be present, especially in cases of infringement by broadcast.[209]   Mr. McClure said as to the elimination of minimum damages in the Duffy bill:

In providing * * * for the elimination of the minimum statutory damage fee, there was no thought of leaving the copyright holder unprotected. Under the Duffy bill, the holder * * * has [in civil actions] effective injunctive relief,

---

[197] Sec. 25(a)(3).
[198] Ibid.
[199] Sec. 25(b).
[200] Sec. 25(c) of the bill called these exceptions "immunity".
[201] Sec. 25(c).
[202] Ibid.
[203] Sec. 25(d).
[204] Sec. 25(e).
[205] Supra, note 188.
[206] Hearings, 1075, statement by William L. Brown, Register of Copyrights.
[207] Hearings, 260; Membership of Committee, Hearings, 1065.
[208] Hearings, 1072. See also statement endorsed by Assistant Secretary of State Moore, Hearings, 265 at 266.
[209] Hearings, 269.

unlimited damages * * * on proof of loss, and provisions for statutory damages on mere showing of infringement, regardless of loss, with a maximum |of $20,000.

The minimum statutory damage fixed by the Duffy bill is that the court must award, where infringement, though no loss, is proved, an amount sufficient to make it unprofitable for infringement to continue and such shall be just, proper and adequate * * *.

This should operate as full protection to the copyright holder, but is not calculated to give him subsidized bargaining power.

The representative of the National Association of Broadcasters [210] stated:

It is a curious paradox that the minimum fine [under the criminal provision of the copyright law] is $100 in a criminal proceeding, where willfulness is an essential ingredient, and $250 in a proceeding where intent is immaterial.

On the distinction between willful and innocent infringement, Mr. Caldwell said: [211]

When the Copyright Act of 1909 was enacted the line between innocent * * * and willful infringement was clear. All the known methods of infringement involved using a published copy of the copyrighted work * * *.

Except in rare cases, the mere fact of infringement demonstrated automatically that it had been willful, and Congress was justified in acting accordingly.

Scientific advances have changed all that * * *. A deliberate, willful infringement, at least in radio, is a rare thing and, in the great majority of cases, any intent to infringe is completely absent.

(ii) *In favor of the Sirovich bill.*—Mr. Burkan, in supporting the $250 minimum provision [212] stated the purpose of fixed statutory minimum damages as twofold: (1) to prevent the award of nominal damages and (2) to act as a deterrent to prevent the defendant and others from pirating. Mr. Burkan argued that the fine of from $100 to $1,000 and threat of imprisonment [213] was open to the same objection, namely that it might be used for bargaining purposes. He stated that the actual ASCAP license fees had no relation to the $250 minimum provision and were not based on it.

Mr. Burkan quoted the case of *Brady* v. *Daly* [214] to the effect that a statutory minimum provision did not make the statute a penal one and that, in its absence, it would often be difficult to give any remedy where proof of damages was not possible. Mr. Burkan held that the lack of a general minimum damage provision before the act of 1909 encouraged piracy and discouraged intellectual production. As an example, Mr. Burkan mentioned the compulsory license clause: [215]

The minimum damage provision is not extended to cover infringement by this means of reproduction of a work. In consequence composers were cheated and defrauded of the remuneration that the law entitled them to, and legitimate manufacturers suffered from keen and unfair competition because * * * the pirate made no payment whatsoever. [216]

Mr. Hess stated [217] that minimum damages were used from the time of the first copyright statutes—

because Congress realized that it was facing a unique problem in legislating for intangible property rights in intellectual creations.

Mr. Hess was of the opinion that the drafters of the Duffy bill were unrealistic in hoping to enforce licensing of copyrighted works without

---

[210] Statement by Louis C. Caldwell, Hearings, 465 at 481.
[211] Hearings, 465 at 477.
[212] Information furnished by Nathan Burkan, Hearings, 1093 at 1107.
[213] 17 U.S.C. 104.
[214] 175 U.S. 148 (1899) at 154.
[215] 17 U.S.C. 1(e).
[216] Burkan, Hearings at 1109.
[217] Statement of Gabriel L. Hess, in behalf of Motion Picture Distributors, Hearings, 1297 at 1312.

a minimum damage provision.[218] However, Mr. Hess was ready to agree to a minimum damage clause of $125 in the case of infringement of "small" rights in musical works.[219] He said:[220]

Statutory damages are compensatory damages, not primarily for the use made or the license fee withheld, but for the actual invariably existing indirect damages due to the expense of policing the copyright to detect and take action against those who will not negotiate licenses. This damage * * * is not susceptible of allocation to the particular infringement * * * under ordinary rules of evidence, so that Congress takes legislative notice of their existence by providing a minimum.[221]

Mr. Kilroe[222] stated that minimum damages did not control the bargaining for the price to be paid for the use of a work, but prevented unauthorized use made in the hope that, if discovered, only the actual value of the license would have to be paid:

In other words, the specified minimum damage provision of $250 is a necessary alternative to "compulsory licensing."

And further:

Minimum damages are vastly more important as a guide to users contemplating infringement, than they are to any Court concerned with assessing damages in the rare case of a claim actually brought before it * * * . An adequate minimum statutory damage serves to prevent abuses. Unspecified damages are an invitation to infringement and to litigation.[223]

3. The Shotwell bill

(a) The views of the interests

As part of the "Shotwell papers"[224] a comparative table was drafted setting forth the proposals of the various interest groups for a new copyright law.[225] This table contained drafts for a damage provision by the following groups: Authors, Book Publishers, Radio, Motion Pictures.[226] The various proposals compare as follows:

As to minimum and maximum damages:

    1. Authors:
        (a) Minimum: $250; $50 for reproduction of photograph in newspaper.
        (b) Maximum: $25,000; $200 for reproduction of photograph in newspaper.
    2. Book Publishers:
        (a) Minimum: None, except damages must be sufficient to prevent their operation as a license.
        (b) Maximum: $20,000; $200 for reproduction of a photograph in a newspaper.

---

[218] Id. at 1313.
[219] Id. at 1315 (see his proposal for a damage section, ibid.)
[220] Id. at 1320.
[221] For minimum damages in other laws see the list compiled by Edward A. Sargoy, Hearings, 1326 at 1329.
[222] Statement by (the late) Edwin P. Kilroe, Memorandum in Behalf of the Motion Picture Producers and Distributors, Hearings, 1185 at 1187.
[223] The committee report on S. 3047 (No. 896, May 13, 1935, 74th Cong., 1st sess.) pointed, as the principal invocation in the Duffy bill, to the elimination of statutory minimum damages:
"So many palpable injustices have arisen from the present law that courts have acquired a dislike for handling such cases and have come to feel that the law is wrong."
[224] Studies on the Shotwell bill were begun in 1938 by a Committee for the Study of Copyright of the National Committee of the United States on International Intellectual Cooperation and the bill was introduced as S. 3043 by Senator Thomas of Utah on Jan. 8, 1940, under the title "Act for the Protection of Literary and Artistic Works." No hearings were held and no action was taken on this bill.
[225] The table probably was drafted in 1939. It is understood to represent only tentative views which were changed to some extent during the discussions on the Shotwell bill. However, there seems to be no later comparative table.
[226] The draft by the group called "Scholarship" is omitted here.

3. Radio:

   (*a*) Minimum: None, except damages must be sufficient to prevent their operation as a license.

   (*b*) Maximum: $20,000.

4. Motion Pictures:

   (*a*) Minimum: $250; $50 for reproduction of photograph in newspaper; special—presumably lesser—amount for infringement of musical composition not component part of motion picture or dramatico-musical work; same for infringement by mechanical reproduction.

   (*b*) Maximum: $5,000.

As to multiple infringements:

1. Authors: No change from act of 1909.

2. Book Publishers: Unauthorized performance by network broadcasting considered single infringement.

3. Radio: Same as book publishers.

4. Motion Pictures: Increase of $50 over minimum for each similar act of infringement, not exceeding maximum of $5,000. However, all infringements by motion picture or by network broadcast considered single infringement.

As to limitations on liability:

1. Authors: None.

2. Book Publishers: Plaintiff must prove registration and copyright notice, or be limited to injunction, and value of license not exceeding $1,000. A printer innocently infringing by printing infringing work, subject only to injunction, except where he is also publisher of the work. No liability for—

   (1) charitable performances of music;

   (2) auditory reception by broadcasts, or coin-operated machine, or by a mechanical instrument or film made with the consent of the copyright owner, except where admission, cover, or minimum fee is charged;

   (3) incidental inclusion of copyrighted work in newsreel or news broadcast.

3. Radio: Plaintiff must prove registration and copyright notice, or be limited to injunction, and value of license not exceeding $1,000. Innocent infringer by including advertising matter in newspaper, periodical or broadcast, subject only to injunction against repetition. No liability for: (1), (2), and (3): Same as Book Publishers. Innocent infringer liable only for a sum which equitably compensates owner of right for use, but such sum to be sufficient to prevent its operation as a license, and to be just, proper and adequate; court may receive testimony as to current prices for like works.

(b) The damage provisions of the Shotwell bill

Section 19 of the Shotwell bill gave the copyright owner an option to recover (1) actual damages; or (2) all or such part of the profits as the infringer made from the infringement; or (3) statutory damages. For statutory damages the minimum was $250, and the maximum $10,000, except in the case of reproduction of a photograph the amounts were $50 and $250, respectively, and in the case of an infringing performance of a musical work the amounts were $150 and $2,500. The Shotwell bill had elaborate provisions regarding statutory damages for multiple infringement by motion picture or network broadcasting, the minimum damages were increased by $25 for each—

similar act of infringement proved to have been committed at a different place by the act of one infringer * * *

not to exceed a total of $2,000; and this amount could be increased, in the discretion of the court, up to the normal maximum amount of damages. The court could ignore the maximum limitations where an infringement was committed after commencement of suit.

B. Costs and Attorney's Fees

I. HISTORY OF PROVISIONS ON COSTS AND ATTORNEY'S FEES

1. Colonial copyright statutes

Two of the colonial copyright statutes contained provisions on costs. The act of March 26, 1784, of South Carolina provided that if a verdict were given for the defendant, or the plaintiff became nonsuited or discontinued his action, then the defendant should recover his full costs. The act of April 29, 1786, of New York permitted an author or copyright proprietor to recover damages for infringement "with costs."

2. The Federal copyright statutes

Section 12 of the act of February 3, 1831, provided that in all recoveries under the act full costs should be allowed. The act of August 18, 1856, provided that the plaintiff should recover costs of suit. Section 108 of the act of July 8, 1870, provided that in all recoveries under the copyright laws full costs should be allowed, and section 972 of the Revised Statutes, 1873 (Rev. Stat. (1878) 183) had an identical provision.

II. THE PRESENT PROVISIONS [227]

Section 116 provides as follows:

In all actions, suits, or proceedings under this title, except when brought by or against the United States or any officer thereof, full costs shall be allowed, and the court may award to the prevailing party a reasonable attorney's fee as part of the costs.

Under section 1(e) the court may award taxable costs to the plaintiff and a reasonable counsel fee, where a manufacturer of mechanical reproductions fails to pay royalties in accordance with section 1(e).

1. Costs

Section 116 makes award of full costs preemptory.[228] Although section 116 does not expressly so provide, the award is, of course, made to the prevailing party.[229]

---

[227] Title 17, U.S.C., as amended.
[228] Judge Learned Hand, in *Marks Music* v. *Foullon*, 171 F. 2d 905 (2d Cir. 1949). But see *Vernon* v. *Shubert*, infra, note 6.
[229] *Amsterdam* v. *Triangle Publications, Inc.*, 189 F. 2d 104 (3d Cir. 1951), modifying and affirming 93 F. Supp. 79 (E.D. Pa. 1950); *Official Aviation Guide Co.* v. *Amer. Aviation Assoc.*, 162 F. 2d 541 (7th Cir. 1947); *Corcoran* v. *Columbia Broadcast. System*, 121 F. 2d 575 (9th Cir. 1941). As to division of cost see *Witmark and Sons* v. *Standard Music Roll Co.*, 221 Fed. 376 (3d Cir. 1915); *Record and Guide Co.* v. *Bromley* (3d Cir. E.D. Pa. 1909).

Award of costs apparently is mandatory even where the prevailing party recovers less than $500, and costs may be awarded where he recovers nothing at all.[230] In *Official Aviation Guide* v. *American Aviation Associates*,[231] the defendant had entered a counterclaim contingent on a finding that the complainant had rights under the asserted copyrights. Judgment was entered dismissing both the complaint and the counterclaim with prejudice. But the court held that the defendant's counterclaim was merely an instrumentality of defense, and that despite its dismissal the defendant was the prevailing party. The court awarded him full costs.

In *Vernon* v. *Shubert, Inc.*,[232] the court gave judgment for the defendant, but ignored the rule of mandatory award of costs because the plaintiff—

by a combination of circumstances, was led to the belief that his work had been appropriated, and * * * therefore, the suit was earnestly brought and in good faith.[233]

In *Fisher, Inc.* v. *Dillingham*,[234] Judge Learned Hand awarded full costs, despite his reluctance to award minimum damages.[235] In *Marks Music Corp.* v. *Foullon* [236] Judge Learned Hand awarded full costs to two prevailing defendants, stating that the lack of such award in the lower court was apparently an oversight "for * * * [sec. 116] makes them preemptory." In other jurisdictions costs have also been awarded despite the court's reluctance to impose minimum damages.[237]

In *Witmark and Sons* v. *Standard Music Roll Co.*,[238] where the complaint was dismissed as to one infringement, and sustained as to another, partial costs were awarded:

as the complainant prevailed in part and failed in part, the [district] court did not abuse its discretion in making a division of costs.

As to the philosophy of mandatory award of full costs to the prevailing party, it was obviously the congressional intent to allow costs reguardless of any intent of the infringer, or the severity of the infringement.[239] Discretion has been allowed for an adjustment of expenses for the proceedings in view of these and similar factors by making award of attorney's fees discretionary with the court.[240] Further discretion may possibly be given to the courts by revising the minimum damage provision, or the award of costs may also be made discretionary.[241]

---

[230] Under Civ. Proc. R. 41 (d), 42(a), 54 (d) see also former sec. 815, (title 28, U.S.C.) award of costs in the case of recovery of less than $500 exclusive of cost is discretionary. See also H.R. Rep. No. 2222, on sec. 40, act of 1909.

[231] Supra, note 3.

[232] 220 Fed. 694 (S.D.N.Y. 1915). The decision apparently has not been followed or even been cited on the point of costs.

[233] Ibid. at 696.

[234] 298 Fed. 145 (S.D.N.Y. 1924).

[235] See supra, note 98.

[236] 171 F. 2d 905 (2d Cir. 1949) affirming 79 F. Supp. 664 (S.D.N.Y. 1948).

[237] *Witmark and Sons* v. *Pastime Amusement Co.*, 298 Fed. 470 (E.D.S.C. 1924); *Witmark and Sons* v. *Calloway*, 22 F. 2d 412 (E.D. Tenn. 1927).

[238] 213 Fed. 523 (N.J. 1914), affirmed 221 Fed. 376 (3d Cir. 1915).

[239] See H.R. Rep. No. 2222 to sec. 40, act of 1909.

[240] See B, II, infra.

[241] Sec. 6(2) of the British and sec. 20(2) of the Canadian Copyright Acts make the awards of costs in any infringement proceeding discretionary with the court. See Copinger, "Law of Copyright," 177, 178 (1948) and Fox, "Can. Law of Copyright," 488 to 493 (1944) for exercise of judicial discretion as to costs in Great Britain and Canada. In *Scheff* v. *Columbia Pict. Corp. Ltd.* (1938) 4 All E.R. 318, the expense incurred in employing experts to examine the works in question and investigate common owners was allowed. Award of attorney's fees is not mentioned in these statutes, nor is it discussed by either Copinger or Fox.

2. Attorney's fees

Weil stated the reason for discretionary awarding of attorney's fees as follows:

> The amount of money frequently involved in copyright letigation, especially on the part of the defendant is trifling. The expense of any letigation is considerable. Unless, therefore, some provision is made for financial protection to a litigant, if successful, it may not pay a party to defend rights, even if valid, a situation opposed to justice * * *. It is increasingly recognized that the person who forces another to engage counsel either to vindicate, or defend, a right should bear the expense of such engagement and not his successful opponent * * *.[242]

The Vestal, Sirovich, Daly, Duffy, and Shotwell bills contemplated no changes in the provision concerning costs and attorney's fees.

The cases indicate that this discretion has been judiciously exercised by the courts.[243]

C. RECAPITULATION OF MAJOR ISSUES

In a general revision of the copyright law, the following major issues regarding damages should be considered.

1. Should actual damages and the infringer's profits be cumulative or alternative?

2. Should the law continue to provide for minimum and maximum amounts as statutory damages in lieu of actual damages and profits?

3. (a) Should statutory damages be allowable when (i) actual damages are ascertainable? (ii) profits are ascertainable? (iii) both are ascertainable?

(b) If so, should statutory damages be allowable (i) in the discretion of the court, or (ii) at the plaintiff's option?

4. Should the present minimum amount of statutory damages ($250) be retained, increased, or reduced?

5. Should a special minimum amount of statutory damages be provided, and if so in what amount, for—

(a) Newspaper reproduction of a copyrighted photograph (present minimum of $50)?

(b) Any other particular infringements?

6. Should the present maximum amount of statutory damages ($5,000) be retained, increased, or reduced?

7. Should a special maximum amount of statutory damages be provided, and if so what amount, for—

(a) Innocent infringement of nondramatic work by means of motion pictures (present maximum of $100)?

(b) Innocent infringement of nondramatic literary work by broadcast (present maximum of $100)?

[242] Weil, "Law of Copyright," 530, 531 (1917).
[243] Jewell LaSalle Realty Co. v. Buck, 283 U.S. 202 (1931); Ziegelheim v. Flohr, 119 F. Supp. 324 (E.D.N.Y 1954); Overman v. Loesser, 205 F. 2d 521 (9th Cir. 1953); Marks v. Borst, 110 F. Supp. 913 (N.J. 1953); Metro Associated Services v. Webster City Graphic, 117 F. Supp. 224 (N.D. Iowa 1953); Stein v. Rosenthal, 103 F.Supp. 227 (S.D. Cal. 1952); White v. Kimmell, 94 F.Supp. 502 (S.D. Cal. 1950); Rosen v. Lowe's Inc., 162 F. 2d 785 (2d Cir. 1947; Lowenfels v. Nathan, 2 F. Supp. 73 (S.D.N.Y. 1932). Also: Advertisers Exchange v. Hinkley, 199 F. 2d 313 (8th Cir. 1952), cert. den. 344 U.S. 921 (1953); Lewys v. O'Neill, 49 F. 2d 603 (S.D.N.Y. 1931); Northern Music Corp. v. King Record Distrib. Co., 105 F. Supp. 393 (S.D.N.Y. 1952); Official Aviation Guide Co. v. Amer. Aviation Assoc., 162 F. 2d 541 (7th Cir. 1947); Jerome v. Twentieth Century Fox, 67 F. Supp. 736 (S.D.N.Y. 1946), 71 F. Supp. 914, 916 (S.D.N.Y. 1946), 7 F.R.D. 190 (S.D.N.Y. 1947), aff'd 165 F. 2d 784 (2d Cir. 1948); Advertisers Exchange v. Anderson, 144 F. 2d 907 (8th Cir. 1944); Witmark and Sons v. Pastime Amusement Co., 298 Fed. 470 (E.D.S.C. 1924).
Sec. 285, title 35, U.S.C., provides, with respect to patent infringement suits, as follows: "The court in exceptional cases may award reasonable attorney fees to the prevailing party (July 19, 1952, ch. 950, 66 Stat. 813.)"

(*c*) Newspaper reproduction of a copyrighted photograph (present maximum of $200)?

(*d*) Any other particular infringements?

8. Should the maximum limitation on statutory damages not be applicable to—

(*a*) Infringements occurring after actual notice to the defendant, as provided in the present law?

(*b*) Willful infringements for profit?

9. Within the minimum and maximum limits, should the law continue to specify, as it now does, an amount per infringing copy or per infringing performance? If so, should the amounts be those now specified in section 101(b)?

10. (*a*) Should innocent secondary infringers (vendors, printers and other processors) be absolved from liability (i) for actual damages, (ii) for profits, (iii) for statutory damages?

(*b*) Should other innocent infringers (who show that they were not aware that they were infringing and that such infringement could not have been reasonably foreseen) be absolved from liability (1) for actual damages, (2) for profits, (3) for statutory damages?

11. For the purpose of assessing statutory damages, should multiple infringements be treated as a single infringement:

(*a*) In the case of simultaneous broadcasts over a number of stations?

(*b*) In the case of multiple distribution and exhibitions of a motion picture?

(*c*) In any other cases?

12. Should the present provisions of section 116 for the mandatory allowance of full costs, with the court having discretion to award a reasonable attorney's fee, be retained?

STUDY NO. 24

REMEDIES OTHER THAN DAMAGES
FOR COPYRIGHT INFRINGEMENT

By William S. Strauss

March 1959

REMEDIES OTHER THAN DAMAGES FOR COPYRIGHT INFRINGEMENT

Scope of This Study

Civil remedies and criminal penalties for infringement of copyright are dealt with in chapter 2 of our copyright law entitled "Infringement Proceedings." [1] Since the provisions on damages and profits have been treated previously,[2] this study deals only with civil remedies other than damages and profits: that is, with injunctions,[3] impounding during action,[4] and destruction of infringing copies and devices;[5] and also with criminal penalties for infringement.[6]

I. Equitable Remedies

1. Injunction

(a) History of injunctive relief in the copyright law

Under the Copyright Acts of 1790 [7] and 1802 [8] remedies for copyright infringement were limited to an action in debt for forfeiture of copies and for statutory penalties,[9] and to a special action on the case for recovery of all damages occasioned by the infringement.[10] The Copyright Act of 1819 [11] first conferred on the circuit courts of the United States—

jurisdiction as well in equity as at law of all actions, suits, controversies, and cases, arising under any law of the United States, granting or confirming to authors or inventors the exclusive right to their respective writings, inventions, and discoveries.

Upon bill in equity the circuit courts had authority to grant injunctions, "according to the course and principles of courts of equity." Provisions empowering the courts to grant injunctions have been part of the copyright law ever since,[12] and no question as to the appropriateness of this remedy as a general matter has been raised. Indeed, an authority on equity has stated as follows: [13]

When the existence of a * * * copyright is conceded or has been established by an action at law, the jurisdiction of equity to restrain an infringement is too well settled and familiar to require the citation of authorities in its support.

---

[1] Title 17, U.S.C., ch. 2.
[2] Strauss, "The Damage Provisions of the Copyright Law" [Study No. 22 in the present Committee Print]. That study also dealt with the award of costs and attorney's fees.
[3] 17 U.S.C. 101(a); for recordings of music, sec. 101(e).
[4] 17 U.S.C. 101(c).
[5] 17 U.S.C. 101(d).
[6] 17 U.S.C. 104. Sec. 105, providing a criminal penalty for fraudulent copyright notice does not relate to infringement and is outside the scope of this study.
[7] 1 Stat. 124 (1790).
[8] 2 Stat. 171 (1802).
[9] Act of 1790, sec. 2; act of 1802, sec. 3.
[10] Act of 1790, sec. 6.
[11] 3 Stat. 481 (1819).
[12] Act of Feb. 3, 1831, (4 Stat. 436) sec. 9; act of July 8, 1870, (16 Stat. 212) sec. 106; act of Dec. 1, 1873 (Rev. Stat. 1878, 957), sec. 4970; act of Jan. 6, 1897 (29 Stat. 481); act of Mar. 3, 1897 (29 Stat. 694) revising sec. 4963 of the Rev. Stat.; act of Mar. 4, 1909 (35 Stat. 1075) secs. 25, 36.
[13] Pomeroy, "Equity Jurisprudence" (1941), sec. 1352.

From the nature of the right and of the wrong—the violation being a continuous act—the legal remedy is necessarily inadequate.

The Second Circuit Court has indicated that the remedy of injunction in copyright matters may well be available even if the copyright law did not expressly provide for it:[14]

In cases of infringement of copyright as injunction has been recognized as a proper remedy, because of the inadequacy of the legal remedy. The remedy by injunction exists independently of exepress provision therefor in the copyright statutes, it being granted on the well-established principle that a court of equity will protect a legal right where the remedy at law is inadequate.

Since the copyright statute provides that the question of granting or withholding an injunction is decided by the court "according to the course and principles of the courts of equity,"[15] it is in the sound discretion of the trial court to determine whether or not an injunction should be granted; and "an order granting the same will not be set aside on appeal, unless it is clearly shown that the court abused its discretion, or was mistaken in the view it took of the situation."[16] In other words, the principles upon which injunctions are granted or withheld in the field of copyright law are those followed in all other fields of law. The cases, in this respect, show no problems peculiar to copyright jurisprudence.

(b) Injunctive relief in the present copyright statute

Section 101(a) provides, without any limitation, for injunctions restraining copyright infringement. The only instance in which the statute expressly restricts the courts' discretion in issuing an injunction is the very special situation in which an infringer has been misled by the accidental omission of the copyright notice from a particular copy or copies.[17] In such a case—

no permanent injunction shall be had unless the copyright proprietor reimburses to the innocent infringer his reasonable outlay innocently incurred if the court, in its discretion, shall so direct.

Even this is not an absolute prohibition of an injunction: the court is to exercise its discretion as to whether or not it will require reimbursement; and only if it orders reimbursement and the copyright proprietor does not comply with the order, will the court be precluded from issuing a permanent injunction. Presumably, if the court saw fit, it could issue an injunction without imposing that condition. Also, this prohibition does not come into play if the copyright propretor has taken no steps toward compliance with the notice requirement[18] or if the infringer had actual notice of the copyright despite the lack of notice on the infringed copy.[19]

Apart from this special rule in section 21, there exists no provision in the copyright statute preventing an injunction, temporary or permanent, to issue in any case where a court deems it appropriate, even in cases where the infringer did not know, and could not reasonably foresee, that he was infringing. The present law, in stating that "any person" who infringes is liable to an injunction,[20] offers no statutory protection to the innocent infringer against the possibility that he may

---

[14] *American Code Co.* v. *Bensinger*, 282 Fed. 829 (2d Cir. 1922).
[15] Title 17, U.S.C., sec. 112.
[16] Supra, note 14.
[17] Title 17, U.S.C., sec. 21.
[18] *Nat'l Comics Publications, Inc.* v . *Fawcett Publications, Inc.*, 191 F. 2d 594 (2d Cir. 1951).
[19] *W. H. Anderson Co.* v. *Baldwin Law Pub. Co.*, 27 F. 2d 82 (6th Cir. 1928); *Schellberg* v. *Empringham*, 36 F. 2d 991 (S.D.N.Y. 1929).
[20] 17 U.S.C. sec. 101, first sentence in conjunction with sec. 101(a).

be enjoined. But the issuance of an injunction is a matter of the court's discretion,[21] and the courts may be expected to take into account the circumstances of the particular case, including the "innocence" of the infringer and the comparative effect of an injunction on him and on the complainant.

In what manner have the courts applied the provision on injunction? In *Markham* v. *A. E. Borden Co.*[22] the court said that where the infringement has come to an end before suit was commenced and there is little likelihood of its future renewal, an injunction will be denied.[23] An injunction will not be granted merely to allay litigants' fear without clear proof of the imminence of real injury.[24] As to the granting of injunctions in general, it has always been the rule of the courts that their power to issue injunctions is an extraordinary one which should be used with moderation and then only in clear and unambiguous cases.[25] The courts generally take great care in judiciously weighing the legitimate interest of the plaintiff in the issuance of an injunction against the possibility of undue injury to the defendant in the case that the injunction should issue. This is quite evident from the reported cases. Nevertheless, legislative proposals have purported to withhold from the courts the injunctive power under certain circumstances. These proposals will now be discussed.

(c) Legislative proposals regarding the remedy of injunction

A number of the general copyright revision bills submitted to Congress between 1924 and 1940 contained provisions limiting or denying altogether the remedy of injunction in some situations where the infringement was innocent, and restricting it in other cases to an injunction preventing future infringement.

Section 26(b) of the Dallinger bill[26] provided that the copyright proprietor of a work of architecture could not obtain an injunction restraining the construction of an infringing building if substantially begun, nor an order for its demolition or seizure.[27] A similar provision appeared in the Duffy bill.[28]

The first Vestal bill,[29] which limited the remedies available for innocent infringements by persons engaged solely in printing, binding, or manufacturing printed copies (except of dramatic-musical or musical works), permitted injunctions against them only as to future printing, binding, or manufacturing of printed copies.[30] This limita-

---

[21] By contrast, courts have expressed their dissatisfaction with the provision in sec, 101(b) which makes it mandatory to impose statutory minimum damages on innocent infringers. Cf. *Dreamland Ballroom* v. *Shapiro, Bernstein & Co.*, 36 F. 2d 354 (7th Cir. 1929); *Fisher* v. *Dillingham*, 298 Fed. 145 (S.D.N.Y. 1924). Cf. Strauss, op. cit. supra, note 2.

[22] 108 F. Supp. 695 (D. Mass. 1952), rev'd on other grounds 206 F. 2d 199 (1st Cir. 1953), aff'd 221 F. 2d 586 (1st Cir. 1955).

[23] Accord: *Trifari, Krussman and Fishel, Inc.* v. *B. Steinberg-Kaslo Co.*, 144 F. Supp. 577 (S.D.N.Y. 1956). However, if the plaintiff alleges he will suffer irreparable harm in the event that defendants are not restrained from pursuing their present course, a detailed showing of irreparable harm in the absence of relief is not a prerequisite to a preliminary injunction if the infringement is plain. *Geo-Physical Maps, Inc.* v. *Toycraft Corp.*, 162 F. Supp. 141 (S.D.N.Y. 1958); see also: *Rushton* v. *Vitale*, 218 F. 2d 434 (2d Cir. 1955); *Houghton Mifflin Co.* v. *Stackpole Sons*, 104 F. 2d 306 (2d Cir. 1939), cert. denied 308 U.S. 597 (1939); *Inge* v. *20th Century Fox Film Corp.*, 143 F. Supp. 294 (S.D.N.Y. 1956). Inconvenience or loss to the defendant arising from the issuance of a preliminary injunction will not prevent its being granted where the infringement is blatant. *Geo-Physical Maps, Inc.* v. *Toycraft Corp.*, supra, citing *L. C. Page and Co.* v. *Fox Film Corp.*, 83 F. 2d 196 (2d Cir. 1936).

[24] *Worthington Pump and Machinery Corp.* v. *Charles Douds*, 97 F. Supp. 656 (S.D.N.Y. 1951); *Northrop Corp.* v. *Madden*, 30 F. Supp. 993 (S.D. Cal. 1937). And see the very recent case of *Christie* v. *Raddock*, 169 F. Supp. 48 (S.D.N.Y. 1959).

[25] *Leland* v. *Morin*, 104 F. Supp. 401 (S.D.N.Y. 1952).

[26] H.R. 9137, 68th Cong., 1st sess., introduced May 9, 1924.

[27] Sec. 15(n) of this bill protected works of architecture.

[28] S. 3047, 74th Cong., 1st sess. (1935), sec. 17.

[29] H.R. 10434, 69th Cong., 1st sess., introduced Mar 17, 1926.

[30] Sec 16(e). The same provision was contained in H.R. 6990, 71st Cong., 2d sess., introduced Dec. 9, 1929, by Mr. Vestal.

tion did not apply where the infringer was also engaged in publishing, selling, or distributing the work or was interested in any profits from these operations.[31]

A subsequent Vestal bill [32] contained the above limitation,[33] and provided further that injunctions against a newspaper publisher would be granted only against the continuation or repetition of the infringement in future issues of the newspaper, but not against the completion of publication and distribution of any issue where actual printing had commenced.[34] This bill further provided that no temporary restraining order should issue which would prevent publication of a newspaper or periodical, and that in the case of a newspaper or periodical reproduction of a copyrighted photograph no injunction should issue.[35]

This last Vestal bill, H.R. 12549, also contained liminations on the courts' power to grant injunctions in the case of innocent infringement by way of advertising matter printed in a newspaper or periodical.[36] In such cases an injunction might be granted before manufacture of an issue had commenced, or against the continuation or repetition of infringement in future issues, but not against completion of the publication and distribution of an issue where manufacture had already commenced. The remedy of injunction was, however, fully available against the advertiser or other person responsible for the infringement,[37] or against the publisher if he was also interested in the advertising matter in a capacity other than as publisher.[38]

H.R. 12549 also generally provided [39] that if a defendant proved that he had acted innocently (in the situation where no copyright registration had been made and the work infringed bore no copyright notice), the plaintiff should not be entitled "to any remedy * * * other than to recover an amount equivalent to the fair and reasonable value of a license, but not less than $50 nor more than $2,500 * * *," thus denying in the stated circumstances the right to all remedies (including an injunction) except monetary recovery as stated.[40]

The Dill bill,[41] which proposed to subject performing rights' organizations to statutory control, provided that, in any action brought by an organization or by an individual whose infringed work was controlled by an organization, injunctions would be limited to works proved to have been infringed.

The first Sirovich bill[42] limited the remedy of injunction as follows: in respect to infringement by printing to an injunction against future printing; [43] in respect to infringement by presentation of advertising matter to an injunction against future public presentation of the

---

[31] Sec. 16(e).
[32] H.R. 12549, 71st Cong., 2d sess., introduced May 22, 1930, superseding H.R. 9639, 71st Cong., 2d sess., introduced Feb. 7, 1930. H.R. 12459 was passed by the House, and reported favorably with amendments (not germane here) by the Senate committee, but died on the Senate floor at the close of the 71st Cong.
[33] See 15 (e).
[34] Sec. 15 (e), second proviso.
[35] Sec. 15 (a), provisos.
[36] Sec. 15 (f).
[37] Sec. 15 (f), second proviso.
[38] Sec. 15 (f), third proviso.
[39] The provisions of sec. 15 in H.R. 12549 were substantially repeated in sec. 14 of H.R. 139, 72d Cong., 1st sess., introduced Dec. 8, 1931, by Mr. Vestal, and in sec. 14 of S. 176, 72d Cong., 1st sess., introduced by Senator Hebert.
[40] During the hearings, Mr. Fenning, a well-known Washington attorney, said: "* * * sec. (d) is a provision with respect to a man who infringes innocently and [against whom the copyright owner] is entitled to no remedy excepting a money remedy. It seems to me an injunction should be granted against his repeating that offense." Hearings on H.R. 12549, January 1931 at 22.
[41] S. 3985, 72d Cong., 1st sess., introduced Mar. 2, 1932, sec. 21(c).
[42] H.R. 10364, 72d Cong., 1st sess., introduced Mar. 10, 1932.
[43] Sec. 10(a).

infringing matter;[44] and in respect to infringement by publication of a newspaper or periodical to an injunction against publication of future issues.[45]

In 1935–36 three more general revision bills were introduced in Congress.[46] The Duffy bill[47] limited the remedy of injunction in a manner similar to that previously employed in the last Vestal bill, H.R. 12549. It also provided[48] that a broadcast of infringing advertising matter was not to be enjoined after the broadcaster had innocently begun the rehearsal of the program, and that no temporary restraining order was to issue preventing the production of a motion picture innocently commenced or its distribution or exhibition. The Sirovich bill[49] contained the same limitations as the bills submitted by Mr. Sirovich in 1932. The Daly bill[50] did not propose to change the provision on injunction in the act of 1909.[51]

The Thomas bill of 1940,[52] although it contained very elaborate and special provisions on damages, did not in any way impose limitations on the remedy of injunction.

The discussion of a limitation on the remedy of injunction during the hearings held on the various bills mentioned above began in April 1926 on the first Vestal bill, H.R. 10434.[53] Mr. Lucas, executive secretary of the National Publishers' Association, proposed the addition of a further limitation on the availability of injunctions in regard to advertising matter carried by a newspaper or periodical.[54] Such a limitative provision was incorporated in the later Vestal bills, H.R. 9639 and H.R. 12549.[55]

In the hearings on another Vestal bill, H.R. 6990, in April 1930,[56] W. B. Warner, representing the National Publishers' Association, again emphasized the need of special protection of newspapers and periodicals against enjoining publication of a whole issue where only one item contained therein was infringing. Elisha Hanson, attorney for the American Newspaper Publishers' Association, requested that a proviso be added to section 16(a) of the bill to the effect that no temporary restraining order should issue which would prevent the publication of a daily newspaper. This was incorporated in the later Vestal bill, H.R. 12549.[57]

During its efforts toward a new copyright law, the Shotwell committee,[58] early in its meetings,[59] considered draft proposals of the various interested groups. As regards the remedy of injunction, the radio

---

[44] Sec. 10(b).
[45] Sec. 10(c). The same provisions appeared in sec. 10 of H.R. 10740, 72d Cong., 1st sess., introduced Mar. 22, 1932; in sec. 11 of H.R. 10976, 72d Cong., 1st sess., introduced Mar. 30, 1932; in sec. 11 of H.R. 11948, 72d Cong., 1st sess., introduced May 7, 1932; in sec. 11, of H.R. 12094, 72d Cong., 1st sess., introduced May 16, 1932; and in sec. 11 of H.R. 12425, 72d Cong., 1st sess., introduced June 2, 1932; all by Mr. Sirovich.
[46] S. 3047, 74th Cong., 1st sess. (1935), introduced by Senator Duffy; H.R. 11420, 74th Cong., 2d sess. (1936), introduced by Mr. Sirovich; H.R. 10632, 74th Cong., 2d sess. (1936), introduced by Mr. Daly.
[47] S. 3047, sec. 17 amending sec. 25 of the act of 1909.
[48] In the form as passed by the Senate on May 13 (calendar day, June 17), 1935, sec. 25(a) (1).
[49] H.R. 11420, 74th Cong., 2d sess., sec 25.
[50] H.R. 10632, 74th Cong., 2d sess.
[51] Act of 1909, sec. 25(a).
[52] S. 3043, 76th Cong., 3d sess. introduced Jan. 8, 1940; also known as the Shotwell bill. No hearings were held on this bill, nor was any further action taken on it.
[53] Supra, note 29.
[54] This provision was to be added in sec. 16 before (d), or after (e).
[55] Supra, note 32.
[56] This bill preceded H.R. 9639, supra, note 32.
[57] Supra, notes 32 and 35.
[58] National Committee of the U.S.A. on International Intellectual Cooperation, Committee for the Study of Copyright, 1938–41. The papers of the Shotwell committee are collected in the Copyright Office.
[59] November 1938.

broadcasters' and the book publishers' proposals contained a limitation on the remedy of injunction as follows:

Under the broadcasters' proposal, infringers would be liable to an injunction except—

* * * That no temporary restraining order shall be issued which would prevent the broadcasting of a program by radio or television, the publication of a newspaper, magazine, or periodical, or the production substantially commenced or the distribution or exhibition of a motion picture.[60]

The broadcasters further proposed the following paragraph for section 25:

(e) In the event that advertising matter of any kind carried by a newspaper, magazine or periodical, or broadcast by radio, shall infringe any copyright work, where the publisher of the newspaper, magazine, or periodical, or the broadcaster, shall show that he was not aware that he was infringing and that such infringement could not reasonably have been foreseen, the person aggrieved shall be entitled to an injunction only before work of manufacture of the issue has commenced, or, in the case of broadcasting, before the rehearsal of the program has begun, and only against a continuation or repetition of such infringement in future issues of such newspaper, magazine, or periodical, or in future broadcasts; but shall not be entitled to any profit made by such publisher or broadcaster from his contract or employment to carry such advertising matter, nor to damages, actual or statutory, against him: *Provided, however,* That no injunction shall lie against the completion of the publication and distribution of any issue of such newspaper, magazine, or periodical, or the broadcast of any radio program, containing alleged infringing matter where the work of manufacture of such issue has commenced, or, in the case of broadcasts, where rehearsals have begun.

The book publishers in turn proposed the following provision in regard to injunctions:

(d) In any action against publishers, distributors, or sellers of periodicals, magazines, or newspapers for infringement of copyright, the plaintiff shall not be entitled to enjoin the alleged infringement as to any matter claimed to infringe such copyright when any part of such material has, prior to the time when action was commenced, been included in any issue of such periodicals, magazines, or newspapers upon which the work of manufacture has actually begun, or to sequester, impound or destroy any issue containing such alleged infringing matter, or the means for publishing such issue except upon proof to the satisfaction of the court that the manufacture of the issue containing such alleged infringing matter or the first installment thereof was commenced with actual knowledge that copyright subsisted in the work alleged to have been infringed.

During a meeting of the committee, held on March 28, 1939, Mr. Paine [61] pointed out that—

We have * * * scouted the possibility of an innocent infringement clause, but as yet have been unable to come to any agreement as to that * * * . The broadcast interests are going to take up the proposals with their principals, and Mr. Sargoy was going to discuss it with the motion picture people * * * ·

The next following draft bill [62] contained no limitation on the remedy of injunction.[63] Apparently, there was no further discussion of the problem by the committee.

Thus, after limitations on the remedy of injunction had been included in a number of revision bills over a period of nearly 15 years, the question must have been dropped, for the later Shotwell draft bills and the Thomas bill contained no limitation on this remedy. It is not apparent from the transcript of the committee discussions whether the reason for this omission was that the interests concerned

---

[60] Proposed amendment to sec. 25(a), draft bill of November 1938.
[61] ASCAP representative.
[62] Presumably of Apr. 15, 1939.
[63] Nor did subsequent draft bills contain such a limitation. For instance, the draft bill of June 14, 1939, contained a marginal note that the provision on injunction was the same as sec. 25 (a) of the act of 1909 (now sec. 101 (a), title 17, U.S.C.). So did the following draft bills.

were "unable to come to any agreement as to that" [64] or whether a limitation on the remedy of injunction was considered unnecessary because the courts could be expected to exercise their injunctive power in a judicious manner. This question remains open for further consideration.

2. *Impounding and destruction of infringing copies and devices* [65]

(a) *Impounding*

This remedy is available "during the pendency of the action, upon such terms and conditions as the court may prescribe * * *." [66] These "terms and conditions" have been further defined in the Rules of the Supreme Court [67] in order to prevent any undue injury to the defendant.

Under rule 3, the complainant must file a bond together with his affidavit stating the number and location of infringing articles or devices. Under rule 4, the bond may not be less than twice the reasonable value of the infringing articles or devices, and only upon filing of such bond may the court issue a writ to seize and hold the infringing articles or devices. Under rule 7, the defendant may, within 3 days after seizure, except to the amount of the penalty of the bond, and the court may order a new bond to be executed.

Award of this remedy is within the discretion of the court. In *Miller* v. *Goody* [68] the Court said that—

Since the defendant has openly appropriated the benefit of the copyrighted composition without giving statutory notice [of intention to record] or paying the royalties, I believe that it is within my power, as a matter of discretion, * * * to include in the injunction a provision that the matrices, plates, molds, stamps, discs, tapes, and other matter upon which the copyrighted musical composition may be recorded or transcribed, * * * shall be impounded until the defendant shall have paid the royalties and damages provided in the final decree * * *.

In the *Goody* case impounding was used as a temporary remedy until the defendant complied with a decree of the court for the payment of royalties. A second purpose for the impounding provision was stated by Judge Learned Hand in *Jewelers' Circular Pub. Co.* v. *Keystone Pub. Co.*: [69]

Section 25(c) [now sec. 101(c), title 17, U.S.C.] * * * is ancillary to section 25(d) [now sec. 101 (d)], for I take it as patent that the "impounding" is only to assure the eventual destruction of the infringing articles.

Under *Miller* v. *Goody, supra,* it would seem that when impounding is used as a method of compelling compliance with the court's decree, the impounded articles may be returned to the defendant upon his compliance.

As to possible return of the seized articles, the court said in *Crown Feature Film Co.* v. *Bettis Amusement Co.* [70] that a motion for an order to show cause why articles impounded as allegedly infringing should not be returned, presupposes a showing that the seized articles are not infringing. In *Universal Film Mfg. Co.* v. *Copperman,* [71] the court

---

[64] See the statement of Mr. Paine, supra, at note 61.
[65] Title 17, U.S.C., sec. 101(c) (d).
[66] Title 17, U.S.C., sec. 101 (c). See *Foreign & Domestic Music Corp.* v. *Licht.,* 196 F. 2d 627 (2d Cir. 1952).
[67] 214 U.S. 533 (1909), as amended by 307 U.S. 652 (1939).
[68] 125 F. Supp. 348, 351 (S.D.N.Y. 1954). On this point see also: *Miller* v. *Goody,* 139 F. Supp. 176 (S.D. N.Y. 1956).
[69] 274 Fed. 932 (S.D.N.Y. 1921), aff'd 281 Fed. 83 (2d Cir. 1922), cert. denied, 259 U.S. 581.
[70] 206 Fed. 362 (N.D. Ohio 1913).
[71] 206 Fed. 69, 70 (S.D.N.Y. 1913).

stated the purpose and application of the impounding provision as follows:

> Congress evidently intended * * * to give a very summary remedy to the copyright owner * * * and the Supreme Court by its rules thought it sufficient to protect the interests of the parties, respectively, by requiring bonds adequate in amount and with sufficient sureties * * * . The procedure is that the articles alleged * * * to infringe * * * are to be delivered up to the marshal upon the complainants' giving security to indemnify the defendant * * * and upon the defendant's alleging that the articles seized are not infringements, they may be returned to him upon his giving adequate security to abide the order of the court * * *.

As to proposals regarding this provision in past revision bills, section 15(a) of the Hebert bill[72] and section 20(d) of the Dill bill[73] provided for the usual method of impounding allegedly infringing articles, but with the proviso:

> that in case the judgment is adverse to the complainant, the respondent shall be entitled to such damages as he may have suffered on account of such impounding and have judgment therefor rendered by the court.

As will be noted below, several of the past revision bills would have excluded the remedies of impounding and destruction in certain situations.[74]

(b) Destruction

This remedy is available after the fact of infringement has been judicially established, and is applicable only against copies or devices for making copies in the hands of the infringer. Thus, it was said in *Foreign and Domestic Music Corp.* v. *Licht et al.*,[75] that "the remedy of forfeiture and destruction is given only against *an infringer*[76] * * *," and the court held that this remedy did not apply against one who was not an infringer. The cases,[77] would seem to indicate that delivery up for destruction of infringing articles may be awarded, together with an injunction restraining further infringement, or in conjunction with both legal and equitable remedies.[78]

Some of the past revision bills would have limited the remedies to an injunction or a reasonable license fee only, thereby by implication excluding impounding and destruction, where notice and registration were lacking, or in other cases of innocent infringement. Thus, the Dallinger bill provided that an injunction as to future infringement was to be the only remedy against an innocent infringer of an unregistered work.[79] Under the Vestal bill which passed the House in 1931, an amount equivalent to a reasonable license fee was to be the only remedy against an innocent infringer unless the work had been registered or published with copyright notice.[80] The Dill bill[81] and the Duffy bill which passed the Senate[82] both provided that if the

---

[72] S. 176, 72d Cong., 1st sess., introduced Dec. 9, 1931.
[73] S. 3985, 72d Cong., 1st sess., introduced Mar. 2, 1932.
[74] See infra at notes 79–88.
[75] 196 F. 2d, 627, 629 (2d Cir. 1952).   Accord: *Lampert* v. *Hollis Music, Inc.*, 105 F. Supp. 3 (E.D.N.Y. 1952).
[76] Italic in original.
[77] In *Midcontinent Map Co.* v. *Kintzel*, 50 U.S.P.Q. 495 (E.D. Ill. 1941) plaintiff was awarded an injunction restraining the defendant from further infringement, the profits realized by defendant from the infringement and the damages the plaintiff had sustained.   Defendant had to deliver up to plaintiff all copies, photostats and negatives of the infringing maps.   See also: *Edward B. Marks Music Corp.* v. *Borst Music Pub. Co.*, 110 F. Supp. 913 (D.N.J. 1953); *Markhan* v. *A. E. Borden Co.*, 108 F. Supp. 695 (D.C. Mass. 1952), rev'd on other grounds, 206 F. 2d 199 (1st Cir. 1953), aff'd 221 F. 2d 586 (1st Cir. 1953); *Northern Music Corp.* v. *King Record Distributing Co.*, 105 F. Supp. 393 (S.D.N.Y. 1952).
[78] *Local Trademarks Inc.* v. *Grantham*, 117 U.S.P.Q. 335 (D. Neb. 1957).
[79] H.R. 9137, 68th Cong., 1st sess. (1924), sec. 26(a).
[80] H.R. 12549, 71st Cong., 3d sess. (1931), sec. 14(d).
[81] S. 342, 73d Cong., 1st sess. (1933), sec. 20(e), proviso.
[82] S. 3047, 74th Cong., 1st sess. (1935), sec. 17 amending sec. 25(b) of the act of 1909.

work had not been registered or published with copyright notice, the remedy for any infringement was to be limited to an injunction or a reasonable license fee.

Some of the past revision bills contained express limitations on impounding and destruction. Thus, the Dallinger[83] and Duffy[84] bills provided that an infringing architectural building substantially begun was not to be subject to demolition or seizure. The Vestal bill provided that no order was to be granted to impound or destroy an issue of a newspaper containing infringing matter where actual printing had commenced.[85] Under the Duffy bill the remedies of impounding and destruction were not to apply to an innocent infringement by a publisher or distributor of a newspaper, magazine, or periodical, by a broadcaster, or by a motion-picture producer or distributor.[86]

It is interesting to note that while the Vestal[87] and Duffy[88] bills would have absolved innocent printers from liability for damages and profits, they would have been liable to "the delivery up" of the printed material as well as to an injunction against future printing.

The Sirovich bills of 1932[89] provided[90] that, upon the conclusion of the action resulting in a judgment in favor of the copyright owner, all infringing articles owned by the infringer should be destroyed if the copyright owner established that the infringer acted with intent to infringe.[91] In all other cases, the court was given discretion to direct the destruction of infringing articles.

The Thomas bill[92] contained no restriction on this remedy and included among the articles to be delivered up "for destruction or such other disposition as the court may order"[93] the following: all infringing copies, records, rolls, films, prints, discs, and other contrivances or devices, as well as all plates, molds, matrices, or other means for making such infringing copies, contrivances, or devices.

3. Provisions in foreign laws on injunction, impounding and destruction of copies

(a) Injunction

Under article 66 of the French copyright law[94] the president of the court of jurisdiction may enjoin continued manufacture of infringing articles. Section 36 of the German copyright law[95] in conjunction with section 823, paragraph 2, of the German Civil Code, permits an injunction against infringement. Section 17 of the British Copyright Act, 1956[96] provides for an injunction in the same manner "as is available in any corresponding proceedings in respect of infringements of other property rights." Section 20 of the Canadian Copyright Act, 1921[97] provides for relief by way of an injunction; this

[83] H.R. 9137, 68th Cong., 1st sess. (1924), sec. 26(b).
[84] S. 3047, 74th Cong., 1st sess. (1935), sec. 17 amending sec. 25(a)(1) of the act of 1909.
[85] H.R. 12549, 71st Cong., 3d sess. (1931), sec. 14(e), proviso.
[86] S. 3047, 74th Cong., 1st sess. (1935), sec. 17 amending sec. 25(e) of the act of 1909.
[87] H.R. 12549, 71st Cong., 3d sess. (1931), sec. 14(e).
[88] S. 3047, 74th Cong., 1st sess. (1935), sec. 17 amending sec. 25(c) of the act of 1909.
[89] H.R. 10364, H.R. 10740, H.R. 10976, H.R. 11948, H.R. 12094, H.R. 12425, 72d Cong., 1st sess., introduced Mar. 10, 22, 30, May 7, 16, June 2, 1932, respectively.
[90] Sec. 9(d), H.R. 10740; sec. 10(d), H.R. 10976, H.R. 11948.
[91] Sec. 10(d) H.R. 11948, H.R. 12094 reads: "if the infringer has not acted in good faith." Sec. 10(d), H.R. 12425 reads: "unless the defendant establishes that he was an innocent infringer." The Sirovich bill of 1936, H.R. 11420, 74th Cong., 2d sess., had a similar provision in sec. 24(d).
[92] S. 3043, 76th Cong., 3d sess. (1940).
[93] Sec. 19(c).
[94] Law of Mar. 11, 1957.
[95] Law of June 19, 1901.
[96] 4 and 5 Eliz., ch. 74.
[97] Can. Rev. Stat., ch. 2 (1952).

remedy, in some cases of innocent infringement is in fact the only remedy.[98]

(b) Impounding and destruction of copies

Some foreign copyright laws make a decree for destruction of infringing copies mandatory on the court. Thus, section 42 of the German copyright law requires destruction of infringing copies or devices after final judgment even where infringement in the production or distribution of such copies was neither intentional nor negligent, and whether the production was completed or not. The French copyright law provides in article 72 that in the case of conviction for repeated infringements the place of business of the infringer may be closed temporarily or permanently, and the employees of the infringer must be paid their regular salaries during the period of closing and for 6 months thereafter. In addition under article 23 all infringing articles are to be destroyed. The British Copyright Act provides in section 21(g) that—

the court before which a person is charged with an offense under this section [i.e., that he knowingly infringed] may, whether he is convicted of the offense or not, order that any article in his possession which appears to the court to be an infringing copy, or to be a plate used or intended to be used for making infringing copies, shall be destroyed or delivered up to the owner of the copyright in question or otherwise dealt with as the court may think fit.

II. Criminal Penalty for Infringement [99]

1. Effect and application of section 104

Section 104 makes it a misdemeanor willfully and for profit to infringe a copyright, or knowingly and willfully to aid or abet such infringement. The punishment in both cases may be imprisonment not exceeding 1 year, or a fine of not less than $100 nor more than $1,000 or both.

This section has rarely been invoked. The infrequency of its use, however, does not disprove its efficacy as a deterrent to willful and reckless infringements. It may be that civil actions are preferred by injured copyright owners since they offer a more lucrative result. To "charge an author with willfully infringing a copyright by plagiarism is to charge him with a crime,"[100] and though charges of that nature are sometimes made in civil actions there is seldom any resulting criminal prosecution.

The problems arising in the reported cases dealing with section 104 seem to be largely of a procedural nature.

In *United States* v. *Schmidt*,[101] the court denied a motion to quash an indictment which did not strictly follow the wording of section 104. It was alleged in the indictment that one defendant—

did knowingly, willfully, and for profit, and without securing permission or license so to do, print and publish certain [copyrighted] publications * * *—

that another defendant—

did knowingly, willfully, unlawfully, and for profit, aid, abet, incite, counsel, and procure the [first defendant] * * * to knowingly, willfully, unlawfully and for profit, infringe * * *.

---

[98] Sec. 22.
[99] The only section on criminal penalties of title 17, U.S.C., discussed here is sec. 104.
[100] *Cloth* v. *Hyman*, 146 F. Supp. 185 (S.D.N.Y. 1956).
[101] 15 F. Supp. 804 (M.D. Pa. 1936).

Defendants urged that all counts were bad for duplicity, and were vague, indefinite, and uncertain. The court, setting out in detail that the indictment was sufficient, denied the motion.

In *Marx* v. *United States* [102] one of the defendants' arguments on appeal was also that the indictment was insufficient. In this case the indictment was worded in the language of the statute, but did not allege copying and did not expressly negative the possibility that the composition alleged to be infringing was an original conception. The court held that the indictment charged—

a willful infringement of the copyrighted drama by broadcasting the same to the general public. An intentional copying is sufficiently alleged.[103]

As to the question of willfulness, it was claimed by defendants that the evidence was insufficient to show willful infringement. The court said that admittedly defendants were familiar with the infringed work and whether they had forgotten it as they claimed, or whether they remembered but chose to disregard the rights of the proprietors, were problems for the determination of the jury.

In *United States* v. *Backer*,[104] one of the errors charged on appeal again concerned the trial court's interpretation of the word "willful." The court of appeals held that a comparison of the infringing and the infringed copies—

leaves no doubt, in view of other evidence in the case, that they [the infringing copies] are in most respects copies of the [copyrighted works] as charged in the indictment. Nor can there be any fair doubt that the appellant had the copies made and deliberately sold them for profit.[105]

In addition to the few reported cases, there have been several unreported criminal prosecutions for willful infringements of copyright for profit.

2. *Brief history of provision on criminal penalty for infringement*

By the act of January 6, 1897,[106] section 4966 of the Revised Statutes [107] was amended to provide, in part, as follows:

If the unlawful performance and representation [of a copyrighted dramatic or musical composition] be willful and for profit, such person or persons shall be guilty of a misdemeanor and upon conviction be imprisoned for a period not exceeding 1 year.

Section 28 of the act of 1909, which was identical with the present section 104, extended the scope of the criminal provision in two respects: instead of covering only infringing performances of dramatic or musical works as in the previously existing law, the new section applied to all willful infringements for profit,[108] and the penalty was made alternative, i.e., imprisonment or a fine, or both, could be imposed.

In several of the bills to revise the Copyright Act of 1909, changes, principally of form, were proposed in the provision on criminal penalty for infringement; in some bills the section on criminal penalty for infringement was altogether omitted. In the latter group was

---

[102] 96 F. 2d 204 (9th Cir. 1938).
[103] Ibid.
[104] 134 F. 2d 533 (2d Cir. 1943).
[105] Ibid.
[106] 29 Stat. 481.
[107] Act of July 8, 1870, 16 Stat. 214.
[108] See the explanation in the committee report, H.R. Rept. No. 2222, 60th Cong., 2d sess., on the bill enacting the Copyright Act of 1909, on sec. 28

H.R. 12549 [109] in which remedies for infringement were limited to civil actions.[110]

The changes proposed varied considerably. In a bill introduced in 1931 [111] to amend sections 23, 25, and 28 of the Copyright Act of 1909, imprisonment for willful infringement for profit was limited to 6 months and the fine to $500, but no other substantive changes were proposed. A criminal provision of considerably enlarged scope was proposed in the first Sirovich bill.[112] It provided criminal penalties for other acts (involving fraudulent misrepresentations) as well as for willful infringement for profit. Section 38 of this bill read as follows:

> Any person who, with intent to defraud, shall assign a copyright or grant any license thereunder, knowing that he has previously assigned and/or licensed the same right to others, or knowing that he has no right or authority to make such assignment or license, or who willfully and for profit shall infringe or conspire to infringe any copyright secured by this Act, or who, with fraudulent intent, shall institute or threaten to institute any action or other proceeding under this Act, knowing such action or other proceeding to be without foundation, or who shall register or cause to be registered a pirated work with knowledge that such work is pirated, or who shall record or cause to be recorded a false or fraudulent assignment or license with the knowledge that such assignment or license is false or fraudulent, or who shall make a false and fraudulent statement in any affidavit or other writing filed in the Copyright Office shall be deemed guilty of a misdemeanor, and upon conviction thereof, shall be punished by a fine of not more than $2,000 and/or imprisonment for not more than six months.[113]

The Thomas bill [114] similarly combined the criminal provisions on willful infringement for profit with provisions imposing criminal penalties for other acts (involving fraudulent misrepresentations) as follows: [115]

> Any person who willfully and for profit shall infringe any right secured by this Act, and who shall knowingly aid or abet such infringement, or who shall insert, impress, or affix any notice of copyright upon any article with knowledge that such notice is false, or any person who shall knowingly issue, publish, sell, distribute, or import into the United States any such article containing such false notice, or who shall remove or alter with fraudulent intent the copyright notice upon any article duly affixed by the persons entitled so to do, or who shall register or cause to be registered a pirated work with knowledge that such work is pirated, or who shall record or cause to be recorded a false or fraudulent grant with the knowledge that such grant is false or fraudulent, or shall knowingly make a false and fraudulent statement in any affidavit or other writing filed in the Copyright Office, shall be deemed guilty of a misdemeanor, and upon conviction thereof shall be punished for each offense by imprisonment for not exceeding one year, or by fine of not less than $100 nor more than $1,000, or both such fine and imprisonment.

3. Provisions in foreign laws on criminal penalties for infringement

The copyright laws of practically all foreign countries contain provisions for criminal penalties for infringement of copyright. These provisions are used to a much greater extent, particularly in the "civil law" countries, than is the case in this country. One of the reasons for this more frequent application of criminal provisions

---

[109] 71st Cong., 3d sess., Jan. 21, 1931, as it came to the Senate from the House (passed by the House Jan. 13, 1931). H.R. 12549, 71st Cong., 2d sess., as introduced May 22, 1930, by Mr. Vestal contained, in sec. 26, a criminal provision. This provision was restored in S. 176, 72d Cong., 1st sess., introduced Dec. 9, 1931, by Mr. Hebert. Also in this group was the Dill bill, S. 3985, 72d Cong., 1st sess., introduced Mar. 2, 1932.
[110] Under sec. 32 of H.R. 12549 use of a fraudulent copyright notice was a misdemeanor.
[111] S. 5687, 71st Cong., 3d sess., introduced Jan. 5, 1931, by Mr. King.
[112] H.R. 10364, 72d Cong., 1st sess., introduced Mar. 10, 1932.
[113] The fine was reduced to $1,000 in sec. 39 of H.R. 10976, 72d Cong., 1st sess., introduced on Mar. 30,1932, by Mr. Sirovich, committed to the Committee of the Whole House on the State of the Union, Apr. 5, 1932 (Union Cal. No. 190).
[114] S. 3041, 76th Cong., 3d sess., introduced Jan. 8, 1940.
[115] Sec. 18. The note on the draft bills preceding the Thomas bill states as to sec. 18: "This section combines and revises secs. 28 and 29 of the law of 1909."

would seem to be that, under these foreign laws, criminal penalties and civil damages are frequently imposed in one action and both may accrue to the benefit of the plaintiff.[116]   Another reason may be that civil damage awards are usually for smaller sums in foreign countries than in the United States.   It therefore appears difficult to compare the criminal provisions of the foreign and U.S. copyright laws.

The British Copyright Act, 1956,[117] provides, in section 21, for penalties and summary proceedings in respect of dealings which infringe copyright.   Under this section fines may be imposed from a minimum of 40 shillings for each infringing article to a maximum of 50 pounds, and in cases of repeated infringement, imprisonment not exceeding 2 months.   Acts which are punishable under this section of the British Copyright Act, 1956, include, e.g., knowingly making for sale or hire, selling, exhibiting, or distributing infringing copies, making or possessing plates knowing they are to be used for making infringing copies, or knowingly and without authority performing a copyrighted work.

The Canadian Copyright Act [118] contains a criminal provision [119] which is similar to that of the British Copyright Act.

III. Issues Presented

1. Analysis

Two subjects are analyzed in this paper: civil remedies other than damages, and criminal penalties for infringement.   What are the problems raised in connection with these subjects?

(a) Injunction

The present law leaves it to the discretion of the court whether an injunction will be granted or denied.   It has always been the rule of the courts that an injunction is an extraordinary remedy to be used only where further injury to the plaintiff is likely and the equities of the situation are on the side of injunctive relief, and the courts have denied an injunction in cases where it was thought that this remedy would be unduly harsh on the defendant.

Some of the past bills for general revision of the copyright law contained proposals to limit the power of the courts to grant injunctions in certain instances, particularly where an infringing undertaking had been innocently begun.   Thus, it was proposed that no injunction shall be issued against the completion of a building or of printing innocently begun, or against the publication of a newspaper or periodical, or against the publication or broadcasting of infringing advertisements for which preparation had been innocently begun. A provision was also proposed that no temporary restraining order shall be issued against the production of a motion picture substantially begun or its distribution or exhibition.

The question whether in these or other circumstances, there should be in a revised law any express limitations on the injunctive power of the courts.   It should be noted that no reported case has been

---

[116] For details see Strauss, "The Damage Provisions of the Copyright Law" [Study No. 22 in the present Committee Print, pt. A—III].
[117] 4 and 5 Eliz. 2, ch. 74.
[118] Can. Rev. Stat., 1952, ch. 55.
[119] Sec. 25.

found where a court has issued an injunction that the revision proposals mentioned above would have prevented.

(b) *Impounding and destruction*

Impounding is a temporary remedy to be used either to insure defendant's compliance with a decree of the court, or as a measure preliminary to possible destruction of the infringing articles. Such destruction may be ordered only after the fact of infringement has been judicially established and only against a proven infringer. Impounding and destruction are matters for the court's discretion.

As to impounding, two of the past revision bills proposed an added provision granting a successful defendant an award of such damages as he may have incurred due to the impounding. The Supreme Court Rules requiring the plaintiff to file a bond would seem to take care of this.

Some of the past revision bills provided variously that the remedies of impounding and destruction were not to be available in regard to a building under construction or an issue of a periodical or newspaper of which manufacture had innocently begun, or against an innocent broadcaster or motion picture producer or distributor, or against innocent infringers generally.

Impounding and destruction, like injunctions, are extraordinary remedies which courts, in their discretion, apply as the situation in each case seems to require in order to prevent further injury to the plaintiff; and these remedies are not applied where the court feels that they would be unduly injurious to the defendant. The proposals in past revision bills to deny these remedies in certain situations were apparently prompted by an abundance of caution. No reported case has been found in which impounding or destruction was ordered in a situation where it would have been precluded by these proposals.

(c) *Criminal penalties*

Though infrequently invoked, the criminal provision in section 104 of the present law may serve as a deterrent to willful infringement. It does not appear to have created any special difficulties in its application.

Two of the past revision bills omitted this provision entirely, without explanation; perhaps it was considered unnecessary. In other revision bills the provision was left intact, or was merely changed in form to combine this with other criminal provisions relating to fraudulent misrepresentations. Some bills proposed to change the penalties: maximum imprisonment for 6 months, instead of the present 1 year; or a maximum fine of $500 in one bill, of $2,000 in another, instead of the present $1,000.

2. Summary of issues

(a) Should any limitations be imposed by the statute on the issuance of injunctions against copyright infringements? If so, what limitations?

(b) Should any limitations be imposed by the statute on the impounding or destruction of infringing copies and devices? If so, what limitations?

(c) Should the criminal penalty for willful infringement for profit, or for knowingly and willfully aiding or abetting such infringement, be retained, eliminated, or modified?

STUDY NO. 25

LIABILITY OF INNOCENT INFRINGERS OF COPYRIGHTS

By Alan Latman and William S. Tager

January 1958

LIABILITY OF INNOCENT INFRINGERS OF COPYRIGHTS

I. INTRODUCTION

Copyright infringement consists of interference with any of a variety of rights and justifies resort to a number of remedies. Such interference may be intentional, negligent or accidental.

The law of torts, from which these terms are borrowed, considers intention relevant in several respects. For example, liability for conversion depends upon an intentional use of a chattel in such a way as to interfere with another's right to possession.[1] The defendant is liable even though he is under the reasonable but erroneous impression that the chattel is his and accordingly intends no such interference;[2] such good faith, however, may permit him to tender the chattel to the plaintiff and thus mitigate damages.[3]

Inasmuch as copyright infringement has been held to be an action "sounding in tort,"[4] the question is raised whether copyright law recognizes or should recognize similar distinctions based on the "innocence" of the infringer. Should one who copies, performs, or sells a copyrighted work unintentionally and in the exercise of due care be considered an infringer at all? Or should the remedies against him be limited? To what extent should a new Federal copyright statute modify existing law in this regard?

It is apparent that any answer to these questions is complicated by the great variety of copyright infringements. Innocent infringement occurs in various situations in which the opportunity to avoid infringement, and the impact of the infringement and of the imposition of certain remedies, differ. The innocent infringer might, for example, be shielded from liability for interfering with certain rights and not others. The copyright owner might be restricted in his choice of remedies against the innocent infringer or in the scope of any particular remedy. Many of the possible permutations have been attempted or proposed in this country or abroad. Of course, a balancing of policy considerations must dictate the relevance of intention or negligence in each situation. Moreover, the wide range of factual situations encompassed by the general concept of "innocent infringement" must be appreciated. The variety of factual or legal knowledge of which the "infringer" may be "innocent" may, where applicable, call for different answers to the broad questions posed above.

---

[1] Restatement, Torts, sec. 222 (1934).
[2] Id. at sec. 222, comment *d*.
[3] Id. at sec. 247.
[4] *Turton* v. *United States*, 212 F. 2d 354 (6th Cir. 1954); Howell, "The Copyright Law" 165 (1952).

II. History of the Treatment of Innocent Infringers in the United States

A. COLONIAL STATUTES, 1783–86

The 12 colonial copyright statutes,[5] enacted largely as a result of the recommendation of the Continental Congress,[6] took three different approaches to the problem of intention and its relation to civil liability for infringement.

1. *No distinction between innocent and willful infringement*

Four States [7] did not distinguish in their statutes between innocent and intentional infringement. Neither by limiting language in the specifications of infringement nor by proviso was state of mind made relevant. Thus, the innocent infringer was to be made liable to the same extent as one who purposely infringed. It should be noted, however, that the sole remedy afforded by three of these statutes [8] was recovery of a sum, limited by a stated minimum and maximum. In determining the amount of such sum which the defendant was to "forfeit and pay," it is conceivable that the courts were expected to take into consideration the degree of the defendant's culpability.

2. *Liability of distributor conditioned on knowledge that consent had not been obtained to "publish, vend, utter, and distribute" protected work*

The statutes of five States [9] appear to distinguish between those who introduce a work into circulation, without the consent of the author, and those who aid in its distribution. Liability attached to anyone who, without such consent, printed or imported the work, but only to one who—

shall *knowingly* publish, vend, and utter or distribute the same, without the consent of the proprietor thereof in writing * * *. [Emphasis added.]

The distributor, to be liable, must know that his sale was unauthorized; the initiator was liable, whether he knew of his lack of authorization or not.

3. *Liability of distributor conditioned on knowledge that printing or importation was unauthorized*

The statutes of Virginia, Maryland, and South Carolina may not have differed in basic approach from the five statutes discussed immediately above. The different language chosen is significant, however, for it served as a model for the first Federal copyright statute. The liability for undertaking to "sell, publish, or expose to sale" was limited to a person "knowing the same to be so printed, reprinted, or imported, without such consent first had and obtained." Thus, a seller who did not know that the *printing* of his copies was unauthorized was not liable.

---

[5] All the Original Colonies except Delaware enacted copyright statutes.
[6] Resolution of Continental Congress, May 2, 1783. This resolution, in addition to the colonial statutes, are reproduced in "Copyright Laws of the United States of America, 1783–1956," a publication of the Copyright Office.
[7] Massachusetts, New Hampshire, Rhode Island and Pennsylvania.
[8] The Pennsylvania statute provided for recovery of "double the value" of the infringing copies, without apparent variation.
[9] Connecticut, Georgia, New Jersey, New York and North Carolina.

B. ACT OF 1790

Section 2 of the first Copyright Act passed by the Congress of the United States [10] provided in pertinent part:

That if any other person or persons * * * shall print, reprint, publish, or import, or cause to be printed, reprinted, published, or imported from any foreign Kingdom or State, any copy or copies of such map, chart, book or books without the consent of the author or proprietor thereof, first had and obtained in writing * * *; or *knowing the same to be so printed, reprinted, or imported, shall publish, sell, or expose to sale or cause to be published, sold, or exposed to sale,* any copy of such map, chart, book or books, without such consent first had and obtained in writing as aforesaid, then such offender shall forfeit all and every copy * * *: And every such offender and offenders shall also forfeit and pay the sum of fifty cents for every sheet * * *. [Emphasis added.]

Thus, persons who printed, published, or imported copies without consent were liable without regard to their innocence; but those who published or sold copies were liable only if they knew that the copies were printed or imported without consent. The statute was ambiguous in its reference to "publish" in both contexts.

C. ACT OF 1870

Sections 99 and 100 of the 1870 act [11] retained the distinction between persons who printed, published, or imported copies, and those who sold copies; but removed the ambiguity in the dual use of the term "publish" in earlier statutes by deleting that word from the description of acts which, if innocent, did not constitute infringement.

Subsequent amendments of the law relating to copyrights prior to the 1909 act continued the requirement of knowledge on the part of the vendor.

III. THE PRESENT LAW

A. THE STATUTE

The general features of the law of innocent infringement were shaped prior to 1909. Except for the innocent vendor, innocence or lack of intent to infringe was not generally a defense to an action for infringement.[12] There is considerable evidence that this situation was realized by those participating in the drafting and enactment of the 1909 act;[13] although the problem of the innocent infringer was considered at some length in the hearings, the 1909 statute contained no broad provisions excusing innocent infringers.[14] Moreover, the act eliminated the provision in earlier statutes expressly protecting the innocent seller.

However, several provisions limiting available remedies in certain instances of innocent infringement were inserted. These provisions were supplemented by amendments in 1912 [15] and 1952.[16]

---

[10] Act of May 31, 1790, ch. 15, 1 Stat. 124.
[11] 16 Stat. 198.
[12] Drone, "Copyrights" 401–403 (1879); Spalding, "The Law of Copyright" 55 (1878); Morgan, "The Law of Literature" 240, 665, (1875).
[13] E.g., Hearings Before Committees on Patents on H.R. 19853, and S. 6330, 59th Cong., 1st sess. 17, 137 (June 1906).
[14] These developments were considered significant in *DeAcosta* v. *Brown*, 146 F. 2d 408, 411 (2d Cir. 1944).
[15] 37 Stat. 489.
[16] 66 Stat. 752.

1. *Accidental omission of notice and the innocent infringer: Section 21*

The only section in the present copyright act which uses the term "innocent infringer" deals with only a narrow area of the problem. Section 21 seeks generally to protect the copyright proprietor from the loss of copyright where notice has been omitted by accident or mistake from a limited number of copies. The section provides that such omission shall not invalidate the copyright or prevent recovery for infringement against any person who, after actual notice of the copyright, begins an undertaking to infringe it—

* * * but shall prevent the recovery of damages against *an innocent infringer* who has been misled by the omission of the notice; and in a suit for infringement no permanent injunction shall be had unless the copyright proprietor shall reimburse to the innocent infringer his reasonable outlay innocently incurred if the court in its discretion, shall so direct. [Emphasis added.]

This section appears only to bar the recovery of damages and, in some circumstances, the granting of injunctive relief against an innocent and misled infringer. The profits of an innocent infringer may apparently still be recovered even though he has been misled by the omission of the notice.[17]

2. *Innocent infringement by means of motion pictures: Section 101(b)*

The rapidity and frequency of the exhibition of a motion picture were considered to pose special problems as to innocent infringement. If a motion picture infringed a copyrighted work, the number of infringements in its repeated exhibitions could lead to the cumulative recovery of a potentially staggering amount of statutory damages. If such infringement were innocent, it was felt that this recovery would be unjustified.[18] Accordingly, in 1912, when Congress amended the 1909 act to enumerate motion pictures as a class of copyrightable works, it limited the amount of statutory damages recoverable for infringement by means of motion pictures.

(a) *Infringement of a nondramatic work*

Section 101(b) provides in part:

* * * and in the case of the infringement of an undramatized or nondramatic work by means of motion pictures, where the infringer shall show that *he was not aware that he was infringing, and that such infringement could not have been reasonably foreseen,* such [statutory] damages shall not exceed the sum of $100; * * *. [Emphasis added.]

(b) *Infringement of a dramatic work*

Congress took a slightly different approach with respect to infringement in a motion picture of a work in dramatic form. Innocent infringement of such a work was to be subject to the same scale of statutory damages as an ordinary infringement, but the entire process of making the motion picture and distributing it to exhibitors was to be considered a single infringement.

Thus, in another portion of section 101(b), it was provided:

* * * and in the case of an infringement of a copyrighted dramatic or dramatico-musical work by a maker of motion pictures and his agencies for distribu-

---

[17] *Strauss* v. *Penn. Printing & Publishing Co.*, 220 F. 977 (E.D. Pa. 1915). Sec. 21 is discussed at length in Weil, "American Copyright Law" 351–354 (1917); see also Ball, "Law of Copyright and Literary Property" 327 (1944).
[18] H.R. Rept. No. 756, 62d Cong., 2d sess., 3 (1912).

tion thereof to exhibitors, where such infringer shows that *he was not aware that he was infringing a copyrighted work, and that such infringements could not reasonably have been foreseen*, the entire sum of such damages recoverable by the copyright proprietor from such infringing maker and his agencies for the distribution to exhibitors of such infringing motion pictures shall not exceed the sum of $5,000 nor be less than $250 * * *. [Emphasis added.]

3. *Innocent infringement of a nondramatic literary work by broadcasting: Section 1(c)*

In 1952, section 1(c) was amended to extend public performance rights to nondramatic works.[19] Included in the amendment was the following provision:

* * * The damages for the infringement by broadcast of any work referred to in this subsection shall not exceed the sum of $100 when the infringing broadcaster shows that *he was not aware that he was infringing and that such infringement could not have been reasonably foreseen; * * *.* [Emphasis added.]

It should be noted this limitation is almost identical to the provision of section 101(b) limiting the remedy for infringement of a nondramatic work by motion pictures.

4. *Discretion of the court in granting remedies: Sections 101(b), 101(c), 101(d), and 116*

Section 101(c) provides for the impounding of infringing articles during the pendency of an action for infringement "upon such terms and conditions as the court may prescribe." Section 101(d) provides for delivery for destruction of all infringing copies or devices for making such copies "as the court may order." There is some indication in the legislative hearings that the discretion given to the court in these provisions may have been intended to give some measure of protection to the innocent infringer.[20] Similarly, section 101(b) provides, in lieu of actual damages and profits, for "such [statutory] damages as to the court shall appear to be just," within a specified range of minimum and maximum amounts;[21] and section 116 contains a provision by which "the court may award to the prevailing party a reasonable attorney's fee as part of the costs." In granting these various remedies, the courts may mitigate the remedies accorded against an innocent infringer.

5. *Criminal provision and innocent intention: Section 104*

Section 104 makes willful infringement for profit a misdemeanor. The requirement of willfulness thus expressly excludes the innocent infringer from the sweep of this criminal provision.

---

[19] 66 Stat. 752 (1952).

[20] See discussion in Hearings (December 1906) 178–179 and Hearings (June 1906) 177.

[21] The limitations on the amount of such statutory damages are made inapplicable to: "* * * infringements occurring after the actual notice to a defendant either by service of process in a suit or other written notice served upon him." The willful infringement after notice at which this provision is directed might include certain types of infringements which would otherwise be considered "innocent." Thus, one who reasonably but erroneously relies upon the supposed invalidity of a claim to copyright after written notice of the claim might not be protected by his good faith.

B. THE TREATMENT OF THE INNOCENT INFRINGER IN THE COURTS

1. *Innocence or lack of intention as a defense*

The rule is well established that lack of intention to infringe is generally no defense to an action for infringement.[22] This was the general rule prior to the present statute [23] subject, of course, to the statutory exceptions in favor of the innocent distributor; the provisions and legislative history of the 1909 act left little room for judicial modification. Thus, no less applicable under present law are the views expressed in the early case of *Lawrence* v. *Dana* [24] to the effect that—

> Mere honest intention on the part of the appropriator will not suffice * * * as the court can only look at the result, and not at the intention in the man's mind at the time of doing the act complained of, and he must be presumed to intend all that the publication of his work effects * * *.[25]

This principle has been recognized by the Supreme Court which stated, by way of dictum, in *Buck* v. *Jewell-LaSalle Realty Co.*: [26] "Intention to infringe is not essential under the act."

Direct copying of copyrighted material will give rise to liability even if committed under the reasonable but erroneous assumption that the portion of the work being copied is in the public domain.[27] Neither is copying excused by reason of a notice in exceedingly small type,[28] or even by the omission of notice on the part of a licensee of the copyright owner.[29] And even where the user obtains the permission of the publisher of the magazine carrying an article copyrighted by the author, he cannot escape liability.[30]

There are still other situations in which the defendant has not consciously copied the plaintiff's work but the question of infringement is nevertheless raised. Here the defendant may be "innocent," to a varying extent, of different facts or legal results. These situations will be discussed separately in an attempt to describe the operation, in each of them, of the general rule that innocence of intention to infringe is no defense.

(a) *Indirect copying*

Copying from a publication which was itself copied from a copyrighted work constitutes infringement and is usually designated as "indirect" copying.[31]

Whatever doubts may exist as to the appropriate remedies to be applied, there is agreement among courts and writers that the copyist of an infringing copy is liable as an infringer, even if ignorant of the fact of copyright.[32] This rule was applied in *DeAcosta* v. *Brown* [33] to common law literary property. And while the Supreme Court has not specifically decided the point, it has considered a similar factual situation. In *Douglas* v. *Cunningham*,[34] the defendant pub-

---

[22] Howell, op. cit., note 4, supra, 122; Peck, "Copyright Infringement of Literary Works," 38 Marquette L. Rev. 180, 187 (1955).
[23] See note 12, supra.
[24] 15 Fed. Cas. 26, Case No. 8, 136 (C.C.D. Mass. 1869).
[25] Id. at 60.
[26] 283 U.S. 191, 198 (1930).
[27] *Toksvig* v. *Bruce Pub. Co.*, 181 F. 2d 664 (7th Cir. 1950).
[28] *Advertisers Exchange, Inc.* v. *Laufe*, 29 F. Supp. 1 (W.D. Pa. 1939).
[29] *American Press Ass'n* v. *Daily Story Publishing Co.*, 120 Fed. 766 (7th Cir. 1902).
[30] *Insurance Press* v. *Ford Motor Co.*, 255 Fed. 896 (2d Cir. 1918).
[31] Amdur, "Copyright Law and Practice" 688 (1936).
[32] *Altman* v. *New Haven Union Co.*, 254 Fed. 113 (D. Conn. 1918). See *American Press Ass'n* v. *Daily Story Publishing Co.*, 120 Fed. 766 (7th Cir. 1902); Weil, "American Copyright Law" 400 (1917); Shafter, "Musical Copyright" 238 (1939).
[33] 146 F. 2d 408 (2d Cir. 1944).
[34] 294 U.S. 207 (1935).

lished the plaintiff's copyrighted story in the belief that the material which had been orally related to defendant's employee by a third person represented an original recounting of actual happenings. The Court, in finding improper the interference by the court of appeals with the discretion of the trial court in fixing statutory damages, apparently accepted the liability of the defendant, notwithstanding his innocence.

(b) Innocent printers

During the hearings preceding the 1909 act, George W. Ogilvie, a Chicago publisher, stated:

> * * * There is no printer in the United States whom I cannot get in trouble—serious trouble—so serious that it might put him out of business. I take to him a set of plates about which he knows nothing as to the existence of copyright on them. He prints them for me * * * and then the owners of the copyright can get after him and collect damages * * *.[35]

Mr. Ogilvie thought the law should be changed to protect a printer who unwittingly prints infringing copies; but the law was not changed and the innocent printer has been held liable by the courts.[36] Insofar as the printer, innocent or not, is independent of the publisher and in no way a coadventurer, it has been held that he is not jointly liable for the publisher's profits, but is accountable only for his own.[37]

(c) Innocent vendors

Since the removal in 1909 of the protective provision of earlier statutes, innocent nonmanufacturing vendors have also been held to be infringers.[38] The good faith of the defendants in the recent *Woolworth* litigations [39] was acknowledged by both the majority [40] and dissent [41] in the Supreme Court, without apparently casting doubt on the vendor's status as an infringer. Thus, it is not surprising that in recent litigation,[42] the defendant dealers conceded that—

> the sale or vending of an unauthorized copy of a copyrighted article by anyone is an infringement of the copyright irrespective of the position of the vendor in the distributive process, his bona fides, his innocence, or the unknown peril to which he may have been subjected.[43]

And the court, relying in part on the *Woolworth* case, found that "this is undoubtedly the law."

(d) Vicarious liability

The normal agency rule that a master is liable for his servant's wrongful acts committed within the scope of employment has been considered applicable to copyright infringement.[44] A few courts have refused to apply this rule where its effect would have been, in the court's view, essentially penal. Thus, in *Taylor* v. *Gilman*,[45] the court regarded as a penalty the statutory amount required by a former provision to be divided equally between the plaintiff and the U.S. Government. Although the court refused to consider the em-

---

[35] Hearings (December 1906) at 49.
[36] See *American Code Co.* v. *Bensinger*, 282 Fed. 829, 834 (2d Cir. 1922).
[37] *Sammons* v. *Larkin*, 126 F. 2d 341 (1st Cir. 1942).
[38] E.g., *McCulloch* v. *Zapun Ceramics, Inc.*, 97 U.S.P.Q. 12 (S.D.N.Y. 1953).
[39] *F. W. Woolworth Co.* v. *Contemporary Arts, Inc.*, 193 F. 2d 162 (1st Cir. 1951), rev'd, 344 U.S. 228 (1952)
[40] 344 U.S. 229.
[41] Id. at 234–235.
[42] *Miller* v. *Goody*, 139 F. Supp. 176 (S.D.N.Y. 1956), rev'd sub nom *Shapiro, Bernstein* v. *Goody*, 248 F. 2d 260 (2d Cir. 1957). The court of appeals apparently extended this principle to the sale of unauthorized phonograph records.
[43] 139 F. Supp. 180.
[44] See *M. Witmark & Sons* v. *Calloway*, 22 F. 2d 412, 414 (E.D. Tenn. 1927).
[45] 24 Fed. 632 (S.D.N.Y. 1885).

ployer liable for such amount, it was conceded that the defendant "might be civilly liable." And in an isolated instance under the present statute, though it provides in section 101(b) that statutory damages "shall not be regarded as a penalty," the court relied upon *Taylor*, the absence of actual damage, and what the court considered the "accidental" copying of the plaintiff's work, to deny recovery of statutory damages.[46] Despite these two cases, the rule seems well established that an employer may be held liable for infringing acts committed by his employees.[47]

An interesting application of the theory of vicarious liability to copyright law results in the liability of innocent proprietors of theaters and dance halls for infringements committed by hired musicians. Such liability apparently goes beyond the ordinary rules of *respondeat superior* and does not require a strict common law master-servant relationship. Thus, in *Dreamland Ballroom, Inc.*, v. *Shapiro, Bernstein & Co.*,[48] the court stated:

> The authorities are, we believe, unanimous in holding that the owner of a dance hall at whose place copyrighted musical compositions are played in violation of the rights of the copyright holder is liable, if the playing be for the profit of the dance hall. *And this is so, even though the orchestra be employed under a contract that would ordinarily make it an independent contractor.* [Emphasis added.]

2. *Innocence or lack of intention and remedies for infringement*

Innocence or lack of intention is of greater relevance to the fashioning of remedies for infringement than it is to the substantive question whether infringement has taken place. The copyright statute provides a battery of remedies for infringement; and the culpability of the defendant has played a significant role in judicial selection and adaptation of these remedies.

(a) *Damages*

It has been noted that one court considered the remedy of awarding statutory damages sufficiently penal to warrant denial of the remedy for an "accidental" use of plaintiff's work by defendant's agent where no actual damage to the plaintiff resulted.[49] More typically, a court is concerned with the amount of the statutory damages to be selected between the statutory maximum and minimum and may use the defendant's culpability as a guide to making such a selection.

In some of the cases discussed earlier, the innocence of the defendant, while insufficient to excuse his infringement, was a factor in the court's refusal to award more than the statutory minimum.[50] However, several Supreme Court decisions have made it clear that where the trial court has fixed a higher amount of statutory damages, the amount awarded may not be reduced by an appellate court, however innocent the infringer might have been.[51]

It has long been accepted that all who participate in an infringement are jointly and severally liable for all the damage sustained by the copyright owner.[52] There have been recent instances, however, where courts influenced by one defendant's innocence have ignored

---

[46] *Norm Co.* v. *John A. Brown Co.*, 26 F. Supp. 707 (W.D. Okla. 1939).
[47] Warner, "Radio and Television Rights," 609 (1953).
[48] 36 F. 2d 354, 355 (7th Cir. 1929).
[49] See note 46, supra.
[50] See, e.g., *Altman* v. *New Haven Union Co.*, 254 Fed. 113 (D.C. Conn. 1918); *Sammons* v. *Larkin*, 38 F. Supp. 649 (D.C. Mass. 1940); judgment vacated and cause remanded sub nom *Sammons* v. *Colonial Press*, 126 F. 2d 341 (1st Cir. 1942).
[51] *F. W. Woolworth Co.* v. *Contemporary Arts, Inc.*, 344 U.S. 228 (1952); *Douglas* v. *Cunningham*, 294 U.S. 207 (1935).
[52] Ball, "Law of Copyright and Literary Property" 332 (1944); Warner, op. cit., note 47, supra, at 646.

or modified this rule.   Thus, in *Northern Music Corp.* v. *King Record Distributing Co.*, [53] the corporate defendants made and distributed recordings of a song actually copied by other defendants from the plaintiff's copyrighted song.   The corporate defendants had no knowledge or reason to know of the plaintiff's copyright and were held liable for only "that portion of the damage which is attributable to their individual infringements of plaintiff's copyright."   And in *Gordon* v. *Weir*,[54] the court refused to hold innocent infringers, misled by a certificate of registration issued to the original willful infringer, liable for the damages inflicted by the original infringer.

These decisions go further than the earlier decision in *Detective Comics, Inc.* v. *Bruns Publications*,[55] which found joint liability but modified its enforcement in favor of innocent infringers.   The distributors of the infringing articles were there to be held accountable for damages, profits, and counsel fees only if the principal infringer could not answer therefor.   It remains to be seen whether the *Northern Music* and *Gordon* cases represent a trend against applying general principles of joint liability for tort to copyright infringement.[56]

It should be noted that in *DeAcosta* v. *Brown*, which involved the question of the liability of one who innocently published a story which infringed a common law right of literary property, the issue which divided the dissenting Judge Learned Hand from the majority was the liability of such innocent infringer for damages.   Judge Learned Hand believed that while injunction and recovery of the innocent infringer's profits were appropriate, an award of damages was not.

(b) Profits

An innocent infringer may partially escape liability for profits if the copyright owner, though aware of the infringement, fails to notify the infringer within a reasonable time.   In *Haas* v. *Leo Feist, Inc.*,[57] the court provided for reduction of the plaintiff's recovery in accordance with the length of time each plaintiff knew of the infringement and yet allowed the defendant to continue infringing.   The court stated:

> If the defendant be a deliberate pirate, this consideration might be irrelevant * * *; but it is no answer to such inequitable conduct, if the defendant Feist is innocent, to say that its innocence alone will not protect it.   It is not its innocence, but the plaintiff's availing himself of that innocence to build up a success at no risk of his own, which a court of equity should regard.

(c) Injunction

Innocence alone will not preclude a court's granting an injunction against a defendant.   Nevertheless, in some situations innocence combines with other factors to lead a court to deny or modify injunctive relief.

A recent illustration of this approach is found in *Trifari, Krussman & Fishel, Inc.* v. *B. Steinberg-Koslo Co.*,[58] in which a preliminary

---

[53] 105 F. Supp. 393 (D.C.N.Y. 1952).
[54] 111 F. Supp. 117 (E.D. Mich. 1953) aff'd, 216 F. 2d 508 (6th Cir. 1954).
[55] 111 F. 2d 432 (2d Cir. 1940).
[56] In *Shapiro, Bernstein & Co.* v. *Goody*, 248 F. 2d 260 (2d Cir. 1957), the court decided that the release of the manufacturer of unauthorized recordings did not release the sellers of the recordings, on the ground that "the liability of each infringer, whether he be manufacturer, distributor or seller is several." Id. at 267. It is not clear that this interpretation of sec. 101(e) would be extended to sec. 101(b).
[57] 234 Fed. 105, 108 (S.D.N.Y. 1916). It is generally accepted on the basis of principles of equity that coinfringers are not jointly liable for profits. *Alfred Bell & Co.* v. *Catalda Fine Arts, Inc.*, 86 F. Supp. 399 (S.D.N.Y. 1949), modified, 191 F. 2d 99 (2d Cir. 1951); *Washingtonian Publishing Co.* v. *Pearson*, 140 F. 2d 465 (D.C. Cir. 1944).
[58] 144 F. Supp. 577 (S.D.N.Y. 1956).

injunction was denied where the defendants had no notice of plaintiff's copyright and did not intend to infringe during the pendency of the action. There have also been instances of denial of an injunction against an innocent defendant where the plaintiff was guilty of laches,[59] or where it would have been difficult to distinguish between infringing and noninfringing parties of the work.[60] And the court in *Lawrence v. Dana* observed—

* * * but cases frequently arise in which, though there is some injury, yet equity will not interpose by injunction to prevent the further uses, as where the amount copied is small and of little value, if there is no proof of bad motive.[61]

(d) Counsel fees and costs

A court may be influenced by a defendant's innocence in determining the amount to be awarded as attorney's fees or in refusing to give attorney's fees at all.[62] And in *Gross* v. *Van Dyk Gravure Co.*,[63] the court refused to award not only counsel fees against an innocent infringer, but other costs as well. An occasional decision has gone even further and refused to award costs against an innocent infringer who was the only party defendant, despite the apparently mandatory statutory language concerning the award of costs in general, as opposed to attorney's fees.[64]

The cases considered above indicate that innocence can be of some importance, in the selection of remedies in a particular case. It should be noted, however, that in most of the cases other factors— such as mere technical character of an infringement involving little or no loss to the plaintiff, laches on the part of the plaintiff, or the presence of willful infringers who could be taxed to compensate the plaintiff—combined with the defendant's innocence in influencing the court's decision.

3. Innocence or lack of intent and contributory infringement

It has been stated that with respect to—

* * * parties who aid, induce, or contribute to the infringement * * *, guilty knowledge is the basis of liability for contributory infringements * * *.[65]

In other words, one who unwittingly aids the commission of infringement is not liable.[66] This is one area where knowledge or intention is required for liability.[67] Such intention was found by the Supreme Court in *Kalem* v. *Harper Bros.*,[68] where the producer-distributor of a plagiarizing motion picture expected it to be exhibited in violation of copyright; the producer was held liable as a contributory infringer.

---

[59] *West Pub. Co.* v. *Edward Thompson Co.* 176 Fed. 833, 838 (2d Cir. 1910).
[60] *Webb* v. *Powers*, 29 Fed. Cas. 511, Case No. 17,323 (C.C.D. Mass. 1847).
[61] 15 Fed. Cas. 26, 60, Case No. 8,136 (C.C.D. Mass. 1869).
[62] E.g., *Haas* v. *Leo Feist, Inc.*, 234 Fed. 105 (S.D.N.Y. 1916).
[63] 230 Fed. 412 (2d Cir. 1916).
[64] *Altman* v. *New Haven Union Co.*, 254 Fed. 113 (D.C. Conn. 1918).
[65] 45 Colum. L. Rev. 644, 645, n. 6 (1945).
[66] *Harper* v. *Shoppell*, 26 Fed. 519 (S.D. N.Y. 1886), motion for new trial denied, 28 Fed. 613.
[67] See Amdur, op. cit., note 31, supra, at 968; 38 Marquette L. Rev. 180, 187.
[68] 222 U.S. 55 (1911).

4. *Probative effect of intention or innocence*

(a) *Copying*

In *Harold Lloyd Corporation* v. *Witwer*,[69] the court stated:

In considering the weight of the circumstantial evidence of copying derived from an analysis of similarities between the play and the story, the question of intent to copy is an important factor, although, as has been stated, an intentional copying is not a necessary element in the problem * * *.

Thus, evidence of an intent or willingness to infringe may be a link in the chain of circumstantial evidence indicating copying.[70] Moreover, in *Meccano, Ltd.* v. *Wagner*,[71] the court took into consideration defendant's intentional acts of unfair competition in determining whether or not he had infringed plaintiff's copyright.

(b) *Fair use*

The state of mind of the user of copyrighted material is of significance in determining whether his copying constituted infringement or "fair use." [72]   For example, in *New York Tribune, Inc.* v. *Otis & Co.*,[73] defendant contended that its distribution of a photostatic copy of a copyrighted newspaper editorial was for noncommercial purposes. The court, in declining to rule on this issue on motion, recognized the relevance of the purpose of the claimed fair use and the defendant's intention.

IV. Legislative Proposals Since 1909 [74]

As indicated earlier,[75] a significant legislative development with respect to innocent infringers occurred in 1912. It was in that year that the Townsend Act [76] furnished the special limitation applicable to infringements by means of motion pictures presently in section 101(b) of the Copyright Act. Other attempts to cover the problems of innocent infringement were made in the series of general revision bills introduced from 1924 to 1940.

A. DALLINGER BILLS, 1924

The Dallinger bills,[77] maintained the provision, presently in section 101(b), which removes the statutory damage limitations in the case of infringements after actual written notice.[78] The second bill main-

---

[69] 65 F. 2d 1, 17 (9th Cir. 1933).

[70] Peck, "Copyright Infringement of Literary Works," 38 Marquette L. Rev. 180, 188 (1955). Warner, op. cit., note 47, supra, 606. See also Howell, "The Copyright Law" 122 (1952).

[71] 234 Fed. 912 (S.D. Ohio 1916), modified on other grounds 246 Fed. 603 (6th Cir. 1918).

[72] Peck, op. cit., note 70, supra at 187. Warner op. cit., note 47, supra. The relevance of intent in this area was recognized prior to the present statute. See, e.g., *Lawrence* v. *Dana*, note 61, supra, at 60. "Innocent intention" in this context has been roughly equated by one writer with "good faith." Cohen, "Fair Use in the Law of Copyright," Copyright Law Symposium No. 6, 43, 60 (1955). In *Broadway Music Corp.*, v. *F-R Pub. Corp.*, 31 F. Supp. 817, 818 (S.D. N.Y. 1940), the court found the absence of an "intent to commit an infringement" to "go to fill out the whole picture" with respect to fair use.

[73] 39 F. Supp. 67 (S.D. N.Y. 1941).

[74] In addition to the general copyright revision bills to be discussed, a number of bills proposed granting to designs for useful articles protection based on copyright principles. These bills generally provided for more generous treatment of the innocent infringer than the copyright revision bills. For example, sec. 10(b) of H.R. 11852, 71st Cong., 2d sess. (1929), authorized the court to dispense with an accounting for damages and profits "in cases where the copying complained of was without knowledge or notice of copyright." In addition extensive protection was granted to distributors. This basic philosophy apparently continues to guide the drafting of design proposals. For example, see exceptions in the definition of infringement in sec. 9(b) of H.R. 8873, 85th Cong., 1st sess. (1957).

[75] See pp. 141-142, supra.

[76] See note 15, supra.

[77] H.R. 8177 and H.R. 9137, 68th Cong., 1st sess. (1924).

[78] See note 21, supra.

tained the Townsend limitations as well, as did most of the revision bills. In addition, section 26(a) of both Dallinger bills provided:

> In any action for infringement of copyright of any work, if the defendant proves that he was not aware that he was infringing and that he acted in good faith, or has been subjected to fraud, or substantial imposition by any third person or persons, the plaintiff shall not be entitled to any remedy other than an injunction in respect to future infringement: *Provided*, That this provision shall not apply in the event of registration of copyright or of any instrument affecting the same prior to defendants entering into or upon the undertaking which results in such infringement: *And provided further*, That the mere failure to register a work or to affix a notice shall not, per se, be deemed to create either a presumption of innocence in infringement or be deemed evidence of such innocence.

Thus, the innocent infringer of an unregistered work was to escape such remedies as liability for damages and for profits. This provision does not appear to have been specifically discussed in the hearings on the second Dallinger bill.

B. THE PERKINS BILLS, 1925

The Perkins bills [79] offered no innovations with respect to innocent infringement. The Townsend damage limitations in the case of innocent infringement by motion pictures were retained. Otherwise, the bills made no distinctions based upon the state of mind of the infringer. Thus, the Perkins bills represent an adherence to the 1909 postion, in contrast with the more sweeping exculpatory approach of the Dallinger bills.

C. THE VESTAL BILLS, 1926–31

The Vestal bills reverted generally to the Dallinger approach of limiting the remedies against innocent infringers. A refinement of the provision in the Dallinger bills set forth above, appeared in section 16(d) of H.R. 10434,[80] the first Vestal bill. This section, which seemed to be restricted to infringement of copyright in dramatic works, also limited the remedy against the innocent infringer to an injunction. But the section was made inapplicable not only where the plaintiff's work had been registered, but also where it had been published with notice, or performed in a "first class public production." Register of Copyrights Solberg expressed the view that the notice proviso imposed an undue burden on the copyright owner in a bill that provided for only optional notice;[81] but the section was favored by representatives of the motion picture industry.[82] The provision was modified in the amended Vestal bill which passed the House.[83] It then clearly applied to all copyrighted works but substituted for the injunctive remedy recovery of "an amount equivalent to the fair and reasonable value of a license, but not less than $50 nor more than $2,500."

The Vestal bills also included the protection of the innocent printers sought in the 1909 hearings. Section 16(e) of H.R. 10434 protected the printer who "was not aware that he was infringing and * * * was acting in good faith" as long as he did not participate in the publishing, distributing or selling activities. The remedies against such innocent printers included only injunction and forfeiture of the infringing copies.

---

[79] H.R. 11258 and S. 4355. 68th Cong., 2d sess. (1925) and H.R. 5841, 69th Cong., 1st sess. (1925).
[80] 69th Cong., 1st sess. (1926).
[81] Hearings Before House Committee on Patents on H.R. 10434, 69th Cong., 1st sess. 237 (1926).
[82] Id. at 249–250.
[83] H.R. 12549, 71st Cong., 2d sess. (1931), sec. 15(d).

Notwithstanding the objections raised by Mr. Solberg to the proposed protection to different classes of infringers in derogation of the rights of the copyright owner,[84] the provisions in favor of innocent infringers were extended even further in the later Vestal bills, with respect to newspapers and periodicals. Thus, section 16(f) of H.R. 12549, included a special immunity as to advertising matter in newspapers and periodicals. The publisher who showed that he "was not aware that he was infringing and that such infringement could not reasonably have been foreseen" was to be subjected to an injunction only with respect to issues the manufacture of which had not been commenced. This immunity was inapplicable if the publisher was interested in the advertising phase of the enterprise. This provision had been proposed at earlier hearings by the periodical publishers on the ground that they, like the printers, are merely a medium for the advertiser.[85] Support was finally obtained from the Authors' League in 1930.[86]

D. THE DILL AND SIROVICH BILLS, 1932

The proposed revision bills in 1932 were not as sweeping as the Vestal bills with respect to the question of innocent infringers. The Dill bill [87] even retreated from the position taken in the amended 1909 act with respect to motion pictures; it included only the accidental omission of notice provision of section 21 of the 1909 act. The Sirovich bills [88] followed the Vestal bills in protecting innocent printers and periodical publishers of advertising matter.[89] In addition, the Sirovich bills, in effect, exempted the infringer who acted "without intent to infringe" or "in good faith" from liability for profits, but not for damages.[90]

The House committee considered the provisions of the 1909 act too harsh as against the innocent infringer. Thus, in its report on H.R. 10976,[91] one of the Sirovich bills, the committee stated:

> The present law further imposes upon an infringer, whether innocent or guilty, a tremendous penalty by awarding all the profits made by the infringer to the injured party contrary to the usual measures of compensation in force throughout the country. It is even possible that courts have hesitated with good reason before decreeing an infringement because of the very heavy penalties involved.[92]

The committee also explained:

> The present law, except in the case of certain infringements by motion-picture producers, takes no account of innocence in the matter of infringements. The new bill takes account of innocence—for instance, innocent printers who act merely to print a work, and who have no other interest in it are subject only to injunctions against future printing.
> Aside from these specific instances, all innocent infringers are treated alike under the provisions of the bill and are protected by provisions which limit the amount of recovery and the character of the remedy, according to the registration or non-registration of the work. Under the present copyright law all profits are taken from an infringer, whether innocent or otherwise. As pointed out, we believe that the success of infringement suits has been hampered by the drastic provisions of this kind in the law.[93]

---

[84] Hearings, note 81, supra, 235–237.
[85] Id. at 169.
[86] Hearings Before House Committee on Patents on H.R. 6990, 71st Cong., 2d sess. 139 (1930).
[87] S. 3985, 72d Cong., 1st sess. (1932); S. 342, 73d Cong., 1st sess. (1933).
[88] H.R. 10364, 72d Cong., 1st sess. (1932); H.R. 10740; H.R. 10976; H.R. 11948; H.R. 12094; H.R. 12425.
[89] E.g., sec. 10, H.R. 10364.
[90] E.g., sec. 10(b), H.R. 12094.
[91] H.R. Rep. No. 1008, 72d Cong., 1st sess. (1932).
[92] Id. at 2.
[93] Id. at 4.

E. DUFFY, DALY AND SIROVICH BILLS, 1935–36

The first Duffy bill [94] contained comprehensive provisions mitigating the effects of innocent infringement. Section 17 included: (1) General limitation of available remedies against an innocent infringer to recovery, "for all infringements by such defendant up to the date of judgment, [of] an amount equivalent to the fair and reasonable value of a license," unless the work had been registered or published with notice; (2) limitation of remedies against innocent printers to injunction and forfeiture of infringing copies and devices; (3) limitation of remedy to injunction with respect to advertising matter innocently broadcast or published in a newspaper, magazine or periodical, and (4) immunity from delivering up infringing copies and devices for the publisher of a newspaper, magazine, or periodical, a broadcaster, or a motion-picture producer or distributor, who has acted in good faith.

In addition, an injunction and a reasonable license fee not in excess of $1,000 were the only remedies available against *any* infringer if the work was not registered or published with notice. The provision described in (1) above was omitted in the second Duffy bill.[95]

In contrast to the Duffy bill, the Daly bill,[96] contained no provision modifying the 1909 act with respect to innocent infringers. The 1936 Sirovich bill,[97] as did earlier Sirovich bills, contained provisions absolving the innocent periodical publisher of advertising matter, and the innocent printer, from liability for profits.

Although the Duffy bill, which passed the Senate, was strongly opposed as "an infringer's bill," [98] the radio broadcasters felt that it did not go far enough in protecting the innocent infringer, and that there should be no liability whatsoever for certain types of infringement, by radio.[99]

F. THOMAS (SHOTWELL) BILL, 1940

Despite the great variety of treatment of the problem under consideration in revision attempts from 1924 to 1936, the Shotwell committee apparently adopted the approach of relying upon the discretion of the trial judge in awarding damages to protect the innocent infringer. In any event, section 12(b) of the Thomas bill [100] excused "the incidental and not reasonably avoidable infringement of a copyrighted work in the depiction or representation of current news events." This exemption was made inapplicable to any use for advertising purposes. In addition, section 19(e) reduced the possible recovery for infringement by motion pictures and radio by considering multiple infringements in certain situations as a single infringement.

[94] S. 2465, 74th Cong., 1st sess. (1935).
[95] S. 3047, 74th Cong., 1st sess. (1935).
[96] H.R. 10632, 74th Cong., 2d sess. (1936).
[97] H.R. 11420, 74th Cong., 2d sess. (1936). The relevant provisions are found in secs. 24 and 25.
[98] See Hearings Before House Committee on Patents on Revision of Copyright Laws, 74th Cong., 2d sess. 1087 (1936); 47 Yale L. J. 433, 436 (1938).
[99] Hearings, note 98, supra at 478. Thus, it was argued that the liability for network programs should be restricted to the originating broadcaster. Limited relief was also sought with respect to broadcasts by remote control.
[100] S. 3043, 76th Cong., 3d sess. (1940).

V. Laws of Foreign Countries [101]

The interrelation of civil and criminal remedies for copyright infringement found in the laws of many foreign countries complicates consideration of foreign treatment of the problem of innocent infringement.

For example, in the Greek law,[102] the sole pecuniary remedy of the copyright owner is through disposal of infringing copies after conviction of the infringer. Such conviction must be based on "willful or fraudulent" infringement. Confiscation may often be effected in the course of a criminal action. This is the rule in France where the proceeds of such confiscation may be used to indemnify the copyright owner, with no statutory mention of intent or innocence. In Belgium, confiscation is the core of civil remedies with respect to which nothing is said about intent; the Belgian criminal provision [103] is made applicable to "any willful or fraudulent violation of copyright."

In view of the interrelation of remedies noted above, the laws of many foreign countries apparently do not distinguish between innocent and willful infringers for the purposes of civil liability. These include France, Italy, Switzerland, Argentina, Brazil, Peru, Portugal, Monaco and Mexico. At the other extreme, the German law [104] appears to require intent or negligence for every case of infringement. Between the extremes are varied approaches and different limitations of the remedies available against the innocent infringer.

Innocence is quite relevant to liability under the Spanish law. Article 45 makes the author of an infringing work "responsible in the first instance" for copyright infringement. It is further provided that if such approach is not successful, liability is fastened on "the publisher and printer, successively, *unless they are able to prove their respective innocence.*" The law of Chile similarly protects those deemed less directly responsible for infringement. Article 19 excuses "utilization for profit" of infringing copies if "good faith can be proved in the acquisition and use of the copies."

One approach to the problem of remedies is to absolve the innocent infringer from liability for damages. For example, section 18 of the Hungarian law grants immunity from any pecuniary remedy except profits to the infringer who is not guilty of either "willfulness or negligence." The Polish law [105] imposes liability for damages only "in the case of willful infringement." And article 21(4) of the Guatemalan law specifically limits the remedy of damages to willful and negligent violations. Article 21 of the Norwegian law of 1930 permits damages only where infringement has been committed "willfully or by gross negligence." Profits are expressly made available "in any case" even where good faith is shown.

Denmark modifies the remedy of delivery and destruction of infringing copies where the infringement was committed "in good faith." In such a case, the infringer is permitted by section 16 to place copies in public custody until the expiration of the copyright term.

[101] The statutes of foreign countries are translated in "Copyright Laws and Treaties of the World" (1956). which collection, including its 1957 supplement, is the basis for the discussion of all foreign laws except the recent statutes of France (Law No. 57-298), India (Law No. 14 of 1957), and the United Kingdom, 1956 (4 and 5 Eliz. 2, ch. 74).
[102] Art. 16.
[103] Art. 22.
[104] Secs. 36 and 37.
[105] Art. 56.

The laws of the British Commonwealth nations are most elaborate in this area and afford considerable protection to the innocent infringer in certain situations. The United Kingdom Act of 1956 has not significantly altered the approach, and may serve as an example: (1) Under various provisions of section 5, one who does not know of the infringing nature of an article is not guilty of infringement at all by reason of his unauthorized importation, sale, or exhibition; nor is one an infringer who permits the use of his premises for an infringing public performance if he had no reason to suspect the performance would be infringing or if he received no profit from granting such permission; (2) one "who was not aware and had no reasonable grounds for suspecting that copyright subsisted" is absolved by section 17(2) from liability for damages arising out of the infringement, but is liable for profits; (3) section 18 precludes any pecuniary remedy for conversion or detention of infringing copies not only where the defendant did not and could not reasonably know of the existence of copyright protection, but also if he reasonably believed that the copies were not infringing copies.

Apparently, the British courts had interpreted the clause "was not aware, and had no reasonable ground for suspecting, that copyright subsisted in the work" quite narrowly under the 1911 act.[106] It, therefore, did not furnish as much assistance to the innocent infringer as the language might suggest. In addition, the Canadian statute imposes another limitation on the immunity of the innocent infringer. Section 22 provides that where a work has been duly registered under the act, "the defendant shall be deemed to have reasonable ground for suspecting that copyright subsisted in the work." [107]

The Indian copyright law of 1957 accepts generally the philosophy of the United Kingdom Act. At least one significant modification has been introduced, however. While one who innocently permits, though for profit, the use of his premises for an unauthorized performance of a copyrighted work is excused from liability for infringement, the innocent seller, importer, and exhibitor are apparently considered infringers.[108] As in the United Kingdom Act, injunction and an award of profits are the only remedies available against anyone who "was not aware and had no reasonable grounds for believing that copyright subsisted in the work." [109]

Provisions concerning the state of mind of the defendant are found more frequently in criminal sanctions where such provisions are separated from civil remedies. Thus, the Swiss law [110] specifically provides that the penal law applies only if the infringement is "inten-

---

[106] See Copinger, "The Law of Copyright" 170-171 (1948) wherein the author states:

"Judging from its marginal note, the section is intended to afford protection to innocent infringers, but is framed in such language that it is difficult to imagine a case in which it can be invoked in aid. The section must be specifically pleaded, and the burden is upon the defendant to prove that 'at the date of the infringement he was not aware, and had no reasonable ground for suspecting, that copyright subsisted in the work' * * * Nor is it, under section 8, sufficient to prove mere innocence and absence of carelessness; the innocence that must be proved is ignorance that 'copyright subsisted in the work', i.e., the work which has, in fact, been pirated. * * *

"In what cases, then can the section apply? What 'reasonable ground' can a direct copyist have for not suspecting the work he copies to be the subject of copyright? It is submitted that the proper attitude of mind of a copyist toward a work that he copies is that copyright in the latter subsists unless he has evidence to the contrary. The only grounds for not suspecting copyright appears to be either (a) that the period of protection has run out; (b) that he thinks that the work is of such a character that it ought not to be a subject of copyright; or (c) that the work is a foreign work."

[107] For a discussion of the Canadian provisions, see Fox, "Evidence of Plagiarism in the Law of Copyright," 6 U. of Toronto L.J., 414, 446 (1946).

[108] Sec. 51(a)(ii).

[109] Sec. 55.

[110] Art. 46.

tionally committed." And the Monaco law requires "bad faith" for the imposition of criminal penalties.[111] Section 17 of the Danish law limits criminal penalties to a willful or grossly negligent violation.

Such express provisions are not universal even in those countries making every infringement a criminal offense. For example, the laws of France, Portugal, and Argentina do not specify intent or willfulness as an element of the offense of infringement. The Italian law[112] clearly indicates that negligence is sufficient to invoke the criminal provisions, but reduces the fine in such a situation.

VI. Review of Underlying Problems

As indicated by the foregoing, innocent infringement is not a unitary concept. As broadly understood, the term encompasses a number of factual stituations in which infringement is not intended, for example: (1) use of material on which notice has been omitted; (2) belief that certain material in a copyrighted publication is in the public domain; and (3) a variety of secondary infringements where infringing material has been received for reproduction or distribution with the reasonable assumption of its originality.

Statutory provisions dealing generally with the problem of the culpability of the defendant also vary greatly in their approach. Thus, to enjoy the limitations on recovery for infringement by motion pictures imposed by section 101(b) of the present law, an infringer must establish freedom from negligence as well as lack of intent. Negligence would not seem to be sufficient for liability under a strict reading of section 5 of the British Act. On the other hand, in some of the revision bills, even good faith and freedom from negligence would not have shielded the infringer from the full battery of remedies, if the work in question had been registered or published with notice.[113]

A possible general definition of the innocent infringer is one who invades the rights of the copyright owner without intending to do so and without having reason to suspect that he is doing so. The basis for the innocent infringer's ignorance will vary according to the factual situation. The consequences attached to his innocence will similarly vary.

The problem basic to all the variations discussed above is the conflict between the full enjoyment of rights by the copyright owner on the one hand, and the interests of users who, even though scrupulously attempting to respect such rights, commit infringement. Thus, Mr. Solberg argued that the provisions of the Vestal bill—

are virtually inroads upon the author's right to the protection of his exclusive privileges, and they have the regrettable effect of cutting down the powers of the courts to properly adjudicate the trespass committed.[114]

On the other hand Representative Townsend viewed his ultimately successful proposal to limit damages for infringement by motion picture as a bill which "merely seeks to make the damage reasonable," rather than one which "excuses" infringers.[115]

Some judges and commentators have expressed disapproval of certain applications of the rule that innocence is no defense. In

[111] Art. 21.
[112] Art. 172.
[113] E.g., Vestal bill, H.R. 10434, 69th Cong., 1st sess. (1926), see pp. 150–151, supra.
[114] Hearings, note 81, supra, at 237 (1926).
[115] Hearings Before Committee on Patents on H.R. 15263 and H.R. 20596 at 5 (1912).

DeAcosta v. *Brown*,[116] Judge Learned Hand, accepting the majority's analogy of conversion, likened the innocent indirect infringer to one who carries off a watch in his bag without any knowledge that it is there. This is to be contrasted with the innocent direct infringer who, by analogy, intentionally takes the watch believing that it was not the property of the plaintiff. Judge Hand felt that only an injunction and accounting for profits should be imposed against an innocent indirect copyist. Similar views were expressed in a dictum by the court in *Barry* v. *Hughes*.[117] Others have pointed out that the blanket imposition of liability in the indirect infringement situation fails to take into account the problems faced by the radio, television, and motion picture industries, and the complex problems of publication where the author is no longer identified with the publisher or the artist with the lithographer.[118]

Mr. Solberg's remarks suggest an argument against any extensive legislation in this area. The flexible powers of a court in granting remedies, rather than a legislative attempt to provide for an infinite variety of factual situations, may arguably represent the more appropriate technique for solving the problems raised by innocent infringement. The court may consider all the factors involved and fashion a tailormade remedy within such areas of discretion as the statute provides. For example, the power of the court to withhold an award of counsel fees in the absence of willfulness was considered by the representative of the book publishers, in the hearings on the amendment of section 1(c), to represent an effective tool with which to adjust problems raised by innocent infringement.[119]

The problems common to a particular group, such as vendors, printers, periodical publishers or broadcasters, may call for special treatment. Mr. Ogilvie pointed out at the hearings leading to the 1909 act that "it is utterly impossible" for the printer to "read everything that goes into his place" and that he is not in a position to guard against copyright infringement.[120] Vendors are also "secondary infringers" who must rely on their publishers. This relationship may have motivated the court's action in *Detective Comics, Inc.* v. *Bruns Publications, Inc.*,[121] whereby the liability of the distributor of the infringing work was made secondary to that of the publisher. This general approach has been codified by the Spanish law where a hierarchy of liability is established subject to a showing of innocence by the publisher or printer.[122] This approach recognizes the importance of permitting the plaintiff to have recourse against several defendants, in order to facilitate enforceability of a judgment. It may be argued that to immunize printers and vendors from liability might remove the only financially responsible parties from the plaintiff's reach.[123]

Similar considerations apply in the case of newspaper or periodical publishers with respect to advertising matter. Their ability to guard against secondary infringement through the publication of such matter would seem slight.

[116] 146 F. 2d 408, 413 (2d Cir. 1944) (dissenting opinion).
[117] 103 F. 2d 427 (2d Cir.), cert. denied, 308 U.S. 604 (1939).
[118] See 45 Colum. L. Rev. 644, 648 (1945).
[119] Hearings Before Subcommittee of Committee on the Judiciary on H.R. 3589, 82d Cong., 1st sess. 34 (1951).
[120] See note 35, supra.
[121] 28 F. Supp. 399 (S.D.N.Y. 1939). See p. 147, supra.
[122] See p. 153, supra.
[123] Cf. *Miller* v. *Goody*, 139 F. Supp. 176, 182 (S.D.N.Y. 1956) rev'd sub nom, *Shapiro, Bernstein & Co.* v. *Goody*, 248 F. 2d 260 (2d Cir. 1957) (effects of insolvency of disk pirates).

The broadcasters pose a slightly different problem. They are primary, rather than secondary users, of copyrighted material. Nevertheless, the relative speed with which a great mass of material is used is said to create special problems.[124] The broadcasters themselves have gone so far as to say that "a deliberate, willful infringement by a broadcasting station is a very rare thing, and in practically every infringement case, an intent to infringe is completely absent.' [125] On the other hand, broadcasters are a principal user of copyrighted material and the representatives of authors and publishers have resisted any special treatment for them.[126]

Even as to special groups such as printers or vendors, the remedial problems may be more significant than the general question of liability. In other words, state of mind might be considered irrelevant to the question of infringement but might be made determinative of the remedies available against the infringer. This is basically the approach of the Lanham Act[127] with respect to trademark infringement. Under that act, an innocent printer or an innocent periodical publisher who publishes infringing advertising matter is subject only to injunction.[128] The statutory provision uses the description "innocent infringers" rather than any more detailed standard.

Perhaps the problem might be analyzed in terms of which of two innocent parties can more appropriately protect against the infringement. This analysis would suggest, for example, expansion of section 21 so as to shield the innocent infringer from liability where the notice was omitted by a licensee of the copyright owner. Such a result would be based on the fact that the copyright owner is better equipped than the infringer to prevent the infringement; at least he might secure indemnification from his licensee for any loss. On the other hand, the infringer would be made to bear the loss imposed on the copyright owner where such infringer receives infringing material from a third person with assurances that the material is original.

Even under this approach, the loss need not be completely imposed on one party. The remedy of injunction could, as in the Vestal bills, be available in any event; but the compromise in available remedies or selection of damage limitations might be weighted against the person whose contractual or other dealings would permit protection against unintended infringements.

The problem of innocent infringement is obviously part of the larger question of liability and remedies for infringement in general. Perhaps less obvious is its potential relationship with the question of formalities. The history of previous attempts at revision of the statute illustrate how close this relationship could be. For exemple, in some proposals, formalities replace provisions concerning good faith. Thus, the second Duffy bill[129] limited the remedies against infringement of a work which had not been registered, published with notice or publicly performed, regardless of the good or bad faith of the infringer. This development is to be contrasted with earlier pro-

---

[124] See e.g., Hearings Before Committee on Patents, 74th Cong., 2d sess. 478–480 (1936).
[125] Hearings. note 119, supra, at p. 19.
[126] Id. at 5, 32.
[127] 60 Stat. 427 (1946), as amended 15 U.S.C. 1051–1127 (1952), as amended 68 Stat. 509 (1954).
[128] Sec. 1114(2). In addition sec. 1114(1) provides—
"Any person who shall, in commerce, * * * (b) reproduce, counterfeit, copy or colorably imitate any such [registered] mark and apply such reproduction, counterfeit, copy, or colorable imitation to labels, signs, prints, packages, wrappers, receptacles, or advertisements intended to be used upon or in connection with the sale in commerce of such goods or services, shall be liable * * * [for damages and profits only if] the acts have been committed with knowledge that such mark is intended to be used to cause confusion or mistake or to deceive purchasers."
[129] S. 3047, 74th Cong., 1st sess. (1935).

posals, such as in the Dallinger bills,[130] whereby registration merely precluded the immunity which good faith might otherwise have warranted.   In other words, the Dallinger bills focused on good faith but made registration a factor which could negate good faith.   The question of good faith or innocence was irrelevant in the approach of the second Duffy bill.   More objective criteria there determined results which were primarily dependent in the Dallinger bills on the question of good faith.[131]

VII. Summary of Major Issues in Revision of Law

Examination of present statutory and case law, previous proposals for revision of the law, and provisions in foreign laws reveals several major issues for policy decision.   These issues are posed most sharply in particular areas which will be suggested below.   Although the issues may be isolated for discussion purposes, it is apparent that the problem of the innocent infringer might be solved by an infinite combination of different provisions.   The major issues may be posed as follows:

A. Should all innocent infringers (i.e., all those who act in good faith without knowing or having reason to suspect that they are infringing) either be absolved from liability, or be subjected only to limited remedies?

B. If not, should immunity be given, or the remedies be limited for innocent infringements in the case of—
    1. Printers?
    2. Vendors?
    3. Periodical publishers with respect to advertisements?
    4. Motion picture producers?
    5. Broadcasters?
    6. Any others?

C. Should innocent infringement be related to formalities so that—
    1. A copyright notice, or registration, will preclude the defense of innocence?
    2. Reliance in good faith upon the absence of a copyright notice, or of registration, will constitute innocence?

D. Under A or B or C–2, above, what remedies should be available against the innocent infringer:
    1. Actual damages?
    2. Profits?
    3. Statutory damages in the usual amounts or in reduced amounts?
    4. Reasonable license fees, with or without a stated minimum and maximum?
    5. Injunction?
    6. Impounding and destruction of infringing copies?
    7. Costs?

---

[130] H.R. 8177, H.R. 9137, 68th Cong., 1st sess. (1924).
[131] The Lanham Act, note 127, supra, also attempts to deal with this problem.   Damages are recoverable only if the defendant had notice, actual or through a mark on the goods, that the goods are protected by a mark registered under the act.

STUDY NO. 23

THE OPERATION OF THE DAMAGE PROVISIONS OF THE COPYRIGHT LAW: AN EXPLORATORY STUDY

By Prof. Ralph S. Brown, Jr., with the assistance of William A. O'Brien and Herbert Turkington

March 1958

THE OPERATION OF THE DAMAGE PROVISIONS OF THE COPYRIGHT LAW: AN EXPLORATORY STUDY

I. INTRODUCTION

This study is an imperfect and experimental attempt to cast some light on the actual operation of the damage provisions of the Copyright Act. Those provisions, as is well known, are extraordinarily elaborate, indeed uniquely so. They include the following elements: [1]

(1) "such damages as the copyright proprietor may have suffered due to the infringement";

(2) "as well as all the profits which the infringer shall have made from such infringement * * *."

(3) "or in lieu of actual damages and profits, such damages as to the court shall appear to be just," a broad grant of discretion guided in these ways:

(a) by the permissive schedule of items "First" through "Fourth" (here set out in a footnote),[2] of which the most used is "$1 for every infringing copy" of works other than paintings, statues, or sculptures.

(b) by a general maximum of $5,000 and a general minimum of $250.

(c) by a special minimum of $50 and maximum of $200 "in case of a newspaper reproduction of a copyrighted photograph."

(d) by a special maximum of $100 for innocent infringement of an "undramatized or nondramatic work by means of motion pictures."

(e) by a special maximum of $5,000 for innocent infringement "of a copyrighted dramatic or dramatico-musical work by a maker of motion pictures and his agencies for distribution thereof to exhibitors"—which presumably differs from the general $5,000 maximum in that only one such $5,000 recovery is permitted against the maker and his distributors.

(f) a special maximum of $100 for innocent infringement "by broadcast" of a "lecture, sermon, address, or similar production, or other nondramatic literary work" is found in a 1952 amendment to section 1(c).[3]

---

[1] 61 Stat. 652, 661, 17 U.S.C. 101(b), (1952), except as otherwise indicated.
[2] First. In the case of a painting, statue, or sculpture, $10 for every infringing copy made or sold by or found in the possession of the infringer or his agents or employees; Second. In the case of any work enumerated in section 5 of this title, except a painting, statue, or sculpture, $1 for every infringing copy made or sold by or found in the possession of the infringer or his agents or employees; Third. In the case of a lecture, sermon, or address, $50 for every infringing delivery; Fourth. In the case of a dramatic or dramatico-musical or orchestral composition $100 for the first and $50 for every subsequent infringing performance; in the case of other musical compositions $10 for every infringing performance.
[3] 66 Stat. 752, 17 U.S.C. (1) (1952).

(g) "the limitation as to the amount of recovery [shall not] apply to infringements occurring after the actual notice to a defendant * * *."

(4) Another form of statutory damages is found in section 1(e) and section 101(e), with respect to mechanical recordings. The court may require infringers to pay up to four times the statutory royalty. This subject will not be treated in this study.[4]

(5) "the court may award to the prevailing party a reasonable attorney's fee as part of the costs" (sec. 116).

In short, there are three major elements of the damage provisions with which this report is concerned: (1) actual damages and profits, (2) statutory damages, including all the refinements listed in items (a) to (g) above, (3) costs and attorney's fees.

Actual damages are of course the cornerstone of commonlaw remedies; infringer's profits are an equally familiar concept from equity practice. Their statutory embodiment is, however, not free of ambiguities. For example, there is the question whether the phrase "as well as" is to be read literally so as to permit the recovery of damages *and* profits, or whether it can be taken in what is usually considered a more rational disjunctive meaning.[5] Such questions of interpretation are not our concern, unless they seem to affect the practical administration of the statute either by the courts or by lawyers in settling cases. We will instead ask: To what extent are actual damages and profits determinable in copyright cases? To what extent are they awarded?

Similar questions should be asked about statutory damages. To what extent do parties and courts resort to them because of the supposed indeterminacy or inadequacy of actual damages? If they are preferred by plaintiffs, do they appear to contain inequities for defendants? What parts of the statutory damage scheme are actually used, and by whom? Here we have to consider the general $250 minimum, the general $5,000 maximum, the various special minima and maxima, and the suggested schedules "First" through "Fourth."

With respect to attorney's fees, how often are they awarded, in what amounts, and in what circumstances? What role does their possible availability play in settlements?

Partial answers to these questions have been sought from three sources. First, the reported cases; second, a questionnaire; third, interviews and correspondence which amplified the questionnaires, or which were independently initiated. We interviewed about 25 lawyers experienced in copyright matters, and had helpful letters from perhaps 10 more. Information derived from these last sources, and from the cases, will be drawn upon at appropriate places. The questionnaire requires separate analysis. It is reproduced below.

[4] See Henn, The Compulsory License Provisions of the United States Copyright Law [Study No. 5 in the present series of Committee Prints, pp. 13–21]; Shapiro, Bernstein & Co. v. Goody, 248 F. 2d 260 (2d Cir. 1957), holding, inter alia, the $250 minimum damage provision of sec. 101(b) inapplicable to an infringing phonograph record, because secs. 1(e) and 101(e) create a separate statutory scheme of damages. An interviewee stated that "the provisions for discretionary awards of three times the statutory license fee, in addition to the basic two cents per "part" manufactured, are not invoked in practice.
[5] See Strauss, "The Damage Provisions of the United States Copyright Law" [Study No. 22 in the present Committee Print, p. 5].

COPYRIGHT DAMAGES SURVEY

MARCH 1957.

(All estimates can be approximate. Please confine yourself to the postwar period.)

1. Approximately how many cases have you handled in the last 10 to 12 years that involved copyright money damage claims?

    1 to 5 _____ _____

    6 to 10 _____ _____

    If more than 10, about how many _____ _____

       (By case, we mean any matter that involved communication with an opposing party, not just advice to a client.)

2. Have you handled any common law literary property cases that involved damage claims? (approximate number) _____ _____

3. In what rough percentage of those cases in questions 1 and 2 were you representing—Plaintiffs? (include counterclaiming defendants) _ _____

    Defendants? _____ _____

4. How many of these cases were settled or otherwise disposed of before judgment? _____ _____

5. Of the cases closed before judgment, how many would you say were concluded on the basis of

    (a) Cessation (by license or otherwise) of infringement _____

    (b) Money settlement based on—

        (i) Actual damages _____ _____

        (ii) Infringer's profits _____ _____

    (c) Money settlement based on statutory damages _____ _____

    (d) Money settlement based on expenses of suit, including attorney's fees _____ _____

6. How many of your cases were carried to judgment? _____ _____

7. In those cases carried to judgment in which there was a recovery, in how many was recovery—

    (a) Based on actual damages _____ _____

    (b) Based on infringer's profits _____ _____

    (c) Based on statutory damages _____ _____

    (d) In how many was the successful party awarded an attorney's fee _____ _____

8. If you had any cases involving the award of statutory damages (item 7(c) above), did any of them involve the application of (or departure from) the statutory scheme of damages in sec. 101(b) "First" through "Fourth" _____ _____

    (If so, could you describe them briefly on a separate sheet?)

  How many, if any, of the statutory damage cases resulted in the award of the $250 minimum statutory damages? _____ _____

9. Have you had any cases, either settled or tried, that involved statutory damages in excess of $5,000 (because of infringement with notice, or because of a finding of multiple infringements)? _____ _____

    (If so, could you describe them briefly on a separate sheet?)

10. Have you had any cases, either settled or tried, that involved the special minimum and maximum statutory damages, as follows:

    (a) Newspaper reproduction of a copyrighted photo ($50 minimum, $200 maximum)? _____ _____

    (b) Innocent infringement of nondramatic work by motion picture ($100 maximum)? _____ _____

    (c) Innocent infringement of nondramatic work by broadcast (sec. 1(c); $100 maximum)? _____ _____

    (If so, could you describe them briefly on a separate sheet?)

The information in this questionnaire will be used in attempting to reach conclusions about the use and usefulness of the damage provisions. It will not be ascribed to you. May we communicate with you further about your experience with the damage provisions? Yes _____. No _____. Whether any further information is to be ascribed to you or quoted from you will be determined by mutual agreement in each case.

_____   _____

      Your name   Address

II. THE QUESTIONNAIRE

A little more than 500 copies of the questionnaire reproduced on the foregoing pages were sent out, of which about 480 went, in late March 1957, to the members of the Copyright Society of the U.S.A., through the kindness of its then President Joseph A. McDonald, and Mr. Fred B. Rothman.

Eighty-eight questionnaires were returned, of which 30 reported no "cases," as defined in the questionnaire—"any matter that involved communication with an opposing party, not just advice to a client." Five returns from performing-right societies or their counsel will be treated separately. This leaves 53 reporting one or more cases. Thirteen of these respondents, with a total of approximately 50 cases, reported that none of their cases had resulted in any monetary payments. These respondents are not included in the tabulations that follow. If they were included, the only effect would be to increase to some extent the number of settlements based on cessation of the claimed infringement—a figure which, though large, could not be tabulated (see p. 67 below). Another respondent, who had been connected with about 50 cases, was unable to provide any numerical breakdown of his cases; so his return is also omitted.

The remaining 39 respondents are those whose experience (in the postwar period) included some cases in which money payments were made, as well as those that were otherwise disposed of. This is less than half of all those responding, and less than 10 percent of those approached, not a very rewarding return, even if one considers that many of the members of the Copyright Society are libraries and others not in active practice. Nevertheless, the 39 respondents listed a total of roughly 850 cases, so the results are not altogether insignificant, even after the following qualifications are emphasized.

1. A glance at the questionnaire will show that estimates and approximations were all that was requested in most instances, and indeed all that could be provided without great difficulty. Most of the totals given here are rounded, and are the rough medians of the range of cases reported under a given question.

2. The questionnaire was apparently unclear at some points. This was of course not intended. On the other hand, deliberate effort to encourage responses by keeping the questions as simple as possible resulted in our seeking no information about the kinds of infringements reported. When it became apparent that music performing rights cases should be separated, we were able to identify plaintiffs with fair accuracy, defendants with less.

3. A few respondents account for a great many cases. Particularly, one west-coast firm reported, under question 1, 100 cases, mostly on behalf of plaintiffs and with a large preponderance of common-law cases. A New York firm reported 150 cases with a similar disproportion. Another New York firm reported more than 50 cases, usually on behalf of defendants. These three respondents thus accounted for about one-third of all the cases reported. Their special patterns must be kept in mind.

A. GROSS RESULTS

Of the total of 850 cases, about 250 were common-law literary property cases (question 2). Half of the common-law cases came from the two respondents mentioned above with the largest numbers of cases. For this reason no inference should be drawn that common-law cases amount to almost one-third of copyright claims in actual practice. But they do so figure in these tabulations.

Representation of plaintiffs was reported in about 400 cases, for defendants in about 450 (question 3). Half of the total plaintiffs' representations are accounted for by the same two firms; representation of defendants was much more widely dispersed.

The ratio of settlements to judgments was elicited by questions 4 and 6. Of the 850 cases ("controversies" might have been a better term), about 700 were settled, and 90 were carried to judgment. Sixty were either pending, discontinued without any definite settlement, or unaccounted for because of discrepancies in reporting.

B. BASES FOR SETTLEMENTS

The settlement of seven cases out of eight will presumably come as no surprise. What was sought in question 5 was an indication of the elements that went into these settlements. The question was not well expressed, and there was much inconsistency in the responses. Still, certain conclusions emerge. Cessation of the claimed infringement, with no money payment, was the outcome of a very substantial number of cases, for which a meaningful number cannot be given because of uncertain estimates. Many of these cases were accompanied by negotiation of a license for further use. Sixty settlements were described as based on actual damages, and only 10 on defendant's profits. Together these two factors, which would probably be influential whether or not they were explicitly sanctioned by the statute, formed the basis for only 10 percent of the settlements. Thirty-two settlements were reported to be based on "statutory damages" (we did not ask for further specification). This is less than 5 percent of the total. If we now take into account the likelihood that about one-third of the settlements occurred in common-law copyright cases where statutory damages would be inapplicable, the percentage is still only 7. Furthermore, 2 respondents, 1 listing 15 and the other 10 such cases, made up three-fourths of the modest total of 32.

Under the heading "Money Settlement Based on Expenses of Suit, Including Attorney's Fees," 135 cases were reported, 20 percent of the total. This response occurred despite some ambiguity in the question, which was intended to refer to what the *expected* expenses of litigation would be. Finally, six respondents volunteered "general bargaining power," or its equivalent, as the basis for settlement in 93 cases, 13 percent of the total.

It is apparent that statutory damages played only a minor role in the attainment of the settlements enumerated by these 40 respondents who, it should be remembered, are not intended to include parties to claims based on music performing rights. However, the possibility of statutory damages, particularly minimum damages and attorney's fees, may have been influential in the many cases

(1073)

where the defending party gave some sort of undertaking that the alleged infringement would not be continued or repeated.

C. BASES FOR JUDGMENTS

In the replies to item 7 on the questionnaire, actual damages were reported as the basis for 40 of the 54 judgments in which recoveries were reported (the remaining 36 judgments out of the total of 90 apparently went for defendants. In some only injunctive relief may have been sought). Profits were awarded in five. For this purpose it is unnecessary to separate common-law from statutory cases, since the availability of actual damages or profits is essentially the same in either kind of action.

Statutory damages were reported to underlie. nine judgments. If the assumption is made that one-third (18) of the judgments were in common-law cases (following the overall ratio of common-law to statutory copyright matters in the entire sample), then statutory damages were the basis for about 25 percent of the 36 plaintiff's judgments assumed to have been awarded under the Copyright Act. This 25 percent is still subject to considerable error; the reader should not be misled by the apparent exactness of the small numbers we are now reviewing, for they also are partly estimated and contain various discrepancies. But the role of statutory damages in judgments is by any measure significantly greater than their apparent influence on settlements.

This is the one area in which the questionnaire results can meaningfully be compared with reported decisions, and such a comparison is rather startling. In the same decade to which the questionnaire was directed, there are 24 reported decisions in which plaintiffs were successful (not counting one performance right case.)[6] In two of these an injunction only was awarded. Two cases awarded actual damages, four profits. Four used a combination of elements for different counts—profits and statutory damages, actual damage and profits, actual and statutory damages, and (in one case) all three. It will be noted that statutory damages figured in three of these "combination" cases. The remaining 12 cases were all awards of statutory damages. Thus statutory damages appeared in 15 out of 24 cases, or about 60 percent. This ratio is so much greater than that shown by the questionnaire that some explanation is called for. Indeed, the proportion of actual damage and statutory damage cases is, between the questionnaire and the reported decisions, in effect reversed. Perhaps there are a large number of cases involving actual damages that raise no important questions of law, and are not reported.

Next, the questionnaire returns show that attorney's fees were awarded in 18 cases, 30 percent of the 60 cases going to judgment that are assumed to have been brought under the Copyright Act.

The attempt to get specific information, in questions 8, 9, and 10, about the application of the numerous components of statutory damages, did not yield any statistically meaningful returns, except in a negative way. That is, only occasional references were made to any one of the specifications of statutory damages, with the single exception of claims for "statutory damages in excess of $5,000 (because of

---

[6] The cases were taken from "Copyright Decisions" through Copyright Office Bulletin No. 29 (1953–54) and thereafter from U.S.P.Q. through May 1957.

infringement with notice, or because of a finding of multiple infringements)" (question 9). Twelve such *claims* were reported. The information that was obtained under these headings, as supplemented by correspondence and interviews, will be discussed below.

In sum, the questionnaire results that could be tabulated, while they must be taken with caution because of the narrow base on which they rest, point to the following findings:

(1) There is an expectably high ratio of settlements to judgments (7 to 1).

(2) The statutory damage provisions (those other than actual damages and profits) seem to play a minor part in the negotiation of settlements.

(3) In a small group of cases going to judgment, the statutory damage provisions were used to a significant extent (about 25 percent). (In reported decisions of the same period, their use is much higher—60 percent.)

(4) Attorney's fees, stemming from another statutory provision, were awarded in a significant number of the judgments (about 30 percent). The basis for these awards is another matter which will be discussed below.

It should be reiterated that these observations do not apply to performance-right cases.

III. Actual Damages

This section and the following one on profits are, to a greater extent than the rest of this study, simply supplementary to "Copyright Law Revision Study No. 22" by William Strauss [in the present committee print].

Though it appeared that actual damages were the basis for a substantial number of recent judgments, according to questionnaire respondents, they appear in few reported decisions. One shortcoming of actual damages as a remedy in copyright cases, it has long been considered, is the supposed difficulty of computing them. Since works subject to copyright are by and large differentiated from each other, it is difficult to establish values. If the value of the work before the infringement and its diminished value afterward are sought, in accordance with one approved technique of damage law, two valuations are necessary. Or, if the plaintiff's lost profits are proposed as a measure of his damages, there is the problem of establishing with reasonable certainty what they would have been.

On the other hand, it is suggested that where valuations are called for, expert testimony is admissible, in line with the admissibility of such testimony in cases where profits have to be apportioned. As for lost profits, the trend in damage law in recent decades has been to relax the requirements of exactness. Once the fact of damage has been established, some freedom is left to the trier to estimate the amount.[7]

The application of both these principles is illustrated by the well-known case of *Universal Pictures Co.* v. *Harold Lloyd Corp.*[8] There the defendant, Universal, and the codefendant, Bruckman, a scriptwriter employed by Universal, were found to have appropriated, in

---

[7] See note, "The Requirement of Certainty in the Proof of Lost Profits," 64 Harv. L. Rev. 317 (1950).
[8] 163 F. 2d 354 (9th Cir. 1947).

1943, an extensive comedy sequence from Lloyd's "Movie Crazy," in the production of which Bruckman had been employed by Lloyd in 1931–32. The trial court awarded Lloyd actual damages of $40,000 (along with an injunction, and attorney's fees of $10,000). This sum was considerably greater than Universal's profits attributable to the infringement: and profits as such were not included in the award.

To fix damages it was necessary to determine the value of Lloyd's movie if it were reissued or remade, and the extent to which the infringement had impaired that value. For this purpose the court heard testimony about the profitability of the movie on its initial run—$400,000 during a period of economic depression. Harold Lloyd and two experts testified as to its possible profitability as a reissue or a remake, and to the considerable impairment of that value by the defendant's widely distributed infringement of a major component (the "magician's coat" sequence in issue accounted for about 30 percent of the original cost of production of "Movie Crazy"). Experts for the defendant gave opposing testimony—that "Movie Crazy" was obsolete and of no value. The trial court had to take into account these conflicts of testimony, and also the effect on the reissue value of "Movie Crazy" resulting from another infringement by Columbia Pictures, in a short comedy, of the same material.

The judgment withstood attack from both parties. Defendants asserted that the damages were too uncertain and speculative, and attacked the plaintiff's use of experts. Plaintiff claimed, on the one hand, that the actual damages were $400,000, and, on the other, that the court should have given consideration to statutory damages, which according to his calculations, would be $50 for each of the 6,636 theaters in which the infringing picture was exhibited, or $331,800. The circuit court upheld the trial court's exercise of discretion in awarding actual damages rather than profits or statutory damages, its admission of testimony of "alleged experts," and its final figure.

It is quite possible that the use of expert testimony might be too costly a method of proof except where the amounts involved are large. There is another type of case in which actual damages may also be appropriate, and in which they are more readily computed. As distinct from plagiarism cases like *Universal Pictures*, these cases raise no issue whether the defendant used the plaintiff's material. The questions turn rather on the defendant's right to use the material, in the light of earlier or incomplete contractual relations between plaintiff and defendant. These may be called "contractual" cases. An apt illustration is the very recent case of *Szekely* v. *Eagle Lion Films, Inc.*[9] There the defendant Eagle Lion used a screenplay for which the plaintiff, under the terms of a contract with a codefendant, Geiger, was to receive $35,000, of which only $10,000 had been paid. The court held that the defendant's appropriation had made plaintiff's interest in the play valueless, and that plaintiff was entitled to the unpaid $25,000 as compensatory damages.

Another recent case which illustrates the use of an earlier contract price as the measure of damages is *Advertisers Exchange* v. *Hinkley.*[10]

[9] 242 F. 2d 266 (2d Cir. 1957).
[10] 199 F. 2d 313 (8th Cir. 1952), cert. denied, 344 U.S. 921 (1953) affirming 101 F. Supp. 801 (W.D. Mo. 1951). See also *Gordon* v. *Weir*, 111 F. Supp. 117 (E.D. Mich. 1953). Plaintiff's recovery was computed in part on the basis of his income from previous dealings with the defendant in similar copyrighted material used in a newspaper contest. For other infringements in the same case minimum damages were awarded, and for still others, defendant's profits.

There a merchant had had a 1-year contract with the plaintiff for the use of the plaintiff's copyrighted advertising services, at a price of $156. After the year was up the defendant merchant continued to use plaintiff's copyrighted mats for advertising in a local paper for almost 2 years. The court, rejecting plaintiff's contention that it was entitled to statutory damages of about $90,000 (computed by plaintiff at the rate of $1 for each copy of the newspaper in which the advertisements were published), said that the only damage the plaintiff could have suffered was $312—2 years' income at the contract price. Judgment was awarded for this amount. Though the discussion, especially in the court of appeals, is largely in terms of statutory damages, since the plaintiff did not claim actual damages, it is clear that the computation reflected putative actual damage, measured by the contract price.

It thus appears that in appropriate cases techniques are available for determining actual damages. To the extent that these techniques seek to overcome the uncertainty of valuing a unique creation by permitting rather free estimates, they raise one further question. Suppose the plaintiff demands a jury trial on the issue of damages. Some fears have been expressed, derived from experience in unfair competition and common-law copyright cases, especially in California, that juries may make excessively large awards.[11]

Thus far there seem to be not enough instances to support a generalization that juries are overgenerous in this field. No cases reported under the Copyright Act seem to have resulted in large awards by juries. Awards that are "grossly excessive" or that fail to meet other measuring sticks of judicial discretion may of course be cut down by remittitur (unless the plaintiff chooses the alternative of a new trial). The scope of remittitur in the Federal courts is narrower than in many State courts, at least at the appellate level, where the courts of appeal have long deferred to the discretion of the trial judge and to the command of the seventh amendment that "no fact tried by a jury, shall be otherwise reexamined in any court of the United States, than according to the rules of the common law." But there seems to be no question that the Federal trial judge has some power to set aside excessive verdicts.[12] And reviewing courts are said to be more perceptive of reversible error when verdicts are swollen.

IV. Profits

The award of "all the profits which the infringer shall have made from such infringement" is a subject which seems to have been well developed in the case law, as outlined in the Strauss memorandum and elsewhere.[13] There may be practical difficulties in making an accurate accounting of profits in cases where an irresponsible infringer keeps inadequate records;[14] and any accounting may be complicated

[11] On the availability of jury trial, see Karp, "Copyright Litigation," in 7 Copyright Problems Analyzed 171 (1952) on their frequency in California; Carman, "The Function of Judge and Jury" in the "Literary Property" Lawsuit, 42 Calif. L. Rev. 52 (1954). Much of the California litigation has been brought in the State courts on an implied contract theory (one correspondent says this is so even when the material is copyrighted). See Kaplan, "Implied Contract and the Law of Literary Property," 42 Calif. L. Rev. 28 (1954), reporting (notes 5-6) judgments of $25,000 and $35,000 in the *Golding* and *Stanley* cases. Much larger jury verdicts have been reported in the trade press in cases which were not appealed and in which there was probably a settlement for a lesser sum.
[12] See Moore, "Federal Practice," par. 59.05(3), 59.08(6); *Neese* v. *Southern Ry. Co.*, 350 U.S. 77 (1950).
[13] Strauss, op. cit., supra, note 5 at 5-7; Warner, "Radio and Television Rights," sec. 162 (1953). Warner also discusses many of the other cases and problems treated in this study.
[14] But the statute, by requiring the plaintiff to "prove sales only," puts most of this burden on the defendant; see *Whitman Publishing Co.* v. *Writsell*, 83 U.S.P.Q. 535 (S.D. Ohio 1949).

by difficulties, not peculiar to this field, of allocating overheads or other joint costs.[15]

A major anomaly in the award of profits was ended by the *Sheldon* case in 1940, when the Supreme Court affirmed the decision of the second circuit [16] that profits could be apportioned, thus, giving effect to the seemingly clear statutory mandate quoted above. The earlier rule compelling an award of all profits on an infringing production, without determining the contribution of the work infringed to the final product, may have resulted in a denial of relief in cases where the courts were unwilling to bestow a huge windfall on the plaintiff.[17]

The *Sheldon* case calls for liberality to the plaintiff where the extent of his contribution cannot be accurately determined. The few apportionments made in the cases since *Sheldon*, apparently influenced by the 20 percent of profits from a motion picture awarded to the author in that case, seem to have followed that admonition.[18] Such liberality may be misplaced when the profits of an innocent infringer are taken. After his success in the case against MGM, Sheldon sued the operators of the Capitol Theater in New York for their profits from a 2-week run of the picture. The court in this case probably had no alternative to adopting the same percentage used in the main case, with the result that the defendant had to pay over $3,099 profits (plus $1,500 attorney's fees, and a $1,000 allowance to a special master), even though the court found that the respondent "is unquestionably an innocent infringer." The plaintiff had already been awarded, as his share of the profits of the producer, far more than the probable commercial value of his play. He was now in a position to exact a reward from thousands of exhibitors who ordinarily would make no direct contribution to the author.[19] However, an apportionment such as was made in the *Capitol Theater* case is clearly preferable to taking all the profits of an innocent infringer. The situation of the innocent infringer with respect to statutory damages will be discussed in part V below.

V. STATUTORY DAMAGES

A. MUSIC PERFORMING RIGHTS AND THE MINIMUM DAMAGE PROVISION

It has been previously suggested that performing rights cases stood somewhat apart from other claims for damages. There are two related reasons for this. First, the existence of powerful collective licensors of performing rights in musical compositions has permitted a vigorous enforcement of those rights. Second, in such enforcement the statutory $250 minimum damage provision has been an important and controversial weapon.

There are three licensors of performing rights whose practices are of interest. ASCAP, the American Society of Composers,

---

[15] Consult note, "Monetary Recovery for Copyright Infringement," 67 Harv. L. Rev. 1044, 1049 (1954).

[16] *Sheldon* v. *Metro-Goldwyn Pictures Corp.*, 106 F. 2d 45 (1939), aff'd 309 U.S. 390 (1940).

[17] E.g. *Witwer* v. *Harold Lloyd Corp.*, 46 F. 2d 792 (S.D. Cal. 1930), rev'd 65 F. 2d 1 (9th Cir. 1933); see dissenting opinion at pp. 44–47. The circuit court, in reversing the district court, found no infringement of plaintiff's story in a movie which made profits of $1 to $2 million, though access was proved and similarities were plausible. The plaintiff had never got more than $1,000 for a movie story.

[18] *Harris* v. *Miller*, 57 U.S.P.Q. 103 (S.D.N.Y. 1943) (35 percent of profits of play allocated to script); *Stonesifer* v. *20th-Century Fox Film Corp.*, 48 F. Supp. 196, (S.D. Cal. 1942) aff'd 140 F. 2d 579 (9th Cir. 1944) (20 percent of movie profits).

[19] *Sheldon* v. *Moredall Realty Corp.*, 29 F. Supp. 729 (S.D.N.Y. 1939); cf. *Washingtonian Pub. Co.* v. *Pearson*, 140 F. 2d 465 (D.C. Cir. 1944). There a 10-percent apportionment was made for a few pages of a book that were unintentionally infringing. But the publisher, who had made substantial profits, was bankrupt; the judgment against the authors, who had not received most of their royalties, was for $15.46; the printer had made no profits.

Authors & Publishers, is the oldest and largest. Broadcast Music, Inc., a rival to ASCAP formed in 1940 and controlled by broadcasters, has steadily grown in importance. SESAC, Inc., does not compare with the other two in size; it is apparently the only significant independent survivor of a number of privately owned licensors that once existed.[20]

For all three organizations the largest market by far is in broadcasting, and here it may be said that the statutory damage provisions are only of theoretical significance. Broadcasters negotiate licenses with the licensors, and if, as occurred in the famous dispute in 1940–41, no contract is in effect, the broadcaster avoids using the works of the licensor pending a new contract. Infringements by networks would be easily detected. However, ASCAP advises that whereas in 1940–41 there were only about 800 radio stations, and no television stations, there were as of December 1, 1956, 3,515 radio stations and 511 television stations. This presents an ever-present problem with non-network stations which may not have the necessary licenses to perform copyrighted works. In such cases, ASCAP advises, it incurs substantial expense in detecting and obtaining evidence of infringements by means of taping broadcasts throughout the country.

Among the vast number of what may be called miscellaneous users, however, there are always new or old enterprises that either through ignorance or design do not take out licenses. Miscellaneous users include—

Restaurants, taverns, dance halls, hotels, department stores, and such wired music concerns as Muzak. Of late, factories and similar industrial establishments have become important users of music.[21]

Licenses are always available at rates of which some representative current examples are given in table A [at page 90].

Since ASCAP pioneered in the enforcement of performing rights against such infringers, its technique may be summarized first. The practice appears not to have changed substantially from a description given in the Yale Law Journal 20 years ago, based on 1936 congressional hearings.*

When the society is informed through its extensive network of investigators throughout the country that some unlicensed theatre or cafe or hotel is using copyrighted music, it writes a letter informing the proprietor that he is violating the law and suggesting that he take out a license. The relevant sections of the copyright law are quoted, the leading cases cited, and the definition of "performance for profit" as laid down by the Supreme Court in *Herbert* v. *The Shanley Co.*, reported in full. If there is no response, additional letters in much the same tone follow, with perhaps more emphasis on the possibility of a suit. Finally, if the proprietor persists in disregarding these warnings, suit is brought for infringement. Realizing that under the minimum damage provision there can be no defense to this action, however, the proprietor will usually capitulate before trial and obtain a license from the Society. But even when judgment has been finally entered, the Society very rarely attempts to recover upon it, and generally compromises for the cost of a license to the infringer from the time the infringement was first discovered plus the expenses of the investigation and suit.[22]

Through its field offices and the lawyers who represent it throughout the country, ASCAP keeps a substantial number of these enforcement

[20] See Warner, "Radio and Television Rights" (1953), ch. 13, especially pp. 361–366 (SESAC and minor licensors).
[21] Finkelstein, "Public Performance Rights in Music and Performance Rights Societies," in 7 Copyright Problems Analyzed 69, 78 (1952).
* [Editor's note: A description of the present practice of ASCAP is given by Mr. Herman Finkelstein in his comments appearing on pp. 107–109 of the "Comments and Views" attached hereto.]
[22] Comment, "Copyright Reform and the Duffy Bill," 47 Yale L.J. 433, 443 (1938).

proceedings underway at all times. In response to the questionnaire, ASCAP reported about 700 cases in the last decade, of which 400-odd were settled. "Cases are usually settled," we were advised, "on the basis of the defendant paying an amount equal to what his license fee would have been during the period of infringement plus out-of-pocket expenses in ascertaining infringement." Something around 40 cases was discontinued for a variety of reasons; 131 were carried to judgment, in all of which statutory minimum damages were awarded. About 125 cases were pending. ASCAP has no central records with respect to attorney's fees, but replies from four of its representatives indicate that an award of attorney's fees is almost invariable. A great many such cases were reported in the 1930's; at that time the attorney's fees were in the range of $50 to $150.

A recent case history supplied by the society illustrates the process of adapting suits and judgments to the enforcement of the prescribed licensing rates. An establishment for which the license rate is $480 a year had started unlicensed performances in September 1956. Suit was filed in December 1956, alleging infringement of two copyrights. A default judgment was entered which formed the basis for a settlement in March 1957. The judgment was for $657, composed of minimum damages of $250 on each copyrighted composition, costs of $57, and an attorney's fee of $100. The settlement provided for a license commencing March 1, and for payments totaling $417, of which $240 represented the license fees that would have been paid for the 6 months from September 1956 through February 1957, $120 the first quarter's fee under the new license, and $57 the statutory costs. No attorney's fee was included in the settlement.

Broadcast Music, Inc., appears to follow enforcement policies that are generally similar, though on a less extensive scale. Their counsel reported that, in addition to 125 to 150 licensing contracts obtained as the result of legal demand letters, 80 settlements were made which involved acceptance of a license and a money payment based on expenses including attorney's fees. Ten cases carried to judgment all resulted in statutory minimum damages, and in nine of them an attorney's fee was awarded.

If it is necessary to bring suit, however, BMI does not confine itself to a number of infringements that will roughly approximate unpaid license fees, taking each infringement at $250. Offenders have by this time been repeatedly warned of their infringement and have had ample opportunity to take a license. In one recent instance BMI sued a metropolitan theatre which, without a license, had performed 16 BMI-held compositions. All 16 infringements were pleaded. However, the case was settled before trial.

SESAC reports no completed litigation since the 1930's, when it carried two cases to judgment to establish unsettled rights.[23] It attempts to persuade groups of users through trade associations, or individual users through a small staff of field representatives, of the necessity and desirability of having a license. Its spokesmen state that practically all negotiations for licensing are ordinary business negotiations in which the existence of copyright remedies does not figure.

---

[23] *SESAC* v. *Hotel Statler*, 19 F. Supp. 1 (S.D.N.Y. 1937); *SESAC* v. *WCAU Broadcasting Co.*, 39 U.S.P.Q. 261 (E.D. Pa. 1938); 46 U.S.P.Q. 198 (E.D. Pa. 1940); 47 U.S.P.Q. 310 (E.D. Pa. 1940) (preliminary issues only reported).

It may be observed that the users with whom SESAC deals have probably been made aware of the statutory remedies by the vigorous policing activities of ASCAP and BMI.

The availability of the $250 minimum damages for a single infringement of a performing right has been a source of recurrent complaint by users. These complaints were most emphatic in the 1930's, when ASCAP was the only major licensing organization, and were extensively voiced in the 1936 hearings on the Duffy and Daly bills.[24]

Objections to the minimum damage provision seem to have two bases. One is that it gives licensors too powerful a weapon in demanding licenses at rates which users consider excessive. Behind this objection may lie dissatisfaction with having to recognize performing rights at all. For example, jukeboxes are exempt; but any establishment which makes broadcast music available to its customers can presumably be required to have a license. Again, court decisions establish that for a hotel to make broadcast music available to its patrons either in public rooms or in bedrooms is a public performance for profit, and thus within the act.[25] Hotel interests, according to an interview source, resist this interpretation, especially in its application to bedrooms. They would therefore naturally be critical of a damage provision which facilitated its enforcement. Whether the cost of licenses is excessive is of course not abstractly determinable. Under the 1950 amendments to the ASCAP consent decree, any user who objects to a rate quoted by the Society can apply to the U.S. District Court for the Southern District of New York to have a fair rate fixed by the court.

The other basic objection to the use of the minimum damage provision in music performing-right cases is that it exposes an innocent infringer to the threat of inordinate multiple damages, since each performance of a copyrighted composition may be the foundation for a claim of $250. Note that a regular user of music has no occasion to make this objection against the major performing-right licensors, for if he takes a blanket license he will avoid infringement of anything in their catalogs. The fear of such users seems to be that they will be held for successive performances of some composition not licensed. Checking the catalogs of the three licensing organizations is laborious. Phonograph records, the most used means of performance, may or may not indicate the licensor, as is also true of sheet music; and there is no statutory or other requirement that such notice be given.

Reported decisions and cases described to us do not disclose any recent instances of successful damage claims for multiple infringements of copyrighted music, except for the well-known case of *Law* v. *N.B.C.*[26]

In the case of the user who does not have any licenses and who, if he is a regular user, presumably infringes dozens of copyrights in his normal operation, we have seen that he is urged to accept a license retroactively, in settlement of any damage claims. If he persists in infringement and is sued, the probability is that he has been put on notice and that the $5,000 maximum would be lifted. Yet the standard procedure in suits by ASCAP is to sue on only enough infringements to cover the claimed license fees and other expenses. Another

[24] See comment, note 22, supra; Strauss, supra, note 5 at 25–27.
[25] *Buck* v. *Jewell-LaSalle Realty Co.*, 283 U.S. 191 (1931); *SESAC* v. *Hotel Statler*, 19 F. Supp. 1 (S.D.N.Y. 1937).
[26] 51 F. Supp. 798 (S.D.N.Y. 1943).

questionnaire respondent mentioned "two or three" cases where claims were made in excess of $5,000 against unlicensed radio stations, but they were settled without suit. BMI sometimes sues and recovers larger amounts than the minimum $250.

No reported decision describes a large judgment in favor of a licensing organization. Even if self-restraint did not dictate abstention from such claims, there are other reasons for selecting only a few infringements as the cause of action. One basis for the ready availability of the $250 minimum is that the actual damages for a single infringement of a single copyright are unascertainable. If a large number of infringements were sued on, the court could more readily resort to actual damages.

References to the availability of statutory minimum damages are conspicuous in the publications of another type of licensing organization which may be described as borderline. Two such licensors have circularized radio stations in recent years offering licenses to perform listed compositions or arrangements. The lists contain a high proportion of works that are patently in the public domain. The list of one of these licensors appeared to include all the major works of Stephen Foster; the other included, among 83 entries under the letter A, the following: "Abide With Me," "Adeste Fidelis," "All Through the Night," "America," "America the Beautiful," "Angels We Have Heard," "Annie Laurie," "Asleep in the Deep," "Au Clair de la Lune," "Auld Lang Syne," "Away in a Manger," and a number of others which, though not of such unchallenged antiquity, are surely not subject to copyright. If the licensor was offering anything with respect to these works, it must have been a particular arrangement, a fact that was, however, certainly not made clear.

B. OTHER USES OF MINIMUM DAMAGES

There are several other fields, besides that of music performing rights, in which copyright proprietors have found the minimum damages provision especially useful.

1. Motion pictures.—In the 1930's a concerted effort was made in the motion picture industry to deter exhibitors from evading rental fees. Many exhibitors were apparently guilty of a variety of trade practices which resulted in exhibitions at unauthorized times and places for which no compensation was paid to the producer. The usefulness of the minimum damage provision in this campaign is succinctly described by an expert on the subject, Edward A. Sargoy, Esq., in his comments to the Strauss study, and need not be repeated here. Mr. Sargoy writes that "the practice was virtually almost stamped out."[27] It should be mentioned that the recoverable actual damages or profits in these cases are rather more substantial than would ordinarily be the case for a single infringement of a musical performing right.

2. Sheet music publishers.—The music-publishing industry has been plagued with infringers of sheet music. Sometimes both words and music were copied; more commonly, the words of popular songs were collected in pamphlets or other publications, which were widely sold on newsstands. A systematic campaign in which the $250 minimum was effectively invoked, was directed in the 1930's against

---

[27] Sargoy comments, p. 50.

this particular form of infringement. Newsstands were first generally warned; then infringing songbooks were purchased to fix liability; a specific warning was given, and finally, if the infringing sales continued, suit was instituted for $250. An attorney active in this campaign reports that it was highly successful.[28] Nevertheless, leaflets incorporating copyrighted lyrics still are circulated for use in taverns and other places of entertainment. A more elaborate form of infringement is the clandestine preparation and sale, at a price of $20 to $25, of extensive compilations of copyrighted music and lyrics. An example of this sort of collection which the writer has seen bore no indication of its origin and included no notices of copyright.

3. *Packaged advertising.*—There are a number of reported cases in which suppliers of copyrighted advertising material have resorted to the $250 minimum against defendants who continued to use the material after the contract period on their license expired or who had copied without having had a license. As the result of the Supreme Court's decision in *L. A. Westermann Co.* v. *Dispatch Printing Co.*,[29] which decided that each illustration in a packaged advertising series could be the subject of a copyright and that the $250 minimum was recoverable for each copyright infringed, plaintiffs in these cases have on several other occasions also been awarded multiples of $250, not without expressions of dissatisfaction by the judges. In *Advertisers Exchange* v. *Hinckley*, previously discussed, the court rejected the plaintiff's large claims for statutory damages and awarded what in effect were actual damages based on the contract price.[30]

C. MULTIPLE INFRINGEMENTS; THE $5,000 GENERAL MAXIMUM AND ITS AVOIDANCE BY "ACTUAL NOTICE"

Though there have been cases where an award of statutory damages in the maximum amount of $5,000 has provoked criticism, for example, Justice Black's dissent in *F. W. Woolworth Co.* v. *Contemporary Arts, Inc.*,[31] this provision does not seem to have created much difficulty in administration. The possibility of awards greater than $5,000, based on "infringements occurring after the actual notice to a defendant, either by service of process in a suit or other written notice served upon him," does create concern among large users of material subject to copyright. Magazine and newspaper publishers, broadcasters, and the advertisers who support all of them, consider that their potential liability is alarming. Each has special problems.

Modern advertising campaigns are often saturation affairs that employ all media simultaneously and intensively for a limited period. A campaign, once started, cannot feasibly be stopped. If an advertiser receives notice early in the campaign that an illustration or piece of copy infringes a copyright, he has little choice but to continue, at the risk of losing the protection of the $5,000 maximum. Larger damages than $5,000 might be found, either by multiplication of mini-

---

[28] For a reported example, see *Johns & Johns Printing Co.* v. *Paull-Pioneer Music Corp.*, 102 F. 2d 282 (8th Cir. 1939).

[29] 249 U.S. 100 (1919).

[30] See note 10, supra. Multiples of $250 were awarded in *Advertisers Exchange, Inc.* v. *Lauffe*, 29 F. Supp. 1 (W.D. Pa. 1938); *Krafft* v. *Cohen*, 32 F. Supp. 821 (E.D. Pa. 1940); *Zuckerman* v. *Dickson*, 35 F. Supp. 903 (W.D. Pa. 1940); *Advertisers Exchange, Inc.* v. *Bayless Drug Store, Inc.*, 50 F. Supp. 169 (D.N.J. 1943); *Amsterdam Syndicate, Inc.* v. *Fuller*, 154 F. 2d 342 (8th Cir. 1946) though plaintiff's demand characterized as "harsh and unreasonable"); single awards of $250 were made reluctantly in *Doll* v. *Libin*, 17 F. Supp. 546 (D. Mont. 1936); *Lindsay & Brewster, Inc.* v. *Verstein*, 21 F. Supp. 264 (D. Md. 1937).

[31] 344 U.S. 228, 334 (1952); cf. *Douglas* v. *Cunningham*, 294 U.S. 207 (1935) (unanimous opinion that award up to $5,000 is within discretion of trial court).

mum damages for separate infringements in many different outlets or by application of the statutory schedule of $1 a copy ($10 a copy in the case of a painting).

Broadcasters, besides being jointly liable with advertisers for the latters' infringements, have their own programs to consider. These also are advertised in advance; often some kind of synopsis will be given. Network broadcasters report that they are accustomed to receiving a number of telegrams and other communications purporting to give notice of infringement before every television spectacular. There will be insufficient time to check the claimed invasion; the show must go on. If each station outlet is considered to be the source of an "infringing performance," as *Law* v. *NBC* [32] held, substantial damages can result from the application of paragraph "Fourth" of the statutory schedule. However, for these damages to exceed the $5,000 maximum would require 100 outlets in the case of a "dramatic or dramatico-musical or a choral or orchestral composition," and more than 500 in the case of "other musical compositions." Such a situation is unlikely to occur unless the infringement is continued through a series of programs.

Publishers of magazines and newspapers also share legal responsibility for infringing advertisements. Against these infringements, however, they (and the broadcasters, too) will ordinarily be indemnified. Most of the editorial content of a newspaper is either written by its own employees or supplied by news associations or syndicates who presumably stand behind their material. There seems to be little concern about copyright liability in the newspaper industry. Magazine publishers, however, use material from a variety of sources. They may buy material from an author who is himself a plagiarist, or they may become liable as infringers to an author if, under pressure of a deadline, they use his work while negotiations are incomplete, and have not ripened into a valid license. The publishers then, if they receive notice of infringement when the presses are already rolling, have to contemplate the theoretical possibility of damages measured at $1 a copy for a circulation that may amount to millions.

However, all these possibilities of astronomical damages do appear to be quite theoretical. In the first place, "in lieu" damages are defined in the statute as "such damages as to the court shall appear to be just," and though the trial court's statutory discretion is extensive, the Supreme Court, in confirming that discretion in two modern cases, has in both made the point that the area of discretion lay between the $250 and $5,000 minimum and maximum. [33] Second, it has long been settled that the schedules "First" through "Fourth," which form the basis for the most exaggerated hypothetical calculations, need not be resorted to by the court; they are simply guides to discretion. [34] Third, there appear to be only three reported cases under the 1909 act—all from district courts—in which statutory awards greater than $5,000 were made. In *Schellberg* v. *Empringham* [35] the total award was $8,500, $8,000 of which was computed at $1 per copy for two infringing editions of a book. Four thousand dollars of this was against the publisher who participated in the second edition with knowledge of the infringement. The rest was against the plagiarist and his business. The $5,000 maximum was not discussed. A

[32] 51 F. Supp. 798 (S.D.N.Y. 1943).
[33] Cases cited note 31, supra.
[34] *Turner and Dahnken* v. *Crowley*, 252 Fed. 749 (9th Cir. 1918).
[35] 36 F. 2d 991 (S.D.N.Y. 1929).

similar omission mars *Select Theatres* v. *The Ronzoni Macaroni Co.*[36] There the principal defendant plagiarized from two copyrighted versions of "Death Takes a Holiday," the Italian original and the English adaptation. Other defendants were the sponsor of the radio program in which the infringing play was presented in 20 install-ments, and the 2 stations over which it was presented. There was no indication that the other defendants were aware of the infringements, nor any suggestion that the plaintiffs had given them actual notice. Nevertheless, the court treated each of the 20 installments as a separate infringement, and held the $250 minimum applicable to each. A judgment for $5,000 was entered jointly against the plagiarist, the sponsor, and the originating station, and judgment for an equal amount was imposed on the other station. The plagiarist was also found to have committed three infringements against each of the two copyright owners in three stage presentations, making him liable for $1,500 more.

This is not a well-considered case. There were two copyrights involved, and it might be argued that damages not exceeding $5,000 for the radio infringement of each of them would be within the stat-ute; but the actual division of the damages between the plaintiffs, made on the basis of the source of the material used in the various broadcasts, was $1,500 to one plaintiff and $8,500 to the other.

A more careful consideration of the nature of a copyright and of an infringement appears in the third case, *Harry Alter Co.* v. *A. E. Borden Co.*[37] Defendant had, in two of its catalogs, copied exten-sively from two of plaintiff's copyrighted catalogs. One dollar a copy was awarded for a total of 6,000 infringing catalogs. For two other infringements of less magnitude minimum damages of $250 each were awarded.

In the questionnaire returns only 12 instances were reported of *claims* for statutory damages in excess of $5,000. Most of these, when further explored by interviews or correspondence, turned out to be unsuccessful.[38] One settlement for slightly more than $5,000 was described to us, resulting from an infringing series of 39 weekly network radio programs; the plaintiff had claimed $250 for each program.

Though instances of recoveries going beyond the $5,000 maximum are thus few, it must be conceded that the state of the law is uncertain. It is not clear what constitutes an "actual notice"—that is, whether an unsupported assertion of infringement is enough to put on guard a broadcaster or other user who receives many such claims, mostly empty. It is not clear how many infringements are involved when a copyrighted work or components of it are used in successive editions or broadcasts, or in simultaneous broadcasts. The definition of a "case," to which the $5,000 maximum applies, is unsettled. These questions have been present in the decisions summarized above, and in a few others;[39] but it cannot be said that they have been answered in a satisfactory manner. There is therefore good reason for some uncertainty about the extent of statutory liability for multiple in-

[36] 59 U.S.P.Q. 288 (S.D.N.Y. 1943). Cf. Warner, op. cit., supra, sec.163, note 13, on the three cases last cited
[37] 121 F. Supp. 941 (D. Mass. 1954).
[38] Decided and reported cases in which defendants won include *Twentieth Century-Fox Film Corp.* v. *Deckhaus*, 153 F. 2d 893 (8th Cir. 1946), *Jerome* v. *Twentieth Century-Fox Film Corp.*, 165 F. 2d 784 (2d Cir. 1948).
[39] *Markham* v. *Borden*, 221 F. 2d 586 (1st Cir. 1955) $2,250 (9×$250) award upheld in catalog case; *Cory* v. *Physical Culture Hotel, Inc.*, 14 F. Supp. 977 (W.D.N.Y. 1936), aff'd 88 F. 2d 411 (2d Cir. 1937); cf. note 15, supra, note, 67 Harv. L. Rev. at 973.

fringements, even though no instances are known of recovery much in excess of $10,000.

D. THE SPECIAL MINIMUMS AND MAXIMUMS

This part deals with items (3) (c) through (f) in the breakdown of section 101(b) set forth in the introduction.

1. "In case of a newspaper reproduction of a copyrighted photograph, such damages shall not exceed the sum of $200 nor be less than the sum of $50."

There are no reported cases giving effect to this provision.[40] Four respondents to the questionnaire reported having had "cases" to which it would apply, but the one settlement mentioned was in a suit brought in a New York State court, on a common-law claim coupled with a charge of unfair competition. There the plaintiff was able to obtain a sum much larger than the statutory maximum.

It seems fairly probable that the statutory limits have discouraged litigation. A lawyer with long experience in representing newspapers writes that—

Prior to the enactment of the * * * provision * * * there were innumerable controversies, many of which reached the court, but practically all of these were prior to 1909. In some of those cases, the damages allowed by the courts appeared to be excessive. Since the enactment of this provision there have been practically no cases that have gone to litigation, because it has been the practice of newspapers, where infringement has been shown, to negotiate a settlement somewhere within the $50–$200 limit, thereby avoiding the expense of litigation.[41]

The inapplicability of this special limitation to a monthly magazine was established by *Cory* v. *Physical Culture Hotel, Inc.*[42]

It will be noted that, unlike the other special provisions, this limitation is not conditioned on the innocence of the infringement. It is therefore a sort of a compulsory license, which sets $200 as the maximum amount that a newspaper will have to pay for the use of a copyrighted photograph. We have no information whether a photograph would ever have a higher market value to a single newspaper user. The photographer can presumably protect the valuable right of exclusive first publication by reliance on common-law copyright. He might also in some circumstances make out a claim for actual damages or profits.

2. "In the case of the infringement of an undramatized or non-dramatic work by means of motion pictures, where the infringer shall show that he was not aware that he was infringing, and that such infringement could not have been reasonably foreseen, such damages shall not exceed the sum of $100; and in the case of an infringement of a copyrighted dramatic or dramatico-musical work by a maker of motion pictures and his agencies for distribution thereof to exhibitors, where such infringer shows that he was not aware that he was infringing a copyrighted work, and that such infringements could not reasonably have been foreseen, the entire sum of such damages recoverable by the copyright proprietor from such infringing maker and his agencies for the distribution to exhibitors of such infringing motion picture shall not exceed the sum of $5,000 nor be less than $250."

These provisions, added in 1912 when motion pictures were included among the statutory classifications of copyright in section 5 of the act, appear to have had no practical effect. There have been

---

[40] Cf. *Hoyt* v. *Daily Mirror*, 31 F. Supp. 89 (S.D.N.Y. 1939) (complaint for newspaper infringement dismissed because no copyright notice on the photograph in suit).

[41] The claims referred to before 1909 would presumably have arisen under 28 Stat. 965 (1895), amending R.S. sec. 4965, and limiting damages for infringement of a photograph to a $100–$5,000 range. There are no reported cases under this provision involving newspapers, but the correspondent quoted is certain that claims were frequent.

[42] See note 39, supra.

no reported cases, and no questionnaire respondent had had any experience with claims controlled by them. In practice authors suing motion picture producers ask for actual damages or profits. In any event, the special limits are available only if the defendant establishes the innocence of his infringement.[43]

3. "The damages for the infringement by broadcast of any work referred to in this subsection shall not exceed the sum of $100 where the infringing broadcaster shows that he was not aware that he was infringing and that such infringement could not have been reasonably foreseen."

This amendment, which relates to nondramatic literary works, has been effective only since January 1, 1953. The standard of innocence which the infringer must meet is obviously patterned on the 1912 amendments to section 101(b) just discussed. There are no reported cases on this amendment. Questionnaire responses supplemented by interviews turned up three controversies which might have fallen within the terms of the provision and which were settled for amounts within the prescribed maximum. In a fourth case, involving a performance of a copyrighted musical composition in a dramatic setting, the limitation was interposed as a defense; but it was apparently not applicable, since the case was settled for a sum quite substantially in excess of the $100 maximum.

The placing of this limitation in section 1(c) raises unresolved questions about its relation to the other damage provisions. For example, does it preclude an award of actual damages or profits? This limitation is not, like the others, part of the "in lieu" provisions. With respect to the determination of multiple infringements by a network broadcast, will the $100 limitation be controlling, or will "the infringing broadcaster" be held to refer to each outlet? If there are multiple infringements in such a situation, would each outlet have to be sued separately, precluding recovery from the network for all the claimed infringements?

These questions are related to the overall problem of the extent of liability of the "innocent infringer." [43a] The provisions just discussed, with the exception of the atypical limitation for newspaper use of photographs, represent a piecemeal attempt to limit the liability of motion picture producers and broadcasters when they do not know or have reason to know they are infringing. This can be the situation of many others dealing with copyrighted material. The broadcaster himself when he mistakenly relies on a song's listing in a licensor's catalog;[44] the magazine or other publisher who buys or licenses material from an author who is in fact a plagiarist;[45] the contract printer of an infringing work; all these are supposedly subject to the full sweep of section 101(b). It is true that, so far as statutory damages are concerned, the $5,000 maximum would be applicable; for an infringer who has been given the "actual notice" that removes the ceiling is no longer "innocent." But this slight comfort does not take account of the possibility that several copyrights may be in-

---

[43] Warner, op. cit., supra, note 13, p. 650, says that, "The maximum of $5,000 was prescribed to cover the unique situation of the manufacture and distribution of a motion picture plagiarizing another form of dramatic work, viz.,'a stage play. This provision was intended to rectify the Supreme Court's decision in *Kalem Co.* v. *Harper* [222 U.S. 55 (1911)] where the exhibition of the motion picture by 10,000 innocent exhibitors resulted in 10,000 separate infringing performances."

[43a] The Copyright Office is preparing a separate study on the liability of innocent infringers.

[44] *Law* v. *NBC*, 51 F. Supp. 798 (S.D.N.Y. 1943). The broadcaster in this case was indemnified by the performing right licensor.

[45] *De Acosta* v. *Brown*, 146 F. 2d 408 (2d Cir. 1944); cert. denied 325 U.S. 862 (1945).

volved, with the result that each may form the basis for a calculation of statutory damages; or that compliance with a notice may be unfeasible, because of close deadlines; or that a trial court's reckoning of statutory damages, which may be mechanical and quite out of proportion to the values involved in a minor case, is nevertheless almost unassailable if it is within the $250–$5,000 range.

The only general protection that the act gives the "innocent infringer" is in section 21, which, dealing with accidental omission of notice, states that "it shall prevent the recovery of damages against an innocent infringer who has been misled by the omission of the notice."

The supposed plight of the innocent infringer heightens the apprehensions already discussed about the possible impact of multiple infringements and calculations based on the schedules "First" through "Fourth." So far as can be determined, these apprehensions have only limited foundation in actual practice. A few reported cases do seem to deal harshly with infringers who may be innocent, and who can be described as "secondary"—a term which has no present statutory significance, but which loosely refers to persons who perform an infringing act, such as reselling, but who are not the principal actors in the infringing enterprise.[46]

One cannot say with assurance, however, that because an infringer is "secondary" he is innocent. For example, a printer may very well be a knowing participator with the publisher in a plagiarism, or he may be truly innocent. Since legal liability has not turned on these distinctions, except with respect to the little-used special maximums and minimums, the courts have not been obliged to make them.

"Secondary" infringers are often in a contractual relationship with "primary" infringers, so that indemnification may be available. This subject will be discussed in section VII of this paper.

E. SUMMARY ON STATUTORY DAMAGES

If we piece together the information and inferences derived from the questionnaires, interviews, and reported cases, the following general observations may be made about the operation of the statutory damage provisions:

1. The $250 minimum is rigorously followed, and gives the successful litigant at least the assurance of that much recovery. Attempts to multiply the $250 in a single case, for which there are various theoretical bases in the counting of infringements and of the number of copyrights infringed, are occasionally successful. But it does not appear that the courts will follow extreme computations blindly. The $250 minimum continues to be most effective as a policing and deterrent device for performing rights licensors. At this time it seems to have lesser importance for motion picture producers and sheet music publishers.

2. The $5,000 general maximum is rarely reached and hardly ever pierced. Though it is removed by a showing of "actual notice," and though (as with minimum damages) causes of actions may be multiplied so that in theory several awards of $5,000 might be made in a single proceeding, the potential hazard of these events for defendants is much greater than their apparent actuality.

---

[46] E.g. *McCulloch* v. *Zapun Ceramics, Inc.*, 97 U.S.P.Q. 12 (S.D.N.Y. 1933).

The chief means of ascending to stratospheric damages, in a case of "actual notice," would be a mechanical resort to the suggested schedules "First" through "Fourth." Of these the only one that is ever used at all seems to be the "Second": $1 a copy for other than graphic works, and this not for very large sums.

3. The special minimums and maximums have very little or no application, except as they discourage claims altogether.

4. A number of reported statutory damage cases award round sums well within the limits, such as $1,000 or $2,000, without explanation.[47] To the parties these may be quite substantial recoveries, in view of the dimensions of the case; but there is no way of estimating whether they are out of line with actual damages or profits, since presumably neither can be determined. If the case is one of considerable magnitude, in dollar terms, the plaintiff appears to be more likely to aim for, and, if successful, to get actual damages or profits.

These observations refer to litigated cases. The final inquiry goes to the influence of the statutory damage provisions on settlements. We have already noted in analyzing the questionnaire results in part II that statutory damages were considered the basis for less than 10 percent of the settlements reported. Opinions derived from interviews and correspondence are less one-sided, and indeed quite divergent. Attorneys agreed that the only damage provision which invariably affected settlements was the 2-cent-per-record compulsory royalty provision of section 1(e). It operates as a ceiling. An attorney prominent in broadcasting thought statutory damages extremely important in settlements of musical-plagiarism cases; an attorney the bulk of whose practice concerns musical plagiarism thought they were most unimportant, because the expenses of collecting them, plus the fact that attorney's fees (if awarded) tend to follow damages and tend to prove inadequate, made them of dubious bargaining utility. An attorney who represents various underwriters thought the $5,000 statutory maximum damage provision influenced all substantial settlements of single infringements; an attorney prominent in musical controversies thought it of no influence.

Opposing points of view are best summed up by the comments of two lawyers of extensive and varied experience. One wrote:

We settle all cases on the basis of what we can get away with when we are the defendant and what the traffic will bear when we are the plaintiff.

The other reported his practice in negotiating settlements was to—

determine the maximum statutory damages which might be awarded, with a reasonable attorney's fee, and offer to settle for an amount substantially less * * *. In practically every case I have had the final reliance has been on statutory damages.

Attitudes toward techniques of settlement, one suspects, are as variable as the temperaments of individual lawyers. The factors that enter into the amount of a settlement (if there is any money payment; often there is not) are intimately connected with the degree of willingness to settle at all. Though most controversies do get settled, some attorneys are obviously much more resistant than others to settlement. Considerations of temperament are reinforced, in the

---

[47] E.g. *General Drafting Co.* v. *Andrews*, 37 F. 2d 54 (2d Cir. 1930) (road maps; $2,000 damages, $4,000 attorney's fees); *Zenn* v. *National Golf Review, Inc.*, 27 F. Supp. 732 (S.D.N.Y. 1939) (print used in magazine with 50,000 circulation; $1,000 awarded); *M. J. Golden & Co.* v. *Pittsburgh Brewing Co.*, 137 F. Supp. 455 (W.D. Pa. 1956) (7,500 advertising plaques; $1,000 awarded); cf. *Tokvig* v. *Bruce Publishing Co.*, 181 F. 2d 664 (7th Cir. 1950) ($1,000 award, though substantial profits determinable).

case of some of those representing users of copyrighted material, by the belief that a settlement with plaintiffs charging plagiarism, even for an amount justified by "nuisance value," is imprudent. It is thought that word gets around; and that more claims result. Consequently some clients are advised never to settle. This leads to occasional avoidable litigation: but it doubtless also disposes of many claimants who will not or cannot finance litigation.

Most lawyers will incline toward settlement, motivated largely, it appears, by the same considerations that apply in other branches of the law, notably the great expense of litigation. In some cases, and to an undeterminable extent, either the real hazard of substantial statutory awards, or the imagined hazard of enormous ones, is a factor in reaching and in putting a price on a settlement.

VI. Costs and Attorney's Fees

Section 116 directs that—

In all actions, suits, or proceedings under this title, except when brought by or against the United States or any officer thereof, full costs shall be allowed, and the court may award to the prevailing party a reasonable attorney's fee as part of the costs.

The mandatory award of costs is sufficiently described in the Strauss study.[48] It raises no problems special to copyright, and is not ordinarily of substantial magnitude unless there has been a reference to a special master.

The discretionary power to award attorney's fees to the prevailing party is, however, an element that should always be taken into account in appraising the substantiality of recovery in a copyright case. Awards of attorneys' fees are not unique in copyright practice; a variety of Federal regulatory and welfare legislation includes such provisions.[49] In fields closely related to copyright they are also found, but with significant variations. In private antitrust actions a successful plaintiff, in addition to triple damages, is apparently entitled to attorney's fees as a matter of right.[50] On the other hand, the patent law authorizes attorney's fees only "in exceptional cases." [51] The Lanham Trade Mark Act permits the plaintiff to recover, "subject to the principles of equity," damages, profits, and "costs of the action." [52] As recently as 1937 the Second Circuit Court of Appeals held that attorney's fees could not be awarded in trademark cases, but more recently a practice has developed of making such awards to plaintiffs where "there is a showing of fraud." The award is apparently justified on general equitable principles.[53]

The Copyright Act differs from all these neighboring fields in that the allowance to the prevailing party is entirely a matter of judicial discretion—a discretion that is, however, reviewable by the courts of appeals (in contrast to the supposed impregnability of statutory dam-

[48] See note 5, supra 29–31.
[49] 6 Moore, Federal Practice, sec. 54.71(2).
[50] Sherman Act, 26 Stat. 209, 15 U.S.C. sec. 7.
[51] 66 Stat. 813, 35 U.S.C. sec. 285.
[52] 60 Stat. 439, 15 U.S.C. sec. 1117. This is substantially an amalgamation of secs. 16 and 19 of the 1905 act.
[53] *Gold Dust Corp.* v. *Hoffenberg*, 87 F. 2d 451 (2d Cir. 1937); *Century Distilling Co.* v. *Continental Distilling Corp.*, 205 F. 2d 140, 149 (3d Cir. 1953); *Admiral Corp.* v. *Penco, Inc.* 106 F. Supp. 1015 (W.D.N.Y. 1952); aff'd 203 F. 2d 517 (2d Cir. 1953) (flagrant violation); compare 4 Callmann, Unfair Competition and Trade Marks (1950) 1902 with id., 1956 supplement. There is a general equitable power to award attorney's fees to *defendants* where an action is "brought or maintained vexatiously, wantonly, or for oppressive reasons." 6 Moore, sec. 54.77(2).

age awards).[54]　That discretion may be exercised to withhold an allowance altogether if the courts consider the statutory damage award adequate—or excessive.　On the other hand, a liberal allowance may be made that has the effect of substantially enhancing any other form of recovery.

The accompanying table B [at page 91] shows the relation of fee allowances to damage awards in cases decided in the 20-year period 1938–57.

Treated as an enhancement of damages, some of the amounts listed are substantial, at least when they are contrasted to the usual American civil practice of making no provision for the successful party's legal expenses.[55]　But if their purpose is to provide for the *actual* reasonable expenses of prosecuting or defending an infringement, the prevailing opinion among lawyers interviewed was that fee allowances rarely are sufficient.　For one thing, they are likely to be scaled roughly in proportion to the amount recovered by successful plaintiffs; and though this approach may not be inconsistent with lawyers' own habits in billing clients, it may bear little relation to the time and energy expended on a case.　Second, courts do not usually make an allowance at all if an unsuccessful plaintiff's claim was not "synthetic, capricious or otherwise unreasonable," or if the losing defendant raised real issues of fact or law.[56]　Several experienced practitioners said that they seldom received fee allowances, nor were their clients compelled to pay allowances, because the only cases they took to court involved unsettled questions of law or fact, and they did not expect the court to make an allowance to either side.　Finally, there does not yet appear to be any discernible trend to adjust allowances to take account of the postwar inflation.

One expense of litigation that attorney's fees do not attempt to meet is the time lost by parties and witnesses, the cost of investigations undertaken by the client rather than the lawyer, and all the other peripheral but often major outlays attending litigation.　However, no provision is ever made in our system for the recovery of such costs, except possibly in punitive damages.　A few lawyers interviewed thought that fees were sometimes awarded punitively.　This may be true in the sense that the court may grant fees rather than deny them because it reaches an unfavorable conclusion about the good faith of the losing party.[57]　But there is no indication that fee allowances include any amounts beyond actual fees and disbursements.

The expected cost of litigation is, as we saw in part II, one of the factors that influence willingness to settle and the amounts acceptable in settlement.　But the likelihood of getting a fee allowance at the end of litigation is so problematical that, according to our interview sources, it is not a factor that they will count on in deciding whether to settle or litigate.[58]

These observations about attorney's fees are not intended as an exhaustive treatment of the subject.　The cases disclose a variety of

---

[54] *Hartfield* v. *Peterson*, 91 F. 2d 998 (2d Cir. 1937). The circuit courts also exercise discretion to award a further allowance for fees on appeal.

[55] Except by way of exemplary or punitive damages. See note, "Exemplary Damages in the Law of Torts," 80 Harv. L. Rev. 517, 519 (1957).

[56] *Cloth* v. *Hyman*, 146 F. Supp. 185 (S.D.N.Y. 1956), quotation at 193. This opinion, awarding fees to a successful defendant, include a helpful discussion of the considerations involved. See also *Eisenschiml* v. *Fawcett Publications, Inc.*, 246 F. 2d 598, 604 (7th Cir., 1957); *Marks* v. *Leo Feist, Inc.*, 8 F. 2d 460 (2d Cir. 1925).

[57] See *Caruthers* v. *RKO Radio Pictures*, 20 F. Supp. 906 (S.D.N.Y. 1937) ("The allowance of fees * * * constitutes a sanction which tends to be a deterrent both on infringers of copyright, and on wholly unfounded copyright claims").

[58] Performing-right licensors' cases seem to be the only area in which fees are routinely awarded.

miscellaneous reasons for denying fees, or for setting them at a particular figure, within a rubric that—

the court should take into account the following elements, among others: the amount of work necessary; the amount of work done; the skill employed; the monetary amount involved; and the result achieved.[59]

The relevance of fee allowances to the overall operation of the damage provisions is that, as an exception to the general proposition that parties pay their own legal expenses, these allowances when made increase a prevailing plaintiff's recovery. Their deterrent effect on ill-founded litigation, whether by plaintiffs or defendants, is outside the scope of this inquiry.

VII. INDEMNITY AND INSURANCE

The incidence of damage awards may be shifted by indemnity agreements and distributed by insurance; therefore these two insitutions deserve some attention.

A. INDEMNITY

A right to indemnity may arise either from express warranties made by an author, from express contracts of indemnity made in the course of any dealings with copyright material, or from implied warranties and obligations to indemnify. Typical of the kind of warranty that may be made by an author is this provision in the uniform popular songwriters contract:

The writer hereby warrants that the composition is his sole, exclusive, and original work, that he has full right and power to make the within contract, and that there exists no adverse claim to or in the composition. * * *

(with exceptions respecting ASCAP licenses and any other rights specifically excepted).

As a musical or other work moves into commercial channels of use, the person who supplies it usually agrees to indemnify the user against any liability arising from its use. These indemnities are elaborately developed in the complex of relationships among advertising agencies, producers of programs, licensors of musical performing rights, and broadcasters.

An illustration of the precise allocation of responsibility as between agency and broadcaster is found in a contract form approved by the American Association of Advertising Agencies and the National Association of Radio & Television Broadcasters for spot telecasting:

(a) *Indemnification by Agency.*—Agency agrees to hold and save Station harmless against any or all liability resulting from the telecast of programs or program material prepared, produced or furnished by Agency excepting such liability as may result from the telecast on Agency-produced telecasts of material furnished by Station and musical compositions, the performances of which are licensed by a music licensing organization of which Station is a licensee.

(b) *Indemnification by Station.*—Station will hold and save Agency and Advertiser harmless against all such liability on Station-produced telecasts excepting only such liability as may result from the telecast of commercial credits, and other material furnished by Agency. In addition, Station will hold and save Agency and advertiser harmless with respect to material furnished by Station for Agency-produced telecasts and the performances of musical compositions on Agency-produced telecasts provided the performances of such musical compositions are licensed for telecasting by a music licensing organization of which Station is a licensee.[60]

---

[59] *Cloth* v. *Hyman,* note 56, supra.
[60] Both this form, and the songwriters contract quoted above, are copyrighted.

Magazine publishers, it appears, routinely require indemnity from agencies and advertisers with respect to material supplied by them. Major newspaper publishers do also. A publication called Standard Rate and Data Service for newspapers includes an indemnity clause as No. 34 in a long list of suggested contract provisions and copy regulations. Newspapers using the service indicate by number which of these clauses they considered applicable. An interviewee reports, on the basis of a random sampling of this service, that smaller newspapers sometimes do and sometimes do not include No. 34.

The enforcibility of express warranties or indemnity agreements seems to be taken as a matter of course; we have not found any reported cases on indemnity undertakings relating directly to copyright, except for the extreme and unsuccessful claims of the indemnitee in *Loew's Inc.* v. *Wolff.*[61]

There seems to be no modern case considering the rights of an assignee or licensee of copyrighted material when no express warranty or agreement to indemnify has been given. If the user has been held liable to a third party for infringement, it would seem that the supplier of the infringing material might, by analogy to sales law, be held to an implied warranty of title and of fitness for the intended use. Another approach, where the supplier of the material is a consciously plagiarizing author or proprietor, would be to recognize that though both the supplier and the infringing user are tort feasors as against the owner of the material, between themselves the "active" infringer— i.e., the plagiarist—would be liable over to the "passive" infringer— i.e., the secondary and presumably innocent user. If both infringers were "active," which in this context one would take to mean that both were aware of the copying of the original plaintiff's work, or if they were both "passive," then there would be presumably no common-law right of indemnity, and perhaps no right even to contribution.[62]

However, it is not the purpose of this study to speculate about liabilities which seem not to arise in practice. The prevalence of express warranties and indemnity agreements, in fields where infringement claims are common, and their accepted enforceability, have already been mentioned. We are informed that indemnity agreements are enforced, as a matter of course, among business enterprises. Some variation occurs when the process of recovery overreaches the individual author. In the music-publishing world, we are advised, the erring composer is held to his SPA contract. In the book-pub-

---

[61] 101 F. Supp. 981 (S.D. Cal. 1951). This case involved an assignment of an unpublished manuscript, accompanied by extensive warranties of title and originality, and an agreement to indemnify the purchaser "against any and all loss, damage, costs, charges, legal fees, recoveries, judgments, penalties, and expenses which may be obtained against, imposed upon, or suffered by the purchaser by reason of any infringement or violation or alleged violation of any copyright or any other right * * * or from any use which may be made of said work by the purchaser." The assignors were sued by a person claiming an interest in the work, and successfully defended. The assignee, having attempted to rescind while this other suit was pending, now asserted that the seller had breached a warranty of "marketable and perfect title", by analogy to real estate title warranties. The court held that the assignor had given no such warranty, and that the warranties he did give were no more extensive than those ordinarily implied in a sale of personal property, in which the doctrine of "marketable title" had no place. The assignee also claimed that he was entitled to recover, under the indemnity agreement, his expenses in the instant case. The court held that these expenses were self-imposed, and not within the contemplation of the indemnity agreement.

See *Alfred Bell & Co.* v. *Catalda Fine Arts*, 86 F. Supp. 399, 409 (S.D.N.Y. 1949), aff'd 191 F. 2d 99 (2d Cir. 1951), where the court points out that the defendant printer had been given judgment over against the principal defendant on an indemnity agreement, and therefore had little reason to complain about certain aspects of the judgment against him.

[62] See *Pacific Iron Works* v. *Newhall*, 34 Conn. 67 (1867) (common-law indemnity by patent licensee against licensor); *Duke of Queensberry* v. *Shebbeare*, 2 Eden 329 (1758) (reporters's notes re recovery by defendant who was enjoined from printing a manuscript of Lord Clarendon's "History," for misrepresentation by his assignor of latter's right to publish); Weil, "Copyright Law," 558 (1917).

On indemnity to "passive" from "active" tort feasors, see *Schwartz* v. *Merola Bros. Constr. Corp.*, 290 N.Y. 145, 48 N.E. 2d 299 (1943).

lishing world, and among other users of literary material, resort to the author depends on the relationship between him and the publisher or other user of this material. Sometimes authors are expected to pay; sometimes they are not. Of course, the practical limit of claims against authors (and for that matter, against small enterprises) is a question of solvency. Authors are often able to make contracts that limit their liability on warranties to the amount received in royalties, or some small multiple thereof.[63]

To the extent that indemnity agreements exist and are enforced, they of course mitigate the situation of the innocent infringer. A "hold harmless" provision that includes expenses, legal fees, and the like, lifts his burden almost entirely.

B. INSURANCE

The form of insurance which is applicable to copyright damages is commonly referred to as "errors and omissions" insurance. Its coverage is far more extensive than claims of copyright infringement. Policies issued by one leading company, which seem representative in coverage, protect against liability for—

(a) Libel, slander, defamation, or
(b) Any infringement of copyright of or title or of slogan, or
(c) Piracy, or unfair competition or idea misappropriation under implied contract, or
(d) Any invasion of rights of privacy.

The language of the undertaking in this policy is that of indemnity against loss resulting from a judgment; but the insurer also undertakes to defend any suits brought against the insured, "even if such suit is groundless, false, or fraudulent." The insurer has power to settle any suit. Another form of policy indemnifies against "claims" rather than judgments. The insurer has the power to take over the defense of a case, but is not bound to contest a claim unless a neutral attorney so advises; the approval of the insured is required for a settlement.

The practical consequence of either type of contract is that any claim is referred to the insurer; and most claims are settled by the insurer.

The industries which make extensive use of this insurance protection are about the same as those which have thoroughly systematized the use of indemnity agreements: broadcasters, producers for broadcasting, advertising agencies, advertisers. However, insurance seems to be little used in the music field. Apparently only one major recording company is insured. Producers of feature motion pictures sometimes obtain insurance, especially for film libraries used on television, and recently for current production. One carrier writes insurance for newspapers, but its use is apparently not widespread in that field, nor in magazine publishing. Apparently book publishers do not insure at all.

The fact that this form of insurance is concentrated among a few carriers, with one of them seemingly dominant in fields related to broadcasting, means that the administration of the indemnities described in the first part of this section is often a matter of concern primarily to the insurer, since the same company may insure all the

---

[63] Colton, "Contracts in the Entertainment and Literary Field," "1953 Copyright Problems Analyzed," 144 (1953).

parties in a chain of indemnity agreements. However, individual authors, who theoretically are ultimately responsible in many cases, do not carry insurance, though at least one carrier offers to insure them. Insurers do not find it practical to press claims to which they are subrogated against authors.

The policies in use have a variety of provisions to protect the insurer against having to pay for liability willfully incurred by the insured. These provisions are cast sometimes in terms that except claims for acts made with knowledge that they are infringing; another form excepts acts committed "after actual notice of an infringement." The latter variation raises the question whether the notices of alleged infringement that are said to be so common in the broadcasting field, and that may operate to remove the $5,000 limit on statutory damages, would at the same time remove the insurance protection. However, we are advised that the contracts are not so interpreted. These notices in fact form the basis of many of the claims that are accepted and processed by the insurer.

The contract written by another carrier excepts acts or omissions of the insured with knowledge "that such act or omission *might* form the basis for a claim * * *." [Emphasis supplied.] This condition if literally read would make the insurance of very limited application; but apparently a literal construction is avoided.

Though no figures are available, it is probable that the legal and other expenses of the insurer in contesting claims, even though very few are litigated, are greater than the actual payments to claimants. Some expense is also incurred by insureds in that their own counsel may participate to a greater or less extent in the analysis and disposition of claims. With these considerations in mind, some indication of the amount of risk that is distributed by this form of insurance may be gained from some representative rates supplied by a leading carrier, reproduced as table C [at page 92]. However, it is not possible to say what part of these costs are attributable to claims arising under the Copyright Act, since liability arising from the whole range of interests that a literary or musical work is likely to invade are covered by "errors and omissions" insurance.

TABLE A.—*Representative ASCAP License Rates (based on material supplied by ASCAP)*

1. The license fee for ballrooms is eight-tenths of 1 percent of the annual gross receipts for admission (with an annual minimum of $60).

2. For hotels, the fee is based on the "annual expenditure for all entertainment at hotel," as defined in a form agreement. A scale of rates is provided, of which the following are examples:

Entertainment expenditure:	Annual rate
Less than $1,500	$60
$10,000 to $14,999.99	240
$65,000 to $79,999.99	900
$160,000 to $179,999.99	2, 400
$300,000 and over	3, 600

3. For roller skating rinks, a scale of rates is related to "annual gross receipts for admissions," of which the following are examples:

Annual gross receipts:	Annual rate
Up to $7,500	$60
$10,001 to $50,000	120
$50,001 to $75,000	360
Over $100,000	480

4. In determining the appropriate rate for other establishments such as bars, grills, and taverns, lounges, restaurants, etc., the following factors are taken into account: Seating capacity of the establishment; the number of nights in a week during which it operates; the number and nature of the performers; for example, a single instrumentalist on the one hand, and a "name" band on the other.

For example, the license rate for a single instrumentalist playing 7 nights each week in a bar, grill, or tavern, with seating capacity up to 75, would be $5 per month.

5. In determining the appropriate rate for nightclubs, the following factors, in addition to seating capacity and number of nights of operation in a week, are considered: A charge for admission or a cover or minimum charge; floor shows; a seminame band or talent; whether there is an alternate or relief band; and whether there are more than two complete programs of entertainment per night. The most elaborate nightclub with a seating capacity of over 600 persons, operating every night and employing all the above factors would pay a maximum fee of $250 per month. However, the average nightclub with a seating capacity up to 150 and with a full orchestra, but with no floor show or minimum or cover charge, would pay $20 per month.

6. During the year 1956, the Society's receipts from license fees from users other than radio and television were approximately $3 million. Total receipts from license fees during 1956 were approximately $24,800,000.

TABLE B.—*Fee Awards to Prevailing Plaintiffs, 1933–57*

	Damages (or Profits)	Attorney's fees
Davilla v. *Brunswick Balke Collander Co.*, 19 F. Supp. 819, mod. 94 F. 2d 567 (2d Cir. 1938)	$1,057	$1,000
Eliot v. *Geare-Marston, Inc.*, 30 F. Supp. 301 (E.D. Pa. 1939)	500	250
Sheldon v. *Moredall Realty Corporation*, 29 F. Supp. 729 (S.D.N.Y. 1939)	3,099	1,500
Zenn v. *National Golf Review, Inc.*, 27 F. Supp. 732 (S.D.N.Y. 1939)	1,000	400
Burndy Engineering Co. v. *Penn Union Elec. Corp.*, 32 F. Supp. 671 (W.D. Pa. 1940)	4,000	1,000
Krafft v. *Cohen*, 32 F. Supp. 821 (E.D. Pa. 1940)	750	300
Sheldon v. *Metro-Goldwyn Pictures Corp.*, 106 F. 2d 45, aff'd 309 U.S. 390, (1940)	63,000	33,000
Adventures in Good Eating, Inc. v. *Best Places to Eat, Inc.*, 131 F. 2d 809 (7th Cir. 1942)	3,500	1,700
Burndy Engineering Co. v. *Sheldon Service Corp.*, 39 F. Supp. 274, (1941) aff'd 127 F. 2d 661, (2d Cir. 1942)	3,500	2,000
Sammons v. *Colonial Press, Inc.*, 126 F. 2d 341 (1st Cir. 1942)	7,486	1,500
Advertisers Exchange, Inc. v. *Bayless Drug Store, Inc.*, 50 F. Supp. 169 (D.N.J. 1943)	250	150
Law v. *NBC*, 51 F. Supp. 798 (S.D.N.Y. 1943)	2,180	250
Rudolf Lesch Fine Arts, Inc. v. *Metal*, 51 F. Supp. 69 (S.D.N.Y. 1943)	1	300
Select Theatres Corp. v. *The Ronzoni Macaroni Co.*, 59 U.S.P.Q. 288 (S.D.N.Y. 1943)	11,500	2,000
Remick Music Corp. v. *Interstate Hotel Co.*, 58 F. Supp. 523 (D. Neb. 1944)	4,750	2,400
Stonesifer v. *Twentieth Century Fox*, 48 F. Supp. 196 (S.D. Cal. 1942), aff'd 140 F. 2d 579 (9th Cir. 1944)	3,960	1,000
Gumm v. *Jerry Vogel Music Co.*, 53 F. Supp. 191 (S.D.N.Y. 1943), aff'd 158 F. 2d 516 (2d Cir. 1946)	(*)	10,000
Phillips v. *The Constitution Publishing Co.*, 72 U.S.P.Q. 69, (N.D. Ga. 1947)	250	250
Whitman Publishing Co. v. *Writsell*, 83 U.S.P.Q. 535 (S.D. Ohio 1949)	10,850	1,500
Toksvig v. *Bruce Publishing Co.*, 181 F. 2d 664 (7th Cir. 1950)	1,000	500
F. W. Woolworth Co. v. *Contemporary Arts, Inc.*, 93 F. Supp. 739 (D. Mass. 1950), aff'd 344 U.S. 228 (1952)	5,000	2,500
Alfred Bell & Co. v. *Catalda Fine Arts, Inc.*, 86 F. Supp. 399 (S.D.N.Y. 1949), mod. and aff'd 191 F. 2d 99 (2d Cir. 1951)	10,800	7,750
Malsed v. *Marshall Field & Co.*, 96 F. Supp. 372 (W.D. Wash. 1951)	100	500
Gordon v. *Weir*, 111 F. Supp. 117 (E.D. Mich. 1953)	3,874	1,000
Barry Alter Co. v. *A. E. Bordon Co.*, 121 F. Supp. 941 (D. Mass. 1954)	6,500	1,000
Hollywood Jewelry Mfg. Co. v. *Dushkin*, 136 F. Supp. 738 (S.D.N.Y. 1955)	3,500	500
Royal v. *RCA*, 107 U.S.P.Q. 173, (S.D.N.Y. 1955)	510	150
M. J. Golden & Co. v. *Pittsburgh Brewing Co.*, 137 F. Supp. 455 (W.D. Pa. 1956)	1,000	300
Nikanov v. *Simon & Schuster, Inc.*, 144 F. Supp. 375 (S.D.N.Y.), aff'd 246 F. 2d 501 (1956)	5,000	1,000

* Accounting ordered.

TABLE C.—*Representative Schedule of Representative Rates (as of Dec. 2, 1957)*

(a) Rates, BL form (all limits in thousands):

Radio stations, class A time charge $200 per hour: *Dollars*

25/50 limits premium	400
100/200 limits premium	568
250/500 limits premium	760

Radio stations, class A time charge $75:

25/50 limits premium	300
100/200 limits premium	426
250/500 limits premium	570

TV station, class A time charge $1,000:

25/50	950
100/200	1,349
200/400	1,805

TV station, class A time charge $400:

25/50	800
100/200	1,136
250/500	1,520

(b) TV show ½ hour once a week, dramatic show, new, 39 weeks:

Per show:

Premium $22.50 base limits 100/200 times 39	877.50
Minimum premium 35 percent of annual	409.50

TV show 1 hour once a week, variety 52 weeks:

Per show:

Premium $52 base limits 100/200 times 52	2,704
Minimum premium 35 percent of annual	846.40

Radio program, 15 minutes 5 times a week, on air 2 years, 52 weeks:

Base premium	10.20
35 percent for 5 times per week	3.57
Per week cost	13.77
Times 52	716.04
Minimum premium 35 percent	250.61

Increased limits on above:

200/400	1.30
250/500	1.40

(c) Advertiser, premium based on actual advertising expenditures in latest completed fiscal year or calendar year.

Maximum limit policy	100,000
Expenditure under $100,000	75
" between $100,000 and $250,000	100
" between $250,000 and $500,000	250
" between $3,000,000 and $4,000,000	1,000

Higher limits of liability: *Percent of base*

$200,000	125
$300,000	135
$500,000	145
$1,000,000	175

(d) Advertising agency, premiums based on agency's gross billings in latest completed fiscal or calendar year.

Minimum limit policy	100,000
Billings under $1,000,000	250
" between $1,000,000 and 2,000,000	350
" between $5,000,000 and 7,500,000	750
" between $10,000,000 and 20,000,000	1,000

Higher limits of liability: *Percent of base*

$200,000	125
$300,000	140
$500,000	155
$1,000,000	190

PART IX

GENERAL REVISION OF THE COPYRIGHT LAW

History, Manufacturing Clause, Register's Report

The first published revision study successfully places the present program in historical perspective. Beginning with a summary of the 1909 general revision, this study traces subsequent revision efforts of the twentieth century, indicating the genesis, progress and obstacles of the various attempts to overhaul comprehensively the 1909 Act. To supplement this survey, a brief historical summary of recent revisions of the patent and trademark laws is included.

The present revision program began with the preparation and circulation of the 34 revision studies included in these volumes. Also included in the present work is a study of the requirement to print and bind English-language books and periodicals in this country. A study of this so-called "manufacturing clause," which was not among the 34 studies originally published in the series of Senate Subcommittee prints, is included in the present work.

The revision studies, after reviewing and analyzing the history and interpretation of present provisions, prior attempts to revise them, and comparable provisions of foreign laws, discuss and pose the basic issues raised in any general revision. The studies carefully attempt to refrain from resolving these issues. It is this resolution, in the form of the Register's tentative recommendations, which is the essence of the Report of the Register. The concise summary of pertinent legal and factual developments, as well as the careful balancing of conflicting considerations, make this Report a remarkable document irrespective of the degree to which one agrees with the various recommendations. The Report has been widely distributed to encourage the submission of views and suggestions to the Register of Copyrights. It is hoped that this process will crystallize in the near future into a new United States copyright law.

STUDY NO. 1

THE HISTORY OF U.S.A. COPYRIGHT LAW REVISION FROM 1901 TO 1954

By ABE A. GOLDMAN

July 1955

(1101)

THE HISTORY OF U.S.A. COPYRIGHT LAW REVISION FROM 1901 TO 1954

The first copyright law of the United States was enacted by the First Congress in 1790. Comprehensive revisions were enacted, at intervals of about 40 years, in 1831, 1870, and 1909. The present copyright law, title 17 of the United States Code, is basically the act of 1909 with a number of subsequent amendments of individual provisions.

I. General Revision of 1909

The history of copyright law revision in modern times begins with the general revision accomplished in the act of 1909.

In his annual report for each of the years from 1901 through 1904, Thorvald Solberg, then Register of Copyrights, mentioned the need for a general revision of the copyright law, and suggested the appointment by Congress of a commission, representing the different interests concerned, to prepare a draft of a new integrated copyright law. The Senate Committee on Copyrights, however, was dubious of the efficacy of such a commission and suggested instead that the Librarian of Congress, Dr. Herbert Putnam, call into conference representatives of the various interests concerned with copyright and draft a bill for general revision.

In December 1905, the President transmitted a message to the Congress reading in part as follows:

Our copyright laws urgently need revision. They are imperfect in definition, confused and inconsistent in expression; they omit provision for many articles which, under modern reproductive processes, are entitled to protection; they impose hardships upon the copyright proprietor which are not essential to the fair protection of the public; they are difficult for the courts to interpret and impossible for the Copyright Office to administer with satisfaction to the public. Attempts to improve them by amendment have been frequent, no less than twelve acts for the purpose having been passed since the Revised Statutes. To perfect them by further amendment seems impracticable. A complete revision of them is essential. Such a revision, to meet modern conditions, has been found necessary in Germany, Austria, Sweden, and other foreign countries, and bills embodying it are pending in England and the Australian colonies. It has been urged here, and proposals for a commission to undertake it have, from time to time, been pressed upon Congress.

The inconveniences of the present conditions being so great an attempt to frame appropriate legislation has been made by the Copyright Office, which has called conferences of the various interests especially and practically concerned with the operation of the copyright laws. It has secured from them suggestions as to the changes necessary; it has added from its own experience and investigations, and it has drafted a bill which embodies such of these changes and additions as, after full discussion and expert criticism, appeared to be sound and safe. In form this bill would replace the existing insufficient and inconsistent laws by one general copyright statute. It will be presented to the Congress at the coming session. It deserves prompt consideration.

Pursuant to the suggestion of the Senate committee, the Librarian of Congress invited representatives of some 30 organizations to meet with him and the Register of Copyrights in a series of conferences

1

held in June and November of 1905 and March of 1906. The organization participating in the conferences represented authors, dramatists, theater managers, architects, artists, composers, book publishers, directory publishers, newspaper publishers, periodical publishers, photoengravers, photographers, print publishers, lithographers, music publishers, printers, educational institutions, public libraries, advertising agencies, bar associations, and a few other miscellaneous groups. (For a full list of the participants, see June 1906 hearings on H.R. 19853, 59th Cong., pp. 4 and 5.)

The Copyright Office, serving as a secretariat during, between, and after the conferences, assembled data, prepared memos on the major issues, consulted and carried on a great volume of correspondence with the participants, kept them advised of the various proposals, received their comments and suggestions, and coordinated their views. Following the conferences, the Register of Copyrights prepared a draft of a bill which was sent to all the participants for comment and suggestion. After further correspondence and discussion with the participants, the Register of Copyrights redrafted the bill.

The bill was introduced on May 31, 1906, as H.R. 19853 and S. 6330 in the 59th Congress. Hearings were held before a joint committee of members of the House and Senate Committees on Patents on June 6, 7, 8, and 9, and December 7, 8, 10, and 11, of 1906.

The history of these conferences and their results are summarized in the testimony of the Librarian of Congress at the opening of the hearings in June 1906:

[The message of the President] did not contain what was the fact as to the origin of this project, that it did originate in an informal suggestion on the part of the chairman of this committee.

The conferences to which it refers were not open, public meetings; they were not conventions; they were conferences, and conferences of organizations—that is to say, associations representing a group of interests; and those organizations were specially invited, additions being made to the list later as suggestions were made of others that should be added.

The organizations selected were the most representative organizations that we could think of or that were brought to our attention as having practical concern in the amelioration of the law, but especially, of course, those concerned in an affirmative way—that is to say, in the protection of the right. They were nearly thirty in number.

    •   •   •   •   •   •   •

The conference held three meetings in June and November of last year and in March of this year, but, of course, as a conference it included various minor consultations and much correspondence. At the outset of the meeting last June each organization was invited to state the respects in which it deemed the present law defective, or injurious, either to its own interest, or, in its opinion, to the general interest. The second conference had before it a memorandum prepared by the register embodying provisions deemed by the office important for consideration at that stage. The third conference, in March of this year, had before it a revision of this memorandum. The last conference, this third, resulted in the draft of a bill, which was sent to each participant for comment and suggestion, and the bill itself is before you.

We would have no misunderstanding as to what this bill is. It is a bill resulting from the conference, but it is not a conference bill; for the conference did not draw it, nor did it by explicit vote or otherwise determine its precise provisions. It is rather a copyright office bill. The office submits it as embodying what, with the best counsel available including the conferences, it deems worthy of your consideration, in accordance with your previously expressed desire. In calling the conferences and in submitting the draft it has proceeded upon your suggestion. Apart from the chapter relating to its own administration, it has no direct interest in the bill, except its general interest to secure a general amelioration of the law. It does not offer the bill to you as the unanimous decision of a council of experts, for it contains certain provisions as to which expert opinion as well as substantial interest was divided. It does not offer to you the bill as one that has passed the test of public discussion, for it has only now come before the public. It knows already of objection to certain of its provisions—objection which will be entitled to be heard by your committee; and it is informed by one critic that his objections are sufficient to cover fully one-half of the provisions of the bill.

[The bill] is not an attempt at abstract and theoretic perfection, nor is it an attempt to transplant to this country theoretic or what might be charged to be sentimental provisions of foreign law. It tries to be a bill possible for this country at this time and under conditions local here. It contains, therefore, some provisions which are, in our judgment, neither theoretically sound nor according to modern usage abroad nor satisfactory to particular participants in the conference. These are a compromise between principle and expediency or between one interest and another at the conference, beween which we could not decide for either extreme—I mean decide in the sense of bringing before you a suggestion in this particular form. We had not any decision in any other sense; we were not a commission. The bill is a compromise. I doubt if there is a single participant in the conferences whom it satisfies in every particular.

    *   *   *   *   *   *   *

Finally, Mr. Chairman, notwithstanding the labor put upon it, the bill is doubtless still imperfect in expressing its intentions; and I have no doubt that while it is under consideration those especially concerned will ask leave to submit to you some amendments of phraseology. I understand that any such amendments proposed by participants in the conferences will be communicated first to the copyright office, so that they may be formulated by the register for your convenient consideration; and the office will gladly do the same for any that may reach it from any other source.

Representatives of the great variety of interests concerned with copyright, as exemplified by the variety of organizations participating in the Librarian's conferences, testified at the 1906 hearings. Some were willing to accept the bill in toto as a reasonable compromise on the numerous controversial issues; but many of the witnesses raised objections to particular features of the bill, mostly on relatively minor points. Two issues were the subject of major controversy: the use of copyrighted music on mechanical instruments such as piano rolls and phonograph records, and the importation by public libararies of books printed abroad.

After the close of the hearings, the Register of Copyrights collaborated with the House and Senate committees in redrafting the bill to meet some of the objections presented at the hearings, and a revised bill was introduced on January 29, 1907, as H.R. 25133 and S. 8190. These bills were reported favorably by the committees on January 30, 1907 (H. Rept. No. 7083, S. Rept. No. 6187, 59th Cong.), with a minority report in each case opposing principally the provision to give the copyright owner of music the right to record his music for use on mechanical instruments. No further action on the bills was taken in the 59th Congress.

In the 60th Congress, the bills favorably reported in the 59th Congress were reintroduced in the House on December 2, 1907 (H.R. 243) and in the Senate on December 16, 1907 (S. 2499) by the committee chairmen, Representative Currier and Senator Smoot. Bills reflecting the minority report in the 59th Congress were also introduced (H.R. 11794 on January 6, 1908, by Representative Barchfield, and S. 2900 on December 18, 1907 by Senator Kittredge). Hearings on these bills were held by the two committees meeting jointly on March 26, 27, and 28 of 1908. Again a large number of witnesses were heard and expressed opposing views on a number of features in the several bills.

the most important controversy being that regarding the use of music on mechanical instruments. At the close of the hearings the chairman, Representative Currier, suggested that the differing groups on this last issue meet and attempt to work out a compromise proposal.

After the hearings, a series of eight revised bills were introduced in the House: two by Representative Washburn (H..R. 21592 on May 4, 1908, and H.R. 27310 on January 28, 1909), two by Representative Sulzer (H.R. 21984 on May 12, 1908, and H.R. 22071 on May 12, 1908), one by Representative Barchfield (H.R. 24782 on December 19, 1908), and two by Representative Currier (H.R. 22183 on May 12, 1908, and H.R. 28192 on February 15, 1909). These bills were all similar in most respects but each contained some features of its own. On February 22, 1908, the House committee reported favorably (H. Rept. No. 2222, 60th Cong.) Representative Currier's last bill, H.R. 28192; and on that same day Senator Smoot introduced a companion bill, S. 9440, which the Senate committee reported favorably on March 1, 1909 (S. Rept. No. 1108, 60th Cong.).

On March 2, 1909, the Committee of the Whole House agreed to certain amendments of the Currier bill, H.R. 28192, and the bill as so amended was passed by the House on March 3 and by the Senate on March 4, the last day of the 60th Congress. It was approved by the President on March 4 and became Public Law 349, the Copyright Act of 1909.

II. Revision for Adherence to Berne Convention

Between 1909 and 1924 a number of bills to amend particular provisions of the copyright law were introduced and four amendments were enacted.[1] None of these bills involved any broad revision of the law.

After the First World War, the growing market for American works abroad emphasized the shortcomings in our international copyright relations and gave impetus to a broad movement to have the United States adhere to the International Copyright Convention, commonly known as the Berne Convention, to which most of the European countries and a number of important countries in other parts of the world were parties. Bills for this purpose were first introduced in the 67th Congress in 1922 [2] at the behest of the Authors' League of America; and similar bills were introduced during 1923 in the 67th Congress,[3] and in the 68th Congress.[4] These bills purported to amend the copyright law to the minimum extent thought necessary to permit adherence to the Berne Convention. No action was taken on any of these bills.

DALLINGER, PERKINS, AND VESTAL BILLS

Adherence to the Berne Convention required many fundamental changes in the copyright law, and some of the interests concerned felt that the revision of the law for that purpose should be extended

---

[1] Act of Aug. 24, 1912, 37 Stat. 488, ch. 356; act of Mar. 2, 1913, 37 Stat. 724, ch. 97; act of Mar. 28, 1914, 38 Stat. 311, ch. 47; act of Dec. 18, 1919, 41 Stat. 369, ch. 11.
[2] H.R. 11476 by Representative Tincher and S. 4101 by Senator Lodge.
[3] H.R. 13676 by Representative Davis, H.R. 14035 by Representative Tincher.
[4] H.R. 573 by Representative Tincher, S. 74 by Senator Lodge, H.R. 2663 by Representative Bloom, and H.R. 2704 by Representative Lampert.

to cover also other issues that had arisen. With this broader purpose in view, attorneys for the motion picture industry in 1924 drafted a complete revision of the law, modeled after the British Copyright Act, designed to adopt the principles of the Berne Convention and to amend the law in other respects. Representative Dallinger introduced this draft on March 24, 1924, as H.R. 8177, and introduced a modified version on May 9, 1924, as H.R. 9137. Some consideration was given to H.R. 9137 in hearings devoted principally to other bills for special amendments of the copyright law. At the hearings, objections to portions of the Dallinger bill were voiced by the Register of Copyrights and by representatives of authors, composers, and book and music publishers. No further action was taken on the bill.

In the following year, 1925, another version of a general revision bill including the major changes necessary to bring our law into conformity with the Berne Convention was introduced by Representative Perkins. This bill, H.R. 11258, 68th Congress, was sponsored by the Authors' League of America and had been drafted by the Register of Copyrights, Thorvald Solberg, at the request of the Authors' League. Hearings were held at which the bill was favored by representatives of authors, composers, artists, music publishers, and libraries, and by the Register of Copyrights; and opposed as to various features by representatives of the printers, book publishers, motion picture producers and exhibitors, periodical publishers, phonograph manufacturers, piano roll and record manufacturers, radio broadcasters, and art dealers.

At the close of these hearings, a subcommittee was appointed to attempt, during the summer recess of Congress, to reconcile the divergent views. The subcommittee arranged for a meeting of representatives of the various interested groups, most of whom had testified at the hearings, and at this meeting the representatives of those groups organized themselves into an informal "Committee on Copyright Revision" which held a number of further meetings and reconciled some, but not all, of the conflicts. The work of this informal committee resulted in a new draft bill which was introduced in March 1926 by Representative Vestal, chairman of the House Committee on Patents in the 69th Congress, as H.R. 10434. Meanwhile the Perkins bill had been reintroduced in the 69th Congress as H.R. 5841.

At the hearings in April 1926, the Vestal bill was supported by representatives of authors, composers, artists, book publishers, book sellers, printers, and motion picture producers and distributors. Some features of the bill were opposed by art groups, libraries, scholars, motion picture exhibitors, phonograph and record manufacturers, theatrical producers, and other miscellaneous persons. Two groups—the radio broadcasters and some of the periodical publishers—were opposed to any legislation adopting the Berne Convention system of automatic copyright without formalities. The American Bar Association favored the Perkins bill. No further action was taken in the 69th Congress.

Representative Vestal reintroduced his bill in the 70th Congress, H.R. 8912, but there were no further proceedings in that Congress. He again introduced the bill in the 71st Congress as H.R. 6990, and hearings were held in April and May 1930, at which the more important controversies manifested in the 1926 hearings were aired again and various proposals were presented for modification of the bill to resolve these controversies.   After the hearings Representative Vestal introduced a revised bill, H.R. 12549, which was reported out by the House Committee on Patents (H. Rept. No. 1689, 71st Cong.) [5]   The report summarized the development of the bill as follows:

> H.R. 6690, introduced in the House of Representatives during the first session of the Seventy-first Congress, is a general revision of the national copyright law. A similar bill was introduced in the year 1926 and has been before the Patents Committee ever since its introduction in that year; and there have been many hearings upon it before the committee, a large amount of testimony taken and a multitude of conferences between various interests held.   The committee has successfully reconciled the differences.   The context of the bill has been changed in various particulars from time to time to meet valid suggestions on the part of one interest or another and the present bill, H.R. 12549, combines the results of all hearings and all conferences.
>
> It has been found that practically all the industries and all the authors have united in support of this revision.   The authors, playwrights, screen writers, composers, and artists support it.   The book publishers, the motion picture producers, the newspapers and magazines, the allied printing trades unions, the librarians, the majority of the theatrical managers, all of these have appeared at the hearings and have supported the principles of the bill.
>
> This general revision of the copyright law provides for—
>> (1) Automatic copyright by which the copyright is conferred upon the author upon creation of his work, a right so limited by various provisions of the bill as to be made a privilege;
>> (2) Divisible copyright, which permits the assignee, grantee, or licensee to protect and enforce any right which he acquires from an author without the complications incident to the old law;
>> (3) International copyright, which enables American authors merely by complying with the provisions of this act, to secure copyright throughout all of the important countries of the world without further formalities.

One member of the House committee, Representative Sirovich, filed a minority report in opposition to the provision for divisible copyright which the theatrical producers opposed.   After the debate [6] the bill was passed by the House on January 5, 1931.

When the bill as passed by the House was referred to the Senate Committee on Patents, further hearings were requested by a few interested groups that continued to oppose some features of the bill. The chief opponents at the Senate hearings in January 1931 were the radio broadcasters who were opposed to the fundamental principle of automatic copyright; the theatrical producers who opposed divisible copyright; and the manufacturers of coin-operated phonographs who objected to the elimination of the jukebox exemption.   Amendments to specific provisions were also urged by representatives of libraries, scholars, and motion picture exhibitors, and by the Register of Copyrights and a few other witnesses of miscellaneous affiliation.   The Senate committee reported the bill on February 23, 1931 (S. Rept. No. 1732, 71st Cong.) with a number of minor amendments. [7]   Debate in the Senate began on February 26 and continued intermittently through March 2; [8] but further debate was blocked by a filibuster on

---

[5] The bill was twice recommitted for technical reasons and reported out anew in H. Rept. Nos. 1898 and 2016, 71st Cong.

[6] Congressional Record, vol. 72, pp. 11994, 11996, 12018, 12473, 12474; vol. 74, pp. 2006, 2019, 2022, 2037, 2080, 2081.

[7] Meanwhile, on Jan. 21, 1931, President Hoover had transmitted to the Senate, for advice and consent to ratification, the 1908 Berlin Revision of the Berne Convention. The Senate Committee on Foreign Relations voted to report it favorably but deferred further action pending approval of H.R. 12549.

[8] Congressional Record, vol. 74, pp. 6102, 6234, 6237, 6244, 6449, 6458, 6463, 6470, 6474, 6480, 6486, 6640, 6654, 6706, 6709, 6712, 6717, 6721, 6722.

another matter and the session ended before the bill could be brought to a vote.

The Vestal bill, coming so near to enactment in the 71st Congress, marked the high tide of the efforts to revise the law for adherence to the Berne Convention. Up to that time the 1908 Berlin Revision of the Convention had been open to adherence with reservations which had been embodied in the bill. Thereafter only the 1928 Rome Revision of the Convention, which permitted no reservations, was open to adherence.

THE SIROVICH BILL

In the 72d Congress Representative Vestal reintroduced his bill as H.R. 139 and Senator Hébert introduced the Senate version as S. 176. Representative Vestal died shortly thereafter and no action was taken on these bills. Instead, the new chairman of the House Committee on Patents, Representative Sirovich, began anew. He called hearings to discuss the problems involved in copyright law revision without reference to any particular bill, apparently to acquaint the new members of the committee with the subject. All the interested groups were invited to present their views at the extended hearings held intermittently from February 1 to March 14, 1932. On March 10 Representative Sirovich introduced a bill, H.R. 10364, which was similar to the Vestal bill with respect to the fundamental changes in the law to conform with the Berne Convention, but differed from the Vestal bill on a number of other points.

Hearings on the bill were held on March 21, 24, and 25. On March 22, during the course of the hearings, Representative Sirovich introduced a revised bill, H.R. 10740. At the hearings, the bill was generally supported by representatives of authors, artists, book publishers, periodical publishers, and photographers. Various features of the bill were opposed by representatives of map publishers, scholars, motion picture producers and distributors, motion picture exhibitors, phonograph and record manufacturers, broadcasters, and ASCAP. After these hearings, on May 30, Representative Sirovich introduced another revised version of the bill as H.R. 10976, which the Committee on Patents reported out on April 5 (H. Rept. No. 1008, 72d Cong.) ; however, a few of the interested groups—particularly the map publishers, the motion picture exhibitors, and ASCAP—indicated their objections to some of the last revisions and asked for further hearings. Representative Sirovich then introduced another version of the bill, H.R. 11948 on May 7, designed to meet some of these last objections, and supplemental hearings were held on May 12. At these hearings, the map publishers and motion picture exhibitors indicated their satisfaction with the bill as revised, but the motion picture producers and distributors objected to the new revisions, and ASCAP was still opposed to some features of the bill.

After these hearings, on May 16, Representative Sirovich once more revised his bill as H.R. 12094, which was reported out of the committee on May 18 (H. Rept. No. 1361, 72d Cong.), and a special order was requested (H. Res. 229). In the ensuing debate on the order Representative Lanham, who had been the ranking minority member of the Committee on Patents during Representative Vestal's chairmanship, attacked the Sirovich bill as a hasty and ill-considered measure, and argued that the committee should have taken up the

Vestal bill which represented 8 years of work "to reconcile and harmonize the divergent interests affected by copyright legislation," and which the House had passed at the preceding session.[9] After the debate the bill was recommitted to the committee.

On June 2, 1932, Representative Sirovich introduced a fifth version of his bill as H.R. 12425, but no further action was taken in the 72d Congress.

THE DUFFY BILL

In the 73d Congress a movement was started to return to the objective that had first prompted the revision efforts 10 years earlier in the 67th Congress, namely, revision of the law only in those respects necessary for adherence to the Berne Convention. A bill for that purpose was introduced in 1933 by Representative Luce as H.R. 5853 and by Senator Cutting as S. 1928. On February 19, 1934, President Roosevelt transmitted to the Senate, for its advice and consent to adherence, the Berne Convention as revised at Rome in 1928 (Ex. E, 73d Cong.). On March 28 and on May 28 and 29, 1934, hearings were held before a subcommittee of the Senate Foreign Relations Committee on the Cutting bill and the convention. At the hearings adherence to the convention was favored by representatives of the State and Commerce Departments and the Copyright Office, and by representatives of authors, book publishers, educators, and map publishers, but was opposed by representatives of the motion picture producers, motion picture exhibitors, radio broadcasters, and periodical publishers. Changes in the Cutting bill were urged by the printing trades unions, by some of the proponents of adherence (particularly the book and map publishers), and by the various opponents of adherence; and a number of the witnesses urged that the efforts to revise the law completely be renewed along the lines of the earlier Perkins, Vestal, or Sirovich bills.

In explanation of the opposition to adherence to the Berne Convention by groups that had formerly favored adherence, it should be noted that the Berne Convention had previously permitted adherence with reservations, which was no longer possible, and that the 1928 Rome Revision of the Convention had added certain new features which some of the groups found unacceptable.

After the hearings on the Cutting bill, the Senate Committee on Foreign Relations, adopting a suggestion made at the hearings, requested the State Department to organize an informal interdepartmental committee to confer with the various interests in an endeavor to reconcile their divergent viewpoints as far as possible. This committee consisted of two representatives of the State Department, two of the Copyright Office, and one of the Commerce Department. The committee held a series of conferences with representatives of the various interests that had appeared at the hearings, drafted a bill which was circulated among the different interests for comment, and then prepared a revised draft which was introduced by Senator Duffy in the 74th Congress on March 13, 1935, as S. 2465.

On April 18, 1935, the Senate Committee on Foreign Relations reported favorably on adherence to the Berne Convention (Ex. Rept.

---

[9] Congressional Record, vol. 75, pp. 11065–11066.

No. 4, 74th Cong.), and on April 19 the Senate voted to ratify the Convention; but this vote was reconsidered on motion by Senator Duffy on April 22 and the Convention was put back on the Executive Calendar by unanimous consent to await action on the Duffy bill.

On June 17, 1935, Senator Duffy introduced a revised version of his bill as S. 3047,[10] and this bill was reported favorably by the Senate Committee on Patents (S. Rept. No. 896, 74th Cong.). During the debate in the Senate, provisions known as the "Vandenberg amendment" were added to the bill to provide copyright protection for industrial designs; and another amendment restored the requirement of domestic manufacture for foreign works, which would apparently have precluded adherence to the Berne Convention. On August 7, 1935, in the closing days of the 1st session of the 74th Congress, the Senate passed the bill with these amendments.

In the second session on January 27, 1936, Representative Daly introduced H.R. 10632, which was similar to the Duffy bill as passed by the Senate, plus additional new provisions to give performing artists copyright in their recorded renditions of music. On February 24, 1936, Representative Sirovich introduced a new bill, H.R. 11420, making a number of revisions in the law but abandoning some of the changes necessary for adherence to the Berne Convention, and this bill, too, included new provisions for the copyright protection of performing artists.

Extensive hearings on the Duffy, Daly, and Sirovich bills were held before the House committee on 27 days during the period of February 25 to April 15, 1936. The wide variety of controversial issues and divergent views presented at previous hearings on copyright revision bills was now complicated further by the interjection of the new issues involved in the two broad proposals to provide copyright protection for industrial designs and for recorded renditions of music. A number of new groups were now brought into the hearings and the conflicts of interest were multiplied.

Taking the Duffy bill alone without the Vandenberg amendment, it was generally favored at the hearings by representatives of the State Department, broadcasters, hotel owners, libraries, periodical publishers, jukebox manufacturers, and motion picture exhibitors. Some of the features of the Duffy bill (excluding the Vandenberg amendment) were opposed by representatives of the authors, composers, music publishers, phonograph record manufacturers, motion picture producers, book publishers, periodical publishers, and map publishers. It became apparent at the hearings that additional groups formerly advocating adherence to the Berne Convention—notably some of the author, composer, and publisher groups—had now become indifferent or opposed to adherence.

At these same hearings, representatives of the performing artists and the phonograph record manufacturers urged enactment of the provisions in the Daly and Sirovich bills to give copyright protection to recorded renditions of music, while the radio broadcasters opposed

---

[10] No report of hearings on the original Duffy bill, S. 2465, has been found. Apparently the Committee on Patents held informal conferences on that bill before its revision as S. 3047. In the Congressional Record, vol. 79, p. 12188, Senator Duffy stated that the Committee on Patents had "held hearings and had conferences" on S. 2465. A companion bill to S. 3047 was also introduced in the House on June 19, 1935, by Representative Bloom as H.R. 8557.

those provisions and the other groups were generally noncommittal on this issue. The Vandenberg amendment in the Duffy bill was favored by representatives of the designers and of the manufacturers of silk and rayon fabrics, leather, pottery, furniture, upholstery and drapery fabrics, and women's apparel; and was opposed by representatives of the railroads, the manufacturers of automobiles, machine parts, glass containers, and popular price dresses, groups of retail merchants, and the Farm Bureau Federation.

After the hearings, a special subcommittee of the House Committee on Patents held several meetings, but the groups concerned showed little interest and no further action was taken in the 74th Congress.

The 1936 hearings were the last held on bills for general revision of the law. Senator Duffy reintroduced his bill in the 75th Congress as S. 7 and companion bills were introduced in the House by Representative Moser (H.R. 2695) and Representative Bloom (H.R. 3004). Representative Daly also introduced a somewhat modified version of his bill as H.R. 5275, and a companion bill was introduced by Senator Guffey as S. 2240. No action was taken on any of these bills. Likewise, no action was taken on similar bills introduced in the 76th Congress (H.R. 926 and 4871 by Representative Daly, and H. R. 6160 and 9703 by Representative McGranery).

THE SHOTWELL BILL

The last chapter in the attempts to revise the copyright law to conform with the Berne Convention was an undertaking by the National Committee of the United States of America on International Intellectual Cooperation, one of several such committees organized in various parts of the world in the early 1920's to collaborate with the Organization on Intellectual Cooperation of the League of Nations. In 1938 this national committee, of which Prof. James T. Shotwell of Columbia University was then chairman, activated a subsidiary Committee for the Study of Copyright to promote international copyright relations. Professor Shotwell and later Dr. Waldo G. Leland, director of the American Council of Learned Societies, acted as chairman of this latter committee, and Dr. Edith T. Ware served as its executive secretary. In 1938 the Committee for the Study of Copyright, commonly known as the Shotwell committee, inaugurated a series of conferences with the various groups concerned with copyright in an effort to work out revisions of the law looking toward adherence to the Berne Convention and the establishment of a better basis for a future Pan American Copyright Convention. Participating in these conferences were representatives of authors, publishers, the printing trades, motion picture producers, radio broadcasters, record manufacturers, libraries, and scholars. The Shotwell committee secured from each group a statement of the changes it desired in the law, circulated these statements among the various groups for comment, and then designated a number of smaller committees to attempt to reconcile the major conflicts. These conferences continued until the latter part of 1939 when the Shotwell committee drafted a bill for a complete revision of the law. The various groups agreed that the bill might be introduced, but a number of them indicated their intention to present objections to various features of the bill. The bill was introduced by Senator Thomas as S. 3043 in the 76th Congress on January 8, 1940.

Meanwhile, on April 11, 1939, at the behest of Senator Thomas, the Senate Committee on Foreign Relations had again reported favorably on ratification of the 1928 Rome revision of the Berne Convention (Ex. Rept. No. 2, 76th Cong.), but further action on the report was deferred pending the necessary amendments of the law on which the Shotwell committee was working.

No hearings were held on the "Shotwell bill" introduced by Senator Thomas. According to a report in the January 24, 1940, issue of Variety, a leading journal of the entertainment industries, the bill was favored by the authors and book publishers, but opposed by the radio broadcasters, motion picture producers, periodical publishers, and record manufacturers.

The Register of Copyrights, who had not participated in the activities of the Shotwell committee, submitted his views on the bill at the request of Senator Bone, then chairman of the Committee on Patents, and expressed his opposition to many features of the bill.

No further action was taken on the bill.

SUMMARY OBSERVATIONS

It may be of interest to mention briefly the major issues on which the groups concerned differed during the efforts between 1924 and 1940 to revise the law.

Among the most important differences were those concerning provisions deemed essential for adherence to the 1928 Rome Revision of the Berne Convention: Automatic copyright in the author upon creation of the work (i.e., without formalities such as notice, deposit of copies, and registration); removal of the requirement for domestic manufacture of foreign books and periodicals; retroactive copyright protection of foreign works; the duration of copyright for the life of the author and a period of years after his death; copyright in oral speeches; and the "moral" rights of authors. Other important issues of controversy were proposals for divisible copyright (i.e., the assignment of separate rights); the removal of the "compulsory license" for the recording of music; the removal or diminution of the statutory minimum damages; the protection of "innocent" infringers; the removal of the privilege of scholars and libraries to import copies; and the restriction of performance rights. In the middle 1930's the proposals to extend copyright protection to industrial designs and to recorded performances of music opened up new areas of controversy.

It may be said in general that the major controversies were rooted in the conflicting interests of the various author and publisher groups on the one hand, and the users of copyright material—such as broadcasters, motion picture producers, and record manufacturers—on the other hand. Each effort to revise the law resolved itself into an attempt to reconcile this conflict of interests through extended discussion and negotiation with the various groups concerned in order to work out compromise solutions to the controversial issues. Such an attempt was successful in the enactment of the 1909 revision and almost succeeded with the Vestal bill in 1931.

Between 1926 and 1941, five acts were passed amending individual provisions of the copyright law: Act of July 3, 1926, 44 Stat. 818; act of May 23, 1928, 45 Stat. 713; act of July 31, 1939, 53 Stat. 1142; act of March 15, 1940, 54 Stat. 51; and act of September 25, 1941, 55 Stat. 732.

III. REVISION FOR ADHÉRENCE TO THE UNIVERSAL COPYRIGHT CONVENTION

After World War II, with the further expansion of the foreign market for U.S. copyright material, a movement for more effective international copyright relations was revived. It was now clear that the United States would not adhere to the Berne Convention. As stated in the report of the Senate Committee on Foreign Relations dealing with the Universal Copyright Convention (Ex. Rept. No. 5, 83d Cong., June 11, 1954):

> [The United States] has found it impossible to subscribe to the [Berne] Convention * * * because it embodied concepts at variance with American Copyright Law. These concepts involved such matters as the automatic recognition of copyright without any formalities, the protection of "moral" rights and the retroactivity of copyright protection with respect to works which are already in the public domain in the United States. This revival of copyright under the retroactivity doctrine would have worked considerable prejudice to American motion picture, music, and publishing houses * * *. Finally it was claimed that Berne's protection of "oral" works, such as speeches, would have conflicted with Article I, Section 8 of the Constitution, which refers only to "writings" as material to be protected.

The new effort was directed at preparing a new international convention to which both the member countries and the nonmembers of the Berne Union might adhere. In September 1947, an intergovernmental committee of copyright experts assembled by the United Nations Educational, Scientific, and Cultural Organization (UNESCO) at a meeting in Paris, proposed that UNESCO undertake a survey of the international copyright relations of all the countries of the world. Beginning in 1948, UNESCO assembled information on the international copyright situation in all countries by means of questionnaires sent to the various countries. UNESCO submitted its report to an intergovernmental Committee of Experts which met in Paris in July 1949. This second Committee of Experts proposed the preparation of a new Universal Copyright Convention and formulated the basic principles for such a convention. This proposal and statement of basic principles was then sent to the governments of all countries for comment. The replies of the governments were submitted to a third Committee of Experts meeting in Washington in October and November 1950, and this Committee developed a revised and more detailed statement of principles to be embodied in the new convention. This second statement of principles was circulated among all the governments; and on the basis of their comments, a fourth Committee of Experts met in Paris in June 1951 and prepared a preliminary draft of the convention which was submitted to all the countries. A special committee of representatives of the pan-American countries met in Washington early in 1952 to consider the effect of the new draft convention on copyright relations among the American Republics.

An Intergovernmental Conference was held in Geneva in August and September 1952 at which the Universal Copyright Convention was drafted in final form. The new Convention was signed by 40 countries including the United States, and was open to adherence by other countries as well.

Throughout this process of formulating the Convention, the Librarian of Congress, the Register of Copyrights, and the State Department, working through a Panel on International Copyright, met and consulted with representatives of all the various interests in the United States concerned with copyright. This Panel was established as an auxiliary of the State Department's U.S. National Commission for UNESCO, with the Librarian of Congress as chairman of the Panel. At each stage of the development of the Convention, before and after each meeting of the international Committee of Experts, the views of all the interests were secured and exchanged at meetings of the Panel and through informal conferences and correspondence carried on by the State Department and the Register of Copyrights. From 1948 to 1953 fourteen meetings of the Panel were held. In addition to more than 60 representatives of the various industries and interests concerned, representatives of other Government agencies, including the Justice, Commerce, and Labor Departments, attended some of the Panel meetings. On the basis of these meetings and other exchanges of views, the position of the U.S. Government was developed before each meeting of the international Committee of Experts and before the Geneva Conference in 1952. Every effort was made to secure the agreement of the various interests on the position to be taken by the U.S. Government at each stage of the development of the Convention.

The Librarian of Congress, the Register of Copyrights, a representative of the State Department, and some of the attorneys representing various interests participated in the several international meetings of experts. At the Geneva Conference in 1952 which completed the Convention, the U.S. delegation consisted of the Librarian of Congress as chairman, the Register of Copyrights, a representative of the State Department, two Congressmen, and four leading copyright attorneys who represented a diversity of private interests. The position taken by the U.S. delegation at the conference had the unanimous approval of the members of the delegation on every point.

On June 10, 1953, President Eisenhower submitted the Universal Copyright Convention to the Senate for its advice and consent to ratification (Ex. M, 83d Cong.). Ratification required major changes in the copyright law to make it conform with the Convention in respect to the protection afforded works created by citizens of, or first published in, other member countries. A bill to amend the law accordingly was drafted by the Copyright Office in collaboration with the State Department, and was introduced by Representative Crumpacker (H.R. 6616), Representative Reed (H.R. 6670), and Senator Langer (S. 2559) during July and August 1953.

On March 15 and 17 and April 9, 1954, hearings on the House bills were held before a subcommittee of the House Judiciary Committee. On April 7 and 8, 1954, hearings on the Convention and the Senate bill were held before a joint subcommittee of the Senate Foreign Relations and Judiciary Committees. At these hearings, the Convention and the bills were supported by representatives of the authors, composers, book publishers, music publishers, periodical publishers, bar associations, libraries, scholars, radio and television broadcasters, record manufacturers, motion picture producers and exhibitors, and photographers. Adoption of the Convention and bills was also urged by the Librarian of Congress, the Register of Copyrights, and representatives of the State, Commerce, and Labor Departments.

The Convention and bills were opposed only by the printing and binding trades unions of the American Federation of Labor because of the removal of the requirement for domestic manufacture of books by foreign authors published in other member countries of the Convention. The removal of this requirement was essential for adherence to the Convention. The Congress of Industrial Organizations, however, filed a statement favoring adoption of the Convention and bills. After the hearings, representatives of some of the motion picture producers indicated their objection to one feature of the Convention; but as indicated in the Senate report (No. 1936, 83d Cong.), they subsequently withdrew their objection and favored adoption of the Convention and bills.

The Senate Committee on Foreign Relations reported favorably on ratification of the Convention on June 11, 1954 (Ex. Rept. No. 5, 83d Cong.), and on June 25, 1954, ratification of the Convention was approved by a 65–3 vote of the Senate.

On July 19, 1954, the Senate Judiciary Committee reported S. 2559 favorably (S. Rept. No. 1936, 83d Cong.). On August 3, 1954, the House Judiciary Committee reported H.R. 6616 favorably (H. Rept. No. 2608, 83d Cong.), and on that same day the House passed the bill. On August 18, 1954, the Senate passed H.R. 6616. It was signed by the President on August 31, 1954, as Public Law 743. On December 6, 1954, the President deposited with UNESCO the instrument ratifying the Convention.

The almost unanimous support of the Convention and bill by the many diverse interests concerned, was summarized by Senator Hickenlooper, in presenting the Convention to the Senate on June 25, 1954, as follows:

Few treaties which have been presented to the Senate have had such widespread endorsement by so many different elements of the American public as this Convention has received * * *. The Convention has been drafted with the greatest of care and skill. Its clauses were painstakingly developed in extensive consultations between copyright experts here and abroad * * *. The result of the [Geneva] Conference was a document which not only embodies the most acceptable concepts of American and European practice, but which recognizes the basic principles governing the Law of Copyright in the United States.

INDIVIDUAL AMENDMENTS

No copyright legislation was enacted during the years 1942 to 1946. By the act of July 30, 1947 (61 Stat. 652), the Copyright Act of 1909, as amended, was codified and enacted into positive law as title 17 of the United States Code. Since then five acts have been passed amending individual provisions of the copyright law, some of considerable substantive importance: Act of April 27, 1948, 62 Stat. 202; act of June 3, 1949, 63 Stat. 153; act of October 31, 1951, 65 Stat. 710; act of July 17, 1952, 66 Stat. 752; and act of April 13, 1954, 68 Stat. 52.

The act of August 31, 1954, 61 Stat. 655, amending the copyright law to implement the Universal Copyright Convention, has already been mentioned.

(1116)

SUPPLEMENTARY NOTE
REVISION OF PATENT AND TRADEMARK LAWS

In a number of respects the patent and trademark laws parallel the copyright law. The patent and copyright laws are founded on the same provision of the U.S. Constitution, article I, section 8, eighth clause; the trademark law is founded on article I, section 8, third clause (the commerce clause). All three laws deal with intangible property rights of a special character. All three are under the jurisdiction of the same subcommittee of the Judiciary Committee of the respective Houses of Congress.

In connection with the history of copyright law revision, therefore, it may be enlightening to summarize briefly the history of the recent revisions of the patent and trademark laws.

I. PATENT LAW REVISION

The first patent law of the United States, like our first copyright law, was enacted in 1790 by the First Congress. Aside from amendments of particular items, general revisions of the patent law were made in 1836 (5 Stat. 117), in 1861 (12 Stat. 246), and in 1870 (16 Stat. 198). After 1870 there was no general revision until the recent act of July 19, 1952 (66 Stat. 792) which enacted the new patent law as title 35 of the United States Code.[11]

For some years prior to 1952 the patent bar had been urging that the existing law—basically the law of 1870 with a number of amendments—had become outmoded and should be revised in a number of respects. At the same time, the codification of the patent statutes was being contemplated as a part of the general program for codification of all the laws of the United States. These two movements came to a head in 1949 when the Subcommittee on Patents of the House Judiciary Committee, under the chairmanship of Representative Bryson, inaugurated a comprehensive study of the patent law with a view to its complete revision and codification. The subcommittee enlisted the aid of Mr. P. J. Federico of the Patent Office to assemble reports on prior laws and legislative proposals and suggestions which had been made by various groups for changes in the law, and to draft preliminary alternative proposals for a new law as a basis for discussion. In February 1950, these reports and proposals were circulated by the subcommittee to a great number of patent attorneys and others interested for their comments and suggestions.

---

[11] The history of this act of 1952 is summarized in the hearings on H.R. 3760, 82d Cong., June 13–15, 1951, and in the House and Senate reports on H.R. 7794, 82d Cong. (H. Rept. No. 1923; S. Rept. No. 1979). Its history is also summarized in pp. 6–9 of the "Commentary on the New Patent Act" by P. J. Federico, Examiner-in-Chief of the U.S. Patent Office, appearing in title 35 of the United States Code Annotated.

15   (1117)

The various patent law associations organized a coordinating committee of patent attorneys which coordinated the views of the patent groups on the preliminary proposals and the subsequent draft bills. This coordinating committee prepared reports and recommendations which it submitted to the subcommittee of the House Judiciary Committee.

On the basis of the comments and suggestions received on the preliminary proposals, the subcommittee, with the technical assistance of Mr. Federico and others, prepared a bill which was introduced by Representative Bryson on July 17, 1950, as H.R. 9133, 81st Congress.[12] Over 6,000 copies of this first bill were distributed by the subcommittee to all who were thought to be concerned for their further comment and suggestions, after which the bill was revised and reintroduced by Representative Bryson on April 18, 1951, as H.R. 3760, 82d Congress.

Hearings on H.R. 3760 were held before the subcommittee of the House Judiciary Committee on June 13, 14, and 15, 1951. A large number of persons representing Government agencies, bar groups, inventors, industries, and other miscellaneous interests concerned with patent law, presented their views at the hearings.

On the basis of these hearings and further comments received thereafter, the subcommittee prepared another revised bill. Representative Bryson introduced this revised bill on May 12, 1952, as H.R. 7794, 82d Congress, and on the same day the bill was reported favorably by the House Judiciary Committee (H. Rept. No. 1923, 82d Cong.). The bill was passed by the House on May 19, 1952, by unanimous consent. The Senate Judiciary Committee reported the bill favorably, with a few minor amendments, on June 27, 1952 (S. Rept. No. 1979, 82d Cong.), and the bill was passed by the Senate on July 4, 1952, by unanimous consent. The House concurred in the Senate amendments later the same day, and the bill was signed by the President on July 19, 1952, becoming Public Law 593, 82d Congress.

II. Trademark Law Revision

The first trademark law of the United States was enacted in 1870 as part of an act to revise and consolidate the patent and copyright laws (16 Stat. 198, at 210). Based on the patent and copyright clause of the Constitution (art. I, sec. 8, eighth clause), the trademark provisions of that act were held unconstitutional by the U.S. Supreme Court in 1879 (*Trademark Cases*, 100 U.S. 82). In 1881 a new trademark law was enacted (21 Stat. 502) limited to trademarks used in commerce with foreign nations or with the Indian tribes. It was not until 1905 (33 Stat. 724) that a trademark statute was enacted covering interstate commerce generally, and for 42 years this was the basic Federal statute on trademarks. The 1905 act was amended a number of times, and was supplemented by a statute enacted in 1920 (41 Stat. 533) to provide for the registration of certain trademarks not otherwise registrable, in order to qualify them for protection in foreign countries under international conventions.

---

[12] It should be noted that in drafting the bill, some of the earlier proposals for substantive changes in the law were eliminated as too controversial for consideration in the general revision and codification.

The act of 1905 was merely a procedural statute providing for registration of trademarks to establish prima facie evidence of ownership and for remedial actions in the Federal courts. The substantive rights of trademark owners were left to the common law or statutes of the several States. By the 1920's, many people had become dissatisfied with the act of 1905 and a movement began to revise and enlarge the Federal trademark law. Committees of several bar associations worked together in drafting a bill for complete revision of the law, which was first introduced in 1924 in the 68th Congress, and successive bills were introduced in the 69th through the 72d Congresses.[13] Hearings were held in each Congress before the House or Senate Committee on Patents at which many of the features of the bills were in controversy. In the 69th and 70th Congresses, bills introduced by Representative Vestal, as redrafted and reintroduced after the hearings, passed the House but died in the Senate committee. In the 71st Congress in 1931, the Vestal bill passed the House; it was reported by the Senate committee and brought under debate in the Senate, but was not reached for a vote before adjournment.[14]

In the 72d Congress Representative Vestal reintroduced his bill as H.R. 7118 and hearings were held but, after his death during that session, no further action was taken.

No bills to revise the trademark law were introduced during the 73d or 74th Congress. Some of the bar groups, however, becoming disturbed at the trend in the States to enact laws requiring local registration of trademarks, reactivated their committees on revision of the Federal trademark law and these committees drafted a bill for complete revision which Representative Lanham introduced in the 75th Congress in 1938 as H.R. 9041. Hearings were held before the House Committee on Patents on March 15–18, 1938, at which this bill was discussed section by section in order to apprise the House committee of the different views of the various groups concerned. Differences of opinion on a number of important issues were brought out at the hearings. On the basis of these hearings the bar committees prepared a revised draft which Representative Lanham introduced in the 76th Congress as H.R. 4744. Hearings on this bill were held on March 28–30, 1939, after which it was revised to reconcile differences of opinion and reintroduced as H.R. 6618, 76th Congress. Further hearings were held on June 22, 1939, and H.R. 6618 was reported favorably by the House committee on June 27, 1939 (H. Rept. No. 944, 76th Cong.), and was passed by the House on July 17, 1939. The Senate Committee on Patents, after extended consultation with the members of the House committee, reported the bill on May 1, 1940, with several amendments including some on controversial points (S. Rept. No. 1562, 76th Cong.). The Senate first voted to pass the bill but then adopted a motion to reconsider. No further action was taken.

---

[13] In the 68th Cong., S. 2679. In the 69th Cong., H.R. 6248, H.R. 13486, S. 2547, and S. 4811. In the 70th Cong., H.R. 6683, H.R. 11988, H.R. 13109, and S. 2744. In the 71st Cong., H.R. 2828. In the 72d Cong., H.R. 7118 and S. 2679.

[14] It is interesting to note the parallel between these efforts to revise the trademark law during this period of 1924–31 and the efforts during the same period by the same House committee under the leadership of Representative Vestal to revise the copyright law. See pp. 4–7 of the accompanying "The History of U.S.A. Copyright Law Revision From 1901 to 1954."

In the 77th Congress in 1941, Senator Bone introduced S. 895, the bill as modified by the Senate committee in the preceding Congress, and Representative Lanham introduced an identical bill as H.R. 102. The Senate bill was reported out on July 22, 1941 (S. Rept. No. 568, 77th Cong.), and was passed by the Senate on September 17, 1941.

Meanwhile, in the autumn of 1940, a number of trade associations (the National Association of Manufacturers, the Association of National Advertisers, the United States Trademark Association, and others) had joined with the trademark bar groups in organizing a coordinating committee to reconcile the differing views on the remaining points of controversy and draft a revised bill that all might support. That draft, with some changes, was introduced by Representative Lanham on July 31, 1941, as H.R. 5461. In November 1941, after the Senate had passed S. 895, hearings were held before the House committee on the three bills (H.R. 102, H.R. 5461, and S. 895) at which a number of amendments to H.R. 5461 were suggested. The House committee adopted some of those suggestions, revised S. 895 in numerous respects to conform with the amended version of H.R. 5461, and reported out S. 895 as so revised on June 25, 1942 (H. Rept. No. 2283, 77th Cong.). The revised S. 895 was passed by the House on September 24, 1942.

In the 78th Congress, Representative Lanham introduced, as H.R. 82, the bill passed by the House in the preceding Congress with a few amendments that had been suggested by the Senate committee. Hearings before the House committee on April 7 and 8, 1943, were confined to a few particular points of controversy in view of anticipated hearings by the Senate committee. H.R. 82 was reported favorably by the House committee on June 25, 1943 (H. Rept. No. 603, 78th Cong.), and passed the House on June 28, 1943. The Senate committee held hearings on November 15 and 16, 1944, and reported the bill with several amendments on December 4, 1944 (S. Rept. No. 1303, 78th Cong.). The bill was not reached for a vote in the Senate before adjournment.

Representative Lanham reintroduced his bill on January 22, 1945, in the 79th Congress as H.R. 1654. On February 26, 1945, the House committee reported the bill with a few minor amendments (H. Rept. No. 219, 79th Cong.), and the bill was passed by the House on March 5, 1945. The Senate committee reported the bill with several amendments on May 14, 1946 (S. Rept. No. 1333, 79th Cong.), and the Senate passed the bill on June 14, 1946, with some further amendments. A conference committee met on June 21 and filed its report on June 24 (H. Rept. No. 2322, 79th Cong.), which was agreed to by the House on June 25 and by the Senate on June 28, 1946. The act was signed by President Truman on July 5, 1946, and became Public Law 489, 79th Congress, effective July 5, 1947.

As stated in the House report (No. 219, 79th Cong.) submitted by Representative Lanham on H.R. 1654, on the bill finally enacted:

Besides the official recorded action of Congress concerning the proposed legislation, many hours of time were devoted to the perfecting of this legislation by the Members of Congress in conference with officials of various Government departments, lawyers, trademark owners, manufacturers, and others interested in securing the enactment of a modern concise trademark statute. It might also be mentioned that various committees (of bar and trade associations) studied and debated the various bills, and presented their conclusions for official consideration at various times.

The activities of the bar and trade associations and of the committees organized by them have been outlined in the foregoing summary. The Government agencies that participated in various hearings and presented their views to the congressional committees included the Justice Department, the Federal Trade Commission, the Food and Drug Administration, and the Navy Department, as well as the Patent Office. Officials of the Patent Office were consulted by the bar and trade associations in the drafting of proposed bills, were present at the various hearings as advisers of the congressional committees, and assisted the committees in revising the successive bills.

THE MANUFACTURING CLAUSE
OF THE U. S. COPYRIGHT LAW

By Marjorie McCannon

Assistant Chief, Reference Division
Copyright Office

with the assistance of

Benjamin W. Rudd, General Attorney-Librarian,
Copyright Office

February, 1963

THE MANUFACTURING CLAUSE
OF THE U. S. COPYRIGHT LAW

I. Introduction

A strange marriage of crafts is sheltered under the cloak of copy-right. Copyright was constitutionally espoused to secure the rights of authors for the purpose of promoting the "Progress of Science and useful Arts."[1] Although the craft of printing is perhaps not one of the "arts" contemplated by the Constitution, yet it is one on which authors depend for the multiplication of copies of their works; and the printing trades, in order to protect themselves against foreign competition, have bound authors to a sort of servitude fixed in the copyright law many years ago. Ironically, it was against printers that the Statute of Anne,[2] on which our copyright law was based, purported to protect authors.[3]

The "tie that binds" is the manufacturing clause requiring that books in English be entirely manufactured in the United States to be accorded full U. S. copyright protection, and limiting the number of copies of foreign-made books in English that can be imported. Query, whether the copyright protection of authors should continue to depend upon the manufacture of copies in the United States. Query further, whether the import limitation is still justified or is an impediment to progress in the arts and sciences.

This study undertakes, with the aid of much that has already been written, to show how this anomaly came to be and how it has worked, with a view to determining whether the parties can now afford a divorce.

II. The Present Law: what the "Manufacturing Clause" is

Interspersed throughout the copyright law (Title 17 of the U. S. Code) are references to the manufacturing requirements. The "manu-facturing clause" as last amended in 1954 (effective September 16, 1955), is found in section 16 of the statute and is supplemented by sections 17, 18, 22, 23, and 107, with related references to it in sections 9(c) and 13, forming an intricate tangle of general require-

---

[1] Art. I, § 8, cl. 8.
[2] 8 Anne, c. 19 (1710). For a discussion of the origins of this Act, see RANSOM, THE FIRST COPYRIGHT STATUTE (1956).
[3] See BOWKER, COPYRIGHT—ITS HISTORY AND ITS LAW 24 (1912).

ments, exceptions, special procedures for proof of compliance, special provisions for "ad interim" copyright, and import prohibitions and exceptions. These provisions abound in abstruse or ambiguous terms, making enforcement extremely difficult. The basic provision is set forth below:

SEC. 16. MECHANICAL WORK TO BE DONE IN UNITED STATES.—Of the printed book or periodical specified in section 5, subsections (a) and (b), of this title, except the original text of a book or periodical of foreign origin in a language or languages other than English, the text of all copies accorded protection under this title, except as below provided, shall be printed from type set within the limits of the United States, either by hand or by the aid of any kind of typesetting machine, or from plates made within the limits of the United States from type set therein, or, if the text be produced by lithographic process, or photoengraving process, then by a process wholly performed within the limits of the United States, and the printing of the text and binding of the said book shall be performed within the limits of the United States; which requirements shall extend also to the illustrations within a book consisting of printed text and illustrations produced by lithographic process, or photoengraving process, and also to separate lithographs or photoengravings, except where in either case the subjects represented are located in a foreign country and illustrate a scientific work or reproduce a work of art: Provided, however, That said requirements shall not apply to works in raised characters for the use of the blind, or to books or periodicals of foreign origin in a language or languages other than English, or to works printed or produced in the United States by any other process than those above specified in this section, or to copies of books or periodicals, first published abroad in the English language, imported into the United States within five years after first publication in a foreign state or nation up to the number of fifteen hundred copies of each such book or periodical if said copies shall contain notice of copyright in accordance with sections 10, 19, and 20 of this title and if ad interim copyright in said work shall have been obtained pursuant to section 22 of this title prior to the importation into the United States of any copy except those permitted by the provisions of section 107 of this title: Provided further, That the provisions of this section shall not affect the right of importation under the provisions of section 107 of this title.

In substance, section 16 provides that the various steps in the manufacture of English-language books and periodicals must be performed in the United States, and that with certain exceptions the same requirements apply to lithographs and photoengravings. It goes on to provide that these requirements of manufacture in the United States "shall not apply to works in raised characters for the use of the blind, or to books or periodicals of foreign origin in a language or languages other than English"; and it permits the importation of not more than 1,500 copies of an English-language book or periodical first published abroad for which an ad interim copyright has been obtained under section 22.

Section 17 provides that the deposit for registration of copies of a book subject to the manufacturing requirements shall be accompanied by an affidavit setting forth certain facts to show compliance with those requirements.

Section 18 prescribes a criminal penalty and forfeiture of copyright for knowingly making a false affidavit.

Section 22 provides that in the case of an English-language book or periodical first published abroad, ad interim copyright may be secured upon deposit of a copy of the foreign edition for registration in the Copyright Office within six months after such publication, the ad interim copyright to endure for five years from such publication. During the five-year period of ad interim copyright, up to 1,500 copies of the foreign edition may be imported (as provided in section 16). The theory of these provisions is to give the author (or other owner) copyright protection for a period of five years during which he can test the market in the United States and decide whether to incur the expense of having an edition manufactured in the United States.

Section 23 then provides that if an edition is manufactured and published in the United States within the five-year period, the ad interim copyright can then be extended to endure for the regular term of twenty-eight years (renewable for another twenty-eight years). If an edition has not meanwhile been manufactured and published in the United States, and the claim registered, the copyright ceases at the end of the five-year ad interim term.

Section 107 prohibits the importation into the United States of foreign editions of copyrighted books required by section 16 to be manufactured in the United States, with, however, specified exceptions for individual copies brought in for private use or for educational institutions, libraries, etc. Sections 108 and 109 provide enforcement procedures for all articles prohibited importation.

Section 9(c), an amendment effective September 16, 1955, was enacted to implement the Universal Copyright Convention. It exempts foreign works protected under the Universal Copyright Convention from the manufacturing requirements, the ad interim provisions, and the importation restrictions, provided the copies bear the U.C.C. notice.

Section 13, which specifies what shall be deposited in the Copyright Office for registration purposes, provides that "if the work be a book or periodical, [the copies or copy deposited] shall have been produced in accordance with the manufacturing provisions specified in section 16 * * *."

These are, currently, the sections of the copyright law relating to the manufacturing requirements.

III. History of the Manufacturing and Import Provisions

A. How the Manufacturing and Import Provisions Developed

1. *The copyright law of 1790*

The first federal copyright law of the United States of America was enacted in 1790 when there were few American printers and most of the public's reading matter was necessarily imported. In fact, to assure a supply, the copyright law encouraged importation and sanctioned piracy of foreign works by providing:

* * * That nothing in this act shall be construed to extend to prohibit the importation or vending, reprinting, or publishing within the United States, of any map, chart, book or books, written, printed, or published by any person not a

citizen of the United States, in foreign parts or places without the jurisdiction of the United States.[4]

The protection of the 1790 law extended to works by citizens or residents of the United States only. For over 100 years there were no restrictions upon the free use of foreign works in the United States.[5]

2. Origin of the international copyright movement

Piracy worked both ways, however, and American authors found themselves deprived of compensation both at home and abroad. Their works were slighted at home because publishers could more profitably handle foreign works which were royalty-free, and their works were pirated abroad because there were no reciprocal copyright arrangements.[6]

In 1837 Henry Clay submitted a bill to Congress[7] which would have granted American copyright to foreign authors under certain conditions. One of the conditions of U. S. copyright for foreign works was that they be printed and published in this country. This "manufacturing clause" would have provided income for the struggling American printers whose principal business depended on the availability of foreign works to print. The same bill was presented in several successive Congresses but was never acted upon. The printing and publishing industries were not ready to open the copyright door to foreign works.

Lacking international copyright protection, American authors were obliged to submit to the republication of their books abroad without compensation, and agitation for copyright on an international scale increased during the years that followed Clay's effort to admit foreign works to copyright protection. At the same time, prominent literary men were compelled by economics to align themselves with their American publishers on the problem of foreign book competition and a protectionist tariff. There was sharp division between scholars and intellectuals on one side, and the publishers and book manufacturers on the other, on the matter of importing foreign books and other articles of cultural exchange. The former wanted unrestricted access to foreign material and urged that all such material coming from abroad be admitted duty-free; the book manufacturers and publishers, on the other hand, insisted on a substantial tariff to discourage foreign competition. In 1876, for example, America was importing from England $940,000 worth of books and related items, whereas American exports to England amounted to only $93,000.[8]

---

[4] Act of May 31, 1790, ch. 15, 1 Stat. 124. Existing state laws provided the pattern for the federal provision.

[5] This point was made even more explicit by the Act of July 8, 1870, ch. 230, § 103, 16 Stat. 215, which provided:

* * * That nothing herein contained shall be construed to prohibit the printing, publishing, importation, or sale of any book, map, chart, dramatic or musical composition, print, cut, engraving, or photograph, written or composed, or made by any person not a citizen of the United States nor resident therein.

[6] See Dozer, *The Tariff on Books,* 36 MISS. VALLEY HIST. REV. 73, 83 (1949).

[7] S. 32, 25th Cong., 2d Sess.

[8] H.R. MISC. DOC. NO. 6, 47th Cong., 2d Sess. 1071 (1882-83).

Leading American publishers procured the signatures of Thomas Bailey Aldrich, editor of *Atlantic Monthly,* Oliver Wendell Holmes, and John Greenleaf Whittier, among others, on a petition to Congress in 1883 to retain the high 25 percent ad valorem tariff on printed books.[9] Commentators suggested that the literary men who signed the petition were probably motivated, in part at least, by a desire to discourage the entry of pirated editions of their own books into the American market.[10]

The question of tariff on books has always been inextricably tied up with the question of international copyright and the related manufacturing clause in the copyright law. There has always been a fear that too many foreign books produced at lower cost would displace the market for American books. Protectionist sentiments have largely prevailed. Then, too, nationalism and the proud desire to foster American literature and keep out alien philosophies, politics, and religion have influenced Congress.[11]

The international copyright movement reached a climax in the 1880's. In 1886 at Berne, Switzerland, an international copyright union was formed on the concept that each member country should give copyright protection to works originating in any other member country. The United States could not join this union because its law offered no protection for foreign works.

3. The international copyright bills of the 1880's

Bills for international copyright were placed before the Senate Committee on Patents in 1885 and 1886. Of these, the Hawley bill[12] contained no manufacturing clause, while the Chace bill[13] required American printing of any copyrighted book, musical composition, or photograph of foreign authorship. The importation of plates would have been permitted under the Chace bill. Restriction on the foreign manufacture of books and certain other items seemed inevitable in order to secure legislation authorizing protection of foreign works, and compromise became necessary. G. P. Putnam, writing on this point, said:

* * * It was the opinion of Senator Chace, and of other of the congressional friends of copyright that the co-operation of the unions would be very important, while their influence against the bill in committee and through their friends in the House would probably be sufficiently powerful to prevent its passage, at least at any early date.

It was, therefore, decided by the authors and publishers of the two leagues to meet the views of the typographers on this point * * *.[14]

Henry C. Lea, an author and publisher of Philadelphia, is considered the author[15] of the manufacturing clause as it appeared in an 1888 version of the international copyright bill[16] introduced by

---

[9] See Dozer, *supra* note 6, at 81.
[10] See *id.* at 83.
[11] See *id.* at 79.
[12] S. 191, 49th Cong., 1st Sess. (1885).
[13] S. 1178, 49th Cong., 1st Sess. (1886).
[14] PUTNAM, THE QUESTION OF COPYRIGHT 51, n. 4 (3d ed. 1906).
[15] See *id.* at 53.
[16] S. 554, 50th Cong., 1st Sess. (1888). For a chronological record of Congressional action on

Senator Chace at the instance of the typographers. According to Mr. Putnam:

He [Mr. Lea] was a strong believer in the principles of international copyright, but he was equally clear in his conviction that it would be contrary to the interests of the community to permit any injury to the business of the American book-making trades, or to transfer to English publishers any control of the American book market. He contended, therefore, that the total American manufacture of books copyrighted must be made an essential condition of the concession of American copyright to foreign authors. His contention, backed up by the printers, was finally accepted by the authors, and the "type-setting" and "non-importation" clauses were inserted in the bill.[17]

The Chace bill passed the Senate on May 9, 1888,[18] but was allowed to die in the House.

4. The International Copyright Act of 1891

There followed a flood of petitions favoring the principles of the Chace international copyright bill, including petitions from various typographical unions, and at the beginning of the 51st Congress the President of the United States urged enactment of such a law.[19] As Senator Chace had resigned his seat on April 9, 1889, others reintroduced his bill several times with various amendments in both Houses.[20] The manufacturing clause in the bill[21] as finally passed, becoming the Act of March 3, 1891,[22] stipulated in section 3 (amending section 4956 of the Revised Statutes):

* * * *Provided*, That in the case of a book, photograph, chromo, or lithograph, the two copies of the same required to be delivered or deposited as above shall be printed from type set within the limits of the United States, or from plates made therefrom, or from negatives, or drawings on stone made within the limits of the United States, or from transfers therefrom * * *.

The manufacturing requirement was confined to books, photographs, chromos, and lithographs; excluded were engravings, cuts, and musical and dramatic compositions. The Music Engravers Union of America proposed to add "musical compositions" and "music plate engraving process" to the clause, but these were omitted by compromise, as were "dramatic compositions."[23]

5. Proposal for affidavit of manufacture

An amendment to section 4956 of the Revised Statutes (the Act of March 3, 1891) was proposed in 1904[24] to require that the deposit of American-made copies of books, photographs, chromos, or lithographs be accompanied by an affidavit that they had been produced in the United States. The bill further provided penalties for a false affidavit of compliance. The report on the bill stated:

this bill, see U.S. COPYRIGHT OFFICE, BULL. NO. 8, COPYRIGHT IN CONGRESS, 1789-1904, at 259-64 (1905).
[17] PUTNAM, *op. cit. supra* note 14, at 53.
[18] See 50 CONG. REC. 3882 (1888) and note 16, *supra*.
[19] See H.R. JOUR., 51st Cong., 1st Sess. 7, 10 (1890).
[20] For a legislative history of the Chace Act, see BOWKER, *op. cit. supra* note 3, at 358-64.
[21] H.R. 10881, 51st Cong., 1st Sess. (1891).
[22] 26 Stat. 1107.
[23] See 22 CONG. REC. 3848 (1891).
[24] H.R. 13355, 58th Cong., 2d Sess.

After investigation your committee has reason to believe that it is not only possible, but that in some instances the present law has been evaded and violated to the injury of American labor, and that this can be done with comparative ease under the existing law; that there is no remedy and no means of enforcing this condition as to printing from type set by American labor and within our own country. That being the case, your committee is of the opinion that the person applying for a copyright should be required as a condition precedent to furnish proof in the form of an affidavit that all of these conditions with respect to the labor employed in the printing and the place of printing the copies of books to be deposited have been complied with, and in the event that any false statement is made in said affidavit concerning a material fact, and upon conviction thereof, the person thus attempting to obtain a copyright should be punished and the copyright forfeited.[25]

The bill passed the House[26] but not the Senate. It was not until the Act of July 1, 1909 that the affidavit provisions, in slightly amended form, became law.

6. *Proposals for interim protection*

The Act of March 3, 1891 provided that the citizens of any foreign country in whose favor a copyright proclamation had been made could obtain copyright in the United States. Fourteen such proclamations had been issued by the time of the Register's Report for the fiscal year 1903-1904. Concerning the effect of the proclamations, Mr. Solberg, the Register, said in that Report:

While copyright entries have been made under the proclamations * * * to secure protection upon foreign works of art, music, dramas, engravings, etc., there have been scarcely any entries for books by the living authors of continental Europe. The reason for this is that foreign authors of books in other languages than English have found it practically impossible to comply with the statutory provisions * * *.[27]

A work must have been printed and published in the United States not later than the date of publication in any other country, and the editions in this country must have been manufactured from type set within the limits of the United States. "On account of this difficulty," he continued, "foreign authors, except English authors, have secured practically no advantage from the international provisions in the present copyright statute * * *."

The Register reported that Germany and France were considering repeal of copyright relations in force between them and the United States. "The obvious remedy," he said, "would be to allow a reasonable period of time during which the foreign author might arrange to comply with the requirements of American manufacture."

In 1902 Senator Platt introduced a bill[28] from which later legislation stemmed. This bill would have permitted deposit of foreign books in a foreign language within thirty days after publication abroad and would have allowed twelve months from first publication abroad to bring out an American edition. This American edition could be either in the language of the original or in a version or

---

[25] H.R. REP. NO. 2857, 58th Cong., 2d Sess. 2 (1904).
[26] 38 CONG. REC. 5834-35 (1904).
[27] 1903-04 REGISTER OF COPYRIGHTS REP. 142 [hereinafter cited as REG. COP.].
[28] S. 2894, 57th Cong., 1st Sess.

translation thereof in English or some other language. During this interval the importation of copies of the original foreign work (without notice of copyright) was to be permitted.

A substitute bill was introduced in the next Congress,[29] which proposed to allow a foreign author twelve months after first publication abroad to produce an authorized translation into English printed from type set in the United States or from plates made therefrom, provided that his translation was the first registered for copyright since the publication of his original book. The proposal was ordered to "go over without prejudice" on February 8, 1904.[30] The bill went through several amendments before passage and approval on March 3, 1905.[31] The act as approved stressed the reciprocal basis for copyright in foreign books; the pertinent text (amending section 4952 of the Revised Statutes) reads as follows:

Whenever the author or proprietor of a book in a foreign language, which shall be published in a foreign country before the day of publication in this country, or his executors, administrators, or assigns, shall deposit one complete copy of the same, including all maps and other illustrations, in the Library of Congress, Washington, District of Columbia, within thirty days after the first publication of such book in a foreign country, and shall insert in such copy, and in all copies of such book sold or distributed in the United States, on the title page or the page immediately following, a notice of the reservation of copyright in the name of the proprietor, together with the true date of first publication of such book, in the following words: "Published ————, nineteen hundred and ———— Privilege of copyright in the United States reserved under the Act approved————, nineteen hundred and five, by————," and shall, within twelve months after the first publication of such book in a foreign country, file the title of such book and deposit two copies of it in the English language, printed from type set within the limits of the United States, or from plates made therefrom, containing a notice of copyright, as provided by the copyright laws now in force, he and they shall have during the term of twenty-eight years from the date of recording the title of the book or of the English translation of it, as provided for above, the sole liberty of printing, reprinting, publishing, vending, translating and dramatizing the said book: PROVIDED, That this Act shall only apply to a citizen or subject of a foreign State or nation when such foreign State or nation permits to citizens of the United States of America the benefit of copyright on substantially the same basis as to its own citizens.

The Louisiana Purchase Exposition, a World's Fair held in St. Louis in 1904, had posed a problem with respect to the mass of foreign materials coming in for exhibition. To cope with this influx without engendering international ill will, legislation was enacted to permit temporary, two-year copyright protection and unhindered sale in the United States for foreign works by registering them up to November 30, 1904.[32] In the case of a book, deposit in the Copyright Office, during the two-year term of protection, of two copies of the original text or of an English translation, was to extend protection to the full term of the copyright law, if the copies deposited were "printed from type set within the limits of the United States or from plates made therefrom." In the case of a photograph,

---

[29] S. 849, 58th Cong., 1st Sess. (1903), reprinted to correct an error as S. 2229, 58th Cong., 2d Sess. (1903).
[30] 38 CONG. REC. 1714 (1904).
[31] 33 Stat. 1000.
[32] Act of Jan. 7, 1904, ch. 2, 33 Stat. 4.

chromo, or lithograph, the two copies to be deposited were to be "printed from negatives, or drawings on stone made within the limits of the United States or from transfers made therefrom."

After the passage of that Act, the question was raised whether it removed the importation prohibitions of the 1891 law. An exchange of official notes settled the matter—the prohibitions were declared not applicable to the articles named in the Act of March 3, 1891.[33]

Thus, for a brief period, there was a free flow of some foreign books and other articles into the United States under copyright protection. This was the first "ad interim" copyright.

Under both the Louisiana Purchase Exposition amendment and the Act of March 3, 1905, quoted above, interim protection was provided—two years in the first case and one year in the latter—and the extension of the protection to the full term of copyright could be secured if an American edition of an English translation of the original foreign work was produced within the interim period. Not until the Act of March 4, 1909 was there an exception to the reprinting requirement for "a book of foreign origin in a language or languages other than English."

7. Development and provisions of the Act of 1909

Language sounding very familiar to those who are presently concerned with revising the copyright law appears in the Register's Report for the fiscal year 1905-1906. Mr. Solberg then said, "During the fiscal year covered by this report important action has been taken in the direction of a revision of the copyright laws."[34] He had reference to the series of conferences called by the Librarian of Congress for the purpose of drafting a new copyright act. The three-volume stenographic record of these conferences, in which various interests participated, has never been published, but the copy in the Copyright Office furnishes an interesting parallel to present efforts to revise the copyright law. In preparation for this study parts relating to the manufacturing clause were excerpted, and the fact that there were over 200 pages of typescript on this subject indicates its importance in past revision efforts. From the conferences and from subsequent congressional hearings[35] on a number of bills introduced between 1906 and 1909, gradually evolved the Act approved March 4, 1909 containing what are basically the manufacturing and importation clauses in effect today.

On May 22, 1908, a bill (H.R. 22098, 60th Cong., 1st Sess.) was introduced to exempt books in foreign languages from the requirement of typesetting in the United States. No action was taken on this bill but the language underscored in the following provision of the bill was embodied in the 1909 act:

---

[33] See 1903-04 REG. COP. 113.
[34] 1905-06 REG. COP. 98.
[35] *Arguments on S. 6330 and H.R. 19853 Before the Senate and House Committees on Patents,* 59th Cong., 1st Sess. (June 1906); *Arguments on S. 6330 and H.R. 19853 Before the Senate and House Committees on Patents,* 59th Cong., 1st Sess. (Dec. 1906); *Hearings on Pending Bills to Amend and Consolidate the Acts Respecting Copyright Before the Senate and House Committees on Patents,* 60th Cong., 1st Sess. (1908).

* * * provided, that in the case of a book, photograph, chromo, or lithograph, *except the original text of a book of foreign origin in a language or languages other than English.*[36] [Emphasis supplied.]

The manufacturing clause as embodied in the Act of 1909 differed from the original 1891 provision in requiring that, for a book, not only the setting of type but also the making of plates, the printing, and the binding should all be done within the United States. It also differed in adding periodicals, in omitting photographs and dropping the word "chromo," and in including photo-engravings as well as lithographs. The inclusion of binding in the manufacturing clause met with opposition[37] but survived. Some exceptions were specified. Following is the text of the 1909 manufacturing provision:

SEC. 15. That of the printed book or periodical specified in section five, subsections (a) and (b) of this Act, except the original text of a book of foreign origin in a language or languages other than English, the text of all copies accorded protection under this Act, except as below provided, shall be printed from type set within the limits of the United States, either by hand or by the aid of any kind of typesetting machine, or from plates made within the limits of the United States from type set therein, or, if the text be produced by lithographic process, or photo-engraving process, then by a process wholly performed within the limits of the United States, and the printing of the text and binding of the said book shall be performed within the limits of the United States; which requirements shall extend also to the illustrations within a book consisting of printed text and illustrations produced by lithographic process, or photo-engraving process, and also to separate lithographs or photo-engravings, except where in either case the subjects represented are located in a foreign country and illustrate a scientific work or reproduce a work of art; but they shall not apply to works in raised characters for the use of the blind, or to books of foreign origin in a language or languages other than English, or to books published abroad in the English language seeking ad interim protection under this Act.[38]

To enforce the requirements of section 15, as first proposed by the bill introduced in 1904,[39] the 1909 Act provided for an affidavit of American manufacture and penalty and forfeiture for a false affidavit. These clauses have remained substantially the same to date.[40]

To further enforce and give practical effect to the manufacturing requirements, the 1909 Act incorporated import prohibitions, in sections 31, 32, and 33, which became sections 107, 108, and 109 when the law was codified in 1947.[41]

But import prohibition as a part of the copyright law was not new in 1909. Section 3 of the Act of March 3, 1891 (amending section 4956 of the Act of July 8, 1870) prohibited importation of any of the enumerated copyright articles:

During the existence of such copyrights the importation into the United States of any book, chromo, lithograph, or photograph, so copyrighted, or any edition or editions thereof, or any plates of the same not made from type set, negatives,

---

[36] See H.R. REP. NO. 2222, 60th Cong., 2d Sess. 14-15 (1909).
[37] See *Hearings on Pending Bills to Amend and Consolidate the Acts Respecting Copyright Before the Senate and House Committees on Patents,* 60th Cong., 1st Sess. 66-72 (1908).
[38] 35 Stat. 1078 (1909).
[39] H.R. 2857, 58th Cong., 2d Sess.
[40] Act of Mar. 4, 1909, ch. 320, 35 Stat. 1079, §§ 16, 17, now 17 U.S.C. §§ 17, 18 (1958).
[41] 61 Stat. 663-64, 17 U.S.C. §§ 107-09.

or drawings on stone made within the limits of the United States, shall be and it is hereby, prohibited, except in the cases specified in paragraphs 512 to 516, inclusive, in section 2 of the act entitled "An act to reduce the revenue and equalize the duties on imports, and for other purposes," approved October 1, 1890 and except in the case of persons purchasing for use and not for sale, who import subject to the duty thereon, not more than two copies of such book at any one time; and except in the case of newspapers and magazines, not containing in whole or in part matter copyrighted under the provisions of this act, unauthorized by the author, which are not hereby exempted from the prohibition of importation: *Provided, nevertheless,* that in the case of books in foreign languages, of which only translations in English are copyrighted the prohibition of importation shall apply only to the translation of the same, and the importation of the books in the original language shall be permitted.[42]

The "paragraphs 512 and 516 inclusive," referred to in section 3 above, were taken almost bodily from section 2 of the Tariff Act of 1890[43] listing duty-free items. They were added as section 31 (now 107) of the copyright law, forming exceptions to the import prohibitions. This was to satisfy the academic, scientific, religious, and foreign language interests which had been petitioning Congress since 1872 for tariff reform.[44]

These cosmopolitan groups sought free interchange of culture and, to that end, reduction of tariff barriers. The book manufacturers and publishers insisted upon protecting the American book manufacturing industry. The conflict between these groups brought the "ad interim" compromise, an outgrowth of the stringent manufacturing requirements of the Act of 1891. Both the Act of March 3, 1905 and the 1909 Act allowed only thirty days from the date of publication abroad for depositing foreign books, and protected such books for a limited time after their deposit in the Copyright Office. Extension to the full term under both Acts was conditioned upon the printing, publication, and registration of an American edition within a stated time limit.[45] The 1905 law applied to foreign books in a foreign language and allowed twelve months for the manufacture of an American edition or an English translation; the 1909 law applied to foreign books in the English language and allowed only thirty days for printing, publishing, and registering an American edition.

B. PROPOSALS FOR REVISION SINCE 1909

1. In general

It was admitted by the framers of this involved law that there were loopholes,[46] and it was argued that anyone could appropriate the author's book and bring out a piratical edition during the time necessary to produce and print an authorized edition of the original or a translation in the United States.[47] It was expected that the new law would give rise to questions of interpretation.[48] Fifty-three of

---

[42] 26 Stat. 1107-08.
[43] Act of Oct. 1, 1890, ch. 1244, 26 Stat. 604.
[44] See Dozer, *supra* note 6, at 91.
[45] Act of Mar. 3, 1905, 33 Stat. 1000; Act of Mar. 4, 1909, ch. 320, § 22, 35 Stat. 1080.
[46] See *Arguments on S. 6330 and H.R. 19853, supra* note 35, at 196 (Putnam statement); see also HOWELL, THE COPYRIGHT LAW 96-97 (3d ed. 1952).
[47] *Cf.* HOWELL, COPYRIGHT LAW 103 (rev. [4th] ed. Latman 1962).
[48] 1909-10 REG. COP. 12.

the sixty-three opinions requested from the Attorney General and the Treasury Department within three years after the new law became operative ruled on situations involving the manufacturing and importation clauses of the new law. Digests of the opinions are printed as Addenda to the Register's Report for the fiscal year 1912-1913.[49]

There were many proposals for amendatory legislation through the years, especially after the Rome Convention of 1928 when activity was renewed for U. S. ratification of the International Copyright Union. Six proposed amendments to the copyright statute affecting foreign-manufactured works became law. The first change eased the deposit requirements for foreign works but did not alter the manufacturing provisions.[50] Other proposed amendments that became law will be reported as they fit into the following historical survey of legislative action bearing on the manufacturing and importation clauses.

2. Proposals for amendment, 1915-1918

On December 6, 1915 a bill[51] was introduced by Mr. William S. Bennett to amend section 15 of the Act of 1909 to except foreign periodicals from the requirement of typesetting within the United States. There was a public hearing in the House Committee on Patents,[52] but no further action developed.

In regard to the operation of the Act of 1909, Mr. Solberg observed, in his report for the fiscal year 1916-1917:

> During the eight years or more since the Act of 1909 went into effect, some 3,000 ad interim registrations have been made, or for about 300 different books each year. While these 30-day ad interim provisions may be advantageous and sufficient in the case of a few well-known authors having established relations with American publishers who are accustomed to publish English books, they are of little or no value to the new, unknown, or little known English author who cannot hold back the date of publication of his book in London, and who fails to secure promptly a publisher in the United States. The Copyright Office records clearly demonstrate that both 30-day terms are too short to be really helpful. In about 5% of the applications received there has been failure to make deposit within the prescribed 30-days after first publication; and of the English books actually registered for ad interim protection hardly more than one-third have been finally republished in the United States. A certain proportion of the books which were reprinted, moreover, have not been published in the United States within the thirty-days of the ad interim term and therefore have not fully complied with the law's requirements. It is to be observed that in all cases where the ad interim registration is followed by an American edition, two registrations must be made, two fees paid, and three copies, in all, of each book must be deposited. The special requirements * * * actually result, therefore, in barring foreign authors from securing copyright in the United States for the greater number of their literary productions.[53]

---

[49] 1912-13 REG. COP. 219-26.

[50] Act of Mar. 28, 1914, ch. 43, § 1, 38 Stat. 311. Deposit of only one copy of a foreign work was required.

[51] H.R. 588, 64th Cong., 1st Sess.

[52] *Hearing on a Bill [H.R. 588] to Amend the Copyright Laws Relating to Printing of Periodicals Before the House Committee on Patents*, 64th Cong., 1st Sess. (1915).

[53] 1916-17 REG. COP. 20-21.

A bill which was introduced in 1915[54] and reintroduced in 1916[55] would have increased the ad interim term of protection from 30 to 90 days. The bill also would have prohibited the importation of authorized copies of English books (then permitted for private use and for libraries) without the "consent of the proprietor of the American copyright or his representative."[56]

Conditions growing out of World War I led to further attempts to alleviate the rigid time limits for copyrighting foreign books in English.[57] It was estimated that less than 1% of such books were reprinted and copyrighted in the United States, and books were becoming increasingly important for use in the growing motion picture industry.[58] It was urged that something be done to insure protection for all books in English; it was argued that this would be profitable for American printers and publishers because they would be called upon to reprint and publish foreign books that simply were not coming into the country.

3. Amendment extending ad interim time limits

A longer period for foreign claimants to comply with the ad interim and manufacturing requirements was achieved late in 1919 by the amendment of section 21 of the 1909 Act.[59] Books published abroad in the English language after December 18, 1919, the effective date of the amendment, could be deposited in the Copyright Office for registration within *sixty* (instead of thirty) days after first publication, to secure ad interim copyright in the United States for *four* months (instead of thirty days) from the date of receipt of the deposited copy and registration. As amended, section 21 read:

> That in the case of a book first published abroad in the English language on or after the date of the President's proclamation of peace, the deposit in the copyright office, not later than sixty days after its publication abroad of one complete copy of the foreign edition, with a request for the reservation of the copyright and a statement of the name and nationality of the author and of the copyright proprietor and of the date of publication of the said book, shall secure to the author or proprietor an ad interim copyright, which shall have all the force and effect given to copyright by this Act, and shall endure until the expiration of four months after such deposit in the copyright office.

4. Developments, 1920-1923

In his 1920-1921 report, Mr. Solberg referred to the new Canadian Copyright Act of June 4, 1921,[60] which provided for certain printing and import limitations, and its possible effect on United States publishers, saying:

> When its provisions are put into effect they will seriously embarrass the publishers of books and periodicals in the United States. The enactment of this Canadian statute makes it imperative that some action be promptly taken to secure more satisfactory relations between the United States and Canada, The fundamental

---

[54] H.R. 20695, 63d Cong., 3d Sess.
[55] H.R. 10231, 64th Cong., 1st Sess.
[56] Section 2(d).
[57] See 1917-18 REG. COP. 137-38; 1918-19 REG. COP. 131-33.
[58] See 1918-19 REG. COP. 132.
[59] Act of Dec. 18, 1919, ch. 11, 41 Stat. 369.
[60] 11 & 12 Geo. 5, c. 12.

difficulty heretofore has been the obligation to print in the United States books and periodicals and to manufacture here lithographs and photoengravings, and the first step clearly indicated is the elimination by law of this requirement of American manufacture. The Authors' League of America is proposing the introduction of an amendatory act limited to the abrogation of all provisions of the Copyright Act of March 4, 1909, relating to American typesetting, etc., and to urge its prompt enactment by Congress. When that has been accomplished satisfactory reciprocal copyright protection between the two countries may be discussed and arranged for.[61]

In succeeding years a dozen or more bills were introduced for the purpose of permitting U. S. entry into the International Copyright Union. Most of these either eliminated or modified the manufacturing and importation provisions of the copyright law. There were three bills introduced by Representative J. N. Tincher; the first would have repealed the manufacturing requirements[62] and the other two, which were identical, would have excepted books or periodicals of foreign origin.[63] The exceptions to the import prohibitions were stated in language now embodied substantially in section 107. The text of the manufacturing and importation provisions in the first version appears as Appendix A to this study.

Three identical bills,[64] providing for such minimum amendment of the existing law as would permit entry into the International Copyright Union, were introduced on the same date in 1923 by Senator Henry Cabot Lodge and by Representatives Sol Bloom and Florian Lampert. Section 6 in each of these bills provided:

* * * that the enjoyment and exercise by such authors [foreign authors claiming copyright by virtue of the Berne Union] of the rights and remedies accorded by the copyright laws of the United States and the provisions of this Act shall not be subject to the performance of any formalities in order to secure copyright, and such authors shall not be required to comply with the provisions of the copyright laws of the United States as to publication with notice of copyright, deposit of copies, registration of the copyright, or *manufacture within the limits of the United States.* * * * that the provisions of section 31 of the said act of 1909 [prohibiting import of certain books] shall not apply to a book by any author described in section 4 of this Act [Berne works] unless, under an assignment recorded in the Copyright Office at Washington of the copyright for the United States in such book, an American edition thereof shall have been produced which complies with the requirements of the said Act as to manufacture, publication, deposit of copies, and registration. [Emphasis supplied.]

5. General revision bills, 1924-1925

The Dallinger general revision bills of 1924[65] contained similar provisions for exempting foreign authors from the manufacturing requirements. Under section 18 of these bills, the import prohibition would not have applied to—

* * * books of foreign origin in a language or languages other than English, or to books of foreign origin published abroad in the English language, in which United States copyright may exist by virtue of international agreement for reciprocity in the granting of copyright to which the United States might become a

---

[61] 1920-21 REG. COP. 124-125.
[62] H.R. 11476, 67th Cong. 2d Sess. § 4 (1922).
[63] Section 6 of H.R. 14035, 67th Cong., 4th Sess. (1923) and H.R. 573, 68th Cong., 1st Sess. (1923).
[64] S. 74, H.R. 2663, H.R. 2704 (68th Cong., 1st Sess.).
[65] H.R. 8177, H.R. 9137 (68th Cong., 1st Sess.).

party except, in the latter case, during any period of time during which the United States copyright, or the right to publish, print and vend said work is owned in law or in equity by a citizen or resident of the United States.

In the following year, 1925, there were the Perkins bills,[66] and in 1926 the Vestal bills,[67] having the same basic purpose. Under the former, no deposit was required for books by foreign authors unless republished in the United States under an assignment of the copyright for the United States or under a license to print and sell such books in the United States. Registration and deposit were made optional.

6. Amendment concerning processes of manufacture, 1926

H.R. 10774 (69th Congress, 1st Session), introduced by Representative Albert H. Vestal on March 27, 1926, became law on July 3, 1926.[68] This Act amended section 15 of the Act of 1909 which sets out the specific requirement of manufacture within the United States in the case of books, periodicals, and lithographs or photoengraved prints. In regard to such requirements of American manufacture the Act of 1909 provided, however, that "they shall not apply to—"

* * * books of foreign origin in a language or languages other than English, or to books published abroad in the English language seeking ad interim protection under this act,

and the amendatory act added—

* * * or to works printed or produced in the United States by *any other process* than those above specified in this section. [Emphasis supplied.]

The Register explained this amendment in his Report for the fiscal year 1925-1926, as follows:

The difficult situation brought about by the World War in regard to printing made it necessary or convenient in substitution for printing from typeset, to resort to other methods for the production of many classes of books and periodicals. * * * University professors and other teachers have suffered seriously by this loss of copyright for their books because they were not printed from "type set." This amendatory act allows the author * * * to select his own method of production, and still be sure of adequate protection from the time his work is actually published in the United States by any process of production. The enactment of this measure of relief from the restrictive type-setting requirements, in behalf of university professors and others, will also prove a considerable relief to the copyright office.[69]

Thus, the premise of the 1926 amendment was that, under section 15 of the Act of 1909, no book or periodical produced by any process other than those enumerated (typography, lithography, and photoengraving) could be copyrighted at all, even if produced in the United States. Since there is no record of any intent, in the legislative history of the 1909 Act, to establish such a condition of copyright protection, the premise of the 1926 amendment is highly dubious, and its effect questionable. It remains unclear whether an English-

[66] H.R. 11258, 68th Cong., 2d Sess.; H.R. 5841, 69th Cong., 1st Sess.
[67] H.R. 6249, H.R. 10353, H.R. 10434 (69th Cong., 1st Sess.).
[68] 44 Stat. 818.
[69] 1925-26 REG. COP. 238. See also H.R. REP. NO. 1100, 69th Cong., 1st Sess. (1926).

language book or periodical produced by a process not enumerated in the statute (mimeographing or typewriting, for example) would have to be manufactured in the United States to be copyrighted here.

7. Vestal bills, 1928-1930

Mr. Vestal tried again and again, at the behest of such organizations as the Authors' League of America, ASCAP, the Drama League of New York, the National Association of Book Publishers, the Motion Picture Producers and Distributors of America, and others, to revise and update the copyright law and bring it into harmony with the requirements for entry into the International Copyright Union. In fact, he introduced so many bills that it is difficult to keep them straight. The first one in 1928[70] included the following provisions affecting manufacture and importation of works by foreign authors who secured copyright under the International Copyright Convention:

SEC. 6. * * * enjoyment and exercise of rights and remedies * * * shall not be subject to the performance of any formalities in order to secure copyright, and such authors shall not be required to comply with the provisions of the copyright laws of the United States as to publication with notice of copyright, deposit of copies, registration of copyright, or manufacture within the limits of the United States.

SEC. 7. That the provisions of section 31 of the said act of 1909 shall not apply to a book by any author described in section 4 of this act unless, under an assignment recorded in the copyright office at Washington of the copyright for the United States in such book, an American edition thereof shall have been produced which complies with the requirements of the said act as to manufacture, publication, deposit of copies, and registration.

Another bill authorized the President of the United States to effect adherence to the Rome Convention of 1928 without any amendment of the existing law,[71] but the one Mr. Vestal introduced on May 22, 1930 was a comprehensive general revision bill.[72] (See excerpts in Appendix B.) Although this bill, which would have eliminated the manufacturing requirements as a condition for copyright but not as a condition for bringing suit in certain cases, managed to pass the House,[73] like all the other Vestal bills it failed of enactment. However, according to the Senate Committee Report,[74] the opposition of the printing trades appeared to have been met. The report said:

* * * American printers are protected against foreign importations by the provisions in section 28. This section is believed to be entirely satisfactory to the printing trades, and provides that the works of American authors, which are the subject of copyright in the United States, shall be printed in this country.[75]

8. General revision bills and other developments, 1931-1934

A proliferation of general revision bills came up for consideration in the next Congress, and there continued to be sharp differences of

---

[70] H.R. 9586, 70th Cong., 1st Sess.
[71] H.R. 6988, 71st Cong., 2d Sess. (1929).
[72] H.R. 12549, 71st Cong., 2d Sess. (1930). This was a rewritten version of H.R. 6990, same Congress and session, which in turn was a reprint of H.R. 8912, 70th Cong., 1st Sess. (1928).
[73] 74 CONG. REC. 2081 (1930).
[74] S. REP. NO. 1732, 71st Cong., 3d Sess. (1931).
[75] Id. at 26.

opinion about the manufacturing and importation provisions, among other controversial aspects of the bills. Mr. Vestal introduced another bill[76] substantially identical to the last one he had introduced in the 71st Congress,[77] but it fell by the wayside along with similar bills offered by Senator Herbert,[78] Senator Dill,[79] and Mr. Sirovich.[80]

Mr. Vestal died the following April, 1932, and copyright law revision lost another champion.

As in 1904 for the Louisiana Purchase Exposition,[81] some relaxation was needed for importing and protecting foreign books to be shown at the Chicago World's Fair Centennial of 1933 ("A Century of Progress"). Temporary copyright and issuance of a certificate of copyright registration was authorized for works of foreign authors without compliance with any conditions or formalities.[82]

9. The Duffy, Sirovich, and Daly bills, 1933-1937

In 1933, toward the close of the first session of the 73rd Congress, companion bills were introduced[83] aimed at doing the minimum necessary to permit adherence to the Rome Convention. On February 19, 1934, President Roosevelt transmitted the Convention to the Senate.[84] As an outgrowth of hearings in the spring of 1934,[85] an Interdepartmental Committee was organized, composed of representatives of the Departments of State and Commerce and the Copyright Office, to prepare a draft bill with a view to facilitating approval of the Convention.[86] The committee held conferences[87] which culminated in the introduction of the Duffy bill.[88] Section 11 of this bill proposed to amend the proviso specifying exceptions to the manufacturing clause in section 15 of the Act of 1909 by the following language:

Provided, however, that said requirements shall not apply to (1) works printed or produced in the United States by any other process than those above specified in this section; (2) works in raised characters for the use of the blind; (3) books or periodicals of foreign origin in a language or languages other than English; (4) works by nationals of the United States copies of which are distributed only in foreign countries; or (5) works in any language by foreign authors, first published in a foreign country party to the Convention for the Protection of Literary and Artistic Works.

The report on the conferences and the draft bill resulting therefrom[89] made it clear that it would be desirable to wipe out the clause

---

[76] H.R. 139, 72d Cong., 1st Sess. (1931).
[77] See note 72, *supra.*
[78] S. 176, 72d Cong., 1st Sess. (1931).
[79] S. 3985, 72d Cong., 1st Sess. (1932).
[80] H.R. 10976 and H.R. 12094, 72d Cong., 1st Sess. (1932). Mr. Sirovich introduced five general revision bills at this session. For a legislative history of these bills, see Goldman, *The History of the U.S.A. Copyright Law Revision,* COPYRIGHT LAW REVISION STUDY NO. 1, SUBCOMM. ON PATENTS, TRADEMARKS, AND COPYRIGHTS, SENATE COMM. ON THE JUDICIARY, 86TH CONG., 1ST SESS. (Comm. Print. 1960).
[81] See note 32 *supra* and accompanying text.
[82] See Act of July 19, 1932, ch. 509, 47 Stat. 703. Similar legislation has been adopted for subsequent international exhibitions.
[83] H.R. 5853, S. 1928.
[84] EXEC. E, 73d Cong., 2d Sess.
[85] *Hearing on S. 1928 Before the Senate Committee on Foreign Relations,* 73d Cong., 2d Sess. (1934).
[86] See EXEC. REP. NO. 4, 74th Cong., 1st Sess. 4 (1935).
[87] *Ibid.*
[88] S. 2465, 74th Cong., 1st Sess. (1935).
[89] The report of the interdepartmental group was printed as an exhibit to the Senate Committee report on the Convention. See EXEC. REP. NO. 4, 74th Cong., 1st Sess. 9-18 (1935).

completely, but that caution dictated change only insofar as necessary to comply with the treaty. The report stated that "the only argument against the elimination of the manufacturing clause lies in the suggestion that it might reduce the amount of work being done in American shops at this time when there is widespread unemployment." Employment figures cited indicated that about 300 people in this country were given employment because of the manufacturing clause; that more than 70,000 people were normally engaged in printing, publishing and engraving in the United States and more than 12,000 in the book-publishing trades alone. On the basis of the figures available, the committee felt that the repeal of the clause could have no perceptible effect on the employment situation; that there was every reason to believe that much of the work accredited to the manufacturing clause would, for reasons of convenience or economy, continue to be done in the United States even if the provision were repealed; and that possible retaliation by other nations could cause far more unemployment.

On April 19th, 1935, the Rome Convention of 1928 was ratified by the Senate without a record vote.[90] On the next legislative day, at the request of Mr. Duffy, the vote was reconsidered and the treaty was restored to the Executive Calendar pending action on the enabling legislation, which Mr. Duffy had intended should be taken up before ratification of the treaty.[91]

Shortly thereafter Senator McAdoo, chairman of the Senate Committee on Patents, held an "informal conference" on the Duffy bill,[92] as a result of which the bill was amended and a clean bill introduced.[93] The new bill, however, did not include any change in the amendment to the manufacturing provisions as proposed in the original Duffy bill. The Senate Report, submitted by Senator McAdoo, included this prophecy about elimination of the manufacturing requirement:

Among the other important provisions of the bill growing out of its relations to the treaty is the elimination of the requirement for the domestic manufacture in the United States of books and similar publications, if in the English language, in order to be eligible to copyright in the United States. This provision in the present law has been a constant source of irritation and of danger to the interests of American exporters of literary and artistic works. Its elimination will, according to perfectly reliable evidence, create no adverse effect upon American industry, but the protection to American exporters accorded by the treaty promises to stimulate the manufacture of books and so to increase employment in this country.[94]

The Duffy bill passed the Senate on August 7, 1935,[95] but with an amendment, proposed by Senator Trammell,[96] which restored the requirement of American manufacture for all works distributed in

---

[90] 79 CONG. REC. 6032 (1935).
[91] Id. at 6099.
[92] A transcript of the proceedings is printed in *Hearings on Revision of Copyright Laws Before the House Committee on Patents*, 74th Cong., 2d Sess. 1402-19 (1936).
[93] S. 3047, 74th Cong., 1st Sess. (1935).
[94] S. REP. NO. 896, 74th Cong., 1st Sess. 3 (1935).
[95] 79 CONG. REC. 12615.
[96] The Trammell amendment is reproduced in Appendix C. This amendment imperilled the chief purpose of the bill, which was to prepare the way for adherence of the United States to the International Copyright Union.

the United States in book, pamphlet, map, or sheet form. The bill, as amended, was introduced in the House the next day,[97] but Congress adjourned before final action could be taken.

Modelled after the Duffy bill, which had been "through the mill" and passed the Senate in the previous session of the 74th Congress,[98] was the Sirovich bill[99] of the second session. However, it contained the drastic Trammell amendment[100] requiring American manufacture for all works distributed in the United States in book, pamphlet, map, or sheet form. The bill's ad interim provisions were the same as those then in effect. The importation prohibition of the 1909 law was unchanged by this bill. The Daly bill contained the same manufacturing provision as the Sirovich bill, but extended it to "all records, discs, sound tracks, or other mechanical means of the reproduction of renditions and interpretations."[101]

Extensive hearings on the Duffy, Daly, and Sirovich bills were held in February, March, and April, 1936 before the House Committee on Patents.[102] At these hearings objections were voiced by author and publisher groups to United States adherence to the Berne Convention and to the fact that American authors would be subjected to formalities—including manufacturing requirements—from which foreign authors would be exempt.

The 1936 hearings were the last to be held on bills for general revision of the copyright laws. In 1937, during the 75th Congress, Senator Duffy reintroduced his bill,[103] and identical bills were introduced in the House by Mr. Moser[104] and Mr. Bloom.[105] Representative Daly also introduced a somewhat modified version of his bill,[106] and a companion bill was introduced by Senator Guffey.[107] No action was taken on any of these bills, nor on similar bills introduced in the 76th Congress.[108]

10. The Shotwell bill and other developments, 1939-1940

The last important attempt to revise the copyright laws to permit United States adherence to the Berne Convention was a general revision bill introduced on January 8, 1940 by Senator Thomas of Utah.[109] This bill, commonly known as the "Shotwell Bill," drafted by a national committee under the chairmanship of Professor James T. Shotwell of Columbia University, met with considerable opposition, according to an article in the January 24, 1940 issue of *Variety*. Under section 29 of the bill, domestic manufacture was not made a condition

---

[97] 79 CONG. REC. 12904.
[98] See note 95 *supra,* and accompanying text.
[99] H.R. 11420, 74th Cong., 2d Sess. (1936).
[100] See Appendix C.
[101] H.R. 10632, 74th Cong., 2d Sess. § 14 (1936).
[102] *Hearings on Revision of Copyright Laws Before the House Committee on Patents,* 74th Cong., 2d Sess.
[103] S. 7.
[104] H.R. 2695.
[105] H.R. 3004.
[106] H.R. 5275.
[107] S. 2240.
[108] H.R. 926 and 4871 by Mr. Daly, and H.R. 6160 and 9703 by Mr. McGranery.
[109] S. 3043, 76th Cong., 3d Sess.

of copyright, but importation of a foreign-manufactured work in English was limited to 500 copies.[110]

The authority of the Secretary of the Treasury and the Postmaster General to make rules and regulations to enforce the law's importation prohibitions was amplified by the Act of April 11, 1940. As a condition for exclusion, a certificate of compliance with the copyright law, including the manufacturing provisions, was required to be filed with the Post Office Department or the Treasury Department, to give notice to postal and customs authorities of such compliance.[111]

11. Manufacturing clause amendment, 1949

After World War II, European countries were finding it increasingly difficult to comply with the requirements for U. S. copyright because of the dollar shortage and the inadequate time limits,[112] and foreign registrations fell off sharply. Desiring to make more foreign works available for cultural use in the United States, the Register of Copyrights, Sam B. Warner, was instrumental in procuring the enactment of Public Law No. 84, approved June 3, 1949.[113] This law amended sections 16, 22 and 23 of the copyright law by extending the time period for ad interim registration and U. S. manufacture of foreign works in English.

In his annual report for the fiscal year ending June 30, 1949, Mr. Warner predicted the principal benefits of this amendment as follows:

Even more important are the changes wrought by this act in provisions of the copyright law regarding books and periodicals in the English language. Prior to passage of Public Law 84 a book published abroad in the English language had to be registered in the Copyright Office within 60 days of publication and was required to be manufactured in the United States within four months thereafter in order to secure U. S. copyright protection. With a few exceptions no copy manufactured abroad could be imported into the U. S. while the American copyright subsisted.

The effect was to deprive almost all works published abroad in the English language of American copyright protection. During the last few years only a few hundred books and periodicals were so registered and many less were in fact manufactured in this country.[114]

Public Law 84 allowed six months from publication abroad within which to register, and five years within which to manufacture in the United States. It also authorized the importation of 1,500 copies without loss of copyright. The Register said further:

It is expected that the new law will increase the number of English language books reprinted in the U. S. The extension of the period to five years should make it possible for an American publisher to determine whether a book is a success in England and Canada before deciding whether to publish it here. The right to import 1,500 copies to test the American market should greatly assist in determining

---

[110] For the text and importation provisions of this bill, see Appendix D.
[111] See 54 Stat. 106 (1940), 17 U.S.C. § 109 (1958).
[112] 1948-49 REG. COP. 2.
[113] 63 Stat. 153. See statement of Mr. Warner, *Hearings on H.R. 2285 (Relaxation of Copyright Law as to Foreign Works) Before Subcommittee No. 4 of the House Committee on the Judiciary*, 81st Cong., 1st Sess. 38-44 (1949).
[114] 1948-49 REG. COP. 3.

whether the Act will appeal to American as well as to British and Canadian tastes.[115]

As predicted, there was an unusual increase in the number of foreign registrations for the next year. By 1951 registrations for foreign books in English rose 43%; in foreign languages, 36%.[116]

12. Universal Copyright Convention and implementing legislation

By this time the movement begun in 1947 under the auspices of Unesco for a new international copyright convention was making headway. To pave the way for adherence by the United States, efforts were renewed to remove from the copyright law the manufacturing requirements for foreign works, always a block to U. S. participation in world-wide copyright arrangements. The basic proposal, which was eventually adopted in the Universal Copyright Convention of 1952, involved the provision that a simple copyright notice on published copies should be deemed to satisfy all formalities—including domestic manufacture—on which copyright might be conditioned under national laws. Corresponding amendments of the U. S. law would, of course, be necessary for ratification of a convention containing such a provision.

In May 1951, before the final form of the Universal Copyright Convention had been drafted, Representative Celler of New York introduced a bill[117] to modify the manufacturing clause as an essential step toward establishment of a workable international copyright relationship, compatible with the plans then developing for a new copyright convention.[118] The bill provided for removal of the domestic manufacturing requirements then applicable to foreign books and periodicals in the English language, but did not propose to change the requirements as to domestic works. The bill was favorably reported with amendments by Subcommittee No. 3 of the House Judiciary Committee on February 28, 1952.[119] On March 22 of that year, the full Judiciary Committee voted not to report the bill to the floor of Congress.[120] Mr. Celler reintroduced his bill early in 1953[121] but no further action was recorded.

In September 1952, the Universal Copyright Convention was signed at Geneva by forty nations, including the United States. Thereafter, in 1953, several bills were introduced to revise the copyright law to conform with the standards prescribed by the Convention.[122] The hearings[123] held April 7 and 8, 1954 on these bills are replete with

---

[115] *Ibid.*

[116] See 1950-51 REG. COP. 1.

[117] H.R. 4059, 82d Cong., 1st Sess.

[118] See, *e.g.*, statement of Dr. Luther E. Evans, Librarian of Congress, *Hearings on H.R. 4059 before Subcommittee No. 3 of the House Committee on the Judiciary*, 82d Cong., 2d Sess. 2-5 (1952).

[119] See 1951-52 REG. COP. 6; *Sub-Committee Votes Change in Manufacturing Clause*, 161 PUBLISHERS' WEEKLY 1197 (1952).

[120] See 1951-52 REG. COP. 6; Editorial, *We Deplore the Shelving of the Celler Bill*, 161 PUBLISHERS' WEEKLY 1550 (1952).

[121] H.R. 397, 83d Cong., 1st Sess.

[122] H.R. 6616, H.R. 6670, S. 2559, 83d Cong., 1st Sess. (1953). See GOLDMAN, *op. cit. supra* note 80, at 13.

[123] *Hearings on Executive M, 83d Cong., 1st Sess., the Universal Copyright Convention and S. 2259 Before a Subcommittee of the Senate Committee on Foreign Relations and a Subcommittee of the Senate Committee on the Judiciary*, 83d Cong., 2d Sess. (1954).

testimony dealing with the manufacturing clause and the question of its complete repeal or modification. For a number of years, the annual reports of the International Typographical Union, A.F.L., which was still zealously opposing repeal of the manufacturing clause, had contained strongly worded resolutions and recommendations supporting its position.[124] As the United States tended toward fewer and lower tariff restrictions, the printing industries feared eventual elimination of the copyright barrier and consequent foreign competition and jeopardy of U. S. wage standards.[125]

The Senate Committee on the Judiciary was obviously impressed by the economic analysis which the American Book Publishers Council presented on the potential economic effect of the proposed amendment of the manufacturing clause. The Committee said:

> This analysis tended forcefully to establish that even if the entire segment of book publication involved were to be wiped out because of the injurious impact of competition from foreign manufacture, not more than 200 workmen would be affected.
> * * * The Committee is, of course, concerned with any segment of labor. In the present case, however, it is not convinced that such an eventuality may result from enactment of this legislation, and therefore concludes, as regards the modification of the manufacturing clause that no harm will be done either to American labor or to American industry.[126]

The outgrowth of these legislative efforts was Public Law 743, approved August 31, 1954.[127] P.L. 743 provided the legislation enabling the Universal Copyright Convention to come into effect in the United States three months after twelve countries (including four non-members of the Berne Union) deposited their ratifications with Unesco. Among the changes in the domestic law were the addition of subsection (c) to section 9, exempting foreign works qualifying for Universal Copyright Convention protection and published with the U.C.C. notice from: (1) the manufacturing requirements of section 16, (2) the affidavit requirements of sections 17 and 18, and (3) the import prohibitions of section 107 to the extent that they relate to the manufacturing requirements.

Public Law 743 also modified section 16 by substituting the words "first published abroad" for the words "of foreign origin" in the first proviso. Since the phrase "of foreign origin" had been understood to refer to foreign authorship,[128] the effect of this change was to extend to an American author, who first published his book abroad in the English language, the limited import privilege (up to 1,500 copies) heretofore available only to foreign authors first publishing their English-language books outside the United States. Testimony

---

[124] See, e.g., the resolution of the union's Committee on Organization and Allied Trades, INTERNATIONAL TYPOGRAPHICAL UNION, PROCEEDINGS OF THE NINETY-SECOND SESSION, WASHINGTON, D.C., AUGUST NINETEENTH TO TWENTY-FIFTH, NINETEEN FIFTY, at 133 (1950), which was published as a supplement to the Sept. 1950 issue of The Typographical Journal.

[125] See EXEC. M, 83d Cong., 1st Sess. (1954); S. EXEC. REP. NO. 5, 83d Cong., 2d Sess. (1954).

[126] S. REP. NO. 1936, 83d Cong., 1st Sess. 7-8 (1953).

[127] 17 U.S.C. §§ 9, 16, 19 (1958). These amendments were based on H.R. 6616, 83d Cong., 1st Sess. (1951).

[128] See Cary, The United States and Universal Copyright—An Analysis of Public Law 743, in UNIVERSAL COPYRIGHT CONVENTION ANALYZED 85 (Kupferman & Foner ed. 1955).

in the hearings urged that American authors ought to have the same privilege.[129]

Thus, for the first time books of foreign authorship, in the English language, first published abroad, did not need to be manufactured in the United States in order to achieve full-term U. S. copyright protection, and were freed from restrictions on importation. Furthermore, on the coming into force of the Universal Copyright Convention in a foreign nation, the period of protection for ad interim copyrights then subsisting in works of its nationals was extended to the full term of twenty-eight years from the date of first publication abroad, without the need for complying with the further formalities (including manufacture in the United States) specified in section 23 of the copyright law.

13. Conclusion

The Universal Copyright Convention came into force in the United States on September 16, 1955. Since that date efforts to amend the copyright law have been confined to emergency needs, and the manufacturing and importation clauses as amended have been allowed to rest, to see how they work. A carefully planned program for general revision was undertaken—one which would avoid, if possible, the pitfalls of previous general revision efforts.

As is apparent from the legislative history of the manufacturing clause of the copyright law, this feature has probably been one of the major stumbling blocks to the success of any general revision bill. Therefore, it is obviously important to consider how this traditional, but gradually eroded provision of the copyright law fits into the present-day scheme of domestic and international copyright and related enterprise. As one commentator has said recently:

> Compromise has been the bloodline of the manufacturing requirement. It was compromise that originally injected the clause into the law, and as demonstrated through its long history, it was compromise after compromise that sustained it.
> * * * It is difficult to see how the remaining shell of the once powerful manufacturing clause can survive further revision of the act, as is presently contemplated.[130]

IV. SOME PROBLEMS IN ADMINISTERING THE PROVISIONS

A. COPYRIGHT OFFICE: REGISTRATION PROBLEMS

Reference has already been made to the numerous perplexing questions of interpretation referred to the Attorney General and the Secretary of the Treasury after the 1909 Act became operative.[131] The problems involved in the construction of the manufacturing clause could form the basis of a lengthy treatise, for the clause, complicated by involved sentence structure, is replete with undefined words and ambiguous phrases, admitting all sorts of evasions. Only a small

---

[129] See *Hearings, supra* note 123, at 76-77.
[130] Paul, *A Reappraisal of the Manufacturing Clause of the Copyright Act in Light of its History and the Universal Copyright Convention,* 13 U. MIAMI L. REV. 315, 319 (1959).
[131] See note 48 *supra* and accompanying text.

fraction of the continuing problems can be described in this paper as examples. The Copyright Office has had to devise special forms, regulations and examining procedures for works affected by the manufacturing and importation provisions, and to evaluate many borderline cases. The public is bewildered by these special forms, regulations and procedures, and by the technical distinctions involved in their application.

1. Scope of clause

Stated in the broadest possible terms, the domestic manufacturing requirements apply, with certain exceptions, to books and periodicals, to illustrations in books, and to separate lithographs or photoengravings. These categories of works are not defined in the manufacturing clause.

(a) Books and periodicals

Not all works published in "book form" are subject to the requirement; musical compositions, either in sheet or bound form, have been held not to fall within the terms "book" or "lithograph."[132] Nor is a published drama a "book."[133] Yet a published lecture is considered a "book" under the Copyright Office Regulations.[134]

The enforcement provisions of the law do not apply to periodicals. No affidavit of domestic manufacture is required for them, and a foreign-printed "newspaper or magazine" is not denied entry through Customs, even though it contains contributions separately copyrighted in the United States.[135]

The manufacturing must be performed "within the limits of the United States." This phrase is used four times in the manufacturing clause, but is not explicitly defined anywhere in the Act. Moreover, there has been no reported court decision on the question of whether these terms include territorial dependencies and possessions of the United States.[136] For purposes of registration, the Copyright Office has construed this geographic limitation to mean not only the continental United States but also incorporated territories and organized unincorporated territories and possessions under the jurisdiction of the United States.[137]

---

[132] See Littleton v. Oliver Ditson Co., 62 Fed. 597 (C.C.D. Mass. 1894), aff'd per curiam, 67 Fed. 905 (1st Cir. 1895). The opposite result was reached in 22 OPS. ATT'Y GEN. 29 (1898). The 1898 ruling was shortly thereafter reversed in 1 TREAS. DEC. 792 (1899), and this reversal of practice was later confirmed in 23 OPS. ATT'Y GEN. 445 (1901).
[133] See Hervieu v. J. S. Ogilvie Pub. Co., 169 Fed. 978 (C.C.S.D.N.Y. 1909).
[134] See 37 C.F.R. § 202.6 (1960).
[135] See 17 U.S.C. § 107(b) (1958).
[136] For a discussion of territories as geographical parts of the United States for purposes of the copyright law, see Varmer, *Copyright in Territories and Possessions of the United States*, COPYRIGHT LAW REVISION STUDY NO. 34, SUBCOMM. ON PATENTS, TRADEMARKS, AND COPYRIGHTS, SENATE COMM. ON THE JUDICIARY, 86th CONG., 2d SESS. 49-50 (Comm. Print 1961).
[137] This construction appears to be justified for those territories to which the copyright laws specifically, or all the laws of the United States in general, have been extended. See, *e.g.*, Organic Act of Guam § 24, 70 Stat. 911 (1956), 48 U.S.C. § 1421n (Supp. V, 1958). Hence, claims to copyright in books manufactured in the Panama Canal Zone, Guam, Puerto Rico, or the Virgin Islands are considered registrable. It is probable that a court would hold such claims valid, but the status of works manufactured in other areas under the jurisdiction of the United States is doubtful.

The manufacturing provision attempts to specify the processes which must be performed in the United States, but without defining them. The named processes are: typesetting, platemaking, lithography, photoengraving, printing, and binding. The law says, "printed from type set within the United States * * * or from plates made within the United States from type set therein * * *." There can be little doubt that, for any work for which domestic typesetting is required, the plates made from such type must also be manufactured in the United States. The language of the domestic manufacturing requirements would presumably not cover plates made by photogravure, hand engraving, or any other intaglio (engraving) process, because such plates are not made from type and do not fall within the "lithographic"[138] or "photoengraving"[139] processes. In 1926, however, the clause was amended to provide for copyright in books produced "by any other process" than those enumerated,[140] and, as will be pointed out below,[141] this amendment raises a question as to the status of works manufactured abroad by one of these methods.

The part reading "* * * if the text is produced by lithographic process, or photoengraving process, then by a process wholly performed within the limits of the United States" applies generally to text that has been printed from a plane surface by a chemical process based on the antipathy between grease and water, or from a raised surface produced by photography. An increasingly common and difficult question arises when the text of a book is printed abroad, and then an American offset edition is reproduced from the foreign book, plates, or unbound sheets. The language of section 16 is ambiguous as to whether the American edition satisfies the manufacturing requirements in such a case. The first part of the provision could be read to mean that, if typesetting, platemaking, or printing from type are involved anywhere in the manufacture of the book, they must be done in the United States. On the other hand, it could be argued that the clause

* * * or, if the text be produced by a lithographic process, or a photoengraving process, then by a process wholly performed within the limits of the United States, * * *

means that production of the particular text of the American edition by a lithographic process wholly performed in the United States is sufficient, even if the text was duplicated from material printed abroad.

A possible rationale of the second theory would be that at least one segment of the American printing industry has benefitted from the production of the book. The legislative history on the question, while inconclusive, includes a few passages in the debates on the 1891

---

[138] Lithography has been defined as "the art or process of putting writing or designs on stone with a greasy material, and of producing printed impressions therefrom; also, any process based on the same principle, as one using zinc, aluminum, or some other substance instead of stone." WEBSTER, NEW COLLEGIATE DICTIONARY 491 (1956).

[139] Photoengraving has been defined as "engraving by the aid of photography; specif. and usually, any photomechanical process for reproducing pictures, etc., in which the printing surface is in relief, as contrasted with photolithography and photogravure." *Id.* at 634.

[140] Act of July 3, 1926, ch. 743, 44 Stat. 818.

[141] See notes 164-66 *infra* and accompanying text.

Act[142] that might lend support to this theory. These factors, together with the doctrine of narrow construction of statutory provisions, has led the Copyright Office to accept the American edition for deposit in fulfillment of the manufacturing and ad interim requirements. It seems clear, however, that if any part of the "lithographic process" itself—such as the photography involved in using "repro proofs"— takes place abroad, registration could not be considered.

The last process of manufacture specified, i.e., binding, was new in the 1909 Act. The reasons for including this step in book manufacture are discussed in the 1908 Committee hearings.[143] Generally, "binding" means any process involving the fastening together of the sheets and enclosing them within covers; such work must be performed in the United States.[144] The requirement applies only to "printed books"; it does not apply to periodicals or to books produced by some process other than printing (presswork), under the narrow definition of that term.

(b) Pictorial works

A distinct category of works in addition to books and periodicals is made subject to the manufacturing requirements by the so-called "graphic arts" clause, reading:

* * * which requirements shall extend also to the illustrations within a book consisting of printed text and illustrations produced by lithographic process, or photoengraving process, and also to separate lithographs or photoengravings, except where in either case the subjects represented are located in a foreign country and illustrate a scientific work or reproduce a work of art: * * *.

Here again, as in the case of periodicals, the enforcement provisions of the copyright law do not expressly include lithographs and photoengravings; they do not fall within the ad interim or affidavit requirements, and, if produced abroad, they are not barred entry into the United States for failure to comply with the manufacturing requirements.

During the pre-1909 hearings the lithographers indicated that they could not possibly compete with the German artisans in the pictorial arts, and urged that the manufacturing requirements be extended to illustrative material.[145] The term "illustrations" needed refinement, however. There had been a debate about including photographic negatives[146] which were ultimately omitted to facilitate international commerce in photography,[147] and "chromos" were omitted because chromolithography was comprehended in the term "lithography," which generally refers to a planographic method.[148] In the evolution

---

[142] See 22 CONG. REC. 2673-74, 2790 (1891).
[143] See statement of Mr. Feeney representing the International Brotherhood of Bookbinders, *Hearings on Pending Bills to Amend and Consolidate the Acts Respecting Copyright Before the Senate & House Committees on Patents*, 60th Cong., 1st Sess. 66-68 (1908) [hereinafter cited as 1908 *Hearings*].
[144] For a ruling on rebinding abroad, see 28 OPS. ATT'Y GEN. 209 (1910).
[145] See 1908 *Hearings* at 109-15.
[146] See *Arguments on S. 6330 and H.R. 19853 Before the Senate & House Committees on Patents*, 59th Cong., 1st Sess. 8, 10, 60 (June 1906) and 100, 110 (Dec. 1906).
[147] See *id.* (Dec. 1906) at 194.
[148] See *id.* at 10.

of the graphic arts clause all sorts of ramifications appeared in drafts, such as:

> * * * which requirements shall extend also to the illustrations produced by lithographic process within a printed book consisting of text and illustrations, and also to separate lithographs, except where in either case the subjects represented are located in a foreign country * * *.[149]

There was objection to the exception in favor of "subjects * * * located in a foreign country."[150] The lithographers felt that this would give the European lithographers all work relating to foreign subjects; they suggested that the exception should be confined to works of art and scientific material which required the foreign artist's or scientist's personal supervision. The "photo-engraving" process was inserted, and the phrase "and illustrate a scientific work or reproduce a work of art" was added.[151]

Under the rule of strict construction applicable to statutes which specify their coverage, pictures made in a foreign country by a process of reproduction other than a "lithographic" or "photoengraving" process would be exempt from the manufacturing requirements.[152] Therefore, this exemption would seem to include photogravures, collotypes, line engravings, etchings, mezzotints, stipple and crayon engravings, and wood cuts.

However, the popular process commonly known as "offset" or "photo-offset" is clearly a lithographic process and therefore subject to the manufacturing requirement. These technical distinctions point up the need to know and recognize the various manufacturing processes in order to decide the applicability of the graphic arts clause, and there are many new processes to consider.

Since the graphic arts clause says that the manufacturing requirements extend to "illustrations within a book * * * ," apparently they do not apply to illustrations in periodicals or in musical or dramatic works published in book form.

The following case points up some of the difficult technical questions presented by the graphic arts clause: A book in English by a foreign author had been manufactured and copyrighted in this country. Later, a better edition containing photoengraved illustrations was produced abroad. The publisher, desiring to import and sell the foreign edition, abandoned his U. S. copyright in the text in order to copyright the illustrations, which did not fall within the exceptions in the graphic arts clause. Registration could be made for the illustrations, without regard to the place of manufacture, if it were assumed (1) that illustrations and text are to be treated separately and (2) that the term "book" in the graphic arts clause refers only to a book covered by the restrictions in the first part of section 16 on the printing of textual matter. On these

---

[149] *E.g.,* Section 13 in the companion bills, S. 6330 & H.R. 19853, 59th Cong., 1st Sess. (1906).

[150] See 1908 *Hearings* at 112-13.

[151] See, *e.g.,* H.R. 11794, 60th Cong., 1st Sess. § 16 (1908); H.R. 22183, 60th Cong., 1st Sess. § 16 (1908).

[152] 2 LADAS, THE INTERNATIONAL PROTECTION OF LITERARY AND ARTISTIC PROPERTY 765 (1938).

assumptions there would be no restrictions on the manufacture of illustrations in a book, the text of which was not "accorded protection under this title." By such mental gymnastics it is possible to avoid the precise specifications of the manufacturing clause.

The exception tacked onto the graphic arts clause was hastily drafted and does not say what was probably intended. The hearings indicate an intention to exempt pictorial representations of material located abroad which it would be impossible or impractical to transfer to the United States for purposes of reproduction by lithography or photoengraving.[153] Examples given included anatomical drawings sketched at the surgeon's operating room of a European hospital, or a reproduction made at the Louvre of the Mona Lisa. However, the clause says that the "subjects represented" must be "located in a foreign country" and that these "subjects" must either "illustrate a scientific work" or "reproduce a work of art." The confused language of this clause has been authoritatively construed as permitting the making abroad of lithographs or photoengravings that reproduce any scientific drawing or any "work of art" (which might be a mere sketch) located abroad.[154] In other words, a reproduction of any art work prepared abroad solely for the purpose of being reproduced would fall outside the manufacturing clause, regardless of the subject shown in the picture. This construction makes the exception vastly broader than may have been intended.

Query whether it would be permissible under the exception to transport an American painting to a foreign country for the express purpose of reproducing it there.[155] And should the United States deny copyright to a Dutch lithographer for his work of imagination drawn directly onto a plate, because the "subject" did not "reproduce" a work of art?

2. Exceptions to the manufacturing clause

(a) Implied exceptions

Aside from the exceptions implied from narrow definition of the named processes and the exceptions stated in the graphic arts clause, there are many other implied exceptions to the manufacturing requirements.

Only "copies accorded protection under this title" must be manufactured in the United States. This would, of course, exclude all public domain books. It would also exclude books which are not subject to copyright because of the nationality of the author.

A practice developed shortly after 1909 whereby parts of books (without any indication of incompleteness) were deposited for copyright registration. These were subsequently included in books, the remainder of which had been printed abroad and imported as uncopyrighted material. Thus, although not legally entitled to copyright, the portions printed abroad would have been useless to anyone

---

[153] See 1908 *Hearings* at 113.
[154] See 28 OPS. ATT'Y GEN. 150 (1910); *id.* at 557 (1911).
[155] The 1910 opinion of the Attorney General cited in note 134, *supra*, casts doubt on the permissibility of this.

unless permission were obtained to include the "copyrighted" portions. The Attorney General ruled out this evasion of the manufacturing requirements by holding that the word "book" as used in the law meant only complete works, not mere fragments, and that registration in any such case should be refused.[156]

The phrase, "the *text* of all copies accorded protection under this title" [emphasis supplied], which text must be manufactured within the United States, has been held to exclude a catalog of paintings. In *Basevi v. Edward O'Toole Co.*[157] the court held that a catalog produced abroad containing copyrightable reproductions of certain religious paintings located abroad, with very minor, incidental text, was properly registrable as a "book" but that, since the illustrations were within one of the excepted classes, and there was no copyrightable text, domestic manufacture was not required.

On the other hand, a work such as a picture history of the Civil War, containing illustrations which were made abroad and which were *not* excepted, could be registered if the notice of copyright were limited to the text printed in the United States.

(b) Expressed exceptions

The foregoing exceptions are not expressly stated as such in section 16, but the following are: (1) works in raised characters for the use of the blind; (2) books or periodicals of foreign origin in a language or languages other than English; (3) works printed or produced in the United States by any other process than those specified in the section; and (4) copies of books or periodicals imported into the United States under the ad interim provisions of the law.

The first-named exception concerning books for the blind had its origin in item 513 in the "first list" under section 2 of the Tariff Act of 1890,[158] and was evidently perpetuated because such imports cause no real problem. This exception is repeated in section 107, one of the importation provisions of the copyright law.

The second specific exception covers "books or periodicals of foreign origin in a language or languages other than English." This exception appears not only in the proviso clause but also in the main body of section 16. In 1909 it was agreed that the benefits of copyright for the unrestricted importation of foreign-language works, which were desired by scholars, outweighed any loss to American printing interests; they would be printing the English translations.[159]

The phrase "of foreign origin," in common with most of the language in the manufacturing provision, is not explained anywhere in the Act. "It seems that * * * [it] was meant to include only books of foreign authorship even though printed in a foreign language."[160] In other words, this would mean that Americans writing in foreign

---

[156] 28 OPS. ATT'Y GEN. 176 (1910).
[157] 26 F. Supp. 41 (S.D.N.Y. 1939).
[158] Act of Oct. 1, 1890, ch. 1244, 26 Stat. 604.
[159] See H.R. REP. NO. 2222, 60th Cong., 2d Sess. 14 (1909).
[160] HOWELL, COPYRIGHT LAW 102 (Latman ed. 1962).

languages are bound by the domestic manufacturing requirements,[161] a construction which is followed by the Copyright Office.[162] This phrase also creates difficult problems in regard to composite works including articles by both American and foreign authors.

A difficulty with the wording "in a language or languages other than English," is deciding whether books or periodicals containing some English fall within the exemption. A scattering of English phrases, English footnotes, or English titles probably would not disqualify a book or periodical that was mainly in a foreign language, but bilingual and multilingual books and periodicals have posed difficult registration problems. Dual registration, both on the ad interim application form and on the form for foreign books in a foreign language, has been resorted to in cases of doubt involving such works.

As noted above,[163] the "any other process" exception[164] has an almost incredible history. It was added to the copyright law in 1926 to establish the basic copyrightability of works produced by mimeograph, typewriter, or other processes not enumerated in the section.[165] However, the addition—or rather the manner in which it was added—raised new doubts.

In a ruling in 1910,[166] the Attorney General construed the language of the manufacturing clause to permit copyright in typewritten or mimeographed material, regardless of the place of manufacture. Later, however, the Register of Copyrights adopted the position on the basis of a literal interpretation of the phrase in the section, "of the printed book or periodical," that such works were completely outside the scope of statutory copyright.

It was to clarify this point that legislation was urged. However, by making "works printed or produced *in the United States* by any other process than those above specified in this section" an *exception* to the basic manufacturing requirements, the amendment could be said to imply that such works must be manufactured in the United States. The result of this reasoning could be denial of copyright to every book or periodical produced abroad by any process other than "printing."

This was certainly not the basic intent of the amendment, and the Copyright Office, as a matter of practice, registers published mimeographed, typewritten, or similarly produced books and periodicals regardless of the place of manufacture, if the work is otherwise eligible for registration. Because of the uncertainty, however, an affidavit is requested for books manufactured in the U. S. A. by any process.

Finally, the complicated ad interim exception introduces all sorts of problems and requires elaborate administrative machinery. The full statement of the exception reads as follows:

---

[161] See *id*. at 102-03, and authorities cited therein, in support of this construction.
[162] See Younger, *Citizens Who Publish Abroad*, 44 CORNELL L. Q. 215, 226 (1959), reprinted in 6 BULL. CR. SOC. 114, 127 (1959).
[163] See notes 140-44 *supra* and accompanying text.
[164] 44 Stat. 818.
[165] See 1925-26 REG. COP. 237-39 published as Appendix II, U.S. LIBRARY OF CONGRESS, REPORT OF THE LIBRARIAN OF CONGRESS FOR THE FISCAL YEAR ENDING JUNE 30, 1926 (1926).
[166] 28 OPS. ATT'Y GEN. 265.

* * * or to copies of books or periodicals, first published abroad in the English language, imported into the United States within five years after first publication in a foreign state or nation up to the number of fifteen hundred copies of each such book or periodical if said copies shall contain notice of copyright in accordance with sections 10, 19, and 20 of this title and if ad interim copyright in said work shall have been obtained pursuant to section 22 of this title prior to the importation into the United States of any copy except those permitted by the provisions of section 107 of this title * * *.

It must be ascertained, among other things, that the work is in the English language; that it was first published as well as printed abroad; that the statutory time limit (fixed in section 22) for deposit and registration has not been exceeded; that such books or periodicals are by authors who are citizens of either the United States or of a country with which the United States has copyright relations; and whether an import statement can òr should be issued authorizing the designated party to import a maximum of 1,500 copies of the foreign edition.[167] Since the amendment of 1954,[168] the limitation on importation applies only to books by U. S. authors and books by foreign authors not eligible for Universal Copyright Convention exemptions.

United States citizens who write for publication in foreign books or periodicals are often shocked upon learning, perhaps too late, that their English-language works published abroad are not protected in the United States if they fail to make ad interim registration within six months, or fail to reprint and publish the work in the United States within five years. The shock is even greater when a U. S. citizen who writes in a foreign language learns that his work, having been printed and published abroad, cannot get any protection at all in the United States. Many persons are appalled that such a drastic penalty as copyright forfeiture is exacted against learned and influential Americans who write for a foreign market.

There have been cases where books in a foreign language were written by authors who had become U. S. citizens but who continued to write for publication in the country from which they came. In order to secure U.S. copyright for such foreign-language books, the procedure was adopted of issuing mimeographed copies in the United States before having the book published abroad. Similar legal evasions are not uncommon.

Since ad interim copyrights are still needed for works in the English language that do not fall within the Universal Copyright Convention exemptions from the manufacturing requirements, such as books in English written by U. S. citizens and first published abroad, it is necessary to observe very carefully the conditions for extending the temporary rights or they will be cut off. For extension to the full term there must be compliance, under section 23, with the manu-

---

[167] Although enforcement of the importation prohibitions of section 107 is the responsibility of the Bureau of Customs, the Copyright Office is concerned to the extent that issuance of an import statement may be involved. For example, section 107(b) exempts from the prohibition "a foreign newspaper or magazine." An unlimited number of copies of such works can be imported and no import statement need be issued. However, it may be necessary for the Copyright Office to determine whether or not a given work is "a foreign newspaper or magazine"; it may be neither "foreign," a "newspaper," nor a "magazine."

[168] 17 U.S.C. § 9(c).

facturing, notice, publication, registration, affidavit, and deposit provisions of the United States law within the five-year period of ad interim protection provided by section 22.[169] Consequently, Copyright Office regulations provide that a copyright may not be renewed unless an American edition has been registered within the ad interim period,[170] and that an American edition may not be registered after the ad interim term has expired,[171] or if there has been no ad interim registration.[172]

Thus, the machinery for allowing authors who must rely on the interim provisions of the law the full benefit of copyright is not only burdensome for all concerned, but one slip may actually cause forfeiture of property rights that might have been very valuable over a period of more than fifty years.

B. BUREAU OF CUSTOMS: ENFORCEMENT PROBLEMS

Administering the complex manufacturing provisions from the registration standpoint is only one aspect of the whole picture. Enforcement of the import restrictions burdens customs officials with difficult technical details to be handled in *ex parte* proceedings.[173]

Section 107 of the copyright law prohibits, with minor exceptions, the importation, during the existence of copyright, of copies not produced in accordance with the domestic manufacturing requirements of section 16. However, under section 16, books registered ad interim may be imported to the extent of 1,500 copies; books of foreign authors qualifying under the Universal Copyright Convention and published with the U.C.C. notice are, by section 9(c), exempt from this limitation.

Section 109 of the copyright law empowers the Secretary of the Treasury (under whose jurisdiction the Bureau of Customs operates) and the Postmaster General to make regulations for the exclusion of articles prohibited importation by the copyright law. The postal regulations[174] are of little practical significance for purposes of this study, since enforcement problems have generally been the primary concern of the Bureau of Customs. The governing customs regulations are found in Title 19 of the Code of Federal Regulations, Parts 9 and 24, particularly sections 11.18 to 11.21 inclusive, and are based on sections 9(c), 16, 106, 107, and 108 of the copyright law.

---

[169] Sections 22 and 23 have been summarized in Part II, *supra*.

[170] See 37 C.F.R. § 202.4(b)(3)(1960), which reads in part:
> Since by law ad interim copyright expires at the end of the ad interim term unless an American edition is published during that term, a renewal application covering a work registered only under the ad interim provisions will be rejected.

[171] See 37 C.F.R. § 202.4(b)(2)(1960), which reads:
> When a book or periodical has been registered under the ad interim provisions, an American edition of the same work, to be registrable, must be manufactured and published in the United States within five years after the date of first publication abroad.

[172] See 37 C.F.R. § 202.4(b)(1)(1960), which reads:
> An American edition of an English-language book or periodical identical in substance to that first published abroad will not be registered unless an ad interim registration is first made.

[173] See Publishers' Weekly, July 18, 1960, p. 38, for a comprehensive discussion of importation problems.

[174] The relevant postal regulations are covered by various sections of 39 C.F.R. (rev. as of Jan. 1, 1962).

The customs regulations prohibit importation of copies of books or periodicals not produced in accordance with the manufacturing requirements, as follows:

11.21 **United States manufacturing requirements; copies not produced in accordance with 17 U.S.C. 16.** (a) Copies of books or periodicals for which manufacture in the United States is required by 17 U.S.C. 16 may not be imported during the existence of the United States copyright, unless importation is permitted under 17 U.S.C. 107, or unless protection was secured under 17 U.S.C. 9(c) by virtue of the Universal Copyright Convention or an ad interim copyright was extended to the full term by the provisions of 17 U.S.C. 9(c).

(b) Up to 1,500 copies of a book or periodical covered by ad interim copyright, when imported pursuant to the quantitative exception in 17 U.S.C. 16, may be released upon compliance with usual customs requirements if there is presented in connection with the entry an "Import Statement" issued by the Register of Copyrights on Copyright Office Form C-100, and such copies are otherwise admissible. The reverse side of the statement shall be completely filled in by the customs officer concerned and mailed at once to the Register of Copyrights as directed in the form.

(c) When an ad interim coypright is extended to a full term copyright, as provided for in 17 U.S.C. 23, notice of such extension, together with the full-term registration number and the date thereof, shall be communicated by the copyright proprietor to the Commissioner of Customs, Washington 25, D.C., within 30 days after such date.

Among the many copyright details for which customs officers are responsible because of the manufacturing requirements are:

1. Inspection of books and periodicals and accompanying documents, to check the following points:
   (a) whether the copies bear a copyright notice;
   (b) the language in which the book or periodical is written;
   (c) the country in which the work was first published;
   (d) the country of which the author is a citizen;
   (e) the country in which the author is domiciled.
   Of course the customs officer does not have time to examine each book or periodical in a bulk shipment; he must rely on invoices or other documents furnishing operative facts.

2. Determining whether books or periodicals (and separate lithographs or photoengravings) are exempt from the manufacturing requirements and the importation restrictions, i.e., whether they come within the exceptions of sections 107, 16, or 9(c). Knowledge of these excepted categories is essential.

3. Determining whether an import statement is required. The customs officer needs a knowledge of ad interim copyright and the Universal Copyright Convention exemptions. An import statement (issued by the Register of Copyrights upon ad interim registration) is necessary for importation under section 16 of up to 1,500 copies of a book in English manufactured and first published outside the United States where—
   (a) the author is a United States citizen, or is domiciled in the United States, or
   (b) neither the country of the author's nationality nor the country of first publication is a party to the Universal Copyright Convention.

(1157)

4. Limiting the number of copies imported to 1,500 in the case of ad interim copyrights, and keeping records of partial shipments; this involves handling and correspondence concerning the import statement issued by the Copyright Office.
5. Recognizing when Universal Copyright Convention protection has been secured.
6. Accepting and acting on statements of abandoned claims of copyright.[175]
7. Seizure and detention of books and periodicals prohibited importation.
8. Collecting storage fees when shipments are temporarily detained.
9. Handling the notification cards and other identifying documents filed with Customs by copyright claimants, against which Customs offices must check incoming merchandise, to prevent unauthorized or infringing copies.[176]

On September 12, 1957, the Bureau of Customs issued a circular having as its subject "Instructions for the new situation which will prevail when, on September 27, 1957, the Universal Copyright Convention comes into force for the United Kingdom."[177] These instructions are equally applicable to any other U.C.C. member country, and are reflected to some extent in the customs regulations.

Accordingly, if there is submitted to the Collector of Customs a statement that the author of a book is a national of a foreign country adhering to the U.C.C., or that the book was first published in such a country, importation in unlimited quantity is permitted, without regard to the manufacturing clause. Although the Collector generally accepts the statement at face value, he must, nevertheless, inspect a copy for other reasons, and he must know that the particular country is a U.C.C. adherent. He must be alert to U.S. authorship, too, since U.S. citizens are still bound by the manufacturing requirements and the limitation on importation of copies regardless of where their works are published.

There are many cases of simultaneous publication in two or more countries, aimed at securing the broadest geographical protection possible under the Universal Copyright and Berne Conventions. In such cases it sometimes becomes necessary for the collector to decide which was the country of first publication before he can allow entry. A variety of other problems—having to do with such matters as unbound sheets folded and gathered for importation, circulation of

---

[175] When a copyright proprietor has had copies made abroad of his book on which U.S. copyright is subsisting, the Customs officials will bar entry of such copies, as authorized by section 107 of the copyright law and section 11.21 of 19 C.F.R. The copyright proprietor must make a difficult choice between preserving his copyright or importing the foreign-made copies in which he has invested. If he chooses the latter, his copyright must be sacrificed. There is no specific statutory procedure for "abandoning" a copyright. There is, however, machinery for recording documents relating to copyrights, and the practice, for a copyright owner faced with this dilemma, is to record in the Copyright Office a statement of abandonment of the copyright. After recording the statement in the Copyright Office, he presents the certificate of recordation to the Customs authorities at the port of entry, whereupon importation may be permitted, provided the notice of copyright is deleted from all copies to be circulated in the United States.
[176] See 19 C.F.R. § 11.19(a) (rev. as of Jan. 1, 1961).
[177] U. S. BUREAU OF CUSTOMS, COPYRIGHT, TRADEMARK, AND TRADE NAME CIRCULAR NO. 664. The complete text of this circular is reproduced in Appendix E.

foreign editions in large quantities to individual U.S. consignees (thus in certain cases exempt from import limitation),[178] abandonment of copyright to allow importation without benefit of copyright, and the cumbersome records requirements for preventing importation—all these continually beset the beleaguered Collector.

Many of the problems encountered in the registration process must also be considered by customs authorities. For example, they must decide whether the authorship of a book or periodical is foreign, which decision is complicated by multiple authorship, and they must determine whether a bilingual or multilingual work is "in a language or languages other than English." In some cases they are required to determine whether the author was a United States citizen on the date of publication. Some of these problems stem from varying tariff rates as well as from copyright restrictions, and the customs officials must keep the distinctions in mind. Close cooperation has at all times been necessary between the Copyright Office and the Bureau of Customs in the drafting of regulations, in their enforcement through the widely scattered ports, and in consultation on specific cases. It is remarkable that the machinery works as well as it does; doubtless many violations, innocent or otherwise, elude customs examiners. Preventing improper or excessive importation will remain an administrative burden as long as there are any manufacturing or quota provisions in the copyright law, even with broadened exemptions.

V. International Considerations

A. Foreign Laws and Agreements Which Restrict Book Trade

Although the United States is the only nation having a requirement in its copyright law that books and periodicals be manufactured within the country as a condition of full copyright protection,[179] it is by no means the only country that restricts importation of books. Import barriers, many more onerous than our own, exist elsewhere in the form of duties, quotas, fees, documentation, and other administrative requirements.

1. Customs laws

In 1956[180] thirty countries were imposing import duties on books. Canada maintained a 10% levy on books from the United States. Italy and Portugal imposed duties on books bound in leather. Spain

---

[178] This problem stems from the fact that section 107(d) of the copyright law lists as one of the exceptions to the importation prohibitions "any book published abroad with the authorization of the author or copyright proprietor when imported * * * not more than one copy at one time, for individual use and not for sale."

[179] *But see* notes 200-01 *infra* and accompanying text.

[180] The information for this paragraph was taken from the Unesco publications, BARKER, BOOKS FOR ALL—A STUDY OF INTERNATIONAL BOOK TRADE (1956) and U.N.E. S.C.O. DEP'T OF MASS COMMUNICATIONS, DIV. OF FREE FLOW OF INFORMATION, TRADE BARRIERS TO KNOWLEDGE (new & rev. ed. 1955). For further recital of arbitrary import restrictions by foreign countries, see statement of G. P. Van Arkel, representing the International Typographical Union, *Hearings on Executive M, 83d Cong., 1st Sess., the Universal Copyright Convention and S. 2559 Before a Subcommittee of the Senate Committee on Foreign Relations and a Subcommittee of the Senate Committee on the Judiciary*, 83d Cong., 2d Sess. 82-83 (1954).

and Denmark imposed duties on books printed in their domestic languages. Brazil maintained a restriction on the importation of books in the national language; books translated from other languages into Portuguese were not allowed entry under any condition. Austria charged importers a 5¼% "equalization" tax calculated on the invoice value. Some countries imposed a tax on remittances to pay for books. There was something resembling a sales tax on imported books in the German Federal Republic, the Netherlands, Norway, and in certain states of India. Brazil, Switzerland, and Iceland imposed a "handling" charge; Belgium charged a "taxe de transmission." Over sixty countries operated import licensing systems which affected books. For a time the United Kingdom restricted book imports from the dollar area.

Such restrictions have a long historical background. In John Milton's day, the problem evoked his celebrated attack in *Areopagitica— A Speech for the Liberty of Unlicensed Printing*. He said:

> Truth and understanding are not such wares as to be monopolized and traded in by tickets, and statutes and standards. We must not think to make a staple commodity of all the knowledge in the land, to mark and license it like our broadcloth, and our wool packs.[181]

The situation is gradually improving. Unesco studies and conferences and resulting agreements for international cooperation have wrought many gratifying changes. There is more flexibility for adjustment to fluctuating economic conditions. Books are now duty-free in many countries, and they are entitled to special postage rates if sent by mail. Legalized documentation is required by relatively few countries.

Currently available information on foreign trade restrictions[182] furnishes a good indication of the gradual relaxation of import controls by the various countries. Many new tariff laws have been passed in recent years which have reduced duties and administrative procedures and extended the opportunity for trade under open general license. Tariff rates for tens of thousands of items entering into world commerce have been reduced, or maximums established, as a result of the system of complaint, conference, and consultation set up in connection with the General Agreement on Tariffs and Trade.[183]

There is also a tendency of neighboring or related nations to unite in trade arrangements for their common benefit. Most of the British Commonwealth nations offer preferential customs treatment to each other. The British Book Export scheme has provided a number of European countries with sterling for the books they need. The Unesco Book Coupon program has helped book trade. The Organization for European Economic Cooperation (OEEC), familiarly known as the Common Market, has been active in freeing books from currency

---

[181] Quoted in BARKER, *op. cit. supra* note 180, at 31.
[182] The Bureau of Foreign Commerce, U.S. Dep't of Commerce, publishes an information service on changes in duties, taxes, and other foreign trade requirements in FOREIGN COMMERCE WEEKLY and also publishes "Operations Reports," a leaflet service containing changes as they occur in international trade requirements. The EXPORTERS' ENCYCLOPEDIA, published annually by Thos. Ashwell & Co., New York, includes a bulletin service containing summaries of customs laws and regulations, and other trade information.
[183] For a discussion of the General Agreement, see text accompanying notes 213-23 *infra*.

restrictions, and every OEEC country makes available all the foreign exchange needed for books.[184] A similar grouping of Latin American countries as a free trade area is under consideration.[185] The United States receives "most-favored-nation"[186] treatment under trade agreements with many countries.[187]

The lack of common definition for the terms "book" and "periodical" as used in our manufacturing clause and in other laws complicates any analysis or comparison of tariff laws affecting these articles of commerce. There have been international efforts to clarify the matter.[188] Notwithstanding definitional difficulties, it is apparent that, despite progress, much remains to be done in freeing the circulation of books. A few examples of continuing restrictions and discriminations are cited in the paragraphs that follow.[189]

Under a new tariff law, in effect since August, 1957, Brazil no longer requires consular invoices for books, and books receive some preferential treatment, whether shipped by freight or parcel post. However, legalized documentation is still required, and there remain exchange quotas and controls, and certain duties, taxes, and penalties. Books in Portuguese printed outside Portugal are not in the preferential class.

For the importation of books and periodicals, the overall tariff law of Colombia requires not only a detailed commercial invoice, with a declaration in Spanish, but also a consular legalization and an import license. Mexico, Nicaragua, and Paraguay also require import licenses, and most Latin-American countries have rather elaborate documentation regulations. Colombia, Nicaragua, and Paraguay impose exchange control. Venezuela introduced exchange control on November 9, 1960, and its law also imposes surtaxes, consular fees, fines, and taxes. Haiti's new law of September, 1960, authorizes the imposition of import quotas and has a surtax of 20% of the duty, plus a consumption tax and holding and stamping charges. El Salvador requires commercial invoices visaed by consul, plus a certificate of origin, but gives preferential duty to imports from the United States.

Canada has a sales tax of 11% on the duty-paid value of dutiable goods. However, under a Canadian-American trade agreement, printed matter is free of duty and sales tax "when in packages valued at no more than $1 each addressed to different persons or firms in Canada and when not imported for sale or in a manner designated to evade payment of customs duties." Reprints of Canadian copyrighted

---

[184] See BARKER, *op. cit. supra* note 180, at 34-39.
[185] See PAN AMERICAN UNION, ESTUDIOS BIBLIOTECARIOS 2, BOOKS IN THE AMERICAS—A STUDY OF THE PRINCIPAL BARRIERS TO THE BOOK TRADE IN THE AMERICAS 62-63 (1960).
[186] "Most favored nation clause" is defined as "a clause found in most treaties providing that the citizens or subjects of the contracting states may enjoy the privileges accorded by either party to those of the most favored nations." BLACK, LAW DICTIONARY 1164 (4th ed. 1951).
[187] See, *e.g.*, Treaty of Friendship and Commerce With Pakistan, Nov. 12, 1959 [1961], art. XIV, 1 U. S. T. & O. I. A. 110, T. I. A. S. No. 4683 (effective Feb. 12, 1961).
[188] The Brussels Convention on Nomenclature for the Classification of Goods in Customs Tariffs establishes common headings for tariffs, chapter 49 of which covers "printed books, newspapers, pictures and other products of the printing industry." BARKER, *op. cit. supra* note 180, at 37. Unesco has proposed a standard definition of a "book" as a "non-periodical publication containing 49 or more pages not counting the covers." *Id.* at 17.
[189] The examples which follow were drawn mainly from summaries in various editions of EXPORTERS' ENCYCLOPEDIA. See note 182 *supra*.

works, and reprints of British copyrighted works which have been copyrighted in Canada, are prohibited importation.

Australia has a three-column customs tariff, with preferential rates for the United Kingdom. There is a duty on books, but they can come in under open general license.

Controls on imports from the United States were largely eliminated by the United Kingdom on November 9, 1959, and a new tariff went into effect on January 1, 1959. Books enter under open general license.

In West Germany products of the book trade and the graphic arts industry, up to a value of 1,000 marks, can come in under general license from all but Soviet bloc countries. Italy has a general entry tax on most imports, but gives the United States most-favored-nation treatment. Portugal requires a prior registration of all imports, and there are consular regulations. ·

A new customs tariff went into effect in Spain on January 8, 1960. Most printed matter is dutiable and subject to tax. The fees for documents are rather high. About 200 classes of goods have been freed from quantitative controls and import licenses. (It is not clear whether books were freed.) Minor errors may invalidate the certificate of origin.

In Poland all transactions involving foreign exchange are controlled by license requirements. Import permits must be secured from the agency Amtorg for imports to Russia.

Pakistan permits books, magazines, etc., to be imported through the post duty-free for personal use up to a maximum value of 150-rupees.

The Philippine Republic did have a reciprocal duty-free arrangement with the United States, but starting January 1, 1956 gradual imposition of customs duties by both countries on a percentage basis was agreed upon, with the objective of eventual reduction or elimination of duties.[190]

In the United States, the first tariff act was passed in 1789.[191] The Tariff Act of 1930,[192] which imposed the highest tariff in United States history, is the latest general tariff revision by the Congress that is currently in effect, and, significantly, was enacted during the depression years. Only a few years later, the pendulum began to swing in the other direction with the enactment of the Trade Agreements Act of 1934.[193] Under that Act the President was authorized to negotiate trade agreements with other countries and to implement them by raising or lowering tariffs by as much as fifty percent of the existing level. Later extensions of the 1934 Act[194] authorized further reductions.[195]

---

[190] See 1962 CUSTOM HOUSE GUIDE 654-55.
[191] Act of July 4, 1789, ch. II, 1 Stat. 24. For a general discussion of United States tariff history, see SNIDER, INTRODUCTION TO INTERNATIONAL ECONOMICS 422-27 (rev. ed. 1958).
[192] Act of June 17, 1930, ch. 497, 46 Stat. 490, 19 U.S.C. §§ 1001-1654 (1959).
[193] Act of June 12, 1934, ch. 474, 48 Stat. 943.
[194] Act of June 21, 1955, 69 Stat. 162, as amended; Act of Aug. 20, 1958, 72 Stat. 673.
[195] See Clubb & Reischer, *The Trade Adjustment Bills: Their Purpose and Efficacy*, 61 COLUM. L. REV. 490 (1961).

Since 1934, the tariff on books and related materials has been progressively reduced by the negotiation and implementation of bilateral and multilateral trade agreements. A comparison of the 1930 rates with those in effect as of July 1, 1962[196] reveals, for example, that the duty on books of bona fide foreign authorship has been reduced from fifteen percent ad valorem to four percent and the rate on books of American authorship has been reduced from twenty-five percent to ten percent. Further reductions have been projected to take effect on July 1, 1963.[197]

As can be seen from the foregoing, on the whole, substantial tariff reduction has been accomplished in recent years throughout the world. Although customs red tape has been reduced, considerable documentation is still required.

2. Restrictions in copyright laws

The copyright laws of approximately twenty-four countries contain some bar against importation of books or other literary properties.[198] The ban, however, is generally against piratical copies rather than against copies of foreign manufacture as such. Most laws merely provide that infringing copies are barred, but several provide that the act of importing unauthorized copies may itself constitute infringement.[199] Thus, copies of books made abroad without the consent of the owner of the domestic copyright may be regarded as unlawful imports, either because they violate one or more of the copyright owner's exclusive rights or because they violate an express ban against importation of infringing copies. However, such restrictions are not to be confused with a restriction based on a domestic manufacturing requirement.

A bill was introduced by Congressman Gonzales in the Philippines in 1959 which would have amended their copyright law by adding a manufacturing provision much like the one in the U. S. law.[200] Fortunately, this retaliatory legislation did not pass.

The present Canadian copyright statute contains a compulsory licensing provision with respect to books not printed in Canada, if written by an author who is a national of Canada or of a foreign country not a member of the Berne Union.[201] The Minister of the Crown is empowered to grant licenses if the owner of such a book

---

[196] See 1962 U.S. TARIFF COMM'N, TC PUBLICATION 63, UNITED STATES IMPORT DUTIES 232.

[197] Telephone information from U.S. Tariff Comm'n.

[198] The summaries which follow are drawn mainly from the loose-leaf publication, U.N.E.S.C.O., COPYRIGHT LAWS AND TREATIES OF THE WORLD (1956, Supp. 1957-61).

[199] Rather typical of statutory import restrictions is the following: "Copies made out of New Zealand of any work in which copyright subsists which if made in New Zealand would infringe copyright and as to which the owner of the copyright gives notice in writing by himself or his agent to the Ministry of Customs that he is desirous that such copies should not be imported into New Zealand, shall not be so imported, and shall, subject to the provisions of this section, be deemed to be prohibited importation within the meaning of the Customs Law Act of 1908 . . . ." Copyright Act, 1913, 4 Geo. V, No. 4 of 1913 § 21 (1) (N.Z.).

[200] H. No. 1502, 4th Cong., 1st Sess.

[201] Copyright Act, 1921, 11 & 12 Geo. V, c. 24, § 14, CAN. REV. STAT. c. 55, § 14 (1952). "This provision has remained practically a dead letter, for if the demand for the book in Canada is sufficient to justify the expense of reprinting, the author or publisher may give the prescribed undertaking to bring out a Canadian edition of the work, whereupon the license is withheld." HOWELL, *op. cit. supra* note 160, at 99.

declines to produce an edition in Canada. Section 28 makes unlawful the importation of copies of books so licensed.

A report issued in 1957 by a Canadian Royal Commission,[202] under the chairmanship of J. L. Ilsley, appointed to study problems of legislation in the field of intellectual and industrial property, included a recommendation for repeal of the printing clauses in the Canadian copyright law.[203] Following is a summary of the Commissions' reasoning behind the recommendation:

1. One of the reasons for the printing clauses was the existence since 1891 of the manufacturing provisions in the United States copyright statute. The restrictions can no longer be justified, by virtue of United States adherence to the Universal Copyright Convention and the resulting opportunity, by joining the Convention, of securing complete protection without manufacture in the United States.

2. The compulsory license technique for the enforcement of the printing clauses is inconsistent with Canada's obligations under the Berne Convention.

3. Only two licenses have ever been applied for under the compulsory licensing provisions, so that, as a practical matter, the printing clauses have not presented any real problem.

In addition to the copyright legislation mentioned above, several bilateral copyright treaties in force between Spain and other countries include provisions which make unauthorized foreign printing and importation illegal but do not bar copyright.[204]

3. Private agreements

Probably the most common method of seeking to restrict imports of books is by contract. Publishers of different countries will often acquire exclusive rights of sale in other territories. For example, a publisher in the United States and another publisher of the same work in the United Kingdom may each agree not to sell his edition in the other's territory. Prior to British ratification of the Universal Copyright Convention (effective September 27, 1957), United States book publishers relied principally on the manufacturing clause and the related import prohibitions of section 107 of the copyright law to enforce these agreements. Now, of course, British books copyrighted under the U.C.C. come in freely.

United States publishers have repeatedly expressed concern about the volume of British books, including paperbacks, being imported in direct competition with U. S. editions of the same works. However, even if U. S. publishers have contractual arrangements with the British publishers not to invade, there would appear to be no way for them legally to prevent British jobbers from supplying American bookstores. It has been suggested that the import ban on piratical copies[205] be extended to bar importation of foreign-made editions in

---

[202] CANADA, ROYAL COMM'N ON PATENTS, COPYRIGHT, TRADE MARKS AND INDUSTRIAL DESIGNS, REPORT ON COPYRIGHT (1957).

[203] See *id.* at 30-31.

[204] See, *e.g.,* Copyright Treaty Between Spain and Colombia, Nov. 28, 1885, art. 7, Gaceta de Madrid, Jan. 19, 1887 (effective Jan. 1, 1887).

[205] "Piratical copies" are defined in the customs regulations as "actual copies or substantial

contravention of an agreement to divide international markets.[206] However, to do so would impose the territorial restrictions in a private contract upon third persons with no knowledge of the agreement. Even as between the parties, Customs does not seem to be an appropriate agency for the enforcement of private contracts.

Most of the large publishing houses, here and abroad, have foreign affiliates to coordinate activities. In fact, a recent article explained how U. S. publishers are finding it profitable to have agencies for American paperbacks abroad for the tourist trade, particularly in Paris.[207] International competition works both ways.

Exclusive territorial contracts to prevent international competition and maintain price levels may be questionable under the antitrust laws. This possibility has been raised by a federal court in a trademark case.[208]

B. MULTIPARTY TRADE AGREEMENTS

A few specialized international trade agreements have been mentioned previously.[209] The following are the major agreements affecting the book trade.

1. The Havana Charter

In 1947 a preparatory committee drafted a charter which formed the basis for the work of the United Nations Conference on Trade and Employment held in Havana, Cuba, from November 1947 to March 1948.[210] Fifty-seven nations, including the U.S.A., participated in the Conference, which culminated in a lengthy multilateral charter for an International Trade Organization and established an Interim Commission for the International Trade Organization. In article 1 of chapter I of the Charter, entitled "Purposes and Objectives," one of the purposes listed was the promotion of national and international action, on a reciprocally and mutually advantageous basis, designed to attain "reduction of tariffs and other barriers to trade and the elimination of discriminatory treatment in international commerce."

Although the Havana Charter has not been accepted,[211] some of its provisions regarding imports are interesting in tracing the evolution of provisions in later trade agreements.

Article 20, specifically relating to import quotas, reads in part:

1. No prohibitions or restrictions other than duties, taxes or other charges, whether made effective through quotas, import or export licenses or other measures, shall be instituted or maintained by any Member on the importation of any product

---

reproductions of legally copyrighted works produced and imported in contravention of the rights of the copyright proprietor." 19 C.F.R. § 11.20(a) (1961).

[206] See U.S. COPYRIGHT OFFICE, REPORT OF THE REGISTER OF COPYRIGHTS ON THE GENERAL REVISION OF THE COPYRIGHT LAW [submitted to the House Comm. on the Judiciary, 87th Cong., 1st Sess.] 125-26 (Comm. Print 1961). "The import ban on 'piratical copies' does not seem to apply to authorized copies." *Id.* at 126.

[207] Publishers' Weekly, May 22, 1961, p. 44.

[208] United States v. Guerlain, Inc., 155 F.Supp. 77, 97-98 (S.D.N.Y. 1957).

[209] See note 179 *supra* and accompanying text.

[210] UNITED NATIONS CONFERENCE ON TRADE AND EMPLOYMENT, FINAL ACT AND THE HAVANA CHARTER FOR AN INTERNATIONAL TRADE ORGANIZATION (1948).

[211] See Note, *United States Participation in the General Agreement on Tariffs and Trade,* 61 COLUM. L. REV. 505, 506 n. 3 (1961).

of any other Member country or on the exportation or sale for export of any product destined for any other Member country.

Exceptions were made for export prohibitions or restrictions to prevent or relieve critical shortages of essential products; excepted also were restrictions necessary to the "application of standards or regulations for the classification, grading or marketing of commodities in international trade."

Then, in Article 21, paragraph 2,

Notwithstanding the provisions of paragraph 1 of Article 20, any Member, in order to safeguard its external financial position and balance of payments, may restrict the quantity or value of merchandise permitted to be imported * * *.

This permitted restriction, however, was subject to progressive relaxation and ultimate elimination as the financial position improved.

Members were to undertake, according to paragraph 3(c) of Article 21,

(i) not to apply restrictions so as to prevent unreasonably the importation of any description of merchandise in minimum commercial quantities the exclusion of which would impair regular channels of trade, or restrictions which would prevent the importation of commercial samples or prevent the importation of such minimum quantities of a product as may be necessary to obtain and maintain patent, trademark, copyright or similar rights under industrial or intellectual property laws.

Consultations were invited concerning proposed restrictions, withdrawals, or modifications, or if financial or balance-of-payment difficulties developed.

As a result of a lack of acceptance of the Havana Charter, it became evident that the establishment of the International Trade Organization would be indefinitely postponed. With the decision to provide for the establishment of an organization to administer the General Agreement on Tariffs and Trade (GATT), next to be discussed, there was "tacit recognition that establishment of ITO has been abandoned."[212]

2. GATT

The General Agreement on Tariffs and Trade,[213] referred to as GATT, was a logical product of post-war planning in the economic sphere through the United Nations. The Agreement was negotiated on April 10, 1947, signed at Geneva on October 30, 1947 by representatives of 23 nations, including the United States of America, and came into force on November 15, 1947.[214] As of March, 1960, there were thirty-seven contracting countries, representing over four-fifths of the total world trade.[215]

---

[212] EVERYMAN'S UNITED NATIONS 530 (6th ed. 1959).
[213] The official text of GATT is issued as III THE CONTRACTING PARTIES TO THE GENERAL AGREEMENT ON TARIFFS AND TRADE, GENERAL AGREEMENT ON TARIFFS AND TRADE BASIC INSTRUMENTS AND SELECTED DOCUMENTS (1958) [hereinafter cited as BASIC INSTRUMENTS].
[214] See Proclamation No. 2671 A, 12 Fed. Reg. 8863 (1947) ("Carrying Out General Agreement on Tariffs and Trade Concluded at Geneva, Oct. 30, 1947").
[215] See THE CONTRACTING PARTIES TO THE GENERAL AGREEMENT ON TARIFFS AND TRADE, WHAT GATT IS AND WHAT GATT HAS DONE 22 (9th ed. 1960). The information on GATT is drawn mainly from this publication.

GENERAL REVISION

GATT was intended as a stop-gap arrangement, pending the entry into force of the Havana Charter and the creation of the International Trade Organization. It does not contain provisions for an organization. As events have worked out, GATT has stood alone since 1948—a de facto organization—as the first and only international instrument which lays down rules of conduct for trade on a world-wide basis, and which has been accepted by a high proportion of the major trading nations.

The objectives of this Agreement are stated in the introductory resolution as follows:

Recognizing that their relations in the field of trade and economic endeavor should be conducted with a view to raising standards of living, ensuring full employment and a large and steadily growing volume of real income and effective demand, developing the full use of the resources of the world and expanding the production and exchange of goods;

Being desirous of contributing to these objectives by entering into reciprocal and mutually advantageous arrangements directed to the substantial reduction of tariffs and other barriers to trade and to the elimination of discriminatory treatment in international commerce * * *.

Formalities connected with importation and exportation were to be minimized and simplified, and there was to be general relaxation and elimination of quotas or other quantitative restrictions,[216] with due regard for safeguarding financial position and resources.

There is an emergency clause which provides that:

If, as a result of unforeseen developments and of the effect of the obligations incurred by a contracting party to this Agreement, including tariff considerations, any product is being imported into the territory of that contracting party in such increased quantities and under such conditions as to cause or threaten serious injury to domestic producers in that territory of like or directly competitive products, the contracting party shall be free, in respect of such product, and to the extent and for such time as may be necessary to prevent or remedy such injury, to suspend the obligation in whole or in part, or to withdraw or modify the concession * * *.[217]

The following clause is among the general exceptions to the provision for emergency measures to remedy or prevent injuries:

* * * subject to the requirement that such measures are not applied in a manner which would constitute a means of arbitrary or unjustifiable discrimination between countries where the same conditions prevail, or a *disguised restriction on international trade*, nothing in this Agreement shall be construed to prevent the adoption or enforcement by any contracting party of measures: * * * necessary to secure compliance with laws or regulations which are not inconsistent with the provisions of this Agreement, including those relating to customs enforcement, the enforcement of monopolies operated under paragraph 4 of Article II and Article XVII, the protection of patents, trademarks and copyrights, and the prevention of deceptive practices; * * * [Emphasis supplied].[218]

In regard to the general elimination of quantitative restrictions, Article XI provides:

No prohibition or restrictions other than duties, taxes or other charges, whether made effective through quotas, import or export licenses or other measures,

---

[216] See GATT, arts. VIII, XI.
[217] GATT, art. XIX.
[218] GATT, art. XX (I).

shall be instituted or maintained by any contracting party on the importation of any product of the territory of any other contracting party * * *.[219]

Under a Protocol of Provisional Application, the United States, along with several other GATT signatories, accepted application of the quota prohibition, and other articles, only to the extent to which they did not conflict with existing legislation.[220]

Tariff schedules in effect in 1939 were appended to and made part of the Agreement, with the understanding that the items listed would be exempt from ordinary customs duties in excess of those set forth and provided for therein, and that any contracting party could maintain its requirements existing on the date of the Agreement as to the eligibility of goods for entry at previous rates of duty.

On October 11, 1962 the President of the United States signed as Public Law 87-794 the Trade Expansion Act of 1962[221] "to stimulate the economic growth of the United States and maintain and enlarge foreign markets for the products of the U. S. agriculture, industry, mining, and commerce; to strengthen economic relations with foreign countries through the development of open and nondiscriminatory trading in the free world; and to prevent Communist economic penetration."[222] The Act gives the President powers to cut most tariffs up to fifty percent and to abolish others, in return for similar trade concessions from other nations. As the law's provisions are carried out, a comprehensive new system of classification of articles by categories may be expected and rates will be based upon a new evaluation of values.[223] Modifications or continuance of existing trade agreements may be proclaimed as determined appropriate.

3. The "Florence Agreement"

The International PEN Club, at its first Congress held in Paris in 1896, examined the import regulations of 110 countries and found only sixty-nine of them innocent of "sins" against books.[224] Another survey was presented in 1954 as a report to the International Publishers Association, at its 13th Congress, in Zurich, Switzerland.[225] A comparison of these surveys has proved useful in studying the problem of eliminating barriers to the international flow of knowledge. Unesco has also undertaken studies, and has had notable success in its remedial efforts.

In 1949 Unesco prepared, in cooperation with the Contracting Parties to GATT, the "Agreement on the Importation of Educational, Scientific and Cultural Materials," also known as the "Florence Agreement."[226] This Agreement, which came into force on May 21, 1952[227]

---

[219] GATT, art. XI (1).
[220] The protocol is printed in 1 BASIC INSTRUMENTS 77 (1952).
[221] 76 Stat. 872.
[222] Section 102.
[223] Section 211.
[224] See BARKER, *op. cit. supra* note 180, at 34-35.
[225] Vallardi, *Traitement accordé au livre dans les différents pays sur le plan des impôts et taxations*, UNION INTERNATIONALE DES EDITEURS, XIII CONGRES, ZURICH, 21-25 JUIN 1954, RAPPORTS 215.
[226] For the text of the agreement, which was adopted unanimously by the General Conference of UNESCO at its fifth session in Florence in July 1950, see the UNESCO publication, MC/12 (1950).
[227] See SEN. EXEC. REP. NO. 1, 76th Cong., 2d Sess. 1 (1960).

with ten adherents, exempts books, newspapers, periodicals, travel literature, manuscripts, book catalogs, printed music, maps, charts, and various other informational materials from "customs duties and other charges." In addition, contracting states undertake to grant import licenses and foreign exchange for publications required by public libraries, for official government publications, and for publications of the United Nations and its specialized agencies. The Agreement places a ceiling on taxes and other fees. Contracting states furthermore undertake to abolish or reduce any restrictions to the free circulation of educational, scientific, or cultural materials, to simplify administrative procedures affecting such materials, and to facilitate their safe and expeditious clearance through Customs.

By November 1960, thirty-three countries, including the United States, had signed this Agreement.[228] The U. S. Senate approved its ratification by the United States on February 23, 1960.[229] Enabling legislation, introduced early in 1961,[230] has not yet been passed.

There is a protocol to the Agreement under which the United States (or any other contracting country) could suspend application of the Agreement in regard to books if their importation caused or threatened serious injury to the printing trades.

A report on the tenth anniversary of the Florence Agreement attributes to it considerable success in reducing the costs of the international flow of informational materials, and also elimination of complex procedures which delay and block this flow. The Agreement has spread its influence downward from the lofty level of international conferences to the fabric of day-to-day life in many countries.[231]

4. Universal Postal Union

Although the series of international postal conventions, to which the United States has been a party for many years, contain general provisions which affect the importation of books, their relevance to the problem of import restrictions due to the manufacturing clause is negligible. The current Universal Postal Convention[232] is mentioned merely because many books are imported by mail, and procedures under the Convention are established for prohibiting importation of "articles whose admission or circulation is prohibited in the country of destination."[233] Violations of the copyright law would be comprehended in such prohibitions. This Convention has been effective in encouraging the widespread adoption of special parcel post rates and customs duty exemptions for books.

---

[228] See Press release, UNESCO/NYO/33 (1960).
[229] 106 CONG. REC. 3209 (1960).
[230] H.R. 2537, 87th Cong., 1st Sess. (1961).
[231] See *Free Flow Agreement Marks Tenth Year*, 6 UNESCO CHRONICLE 273 (1960).
[232] Universal Postal Convention, Oct. 3, 1957 [1960] 1 U.S.T. & O.I.A. 413, T.I.A.S. 4202 (effective April 1, 1959).
[233] Art. 60 (1) (d).

VI. The Economics of Book Manufacture and Importation

A. PREDICTIONS

Experts predicted, when the implementing legislation for the Universal Copyright Convention was being considered in 1952[234] and 1954,[235] that elimination of the manufacturing requirement for foreign books would have negligible effect on the American printing and publishing industries, and that there would be no flooding of the American market with foreign books. They suggested that Americans would prefer advanced U. S. technology for their printing needs; this would be true particularly for large editions, and for textbooks and other similar publications requiring constant editing, since overseas negotiations for such works would be inconvenient and expensive, considering the shipping, insurance, and duty costs. They pointed out the continued growth of the American publishing industry, and the relatively small segment of the printing industry actually affected by the book-manufacturing requirement in the copyright law. They also ventured the prediction that American book exports would greatly increase, and that one of our greatest fields for expansion would be the foreign market.

We can now view with the eye of history what has actually happened in the book industry since the relaxation of the manufacturing requirements in 1955, when the Universal Copyright Convention came into force, and particularly since 1957, when the United Kingdom became the first major English-speaking nation outside the United States to ratify the Convention.

B. PRINTERS' VIEWS

First, it must be recorded that printers did not share the optimism of the more internationally-minded elements of the economy. Printing interests have pointed to the low wage scales of foreign countries in comparison with those of the United States. They have viewed with grim apprehension an anticipated flood of imported cheap foreign editions with which U. S. manufacturers could not compete.

They were fearful when, in 1933, a bill to permit adherence to the Berne Union proposed to eliminate the ad interim provisions of the copyright law, and exempt from the manufacturing clause "works in any language, by foreign authors, first published in a foreign country party to the Convention for the Protection of Literary and Artistic Works."[236] The Edition Book Manufacturers cited some rather unpersuasive statistics to show the loss of man hours that might result from elimination of the requirement for U. S. remanufacture of foreign editions granted temporary U. S. copyright.[237] At that

---

[234] See *Hearings on H.R. 4059 Before Subcommittee No. 3 of the House Committee on the Judiciary*, 82d Cong., 2d Sess., ser. no. 13 (1952). Note particularly "Memorandum on the Celler Bill, H.R. 4059" and accompanying charts at 217-23.

[235] See *Hearings on Executive M, Eighty-third Congress, First Session, the Universal Copyright Convention and S. 2559*, 83d Cong., 2d Sess. (1954).

[236] See notes 93-97 *supra* and accompanying text.

[237] U.S. INTERDFPARTMENTAL COMM. ON COPYRIGHT, MEMORANDUM URGING RETENTION OF IMPORT RESTRICTIONS AND APPROPRIATE MANUFACTURING

time the National Industrial Recovery Act was in effect; industry records showed that in 1934 there were 123 establishments primarily engaged in edition book manufacture, with a $13,435,000 payroll, and about 12,600 skilled mechanical employees producing $30 million in net sales.[238] Speaking on behalf of this segment of industry, and in opposition to the proposed bill, the NIRA Code Director, who was a representative of the book manufacturers, said:

> * * * without assurance of protection from importations of foreign-manufactured copies, there would be little, if any, incentive for an American publisher to produce an edition in this country, especially in view of the ordinary hazards of successful distribution. Thus, it may be anticipated that the foreign authors of English-speaking countries who now are afforded an opportunity of selling the American rights to publishers in the United States would no longer enjoy a vast market in this country for his [sic] works.
>
> Not only would this situation create havoc among those American publishers who have succeeded in building a reputation for foreign titles and necessitate a long period of readjustment in the publishing industry, but the foreign authors would be deprived of substantial benefits of his work.[239]

The Code Director cited the following figures:

> The fact has been ascertained by our industry that in the year 1934 approximately 1600 titles of foreign authorship first published abroad in the English language were imported into the United States. Of this number it is conservatively estimated that approximately 855 titles, averaging 2000 books per title, were manufactured in the United States during ad interim periods in order to comply with the present copyright law. Hence a total of about 1,710,000 books were manufactured by our edition book manufacturing industry as a direct result of the existing provisions of the manufacturing section during the year 1934.[240]

This work, he said, provided about 600,000 hours of American labor.[241] He was pessimistic about the export market compensating for this loss of work:

> While certain edition book manufacturers do value the export market and do manufacture for exportation to countries of the Union, the majority of the establishments identified with the book manufacturing industry do not recognize the export market as presenting material advantages comparable to the quantity of work resulting from the present manufacturing requirements.[242]

In 1939 the book manufacturers were saying, "We are being sold down the river by the Treaty route."[243] They pointed to the statistics on imports and exports for the years 1937 and 1938, which showed that imports exceeded exports of books and other printed matter. In 1937, they said, exports of books amounted to $5,514,063 and imports $7,236,049; in 1938, the value of exports totalled $5,543,646; imports $6,014,530.[244] (See Appendix G for figures on later years.)

REQUIREMENTS (mimeographed), submitted by the Code Director, National Code Authority, Book Manufacturing Industry on behalf of Edition Book Manufacturers (1935).

[238] See *id.* at 3.
[239] *Id.* at 8-9.
[240] *Id.* at 14-15.
[241] *Id.* at 15.
[242] *Ibid.*
[243] Editorial, *The Argentine Beef of Copyright,* Book Manufacturers' Monthly, May 1939, p. 4, 5. This had reference to the then-pending efforts to make United States a party to the Berne Convention.
[244] *Ibid.* The campaign by book manufacturers against bills to permit U.S. adherence to the Berne Convention was continued in 1940-41 issues of this monthly.

Notwithstanding this apprehensive position on the part of printers, they allowed the ad interim provisions of the copyright law to be modified in 1949.[245] As noted above,[246] the 1949 amendment provided five years' copyright protection for books in English, written by foreign authors and manufactured and first published outside the United States, with the privilege of importing up to 1,500 copies to test the American market. The printers agreed that imports of that quantity would pose no great threat to the printing industry, since an edition of that size would be too costly to produce in the United States.

After a trial period of a year and a half under the 1949 relaxation of the manufacturing clause, the Register reported the following significant statistics from Copyright Office records for the period from July 1, 1949 through December 31, 1951 :[247]

Import statements 2,644
Number of books importable
    (2,644 x 1,500) 3,966,000
Number of books actually imported 174,183
Percentage of potential imported 4.3%
Number of foregoing separate titles
    manufactured in the United States 369

The remanufacture of 369 titles would not provide many hours of work for that period of time. This small volume of reprint work did not, however, seem to retard employment in the industry. Labor statistics since 1948 have shown progressive employment gains in book manufacturing.[248]

At the annual conventions of the American Federation of Labor, reports and resolutions have been adopted protesting, on behalf of the printing trades, attempts to reduce tariffs on books (referring to the Havana Charter and the Florence Agreement), and to remove the manufacturing requirements from the copyright law. Labor could not agree that

the free flow of ideas is synonymous with free competition of goods produced by cheap labor * * *,[249]

and declared,

We shall support a copyright treaty only if and when such treaty does not include a provision for destroying American wage standards.[250]

A representative of the printing industry testifying at the 1952 hearings on implementing legislation for the Universal Copyright Convention said it appeared to him that the proposed legislation was part of the general technique that began by getting a foot in the

---

[245] Act of June 3, 1949, ch. 171, §§ 1-3, 63 Stat. 153-54, 17 U.S.C. §§ 16, 22, 23 (1958).
[246] See notes 112-16 *supra* and accompanying text.
[247] See statement by Arthur Fisher, Register of Copyrights, *Hearings, supra* note 201, at 213.
[248] This information is drawn from releases of the Bureau of Labor Statistics on employment, hours, and earnings in the Printing, Publishing and Allied Industries Group.
[249] AFL, REPORT OF PROCEEDINGS OF THE SEVENTY-FIRST CONVENTION, HELD AT NEW YORK, N.Y., SEPTEMBER 15 TO 23, INCLUSIVE, 1952, at 548.
[250] *Ibid.*

door.[251] He condemned the bill, saying " * * * we have been offered nothing but unsupported assertions, conjectures, and predictions by the proponents."[252]

Another printers' representative at the 1954 hearings commented that the "very generous" concessions of 1949 should have been sufficient to put the matter at rest.[253]

The vigilant Book Manufacturers Institute, at its 28th annual convention in 1960, noted its keen awareness of competition from Japan, Hong Kong, and Taiwan, as well as Europe. It also took note of the recent approval of the Florence Agreement, which would tend to make book imports duty-free; its spokesman repeated the phrase about being "sold down the river":

> Constant watch should be maintained both here and in Washington to be sure that the industry of book manufacturers in this country is not sold down the river to foreign competition, which has been only too true in other branches of our national economy.[254]

The campaign to preserve the manufacturing clause has been waged through industry publications as well as through committee activities, reports to annual conventions, and contacts with Congress. Industry leaders repeatedly warn through these media of the dire consequences of elimination of the manufacturing clause from the copyright law. The substantive part of a full-page editorial issued in October of 1961 reads:

> * * * a quick comparison of labor costs in the United States with those of England, Holland, Germany, Japan, Nationalist China, and other countries indicates serious complications. Were all restrictions to be eliminated what would be the fate of the book manufacturing industry when faced with the competition of overseas printers and binders whose wages range from ¼th to 1/20th that of American workmen? In addition would we see a complete deterioration in commodity standards, specifications, and overall quality of the finished book, as has so unfortunately occurred in other industries, such as toys and textiles, when faced with over-whelming overseas competition?
>
> The issues are complex. In a changing world, determined adherence to conditions pertinent in 1891 may be ill advised—but neither can the immense damage implied in a copyright change in 1962 be ignored.
>
> Whatever position the book industry takes upon this controversial question must be based on a scrupulous and impartial study of the facts. This we propose to do in future issues, and we invite the comments of all serious leaders of the industry.[255]

The need for protection from low-cost foreign competition was again stressed at the 1962 annual meeting of the Book Manufacturers' Institute.[256] Mr. Malcolm Frost, General Counsel and Executive Director, reporting for the Copyright, Tariff and Legislative Committee of BMI, proposed that BMI as a leader in the industry enthusiastically support the implementation of the Florence Agreement. This support, however, should be subject to a condition that "books by

[251] See statement of O. R. Strackbein, International Allied Printing Trades Ass'n, *Hearings*, *supra* note 234, at 57.

[252] *Ibid.*

[253] See statement of Gerhard P. Van Arkel, International Typographical Union, *Hearings*, *supra* note 235, at 79.

[254] Publishers' Weekly, Nov. 7, 1960, p. 60.

[255] Kubilios, *The Copyright Law—A Warning*, Book Production, Oct. 1961, p. 53.

[256] See Publishers' Weekly, Nov. 5, 1962, p. 50-55, 68-69; Dec. 24, 1962, p. 14-16.

(1173)

American authors, or by foreign authors resident or domiciled in the United States, in the English language, must be manufactured from type set and wholly produced in our country." This condition, he said, would preclude "commercial transactions, where such a book by an American author might be manufactured abroad, at lower cost, for reentry and sale in this country." Mr. Frost said that this policy had been agreed to in principle by the publishers' representatives, subject to confirmation by their respective Boards of Directors. He reported that he had asked the House Ways and Means Committee for public hearings on this controversial matter.[257]

Mr. Frost also commented on the recommendation in the Register's Report on General Revision in regard to the manufacturing clause,[258] reminding those present at the meeting that BMI had issued a statement of policy[259] sharply resisting elimination of the manufacturing clause from a new copyright law. He referred to real "peril point" competition from England, the Common Market, Japan, Formosa, and Hong Kong and to past time-consuming and damaging delays in getting remedies. He urged use and preservation of the law already on the books.[260]

Mr. Frost said the practice had developed of importing, at a negligible tariff rate, "repro proofs" of type matter composed abroad for use in making printing plates in the United States. He argued that the Copyright Office ought not register claims in this situation "even though the application is silent about where the type was set * * *."[261]

Concern about tariff concessions has been framed in words of criticism about the Trade Expansion Act of 1962.[262] Mr. David W. Kendall, BMI's Washington Counsel, observed that present United States tariffs "afford almost no protection" and criticized the 1962 Trade Expansion Act as "too narrow, dealing solely with tariffs and customs and neglecting the full spectrum of international banking, cartels, monetary policy, labor rates and business understanding."[263] He claimed that "it moved too fast too far in a narrow front, giving unprecedented powers to an executive without needed legal guidelines."[264]

---

[257] See *id.*, Nov. 5, 1962, p. 52-54.

[258] U. S. COPYRIGHT OFFICE, REPORT OF THE REGISTER OF COPYRIGHTS ON THE GENERAL REVISION OF THE COPYRIGHT LAW [submitted to the House Comm. on the Judiciary, 87th Cong., 1st Sess.] 124 (Comm. Print 1961). The recommendation reads as follows:

> (a) The requirement of manufacture in the United States as a condition of copyright (sec. 16) and the related provisions dealing with affidavits (secs. 17 and 18) and ad interim copyright (secs. 22 and 23) should be eliminated.
>
> (b) The prohibition against the importation of copyrighted English-language books manufactured abroad (sec. 107) and the provision for importing up to 1,500 copies under ad interim copyright (sec. 16) should be eliminated. If Congress finds that an import limitation on English-language books is necessary for the protection of the U.S. printing industry, the limitation need not be confined to copyrighted books, and it should be provided for in legislation other than the copyright statute.

[259] This statement is printed in Book Production, Sept. 1962, p. 47.

[260] See Publishers' Weekly, Nov. 5, 1962, p. 55.

[261] *Ibid.*

[262] See note 221 *supra* and accompanying text.

[263] Publishers' Weekly, Nov. 5, 1962, p. 68.

[264] *Id.* at 69.

This strong and unabating resistance to any proposed elimination of the manufacturing clause from the copyright law emphasizes its relationship to the tariff laws. When tariff reductions are proposed to implement the Florence Agreement and to effectuate the purposes of the Trade Expansion Act of 1962, the manufacturing clause may become a bargaining tool of those who seek to maintain protection from competitive foreign imports. A serious question arises as to whether the copyright condition can stand in the face of our international obligations in the interest of freer trade.[265]

C. ECONOMIC SURVEYS

Through the years the protectionist position embodied in the copyright law seems to have been based more on surmise and fear of competition than on factual data. There had been at least one comprehensive economic survey of the book industry before the U.C.C.,[266] but it did not analyze international trade data. It was not until the printing interests challenged the proponents of the Universal Copyright Convention implementing legislation to produce more than "unsupported assertions and conjectures,"[267] that full-scale economic studies were undertaken which related the manufacturing requirements and import restrictions to the book industry.

The Legislative Reference Service of the Library of Congress was asked to prepare a report, for use in the 1952 hearings on H.R. 4059,[268] on the relationship between book imports and exports and domestic production. The following chart from the Legislative Reference Service study reflects the situation as of 1950:[269]

---

[265] See law review article, *supra* note 211, at 556. The author expresses the opinion that the manufacturing clause is clearly inconsistent with art. III of GATT, entitled "National Treatment on Internal Taxation and Regulation." *Ibid.*

[266] CHENEY, ECONOMIC SURVEY OF THE BOOK INDUSTRY, 1930-31 (1931). This survey, commonly known as the Cheney Report, was reprinted in 1960 with an introduction by Robert W. Frase.

[267] See note 252 *supra* and accompanying text.

[268] *Hearings, supra* note 234.

[269] *Id.* at 221.

COMPARISON OF IMPORTS OF BOOKS
WITH DOMESTIC PRODUCTION
UNITED STATES, 1950

DOMESTIC PRODUCTION[*]

Value of product of
U. S. book publishing
industry (receipts)

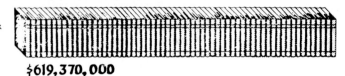

$619,370,000

IMPORTS[†]

Books and pamphlets
that might be affected
by the "manufacturers' clause."

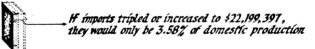

*If imports tripled or increased to $22,199,397,
they would only be 3.58% of domestic production*

$7,399,799 (Actual Imports)
(1.19% of domestic production)

* American Book Publishers Council

† Department of Commerce

ONE BOOK REPRESENTS TEN MILLION DOLLARS

CHART A, VALUE OF IMPORTS AND DOMESTIC PRODUCTION OF BOOKS IN 1950

The figure $7,399,799 for books imported includes all books imported into the United States except those which are not affected by the manufacturing clause, that is, books printed wholly or chiefly in languages other than English, books imported for use of the United States Government, Bibles and Testaments, and prayer books. The figure for domestic production is an estimate from the American Book Publishers Council and is the value of product of United States book publishing industry (receipts).

This chart shows that, in 1950, imports of books that might be affected by the manufacturing clause amounted to $7,399,799. This represented 1.19% of the total domestic production of books in 1950. The total volume of books imported into the United States in 1959, exclusive of postal and freight shipments, rose to $20,282,699, less than the triple increase projected in the chart. During the same period the dollar value of domestic production rose about 158%, and that of exports rose about 224%.[270]

At the 1954 hearings on implementing legislation for the Universal Copyright Convention Robert W. Frase, Economic Consultant for the American Book Publishers Council, Inc., testified that he had been engaged by the Book Manufacturers' Institute and the Book Publishers Council to conduct an independent study of the possible disadvantages to the U. S. economy resulting from books in English being manufactured abroad and published in the United States.[271] Mr. Frase's testimony,[272] based on his study,[273] showed that, for a variety of practical reasons, many kinds of books are not affected

[270] See Publishers' Weekly, August 15, 1960, p. 27-28. Postal and freight shipments would probably increase these figures by fifty percent according to the American Book Publishers Council. *Id.,* Jan. 16, 1961, p. 86.
[271] See *Hearings, supra* note 235, at 132-33.
[272] See *id.* at 132-41.
[273] The study, entitled "An Economic Analysis of the Universal Copyright Convention," is printed in *id.* at 141-147.

by the manufacturing clause. Among the categories unaffected, he said were book-club books, produced monthly in enormous editions of 200,000 to 400,000 copies for immediate shipment from the manufacturing plant; paperback books, produced in great quantities in the United States far cheaper than abroad (about 10¢ apiece for a 25¢ retail copy), on a split-second distribution schedule which would allow no time for overseas negotiations or transportation; textbooks, written mostly by American scholars and generally produced in large editions· for the American market; Bibles in the public domain or commentaries on the Bible by Americans; scientific and technical books, written primarily by American scientists and slanted toward American conditions and vocabulary; and encyclopedias directed primarily toward the American market, produced in large editions and generally by American authors. The *Encyclopedia Britannica*, he revealed, was printed in the United States. Cookbooks, dictionaries, and the like, were also generally printed in the United States in large editions.

These economic studies went a long way toward answering the printers' protests. Presented with climactic impact toward the end of the 1954 hearings,[274] Mr. Frase's analysis of the statistics contained in these studies made the possibility of real harm to the printing industry seem quite unlikely. According to testimony at the 1952 and 1954 hearings, it was not economically feasible to print these books outside the United States for the U. S. market.[275] Small editions would hardly be worthwhile in the United States from the financial standpoint; editions would have to be in runs of over 5,000 to be profitable.[276]

A reasonable conclusion to be derived from the Legislative Reference Service and Frase surveys, as well as from other testimony at the hearings,[277] was that a relatively small segment of the printing industry—book manufacturers only, and not too many of them—would be affected by the relaxation of the manufacturing clause, and that the stimulus of the Universal Copyright Convention should substantially expand the sale of U. S. books abroad. This is exactly what has happened. Exports of books have grown well beyond 1950 expectations.

D. CUSTOMS REPORTS

In anticipation of the new situation that would prevail when the Universal Copyright Convention came into force for the United Kingdom, arrangements were made prior to that date (September 27, 1957) for the Bureau of Customs to keep the Register of Copyrights informed of the number of titles and copies of English-language books imported bearing copyright notice after that date.[278] Under these arrangements separate reports are sent to the Bureau of Customs

---

[274] *Id.* at 141.
[275] See, *e.g., id.* at 134-36, 144-46.
[276] Cost and quality comparisons are discussed in *Hearings, supra* note 234, at 55-73.
[277] See, *e.g., Hearings, supra* note 235, at 143-45.
[278] See Appendix E.

from the various ports of entry and then forwarded monthly to the Register of Copyrights for consolidation and analysis. The figures furnished are, of practical necessity, based more on sampling and calculation than on actual count.

The figures available for 1957 cover only three months. The 1958 figures, the first covering a full year of U.C.C. operation, report the number of copies, not value; hence, they cannot be compared with import or export figures supplied by the Department of Commerce (Bureau of the Census). In that year a million-and-a-half copies of books in English were imported. The volume of book imports had increased by the end of 1962 to more than seven million copies. The total import figures furnished by Customs through December 1962 show that about eight out of every ten titles are imported in a quantity under 1,500 copies.

As most titles are imported in quantities of less than 1,500, this might indicate ad interim restriction. However, the fact probably is that these shipments are responsive to specific orders for limited quantities, and that they come in under the Universal Copyright Convention without import restriction.

The following table, based on Customs reports to the Copyright Office, gives a breakdown of book imports since the U.C.C. came into force in the United Kingdom on September 12, 1957 and through December 1962:

CONSOLIDATED CUSTOM REPORTS

Year	1,500 and Under	Over 1,500	Total Copies
1957 (3 months)	44	26	107,612
1958	1,222	318	1,576,023
1959	2,022	426	2,639,980
1960	3,055	693	4,561,274
1961	2,727	551	3,817,549
1962	7,580	996	7,059,731
Totals	16,650	3,010	19,762,169

The separate reports from the various ports of entry show that the largest proportion of book imports (70%) come through New York, with Baltimore handling 17%. Boston, which receives the next largest number, has reported only 601,797 books in English for the entire period under study. Very few books in English come through the West Coast ports; this indicates that Europe, and particularly the United Kingdom, is still the primary source.

E. COMMERCE FIGURES

On the basis of figures released by the U. S. Department of Commerce, the American Book Publishers Council regularly tabulates and analyzes the data on book production and distribution, and the information is published annually in *Publishers' Weekly*. The annual summary for 1961 confirms the established upward trend for book production, imports, and exports.[279] The rate of growth for the book industry is indicated by the increase from 13,462 books published in 1958 to 18,060 for 1961[280] and publishers receipts of $1,010,713,000 in 1958 contrasted with receipts expected to exceed $1.5 billion when final 1961 receipts have been tabulated.[281] The estimated value of book printing for 1961 amounted to $551,053,000, an increase of 30.3% over the previous three years.[282]

The Bureau of the Census statistics show a steady increase both in imports and exports of printed matter, consistent with the expanding market. Although exports in recent years have far exceeded imports, three times or more, the ratio is decreasing. Printed matter imported during 1961 is valued at $43,367,472, while exports are valued at $149,102,384. For 1959 the import figure was $33,062,907 as against $124,338,740 for exports.[283] The Common Market may be responsible for this trend. Exports to the six countries comprising the European Common Market have increased 27% since 1959, while imports from those countries over the same period have risen 40%.[284]

It should be noted, however, that the United States appears to be moving toward a substantially favorable balance of trade in books. In fact, books and printed matter have been listed among the limited number of export items that have increased more than the increase in gross national product in the past few years, in a period when exports have generally fallen off and there has been much concern over the balance of payments deficit.[285]

F. REGISTRATION STATISTICS

Also to be considered are copyright registration records, which are reported on a fiscal year basis. For example, of the 66,571 books registered in fiscal 1962, 4,784 of which were foreign books, only 777 were registered ad interim, in the dwindling number of ad interim registrations. In 1957 there were 1,777 ad interim registrations.[286]

For each ad interim registration made in fiscal year 1962 (777) an import statement was issued by the Copyright Office authorizing the importation of 1,500 copies. Copies imported as a result of these authorizations in fiscal 1962 totalled 59,686, or an average of only 77 copies per import statement. For the fiscal years 1958-1962 the aver-

[279] See Publishers' Weekly, Jan. 15, 1962, p. 45-48, 64-66.
[280] See 1962 THE BOWKER ANNUAL OF LIBRARY AND BOOK TRADE INFORMATION 92. State and Federal Government publications, subscription books, dissertations, reprints, and pamphlets of under 49 pages are not included in the count.
[281] See Publishers' Weekly, Jan. 15, 1962, p. 64.
[282] See *Growth Patterns in Printing and Publishing,* U.S. DEP'T OF COMMERCE, BUSINESS AND DEFENSE SERVICES ADMINISTRATION, PRINTING AND PUBLISHING DIV., PRINTING AND PUBLISHING INDUSTRY REP'T VOL. 4, NO. 5 (Oct. 1962).
[283] See *Market Distribution of U. S. Foreign Trade in Printed Matter and Printing Plates, id.* VOL. 4, NO. 4, at 2 (Sept. 1962). The import and export figures cover periodicals and other "printed matter" in addition to books.
[284] See *id.* at 2, 5.
[285] See U. S. LIBRARY OF CONGRESS, LEGISLATIVE REFERENCE SERVICE, GOLD AND THE UNITED STATES BALANCE OF PAYMENTS DEFICIT, PREPARED FOR THE HOUSE COMM. ON FOREIGN AFFAIRS, 87th Cong., 1st Sess. 21 (Comm. Print 1961).
[286] For chart showing five-year comparison, see 1960/61 REG. COP. 10.

age number of copies imported per statement issued was 117,[287] a record hardly justifying the administrative trouble of handling import statements.

A count based on a random sample of 1,000 recent ad interim registrations showed that approximately 75% of the authors are U.S. citizens, 10% British, 7% Canadian, 4% Australian, and the rest other nationals. Special ad interim copyright has lost much of its former importance for foreign authors, since their works may be exempt from the manufacturing clause, if their country is a party to the Universal Copyright Convention or if their works are published first in a U.C.C. country.

Comparison of the ad interim registrations and importation figures with the figures furnished by the Bureau of Customs for imports of books in English will show a vast discrepancy. For example, Customs reported a total of 4,561,274 copies of books imported for the calendar year 1960 as against 97,128 ad interim imports. It should be borne in mind that public domain books can come in without limit, as well as books copyrighted under the Universal Copyright Convention. Only about 2% of the books in the English language that are imported are imported "ad interim."

In the category of books manufactured abroad and coming in without limit, 4,007 registrations were made in fiscal 1962; 3,819 in 1961. The number of such registrations is increasing every year.[288]

G. BOOK PRODUCTION AND DISTRIBUTION

1. Developments in the United States

The growth of the book industry in the United States has closely paralleled the population increase. In 1930 book titles produced totalled 10,807; in 1960, 15,012—a 48 percent increase. The population increase for that same period was 47 percent.[289]

Recent years have been notable in the industry for activities designed to attract capital and eliminate competition, such as mergers, centralization of plant, improved fiscal policies, establishment of foreign affiliates, "going public" by the issuance of shares of stock to the public, development of paperbacks, and utilization of modern production, distribution, and advertising methods. Publishing has become big business.[290]

---

[287] See *id.* for figures on ad interim registration. The following figures have been furnished by the Accounting Section of the Copyright Office on the basis of endorsements by Customs on the import statements:

Fiscal Year	Import Statements	Copies Imported
1962	777	59,686
1961	802	143,092
1960	581	97,128
1959	583	64,261
1958	1030	87,575

[288] See chart, Appendix F, which covers only years for which comparable Census statistics were found.

[289] See CHENEY, *op. cit. supra* note 266, at 339; Publishers' Weekly, Jan. 16, 1961, p. 56.

[290] This is illustrated by comparative tables on the value of shipments of "books, publishing and printing" for the years 1958 to 1960, in U. S. BUREAU OF THE CENSUS, DEP'T OF COMMERCE, SER.: M60(AS)-2, 1960 ANNUAL SURVEY OF MANUFACTURES 11 (1962). See also *1960 in Review—News, Trends and Statistics in the American Book Industry,* Publishers' Weekly, Jan. 16, 1961, p. 79-91.

Despite all this—despite faster printing techniques and greater automation, and despite higher wages—there is reported to be a serious manpower shortage in the printing industry. This was the subject of a recent industrial relations conference of the Printing Industry of America.[291]

New production techniques are changing the whole economy of the book manufacturing industry. Among the many technological changes in the manufacture of books has been development of the highspeed rotary offset process which has been so improved in recent years that it can—in the lingo of the industry—"run high quality process work with close register and accurate reproduction up to 1,000 feet and more per minute, with the immense advantage of 6 to 8 hours make-ready on 8-color work, compared with 24 to 36 hours make-ready on equivalent letterpress." The "break-even point," the point beyond which profits can be measured, is for this process somewhere between 25,000 and 30,000 copies.[292]

This development was discussed at a meeting in 1960 of the Lithograph Book Manufacturers' Committee of the Lithographers' and Printers' National Association.[293] Statistics presented at the meeting made it evident that offset and gravure are growing at the expense of letterpress. For example, in 1947, eighty-eight percent of all bound books were printed by letterpress and about twelve percent by offset; in 1954, eighty-one percent were letterpress-printed and seventeen percent offset-printed and two percent gravure-printed. In 1958 the number of employees in all letterpress printing was one percent fewer than in 1954, while employment in offset printing increased by twenty-six percent. Employment in electro-typing and stereotyping (for letterpress) dropped fifteen percent from 1954 to 1958. During that period there was an increase of more than thirty-six percent in the volume of books printed.[294]

As was brought out above,[295] it is unclear whether, in the manufacture of an American edition by offset process, the use of "repro proofs" made from material printed abroad constitutes a violation of the manufacturing requirements. While no figures exist that would indicate the extent of this practice, the growing concern with the problem among book manufacturers would suggest that the practice is fairly common.[296] Although American compositor interests may be adversely affected by this practice, it would seem that another segment of the domestic printing industry—the lithographers—might be the gainer. In any event, the wording of the manufacturing clause would seem to be outmoded by the increasing trend away from letterpress to offset printing.

---

[291] See Hadley, *U.S. Printing Industry Warned It Must End Manpower Shortage,* The Evening Star (Washington, D. C.), Mar. 8, 1961, p. B 10, col. 1.
[292] See *Books and the Future of Printing,* Publishers' Weekly, Nov. 7, 1960, p. 89.
[293] See *id.* at 75.
[294] See *id.* at 89. For chart showing receipts and the share of lithographers and typesetters in relation to other processes, see Appendix F.
[295] See Part IV *supra.*
[296] See *e.g., Florence Treaty and Copyright—BMI and ABPC Views Are Aired,* Publishers' Weekly, Dec. 24, 1962, p. 14.

Cost saving in book production has been achieved to a considerable extent by concentration of plant, i.e., by combining manufacturing in all of its phases with shipping, making the one plant serve as a place for manufacture of large printings, for warehousing, and for shipping into or out of the country. This plan was inaugurated by the British Book Centre, in New York, in 1954[297] and has been adopted by several book manufacturing or publishing firms in recent years. Among other savings, consolidation of plant eliminates trucking costs and much time.

2. Comparative wages and unit costs

The wage levels in the printing industry in the United States are much higher than in other countries. According to a survey of the printing industry conducted by the Bureau of Labor Statistics,[298] as of July 1, 1960, the average hourly wage scales in book and job printshops ranged from $2.75 for press assistants and feeders to $3.94 for photoengravers. The average work week in book and job shops was 36.6 hours.

Statistics furnished by the Minister of Labour covering rates of wages and hours of work in the printing and book binding industry in Great Britain[299] indicate that as of April, 1961 the weekly wage ranges somewhere between 148 and 324 shillings, with many variations for grade of work, types of machine operated, day or night shift, location of plant, and sex of worker. This amounts to a rough average of about 250 shillings or $35 a week. The normal work week is forty-one or forty-two hours. The wages range higher for lithographic printing and photo-gravure.

British wages are higher than on the European continent and much higher than in Asian countries. Labor can be had in India at 50¢ a day,[300] so that labor-saving machinery would have to save a great deal to be worth anything at all, and importing machinery is expensive; even paper is expensive there and space is at a premium.

As Mr. Frase pointed out at the 1954 hearings on the Universal Copyright Convention,[301] the unit cost of books in editions of 2,500 or more is lower in the United States than elsewhere, notwithstanding lower wages everywhere else, due to more highly mechanized U.S. processes of manufacture. Low labor costs do not necessarily mean manufacturing economy. It is to be noted that most imported books come in editions of 1,500 or less,[302] and U.S. printers have not been concerned about small editions.

---

[297] See *British Book Centre in New Production, Shipping Plan,* 165 PUBLISHERS' WEEKLY 2057 (1954).

[298] U. S. BUREAU OF LABOR STATISTICS, DEP'T OF LABOR, BULL. NO. 1292, UNION WAGES AND HOURS, JULY 1, 1960 AND TREND, 1907-1960, at 6-7 (1960). The comparative union hourly wage index figures for each year from 1907 reflect the typical inflationary trend. For example, the index for book and job wage scales in 1909 was 17.8; in 1948 it was 94.3; by 1955, figures were available for various categories of workers; the "averaged" index was 131.9; in 1960 it was 155.6. Variations in wages are also shown by area and by type of employment in the industry.

[299] GR. BRIT. MINISTRY OF LABOUR AND NATIONAL SERVICE, TIME RATES OF WAGES AND HOURS OF WORK 148-57 (1st Apr. 1961).

[300] Personal communication from a staff member from India of the World Bank.

[301] *Hearings, supra* note 235, at 135.

[302] See "Consolidated Custom Reports" (table) under Part VI, D. 3 *supra.*

3. Competition with the United Kingdom

Foreign competition in the book industry is mainly from the United Kingdom, which is the largest producer of English-language books in the world. About three-fourths of all titles published throughout the world come from ten countries;[303] it is books in English which have heretofore caused concern to the United States printing industry, and most of those books are published in Great Britain.

In 1960 Great Britain published 23,783 titles (22,045 exclusive of government publications), a record high;[304] as previously mentioned,[305] the United States published 15,012 titles, (exclusive of government publications), also a record. The per capita book production in Great Britain was very much greater than in the United States in 1952; there were 375 books per million population in Great Britain, whereas in the United States there were 74.[306] Exports of United Kingdom books to the United States exceeded those of any other country; in 1952 the value of United Kingdom books imported into the U.S. was $7,640,000.[307] In 1960, imports to the U.S. from the United Kingdom amounted to $12,527,739.[308]

At the same time, the British are becoming concerned that their traditional domination of the world market for English-language books is being seriously threatened by the United States. Comment on this in the leading British publishers' weekly goes like this:

* * * competition from foreign books in the English language (principally but not only from the U.S.) is becoming ever more intense in Commonwealth countries where the large and still growing market for books had hitherto been developing chiefly by the enterprise and investment of British publishers. Second, although it is confidently hoped that the last quarter of the year will prove to have been a very good one in the home market (despite increased foreign competition even here), there can be little doubt that, school books apart, home sales have declined.[309]

Further,

The report [of the British Publishers Association] refers to anxieties about market infringements felt by both American and British publishers during the year. Ratification by the U.S. Senate of the Unesco Florence Agreement, which obligates signatory countries to remove all tariffs on books and other educational material, increased American publishers' anxieties about "buying round." The report says, "The Americans are understandably concerned at the thought of their editions meeting competition from lower-priced British editions in their home market, just as British publishers are concerned about their hard-cover editions suffering from the illegal importation of infringing American paperback editions in many parts of the world."

Many members of the P.A. reported that strong complaint to the American publishers had brought prompt withdrawal and amends in such cases, and the Advisory Council in India obtained an order from the Registrar of Copyrights in India forbidding the importation of an American paperback edition of a title for which the market was controlled by the British publisher.[310]

---

303 See BARKER, BOOKS FOR ALL 18 (1956).
304 See Publishers' Weekly, Jan. 16, 1961, p. 101.
305 See text accompanying note 288 supra.
306 See BARKER, op. cit. supra note 301, at 21.
307 See id. at 25.
308 See Publishers' Weekly, Sept. 25, 1961, p. 40.
309 The Bookseller, Mar. 18, 1961, p. 1355.
310 Id. at 1356.

The dramatic increase in United States competition with Great Britain has probably been due to broader distribution of American paperbacks. Many importing countries cannot afford the higher-priced books, and U.S. publishers have turned to paperbacks as a means of taking advantage of the world market. To lessen production costs, U.S. publishers are also printing facsimile editions in Japan of those titles that have a strong potential sale in Asia. As the British weekly reports a Unesco survey of this development:

* * * By printing in Japan, in cooperation with a local publisher there, the American publisher is able to reduce the costs of production, which are high in the United States, to the point where the books can be sold at one-half to one-third of the American price list. So far, the survey states, almost 200 scientific, medical and technical books have been reproduced in this way for sale in Asian countries.[311]

4. Programs to encourage wider dissemination

There are various government programs, here and abroad, to encourage the widest possible dissemination of books. The language barrier is being attacked and, in some cases, overcome by translation programs. The program authorized by Public Law 480, 83d Congress,[312] makes possible translation and publication of American textbooks at low prices for overseas distribution, and the Informational Media Guaranty Program[313] facilitates monetary exchange. The U.S.I.A. has various translation programs, and a total of 55,-000,000 copies of American books in fifty languages have been shipped overseas as a result of them.[314] Great Britain has an official low-priced book scheme to encourage exports, under the direction of the Central Office of Information.

Among private organizations working toward the same end, there is the Asia Foundation.[315] Shipments of books under its book-for-Asian-students program are approaching one million copies to more than a thousand colleges, universities, and libraries in sixteen Asian countries; the Foundation pays the translation costs. The American-Korean Foundation has collected books for Korean rehabilitation. There is also Franklin Publications in New York,[316] which serves as an outlet for translations.

The university presses are cooperating in programs to encourage international exchange of books; their national association has a committee on international trade. They have proposed translation into Spanish and Portuguese, and offset printing of English-language editions, by Latin-American publishers, with Latin-American scholars selecting the titles.[317] They have also made similar proposals for Asian and African studies.

[311] *Id.*, Apr. 15, 1961, p. 1604.
[312] Act of July 10, 1954, ch. 469, 68 Stat. 454.
[313] A program instituted in 1952 to provide currency convertibility for imports of American books into the several foreign countries where the program operates. Publishers' Weekly, Jan. 16, 1961, p. 86.
[314] See The Bookseller, Apr. 15, 1961, p. 1604.
[315] *Ibid.*
[316] A quasi-private, long-established organization devoted to the translation and publication of American books primarily for the Muslim world, though its operations have been expanded to Latin America and parts of Africa. Publishers' Weekly, Jan. 15, 1962, p. 68.
[317] See *University Presses Emphasize Programs for International Cooperation,* Publishers' Weekly, June 19, 1961, p. 18.

GENERAL REVISION

The Department of State is cooperating with a working group consisting of forty book, magazine, and newspaper publishers and individuals from foundations, universities and the Federal Government, in an effort to plan educational and cultural programs.[318]

Barriers to the exchange of cultural materials are rapidly being swept aside. It is being realized that the entire world is affected in many significant ways by the printed word available in the remotest places. Meanwhile, U.S. book exports have increased faster than imports, and the economic trend for the book printing and publishing industry suggests that there are now effective substitutes for the present manufacturing and import restrictions of the copyright law.

H. ECONOMISTS' VIEWS

Scholars in the field of economics insist that the long view, and the one in the ultimate best interest of the American economy, requires more and freer international trade. Maintaining the proper balance is, of course, a delicate and difficult task, and that balance must support two major goals. There is the goal of more widespread economic well-being, and there is the goal of international understanding; books play an important role in the achievement of both.

As Dr. Howard S. Picquet, Economist of the Legislative Reference Service, reported to Congress in a study dated September 13, 1961,[319] the balance of payments is a composite of many variables and "it is easy to blame the adverse balance on the variable that one likes the least. * * * Those who dislike competition from commodity imports are disposed to blame them." However, a chart reproduced in the study shows that books and printed matter are blameless, for they are listed among the exported commodities that increased more than the increase in gross national product during a time of deteriorating export surplus.[320]

The economic forces of adjustment seem to be at work. Again quoting Dr. Picquet:

There is no doubt that increases in some imports of manufactured goods have caused difficulty for certain domestic producers * * * Countries with abnormally low wage scales but which are equipped with highly efficient modern machinery, can compete successfully with American industry in similar lines of produce. Again, however, perspective is essential. * * * Competition from imports can serve as an important stimulus to domestic producers. Finally, wages in countries that only recently have become exporters of manufactured goods have a tendency to rise. * * * When this occurs the competitive advantage * * * will be diminished. * * * Trade restrictions which, superficially, seem to offer a solution would not really solve the balance of payments problem. Expansion of trade and the reduction of quantitative restrictions imposed by foreign countries against United States exports offer hope for continuing a reasonable export surplus to cushion the current pressure on the dollar. * * * Restrictive trade policies would aggravate, rather than solve, the gold problem.[321]

---

[318] See 20 U. S. LIBRARY OF CONGRESS, INFORMATION BULLETIN 341 (1961).
[319] See note 285 *supra* and accompanying text.
[320] *Id.* at 21.
[321] *Id.* at 25.

He says, further:

Governmental restriction of importation would widen the export trade surplus by reducing imports. Within a short time the effect would be to throttle exports also. For more than 25 years the United States has led the movement for the mutual reduction of tariffs and other trade barriers. It has done so through the reciprocal trade agreements program and by leadership in the formation of the General Agreement on Tariffs and Trade. The imposition of intensified restrictions against importation would be an announcement to the world that the United States has abandoned leadership with respect to international economic cooperation. Other countries would follow suit and world trade would become engulfed in a contracting spiral that would aggravate economic problems everywhere.[322]

Other economists have expressed the same viewpoint, and, of course, that is the general idea behind GATT. The author of a study on American imports, undertaken under the sponsorship of the Twentieth Century Fund says:

Although expansion of imports may be more difficult to achieve and temporarily more painful, it would lead ultimately to greater benefits. * * * If American imports were to rise more rapidly than exports it would assist other countries to eliminate exchange controls and other measures that discriminate against dollar goods. * * * This offers the best pattern of adjustment.[323]

He adds:

A reduction of American trade barriers would be one of the most effective means for counteracting Soviet economic offensive against the free world and for cementing more strongly the unity of the free countries * * *.[324]

It appears from the foregoing that advances in the production, translation, and dissemination of books have made it possible to compete successfully and to develop new channels of trade. With the support of governments and private enterprise, these advances could bring the heritage of the world's literature to vast new audiences and thus aid in accomplishing the two-fold objective of greater economic stability and international understanding. Books convey "know how" as well as culture and encourage improvement in all human relations. Restrictions on their international dissemination, whether by tariff or import quota, can hamper progress.

VII. Conclusions

A. U. S. Manufacture as a Condition of Copyright Protection

To deny copyright protection to authors whose works are printed abroad seems to violate the fundamental purposes of the copyright law. That law is intended to benefit authors, but the manufacturing requirement subordinates their protection to that of the printers. And even aside from this, is there sufficient corresponding practical benefit to printers, whom authors admittedly need, to override the apparent inequity? Facts seem to deny this.

While authors will usually have their works printed and published first in their own country, valid reasons may make it necessary or

---

[322] *Id.* at 49-50.
[323] HUMPHREY, AMERICAN IMPORTS 456 (1955).
[324] *Id.* at 512-13.

expedient in some cases to employ a foreign manufacturer. The following are some of the situations that could justify foreign manufacture: (1) a U.S. author is residing abroad or writing in a foreign language or for a foreign market; (2) a foreign publisher is the only one offering to publish a technical or scholarly work; (3) the market for a special work is so limited that printing must be procured wherever the cost is lowest; (4) the superior quality afforded by a foreign artisan is a primary consideration. The penalty for foreign manufacture in such cases—either total deprivation of property rights or severe limitations on them—seems unduly harsh and discouraging for the writers. As a direct consequence of the manufacturing provisions, there are many and serious forfeitures.

There are no reliable statistics to show how many forfeitures have resulted from failure to have books manufactured in the United States. Customs authorities estimate that perhaps ten or twelve statements of copyright abandonment are presented during the course of a year in order to gain admittance of books otherwise ineligible for importation. The reasons, they surmise, are that the ad interim quota of 1,500 copies has been used up and the copyright owner wants to bring in additional copies of the work, or that, in a case where a full term copyright has been secured, the copyright owner wants to import copies of a foreign edition. These documents of "abandonment," for which there is no statutory provision, must be recorded in the Copyright Office before they will be accepted by the Customs officials. However, a perusal of a random selection of recorded abandonments does not readily reveal their purpose; several of those examined refer merely to the restrictions of section 107 of the copyright law.

Abandoning or disclaiming copyright is no doubt a less frequent occurrence than the failure to claim copyright by the deliberate, though not exactly voluntary, omission of copyright notice because of the manufacturing requirements. There is no way of estimating how many such cases there have been. Authors have had to weigh the advantages of getting their books printed and on the market against the loss of valuable rights in them. Perhaps they hope to bring their work to the attention of a U.S. publisher who will bring out a new and copyrightable edition. Nevertheless, it is questionable that this is a gamble that an author should be forced to take.

The effect on authors is severe not only because they lose the exclusive right to reproduce their works in printed form, but also because they lose many other rights often much more remunerative, such as motion picture and television rights, dramatization, serialization, translation, and adaptation rights. Some idea of revenues from the exploitation of copyrights in books may be gained from a Copyright Office study.[325] Citing 1954 Census of Business figures, the study showed that nearly $70 million was paid by book publishers in

---

[325] Blaisdell, *Size of the Copyright Industries*, COPYRIGHT LAW REVISION, STUDY NO. 2, PREPARED FOR THE SUBCOMM. ON PATENTS, TRADEMARKS, AND COPYRIGHTS, SENATE COMM. ON THE JUDICIARY, 86th Cong., 1st Sess. 21-59 (Comm. Print 1960).

royalties to authors.[326] Besides the financial return to the individual author, the impact of his creative efforts on the total economy is something to be considered. When an author's work is put into the hopper of industry, the diversified uses of that work radiate income to many others. The study includes a table[327] indicating that the national income originated by books in 1954 amounted to $390 million.

The benefits, if any, which may accrue to the printing industry because of the manufacturing requirements are more than offset by the resultant losses to the author. It has been shown that the amount of American labor employed in reprinting foreign-made books does not appear to be significant, and that the manufacturing clause does not seem to have forced any appreciable number of authors to employ U.S. printers. High prices have sometimes driven authors and scholars to foreign manufacture, and this additional business for the foreign printer may have made him a stronger competitor to some extent. However, foreign competition apparently has not been damaging, for, with every relaxation of the manufacturing requirement, whether incidental or not, there has been a concomitant increase in the volume of U.S. printing.

Foreign competition has not depressed wages or prices or income, or reduced employment; as previously mentioned, there is reported to be a shortage of skilled workers in the industry. It has not interfered with the more profitable large-edition, mass-produced book manufacture. On the contrary, foreign competition has challenged the U.S. printing industry to improve methods of production and distribution, with the result that a tremendously valuable export market has been developed which more than compensates for such printing business as has been driven outside the country. In recent years there has been a complete reversal of the large import surplus of the early years, which suggests that removal of the manufacturing requirements as a condition of copyright would not affect the economic interests of the now mature and thriving domestic printing industry.

B.   IMPORT RESTRICTIONS AND THE COPYRIGHT LAW

Relatively few foreign books in English are any longer subject to the 1,500 copy import limitation. The import limitation, as well as the manufacturing requirement itself, were eliminated in 1955 for foreign works protected under the Universal Copyright Convention. More than forty countries have now adhered to the Convention; one of these is the United Kingdom, traditionally the largest producer of books in English. Canada, another large producer, has recently deposited its instrument of ratification, and the few countries producing English-language books that have not yet adhered to the Convention may be expected to do so within the next few years. It can be expected that, eventually, almost the only books to which the import limitation will apply are those by U. S. authors, and the vast

---

[326] *Id.* at 48.
[327] *Id.* at 38.

bulk of their books are printed in the United States for reasons unrelated to the manufacturing clause or the import restriction.

Furthermore, there are many kinds of "books" in English to which the import limitation has never applied, such as public domain works or books of music or drama. The proportion of books that come in without limitation is so much greater in volume now than for books still limited by the copyright law that any distinction in treatment seems illogical. For example, the number of copies imported with import authorizations during fiscal 1961 totalled 143,092,[328] whereas 3,817,549 copies of books of all kinds were imported.[329] This disparity implies that the import restriction is not achieving much protection for the domestic printing industry.

Even if it could be shown that the printing industry needs protection from foreign books imports, it would be difficult to explain why this protection is limited to certain classes of copyrighted works —which represent a small segment of book imports.

The last three decades have witnessed efforts to effect general tariff reductions in all commodities with a view to achieving a maximum expansion of international trade. The manufacturing clause, which in the last analysis is merely a substitute for a tariff, seems incongruous in a world dedicated to the removal of trade barriers of all kinds, especially to the exchange of knowledge.

---

[328] Copyright Office figures based on Customs endorsements on import statements issued.
[329] Consolidated Customs Reports furnished the Copyright Office.

APPENDIX

A. TINCHER BILL, 1922: §§ 4, 6

SEC. 4. That sections 15, 16, 17, 21 (as amended December 18, 1919), 22, and 31 of the said copyright act of 1919 are hereby repealed, and that the said act is further amended by striking out from section 9 the words "except in the case of books seeking an ad interim protection under section 21 of this act"; by striking out from section 12 the words "which copies, if the work be a book or periodical, shall have been produced in accordance with the manufacturing provisions specified in section 15 of this act"; and by striking out from section 55 the words "in the case of a book the certificate shall also state the receipt of the affidavit, as provided by section 16 of this act, and the date of the completion of the printing, or the date of the publication of the book, as stated in the said affidavit."

SEC. 6. That during the existence of the American copyright in any book the importation into the United States of any copies thereof shall be, and is hereby, prohibited, except with the assent of the proprietor of the American copyright subsequent to the registration of American publication and the deposit in the copyright office at Washington, District of Columbia, of two copies of any such book: *Provided, however,* That, except as regards piratical copies, such prohibition shall not apply: (a) To any book as published in the country of origin with the authorization of the author or copyright proprietor when imported, not more than one copy at one time, for individual use and not for sale, or when imported for use and not for sale, not more than one copy in any one invoice, in good faith, by or for any society or institution incorporated for educational, literary, philosophical, scientific, or religious purposes, or for the encouragement of the fine arts, or for any college, academy, school, or seminary of learning, or for any State, school, college, university, or free public library in the United States, provided the publisher of the American edition of such book has (within ten days after written demand) declined or neglected to agree to supply the copy demanded; (b) to books which form parts of libraries or collections purchased en bloc for the use of societies, institutions, or libraries designated in the foregoing paragraph, or form parts of the libraries or personal baggage belonging to persons or families arriving from foreign countries and are not intended for sale; (c) to works in raised characters for the use of the blind; (d) to works imported by the authority or for the use of the United States; (e) to the authorized edition of a book in a foreign language or languages of which only a translation into English has been published in this country; (f) to a foreign news-

(1190)

paper or magazine, although containing matter copyrighted in the United States printed or reprinted by authority of the copyright proprietor, unless such newspaper or magazine contains also copyright matter printed or reprinted without such authorization: *Provided,* That copies imported as above may not lawfully be used in any way to violate the rights of the proprietor of the American copyright or annul or limit the copyright protection secured by this act, and such unlawful use shall be deemed an infringement of the copyright.

B. Vestal Bill, 1930: §§ 28-29

SEC. 28. Except as in this act otherwise expressly provided, all copies of any copyright material which shall be distributed in the United States in book, pamphlet, map, or sheet form shall be printed from type set within the limits of the United States or its dependencies, either by hand or by the aid of any kind of typesetting machine, and/or from plates made within the limits of the United States or its dependencies from type set therein; or, if the text be produced by lithographic, mimeographic, photogravure, or photo-engraving, or any kindred process or any other process of reproduction now or hereafter devised, then by a process wholly performed within the limits of the United States or its dependencies; and the printing or other reproduction of the text, and the binding of said book or pamphlet, shall be performed within the limits of the United States or its dependencies. Said requirements shall extend also to any copyright illustrations within any book, pamphlet, or sheet, except where the subjects represented are located in a foreign country and/or illustrate any scientific or technical work or reproduce a work of art. Said requirements shall not apply to works in raised characters for the use of the blind, nor to works by authors who are nationals of a foreign country.

SEC. 29. That whenever manufacture is required in the United States or its dependencies under the preceding section, an affidavit under the official seal of any officer authorized to administer oaths within the United States or its dependencies, duly made by the author himself; or by the owner of any right to print or publish such work in the United States in book, pamphlet, map, or printed sheet form; or by any agent of such author or owner duly authorized for that purpose residing in the United States or its dependencies, shall be filed in the copyright office within sixty days after such publication setting forth the manner in which compliance has been had with all requirements of the preceding section. Such affidavit shall state also the place where, and the establishment or establishments in which, such type was set and/or plates where made or where lithograph, photogravure, photo-engraving, or reproduction of any kindred process or any other process of reproduction now or hereafter devised, and/or printing and binding, were performed, and the date of completion of printing of the work or the date of publication. At any time

(1191)

or times when compliance with such preceding section is requisite, unless said affidavit shall be filed or the court shall find the failure to file said affidavit was due to excusable neglect, no action in respect to an infringement of copyright in said work or any right or rights therein shall be instituted or maintained by any person who, under the provisions of this section, might have filed this affidavit. But nothing herein contained shall limit or suspend the right of the assignee or licensee of the author of any right under such copyright other than those in this section specified to bring any action or proceeding for the infringement of the rights which such assignee or licensee may own.

C. TRAMMELL AMENDMENT TO DUFFY BILL, 1935: § 11

SEC. 11. The proviso of section 15 of such Act, as amended, is hereby amended, to read as follows: *"Provided, that* all copies of any copyrighted material which shall be distributed in the United States in book, pamphlet, map, or sheet form shall be printed from type set within the limits of the United States, either by hand or by the aid of any kind of typesetting machine, and/or from plates made within the limits of the United States; or if the text be produced by lithographic, mimeographic, photogravure, or photoengraving, or any kindred process or any other process of reproduction now or hereafter devised, then by a process wholly performed within the limits of the United States; and the printing or other reproduction of the text, and the binding of the said book or pamphlet, shall be performed within the limits of the United States. Said requirements shall extend also to any copyright illustrations, maps, or charts within any book or pamphlet, or in sheet form. Said requirement shall not apply to works in raised characters for the blind."

D. "SHOTWELL BILL," 1940: §§ 29-31

SEC. 29. (1) Except as in this Act otherwise expressly provided, all copies of any copyrighted work which shall be distributed in the United States in book, pamphlet, map, or sheet form, including any copyrighted illustrations therein, shall be printed from type set within the limits of the United States or its dependencies, either by hand or by the aid of any kind of typesetting machine, or from plates made within the limits of the United States from type set therein; or, if said copies be produced by lithographic, mimeographic, photogravure, or photoengraving, or any kindred process of reproduction now known or hereafter devised, then by type set, or by such process wholly performed, within the limits of the United States or its dependencies, and the printing or other reproduction of said copies, and the binding of any book, pamphlet, collection of maps, or sheets, shall be performed within the limits of the United States or its dependencies.

(1192)

(2) The aforesaid provisions of this section shall not apply—

(a) to copies imported in personal baggage and not for sale or hire: PROVIDED, That no more than one copy of any work is imported in the baggage of any one person;

(b) to importation through ports of entry or through the mails, of not more than one copy of any work on any one invoice for personal use of the consignee and not for sale or hire: PROVIDED, HOWEVER, That no person in the United States other than a retail bookdealer shall act as the agent of the consignee in the acquisition of such copy;

(c) to two copies imported for the author's own use;

(d) to copies imported for libraries;

(e) to works which form parts of private collections purchased en bloc in a foreign country and which are not intended for sale or hire;

(f) to foreign newspapers, periodicals, or magazines;

(g) to an authorized translation in a foreign language of a work previously published in the United States;

(h) to works in a foreign language by authors not resident or domiciled in the United States at the time of the creation of the work;

(i) to works in raised characters for the use of the blind;

(j) to illustrations of a scientific work or reproductions of a work of art where the subjects represented are located in a foreign country;

(k) to not more than twelve copies of an unprinted work in manuscript, typescript, mimeographic, or photostatic form;

(l) to motion pictures with or without sound.

(3) Nor shall the provisions of subdivision (1) apply to the first five hundred copies, other than copies imported as provided in subdivision (2), of any work imported into the United States through the ports of entry or in the mails: PROVIDED, That such number of copies shall not include the copies importation of which is permitted under the provisions of subdivision (2), and that this privilege of importation of such five hundred copies shall not extend to works of authors, citizens of, or aliens resident or domiciled in, the United States of America at the time of creation, printing, or first publication:

AND PROVIDED FURTHER, That—

(a) every such importation is accompanied by a written authorization, specifying the title of the work and the number of copies imported thereunder, signed by the author or the owner of the publication rights for the United States with respect to said work, together with an affidavit of the importer certifying that a duplicate copy of said authorization has been mailed to or deposited with the Register of Copyrights; and that

(b) if copies in excess of five hundred are imported except as provided in this section with the consent of the author or anyone authorized to act on behalf of the author, then no remedies shall be available under this Act for the printing, reprinting, publication, distribution, or vending of copies of such work made by any process set forth in subsection 1.

MANUFACTURING CLAUSE

SEC. 30. (1) The importation into the United States without the written consent of the author, or any authorized agent to act on behalf of the author of copies of works produced in violation of section 29 of this Act is hereby prohibited and such copies shall be seized by the customs or post-office officials.

(2) When an edition of a copyrighted work is manufactured in the United States, pursuant to the provisions of section 29, and is published either by the author, or by the grantee of exclusive publication rights, in the United States pursuant to a written grant recorded in the Copyright Office, then during the period of said exclusive publication rights or the term of copyright therein, whichever terminates sooner, importation of copies in violation of section 29 is prohibited.

(3) The importation into the United States, except as otherwise herein permitted, of a copy of the whole or any part of any copyrighted work, which if published in the United States would infringe such copyright, shall be deemed an infringement, and is hereby prohibited.

SEC. 31. Any and all copies of which importation is prohibited by this Act brought into the United States from any foreign country shall be seized and forfeited by like proceedings as those provided by law for the seizure and condemnation of property imported into the United States in violation of the customs revenue laws. Such articles when forfeited shall be destroyed in such manner as the Secretary of the Treasury or the court, as the case may be shall direct: PROVIDED, however, That all copies of authorized editions of copyrighted works imported in violation of the provisions of this Act may be exported and returned to the country of export whenever it is shown to the satisfaction of the Secretary of the Treasury, in a written application that such importation does not involve gross negligence or fraud.

The Secretary of the Treasury and the Postmaster General are hereby empowered and required to make and enforce such rules and regulations as shall prevent the importation into the United States through the ports of entry or in the mails of articles importation of which is prohibited under sections 29 and 30 of this Act, but the Treasury Department, as the case may be, shall not be required to prevent such importation unless the copyright owner or other injured party shall have filed a written claim of copyright pursuant to said rules and regulations.

E. CUSTOMS INSTRUCTIONS

Instructions for the new situation which will prevail when, on September 27, 1957, the Universal Copyright Convention comes into force for the United Kingdom.

The following instructions relate exclusively to section 11.21 of the Customs Regulations and have no bearing on cases involving piratical copies or false notice of copyright.

(1194)

GENERAL REVISION

Upon the coming into force of the Universal Copyright Convention for the United Kingdom many books for which we would ordinarily have required import statements will be entitled to importation without statements and in unlimited quantities. The purpose of these instructions is to help you determine whether or not you must require an import statement for a particular book and limit its importation to 1,500 copies.

With respect to the importation of books, the practical effect of the Convention is limited to those in the English language. The following procedures, therefore, apply only to such books.

PROCEDURE

1. If the book is in English and bears a copyright notice, require the importer to supply in writing the following items of information:
   a. The country in which the book was first published.
   b. The country of which the author is a citizen.
   c. The country in which the author is domiciled.

2. No import statement will be required and copies may be imported in unlimited quantities if:
   a. The country in which the book was first published is a Convention country; or
   b. The country of which the author is a citizen is a Convention country;

   Provided, the author is neither a United States citizen nor domiciliary, and provided the work was not first published in the United States.

   The countries presently adhering to the Universal Copyright Convention are: Andorra, Austria, Cambodia, Chile, Costa Rica, Cuba, Ecuador, France, German Federal Republic, Great Britain, Haiti, Holy See, Iceland, Israel, Italy, Japan, Laos, Liberia, Luxembourg, Mexico, Monaco, Pakistan, Philippines, Portugal, Spain, Switzerland, and United States of America. You will be notified as additional countries ratify the Convention.

3. Keep a written record of the titles of English language books bearing copyright notice which are imported after September 27, 1957, and the number of copies of each. Forward this record to the Register of Copyrights, Washington 25, D. C., on the first of each month, beginning November 1, 1957.

Refer any questions which arise concerning the Universal Copyright Convention to the Bureau.

B. H. FLINN
Chief, Division of Entry,
Value, and Penalties

(1195)

F. Data on Book* Manufacture and Distribution (Chart)

	1891	1930	1939	1947	1958	1959	1960
Domestic Production:							
No. titles[1]	4,665	10,027	10,640	9,182	13,462	14,876	15,012
Publishing & Printing (value)[2]	$33,753,000[9]		$103,708,000	$262,903,000	$1,010,713,000	$1,134,270,000	$1,276,080,000
Printing[3]			$ 24,477,000	$ 57,659,000	$ 422,907,000	$ 472,458,000	$ 531,708,000
Printing & binding (lithography)[4]			$ 99,910,000	$313,462,000	$ 167,586,000	$ 208,676,000	$ 253,236,000
" " (other processes)[4]					$ 263,153,000	$ 258,878,000	$ 263,153,000
Typesetting[4]			$ 22,044,000	$ 66,842,000	$ 175,466,000	$ 185,645,000	$ 188,267,000
Photoengraving[4]			$ 48,258,000	$116,131,000	$ 208,510,000	$ 212,239,000	$ 208,722,000
Electrotyping & stereotyping[4]			$ 22,141,000	$ 47,937,000	$ 81,479,000	$ 80,467,000	$ 79,150,000
Employment in book printing:							
No. production workers			7,628	9,280	33,700	35,500	38,100
Average weekly wage[5]		$21.76	$34.25[12]	$54.06	$85.80	$90.52	$93.43
Imports:							
No. copies[6]					1,576,023	2,639,980	4,561,274
No. import statements issued by C.O.[7]			—	712	841	583	581
Ad interim copies imported[8]			—		87,575	64,261	97,128
Value, all book imports[11]	$ 3,996,085[9]	$11,848,315	$ 8,224,145	$ 12,902,601	$ 17,108,198	$ 20,282,699	$ 22,247,677
Exports:[11]							
Value, all books	$ 1,943,228[9]	$12,443,626	$ 5,727,959	$ 25,977,759	$ 44,010,431	$ 50,904,214	$ 57,142,142
Registrations:[8]							
All books	11,000[10]	15,221	44,693	49,243	57,242	55,967	60,034
Ad interim (English language, mfd. abroad)	—	1,228	1,122	712	1,030	583	581
Foreign-mfd. books (except ad interim)	—	4,664	4,086	3,970	2,937	3,549	3,740

* The term "book" as used in this chart, with the exceptions of lines 13-17 and 20-23 (which relate to the broader copyright classification), is defined as a non-periodical publication of 49 or more.

Numbered explanatory notes appear on page following chart.

GENERAL REVISION

Notes to Chart

[1] Figures from issues of Publishers' Weekly.

[2] Includes printing by publisher, in his own establishment and contracted out.

[3] Printing conducted separately from publishing function.

[4] Included in printing total.

[5] Figures from Bureau of Labor Statistics, Dep't of Labor.

[6] Bureau of Customs reports to Copyright Office for all books.

[7] Copyright Office authorizations to import copies, issued at time of ad interim registration (fiscal year).

[8] Copyright Office accounting records. Figures for "all books" include ad interim and foreign-language registrations.

[9] Figures from *Hearings on H.R. 4059 Before Subcommittee No. 3 of the House Committee on the Judiciary,* 82d Cong., 2d Sess. 218 (1952).

[10] Estimated on basis of Reports of the Librarian of Congress for 1889-97.

[11] Figures from foreign trade reports of Dep't of Commerce.

[12] Figures from Book Manufacturers' Monthly, Apr. 1940, p. 4.

REPORT OF THE REGISTER OF COPYRIGHTS ON THE GENERAL REVISION OF THE U.S. COPYRIGHT LAW

Chapter I

THEORIES OF COPYRIGHT

OUTLINE OF CHAPTER

CHAPTER I

THEORIES OF COPYRIGHT

A. Introduction

Before embarking upon a discussion of the provisions of the copyright law, we are devoting this first chapter to a sketch of the underlying theories on which we believe the law has been and should be based.

We realize that any abstract statement of the nature and purposes of copyright is likely to be disputed, and is unlikely to resolve concrete questions as to what the law should provide. Also, in trying to outline our theories briefly, we run the risk of oversimplification. Nevertheless, we believe that a statement of our basic approach will help to explain the proposals made in the succeeding chapters.

B. The Nature of Copyright

1. IN GENERAL

In essence, copyright is the right of an author to control the reproduction of his intellectual creation. As long as he keeps his work in his sole possession, the author's absolute control is a physical fact. When he discloses the work to others, however, he makes it possible for them to reproduce it. Copyright is a legal device to give him the right to control its reproduction after it has been disclosed.

Copyright does not preclude others from using the ideas or information revealed by the author's work. It pertains to the literary, musical, graphic, or artistic form in which the author expresses intellectual concepts. It enables him to prevent others from reproducing his individual expression without his consent. But anyone is free to create his own expression of the same concepts, or to make practical use of them, as long as he does not copy the author's form of expression.

2. COPYRIGHT AS PROPERTY

Copyright is generally regarded as a form of property, but it is property of a unique kind. It is intangible and incorporeal. The thing to which the property right attaches—the author's intellectual work—is incapable of possession except as it is embodied in a tangible article such as a manuscript, book, record, or film. The tangible articles containing the work may be in the possession of many persons other than the copyright owner, and they may use the work for their own enjoyment, but copyright restrains them from reproducing the work without the owner's consent.

3

Justice Holmes, in his famous concurring opinion in *White-Smith Music Publishing Co.* v. *Apollo Co.* (209 U.S. 1 (1908)), gave a classic definition of the special characteristics of copyright as property:

> The notion of property starts, I suppose, from confirmed possession of a tangible object and consists in the right to exclude other from interference with the more or less free doing with it as one wills. But in copyright property has reached a more abstract expression. The right to exclude is not directed to an object in possession or owned, but is now in vacuo, so to speak. It restrains the spontaneity of men where, but for it, there would be nothing of any kind to hinder their doing as they saw fit. It is a prohibition of conduct remote from the persons or tangibles of the party having the right. It may be infringed a thousand miles from the owner and without his ever becoming aware of the wrong.

3. COPYRIGHT AS A PERSONAL RIGHT

a. *Generally*

Some commentators, particularly in European countries, have characterized copyright as a personal right of the author, or as a combination of personal and property rights. It is true that an author's intellectual creation has the stamp of his personality and is identified with him. But insofar as his rights can be assigned to other persons and survive after his death, they are a unique kind of personal rights.

b. *Moral rights* [1]

On the theory of personal right, some countries have included in their copyright laws special provisions for "moral rights" of authors. These provisions are intended to protect the author against certain acts injurious to his personal identity or reputation. They give the author the following rights:

- To have his name appear on copies of his work;
- To prevent the attribution to him of another person's work;
- To prevent the reproduction of his work in a distorted or degrading form.

These moral rights are regarded as not assignable, but the author may sometimes agree to waive them in particular cases. In some countries the moral rights survive the author's death and may be enforced by his heirs or representatives.

In the United States the moral rights of authors have never been treated as aspects of copyright. But authors have been given much the same protection of personal rights under general principles of the common law such as those relating to implied contracts, unfair competition, misrepresentation, and defamation.

c. *Assignability of copyright*

On the theory that copyright is essentially a personal right of the author, there is a tendency in some countries to declare that only the author or his heirs can own the copyright, and that they cannot assign it. Nevertheless, they may give exclusive licenses to use the work, and the practical result is substantially the same as an assignment of the particular right covered by the license.

The assignability of copyrights has always been a fundamental feature of the law in the United States. To make them unassignable would conflict with the whole structure of the law and established practice.

The U.S. law, however, has recognized the principle of limiting assignments for the benefit of authors and their heirs, by providing

---

[1] See "Copyright Law Revision Study No. 4".

for the reversion to them of the right to renew the copyright beyond an initial term of years.

4. COPYRIGHT AS A MONOPOLY

Copyright has sometimes been said to be a monopoly. This is true in the sense that the copyright owner is given exclusive control over the market for his work. And if his control were unlimited, it could become an undue restraint on the dissemination of the work.

On the other hand, any one work will ordinarily be competing in the market with many others. And copyright, by preventing mere duplication, tends to encourage the independent creation of competitive works. The real danger of monopoly might arise when many works of the same kind are pooled and controlled together.

C. THE PURPOSES OF COPYRIGHT

1. CONSTITUTIONAL BASIS OF THE COPYRIGHT LAW

The copyright law of the United States must be founded on the provision of the Constitution (art. I, sec. 8) which empowers Congress—

> * * * To Promote the Progress of Science and useful Arts, by securing for limited Times to Authors and Inventors the exclusive Right to their respective Writings and Discoveries.

As reflected in the Constitution, the ultimate purpose of copyright legislation is to foster the growth of learning and culture for the public welfare, and the grant of exclusive rights to authors for a limited time is a means to that end. A fuller statement of these principles was contained in the legislative report (H. Rept. No. 2222, 60th Cong., 2d sess.) on the Copyright Act of 1909:

> The enactment of copyright legislation by Congress under the terms of the Constitution is not based upon any natural right that the author has in his writings, for the Supreme Court has held that such rights as he has are purely statutory rights, but upon the ground that the welfare of the public will be served and progress of science and useful arts will be promoted by securing to authors for limited periods the exclusive rights to their writings. The Constitution does not establish copyrights, but provides that Congress shall have the power to grant such rights if it thinks best. Not primarily for the benefit of the author, but primarily for the benefit of the public, such rights are given. Not that any particular class of citizens, however worthy, may benefit, but because the policy is believed to be for the benefit of the great body of people, in that it will stimulate writing and invention to give some bonus to authors and inventors.
>
> In enacting a copyright law Congress must consider * * * two questions: First, how much will the legislation stimulate the producer and so benefit the public, and, second, how much will the monopoly granted be detrimental to the public? The granting of such exclusive rights, under the proper terms and conditions, confers a benefit upon the public that outweighs the evils of the temporary monopoly.

2. THE RIGHTS OF AUTHORS AND THE PUBLIC INTEREST

a. *In general*

Although the primary purpose of the copyright law is to foster the creation and dissemination of intellectual works for the public welfare, it also has an important secondary purpose: To give authors the reward due them for their contribution to society.

These two purposes are closely related. Many authors could not devote themselves to creative work without the prospect of remuneration. By giving authors a means of securing the economic reward afforded by the market, copyright stimulates their creation and dissemination of intellectual works. Similarly, copyright protection enables publishers and other distributors to invest their resources in bringing those works to the public.

b. Limitations on author's rights

Within reasonable limits, the interests of authors coincide with those of the public. Both will usually benefit from the widest possible dissemination of the author's works. But it is often cumbersome for would-be users to seek out the copyright owner and get his permission. There are many situations in which copyright restrictions would inhibit dissemination, with little or no benefit to the author. And the interests of authors must yield to the public welfare where they conflict.

Accordingly, the U.S. copyright law has imposed certain limitations and conditions on copyright protection:

• The rights of the copyright owner do not extend to certain uses of the work. (See ch. III of this report.)

• The term of copyright is limited, as required by the Constitution. (See ch. V.)

• A notice of copyright in published works has been required. (See ch. VI.) The large mass of published material for which the authors do not wish copyright is thus left free of restrictions.

• The registration of copyrights and the recordation of transfers of ownership have been required. (See ch. VII and VIII.) The public is thus given the means of determining the status and ownership of copyright claims.

c. The author's reward

While some limitations and conditions on copyright are essential in the public interest, they should not be so burdensome and strict as to deprive authors of their just reward. Authors wishing copyright protection should be able to secure it readily and simply. And their rights should be broad enough to give them a fair share of the revenue to be derived from the market for their works.

D. Summary

Copyright is a legal device to give authors the exclusive right to exploit the market for their works. It has certain features of property rights, personal rights, and monopolies, but it differs from each of these. The legal principles usually applicable to property, personal rights, or monopolies are not always appropriate for copyright.

The primary purpose of copyright is to stimulate the creation and dissemination of intellectual works, thus advancing "the progress of science and useful arts." The grant of exclusive rights to authors is a means of achieving this end, and of compensating authors for their labors and their contributions to society.

Within limits, the author's interests coincide with those of the public. Where they conflict, the public interest must prevail. The ultimate task of the copyright law is to strike a fair balance between the author's right to control the dissemination of his works and the public interest in fostering their widest dissemination.

Chapter II

COPYRIGHTABLE WORKS

Outline of Chapter

CHAPTER II

COPYRIGHTABLE WORKS [1]

A. General Standards of Copyrightability

1. THE BASIC REQUIREMENTS

It is well established, by a long line of court decisions, that in order to be copyrightable under the statute a work must meet the following requirements:

(*a*) The work must be in the form of a "writing," i.e., it must be fixed in some tangible form from which the work can be reproduced.

(*b*) The work must be a product of original creative authorship. Two interrelated elements are involved here: originality and creativity.

(1) The work must be original in the sense that the author produced it by his own intellectual effort, as distinguished from merely copying a preexisting work. It need not be novel (as a patentable invention must be); in theory at least, it could be precisely the same as a preexisting work as long as it was created by the author independently.

(2) The work must represent an appreciable amount of creative authorship.

These basic requisites of copyrightability are not mentioned explicitly in the statute. While they are generally recognized by copyright specialists, the absence of any reference to them in the statute seems to have led to misconceptions as to what is copyrightable matter. We believe it would be desirable for the new statute to mention these basic requisites in general terms.

2. THE COPYRIGHTABILITY OF NEW VERSIONS

Misunderstanding as to what is copyrightable matter has arisen particularly in regard to "new versions" of preexisting works. A new version may be an adaptation of an earlier work (e.g., a translation, a dramatization of a novel, or a new arrangement of music), or an original compilation of preexisting materials, or it may consist of preexisting material with the addition of new material.

The present statute (sec. 7) specifies that new versions "shall be regarded as new works subject to copyright," but that the copyright in the new work as such pertains only to the new elements, and does not affect the copyright or public domain status of the preexisting material. What the present statute fails to make clear is the basic requirement that the new elements must in themselves represent original creative authorship.

---

[1] See "Copyright Law Revision Study No. 3"

9

3. RECOMMENDATIONS

(*a*) The statute should mention the general requirements that any work, in order to be copyrightable, must be fixed in some tangible form and must represent the product of original creative authorship.

(*b*) The statute should make it clear that these requirements apply to new versions of preexisting works.

B. SPECIFICATION OF CLASSES OF COPYRIGHTABLE WORKS

1. DEVELOPMENT AND PROVISIONS OF THE PRESENT LAW

The copyright statutes before 1909 specified the classes of works that were copyrightable. The first copyright statute of 1790 provided protection for "maps, charts, and books." Revisions during the 19th century expanded the classes of copyrightable works to include dramatic works, musical compositions, photographs, and certain works of the fine and graphic arts.

In the present law, which is the act of 1909 with some amendments, a different approach was taken. Section 4 provides:

> The works for which copyright may be secured under this title shall include all the writings of an author.

Section 5 then sets out 13 classes of copyrightable works—books, periodicals, music, and so forth—but provides that these classes are to be used in applying for registration, and "shall not be held to limit the subject matter of copyright as defined in section 4."

2. EFFECT OF THE PRESENT LAW

Since the phrase "all the writings of an author" in section 4 is substantially the same as the constitutional language, it has sometimes been said that the present law purports to cover the entire field of works that could be made copyrightable under the Constitution. And the 13 classes listed in section 5 have been said to be a mere classification for the convenience of the Copyright Office and claimants in making registration. Since section 5 states that the 13 classes "shall not be held to limit the subject matter of copyright as defined in section 4," the scope of copyrightable works under section 4 would appear on its face to be broader than the 13 classes listed in section 5.

Nevertheless, section 4 has not been so broadly construed by the courts. In 1955, for example, the Second Circuit Court of Appeals held that although a sound recording of a singer's performance could be made the subject of copyright under the Constitution, Congress had not chosen to make such a recording copyrightable under the present statute. *Capitol Records Inc.* v. *Mercury Record Corp.*, 221 F. 2d 657 (2d Cir. 1955). Thus, there are certain works which appear to be the "writings" of an "author" within the scope of the Constitution, but which do not come within the scope of the copyright statute.

At the same time, all works that have been held copyrightable under the statute can be fitted into the classes enumerated in section 5. And those classes have been broad enough to include works produced in the new forms developed by technological advances. For example, a microfilm may qualify as a "book," and a television film or video tape as a "motion picture." For all practical purposes, section 5 has operated as a list of the categories of works capable of being copyrighted.

3. PROPOSAL FOR SPECIFICATION IN A NEW LAW

We believe that the all-embracing provision of section 4 is undesirable for two reasons:

(*a*) As already noted, this provision has been construed as not meaning what it appears to say. What kinds of works it might include, beyond those listed in section 5, is uncertain.

(*b*) The possible scope of the constitutional concept of the "writings" of an "author" will expand with the passage of time. This is illustrated by two developments: (1) the steady expansion since 1790 in the statutory specification of the classes of copyrightable works, and (2) the recent emergence of questions as to the protection available to creations such as sound recordings and the ornamental designs of useful articles.

We believe the scope of the statute should be broad enough to include not only those forms in which copyrightable works are now being produced, but also new forms which are invented or come into use later. At the same time, we do not think that the language of the statute should be so broad as to include some things—typography, broadcast emissions, and industrial designs are possible examples— that might conceivably be considered the "writings of an author" but are not intended by Congress to be protected under the copyright law. We believe that the extension of the copyright statute to entirely new areas of subject matter should be left to the determination of Congress rather than to the chance interpretation of an omnibus provision.

Instead of the omnibus provision in section 4, we believe that the statute should specify the categories of copyrightable works. This specification should cover all of the classes now included in section 5 and any others that Congress may wish to add, and should be stated in broad terms to allow coverage of similar works in new forms or media.

Clarification of the scope of some of the categories as now listed in section 5, and the possible addition of other categories, will be considered in part C of this chapter.

4. SEPARATE CLASSIFICATION FOR ADMINISTRATIVE PURPOSES

Apart from the specification of copyrightable works, the Copyright Office, in administering the deposit and registration system, needs to divide the works deposited into class groups. The Office now receives deposits for the registration of over 250,000 works a year, and the various kinds of material deposited require division into groups for efficient processing, examining, cataloging, Library selection, storage, and reference. The criteria for administrative classification are not necessarily the same as those for specifying the categories of copyrightable works.

The present section 5 prescribes a fixed scheme of classification for administrative purposes. The experience of the Copyright Office has shown that this classification scheme is too rigid for the most effective accommodation to changing conditions and procedures. Although the Copyright Office has combined or subdivided some of the pre-

scribed classes over the years, the adaptability of the statutory specification in section 5 has been limited.

A classification scheme intended solely for administrative purposes
should be flexible so as to permit alteration from time to time in the
light of experience and changing needs. We propose that the Register of Copyrights be authorized to provide by regulation for the
scheme of administrative classification.

5. RECOMMENDATIONS

(*a*) The provision of section 4, making "all the writings of an
author" copyrightable, should be eliminated.

(*b*) Section 5, which now lists the classes of works for purposes of
registration, should be reformulated as a specification of the categories of works copyrightable under the statute. The categories should
be stated in broad terms to cover all the classes of works now included
under section 5 and any others that Congress may wish to add, and
to allow coverage of these general categories in any new forms or
media that may be developed.

(*c*) The clasisfication of works for purposes of administering the
deposit and registration system should be left to administrative regulation by the Register of Copyrights with approval of the Librarian
of Congress.

C. COPYRIGHTABILITY OF CERTAIN WORKS

1. WORKS OF "APPLIED ART"

a. Recent developments

In recent years an important problem has arisen as to whether ornamental designs of useful articles (also referred to as "applied art" or
"industrial designs") come within the category of copyrightable
"works of art." In *Mazer* v. *Stein* (347 U.S. 201 (1954)), the Supreme Court held that, where a statuette had been copyrighted as a
"work of art," its copyright protection was not lost or diminished because it was intended to be used, and was used, as a lamp base; an unauthorized maker of lamps, the bases of which were copies of the
statuette, was held an infringer of the copyright. Since the *Mazer*
decision the courts have sustained copyright claims in "works of art"
embodied in costume jewelry, textile fabrics, toys, and dinnerware.

In the light of the *Mazer* case, the Copyright Office has registered a
rapidly increasing number of claims in "works of art" that are embodied in useful articles, including fabrics, jewelry, lace, dishes, glassware, silverware, lamps, clocks, ashtrays, and the like. But there have
also been a number of copyright claims in designs of useful articles
that the Copyright Office has refused to register on the ground that
they were not "works of art." The denial of registration for some
of these claims has been challenged, and it can be expected that copyright claims in the design area will continue to grow.

The borderline between copyright protection for "works of art"
and separate protection for the ornamental designs of useful articles
has been the subject of much discussion in connection with a recent
series of bills for the sui generis protection of designs. The most
recent bills in this series, which were introduced in May 1961, include
an amendment to the present copyright statute reaffirming and im-

plementing the principle of the *Mazer* decision, and also defining its application. For the reasons explained below, we are in accord with the revisions in the copyright statute proposed in these bills.

b. The need for sui generis protection of designs of useful articles as such

We believe that, as the Supreme Court held in the *Mazer* case, the protection now accorded by the copyright statute should continue to be available for "works of art"—that is, pictorial, graphic, and sculptural works—even after they have been employed as a design or decoration of a useful article. But we would not extend the copyright statute to designs of useful articles as such—automobiles, sewing machines, wearing apparel, etc. We would favor granting reasonable protection against the copying of these designs under a sui generis statute, but we do not believe they should be given protection of the length and breadth afforded by the copyright statute.

In the years since the *Mazer* decision, full protection under the copyright law has not proved inappropriate for "works of art" used as a design or decoration of useful articles. We do not believe, however, that it would be appropriate to extend the copyright law to industrial designs as such. In this area there is a delicate balance between the need for protection on the part of those who originate and invest in a design, and the possible effect of protection, if overextended, in restraining competition. The term of copyright (which is now up to 56 years and would be even longer under the proposal made in ch. V of this report) is too long for ordinary design protection. And there are other fundamentals of the copyright statute—the provisions on notice, deposit, registration, publication, and liability of innocent distributors of infringing articles, for example—that are not suitable for the entire range of industrial designs.

As noted above, special bills for the protection of "ornamental designs of useful articles"—S. 1884, H.R. 6776, H.R. 6777, 87th Congress, 1st session—were introduced in Congress in May 1961. These bills, which are identical, provide for a short term of protection and differ in other significant respects from the copyright statute. However, they specifically preserve the full copyright protection now available to "works of art" under the *Mazer* decision. They are the outgrowth of similar bills introduced in the 86th Congress (S. 2075, S. 2852, H.R. 9525, H.R. 9870), and result from a reconciliation of the differences between those earlier bills.

c. Relationship between copyright and the designs of useful articles

The principal administrative problem now faced by the Copyright Office in this field derives from the deposit of useful articles for copyright registration, and the difficulties in determining whether or not they embody or constitute copyrightable "works of art.". As a practical matter this problem might be partially solved by the enactment of a sui generis design protection statute, which many applicants would invoke in preference to the copyright law. However, in order to achieve a fully effective solution to this problem, we propose that registration under the copyright statute should be confined to pictorial, graphic, or sculptural works, and that useful articles should not be acceptable for deposit. This would not, of course, preclude registration for drawings, models, photographs, or the like that portray useful articles, or that are obviously going to be used in the manufacture of useful articles.

There remains the question of protection to be given to a copyrighted work of art that is utilized as a design in the manufacture of useful articles. We believe that, where the copyrighted work is used as a design or decoration of a useful article, it should continue, as under the present law, to be protected by copyright if the owner wishes. In this situation the copyright owner should be given the option of securing protection under the design patent law or under special design legislation; but, if he does not do so, his copyright protection should remain unaffected. However, where the "work of art" actually portrays the useful article as such—as in a drawing, scale model, advertising sketch, or photograph of the article—existing court decisions indicate that copyright in the "work of art" does not protect against manufacture of the useful article portrayed. We agree with these decisions and the distinctions made in them.

Some examples will illustrate these points.

(1) The following would be accepted for deposit and registration by the Copyright Office, since they would not be considered "useful articles":

- A painting showing a floral pattern, submitted by a manufacturer of textile fabrics; a statuette in the form of a human figure, submitted by a lamp manufacturer;
- A technical drawing or scale model of an airplane;
- A jewelry design embodied in earrings.

(2) The following would not be accepted for deposit and registration by the Copyright Office, since they constitute useful articles as such:

- A rug; a yard of dress material;
- A lamp;
- A chair; a dress; a frying pan.

(3) Since the protection available to a copyrighted pictorial, graphic, or sculptural work is not affected by use of the work as a design or decoration of a useful article, the following works would continue to be accorded full protection under the copyright statute (unless the owner chooses to secure protection under the patent law or special design legislation):

- A copyrighted painting reproduced on textile fabrics;
- A copyrighted cartoon drawing or photograph reproduced on fabrics or in the form of toys or dolls;
- A copyrighted drawing of a chair reproduced on a lampshade;
- A copyrighted sculptured figure used as a lamp base.

(4) Under distinctions indicated in existing court decisions, that the copyright in a work portraying a useful article as such would not protect against manufacture of that article, copyright protection would not extend to the following cases:

- A copyrighted drawing of a chair, used to manufacture chairs of that design;
- A copyrighted scale model of an automobile, used to manufacture automobiles of that design;
- A copyrighted technical drawing showing the construction of a machine, used to manufacture the machine;
- A copyrighted picture of a dress, used to manufacture the dress.

d. Recommendations

(1) The copyright statute should make it clear that, for purposes of registration, the "works of art" category includes pictorial, graphic, and sculptural works even though they may portray or be intended for use in useful articles, but that useful articles, as such, are not acceptable for deposit.

(2) When a copyrighted work of art is used as a design or decoration of a useful article, it should continue to have all the protection afforded by the copyright law. If the work is registered as a design under the patent law or special design legislation, copyright protection should terminate insofar as it relates to useful articles, but if patent or design registration is not made, copyright protection should continue unaffected.

(3) The statute should not alter the distinctions drawn in this area by existing court decisions—that copyright in a pictorial, graphic, or sculptural work, portraying a useful article as such, does not extend to the manufacture of the useful article itself.

2. ARCHITECTURAL DRAWINGS AND STRUCTURES [2]

a. The present law

Architectural drawings are copyrightable under the present law within the general category of technical drawings. The copyright in an architectural drawing protects it against the unauthorized making and distribution of copies of the drawing.

When an architectural structure, such as a monument, is itself a "work of art," copyrighted drawings of the structure are protected against their "execution" by erecting the structure. This is merely an application of the provision in section 1(b) protecting "a model or design for a work of art" against its "execution." But the courts have held that the drawings of a functional structure, which is not a "work of art," are not protected against their use in building the structure.

Architectural structures themselves are not mentioned in the present statute. If a structure constitutes a "work of art" (e.g., a piece of sculpture or an artistic monument), the structure itself may now be copyrighted under the general category of "works of art." But copyright protection has been denied to functional structures that do not qualify as "works of art."

b. Protection for the artistic features of functional structures

It seems clear that a structure designed solely for esthetic effect should be entitled to copyright protection on the same basis as any other nonutilitarian work of art. It seems equally clear, at the other extreme, that a functional structure having no artistic features is not an appropriate subject for copyright protection, even though it embodies original ideas as to technical methods of construction. The more difficult question is whether copyright protection should extend to structures that are functional in purpose but also display nonfunctional features of "artistic" design.

We believe that what we have said above in regard to the ornamental design of useful articles applies also to the "artistic" design of

---

[2] See "Copyright Law Revision Study No. 27"

functional architectural structures. In the case of architecture particularly, it would often be difficult to differentiate between the functional and the "artistic" features of a design. While we are inclined to the view that a limited measure of protection should be afforded to the designs of functional structures, we do not believe that the copyright statute provides the appropriate framework for their protection. We would leave this protection to be dealt with in the separate legislation proposed for the protection of ornamental designs of useful articles.

It should be understood, of course, that a nonutilitarian work of art, such as a piece of sculpture or a mural, which is superimposed upon a functional structure but retains its separate identity, remains copyrightable as a work of art apart from the structure.

c. Recommendations

(1) The copyright law should continue to protect—
(*a*) Architectural drawings, against the unauthorized making and distribution of copies;
(*b*) Nonfunctional architectural structures that constitute works of art, on the same basis as sculptural works of art;
(*c*) Drawings for such a nonfunctional structure, on the same basis as drawings for a sculptural work of art.

(2) The copyright law should not be extended to the design of functional architectural structures. Protection for these designs on a more limited basis should be considered in separate legislation for the protection of ornamental designs of useful articles.

3. CHOREOGRAPHIC WORKS [3]

a. Choreographic works as proper subject of copyright

Choreographic works, such as ballets, represent a recognized art form, and undoubtedly constitute works of authorship. Until fairly recent times it was difficult to secure copyright protection for choreographic works because of the absence of practical means of fixing them in a tangible form. Fixation is now feasible in the form of systems of notation recently developed or in the form of motion pictures.

For purposes of copyright at least, the term "choreographic works" is understood to mean dance works created for presentation to an audience, thus excluding ballroom and other social dance steps designed merely for the personal enjoyment of the dancers. This distinction is important because the copyright protection of choreographic works is concerned mainly with their public performance.

b. Coverage under the present law

Although not mentioned by name in the present copyright statute, choreographic works have been regarded as copyrightable if they qualify as "dramatic compositions." There are some old court decisions indicating that a dance which presents a story or definite theme qualifies as a "dramatic" work.

The treatment of choreographic works as a species of "dramatic compositions" for copyright purposes has had two virtues: (1) It has served to define the choreographic works protected as being dance works created for presentation to an audience; and (2) it has placed

---

[3] See "Copyright Law Revision Study No. 28"

choreographic works in an existing category in which the rights of the copyright owner are established.

c. *Choreographic works as distinct from dramatic works*

Treating choreographic works as a species of "dramatic compositions," however, has one serious shortcoming. Many choreographic works present "abstract" dance movements in which, aside from their esthetic appeal, no story or specific theme is readily apparent. Whether such "abstract" dances qualify as "dramatic compositions" is uncertain. We see no reason why an "abstract" dance, as an original creation of a choreographer's authorship, should not be protected as fully as a traditional ballet presenting a story or theme.

In view of the doubt as to whether "abstract" dances would come within the category of "dramatic compositions," we believe that choreographic works should be designated as a separate category. The statute should make it clear that this category covers only dances prepared for presentation to an audience. We believe that the rights of the copyright owner in dramatic works are appropriate for choreographic works.

d. *Recommendations*

(1) Choreographic works prepared for presentation to an audience should be mentioned specifically in the statute as a category of copyrightable works.

(2) They should be given the same protection as is accorded to dramatic compositions.

4. SOUND RECORDINGS [4]

a. *Recent developments*

During the past several years there has been considerable discussion here and abroad of proposals to provide some protection for performing artists and for record producers in their sound recordings. It has been proposed that performers or record producers, or both, be given the right to prevent the unauthorized reproduction of their sound recordings. It has also been suggested that their rights might extend to the collection of royalties for the use of their recordings in broadcasts and other public performances. These proposals have been the subject of a series of international meetings to consider the development of a convention for the international protection of "neighboring rights." A diplomatic conference to develop the final text of a convention is to be held in Rome in October 1961.

b. *The present legal situation*

It is important to an understanding of the problems involved here to distinguish between: (1) the literary or musical composition of an author embodied in a recording, (2) the recorded rendition of the performer, and (3) the recording as a work in itself. All three of these elements are present in most recordings, but only the author's composition is given statutory copyright protection in the United States. The laws of some foreign countries have provisions for the protection of the performer in his recorded rendition, or for the protection of the record producer in the sound recording as a work in

---

[4] See "Copyright Law Revision Study No. 26"

itself. These provisions in the foreign laws usually appear as adjuncts to the copyright statute, but they frequently differ—as to the scope and duration of protection and in other respects—from the provisions governing copyright works in general.

Recent disclosures indicate that the unauthorized reproduction of sound recordings has reached serious proportions. While there are no statutory provisions in the United States protecting performers or record producers against the unauthorized reproduction of their sound recordings, several recent court decisions have accorded protection under common law doctrines of literary property rights and unfair competition. The lack of any statutory specification of the rights of performers and record producers may be leading to establishment of common law rights that are unlimited in scope and duration.

A bill aimed at combating the counterfeiting of records—H.R. 6354, 87th Congress, 1st session—was introduced on April 17, 1961. It would impose criminal penalties on anyone who, knowingly and with fraudulent intent, transports or receives in interstate or foreign commerce a reproduction of a sound recording made without permission of the "owner of the master recording."

c. Exploration of statutory solution

All of this suggests that the present legal situation with respect to the unauthorized reproduction of sound recordings is unsatisfactory, and that Federal statutory protection should be accorded within appropriate limits. Although we believe that the principles of the copyright law offer the most appropriate basis for this protection, there are many complex issues that have not yet crystallized sufficiently for us to make detailed recommendations at this time. Among the unresolved questions are: (1) whether rights should be given to the performer or to the record producer or both; (2) whether formalities such as the copyright notice, deposit, and registration should be applied to sound recordings; and (3) the scope and duration of protection to be accorded.

We hope that continuing study will develop proposals for the solution of these problems in the not too distant future.

d. Recommendation

Sound recordings should be protected against unauthorized duplication under copyright principles, but detailed recommendations are being deferred pending further study.

Chapter III

RIGHTS OF COPYRIGHT OWNERS

OUTLINE OF CHAPTER

19

CHAPTER III

RIGHTS OF COPYRIGHT OWNERS

A. Rights Specified in the Present Law

1. Development of Present Rights

Copyright was originally concerned with printed matter, chiefly in the form of books. It meant the exclusive right of the copyright owner to make and publish copies. In the course of time, the concept of copyright expanded in two directions: (1) to cover other works of authorship such as dramatic, musical, and art works; and (2) to grant exclusive rights to the copyright owner to disseminate the work by other means such as public performance and the making and distribution of sound recordings. Copyright is now a bundle of several rights pertaining to the various means of reproducing and disseminating works of authorship.

2. Summary of Present Rights

The exclusive rights of a copyright owner now specified in section 1 of the copyright law may be summarized as follows:

(a) All categories of copyrighted works are protected against the making and publication of copies.

(b) Literary, dramatic, and musical works are protected against the making of new versions; models or designs for works of art are protected against the execution of the work of art.

(c) Nondramatic literary and musical works are protected against public delivery or public performance "for profit" (except for performances of music on coin-operated machines); dramatic works are protected against public performance, whether or not for profit.

(d) Literary, dramatic, and musical works are protected against reproduction in any transcription or record (subject, in the case of music, to the compulsory license for the making of sound recordings).

3. Analysis of Present Rights

a. The right to make and publish copies

Section 1(a) of the present law provides for the exclusive right of the copyright owner "to print, reprint, publish, copy, and vend the copyrighted work." These various terms are redundant. Printing and reprinting are modes of copying, and vending is a mode of publishing. As to vending, it is well settled that when publication has been authorized, the right to vend pertains only to the initial sale of a copy; the purchaser of the copy is then free to resell or otherwise dispose of it. On the other hand, when publication is not authorized, any vending of a copy is an infringement of the right to publish. In substance,

21

as several courts have observed, the right embraced in the repetitive terms of section 1(a) is the twofold right to make and to publish copies.

This right is the historic basis of copyright and pertains to all categories of copyrighted works. The "copying" embraced in this right is a broad concept. "Copying" is not confined to complete and literal reproduction. While anyone is free to use the ideas disclosed in a work, and to use the same source material in creating another work, the reproduction of the essential substance of an author's expression constitutes "copying," even though his work is altered in the reproduction or is reproduced in a different medium or form.

In *White-Smith Music Publishing Co.* v. *Apollo Co.* (209 U.S. 1 (1908)), the Supreme Court held that "copying" implied a visual reproduction from which the work could be read; the making of a mechanical sound recording was held not to constitute "copying." By the same token, a public performance would not appear to be "copying" in this sense. The present statute provides separately for the rights to make sound recordings and to give public performances.

b. *The right to make new versions*

Section 1(b) of the present law provides for the exclusive right of the copyright owner to make new versions (translations, adaptations, etc.) of the copyrighted work. The making of a new version would appear to be a form of "copying," and there are court decisions so indicating. Nevertheless, provisions expressly granting the right to make translations and dramatizations, and to execute models or designs for works of art, have been incorporated in our copyright statutes since 1870; the remaining rights specified in section 1(b)—to make any other versions of a literary work, to convert a drama into a novel or other nondramatic work, and to arrange or adapt a musical work— were added in 1909.

Although section 1(b) probably covers the most common forms of new versions, there are other types of works and forms of new versions not specifically mentioned. For example, a painting may be remade as a sculpture or vice versa, a photograph may be reproduced as a painting, or a motion picture may be converted into a stage play.

Perhaps section 1(b) is unnecessary, since the courts might well hold that any new version is a "copy" of the original work under section 1(a). However, section 1(b) has been relied on as the basis for some court decisions; and to avoid any doubt, we would retain a specific reference in the statute to the right to make new versions. We suggest, though, that the present language of section 1(b) be both simplified and broadened to refer to all classes of works and all forms of new versions.

c. *The right of public performance*

This right is now provided for in three separate subsections of section 1:

- Subsection (c) specifies the right "to deliver, authorize the delivery of, read, or present the copyrighted work in public for profit if it be a lecture, sermon, address or similar production, or other nondramatic literary work."
- Subsection (d) specifies the right "to perform or represent the copyrighted work publicly if it be a drama."

- Subsection (e) specifies the right "to perform the copyrighted work publicly for profit if it be a musical composition." This right is subject to a special exemption for performances on coin-operated machines, to be discussed later.

Note that for nondramatic literary and musical works the right is limited to public performance "for profit"; while for dramas (which include dramatico-musical works) the right extends to any public performance whether or not for profit. This distinction will be discussed below.

It is now well established by a long line of court decisions that radio and television broadcasting is a form of public performance.

It seems odd that motion pictures are not designated among the categories of works to which performance rights are accorded, especially since performance (i.e., exhibition) is almost the only practical means of disseminating motion pictures. We shall discuss this in a later section.

d. The right to make records

This right is now provided for in the same three subsections as the public prformance right:

- Subsection (c) specifies, for a nondramatic literary work, the right "to make or procure the making of any transcription or record thereof by or from which, in whole or in part, it may in any manner or by any method be exhibited, delivered, presented, produced, or reproduced."
- Subsection (d) specifies substantially the same right for a dramatic work.
- Subsection (e) provides, for a musical work, the right "to make any arrangement or setting of it or of the melody of it in any system of notation or any form of record in which the thought of an author may be recorded and from which it may be read or reproduced."

The principal effect of these provisions is to give copyright owners the exclusive right to made sound recordings—the right which the Supreme Court in the *White-Smith* case had held was not embraced in the right to make copies. In addition to sound recordings, these subsections cover the making of any form of visual record, such as a stenographic transcription or a motion picture of a performance. They also provide that the performance right extends to performances given by means of records.

The three subsections dealing with the recording right seem unnecessarily repetitious and confusing. We suggest that this right be restated more simply and clearly—as the right to make any form of transcription or record, visual or aural, from which the work can be performed or reproduced.

Section 1(e) also contains the long and complex "compulsory license" provisions, which we shall discuss later. In sum, these provide that when the copyright owner of a musical work has once permitted the making of a mechanical sound recording of the music, any other person may make such a recording upon giving notice and paying a specified royalty.

4. RECOMMENDATIONS

(*a*) Subject to certain limitations and exceptions to be discussed below, the statute should continue to accord to copyright owners the exclusive rights to exploit their works by (1) making and publishing copies, (2) making new versions, (3) giving public performances, and (4) making records of the work.

(*b*) The present provisions of section 1 granting these rights should be redrafted in simpler and clearer language.

B. SPECIAL RIGHTS, LIMITATIONS, AND EXCEPTIONS

1. FAIR USE IN GENERAL [1]

a. What is "fair use"?

Nothing is said in the statute as to the "fair use" of copyrighted works. The doctrine of "fair use," however, has been developed by the courts over a period of many years and is now firmly established as an implied limitation on the exclusive rights of copyright owners.

Copyright does not preclude anyone from using the ideas or information disclosed in a copyrighted work. Beyond that, the work itself is subject to "fair use." That term eludes precise definition; broadly speaking, it means that a reasonable portion of a copyrighted work may be reproduced without permission when necessary for a legitimate purpose which is not competitive with the copyright owner's market for his work.

The general scope of fair use can be indicated by the following examples of the kinds of uses that may be permitted under that concept:

- Quotation of excerpts in a review or criticism for purposes of illustration or comment.
- Quotation of short passages in a scholarly or technical work, for illustration or clarification of the author's observations.
- Use in a parody of some of the content of the work parodied.
- Summary of an address or article, with brief quotations, in a news report.
- Reproduction by a library of a portion of a work to replace part of a damaged copy.
- Reproduction by a teacher or student of a small part of a work to illustrate a lesson.
- Reproduction of a work in legislative or judicial proceedings or reports.
- Incidental and fortuitous reproduction, in a newsreel or broadcast, of a work located at the scene of an event being reported.

Whether any particular use of a copyrighted work constitutes a fair use rather than an infringement of copyright has been said to depend upon (1) the purpose of the use, (2) the nature of the copyrighted work, (3) the amount and substantiality of the material used in relation to the copyrighted work as a whole, and (4) the effect of the use on the copyright owner's potential market for his work. These criteria are interrelated and their relative significance may vary, but

---

[1] See "Copyright Law Revision Study No. 14"

the fourth one—the competitive character of the use—is often the most decisive.

b. Statutory recognition of fair use

Since the fair use doctrine may be applied in any number and variety of circumstances, it would be difficult to prescribe precise rules suitable for all situations. For example, the amount of a work that may be properly used under that doctrine will vary according to the nature of the work, the essential character of the portion used, and the purpose and competitive effect of the use.

Nevertheless, the doctrine of fair use is such an important limitation on the rights of copyright owners, and occasions to apply that doctrine arise so frequently, that we believe the statute should mention it and indicate its general scope. It seems anomalous to have the statute specify the rights of copyright owners in absolute terms without indicating that those rights are subject to the limitation of fair use.

c. Recommendation

The statute should include a provision affirming and indicating the scope of the principle that fair use does not infringe the copyright owner's rights.

2. PHOTOCOPYING BY LIBRARIES [2]

a. Statement of the problem

The application of the principle of fair use to the making of a photocopy by a library for the use of a person engaged in research is an important question which merits special consideration. This question has not been decided by the courts, and it is uncertain how far a library may go in supplying a photocopy of copyrighted material in its collections. Many libraries and researchers feel that this uncertainty has hampered research and should be resolved to permit the making of photocopies for research purposes to the fullest extent compatible with the interests of copyright owners.

Scholars have always felt free to copy by hand from the works of others for their own private research and study. Aside from the impossibility of controlling copying done in private, the acceptance of this practice may have been based on the inherent limitation of the extent to which copying could be done by hand. But copying has now taken on new dimensions with the development of photocopying devices by which any quantity of material can be reproduced readily and in multiple copies.

Researchers need to have available, for reference and study, the growing mass of published material in their particular fields. This is true especially, though not solely, of material published in scientific, technical, and scholarly journals. Researchers must rely on libraries for much of this material. When a published copy in a library's collections is not available for loan, which is very often the case, the researcher's need can be met by a photocopy.

On the other hand, the supplying of photocopies of any work to a substantial number of researchers may diminish the copyright owner's market for the work. Publishers of scientific, technical, and scholarly

---

[2] See "Copyright Law Revision Study No. 15"

works have pointed out that their market is small; and they have expressed the fear that if many of their potential subscribers or purchasers were furnished with photocopies, they might be forced to discontinue publication.

b. Approach to a solution: single photocopies for research use

As a general premise, we believe that photocopying should not be permitted where it would compete with the publisher's market. Thus, when a researcher wants the whole of a publication, and a publisher's copy is available, he should be expected to procure such a copy.

In situations where it would not be likely to compete with the publisher's market, however, we believe that a library should be permitted to supply a single photocopy of material in its collections for use in research. Thus, when a researcher wants only a relatively small part of a publication, or when the work is out of print, supplying him with a single photocopy would not seriously prejudice the interests of the copyright owner. A number of foreign laws permit libraries to supply single photocopies in these circumstances.

c. Multiple and commercial photocopying

The question of making photocopies has also arisen in the situation where an industrial concern wishes to provide multiple copies of publications, particularly of scientific and technical journals, to a number of research workers on its staff. To permit multiple photocopying may make serious inroads on the publisher's potential market. We believe that an industrial concern should be expected to buy the number of copies it needs from the publisher, or to get the publisher's consent to its making of photocopies.

Similarly, any person or organization undertaking to supply photocopies to others as a commercial venture would be competing directly with the publisher, and should be expected to get the publisher's consent.

There has been some discussion of the possibility of a contractual arrangement whereby industrial concerns would be given blanket permission to make photocopies for which they would pay royalties to the publishers. Such an arrangement, which has been made in at least one foreign country, would seem to offer the best solution for the problem of multiple and commercial photocopying.

d. Recommendations

The statute should permit a library, whose collections are available to the public without charge, to supply a single photocopy of copyrighted material in its collections to any applicant under the following conditions:

(a) A single photocopy of one article in any issue of a periodical, or of a reasonable part of any other publication, may be supplied when the applicant states in writing that he needs and will use such material solely for his own research.

(b) A single photocopy of an entire publication may be supplied when the applicant also states in writing, and the library is not otherwise informed, that a copy is not available from the publisher.

(c) Where the work bears a copyright notice, the library should be required to affix to the photocopy a warning that the material appears to be copyrighted.

3. LIMITATIONS ON THE PERFORMANCE RIGHT [8]

a. Nondramatic literary and musical works

(1) *The "for profit" limitation.*—In the case of nondramatic literary and musical works the present law limits the copyright owner's performance right to public performances "for profit." The phrase "for profit" has been construed in a number of court decisions, and now has a fairly well-defined meaning.

A public performance may be "for profit," even though no admission fee is charged, if it is given in furtherance of a commercial enterprise. Thus, the playing of music in a hotel or restaurant has been held "for profit" since its purpose is to attract patronage. The same has been held for broadcasts of music by stations that carry commercial advertising, even if the particular program was noncommercial, or if the station itself was a nonprofit enterprise.

On the other hand a public performance given by a charitable, educational, or similar organization, with no motive of private gain, has been regarded as not "for profit," even though the performance was part of a fund-raising event.

(2) *Alternatives to the "for profit" limitation.*—Some of the revision bills of 1924–40 proposed to specify, in addition to or instead of the general "for profit" limitation, particular situations in which a public performance could be given without permission of the copyright owner. Most foreign laws do not contain an express "for profit" limitation on the public performance right, but specify in considerable detail the situations in which a public performance is freely permissible (e.g., for charitable, educational, religious, or civic purposes where no one derives financial gain). These specifications have substantially the same effect as the "for profit" limitation in our present law.

We believe that the principle of the "for profit" limitation on the right of public performance in nondramatic literary and musical works, and the application given to that principle by the courts, strike a sound balance between the interests of copyright owners and those of the public. There will undoubtedly be some specific instances in which the application of that general principle is uncertain until ruled on by the courts. We believe, however, that any attempt to specify the various situations in which the principle applies would be likely to include too much or too little, and to raise new uncertainties.

Incidentally, section 104 of the present statute contains a proviso to the effect that certain musical works may be performed freely by public schools, church choirs, or vocal societies, "provided the performance is given for charitable or educational purposes and not for profit." Since all nonprofit performances of music are exempt under the general provision of the law, this proviso (a vestige of an earlier draft of the bill that became the act of 1909) is entirely superfluous.

b. Dramatic works

In the case of dramatic works (including dramatico-musical works), the copyright owner's performance right extends to all public performances, whether for profit or not. This has been true since the

---

[8] See "Copyright Law Revision Study No. 16"

right of public performance was first accorded to dramatic works in 1856.

The reasons given for this difference in treatment between dramatic and nondramatic works are:

- The audience at a nonprofit performance of a dramatic work is less likely to pay to attend another performance than is the case with nondramatic works.
- Public performance is usually the main source of revenue from a dramatic work; in the case of nondramatic works, revenue is also available from the sale of copies and sound recordings.
- Dramatic works are not as readily or as frequently performed for charitable, educational, and similar purposes as are nondramatic works.

We believe these reasons warrant continuing the public performance right in dramatic works with no "for profit" limitation.

c. Recommendations

(1) For nondramatic literary and musical works, the right of public performance should continue to be limited to such performances "for profit."

(2) For dramatic works, the right of public performance should continue to apply to all such performances, whether for profit or not. (As recommended in ch. II, C 3, this would be extended to choreographic works.)

4. EXTENSION OF THE PERFORMANCE RIGHT TO MOTION PICTURES [4]

a. The present law

The present statute does not provide explicitly for the right to perform (i.e., to exhibit) a copyrighted motion picture. Motion pictures were not mentioned in the act of 1909. By an amendment in 1912, they were added to the classes of works enumerated in section 5, but no corresponding amendment was made in section 1 to provide for the right to perform motion pictures.

The courts have attempted to fill this gap by applying the terms of section 1 to the performance of motion pictures. In several decisions the courts have held that dramatic motion pictures (photoplays) are a species of dramatic works and are therefore accorded the right of public performance given to dramatic works by section 1(d). The more difficult problem of nondramatic motion pictures was presented to the Second Circuit Court of Appeals in *Patterson* v. *Century Productions* (93 F. 2d 489 (1937)), in which an infringing copy of a documentary (nondramatic) motion picture had been made and exhibited publicly in a theater. The court held that the exhibitor had infringed the copyright, on the ground that the projection of the motion picture on the theater's screen constituted the making of a "copy" under section 1(a).

We believe this last decision is an example of the maxim that "hard cases make bad law." In reaching what was no doubt a just result, and apparently seeing no other provision in the statute that would fit the case, the court stretched the concept of "copying" to new lengths. While that case involved a public exhibition, the theory of

---

[4] See "Copyright Law Revision Study No. 16"

"copying" on which the decision was based, if followed to its logical conclusion, would have a far-reaching effect: any unauthorized projection of a motion picture, private as well as public, would be an infringement of the copyright. Whether the courts would so hold in a case involving a private projection is still a matter of conjecture.

b. *Public performances*

We believe that the statute should provide explicitly for the performance right in motion pictures. We see no reason to distinguish between dramatic and nondramatic motion pictures in this regard. They are alike in physical form and in the manner of their performance.

It has been suggested that the performance right in motion pictures should not extend to nonprofit exhibitions given solely for educational purposes. However, the reasons given above for omitting the "for profit" limitation as to public performances of dramatic works apply equally to public exhibitions of motion pictures. We would extend to all motion pictures the same right of public performance, with no "for profit" limitation, as is now accorded to dramatic works.

c. *Performances in "semipublic" places*

The producers and distributors of motion pictures have been concerned about unauthorized performances in what might be called "semipublic" places—such as social clubs, lodges, camps, schools, and factories—where the audience may be large but is limited to a special group. Since the general public is not invited to attend, it might be argued that these are not "public" performances.

This question has not been resolved by the courts. In one case— *Metro-Goldwyn-Mayer Distributing Corporation* v. *Wyatt and Maryland Yacht Club* (21 C.O. Bull. 203 (D. Md. 1932))—a Federal district court held (erroneously, we believe) that the performance of a motion picture at a social club for its members and their guests was not a public performance. The courts in Great Britain and several other countries have held that musical performances given in such places are public performances.

We are sympathetic with the view that performances—not only of motion pictures but also of other works—given at places such as clubs, lodges, and camps, should ordinarily be considered public performances. We have given some thought to defining "public performance" in the statute, but we believe it would be virtually impossible to formulate a definition that would draw an appropriate line between public and private performances. We would prefer to rely upon the courts to reach the proper result in particular situations.

d. *Private performances*

Motion picture producers and distributors have urged that the performance right in motion pictures should extend to what are clearly private performances, including performances given in private homes. They point to *Patterson* v. *Century Productions*, and its concept that exhibition is a form of "copying," to support their position. Motion picture films are commonly leased for exhibition at specified places and dates. Most leases are for commercial exhibitions, but many films are also leased for home use. It is argued that in either case private exhibitions beyond the terms of the lease should constitute an infringement of copyright.

This argument may have some theoretical plausibility, but we would question it for several reasons:

- Injury to a copyright owner from private performances beyond the terms of a lease would be minimal. He may be entitled to the usual license fee as damages for a breach of contract, but the statutory damages for copyright infringement would be grossly excessive.[5]
- As a practical matter, unauthorized private performances could rarely be discovered or controlled.
- Many motion picture films are sold for use in homes, schools, libraries, and the like. The purchaser should not be subjected to the risk of liability for private performances that the copyright owner might contend are not authorized.
- New technical devices will probably make it practical in the future to reproduce televised motion pictures in the home. We do not believe the private use of such a reproduction can or should be precluded by copyright.
- Libraries, museums, and other collectors of motion pictures should be free to have private showings for purposes of research or scholarship.

e. Recommendation

The statute should provide explicitly that the copyright owner of any motion picture shall have the exclusive right to perform (or exhibit) it in public, with no "for profit" limitation.

5. PUBLIC RECEPTION OF BROADCASTS

a. The problem presented

There is now no doubt, under a line of court decisions, that a radio or television broadcast of a copyrighted work is a public performance. The courts have had more difficulty with the further question of whether the reception of a broadcast by means of a receiving set in a public place, such as a hotel or restaurant, is a separate public performance for which the copyright owner may require a license. After some lower court decisions to the contrary, the Supreme Court, in *Buck* v. *Jewell-La Salle Realty Co.* (283 U.S. 191 (1931)), answered this question affirmatively, holding that the unlicensed reception in a hotel of a broadcast of copyrighted music, which the hotel retransmitted to its various rooms, constituted an infringement of the copyright.

Although the *Jewell-La Salle* case involved a retransmission, the effect of this decision may be that any business establishment that operates a radio or television receiving set for the entertainment of its patrons—including hotels, restaurants, taverns, barber shops, etc.—could be required to procure performing licenses for all copyrighted works in the broadcasts it receives.

As a practical matter this problem has been confined so far to broadcasts of music, though it could conceivably arise also as to broadcasts of dramatic and literary works and even of motion pictures. We understand that the two principal organizations controlling the performing rights in music (ASCAP and BMI) have generally followed

---

[5] Statutory damages are discussed below in ch. IX, pt. B 2.

the policy of confining their demands for license fees to those establishments, such as the hotel in the *Jewell-La Salle* case, that retransmit broadcasts to their various rooms. Other similar organizations, however, may not have the same policy. And there have been complaints from some small establishments that they were asked to obtain performing licenses for the mere operation of receiving sets. In any event, the free use of receiving sets should not be left to the grace or forbearance of the performing rights organizations or other copyright owners.

In several of the previous revision bills of 1924-40, it was proposed to exempt the reception of broadcasts from the public performance right, except where a charge is made for such reception. Hotel operators, in particular, have sought such an exemption.

b. *The principle of "clearance at the source"*

It is now established practice, reinforced by consent decrees against ASCAP and BMI, that the use of copyrighted music in network broadcasts is "cleared at the source," i.e., the license to perform the music is obtained by the network broadcaster and no further license is required of local stations for their retransmission of the broadcast. The same principle of "clearance at the source" is applied to the performance of music in the public exhibition of motion pictures: the producer obtains a license and no further license is required of the exhibitors. Likewise the license obtained by the operator of a wired music service covers its public performance in the hotels, restaurants, and other places where the music is heard.

We believe this principle of clearance at the source should apply to the reception of broadcasts. The performing license obtained by the broadcaster should suffice, with no further license required of those who merely receive the broadcast. We would, however, require the receiver to obtain a performing license if he makes a charge to the public for the reception of the broadcast—for example, by charging an admission fee, or by requiring a payment for operation of the receiving set.

c. *Recommendation*

The statute should exempt the mere reception of broadcasts from the public performance right, except where the receiver makes a charge to the public for such reception.

6. THE JUKEBOX EXEMPTION

a. *The present status of the problem*

Section 1(e) of the present law provides:

> The reproduction or rendition of a musical composition by or upon coin-operated machines shall not be deemed a public performance for profit unless a fee is charged for admission to the place where such reproduction or rendition occurs.

This exempts the operators of "jukeboxes" from any obligation to pay royalties for the public performance of music, though their operation is clearly for profit and the public pays for the performance.

Bills to repeal or modify this exemption have been and are now before Congress, and have been the subject of repeated and exhaustive hearings. In the course of those hearings we have expressed our view that this exemption should be repealed, or at least should be replaced by a provision requiring jukebox operators to pay reasonable royalties.

The jukebox exemption is a historical anomaly. The exemption was placed in the law in 1909 at the last minute with virtually no discussion. The coin-operated music machines of that day were apparently a novelty of little economic consequence. The jukebox industry is now among the largest commercial users of music, with an annual gross revenue of over a half-billion dollars.

Jukebox operators are the only users of music for profit who are not obliged to pay royalties, and there is no special reason for their exemption. No such exemption is made in any other country, except that in Canada the playing of music on jukeboxes comes within a general exemption of performances by means of a gramophone. A Canadian commission appointed to review its copyright law recently declared that the exemption of jukeboxes is not warranted; but that since the royalties collected in Canada would go mainly to copyright owners in the United States, the withdrawal of the exemption in Canada might await like action in our country.

Since the jukebox exemption has been thoroughly explored by the congressional committees, and proposals for the solution of the problem are presently under consideration by those committees, we are not reviewing the matter further in this report.

b. Recommendation

The jukebox exemption should be repealed, or at least should be replaced by a provision requiring jukebox operators to pay reasonable license fees for the public performance of music for profit. The consideration of legislation proposed for this purpose should continue without awaiting a general revision of the law.

7. THE COMPULSORY LICENSE FOR THE RECORDING OF MUSIC [6]

a. The present law and its history

Sections 1(e) and 101(e) of the present statute contain elaborate and complex provisions for what is commonly known as the "compulsory license" for the making of sound recordings of music. In brief, they provide that when the copyright owner of a musical work has once permitted it to be recorded, any other person may record the work upon (1) giving notice to the copyright owner of his intention to do so and (2) paying a royalty of 2 cents for each record manufactured.

These provisions were inserted in the act of 1909 in view of the special conditions existing at that time. The Supreme Court, in the *White-Smith* case mentioned above, had held that the pre-1909 law gave no exclusive right to the copyright owner to make a sound recording of his musical work. In the general revision bills leading up to the act of 1909 it was proposed to give the copyright owner such an exclusive right.

As stated at some length in their reports (H. Rept. No. 2222, S. Rept. No. 1108, 60th Cong., 2d sess.) the congressional committees felt that composers should be given adequate compensation for the use of their music in sound recordings. They were first inclined to

---

[6] See "Copyright Law Revision Studies Nos. 5 and 6"

give the copyright owner the exclusive right to make sound recordings, in the same way that all other rights are given exclusively. During the course of the hearings, however, it was learned that one dominant record company, anticipating the establishment of an exclusive recording right, had contracted with the leading music publishers for the exclusive right to record all their music. To forestall the danger that this company would acquire a monopoly in the making of records, the committees adopted the device of the compulsory license.

b. Practical effect of the compulsory license

The compulsory license provisions are rather severe in their effect upon the copyright owner. Once he exploits his right to record his music, he is deprived of control over further recordings. He cannot control their quality nor can he select the persons who will make them. There have been many complaints of inferior recordings and of recordings by financially irresponsible persons. What is perhaps even more important, the statute places a ceiling of 2 cents per record on the royalty he can obtain. In essence, the compulsory license permits anyone indiscriminately to make records of the copyright owner's music at the 2-cent rate fixed in the statute.

In practice the authors of musical works generally assign their recording and other rights to publishers, under an agreement for the division of royalties. In most instances the record companies secure licenses from the publishers, thereby avoiding some of the mechanics of notice and accounting required by the statute for exercise of the compulsory license. But the statutory rate of 2 cents per record operates as a ceiling on the royalty rate paid, even as to the first recording. For records of popular music, the royalty rate paid is commonly less than 2 cents.

c. Need for the compulsory license

The danger of a monopoly in the situation existing in 1909 was apparently the sole reason for the compulsory license. There are now hundreds of recording companies competing with one another, and the music available for recording is widely scattered among hundreds of competitive publishers. The market for recordings and the number and variety of compositions recorded have increased tremendously. The volume of music available for recording is immense and constantly growing. Much of the new music available remains unrecorded, and no one can foretell whether a recording of a particular composition will strike the public fancy.

Author and publisher groups have urged strenuously that, since the compulsory license is no longer justified as an antimonopoly measure, it should now be eliminated. They argue that the fundamental principle of copyright—that the author is to have the exclusive right to control the commercial exploitation of his work—should apply to the recording of music, as it is applied to all other kinds of works and to other means of exploiting music.

d. Analysis of arguments for retaining the compulsory license

Representatives of the record industry argue that even though the antimonopoly reason for the compulsory license is gone, there are now other reasons for retaining it. They contend that, by giving all record companies the opportunity to make records of the music recorded by any one company, the compulsory license is beneficial in the following respects:

(1) It provides the public with a variety of recordings of any particular musical work, which might not be true if the copyright owner could give an exclusive license to one record company.

(2) It enables smaller record companies to compete with the larger ones by offering other recordings of the same music.

(3) It benefits authors and publishers by giving their works public exposure through several different recordings, thereby increasing their revenue from royalties.

All of these asserted benefits flow from multiple recordings of a musical work by several companies under nonexclusive licenses, as opposed to a single recording by one company under an exclusive license. The removal of the compulsory license, however, would not necessarily result in exclusive licenses being given. If it is true that authors and publishers benefit from multiple recordings, they would presumably seek to give nonexclusive licenses to several companies. We understand that in those foreign countries having no compulsory license, the recording of musical works is usually licensed nonexclusively to any reputable company.

It seems likely that in the absence of the compulsory license, multiple recordings would still be licensed nonexclusively. If so, the three benefits attributed to the compulsory license by the record industry would still exist, but with these differences: the author or publisher could refuse a license to a recorder whom he considered irresponsible or for a recording he considered undesirable, and the royalty rate would be fixed by free negotiation.

Even assuming that removal of the compulsory license would result in the granting of exclusive licenses, we believe that any loss of the three benefits flowing from multiple recordings would be offset by other considerations:

(1) The public now gets a variety of recordings of certain musical works because, when a record made by one company promises to be a hit, other companies make records of the same music. Under a regime of exclusive licenses, each company would have to record different music; while the public would not get several recordings of the same music, it would probably get recordings of a greater number and variety of musical works.

(2) A small record company may now make a competing record of a musical work with which a large company has made a prospective hit, but this also works the other way. Many hits are now originated by small companies; and their prospective hits are often smothered by records of the same music brought out by larger companies having better known performers and greater promotional facilities. Under a regime of exclusive licenses, the companies would not compete with various recordings of the same music, but they would compete with recordings of different music. There is little danger that the large companies would get all the hits: in the popular field the number of compositions available for recording is virtually inexhaustible, and which of them may become hits is unpredictable.

(3) The authors and publishers believe they would benefit from removal of the compulsory license. They would no doubt

take care of their own interests in deciding whether nonexclusive or exclusive licenses are better for them. Nonexclusive licenses might be more profitable for those authors who have already achieved success. The possibility of granting an exclusive license might give new and unknown authors more opportunity to have their works recorded.

Representatives of the record industry have also argued that the enormous growth since 1909 in the volume of the records manufactured and sold has proved the worth of the compulsory license. They point out that the record industry has prospered, authors and publishers have received more royalties, and the public has been supplied with more records of a better quality at a lower price. We do not see why this expansion of the record industry, coincident with technical improvements and rising public demand, should be attributed to the compulsory license. Other entertainment industries have enjoyed a similar growth. And we understand that the record industry has also expanded in foreign countries where there is no compulsory license.

e. General observations

Removal of the compulsory license would be likely to result in a royalty rate, fixed by free negotiation, of more than the present statutory ceiling of 2 cents. The record companies would, of course, lose the advantage of the lower rate. The price of records to the public might be increased by a few cents, though this is not certain since many factors enter into the pricing of records. If it is true that a freely negotiated rate would exceed 2 cents, we would conclude that the 2-cent ceiling denies authors and publishers the compensation due them for the use of their works.

We have previously mentioned the fundamental principle of copyright that the author should have the exclusive right to exploit the market for his work, except where this would conflict with the public interest. In the situation prevailing in 1909, the public interest was thought to require the compulsory license to forestall the danger of a monopoly in musical recordings. The compulsory license is no longer needed for that purpose, and we see no other public interest that now requires its retention.

For these reasons we favor complete elimination of the compulsory license provisions. However, we recognize that the present practices in the record industry are based on the compulsory license, and that its elimination would require some major adjustments and new contractual relationships. We therefore propose that the present compulsory license provisions be left in effect for a reasonable time after the new statute is enacted.

If Congress, after considering this highly controversial question, determines that the principle of the compulsory license should be retained, we believe that substantial changes should be made in the present provisions. Among the problems that would need to be considered are:

- The royalty rate and the basis on which it is to be computed;
- The present requirement that the copyright owner file a notice of use as a condition to recovery for infringement;
- The mechanics for assuring payment of the royalties;

• The copyright owner's remedies against those who make records without permission and without complying with the compulsory license requirements.

f. Recommendations

(1) The compulsory license provisions in sections 1(e) and 101(e) of the present statute should be eliminated.

(2) Since elimination of the compulsory license would require negotiations between music publishers and record companies to make new contractual arrangements as to royalty rates, etc., we propose that the present compulsory license provisions be left in effect for one year after the enactment of the new law.

Chapter IV

UNPUBLISHED WORKS: COMMON LAW AND STATUTORY PROTECTION

Outline of Chapter

37

(1237)

CHAPTER IV

UNPUBLISHED WORKS: COMMON LAW AND STATUTORY PROTECTION [1]

A. Historical Background and the Present Law

1. Unpublished Works Protected by Common Law

Even before the adoption of our first Federal copyright statute in 1790, the common law protected authors against the unauthorized publication of their manuscripts. But when the author published his work by issuing copies, his common law rights ended and, in the absence of statutory copyright, the work went into the public domain. The first and succeeding Federal copyright statutes were designed to supplement the common law by giving authors the opportunity to secure copyright protection for their works for a limited time after publication.

This concept has largely been retained in the present copyright law. Except when voluntarily registered, unpublished works are protected by the common law (sec. 2). When a work is published, common law protection ceases and statutory copyright is secured by placing a notice of copyright on the published copies (sec. 10). Generally speaking, publication of copies without the prescribed notice puts the work in the public domain.

2. Statutory Copyright Available for Some Unpublished Works by Voluntary Registration

An innovation made in 1909 now permits certain kinds of unpublished works to be copyrighted under the statute by voluntary registration in the Copyright Office (sec. 12). This privilege of substituting statutory copyright for common law protection is extended to those classes of unpublished works that are commonly performed or exhibited in public: Lectures, dramas, music, photographs, drawings, art works, and motion pictures.. It is not available, however, for other unpublished works, notably book material.

B. Absence of Limitations on Common Law Protection of Unpublished Works

Under our present copyright law, "publication" means making copies of a work available to the public. The important point here is that public performances, such as broadcasts and stage presentations, do not constitute "publication." And, although recent court decisions throw doubt on this assumption, it has traditionally been

---

[1] See "Copyright Law Revision Study No. 29"

thought that the sale of phonograph records is not "publication" of the recorded work.

Consequently, as long as a work is neither published in copies nor voluntarily registered, the exclusive rights under the common law continue with no time limit, even though the work is used commercially and widely disseminated. This result—perpetual protection for works disseminated in any manner other than publication—seems contrary to the principle embodied in the provision of the Constitution (art. I, sec. 8) empowering Congress "to promote the progress of science and useful arts, by securing *for limited times* to authors * * * the exclusive right to their * * * writings * * *." [Emphasis added.]

Unpublished works under common law protection are also immune from limitations on the scope of statutory protection that have been imposed in the public interest. These limitations are discussed in chapter III, part B. They include the "fair use" doctrine, the "for profit" limitation on the public performance right in nondramatic literary and musical works, and the compulsory license for the recording of music.

C. Public Dissemination as the Present Equivalent of Publication

1. IN REGARD TO LIMITATIONS ON STATUTORY COPYRIGHT

In the 19th century copyright was concerned principally with printed material, and the publication of copies was virtually the only means of making a work available to the public. At that time it was justifiable to make publication the event at which to terminate common law protection and apply the statute. Today the publication of copies is only one of several methods of public dissemination.

The constitutional provision contemplates that the public interest will be served by giving authors exclusive rights in their works for a limited time, after which the works go into the public domain. We believe that the constitutional principle of a time limitation should be applied when a work is disseminated to the public, whether by the publication of copies or registration, as under the present law, or by public performance or the public distribution of sound recordings. We also believe that any statutory limitations imposed in the public interest on the scope of copyright protection should apply when a work has been publicly disseminated in any of these ways.

2. IN REGARD TO ADVANTAGES OF STATUTORY COPYRIGHT

Although statutory copyright is subject to time and other limitations, it also affords to the author certain advantages over common law protection: (1) registration under the statute provides prima facie proof of the facts stated in the registration certificate, and (2) the statute affords better and more precise remedies for infringement. We see no reason why these advantages should not be accorded to all works when they are publicly disseminated.

3. CONCLUSION

We propose that the statute should apply to works that are publicly disseminated by the publication of copies, by registration, by public performance, or by the public distribution of sound recordings.

As stated in chapter II, part A, fixation of a work in some tangible form would be a requirement of its copyrightability. Hence, the statute would not apply to a work created in the process of its performance—such as an impromptu speech or a musical improvisation—which the author has not fixed in any tangible form.

D. Protection of Undisseminated Works

1. COMMON LAW OR STATUTORY PROTECTION

We have given considerable thought to the suggestion that the protection of all copyrightable material should be governed exclusively by the Federal statute. This would mean the complete elimination of protection for undisseminated works under the common law, and the extension of the Federal statute to all copyrightable material as soon as it comes into existence.

This approach is said to have the advantages of simplifying our present dual system of protection and of providing greater assurance of national uniformity. We agree that a uniform Federal copyright system is desirable for the protection of works that have been publicly disseminated. But we believe there are overbalancing reasons to preserve the common law protection of undisseminated works until the author or his successor chooses to disclose them.

2. TIME LIMITATION ON PROTECTION OF UNDISSEMINATED WORKS

Undisseminated material consists largely of manuscripts of a private nature, such as letters, memoranda, personal diaries, journals, and family photographs. Authors and their heirs may not wish to have their private papers disclosed to the public. The common law now protects them against unauthorized disclosure, without a time limit.

For protection under the Federal statute, however, the Constitution would necessarily require a time limitation. We believe that a fixed time limit for the protection of private papers against unauthorized disclosure would be undesirable. The right of privacy should be paramount in this situation.

We realize that, after some period of time, the need for privacy diminishes and private papers may become valuable sources of information for historians and other scholars. But we would not, for this reason, throw all such papers into the public domain after the lapse of a fixed period. To do so might induce the holders of private papers to destroy them. We believe that the right of privacy and the interests of scholarship can be balanced by a special provision for the use of manuscript material that is made accessible to the public in a library or other archive. We shall discuss this below.

3. EXCLUSIVE FEDERAL JURISDICTION

Extension of the Federal statute to all undisseminated works would preclude the protection of copyrightable material under common law or State statutes. It would also mean that all suits involving rights in copyrightable material would be tried exclusively in the Federal courts.

Undisseminated works would generally be matters of private and local concern until they are disclosed to the public. We therefore see no compelling reason to oust the State law and State courts from jurisdiction over questions concerning the private rights in these works.

4. STATUTORY COPYRIGHT AVAILABLE VOLUNTARILY

Many voluntary registrations are now made for unpublished works, to attain the advantages of the prima facie evidence afforded by the registration certificate and the stronger statutory remedies against infringers. Under the present law, however, this privilege of voluntary registration is limited to certain types of works. It does not extend to nondramatic literary material such as the manuscripts of books, stories, poems, and articles. The Copyright Office receives a considerable number of applications and inquiries seeking registration for unpublished material of this kind, which it must refuse. We believe that the privilege of securing statutory copyright by voluntary registration should be extended to undisseminated works of all types.

5. MANUSCRIPTS PLACED IN ARCHIVES

We have mentioned above the problem of permitting scholars to use manuscripts that have been made accessible to the public in a library or other archival institution. There is ordinarily no difficulty where the author or his heirs have deposited the manuscripts: They can authorize use of the manuscript material and can specify any restrictions they wish to impose. But many manuscripts are deposited by other persons, such as the recipients of letters or their successors. In these cases the depositor can impose restrictions on use of the manuscripts; but where the literary property rights are still owned by the author or his heirs, the depositor's authorization to use the material is probably ineffectual. Scholarly use of the manuscripts in a library is often handicapped by the uncertainty as to whether they are still subject to the authors' common law rights, and by the impracticality of seeking permission from numerous authors or heirs.

Authors who place their manuscripts in the possession of other persons take the risk that those persons, even when not authorized to disclose the manuscripts, may in fact do so. When the holder of manuscripts has made them accessible to the public in a library they are no longer private in fact. We believe they should then be available for scholarly use.

For the same reasons we believe that the manuscript material in a library should eventually become available for publication. On the other hand, when a manuscript has been placed in a library by someone other than the author or his heirs, their literary property rights should be preserved for a reasonable period of time. We propose that these rights endure until the manuscript is 50 years old and has been in the library for more than 10 years. During that time the author or his heirs could extend the period of their protection, if they so desired, by registering a copyright claim.

In regard to manuscripts placed in a library before the new law comes into effect, we propose that the rule terminating literary property rights in 50-year-old manuscripts should not apply until 10 years after the effective date of the new law.

Provisions of this character would enable scholars to determine whether old manuscripts accessible to them in libraries are available for publication, without having to seek out the authors or their heirs. We believe this would achieve a fair balance between the interests of authors and those of scholars.

E. RECOMMENDATIONS

1. The statute should apply, and common law rights should end, when a copyrightable work is publicly disseminated by the publication of copies, registration in the Copyright Office, public performance, or the public distribution of sound recordings.

2. Common law protection should be left in effect for copyrightable works not publicly disseminated. The privilege of securing statutory copyright in lieu of common law protection, by voluntary registration in the Copyright Office, should be extended to all copyrightable works.

3. When any holder of a manuscript has made it accessible to the public in a library or other archival institution:

   (a) The institution should be permitted to supply any applicant with a single copy of the manuscript for his use in research.

   (b) The manuscript should be subject to fair use.

   (c) The manuscript material should go into the public domain when it is 50 years old and has been in the institution for more than 10 years, unless the owner of the literary property rights has registered a claim of copyright which is still subsisting. With respect to manuscripts placed in an institution before the effective date of the new law, this rule should not become applicable until 10 years after the effective date.

Chapter V

DURATION OF COPYRIGHT

Outline of Chapter

CHAPTER V

DURATION OF COPYRIGHT [1]

A. The Present Law; Revision Necessary

Under the constitutional requirement that Federal copyright protection be limited in time, the present statute (sec. 24) provides for two successive copyright terms totaling 56 years. Copyright endures for 28 years from the date of first publication of the work, and may be renewed by certain persons for a second term of 28 years. If the work is first registered in unpublished form, the 28- or 56-year term is measured from the date of registration, even if the work is later published.

We have recommended in chapter IV that the copyright statute apply to works that are publicly performed or publicly distributed in the form of sound recordings, as well as to those published or registered. This would require a new term provision applicable to works that are publicly disseminated in any of these ways. There are also other changes in the present term provisions that we believe should be considered.

B. Base Point for Computing the Term

1. ALTERNATIVE APPROACHES

In fixing the base point from which to compute the term, either of two general approaches may be taken:

(*a*) To measure the term from the inception of copyright. This is the approach taken in our present law.

(*b*) To measure the term from the death of the author. Most foreign laws adopt this approach.

2. TERM BASED ON INCEPTION OF COPYRIGHT

Under the present law, publication or earlier registration begins the copyright and is also the base point from which the term is computed. If copyright is to begin upon public dissemination—that is, upon publication, registration, public performance, or the public distribution of sound recordings—a logical adaptation of the present law would be to compute the term from first public dissemination.

3. TERM BASED ON DEATH OF THE AUTHOR

In most foreign countries copyright begins upon creation of the work, and the term for works in which the author is identified is computed from the date of the author's death. A number of persons have urged that a term based on the author's death be adopted in our law.

---

[1] See "Copyright Law Revision Study No. 30"

For many works, however, the date of the author's death could not be used as the base for computing the term. About 40 percent of all works registered in the Copyright Office are "corporate works"—that is, works prepared for corporations or other organized bodies by their employees. Many works of individual authors are also disseminated anonymously. The term for corporate and anonymous works would have to be based on something other than the death of the author. In most foreign countries the term for these works is computed from first publication, and no term provision is made for corporate or anonymous works that are not published.

4. COMPARISON OF THE ALTERNATIVES

a. *Advantages of each alternative*

Basing the term on dissemination would have the following advantages:

(1) The date from which the term is measured could be shown in the registration records and in the published copies of the work. Also, the term could be computed at any time after the copyright begins. (None of this would ordinarily be true of a term based on the author's death, and the death date of many authors would be difficult to ascertain.)

(2) The same term could be applied to all works. (A term based on the author's death would not apply to corporate and anonymous works, and some special provision would also be necessary for the joint works of two or more authors.)

(3) The term provisions would require little change in the established practices of the industries dealing with copyright materials. (A term based on the author's death would require a much greater adjustment.)

Basing the term on the death of the author—with a different basis for corporate and anonymous works—would have the following advantages:

(1) It would bring our term in line with that in most foreign countries.

(2) The author would be assured of the benefit of copyright during his entire life, and his family would benefit after his death. (A term based on dissemination might expire during the author's lifetime—unless it ran for longer than any author could be expected to live.)

(3) All of an author's works—except joint or anonymous works and works made for hire—would go into the public domain at the same time. (Under a term based on dissemination, each of his works would go into the public domain at a different date.)

b. *Evaluation of advantages*

(1) *Determination of controlling date.*—We believe the most important factor in deciding the base point for computing the term is the ability of the public to determine the date of that event. From this standpoint, basing the term on dissemination seems preferable. The death date of authors who are not well known would often be difficult to ascertain.

It has been suggested that this difficulty could be overcome by requiring that the date of the author's death be recorded in the Copyright Office within a specified period. But if the copyright were terminated for failure to record in due time, the purpose of basing the term on the death of the author would be defeated. And when there was a failure to record, the public would not know whether or when the author had died.

(2) *Same basis of term for all works.*—A term based on dissemination also seems preferable from the standpoint of uniformity and simplicity. It would be applicable to all works, while a term based on the author's death could not be applied to the large volume of corporate and anonymous works.

(3) *Protection for the author's lifetime and beyond.*—We believe that the benefits of copyright should be available to an author for his lifetime and to his dependents if he dies prematurely. This appears to be the premise that has led most foreign countries to adopt a term enduring for the life of the author and a number of years after his death. But, as we shall point out below, this objective can also be achieved by making the term based on dissemination sufficiently long.

(4) *Correspondence of U.S. term with that of foreign countries.*— In most foreign countries the term for works of an identified individual author runs for his life (or, if there is more than one author, for the life of the last survivor), and a stated number of years after his death. For corporate or anonymous works, and also for works first published after the author's death, the term runs for a like number of years after first publication. Though the specified period varies in the foreign laws, ranging from 15 to 80 years, the most prevalent pattern is a term expiring 50 years after the death of the author or after publication.

It would, of course, simplify international copyright protection if the term in all countries were the same. And there is much weight to the argument that the United States should give foreign works protection equal to that given by foriegn countries to the works of U.S. authors. In our discussion below of the length of the term, we adopt the approach of making our term equivalent in length with the term most prevalent in other countries.

5. CONCLUSION

We believe that a term based on dissemination has the greater advantages for the public, and that the principal purposes of a term based on the death of the author can be achieved by a sufficiently long term based on dissemination.

C. LENGTH OF TERM

1. MAXIMUM TERM FOR ADEQUATE BENEFIT TO AUTHORS AND THEIR DEPENDENTS

Many persons have argued that the present maximum term of 56 years is too short. Those who advocate a term based on the author's death are concerned primarily with a longer term for the benefit of authors and their dependents.

A substantial number of works—though they constitute a small percentage of all copyrighted works—continue to have commercial value beyond the present term of 56 years. In some of these cases the author is still living or there are still dependents of a deceased author when the term expires. We are sympathetic to the view that the author during his old age, or his dependents if he dies prematurely, should continue to have the benefits afforded by copyright. A maximum term of 56 years is not enough to assure this in all cases.

2. TERM EQUIVALENT IN LENGTH TO THAT IN OTHER COUNTRIES

We are also sympathetic to the view that our maximum term should be generally comparable to the term given our works in most other countries. The term of 56 years, measured from first public dissemination, is considerably shorter on the average than the term of 50 years after the author's death. In most instances dissemination will precede the author's death by substantially more than 6 years.

For any particular work, a term based on dissemination will hardly ever coincide with a term based on the author's death. But the length of the two terms can be roughly equated on the basis of an average span of time between dissemination and the author's death.

From the information given in the 1942 and 1955 editions of "Twentieth Century Authors," we have extracted the following data on 673 authors of English-language books who died between 1930 and 1955:

	Years
Average age of authors at death	68
Average age of authors—	
When first book published	32
When last book published	64
Average age at median between first and last books	48
Average span between median age at publication and age at death	20

A survey of 61 composers of serious music, based on 3 standard reference works, brought closely similar results. A survey [2] of 191 authors of popular music who died between 1930 and 1950 indicates that, although the average life expectancy and creative period of this group may be somewhat shorter, the average span between the author's median age at publication and his age at death is also about 20 years.

On the basis of these figures, it might be assumed that a copyright term of 70 years after first publication would approximate, on the average, a term of 50 years after the author's death. However, this result is based on an average age of 68 years at death, while the last available census indicates that this figure for all men and women had reached almost 70 years in 1950, and it has steadily been rising. Also, publication will sometimes come later than dissemination in another manner. We therefore propose that the maximum term computed from first public dissemination be fixed at 76 years, which would add 20 years to the present maximum term.

---

[2] Since there are no comprehensive biographical reference works dealing with the authors of popular music, our survey was based on the 1,344 songwriters of the approximately 4,600 songs published between 1900 and 1950 which are listed in the 1950 edition of "Variety Music Cavalcade." By checking through the obituaries in the 1,500 weekly issues of Variety from 1930 through 1958, we found the death dates of 215 of the 1,344 songwriters; death dates of an additional 80 of the authors were found in the "ASCAP Dictionary of Composers, Authors, and Publishers" (1948). Of the total of 295 songwriters whose dates of death were found, 191 died within the sample period 1930–50.

3. CONCLUSION

A term of 76 years from first public dissemination would be generally equivalent to the term most prevalent in foreign countries. And it would virtually assure protection for the author's lifetime or, if he dies prematurely, for his dependents during a reasonable period after his death. Thus, in addition to the advantages of being based on ascertainable events and of being applicable to all works, this term would achieve the main purposes of those who have advocated a term of 50 years from the death of the author.

D. RENEWABLE TERM [3]

1. THE PRESENT RENEWAL SYSTEM

Under the present law (sec. 24) the maximum term of 56 years is divided into two periods of 28 years each. Copyright expires after the initial term of 28 years, unless it is renewed during the last year of that term. For some kinds of works—posthumous works, composite works, and works made for hire—the renewal for the second term of 28 years may be secured by the owner of the copyright at the time of renewal. For all other works, the renewal may be secured (a) by the author; (b) if the author is not living, then by his widow and children; (c) if there be no widow or children, then by his executors or, if he left no will, by his next of kin.

2. RENEWAL SYSTEM AS A LIMITATION ON THE TERM

a. Maximum term not needed for most works

We do not believe that the maximum term of copyright—which we are proposing be 76 years from first public dissemination—is necessary or advisable for all works. Experience indicates that the present initial term of 28 years is sufficient for the great majority of copyrighted works: less than 15 percent of all registered copyrights are being renewed at the present time.

The percentage of renewals varies from one class of works to another. During a recent year, for example, renewals ranged from 70 percent of the eligible motion pictures, down through 35 percent for music, 11 percent for periodicals, 7 percent for "books" (which includes text material published in various forms), to less than 1 percent for technical drawings.

b. Arguments in opposition to a renewable term

A number of persons have argued that a renewable term is undesirable because (1) it imposes on authors and other renewal claimants the burden of filing a renewal application and (2) it subjects them to the risk of losing their copyrights if they forget to file the application in time.

Some of the opponents of a renewable term recognize that certain works do not need as long a term as others; they suggest that the law provide single terms of different lengths for various classes of works. Others suggest that a uniform single term be provided for all works.

---

[3] See "Copyright Law Revision Study No. 31"

(1) *Various single terms as an alternative to a renewable term.*— Only two foreign countries divide the term of copyright by a renewal device, though many of them have renewable terms for patents and trademarks. However, the copyright laws of a number of foreign countries provide special terms, shorter than the usual term, for certain classes of works—e.g., photographs, motion pictures, sound recordings, translations, and collective works.

For the following reasons, we believe that a uniform renewable term for all works is preferable to various single terms for different classes of works:

- A uniform term for all works is simpler. Different terms for various classes of works would raise questions as to the scope of each class, and as to the appropriate class for a particular work.
- A renewal system tailors the term to the need felt by the copyright owner. A single term for all works of a given class would be unnecessarily long for some works or not long enough for others of that class.
- Renewal registrations provide a fresh record of copyright ownership after the lapse of many years.

(2) *Uniform single term for all works.*—Advocates of a uniform single term contend that, even though most works have little or no commercial value beyond 28 years, it would do no harm to let their protection continue for the maximum term. They argue that no one is interested in using a work after it has ceased to have commercial value, so the continuation of copyright would be of no practical consequence.

We believe that this argument is fallacious on two grounds:

- Many works that have ceased to have substantial commercial value in themselves are still useful to scholars, researchers, historians, and educators, as well as to authors of new works based on preexisting ones.
- The argument seems to assume that the public derives no benefit from having works in the public domain. Copyright protection for a certain period is essential to foster the creation and dissemination of intellectual works and to give authors their due reward. But on the other hand, there are many circumstances in which copyright restrictions inhibit the dissemination of works or their use in the creation of new works.

We believe that, when authors or other copyright owners feel that they have no need for a longer term, the termination of copyright restrictions after 28 years is in the public interest.

(3) *Renewal as a burden; the danger of inadvertent failure to renew.*—The filing of a renewal application is a simple process. We do not believe it is too great a burden for those copyright owners who wish to have their protection extended beyond the initial term of 28 years.

It is nevertheless true that some renewals have been lost because the application was not filed within the 1 year allowed by the present law. A survey covering a recent period of 6 months showed that, out of a total of more than 10,000 renewal applications received, 102 had to be rejected because they were filed too late. There were undoubtedly other instances in which the claimant did not submit a renewal application because he realized that it was too late to do so.

To reduce the danger that the period for filing renewal applications may be overlooked, we propose that renewal be permitted at any time within the last 5 years of the initial 28-year term.

c. *Conclusions*

We believe that the copyright term should continue to be divided, so that copyrights not renewed would terminate 28 years after first publication or other dissemination. Copyright owners should have the privilege of extending their protection to the maximum term of 76 years from first public dissemination, by filing an application for renewal during the last 5 of the initial 28 years.

Note that these conclusions relate only to the length of the term. The questions of who may apply for renewal and who owns the copyright during the renewal term will be considered next.

3. REVERSION OF RENEWAL COPYRIGHT TO THE AUTHOR OR HIS HEIRS

a. *The reversionary provision and its purpose*

With certain exceptions, the present law gives the renewal copyright to the author or to specified heirs of a deceased author. The primary purpose of this provision was to protect the author and his family against his unprofitable or improvident disposition of the copyright. The renewal copyright was intended to revert to them so that they could negotiate new contracts for the further exploitation of the work.

The present provision also operates to change the usual rules, under State laws, of succession to a deceased person's property. For example, it gives the right to obtain a renewal copyright to a deceased author's widow and children, even if the author purports to leave his rights to others in his will.

b. *Practical effect of the reversionary provision*

In practice, this reversionary feature of the present renewal system has largely failed to accomplish its primary purpose. It has also been the source of more confusion and litigation than any other provision in the copyright law.

The courts have held that an assignment of future renewal rights by the author is binding if he lives into the 28th year and renewal registration is then made in his name. In that situation the author's renewal rights become the property of the assignee as soon as the renewal term begins. It has become a common practice for publishers and others to take advance assignments of future renewal rights. Thus the reversionary purpose of the renewal provision has been thwarted to a considerable extent.

Moreover, the assignees are themselves in an uncertain position. The person entitled to secure the renewal copyright cannot be ascertained until the 28th year. If the assignor dies before then, an advance assignment will fall. A considerable amount of trafficking in the possible future renewal right of authors and their prospective heirs has grown up. An assignee can never be sure of his right to use the work during the renewal term until the time for renewal registration actually arrives.

To give full effect to the primary purpose of the reversionary provision would seem to require that the renewal right be made unassignable in advance. Whether this would operate to the benefit of authors and their heirs is questionable. The commercial value of their copyrights might be diminished in many instances if they were unable to contract for the use of their works beyond the end of the first 28-year term. And, during the later years of that term, they might well find that publishers, motion picture producers, and other users who need assurance of continued use for an extended period, would be reluctant to undertake exploitation of the work.

c. Arguments for elimination of the reversionary provision

It has been argued that most authors do not need or want to be treated as incompetent to handle their business affairs. Many of them have banded together in organizations which negotiate standard contracts providing for continuing royalties. Their assignments can be and often are given for limited periods of time.

It is still true, however, that most authors are not represented by protective organizations and are in a relatively poor bargaining position. Moreover, the revenue to be derived from the exploitation of a work is usually unpredictable, and assignments for a lump sum are still common. There are no doubt many assignments that give the author less than his fair share of the revenue actually derived from his work. Some provision to permit authors to renegotiate their disadvantageous assignments seems desirable.

It has also been argued that the present provision for reversion of the renewal right should be eliminated for the following reasons:

(1) Authors would often be in a better bargaining position if they could assign their rights unconditionally beyond the 28th year.

(2) Assignees should have assurance that the rights acquired by them will not be cut off by the death of the author.

(3) An author's copyrights, like his other personal property, should be subject to his bequest by will or, if he leaves no will, should go to his heirs under the general law of intestate succession.

The widespread sentiment for elimination of the present renewal system seems to be prompted largely by the welter of confusion and uncertainty caused by the reversionary provision.

d. Conclusions

We believe that the provision of the present law for reversion of the renewal right to the author or specified heirs should be eliminated. We propose that the law simply provide for the extension of the first 28-year period to the maximum term upon the filing of a renewal application by any person claiming an interest in the copyright. This is in contrast with the present law, under which the copyright can be renewed only in the name of the particular claimant specified in the statute. Our proposal would mean that the renewal becomes a mere extension of term without affecting ownership of rights under existing contracts. Any person claiming an interest in the copyright—author, executor, heir, employer, assignee, licensee, etc.—could make renewal registration. The renewal would extend all rights under the copyright to the full 76-year term, for the benefit of everyone having any interest in the copyright.

Instead of the present reversion of the renewal right, we believe that some other provision should be made to permit authors and their heirs to renegotiate their assignments in certain situations. We shall consider this later in chapter VIII, part D 3.

E. Minimum Term for Published Works

Our proposal that the term run for 28 years or, if renewed, for 76 years, from the first public dissemination of the work may raise a question as to foreign works protected under the Universal Copyright Convention. The Convention requires that the term run for at least 25 years from first publication (or earlier registration). And "publication" is defined in the Convention as "the reproduction in tangible form and the general distribution to the public of copies of a work from which it can be read or visually perceived." It is doubtful whether a term of 28 years from first public dissemination in some other manner—that is, by public performance or by the public distribution of sound recordings—would satisfy the U.C.C. requirement in all cases.

The term of 28 years from first public dissemination could be made to conform with the U.C.C. by adding a proviso as follows: if a work is first disseminated otherwise than by publication and is later published before the term expires, the term would continue for a period of years—not less than 25—after first publication.

In addition to conforming our law with the U.C.C., this proviso would have the advantage of allowing established practices to be continued, particularly in regard to the copyright notice. Publishers could continue to use the year date of first publication in the notice, even if the work had previously been disseminated otherwise. And the date of publication is usually more significant to libraries and scholars than the date of an earlier dissemination in some other manner. Publication is also significant in many cases for purposes of international copyright protection.

We would favor a proviso of this sort for all works, foreign and domestic. And for the sake of uniformity—since a work first disseminated by the publication of copies would have a basic term of 28 years from publication—we would also have the alternative term under the proviso run for 28 years after publication. The term provisions would then operate as follows:

1. The basic copyright term in all cases would be 28 years from first public dissemination.

2. Renewal during the last 5 years of this basic term would extend the copyright for a further period of 48 years. The maximum term in all cases would be 76 years from first public dissemination.

3. An exception would be made for a work that (a) was first disseminated in some manner other than the publication of copies and (b) is published during the basic 28-year term. In this case the copyright would continue for 28 years from first publication, but would then expire if the copyright had not been renewed before the end of the basic term.

The following hypothetical cases will illustrate the effect of these provisions:

• A work is first disseminated by the publication of copies. The basic term of 28 years, the 5-year period for renewal, and the maximum term of 76 years would all be measured from the year of publication.

• A work is first disseminated by a television broadcast in 1970. Copies are published in 1980.

> (*a*) The copyright would be eligible for renewal between 1993 and 1998.
>
> (*b*) If renewed, the term would run for 76 years from 1970.
>
> (*c*) If not renewed, the term would run for 28 years from 1980.

A work is first disseminated by a television broadcast in 1970. Copies are first published in 1999. This publication would have no effect on the term. The copyright would expire in 1998 if not renewed, or in 2046 if renewed.

F. Year-End Expiration of Term

The copyright term now expires 28 or 56 years from the precise day of first publication or earlier registration.

We propose that in all cases the term should run until the end of the calendar year in which it would otherwise expire. This provision, found in most foreign laws, would simplify the computation of the term. It would then be enough to determine the year, rather than the exact date, of the event from which the term is computed.

G. Recommendations

With respect to copyrights secured under the new law:

1. The copyright should endure for an original term of 28 years from the first public dissemination of the work (i.e., publication of copies, registration, public performance, or public distribution of sound recordings).

2. Any person claiming an interest in a copyright should be entitled to renew it by filing an application for renewal in the Copyright Office during the last 5 years of the original term. Renewal by any interested person should extend all rights in the copyright to endure for a total of 76 years from first public dissemination.

3. An alternative term should be provided in cases where a work (1) is first publicly disseminated otherwise than by the publication of copies, (2) is later published during the original 28-year term, and (3) is not renewed before the end of the original 28-year term. In such cases the copyright should continue for 28 years from first publication and then expire.

4. All terms should run to the end of the calendar year in which they would otherwise expire.

H. Application of New Term Provisions to Preexisting Works

1. IN GENERAL

There remain the questions of how the new term provisions should apply to (1) works under common law protection at the effective date of the new law, and (2) works in which copyright is subsisting at that date.

The new law would not, of course, restore protection to works that had gone into the public domain before its effective date.

2. WORKS UNDER COMMON-LAW PROTECTION

Preexisting works that had neither been published nor registered should continue under common-law protection until their first public dissemination after the effective date of the new law, and should then come under the statute.

A question arises as to works that had not been published or registered but, on the effective date, were in the process of a continuous dissemination. Examples are the run of a stage play or the sale of phonograph records, begun before and continuing after that date. We believe it would create practical difficulties to shift from common-law to statutory protection in this situation. Therefore, the continuation of a series of disseminations begun before the new law comes into effect should be excluded from the rule that the new law applies upon the first public dissemination after its effective date.

3. SUBSISTING COPYRIGHTS

a. Length of term

We believe that, as far as feasible, the term provisions of the new law should be applied to subsisting copyrights. Thus, (1) we would have the term of subsisting copyrights run to the end of the calendar year, (2) we would extend the period for renewal registration to 5 years, and (3) we would lengthen the renewal term from 28 to 48 years. However, the base point for computing the term under the present law (publication or earlier registration) should remain unchanged for subsisting copyrights.

b. Ownership of future renewal rights

The new law would change the present renewal system in regard to the persons entitled to copyright for the renewal term. Where a subsisting copyright is in its first term at the effective date of the new law, who is to have the future renewal rights?

Certain persons will have acquired expectancies of the future renewal rights under the present law—expectancies that might accrue to them when the time for renewal arrives, depending upon who is living at that time. Substantial sums have been invested in some of these expectancies. To apply the new law would deprive potential claimants and their assignees of their expectancies in many cases.

Consequently, we believe that the present provisions as to who may renew should remain in effect for preexisting copyrights in their first term. It is unfortunate that the highly troublesome provisions for the reversion of renewal rights should continue in effect for 28 years longer, but we believe this is preferable to the confusion and unfairness that would result if existing renewal expectancies were cut off.

c. Ownership of renewal copyright for extended period

Under our recommendations, the new law would extend the renewal term of subsisting copyrights from 28 to 48 years, whether renewed before or after the effective date of the new law. Where the author or his heirs assigned their renewal rights before the effective date of the new law, who should have the copyright for the added 20 years? We believe there would be little justification for lengthening the term unless the author or his heirs were to receive some benefit from it. At the same time, the interests of their assignees must also be considered.

If the assignee is obligated to continue paying royalties or a part of his revenue to the author or his heirs during the entire life of the copyright, we would allow the assignment to remain in effect during the added 20 years. On the other hand, if the author or his heirs would otherwise receive no benefit from the lengthened term, we would terminate the assignment at the end of the 28th year of the renewal term, even if it purported to convey ownership for the length of the copyright "and any extensions thereof"; the copyright for the remaining 20 years would then revert to the author or his heirs.

4. RECOMMENDATIONS

a. With respect to preexisting works not under copyright at the effective date of the new law—

(1) Works in the public domain on that date should stay in the public domain.

(2) Preexisting works that have not been published or registered before the effective date should come under the new law upon their first public dissemination after that date. But this should not apply to a dissemination that merely continues a series of disseminations begun before that date.

b. With respect to copyrights subsisting at the effective date of the new law—

(1) The term should continue to be computed from the first publication or earlier registration of the work. The new law should apply in the following respects:

(*a*) The term should run to the end of the calendar year.

(*b*) The period for renewal registration should be the last 5 years of the original 28-year term.

(*c*) The renewal term should be lengthened to 48 years.

(2) Subsisting copyrights that are still in the original term on the effective date should be renewable by the persons entitled to renew under the present law.

(3) Assignments of renewal rights, executed by an author or his representatives or heirs before the effective date, should expire at the end of the 28th year of the renewal term, and the copyright for the additional 20 years should revert to the author or his heirs, except where the assignee is obligated to continue paying royalties or a part of his revenue to the author or his heirs during the entire life of the copyright.

Chapter VI

NOTICE OF COPYRIGHT

Outline of Chapter

59

CHAPTER VI

NOTICE OF COPYRIGHT [1]

A. The Present Law

1. NOTICE IN PUBLISHED COPIES REQUIRED

The requirement that published copies of copyrighted works bear a notice of copyright has been in the U.S. copyright law since 1802. Before that, the first U.S. copyright law enacted in 1790 required that notice of copyright be given by publishing the record of copyright registration in one or more newspapers.

The present law (sec. 10) requires, as a condition of copyright, that "the notice of copyright * * * shall be affixed to each copy [of the work] published or offered for sale in the United States by authority of the copyright proprietor." The notice must be in a prescribed form (sec. 19) consisting of (1) the word "Copyright" or the abbreviation "Copr." or the symbol ©, accompanied by (2) the name of the copyright proprietor and (3) the year in which copyright was secured. An alternative form without the year date is permitted for certain artistic or graphic works. The notice must be placed in specified positions (sec. 20) varying for different classes of works.

The copyright notice is designed to apprise persons coming into possession of a published copy that the work is copyrighted, who owned the copyright at the time of publication, and, where required, the year in which the copyright term began to run.

2. EFFECT OF OMISSION OF NOTICE

The absence of a notice in the published copies of a work can ordinarily be taken to mean that the work is in the public domain. This is not always true, however. For example, the absence of a notice in copies published without the consent of the copyright owner will not invalidate the copyright. And under section 21 of the present law, the omission of the notice from a few copies by accident or mistake will not invalidate the copyright; but an innocent infringer who has been misled by the omission is absolved from liability.

3. EFFECT OF ERRORS IN FORM OR POSITION OF NOTICE

Errors in the form or position of the notice, as well as its complete omission, may result in the loss of copyright. Earlier court decisions tended to require precise compliance with the statutory specifications as to the form and position of the notice. However, the trend of the more recent decisions has been to uphold notices which, though falling short of literal compliance with the statute, are adequate to apprise the public of the information required.

---

[1] See "Copyright Law Revision Studies Nos. 7–9"

61   (1261)

4. PROVISION FOR NOTICE IN THE UNIVERSAL COPYRIGHT CONVENTION

The Universal Copyright Convention, to which the United States adheres, permits any member country to require a copyright notice in the published copies of foreign works as a condition of their protection. If the prescribed notice is used, no other formality—such as deposit, registration, or domestic manufacture—is to be required for copyright protection.

The notice prescribed by the Convention differs in one important respect from that prescribed by our statute: Instead of specifying the position of the notice, the Convention provides that it be "placed in such manner and location as to give reasonable notice of claim of copyright." This liberalized provision has been inserted in section 9(c) of our statute, but it applies only to foreign works protected under the Convention.

B. ARGUMENTS FOR AND AGAINST THE NOTICE REQUIREMENT

1. VALUE OF THE NOTICE

a. *Placing published material in the public domain*

The notice requirement serves to place most of the great mass of published material in the public domain, while giving authors the opportunity to secure copyright when they want it.

Most published material bears no notice, and is therefore in the public domain, because the author is not interested in securing copyright. This uncopyrighted material includes, for example, most pamphlets, circulars, corporation and society reports, manuals, advertising matter, newspapers, etc., which have little or no commercial value for copyright exploitation. It also includes scholarly, scientific, and other informational matter which the author is willing to make freely available for reproduction and circulation by anyone.

b. *Showing whether a work is under copyright*

The notice on a published work serves to inform the public that the work is under copyright. Its absence generally indicates that the work is in the public domain.

c. *Identifying the copyright owner*

The notice indicates who is the copyright owner at the time of publication. In foreign countries where no notice is required, the laws commonly provide that if the author is identified in the copies of the work, he is presumed to own the copyright; otherwise the publisher named in the copies is presumed to be the copyright owner. In a substantial number of instances, however, the notice required by our law shows that the copyright owner is someone other than the person to whom such a presumption would apply.

It is true, of course, that the copyright owner named in the published copies may later assign the copyright to another person. For this reason it is often necessary to search the assignment records in the Copyright Office to determine ownership with certainty. But the notice, by naming the owner at the time of publication, provides a starting point from which further transactions can be traced.

d. *Showing the year of publication*

The year date in the notice gives the public a basis for determining when the copyright expires. The notice will not usually show whether the copyright has been renewed; a search of the Copyright Office records will be necessary to determine that fact. But the public will know that the copyright expires 28 years after the date in the notice if not renewed, and—under the term proposals we are making—that it expires 76 years after that date at the most. The year date of publication is also of value to the public for other purposes, as in showing the age of a particular work or edition.

2. OBJECTIONS TO THE NOTICE REQUIREMENT

a. *In general*

There has been considerable sentiment, particularly among some author and publisher groups, for complete elimination of the notice requirement. Others, especially those who use copyright material, have been no less firm in urging that the notice is of great value and should be retained. It seems generally agreed that if a notice requirement is retained, the rigid specifications of the present law as to its form and position should be relaxed.

The elimination of the notice requirement would mean that everything potentially copyrightable is under copyright protection. With some exceptions for particular kinds and uses of works, this is the state of the law in most foreign countries. Advocates of eliminating our notice provision argue that, as a matter of principle, all authors are entitled to have copyright in all their works without any requirement that they assert their desire for copyright protection. They urge that it is unjust to deprive an author of copyright because of his failure to comply with a technical notice requirement.

b. *Inadvertent loss of copyright*

The chief objection to the present notice requirement is that copyright may be—and in a significant number of instances has been—lost unwittingly because, through mistake or inadvertence, the notice has been omitted or a fatal error has been made in its form or position.

We believe that the inadvertent forfeitures of copyright that occur under the present notice requirement should and can be avoided by appropriate modifications of the present provisions.

3. CONCLUSIONS

We believe the public interest is served by keeping free of copyright restrictions the great bulk of published material in which the authors do not wish to secure copyright. The copyright notice is a simple and highly useful device to accomplish that purpose, and also to give the public information as to the copyright status and ownership of any work. We would therefore continue to require a copyright notice in published copies, but with certain changes in the present law to avoid the forfeiture of copyright through inadvertent omission of or errors in the notice.

As under the present law, the notice requirement should be confined to published copies, although copyrighted works are also disclosed to the public by other means of disseminatiton. It would not be practicable to require that a copyright notice be given, for example, at each public performance of a work. Nor does there seem to be the same need for a notice on such occasions. A notice is needed more particularly when copies of the work, from which it can readily be reproduced, are placed in the hands of the public.

C. Proposed Changes in the Notice Provisions

1. INADVERTENT OMISSION OF NOTICE

Section 21 of the present law provides that when the copyright owner has sought to comply with the notice requirement, the omission of the notice "by accident or mistake * * * from a particular copy or copies" shall not invalidate the copyright. However, an innocent infringer who has been misled by the omission of the notice is absolved from liability for damages, and his infringement is not to be enjoined unless he is reimbursed for his outlay.

This provision applies only where the notice is affixed to most of the published copies, but is omitted from a few copies by accident or mistake. We believe that section 21 has served a valuable purpose, and we would retain it in substance.

We believe further that the same principles should be extended to cover the inadvertent omission of the notice from more than a few or from all of the copies in a published edition or printing. We would not sanction a deliberate omission of the notice, but we would avoid forfeiture where the claimant indicates his desire for copyright protection and shows that omission of the notice was inadvertent.

We propose that the inadvertent omission of the notice from more than a few copies or from an entire edition or printing should not invalidate the copyright if (a) the work has been registered before, or is registered within 1 year after, the publication of copies without the notice, and (b) within that 1 year the claimant files a statement of the circumstances causing the omission.

However, since the absence of notice is an indication to the public that the work is not under copyright, an innocent infringer who is misled by the absence of notice should be shielded from liability. We therefore propose that anyone who, relying on the absence of the notice, innocently begins an infringing undertaking before he is actually informed that a copyright claim has been registered, should not be held liable for infringement. Nor should he be enjoined from completing the undertaking innocently begun unless he is fully reimbursed for his outlay.

2. ERRORS IN FORM OF NOTICE

The most common errors in the form of the notice that have forfeited or jeopardized copyrights occur in (a) giving the wrong name or year date in the notice, and (b) giving the name or date elsewhere than in conjunction with the copyright word or symbol.

a. Wrong name or date

We propose that an erroneous name or date in the notice should not invalidate the copyright, but that any person not actually informed otherwise should be entitled to act on the assumption that the name and date given in the notice are correct.

In the case where the year date given is later than the correct one, this assumption would not be enough to protect the public. The later date will indicate that the copyright term extends beyond its actual duration. It frequently occurs, however, that a work is published near the end of a year bearing the date of the next year; this error is not serious. We propose that where the notice is post-dated by more than 1 year, the claimant should be required to record in the Copyright Office, within 1 year after publication with the erroneous date, the correct date with a statement of the circumstances in which the later date was given.

b. Separated name or date

Where one or more names or dates appear in the copies but are so separated from the copyright word or symbol as not to be clearly identified as part of the notice, the copyright should not be invalidated; but certain presumptions should be established as to the name or date to be considered part of the notice.

3. POSITION OF THE NOTICE

The specifications in the present law (sec. 20) as to the position of the notice are unnecessarily rigid. The purpose would be served by a general requirement that the notice be so placed that it will reasonably come to the attention of the public. In accordance with this principle the Universal Copyright Convention provides that the notice may be "placed in such manner and location as to give reasonable notice of claim of copyright," and this provision has been inserted in our law (sec. 9(c)) in respect of foreign works protected under the Convention. We propose that a similar provision be adopted for all works.

4. NOTICE IN COLLECTIVE WORKS

A special problem is presented as to the notice in collective works (such as periodicals and anthologies) containing a number of component works that might be copyrighted separately. In some situations it is doubtful whether a single notice giving the copyright owner and year date of the collective work as a whole satisfies the notice requirement as to the individual component works, particularly where a component work was previously copyrighted.

We propose that a single notice for a collective work as a whole should suffice also for the individual component works. This should apply to component works previously copyrighted, but without extending the copyright term for those works. The public should be entitled to rely upon the single notice as to any component work for which no separate notice is given. (In dealing with the public, the person named in the notice would act as trustee for others having rights in the component works: see ch. VIII, pt. B 4 b.)

5. YEAR DATE

a. To be required on all published works

"The year in which the copyright was secured by publication" is now required in the notice on literary, musical, and dramatic works (sec. 19). For graphic and art works, however, the present law permits the use of a special short form of notice which omits the year date. This short form was provided for in the act of 1909 because of objections that the longer form then required for other works, if placed on the face of a graphic or art work, would disfigure it. Our proposals as to the form and position of the notice would go far toward eliminating the basis for this objection. Since the year date gives important information to the public, we believe it should be required in the notice for all classes of published works.

b. *Date to be year of publication*

Where copyright is secured by registration of an unpublished work, and the work is later published with no change in substance, the present law has been construed as requiring that the date in the notice be the earlier year of registration. This has caused confusion and has resulted in erroneous notices in some cases.

We have proposed in chapter IV that copyright begin upon the first public dissemination of a work in any of several ways (including registration). However, a requirement that published copies contain the year of an earlier dissemination would upset existing practices and aggravate the present confusion. Under our recommendations in chapter V the copyright term of published works, if not renewed, would be measured from their first publication. The date of publication is also meaningful for other purposes.

For these several reasons, the date required in the notice should be the year of first publication in all cases.

D. RECOMMENDATIONS

1. A notice of copyright, consisting of either the word "copyright" or the symbol ©, accompanied by the name of the copyright owner and the year date of first publication, should be required in all published copies of copyrighted works.

2. With respect to inadvertent omission of the notice:

(a) If the notice is omitted inadvertently from a few copies only, and other copies bear the notice, the copyright should not be invalidated.

(b) If the notice is omitted inadvertently from more than a few copies or from an entire edition or printing, the copyright should not be invalidated if:

(1) a copyright claim is registered before, or within 1 year after, publication of the copies without notice, and

(2) a statement of the circumstances of the omission is filed within that 1-year period.

(c) In any case, an innocent infringer who is misled by the omission should not be liable for an infringement begun before he is actually informed that a copyright claim has been registered, and should not be enjoined from completing the infringement innocently begun unless he is fully reimbursed for his outlay.

3. An erroneous name or date in the notice should not invalidate the copyright. However:

(a) Any person not actually informed otherwise should be entitled to act on the assumption that the name and date given in the notice are correct.

(*b*) Where the year date in the notice is more than 1 year later than the date of first publication, the claimant should be required to record in the Copyright Office, within 1 year after the publication of copies bearing the later date, a statement showing the correct year date and the circumstances in which the later date was given.

4. Where there is no name or no date accompanying or clearly associated with the rest of the notice, it should be presumed that, for purposes of the notice:

(*a*) The author named in the copy, or the publisher if no author is named, is the copyright owner.

(*b*) The imprint or issue date in the copy is the date of first publication.

5. The statute should not require that the notice be placed in a specified position. Instead, it should merely require that the notice be so placed that a reasonable inspection of the copy will reveal it.

6. A single notice in a collective work should be a sufficient notice for the work as a whole and for each of the component works, including those previously copyrighted. The single notice should be presumed to apply to all the component works for which no separate notice is given.

Chapter VII

REGISTRATION AND DEPOSIT OF COPIES

OUTLINE OF CHAPTER

CHAPTER VII

REGISTRATION AND DEPOSIT OF COPIES [1]

A. The Present Law

1. HISTORICAL DEVELOPMENT

A system of copyright registration has been a basic feature of our copyright law from its beginning in 1790, and the deposit of material to identify the work being registered has always been required. Since 1846 (except for one interval of a few years) copies of published works under copyright have also been required to be deposited in the Library of Congress for its collections.

Until 1909, copyright was secured by a registration made before the work was published. The deposit of certain material identifying the work was required for registration. After the work was published, copies of the published edition were required to be deposited.

The pre-1909 law resulted in the forfeiture of copyright when works were inadvertently published before being registered. To avoid these forfeitures, the act of 1909 inaugurated the present system: copyright is now secured by publication of the work with the copyright notice, and registration is made later when copies of the work as published are deposited. The one deposit now serves both to identify the work for the registration record and to enrich the collections of the Library of Congress.

2. PROVISIONS OF THE PRESENT STATUTE

The present statute provides that after copyright has been secured by publication of the work with the notice, copies of the work, accompanied by a claim of copyright, shall be "promptly" deposited in the Copyright Office (sec. 13). When the deposit has been received, the Copyright Office is to make registration and issue a certificate (secs. 11, 208, 209). Deposit and registration are prerequisites to the institution of an infringement suit (sec. 13). The certificate of registration is to be "admitted in any court as prima facie evidence of the facts stated therein" (sec. 209).

Copyright may also be secured for certain classes of unpublished works by a voluntary deposit and registration. Where a work registered in unpublished form is later published, copies of the published edition must be deposited promptly (sec. 12).

If the required deposit is not made promptly after publication, the Register of Copyrights may demand it. Failure to comply with the demand within certain time limits will subject the copyright owner to a fine and will void the copyright (sec. 14).

---

[1] See "Copyright Law Revision Studies Nos. 17, 18, and 20"

3. THE REQUIREMENT OF "PROMPT" DEPOSIT

Instead of specifying a time period for the deposit, the present statute provides that deposit shall be made "promptly" after publication. What constitutes a "prompt" deposit, and the consequences of failure to deposit "promptly," remained open questions until the decision of the Supreme Court in *Washingtonian Publishing Co.* v. *Pearson* (306 U.S. 30 (1939)). It is now settled by that decision that a long delay in making the deposit does not affect the validity of the copyright or its enforcement against an infringement occurring before the deposit. Consequently, deposit may be deferred until (1) the Register of Copyrights makes a demand or (2) the copyright owner needs to institute an infringement suit.

As a practical matter, the Register cannot ascertain all works published with a copyright notice, and most copyrights are never involved in litigation. The result is that for many copyrighted works deposit and registration may be withheld indefinitely or never made.

B. THE REGISTRATION SYSTEM

1. VALUES OF REGISTRATION

a. *Value to copyright owners*

Registration provides, for authors and other copyright owners, a permanent and official record of their copyright claims. It furnishes them with proof of the existence of their works at a particular time and the facts supporting their copyright claims. Particularly important to them is the certificate of registration, which constitutes prima facie evidence of the stated facts and is generally accepted in trade circles as proof of copyright.

b. *Value to users*

Registration serves other purposes, perhaps even more important, for persons who wish to use copyright materials. It provides acccessible official records from which they can obtain information regarding the existence and basis of a copyright claim, the extent of the claim (e.g., in a new version of a preexisting work), its duration, and its initial ownership. In conjunction with the records of assignments and other transfers of ownership, it enables users to trace title to the copyright.

c. *Other values*

A registration system also has other values:

(1) It provides a means for securing the automatic deposit of copies for the collections of the Library of Congress.

(2) It provides an administrative review of copyright claims whereby—

- Many unfounded claims, usually resulting from a lack of understanding or knowledge of the law, are weeded out, thus avoiding needless controversy and litigation;
- Authors and other claimants not familiar with the law are informed of the requirements for copyright protection;

The courts and the public are assisted in construing the law.

(3) It facilitates the enforcement of certain requirements and restrictions in the law, such as those pertaining to domestic manufacture and imports (discussed below in ch. X, pts. B and C).

In the major foreign countries that have no public registry for copyrights, private organizations find it necessary to maintain much the same kind of copyright records for their own use. This is indicative of the value of a registration system, but we believe that a public registry is greatly preferable: it provides a single, comprehensive record that is official, based on an administrative review, and freely accessible to the public. Private records may serve the purpose of the particular groups that maintain them, but they do not provide, for users of copyright materials and for the public, the accessible source of authoritative information afforded by a central public registry.

2. PROPOSALS FOR A REVISED REGISTRATION SYSTEM

a. Basis of proposed system

Most interested groups in the United States appear to favor a public registration system that would provide the most complete and dependable record possible. At the same time most groups feel that failure to register should not entail forfeiture of copyright. No such forfeiture results under the present law, except where a demand by the Register of Copyrights is not complied with.

We agree with this approach. Accordingly, we propose that registration should not be required to sustain a copyright secured by publication or other public dissemination of the work, but that strong inducements to make registration within a reasonable time should be provided.

The problem of securing copies for the Library of Congress when they are not deposited for registration will be dealt with later in this chapter.

b. Inducements to register

(1) *Benefits of registration to copyright owners.*—The inherent value of the registration record to the copyright owner, and the prima facie proof afforded by the registration certificate, would probably induce a substantial number of registrations. But in those foreign countries having a wholly voluntary system of registration, where similar benefits are the only inducement, most copyrights are not registered. More compelling inducements are also needed to achieve the objective of fairly complete coverage of all copyright claims in the registration records.

(2) *Certain remedies dependent upon registration.*—We propose that these other inducements be provided by making certain remedies for infringement available only for registered copyrights.

The remedies available against copyright infringers (discussed below in ch. IX) include those comparable to the remedies usually accorded for torts in general—namely, (*a*) an injunction to prevent future infringement and (*b*) recovery of the actual damages suffered by the copyright owner. The other remedies are somewhat unusual— (*c*) an award of the infringer's profits, (*d*) an award of statutory damages in lieu of a lesser amount of actual damages and profits, and (*e*) the impounding and destruction of infringing articles.

We propose that where a copyright has not been registered within a prescribed period of time, the remedies available for an infringement commenced before registration should be limited as follows:

(*a*) The copyright owner should recover the actual damages shown to have been suffered by him.

(*b*) No award of profits as such or of statutory damages should be allowed. (In some cases the infringer's profits may be a measure of the actual damages.)

(*c*) The court should have discretion to enjoin future infringements.

(*d*) The court should also have discretion to enjoin the completion of an infringing undertaking commenced before registration, or to order the impounding and destruction of infringing articles, but only on condition that the infringer be fully reimbursed for his outlay.

We believe that the matter of awarding costs and attorney's fees to the prevailing party (see ch. IX, pt. D) should be left to the court's discretion in any case.

In addition to these civil remedies, a willful infringement for profit would be subject to criminal penalties (see ch. XI, pt. B 1) even though the copyright had not been registered.

c. Time period for registration

To be most useful and reliable as a source of information, registratration should be made shortly after the first public dissemination of the work. We believe that a period of 3 months after dissemination in the United States, or 6 months after dissemination abroad, would allow the copyright owner a reasonable period of time to apply for registration.

All the remedies for infringement—including the infringer's profits, statutory damages, and injunctions without reimbursement—would be available where the copyright is registered within the 3- or 6-month period. Where registration is delayed beyond that period, all the remedies would still be available for an infringement commenced after registration, but only the limited remedies would be available for an infringement commenced before registration.

d. Exemption for U.C.C. works

The Universal Copyright Convention provides that foreign works covered under the convention, if they are unpublished or if they are published with a prescribed notice, are to be protected without deposit or registration. Their registration may be required, however, as a prerequisite to suit. The statute (sec. 9(c)) exempts these works from the present registration requirements, except before suit.

It might be argued that as long as registration is not a condition of copyright protection, and reasonably adequate remedies are provided for infringement of unregistered works, the withholding of additional remedies where the work is not registered would be consistent with the U.C.C. This, however, may be open to some question. It would comport better with the spirit of the U.C.C., if not its letter, to continue exempting foreign works covered under the convention from the consequences of failure to register. These works should therefore be excluded from the proposed limitations on the remedies for infringement of unregistered works.

e. Registration as prerequisite to suit

The present law (sec. 13) provides that no infringement action shall be maintained until the work has been registered. Since the registration process identifies unfounded claims and assists the courts in establishing presumptive facts and applying the law, we believe the requirement of registration before suit should be maintained, but with one important modification.

Where registration has been applied for, but has been refused by the Register of Copyrights on the ground that the claim is invalid, the claimant may now bring an action in the nature of mandamus against the Register, seeking to establish that the claim is valid and entitled to registration. In *Vacheron & Constantin-Le Coultre Watches, Inc.* v. *Benrus Watch Co.* (260 F. 2d 637 (1958)), the Second Circuit Court construed the present law as meaning that the claimant whose application had been refused could not maintain a suit against an infringer until registration had been secured through an action against the Register.

We believe this result is unfortunate. If the infringement continues, the delay involved in proceeding first against the Register may aggravate the injury. And two successive actions—usually in different jurisdictions—may be an expensive burden.

Where a claimant has deposited the required copies, application, and fee, and registration has been refused, we believe he should be entitled to maintain a suit against an infringer. The validity of the claim would be determined in that suit. But the Register should be notified of the suit and given the opportunity to advise the court of the reasons for refusing registration.

f. Probative effect of registration

The present law (sec. 209) makes the certificate of registration prima facie evidence in any court of the facts stated. The certificate is not conclusive proof but, if not controverted, the facts stated supply the basis for determining the subject matter, ownership, and subsistence of the copyright.

The facts shown in the certificate are derived from the claimant's application, after an administrative examination of the application and deposit copies. They have generally proved to be reliable, and the prima facie proof afforded by the certificate simplifies judicial proceedings.

The reliability of the facts supplied by the claimant, however, is less certain when registration is made long after the copyright claim originated. This is true particularly when registration is made on the eve of an infringement suit, or is made by a claimant who is not the original owner.

We propose that registration certificates should continue to be prima facie proof when registration is made within 1 year after the first public dissemination of the work. When registration is delayed for more than 1 year, the probative effect of the certificate should be left to the discretion of the court.

g. Authority of the Register of Copyrights to refuse registration

The Register of Copyrights has for many years exercised the authority to refuse registration when he finds that the article deposited is not copyrightable, or that the requirements for securing copyright or for registration have not been fulfilled. A recent survey shows, in round figures, that out of 250,000 applications received in a year, 6,000 or 2.4 percent were rejected. Of the rejections, 40 percent were for articles considered not copyrightable, 35 percent for articles not bearing the required notice, 17 percent for unpublished material of classes not eligible for registration, and the remaining 8 percent for miscellaneous reasons.

There have been several mandamus actions against the Register. In two cases, where he had refused registration on the ground that the materials deposited were not the copies required by the statute, the court held the deposit adequate and ordered registration. In other cases the courts have sustained his refusal to make registration on the ground that the articles were not copyrightable. Because the Register's authority to refuse registration is not stated explicitly in the statute, unsuccessful claimants have sometimes challenged his authority to reject applications for any reason.

We believe that if claims were registered without regard to their validity, the registration records and certificates would lose much of their probative value to claimants, the public, and the courts.

We suggest that the statute should state explicitly what we believe it now implies: (1) That the Register is required to make registration of any claim appearing to be valid under the statute, upon compliance with the procedural requirements for registration; and (2) that he is authorized, subject to review by the courts, to refuse registration for any claim he finds invalid.

As indicated above, his refusal should not prevent the claimant from bringing an infringement suit in which the validity of the claim can be determined by the court.

3. RECOMMENDATIONS

(*a*) Registration should not be a requirement for copyright protection, but it should be available for any valid copyright claim.

(*b*) The Register of Copyrights should be required to make registration of any copyright claim that appears to be valid, upon deposit of the prescribed copies, application, and fee. His authority to refuse registration of any claim he finds invalid, subject to review by the courts, should be stated expressly.

(*c*) Registration should continue to be a prerequisite to an action for copyright infringement. But where the procedural requirements for obtaining registration have been fulfilled and the Register of Copyrights refuses registration, the claimant should be entitled to bring an infringement suit if the Register is notified and permitted to become a party to the suit.

(*d*) The certificate of registration should continue to be admitted in any court as prima facie evidence of the facts stated, if registration is made within 1 year after the first public dissemination of the work. In the case of a later registration, the probative weight to be given to the certificate should be left to the discretion of the court.

(*e*) If registration is made within 3 months after the first public dissemination of the work in the United States, or within 6 months after its first public dissemination abroad, or at any time before an infringement is commenced, all remedies for the infringement should be available to the copyright owner. If registration is not made within that time, the civil remedies for an infringement commenced before registration should be limited to the following:

(1) The actual damages suffered by the copyright owner.

(2) In the discretion of the court, an injunction against future infringements.

(3) In the discretion of the court, an injunction against completion of the infringing undertaking commenced before registration, and the impounding and destruction of infringing articles made in the course of the undertaking, but only on condition that the infringer be fully reimbursed for his outlay.

(f) Foreign works entitled to protection under the Universal Copyright Convention, if they are unpublished or if published with the notice prescribed by the convention, should have all remedies for infringement without regard to the time of registration.

(g) An award of costs and attorney's fees to the prevailing party should be left to the court's discretion in all cases.

(h) The criminal penalties against a willful infringement for profit should be applicable without regard to the time of registration.

C. Deposit of Copies

1. PURPOSES OF DEPOSIT

Under the present law, the deposit of copies of copyrighted works is required for two purposes: (1) to identify the work being registered, and (2) to enrich the collections of the Library of Congress. A single deposit, accompanied by an application for registration, now serves both purposes.

2. DEPOSIT FOR THE LIBRARY OF CONGRESS

Most of the major countries of the world have established a deposit system of some kind to obtain copies of domestically published works for one or more libraries. In those countries having no copyright registration or a purely voluntary registration system, the deposit of copies is required apart from copyright. In other countries, as in the United States, copyright registration is a means of obtaining copies for the national library.

The deposit of copies in conjunction with copyright registration has been a principal source of acquisitions for the Library of Congress. Since 1909 about 7 million copies of various kinds of works have been supplied for the Library's collections out of copyright deposits. While the Library must acquire many uncopyrighted works from other sources—by gift, exchange, or purchase—the great bulk of the significant works published commercially in the United States have come to the Library through the copyright registration system.

3. DEPOSIT REQUIRED FOR REGISTRATION

a. In general

We believe that under the registration system recommended above most copyrighted works published in the United States will be registered. And it is economical for all concerned to have a single deposit that serves both for registration and for the Library of Congress.

The deposit required for registration should therefore continue to include the copies to be obtained for the Library.

b. Present requirements

For the purpose of copyright registration alone, the deposit of one copy of the work is sufficient; and where it is not practicable to deposit a copy of the work itself, other material identifying the work is usually an adequate substitute. Accordingly, for the registration of unpublished works, which are not generally wanted by the Library, the present law requires the deposit of one copy only or, in some cases, other identifying material (sec. 12).

Since most categories of published works are wanted by the Library, the present law requires, with certain exceptions, that two copies of the best edition of published works be deposited for registration (sec. 13). The exceptions—other than that for foreign works to be discussed below—pertain to categories of published works not generally wanted by the Library:

(1) For a separately copyrighted contribution to a periodical, only one copy of the periodical issue is required.

(2) For certain published works in the art classes, the Register of Copyrights may permit the deposit of photographs or other identifying reproductions in lieu of copies.

c. Need for flexibility

We believe that the basic approach of the present law—requiring, for registration, the deposit of two copies of a published work or one copy of an unpublished work, with exceptions to meet special situations—is sound. But the present statute does not permit exceptional treatment in a number of situations where exceptions are needed or warranted. For example:

• Under the present statute two complete copies of a published motion picture film must be deposited. The films are heavy, expensive, and inconvenient to handle. Other identifying material would suffice for registration, and the Library wants only one copy of selected motion pictures. In practice, the two films are usually returned to the depositor immediately after registration upon his agreement to supply one film for the Library if later requested.

• The requirement that each issue of a newspaper be deposited for separate registration has discouraged the copyrighting of daily newspapers.

• Similarly, the copyrighting of photographs has been hampered by the requirement that each separately published photograph be deposited for separate registration.

• A sound recording is not now acceptable as a deposit for a musical work. In some instances the work is first produced in the form of a sound recording, and transcription into the written notation required for deposit is difficult and expensive.

• For some categories of published works not wanted for the Library's collections, the deposit of one copy would suffice for registration where two copies are now required.

• The Copyright Office may now permit, but cannot require, the deposit of identifying photographs in lieu of copies of unwieldly or fragile art objects; it must accept actual copies when submitted though photographs would be preferable for storage, preservation, and reference.

An attempt could be made to specify in the statute the various exceptions to the basic requirement that two copies of a published work and one copy of an unpublished work be deposited for copyright registration. But we believe that the detailed exceptions should be left flexible to meet new and changing conditions. We propose that the Register of Copyrights, with the approval of the Librarian of Congress, be authorized to make exceptions by administrative regulation.

d. *Special provisions for foreign works*

Since it is not feasible to demand the deposit of works published in foreign countries, many of which are wanted by the Library, the present law seeks to facilitate and encourage their deposit. Thus, the deposit of one copy only is required for registration (sec. 13), or the registration fee is waived if two copies are deposited with a catalog card (sec. 215).

During the fiscal year 1960, a total of 12,785 works published in foreign countries were registered, 2,435 on deposit of one copy with the registration fee, and 10,350 on deposit of two copies without the fee. We believe the special deposit provisions have been a substantial factor in inducing the deposit and registration of foreign works.

We propose that these special provisions be retained with one minor change. The catalog cards deposited with the two copies for no-fee registration have proved to be of little or no use. The requirement of a catalog card should therefore be eliminated.

4. DEPOSIT FOR THE LIBRARY OF PUBLISHED WORKS NOT REGISTERED

a. *Deposit to be mandatory*

The registration system alone cannot be relied upon to obtain the copies of all copyrighted works published in the United States that are wanted by the Library. As long as registration is not mandatory, it can be expected that some copyrighted works will not be registered. Also, registration may be long delayed while the copies are needed by the Library at the earliest possible date.

We therefore propose that the statute should require the deposit of copyrighted works wanted by the Library within 3 months after they are published in the United States. This requirement would be fulfilled if the deposit were made in due time in conjunction with an application for registration, but the deposit would still be required if registration is not applied for.

b. *Changes in present law*

To carry out this proposal, we suggest that the present statute should be changed in the following respects:

- Instead of the present requirement that deposit be made "promptly" after publication (sec. 13), a time period of 3 months should be specified.
- The present law (sec. 13) is understood as requiring that each deposit of a published work be accompanied by an application for registration. Only the deposit of copies should be mandatory, with registration being optional.

• Since some categories of copyrighted works are not wanted by the Library, we propose that the Register of Copyrights, with the approval of the Librarian of Congress, be authorized to exclude any categories from the deposit requirement.

c. Penalty for failure to deposit after demand

When the Register makes a written demand for the required deposit, the penalty for failure to comply under the present law is forfeiture of the copyright and a fine of $100 plus twice the retail price of the work (sec. 14). It has been suggested that the forfeiture be eliminated and the fine increased to $200 plus twice the retail price of the work. There are differences of opinion on this question. Some believe that forfeiture is too drastic a penalty, while others are fearful that a fine alone might not be adequate to compel deposit. Under the present law, forfeiture cannot occur until 3 months after a specific demand has been made on the claimant, and in actual practice, the Register sends two or three preliminary requests for the deposit before he makes the demand. Forfeiture is rare and occurs in only four or five cases a year.

When foreign works protected under the Universal Copyright Convention are published in the United States, deposit could be demanded of the U.S. publisher. He would be made liable for the fine, but the Convention would preclude forfeiture of the copyright.

5. INCIDENTAL PROVISIONS REGARDING DEPOSITS

a. Mailing receipt

The present law (sec. 15) provides that the postmaster, if requested, shall give a receipt for copyright deposits placed in the mails. This is a vestige of the pre-1909 law under which copyright depended upon the deposit being made or placed in the mails by a certain date. The date of mailing now has little or no practical significance, and anyone wishing a receipt may obtain one for a small charge under general postal procedures. The special provision for a mailing receipt for copyright deposits is therefore superfluous.

b. Free postage

The present law (sec. 15) also provides that copyright deposits shall be mailed free of postage. In practice, the depositors pay the postage in about 70 percent of the cases. Since 1958 the Copyright Office has been required to pay the postage cost of free mailings, out of its appropriations, amounting to about $6,500 annually. We believe that the special procedures for the free mailing of copyright deposits are unnecessary, and that the depositor should pay the postage in the usual manner. We therefore propose that the free mailing privilege be discontinued.

c. Disposition of deposits

The present law (sec. 214) authorizes the Librarian of Congress and the Register of Coyprights to determine, at suitable intervals, which of the deposits not transfered to the Library are no longer needed for the files of the Copyright Office. These deposits may be destroyed after printing a notice in the Catalog of Copyright Entries to permit the copyright owners to reclaim them. A special notice must be sent to the copyright owner before any manuscript of an unpublished work may be destroyed during its term of copyright.

In practice, about half of all the copies deposited for registration are transferred to the Library. Of the remaining half, unpublished works are retained in the Copyright Office for the full copyright term, but most of the published works are disposed of after a few years.

The retention of all deposits for the full copyright term—which might be ideal in theory—is impracticable. Copies are now being deposited for registration at the rate of over 380,000 a year. The space and expense required to retain all deposits for the full copyright term would be prohibitive.

The present practice of disposing of most published works not transferred to the Library, after a few years, is based on the experience that requests for a deposit copy generally come within the first few years after registration. Instances in which a requested deposit was not found in the Library or the Copyright Office have been relatively rare. Moreover, copies of most published works are available elsewhere, and the registration records will usually identify the work deposited.

We propose that the present provisions for the disposition of deposit copies be retained in substance, with one change. The notice now required to be printed in the Catalog of Copyright Entries has almost never brought a request to reclaim a deposit. This useless procedure should be eliminated.

6. RECOMMENDATIONS

(*a*) For copyright registration, the deposit of two copies of the best edition of a published work, or one copy of an unpublished work, should be required, except that—

    (1) The Register of Copyrights, with the approval of the Librarian, should be authorized to make such modifications in these requirements, by regulation, as they find warranted by special circumstances.

    (2) For the registration of a work published abroad, a foreign claimant should have the option of depositing either one copy with the registration fee or two copies without the fee.

(*b*) The copyright owner of any work published in the United States with a copyright notice should be required to deposit two copies of the best edition in the Copyright Office for the Library of Congress, not later than 3 months after the date of publication, if such copies have not meanwhile been deposited for copyright registration.

    (1) The Register, with the approval of the Librarian, should be authorized to exclude any categories of works from this requirement.

    (2) The Register should be authorized to make a written demand for deposit of the copies. Failure to deposit within 3 months after the demand should subject the copyright owner to a fine of $200 plus the retail price of the two copies.

    (3) We make no recommendation at this time as to whether the present provision, that failure to comply with a demand voids the copyright, should be changed. In any event, failure to deposit copies would not affect the copyright in a foreign work protected under the Universal Copyright Convention.

(*c*) Section 15 of the present law—providing for a postmaster's receipt and free mailing of copyright deposits—should be eliminated.

(*d*) Section 214 of the present law—providing for the disposition of deposits not transferred to the Library—should be retained in substance, except for deletion of the requirement that a notice be printed in the Catalog of Copyright Entries before the deposits of published works are destroyed.

Chapter VIII

OWNERSHIP OF COPYRIGHT

OUTLINE OF CHAPTER

83

(1283)

CHAPTER VIII

OWNERSHIP OF COPYRIGHT

A. The Present Law

The present statute (sec. 9) gives the right to secure copyright to "the author or proprietor * * * or his executors, administrators, or assigns." In the case of a "work made for hire," the employer is deemed to be the author (sec. 26).

Under the common law, the author has literary property rights in his work upon its creation. He may assign his common law rights to another person or, if he dies owning them, they will pass on to his legatees or heirs. The owner of the common law rights is the person entitled to secure copyright under the statute.

The owner of a statutory copyright may assign it to another person (sec. 28). When the owner dies, the copyright will pass on to the legatees under his will (sec. 28) or to his heirs under the State laws of intestate succession.

We have discussed above (ch. V, pt. D 3) the special provision in section 24 giving the renewal rights to the author or specified heirs.

B. Initial Ownership

1. IN GENERAL

The right to secure statutory copyright is vested initially in the author, and any other claimant must acquire the right from him. This basic rule, however, is subject to two qualifications:

(*a*) In the case of a work produced "for hire," the employer has the right to secure copyright (sec. 26).

(*b*) In the case of a composite or collective work—such as a periodical or encyclopedia—the publisher has the right to secure copyright. The reference in section 9 to the "proprietor" as a person entitled to secure copyright was apparently intended to cover this situation.

2. WORKS MADE FOR HIRE [1]

a. Ownership of rights

The rule has long been established, both under the common law and under the statute, that the rights in a work produced by an employee in the course of his employment are vested in the employer. This rule has been based on several grounds: (1) the work is produced on behalf of the employer and under his direction; (2) the employee is paid for the work; and (3) the employer, since he pays all the costs and bears all the risks of loss, should reap any gain.

---

[1] See "Copyright Law Revision Study No. 13"

Some commentators have urged that this rule be changed for the benefit of employee-authors. They propose that the employer be given the exclusive right to use the work in his regular business activities, but that the employee should have the rights in other noncompetitive uses. To illustrate how this proposal would work:

- In the case of a story written for a magazine publisher by an employee, the publisher would have the exclusive right to publish the story in any periodical; but the employee would have the exclusive right to use the story in a book, motion picture, broadcast, or any other medium not competitive with the magazine.
- In the case of a script written for a motion picture company by an employee, the company would have the exclusive right to use the script in a motion picture; but the employee would have the exclusive right to publish it in a book or magazine. The employee's right to use the script for a stage or television play would depend upon whether, in the particular situation, that use would compete with the motion picture.

We believe that in some situations there is considerable merit in the argument that an employee-author should share in any commercial value his work may have beyond its use in the employer's business. But we see many practical difficulties in the proposal to divide the rights between employers and employees by a statutory formula:

- Controversial issues would frequently arise as to the scope of the employer's business, and as to the degree of competition between his business and particular uses of the work. No definite rules could be laid down to resolve these issues in the great variety of situations involved.
- The proposal would be unworkable in the common situation where a work is the composite product of many employees.
- It would often be difficult for potential users to know whom to deal with.

It is more practical, we believe, to continue the present rule that all rights vest in the employer. Where employees are in a position to do so, they may bargain—as some have done—for a share of the revenue derived by the employer from subsidiary uses of the work. Most employees are not in this position, but they would probably gain little or nothing from having rights which their employers could require them to assign. In any event, we do not believe that the great variety of situations involved—in which the employment relations, the nature of the works, and their potential uses differ widely—can be fitted into a general statutory formula for the division of rights.

b. *Form of statutory provision*

(1) *Scope of "works made for hire."*—The phrase used in the present statute—"works made for hire"—has been criticized as being inexact, because it might be thought to include works made on special commission. The courts, however, have not generally regarded commissioned works as "made for hire."

It has also been suggested that the statutory language should reflect the holding of the courts that an employee owns the right in a work created on his own initiative outside the scope of his employment.

Instead of the phrase "works made for hire," it was proposed in previous revision bills to substitute "works created by an employee within the regular scope of his employment." We would adopt this more precise language as a definition of "works made for hire."

(2) *Designation of employer as "author."*—The present provision (sec. 26) defining "author" as including "an employer in the case of works made for hire" has also been criticized on the ground that the employer is not in fact the author and should not be designated as such. It has been suggested that the statute, instead of indicating that the employer is the author, should merely provide that the right to secure copyright vests in the employer. We would adopt this suggestion.

3. COMPOSITE WORKS

a. Ownership of the work as a whole

In the case of a composite work—such as a periodical, encyclopedia, dictionary, or symposium—authorship of the work as a whole consists of compilation and editing. Ordinarily, this work is done by employees of the publisher, and the publisher secures the copyright.

The reference in section 9 to the "proprietor"—in addition to "the author * * * or * * * his assigns"—as a person entitled to secure copyright was inserted at the request of publishers of composite works. That reference, however, is cryptic and confusing. The publisher of a composite work acquires the right to secure copyright either as the employer or the assignee of the author. The additional category of "proprietor" as a person entitled to secure copyright is unnecessary. We propose that it be deleted.

b. Ownership of component parts

When the component parts of a composite work are created by the publisher's employees, the publisher acquires the rights in each part as employer. But when the component parts are contributed by independent authors, each author is the initial owner of his contribution, and the publisher must acquire his rights by assignment.

A contribution to a composite work may be copyrighted separately in the name of the author, by placing a separate copyright notice on the contribution. But this is not usually done. The common practice is to place a single notice on the composite work in the name of the publisher. We have recommended above (ch. VI, pts. C 4 and D 5) that the single notice should be deemed to cover all the component parts for which no separate notice is given. Accordingly, the publisher named in the notice should be considered the copyright owner of all the component parts not bearing a separate notice.

However, the author of a contribution may not have assigned all of his rights to the publisher. And in some cases there is no express agreement between them as to the assignment of rights. We propose that the rights not assigned should be held by the publisher in trust for the author. And in the absence of any express agreement, only the right to publish the contribution in a composite work like that of the publisher should be deemed to have been assigned.

4. RECOMMENDATIONS

The statute should provide that copyright may be secured by the author or his representatives, successors, or assigns, except that—

(*a*) In the case of a work made for hire (defined as a work created for an employer by an employee within the regular scope of his employment), the employer should have the right to secure copyright.

(*b*) In the case of a periodical, encyclopedia, or other composite work containing the contributions of a number of authors, the publisher should have the right to secure copyright. The copyright secured by the publisher in the composite work as a whole should cover all of the contributions not separately copyrighted; but the publisher should be deemed to hold in trust for the author all rights in the author's contribution, except the right to publish it in a similar composite work and any other rights expressly assigned.

C. CO-OWNERSHIP [2]

1. IN GENERAL

There are a number of situations in which two or more persons may become co-owners of the same rights in the same work:

* When two or more authors create a work in collaboration, they are usually co-owners of the rights in the first instance;
* When an author transfers to another person an undivided share of his rights, he and his transferee become co-owners;
* When an author transfers all his rights to two or more persons, they become co-owners;
* When a deceased author has two or more heirs, they may succeed to his rights as co-owners;
* Under the present law, when there are several persons in the class entitled to claim a renewal copyright, they take the renewal as co-owners.

Co-ownership must be distinguished from "divisibility," the concept discussed later in this chapter. "Divisibility" concerns the ownership by different persons of different rights in a work, while co-ownership means that two or more persons together own the same rights.

2. RIGHTS OF COOWNERS

The present statute is silent as to the rights of co-owners among themselves and in relation to third persons. The courts have dealt with these questions by adapting the established rules pertaining to the co-ownership of other forms of property by tenants in common. Under the court decisions, any one of the several co-owners of a copyright may use the work or license a third person to use it without the consent of the other owners, but he must share the profits with them.

One co-owner can, of course, assign his interest to a third person who would then become a co-owner in his stead. But since any

---

[2] See "Copyright Law Revision Study No. 12"

co-owner may use the work or license its use, no assignee or licensee of less than all the owners would acquire exclusive rights.

In the United Kingdom and a number of other countries the rule is that a use or license must have the consent of all the co-owners. Some of these countries have a supplemental provision that if one owner refuses his consent, the others may petition a court to arbitrate the dispute. This rule assures the right of every co-owner to control the use of his property. The contrary rule in the United States, on the other hand, facilitates the dissemination of works owned by two or more persons.

As a fundamental principle we believe it is in the public interest to encourage the dissemination of copyrighted works. As long as all co-owners are entitled to share in the profits, the right of any one owner to use or license the work will not ordinarily operate to the detriment of the others. We propose that the rules established by the courts be left undisturbed, and we see no need to restate them in the statute.

3. JOINT AUTHORSHIP

When two or more authors collaborate in creating a single work of joint authorship, they are initially co-owners of the work. When two or more authors independently create separate works, each is the sole owner of his own work even though the works are used collectively.

A clear example of a joint work is a single story written by two authors working together, their contributions being merged insepa-rably in a single whole. A clear example on the other side is that of several stories written independently by different authors and pub-lished together in a periodical. Between these two extremes, how-ever, there are many cases that are not so clear cut.

The present statute provides no basis for determining what con-stitutes a work of joint authorship. Until recently the courts have held rather consistently that the test is whether the authors col-laborated with the object of having their contributions combined into a single integrated work. Thus, where the composer of music and the author of lyrics intended to have their contributions inte-grated as a song, the courts have held the song a joint work even though the music and lyrics could each be used separately.

The test of joint authorship has been thrown into some confusion by a new theory that first emerged in the *Melancholy Baby* case decided by the Second Circuit Court of Appeals in 1946 (161 F. 2d 406), and was carried further in the *Twelfth Street Rag* case decided by the same court in 1955 (221 F. 2d 569, modified in 223 F. 2d 252). In the latter case the composer of a musical composition without words, written as an instrumental piece, had secured copyright in his composition, and had assigned the copyright to a publisher who later commissioned a lyricist to write words for the music. The two authors separately assigned their renewal rights to dif-ferent publishers. Though there was no collaboration between the authors, and the composer did not contemplate or consent to the addition of words to his music, the court held that the music and words together constituted a single work of joint authorship, so that the assignees of the two authors were co-owners of the renewal copyright in the song.

The theory of this decision is that a copyrighted work complete in itself will become a joint work if additions are made later by another author at the request of the copyright owner. This theory is a sharp departure from the view previously taken by the courts. It does not require that the authors collaborate, or that the original author have any intention that his work be combined with that of another author. Under this theory it might even be contended that any new version of a preexisting work is a joint work.

Aside from the uncertainty created by this decision, we believe its theory would lead to inappropriate results. If a new work consisting of a previously copyrighted work by one author and additional material added later by another is considered a work of joint authorship, the two authors (or their successors) become co-owners of the new work. Either of them could then use or license the use of the new work, and each would be entitled to share in the profits from its use. Moreover, the owner of the original work would continue to be a co-owner of the new work after the copyright in the original work had expired.

We believe the question of what constitutes a work of joint authorship should be clarified in the statute. We would not go as far as the theory of the *Twelfth Street Rag* decision, but would adopt the test laid down by the earlier line of cases—that a joint work is one created by two or more authors who intend to have their contributions joined together as a single work.

4. RECOMMENDATIONS

(*a*) The rules established by the court decisions in regard to co-owners of a copyright—that any one co-owner may use or license the use of the work, but that he must account for profits to the other co-owners—should be left undisturbed.

(*b*) A "work of joint authorship" should be defined in the statute as a work created initially by two or more authors with the object of integrating their contributions into a single work.

D. TRANSFER OF RIGHTS

1. IN GENERAL

The author or other owner of the right to secure copyright may transfer that right to another person. Likewise, when copyright has been secured, the copyright owner may transfer any or all of the rights embraced in copyright. Except for an author's right to renew the copyright under the present law, discussed in chapter V, part D 3, the rights not transferred by the owner pass upon his death to his heirs or legatees under State laws. The following discussion is concerned only with inter vivos transfers such as assignments.

Copyright comprises a number of different rights, which are discussed in chapter III. The owner may assign the entire copyright, or he may grant an exclusive license of one or more of the several rights. For example, the copyright owner of a dramatic work may grant to another person the exclusive right to perform it on the stage, while retaining to himself the other rights to publish the work, to convert it into a novel or a motion picture, to broadcast it, etc.

The copyright owner may also grant a nonexclusive license. This is a mere permit to use the work in the manner specified, and does not transfer ownership of any right.

2. DIVISIBILITY OF COPYRIGHT [3]

a. The present theory of "indivisibility"

Transfers covering one right but not others are common in commercial practice. These partial transfers are sometimes designated as exclusive licenses, and sometimes as "assignments." In practical effect an exclusive license of a particular right is equivalent to an assignment of that right. The licensee acquires the right to the exclusion of all other persons, including the licensor.

The theory of the present law, however, has lagged behind the realities of practice. In certain situations the courts have indicated that copyright is an indivisible unit and, consequently, that a transfer of some, but not all, of the rights comprised in a copyright is merely a license and not an assignment. This theory of indivisibility has created a number of troublesome problems:

- It is now uncertain whether the copyright in a periodical, secured by the publisher, covers the individual contributions, unless all rights in the contributions have been assigned to the publisher. (We have dealt with this problem in pt. B 4 b of this chapter.)
- The provisions of the present statute pertaining to transfers of ownership and their recordation (secs. 28–32) refer only to "assignments." It is now uncertain whether they apply to exclusive licenses or other partial transfers. (These provisions will be discussed in pt. D 2 of this chapter.)
- Whether a partial transfer is considered an assignment or a license may determine whether the proceeds are taxed as capital gains or ordinary income. Recent rulings, reversing earlier ones, have generally treated a partial transfer as an assignment for tax purposes.
- A partial transferee cannot now sue for infringement of a right transferred to him without joining the owner of the residual rights as a party to the suit.

This last—the necessity of joining the owner of the residual rights in an infringement suit—is particularly troublesome. Except where the validity of the copyright is challenged, he usually has no interest in the suit, and his joinder becomes a serious obstacle when he is out of the jurisdiction. Many commentators have urged that a partial transferee should be permitted to sue in his own name alone, subject to safeguards against multiple suits where the litigation also involves rights owned by other persons. These safeguards are now provided by rules 19–22 of the Federal Rules of Civil Procedure under which the court may require or permit the joinder or intervention of interested parties when appropriate.

---

[3] See "Copyright Law Revision Study No. 11"

b. *Proposals for divisible copyright*

We believe that the copyright owner should be in a position to assign any one or more of his rights without assigning the entire copyright. And a person who acquires a particular right exclusively should be treated as the owner of that right, though he is not the owner of other rights. This would bring the statute in line with commercial practice. Specifically, we propose that the law provide:

    (1) That any of the rights comprised in a copyright may be assigned separately.

    (2) That the statutory provisions governing "assignments" extend to exclusive licenses and other exclusive transfers of any right.

    (3) That the assignee of any particular right may sue in his own name alone for infringement of that right; but the court, in its discretion, may require or permit the joinder or intervention of any person appearing to have an interest in the suit.

c. *Owner in copyright notice*

Making copyright ownership divisible would raise questions under the present law as to whose name is to appear in the copyright notice on published copies of the work, and the effect of naming the owner of some but not all of the rights.

We believe these questions would be resolved by our recommendations in chapter VI. A notice in the name of any partial owner would protect the copyright. Other owners could establish their rights by recording a transfer from him in the Copyright Office. Third persons could deal safely with the owner named in the notice if no transfer from him is recorded. In dealing with third persons he would act as trustee for any other owner.

Two or more owners could be named in the notice with an indication of the rights held by each, if they wished. But in accordance with the principle that the wrong name in a notice should not invalidate the copyright, we would not require the naming of more than one owner.

3. PROTECTION OF AUTHORS AGAINST UNREMUNERATIVE TRANSFERS [4]

a. *In general*

The present statute has sought to protect authors against transfers of their rights for an inadequate remuneration, by providing for the reversion of the renewal copyright to the author or his heirs. In chapter V, part D 3, we have recommended that this reversion of the renewal right be eliminated, because it has largely failed to accomplish the purpose of protecting authors and their heirs against improvident transfers, and has been the source of much confusion and litigation.

Since authors are often in a relatively poor bargaining position, however, we believe that some other provision should be made to permit them to renegotiate their transfers that do not give them a reasonable share of the economic returns from their works.

---

[4] See "Copyright Law Revision Study No. 31"

b. Possible limitation on transfers

The laws in many foreign countries seek to protect authors and their heirs against disadvantageous transfers, by various provisions such as the following:

- Transfers are effective for not more than a certain period of time.
- Transfers for a lump sum are prohibited except in certain special situations.
- Only those rights specifically enumerated in the written instrument are transferred, with certain limitations on the transfer of all rights.
- Transfer agreements must meet certain statutory standards such as minimum royalties payable to the author and stated periods of time during which the transferee must exploit the work.

We would not favor a statutory specification of the terms and conditions of transfer agreements, or a prohibition of transfers on any particular terms. Transfers are made in a wide variety of situations; terms that may be unfair in some cases may be appropriate in others. And statutory specifications or prohibitions may hamper authors, as well as potential users, in arranging for the exploitation of copyright works.

The situation in which authors are most likely to receive less than a fair share of the economic value of their works is that of an outright transfer for a lump sum. At the time of transfer the revenue to be derived from the work cannot ordinarily be foretold with any degree of certainty. This fact has led to the common practice by which transferees agree to pay authors royalties based on the number of copies sold or performances given, or on a percentage of the revenue. There have been many cases, however, in which authors have sold outright, for a small lump sum, their rights in a work that later proves to be highly popular and lucrative; and lump-sum transfers are still not uncommon.

We would encourage the compensation of authors on a royalty basis, but we would not forbid lump-sum transfers. In some situations—for example, where a contribution is published in a periodical, or where a novel is converted into a motion picture—the payment of a lump sum may be the only or most practical way of remunerating the author.

In several of the revision bills of 1924 to 1940 which proposed to eliminate the reversionary renewal right, it was provided that transfers by an author were not to be effective for more than a certain period of time, after which the rights transferred would revert back to the author or his heirs. Some of those bills would have imposed the time limit on transfers for a lump sum, but not on transfers for which the author or his heirs would receive continuing royalties.

c. Conclusion

We believe this last approach—placing a time limit on transfers that do not provide for continuing royalties—would afford a practical measure of assurance that authors or their heirs will be in a position to bargain for remuneration on the basis of the economic value of their works.

We suggest that a period of 20 years would be ample to enable a lump-sum transferee to complete his exploitation of the work and to realize a fair return on his investment. If he should wish to exploit the work beyond that period, he could then negotiate a new contract with the author or his heirs. We do not believe this time limit would hamper exploitation.

4. RECOMMENDATIONS

(*a*) The statute should recognize the divisibility of copyright ownership. Specifically, it should provide:

(1) That any of the various rights comprised in a copyright may be assigned separately.

(2) That an exclusive license or other exclusive transfer of any particular right constitutes an assignment of that right.

(3) That the assignee of any particular right may sue in his own name alone for infringement of that right; but that the court, in its discretion, may require that notice of the suit be given to other persons appearing to have an interest in the suit, and may require or permit the joinder or intervention of any such person.

(*b*) The statute should provide that any assignment by an author or his representatives or heirs shall not be effective for more than 20 years from the date of its execution, unless it provides for the continuing payment of royalties based on the uses made of the work or the revenue derived from it.

E. EXECUTION AND RECORDATION OF TRANSFERS [5]

1. THE PRESENT LAW

Sections 28–32 of the present statute deal with "assignments" of copyright. Section 28 provides that copyrights may be "assigned, granted, or mortgaged by an instrument in writing signed by the proprietor of the copyright." Section 29 specifies how an "assignment executed in a foreign country" may be acknowledged. Section 30 provides for the recordation of "every assignment" in the Copyright Office within a specified period of time, and states the consequences of failure to record. Section 31 requires the Register of Copyrights to record "such assignment" and to issue a certificate of recordation. Section 32 provides that when an "assignment" has been recorded, the assignee may substitute his name in the copyright notice.

2. SCOPE OF "ASSIGNMENTS"

It is not clear whether the term "assignment," as used in sections 28–32, includes an exclusive license or other transfer of less than all the rights comprised in a copyright. Nor is it clear whether "assignments" includes other instruments—such as wills, trust indentures, decrees of distribution, mortgages and discharges, and corporate mergers—which evidence transfers of copyright ownership.

We propose that the provisions of the statute relating to "assignments" be extended expressly to cover exclusive licenses and all other transfers of any exclusive right under a copyright.

---

[5] See "General Revision Study No. 19"

3. FORM AND EXECUTION OF TRANSFERS

a. *Written and signed instrument*

Since transfers of copyright are important transactions and are to be recorded, they should be required—as "assignments" are now—to be in writing and signed by the transferor.

This requirement should not be extended to nonexclusive licenses. They do not transfer ownership but merely grant permission to use a work. In practice, they are frequently given orally.

b. *Acknowledgment*

The present statute does not require that an instrument transferring copyright ownership be acknowledged, and we see no reason to require it. We believe, however, that an acknowledgment should constitute prima facie evidence of the execution of a copyright transfer.

The only provision in the copyright statute dealing with acknowledgment is section 29, which specifies that an acknowledgment before an authorized consular officer or secretary of legation of the United States shall be prima facie evidence of the execution of an assignment in a foreign country. The comparable provision in the patent law (35 U.S.C. sec. 261) goes farther in two respects:

- Acknowledgment constitutes prima facie evidence of the execution of a patent assignment executed in the United States, as well as of one executed in a foreign country.
- Acknowledgment in a foreign country may be made either before an authorized "diplomatic or consular officer of the United States" or before "an officer authorized to administer oaths whose authority is proved by a certificate of a diplomatic or consular officer of the United States."

We propose that provisions similar to those in the patent law be incorporated in the copyright statute.

4. RECORDATION OF TRANSFERS AND OTHER INSTRUMENTS

a. *Purposes of recordation*

A recordation system for copyright transfers has the same basic purposes as recordation systems for transfers of other forms of property:

(1) To enable a transferee to give constructive notice to all third persons of the transfer of ownership to him; and

(2) To enable third persons to determine from the record who is the owner.

Records of copyright ownership are particularly important in view of the nature of copyright as a form of intangible and incorporeal property not capable of physical possession.

b. *Recordable instruments*

(1) *As to their content.*—In accordance with these purposes, the recordation system should embrace all instruments by which the ownership of a copyright is transferred in whole or in part.

In addition, there are other types of instruments which, though not transferring ownership, have some bearing on the status of a copyright. The Copyright Office now receives and records a number of miscellaneous documents such as nonexclusive licenses, powers of attorney, employment agreements, publishing contracts, changes in names or titles, and court decrees. In the absence of some provision in the statute for recording instruments of this sort, it is doubtful that their recordation operates to give constructive notice.

We do not believe it is necessary or practical to require that instruments other than transfers of ownership be recorded. But we would encourage the recordation of any instruments pertaining to a copyright, by providing that they may be recorded with the effect of giving constructive notice of the information disclosed.

(2) *As to their form.*—There should be practical assurance that the instrument recorded is precisely the same as the one executed. The statute should, therefore, require explicitly that any instrument filed for recordation bear the actual signature of the person executing it or a sworn or official certification that it is a true copy of the original signed instrument.

c. Constructive notice

Recordation serves to give constructive notice to all third persons of the facts disclosed in the recorded instrument. But there are two situations in which there is some uncertainty as to the scope of constructive notice:

(1) *Reference to unrecorded documents.*—In some cases a recorded instrument will refer to another unrecorded document for further information. We believe that third persons should be able to rely on the record as being complete in itself. The statute should, therefore, indicate that constructive notice is confined to the facts specified in recorded instruments.

(2) *Blanket transfers.*—In some cases a recorded transfer will cover "all the copyrights" owned by the transferor with no identification of the individual works. It may be extremely difficult and time-consuming for a third person to ascertain whether the copyright in a particular work is covered by such a blanket transfer. We believe the statute should indicate that constructive notice is confined to the copyrights in works specifically identified by the recorded instrument.

d. Effect of failure to record

(1) *In general.*—It is fundamental to the recordation system that: (*a*) Failure to record has no effect on the validity of the transfer as between the parties to it, but (*b*) third persons not otherwise informed are entitled to rely on the record and to deal with the person who appears from the record to be the owner.

In accordance with this principle, section 30 of the present statute provides that if an assignment is not recorded within 3 months after its execution in the United States, or within 6 months after its execution abroad, "it shall be void as against any subsequent purchaser or mortgagee for a valuable consideration, without notice, whose assignment has been duly recorded."

(2) *The grace period.*—Whether a grace period—now 3 or 6 months—should be allowed for recording a transfer is open to question. The present law assumes that a transferee should be allowed a period of time in which to record before the transfer to him is subject to being defeated by a subsequent transfer to another person. On the other hand, the result of a grace period is that no transferee can be certain of his title for that period of time after the transfer to him.

We believe the arguments for and against a grace period are rather evenly balanced. In that position we are inclined to continue the existing law. However, in view of present methods of rapid transportation, we believe the period of 3 or 6 months is unnecessarily long. We propose that it be reduced to 1 month for transfers executed in the United States and 3 months for transfers executed abroad.

(3) *Priority between conflicting transfers.*—Section 30 provides that, as between two conflicting transfers, the one first executed prevails when it is recorded within the grace period. Otherwise the later transfer, if taken in good faith for value, will prevail when it is the first to be recorded. Section 30 leaves unanswered the question of which prevails when the one first executed is recorded after the grace period but before the recordation of the later one.

The corresponding section in the patent law (35 U.S.C. sec. 261) provides that the first of two transfers of a patent will prevail if it is recorded within 3 months or prior to the date of the subsequent transfer.

We would adopt this principle in clarifying the copyright statute but with one change: We would retain the provision in section 30 that the later transfer must itself be recorded in order to prevail. In sum, we propose that the statute provide that the first of two conflicting transfers will prevail if it is recorded within the grace period or before the later one is recorded.

(4) *Priority of nonexclusive license.*—Another question left in doubt by section 30 is whether a nonexclusive license, obtained in good faith from the copyright owner of record, is effective as against an earlier unrecorded transfer. We believe that a licensee should be able to rely on the record when he seeks permission to use a work. We therefore propose that the statute specify that a nonexclusive license obtained in good faith is effective as against an earlier unrecorded transfer.

Since nonexclusive licenses are not required to be recorded, we believe that they now remain effective without recordation as against subsequent transferees of ownership. In some instances the nonexclusive licenses outstanding may affect the value of a transfer. Nevertheless, we are not proposing that recordation of such licenses be required. It would not be practicable to record the great number and variety of licenses that do not transfer ownership but merely permit the use of a work.

5. NAME OF TRANSFEREE IN COPYRIGHT NOTICE

Section 32 provides that when an assignment has been recorded, the assignee may substitute his name for that of the assignor in the copyright notice. An unfortunate result of this provision has been a judicial holding that, where the assignee's name is substituted before recordation of the assignment, the notice is fatally defective and the copyright is lost.

Our recommendations in chapter VI, concerning the name of the owner in the notice, would preserve the copyright in any case where an assignee is named in the notice, and would eliminate the question dealt with in section 32. That section should therefore be deleted.

6. RECOMMENDATIONS

(*a*) The provisions of the statute regarding "assignments" should be extended to cover exclusive licenses, mortgages, and all other transfers of any exclusive right under a copyright.

(*b*) The present requirement that assignments be in writing and signed by the assignor should be retained.

(*c*) Acknowledgment of the execution of an assignment, whether executed in the United States or abroad, should not be required but, when made, should be prima facie evidence of its execution. Acknowledgment abroad should be permitted before an authorized officer of the United States or before a foreign officer whose authority is certified by an officer of the United States.

(*d*) The statute should provide that an assignment or any other document pertaining to a copyright may be recorded in the Copyright Office, and that recordation will give constructive notice to all persons of the facts contained in the recorded document with respect to the works specifically identified.

(*e*) The statute should require that the document to be recorded must bear either the actual signature of the person executing it or a sworn or official certification that it is a true copy of the original signed instrument.

(*f*) The statute should provide that if an assignment is not recorded within 1 month after its execution in the United States, or within 3 months after its execution abroad, or before the recordation of a subsequent assignment, then the subsequent assignment will prevail when it is taken for a valuable consideration without notice and recorded first.

(*g*) The statute should specify that a nonexclusive license taken without notice of an unrecorded assignment will be valid as against the assignee; and that a nonexclusive license, though not recorded, will be valid as against a subsequent assignment.

Chapter IX

REMEDIES FOR INFRINGEMENT

(1299)

CHAPTER IX

REMEDIES FOR INFRINGEMENT

A. The Present Law

The civil remedies for copyright infringement are now provided in sections 101 and 116 of the statute. The provisions for criminal penalties (secs. 104–105) and those regarding judicial procedures (secs. 112–114) will be discussed below in chapter XI.

The present civil remedies are summarized as follows:

* The court in its discretion may enjoin the infringement (sec. 101(a)).
* The infringer is liable for the actual damages suffered by the copyright owner, "as well as" the infringer's profits. Or, in lieu of a smaller sum of actual damages and profits, the court is to award statutory damages in an amount it deems just; this amount, with certain exceptions, is to be not less than $250 nor more than $5,000 (sec. 101 (b)).
* The court may order the impounding, during the pendency of the action, of all articles alleged to be infringing, and may order the destruction of all infringing copies and devices for making them (sec. 101(c) and (d)).
* In all suits, except those by or against the United States, "full costs shall be allowed, and the court may award to the prevailing party a reasonable attorney's fee as part of the costs" (sec. 116).

B. Damages and Profits [1]

1. ACTUAL DAMAGES AND PROFITS

a. In general

Liability of a wrongdoer for the actual damages suffered by the injured person is a traditional remedy for civil wrongs generally. Actual damages have been one of the remedies for copyright infringement since the first U.S. copyright statute of 1790.

Liability for the profits derived from a wrongful act has also been recognized as a remedy for civil wrongs. The wrongdoer's profits may sometimes be a measure of the damages suffered by the injured person, or they may be awarded to prevent unjust enrichment. Liability for the profits from a copyright infringement was first specified in the act of 1909, but had been imposed by the courts in some earlier cases.

b. Damages and profits as cumulative or alternative remedies

Under the present law there is some question as to whether the copyright owner is entitled to recover both his damages and the in-

---

[1] See "Copyright Law Revision Studies Nos. 22 and 23"

fringer's profits cumulatively, in cases where the profits are more than a measure of the damages. The language of section 101(b) would seem to indicate so. However, the 1909 congressional committee reports (H. Rept. No. 2222, S. Rept. No. 1108, 60th Cong., 2d sess.) show that the intention was to allow the plaintiff to recover either his damages or the infringer's profits, whichever is greater. The few court decisions on this question do not seem to have settled the issue.

We believe the more equitable rule is that under which damages and profits are not cumulative. The statute should be clarified to provide for recovery of either damages or profits, whichever of the two is larger.

c. Problems in awarding profits

In regard to the infringer's profits, the statute now provides that the plaintiff must prove "sales" only, and that the defendant must prove all the elements of cost to be deducted. This provision seems sound in principle. However, since many infringements do not involve "sales," a broader term such as "gross revenue" should be used.

The courts have sometimes had difficulty in determining the elements that are properly deductible as costs. This seems essentially a problem of accounting inherent in the situation and not peculiar to copyright cases. We believe it would be impracticable to attempt any statutory specification of deductible costs.

Another question has arisen as to whether profits are to be apportioned where the infringer has used copyrighted and other materials together. The statute now refers to "all the profits * * * made from such infringement." In some of the earlier decisions the courts said that the infringer is liable to pay over all his profits without apportionment. But more recently the courts have construed the statutory language as meaning only the profits attributable to the infringing use of the copyrighted work, and have apportioned profits accordingly. We believe the statute should be clarified in accordance with these recent decisions, to permit the courts to apportion profits when they find it appropriate to do so.

2. STATUTORY DAMAGES

a. The principle of statutory damages

Statutory damages—stated amounts for which an infringer may be held liable as an alternative to actual damages—have been a feature of the U.S. copyright statutes since 1790. The need for this special remedy arises from the acknowledged inadequacy of actual damages and profits in many cases:

- The value of a copyright is, by its nature, difficult to establish, and the loss caused by an infringement is equally hard to determine. As a result, actual damages are often conjectural, and may be impossible or prohibitively expensive to prove.
- In many cases, especially those involving public performances, the only direct loss that could be proven is the amount of a license fee. An award of such an amount would be an invitation to infringe with no risk of loss to the infringer.
- The actual damages capable of proof are often less than the cost to the copyright owner of detecting and investigating infringements.

- An award of the infringer's profits would often be equally inadequate. There may have been little or no profit, or it may be impossible to compute the amount of profits attributable to the infringement. Frequently the infringer's profits will not be an adequate measure of the injury caused to the copyright owner.

In sum, statutory damages are intended (1) to assure adequate compensation to the copyright owner for his injury, and (2) to deter infringement. A stated minimum amount is to be awarded in any case, and the court may award more, up to a stated maximum, where it considers that the actual damages or profits capable of proof would be inadequate for those purposes. In principle, statutory damages are similar to the liquidated damages frequently provided in contracts, or to statutory amounts specified as damages in various statutes dealing with civil wrongs, such as wrongful death, workmen's compensation, and antidiscrimination laws.

The principle of statutory damages for copyright infringement appears to be acceptable generally to the interested groups. There is considerable sentiment, however, for changing some of the features of the present provisions. The points in issue will be considered below.

b. When statutory damages are awarded

With certain exceptions to be noted later, the amount of statutory damages that may be awarded ranges from $250 to $5,000. Within that range the court has discretion to award the sum it considers just, whenever that sum exceeds the actual damages and profits. Thus:

- If actual damages and profits are both less than $250, the court must award at least $250 and may in its discretion award a higher sum up to $5,000.
- If actual damages or profits are proven in some amount between $250 and $5,000, the court in its discretion may award either the proven amount or any higher sum up to $5,000.
- If actual damages or profits are proven in excess of $5,000, the court will award the proven amount. Statutory damages are not applicable in this case.

c. Mandatory minimum; innocent infringers

In any case the court must award at least $250. The representatives of various groups of copyright owners—authors, book and music publishers, motion picture producers, etc.—have stressed the vital importance to the copyright owner of a mandatory minimum. They argue that a minimum amount is essential to assure the recovery of enough to warrant the expense of detecting infringements, to compensate the owner for his loss, and to deter infringement.

On behalf of certain users of copyright materials—broadcasters, periodical publishers, motion picture exhibitors, etc,—it has been argued that the minimum of $250 can bear too heavily on innocent infringers. In a few cases where the defendant infringed unwittingly, the courts have expressed regret at being compelled to award the statutory minimum. It has been suggested that as against innocent infringers, the mandatory minimum should be eliminated or reduced.[2]

---

[a] As to the liability of innocent infringers, see "Copyright Law Revision Study No. 25"

The present statute reflects a concern for the impact of statutory damages on innocent infringers, in providing three exceptions to the ordinary minimum and maximum amounts:

- Section 101(b) specifies statutory damages of from $50 to $200 for newspaper reproductions of copyrighted photographs.
- Section 101(b) also provides maximum statutory damages of $100 for innocent infringement of nondramatic works in motion pictures.
- Section 1(c) provides for damages of not more than $100 for innocent infringement of nondramatic literary works in broadcasts.

These three exceptions do not absolve innocent infringers from liability for damages, but merely reduce the amount recoverable. If special treatment is justified in these three cases, however, it would seem equally justified in a variety of other situations involving innocent infringement.

The basic principle that an innocent infringer is liable, except where he has been misled through some act or omission of the copyright owner, is firmly established in the copyright law. As between an innocent copyright owner and an innocent infringer, it has generally been agreed that the loss caused by the infringement should be borne by the latter. The question is not whether innocent infringers should be liable; it is whether they should be subject to some minimum amount of damages and, if so, what the minimum should be.

The only purpose of awarding damages for an innocent infringement is to compensate the copyright owner. The other purpose of statutory damages—to deter infringement—is not present as to infringements committed innocently. Statutory damages may still be appropriate in many cases to compensate the copyright owner adequately, but a mandatory minimum of $250 might be excessive in some instances.

We would not attempt to fix special amounts of statutory damages recoverable against innocent infringers, either generally or in specified situations. Rather, we would provide that where an infringer establishes his innocence, the statutory minimum is not mandatory but the court, in its discretion, may award statutory damages in any amount it deems just. Since a plea of innocence may be used as a cloak for negligence and may be difficult to disprove, the infringer should have the burden of proving his innocence.

With the removal of the mandatory minimum as to innocent infringements generally, the three special exceptions in the present statute could be eliminated.

d. Multiple infringements

Another question involves the sum that might be awarded as statutory damages if a single series of events is held to constitute a number of infringements. For example, the production of an infringing motion picture and each of its many exhibitions might be deemed separate infringements. The same is true of an infringing network broadcast and its relay by each of many local stations. The motion picture and broadcasting industries have expressed some concern that statutory damages might be pyramided to an exorbitant total if a court should multiply the statutory minimum by the number of infringements.

We believe that the danger of exorbitant awards in multiple infringement cases is more theoretical than real. In a few cases involving multiple infringements—e.g., where various items in a copyrighted merchandise catalog were reproduced in a series of infringing catalogs—the courts have used this formula of multiplying the number of infringements by $250, but they did so to reach a result they thought just. We know of no case in which the court has felt constrained to use this formula where the resulting total was considered excessive. The present statute, however, is not clear on this point. It is conceivable that a court might construe the statute as requiring the use of this formula in multiple-infringement cases.

We believe that the courts should, as they do now, have discretion to assess statutory damages in any sum within the range between the minimum and maximum. In exercising this discretion the courts may take into account the number of works infringed, the number of infringing acts, the size of the audience reached by the infringements, etc. But in no case should the courts be compelled, because multiple infringements are involved, to award more than they consider reasonable.

We propose that the statute be clarified and made more flexible. It should provide that statutory damages within the minimum and maximum range are to be assessed as the total award for all infringements for which the defendant is liable. The maximum should be sufficiently high to enable the court to award an adequate sum for multiple infringements.

Section 101(b) now provides specially for one case of multiple infringements. It specifies that the total sum of statutory damages recoverable when a motion picture innocently infringes a dramatic work shall be within the range of $250 to $5,000. Our proposal would extend the same principle to all multiple infringements. The special provision could then be dropped.

e. Infringements after actual notice

Section 101(b) now permits the court to exceed the $5,000 maximum, with no limit specified, in the case of "infringements occurring after the actual notice to a defendant, either by service of process in a suit or other written notice served upon him." Some fear has been expressed that this might result in exorbitant awards.

This provision was apparently based on the supposition that any infringement occurring after actual notice would necessarily be willful. But this supposition is questionable. For example, a television network may receive a notice alleging infringement on the eve of a scheduled broadcast when it is too late to defer the program pending an investigation of the claim. Likewise a periodical publisher may receive a notice when an issue is about to be distributed.

The possibility that a court, in its discretion, might award statutory damages greatly exceeding the usual maximum, merely because a notice had been sent, seems remote. In the very few cases where statutory damages of more than $5,000 were awarded, other factors such as willful infringement on a large scale were involved. Nevertheless, we believe the statute is faulty in making the service of notice the basis for exceeding the maximum. A better basis which was proposed in some of the revision bills of 1924–40, would be a showing that the infringement was willful.

We believe, however, that a still better solution was proposed in some of the other revision bills. They would have made the maximum—raised to $10,000 or $20,000—an absolute ceiling, with no special provision for infringements committed after notice or willfully. This would allow the court to take willfulness into account in awarding statutory damages up to the maximum. We favor this approach.

The absolute maximum for statutory damages would not, of course, preclude the recovery of a larger sum of actual damages or profits if proven.

f. Minimum and maximum amounts

The present minimum of $250 and maximum of $5,000 were adopted in 1909. With the depreciation in the value of the currency, those amounts now represent much less than they did then. Some commentators have suggested that these amounts should therefore be raised. Others have suggested, apparently with innocent infringers in mind, that the minimum should be reduced.

In view of our proposal that the minimum not be mandatory against innocent infringers, we see no reason to reduce the present minimum of $250. An award of that amount does not seem unduly severe; anything less would often be inadequate to enable the copyright owner to enforce his rights, and to foster due care by others not to infringe. On the other hand, despite the decreased value of the dollar, the present minimum seems to be enough for these purposes. The court may award more when it considers the minimum inadequate. We would retain the present minimum of $250.

In regard to the maximum, the depreciated value of the dollar seems more significant. In any case where an award of $5,000 would have been appropriate some years ago, an award of $10,000 would be justified now. Any award of more than the minimum is within the court's discretion. And in the light of our proposals to make the maximum an absolute ceiling, even for multiple and willful infringements, we would allow the courts to make awards up to $10,000 as they deem just in the circumstances.

g. Schedule of amounts per copy or performance

Section 101(b) now contains a schedule of amounts for each infringing copy or performance, the amounts varying for different kinds of works. It is understood that this schedule is a mere guide that the courts might use, in their discretion, in fixing the sum to be awarded as statutory damages within the present range between $250 and $5,000.

The schedule has not proved to be a very useful guide, because the amounts are arbitrary and the number of copies or performances is only one of many factors to be considered in assessing damages. In most cases the courts have not applied the mathematical formula of the schedule, and in a few cases where this has been done the results are questionable. To some extent the fear of excessive awards under the present statute is founded on the possibility of a merely mathematical application of the schedule.

The schedule adds a needless complication to the scheme of statutory damages. We would omit it.

3. RECOMMENDATIONS

(*a*) The present provisions of section 101(b) regarding actual damages and profits should be clarified to provide that—

(1) An infringer is liable for the actual damages suffered by the copyright owner, or the profits of the infringer attributable to the infringement, whichever is greater.

(2) In establishing profits, the plaintiff is required to prove only "gross revenue," rather than "sales." The defendant should continue to have the burden of proving deductions.

(*b*) The present provisions of section 101(b) regarding statutory damages should be modified to provide that—

(1) Where an award of actual damages or profits would be less than $250, the court shall award instead, as statutory damages for all infringements for which the defendant is liable, a sum of not less than $250 nor more than $10,000, as it deems just. However, if the defendant proves that he did not know and had no reason to suspect that he was infringing, the court may, in its discretion, withhold statutory damages or award less than $250.

(2) Where an award of actual damages or profits would exceed $250 but would be less than the court deems just, the court in its discretion may award instead, as statutory damages for all infringements for which the defendant is liable, any higher sum not exceeding $10,000.

(*c*) The following provisions of the present statute should be omitted:

(1) The provisions in sections 101(b) and 1(c) fixing special amounts of damages in certain cases.

(2) The provision in section 101(b) for statutory damages in excess of the maximum where notice has been served on the infringer.

(3) The schedule of amounts per copy or performance in section 101(b).

C. REMEDIES OTHER THAN DAMAGES AND PROFITS [3]

1. INJUNCTIONS

a. *Present statutory provisions*

Section 101(a) of the present statute provides simply that a copyright infringer "shall be liable * * * to an injunction restraining such infringements." This provision is reiterated in the first sentence of section 112, which gives the Federal district courts discretionary power "to grant injunctions to prevent and restrain the violation of any right secured by this title, according to the course and principles of courts of equity."

b. *The purpose and effect of injunctions*

The issuance of injunctions to restrain infringements of copyright is merely one instance of the general power exercised by the courts to enjoin civil wrongs. The court may temporarily enjoin the defendant while the suit is pending, or it may issue a permanent injunction when the rights of the parties have been decided.

---

[3] See "Copyright Law Revision Study No. 24"

The general principles of equity followed by the courts in granting or denying injunctions are applicable to copyright infringements. An injunction, by preventing future injury to the plaintiff, is often the most effective remedy, particularly because the damages caused by an infringement may be incapable of accurate assessment. In some situations, however, an injunction may be futile, as where the only injury contemplated has already occurred. In other cases an injunction may be too harsh on the defendant. The courts, in the exercise of their discretion to issue or deny an injunction, balance the plaintiff's need against the consequences the defendant would suffer. The terms of an injunction are tailored to fit the exigencies of the particular case.

c. Proposals to preclude injunctions in certain cases

Some of the revision bills of 1924–40 contained provisions to prevent a court from issuing an injunction in certain cases. For example, various bills specified that no injunction should be issued against the completion of an architectural structure, the publication of a newspaper, the exhibition of a motion picture after its production had innocently begun, or the broadcast of a program after the innocent beginning of its rehearsal.

We see no need for provisions of this kind. If there is any reason why an injunction should not be issued in a particular case, we believe the courts can be relied upon to exercise their discretion appropriately. Moreover, any statutory prohibition against injunctions in a particular situation might prove to be too rigid.

d. Conclusion

We propose that the statute simply provide, as it does now in effect, that the court, in its discretion, may issue an injunction to restrain a copyright infringement.

2. IMPOUNDING AND DESTRUCTION OF INFRINGING ARTICLES

Section 101(c) provides that articles alleged to infringe a copyright may be impounded "during the pendency of the action, upon such terms and conditions as the court may prescribe." The rules of the Supreme Court require that the plaintiff post a bond of at least twice the value of the articles before they may be impounded, to indemnify the defendant for his loss if the articles are later found not to be infringing.

Section 101(d) provides that the court may order an infringer "to deliver up on oath for destruction all the infringing copies or devices, as well as all plates, molds, matrices, or other means for making such infringing copies." Destruction is ordered only after the court has determined that the articles are infringing.

Impounding and destruction are extraordinary remedies which are rather infreqently applied by the courts. Like injunctions they may be a highly effective remedy in some cases, and may be unnecessary or unwarranted in others. These are matters for the court to consider in exercising its discretion.

As mentioned above, some of the revision bills of 1924–40 would have prohibited the granting of injunctions in certain situations. These bills would also have precluded impounding and destruction in similar situations. As in the case of injunctions, we would not attempt to specify situations in which impounding and destruction are not to be ordered, but would leave the application of these remedies to the discretion of the courts.

3. RECOMMENDATIONS

(*a*) The statute should simply provide that injunctions may be issued in the court's discretion.

(*b*) The present provisions for the impounding and destruction of infringing articles should be retained in substance.

D. Costs and Attorney's Fees [4]

1. THE PRESENT STATUTORY PROVISIONS

Section 116 of the present statute provides that in copyright suits "full costs shall be allowed, and the court may award to the prevailing party a reasonable attorney's fee." The costs involved in an infringement action are usually relatively small. But the prosecution or defense of a copyright suit may entail a good deal of work and expense, and an award of attorney's fees can be quite substantial.

The discretionary power of the courts to require the losing party to pay "a reasonable attorney's fee" is intended to discourage unfounded suits and frivolous defenses. The courts have generally denied awards of attorney's fees where the losing party had solid grounds for litigating his claim or defense. This discretionary power of the courts is generally regarded as salutary, and we concur in this view.

The language of section 116 indicates that the allowance of "full costs" is mandatory, and some courts have so held, but others have treated the allowance of costs as discretionary. Section 116 should be clarified in this respect. We believe that the allowance of costs, like the award of attorney's fees, should be left to the discretion of the court.

2. RECOMMENDATION

The statute should provide that the court, in its discretion, may allow costs and a reasonable attorney's fee to the prevailing party.

---

[4] See "Copyright Law Revision Studies Nos. 22 and 23"

Chapter X

INTERNATIONAL ASPECTS OF COPYRIGHT

Outline of Chapter

CHAPTER X

INTERNATIONAL ASPECTS OF COPYRIGHT

A. Works of Foreign Authors [1]

1. BACKGROUND

As first enacted in 1790, the copyright statute afforded protection to published works of citizens and residents of the United States alone. The principal concern at that time was to establish a Federal system of copyright throughout the new Nation, and no effort was made to provide copyright protection for foreign authors. For the next century the works of British and other foreign authors were freely copied and published in the United States, without the need for either authorization or payment. As a result, many 19th-century American authors found it difficult to have their works published, since they were forced to compete with royalty-free works from the rest of the world.

Agitation for the extension of the copyright statute to foreign works began in the 1830's and finally came to fruition in 1891. The act of 1891 (26 Stat. 1106) extended the copyright statute to authors of foreign countries, on certain conditions of reciprocal protection by the foreign country to U.S. authors. Some of the provisions of the 1891 act were changed in 1909 and have been amended since, but the system of protecting foreign authors on the basis of reciprocity has remained fundamentally the same.

2. THE PRESENT LAW

a. In general

The protection now given in the United States to the works of foreign authors differs as between the common law and the copyright statute. Common law protection extends to the unpublished works of all authors, without regard to their nationality. Under the statute, however, the published or registered works of foreign authors are eligible for copyright protection only when certain conditions are met.

The provisions now governing the eligibility of foreign works for statutory copyright are found in section 9, which extends copyright protection to works by "a citizen or subject of a foreign state or nation" only in the following cases:

(1) When the alien author is domiciled in the United States.

(2) When the author is a national of a country designated in a proclamation of the President.

(3) When the work is entitled to protection under the Universal Copyright Convention.

---

[1] See "Copyright Law Revision Study No. 32" As to copyright in territories and possessions of the United States, see "Copyright Law Revision Study No. 34"

b. Domiciled aliens

Section 9(a) extends the statute to the work of an alien who is "domiciled within the United States at the time of the first publication of his work." The principle involved here is the simple one of treating domiciliaries on the same basis as citizens.

The reference in section 9(a) to the time of publication has left a doubt as to whether an alien domiciled in the United States can secure statutory copyright for his unpublished works by voluntary registration. We see no reason to withhold the privilege of voluntary registration from the works of domiciled aliens. Moreover, we have proposed, in chapter IV, that the statute apply upon the first public dissemination of a work in any of several ways, including voluntary registration. If a provision such as section 9(a) is to be retained in the statute, we would propose that it refer to the alien's domicile at the time of first public dissemination.

c. Nationals of proclaimed countries

(1) *The statutory provisions.*—Section 9(b) provides that the President may, "by proclamation made from time to time," extend the statute to the works of the citizens or subjects of a foreign country when he determines that one of the three following conditions exists:

(a) That the foreign country grants copyright protection to U.S. citizens "on substantially the same basis as to its own citizens"; or

(b) That the foreign country grants copyright protection to U.S. citizens "substantially equal to the protection" given by the United States to the authors of that country; or

(c) That the foreign country "is a party to an international agreement which provides for reciprocity in the granting of copyright, by the terms of which agreement the United States may, at its pleasure, become a party thereto."

The first of the three conditions specified in section 9(b) is for "national treatment"—that the foreign country treats U.S. citizens on the same basis as its own citizens. The second is for "reciprocal treatment"—that the foreign country gives U.S. citizens protection equal to that given by the United States to citizens of that country.

The third condition is anomalous. It appears to cover countries that are parties to an international agreement which the United States might join, but to which it has not actually adhered. Until the United States becomes a party to an agreement, there cannot be any assurance of protection for U.S. citizens in the other adhering countries. No Presidential proclamation has ever been issued on the basis of this third condition. If the system of proclamations under section 9(b) is retained, we would omit this condition.

(2) *Present status of proclamations under section 9(b).*—Numerous proclamations have been issued under section 9(b) on the basis of either "national" or "reciprocal" treatment. Individual proclamations have been issued extending our statute to 38 foreign countries now in existence. In addition, general proclamations have been issued declaring the Buenos Aires and Universal Copyright Conventions to be in effect with regard to all adhering countries, and 23 countries not named in any proclamation now adhere to one or both of those conventions.

Section 9(b) provides that the President's determination may be based on the protection given U.S. citizens by a "treaty, convention, agreement, or law" of the foreign country. The existing proclamations for three countries were based on bilateral treaties and the remainder on findings or assurances that the law of the proclaimed country then provided the required protection for works of U.S. citizens. Since the law of a proclaimed country may later be changed, section 9(b) also permits the President at any time to terminate or suspend a proclamation. However, even though there have been one or two instances in which a proclaimed country has curtailed the protection of U.S. citizens on which the proclamation was based, no proclamation has ever been terminated or suspended for that reason.

(3) *Application of formal requirements to foreign works.*—The protection of foreign works by virtue of a proclamation, like the protection of domestic works, depends upon compliance with the general requirements of our statute for securing or maintaining copyright. These include the requirements of a copyright notice on published copies, the deposit of copies for registration of the copyright claim, and the manufacture of copies of certain works in the United States.

Aside from the copyright notice, these requirements impose a much greater practical burden on foreign authors than on domestic authors. As noted below, these formal requirements are mainly eliminated for foreign works protected under the Universal Copyright Convention if they are published with a prescribed notice. And apparently the same result was contemplated under the Buenos Aires Convention.

(4) *Special proclamations as to mechanical recording right.*—For the extension of the mechanical recording right to foreign musical works, section 1(e) requires a special proclamation based on a finding that the author's country grants an equivalent right to the musical works of U.S. citizens. This requirement was placed in the statute in 1909, at a time when the recording right was new to the United States and was not yet provided for in most foreign copyright laws. Today that right is accorded almost universally, and the requirement of a special proclamation seems an unnecessary complication. If the general system of proclamations is retained, this special requirement could well be eliminated.

d. International copyright conventions

(1) *In general.*—Until 1952 the successive conventions of the Berne Union—the first was drafted in 1886 and the most recent in 1948— were the only international copyright conventions designed for worldwide adherence. The members of the Berne Union are predominantly European and British Commonwealth countries; of the countries in the Western Hemisphere, only Canada and Brazil adhere to one of the Berne conventions.

In the United States, as well as in the Latin American countries other than Brazil, the Berne conventions have not been considered acceptable for various reasons. Instead, a series of separate conventions designed for adherence by all the American Republics was developed—the first in 1902 and the latest in 1946. Of these Pan American copyright conventions the United States ratified two: the Mexico

City Convention of 1902, which now governs our copyright regulations with El Salvador only, and the Buenos Aires Convention of 1910, which 16 of the 20 Latin American countries have also ratified.

The Universal Copyright Convention, drafted in 1952 under the auspices of UNESCO, was intended not only as a bridge between the Berne and Pan American groups, but was also designed for worldwide adherence. Ratification by the United States of the Universal Copyright Convention in 1954 was a signal development in our international copyright relations. To date 36 countries in addition to the United States have ratified the UCC, including among others some Berne and Pan American countries. Additional countries will no doubt adhere to this convention in the future.

(2) *The Universal Copyright Convention.*—The underlying principle of the Universal Copyright Convention is "national treatment"— each country is to protect the works originating in other member countries on the same basis as it protects the works of its own nationals. In addition, the UCC specifies certain minimum standards of protection. Section 9(c) was added to our statute in 1954 (effective in 1955) to make it conform with the terms of the Convention.

Section 9(c) extends the statute to the works of authors who are citizens or subjects of a foreign country that is a party to the UCC, and also to the works of any foreign author first published in a Convention country. It also provides that if the published copies of a foreign work eligible for protection under the UCC bear a prescribed copyright notice, the work is exempt from—

    (*a*) The general requirement of deposit and registration (except as a prerequisite to suit) ;

    (*b*) The requirement of domestic manufacture for certain works;

    (*c*) The importation limit of 1,500 copies for certain works; and

    (*d*) The requirement of a special proclamation for the extension of mechanical recording rights to foreign musical works.

(3) *The Buenos Aires Convention.*—The Buenos Aires Convention provides for copyright protection among the adhering American Republics on the general basis of "national treatment" in each country for the works of the citizens or domiciliaries of the other countries. Although it is not clear on this and other points, the Convention appears to apply only to works published in one of the member countries.

There are no provisions in our statute implementing or referring specifically to the Buenos Aires Convention. It was declared to be in effect, however, by a presidential proclamation. The Convention appears to contemplate that, under certain conditions, a work of another member country would be entitled to protection in the United States without compliance with some of the formal requirements of our statute.

As of the date of this report, 7 of the 16 Latin American members of the Buenos Aires Convention have also adhered to the Universal Copyright Convention, and others will undoubtedly join. Until all 16 have done so, however, our copyright relations with some of the Latin American countries will continue to be governed by the Buenos Aires Convention.

e. Special types of foreign works

There are two special types of works—those of stateless authors and those of certain international organizations—which are undoubtedly copyrightable in the United States, though they are not specifically mentioned in the statute. The famous "Mein Kampf" decision, *Houghton Mifflin Co.* v. *Stackpole Sons, Inc.* (104 F. 2d 306 (2d Cir. 1939)), established the copyrightability of works by stateless authors. Protocol 2 of the Universal Copyright Convention requires the United States to extend copyright to works published by the United Nations or its specialized agencies or by the Organization of American States

3. SUMMARY AND ANALYSIS OF THE PRESENT SITUATION

Among the total of 60 countries to which the United States extends copyright protection, the various forms of international relationships can be summarized as follows:

Countries party to international conventions	45
Members of Universal Copyright Convention	36
Members of Buenos Aires Convention	16
Members of both U.C.C. and Buenos Aires	7
Countries party to one or both conventions and also covered by a Presidential proclamation	23
Countries covered by Presidential proclamation only	15
Proclamation based on bilateral treaty	3
Proclamation based on determination of national or reciprocal treatment	12
Total	60

The 60 countries with which the United States has copyright relations comprise almost all of the countries in which copyright materials are of substantial commercial importance at the present time. With a few exceptions, the other 40 or more countries of the world are for the most part relatively underdeveloped or recently established. Of the exceptions the most notable is the Soviet Union, which has no copyright relations with any other nation.

The present arrangements extending protection under our copyright statute to the works of foreign authors are a complex structure of numerous Presidential proclamations and two multilateral conventions. The proclamations and conventions differ as to the standards of eligibility and the conditions for protection, and they overlap for a number of countries. A further complicating factor is the existence of 40 or more countries with which the United States has no copyright relations.

4. POSSIBILITIES OF SIMPLIFICATION AND IMPROVEMENT

a. In general

The Universal Copyright Convention has become the most important and effective means for the permanent establishment of reciprocal copyright protection between the United States and other countries. It goes without saying that our statute should continue to protect foreign works coming under the UCC in accordance with its terms. We must also honor our obligations under the Buenos Aires Convention, at least until all adherents have joined the UCC.

There remain the countries that do not belong to either the Universal or Buenos Aires Conventions—15 "proclaimed" countries and 40 or more countries with which we have no copyright relations. It is here that we may find an opportunity to simplify the protection of foreign works and to improve our international copyright relations.

b. Reciprocity as the basis for international copyright relations

Our present scheme of proclamations is based on the theory of reciprocity: that protection should be extended to foreign authors only if their country grants protection to U.S. authors. The requirement of reciprocity was probably important to us in former years, when our international copyright relations were in the developmental stage and the works of our authors were not yet protected in many foreign markets. Reciprocity still has considerable surface appeal as a means of obtaining protection abroad for works of U.S. citizens. Most foreign countries have likewise based their international copyright relations on this requirement.

As a practical matter, however, the requirement of reciprocity has created an involved complex of protection for some foreign works and no protection for others. The extension of our statute to foreign works generally, without regard to reciprocity, would greatly simplify our international copyright relations and the determination of the copyright status of foreign works.

Our laws dealing with various forms of property other than copyright—chattels, shares of stock, contractual rights, and especially patents—apply generally to the property of citizens and aliens alike. Even in the realm of copyrightable works, our common law now protects the unpublished works of all foreign and domestic authors indiscriminately.

For the purpose of securing protection abroad for U.S. authors, the requirement of reciprocity seems to be of little importance today. The works of U.S. authors are now protected in almost all of the countries where copyright is of commercial value. Removal of our requirement of reciprocity would not be likely to affect this situation adversely. With regard to the 40 or more countries whose works are not now protected under our statute, there is little chance that our withholding of copyright from their authors would encourage them to adopt laws giving protection to our authors. On the contrary, we believe that our recognition of copyright in works emanating from newly established and other underdeveloped countries is more likely to encourage their adoption of copyright laws and their adherence to the Universal Copyright Convention.

France and one or two other countries have extended the protection of their copyright laws to all foreign works without regard to reciprocity. It is noteworthy that French works are protected in at least as many countries as the works of any other nation.

Aside from the matter of securing protection abroad for U.S. authors, we believe that the extension of copyright protection to foreign works generally, without requiring reciprocity, would serve our best interests. U.S. distributors of intellectual works—publishers, motion picture producers, etc.—often need exclusive rights in a work to warrant their investment in its reproduction and distribution. Consequently, copyright protection of foreign works serves to foster their dissemination in the United States. Most important, our adoption of the general principle of affording copyright protection to the works of all authors, regardless of their nationality, would enhance our esteem abroad and give impetus to the development of copyright relations among all nations.

c. Conclusions

As we see it, we have little to lose and much to gain by extending our copyright statute to the works of foreign countries generally, without regard to the existence of reciprocity. There are, however, two qualifications of this principle that we would suggest:

(1) Additional countries should be encouraged to adhere to the Universal Copyright Convention. Works originating in countries belonging to the convention are now exempted from certain formal requirements of our statute, and we would continue to extend these special advantages to U.C.C. works.

(2) The President should be authorized to withhold, suspend, or restrict the statutory protection afforded to the works of a particular country. This power should be available in special situations, or in cases of discrimination against U.S. citizens—although, of course, it would not be exercised in violation of our treaty obligations. There would probably not be many occasions to use this power.

5. RECOMMENDATIONS

(a) Sections 9(a) and 9(b) should be replaced by a provision extending the statute to all foreign and domestic works on the same basis, but with a proviso authorizing the President to withhold, suspend, or restrict statutory protection for the works of nationals or domiciliaries of any country.

(b) The present exemptions enjoyed by foreign works that qualify under the Universal Copyright Convention should be continued in substance.

B. MANUFACTURING AND RELATED PROVISIONS

1. BACKGROUND

Before the International Copyright Act of 1891, the works of foreign authors had been freely and widely pirated in the United States. The piratical printing of foreign works had become such a large part of the domestic printing industry that the printers opposed any extension of copyright to foreign works unless their interests were protected. They insisted upon requiring printing in the United States as a condition of U.S. copyright, not only for foreign works but for the works of U.S. authors as well.

The result was the "manufacturing clause" in the act of 1891 which provided that "in the case of a book, photograph, chromo, or lithograph," the copies which had to be deposited to secure copyright "shall be printed from type set within the limits of the United States" or from other printing devices made in the United States. The act also prohibited the importation of copies of certain types of copyrighted works that had been manufactured abroad.

The manufacturing clause was the price exacted by the printers for the establishment of international copyright protection in the

United States. Its purposes were to preserve for the U.S. printing industry the business it had derived from the piracy of foreign works, and to protect it against foreign competition. Whatever justification may have existed for the manufacturing clause in 1891, however, it is now considered an anomaly in our copyright law. No other country requires domestic manufacture as a condition of copyright protection.

When first enacted the manufacturing clause required that the work be printed in the United States before its publication anywhere. Since foreign works are normally first printed and published abroad, this requirement was so difficult and expensive to meet that it operated to deny copyright protection in a great many cases. The provision has been modified several times since 1891 to ameliorate some of its more drastic effects.

Foreign countries have long protested against the requirement that their works, in order to have copyright protection in the United States, must be printed here. In the preparation of the Universal Copyright Convention they insisted upon the provision, which was adopted, exempting the works of other member countries from any requirement of domestic manufacture. Accordingly, the statute was amended in 1954 (effective in 1955) to exempt foreign works that qualify for protection under the U.C.C.

2. THE PRESENT LAW

The manufacturing clause is found in section 16 of the present statute, supplemented by sections 17, 18, 22, 23, and 107. The provisions of these sections are now an intricate and abstruse tangle of general requirements, exceptions, and special procedures. If the substance of any of these provisions is to be retained in a new statute, the present language is badly in need of clarification and simplification.

In substance, section 16 provides that the various steps in the manufacture of English-language books and periodicals must be performed in the United States, and that with certain exceptions the same requirements apply to lithographs and photoengravings. Sections 17 and 18 require an affidavit of domestic manufacture in the case of books subject to the manufacturing clause, and prescribe penalties for knowingly making a false affidavit. Section 107 prohibits importation, except for certain limited purposes, of copies of copyrighted English-language books manufactured abroad.

Sections 22 and 23 provide a partial exception to the manufacturing requirements. An "ad interim copyright," lasting 5 years, may be secured for English-language books or periodicals first published abroad, by registration in the Copyright Office within 6 months. An ad interim copyright permits the copyright owner to import up to 1,500 copies of the foreign edition during the 5-year period of ad interim protection, so that he may test the U.S. market and determine whether it would be worthwhile to manufacture an edition in the United States. If an edition is manufactured and published in the United States within the 5-year period, the ad interim copyright may be extended to the full copyright term.

Section 9(c) exempts foreign works protected under the Universal Copyright Convention from the manufacturing requirements, the ad interim provisions, and the importation restrictions.

3. EFFECT OF THE PRESENT LAW

a. Books and periodicals in the English language

The manufacturing clause has its most direct impact upon English-language books and periodicals by U.S. authors, or by foreign authors who are not covered by the Universal Copyright Convention. These works are denied full-term copyright unless they are printed in the United States.

If, for example, a U.S. citizen writes a book in English and has it printed abroad, he is faced with a number of difficulties. In order to secure any protection in the United States he must publish his work abroad and register a claim to ad interim copyright within 6 months of publication. Under his ad interim copyright he can import only 1,500 copies; if he wishes to sell more than 1,500 copies in the United States, he must either abandon his copyright or manufacture an edition in the United States. And most important, he will lose copyright protection at the end of the 5-year ad interim term unless he manufactures and publishes a U.S. edition within that period and then registers a full-term copyright claim.

The same difficulties face foreign authors who write works in English that are not covered by the Universal Copyright Convention. And while American authors could normally be expected to have their works manufactured in the United States, this is not the case with most foreign authors. The result in the past has been to deny protection altogether to many foreign works. Foreign countries, however, may now obtain exemption for the works of their authors by joining the U.C.C. Several English-speaking countries, including the United Kingdom, have done so, and others—such as Canada, Australia, and New Zealand—may be expected to join in the future.

b. Books and periodicals in a foreign language

Books and periodicals "of foreign origin" in a language other than English are exempted from the manufacturing requirements and the import prohibitions. The phrase "of foreign origin," however, has an unfortunate and perhaps unforeseen result: a foreign-language book or periodical by a U.S. citizen is denied copyright altogether if the first edition is printed abroad. It is not even eligible for ad interim protection, since the statute makes ad interim copyright available only for English-language books and periodicals.

The domestic printing industry has not been concerned about foreign-language works, and the present requirement has caused hardships in a number of cases. Thus, if the manufacturing requirements are retained, we believe the exemption of foreign-language works should be extended to those by U.S. authors.

c. Lithographs and photoengravings

Many pictorial works are excluded from the provision extending the manufacturing requirements to lithographs and photoengravings:

(1) Foreign works protected under the Universal Copyright Convention are exempted from the manufacturing requirement.

(2) Pictorial works not produced by a lithographic or photoengraving process—including etchings, hand engravings, photogravures, and collotypes—are not affected by the requirement.

(3) Section 16 specifically exempts lithographs and photoengravings where "the subjects represented are located in a for-

eign country and illustrate a scientific work or reproduce a work of art." This ambiguous provision has been construed as exempting any reproduction of an art work or technical drawing located abroad.

In effect, reproductions of pictorial works by artists residing abroad will usually be excluded from the manufacturing clause, while lithographs and photoengravings of works by artists in the United States will be subject to that requirement. We believe that this provision is of no substantial benefit to the U.S. printing industry, but it has been the cause of considerable confusion and of abandonment of some copyright claims. Even if a manufacturing requirement is retained for books and periodicals, we would recommend dropping it for lithographs and photoengravings.

4. CONSIDERATIONS FOR A NEW LAW

a. In general

It is hard to see the basis in logic or principle for denying copyright protection to authors as a means of protecting printers against foreign competition. With the possible exception of the printers themselves, all groups concerned appear to agree that copyright should not be conditioned upon manufacture in the United States.

Foreign authors will usually have their works printed and published first in their own countries. In those instances where there is a large U.S. market for a foreign work, a U.S. edition is likely to be printed. But in most cases it is a burden on foreign authors to require, as a condition of copyright protection, that they have their works reprinted here.

U.S. authors will normally have their works manufactured in the United States, but there are special situations in which their works are manufactured abroad for practical reasons; for example:
- Where the author resides or is stationed abroad;
- Where the work is in a foreign language or is aimed at a foreign market;
- Where a foreign publisher is the only one offering to publish the work;
- Where the market for the work is so small, as in the case of some scholarly or technical works, that printing must be procured wherever the cost is lowest; or
- Where the special quality needed, as in the case of some art reproductions, requires the unique skills of certain foreign artisans.

In these situations it seems unjust to deprive U.S. authors of copyright protection if they do not have their works printed in the United States.

b. Effect on printing industry

In 1891, and in 1909, there was concern about protecting the "infant" printing industry against foreign competition. Even then, however, the device of protecting printers by denying or restricting an author's copyright was questionable. If the printing industry needs this sort of protection today, we believe that a limitation on imports, without depriving authors of copyright, would be sufficient. Moreover, as long as the import limitation is tied to copyright, it will give no protection to printers against foreign editions of works not under copyright.

The present provision for the importation of 1,500 copies of a foreign edition under a 5-year ad interim copyright was adopted in 1949 with the full support of the printers. They were apparently satisfied that the printing industry would not be threatened by permitting a 5-year period of copyright protection for works printed abroad, as long as imports were limited to 1,500 copies. During the hearings in 1954 on the Universal Copyright Convention,[2] however, some representatives of the printers opposed the complete removal of the manufacturing requirement and the import limitation, for foreign works protected under the convention.

It seems apparent that an import limitation, rather than the denial or curtailment of copyright, is the effective method for protecting the printing industry against foreign competition. The limitation of copyright to the 5-year "ad interim" term seems to be of no real benefit to the printers. The copyright owner of a work printed abroad who finds no U.S. market for more than 1,500 copies is not likely to reprint in the United States, though faced with the loss of copyright after 5 years. On the other hand, if there is a U.S. market for substantially more than 1,500 copies, the import limitation is likely to cause the printing of a U.S. edition.

Data presented at the 1954 hearings on the Universal Copyright Convention showed that—

- U.S. book exports greatly exceed imports.
- Even when foreign editions can be imported without limit, as in the case of books in the public domain, U.S. editions are generally preferred in the domestic market, and it is usually more economical to print a domestic edition when there is a market for 2,500 copies or more.

Statistics have been collected on imports of copyrighted English-language books since the United Kingdom joined the Universal Copyright Convention in 1957. They indicate that even though British editions could have been imported without limit under the U.C.C. exemption, no great number has been imported in more than 1,500 copies.

c. Conclusions

We believe that there is no justification for denying copyright protection, or cutting it off after 5 years, for failure to manufacture an edition in the United States. The effect on authors is severe. They lose not only the right to reproduce their works in printed form, but also the other rights, often more remunerative, to use their works in motion pictures, broadcasts, plays, etc. Moreover, withholding or cutting off copyright from works printed abroad has proved to be of little or no benefit to the printing industry. If printers need protection against foreign competition, it should be afforded by other means such as an import limitation.

Whether an import limitation is still needed for the protection of the printing industry against foreign competition is an open question that we consider beyond the province of copyright. We see no reason why import restrictions, if found necessary, should be tied to copyright or confined to copyrighted works. In any event, even if the

---

[2] Hearings before subcommittees of the Senate Committees on Foreign Relations and on the Judiciary, Apr. 7 and 8, 1954, on the "Universal Copyright Convention and Implementing Legislation" (Ex. M and S, 2559, 83d Cong., 1st sess.).

1,500 copy limit on imports is retained, we believe that the copyright protection of authors should not depend upon printing in the United States.

(*a*) The requirement of manufacture in the United States as a condition of copyright (sec. 16) and the related provisions dealing with affidavits (secs. 17 and 18) and ad interim copyright (secs. 22 and 23) should be eliminated.

(*b*) The prohibition against the importation of copyrighted English-language books manufactured abroad (sec. 107) and the provision for importing up to 1,500 copies under ad interim copyright (sec. 16) should be eliminated. If Congress finds that an import limitation on English-language books is necessary for the protection of the U.S. printing industry, the limitation need not be confined to copyrighted books, and it should be provided for in legislation other than the copyright statute.

C. Other Import Provisions

1. UNCOPYRIGHTED WORKS BEARING FALSE NOTICE

a. The statutory provision and its background

Section 106 prohibits the importation of articles bearing "a false notice of copyright when there is no existing copyright thereon in the United States." This prohibition supplements section 105 which provides a criminal penalty for the fraudulent sale or importation of uncopyrighted articles bearing a false notice. The criminal provisions are discussed below in chapter XI.

The false notice provisions of sections 105 and 106 were carried over from pre-1909 statutes under which copyright was secured by registration prior to publication of the work. Before 1909 a copyright notice in published copies was a factual representation that a copyright claim had been registered, and it was possible to determine whether or not a notice was false simply by checking the registration records. This is no longer true.

b. Section 106 now inoperative

Copyright is now secured by publication with notice, and registration is made later. The notice is a declaration that copyright is being claimed, and would not be false as long as a claim could reasonably be asserted. Whether a particular notice is false is now a question involving a legal determination of the copyrightability of the article and the good faith of the claimant.

It is wholly impracticable to expect the customs officers to recognize that a notice may be false, or to exclude articles on this ground. In any case where the question might be raised, the falsity of the notice should be a matter for judicial determination. We believe, therefore, that section 106 is not a suitable method for preventing importation of articles bearing a false notice. This purpose should be accomplished by means of a provision, such as that in section 105, under which a person who knowingly imports an article bearing a false notice is subject to criminal prosecution.

2. PIRATICAL COPIES

a. The present statutory provision and regulations

Section 106 also prohibits the importation of "any piratical copies of any work copyrighted in the United States." Section 107 repeats this prohibition with respect to piratical copies of "any book," but adds nothing to section 106.

The statute does not define "piratical copies," but the phrase has been understood to mean copies made without the authorization of the copyright owner. "Piratical copies" are, of course, infringing copies, and the copyright owner could sue for infringement in the United States after piratical copies made abroad had been imported and distributed here. The statute is designed to prevent the importation of infringing copies in the first instance.

Section 109 directs the Secretary of the Treasury and the Postmaster General to make rules and regulations for enforcement of the import prohibitions. The substance of the regulations now in force (19 C.F.R. secs. 11.18–11.21) is as follows:

(1) Copyright claimants seeking to stop the importation of piratical copies must file an application with customs, accompanied by material identifying the work and a fee of $75.

(2) Customs collectors may bar articles if satisfied that they are piratical. "Piratical copies" are defined in the regulations as "actual copies or substantial reproductions of legally copyrighted works produced and imported in contravention of the rights of the copyright proprietor."

(3) If the importer objects, the copyright claimant may be required to post a bond, and the articles are then detained until the Bureau of Customs determines whether or not they are piratical.

b. Problems of enforcement

The basic policy of prohibiting importation of piratical copies is well established in the United States and other countries. Enforcement of the prohibition, however, has inherent difficulties. It requires customs officers to decide questions of law and fact which are sometimes complex or beyond their ability to investigate. Particularly troublesome are contested claims that commercial art works being imported are piratical copies.

The present customs regulations give the importer the opportunity to show that the articles are not piratical, and seek to safeguard him against loss for a wrongful detention. And he may appeal customs decisions to the courts. At any rate the possible shortcomings in the administrative process do not appear so serious as to require abandonment of the prohibition. Modifications in the present regulations may be called for, but we would rely on the Treasury Department to make them.

3. AGREEMENTS TO DIVIDE INTERNATIONAL MARKETS

When arrangements are made for both a U.S. edition and a foreign edition of the same work, the publishers frequently agree to divide the international markets. The foreign publisher agrees not to sell his edition in the United States, and the U.S. publisher agrees not to sell his edition in certain foreign countries. It has been suggested that the import ban on piratical copies should be extended to bar the importation of the foreign edition in contravention of such an agreement.

Some countries, including the United Kingdom, bar importation in this situation, apparently on the ground that, even though the copies were authorized, their sale in violation of a territorial limitation would be an infringement of the copyright. In the United States, there is no clear decision as to whether the sale of authorized copies beyond a territorial limitation is an infringement. But the import ban on "piratical copies" does not seem to apply to authorized copies.

We assume, without considering the antitrust questions involved, that agreements to divide international markets for copyrighted works are valid and enforcible contracts as between the parties. But we do not believe that the prohibition against imports of piratical copies should be extended to authorized copies covered by an agreement of this sort. To do so would impose the territorial restriction in a private contract upon third persons with no knowledge of the agreement. And even as between the parties, Customs does not seem to be an appropriate agency for the enforcement of private contracts.

4. RECOMMENDATIONS

(*a*) The provision of section 106 prohibiting importation of any article bearing a false notice of copyright should be deleted.

(*b*) The prohibition in section 106 against importation of "piratical copies"—i.e., copies made without authorization of the author or any other copyright owner—should be retained in substance.

(*c*) The provision of section 109, authorizing the Secretary of the Treasury and the Postmaster General to prescribe rules and regulations for the enforcement of the import restrictions, should be retained in substance.

Chapter XI

MISCELLANEOUS PROBLEMS

OUTLINE OF CHAPTER

(1327)

CHAPTER XI

MISCELLANEOUS PROBLEMS

A. Government Publications [1]

1. THE PRESENT LAW AND ITS BACKGROUND

a. The law before 1895

Before 1895 the statutes were silent as to the copyrightability of material emanating from governmental bodies. During the 19th century, however, a series of court decisions had established the rule that, for reasons of public policy, the text of laws, court decisions, governmental proceedings, and similar official documents must be freely available and are therefore not subject to copyright.

At the same time the courts held that a person publishing an official document with his own additions—such as annotations, headnotes, or commentaries—could secure copyright in them. Several cases sustained a State government's copyright in additions of this character prepared by its employees. Hence, although official documents in the nature of governmental edicts and rulings were considered uncopyrightable, there was nothing to prevent governmental bodies, at least of the States, from securing copyright in other kinds of material.

b. The Printing Law of 1895

The 1895 act to centralize printing for the U.S. Government in the Government Printing Office (28 Stat. 608) contained a provision permitting that office to sell duplicate plates "from which any Government publication is printed." This was intended to facilitate the private reproduction of Government publications. To forestall copyright claims in private reproductions it was also provided that "no publication reprinted from such * * * plates and no other Government publication shall be copyrighted." This provision is still in the Printing Law (44 U.S.C. sec. 58) and its substance was incorporated in the copyright statute in 1909.

c. The present copyright law

Section 8 of the present copyright statute provides that "no copyright shall subsist * * * in any publication of the United States Government, or any reprint, in whole or in part, thereof * * *." It also contains a provision intended to preserve the copyright subsisting in a private work when it is reproduced in a publication of the Government.

The ban against copyright in Government publications does not extend to publications of State and local governments. The judicially established rule would still prevent copyright in the text of State laws, municipal ordinances, court decisions, and similar official documents, but other State or local government publications—such as those con-

---

[1] See "Copyright Law Revision Study No. 33"

taining historical, technical, educational, or other informational material—may be copyrighted. Almost every State in the Union has registered copyright claims in some of its informational publications.

2. RATIONALE OF THE PRESENT LAW

Most foreign countries permit copyright in publications of their national governments other than laws, rulings, and similar official documents. In the United States the Government is permitted to obtain patents on inventions made for it by its employees. And, as we have just seen, State and local governments may copyright their informational publications. We have therefore tried to find the reasons why copyright has been prohibited entirely for publications of the U.S. Government.

The legislative history of the initial prohibition in the Printing Law of 1895 indicates that it was aimed at precluding copyright claims by private persons in their reprints of Government publications. It was apparently assumed, without discussion, that the Government itself would have no occasion to secure copyright in its publications. Most Government publications at that time consisted of official documents of an authoritative nature. When the copyright laws were consolidated in the act of 1909, the same provision in substance was incorporated in that act.

During the preliminary consideration of the 1909 act, a suggestion to extend the prohibition to State publications was opposed and dropped. The States generally did not have their own facilities for printing. As a matter of economy, they contracted with private publishers who undertook to print and publish at their own expense as a commercial venture, for which the publishers required copyright protection.

The Federal Government today issues a great variety and quantity of informational material—technical manuals, educational guides, research reports, historical reviews, maps, motion pictures, etc. The basic argument against permitting these publications to be copyrighted is that any material produced and issued by the Government should be freely available to the public and open to the widest possible reproduction and dissemination.

3. WHAT IS A "GOVERNMENT PUBLICATION"

There has been much uncertainty as to what constitutes a "publication of the U.S. Government" in which copyright is prohibited. The word "publication" may mean either of two things:

(a) It may refer to the work itself. In this sense a "Government publication" would be any work produced by the Government—that is, produced for the Government by its employees—regardless of who published it.

(b) It may refer to the act of publishing copies of a work. In this sense a "Government publication" would be any work published by the Government, regardless of who produced it.

It has also been suggested that—

(c) Any work which has either been produced or published by the Government is a "Government publication."

(*d*) Only a work which has both been produced and published by the Government is a "Government publication."

The courts have expressed various opinions, but the weight of authority seems to point to the first meaning: a work produced by the Government. In practice, the Copyright Office and a number of other Government agencies have adopted that construction, with the following conclusions:

- Any work produced by a Government employee within the scope of his employment is not copyrightable, even though issued by a private publisher.
- Any work privately produced may be copyrighted by the author, even though he permits the Government to publish it.
- The Government is not precluded from acquiring copyright in privately produced works by assignment.

Under this construction a number of Government agencies have adopted the following practices:

- They permit private persons who produce works under a Government contract or grant to secure copyright, with the Government obtaining a nonexclusive license to publish.
- They arrange for the private publication of works produced under Government contracts or grants.
- They take assignments to the Government of copyrights secured by private persons.

4. VIEWS OF GOVERNMENT AGENCIES

We have asked a number of Government agencies with extensive publication programs for their experience and views. They agreed generally that the scope of the prohibition should be clarified by defining "Government publications" as meaning works produced for the Government by its employees. Most of them indicated that this would solve their problems, which relate chiefly to works produced under contracts or grants, and that there is no need for copyright in works produced by their employees.

Several agencies, however, indicated that there are exceptional cases in which it would be highly desirable to permit copyright in works produced by their employees; for example:

- Where the agency has special reasons to have a work published commercially, and the publisher wants copyright protection.
- Where a work is the joint product of the agency and a private organization desiring copyright.
- Where a work is produced by the agency under a grant from a private organization desiring copyright.
- Where an agency seeks to operate a self-supporting program for the publication of its research reports.
- Where the agency has reason to believe that reproduction of a publication must be controlled to prevent distortion in a dangerous manner.

These, of course, are unusual situations. The agencies concerned agree that no copyright protection is needed for the great bulk of their publications, but they feel that exceptions to the general prohibition should be authorized in extraordinary cases.

In the past, special legislation has been proposed to permit copyright in individual works of the Government, and a few bills of this character have been enacted.

5. CONCLUSIONS AS TO THE COPYRIGHT PROHIBITION

We agree with the basic principle that works produced by the Government should be open to the widest possible dissemination. We would therefore retain the general prohibition against copyright in "Government publications," with that term being defined as works produced for the Government by its employees.

We believe, however, that provision should be made to permit exceptions in unusual cases, without requiring the agencies to seek special legislation in each instance. It does not seem feasible to spell out the appropriate exceptions in the statute, and we think it would not be advisable to authorize each agency to establish its own standards. A better procedure, we suggest, would be to empower a central agency—possibly the Congressional Joint Committee on Printing or the Bureau of the Budget—to permit exceptions in particular situations. This would provide for the development of uniform standards for the Government as a whole, with controls to assure that copyright is permitted only in special cases where the extraordinary circumstances warrant the departure from the general rule.

The public would be informed of the copyright in any particular case by the copyright notice required to appear in all published copies.

6. TRANSFERS OF GOVERNMENT-OWNED COPYRIGHTS

Ownership of copyrights by the Government raises a problem that has been encountered with Government-owned patents. There is no established procedure enabling Government agencies to grant exclusive licenses to use patents held by them, or to transfer ownership of the patents. We suggest that the central agency empowered to permit the copyrighting of Government publications be further empowered to permit the exclusive licensing or transfer of Government-owned copyrights.

7. PRIVATE WORKS PUBLISHED BY THE GOVERNMENT

A saving clause in the present section 8 is intended to assure that the copyright of a private person is preserved when his work is published by the Government. We believe the saving clause needs to be supplemented in two respects:

(a) It now provides for the preservation of a "subsisting copyright," which might be understood as referring only to a copyright previously secured under the statute. It should be made clear that the rights of a private owner are likewise preserved when his previously unpublished work is published by the Government.

(b) In the absence of a copyright notice in a Government document containing privately owned material, the public may be misled into assuming that the document is a Government publication in the public domain. We propose that when the Government publishes a document containing privately owned material, it should be required to insert a notice identifying that material.

8. RECOMMENDATIONS

(*a*) The general prohibition against copyright in "publications of the U.S. Government" should be retained in the copyright statute, with that term being defined as meaning published works produced for the Government by its officers or employees. To avoid duplication and possible confusion, the similar prohibition in the Printing Law should be deleted.

(*b*) A central Government agency should be empowered to authorize exceptions to the general prohibition in special cases, and to authorize the exclusive licensing or transfer of Government-owned copyrights.

(*c*) The saving clause, preserving the copyright of a private owner when his work is published by the Government, should be clarified to assure copyright protection for the private owner of a previously unpublished work. The Government should be required to insert a copyright notice identifying privately owned material in documents published by it.

B. PHOTOGRAPHS

1. DIFFICULTIES UNDER THE PRESENT LAW

The statutes have designated photographs as copyrightable works since 1865. Some of the general provisions of the law, however, have made it difficult for photographers to secure and maintain copyright in their works:

- Each separately published work is now required to be deposited and registered individually. The economic value of any one photograph is likely to be small. The cost to a photographer of registering each of his published photographs separately is usually prohibitive.
- Many photographs are published in periodicals and the publishers are often unwilling to place a separate copyright notice on individual protographs. Under the present law, it is doubtful whether the general notice for the periodical as a whole will protect a contribution in which copyright has not been assigned to the publisher. Consequently, photographers must either assign all their rights to the publisher or risk the loss of copyright.

2. SOLUTIONS AFFORDED BY PRECEDING RECOMMENDATIONS

We believe that recommendations made earlier in this report would provide solutions for these difficulties.

a. Deposit and registration

In chapter VII we have proposed that the Register of Copyrights be authorized to modify the general specification in the statute as to the deposit required for registration. Photographs were mentioned as an example of the cases for which a departure from the general requirement is desirable. The Register, by regulation, could permit the deposit of a number of photographs collectively for a single registration. In addition, our recommendations in chapter VII would afford protection, though with limited remedies, for unregistered photographs published with notice.

b. *Notice*

In chapter VI we have proposed that a general notice in a composite work be sufficient for all component contributions. We have also proposed that the use of the wrong name in the notice should not invalidate the copyright. Photographs contributed to a periodical would be protected by a general notice in the name of the publisher.

c. *Ownership*

In chapter VIII we have proposed that the publisher who secures copyright in a composite work should be deemed to hold in trust for the contributor all rights not expressly assigned, except the right of publication in a similar composite work. This would apply to a photograph contributed to a periodical.

C. Criminal Provisions

1. Willful Infringement for Profit [2]

In addition to the civil remedies for infringement, discussed above in chapter IX, the statute provides criminal penalties against willful infringement for profit. Section 104 makes it a misdemeanor, punishable by fine, imprisonment, or both, to infringe a copyright "willfully and for profit," or to "knowingly and willfully aid or abet such infringement."

Copyright owners have ordinarily pursued their civil remedies alone; but they have occasionally invoked this criminal provision. The criminal penalties can be effective in deterring flagrant and repeated infringements. We favor retaining them.

2. Fraudulent Use or Removal of Notice [3]

Section 105 provides criminal penalties against the following acts:

    (*a*) Inserting a copyright notice, with fraudulent intent, in "any uncopyrighted article";

    (*b*) Removing or altering, with fraudulent intent, the copyright notice upon "any article duly copyrighted";

    (*c*) Issuing, selling, or importing any article with knowledge that it bears a copyright notice and "has not been copyrighted in this country."

Penalties against the false use of a copyright notice have been provided ever since the notice was first made a requirement in the statute of 1802. Their purpose is to make the notice a reliable indication of the copyright status of a published work, by punishing fraudulent use of a false notice. Since it is not intended to penalize an honest mistake, section 105 makes "fraudulent intent," or knowledge that the notice is false, an essential element of the offense. A notice inserted in an article in good faith does not subject the claimant to criminal prosecution even if the claim is ultimately held invalid.

Although prosecutions for violation of section 105 have been rare, we believe the section has an important deterrent effect which helps insure the reliability of copyright notices. We would retain it in substance, but the present language can be improved. The references to

---

[2] See "Copyright Law Revision Study No. 24"
[3] See "Copyright Law Revision Study No. 10"

uncopyrighted articles bearing a notice are vestiges of the pre-1909 law when copyright had to be secured by registration before any copies could be published with a notice. Since copyright is now secured by the very act of publication with notice, these references are somewhat anomalous. The present language may also be too narrow to cover cases where a false date or name is used in the notice with fraudulent intent.

3. FALSE STATEMENTS IN REGISTRATION AND OTHER DOCUMENTS

Some of the previous bills to revise the copyright law included criminal penalties for knowingly filing in the Copyright Office any documents containing false statements. There is no such provision in the present copyright statute, but the Criminal Code (18 U.S.C. sec. 1001) provides penalties against anyone who knowingly makes false statements or uses false documents "in any matter within the jurisdiction of any department or agency of the United States."

It is, of course, important that the information filed in the Copyright Office for its public records be reliable. It seems clear, however, that the general provision of the Criminal Code applies to documents filed in the Copyright Office. We see no need for a special provision to the same effect in the copyright statute.

4. RECOMMENDATIONS

(*a*) The present criminal penalties against willful infringement for profit should be retained.

(*b*) The provisions of section 105 concerning false use of the copyright notice should be retained in substance, with some improvements in language.

(*c*) No special provisions concerning the filing of false information in the Copyright Office appear to be needed.

D. Provisions Regarding Judicial Procedures

1. IN GENERAL

The Copyright Act of 1909 contained several sections dealing with the jurisdiction, venue, and procedures of the courts in copyright cases. In 1948 some of these provisions were repealed, since they were covered in the Judicial Code (title 28, United States Code) and in the Federal Rules of Civil Procedure. The three remaining sections, 112–114, concern injunctions and appellate review.

2. PROCEDURE INVOLVING INJUNCTIONS

The first sentence of section 112 states that the Federal district courts shall have power to grant injunctions against copyright infringements according to equity principles. As noted in chapter IX, injunctions are mentioned elsewhere in the statute among the remedies to be available for copyright infringement. Nothing of substance is added by the first sentence of section 112.

In contrast, the second sentence of section 112, as supplemented by section 113, provides for procedures not covered otherwise. They make it possible for a copyright owner who has obtained an injunction in one State to enforce it against the defendant when he is located in another State. We believe these provisions should be retained.

3. REVIEW BY APPELLATE COURTS

Section 114 says merely that the decisions of the Federal district courts in copyright cases are reviewable on appeal as provided elsewhere by law. Review of all district courts decisions by the circuit courts of appeals and the Supreme Court are provided for in the Judicial Code.

4. RECOMMENDATIONS

(*a*) The first sentence of section 112 and section 114 should be deleted as superfluous.

(*b*) The second sentence of section 112 and section 113, which provide for the service and enforcement of injunctions anywhere in the United States, should be retained in substance.

E. Performing Rights Organizations

1. THE PURPOSE AND NATURE OF PERFORMING RIGHTS ORGANIZATIONS

In the United States, as in virtually every other major country, copyright owners have found it necessary as a practical matter to place their musical works in a pool for the licensing of public performances. Musical performances are given so widely that no one copyright owner could police all performances of his music or collect the royalties due him. And on the other hand, persons who give performances of many musical works, such as broadcasters, would find it impractical to obtain licenses from, and pay royalties to, each of the many copyright owners individually.

Organizations have therefore been formed to combine the musical compositions of many owners into a single catalog for which the organization issues performing licenses and collects royalties.

Inherent in any organization of this sort is the potential danger of monopolistic control and discrimination, both as to users seeking licenses and as to copyright owners seeking to participate. In this respect a performing rights organization is comparable to a public utility.

2. PERFORMING RIGHTS ORGANIZATIONS ABROAD

In most foreign countries there is only one performing rights organization, operated under some form of government control. The following are some of the typical methods by which these organizations are regulated abroad:

- Government approval must be obtained for the establishment of a performing rights organization;
- Royalty rate schedules must be filed with the government and applied nondiscriminately;
- Royalty rates are made subject to review and adjustment by a tribunal upon complaint;
- Lists of the musical works in the organization's catalog, or lists of its members, must be filed periodically with the government;

• The admission of copyright owners to membership in the organization, and the distribution of its revenue among the members, are made subject to government regulation or review.

3. PERFORMING RIGHTS ORGANIZATIONS IN THE UNITED STATES

a. *Organizations now operating*

In the United States there are now two principal performing rights organizations—the American Society of Composers, Authors, and Publishers (ASCAP), and Broadcast Music, Inc. (BMI). Between them they license the public performance of the great bulk of copyrighted music. A third organization, SESAC, licenses a relatively small catalog of music.

ASCAP is a membership organization of music writers and publishers, started in 1914. In 1958 it had about 4,600 writer and 1,100 publisher members. Its gross revenue for 1960 was about $32 million. Its net revenue, after expenses, is distributed among its members, 50 percent to the writers and 50 percent to the publishers.

BMI was organized in 1939 by the broadcasting industry as a counterweight to ASCAP. In 1958 it licensed the music of about 2,600 publishers, many of which were currently inactive, and a number of individual writers. Its gross revenue for 1960 was about $12 million. BMI is not intended to make a profit. Its royalty schedules are adjusted to produce the revenue needed to defray its expenses, establish a reserve, and make payments to publishers and writers at stipulated rates.

SESAC is a privately owned corporation established in 1930. As of 1958 it licensed the music of 284 publishers with a catalog of about 280,000 works, largely of specialized varieties. It is operated for profit and makes payments to its publisher members at stipulated rates. Its gross revenue is not known.

b. *The present method of regulation*

The copyright statute makes no mention of performing rights organizations, nor is there any other Federal statute for their regulation. Nevertheless, there has been official recognition of the need for these organizations and of the necessity to guard against abuses of their monopolistic position. Antitrust proceedings by the Department of Justice resulted in the acceptance by ASCAP and BMI of consent decrees in 1941, and the ASCAP decree was amended in 1950 and 1960.

These consent decrees contain a variety of requirements designed to prevent discrimination in the licensing of public performances. In addition, the ASCAP decree provides that any user may petition the court to review its royalty rates, and contains provisions regulating its admission of members, its internal organization and voting structure, and its distribution of revenue.

c. *Consideration of other methods of regulation*

The organization and activities of the performing rights organizations in the United States have been the object of much discussion and controversy in congressional hearings and in antitrust proceedings. It has been seriously questioned whether the antitrust procedure is the most appropriate or effective means of regulating their operations, and suggestions have been made that they should be regulated by an administrative agency under statutory provisions.

Whether and how these organizations should be further regulated is a problem that will require extensive investigation and study. Several agencies of the Government have been concerned with some of their activities. We have made no study of this problem since we believe it is beyond the range of the present project for revision of the copyright law, but we suggest that consideration should be given to developing legislation for its solution.

4. RECOMMENDATION

Whether performing rights organizations should be further regulated, and the appropriate method for their regulation, involve problems that are too large and complex to be dealt with in the present program for copyright law revision, but Congress should make it the special subject of comprehensive study.

Chapter XII

ADMINISTRATIVE PROVISIONS

OUTLINE OF CHAPTER

CHAPTER XII

ADMINISTRATIVE PROVISIONS

A. In General

Sections 201–216 of the present law provide for the organization of the Copyright Office in the Library of Congress, and for the administration by that Office of the deposit and registration system. For the most part, these provisions are satisfactory in substance, though they could be improved in form and detail.

We have already proposed, in chapter VII, parts B 2 d and C 5 c, that certain changes be made in sections 209 and 214. The discussion below covers other substantive changes that we believe should be made.

B. Accounting Procedures

1. SECTION 203 NOW OBSOLETE

Section 203, which dates back to 1909, specifies certain procedures under which the fees received by the Copyright Office are to be deposited and accounted for. Since the enactment of the Budget and Accounting Act of 1921, which authorized the General Accounting Office to audit and settle the accounts of all Government agencies, the provisions of section 203 have been superseded by procedures prescribed by the General Accounting Office.

2. RECOMMENDATION

Section 203 should be deleted.

C. Contents of Registration Records and Certificates

1. IN GENERAL

The registration of copyright claims in the Copyright Office is intended to produce a public record that identifies the work and shows facts determinative of the validity, ownership, and duration of the claim. This information is derived from the claimant's application for registration and the deposit copies of the work.

The present law does not specify directly what information is to be given in the application. Section 209 does so indirectly, however, by requiring that specified information be shown in the certificate of registration. Most of this information, for both the public record and the certificate, must be obtained from the application.

2. INADEQUACY OF SECTION 209

Section 209 was designed to enumerate the facts to be shown in the certificate, but this enumeration has proved to be incomplete. For example, it does not include the following:

- The place of publication, which is now pertinent where copyright is claimed under the Universal Copyright Convention.
- The fact that a work is a new version of a preexisting work.
- The limitation of the claim to the new material only, where a work contains both preexisting and new material.
- Data distinguishing the particular work from other editions or versions.

The Copyright Office has sought to fill these gaps by calling for information in the applications beyond that enumerated in section 209, and by including this additional information in its records and in the certificates. It is not clear, however, whether the provision that the certificate is prima facie evidence of the facts stated therein extends to all the facts given in the certificate or only to those enumerated in section 209.

3. NEED FOR FLEXIBILITY

Some of the information needed differs for various kinds of works and various situations. The required information will be changed in some respects when the present law is revised. Further changes will no doubt become necessary in the future as new conditions develop. For these reasons, we believe that the specification of the information to be contained in applications, registration records, and certificates should be broad enough to elicit all relevant information, and flexible enough to fit various and changing conditions.

4. RECOMMENDATIONS

(*a*) In addition to any statutory specification of facts to be included in applications, registration records, and certificates, the Register of Copyrights should be authorized to include any other pertinent information that will identify the work and show facts bearing upon the validity, ownership, or duration of the copyright claim.

(*b*) The certificate of registration should be prima facie evidence of any and all pertinent information it contains if registration is made within 1 year of the first public dissemination of the work.

D. Receipt for Copies Deposited

1. PROVISION IN QUESTION

The last sentence of section 209 provides that, in addition to the certificate of registration, "the Register of Copyrights shall furnish, upon request, without additional fee, a receipt for the copies of the work deposited to complete the registration."

Since the certificate of registration shows that the required copies of the work have been deposited, there is no need for an additional receipt. These receipts have rarely been requested.

On the other hand, a recommendation made earlier in this report (ch. VII, pt. C 6 b) contemplates that some deposits may be made without registration. In such cases the depositor who wishes to have a receipt should be given one. But since no registration fee would be paid in connection with the deposit, we propose that a small fee—possibly $1—be charged for issuance of the receipt.

2. RECOMMENDATIONS

(*a*) The provision in section 209 requiring issuance of a receipt, upon request, for copies deposited in connection with registration should be deleted.

(*b*) The statute should provide that a receipt will be issued, upon request and payment of a small fee, for copies deposited without registration.

E. THE CATALOG OF COPYRIGHT ENTRIES [1]

1. PRINTED CATALOG NOW REQUIRED

Sections 210 and 211 require that an indexed catalog of all copyright registrations be printed at periodic intervals, and that it be distributed to customs and postal officials and offered for sale to the public.

The printed catalog—designated the "Catalog of Copyright Entries"—was originally designed in 1891 to assist customs and postal officials in enforcing restrictions on the importation of copyrighted works. At the same time, it was anticipated that the printed catalog would be useful to the public as a local source of copyright information and as a national bibliography.

When provision was later made for the free distribution of Government documents to depository libraries throughout the Nation (44 U.S.C. secs. 82–89), the "Catalog of Copyright Entries" was included among the documents distributed.

The printed catalog is issued semiannually in eight separate parts, each covering one or more classes of works. The eight parts together cover all copyright registrations made during a 6-month period.

2. USES OF THE PRINTED CATALOG

a. Use by the public

The printed catalog is made available to the public through the sale of all or any parts, and through its distribution to libraries. It is used by the public for two purposes:

    (1) As a local source of copyright information which would otherwise be available only in the Copyright Office.

    (2) As a national bibliography. The parts of the catalog covering certain classes of works—particularly music, motion pictures, and maps—are the most comprehensive national bibliographies now available in their fields. For other classes of works, including books and periodicals, there are other bibliographies of equal or wider coverage.

The extent to which the printed catalog is used by the public varies among its eight parts. During 1959, for example, the sales of the

---

[1] See "Copyright Law Revision Study No. 21"

several parts ranged from a high of 299 for music to a low of 23 each for periodicals and for commercial prints and labels.

Surveys made by the Copyright Office indicate that many libraries use parts of the catalog as bibliographies for their own internal purposes. The surveys indicate further that the public makes extensive use of the catalog in a few libraries located in the major publishing and entertainment centers, but makes little or no use of the catalog in other libraries.

The copyright information given in the printed catalog is, of course, available in the records kept in the Copyright Office. Many persons consult these records in the Office, or have a record search made for them by the Office. But the printed catalog is undoubtedly a great conveniece for subscribers who have constant need for copyright information, and for an unknown number of persons who use the catalog in public libraries.

b. Use in the Copyright Office

The printed catalog is used in the Copyright Office as a source of quick reference, both for its own internal purposes and in making searches for the public. But the same information is available, though sometimes less conveniently, from the primary records in the Office.

The printed catalog has incidental value as a safeguard against the destruction of the primary records. Other less expensive means could be used, however, for preservation of the records. For example, recorded transfers of ownership are now reproduced on microfilm, and a copy of the microfilm is placed in storage as a security measure.

c. Other contemplated uses

The printed catalog has proved to be of little or no use to customs and postal officials in the enforcement of import restrictions. Distribution of the catalog to those officials was discontinued in 1953.

Section 210 provides that the catalog shall be admissible in court as prima facie evidence of the facts stated therein. Certificates of registration are used as such evidence in court; the catalog has almost never been used for this purpose.

3. COST OF THE PRINTED CATALOG; POSSIBLE CURTAILMENT OR SUBSTITUTES

Only a small fraction of the cost of producing the printed catalog is recovered from sales. In 1959, for example, the total cost of assembling, printing, and binding the entire yearly catalog came to about $109,000, while receipts from the year's sales totaled slightly over $4,000. Most of the copies printed are distributed free of charge to libraries and Government agencies.

The parts of the printed catalog that are used widely, either as a local source of copyright information or as a bibliography, provide a public service that is thought to justify their cost. It is questionable, however, whether the cost of the printed catalog is warranted for other parts that appear to be useful to a relatively small number of persons.

The development of new techniques of reproduction may offer possibilities in the future of replacing the printed catalog, as to some or all of its parts, with a less costly substitute. For example, the possibility is now being explored of reproducing the registration records on microfilm; if found to be less costly and equally useful, copies of the microfilm, instead of the printed catalog, might be made available to the public.

We suggest that the Register of Copyrights should be authorized to determine, on the basis of periodic appraisals of their usefulness and cost, whether the various parts of the catalog should be issued and in what form.

4. RECOMMENDATIONS

(a) Instead of requiring that the Register of Copyrights prepare a printed catalog of all copyright registrations, the statute should authorize him to prepare catalogs of registrations in such form and with such content as he may determine.

(b) The catalogs should continue to be available for free distribution to libraries and for sale to the public.

F. FEES

1. FEE RATES IN GENERAL

Section 215 specifies the fees to be paid to the Copyright Office for registrations, for the recording of assignments and other documents, for certifications, and for record searches. The present schedule of fees reflects increases made in 1928 and again in 1948.

In recent years the total of fees received, plus the estimated value of deposits added to the collections of the Library of Congress, has been slightly greater than the total expenditures of the Copyright Office. Leaving aside the value of the deposits, the fees alone have been approximately equal to the expenditures that could be attributed directly to the performance of the services for which fees are charged. The expenditures in excess of the fees can be traced to the governmental functions of the Office—including services performed for the Congress, the Library, other Government agencies, and the general public—which we think the fees should not be expected to cover.

We believe this balance between receipts and expenditures should be maintained. Because of the rising cost of running the Office, it seems likely that some increase in the present fees will be needed to maintain this position. The House Subcommittee on Legislative Appropriations has suggested that the present fees should be raised. We believe the need for higher fees has not yet become urgent, and we therefore propose that changes in the fee schedule be deferred for a brief period until further experience shows what increases may be necessary.

2. REGISTRATION FEES

The present fee for copyright registration is generally $4, but the statute prescribes special fees of $6 for the registration of a commercial print or label, and $2 for a renewal registration.

These special registration fees are not justified by any differences in the registration process. The higher fee of $6 for commercial prints and labels is a holdover from the time before 1940 when they were registered in the Patent Office. The process of registering them in the Copyright Office is now the same as for other classes of works. As to the lower fee of $2 for renewal registrations, their processing requires more time and work, on the average, than the processing of original registrations.

3. FEES FOR SPECIAL SERVICES

The Copyright Office is occasionally requested to furnish special services not mentioned in the statutory fee schedule. For example, copies of some of its catalog cards are being supplied to several persons and groups at the estimated cost of production. We suggest that a general provision be added to the fee schedule authorizing the Register to fix fees, commensurate with cost, for any services not covered by the schedule.

4. RECOMMENDATIONS

(*a*) The fees charged by the Copyright Office should be so fixed that the total of its receipts plus the value of deposits added to the Library's collections is approximately equal to its total expenditures. An increase in the present fees may soon be necessary to maintain this position, but specific recommendations should await further experience in the near future.

(*b*) The fee for all original and renewal registrations should be uniform.

(*c*) The Register of Copyrights should be authorized to fix fees, commensurate with cost, for services not covered by the statutory fee schedule.

FEDERAL CODE ANNOTATED

TITLE 17.—COPYRIGHTS

REPEAL OF PRIOR LAW

Act July 30, 1947, c. 391, § 2, 61 Stat. 668, repealed all of former Title 17 as follows:

§ 1—Act Mar. 4, 1909, c. 320, § 1, 35 Stat. 1075.

§ 2—Act Mar. 4, 1909, c. 320, § 2, 35 Stat. 1076.

§ 3—Act Mar. 4, 1909, c. 320, § 3, 35 Stat. 1076.

§ 4—Act Mar. 4, 1909, c. 320, § 4, 35 Stat. 1076.

§ 5—Act Mar. 4, 1909, c. 320, § 5, 35 Stat. 1076; Aug. 24, 1912, c. 356, 37 Stat. 488; July 31, 1939, c. 396, § 2, 53 Stat. 1142.

§ 6—Act Mar. 4, 1909, c. 320, § 6, 35 Stat. 1077.

§ 7—Act Mar. 4, 1909, c. 320, § 7, 35 Stat. 1077.

§ 8—Act Mar. 4, 1909, c. 320, § 8, 35 Stat. 1077; Dec. 18, 1919, c. 11, 41 Stat. 369; Sept. 25, 1941, c. 421, 55 Stat. 732.

§ 9—Act Mar. 4, 1909, c. 320, § 9, 35 Stat. 1077.

§ 10—Act Mar. 4, 1909, c. 320, § 10, 35 Stat. 1078.

§ 11—Act Mar. 4, 1909, c. 320, § 11, 35 Stat. 1078; Aug. 24, 1912, c. 356, 37 Stat. 488.

§ 12—Act Mar. 4, 1909, c. 320, § 12, 35 Stat. 1078; Mar. 28, 1914, c. 47, § 1, 38 Stat. 311.

§ 13—Act Mar. 4, 1909, c. 320, § 13, 35 Stat. 1078.

§ 14—Act Mar. 4, 1909, c. 320, § 14, 35 Stat. 1078.

§ 15—Act Mar. 4, 1909, c. 320, § 15, 35 Stat. 1078; July 3, 1926, c. 743, 44 Stat. 818.

§ 16—Act Mar. 4, 1909, c. 320, § 16, 35 Stat. 1079.

§ 17—Act Mar. 4, 1909, c. 320, § 17, 35 Stat. 1079.

§ 18—Act Mar. 4, 1909, c. 320, § 18, 35 Stat. 1079.

§ 19—Act Mar. 4, 1909, c. 320, § 19, 35 Stat. 1079.

§ 20—Act Mar. 4, 1909, c. 320, § 20, 35 Stat. 1080.

§ 21—Act Mar. 4, 1909, c. 320, § 21, 35 Stat. 1080; Dec. 18, 1919, c. 11, 41 Stat. 369.

§ 22—Act Mar. 4, 1909, c. 320, § 22, 35 Stat. 1080.

§ 23—Act Mar. 4, 1909, c. 320, § 23, 35 Stat. 1080; Mar. 15, 1940, c. 57, 54 Stat. 51.

§ 24—Act Mar. 4, 1909, c. 320, § 24, 35 Stat. 1080.

§ 25—Act Mar. 4, 1909, c. 320, § 25, 35 Stat. 1081; Aug. 24, 1912, c. 356, 37 Stat. 489. [Also repealed by Act June 25, 1948, c. 646, § 39, 62 Stat. 992.]

§ 26—Act Mar. 4, 1909, c. 320, § 26, 35 Stat. 1082. [Also repealed by Act June 25, 1948, c. 646, § 39, 62 Stat. 992.]

§ 27—Act Mar. 4, 1909, c. 320, § 27, 35 Stat. 1082. [Also repealed by Act June 25, 1948, c. 646, § 39, 62 Stat. 992.]

§ 28—Act Mar. 4, 1909, c. 320, § 28, 35 Stat. 1082.

§ 29—Act Mar. 4, 1909, c. 320, § 29, 35 Stat. 1082.

§ 30—Act Mar. 4, 1909, c. 320, § 30, 35 Stat. 1082.

§ 31—Act Mar. 4, 1909, c. 320, § 31, 35 Stat. 1082.

§ 32—Act Mar. 4, 1909, c. 320, § 32, 35 Stat. 1083.

§ 33—Act Mar. 4, 1909, c. 320, § 33, 35 Stat. 1083; Apr. 11, 1940, c. 81, 54 Stat. 106.

§ 34—Act Mar. 4, 1909, c. 320, § 34, 35 Stat. 1084. [Also repealed by Act June 25, 1948, c. 646, § 39, 62 Stat. 992.]

§ 35—Act Mar. 4, 1909, c. 320, § 35, 35 Stat. 1084. [Also repealed by Act June 25, 1948, c. 646, § 39, 62 Stat. 992.]

§ 36—Act Mar. 4, 1909, c. 320, § 36, 35 Stat. 1084.

§ 37—Act Mar. 4, 1909, c. 320, § 37, 35 Stat. 1084.

§ 38—Act Mar. 4, 1909, c. 320, § 38, 35 Stat. 1084.

§ 39—Act Mar. 4, 1909, c. 320, § 39, 35 Stat. 1084.

§ 40—Act Mar. 4, 1909, c. 320, § 40, 35 Stat. 1084.

§ 41—Act Mar. 4, 1909, c. 320, § 41, 35 Stat. 1084.

§ 42—Act Mar. 4, 1909, c. 320, § 42, 35 Stat. 1084.

§ 43—Act Mar. 4, 1909, c. 320, § 43, 35 Stat. 1084.

§ 44—Act Mar. 4, 1909, c. 320, § 44, 35 Stat. 1084.

§ 45—Act Mar. 4, 1909, c. 320, § 45, 35 Stat. 1085.

§ 46—Act Mar. 4, 1909, c. 320, § 46, 35 Stat. 1085.

§ 47—Act Mar. 4, 1909, c. 320, § 47, 35 Stat. 1085.

§ 48—Act Mar. 4, 1909, c. 320, § 48, 35 Stat. 1085.

§ 49—Act Mar. 4, 1909, c. 320, § 49, 35 Stat. 1085.

§ 50—Act Mar. 4, 1909, c. 320, § 50, 35 Stat. 1085.

§ 51—Act Mar. 4, 1909, c. 320, § 51, 35 Stat. 1085.

§ 52—Act Mar. 4, 1909, c. 320, § 52, 35 Stat. 1085.

§ 53—Act Mar. 4, 1909, c. 320, § 53, 35 Stat. 1085.

§ 54—Act Mar. 4, 1909, c. 320, § 54, 35 Stat. 1086.

§ 55—Act Mar. 4, 1909, c. 320, §§ 55, 64, 35 Stat. 1086, 1088; Mar. 2, 1913, c. 97, 37 Stat. 724.

§ 56—Act Mar. 4, 1909, c. 320, § 56, 35 Stat. 1086.

§ 57—Act Mar. 4, 1909, c. 320, § 57, 35 Stat. 1086; May 23, 1928, c. 704, § 1, 45 Stat. 714.

§ 58—Act Mar. 4, 1909, c. 320, § 58, 35 Stat. 1086.

§ 59—Act Mar. 4, 1909, c. 320, § 59, 35 Stat. 1087.

§ 60—Act Mar. 4, 1909, c. 320, § 60, 35 Stat. 1087.

§ 61—Act Mar. 4, 1909, c. 320, § 61, 35 Stat. 1087; May 23, 1928, c. 704, § 1, 45 Stat. 714.

§ 62—Act Mar. 4, 1909, c. 320, § 62, 35 Stat. 1087.

[§ 63—Act June 18, 1874, c. 301, § 3, 18 Stat. 79, repealed by Act Jan. 31, 1939, c. 396, § 1, 53 Stat. 1142.]

§ 64—Act July 31, 1939, c. 396, § 3, 53 Stat. 1142.

§ 65—Act July 31, 1939, c. 396, § 4, 53 Stat. 1142.

Re-enactment.—Provisions contained in sections of former title were re-enacted in sections of the revised title as follows:

Former Title	Revised Title	Former Title	Revised Title
§ 1	§ 1	§ 33	§ 109
§ 2	§ 2	§ 34	§ 110
§ 3	§ 3	§ 35	§ 111
§ 4	§ 4	§ 36	§ 112
§ 5	§ 5	§ 37	§ 113
§ 6	§ 7	§ 38	§ 114
§ 7	§ 8	§ 39	§ 115
§ 8	§ 9	§ 40	§ 116
§ 9	§ 10	§ 41	§ 27
§ 10	§ 11	§ 42	§ 28
§ 11	§ 12	§ 43	§ 29
§ 12	§ 13	§ 44	§ 30
§ 13	§ 14	§ 45	§ 31
§ 14	§ 15	§ 46	§ 32
§ 15	§ 16	§ 47	§ 201
§ 16	§ 17	§ 48	§ 202
§ 17	§ 18	§ 49	§ 203
§ 18	§ 19	§ 50	§ 204
§ 19	§ 20	§ 51	§ 205
§ 20	§ 21	§ 52	§ 206
§ 21	§ 22	§ 53	§ 207
§ 22	§ 23	§ 54	§ 208
§ 23	§ 24	§ 55	§ 209
§ 24	Obsolete	§ 56	§ 210
§ 25	§ 101	§ 57	§ 211
§ 26	§ 102	§ 58	§ 212
§ 27	§ 103	§ 59	§ 213
§ 28	§ 104	§ 60	§ 214
§ 29	§ 105	§ 61	§ 215
§ 30	§ 106	§ 62	§ 26
§ 31	§ 107	§§ 63, 64	§ 6
§ 32	§ 108	§ 65	§ 25

CHAPTER 1.—REGISTRATION OF COPYRIGHTS

Section
1. Exclusive rights as to copyrighted works.
2. Rights of author or proprietor of unpublished work.

REGISTRATION OF COPYRIGHTS—Continued.
3. Protection of component parts of work copyrighted—Composite works or periodicals.
4. All writings of author included.
5. Classification of works for registration.
6. Registration of prints and labels.
7. Copyright on compilation of works in public domain or of copyrighted works—Subsisting copyrights not affected.
8. Copyright not to subsist in works in public domain, or published prior to July 1, 1909, and not already copyrighted, or Government publications—Publication by Government of copyrighted material.
9. Authors or proprietors, entitled—Aliens.
10. Publication of work with notice.
11. Registration of claim and issuance of certificate.
12. Works not reproduced for sale.
13. Deposit of copies after publication—Action or proceeding for infringement.
14. Failure to deposit—Demand—Penalty.
15. Postmaster's receipt—Transmission by mail without cost.
16. Mechanical work to be done in United States.
17. Affidavit to accompany copies.
18. Making false affidavit.
19. Notice—Form.
20. Place of application—One notice in each volume or number of newspaper or periodical.
21. Effect of accidental omission from copy or copies.
22. Ad interim protection of book or periodical published abroad.
23. Extension to full term.
24. Duration—Renewal and extension.
25. Renewal of copyrights registered in Patent Office under repealed law.
26. Terms defined.
27. Copyright distinct from property in object copyrighted—Effect of sale of object, and of assignment of copyright.
28. Assignments and bequests.
29. Executed in foreign country—Acknowledgment and certificate.
30. Record.
31. Certificate of record.
32. Use of name of assignee in notice.

AMENDMENT NOTE

Act June 3, 1949, c. 171, § 5, 63 Stat. 154, amended the analysis of this chapter by inserting "or periodical" in item 22.

Section 1. Exclusive rights as to copyrighted works. — Any person entitled thereto, upon complying with the provisions of this title, shall have the exclusive right:

(a) To print, reprint, publish, copy, and vend the copyrighted work;

(b) To translate the copyrighted work into other languages or dialects, or make any other version thereof, if it be a literary work; to dramatize it if it be a nondramatic work; to convert it into a novel or other nondramatic work if it be a drama; to arrange or adapt it if it be a musical work; to complete, execute, and finish it if it be a model or design for a work of art;

(c)   To deliver, authorize the delivery of, read, or present the copyrighted work in public for profit if it be a lecture, sermon, address or similar production, or other nondramatic literary work; to make or procure the making of any transcription or record thereof by or from which, in whole or in part, it may in any manner or by any method be exhibited, delivered, presented, produced, or reproduced; and to play or perform it in public for profit, and to exhibit, represent, produce, or reproduce it in any manner or by any method whatsoever. The damages for the infringement by broadcast of any work referred to in this subsection shall not exceed the sum of $100 where the infringing broadcaster shows that he was not aware that he was infringing and that such infringement could not have been reasonably foreseen; and

(d)   To perform or represent the copyrighted work publicly if it be a drama or, if it be a dramatic work and not reproduced in copies for sale, to vend any manuscript or any record whatsoever thereof; to make or to procure the making of any transcription or record thereof by or from which, in whole or in part, it may in any manner or by any method be exhibited, performed, represented, produced, or reproduced; and to exhibit, perform, represent, produce, or reproduce it in any manner or by any method whatsoever; and

(e)   To perform the copyrighted work publicly for profit if it be a musical composition; and for the purpose of public performance for profit, and for the purposes set forth in subsection (a) hereof, to make any arrangement or setting of it or of the melody of it in any system of notation or any form of record in which the thought of an author may be recorded and from which it may be read or reproduced: Provided, That the provisions of this title, so far as they secure copyright controlling the parts of instruments serving to reproduce mechanically the musical work, shall include only compositions published and copyrighted after July 1, 1909, and shall not include the works of a foreign author or composer unless the foreign state or nation of which such author or composer is a citizen or subject

grants, either by treaty, convention, agreement, or law, to citizens of the United States similar rights. And as a condition of extending the copyright control to such mechanical reproductions, that whenever the owner of a musical copyright has used or permitted or knowingly acquiesced in the use of the copyrighted work upon the parts of instruments serving to reproduce mechanically the musical work, any other person may make similar use of the copyrighted work upon the payment to the copyright proprietor of a royalty of 2 cents on each such part manufactured, to be paid by the manufacturer thereof; and the copyright proprietor may require, and if so the manufacturer shall furnish, a report under oath on the 20th day of each month on the number of parts of instruments manufactured during the previous month serving to reproduce mechanically said musical work, and royalties shall be due on the parts manufactured during any month upon the 20th of the next succeeding month. The payment of the royalty provided for by this section shall free the articles or devices for which such royalty has been paid from further contribution to the copyright except in case of public performance for profit. It shall be the duty of the copyright owner, if he uses the musical composition himself for the manufacture of parts of instruments serving to reproduce mechanically the musical work, or licenses others to do so, to file notice thereof, accompanied by a recording fee, in the copyright office, and any failure to file such notice shall be a complete defense to any suit, action, or proceeding for any infringement of such copyright.

In case of failure of such manufacturer to pay to the copyright proprietor within thirty days after demand in writing the full sum of royalties due at said rate at the date of such demand, the court may award taxable costs to the plaintiff and a reasonable counsel fee, and the court may, in its discretion, enter judgment therein for any sum in addition over the amount found to be due as royalty in accordance with the terms of this title, not exceeding three times such amount.

The reproduction or rendition of a musical composition by or upon coin-operated machines shall not be deemed a public performance for profit unless a fee is charged for admission to the place where such reproduction or rendition occurs. (July 30, 1947, c. 391, § 1, 61 Stat. 652; July 17, 1952, c. 923, § 1, 66 Stat. 752.)

Amendment note.—Act July 15, 1952, cited to text, added all that part of subsec. (c) which follows "lecture, sermon, address or similar production."

Effective date.—Section 2 of Act July 17, 1952, cited to text, provided that the amendment of subsec. (c) of this section "shall take effect on the 1st day of January 1953."

Cross reference.—Proclamations extending protection to foreign composers, see § 9 note of this title.

NOTES TO DECISIONS
ANALYSIS

1. In general.

The copyright statutes ought to be reasonably construed, with a view to effecting the purposes intended by Congress. They ought not to be unduly extended by judicial construction to include privileges not intended to be conferred, or so narrowly construed as to deprive those entitled to their benefit of the rights Congress intended to grant. Bobbs-Merrill Co. v. Straus, 210 US 339, 52 LEd 1086, 28 SCR 722, aff'g (CCA 2), 147 Fed 15, 15 LRA(NS) 766, which aff'd 139 Fed 155; Werckmeister v. American Lithographic Co., (CC-NY), 142 Fed 827. Aff'd 148 Fed 1022, which was aff'd 207 US 375, 52 LEd 254, 28 SCR 124; Ford v. Charles E. Blaney Amusement Co., (CC-NY), 148 Fed 642.

R. S. § 4952, as amended by Act Mar. 3, 1891, which secured to authors for a limited time exclusive right to their writings, was not invalid. Kalem Co. v. Harper, 222 US 55, 56 LEd 92, 32 SCR 20, AnnCas 1913A, 1285, aff'g (CCA 2), 169 Fed 61.

Economic philosophy behind clause empowering Congress to grant patents and copyrights is conviction that encouragement of individual effort by personal gain is best way to advance public welfare through talents of authors and inventors in science and useful arts; sacrificial days devoted to such creative activities deserve rewards commensurate with services rendered.

Mazer v. Stein, 347 US 201, 98 LEd 630, 74 SCR 460, 100 USPQ 325, aff'g (CA 4), 204 F(2d) 472, 97 USPQ 310, which rev'd 111 FSupp 359, 96 USPQ 439.

Provisions in the copyright laws should be given a liberal construction in order to give effect to the inherent right of an author in his own work. Myers v. Callaghan, (CC-Ill), 5 Fed 726.

R. S. § 4966 imposing damages for unauthorized performances of copyrighted works was penal in its character. Daly v. Brady, (CC-NY), 69 Fed 285. Aff'd 83 Fed 1007, which was aff'd 175 US 148, 44 LEd 109, 20 SCR 62.

The general intent of Congress, apart from proceedings in equity and from actions at law for damages for unauthorized publication of a manuscript, seems to have been to enforce the copyright laws by penalties, rather than by the ordinary common-law remedies. Daly v. Brady, (CC-NY), 69 Fed 285. Aff'd 83 Fed 1007, which was aff'd 175 US 148, 44 LEd 109, 20 SCR 62.

The copyright law, being a creature of statute and conferring distinct and limited rights which do not exist at common law, must be strictly construed. White-Smith Music Pub. Co. v. Apollo Co., (CCA 2), 147 Fed 226, aff'g 139 Fed 427. Aff'd 209 US 1, 52 LEd 655, 28 SCR 319, 15 AnnCas 70.

The copyright laws should be liberally construed, so as to protect the rights of authors and to promote literature and art. Ford v. Charles E. Blaney Amusement Co., (CC-NY), 148 Fed 642.

The subject of statutory copyright being wholly within the powers of Congress, it has full power to restrict all actions or proceedings dealing with infringement of rights secured by the copyright act. New York Times Co. v. Star Co., (CC-NY), 195 Fed 110.

Repealing section of Copyright Act of 1909 limited the remedy in instances where causes of action arose, or causes were then pending, or where there had been a violation of the statutes which existed prior to July 1, 1909, but which might not be prosecuted until after that date. M. Witmark & Sons v. Standard Music Roll Co., (CCA 3), 221 Fed 376, aff'g 213 Fed 532.

Statute may be applied to new situations not anticipated by Congress, if, fairly construed, such situations come within its intent and meaning. Jerome H. Remick & Co. v. American Automobile Accessories Co., (CCA 6), 5 F(2d) 411, 40 ALR 1511, rev'g 298 Fed 628.

Copyright as distinguished from literary property is wholly creature of statute. Krafft v. Cohen, (CCA 3), 117 F(2d) 579, 48 USPQ 401, rev'g 32 FSupp 82, 44 USPQ 678.

Protection must be sought either in copyright or patent field; it cannot be found in both; there is no overlapping territory, even though line of separation may be difficult of exact ascertainment. Taylor Instrument Cos. v. Fawley-Brost Co., (CCA 7), 139 F(2d) 98, 59 USPQ 384, rev'g 56 USPQ 213.

Fact that copyrighted doll was based on live model does not deprive it of necessary amount of originality. Rushton v. Vitale, (CA 2), 218 F(2d) 434, 104 USPQ 158.

Copyright protects an original work and is not dependent upon novelty. Wihtol v. Wells, (CA 7), 231 F(2d) 550, 109 USPQ 200.

Government officer's written records, executed in discharge of official duties, are public documents owned by government; however, rough notes kept by explorer's associate and later used as basis for associate's private journal belong to associate since they are his private and personal writings, unofficial in character; this is especially true since explorer was carrying out his duty of making official record of expedition. U. S. v. First Trust Co. of Saint Paul, (CA 8), 251 F(2d) 686, 116 USPQ 172, aff'g 146 FSupp 652, 116 USPQ 191.

Mere idea of depicting more common kinds of automobile accidents in form of a story in cartoon form is not copyrightable. American Visuals Corp. v. Holland, (CA 2), 261 F(2d) 652, 119 USPQ 482, aff'g 162 FSupp 14, 117 USPQ 180.

The copyright laws should be liberally construed and the administrative act of the register of copyrights should be so construed, if reasonably possible, as to carry out the intention of the Constitution to protect and encourage creative artists in their work. Southern Music Pub. Co. v. Bibo-Lang, Inc., (DC-NY), 10 FSupp 972, 26 USPQ 321; Basevi v. Edward O'Toole Co., Inc., (DC-NY), 26 FSupp 41, 40 USPQ 333.

Copyright is not defective because author's application for copyright registration erroneously failed to state that book was new edition. Wrench v. Universal Pictures Co., Inc., (DC-NY), 104 FSupp 374, 92 USPQ 350.

Copyright does not extend to idea, but only to execution or development of idea. American Visuals Corp. v. Holland, (DC-NY), 126 FSupp 513, 103 USPQ 139. Aff'd 219 F(2d) 223, 104 USPQ 222.

Copyright laws only protect those parts of author's work which are original and copyrightable; bare facts or "news" are not protected; however, style and form of their presentation are protected. Morse v. Fields, (DC-NY), 127 FSupp 63, 104 USPQ 54.

Copyrights and rights flowing therefrom are entirely creatures of statute. Loew's Inc. v. Columbia Broadcasting System, Inc., (DC-Cal), 131 FSupp 165, 105 USPQ 302. Aff'd 239 F(2d) 532, 112 USPQ 11, which was aff'd 356 US 43, 2 LEd(2d) 583, 78 SCR 667, 116 USPQ 479.

Although ideas as such are not subject to copyright, originality of the slightest degree is sufficient; choice of locale for story does not, necessarily, spell originality; copyrightability lies in manner of developing idea; originality lies in pattern of the work. Bradbury v. Columbia Broadcasting System, Inc., (DC-Cal), 174 FSupp 733, 123 USPQ 10.

New and original plan or combination of existing materials in public domain is sufficiently original to come within copyright protection; however, work must be original in sense that author created it by his own skill, labor, and judgment without directly copying or evasively imitating another's work; plaintiff has burden of establishing these elements when demanding

preliminary injunction. Alva Studios, Inc. v. Winninger, (DC-NY), 177 FSupp 265, 123 USPQ 487.

Cases holding that games, sports, and similar systems and plans are not copyrightable seem to spring from Baker v. Selden, 101 US 99; that case made a clear distinction between writings describing plans, methods, or systems, and the plans or systems themselves; the former were held subject to copyright, the latter, if at all, to patent protection; therefore, court dismisses action for infringement of copyrighted brochure describing betting system and for unfair competition since statutes and court decisions give no protection by copyright to sports, games, or similar systems as distinguished from publications describing them and since sport involved is so elementary and ordinary that it is in public domain and to afford protection would be to give author a monopoly out of proportion to originality involved. Briggs v. New Hampshire Trotting & Breeding Assn., (DC-NH), 191 FSupp 234, 128 USPQ 465.

If copyright law can protect dramas, as it does in subsec. (1) of this section there is no reason why it cannot protect certain forms of public presentations in the form of games or sports involving activity rather than mere words; it is but a question of drawing a line through the spectrum at one end of which is copyrightable television drama, at the other, the T. V. quiz program; in between are various sorts of plans, systems, and games involving varying degrees of originality, imagination, and detail. Briggs v. New Hampshire Trotting & Breeding Assn., (DC-NH), 191 FSupp 234, 128 USPQ 465.

To be copyrightable, work must be original in that the author created it by his own skill, labor, and judgment, contributing something recognizably his own to prior treatments of same subject; requirements are modest; neither great novelty nor superior artistic quality is required; originality in specific three dimensional plastic Santa Claus figure is sufficient. Doran v. Sunset House Distributing Corp., (DC-Cal), 197 FSupp 940, 131 USPQ 94.

Magazine's statements concerning attributes of consumer goods are not copyrightable since they are bald statements of fact which could hardly be stated in any different fashion; they are pedestrian expressions with no independent creative stature; they describe facts and nothing more. Consumers Union of U. S., Inc. v. Hobart Manufacturing Co., (DC-NY), 199 FSupp 860, 131 USPQ 438.

Although flower is creation of nature, its likeness may be copyrighted as work of art; since artificial lilac made of polyethylene reflects originality and a substantial degree of skill and independent judgment, it is proper subject for copyright. Prestige Floral, Societe Anonyme v. California Artificial Flower Co. (Inc.), (DC-NY), 201 FSupp 287, 132 USPQ 350.

Literary work of author is property and is subject to disposal. Tobani v. Carl Fischer, Inc., (DC-NY), 36 USPQ 97. Mf'd 98 F(2d) 57, 38 USPQ 198.

There can be no property right in abstract idea, but there may be literary property in form in which ideas are expressed. Yadkoe v.

Fields, 66 CalApp(2d series) 150, 151 Pac(2d) 906, 63 USPQ 103.

Unpublished literary work is not subject to execution. Dart v. Woodhouse, 40 Mich 399, 29 AmRep 544.

At common law, independently of statute, author has property right in his intellectual production before it is published and is entitled to redress against anyone who interferes with that right. Varconi v. Unity Television Corp., 11 Misc(2d series) 191, 173 NYS(2d) 201, 117 USPQ 107.

2. Nature and extent of rights.

Difference between copyright and letterspatent, see Baker v. Selden, 101 US 99, 25 LEd 341.

Nature and extent of rights, privileges, and powers before and after publication stated, see Harper & Bros. v. M. A. Donohue, (CC-Ill), 144 Fed 491. Aff'd 146 Fed 1023.

A copyright is a property in notion and has no corporeal tangible substance. Stephens v. Cady, 55 US(14 How) 528, 14 LEd 528.

Reporter's copyright does not cover statements of cases, head notes, and opinions prepared by judges in their official capacity. Banks v. Manchester, 128 US 244, 32 LEd 425, 9 SCR 36, aff'g (CC-Ohio), 23 Fed 143.

Unlike a patent, a copyright gives no exclusive right to art disclosed; protection is given only to expression of the idea—not the idea itself. Mazer v. Stein, 347 US 201, 98 LEd 630, 74 SCR 460, 100 USPQ 325, aff'g (CA 4), 204 F(2d) 472, 97 USPQ 310, which rev'd 111 FSupp 359, 96 USPQ 439.

A copyright of a drama, obtained by complying with the terms of the copyright law, gives protection only on the parts that are original with the author. Benn v. Leclercq, (CC-Mass), FedCas 1,308.

The Copyright Acts of 1831 and 1856, when construed together, entitled an author to protection of his composition in whole or in part by representation. Daly v. Palmer, (CC-NY), Fed Cas 3,552, 6 Blatchf 256, 36 HowPrac 206.

An author has a copyright in the plan, arrangement, and combination of his production. Lawrence v. Dana, (CC-Mass), FedCas 8,136, 4 Cliff 1.

The copyright by a state of its judicial reports does not preclude others from publishing the opinions of the judges contained therein, the work of the reporter being the only portion entitled to protection. Banks v. West Publishing Co., (CC-Minn), 27 Fed 50.

Copyright acts protect copyright-owner's plan of sales from interference by other dealers offering surreptitiously obtained copies of the copyrighted work without his consent. Henry Bill Publishing Co. v. Smythe, (CC-Ohio), 27 Fed 914.

Where the copyright upon a dictionary has expired anyone may reprint the work and use the original title thereon. Merriam v. Famous Shoe & Clothing Co., (CC-Mo), 47 Fed 411.

The copyright of a publication consisting of new, original matter incorporated in and with an uncopyrighted publication of a foreign author is not void, but will be afforded protection only as to the original work therein. American Code Co., Inc. v. Bensinger, (CCA 2), 282 Fed 829.

Mere priority in time in obtaining copyright does not confer a monopoly, and two stories, though identical, if each is an original and independent production, may both be entitled to copyright. Harold Lloyd Corp. v. Witwer, (CCA 9), 65 F(2d) 1, rev'g 46 F(2d) 792.

Purpose of copyright to promote literary progress would be frustrated if author could prevent others from using common ideas. Becker v. Loew's Inc., (CCA 7), 133 F(2d) 889, 56 USPQ 455.

Copyright protects only to extent of what is taught or explained; unlike patent, information disclosed is lodged in public domain, where its use is unrestricted. Crume v. Pacific Mut. Life Ins. Co., (CCA 7), 140 F(2d) 182, 60 USPQ 359, aff'g 55 USPQ 267.

Gist of Baker v. Selden, 101 US 99, 25 LEd 841, is that disclosure of copyright is reposed in public to extent necessary to achieve use of what is disclosed, whether disclosure is by descriptive words or diagrams. Crume v. Pacific Mut. Life Ins. Co., (CCA 7), 140 F(2d) 182, 60 USPQ 359, aff'g 55 USPQ 267.

Concrete incidents are protected by copyright law although law gives no monopoly of general ideas. MacDonald v. DuMaurier, (CCA 2), 144 F(2d) 696, 62 USPQ 394, rev'g 60 USPQ 410.

Statutes do not protect intellectual conception apart from thing produced. Christianson v. West Pub. Co., (CCA 9), 149 F(2d) 202, 65 USPQ 263, aff'g 53 FSupp 454, 60 USPQ 279.

Unlike subject matter of patent, copyrighted material need not be new, but only original. Ricker v. General Electric Co., (CCA 2), 162 F(2d) 141, 73 USPQ 458, aff'g 68 USPQ 371.

Copyright is intangible, incorporeal right in nature of privilege or franchise and is independent of any material substance such as manuscript or plate used for printing. Local Trademarks, Inc. v. Price, (CA 5), 170 F(2d) 715, 79 USPQ 344.

Copyright, as its name implies, means making copy of protected work. Foreign & Domestic Music Corp. v. Licht, (CA 2), 196 F(2d) 627, 93 USPQ 272.

Since copyright is intended to protect authorship, essence of copyright protection is protection of originality rather than novelty or invention. Stein v. Mazer, (CA 4), 204 F(2d) 472, 97 USPQ 310, rev'g 111 FSupp 359, 96 USPQ 439. Aff'd 347 US 201, 98 LEd 630, 74 SCR 460, 100 USPQ 325.

A copyright is an intangible, incorporeal right in nature of privilege or franchise and is enjoyable as legal estate, as other movable personal property; it will not be considered a joint estate unless specifically stated. Stuff v. La Budde Feed & Grain Co., (DC-Wis), 42 FSupp 493, 52 USPQ 23.

Copyright of book or periodical does not include cover. Fawcett Publication, Inc. v. Elliot Pub. Co., Inc., (DC-NY), 46 FSupp 717, 54 USPQ 367.

Plaintiff's copyrighted book "Famous First Facts" containing bare statements of historical facts is not infringed by defendant's advertisements entitled "First Facts" each containing one fact obtained from book, since wording of items is not same and plaintiff does not own facts; name "First Facts" is not subject to copyright protection; publications have nothing in common, there is no competition, and plaintiff cannot be injured. Kane v. Pennsylvania Broadcasting Co., (DC-Pa), 73 FSupp 307, 73 USPQ 258.

Right of mechanical reproduction set forth in subsec. (e) of this section is distinct from printing, reprinting rights set forth in subsec. (a) of this section and right to publicly perform for profit set forth in subsec. (e) of this section. Edward B. Marks Music Corp. v. Foullon, (DC-NY), 79 FSupp 664, 77 USPQ 502. Aff'd 171 F(2d) 905, 80 USPQ 56.

Copyright protection cannot be obtained as to ideas which are not novel, but, where idea of collecting and arranging ideas into compact course of study and instruction is novel, originator thereof is entitled to protection under copyright insofar as plan, arrangement, and form of text of publication are concerned. Powell v. Stransky, (DC-SD), 98 FSupp 434, 89 USPQ 310.

Recent trend in copyright actions indicates tendency by courts to afford more liberal protection to copyright owner, who is not denied relief on ground that his work is not of sufficient literary quality to merit copyright protection. Gordon v. Weir, (DC-Mich), 111 FSupp 117, 97 USPQ 387. Aff'd 216 F(2d) 508, 104 US PQ 40.

Unlike patent law, which gives patent owner absolute ownership of patented domain, copyright law gives copyright owner no right other than to prevent copying. Gordon v. Weir, (DC-Mich), 111 FSupp 117, 97 USPQ 387. Aff'd 216 F(2d) 508, 104 USPQ 40.

Copyright gives no protection with respect to techniques and methods; it gives no exclusive right to practice or use arts and methods described in copyrighted work. Dunham v. General Mills, Inc., (DC-Mass), 116 FSupp 152, 99 USPQ 372.

To obtain protection an author's ideas must be novel and original and must be reduced to concrete form in copyrighted writing or article; there is no copyright protection for an idea, although expression of an idea can be protected. Dunham v. General Mills, Inc., (DC-Mass), 116 FSupp 152, 99 USPQ 372.

Valid copyright is not obtained where music as published gives fictitious name for that of composer, although publisher knew that third party had composed music and had not assigned same to publisher. Mills Music, Inc. v. Cromwell Music, Inc., (DC-NY), 126 FSupp 54, 103 USPQ 84.

General copyright in issue of periodical does not protect rights in contributed article therein unless such rights had been previously assigned to publisher; article is protected where author assigned all rights to publisher in the first instance under express condition that, after registration of copyright in publisher's name, publisher would reassign all rights to author. Morse v. Fields, (DC-NY), 127 FSupp 63, 104 USPQ 54.

Although copyright protects against actual copying in the sense of physical reproduction of form, arrangement, and content of original directory, the use, absent copying, of another's directory solely for mail solicitation purposes is not within protection of copyright laws; one who copyrights compilation or directory of names cannot gain monopoly, under copyright statute, over business dealings with those listed. Caldwell-Clements, Inc. v. Cowan Publishing Corp., (DC-NY), 130 FSupp 326, 105 USPQ 116.

Courts have taken broad view of copyright protection in order to give to copyright proprietor the exclusive right to any lawful use of his property whereby he may get a profit out of it. Loew's Inc. v. Columbia Broadcasting System, Inc., (DC-Cal), 131 FSupp 165, 105 USPQ 302. Aff'd 239 F(2d) 532, 112 USPQ 11, which was aff'd 356 US 43, 2 LEd(2d) 583, 78 SCR 667, 116 USPQ 479.

Protection given copyright proprietor extends to other modes or forms of using or exhibiting his work. Loew's Inc. v. Columbia Broadcasting System, Inc., (DC-Cal), 131 FSupp 165, 105 USPQ 302. Aff'd 239 F(2d) 532, 112 USPQ 11, which was aff'd 356 US 43, 2 LEd(2d) 583, 78 SCR 667, 116 USPQ 479.

Author of scientific article published in professional journal is not entitled to monopoly of ideas presented therein. Alexander v. Irving Trust Co., (DC-NY), 132 FSupp 364, 106 USPQ 74. Aff'd 228 F(2d) 221, 108 USPQ 24.

Encroachment upon any one of the rights granted by subsec. (a) of this section gives rise to cause of action. Greenbie v. Noble, (DC-NY), 151 FSupp 45, 113 USPQ 115.

Author may not, through copyright, appropriate and withdraw from public domain an idea, theme, plot, or basic characters. Trailins v. Kaiser Aluminum & Chemical Corp., (DC-Md), 160 FSupp 511, 117 USPQ 79.

Mere idea of basing quiz program on motion pictures, even if it were original, is not subject to protection under copyright laws. Richards v. Columbia Broadcasting System, Inc., (DC-DC), 161 FSupp 516, 117 USPQ 174.

Substantial similarity is not one of ideas as such, but of embodiment of these ideas in written or other form, since author cannot obtain copyright on his ideas apart from their expression; fundamental idea of original work may even be borrowed as long as specific details of author's literary efforts are not copied. Richards v. Columbia Broadcasting System, Inc., (DC-DC), 161 FSupp 516, 117 USPQ 174.

There is clear unmistakable intent in subsec. (e) of this section that number manufactured, not the number sold, is royalty criterion; although copyright holder may agree to accept less than statute entitles him to, custom and usage whereby holder is paid only for phonograph records made and sold, rather than for records manufactured, cannot change meaning of language of statute or add a gloss thereto so as to dilute rights conferred. Southern Music Publishing Co., Inc. v. Seeco Records, Inc., (DC-NY), 200 FSupp 704, 132 USPQ 682.

Only expression of ideas is copyrightable. American Visuals Corp. v. Holland, (DC-NY), 162 FSupp 14, 117 USPQ 180. Aff'd 119 USPQ 482.

Forms, arrangement, and format involved in use of system or method are not protected by copyright. Kanover v. Marks, (DC-NY), 91 USPQ 370.

Exclusive and perpetual grant of any one of "bundle of rights" which go to make up a copyright is "sale" of personal property, rather than mere "license." Herwig v. U. S., 122 CtCls 493, 105 FSupp 384, 93 USPQ 421.

Many of the separate rights of copyright owner may be used as basis for securing new and separate copyrights; for example, copyright owner of novel has right to dramatize it, and he may secure copyright on dramatic scenario based upon the copyright. Herwig v. U. S., 122 CtCls 493, 105 FSupp 384, 93 USPQ 421.

Protectible literary property may be created out of unprotectible material such as historical events; creation in technical sense is not essential to vest one with ownership of rights in intellectual property. Desny v. Wilder, 46 Cal(2d series) 715, 299 Pac(2d) 257, 110 USPQ 433, mod'g (CalApp(2d series)), 286 Pac(2d) 55, 107 USPQ 17.

Charts on which machine records in writing variable temperatures and pressures are not copyrightable since charts function as working mechanical elements of and essential parts of machine which is useless without charts. Brown Instrument Co. v. Warner, 82 AppDC 232, 161 F(2d) 910, 73 USPQ 427, aff'g 68 USPQ 41.

Co-owners of copyrighted work are accountable to each other for profits derived from licensing third party to use work. Jerry Vogel Music Co., Inc. v. Miller Music, Inc., 272 AppDiv 571, 74 NYS(2d) 425, 75 USPQ 205. Aff'd 299 NY 782, 87 NE(2d) 681, 82 USPQ 458.

Except for copyright, published musical composition would be public property usable by any one in any way. Gay v. Robbins Music Corp., (Misc), 38 NYS(2d) 337, 55 USPQ 461.

Copyright is right available only to author or proprietor of literary property; its purpose is to secure to him exclusive right to that property; it is distinct from property copyrighted and its assignment will no more effect transfer of property than sale of property will effect assignment of copyright; it has been described as intangible, incorporeal right in nature of privilege or franchise independent of author's manuscript or printer's plate; in case of copyrighted play, copyright is distinct from play and is exercised by playright or owner for own exclusive benefit. McClintic v. Sheldon, 182 Misc 32, 43 NYS(2d) 695, 59 USPQ 41.

Where parties are equal owners of copyrighted work, in absence of agreement governing their rights in exploitation of work, they are accountable to each other for such exploitation; they are held to standard of dealing befitting their mutual interest in work. Kapplow v. Abelard Schuman, Ltd., 21 Misc(2d series) 306, 193 NYS(2d) 931, 124 USPQ 58.

The Antitrust Laws [15 § 1 et seq.] do not apply to copyrights. Metro-Goldwyn-Mayer Distributing Corp. v. Cocke, (TexCivApp), 56 SW(2d) 489.

3.—Mode of expression.

Copyright of news protects the form of expression but not the facts, since the facts are public property. International News Service v. Associated Press, 248 US 215, 63 LEd 211, 39 SCR 68. 2 ALR 293, aff'g (CCA 2), 245 Fed 244, which mf'd 240 Fed 983; Davies v. Bowes, (DC-NY), 209 Fed 53. Aff'd 219 Fed 178.

Copyright of a book describing a "short hand" system did not give exclusive right to the system, so as to prevent others from describing the same system in their own language. Griggs v. Perrin, (CC-NY), 49 Fed 15.

The system, plan, method, and arrangement of an originator of a compilation of credit ratings derives no protection from the statutory copyright of the book in which they are set forth. Burnell v. Chown, (CC-Ohio), 69 Fed 993.

Copyright of annotator of statutes covers all that may be deemed the result of his labors, such as head notes, marginal references, notes, memoranda, table of contents, indexes, and digests of judicial decisions prepared by him from original sources of information. Howell v. Miller, (CCA 6), 91 Fed 129.

The copyright of a pamphlet describing a plan for organizing and operating a burial association does not confer right to the plan disclosed. Burk v. Johnson, (CCA 8), 146 Fed 209.

Copyright upon a catalogue containing illustrations of a vendor's goods which he offered for sale did not deprive another selling similar goods from issuing a catalogue containing illustrations of his goods, provided such illustrations are not copied from the copyrighted catalogue. National Cloak & Suit Co. v. Standard Mail Order Co., (CC-NY), 191 Fed 528.

Copyright protects means of expressing idea, not idea itself. Dymow v. Bolton, (CCA 2), 11 F(2d) 690; Brunner v. Stix, Baer & Fuller Co., 352 Mo 1225, 181 SW(2d) 643.

It is not the subject that is protected by copyright, it is the treatment of the subject that is protected. Stephens v. Howells Sales Co., Inc., (DC-NY), 16 F(2d) 805.

A lecturer may use ideas expressed in another work, for it is not the subject that is protected, but the treatment of a subject. Nutt v. National Institute, (CCA 2), 31 F(2d) 236, aff'g 28 F(2d) 132.

Where series of events portrayed in book purport to represent real occurrences, the form of expression is the only thing protected by the copyright. Collins v. Metro-Goldwyn Pictures Corp., (CCA 2), 106 F(2d) 83, 42 USPQ 553, rev'g 25 FSupp 781, 39 USPQ 520.

Copyright on work of art does not protect a subject, but only treatment of subject. F. W. Woolworth Co. v. Contemporary Arts, Inc., (CA 1), 193 F(2d) 162, 92 USPQ 4, aff'g 93 FSupp 739, 86 USPQ 476. Aff'd 344 US 228, 97 LEd 276, 73 SCR 222, 95 USPQ 396.

Right to use of certain words is not protected by copyright; copyright secures right to that arrangement of words which author has selected to express his ideas. Funkhouser v. Loew's Inc., (CA 8), 208 F(2d) 185, 99 USPQ 448, aff'g 108 FSupp 476, 96 USPQ 115.

Comic cartoon in magazine embodies conception of humor or surprise or incredulity--whatsoever cartoonist is aiming at—and what owner of copyright is entitled to is protection of that embodiment of his concept. Detective Comics, Inc. v. Bruns Publications, Inc., (DC-NY), 28 FSupp 399, 41 USPQ 182. Mf'd 111 F(2d) 432, 45 USPQ 291.

In the case of literary or artistic works and works of similar character in which form, arrangement, or combination of ideas represents product of labor and skilled effort separate and apart from that entailed in development of intellectual conception involved, the medium of expression is entitled to protection by copyright against its adoption by another in similar form, arrangement, and combination. Long v. Jordan, (DC-Cal), 29 FSupp 287, 43 USPQ 176.

Copyright statute does not give plaintiff monopoly of ideas but merely protects means of expressing ideas. Gropper v. Warner Bros. Pictures, Inc., (DC-NY), 38 FSupp 329, 49 USPQ 17.

Copyright cannot prevent others from using old material; it is not novelty of subject matter, but originality of form of expression, that is important. Lewis v. Kroger Co., (DC-WVa), 109 FSupp 484, 95 USPQ 359.

Although ideas, abstract conceptions, and similar matters are not protectible, author's manner of treatment, expression, incidents and details, and sequence of events by which he works out and develops the abstractions are copyrightable elements of his work and will be protected. Loew's Inc. v. Columbia Broadcasting System, Inc., (DC-Cal), 131 FSupp 165, 105 USPQ 302. Aff'd 239 F(2d) 532, 112 USPQ 11, which was aff'd 356 US 43, 2 LEd(2d) 583, 78 SCR 667, 116 USPQ 479.

Copyright does not pre-empt field as against others who choose different means of expressing same idea; in this respect, it differs from patent which protects inventor against any unauthorized use of discovery itself. Alexander v. Irving Trust Co., (DC-NY), 132 FSupp 364, 106 USPQ 74. Aff'd 228 F(2d) 221, 108 USPQ 24.

Copyright does not cover idea or system of doing business, but only particular mode of expression of idea embodied in copyrighted material; public is free to use idea or method of doing business; while copyrighted description of idea may not be slavishly copied, copyright is not infringed by expression of idea which is substantially similar where similarity is necessary because idea or system being described is the same. Gaye v. Gillis, (DC-Mass), 167 FSupp 416, 119 USPQ 292.

Copyright protects only expression of idea, not idea itself. Doran v. Sunset House Distributing Corp., (DC-Cal), 197 FSupp 940, 131 USPQ 94.

Fact that copyrighted article depicts a figure, theme, or idea in public domain does not in itself void the copyright; test of copyrightability must be the form which author used to express the figure, idea, or theme. Doran v. Sunset

House Distributing Corp., (DC-Cal), 197 FSupp 940, 131 USPQ 94.

Originality in realm of copyright refers to form of the expression, not to novelty of subject matter. Doran v. Sunset House Distributing Corp., (DC-Cal), 197 FSupp 940, 131 USPQ 94.

Abbreviations in publication are not susceptible of copyright protection, since there is nothing unique in their composition or arrangement. Kanover v. Marks, (DC-NY), 91 USPQ 370.

4.—Common-law or statutory.

Common-law right of literary property and statutory copyright distinguished, see Bobbs-Merrill Co. v. Straus, (CCA 2), 147 Fed 15, 15 LRA(NS) 766, aff'g 139 Fed 155. Aff'd 210 US 339, 52 LEd 1086, 28 SCR 722.

Copyright property under the federal law is wholly statutory and depends upon the right created under the acts of Congress passed in pursuance of the authority conferred under § 8, clause 8 of Article I of the Constitution. Bobbs-Merrill Co. v. Straus, 210 US 339, 52 LEd 1086, 28 SCR 722, aff'g (CCA 2), 147 Fed 15, 15 LRA(NS) 766, which aff'd 139 Fed 155.

"Holder of a copyright has no monopoly by virtue of the issued copyright itself, but his rights are measured by the statute." Lydiard-Peterson Co. v. Woodman, (CCA 8), 204 Fed 921, aff'g 192 Fed 67.

Copyright property under federal law is wholly statutory. Metro-Goldwyn-Mayer Distributing Corp. v. Bijou Theatre Co., (CCA 1), 59 F(2d) 70, 13 USPQ 147, aff'g 50 F(2d) 908, 9 USPQ 538.

There is no common-law design copyright, and statute does not permit procuring of design copyright. Chas. D. Briddell, Inc. v. Alglobe Trading Corp., (CA 2), 194 F(2d) 416, 92 USPQ 100.

At common law, author of writing possesses sole and exclusive right to publish it, but upon and after first publication the writing may be published by anyone including author, since writing has gone into public domain; copyright statute extends author's sole and exclusive right by reserving writing from public domain for effective period of the copyright. Warner Bros. Pictures, Inc. v. Columbia Broadcasting System, Inc., (CA 9), 216 F(2d) 945, 104 USPQ 103, mod'g 102 FSupp 141, 92 USPQ 54.

Copyright is wholly statutory. Shapiro, Bernstein & Co., Inc. v. Bryan, (DC-NY), 27 FSupp 11, 41 USPQ 134; Tobani v. Carl Fischer, Inc., (DC-NY), 36 USPQ 97. Mf'd 98 F(2d) 57, 38 USPQ 198.

Common law and copyright statute do not protect intellectual conceptions, however meritorious, until they have been produced; there may be literary property in combination of ideas in form in which ideas are embodied; there can be none in ideas. Grant v. Kellogg Co., (DC-NY), 58 FSupp 48, 63 USPQ 173. Aff'd 154 F(2d) 59, 75 USPQ 301.

Rights possessed by copyright owner are purely statutory. Miller v. Goody, (DC-NY), 125 FSupp 348, 103 USPQ 292.

British composer's common-law rights in his work are recognized in United States even

(1355)

though in Britain those rights appear to have merged in statutory copyright. Mills Music, Inc. v. Cromwell Music, Inc., (DC-NY), 126 FSupp 54, 103 USPQ 84.

Under common law of copyright, once author makes general, as distinguished from limited, publication of his work he loses common-law copyright protection; general publication of arrangement of song, destroying whatever common-law rights arranger had when arranger caused to be sold for unlimited distribution to general public hundreds of thousands of phonograph records of arrangement, placed arrangement in public domain. McIntyre v. Double-A Music Corp., (DC-Cal), 166 FSupp 681, 119 USPQ 106.

Pursuant to agreement with author, publisher published author's articles in book form and took out statutory copyright thereon, thus extinguishing any common-law right to first publication which author may have had in articles; common-law right terminated when statutory right was acquired by publisher by publication of book with notice of copyright thereon. Settel v. Office Appliance Co., (DC-Ill), — FSupp —, 122 USPQ 123.

Where an author acquires under the statute the right to exclusive representation for profit of a dramatic composition deposited with the register, he likewise must be restricted to the remedies provided for the infringement of that right, and the question whether the deposit of the composition with the register amounts to publication is unimportant. Loew's Inc. v. Superior Court, 18 Cal(2d series) 419, 115 Pac(2d) 983, 50 USPQ 641.

Author's right in fruits of his intellectual labor at common law is broader than that which he has under copyright law. Stanley v. Columbia Broadcasting System, Inc., (Cal (2d series)), 208 Pac(2d) 9, 82 USPQ 123, aff'g (CalApp(2d series)), 192 Pac(2d) 495, 77 USPQ 404. Aff'd 35 Cal(2d series) 653, 221 Pac(2d) 73, 86 USPQ 520.

Basic distinction between rights in literary productions as they exist at common law and as they are granted by statutory copyright is that common law protects only a property right while copyright statute grants limited monopolistic privilege. Desny v. Wilder, 46 Cal(2d series) 715, 299 Pac(2d) 257, 110 USPQ 433, mod'g (CalApp(2d series)), 286 Pac(2d) 55, 107 USPQ 17.

Common-law copyright, which is usually referred to as right of first publication, terminates on publication or obtaining of statutory copyright; statutory copyright requires publication plus compliance with copyright statutes; common-law copyright may be regulated by states; statutory copyright solely by federal government; apparently California has regulated common-law copyright by sections 980-985 of the civil code; this statute adopts common-law rule which causes copyright to cease upon publication; type of publication which causes loss of copyright under statute does not differ from type of publication which at common law would cause loss of copyright. Smith v. Paul, 174 Cal App(2d series) 744, 345 Pac(2d) 546, 123 USPQ 463.

No right remains in a literary production which has been made public, except under the federal Copyright Act. State v. State Journal Co., 77 Neb 752, 110 NW 763.

Statutory copyright supersedes the common-law copyright. Jewelers Mercantile Agency, Ltd. v. Jewelers Weekly Pub. Co., 155 NY 241, 49 NE 872, 41 LRA 846, 63 AmSt 666, rev'g 84 Hun 12, 32 NYS 41, 65 NYStRep 198.

Common law prohibits unauthorized use of unpublished manuscript; author has exclusive right to possess, use, and dispose of this literary property. Cantor v. Mankiewicz, — Misc (2d series) —, 203 NYS(2d) 626, 125 USPQ 598.

At common law, rights in literary or artistic work were recognized on substantially same basis as title to other property; rights given by statute supersede those of common law so far as statute applies, but common-law rights in regard to any field of literary or artistic production which does not fall within purview of copyright statute are not affected thereby. Waring v. WDAS Broadcasting Station, 327 Pa 433, 194 Atl 631, 35 USPQ 272.

5.—Prior to registration.

Radio, motion picture, and television have great value, are subject of popular demand, and are as such subject of property rights and deserve the protection of equity. Waring v. Dunlea, (DC-NC), 26 FSupp 338, 41 USPQ 201.

The composer of lyrics or songs has a right to verbally release his product to another before copyright. Khan v. Leo Feist, Inc., (DC-NY), 70 FSupp 450, 73 USPQ 104. Aff'd 165 F(2d) 188, 76 USPQ 27.

All rights to delivered picture are in client who hired photographer to take picture; rule applies to commercial photography as well as to portrait photography; evidence of custom and usage cannot be offered to alter rule; however, contract governs if it provides for retention of rights in photographer. Avedon v Exstein, (DC-NY), 141 FSupp 278, 109 USPQ 376.

United States publisher is not liable to French author for breach of contract even if publisher did not comply with restrictions contained in contract between author and English publisher, from whom United States publisher obtained right to publish in United States, inasmuch as United States publisher never agreed to be so restricted. Rolland v. Henry Holt & Co., Inc., (DC-NY), 152 FSupp 167, 113 USPQ 253.

In the case of a literary work, there is no right which can be protected under the copyright statute until first publication; and upon first publication the right of exclusive property, that is, the right to multiply copies for a limited period, is that afforded by the statute. Loew's Inc. v. Superior Court, 8 Cal(2d series) 419, 115 Pac(2d) 983, 50 USPQ 641.

Whether protectible property interest exists in literary composition reduced to concrete form depends upon originality of form and manner of expression, development of characterizations, and sequence of events; idea alone, the bare, undeveloped story situation or theme, is not protectible. Weitzenkorn v. Lesser, 40 Cal(2d series) 778, 256 Pac(2d) 947, 97 USPQ 545.

Author of any product of mind has exclusive ownership therein and in expression thereof which continues so long as expressions thereof made by him remain in his possession; product of mind is property and is intangible, incorporeal right; there cannot be property in author's idea, but there may be property in particular combination of ideas or in form in which ideas are embodied; although there can be no property in words merely generic or descriptive, person may have property right and right to exclusive use of arbitrary, fictitious, fanciful, artificial, or technical names or titles; they have special significance and are creations of mind. Johnson v. Twentieth Century-Fox Film Corp., 82 CalApp(2d series) 796, 187 Pac(2d) 474, 76 USPQ 131, aff'g 69 USPQ 209.

Literary property in manuscript is separate from manuscript itself, that is, something in nature of chose in action; right to publish may not be inferred from mere possession of manuscript where there is no basis for inference that author transferred manuscript or that, assuming such transfer, transfer was without reservation and that all intermediate transfers carried with it similar transfers of literary property without reservation. Chamberlain v. Feldman, 274 AppDiv 515, 84 NYS(2d) 713, 80 USPQ 85, rev'g 191 Misc 842, 79 NYS(2d) 42, 76 USPQ 203. Aff'd 300 NY 135, 89 NE(2d) 863, 84 USPQ 148.

6.—Titles.

The deposit of a title to a drama, not original with the author, does not secure to him exclusive right thereto. Benn v. Leclercq, (CC-Mass), FedCas 1,308.

Under the copyright laws courts will not protect, independently of the contents of a book, the title thereof. Benn v. Leclercq, (CC-Mass), FedCas 1,308.

Under the Copyright Acts of 1819 and 1831, title of a musical composition would not be protected where the copyright of the work was invalid. Jollie v. Jacques, (CC-NY), FedCas 7,437, 1 Blatchf 618.

A title per se is not protected by copyright. Osgood v. Allen, (CC-Maine), FedCas 10,603, Holmes 185; Donnelley v. Ivers (CC-NY), 18 Fed 592; Black v. Ehrich, (CC-NY), 44 Fed 793; Harper v. Ranous, (CC-NY), 67 Fed 904; Corbett v. Purdy, (CC-NY), 80 Fed 901; Glaser v. St. Elmo Co., (CC-NY), 175 Fed 276; Atlas Mfg. Co. v. Street & Smith, (CCA 8), 204 Fed 398, 47 LRA(NS) 1002; Patten v. Superior Talking Pictures, Inc., (DC-NY), 8 FSupp 196, 23 USPQ 248; Wilson v. Hecht, 44 AppDC 33; Outcault v. Lamar, 135 AppDiv 110, 119 NYS 930; Stringer v. Frohman, (Misc), 152 NYS 935; Dickey v. Mutual Film Corp., (Misc), 160 NYS 609. Mf'd 186 AppDiv 701, 174 NYS 784.

The Copyright Act gives the author a property right in the literary composition, but not in the name or title of it. Corbett v. Purdy, (CC-NY), 80 Fed 901.

The copyright of a book does not prevent others from taking the same title for another book, though the copyright on the original has not expired. Atlas Mfg. Co. v. Street & Smith, (CCA 8), 204 Fed 398, 47 LRA(NS) 1002.

A copyright of a play does not carry with it the exclusive right to the use of the title. Warner Bros. Pictures, Inc. v. Majestic Pictures Corp., (CCA 2), 70 F(2d) 310, 21 USPQ 405.

Copyright of book or play does not give exclusive right to use title; anyone may use it so long as he does not mislead public into thinking it is identical thing which it originally designated; statute protects property in literary composition, not title. Becker v. Loew's Inc., (CCA 7), 133 F(2d) 889, 56 USPQ 455; Martenet v. United Artists Corp., (DC-NY), 56 FSupp 639, 62 USPQ 148.

"Frank Merriwell" copyrights did not include the titles to the stories. Patten v. Superior Talking Pictures, Inc., (DC-NY), 8 FSupp 196, 23 USPQ 248.

Copyright does not carry with it exclusive privilege of using title by which copyrighted material is known. Affiliated Enterprises, Inc. v. Rock-Ola Mfg. Corp., (DC-Ill), 23 FSupp 3, 38 USPQ 35.

Title to a work probably is not protected by copyright law, but it may be protected under law of unfair competition. Loew's Inc. v. Columbia Broadcasting System, Inc., (DC-Cal), 131 FSupp 165, 105 USPQ 302. Aff'd 239 F(2d) 532, 112 USPQ 11, which was aff'd 356 US 43, 2 LEd(2d) 583, 78 SCR 667, 116 USPQ 479.

Copyright of novel or story does not necessarily give author exclusive right to use its title. Meyer v. Universal Pictures Co., Inc., (DC-NY), 89 USPQ 496.

"Queen of the Flat Tops" is arbitrary, fictitious, fanciful, artificial, distinctive, and nondescriptive book title; being nondescriptive, it is product of the mind; owners have right to its exclusive use for all purposes. Johnston v. Twentieth Century-Fox Film Corp., 82 Cal App(2d series) 796, 187 Pac(2d) 474, 76 USPQ 131, aff'g 69 USPQ 209.

There is public or common right to use "Stowaway" as title or the idea or thought conveyed as subject matter of novel, stage play, or screen portrayal. Tamas v. 20th Century-Fox Film Corp., (Misc), 25 NYS(2d) 899, 48 USPQ 573.

7.—Conflict of laws.

The copyright laws of one country have no extraterritorial operation, unless otherwise provided. Ferris v. Frohman, 223 US 424, 56 LEd 492, 32 SCR 263, aff'g 238 Ill 430, 87 NE 327, 43 LRA(NS) 639, 128 AmRep 135; American Code Co., Inc. v. Bensinger, (CCA 2), 282 Fed 829.

A copyright, although derived from the federal government, is the property of the individual, and the copyright or the income derived from it may be taxed by the state. Fox Film Corp. v. Doyal, 286 US 123, 76 LEd 1010, 52 SCR 546, aff'g 172 Ga 403, 157 SE 664.

In suit to enjoin enforcement of state statute against copyright pool, issue is right of copyright owners in association to conduct business of licensing public performances for profit. Gibbs v. Buck, 307 US 66, 83 LEd 1111, 59 SCR 725, 41 USPQ 162.

No abuse was involved in granting preliminary injunction to enjoin enforcement of state statute against copyright pools where state officers were ready to enforce statute and damage would be irreparable. Gibbs v. Buck, 307 US 66, 83 LEd 1111, 59 SCR 725, 41 USPQ 162.

Florida statute prohibiting activities of the unlawful combinations of authors, composers, publishers, and owners of copyrighted musical compositions described in § 1 thereof does not contravene copyright laws or federal Constitution. Watson v. Buck, 313 US 387, 85 LEd 1416, 61 SCR 962, 49 USPQ 468, rev'g (DC-Fla), 34 FSupp 510, 46 USPQ 455.

State law prohibiting activities of unlawful combinations controlling performing rights of copyrighted music did not contravene the copyright laws. Watson v. Buck, 313 US 387, 85 LEd 1416, 61 SCR 962, 49 USPQ 468, mod'g (DC-Fla), 34 FSupp 510, 46 USPQ 455; Marsh v. Buck, 313 US 406, 85 LEd 1426, 61 SCR 969, 49 USPQ 474, rev'g (DC-Neb), 33 FSupp 377, 46 USPQ 354.

State statute setting up complete scheme for regulation of combinations controlling performing rights in copyrighted music was not unconstitutional. Marsh v. Buck, 313 US 406, 85 LEd 1426, 61 SCR 969, 49 USPQ 474, rev'g (DC-Neb), 33 FSupp 377, 46 USPQ 354.

Copyright has no extraterritorial effect. Capitol Records, Inc. v. Mercury Records Corp., (CA 2), 221 F(2d) 657, 105 USPQ 163, aff'g 109 FSupp 330, 95 USPQ 177.

Tennessee statute providing for compulsory licensing of copyrighted musical compositions at prices to be stated in advance, for complicated reports to state officials and prohibiting blanket licensing is unconstitutional; it is class legislation; it is improper exercise of police power as it was enacted, not in public interest, but for benefit of group of users of music; it deprives copyright owners of exclusive rights under Copyright Act; it contravenes treaties relating to copyrights; it impairs obligation of contract; it deprives copyright owners of right of free access to federal courts to maintain infringement suits. Buck v. Harton, (DC-Tenn), 33 FSupp 1014, 47 USPQ 18.

American Society of Composers, Authors, and Publishers has power to fix prices for right to publicly perform copyrighted musical compositions for profit and has restricted substantially all competition in sale of such right since it has substantially all such rights; neither it, nor the members composing it, are entitled to decree for its benefit holding unconstitutional Washington state statute prohibiting pooling of copyrights in order to issue blanket licenses and to collect fees except on per piece system and enjoining its enforcement against them. Buck v. Gallagher, (DC-Wash), 36 FSupp 405, 48 USPQ 316.

Copyright laws do not grant to copyright owners privilege of combining in violation of otherwise valid state or federal laws. Alfred

Bell & Co., Ltd. v. Catalda Fine Arts, Inc., (DC-NY), 74 FSupp 973, 75 USPQ 66. Mf'd 191 F(2d) 99, 90 USPQ 153.

Rights incident to registered copyrights are for determination of federal court, not state court. Stowe v. Croy, (Misc), 124 NYS(2d) 291, 97 USPQ 581. Mf'd 234 AppDiv 302, 130 NYS(2d) 848, 101 USPQ 500.

State court refuses relief since plaintiff has not established any rights based upon common-law copyright; whatever rights plaintiff may have under federal copyright statute must be vindicated in federal court. Hill & Range Songs, Inc. v. London Records, Inc., (Misc), 105 USPQ 302.

8. — Special contracts.

Right of assignor to impose restrictions on use of copyright by assignee, see Coca-Cola Co. v. State, (TexCivApp), 225 SW 791.

Contract between copyright owner and one who has no copyright restraining competitors' distribution of copyrighted articles in open market in order to protect latter from competition is illegal. Interstate Circuit v. U. S., 306 US 208, 83 LEd 610, 59 SCR 467, 40 USPQ 299.

Contract, by which first-run motion-picture exhibitor required distributor and holder of copyrights to impose restrictions as to price and character of exhibition by subsequent run exhibitors, was not protected by such copyrights. Interstate Circuit v. U. S., 306 US 208, 83 LEd 610, 59 SCR 467, 40 USPQ 299.

Distributor of trade-marked articles may not lawfully limit by agreement, express or implied, price at which or persons to whom its purchaser may resell, except as seller moves along route marked by Miller-Tydings Act [15 § 1]; even additional protection of copyright or patent adds nothing to distributor's power to control prices of resale by purchaser; same is true as to restriction of customers. U. S. v. Bausch & Lomb Optical Co., 321 US 707, 88 LEd 1024, 64 SCR 805, 61 USPQ 61, mod'g (DC-NY), 45 FSupp 387, 55 USPQ 343.

Subsection (e) of this section gives only limited protection to musical compositions against reproduction by phonographic records, and evinces unfriendliness towards extending copyright of musical compositions to mechanical reproductions, but parties may substitute for statutory rights any other rights and obligations on which they can agree. Edward B. Marks Music Corp. v. Foullon, (CA 2), 171 F(2d) 905, 80 USPQ 56, aff'g 79 FSupp 664, 77 USPQ 502.

Federal court is without jurisdiction to foreclose mortgage on copyright. Republic Pictures Corp. v. Security-First Nat. Bank, (CA 9), 197 F(2d) 767, 94 USPQ 291, rev'g 97 FSupp 360, 89 USPQ 231.

Plaintiff seeks to restrain defendant from distributing and exhibiting motion picture unless she receives credit; contract providing that defendant would be deemed author of literary property created by plaintiff during employment divested plaintiff of all rights generally known as moral rights of authors, which rights include right to credit as author of a work.

Harris v. Twentieth Century-Fox Film Corp., (DC-NY), 35 FSupp 153, 47 USPQ 11.

9. —Accrual of right to. copyright.

Passage of Copyright Act did not sanction an existing right, but created a new one, dependent upon compliance therewith. Wheaton v. Peters, 33 US(8 Pet) 591, 8 LEd 1055, rev'g (CC-Pa), FedCas 17,486; Caliga v. Inter Ocean Newspaper Co., 215 US 182, 54 LEd 150, 30 SCR 38, aff'g (CCA 7), 157 Fed 186.

The copyright law protected an author's works after its first publication. Bartlett v. Crittenden, (CC-Ohio), FedCas 1,076, 5 McLean 32.

Compliance with § 10 of Act Aug. 10, 1846. 9 Stat. 106, establishing the Smithsonian institute, providing that an author or proprietor of a copyright should deposit a copy of his work with the librarian of the institute was not a prerequisite to the vesting of title of copyright under the Copyright Act of 1831. Jollie v. Jacques, (CC-NY), FedCas 7,437, 1 Blatchf 618.

An author must comply with the copyright laws in order to secure exclusive right to his works. Clemens v. Belford, Clark & Co., (CC-Ill), 14 Fed 728.

There must be a compliance with the conditions prescribed in the copyright law to effect a valid copyright. Holmes v. Donohue, (CC-Ill), 77 Fed 179.

It has become the settled law that protection under the copyright law is granted only to those who perform the conditions essential to a perfect copyright title. Louis DeJonge & Co. v. Breuker & Kessler Co., (CCA 3), 191 Fed 35, aff'g 182 Fed 150. Aff'd 235 US 33, 59 LEd 113, 35 SCR 6.

In order to secure protection of the copyright laws its requisites and conditions must be complied with. Koppel v. Downing, 11 AppDC 93.

10. Exclusive rights acquired.

(Infringement of rights, see § 25 notes of this title.)

A "copyright" is the exclusive right of an author or publisher of multiplying copies of what he has written or printed. Perris v. Hexamer, 99 US 674, 25 LEd 308; Mathews Conveyor Co. v. Palmer Bee Co., (DC-Mich), 41 FSupp 401, 51 USPQ 286. Aff'd 135 F(2d) 73, 57 USPQ 219; Carr v. National Capital Press, 63 AppDC 210, 71 F(2d) 220, 21 USPQ 408; State v. State Journal Co., 77 Neb 752, 110 NW 763.

An author has only a right to multiply copies of his copyrighted works and to be secured against reproduction thereof. Lawrence v. Dana, (CC-Mass), FedCas 8,136, 4 Cliff 1.

Exclusive right to employ a certain advertising method cannot be acquired under the copyright laws. Ehret v. Pierce, (CC-NY), 10 Fed 553.

Copyright is the exclusive right of the owner to multiply and to dispose of copies of an intellectual production. Kennedy v. McTammany, (CC-Mass), 33 Fed 584.

Author's exclusive rights are absolute when perfected. Gilmore v. Anderson, (CC-NY), 38 Fed 846.

Copyright of a pamphlet relating to plans for the formation of burial associations did not confer exclusive right to organize and operate under the plan disclosed in such pamphlet. Burk v. Johnson, (CCA 8), 146 Fed 209.

If no copyright has been obtained, the author has no exclusive right in his production. Bamforth v. Douglass Post Card & Machine Co., (CC-Pa), 158 Fed 355.

The exclusive rights of an author in his "writings" include motion-picture rights. Harper & Bros. v. Kalem Co., (CCA 2), 169 Fed 61. Aff'd 222 US 55, 56 LEd 92, 32 SCR 20.

An author who reworks a previously published plot is not entitled to copyright protection of the plot but is entitled to copyright protection of his manner of stating the plot. Stodart v. Mutual Film Corp., (DC-NY), 249 Fed 507. Aff'd 249 Fed 513.

A copyright owner has exclusive right to the form of his work, but not to the subject thereof. Pellegrini v. Allegrini, (DC-Pa), 2 F(2d) 610.

A copyright protects the exclusive use of a theme presented in an original way with novelty of treatment or embellishment. Roe-Lawton v. Hal E. Roach Studios, (DC-Cal), 18 F(2d) 126; Nutt v. National Institute, Inc., (CCA 6), 31 F(2d) 236, aff'g 28 F(2d) 132.

It is the theme presented in an original way, with novelty of treatment or embellishment, which becomes the property of an author, in the exclusive use of which a copyright will protect him. Roe-Lawton v. Hal E. Roach Studios, (DC-Cal), 18 F(2d) 126.

While composers are given exclusive right of recording their copyright musical compositions and the like right was granted to authors of copyrighted dramatic works, Congress did not give like protection to copyrighted poems, stories, or works of that nature. Corcoran v. Montgomery Ward & Co., Inc., (CCA 9), 121 F(2d) 572, 50 USPQ 274.

Author cannot build story around historical incident and claim exclusive right to use of incident. Echevarria v. Warner Bros. Pictures, Inc., (DC-Cal), 12 FSupp 632, 28 USPQ 213.

Copyright statute affords protection against infringement of copyrighted idea by its manufacture in other media. Jones Bros. Co. v. Underkoffler, (DC-Pa), 16 FSupp 729, 31 USPQ 197.

Owner of copyright is a czar in his own domain, may sell or not as he chooses, may fix such prices as he pleases, and is not required to deal equally or fairly with purchasers. Buck v. Hillsgrove Country Club, Inc., (DC-RI), 17 FSupp 643, 33 USPQ 134; Buck v. Del Papa, (DC-RI), 17 FSupp 645.

Distribution of intellectual property or work is capable of limitation, and restrictions on use of interpretations are not unreasonable or against public policy. Waring v. Dunlea, (DC-NC), 26 FSupp 338, 41 USPQ 201.

Holders of domestic copyrights may refrain from licensing at all, and content themselves with right of excluding others from use of their property. Paine v. Electrical Research Products, Inc., (DC-NY), 27 FSupp 780, 41 USPQ 575.

Copyright Act does not merely codify liability previously existing at common law, since common-law right of copyright protects author only until first publication, whereas right conferred by act is to multiply copies after publication to the exclusion of others. Carew v. Melrose Music, Inc., (DC-NY), 92 FSupp 971, 87 USPQ 84.

Copyright on form of insurance policy does not prevent others from offering insurance coverage similar to that of copyrighted policy. Miner v. Employers Mutual Liability Insurance Co., 97 AppDC 152, 229 F(2d) 35, 108 USPQ 100, aff'g 105 USPQ 357.

Co-ownership in a copyright is a tenancy in common; in dealing with rights of co-owners, courts have relied largely on general principles governing tenancies in common; it is noteworthy that in such cases involving literary property courts have restricted remedy of co-owner to an accounting and have denied injunctive relief. Noble v. D. Van Nostrand Co., Inc., 63 NJSuper 534, 164 Atl(2d) 834, 128 USPQ 100.

Plaintiff and third party jointly compiled research data in preparation for writing a joint book; they own data as tenants in common; neither has a superior right over the other; each can use data without other's consent; hence, plaintiff has no right to obtain injunction against publication by defendant of third party's book based upon such data; if plaintiff has a remedy, it would be in an action for accounting against third party. Noble v. D. Van Nostrand Co., Inc., 63 NJSuper 534, 164 Atl(2d) 834, 128 USPQ 100.

Where plaintiff develops artistic idea used on ashtrays in pursuance of defendant's commission and order, and sells ashtrays to defendant, right to reproduce idea thus created is vested in defendant. Otten v. Curtis Publishing Co., (Misc), 91 USPQ 222.

Design printed on fabric is subject of copyright and is entitled to common law protection if it remains unpublished. Fabrics By Bus Davies, Inc. v. Kay Windsor Frocks, Inc., 25 Misc(2d series) 48, 202 NYS(2d) 467, 125 USPQ 470.

Plaintiffs who designed a method for measuring auto tops and placed same in their copyrighted catalogue did not acquire exclusive right to the methods set forth in the catalogue. Buob v. Brown Carriage Co., 11 OhioApp 266.

11. — Print, publish, and copy.

Right to print does not pass with execution sale of plate. Stephens v. Cady, 14 How(55 US) 528, 14 LEd 528; Stevens v. Gladding, 17 How(58 US) 447, 15 LEd 155, rev'g (CC-RI), FedCas 13,400.

Advertisement in trade-paper was publication. Rigney v. Dutton, (CC-NY), 77 Fed 176.

The literary product of a salaried employee, engaged to compile, prepare and revise, after copyright issued, belongs to the employer, and employee has no more right than a stranger to copy or reproduce. Colliery Engineer Co. v. United Correspondence Schools Co., (CC-NY), 94 Fed 152.

Lending by teacher to his students mimeographed typewritten copies of parts of copyrighted text-book is both a "printing" and "publication" within the meaning of the Copyright Act. Macmillan Co. v. King, (DC-Mass), 223 Fed 862.

The right to novelize a play not resulting in a "copy" did not exist prior to passage of Copyright Act of 1909. Fitch v. Young, (DC-NY), 230 Fed 743. Aff'd 239 Fed 1021.

A "copy" is that which ordinary observation would cause to be recognized as having been taken from or the reproduction of another. King Features Syndicate v. Fleischer, (CCA 2), 299 Fed 533.

Though none of words in this section are specifically applicable to motion picture, it gives owner of copyright exclusive right to print, reprint, publish, copy, and vend the work; in making positive film from plaintiff's negative and then negatives from positive, defendant copied film and infringed. Patterson v. Century Productions, Inc., (CCA 2), 93 F(2d) 489, 35 USPQ 471, aff'g 19 FSupp 30, 33 USPQ 194.

Copyrighting of illustration merely precludes another from copying it, not from making his own. Christianson v. West Pub. Co., (CCA 9), 149 F(2d) 202, 65 USPQ 263, aff'g 53 FSupp 454, 60 USPQ 279.

A copyright owner has right to refuse consent to any compilation, adaptation or arrangement by others of copyrighted work. National Geographic Soc. v. Classified Geographic, Inc., (DC-Mass), 27 FSupp 655, 41 USPQ 719.

"Copy, publish, print, * * * vend" are covered by "publish." American Institute of Architects v. Fenichel, (DC-NY), 41 FSupp 146, 51 USPQ 29.

Absent specific reservation thereof, right to reproduce original painting goes with artist's sale of painting; likewise, if painting is copy of earlier painting by same artist, its sale, without specific reservation of right to reproduce copy, carries with it right to reproduce both copy and original. Grandma Moses Properties, Inc. v. This Week Magazine, (DC-NY), 117 FSupp 348, 99 USPQ 455.

Copyright grants to author the exclusive right of multiplying copies of what he has written or printed. Richards v. Columbia Broadcasting System, Inc., (DC-DC), 161 FSupp 516, 117 USPQ 174.

Copyright embraces the right of one to make copies of a literary work and to publish and vend the same to the exclusion of others. Brunner v. Stix, Baer & Fuller Co., 352 Mo 1225, 181 SW(2d) 643.

12. — Vend.

Exclusive right to print, publish and vend does not create right to impose, by notice in book, a limitation on the price at which the book shall be sold at retail by future purchasers. Bobbs-Merrill Co. v. Straus, 210 US 339, 52 LEd 1086, 28 SCR 722, aff'g (CCA 2), 147 Fed 15, 15 LRA(NS) 766, which aff'd 139 Fed 155.

Notice in a book as to its restricted sale price was ineffectual against one not bound by contract or license agreement. Bobbs-Merrill Co. v. Straus, 210 US 339, 52 LEd 1086, 28 SCR 722, aff'g (CCA 2), 147 Fed 15, 15 LRA(NS) 766, which aff'd 139 Fed 155.

The copyright laws do not confer upon a holder of a copyright any further right after he has exercised his right to "vend." Straus v. American Publishers Assn., 231 US 222, 58 LEd 192, 34 SCR 84, LRA1915A, 1099, AnnCas1915A, 369, rev'g 199 NY 548, 93 NE 1133.

The Copyright Act does not grant the right to fix prices of books at subsequent sales to purchasers from retailers by notice of price limitation inscribed upon the book. Straus v. American Publishers' Assn., 231 US 222, 58 LEd 192, 34 SCR 84, LRA1915A, 1099, AnnCas 1915A, 369, rev'g 199 NY 548, 93 NE 1133.

Dealer, in absence of knowledge of limitation of authority of publishers' agents from whom he purchased, may sell a book for any price he may see fit. Clemens v. Estes, (CC-Mass), 22 Fed 899.

Restriction of sales to subscribers only is protected. Henry Bill Publishing Co. v. Smythe, (CC-Ohio), 27 Fed 914.

One who purchases unbound copyrighted volumes from the copyright owner has the right to bind and resell them. Kipling v. G. P. Putnam's Sons, (CCA 2), 120 Fed 631, 65 LRA 873.

Right to control retail sale prices of books is not protected by the copyright laws. Bobbs-Merrill Co. v. Snellenburg, (CC-Pa), 131 Fed 530.

The copyright law does not give a publisher and owner of a copyrighted book the right to combine with other copyright owners for the purpose of not permitting sale of any books to a cut-price dealer. Mines v. Scribner, (CC-NY), 147 Fed 927.

The phrases "sole liberty to vend" appearing in R. S. § 4952 of the copyright law and "exclusive right to vend" appearing in R. S. § 4884 of the patent law meant the same. Free Sewing Mach. Co. v. Bry-Block Mercantile Co., (DC-Tenn), 204 Fed 632.

Owner of a copyright on a certain set of books which have been sold by him cannot claim exclusive right to subsequent sale of such books when second-hand. Bureau of National Literature v. Sells, (DC-Wash), 211 Fed 379.

The exclusive right to multiply and vend copies of an intellectual work is given by the statutory copyright laws only. Bentley v. Tibbals, (CCA 2), 223 Fed 247.

"Vend" does not enlarge scope of copyright over right granted by the word "copy" in this section. Corcoran v. Montgomery Ward & Co., Inc., (CCA 9), 121 F(2d) 572, 50 USPQ 274.

Lawful monopolist, owner of patent or copyright, cannot prevent purchasers from reselling at whatever prices they please. U. S. v. Aluminum Co., (CCA 2), 148 F(2d) 416, 65 USPQ 6, mod'g 44 FSupp 97.

Statute secures to copyright proprietor exclusive right to multiply copies but right to vend is confined to first sale of any one copy and cannot restrict future sale. Fawcett Publications, Inc. v. Elliot Pub. Co., Inc., (DC-NY), 46 FSupp 717, 54 USPQ 367.

Copyright owner can grant to another the exclusive right to sell the copyrighted right in a specified territory. Davis v. Vories, 141 Mo 234, 42 SW 707.

Where the owner of copyright and plates for book sold a set of plates and agreed that the purchaser could sell the books and that the books should not be sold below a certain price, this contract was binding on one who subsequently bought the copyright and the remainder of the plates. Murphy v. Christian Press Ass'n Pub. Co., 38 AppDiv 426, 56 NYS 597.

13.   — Other versions—Translations.

The publication of a brief synopsis of a copyrighted opera by another than the owner of the copyright thereof not a violation of subd. (b) of this section. G. Ricordi & Co. v. Mason. (DC-NY), 201 Fed 184.

The exclusive right of an author to translate any of his copyrighted works was made an integral part of the copyright itself, by Act Mar. 3, 1891, c. 565, 26 Stat. 1107, amending R. S. § 4952. Atlas Mfg. Co. v. Street & Smith, (CCA 8), 204 Fed 398, 47 LRA(NS) 1002.

Memoranda taken from text books and used in tutoring students constituted "versions" of substantial portions of a book. Macmillan Co. v. King, (DC-Mass), 223 Fed 862.

Former copyright law did not give copyright owner the exclusive right to novelize a play. Fitch v. Young, (DC-NY), 230 Fed 743. Aff'd 239 Fed 1021.

Trust upon translator's copyright will not be implied in favor of the author. Rolland v. Henry Holt & Co., Inc., (DC-NY), 152 FSupp 167, 113 USPQ 253.

Author's grant of right to translate and adapt drama into English, and to perform in that language, does not convey motion-picture rights. Underhill v. Schenck, 114 Misc 520, 187 NYS 589. Mf'd 201 AppDiv 46, 193 NYS 745.

14.   — Dramatization or other exhibition.

"Dramatic composition" defined, see Daly v. Palmer, (CC-NY), FedCas 3,552, 6 Blatchf 256, 36 HowPrac 206; The Mikado, (CC-NY), 25 Fed 183.

Exclusive right to perform is dependent upon existence of copyright. Boucicault v. Hart, (CC-NY), FedCas 1,692, 13 Blatchf 47.

Under Copyright Act of 1856 publication of a play did not give third parties the right to perform it in a theatre without author's consent. Boucicault v. Wood, (CC-Ill), FedCas 1,693, 2 Biss 34.

An exhibition of women "lying around loose" was not a dramatic composition which would entitle the production to the protection of the copyright laws. Martinetti v. Maguire, (CC-Cal), FedCas 9,173, 1 AbbUS 356, Deady 216.

Actors in a play, who later sought to represent such play from memory were not within rule which permits the presentation of a play obtained by process of memory alone. Shook v. Rankin, (CC-Minn), FedCas 12,805.

Mechanical instrumentalities by which scenic effects and situations are produced in presentation of a dramatic composition are not protected by copyright of play in which introduced. Serrana v. Jefferson, (CC-NY), 33 Fed 347.

A stage dance is not a "dramatic composition." Fuller v. Bemis, (CC-NY), 50 Fed 926.

A court cannot decide, upon demurrer, that there is no dramatic right in a series of cartoons. Empire City Amusement Co. v. Wilton, (CC-Mass), 134 Fed 132.

Right of dramatizing a novel can be reserved by its author, when the sole right to print it has been sold to a publisher, who, as proprietor, has taken out a copyright on the novel. Ford v. Charles E. Blaney Amusement Co., (CC-NY), 148 Fed 642.

Sale of story without reservation to a publisher, and copyright by him, carries with it the right of dramatization. Dam v. Kirk La Shelle Co., (CCA 2), 175 Fed 902, 41 LRA(NS) 1002, 20 AnnCas 1173, aff'g 166 Fed 589.

The exclusive right of an author to dramatize any of his copyrighted works was made an integral part of the copyright itself, by Act Mar. 3, 1891, c. 565, 26 Stat. 1107, amending R. S., § 4952. Atlas Mfg. Co. v. Street & Smith, (CCA 8), 204 Fed 398, 47 LRA(NS) 1002.

The copyright laws were liberalized by Act of 1909, particularly by provisions giving right to exhibit and dealing with dramas or dramatic works, but Congress did not intend to add new types of originality to those already within scope of law, or to readjust spheres of copyright and patent laws, respectively. Seltzer v. Sunbrock, (DC-Cal), 22 FSupp 621, 37 USPQ 491.

Where an author acquires under the statute the right to exclusive representation for profit of a dramatic composition deposited with the register, he likewise must be restricted to the remedies provided for in the infringement of that right. Loew's Inc. v. Superior Court, 18 Cal(2d series) 419, 115 Pac(2d) 983, 50 USPQ 641.

Long and continued possession and assertion of exclusive right to the drama raises every presumption of title. Hart v. Fox, (Misc), 166 NYS 793.

15. ——Motion picture, television, and radio.

A photoplay taken from a book constitutes a dramatization. Kalem Co. v. Harper, 222 US 55, 56 LEd 92, 32 SCR 20, AnnCas1913A, 1285, aff'g (CCA 2), 169 Fed 61.

Each distributor of motion pictures, in protection of his own copyright monopoly, may impose present restrictions on his licenses, but he is not free to use copyrights as implements for restraining commerce to protect exhibitor's theater monopoly by suppressing competition with it. Interstate Circuit v. U. S., 306 US 208, 83 LEd 610, 59 SCR 467, 40 USPQ 299.

Owner of copyright of motion-picture film has right to exhibit picture and to grant exclusive or restrictive license to others to exhibit, but he cannot dictate that other pictures may not be shown with licensed film or the admission price which shall be paid for entertainment which includes features other than particular picture licensed. Interstate Circuit v. U. S., 306 US 208, 83 LEd 610, 59 SCR 467, 40 USPQ 299.

The valid copyright of a novel gives the owner thereof exclusive right to make dramatizations of it upon stage or in form of motion pictures. Photo-Drama Motion Picture Co.,

Inc. v. Social Uplift Film Corp., (CCA 2), 220 Fed 449, aff'g 213 Fed 374.

It has become settled by decisions, under the earlier copyright laws, that the copyright of a dramatization covers a photo-play presentation of the same subject. U. S. v. Motion Picture Patents Co., (DC-Pa), 225 Fed 800.

Contract for "exclusive right of producing dramatic version on the stage" does not convey motion-picture rights. Harper Bros. v. Klaw, (DC-NY), 232 Fed 609.

Contract granting "sole and exclusive right to dramatize said book for presentation on stage" does not include motion-picture rights. Klein & Beach, (CCA 2), 239 Fed 108, aff'g 232 Fed 240.

Owners of a copyright on a book or play may make motion pictures of the story, or lawfully assign such right to others. National Picture Theatres, Inc. v. Foundation Film Corp., (CCA 2), 266 Fed 208.

The author of a copyrighted poem is entitled to protection of the name of the production under which it has become known to the public as against one who uses the name alone, and not the body of the work, in the production of a moving picture. Paramore v. Mack Sennett, Inc., (DC-Cal), 9 F(2d) 66.

Exhibition of a moving picture is a "publication." Tiffany Productions, Inc. v. Dewing, (DC-Md), 50 F(2d) 911, 9 USPQ 545.

Motion-picture photoplay is a dramatic work. Tiffany Productions, Inc. v. Dewing, (DC-Md), 50 F(2d) 911, 9 USPQ 545.

Mere motions, voice, and postures of actors and mere stage business are not subject of copyright protection; but sequence having literary quality in that it contains story and has dramatic composition may be protected. Universal Pictures Co., Inc. v. Harold Lloyd Corp., (CCA 9), 162 F(2d) 354, 73 USPQ 317.

New combination and novel arrangement of commonplace materials and acts is protectible by copyright. Universal Pictures Co., Inc. v. Harold Lloyd Corp., (CCA 9), 162 F(2d) 354, 73 USPQ 317.

Photoplay containing "slapstick comedy" is dramatic work and is copyrightable; fact that § 5 of this title lists dramatic compositions and motion pictures separately does not imply that motion pictures are not dramatic compositions. Universal Pictures Co., Inc. v. Harold Lloyd Corp., (CCA 9), 162 F(2d) 354, 73 USPQ 317.

Motion-picture photoplay film is entitled to protection against unauthorized exhibition whether it is a dramatic work or is the dramatization of a nondramatic work. Metro-Goldwyn-Mayer Distributing Corp. v. Bijou Theatre Co., (DC-Mass), 3 FSupp 66, 17 USPQ 124.

Copyright owner's exclusive right to dramatize nondramatic work includes monopoly in presentation of such work in dramatic form on radio broadcast. Warner Bros. Pictures, Inc. v. Columbia Broadcasting System, Inc., (DC-Cal), 102 FSupp 141, 92 USPQ 54. Mf'd 216 F(2d) 945, 104 USPQ 103.

Contract grants sole and exclusive right to make and exhibit motion-picture versions of copyrighted play in any manner and method now or at any time hereafter known; since television is known method of exhibiting motion pictures, right to televise motion pictures is granted unless limitation or reservation is expressly and clearly imposed; "live television" is less competitive than televising motion pictures. Wexley v. KTTV, Inc., (DC-Cal), 108 FSupp 558, 95 USPQ 308. Aff'd 220 F(2d) 438, 105 USPQ 86.

Copyright of a motion picture based on a drama did not constitute a copyright of the drama. O'Neill v. General Film Co., 171 AppDiv 854, 157 NYS 1028, mod'g (Misc), 152 NYS 599.

Copyright of a motion picture based on a published book or drama gives owner of such copyright exclusive right to his motion-picture dramatization, but does not give exclusive right to all motion-picture rights in the book or drama. O'Neill v. General Film Co., 171 AppDiv 854, 157 NYS 1928, mod'g (Misc), 152 NYS 599.

Photographs of scenes of a play used for purpose of advertising do not constitute a representation amounting to a publication of such play. O'Neill v. General Film Co., 171 AppDiv 854, 157 NYS 1028, mod'g (Misc), 152 NYS 599.

The stage performing rights of a drama carry with it the right to produce the play in motion pictures. Hart v. Fox, (Misc), 166 NYS 793.

Under the copyright laws of the United States, an author has the exclusive right to dramatize his works. Gillette v. Stoll Film Co., Ltd., 120 Misc 850, 200 NYS 787.

Copyright owner of play (1) may grant licenses to use play on stage, in motion pictures, or otherwise; he is paid for award of rights to another, proceeds constituting moneys derived from stage production or photoplay exhibition pursuant to contract; (2) he may prevent unauthorized persons from appropriating or using it, or obtain redress from them for such unauthorized use, or both; he is paid for infliction of wrongs on himself, proceeds constituting reparations for injury to his property pursuant to Copyright Act. McClintic v. Sheldon, 182 Misc 32, 43 NYS(2d) 695, 59 USPQ 41.

16. —Musical composition.

Person entitled to copyright for a song which is part of a dramatico-musical composition has the exclusive right to publicly present it. Green v. Luby, (CC-NY), 177 Fed 287.

Extremely brief epitomes of plots of copyrighted operas are not "a version" of copyrighted work. G. Ricordi & Co. v. Mason, (CCA 2), 210 Fed 277.

As a matter of pleading, when the composer composes his composition with an unlimited copyright notice, it may fairly be inferred that he had written the work for the purpose of securing all the rights attainable under the Copyright Act, including the exclusive right publicly to perform it for profit. Hubbell v. Royal Pastime Amusement Co., (DC-NY), 242 Fed 1002.

Right under a copyright to perform musical compositions is not trade or commerce within the Sherman AntiTrust Act [15 §§ 1-7, 15 note]. Harms v. Cohen, (DC-Pa), 279 Fed 276.

Playing any substantial part of composition is a performance. M. Witmark & Sons v. Pastime Amusement Co., (DC-SC), 298 Fed 470. Aff'd 2 F(2d) 1020.

Independent reproduction of a copyrighted musical composition is not infringement; nothing short of plagiarism will serve. Arnstein v. Edward B. Marks Music Corp., (CCA 2), 82 F(2d) 275, 28 USPQ 426.

Monopoly of right to reproduce compositions of any author—his common-law property in them—is not limited to words; pictures are included and court assumes that it covers performances of orchestra conductor and skill and art by which phonographic record maker makes possible proper recording. RCA Mfg. Co., Inc. v. Whiteman, (CCA 2), 114 F(2d) 86, 46 USPQ 324, rev'g 28 FSupp 787, 43 USPQ 114.

It is significant (in case alleging infringement of copyright on poem by setting poem to music and making phonograph record of poem and music) that provisions added to copyright law in 1909 relate only to musical compositions and dramatic works; these changes were in light of Supreme Court decision that making and selling of music rolls for use in player-pianos did not infringe copyrights on sheet music. Corcoran v. Montgomery Ward & Co., Inc., (CCA 9), 121 F(2d) 572, 50 USPQ 274.

Prior statutes afforded no protection against unauthorized mechanical reproduction of copyrighted musical work; as appears from house report, one of purposes of 1909 Copyright Act was to grant such protection. Shilkret v. Musicraft Records, Inc., (CCA 2), 131 F(2d) 929, 55 USPQ 469, rev'g 43 FSupp 184, 52 USPQ 164.

One who copyrights musical composition by publishing written copies thereof with copyright notice has exclusive right under subsec. (e) of this section to make records thereof. Capitol Records, Inc. v. Mercury Records Corp., (CA 2), 221 F(2d) 657, 105 USPQ 163, aff'g 109 FSupp 330, 95 USPQ 177.

Copyright of song protects theme, story, and unique arrangement of words and phrases. Gingg v. Twentieth Century-Fox Film Corp., (DC-Cal), 56 FSupp 701, 62 USPQ 121.

Proprietor has distinct and separable rights, (1) to print and vend published copies of words and music, and (2) to perform copyrighted work publicly for profit. Remick Music Corp. v. Interstate Hotel Co., (DC-Neb), 58 FSupp 523, 63 USPQ 327. Aff'd 157 F(2d) 744, 71 USPQ 138.

Musical composition is made up of rhythm, harmony, and melody, but rhythm and harmony have been in public domain for so long that neither can be subject of copyright, hence originality must be found in melody. Northern Music Corp. v. King Record Distributing Co., (DC-NY), 105 FSupp 393, 93 USPQ 512.

Separate works alike in every respect can be copyrighted without denial of anyone's rights, for copyright does not give monopoly of ideas, but second song must be innocently and independently composed. Northern Music Corp. v. King Record Distributing Co., (DC-NY), 105 FSupp 393, 93 USPQ 512.

As incident to proprietorship over copyrights covering music, proprietor has right to have words written for music. Shapiro Bernstein & Co., Inc. v. Jerry Vogel Music Co., Inc., (DC-NY), 115 FSupp 754, 98 USPQ 438, 99 USPQ 381. Rev'd 221 F(2d) 569, 105 USPQ 178, which was mf'd 223 F(2d) 252, 105 USPQ 460.

Since plaintiff licensed others to reproduce mechanically the words and music of copyrighted song, plaintiff's failure to file notice of use under subsec. (e) of this section bars action wherein complaint charges that defendant mechanically reproduced copyrighted composition. Stasny Music Corp. v. Santly-Joy, Inc., (DC-NY), 156 FSupp 795, 116 USPQ 137. Aff'd 249 F(2d) 957, 116 USPQ 130.

Musical compositions were protected from being copied, under copyright law in force prior to 1909 Act, but they were not protected, as dramatic compositions were, from being performed or represented, or from being caused to be performed or represented by others, by any means, including phonograph records. Beban v. Decca Records, Inc., (DC-Cal), 169 FSupp 829, 121 USPQ 168.

Experimentation by choir director with church choir on one Sunday morning in church cannot constitute performance for profit of copyrighted music within contemplation of this section. Wihtol v. Crow, (DC-Iowa), — FSupp —, 132 USPQ 392.

Orchestra leader has no property interest in his rendition of musical compositions; in absence of palming off or confusion, others may meticulously duplicate or imitate his renditions. Miller v. Universal Pictures Co., Inc., 11 AppDiv(2d series) 47, 201 NYS(2d) 632, 126 USPQ 303, rev'g 18 Misc (2d series) 626, 188 NYS(2d) 386, 121 USPQ 475.

17. ——Public performance for profit.

Playing of copyrighted music in restaurant for entertainment of guests during meal times was a public performance for profit and an infringement. Herbert v. Shanley Co., 242 US 591, 61 LEd 511, 37 SCR 232, rev'g (CCA 2), 221 Fed 229, (CCA 2), 228 Fed 1021, and (CCA 2), 229 Fed 340, which aff'd 222 Fed 344.

A hotel proprietor, in entertaining his guests, through the instrumentality of a radio receiving set and loud speakers installed in the hotel and under his control, is liable for the unauthorized use of a copyrighted musical composition. though he does not select the pieces played from the broadcasting station or have any contractual relation with such station, since his act amounts to a performance within the meaning of the statute. Buck v. Jewell-La Salle Realty Co., 283 US 191, 75 LEd 971, 51 SCR 410, 76 ALR 1266.

Copyright Act gives exclusive right to perform copyrighted musical composition in public for profit. Gibbs v. Buck, 307 US 66, 83 LEd 1111, 59 SCR 725, 41 USPQ 162.

A semicolon should precede the words, "and for the purpose of public performance for prof-

it;" but eliminating the semicolon, the most that the section amounts to is a protection in favor of those persons who do not perform publicly for profit the musical composition—as in the case of street parades, school, educational, or similar public occasions and exhibitions. Hubbell v. Royal Pastime Amusement Co., (DC-NY), 242 Fed 1002.

The playing of excerpts from a copyrighted musical composition, as accompaniment to pictures, in a motion-picture theater charging for admission, was a performance for profit, although no separate charge was made for the music. Harms v. Cohen, (DC-Pa), 279 Fed 276.

Department store maintaining radio department in which it sells at retail radio equipment is liable as for performing "publicly for profit" a copyrighted song, where it maintains a broadcasting station, for which it charges no admission fees to a dining hall connected therewith, and the expense of broadcasting is charged as general expenses of the business; and it is no defense that the song is thereby advertised. M. Witmark & Sons v. L. Bamberger & Co., (DC-NJ), 291 Fed 776.

Playing at motion-picture theater without separate charge for music is performance for profit. M. Witmark & Sons v. Pastime Amusement Co., (DC-SC), 298 Fed 470. Aff'd 2 F(2d) 1020.

Use by operator of player piano on one occasion of copyrighted music rolls, in theater to which admission was charged, rendered the theater owner liable, though the use was without his knowledge and against his orders. M. Witmark & Sons v. Calloway, (DC-Tenn), 22 F(2d) 412.

Person giving public performance of copyrighted musical composition on rolls not showing copyright notice was liable, though the manufacturers of the rolls had paid the fees allowed by law. Lutz v. Buck, (CCA 5), 40 F(2d) 501, 5 USPQ 452.

Cafe owner tuning in on radio for entertainment of his patrons and giving them the rendition of a copyrighted musical composition as to which the broadcasting station had a license was not liable to the copyright owner. Buck v. Debaum, (DC-Cal), 40 F(2d) 734.

Monopoly given copyright owner by subsec. (e) of this section is only to perform work for profit. Associated Music Publishers, Inc. v. Debs Memorial Radio Fund, Inc., (CCA 2), 141 F(2d) 852, 61 USPQ 161, aff'g 46 FSupp 829, 54 USPQ 461.

Publication and sale to public of copyrighted musical compositions in form of sheet music does not confer on purchasers right to publicly perform compositions for profit; right to publish and sell copies of copyrighted musical work and right publicly to perform work for profit granted are separate and distinct rights separately granted; consequently copyright owner may exercise either or both. Interstate Hotel Co. v. Remick Music Corp., (CCA 8), 157 F(2d) 744, 71 USPQ 138, aff'g 58 FSupp 523, 63 USPQ 327.

A hotel proprietor installing a two-channel radio system, making available the programs of two radio stations, with amplifying apparatus, the output of which is led through a cable and fed into distribution wires having termini in some 1900 individual guest rooms, concealed in night tables, on the face of each of which is a switch with a designation plate above, containing the figures 1 and 2, enabling the guest by turning a knob to either figure to tune in on whichever of the two available programs is desired was liable for unauthorized public performance of a copyrighted musical composition broadcast on one of such programs, though the turning of the knob and selection of the program is done by the guest. Society European Stage Authors & Composers, Inc. v. New York Hotel Statler Co., (DC-NY), 19 FSupp 1, 34 USPQ 6.

Although compositions are parts of musical shows, they are musical compositions for purpose of public performance for profit and may not be performed publicly for profit with impunity, although they were copyrighted and published as individual entities separately from copyright of entire shows. Remick Music Corp. v. Interstate Hotel Co., (DC-Neb), 58 FSupp 523, 63 USPQ 327. Aff'd 157 F(2d) 744, 71 USPQ 138.

Published sheet music or orchestral arrangement which alone is "sold" in vending of composition is not the "song" but graphic portrayal of spiritual creation; song remains property of proprietor and to it is attached right of public performance for profit; sale of sheet music or orchestrations does not necessarily suppose or involve their use as instruments in public performance for profit without license, there being other uses. Remick Music Corp. v. Interstate Hotel Co., (DC-Neb), 58 FSupp 523, 63 USPQ 327. Aff'd 157 F(2d) 744, 71 USPQ 138.

Right of public performance for profit assured to proprietor of copyrighted musical composition includes (1) right to perform composition by himself and with no license to others, (2) right to license performance by one and deny privilege to others, (3) right to fix prices and terms on which license is granted, (4) right to limit public performance for profit to certain places, and (5) right utterly to forbid public performance for profit; proprietor may exercise one right and forbear to exercise others. Remick Music Corp. v. Interstate Hotel Co., (DC-Neb), 58 FSupp 523, 63 USPQ 327. Aff'd 157 F(2d) 744, 71 USPQ 138.

Purchase of sheet music or recordings does not carry with it right to publicly perform copyrighted compositions for profit. Taylor v. State, 29 Wash(2d series) 638, 188 Pac(2d) 671, 76 USPQ 275.

18. ——Foreign authors and composers.

Reciprocity proviso as to foreign authors does not affect foreigner domiciled in United States. G. Ricordi & Co., Inc. v. Columbia Graphophone Co., (DC-NY), 258 Fed 72.

Domiciled alien cannot protect under the statute a work of which copies are not reproduced for sale unless his sovereign extends reciprocal rights to Americans. Leibowitz v. Columbia Graphophone Co., (DC-NY), 298 Fed 342.

In the absence of a separate proclamation of the existence of reciprocal conditions as to mechanical production alien cannot avail himself of copyright laws of the United States, and complaint for enforcement of copyright is fatally defective in not alleging affirmatively that a proclamation to that effect was made. Portuondo v. Columbia Phonograph Co., Inc., (DC-NY), 81 FSupp 355.

19. ——License for use.

Maker of mechanical records under compulsory license clause may use copyrighted original composition in their manufacture but he cannot copy and duplicate records made by another licensee. Aeolian Co. v. Royal Music Roll Co., (DC-NY), 196 Fed 926.

Object of compulsory license provision is the prevention of monopoly or favoritism in granting of right to reproduce a musical work mechanically. Standard Music Roll Co. v. F. A. Mills, Inc., (CCA 3), 241 Fed 360, aff'g 223 Fed 849.

The failure to file notice of license to use the music only of a song is no defense to a suit for infringement of copyright of the words. Standard Music Roll Co. v. F. A. Mills, Inc., (CCA 3), 241 Fed 360, aff'g 223 Fed 849.

Correspondence between owner and reproducer did not create a personal license, but was sufficient as notice under § 101 of this title. Leo Feist, Inc. v. American Music Roll Co., (CCA 3), 251 Fed 245.

Compulsory licensee of the right to make phonograph records of a song acquired by such license both the right to make vocal and instrumental recordings of the song. G. Ricordi & Co., Inc. v. Columbia Graphophone Co., (CCA 2), 263 Fed 354.

Notice of intention under § 101 of this title, even if given during pendency of infringement suit, is effective. G. Ricordi & Co., Inc. v. Columbia Graphophone Co., (CCA 2), 263 Fed 354.

The notice required by sec. (e) of this section is not a prerequisite to recovery under § 101 of this title. Irving Berlin, Inc. v. Daigle, (CCA 5), 31 F(2d) 832, rev'g 26 F(2d) 149, 26 F(2d) 150.

Defendants having deliberately frustrated proof of amount of their statutory liability for manufacturing records of copyrighted musical compositions, either by failing to disclose facts reasonably known to them or by failing to keep accurate production records, number of records manufactured may be proven by expert opinion testimony; court has wide discretion in receiving evidence, whether by way of expert opinion or otherwise, where defendants availed themselves of benefits of Copyright Act [§ 1 et seq. of this title], but failed to comply with its burdens; all doubts as to volume of unknown production should be resolved strictly against defendants; court will not permit commercial piracy to produce illegal gains immune from recovery. Shapiro, Bernstein & Co., Inc. v. Remington Records, Inc., (CA 2), 265 F(2d) 263, 121 USPQ 109.

When defendants availed themselves of benefit of compulsory licensing scheme of Copyright Act [§ 1 et seq. of this title] by manufacturing records of musical compositions without following statutory obligations of notice and reports, they placed themselves in much the same posi-

tion as trustee who commingles his own property with like property of others. Shapiro, Bernstein & Co., Inc. v. Remington Records, Inc., (CA 2), 265 F(2d) 263, 121 USPQ 109.

In enacting subsec. (e) of this section and § 101(e) of this title, Congress sought to reach balance between adequate protection for proprietor of musical work and avoiding of music monopoly; to accomplish this, Congress developed statutory scheme of compulsory licensing which gives public valuable privileges which are substantial limitation on what would otherwise be absolute proprietary rights of copyright owner; this limitation imposes collary duty on those desiring to copy copyrighted composition. Shapiro, Bernstein & Co., Inc. v. Remington Records, Inc., (CA 2), 265 F(2d) 263, 121 USPQ 109.

Number of records manufactured, not number sold, is royalty criterion under this section. Shapiro, Bernstein & Co., Inc. v. Remington Records, Inc., (CA 2), 265 F(2d) 263, 121 USPQ 109.

Provisions of Copyright Act [§ 1 et seq. of this title] relating to copying on records of musical composition contemplate obligation upon copier to keep accurate production records; it is mandatory that copier keep records from which statutory statements under oath can be prepared. Shapiro, Bernstein & Co., Inc. v. Remington Records, Inc., (CA 2), 265 F(2d) 263, 121 USPQ 109.

Once copyright owner makes musical work available to any record manufacturer, it becomes subject to compulsory licensing provisions of Copyright Act [§ 1 et seq. of this title] and may be copied by others simply upon giving notice of intention and thereafter paying statutory royalty. Shapiro, Bernstein & Co., Inc. v. Remington Records, Inc., (CA 2), 265 F(2d) 263, 121 USPQ 109.

Parties may substitute private licensing agreements for protection afforded by subsec. (e) of this section; fact that they departed from exact terms of statute by varying accounting period, lowering royalties for songs, and dispensing with notice requirements does not support contention that agreement was private licensing agreement enforceable in state courts only; absent a clear showing that parties did not intend relationship to be governed by statute's compulsory license provisions, it will not be presumed that departure from exact terms of statute was intended as waiver of its protection. Joy Music, Inc. v. Seeco Records, Inc., (DC-NY), 166 FSupp 549, 119 USPQ 460.

Practical effect of subsec. (e) of this section is to limit bargaining rights of copyright proprietor (1) as to persons with whom he may refuse to contract, (2) as to times when he may contract, (3) as to duration of contract, and (4), most importantly, as to maximum royalty he may receive, irrespective of commercial value of particular musical composition. ABC Music Corp. v. Janov, (DC-Cal), 186 FSupp 443, 126 USPQ 429.

Since subsec. (e) of this section fixes precise royalty recoverable for compulsory license, it is just that treble damages should be awarded for violation of subsec. (e) of this section, in absence of showing of good cause to the contrary; burden of making such showing, once violation is proved, rests upon defendant; since § 101(e) of

this title permits anyone to exploit copyright owner's property for commercial advantage and limits royalty payable for such use, those who appropriate a compulsory license, without complying strictly with requirements of subsec (e), do so at their peril, and their liability for failure to perform punctually the obligations imposed may be onerous in the extreme; thus, it is no defense to imposition of treble damages that defendants' failure to pay statutory royalties was merely the result of folly. ABC Music Corp. v. Janov, (DC-Cal), 186 FSupp 443, 126 USPQ 429.

Tendency today is not to look for piracy or willfulness as requisite to increased award under subsec. (e) of this section, but rather to hold that mere violation of statutory obligations imposed upon record manufacturers who appropriate to themselves a compulsory license under § 101 (e) of this title is sufficient to justify treble-damage award. ABC Music Corp. v. Janov, (DC-Cal), 186 FSupp 443, 126 USPQ 429.

Custom and usage may not be invoked to relieve defendant of clear-cut obligations imposed by subsec. (e) of this section; thus, fact that plaintiffs may have accepted payments for a certain period on basis of sales, rather than on basis of records manufactured as required by statute, does not require a continuance of a waiver of payments of royalties on records manufactured but not sold. Famous Music Corp. v. Seeco Records, Inc., (DC-NY), 201 FSupp 560, 132 USPQ 342.

Widow of orchestra leader granted to motion picture producer the right to portray leader in photoplay and to simulate leader's style of playing; agreement made no reference to making recordings from photoplay's sound track; negative covenant, that producer should not so use sound track as to compete with widow's royalty-yielding license to third party to sell original recordings of orchestra, is not implied; producer made sound track under copyright licenses which widow neither controlled nor granted; widow had no protectible interest as such in leader's renditions, and recording of sound tracks for commercial purposes did not involve new medium of entertainment; license to third party was in existence and known to all parties at time of contract with producer and, if widow wished to restrict producer's use of sound track, she should have expressly so provided in contract. Miller v. Universal Pictures Co., Inc., 11 AppDiv(2d series) 47, 201 NYS(2d) 632, 126 USPQ 303, rev'g 18 Misc(2d series) 626, 188 NYS(2d) 386, 121 USPQ 475.

Fact that licensee of copyrighted musical compositions, having right to give performances for profits, gave no performances for profit did not affect his liability for the agreed compensation. Maxwell v. Faust Co., Inc., 90 Misc 702, 154 NYS 224.

20. ——Mechanical reproductions.

Prior to Copyright Act of 1909, perforated player-piano rolls were not infringement on the musical composition recorded thereon. White-Smith Music Publishing Co. v. Apollo Co., 209 US 1, 52 LEd 655, 28 SCR 319, 14 AnnCas 628, aff'g (CCA 2), 147 Fed 226, which aff'd 139 Fed 427.

Prior to Copyright Act of 1909, when copyright covered only "printing, reprinting and vending" a copyright obtained for a musical composition, consisting of music and words, did not protect against the use of the words alone on perforated music rolls. M. Witmark & Sons v. Standard Music Roll Co., (DC-NJ), 213 Fed 532. Aff'd 221 Fed 376.

In fixing punitive damages, the court may take into consideration the intent and acts of the defendant in failing to make payment and its willful disregard of the provisions of the Copyright Act. Leo Feist, Inc. v. American Music Roll Co., (DC-Pa), 253 Fed 860.

Infringing phonograph records which have gone through eight of the nine processes involved in their making, and have then been shipped to Canada for the ninth process, are "manufactured" within the United States and subject to payment of royalty. G. Ricordi & Co., Inc. v. Columbia Graphophone Co., (DC-NY), 270 Fed 822.

Although payment of royalty under § 1(e) of Copyright Act [subsec. (e) of this section] frees record from further contribution, it does not exonerate prior infringers from liability already accrued. Shapiro, Bernstein & Co., Inc. v. Goody, (CA 2), 248 F(2d) 260, 115 USPQ 36, rev'g 139 FSupp 176, 108 USPQ 409.

Relief against seller of unauthorized records of copyrighted music is not restricted to injunction, but seller is liable for royalty as provided in § 1(e) of Copyright Act [subsec. (e) of this section]; however, general damage provisions of § 101(b) [§ 101(b) of this title] are not applicable to infringement of musical copyright by mechanical reproduction; for cases under § 101(e), [§ 101(e) of this title], basic royalty of 2 cents is both maximum and minimum; there is no discretion as to this basic amount. Shapiro, Bernstein & Co., Inc. v. Goody, (CA 2), 248 F(2d) 260, 115 USPQ 36, rev'g 139 FSupp 176, 108 USPQ 409.

Contract whereby orchestra agreed to perform at night club contained clause prohibiting reproduction of such performances; although clause had no self-contained provision for its termination, it does not follow that parties intended, or that contract should be interpreted to mean, that clause should remain in effect in perpetuity; it is more reasonable to infer intent that prohibition at most should be limited to specific term provided for the main affirmative performance bargained for; even if clause could be construed to have any legal effect subsequent to complete performance of affirmative provisions of contract, it does not follow that contract should be interpreted as intended or effective to transfer orchestra's exclusive common-law right to make recordings of its live performances. Walsh v. Radio Corp. of America, (CA 2), 275 F(2d) 220, 124 USPQ 390.

Although "complete defense" provision of subsec. (e) of this section applies by its terms only to actions for "infringement," bar is not avoided by suing for "royalties" under that subsection, rather than for infringement under section 101(e) of this title, which subsection treats "infringement" as embracing "unauthorized manufacture" occurring after copyright pro-

prietor licensed mechanical reproduction; since a once-recorded composition is available to all third parties upon payment of two-cent royalty, manufacture at this point can be "unauthorized" only in that third party fails to make required payments; thus, section 101(e) treats nonpayment of statutory royalty as infringement; therefore, "complete defense" provision applies to all actions for unpaid statutory royalties, however they may be named. Norbay Music, Inc. v. King Records, Inc., (CA 2), 290 F(2d) 617, 129 USPQ 336, rev'g 185 FSupp 253, 126 USPQ 231.

"Notice of use" provision of subsec. (2) of this section is designed to notify all other persons that musical composition has become available for mechanical reproduction; however, statute is silent as to when notice shall be filed beyond the necessary implication that it must be done before suit is instituted if a successful defense is to be avoided; court holds that failure to file timely notice of use bars suit for acts of infringement occurring prior to time notice was filed, but not for acts occurring afterwards. Norbay Music, Inc. v. King Records, Inc., (CA 2), 290 F(2d) 617, 129 USPQ 336, rev'g 185 FSupp 253, 126 USPQ 231.

License to import recordings of copyrighted music from United States or Canada into any other country is really license to export from United States or Canada, and royalty must be paid with respect to exports although the music may be in public domain and not copyrightable in foreign country. Paine v. Electrical Research Products, Inc., (DC-NY), 27 FSupp 780, 41 USPQ 575.

Possession of matrices for making phonograph records does not carry with it right to performance; right to reproduce performances engraved on matrices is intangible and its situs is at domicile of its owner. Capital Records, Inc. v. Mercury Record Corp., (DC-NY), 109 FSupp 330, 95 USPQ 177. Aff'd 221 F(2d) 657, 105 USPQ 163.

Exclusive right given by subsec. (e) of this section to perform copyrighted musical composition for profit is limited by its compulsory license provision, which provides that, once composition is recorded, anyone else may record it on paying two cents for each record manufactured; subsec. (e) of this section puts no condition upon compulsory licensing provision except payment of royalty and provision that court may enter judgment for three times the amount of royalty due, plus costs and counsel fee, if royalty is not paid within 30 days after demand. Miller v. Goody, (DC-NY), 125 FSupp 348, 103 USPQ 292.

21. —Models or designs for works of art.

Use or intended use in industry of statuette eligible for copyright does not bar or invalidate its copyright registration. Mazer v. Stein, 347 US 201, 98 LEd 630, 74 SCR 460, 100 USPQ 325, aff'g (CA 4), 204 F(2d) 472, 97 USPQ 310, which rev'd 111 FSupp 359, 96 USPQ 439.

Purchaser of a painting had right to republish it by chromo. Parton v. Prang, (CC-Mass), FedCas 10,784, 3 Cliff 537.

A photograph of a copyrighted piece of statuary is a "copy" within R. S. § 4952. Bracken v. Rosenthal, (CC-Ill), 151 Fed 136.

Copyright owner cannot acquire such exclusive right to conception expressed in his work as to preclude others from availing selves of any part of general contribution of prior artistic production; if same idea can be expressed in different manners, existence of similarity of composition is not infringement. Allegrini v. De Angelis, (DC-Pa), 59 FSupp 248, 64 USPQ 165.

22. Abandonment, dedication, and loss of copyright.

Copies of a survey chart given to the navy department and placed in the public archives did not effect a public dedication of the chart, so that anyone could copy it. Blunt v. Patten, (CC-NY), FedCas 1,579, 2 Paine 393.

Where there is a question of abandonment of a legal right once existing, the testimony must be reasonably conclusive of the fact before the party will be deprived of his rights under the law. Myers v. Callaghan, (CC-Ill), 5 Fed 726.

If an author has a valid copyright, the fact that his book is bound up in a volume with 50 other books will not invalidate his copyright. Black v. Henry G. Allen Co., (CC-NY), 42 Fed 618, 9 LRA 433.

After owner has transferred his title to copyrighted books under agreement restricting use, he cannot invoke the jurisdiction of the federal courts under the copyright laws to prevent violation of the agreement; and where the court does not have jurisdiction otherwise the suit will be dismissed. Harrison v. Maynard, Merrill & Co., (CCA 2), 61 Fed 689.

Author of a copyrighted book did not abandon his copyright by failing to buy in at execution sale the type plates and impression sheets to be used in publishing his work. Patterson v. J. S. Ogilvie Pub. Co., (CC-NY), 119 Fed 451.

To constitute abandonment there must be a clear, unequivocal, and decisive act of the person entitled to the exclusive rights in a production, showing a determination not to have the rights which he relinquished. Harper & Bros. v. M. A. Donohue & Co., (CC-Ill), 144 Fed 491. Aff'd 146 Fed 1023.

Upon the expiration of a copyright on a book any person has a right to publish the copyright book and fairly use its generic name. G. & C. Merriam Co. v. Ogilvie, (CCA 1), 159 Fed 638, 16 LRA(NS) 549, 14 AnnCas 796, mod'g 149 Fed 858.

When the owner of a copyright licenses the publication of the copyrighted material by the licensee under a new copyright there is an abandonment of the former. West Publishing Co. v. Edward Thompson Co., (CC-NY), 169 Fed 833. Mf'd 176 Fed 833.

On the expiration of the copyright of a novel any person may use the plot for a play, copy or publish it, or make any other use of it. Atlas Mfg. Co. v. Street & Smith, (CCA 8), 204 Fed 398, 47 LRA(NS) 1002.

Where an author copyrights a play under one title and produces it under another, he,

or his assignee do not forfeit the copyright title thereto as to persons with full knowledge of all the facts. Collier v. Imp Films Co., (DC-NY), 214 Fed 272.

The copyright of a 1912 manual did not effect an abandonment of the copyright on a 1911 manual. Meccano Ltd. v. Wagner. (DC-Ohio), 234 Fed 912, 246 Fed 603.

Distribution for instruction purposes of copies of a copyrighted article was not an abandonment of the copyright. Schellberg v. Empringham, (DC-NY), 36 F(2d) 991.

Publication is not limited where 200 mimeographed copies were distributed to interested persons requesting copies without any restrictions as to use or circulation except that manuscript was not to be published in book form. White v. Kimmell, (CA 9), 193 F(2d) 744, 92 USPQ 400, rev'g 94 FSupp 502, 87 USPQ 407.

New York law is that placing of phonograph records of performances by musicians on public sale does not constitute dedication by originator or his assignee of right to copy and sell. Capital Records, Inc. v. Mercury Records Corp., (CA 2), 221 F(2d) 657, 105 USPQ 163, aff'g 109 FSupp 330, 95 USPQ 177.

Rights gained under copyright law may be abandoned; however, abandonment must be manifested by some overt act indicative of purpose to surrender rights and allow public to copy; mere lack of action is insufficient. Hampton v. Paramount Pictures Corp., (CA 9), 279 F(2d) 100, 125 USPQ 623.

Proprietor of copyrighted book of advertisements dedicates specific advertisements to public by furnishing to defendant under contract matrices thereof, on which appears no legible copyright notice, to be published in newspapers, and which are so published; thereafter anyone, including defendant after expiration of contract, may use advertisements freely. Advertising Exchange, Inc. v. Witten Hardware Co., Inc., (DC-Mo), 50 FSupp 137, 56 USPQ 143.

An owner of a manuscript may part with possession of it without parting with his author's rights. O'Neill v. General Film Co., 171 AppDiv 854, 157 NYS 1028, mod'g (Misc), 152 NYS 599.

Intent to abandon common-law rights in literary work in such degree as to afford protection against charge of plagiarism is question of fact. Hirsch v. Twentieth Century-Fox Film Corp., 207 Misc 750, 144 NYS(2d) 38, 105 USPQ 253.

Author's action to enforce common-law rights in motion picture based on his story is barred by laches where he delayed for 18 years, after knowledge of exhibition of picture, in asserting rights. Varconi v. Unity Television Corp., 11 Misc(2d series) 191, 173 NYS(2d) 201, 117 USPQ 107.

23. —Publication.

The serial publication of a book in a monthly magazine prior to any steps taken toward securing a copyright is such a publication as to vitiate a copyright of the whole book, obtained subsequently but prior to the publication of the book as an entirety. Holmes v. Hurst, 174 US

82, 43 LEd 904, 19 SCR 606, aff'g (CCA 2), 80 Fed 514, which aff'd 76 Fed 757; Mifflin v. R. H. White Co., 190 US 260, 47 LEd 1040, 23 SCR 769, aff'g (CCA 1), 112 Fed 1004, 61 LRA 134, which aff'd 107 Fed 708; Mifflin v. Dutton, 190 US 265, 47 LEd 1043, 23 SCR 771, aff'g (CCA 1), 112 Fed 1004, 61 LRA 134 which aff'd 107 Fed 708; Holmes v. Donahue, (CC-Ill), 77 Fed 179.

Use of an author's manuscript by pupils in a school for instructive purpose, did not amount to an abandonment. Bartlett v. Crittenden, (CC-Ohio), FedCas 1,076, 5 McLean 32; Bartlette v. Crittenden, (CC-Ohio), FedCas 1,082, 4 McLean 300.

The publication of a novel adapted from a play is not an abandonment of the right to exclusively re-present the drama. Shook v. Rankin, (CC-Minn), FedCas 12,805, 6 Biss 477.

Delivery of law reports to the state for distribution prior to copyright thereof did not constitute per se a publication. Myers v. Callaghan, (CC-Ill), 5 Fed 726.

Publication of lithographic copies of a copyrighted painting does not effect an abandonment of the exclusive rights to print and vend such copies. Schumacher v. Schwencke, (CC-NY), 30 Fed 690.

After author grants exclusive right to use operetta in United States, author cannot make public dedication by publication preventing protection of rights of grantee. Goldmark v. Kreling, (CC-Cal), 35 Fed 661.

Giving miniature samples of copyrighted photographs to dealers to use in taking orders, where the samples did not contain notice of copyright, was not publication destroying copyright. Falk v. Gast Lithograph & Engraving Co., Ltd., (CCA 2), 54 Fed 890, aff'g 48 Fed 262.

Absolute sale of a book does not amount to a publication which will affect an author's rights therein until the book actually reaches the purchaser. Black v. Henry G. Allen Co., (CC-NY), 56 Fed 764.

Permitting the public to have access to a book constitutes publication, and unless the author completes title to his copyright before publication he is not entitled to protection. Ladd v. Oxnard, (CC-Mass), 75 Fed 703.

The sale of books to the public upon a restrictive agreement not to show them to others, was a publication, and rendered author's copyright void. Larrowe-Loisette v. O'Loughlin, (CC-NY), 88 Fed 896.

Publication with notice of copyright is the essence of compliance with the statute, and publication without such notice amounts to a dedication to the public sufficient to defeat all subsequent efforts at copyright protection. Universal Film Mfg. Co. v. Copperman, (CCA 2), 218 Fed 577, aff'g 212 Fed 301.

It is not such a publication as will constitute an abandonment to the public to give a song to a limited number of artists to sing prior to the date of copyright. McCarthy & Fischer, Inc. v. White, (DC-NY), 259 Fed 364.

Publication of a production without copyrighting it causes it to become dedicated to the public, and any person may thereafter publish it. American Code Co., Inc. v. Bensinger, (CCA 2), 282 Fed 829.

Publication is not limited where 200 mimeographed copies were distributed to interested persons requesting copies without any restrictions as to use or circulation except that manuscript was not to be published in book form. White v. Kimmell, (CA 9), 193 F(2d) 744, 92 USPQ 400, rev'g 94 FSupp 503, 87 USPQ 407.

Manufacturer who published catalogue without copyright and then republished it in following year under copyright was entitled to no protection. W. S. Bessett, Inc. v. Germain, (DC-Mass), 18 FSupp 249, 32 USPQ 550.

Composer's common-law property in musical composition does not survive uncopyrighted phonograph recording and sale of records to general public. Shapiro, Bernstein & Co., Inc. v. Miracle Record Co., Inc., (DC-Ill), 91 FSupp 473, 85 USPQ 39, 86 USPQ 193.

Production and general public sale of phonograph records prior to copyright of musical composition is such publication as to constitute dedication to the public and abandonment of statutory copyright. Shapiro, Bernstein & Co., Inc. v. Miracle Record Co., Inc., (DC-Ill), 91 FSupp 473, 85 USPQ 39, 86 USPQ 193.

Composer's distribution of mimeographed copies of song to members of choral groups whose performances he directed, and his permission to other choral groups to perform song, did not destroy his common-law copyright in song; there was no publication such as would put song in public domain and constitute waiver of right to obtain statutory copyright. Mills Music, Inc. v. Cromwell Music, Inc., (DC-NY), 126 FSupp 54, 103 USPQ 84.

Singing of composition on radio broadcast is not a publication; also, making of single transcription of composition for use by radio station in broadcasting is not a publication since transcription is made for limited specific purpose, not for production of other records for sale to general public. Mills Music, Inc. v. Cromwell Music, Inc., (DC-NY), 126 FSupp 54, 103 USPQ 84.

Copyright proprietor had 100 copies of story mimeographed, but copies were not offered for sale; they were merely distributed to theatrical producers free of charge in effort to induce them to produce story; this was not publication within meaning of Copyright Act. Ilyin v. Avon Publications, Inc., (DC-NY), 144 FSupp 368, 110 USPQ 356.

Common-law copyright is not forfeited by limited distribution for limited purposes. Courts generally are unwilling to deem as limited any but a highly restricted distribution. Continental Casualty Co. v. Beardsley, (DC-NY), 151 FSupp 28, 113 USPQ 181. Mf'd 253 F(2d) 702, 117 USPQ 1.

Copies not bearing copyright notice were distributed to limited group causing forfeiture of copyright since interest in copies was confined to such group and anyone interested could have obtained copy. Continental Casualty Co. v. Beardsley, (DC-NY), 151 FSupp 28, 113 USPQ 181. Mf'd 253 F(2d) 702, 117 USPQ 1.

Article concerning terrestrial globe later copyrighted was not prior publication of globe, since no one reading article could produce globe from what it disclosed, and article did not indicate dedication to public or place globe in public domain. Geo-Physical Maps, Inc. v. Toycraft Corp., (DC-NY), 162 FSupp 141, 117 USPQ 316.

Filing of manuscript for copyright registration does not necessarily place work in public domain so as to extinguish common-law copyright; if valid copyright issues on which author relies, common-law copyright is dead and author's rights are based solely on copyright statute, but, if copyright office refuses to file work submitted or to issue certificate of registration, author's position with respect to common-law copyright is left unimpaired; it cannot be said that filing of plaintiffs' manuscript with copyright office, issuance of certificate of registration, and allegation in complaint that plaintiffs are statutory copyright owners constitute irrevocable abandonment of common-law copyright or operate to extinguish it in event that registration is invalid for failure to comply with copyright law; extinguishment depends not on author's attempt to rely on invalid statutory copyright but on whether there has been such publication as would constitute dedication to public and thus destroy author's common-law right; Congress has not provided that one who seeks to obtain benefits of statutory protection must surrender common-law copyright if statutory protection is not afforded him. Fader v. Twentieth Century-Fox Film Corp., (DC-NY), 169 FSupp 880, 120 USPQ 268.

Publication of author's articles, pursuant to agreement with author, in trade publications, without any notice of restriction of reservation of rights in author, extinguished any common-law right to first publication which author may have had or retained in articles, since common-law right to first publication terminated as of date of first publication. Settel v. Office Appliance Co., (DC-Ill), — FSupp —, 122 USPQ 123.

Manuscript, though not original and protectible, may become subject of protecting contract; although contents of plaintiff's synopsis were within public domain, and defendants were free to use facts there set forth, defendants had to go to original sources for facts and could not, in face of plaintiff's notice of expectation of pay escape liability for use of synopsis. Desny v. Wilder, (CalApp(2d series)), 286 Pac(2d) 55, 107 USPQ 17. Mf'd 46 Cal(2d series) 715, 299 Pac(2d) 257, 110 USPQ 433.

Record was insufficient to uphold contention that printing of 2,500 copies of copyrighted song and gratis distribution of 2,000 of same to broadcasters and musicians, without permission to perform, was general publication. Hirshon v. United Artists Corp., 100 AppDC 217, 243 F(2d) 640, 113 USPQ 110.

Finding that work has been published may have various effects; it may serve to destroy common-law copyright or statutory copyright secured under § 12 of this title; it may serve to validate statutory copyright secured under § 10 of this title, where publication is necessary precondition, or it may invalidate § 10 of this title copyright where alleged publication bears defective notice of copyright; however, it takes more publication to invalidate any copyright, whether statutory or common-law, than to validate it. Hirshon v. United States Artists Corp., 100 AppDC 217, 243 F(2d) 640, 113 USPQ 110.

Television station has no property interest, by copyright or otherwise, in programs broadcast by station or in any signals or programs received on defendant's community antenna system and distributed to defendant's paid subscribers by means thereof; by broadcasting programs on station, and by consenting to their rebroadcast by another station, station intentionally makes them public within meaning of section 67-1107, Revised Codes of Montana; defendant's activities are not infringement upon, or violation of, any rights or privileges of station. Z Bar Net, Inc. v. Helena Television, Inc., — Mont —, — Pac(2d) —, 125 USPQ 595.

Delivery of yardage of fabric bearing design to defendant for express and limited purpose of making sample dresses is restrictive delivery only and does not constitute publication of design. Fabrics By Bus Davies, Inc. v. Kay Windsor Frocks, Inc., 25 Misc(2d series) 48, 202 NYS(2d) 467, 125 USPQ 470.

In determining whether common-law copyright in motion picture films vested in Alien Property Custodian was lost by distribution or exhibition of films, both in United States and abroad, without appropriate copyright notice, court holds appropriate the rationalization and conclusion in cited case wherein it was held that common-law copyright in play or photoplay was not abandoned by performance thereof or by leasing of the film. Brandon Films, Inc. v. Arjay Enterprises, Inc., — Misc(2d series) —, — NYS(2d) —, 133 USPQ 165.

Circulation of a printed musical composition prior to obtaining copyright thereon, though author had told his agents not to sell same for a limited time constituted a complete dedication to the public, and loss of author's exclusive right therein. Wall v. Gordon, 12 Abb Prac(NS)(NY) 349.

Newspaper accounts of the presentation of a play do not constitute a dedication by the owner thereof to the public. O'Neill v. General Film Co., 171 AppDiv 854, 157 NYS 1028, mod'g (Misc), 152 NYS 599.

Editor abandoned common-law rights in his literary work by voluntary publication in his newspaper, there being no intimation or fact presented to raise triable question whether act of dedication was in fact limited reserving that which was not dedicated. Hirsch v. Twentieth Century-Fox Film Corp., 207 Misc 750, 144 NYS(2d) 38, 105 USPQ 253.

Designer of dress loses his right of property in his creation by publishing it without obtaining statutory copyright; embodying design in dress and offering dress for general sale is publication which puts design in public demesne. If disclosure is limited as to both persons and purposes, there is no publication, but disclosure which puts product within reach of general public, so that all may have access to it without further act on part of creator, is publication even though creator attempted to limit use made of thing disclosed by persons to whom it is disclosed and even though there was no sale or even an express offering for general sale. Richard J. Cole, Inc. v. Manhattan Modes Co., Inc., (Misc), 109 USPQ 370. Aff'd 2 AppDiv(2d series) 593, 157 NYS (2d) 259, 112 USPQ 193.

Author's license to motion-picture producer gave latter right to sell and rent motion picture based on author's story as well as right to publish story in magazine or newspaper; this constitutes publication of story and picture adopted therefrom, resulting in loss of author's common-law copyright, which was his until publication was authorized. Varconi v. Unity Television Corp., 11 Misc(2d series) 191, 173 NYS(2d) 201, 117 USPQ 107.

General publication of literary or other intellectual work, by consent of author, terminates all common-law rights; thereafter, any person may publish and use it for his own benefit, unless it is protected by statutory copyright; this is so regardless of author's intent. Varconi v. Unity Television Corp., 11 Misc(2d series) 191, 173 NYS(2d) 201, 117 USPQ 107.

Soldier's letter to minor daughters was not dedicated to public by virtue of his military status, by virtue of necessity for having same read to them, or by virtue of being addressed to them. Property rights (literary property) in contents of letter belong to his estate. In re McCormick, (PaOrCt), 92 USPQ 393.

24. ——Foreign publication.

Public display of painting by artist in London, England, without notice of copyright, voided copyright of assignee in United States to copies of the painting. Werckmeister v. American Lithographic Co., (CC-NY), 117 Fed 360.

Foreign publication of a pianoforte score of songs containing a printed notice that same cannot be used for stage performances did not prevent such publication from being, by our law, an abandonment of the words of the songs. Savage v. Hoffmann, (CC-NY), 159 Fed 584.

Exhibition abroad of foreign-made motion-picture play before copyright registration in the United States renders attempted copyright invalid. Universal Film Mfg. Co. v. Copperman, (DC-NY), 212 Fed 301. Aff'd 218 Fed 577.

Limited publication of a song in Italy does not preclude subsequent American copyright of same song. Italian Book Co. v. Cardilli, (DC-NY), 273 Fed 619.

A play copyrighted in England, unless copyrighted in United States simultaneously, becomes public property here the moment it is published for the purpose of obtaining copyright in England. O'Neill v. General Film Co., 171 AppDiv 854, 157 NYS 1028, mod'g (Misc), 152 NYS 599.

Plaintiff's story was written in Hungarian but his failure to secure copyright protection in United States is conclusive evidence of abandonment of common-law rights and makes story public property in United States even though he had obtained copyright in Yugoslavia. Tamas v. 20th Century Fox Film Corp., (Misc), 25 NYS(2d) 899, 48 USPQ 573.

25. ——Public performance or exhibition.

Proof that complainant's play was performed some six nights before copyright was taken, with author's consent, and for his profit, but while in manuscript form was not evidence of abandonment. Boucicault v. Fox, (CC-NY), FedCas 1,691, 5 Blatchf 87.

Author of a play, who permitted performances of it to be viewed only by licensed witnesses, but did not print, sell, or circulate the play, had not published it, or in any manner abandoned or dedicated it to the public. Boucicault v. Hart, (CC-NY), FedCas 1,692, 13 Blatchf 47.

Facts must exist to indicate that author has allowed a play to be represented for a long period of time without license or objection, before he should be considered as having abandoned it by knowingly dedicating same to public. Boucicault v. Wood, (CC-Ill), FedCas 1,693, 2 Biss 34.

Exhibition of a painting in an art salon would not be a publication unless the public were permitted to make copies thereof. Werckmeister v. Springer Lithographing Co., (CC-NY), 63 Fed 808.

In suit for infringement of copyrighted painting, where the answer alleged that plaintiff exhibited the paintings at the Royal Academy before they were copyrighted, plaintiff could show, without further pleadings or amendment of complaint, that the exhibition was exclusive. Werckmeister v. American Lithographic Co., (CCA 2), 134 Fed 321, 68 LRA 591, rev'g 126 Fed 244.

Copyright upon a large figure of an elk built in a city street was defeated by its free public exhibition which amounted to a publication and a dedication thereof. Carns v. Keefe, (DC-Mont), 242 Fed 745.

Delivery of a lecture before audiences prior to copyright is a limited publication and does not deprive the author of the protection of the copyright statute by later application. National Institute, Inc. v. Nutt, (DC-Conn), 28 F(2d) 132. Aff'd 31 F(2d) 236.

Composer abandoned uncopyrighted song by permitting its wide-spread use since 1908, especially in 1917-1918, and by not objecting in 1917 to eminent composer incorporating song in march whose publication was general publication dedicating song to public use. Egner v. E. C. Schirmer Music Co., (DC-Mass), 48 FSupp 187, 56 USPQ 214. Aff'd 139 F(2d) 398, 60 USPQ 74.

Half-tone reproduction of mezzotint engravings appeared without notice of copyright in widely circulated catalogues, but this was done only for advertising purposes and did not mislead defendants and did not result in abandonment of copyright protection of engravings. Alfred Bell & Co., Ltd. v. Catalda Fine Arts, Inc., (DC-NY), 74 FSupp 973, 75 USPQ 66. Mf'd 191 F(2d) 99, 90 USPQ 153.

Exhibition of literary work for particular purpose, or to limited number of persons does not thereby convert publici juris, and author retains ownership until he relinquishes it by contract or unequivocal act indicating intent to dedicate to public. Stanley v. Columbia

Broadcasting System, Inc., (CalApp(2d series)), 192 Pac(2d) 495, 77 USPQ 404. Aff'd (Cal(2d series)), 208 Pac(2d) 9, 82 USPQ 123, which was aff'd 35 Cal(2d series) 653, 221 Pac(2d) 73, 86 USPQ 520.

Exhibition of motion picture without charge to number of audiences in public places is not publication dedicating picture or material therein to general public. Stanley v. Columbia Broadcasting System, Inc., (CalApp(2d series)), 192 Pac(2d) 495, 77 USPQ 404. Aff'd (Cal(2d series)), 208 Pac(2d) 9, 82 USPQ 123, which was aff'd 35 Cal(2d series) 653, 221 Pac(2d) 73, 86 USPQ 520.

Making of recording of unbroadcast radio program in presence of invited, limited audience is not publication of program to extent of abandoning it to public with right to reproduce it. Stanley v. Columbia Broadcasting System, Inc., (CalApp(2d series)), 192 Pac (2d) 495, 77 USPQ 404. Aff'd (Cal(2d series)), 208 Pac(2d) 9, 82 USPQ 123, which was aff'd 35 Cal(2d series) 653, 221 Pac(2d) 73, 86 USPQ 520.

Public performance of dramatic or musical composition is not abandonment of production to public. Stanley v. Columbia Broadcasting System, Inc., (CalApp(2d series)), 192 Pac (2d) 495, 77 USPQ 404. Aff'd (Cal(2d series)), 208 Pac(2d) 9, 82 USPQ 123, which was aff'd 35 Cal(2d series) 653, 221 Pac(2d) 73, 86 USPQ 520.

Rendering of performance before radio microphone is not abandonment of ownership of literary property or dedication of it to public. Stanley v. Columbia Broadcasting System, Inc., (CalApp(2d series)), 192 Pac(2d) 495, 77 USPQ 404. Aff'd (Cal(2d series)), 208 Pac(2d) 9, 82 USPQ 123, which was aff'd 35 Cal(2d series) 653, 221 Pac(2d) 73, 86 USPQ 520.

Performance of operas by opera company and their broadcast over radio network cannot be deemed a general publication or abandonment so as to divest opera company of all rights to broadcast performances. Metropolitan Opera Ass'n, Inc. v. Wagner-Nichols Recorder Corp., 199 Misc 786, 101 NYS(2d) 483, 87 USPQ 173.

At common law, public performance of play, exhibition of picture, or sale of copy of film for public presentation did not constitute an abandonment or deprive owner of his common-law rights. Dior v. Milton, 9 Misc(2d series) 425, 155 NYS(2d) 443, 110 USPQ 563. Aff'd 2 AppDiv(2d series) 878, 156 NYS(2d) 996, 113 USPQ 210.

Production of a play, delivery of a lecture, playing of musical composition, exhibition of painting, or performance over radio do not constitute publication which operates as abandonment to public use. Waring v. WDAS Broadcasting Station, Inc., 327 Pa 433, 194 Atl 631, 35 USPQ 272.

2. Rights of author or proprietor of unpublished work.—Nothing in this title shall be construed to annul or limit the right of the author or proprietor of an unpublished work, at common law or in equity, to prevent the copying, publication, or use of such unpublished work without his consent, and to obtain damages therefor. (July 30, 1947, c. 391, § 1, 61 Stat. 654.)

NOTES TO DECISIONS
ANALYSIS

1. Nature of common-law rights.
2. Effect of common-law rights on specific property.
3. —Books and literature generally.
4. —Dramatic works.
5. ——Motion picture adaptation or appropriation.
6. ——Radio scripts.
7. ——Musical.
8. —Musical compositions.
9. ——Recordings.
10. —Compilations.
11. —Letters.
12. —Paintings.
13. —Photographs.
14. —Lectures and instruction.
15. —Designs.
16. —Maps and charts.
17. —Abstracts of title.
18. —News.
19. —Commercial uses.
20. —Titles.
21. Persons protected.
22. Manner of protection.
23. Time limitation.
24. Forum.
25. Damages.
26. Effect of copyright statutes.

1. Nature of common-law rights.

Discussion of common-law rights, see Wheaton v. Peters, 33 US(8 Pet) 591, 8 LEd 1055, rev'g (CC-Pa), FedCas 17,486.

Meaning of "proprietor," see Werckmeister v. Springer Lithographing Co., (CC-NY), 63 Fed 808.

Under the common law an author has a right of property in his manuscripts. Little v. Hall, 59 US(18 How) 165, 15 LEd 328; Bartlett v. Crittenden, (CC-Ohio), FedCas 1,076, 5 McLean 32; Stein v. RKO Radio Pictures, Inc., (DC-NY), 53 USPQ 294.

Ownership and right of author to retain and use works for his own benefit, without publication, is a common-law right that exists independently of statutes. Boucicault v. Hart, (CC-NY), FedCas 1,692, 13 Blatchf 47.

Prior to publication, author may make copies of his production and enjoy benefit of limited or restricted publication without forfeiture of right of general publication; limited or restricted publication includes performances of dramatic or musical composition before select audience and private circulation of manuscript. Stanley v. Columbia Broadcasting System, Inc., (Cal(2d series)), 208 Pac(2d) 9, 82 USPQ 123, aff'g (CalApp(2d series)), 192 Pac(2d) 495, 77 USPQ 404. Aff'd 35 Cal(2d series) 653, 221 Pac(2d) 73, 86 USPQ 520.

Author of unpublished manuscript has at common law sole right to decide by whom, when, where, and in what form manuscript shall be published for first time, to restrain others from publishing or using it without his authority, and to recover damages from those publishing or using it without his authority. Golding v. RKO Radio Pictures, Inc., (CalApp(2d series)), 193 Pac(2d) 153, 77 US PQ 415. Aff'd (Cal(2d series)), 208 Pac(2d) 1, 82 USPQ 136, which was aff'd 35 Cal(2d series) 690, 221 Pac(2d) 95, 86 USPQ 537.

Authors are protected in the exclusive use of their literary property by the common law. Ockenholdt v. Frohman, 60 IllApp 300.

The right of a proprietor of a manuscript to publish it or to hold it back from publication is not only a property right, but also an incorporeal right with which the law will not permit interference irrespective of locality. Dart v. Woodhouse, 40 Mich 399, 29 AmRep 544.

In New York separate common-law copyright or control of right to reproduce belongs to artist or author until disposed of by him and will be protected by courts; separate common-law copyright does not necessarily pass with sale of painting. Pushman v. New York Graphic Soc., Inc., 287 NY 302, 39 NE(2d) 249, 52 USPQ 273.

Property rights in a literary production before publication are exclusively in the author, and word "publication" means a general publication as opposed to a limited one. Berry v. Hoffman, 125 PaSuperCt 261, 189 Atl 516.

2. Effect of common-law rights on specific property.

3. —Books and literature generally.

When, with the knowledge and acquiescence of the author, a copyright is obtained by a publisher, the author loses all rights to publish such work. Pulte v. Derby, (CC-Ohio), FedCas 11,465, 5 McLean 328.

Delivery of manuscript to prospective purchaser for perusal and prospective sale is not a publication. Press Pub. Co. v. Monroe, (CCA 2), 73 Fed 196, 51 LRA 353.

Delivery of copies of poem to members of literary committee to enable them to decide whether it is suitable for their acceptance and presentation at public meeting is not publication of poem and does not prejudice owner's common-law rights. Press Pub. Co. v. Monroe, (CCA 2), 73 Fed 196, 51 LRA 353.

The owner of a common-law copyright may communicate the contents of his work to others by a limited publication, without forfeiting any common-law rights. Bobbs-Merrill Co. v. Straus, (CCA 2), 147 Fed 15, 15 LRA(NS) 766, aff'g 139 Fed 155. Aff'd 210 US 339, 52 LEd 1086, 28 SCR 722.

An absolute and unrestricted sale of a printed copy, especially where accompanied by filing similar copies with the register of copyrights is a "publication." Atlantic Monthly Co. v. Post Pub. Co., (DC-Mass), 27 F(2d) 556.

When an unpublished manuscript is levied on by the sheriff, the right of the author is only suspended, and not destroyed. Banker v. Caldwell, 3 Minn 94.

The mere exhibition of a manuscript to others is not sufficient to deprive the author of his common-law rights concerning unpublished manuscripts. French v. Maguire, 55 HowPrac (NY) 471.

Separate common-law copyright, or control of right to reproduce, belongs to artist or author until disposed of by him, and will be protected by courts; since author never intended that it be published, purchaser of manuscript from third party could not have bought publication rights. Chamberlain v. Feldman, 300 NY 135, 89 NE(2d) 863, 84 USPQ 148, aff'g 274 AppDiv 515, 84 NYS(2d) 713, 80 USPQ 85, which rev'd 191 Misc 842, 79 NYS(2d) 42, 76 USPQ 203.

The author of a literary work, has, at common law, a right to its first publication, but this exclusive right is confined to its first publication and when once published it is dedicated to the public. Kortlander v. Bradford, 116 Misc 664, 190 NYS 311.

The owner of a common-law copyright loses his literary property by publishing the same in a magazine, though under agreement with the magazine publisher that the latter shall not license any reproduction of the copyright matter. Van Veen v. Franklin Knitting Mills, Inc., 145 Misc 451, 260 NYS 163.

4. —Dramatic works.

The public representation of a dramatic composition, not printed and published, does not deprive the owner of his common-law right, save by operation of statute. Ferris v. Frohman, 223 US 424, 56 LEd 492, 32 SCR 263, aff'g 238 Ill 430, 87 NE 327, 43 LRA(NS) 639, 128 Am Rep 135.

Until publication literary property in manuscript continues in author, and special use of it by him, in public, is no evidence of abandonment. Boucicault v. Fox, (CC-NY), FedCas 1,691, 5 Blatchf 87.

Where there has been no publication of a play, the author is entitled to the property in his work and full protection thereof under the common law. Boucicault v. Wood, (CC-Ill), Fed Cas 1,693, 2 Biss 34.

The mere representation of unpublished play does not of itself dedicate it to the public. Crowe v. Aiken, (CC-Ill), FedCas 3,441, 2 Biss 208.

Presentation of a theatrical production was a general publication, such as would permit others who heard it to republish from the parts retained in their memory. Keene v. Wheatley, (CC-Pa), FedCas 7,644, 4 Phila 157.

A playright and copyright are distinct, and although a printed publication may forfeit both, an author may reserve his common-law playright from an assignment to a publishing company of the right to print the play in story form. Fitch v. Young, (DC-NY), 230 Fed 743. Aff'd 239 Fed 1021.

Owner of unpublished copyrighted work is not concerned with §§ 10 and 19 of this title relating to copyright notice. Ilyin v. Avon Publications, Inc., (DC-NY), 144 FSupp 368, 110 USPQ 356.

After exhibition of a dramatic work for money, the author can no longer enforce any common-law rights concerning it. Keene v. Kimball, 82 Mass 545, 77 AmDec 426.

Public performance of a play written only in manuscript form was not a publication. Palmer v. DeWitt, 40 HowPrac 293, 32 NYSuperCt 530. Aff'd 47 NY 532, 7 AmRep 480.

Granting of motion-picture rights of an unpublished play and subsequent copyright of motion picture by licensee is not a publication of the play. O'Neill v. General Film Co., 171 AppDiv 854, 157 NYS 1028, mod'g (Misc), 152 NYS 599.

The act of a person who is licensed to produce a motion-picture version of an uncopyrighted play, in publication of the picture or in obtaining a copyright of the picture, will not affect the common-law rights of the author, when such acts were done without his permission. De Mille Co. v. Casey, 121 Misc 78, 201 NYS 20.

5. ——Motion picture adaptation or appropriation.

Owner of a written scenario of a play may perform the play and a motion picture based thereon, and also license others to do the same without prejudicing its common-law ownership. Universal Film Mfg. Co. v. Copperman, (CCA 2), 218 Fed 577, aff'g 212 Fed 301.

Where one acquires the right to elaborate on an original story, he is not given the right to discard the whole story and apply the title and name of the author to a wholly dissimilar tale. Curwood v. Affiliated Distributors, Inc., (DC-NY), 283 Fed 219.

In suit on common-law copyright by author of unpublished play charging defendant with literary larceny in production of motion picture, question of originality is one of fact, not of law, and must be established by proof. Dezendorf v. Twentieth Century-Fox Film Corp., (CCA 9), 99 F(2d) 850, 39 USPQ 467.

Common-law right in work is lost by publication whether or not there be copyright notice. Wrench v. Universal Pictures Co., Inc., (DC-NY), 104 FSupp 374, 92 USPQ 350.

Contract provided for author to write motion-picture script, title to be vested in author until payment of specified sum; he had common-law literary property in script until payment of such sum; author not having received sum and not having consented to utilization of script for production of motion picture, use of his literary ideas in picture constituted plagiarism and deprivation of literary property for which he is entitled to issuance of injunction and award of damages. Szekely v. Eagle Lion Films, Inc., (DC-NY), 140 FSupp 843, 109 USPQ 348. Aff'd 242 F(2d) 266, 113 USPQ 98.

Where plaintiff incorporated in bill synopsis of unpublished uncopyrighted play containing substantially no dialogue but merely rough outline of suggested motion picture and alleged that it was disclosed to defendant who produced play based thereon, and there was no contention that any language had been copied, plaintiff would be entitled to no protection for idea of the plot after he had voluntarily disclosed it to another. Clancy v. Metro-Goldwyn Pictures Corp., (DC-NY), 37 USPQ 406.

Fact that actor expressly accepted literary material submitted by author and invited submission of further material indicates that express contract to pay for material if used could be reasonably implied; only item unexpressed is amount or rate of compensation. Yadkoe v. Fields, 66 CalApp(2d series) 150, 151 Pac(2d) 906, 63 USPQ 103.

An author's rights may be acquired by adverse possession or claim of ownership by another. O'Neill v. General Film Co., 171 App Div 854, 157 NYS 1028, mod'g (Misc), 152 NYS 599.

The common-law rights of an author do not survive publication. Underhill v. Schenck, 201 AppDiv 46, 193 NYS 745.

6. ——Radio scripts.

The rendering of a performance of a radio script before the microphone cannot be held to be an abandonment of ownership to it by the proprietors or a dedication of it to the public. Uproar Co. v. National Broadcasting Co., (DC-Mass), 8 FSupp 358, 23 USPQ 254. Mf'd 81 F(2d) 373, 28 USPQ 250.

7. ——Musical.

A publication of the libretto and vocal score of an English comic opera in London, England, though the authors retained the orchestral score in manuscript, was a dedication to the use of the public of the dialogue, stage business, and the words and melodies of the songs as intended to be sung by one or more persons, or by the chorus, comprising the opera as an entirety, except the instrumental parts. The Mikado, (CC-NY), 25 Fed 183.

An author of an operetta who sells the exclusive rights to its use in America before any publication thereof may not convey any right to a third party to perform it in America, and its subsequent publication cannot effect a dedication to the derogation of the purchasers' exclusive American rights. Goldmark v. Kreling, (CC-Cal), 35 Fed 661.

There is no distinction, independent of statute, between literary property and property of any other description, and the author of literary property possesses the right of sale, and such sale may be absolute or conditional, and with or without qualifications or restrictions. Maurel v. Smith, (CCA 2), 271 Fed 211, aff'g 220 Fed 195.

Owner of English copyright exclusively licensed another in United States; latter obtained United States copyright in own name; his deposit of manuscript with Library of Congress was publication of contents thereof, was authorized by licensor, and destroyed literary property which licensor had at common law; text is in public domain at least since expiration of copyright. Brown v. Select Theatres Corp., (DC-Mass), 56 FSupp 438, 62 USPQ 240.

8. ——Musical compositions.

Author of unpublished work does not lose right to obtain statutory copyright by reason of unauthorized publication of work; he does not lose that right if person, with whom he contracts for publication of work, breaches condition of contract requiring him to comply with copyright law; he does not forfeit statutory copyright already obtained where publisher breaches provision of contract requiring him to affix appropriate copyright notice to each copy of published work. Mills Music, Inc. v. Cromwell Music, Inc., (DC-NY), 126 FSupp 54, 103 USPQ 84.

Composer's distribution of stencil copies of song was among soldier groups for whom song was written and to youth groups who sang it at their gatherings with no sale of copies was not general distribution to any one who might ask for a copy; this was not a publication resulting in loss of common-law copyright. Mills Music, Inc. v. Cromwell Music, Inc., (DC-NY), 126 FSupp 54, 103 USPQ 84.

Creator of musical composition, by performing composition over radio and also performing composition in connection with filming of motion-picture cartoons which were leased and exhibited in commercial theaters throughout world, lost common-law copyright in composition and may not maintain infringement action. Blanc v. Lantz, (CalApp(2d series)), 83 USPQ 137.

9.   — —Recordings.

Orchestra conductor's common-law property in his performances ended with sale of records and legend on records that they could not be used except on phonographs in homes did not save it; even if such restriction did save it, records themselves could not be clogged with a servitude. RCA Mfg. Co., Inc. v. Whiteman, (CCA 2), 114 F(2d) 86, 46 USPQ 324, rev'g 28 FSupp 787, 43 USPQ 114.

Once proprietor avails himself of right provided by statute, common-law right ceases to exist. Supreme Records, Inc. v. Decca Records, Inc., (DC-Cal), 90 FSupp 904, 85 USPQ 405.

Author divests self of common-law remedy by procuring statutory copyright. Lampert v. Hollis Music, Inc., (Misc), 109 NYS(2d) 319, 91 USPQ 325.

Plaintiff played music composed by another for recording and records as sold were marked "Not licensed for Radio Broadcast"; title to physical substance and right to use of literary or artistic property printed upon or embodied in it are distinct and independent of each other; use on radio by one who purchased record and got license from owner of copyright on music was enjoined. Waring v. WDAS Broadcasting Station, Inc., 327 Pa 433, 194 Atl 631, 35 USPQ 272.

10.   —Compilations.

Copyright of compilation of songs does not copyright song in compilation which was printed by publisher merely as licensee of composer, and such publication and sale with composer's consent dedicated song to public and was an abandonment of common-law rights. Egner v. E. C. Schirmer Music Co., (CCA 1), 139 F(2d) 398, 60 USPQ 74, aff'g 48 FSupp 187, 56 USPQ 214.

Inclusion of author's work in compilation gives compiler no copyright thereof; it does not forfeit author's registered copyright or put his unpublished work in public domain, if he did not authorize its publication. Mills Music,

Inc. v. Cromwell Music, Inc., (DC-NY), 126 FSupp 54, 103 USPQ 84.

11.   —Letters.

The recipient of a letter, may, in vindication, publish so much thereof, but no more, without consent of the author, as is required to vindicate his character or reputation or free him from unjust obloquy and reproach occasioned by the author. Any other or further publication breaches the rights of the author. Folsom v. Marsh, (CC-Mass), FedCas 4,901, 2 Story 100.

When letters are valuable as literary productions, they cannot be published without the consent of the author. Hoyt v. Mackenzie, 3 BarbCh(NY) 320, 49 AmDec 178.

The property right of the sender in a letter is well recognized, and publication may be prevented by injunction. In re Ryan's Estate, 115 Misc 472, 188 NYS 387.

12.   —Paintings.

Absolute and unconditional sale and delivery of an uncopyrighted painting carries with it the right of reproduction and sale. Parton v. Prang, (CC-Mass), FedCas 10,784, 3 Cliff 537.

An author has at common law a property in his unpublished works, which he may assign, and which equity will protect until its publication. Parton v. Prang, (CC-Mass), FedCas 10,784, 3 Cliff 537.

When plaintiff (artist) furnishes his art work to defendant for advertisements, he loses common-law rights to copy; his right thereafter to publicize or copy is protected only by Copyright Act, which does not sanction existing right, but creates new one. Grant v. Kellogg Co., (DC-NY), 58 FSupp 48, 63 USPQ 173 Aff'd 154 F(2d) 59, 75 USPQ 301.

Artist's unrestricted sale of copy of original painting ends artist's common-law copyright in original; attempt, years later, to secure statutory copyright on original is invalid. Grandma Moses Properties, Inc. v. This Week Magazine, (DC-NY), 117 FSupp 348, 99 USPQ 455.

At common law, an artist has the exclusive right to make copies of his own paintings. Oertel v. Wood, 40 HowPrac(NY) 10.

The mere fact that an artist gave the right to make copies of his oil painting to another does not dedicate such painting to the public. Oertel v. Wood, 40 HowPrac(NY) 10.

Absolute sale by artist of painting not copyrighted under copyright laws of United States, without reservation of right to reproduce painting, passes such right to vendee. Pushman v. New York Graphic Soc., Inc., 287 NY 302, 39 NE(2d) 249, 52 USPQ 273.

13.   —Photographs.

Where no valid copyright has been obtained, a photographer has no exclusive right to pictures made by him. Lumiere v. Robertson-Cole Distributing Corp., (CCA 2), 280 Fed 550, 24 ALR 1317.

A person does not have property right in image independent of statutory right of privacy, which does not cover a dog or its photograph. Lawrence v. Ylla, 184 Misc 807, 55 NYS(2d) 343, 65 USPQ 342.

Where plaintiff paid photographer to photograph her dog, photographer and his agent are liable for damages for selling photograph to other defendants who used it in advertising. Lawrence v. Ylla, 184 Misc 807, 55 NYS(2d) 343, 65 USPQ 342.

14. —Lectures and instruction.

The use of a person's copyrighted work by such person, in instructing others who are permitted to take copies, does not constitute an abandonment to the public. Bartlette v. Crittenden, (CC-Ohio), FedCas 1,082, 4 McLean 300.

Delivery of lectures before audiences prior to copyrighting was a limited publication not constituting abandonment of common-law rights. Nutt v. National Institute, Inc., (CCA 2), 31 F(2d) 236, aff'g 28 F(2d) 132.

15. —Designs.

Shape and form are only things in common-law copyright for design. Clair v. Philadelphia Storage Battery Co., (DC-Pa), 43 FSupp 286, 52 USPQ 176.

Common-law copyright infringement can only be based on appropriation of copyrightable subject matter. Clair v. Philadelphia Storage Battery Co., (DC-Pa), 43 FSupp 286, 52 USPQ 176.

Reproduction on reduced scale of three-dimensional work of art is copyrightable where it embodies and resulted from reproducer's skill and originality in producing accurate scale reproduction of the original; in a work of sculpture, this reduction requires far more than abridgement of written classic. Alva Studios, Inc. v. Winninger, (DC-NY), 177 FSupp 265, 123 USPQ 487.

A design by an architect is subject to the protection of the common law until it is published by the erection of a building having such design. Gendell v. Orr, 36 LegInt(Pa) 412, 13 Phila 191.

16. —Maps and charts.

Where a person makes a survey of a shoal at his own expense, such survey does not become public property by the fact that it has been deposited in the navy department for the use of the government. Blunt v. Patten, (CC-NY), FedCas 1,579, 2 Paine 393.

17. —Abstracts of title.

Sale, or offer to sell, to any persons for purpose of "examining the title to certain specified property and for no other purpose," constitutes general publication and destroys proprietor's common-law copyrights in abstract of title. Vernon Abstract Co. v. Waggoner Title Co., 49 TexCivApp 144, 107 SW 919.

18. — News.

News distributing agencies have no property interest, as against the public, in uncopyrighted news matter after the moment of its first publication, but among themselves such news must be regarded as quasi property, irrespective of their rights against the public. International News Service v. Associated Press, 248 US 215,

63 LEd 211, 39 SCR 68, 2 ALR 293, aff'g (CCA 2), 245 Fed 244, 2 ALR 317, which mf'd 240 Fed 983.

19. — Commercial uses.

Distribution of copies of a pamphlet in hotel lobbies constitutes a publication and renders subsequently obtained copyright invalid. D'Ole v. Kansas City Star Co., (CC-Mo), 94 Fed 840.

Submission of a novel method of merchandising "for consideration if interested" does not free submittee from obligation not to appropriate without consent. Moore v. Ford Motor Co., (CCA 2), 43 F(2d) 685, aff'g 28 F(2d) 529.

The leasing of uncopyrighted books to the public generally constitutes publication and terminates the common-law copyright. Jewelers' Mercantile Agency, Ltd. v. Jewelers' Weekly Pub. Co., 155 NY 241, 49 NE 872, 41 LRA 846, 63 AmSt 666, rev'g 84 Hun 12, 32 NYS 41, 65 NYStRep 198.

20. — Titles.

At common law, author has exclusive property right in his original intellectual production before it is published; right is absolute, incorporeal property right, and such right may, as an exception to the general rule, include the title of the work where use of the title is unique and would tend to destroy value of the original work. Johnson v. Twentieth Century-Fox Film Corp., 82 CalApp(2d series) 796, 187 Pac(2d) 474, 76 USPQ 131, aff'g 69 USPQ 209.

An author cannot, ordinarily, claim exclusive right to use a title to a book when it is a word denoting virtue, such as "Charity." Isaacs v. Daly, 6 LegGaz(NY) 175, 39 NYSuperCt 511.

21. Persons protected.

Play was literary property of plaintiff, although he wrote it while in employ of another. Boucicault v. Fox, (CC-NY), FedCas 1,691, 5 Blatchf 87.

Under the common law an author, or his assignee, of an unpublished play has a right of property in the manuscript and its incorporeal contents. Crowe v. Aiken, (CC-Ill), FedCas 3,441, 2 Biss 208.

An author may assign his unpublished works to another, and equity will protect the assignee in the enjoyment of such property. Keene v. Kimball, 82 Mass 545, 77 AmDec 426.

A writing need not be the work of one individual, for the author to be entitled to the common-law protection afforded to writers of unpublished manuscripts. French v. Maguire, 55 HowPrac(NY) 471.

22. Manner of protection.

Literary property in a book cannot be protected by trade-mark or otherwise than by copyright. Atlas Mfg. Co. v. Street & Smith, (CCA 8), 204 Fed 398, 47 LRA(NS) 1002.

23. Time limitation.

Common-law copyright exists irrespective of copyright statutes as long as the author does not publish his work. Crowe v. Aiken, (CC-Ill), FedCas 3,441, 2 Biss 208.

Common-law copyright is not limited by time. Continental Casualty Co. v. Beardsley, (DC-NY), 151 FSupp 28, 113 USPQ 181. Mf'd 253 F(2d) 702, 117 USPQ 1.

24. Forum.

Claim based on violation of common-law copyright does not present federal question. Pallant v. Sinatra, (DC-NY), 7 FedRDec 293, 65 USPQ 158.

When one's rights to uncopyrighted literary property has been infringed, equity has jurisdiction to afford redress. Jones v. Thorne, 1 NYLegObs 408.

25. Damages.

In action on implied contract to pay for reasonable value of use of literary material wherein defendant contends that use was trivial, unsubstantial, and insignificant, jury might take into account nature of matter involved and likelihood that, by adoption of fundamental ideas in plaintiff's scripts, particular material was deprived of its substance and rendered of no further value on market. Yadkoe v. Fields, 66 CalApp(2d series) 150, 151 Pac(2d) 906, 63 USPQ 103.

Plaintiff submitted his uncopyrighted but fully developed radio program to defendant, with recording of actual studio broadcast. Defendant subsequently produced and broadcast program found by jury to be based on plaintiff's uncopyrighted program. Verdict for $35,000 was sustained. Stanley v. Columbia Broadcasting System, Inc., (CalApp(2d series)), 192 Pac(2d) 495, 77 USPQ 404. Aff'd (Cal(2d series)), 208 Pac (2d) 9, 82 USPQ 123, which was aff'd 35 Cal(2d series) 653, 221 Pac(2d) 73, 86 USPQ 520.

26. Effect of copyright statutes.

Where the owner of a common-law copyright elects to substitute the protection of the statute for that of the common law, he, upon publication, abandons his common-law rights, including the right under a limited publication. Holmes v. Hurst, 174 US 82, 43 LEd 1086, 19 SCR 606, aff'g (CCA 2), 80 Fed 514, which aff'd 76 Fed 757; Bobbs-Merrill Co. v. Straus, (CCA 2), 147 Fed 15, 15 LRA(NS) 766, aff'g 139 Fed 155. Aff'd 210 US 339, 52 LEd 1086, 28 SCR 722; Caliga v. Inter-Ocean Newspaper Co., (CCA 7), 157 Fed 186. Aff'd 215 US 182, 54 LEd 150, 30 SCR 38; Savage v. Hoffmann, (CC-NY), 159 Fed 584; West Pub. Co. v. Edward Thompson Co., (CC-NY), 169 Fed 833. Mf'd 176 Fed 833; Universal Film Mfg. Co. v. Copperman, (CCA 2), 218 Fed 577, aff'g 212 Fed 301; Photo-Drama Motion Picture Co., Inc. v. Social Uplift Film Corp., (CCA 2), 220 Fed 448, aff'g 213 Fed 374; Societe Des Films Menchen v. Vitagraph Co., (CCA 2), 251 Fed 258; Jewelers' Mercantile Agency Ltd. v. Jewelers' Weekly Pub. Co., 155 NY 241, 49 NE 872, 41 LRA 846, 63 AmSt 666, rev'g 84 Hun 12, 32 NYS 41, 65 NYStRep 198; O'Neill v. General Film Co., 171 AppDiv 854, 157 NYS 1028, mod'g 152 NYS 599; Stowe v. Croy, (Misc), 124 NYS(2d) 291, 97 USPQ 581. Mf'd 234 AppDiv 302, 130 NYS(2d) 848, 101 USPQ 500.

A prose translation of a copyrighted prose romance, when the translation does not paraphrase the original work, does not infringe upon the rights of the author of the original. Stowe v. Thomas, (CC-Pa), FedCas 13,514, 2 WallJr 547.

Dramatic rights may be upheld, not only through rights obtained under the copyright statute, but also because of the protection afforded literary property under the common law. Maxwell v. Goodwin, (CC-Ill), 93 Fed 665.

Common literary property will not be protected by the copyright acts. Hoffman v. Le Traunik, (DC-NY), 209 Fed 375.

This section indicates that the Copyright Act does not displace the common-law rights of an author. Photo-Drama Motion Picture Co., Inc. v. Social Uplift Film Corp., (CCA 2), 220 Fed 448, aff'g 213 Fed 374.

Copyright laws cannot be used to secure exclusive right in article illustrated in copyrighted drawing; copyright proprietor acquires no rights except that no one can copy drawing. Seip v. Commonwealth Plastics, Inc., (DC-Mass), 85 FSupp 741, 81 USPQ 278.

Broadly speaking, statutory copyright operates to divest party of common-law right, but this does not mean that author is divested of all legal rights incident to authorship other than those expressly protected by copyright statutes. Warner Bros. Pictures, Inc. v. Columbia Broadcasting System, Inc., (DC-Cal), 102 FSupp 141, 92 USPQ 54. Mf'd 216 F(2d) 945, 104 USPQ 103.

Even if composer's distribution of stencil copies of music in Palestine would, under United States copyright statute, constitute abandonment of common-law rights if he had done so in United States, it does not follow that he thereby lost right to have music copyrighted under United States statute. Mills Music, Inc. v. Cromwell Music, Inc., (DC-NY), 126 FSupp 54, 103 USPQ 84.

Common-law copyright preceded constitutional grant and was preserved, not established, by copyright statutes. Continental Casualty Co. v. Beardsley, (DC-NY), 151 FSupp 28, 113 USPQ 181. Mf'd 253 F(2d) 702, 117 USPQ 1.

Common-law right exists until Copyright Act has been invoked and rights created thereunder, or common-law right has been abandoned; author has right of election; having elected to secure protection of dramatic rights in unpublished dramatic work under act, author cannot later make different election; act provides system of remedies and no others can be resorted to. Loew's, Inc. v. Superior Court, 18 Cal(2d series) 419, 115 Pac(2d) 983, 50 USPQ 641.

Literary property in intellectual production is afforded protection by common law, federal statute, and Constitution of United States. Literary property which is protected may be created out of unprotected materials. Desny v. Wilder, 46 Cal(2d series) 715, 299 Pac(2d) 257, 110 USPQ 433, mod'g (CalApp(2d series)), 286 Pac (2d) 55, 107 USPQ 17.

The common-law rights of musical composers to their productions have been superseded by statute. Stern v. Rosey, 17 AppDC 562.

By the common law, an author has, until publication, a property in his literary work capable of being held and transmitted, and of which he is not deprived by statute. Palmer v. De Witt, 40 HowPrac 293, 32 NYSuperCt 530. Aff'd 47 NY 532, 7 AmRep 480.

The copyright laws are merely ancillary to the common-law rights of authors, and continue them after publication in print, but in no way impairing such rights, so long as the literary composition remains in manuscript, or is not printed. Palmer v. De Witt, 40 HowPrac 293, 32 NYSuperCt 530. Aff'd 47 NY 532, 7 AmRep 480.

Proprietor, having obtained valid statutory copyright, by that same act gave up and lost forever all common-law rights to operetta. Tams-Witmark Music Library, Inc. v. New Opera Co., Inc., 298 NY 163, 81 NE(2d) 70, 78 USPQ 298, aff'g 74 USPQ 76.

3. Protection of component parts of work copyrighted—Composite works or periodicals.

—The copyright provided by this title shall protect all the copyrightable component parts of the work copyrighted, and all matter therein in which copyright is already subsisting but without extending the duration or scope of such copyright. The copyright upon composite works or periodicals shall give to the proprietor thereof all the rights in respect thereto which he would have if each part were individually copyrighted under this title. (July 30, 1947, c. 391, § 1, 61 Stat. 654; Oct. 31, 1951, c. 655, § 16(a), 65 Stat. 716.)

Amendment note.—Act Oct. 31, 1951, cited to text, substituted the word "title" for "tile" in the first sentence.

NOTES TO DECISIONS
ANALYSIS

1. In general.
2. Titles and arrangement.
3. Pictures, plates, covers, and cuts.
4. Books.
5. —Maps and illustrations.
6. Musical compositions.
7. —Words.
8. Newspapers and periodicals.
9. Dramatic works.
10. Catalogues.
11. Insurance policies.

1. In general.

"Component parts," does not mean subdivision of rights, licenses, or privileges, but refers to the separate chapters, subdivisions, acts, and the like of which most works are composed. New Fiction Pub. Co. v. Star Co., (DC-NY), 220 Fed 994.

This section is but a recognition of law existing long before the statute. Eggers v. Sun Sales Corp., (CCA 2), 263 Fed 373.

"Composite works" defined in this section are those which contain distinguishable parts which are separately copyrightable. Markham v. A. E. Borden Co., Inc., (CA 1), 206 F(2d) 199, 98 USPQ 346, rev'g 108 FSupp 695, 95 USPQ 313.

This section changed pre-existing law as to copyright of composite works containing contributions of different persons by doing away with necessity of obtaining copyright on each contribution. Leigh v. Gerber, (DC-NY), 86 FSupp 320, 82 USPQ 271.

Rights granted upon compliance with Copyright Act [§ 1 et seq. of this title] are separate and independent; they may be retained by owner or disposed of by him to others either singly or in their entirety. Schwartz v. Broadcast Music, Inc., (DC-NY), 180 FSupp 322, 124 USPQ 34.

Only a modicum of originality is required to justify copyright protection; thus, although Egyptian lettering may be but an arrangement of letters which are part of public domain, the distinguishable variation in arrangement and manner of presentation (dark background, particular size of letters, their spacing, their arrangement into three rows) combines to give the product independent authorship worthy of protection against copying; this is even more evident as to drawings of products in catalog which drawings although simple in form, present original effort at illustration of products; having gone to trouble of independently producing these illustration and thereafter copyrighting them, plaintiff is protected against intentional copying by competitor; if it be argued that drawings contain small degree of skill and originality, answer would seem to be that so long as they contain enough skill and originality to justify another's copying them, contrary to copyright notice against such copying, such copying will be enjoined. Amplex Manufacturing Co. v. A. B. C. Plastic Fabricators, Inc., (DC-Pa), 184 FSupp 285, 125 USPQ 648.

2. Titles and arrangement.

Protection cannot be afforded under the copyright laws to a title alone, separate from the book or dramatic composition which it is used to designate. Corbett v. Purdy, (CC-NY), 80 Fed 901.

Copyright of "Visualized American History" did not cover use of "visualized" in title but did include book itself together with arrangement of charts, tabulations, and cartoon illustrations designed to bring information readily to reader's mind. Oxford Book Co., Inc. v. College Entrance Book Co., Inc., (CCA 2), 98 F(2d) 688, 39 USPQ 7.

Although title to song, in itself, is not subject to copyright protection, title should be taken into account when same title is applied to work copied from song. Wihtol v. Wells, (CA 7), 231 F(2d) 550, 109 USPQ 200.

Copyright of musical composition does not protect its title. Arnstein v. Twentieth Century Fox Film Corp., (DC-NY), 52 FSupp 114, 59 USPQ 21.

Copyright of book does not protect owner's exclusive use of title; title alone is not copyrightable; upon publication of book with title, owner ceases to have exclusive common-law right to use title, but owner is protected against competitor where title has secondary meaning. Johnston v. Twentieth Century-Fox Film Corp., 82 CalApp(2d series) 796, 187 Pac(2d) 474, 76 USPQ 131, aff'g 69 USPQ 209.

Court cannot say, as matter of law, that, because literary material in book probably had lost its value, right to use book title also had lost value. Johnston v. Twentieth Century-Fox Film Corp., 82 CalApp(2d series) 796, 187 Pac (2d) 474, 76 USPQ 131, aff'g 69 USPQ 209.

Title of play is subject to ownership, and right in it is established by proof of use, advertising under title, although it is not registered as trade-mark and is not trade name. Johnston v. Twentieth Century-Fox Film Corp., 82 Cal App(2d series) 796, 187 Pac(2d) 474, 76 USPQ 131, aff'g 69 USPQ 209.

Copyright of play or picture does not carry with it exclusive right to use title, especially such broad title as "Invasion." Adventure Films, Inc. v. Twentieth Century-Fox Film Corp., (Misc), 59 USPQ 76.

3. Pictures, plates, covers, and cuts.

(See also note 5 of this section.)

An attempted duplication of a copyright of a painting, in which there was no substantial change, though the title was different was void and of no effect. Caliga v. Inter Ocean Newspaper Co., 215 US 182, 54 LEd 150, 30 SCR 38, aff'g (CCA 7), 157 Fed 186.

Cut not separately copyrighted is not protected by copyright on newspaper alone. Bennett v. Boston Traveler Co., (CCA 1), 101 Fed 445.

A cut and description of a monogram appearing in a copyrighted booklet was not so protected by the copyright on the booklet that others could not lawfully reproduce the cut as a saleable article. Royal Sales Co. v. Gaynor, (CC-NY), 164 Fed 207.

Copyright of periodical protects pictures therein as "component parts." Mail & Express Co. v. Life Pub. Co., (CCA 2), 192 Fed 899.

Upon compliance with copyright law, any person has exclusive right to print and vend copyrighted work which may include prints and pictorial illustrations including prints or labels used for articles of merchandise; prints and labels published in connection with sale or advertising of articles of merchandise are copyrightable; not every commercial label is copyrightable; it must contain appreciable amount of original text or pictorial material; familiar symbols or designs, mere variations of typographic ornamentation, lettering or coloring, and mere listings of ingredients or contents are not copyrightable. Kitchens of Sara Lee, Inc. v. Nifty Foods Corp., (CA 2), 266 F(2d) 541, 121 USPQ 59, mod'g 116 USPQ 292.

Although it is impossible to draw two identical proofs from same mezzotint plate, all proofs carry same interpretation of original work and may be considered same work rather than individual works which must each be copyrighted. Alfred Bell & Co., Ltd. v. Catalda Fine Arts, Inc., (DC-NY), 74 FSupp 973, 75 USPQ 66. Mf'd 191 F(2d) 99, 90 USPQ 153.

Each fashion magazine cover is proper subject of copyright, if each cover is artistic composition, demonstrating originality and good taste, being distinctive of magazine and product of publisher's labor; furthermore, cover of each magazine indicates particular feature emphasized in that issue. Such relation between cover and text makes cover an integral part of magazine falling within protection of copyright of latter as copyrightable component part. Conde Nast Publications, Inc. v. Vogue School of Fashion Modelling, Inc., (DC-NY), 105 FSupp 325, 94 USPQ 101.

4. Books.

Where a book contains several writings, only those that are original are covered by the copyright of the volume, and such copyright does not extend prior copyrights or remove from the public domain the author's works which by his own acts, he has dedicated to the public. Kipling v. G. P. Putnam's Sons, (CCA 2), 120 Fed 631, 65 LRA 873.

United States copyright of work composed partly of original matter and partly of matter pirated from a work copyrighted abroad, but not in United States, protects only the original matter. American Code Co., Inc. v. Bensinger, (CCA 2), 282 Fed 829.

Copyright of collection of works, some of which have been previously copyrighted, protects only what is original in the new collection. Andrews v. Guenther Pub. Co., (DC-NY), 60 F(2d) 555.

Editor may procure successive copyrights on same book, where he has materially revised it; copyright covers whole book and later copyrights cover supplemental material only; there cannot be two copyrights on same material. Adventures in Good Eating, Inc. v. Best Places to Eat, Inc., (CCA 7), 131 F(2d) 809, 56 USPQ 242.

Book containing comic strips printed on one side of paper only and bearing notice of copyright on title page, although each item in book bears separate copyright notice and most of items bear later release date on which date newspapers are first authorized to use material is book and is composite work. King Features Syndicate, Inc. v. Bouve, (DC-DC), 48 USPQ 237.

Copyrights in books, secured by publication with prescribed notice of copyright duly affixed thereto, secure to copyright proprietor copyright in every copyrightable component part of books just as if parts had been separately published with notice of copyright. King Features Syndicate, Inc. v. Bouve, (DC-DC), 48 USPQ 237.

5. —Maps and illustrations.

(See also note 3 of this section.)

Maps in a statistical atlas are covered by copyright of the book as a whole. Black v. Henry G. Allen Co., (CC-NY), 42 Fed 618, 9 LRA 433.

A book and a descriptive map sold with the book were one production; the copyright of the book covering also the map. Lydiard-Peterson

Co. v. Woodman, (CCA 8), 204 Fed 921, aff'g 192 Fed 67.

6. Musical compositions.

Whenever a song is copyrighted as a musical composition, both the words and the music are protected; and, as these do not constitute an indivisible whole, the owner may limit the use of his copyright either to the music or to the words, or he may allow both to be used. Standard Music Roll Co. v. F. A. Mills, Inc., (CCA 3), 241 Fed 360, aff'g 223 Fed 849.

7. —Words.

Copyright of musical composition protects the words of the song. M. Witmark & Sons v. Standard Music Roll Co., (DC-NJ), 213 Fed 532. Aff'd 221 Fed 376.

A license to use a song as may be needed "in the manufacture of sound records in any form whatsoever" does not give the licensee the right to include in the sale of its music rolls printed copies of the words of the song. Standard Music Roll Co. v. F. A. Mills, Inc., (CCA 3), 241 Fed 360, aff'g 223 Fed 849.

The music of a popular ballad, which was written by another than the one who wrote the words was not an independent composition. G. Ricordi & Co., Inc. v. Columbia Graphophone Co., (DC-NY), 258 Fed 72.

Composer transferred all his rights, including renewal rights, in music to publisher which, thereafter, employed another to write lyric for music; publisher then copyrighted resulting song; song is "joint" work, not a "composite" of music and lyric; test is consent, to collaboration of second author, by one who holds copyright on product of first author. Shapiro, Bernstein & Co., Inc. v. Jerry Vogel Music Co., Inc., (CA 2), 221 F(2d) 569, 105 USPQ 178, rev'g 115 FSupp 754, 98 USPQ 438, 99 USPQ 381. Mf'd 223 F(2d) 252, 105 USPQ 460.

The copyright of an adaptation of the English text to Russian music, if valid, does not cover the music. Norden v. Oliver Ditson Co., Inc., (DC-Mass), 13 FSupp 415, 28 USPQ 183.

8. Newspapers and periodicals.

Each infringement of single copyright on entire periodical justifies separate minimal damage award. L. A. Westermann Co. v. Dispatch Printing Co., 249 US 100, 63 LEd 499, 39 SCR 194.

The copyrighting of a magazine under the international Copyright Act of 1891 effects a copyright on all the material therein. Harper & Bros. v. M. A. Donohue & Co., (CC-Ill), 144 Fed 491. Aff'd 146 Fed 1023.

Copyright of a magazine covers articles therein written or owned by the proprietor of the magazine. Ford v. Charles E. Blaney Amusement Co., (CC-NY), 148 Fed 642.

Right of dramatization is included in sale of a story appearing in and covered by copyright of periodical in which it appears. Dam v. Kirk La Shelle Co., (CCA 2), 175 Fed 902, 41 LRA(NS) 1002, 20 AnnCas 1173, aff'g 166 Fed 589.

Publisher's copyright does not attach to commercial advertising and listings in magazine. Official Aviation Guide Co., Inc. v. American Aviation Associates, Inc., (CCA 7), 150 F(2d) 173, 65 USPQ 553, mod'g 62 USPQ 178.

9. Dramatic works.

Copyright may not only protect the dialogue of a drama, but also all such means of expression as the author used to give dramatic significance to the scenes of his work. Sheldon v. Metro-Goldwyn Pictures Corp., (CCA 2), 81 F(2d) 49, 28 USPQ 330, rev'g 7 FSupp 837.

Although it might be possible that author could so carefully delineate character as to secure protectible property interest in character, generally it is held that character is not included within monopoly of copyright. Burtis v. Universal Pictures Co., Inc., 40 Cal(2d series) 823, 256 Pac(2d) 933, 97 USPQ 567.

10. Catalogues.

Copyright of catalogue protects each cut contained therein. Da Prato Statuary Co. v. Giuliani Sanitary Co., (CC-Minn), 189 Fed 90.

A copyright of a catalogue containing trademarks, copyrights the trade-marks as they appear in the catalogue. Jewelers' Circular Pub. Co. v. Keystone Pub. Co., (DC-NY), 274 Fed 932. Aff'd 281 Fed 83, 26 ALR 571.

Protection extends to original achievement in the publication of a trade catalogue. Markham v. A. E. Borden Co., Inc., (CA 1), 206 F(2d) 199, 98 USPQ 346, rev'g 108 FSupp 695, 95 USPQ 313.

Test of material and substantial infringement has no application to catalogues; defendants infringe despite fact that they copied only nine of hundreds of items in copyrighted catalogues. Markham v. A. E. Borden Co., Inc., (CA 1), 206 F(2d) 199, 98 USPQ 346, rev'g 108 FSupp 695, 95 USPQ 313.

Where Italian registration of copyright in picture was subsequent to registration in United States of catalogue containing picture and of course subsequent to date of publication claimed in United States registration, copyright of picture as component part of catalogue was valid. Basevi v. Edward O'Toole Co., Inc., (DC-NY), 26 FSupp 41, 40 USPQ 333.

Each original description and illustration in copyrighted catalogue is component part protected by this section. Harry Alter Co., Inc. v. A. E. Borden Co., Inc., (DC-Mass), 121 FSupp 941, 102 USPQ 2.

Inasmuch as trade catalogue is composite work within meaning of this section, it is infringed by copying of single illustration. Unistrut Corp. v. Power, (DC-Mass), 175 FSupp 294, 121 USPQ 381. Mf'd 280 F(2d) 18, 126 USPQ 82.

11. Insurance policies.

Copyright of insurance policies did not restrict right of defendant to use plans of insurance embraced in copyrighted policies but did restrict use or copying of means of expression selected by author to extent such means of expression were original with him. Dorsey v. Old Surety

Life Ins. Co., (CCA 10), 98 F(2d) 872, 39 USPQ 92, 119 ALR 1250.

4. All writings of author included.—
The works for which copyright may be secured under this title shall include all the writings of an author. (July 30, 1947. c. 391, § 1, 61 Stat. 654.)

Cross references.—Employer included in term "author," see § 26 of this title.

Particular subjects of copyright, see § 5 of this title.

NOTES TO DECISIONS
ANALYSIS
1. In general.
2. Subjects of copyright.
3. —Facts.
4. —Ideas.
5. —Words.
6. Originality of work.
7. Literary and artistic qualities.
8. Illegal or immoral subjects.

1. In general.
A judge acting in his judicial capacity in preparing headnotes, statement of case, and opinion is not an author. Banks v. Manchester, 128 US 244, 32 LEd 425, 9 SCR 36, aff'g (CC-Ohio), 23 Fed 143.

The literary property intended to be protected by the copyrights laws is to be determined by the subject matter of the work only. Clayton v. Stone, (CC-NY), FedCas 2,872, 2 Paine 382.

The property intended to be protected by the copyright acts is exclusive right of an author in his writings. Clayton v. Stone, (CC-NY), FedCas 2,872, 2 Paine 382.

The intent and purpose of Copyright Act may not be limited by private agreement between an author and his publisher. Kipling v. G. P. Putnam's Sons, (CCA 2), 120 Fed 631, 65 LRA 873.

The right of an author to a monopoly of his publications is determined by the copyright statute. American Code Co., Inc. v. Bensinger, (CCA 2), 282 Fed 829.

2. Subjects of copyright.
Cigar labels containing name and cut of a photograph of a dealer are not "writings." M. B. Fahey Tobacco Co. v. Senior, (DC-Pa), 247 Fed 809. Mf'd 252 Fed 579.

In view of this section, the Copyright Act must be understood to cover all compositions which under the Constitution can be copyrighted at all. Reiss v. National Quotation Bureau, (DC-NY), 276 Fed 717.

A chart for analyzing handwriting is copyrightable. Deutsch v. Arnold, (CCA 2), 98 F(2d) 686, 39 USPQ 5, mod'g 22 FSupp 101, 36 USPQ 318; Deutsch v. Felton, (DC-NY), 27 FSupp 895, 41 USPQ 616.

Check is not noncopyrightable merely because it is a check if in specific use it possesses requisite originality or authorship. Cash Dividend Check Corp. v. Davis, (CA 9), 247 F(2d) 458, 114 USPQ 32.

Inseparably included in author's bond and affidavit forms, which constitute means for practice of his insurance plan, is copyrightable language explanatory of plan; hence, forms are copyrightable. Continental Casualty Co. v. Beardsley, (CA 2), 253 F(2d) 702, 117 USPQ 1, mod'g 151 FSupp 28, 113 USPQ 181.

Motion pictures are "writings." Metro-Goldwyn-Mayer Distributing Corp. v. Bijou Theatre Co., (DC-Mass), 3 FSupp 66, 17 USPQ 124.

Ideas, phrases, ordinary English idioms, or words are not protected by copyright. Park v. Warner Bros., (DC-NY), 8 FSupp 37, 23 USPQ 202.

"Writings," which are subject of copyrights and, therefore, of exclusive federal jurisdiction under Constitution, are only such as are original and founded in creative powers of mind of applicant for copyright or his assignee. Cross v. Oneida Paper Products Co., (DC-NJ), 117 FSupp 919, 100 USPQ 141.

3. —Facts.
This section admits to copyright a contribution to a newspaper, but it may not be construed so as to admit to copyright such news elements as are contained in the contribution. International News Service v. Associated Press, 248 US 215, 63 LEd 211, 39 SCR 68, 2 ALR 293, aff'g (CCA 2), 245 Fed 244, 2 ALR 317, which mf'd 240 Fed 983.

Facts of history which necessarily must be dealt with in similar manner by all historians are not copyrightable. Caruthers v. R. K. O. Radio Pictures, Inc., (DC-NY), 20 FSupp 906, 35 USPQ 115, 35 USPQ 542.

One who narrates matters of fact may be protected by copyright as to his arrangement, manner, and style, but not as to material or ideas. Oliver v. Saint Germain Foundation, (DC-Cal), 41 FSupp 296, 51 USPQ 20.

Facts concerning actual life of historic character are in public domain and are not entitled to copyright protection; however, fictionalizing of events in life is author's original treatment of life and is subject to protection. Greenbie v. Noble, (DC-NY), 151 FSupp 45, 113 USPQ 115.

4. —Ideas.
Mere ideas are not protected by copyright, and the fact that two productions display the trend of emotions is not enough to show plagiarism. Nichols v. Universal Pictures Corp., (DC-NY), 34 F(2d) 145, 2 USPQ 139. Aff'd 45 F(2d) 119, 7 USPQ 84.

An author is not entitled to be protected in his ideas, but he is entitled to protection in his expression or illustration of such ideas. Ansehl v. Puritan Pharmaceutical Co., (CCA 8), 61 F(2d) 131, 15 USPQ 38; Eisenschiml v. Fawcett Publications, Inc., (CA 7), 246 F(2d) 598, 114 USPQ 199.

Bank night theater scheme, being in no sense a writing, could not be copyrighted. Affiliated Enterprises, Inc. v. Truber, (CCA 1), 86 F(2d) 958, 32 USPQ 94.

Copyright protects against a copying, but gives no exclusive right to an idea. Caddy-Imler Creations, Inc. v. Caddy, (CA 9), 299 F(2d) 79, 132 USPQ 384.

A theme or idea is not copyrightable. Shipman v. R. K. O. Radio Pictures, Inc., (DC-NY), 20 FSupp 249, 35 USPQ 242. Aff'd 100 F(2d) 533, 40 USPQ 211; O'Rourke v. RKO Radio Pictures, Inc., (DC-Mass), 44 FSupp 480, 53 USPQ 95; Solomon v. RKO Radio Pictures, Inc., (DC-NY), 44 FSupp 780, 53 USPQ 468.

Books describing game or sporting event and rules thereof as ideas are not copyrightable, and system of staging a game or spectacle is not covered. Seltzer v. Sunbrock, (DC-Cal), 22 FSupp 621, 37 USPQ 491.

Idea of staging purportedly transcontinental roller skating race having distinctive treatment of theme ought to be protected by copyright law only if theme be essential part of true dramatic composition. Seltzer v. Sunbrock, (DC-Cal), 22 FSupp 621, 37 USPQ 491.

One cannot get copyright or literary rights to idea of having actors appear in black and white costumes. O'Brien v. Chappel & Co., (DC-NY), 159 FSupp 58, 116 USPQ 340.

Idea of Santa Claus as part of Christmas motif belongs to public domain and cannot be withdrawn by copyright, but reproduction of idea in different combinations, adaptations, arrangements, or mediums of expression which are sufficiently original is protected by copyright laws. Barton Candy Corp. v. Tell Chocolate Novelties Corp., (DC-NY), 178 FSupp 577, 123 USPQ 425.

Idea cannot be protected by copyright. Barton Candy Corp. v. Tell Chocolate Novelties Corp., (DC-NY), 178 FSupp 577, 123 USPQ 425.

Plan, system, or idea is not copyrightable. Crume v. Pacific Mut. Life Ins. Co., (DC-Ill), 55 USPQ 267. Aff'd 140 F(2d) 182, 60 USPQ 359.

5.   —Words.

A list of code words is copyrightable. American Code Co., Inc. v. Bensinger, (CCA 2), 282 Fed 829.

Words in the dictionary, usual English idioms, ideas, and character types are not the subjects of copyrights. Lewys v. O'Neill, (DC-NY), 49 F(2d) 603, 9 USPQ 465.

List of French words with translation included in writings of an author was entitled to copyright. College Entrance Book Co., Inc. v. Amsco Book Co., Inc., (CCA 2), 119 F(2d) 874, 49 USPQ 517, rev'g 33 FSupp 276, 45 USPQ 516.

Copyright or literary rights do not extend to words or phrases isolated from their context. O'Brien v. Chappel & Co., (DC-NY), 159 FSupp 58, 116 USPQ 340.

6.   Originality of work.

A manuscript containing a novel and original system may not be attacked as an improper subject of copyright. Bartlett v. Crittenden, (CC-Ohio), FedCas 1,076, 5 McLean 32.

A work, in order to be copyrighted, must be original in the sense that the author has created it by his own skill, labor, and judgment, without copying or imitating the work of another. Hoffman v. Le Traunik, (DC-NY), 209 Fed 375; Deutsch v. Arnold, (DC-NY), 22 FSupp 101, 36 USPQ 318. Mf'd 98 F(2d) 686, 39 USPQ 5.

Where the features of a plot of a story are old, but an author rewrites and improves thereon, he is protected by copyrighting his work insofar as his embellishments and additions are original. Stodart v. Mutual Film Corp., (DC-NY), 249 Fed 507. Aff'd 249 Fed 513.

United States copyright of work composed partly of original matter and partly of matter pirated from a work copyrighted abroad, but not in United States, protects only the original matter. American Code Co. v. Bensinger, (CCA 2), 282 Fed 829.

Any new or original plan, arrangement, or combination of materials entitled an author to copyright, whether the materials themselves were new or old. Nutt v. National Institute, Inc., (CCA 2), 31 F(2d) 236, aff'g 28 F(2d) 132.

Copyrighted work must be original but need not be new. Sheldon v. Metro-Goldwyn Pictures Corp., (CCA 2), 81 F(2d) 49, 28 USPQ 330, rev'g 7 FSupp 837.

Plaintiff's chart for analyzing handwriting contained matter in prior works but was not copied therefrom and was clearly original work within meaning of Copyright Act. Deutsch v. Arnold, (CCA 2), 98 F(2d) 686, 39 USPQ 5, mod'g 22 FSupp 101, 36 USPQ 318.

To be copyrighted a work must be original in that the author has created it by his own skill, labor, and judgment; if he takes matter which has been published without copyright and adds materials which are result of his own efforts, copyright thereon is not void but is valid as to new and original matter, and the degree of protection is measured by what is actually copyrightable in the publication. Dorsey v. Old Surety Life Ins. Co., (CCA 10), 98 F(2d) 872, 39 USPQ 92, 119 ALR 1250.

Originality in compilation of directory does not mean entirely new conception of directory; any one may produce directory of restaurants, but he must "start from scratch," do own collecting, own appraisal, and own description and editing. Adventures in Good Eating, Inc. v. Best Places to Eat, Inc., (CCA 7), 131 F(2d) 809, 56 USPQ 242.

In determining validity of copyright, starting point is Constitution; as constitutional power to enact Copyright Act derives from § 8 of article 1, act would be void if it went beyond granting monopolies, or exclusive franchises, to authors whose works promote progress of science and useful arts; Constitution does not authorize such grant to one whose product lacks all creative originality. Chamberlin v. Uris Sales Corp., (CCA 2), 150 F(2d) 512, 65 USPQ 544, aff'g 56 FSupp 987, 62 USPQ 375.

Originality cannot be predicated upon similarity of locale. Eschevarria v. Warner Bros. Pictures, (DC-Cal), 12 FSupp 632, 28 USPQ 213.

Originality in manner of treatment of theme, rather than theme, is protected. Eschevarria v. Warner Bros. Pictures, (DC-Cal), 12 FSupp 632, 29 USPQ 213.

It is not novelty but originality of wording that is protected by copyright of book. Seltzer v. Sunbrock, (DC-Cal), 22 FSupp 621, 37 USPQ 491.

Only original work may be copyrighted; there is nothing original in use of "Sons and Daughters of Uncle Sam" or its insignia as applied to corporation of citizens of United States, "Uncle Sam" being descriptive term designating United States. Blish v. National Broadcasting Co., Inc., (DC-Ill), 49 FSupp 346, 56 USPQ 212.

Copyright test of "originality" is not so severe a standard as patent tests of "invention" and "novelty"; nevertheless, courts consistently hold that "originality" requires some element of creativity. McIntyre v. Double-A Music Corp., (DC-Cal), 179 FSupp 160, 124 USPQ 27.

Copyrighted matter must be original with copyright registrant either as author or proprietor as assignee of author; copyrighted score cards contain names of players and their numbers which originated with respective baseball clubs and not with copyright registrant which is therefore not legally entitled to register score card under Copyright Act. Penn Sportservice, Inc. v. Goldstein, (DC-Pa), 46 USPQ 477.

Use of quotation marks by biographer to set out conversations he had with subject of biography, instead of use of narrative form, does not put matter in public domain since no stenographer was present and statement of conversations is biographer's version, the result of his literary effort; if biographer was only trying to reconstruct conversations, that would be authorship; even if conversations were exact repetition, biographer's part in conversations would be original and would have contributed to creation of subject's part. Harris v. Miller, (DC-NY), 50 USPQ 306.

7. Literary and artistic qualities.

The Copyright Act is for the encouragement of learning, and not intended for the encouragement of mere industry, unconnected with learning and the sciences. Clayton v. Stone, (CC-NY), FedCas 2,872, 2 Paine 382.

An article having none of the characteristics of a work of art or of a literary production cannot be the subject of copyright. Ehret v. Pierce, (CC-NY), 10 Fed 553.

The voice, motions, and postures of actors and mere stage business have no literary quality and cannot be copyrighted. Bloom & Hamlin v. Nixon, (CC-Pa), 125 Fed 977; Savage v. Hoffmann, (CC-NY), 159 Fed 584.

A new and original plan, arrangement, or combination of materials may contain literary or artistic merit and entitle the author to a copyright thereon. Hoffman v. Le Traunik, (DC-NY), 209 Fed 375.

To be entitled to copyright an article must have some value as a composition other than as an advertisement. Meccano, Ltd. v. Wagner, (DC-Ohio), 234 Fed 912. Mf'd 246 Fed 603.

Right to a copyright is not affected by the artistic merit of a work. Pellegrini v. Allegrini, (DC-Pa), 2 F(2d) 610.

A plot or the mere concept of a situation around which to build and develop literary or artistic adornment is not copyrightable. Wiren v. Shubert Theatre Corp., (DC-NY), 5 FSupp 358. Aff'd 70 F(2d) 1023.

8. Illegal or immoral subjects.

An immoral production unsuited for public representation is not entitled to the benefit of copyright. Martinetti v. Maguire, (CC-Cal), FedCas 9,173, 1 AbbUS 356, Deady 216.

Articles which may be used for gambling were not immoral or improper in themselves and may be entitled to protection under the copyright laws. Richardson v. Miller, (CC-Mass), FedCas 11,791.

To be entitled to copyright a composition must be free from illegality or immorality. Hoffman v. Le Traunik, (DC-NY), 209 Fed 375.

In determining whether work is indecent or immoral, court adopts tests in cases under postal statutes denying mailing privileges to indecent works; work must be considered as whole and have direct tendency to corrupt morals; mere vulgarity or coarseness of language does not condemn it; narrative can have no immoral tendency where derelictions end in punishment or suffering, and contrition, followed by forgiveness, although author did not have such purpose when writing. Cain v. Universal Pictures Co., Inc., (DC-Cal), 47 FSupp 1013, 56 USPQ 8.

It is unclear whether the register of copyrights has authority to deny registration of a claim to copyright in a work which, while it meets all the formal requirements for registration, contains seditious, libellous, obscene, or other matter which may be illegal or opposed to public policy. The Copyright Act [§ 1 et seq. of this title] imposes no duty upon the register to deny registration of such claims to copyright. It confers discretion upon him to accept for registration works which the courts may ultimately deprive of copyright protection. 41 OAG —, Dec. 18, 1958.

5. Classification of works for registration.—The application for registration shall specify to which of the following classes the work in which copyright is claimed belongs:

(a) Books, including composite and cyclopedic works, directories, gazetteers, and other compilations.

(b) Periodicals, including newspapers.

(c) Lectures, sermons, addresses (prepared for oral delivery).

(d) Dramatic or dramatico-musical compositions.

(e) Musical compositions.

(f) Maps.

(g) Works of art; models or designs for works of art.

(h) Reproductions of a work of art.

(i) Drawings or plastic works of a scientific or technical character.

(j) Photographs.

(k) Prints and pictorial illustrations including prints or labels used for articles of merchandise.

(l) Motion-picture photoplays.

(m) Motion pictures other than photoplays.

The above specifications shall not be held to limit the subject matter of copyright as defined in section 4 of this title, nor shall any error in classification invalidate or impair the copyright protection secured under this title. (July 30, 1947, c. 391, § 1, 61 Stat. 654.)

Cross references.—Registration fees, see § 215 of this title.

Registration of commercial prints and labels, see § 6 of this title.

Regulations for obtaining copyright, see code of regulations of the copyright office in § 207 note of this title.

Rules for registration of claims, see § 207 of this title.

Subjects of copyright in general, see § 4 of this title.

NOTES TO DECISIONS
ANALYSIS

1. In general.
2. Ideas.
3. Books and compilations.
4. —Blank books—Forms.
5. —Title or cover.
6. —Systems and instructions.
7. —Facts and information.
8. —Advertisements, catalogues, and commercial literature.
9. —Letters.
10. —Law reports and digests.
11. —Statutes.
12. Periodicals and newspapers.
13. Lectures, sermons, and addresses.
14. Dramatic or dramatico-musical compositions.
15. Musical compositions.
16. Maps.
17. Works of art, models, and designs.
18. —Utility no bar.
19. Reproductions of works of art.
20. Drawings or plastic works of a scientific or technical character.
21. Photographs.
22. Prints and pictorial illustrations.
23. —Labels.
24. Motion-picture photoplays.
25. Motion pictures other than photoplays.
26. Error in classification.

1. In general.

"Manuscript" did not include a picture. Parton v. Prang, (CC-Mass), FedCas 10,784, 3 Cliff 537.

Playing cards may be the subject of copyright although they are sometimes used for gambling purposes. Richardson v. Miller, (CC-Mass), FedCas 11,791, 15 AlbLJ 340.

To be entitled to copyright the composition must be original, meritorious, and free from illegality or immorality, and it must be original in the sense that the author has created it by his own skill, labor, and judgment, without copying or evasively imitating the work of another. Hoffman v. Le Traunik, (DC-NY), 209 Fed 375.

Dress patterns are not copyrightable. Kemp & Beatley, Inc. v. Hirsch, (DC-NY), 34 F (2d) 291, 2 USPQ 259.

A theme is not subject to exclusive copyright. Shipman v. R. K. O. Radio Pictures, Inc., (CCA 2), 100 F(2d) 533, 40 USPQ 211, aff'g 20 FSupp 249, 35 USPQ 242.

Degree of protection afforded by copyright is determined by what is actually copyrightable in card and not by its entire contents; there is no copyright for toys, badges, or similar articles alone or fastened to a book. Jackson v. Quickslip Co., Inc., (CCA 2), 110 F(2d) 731, 45 USPQ 6, aff'g 27 FSupp 338, 41 USPQ 464.

Copyright may be registered irrespective of novelty of its subject matter if latter is original, that is if it owes its origin to the author. Stein v. Mazer, (CA 4), 204 F(2d) 472, 97 USPQ 310, rev'g 111 FSupp 359, 96 USPQ 439. Aff'd 347 US 201, 98 LEd 630, 74 SCR 460, 100 USPQ 325.

While paints, colors, and subject matter, even as words of English language, are in public domain, when author composes poem of words or artist uses paints to illustrate a subject, resulting creation, if original, may usually be protected by copyright; this does not mean that to the picture there can be added ordinary serving directions, ingredients, and license numbers so as to give copyrightable qualities to these words or to shapes of containers; pictures of cakes used by plaintiff on its labels have sufficient commercial artistry to entitle them to protection against obvious copying, but relief is refused as to shapes of containers, serving directions, ingredients, and dissimilar colors. Kitchens of Sara Lee, Inc. v. Nifty Foods Corp., (CA 2), 266 F(2d) 541, 121 USPQ 359, mod'g 116 USPQ 292.

Brand names, trade names, slogans, and other short phrases or expressions cannot be copyrighted, even if they are distinctively arranged or printed. Kitchens of Sara Lee, Inc. v. Nifty Foods Corp., (CA 2), 266 F(2d) 541, 121 USPQ 359, mod'g 116 USPQ 292.

Classification of copyrights as books or dramatic compositions is not absolutely rigid and is provided partly for convenience of register's office. Seltzer v. Sunbrock, (DC-Cal), 22 FSupp 621, 37 USPQ 491.

When author adds new and original material to matter in public domain, copyright on entire work is valid, but author is entitled to protection only as to such added material. Lake v. Columbia Broadcasting System, Inc., (DC-Cal), 140 FSupp 707, 110 USPQ 173.

In order to be copyrightable, work must (a) represent author's own skill, labor, and judgment and (b) be meritorious in that it must be connected with the fine arts. Surgical Supply Service, Inc. v. Adler, (DC-Pa), — FSupp —, 133 USPQ 510.

Some literary or artistic merit is required to create a copyrightable subject. Surgical Supply Service, Inc. v. Adler, (DC-Pa), — FSupp —, 133 USPQ 510.

2. Ideas.

There may be a valid copyright in the plan, arrangement, combination of materials, and mode of displaying and illustrating the subject, though such materials and subject be common to other writers. Greene v. Bishop, (CC-Mass), FedCas 5,763, 1 Cliff 186.

A new and original plan, arrangement, or combination of materials will entitle the author to a copyright therein, whether the materials themselves be old or new. Lawrence v. Dana,

(CC-Mass), FedCas 8,136, 4 Cliff 1; Hoffman v. Le Traunik, (DC-NY), 209 Fed 375.

Ideas as such and means for expressing ideas, such as warrants to be issued for state insurance, are not proper subjects of copyright. Long v. Jordan, (DC-Cal), 29 FSupp 287, 43 USPQ 176.

Special arrangement of chapters for work on chemistry, that is, idea as to what proper divisions of such work should be, is not copyrightable. Colonial Book Co., Inc. v. Oxford Book Co., Inc., (DC-NY), 45 FSupp 551, 53 USPQ 599. Aff'd 135 F(2d) 463, 57 USPQ 569.

Artist's ideas or conceptions cannot be made subject of copyright or basis of rights; they become such only when executed and in being; when executed and sold, they are gone from his control. Grant v. Kellogg Co., (DC-NY), 58 FSupp 48, 63 USPQ 173. Aff'd 154 F(2d) 59, 75 USPQ 301.

Although there is no copyrightable property right in idea, there may be property rights in particular combination of ideas where combination is reduced to concrete form. Gordon v. Weir, (DC-Mich), 111 FSupp 117, 97 USPQ 387. Aff'd 216 F(2d) 508, 104 USPQ 40.

Neither common law nor statutory copyright extends protection to idea as such; however, ideas may be subject of contract to pay for their use. Desny v. Wilder, 46 Cal(2d series) 715, 299 Pac (2d) 257, 110 USPQ 433, mod'g (CalApp(2d series)), 286 Pac(2d) 55, 107 USPQ 17.

3. Books and compilations.

Where the several parts of a story had been dedicated to the public, through their publication in a magazine, the story could be copyrighted when the several parts were bound together in one book. Holmes v. Hurst, 174 US 82, 43 LEd 904, 19 SCR 606, aff'g (CCA 2), 80 Fed 514.

There may be no copyright in the subject matter of a book which is open to the public, but the book itself may be subject to copyright. Centennial Catalogue Co. v. Porter, (CC-Pa), FedCas 2,546.

Every author of a book has a copyright in the plan, arrangement, and combination of his materials and in his mode of illustrating his subject, if it be new and original in its substance. Emerson v. Davies, (CC-Mass), FedCas 4,436, 3 Story 768.

A plan of a book may be copyrighted. Greene v. Bishop, (CC-Mass), FedCas 5,763, 1 Cliff 186.

An English translation from Hebrew of the books of Moses was a proper subject of copyright. Lesser v. Sklarz, (CC-NY), FedCas 8,276a.

A book may be copyrighted, although it has not been printed. Roberts v. Myers, (CC-Mass), FedCas 11,906.

A pamphlet can be copyrighted. Mutual Advertising Co. v. Refo, (CC-SC), 76 Fed 961.

A monogram appearing in the front of a book is not a subject within the copyright law. Royal Sales Co. v. Gaynor, (CC-NY), 164 Fed 207.

Registered trade-mark "Nick Carter," described as "a weekly periodical devoted to fiction" does not conform to description. It is a book. Literary property in a book cannot be protected by trade-mark; only by copyright.

Atlas Mfg. Co. v. Street & Smith, (CCA 8), 204 Fed 398, 47 LRA(NS) 1002.

Well-known incidents and experiences which are common to all may be the ingredients of a story or play, and although book is copyrighted containing these incidents, they still may be used in a story written by another. Stevenson v. Harris, (DC-NY), 238 Fed 432.

Immoral books are not entitled to copyright protection. Simonton v. Gordon, (DC-NY), 12 F(2d) 116.

Pictorial history of United States, the work of compilers employed by copyright holder is properly a subject of copyright. Yale University Press v. Row, Peterson & Co., (DC-NY), 40 F(2d) 290, 5 USPQ 530.

All writings of author are entitled to copyright and this includes composite and cyclopedic works, directories, gazetteers, and other compilations. College Entrance Book Co., Inc. v. Amsco Book Co., Inc., (CCA 2), 119 F(2d) 874, 49 USPQ 517, rev'g 33 FSupp 276, 45 USPQ 516.

The term "book" is a general term which distinguishes writings from other copyrightable subjects. Sebring Pottery Co. v. Steubenville Pottery Co., (DC-Ohio), 9 FSupp 384.

A gift novelty in the form of a book made of cardboard resembling traveling bag with words "They're Off," with picture of jockey on race horse and "Greetings from Chicago" or some other city and "It's in the Bag," and when its flap was opened there appeared pair of doll's rubber panties marked "So What," was not afforded copyright protection as a book by addition of lettered pants to previous publication. Jackson v. Quickslip Co., (DC-NY), 27 FSupp 338, 41 USPQ 464. Aff'd 110 F(2d) 731, 45 USPQ 6.

Register of copyrights had no power to refuse to register copyright on ground that writing sought to be copyrighted consisted merely of "page proof" of contribution to newspaper; book in question consisted of sheets printed on one side only, each sheet bearing copyright notice; fact that it was apparent from face of book that purpose was to have it published in installments in periodicals does not prevent registration of whole as book. U. S. ex rel. Twentieth Century-Fox Film Corp. v. Bouve, (DC-DC), 33 FSupp 462, 45 USPQ 411. Aff'd 74 AppDC 271, 122 F(2d) 51, 50 USPQ 338.

Where application specified class as book, plaintiff did not protect copyright for works of art or for prints or pictorial illustrations, which may have been contained in book, as it made no application and was issued no certificate therefor. Advertisers Exchange, Inc. v. Anderson, (DC-Iowa), 52 FSupp 809, 59 USPQ 391. Aff'd 144 F(2d) 907, 63 USPQ 39.

Book containing comic strips printed on one side of paper only and bearing notice of copyright on title page, although each item in book bears separate copyright notice and most of items bear later release date on which date newspapers are first authorized to use material, is book within meaning of that term as used in this section and is composite work within meaning of that term as used in § 3 of this title, and this section. King Features Syndicate, Inc. v. Bouve, (DC-DC), 48 USPQ 237.

The word "book" as used in class (a) of this section, means the entire book and not a fragment thereof. 28 OAG 176.

Typewritten pages fastened together and having a printed cover and title page may be copyrighted. 28 OAG 265.

4. —Blank books—Forms.

Blank forms and blank books, usable in themselves, are not copyrightable. Stover v. Lathrop, (CC-Col), 33 Fed 348; Amberg File & Index Co. v. Shea Smith & Co., (CCA 7), 82 Fed 314, aff'g 78 Fed 479; Everson v. Young, 26 WashLawRep 546.

Blank forms of property statements for use of assessors under a state law are not proper subjects of copyright. Carlisle v. Colusa County, (CC-Cal), 57 Fed 979.

Forms illustrating tax bookkeeping system are not copyrightable when included in copyrighted loose-leaf book describing system, since forms embody mechanics of system taught. Aldrich v. Remington Rand, Inc., (DC-Tex), 52 FSupp 732, 59 USPQ 210.

5. —Title or cover.

A title to a book cannot be copyrighted, but if the title is such that it forms a part of the work, it may be included in a copyright of the whole book. Osgood v. Allen, (CC-Maine), FedCas 10,603, 1 Holmes 185.

A title is a mere appendage, which only identifies, and frequently does not in any way describe, the literary composition itself, or represent its character; and the title alone is never protected separate from the book which it is used to designate. Donnelley v. Ivers, (CC-NY), 18 Fed 592.

It is the title in connection with the novel, not the title alone, which the copyright law protects. Harper v. Ranous, (CC-NY), 67 Fed 904.

The copyright of a book does not prevent others from taking the same title for another book, though the copyright has not expired. Atlas Mfg. Co. v. Street & Smith, (CCA 8), 204 Fed 398, 47 LRA(NS) 1002.

Cover ordinarily has no literary copyrightable matter and when individual design is embodied in it, its relation to copyrighted literary content is remote and its authorship and ownership do not prima facie appear as in case of book's contents. Fawcett Publications, Inc. v. Elliott Pub. Co., Inc., (DC-NY), 46 FSupp 717, 54 USPQ 367.

The title of a book or play is not subject to copyright. Isaacs v. Daly, 39 NYSuperCt 511, 6 LegGaz 175; Dickey v. Mutual Film Corp., (Misc), 160 NYS 609. Mf'd 186 AppDiv 701, 174 NYS 784.

6. —Systems and instructions.

Neither a system of bookkeeping nor blank account books is the subject of copyright. Baker v. Selden, 101 US 99, 25 LEd 841.

A ladies' chart for cutting coats and dresses was the legitimate subject of copyright as a

book. Drury v. Ewing, (CC-Ohio), FedCas 4,095, 1 Bond 540.

A copyright of a book describing a new system of stenography, protects the book, but not the system. Griggs v. Perrin, (CC-NY), 49 Fed 15.

Description of a plan or method of a coupon system is subject to copyright, as contrasted with the coupons themselves. Mutual Advertising Co. v. Refo, (CC-SC), 76 Fed 961.

Letter indexes provided with leaves arranged loosely, so that they may be separated, and letters indexed or temporarily filed in their proper places do not constitute a "book," and are not a proper subject of copyright. Amberg File & Index Co. v. Shea Smith & Co., (CC-Ill), 78 Fed 479. Aff'd 82 Fed 314.

A letter file index intended for use is not subject to copyright. Amberg File & Index Co. v. Shea Smith & Co., (CCA 7), 82 Fed 314, aff'g 78 Fed 479.

A pamphlet, containing a plan for the operation of mutual burial associations, may be copyrighted but the plan itself may not. Burk v. Johnson, (CCA 8), 146 Fed 209.

"Meccano Manual," an instruction book accompanying a mechanical toy, was a proper subject of copyright. Meccano, Ltd. v. Wagner, (DC-Ohio), 234 Fed 912. Mf'd 246 Fed 603.

Book of coined words to be used for a private cable code is subject to copyright. Reiss v. National Quotation Bureau, Inc., (DC-NY), 276 Fed 717.

A list of telegraphic code words is copyrightable, so long as it is original matter. American Code Co., Inc. v. Bensinger, (CCA 2), 282 Fed 829.

A list of words for a code book is copyrightable. American Code Co., Inc. v. Bensinger, (CCA 2), 282 Fed 829.

An interest and discount time teller is a "book," and the person designing and producing it is an "author." Edwards & Deutsch Lithographing Co. v. Boorman, (CCA 7), 15 F(2d) 35.

Conventional laws or rules of a game are not copyrightable as such. Whist Club v. Foster, (DC-NY), 42 F(2d) 782; Chamberlin v. Uris Sales Corp., (DC-NY), 56 FSupp 987, 62 USPQ 375. Aff'd 150 F(2d) 512, 65 USPQ 544.

A system of spelling words with less than usual number of letters, such as "Steno-Short-Type System" is not copyrightable, though description of such system might be the subject of copyright. Brief English Systems, Inc. v. Owen, (CCA 2), 48 F(2d) 555, 9 USPQ 20.

One cannot copyright a system or method of selling a product, but may copyright original symbols or designs used as a means of effecting the sale of a product. Kaeser & Blair, Inc. v. Merchants' Ass'n, Inc., (CCA 6), 64 F(2d) 575, 17 USPQ 357.

A person can acquire no exclusive rights in the particular distribution of playing cards, in the problem of play or the principles of contract bridge applicable to its solution. Russell v. Northeastern Pub. Co., (DC-Mass), 7 FSupp 571, 23 USPQ 123.

Article describing bookkeeping system, art, or manufacture created by another is subject to copyright. Aldrich v. Remington Rand, Inc., (DC-Tex), 52 FSupp 732, 59 USPQ 210.

Exclusive right to employ particular method of advertising cannot be acquired under copyright statute and, therefore, is not proper subject matter of a valid copyright. Surgical Supply Service, Inc. v. Adler, (DC-Pa), — FSupp —. 133 USPQ 510.

A system for playing bridge is an idea which cannot be copyrighted, although a book containing the system may be copyrighted. Downes v. Culbertson, 153 Misc 14, 275 NYS 233.

7. —Facts and information.

A compilation of material forming a shipper's guide is copyrightable. Bullinger v. Mackey, (CC-NY), FedCas 2,127, 15 Blatchf 550.

A compilation, made from voluminous public documents, and so arranged as to show readily the date and order of certain historic events, may be copyrighted, because such publications require labor, care, and some skill in their preparation. Hanson v. Jaccard Jewelry Co., (CC-Mo), 32 Fed 202.

A compilation showing the financial standing of local businessmen was not a proper subject of copyright. Burnell v. Chown, (CC-Ohio), 69 Fed 993.

A mere compilation of facts is protected by the copyright law, as well as original matter showing invention. American Trotting Register Ass'n v. Gocher, (CC-Ohio), 70 Fed 237.

A compilation of credit ratings and financial standings is subject to copyright. Ladd v. Oxnard, (CC-Mass), 75 Fed 703.

News and telegraphic market quotations on ticker tape are not subject to copyright. National Tel. News Co. v. Western Union Tel. Co., (CCA 7), 119 Fed 294, 60 LRA 805.

A printed pamphlet, furnishing valuable information as to dimensions of piston rings is subject to copyright. No-Leak-O Piston Ring Co. v. Norris, (CCA 4), 277 Fed 951, aff'g 271 Fed 536.

Jewelry trade directory showing cuts of trademarks used, respectively, by the listed jewelers, was subject to copyright. Jeweler's Circular Pub. Co. v. Keystone Pub. Co., (CCA 2), 281 Fed 83, 26 ALR 571, aff'g 274 Fed 932.

Book containing list of hotels was a "directory" and subject to copyright. American Travel & Hotel Directory Co., Inc. v. Gehring Publishing Co., Inc., (DC-NY), 4 F(2d) 415.

Consolidated index of the tariffs of various carriers on corresponding subject is proper subject of copyright. Guthrie v. Curlett, (CCA 2), 36 F(2d) 694, 4 USPQ 1.

Lists of names, addresses, and other information contained in the applications for registration of motor vehicles in the office of the state commissioner of motor vehicles is copyrightable. New Jersey Motor List Co. v. Barton Business Service, (DC-NJ), 57 F(2d) 353, 13 USPQ 43.

Information as to air travel on file with civil aeronautics authority and distributed by airlines in publicly accessible timetables is not copyrightable per se. Official Aviation Guide Co., Inc. v. American Aviation Associates, Inc., (CCA 7), 150 F(2d) 173, 65 USPQ 553, mod'g 62 USPQ 178.

It is one function of copyright system to clothe with copyright protection a compilation of facts; thus, compiler of directory can, by copyrighting it, obtain protection against competitor who merely copies his work; however, he cannot obtain protection against one who publishes an article upon distribution of residents in relation to national origin and who used compilation from directory for locating concentrations of persons bearing names characteristic of various national origins; directory cases are exceptions to rule that facts are not a proper subject of copyright; exception does not go so far as to prohibit noncompetitive use of facts set forth in copyrighted collection. Consumers Union, Inc. v. Hobart Manufacturing Co., (DC-NY), 189 FSupp 275, 125 USPQ 296.

8. —Advertisements, catalogues, and commercial literature.

A picture may be subject to copyright notwithstanding its use for advertising purposes. Bleistein v. Donaldson Lithographing Co., 188 US 239, 47 LEd 460, 23 SCR 298, rev'g (CCA 6), 104 Fed 993; Ansehl v. Puritan Pharmaceutical Co., (CCA 8), 61 F(2d) 131, 15 USPQ 38.

Specimens of paints attached to a card constitute an advertisement and as such, are not copyrightable. Ehret v. Pierce, (CC-NY), 10 Fed 553.

Cuts of baths, printed in a trade catalogue, were not prints connected with the fine arts and were not subject to copyright. J. L. Mott Iron Works v. J. B. Clow & Son, (CCA 7), 82 Fed 316.

Copyright protection has been extended to the literature of commerce, so that it now includes books, catalogues, mathematical tables, statistics, designs, guide books, directories, and other works of similar character. National Tel. News Co. v. Western Union Tel. Co., (CCA 7), 119 Fed 294, 60 LRA 805.

A catalogue containing illustrations of goods sold is subject to copyright. Da Prato Statuary Co. v. Giuliani Statuary Co., (CC-Minn), 189 Fed 90; J. H. White Mfg. Co. v. Shapiro, (DC-NY), 227 Fed 957.

Advertisements which are misleading and deceptive are not protected by copyright. Stone & McCarrick, Inc. v. Dugan Piano Co., (CCA 5), 220 Fed 837, aff'g 210 Fed 399.

Artistic cuts produced for use in a catalogue are copyrightable matter. Campbell v. Wireback, (CCA 4), 269 Fed 372, 17 ALR 743, aff'g 261 Fed 391.

Labels on which are printed receipts may be copyrighted although intended for advertising purposes. Fargo Mercantile Co. v. Brechet & Richter Co., (CCA 8), 295 Fed 823.

Trade catalogues and tabulations of sizes and dimensions are within the Copyright Act. Burndy Engineering Co., Inc. v. Penn-Union Electric Corp., (DC-Pa), 25 FSupp 507, 39 USPQ 321.

It is matter of common knowledge that many advertisements in American publications of large circulation possess distinctive literary merit and real artistic originality; printed advertisements may be protected by copyright. Deward & Rich, Inc. v. Bristol Savings & Loan Corp., (DC-WVa), 29 FSupp 777, 44 USPQ 26.

Catalogue of plumbers' supplies is copyrightable subject matter and even if all information used in preparing catalogue is public, this does not give defendant right to reproduce photographically any portion of catalogue. R. R. Donnelley & Sons Co. v. Haber, (DC-NY), 43 FSupp 456, 52 USPQ 445.

Catalogue of marine hardware is copyrightable matter. Perkins Marine Lamp & Hardware Co. v. Goodwin Stanley Co., (DC-NY), 86 FSupp 630, 83 USPQ 32.

Mats depicting copyrighted advertisements in copyrighted book are part of copyrighted material where, without mats, copyrighted material is of little value to persons subscribing to right to use advertisements. Advertisers Exchange Inc. v. Hinkley, (DC-Mo), 101 FSupp 801, 92 USPQ 313. Aff'd 199 F(2d) 313, 95 USPQ 124.

Advertisements which exhibit some original intellectual effort as to conception, composition, and arrangement are copyrightable; thus, original advertisement of dot-counting contest, which portrays merchandise given as prize in picture made up of large number of dots, is copyrightable. Gordon v. Weir, (DC-Mich), 111 FSupp 117, 97 USPQ 387. Aff'd 216 F(2d) 508, 104 USPQ 40.

Advertisements, whether in form of words or pictorial illustrations, may be subject of copyright despite absence of any high artistic or literary merit; however, phrases such as "This is Nature's most restful posture" or phrases emphasizing relaxing qualities of chair, which are so purely descriptive of one's product, do not comply even with slight requirement of originality in copyright law as applied to advertisements; also, while one could copyright set of original symbols or designs used as means in sale of his product, a representation, either photographic or linear, of his chair with person in it does not constitute protectible novelty. Laskowitz v. Marie-Designer, Inc., (DC-Cal), 119 FSupp 541, 100 USPQ 367.

Plaintiff expended substantial efforts in gathering, assembling, and synthesizing of data relating to automotive items which it selected for marketing; plaintiff then condensed such data and created for its catalog original descriptions, in text and pictures, of features of items which it stocked and sold; catalog possesses such degree of originality as is required to entitle plaintiff to copyright protection. B & B Auto Supply, Inc. v. Plesser, (DC-NY), — FSupp —, 133 USPQ 247.

Catalogues and directories are copyrightable provided they have some literary or artistic merit. Surgical Supply Service, Inc. v. Adler, (DC-Pa), — FSupp —, 133 USPQ 510.

Mere price list containing only a list of articles, not original with copyright applicant, described by terms used only by manufacturers of articles, and intended only for solicitation of sales, is not copyrightable. Surgical Supply Service, Inc. v. Adler, (DC-Pa), — FSupp —, 133 USPQ 510.

9. —Letters.

Private letters are protected. Bartlett v. Crittenden, (CC-Ohio), FedCas 1,076, 5 McLean 32; Folsom v. Marsh, (CC-Mass), FedCas 4,901, 2 Story 100.

The right to copyright letters after the writer's death is vested in the personal representatives of the writer and not the person who received the letters. Folsom v. Marsh, (CC-Mass), FedCas 4,901, 2 Story 100.

As a general rule the publication of a letter may be restrained by its author or his executor, but in the absence of some special arrangement the recipient of the letter is the owner thereof. Baker v. Libbie, 210 Mass 599, 97 NE 109, 37 LRA(NS) 944, AnnCas 1912D, 551; Ipswich Mills v. Dillon, 260 Mass 453, 157 NE 604, 53 ALR 792.

Private letters are not subject to copyright by the administrator of the receiver. Eyre v. Higbee, 35 Barb(NY) 502, 22 HowPrac 198, rev'g 15 HowPrac 45.

In England the right to copyright a letter unpublished at the time of the writer's death is vested in the receiver of the letter or someone claiming under him. Macmillan & Co. v. Dent & Co., 1 Ch(1906) 101, 3 AnnCas 1113.

10. —Law reports and digests.

Written opinions delivered by United States Supreme Court may not be copyrighted. Wheaton v. Peters, 33 US(8 Pet) 591, 8 LEd 1055, rev'g (CC-Pa), FedCas 17,486; Banks v. Manchester, (CC-Ohio), 23 Fed 143. Aff'd 128 US 244, 32 LEd 425, 9 SCR 36; Connecticut v. Gould, (CC-NY), 34 Fed 319.

Judicial decisions are public property and not protectible by copyright. Little v. Hall, 59 US (18 How) 165, 15 LEd 328.

Court decisions, statements of case and syllabi, prepared by judge in his official capacity are not subject to copyright. Banks v. Manchester, 128 US 244, 32 LEd 425, 9 SCR 36, aff'g (CC-Ohio), 23 Fed 143.

Reporter of a volume of law reports may obtain a copyright for it as an author and such copyright will cover those parts of which he is the author, although he has no exclusive rights in the judicial opinions published. Callaghan v. Myers, 128 US 617, 32 LEd 547, 9 SCR 177, mod'g (CC-Ill), 24 Fed 636.

A reporter obtaining a copyright on a volume of opinions of the court does not obtain a copyright to the headnotes of the opinion, when the headnotes were written by the judges. Chase v. Sanborn, (CC-NH), FedCas 2,628, 4 Cliff 306.

Copyright on law reports does not secure to owner thereof the exclusive privilege to publish opinions of the court. Gould v. Hastings, (CC-NY), FedCas 5,639.

State law forbidding a reporter to secure a copyright in the state law "reports, notes or references" did not deprive reporter of right to copyright in notes or references original with him. Little v. Gould, (CC-NY), FedCas 8,394.

Where a state has taken the copyright of volumes of the opinions of the supreme court of a state, the copyright only covers the completed volume with the syllabi and other work of the reporter, and not the opinions of the judges. Banks & Bros. v. West Publishing Co., (CC-Minn), 27 Fed 50.

Mechanical details of reporter's arrangement of reported cases in sequence, pagination and distribution into volumes are not entitled to copyright protection. Banks Law Pub. Co. v. Lawyers' Co-operative Pub. Co., (CCA 2), 169 Fed 386, 17 AnnCas 957.

The only portions of official law reports which are subject to copyright in the name of an individual are the syllabi or statements by the reporter and any statement of facts produced by original work and not filed as a part of the decision by the court. West Publishing Co. v. Edward Thompson Co., (CC-NY), 169 Fed 833. Mf'd 176 Fed 833.

Works included in a reporter system and digests were duly covered by copyright. West Publishing Co. v. Edward Thompson Co., (CC-NY), 184 Fed 749.

A provision of a state statute that the reporter is entitled to the exclusive copyright of each volume published by him does not and cannot give the reporter any copyright in the volumes, which can only be acquired by taking the steps required for that purpose by the act of Congress. Black v. Merrill, 51 Ind 32.

11. —Statutes.

Use of prior copyrighted statutory compilations prior to independent research constitutes infringement of copyright. Banks v. McDivitt, (CC-NY), FedCas 961, 13 Blatchf 163; George T. Bisel Co. v. Welsh, (CC-Pa), 131 Fed 564, 31 AmSt 451; W. H. Anderson Co. v. Baldwin Law Pub. Co., (CCA 6), 27 F(2d) 82.

A compilation of statutes may be so original as to entitle the author to a copyright on account of skill and judgment displayed in the combination and analysis thereof, but such compiler cannot obtain a copyright for the publication of the laws only, and the legislature cannot confer such exclusive privilege upon him. Davidson v. Wheelock, (CC-Minn), 27 Fed 61.

Statutory legal forms having sufficient originality are the subject of copyright. Brightley v. Littleton, (CC-Pa), 37 Fed 103.

A compiler of a volume of annotated statutes may obtain a valid copyright upon such book to the extent of the matters contained therein which are the product of his work. Howell v. Miller, (CCA 6), 91 Fed 129.

12. Periodicals and newspapers.

(Protection of component parts of work, see § 3 of this title.)

A news article may be copyrighted but news as such cannot be. International News Service v. Associated Press, 248 US 215, 63 LEd 211, 39 SCR 68, 2 ALR 293, aff'g (CCA 2), 245 Fed 244, 2 ALR 317, which mf'd 240 Fed 983.

Newspaper was not copyrightable under Copyright Act of 1790. Clayton v. Stone, (CC-NY), FedCas 2,872, 2 Paine 382.

The copyright of a newspaper was the copyright of a "book." Harper v. Shoppell, (CC-NY), 26 Fed 519.

An "official form chart of races," printed in a daily periodical and containing information and statistics relative to horse racing was a proper subject of copyright. Egbert v. Greenberg, (CC-Cal), 100 Fed 447.

Newspapers composed in large part of non-copyrightable matter were not entitled to a general copyright. Tribune Co. of Chicago v. Associated Press, (CC-Ill), 116 Fed 126.

There can be no copyright of news facts, for such are public property. Davies v. Bowes, (DC-NY), 209 Fed 53. Aff'd 219 Fed 178; Chicago Record-Herald Co. v. Tribune Ass'n, (CCA 7), 275 Fed 797; Gilmore v. Sammons, (TexCiv App), 269 SW 861.

When a periodical contains articles or pictures made by persons who have not transferred their rights to the publisher the publisher's copyright in the periodical does not cover them, the link from the artist to the publisher being missing from the publisher's supposed title. Kaplan v. Fox Film Corp., (DC-NY), 19 FSupp 780, 33 USPQ 469.

Issues of periodicals are original works and therefore copyrightable. Detective Comics, Inc. v. Bruns Publications, Inc., (DC-NY), 28 FSupp 399, 41 USPQ 182. Mf'd 111 F(2d) 432, 45 USPQ 291.

13. Lectures, sermons, and addresses.

Lectures, oral or written, cannot be published without the consent of the lecturer, though taken down when delivered. Bartlett v. Crittenden, (CC-Ohio), FedCas 1,076, 5 McLean 32; Bartlette v. Crittenden, (CC-Ohio), FedCas 1,082, 4 McLean 300.

It cannot be true that the lecturer has no rights of property in his unpublished and unprinted lecture, or that the clergyman has no rights of property in his unpublished sermon merely because he has repeated it to an audience. Crowe v. Aiken, (CC-Ill), FedCas 3,441, 2 Biss 208.

A printed lecture plan of instruction with pictorial illustrations was not copyrightable. Chautauqua School of Nursing v. National School of Nursing, (CCA 2), 238 Fed 151, rev'g 211 Fed 1014.

Delivery of a lecture before audiences prior to copyright does not deprive the author of protection of the copyright laws by later application. Nutt v. National Institute, Inc., (CCA 6), 31 F(2d) 236, aff'g 28 F(2d) 132.

Series of lectures may be copyrighted although they use ideas expressed in another work. Nutt v. National Institute, Inc., (CCA 2), 31 F(2d) 236, aff'g 28 F(2d) 132.

Plaintiff's radio talks were for advertising purposes but were copyrightable as plaintiff had large following to whom lectures may have contributed something of satisfaction and benefit. Vinick v. Charm Publications, Inc., (DC-NY), 46 USPQ 510.

14. Dramatic or dramatico-musical compositions.

A photoplay taken from a book is a dramatization. Kalem Co. v. Harper Brothers, 222 US 55, 56 LEd 92, 32 SCR 20, AnnCas 1913A, 1285, aff'g (CCA 2), 169 Fed 61.

A dramatic composition, composed from old material, but put in a new form, may be copyrighted. Boucicault v. Fox, (CC-NY), FedCas 1,691, 5 Blatchf 87.

A dramatic composition is within the protection of the Copyright Act of 1831. Daly v. Palmer, (CC-NY), FedCas 3,552, 6 Blatchf 256.

A written play, without use of spoken language by the characters is a "dramatic composition." Daly v. Palmer, (CC-NY), FedCas 3,552, 6 Blatchf 256.

Railroad scene from author's composition "Under the Gaslight" was a dramatic composition. Daly v. Palmer, (CC-NY), FedCas 3,552, 6 Blatchf 256.

A patented mechanical contrivance used in a scene in a play cannot be included in a copyright of the play. Freligh v. Carroll, (CC-NY), FedCas 5,092a.

A series of scenes consisting of artists' models in seductive poses is not a "dramatic composition." Martinetti v. Maguire, (CC-Cal), FedCas 9,173, 1 AbbUS 356, Deady 216.

A copyrighted drama cannot be dedicated to the public by the publication of a novel based on such drama. Shook v. Rankin, (CC-Ill), FedCas 12,804, 6 Biss 477.

An imitation river used in connection with a stage play in which real water is used is not a proper subject of copyright. Serrana v. Jefferson, (CC-NY), 33 Fed 347.

A dance consisting solely of a series of graceful movements is not a "dramatic composition" and is not copyrightable. Fuller v. Bemis, (CC-NY), 50 Fed 926.

Scene of a play having literary quality is protectible by copyright. Daly v. Webster, (CCA 2), 56 Fed 483, rev'g 47 Fed 903; Chappell & Co. v. Fields, (CCA 2), 210 Fed 864.

A topical song which is a part of a dramatic composition is a proper subject of copyright. Henderson v. Tompkins, (CC-Mass), 60 Fed 758.

Exhibitions of a woman changing costumes was not a "dramatic composition" subject to a copyright. Barnes v. Miner, (CC-NY), 122 Fed 480.

A dramatic sketch consisting of a series of recitations and songs to be recited or sung by the same person dressed in different costumes was a dramatico-musical composition. Green v. Luby, (CC-NY), 177 Fed 287.

A person has the right to make an independent translation of his own from a French play, although another translation had been made from the same play and copyrighted, provided the new translation does not include parts of the copyrighted one. Stevenson v. Fox, (DC-NY), 226 Fed 990.

Where a song was published and copyrighted separate and apart from a previously copyrighted dramatico-musical composition of which it was a part, and no notice was printed on the republished song that it was taken from a copyrighted comic opera, the benefit of the copyright of a dramatico-musical composition was lost as to that song. Herbert v. Shanley Co., (CCA 2), 229 Fed 340, aff'g 222 Fed 344. Rev'd on other grounds, 242 US 591, 61 LEd 511, 37 SCR 232.

A copyright cannot protect a fundamental plot, which was common property long before the story was written. London v. Biograph Co., (CCA 2), 231 Fed 696.

A copyright extends only to the arrangement of the words and does not give a monopoly to any incident in a play. Eichel v. Marcin, (DC-NY), 241 Fed 404.

Partial invalidity of a copyright for a play does not preclude the valid portion of the copyright from protection. Stodart v. Mutual Film Corp., (DC-NY), 249 Fed 507. Aff'd 249 Fed 513.

Although a song may not be a dramatic composition, the copyright owner has the right to dramatize it. M. Witmark & Sons v. Pastime Amusement Co., (DC-SC), 298 Fed 470. Aff'd 2 F(2d) 1020.

A song, that has dramatic features in it, may be considered a dramatic composition. M. Witmark & Sons v. Pastime Amusement Co., (DC-SC), 298 Fed 470. Aff'd 2 F(2d) 1020.

Mere idea in plot is not copyrightable. Dymow v. Bolton, (CCA 2), 11 F(2d) 690.

An old plot cannot be copyrighted, but a new treatment of an old plot may be protected by copyright. Stephens v. Howells Sales Co., (DC-NY), 16 F(2d) 805.

It is doubtful whether incidents per se can become copyrightable literary property, but it does not take many of them to make what will pass for a plot and constitute the action of a play which can be copyrighted. Frankel v. Irwin, (DC-NY), 34 F(2d) 142.

Content of dramatic or literary composition is not copyrightable, but the form and sequence of its treatment is copyrightable. Rush v. Oursler, (DC-NY), 39 F(2d) 468, 5 USPQ 320.

Copyright of a playwright does not prevent the use of his "ideas." Nichols v. Universal Pictures Corp., (CCA 2), 45 F(2d) 119, 7 USPQ 84, aff'g 34 F(2d) 145, 2 USPQ 139.

The bare outline or theme of a play is not copyrightable. Nichols v. Universal Pictures Corp., (CCA 2), 45 F(2d) 119, 7 USPQ 84, aff'g 34 F(2d) 145, 2 USPQ 139.

A plot or mere concept of a situation around which to build and develop literary or artistic adornment is not copyrightable. Wiren v. Shubert Theatre Corp., (DC-NY), 5 FSupp 358. Aff'd 70 F(2d) 1023.

Distinctive treatment of plot or theme is properly subject of copyright, as dramatic composition and sequence of incidents in plot, taken in conjunction with distinctive locale, and original characterizations, will be protected. Absence of dialogue is not fatal, and theme may be in pantomime, but no broad central dramatic situation in broad outline can be protected. Copyright Act does not protect distinctive locale, mechanical devices used in production, gestures or motions or even movements of dance. Seltzer v. Sunbrock, (DC-Cal), 22 FSupp 621, 37 USPQ 491.

Where pamphlets describing exhibition roller skate race with rules for conduct of race were copyrighted as books, in narrative form with no fixed plot or story, and no distinctive characters possessing individual personalities or names, mere fact that race as staged would be entertaining or thrilling does change essential nature of composition to drama since there is no definite story structure. Seltzer v. Sunbrock, (DC-Cal), 22 FSupp 621, 37 USPQ 491.

Neither choice of distinct locale for play or story is subject of appropriation, nor are mechanical devices used in production, gestures of actors, or movement of dance or spectacle. Supreme Records, Inc. v. Decca Records, Inc., (DC-Cal), 90 FSupp 904, 85 USPQ 405.

Opera based on novel and drama is substantially new and distinct composition, being piece of property wholly separate and independent from novel and drama, and is subject of copyright; copyright on opera does not expire with expiration of copyright on novel. G. Ricordi & Co. v. Paramount Pictures, Inc., (DC-NY), 92 FSupp 537, 86 USPQ 452. Mf'd 189 F(2d) 469, 89 USPQ 289, which was mf'd 190 F(2d) 217, 89 USPQ 564.

Court considers complete text of both plays, including any matter unprotected by statute, as evidence on issue of copying. Burnett v. Lambino, (DC-NY), — FSupp —, 133 USPQ 325.

Test of copyrightability distinguishes between plot ideas used by author and his expression of them; only the latter is copyrightable. Burnett v. Lambino, (DC-NY), — FSupp —, 133 USPQ 325.

15. Musical compositions.

Copyright may be obtained upon music taken from an opera and subsequently rewritten by an arranger to include alterations and additions original with him. Atwill v. Ferrett, (CC-NY), FedCas 640, 2 Blatchf 39.

A musical composition, which is a copy of another piece but with variations which an experienced writer of music might easily make, cannot be copyrighted. Jollie v. Jaques, (CC-NY), FedCas 7,437, 1 Blatchf 618.

A musical composition is not subject to copyright, when it is a combination of parts of older compositions. Reed v. Carusi, (CC-Md), FedCas 11,642, Taney 72.

An orchestral accompaniment for a non-copyrighted oratorio is subject to copyright. Thomas v. Lennox, (CC-Mass), 14 Fed 849.

Pianoforte arrangement of orchestral score of an opera made by a system of selection and culling, creating nothing original, is not protectible by copyright. Carte v. Duff, (CC-NY), 25 Fed 183.

Pianoforte arrangement of the orchestral score of an opera is an original musical composition and subject to copyright. Carte v. Evans, (CC-Mass), 27 Fed 861.

Perforated strip of paper, by which a copyrighted song could be played mechanically on organettes, was not sheet music and therefore did not infringe on the copyright of a musical composition. Kennedy v. McTammany, (CC-Mass), 33 Fed 584.

The word "hottest" as used in the chorus of a song has a vulgar and indelicate meaning preventing the song from being protected by copyright. Broder v. Zeno Mauvais Music Co., (CC-Cal), 88 Fed 74.

Words of a musical composition of an immoral character are not protectible by copyright, although melody will be protected. Broder v. Zeno Mauvais Music Co., (CC-Cal), 88 Fed 74.

A musical composition, as an idea in the concrete, is not copyrightable as such, it is that which gives the conception corporeal and tangible existence which is the subject of copyrighting. White-Smith Music Pub. Co. v. Apollo Co., (CC-NY), 139 Fed 427. Aff'd 147 Fed 226. Aff'd 209 US 1, 52 LEd 655, 28 SCR 319, 14 AnnCas 628.

The addition of an alto to a well-known musical composition is not such a new and original work as entitles the person adding such alto to a copyright. Cooper v. James, (DC-Ga), 213 Fed 871.

An orchestral score of an operetta may be copyrighted separately from the words and music of a song which formed part of the operetta, when such score is a substantially new and distinct composition. Edmonds v. Stern, (CCA 2), 248 Fed 897.

A person having the right to use a copyrighted song has the right to make an orchestration of the song for use in an operetta, and to have such orchestration copyrighted. Edmonds v. Stern, (CCA 2), 248 Fed 897.

Publication in foreign country of song produced and copyrighted there did not prevent later copyright of same song in United States, there having been no intervening rights. Italian Book Co. v. Cardilli, (DC-NY), 273 Fed 619.

New arrangements of the words and music of old song are entitled to protection. Italian Book Co., Inc. v. Rossi, (DC-NY), 27 F(2d) 1014.

Mere fact that copyrighted poem is adapted to be set to music does not make it, in the form written, a musical composition; many prose compositions have been set to music. Corcoran v. Montgomery Ward & Co., Inc., (CCA 9), 121 F(2d) 572, 50 USPQ 274.

Similarity of musical compositions did not preclude copyrights. Arnstein v. Edward B. Marks Music Corp., (DC-NY), 11 FSupp 535, 27 USPQ 127. Aff'd 82 F(2d) 275, 28 USPQ 426.

A composition, to be the subject of a copyright, must have sufficient originality to make it a new work rather than a copy of the old, with minor changes which any skilled musician might make; it must be the result of some original or creative work. Narden v. Oliver Ditson Co., Inc., (DC-Mass), 13 FSupp 415, 28 USPQ 183.

Slight variations in the use of rhythm or harmony, of accent and tempo, may result in a popular song subject of copyright. Hirsch v. Paramount Pictures, Inc., (DC-Cal), 17 FSupp 816, 32 USPQ 233.

Distinctive style in interpretations of musical numbers gives the interpreter a distinct, exclusive, and separable property right in his unique rendition. Waring v. Dunlea, (DC-NC), 26 FSupp 338, 41 USPQ 201.

Before one having limited right to record song may have its recorded musical arrangement thereof protected as a right against competitor, arrangement must have distinctive characteristic, aside from composition itself, of such character that any person hearing it played would become aware of distinctiveness of arrangement. Supreme Records, Inc. v. Decca Records, Inc., (DC-Cal), 90 FSupp 904, 85 USPQ 405.

Specific bass is too simple to be copyrightable; it is mechanical application of a simple harmonious chord; purpose of copyright law is to protect creation, not mechanical skill. Shapiro, Bernstein & Co., Inc. v. Miracle Record Co., Inc., (DC-Ill), 91 FSupp 473, 85 USPQ 39.

Title of musical composition, play, novel, or motion picture cannot be copyrighted, and copyright does not give owner exclusive right to use title. Shapiro Bernstein & Co., Inc. v. Jerry Vogel Music Co., Inc., (DC-NY), 115 FSupp 754, 98 USPQ 438, 99 USPQ 381. Rev'd 221 F(2d) 569, 105 USPQ 178, which was mf'd 223 F(2d) 252, 105 USPQ 460.

Musical composition as an idea or intellectual conception is not subject to copyright, either as to words or music; jingle, as subject of copyright, should be considered as single original work from standpoint of its melody and lyrics, and not disjointedly, or from standpoint of intellectual conception thereby expressed. Smith v. George E. Muehlebach Brewing Co., (DC-Mo), 140 FSupp 729, 110 USPQ 177.

Inconsequential melodic and harmonic embellishments such as are frequently improvised by any competent musician are de minimis contributions and do not qualify for copyright protection since they are technical improvisations in the common vocabulary of music. McIntyre v. Double-A Music Corp., (DC-Cal), 166 FSupp 681, 119 USPQ 106.

Rhythmic annotations indicating manner of performance of chants are integral part of musical composition which may be copyrightable under this section; remedy against unauthorized copying of published literary property must be sought under this law; there is no special reservation of rights in typography of published work, and this may be copied except insofar as copyright makes copying of work itself unlawful. Desclee & Cie v. Nemmers, (DC-Wis), 190 FSupp 381, 128 USPQ 186.

If performer of musical composition, in consummating work by transforming it into sound, contributes by his interpretation something of novel, intellectual, or artistic value, he has participated in creation of product in which he is entitled to right of property which in no way overlaps or duplicates that of author in the musical composition. Waring v. WDAS Broadcasting Station, Inc., 327 Pa 433, 194 Atl 631, 35 USPQ 272.

16. Maps.

Extent of protection afforded maps, charts, and topographical surveys stated, see Emerson v. Davies, (CC-Mass), FedCas 4,436, 1 Woodb&M 21; Gray v. Russell, (CC-Mass), FedCas 5,728, 1 Story 11.

There is no exclusive right to signs and keys on maps. Perris v. Hexamer, 99 US 674, 25 LEd 308.

A chart which corrected an error common to prior like charts, and which was based upon author's own discovery, was copyrightable. Blunt v. Patten, (CC-NY), FedCas 1,580, 2 Paine 397.

A copyright cannot subsist in a map or a chart, as a general subject, though it may in an original and individual work. Blunt v. Patten, (CC-NY), FedCas 1,580, 2 Paine 397.

New editions of maps may be copyrighted. Farmer v. Calvert Lithographing Co., (CC-Mich), FedCas 4,651, 1 Flip 228.

The title of a map cannot be copyrighted. Chapman v. Ferry, (CC-Ore), 18 Fed 539.

A "chart," as used in the original Copyright Act of 1790, was a marine map and would not include sheets of paper containing tabulated or methodically arranged information relating to the popular and electoral votes for President. Taylor v. Gilman, (CC-NY), 24 Fed 632.

Copyright of a statistical atlas covers maps contained therein. Black v. Henry G. Allen Co., (CC-NY), 42 Fed 618, 9 LRA 433.

There is no necessity of copyrighting separately each map in a statistical atlas. Black v. Henry G. Allen Co., (CC-NY), 42 Fed 618, 9 LRA 433.

A map may be copyrighted even though all the material was secured from other uncopyrighted publications, when it constitutes a new arrangement of old material. Woodman v. Lydiard-Peterson Co., (CC-Minn), 192 Fed 67. Aff'd 204 Fed 921.

Automobile road map was proper subject of copyright. General Drafting Co., Inc. v. Andrews, (CCA 2), 37 F(2d) 54, 4 USPQ 72.

One using a government geological survey map and introducing thereon a choice of principal cities was not entitled to a copyright. Andrews v. Guenther Pub. Co., (DC-NY), 60 F(2d) 555.

For map to be copyrightable, its preparation must involve modicum of creative work instead of mere gathering of information from other maps. Amsterdam v. Triangle Publications, Inc., (CA 3), 189 F(2d) 104, 89 USPQ 468, mod'g 93 FSupp 79, 87 USPQ 90.

Although maps as such are entitled to limited copyright protection, court of appeals cannot say as matter of law that plaintiff's map involved such a high degree of creation that, even if copied by defendant, plaintiff's copyright was infringed. Axelbank v. Roney, (CA 9), 277 F(2d) 314, 125 USPQ 262.

Guide material on back of a map is copyrightable as compilation of arrangement of matter in public domain. Freedman v. Milnag Leasing Corp., (DC-NY), 20 FSupp 802, 35 USPQ 184.

Map is copyrightable as original work. Freedman v. Milnag Leasing Corp., (DC-NY), 20 FSupp 802, 35 USPQ 184.

Annual revisions of road map are proper subjects of copyright; copyright attaches only to new matter; design and setting of map are part of presentation or portrayal and are protected by copyright. Crocker v. General Drafting Co., Inc., (DC-NY), 50 FSupp 634, 58 USPQ 60.

Fundamental map outlines of United States are in public domain, not subject to copyright. Christianson v. West Pub. Co., (DC-Cal), 53 FSupp 454, 60 USPQ 279. Aff'd 149 F(2d) 202, 65 USPQ 263.

Plaintiff's original idea of illustrating, by outline map of United States, defendant's national reporter system, is not entitled to protection; only embodiment of idea can be copyrighted; use of arbitrary colors, numbers, or symbols on map, explained by reference to key, is not copyrightable. Christianson v. West Pub. Co., (DC-Cal), 53 FSupp 454, 60 USPQ 279. Aff'd 149 F(2d) 202, 65 USPQ 263.

Copyright of map is void as a duplicate since only change from copyright of proprietor's prior copyrighted map is obvious change of highway route number. Marken & Bielfeld, Inc. v. Baughman Co., (DC-Va), 162 FSupp 561, 117 USPQ 332.

While compilation need not be sole product of maker, something more than compilation of information procured by others is required to make map copyrightable; there must be originality resulting from independent effort of maker in acquiring reasonably substantial portion of information; reduction in size by use of mechanical instrument is not original idea; omission of towns, highways, or other markings superfluous for maker's purpose is no indication of originality; free-hand location of highways is not new information; mere contraction of edge of map to bring in additional area is not sufficient original work. Marken & Bielfeld, Inc. v. Baughman Co., (DC-Va), 162 FSupp 561, 117 USPQ 332.

Although maps are copyrightable, they are entitled to only limited copyright protection; thus, outline of island and names of areas, cities, and hotels are in public domain and not copyrightable; even if copyright proprietor's naming of certain places and descriptions of activities and points of interest can be termed original, originality is so slight that it cannot be basis of valid copyright; moreover, such types of designation and 'description are not within contemplation of statute and are not copyrightable even if original. Carter v. Hawaii Transportation Co., (DC-Hawaii), 201 FSupp 301, 133 USPQ 65.

17. Works of art, models, and designs.

Description of an art is copyrightable, but not the art itself. Baker v. Selden, 101 US 99, 25 LEd 841.

Engraving of a billiard table used for advertisement purposes was not a "work of art." Collender v. Griffith, (CC-NY), FedCas 3,000, 11 Blatchf 212.

An artist cannot acquire such an exclusive right to the conception embodied and expressed in his picture as to preclude others from the exercise of their own creative genius or artistic skill, or from availing themselves of any part of the genial contribution of artistic production. Johnson v. Donaldson, (CC-NY), 3 Fed 22.

A painting about seven inches long by four and one-half inches wide, may be copyrighted. Schumacher v. Schwencke, (CC-NY), 25 Fed 466.

Illustrative engravings of church furniture contained in an advertising book of a manufacturer were not "Works of Art." Lamb v. Grand Rapids School Furniture Co., (CC-Mich), 39 Fed 474.

A painting, if it possess artistic merit and be suitable, also, for use as a design, may, at the owner's election, be protected either by copyright or by patent. Louis Dejonge & Co. v. Breuker & Kessler Co., (CCA 3), 191 Fed 35, aff'g 182 Fed 150. Aff'd 235 US 33, 59 LEd 113, 35 SCR 6.

Representation of an elk of prodigious proportions built of a wooden frame covered with chicken wire, canvassed, plastered and painted, intended for street decoration is not subject to copyright. Carns v. Keefe Bros., (DC-Mont), 242 Fed 745.

Doll head, was assumed, with difficulty, to be a work of art. E. I. Horsman & Aetna Doll Co., Inc. v. Kaufman, (CCA 2), 286 Fed 372.

A design of a statuette of the figures of two saints standing on either side of a crucifix, may be copyrighted, but such copyright does not give an exclusive right to the subject, be it a saint, a crucifix, or anything or any personality which may be the subject of the artist's brush or the sculptor's chisel. Pellegrini v. Allegrini, (DC-Pa), 2 F(2d) 610.

Works of art need not disclose originality to be copyrightable. Gerlach-Barklow Co. v. Morris & Bendien, Inc., (CCA 2), 23 F(2d) 159.

Design for dress goods, whether stamped on paper or on goods itself, is not copyrightable as a design for a work of art. Kemp & Beatley, Inc. v. Hirsch, (DC-NY), 34 F(2d) 291.

Photostatic copies of pencilled art work are in copyrightable form; this section does not warrant any limitation on copyrighting of work merely because it may subsequently achieve more perfect or final form. American Visuals Corp. v. Holland, (CA 2), 239 F(2d) 740, 111 USPQ 288.

Costume jewelry is copyrightable subject matter entitled to protection under Copyright Act. Boucher v. Du Boyes, Inc., (CA 2), 253 F(2d) 948, 117 USPQ 156.

Publication of copyrighted design printed on textiles occurs on sale of textiles to dress manufacturers; notice of copyright at that time is constructive notice to all dress manufacturers, provided notice is sufficient; in that event, copier acts at his peril if he takes design from finished dress; such a result may well be considered necessary to carry out Congressional intent to give copyright protection to reproductions on textiles of works of art; absence of notice is a defense, with burden on copier to show that it could have been embodied in design without impairing its market value. Peter Pan Fabrics, Inc.

v. Dixon Textile Corp., (CA 2), 280 F(2d) 800, 125 USPQ 39.

Although embroidered design, which plaintiff copied on fabric, was in public domain, plaintiff's contribution to reproduction of design sufficed to meet modest requirement made of copyright proprietor that his work contain some substantial, not merely trivial, originality, inasmuch as plaintiff's creation of three-dimensional effect, giving something of the impression of embroidery on a flat fabric, required effort and skill. Millwork Converting Corp. v. Slifka Fabrics, (CA 2), 276 F(2d) 443, 125 USPQ 506, rev'g 180 FSupp 840, 124 USPQ 413.

Design for a cemetery monument was entitled to copyright as a design for a work of art. Jones Bros. Co. v. Underkoffler, (DC-Pa), 16 FSupp 729, 31 USPQ 197.

One who has worked out an embodiment of a design for a work of art or plans for a large building program possesses property right in his original production. Ketcham v. New York World's Fair 1939 Inc., (DC-NY), 34 FSupp 657, 46 USPQ 307. Aff'd 119 F(2d) 422, 49 USPQ 756.

Design printed on fabric from which dresses are manufactured is not copyrightable. Verney Corp. v. Rose Fabric Converters Corp., (DC-NY), 87 FSupp 802, 83 USPQ 386.

Sculpture of animal is copyrightable subject matter. Contemporary Arts, Inc. v. F. W. Woolworth Co., (DC-Mass), 93 FSupp 739, 86 USPQ 476. Aff'd 193 F(2d) 162, 92 USPQ 4, which was aff'd 344 US 228, 97 LEd 276, 73 SCR 222, 95 USPQ 396.

Owner of patentable design on glassware may invoke protection of Copyright Act since design is work of art. William A. Meier Glass Co., Inc. v. Anchor Hocking Glass Corp., (DC-Pa), 95 FSupp 264, 88 USPQ 249.

Statue need not be fine art to be copyrightable. Stein v. Rosenthal, (DC-Cal), 103 FSupp 227, 92 USPQ 402. Aff'd 205 F(2d) 633, 98 USPQ 180.

Relative artistic merit of work is not material in determining eligibility for copyright; costume jewelry may express artistic conception no less than painting or statue; simply because costume jewelry is commonplace fashion accessory, not an expression of "pure" or "fine" art, does not preclude finding that such jewelry is "work of art" within meaning of Copyright Act. Trifari, Krussman & Fishel, Inc. v. Charel Co., Inc., (DC-NY), 134 FSupp 551, 107 USPQ 48.

Costume jewelry is subject to copyright. Hollywood Jewelry Mfg. Co., Inc. v. Dushkin, (DC-NY), 136 FSupp 738, 108 USPQ 354.

If object is clearly a work of art, its utility will not preclude registration; however, wrist watch is not work of art even if it is difficult to tell time by it. Vacheron & Constantin-Le Coultre Watches, Inc. v. Benrus Watch Co., Inc., (DC-NY), 155 FSupp 932, 115 USPQ 115. Mf'd 119 USPQ 189.

Copyright may be obtained for original design of costume jewelry as work of art; fact that design is used in manufacturing cheap jewelry does not deprive original design of benefits of copyright. Dan Kasoff, Inc. v. Palmer Jewelry

Mfg. Co., Inc., (DC-NY), 171 FSupp 603, 120 USPQ 445.

Design printed upon blouse fabric is proper subject of copyright as work of art, although fish, sailor suits, and ice cream parlor trappings are in public domain, designs depicting them are copyrightable since artist's contribution is sufficient to qualify designs as distinguishable variations, that is there is sufficient originality in designs to warrant copyright. Scarves by Vera, Inc. v. United Merchants & Manufacturers, Inc., (DC-NY), 173 FSupp 625, 121 USPQ 578.

Ornamental design, which is reproduction of work of art, printed on dress fabrics is proper subject of copyright; there is sufficient originality in design to warrant copyright; although floral patterns are in public domain, plaintiff has contributed enough originality in design to qualify it as distinguishable variation. Peter Pan Fabrics, Inc. v. Candy Frocks, Inc., (DC-NY), 187 FSupp 334, 126 USPQ 171.

Although it is arguable that none of the differences between plaintiff's copyrighted artificial dahlia and defendant's dahlia when taken alone would be conclusive in establishing that there has been no copying, when taken together the result is that dahlias create different impressions on the court in its ro'e as an inexpert observer; there is no infringement. Prestige Floral, Societe Anonyme v. Zunino-Altman, Inc., (DC-NY), 203 FSupp 649, 133 USPQ 75. Aff'd 133 USPQ 58.

Copyright does not protect dahlia itself but merely creator's impression, treatment, or reproduction thereof in polyethylene. Prestige Floral, Societe Anonyme v. Zunino-Altman, Inc., (DC-NY), 203 FSupp 649, 133 USPQ 75. Aff'd 133 USPQ 58.

Copyright protection extends to plaintiff's designs as productions of originality and novelty, since plaintiff does not claim rights to all toy banks in form of dogs, but only rights in its particular novel and original renditions; by its treatment of the sub'ects, plaintiff has contributed something recognizably its own which is by no means trivial. Royalty Designs, Inc. v. Thrifticheck Service Corp., (DC-NY), — FSupp —, 133 USPQ 148.

Plaintiff performed independent research to locate engravings of famous deceased composers suitable for reproduction on sweatshirts; it found suitable engravings in library, copied them, and produced necessary art work for production of prints on sweatshirts; although engravings were in public domain, plaintiff's art work is sufficiently original and changed from engravings to be copyrightable. Eagle-Freedman-Roedelheim Co. v. Allison Manufacturing Co., (DC-Pa), — FSupp —, 133 USPQ 357.

Ornamental box which presents a novel and original design and which can be used as a container for rings or other small items of jewelry is copyrightable as a work of art under 17 U. S. C. 5(g) [subsec. (g) of this section]. Dan Kasoff, Inc. v. Gresco Jewelry Co., Inc., (DC-NY), — FSupp —, 133 USPQ 438.

"Work of art" in subsec. (h) of this section includes an "applied design." Loomskill, Inc. v. Puritan Dress Co., Inc., (DC-NY), — FSupp —, 134 USPQ 20.

The question as to whether the work presented is a work of art or whether it comes under some other classification is one of fact. 28 OAG 557.

Cardboard star which stands because of folded flaps is not work of art. Bailie v. Fisher, — AppDC —, 258 F(2d) 425, 117 USPQ 334.

18. —Utility no bar.

Congress intended scope of copyright statute to include more than traditional fine arts. Mazer v. Stein, 347 US 201, 98 LEd 630, 74 SCR 460, 100 USPQ 325, aff'g (CA 4), 204 F(2d) 472, 97 USPQ 310, which rev'd 111 FSupp 359, 96 USPQ 439.

Dichotomy of protection for the aesthetic is not beauty and utility but art for copyright and the invention of original and ornamental design for design patents; there is nothing in Copyright Act to support argument that intended use or use in industry of article eligible for copyright bars or invalidates registration. Mazer v. Stein, 347 US 201, 98 LEd 630, 74 SCR 460, 100 USPQ 325, aff'g (CA 4), 204 F(2d) 472, 97 USPQ 310, which rev'd 111 FSupp 359, 96 USPQ 439.

Neither Copyright Act nor any other says that because a thing is patentable it may not be copyrighted. Mazer v. Stein, 347 US 201, 98 LEd 630, 74 SCR 460, 100 USPQ 325, aff'g 204 F(2d) 472, 97 USPQ 310, which rev'd 111 FSupp 359, 96 USPQ 439.

The successive acts, the legislative history of 1909 Copyright Act, and practice of copyright office unite to show that "works of art" and "reproductions of work of art" are terms that were intended by Congress to include authority to copyright statuettes intended primarily for use in form of lamp bases to be made and sold in quantity; individual perception of the beautiful is too varied a power to permit narrow or rigid concept of art; as a standard, court can hardly do better than words of § 202.8 of copyright regulations; they must be original, that is author's tangible expression of his ideas; such expression, whether meticulously delineating model or mental image or conveying meaning by modernistic form or color, is copyrightable. Mazer v. Stein, 347 US 201, 98 LEd 630, 74 SCR 460, 100 USPQ 325, aff'g (CA 4), 204 F(2d) 472, 97 USPQ 310, which rev'd 111 FSupp 359, 96 USPQ 439.

Work of art which may be, and is, utilized for some practical purpose may be protected by copyright. Stein v. Mazer, (CA 4), 204 F(2d) 472, 97 USPQ 310, rev'g 111 FSupp 359, 96 USPQ 439. Aff'd 347 US 201, 98 LEd 630, 74 SCR 460, 100 USPQ 325.

A diagrammatic instruction sheet accompanying a crude model of a steamship, the parts of which are to be assembled according to the instructions, was a proper subject of copyright. Ideal Aeroplane & Supply Co., Inc. v. Brooks, (DC-NY), 18 FSupp 936, 33 USPQ 193.

Statue is properly copyrightable as work of art where photographs deposited with copyright office are photographs of mere statue alone without electrical assemblies, lamp shades, or lamp mounting stubs, even though statues are sold wired with electrical assemblies to which lamp shades are attached. Stein v. Rosenthal, (DC-Cal), 103 FSupp 227, 92 USPQ 402. Aff'd 205 F(2d) 633, 98 USPQ 180.

19. Reproductions of works of art.

Reproduction of painting may be independently copyrightable, and such copyright will support suit for infringement of reproduction. Home Art, Inc. v. Glensder Textile Corp., (DC-NY), 81 FSupp 551, 79 USPQ 12.

Reproductions of work of art constitute distinct class of copyrightable material. Leigh v. Gerber, (DC-NY), 86 FSupp 320, 82 USPQ 271.

Lithographic reproduction of original paintings, in the form of post cards, made in Germany, are subject to registration. 28 OAG 150.

20. Drawings or plastic works of a scientific or technical character.

Inventor obtaining patent cannot extend his monopoly by taking out copyright. Korzybski v. Underwood & Underwood, Inc., (CCA 2), 36 F(2d) 727, 3 USPQ 242.

Chart is copyrightable if it is object of explanation but not if object of use; chart for recording temperature is not copyrightable since it is mechanical element of instrument and is indispensable in its operation, neither teaching nor explaining use of art, but being art itself. Taylor Instrument Companies v. Fawley-Brost Co., (CCA 7), 139 F(2d) 98, 59 USPQ 384, rev'g 56 USPQ 213.

Illustrative drawings of electrical devices in catalogue are proper subject of copyright. Burndy Engineering Co., Inc. v. Penn-Union Electric Corp., (DC-Pa), 25 FSupp 507, 39 USPQ 321.

Drawing interpreting plumbing code shows sufficient originality to sustain copyright which is not defective because it follows interpretation of board of health or because there may be some wrong interpretation. Borthwick v. Stark-Davis Co., (DC-Ore), 38 USPQ 327.

Drawing made to interpret plumbing code, allowed to fall in public domain and later revised to interpret new code and copyrighted, is not demonstrative of bad faith. Borthwick v. Stark-Davis Co., (DC-Ore), 38 USPQ 327.

21. Photographs.

Photographs are entitled to copyright. Burrow-Giles Lithographic Co. v. Sarony, 111 US 53, 28 LEd 349, 4 SCR 79, aff'g (CC-NY), 17 Fed 591; Thornton v. Schreiber, 124 US 612, 31 LEd 577, 8 SCR 618, rev'g (DC-Pa), 17 Fed 603; Falk v. T. P. Howell & Co., (CC-NY), 37 Fed 202; Falk v. Brett Lithographing Co., (CC-NY), 48 Fed 678; Falk v. Donaldson, (CC-NY), 57 Fed 32; Cleland v. Thayer, (CCA 8), 121 Fed 71; American Mutoscope & Biograph Co. v. Edison Mfg. Co., (CC-NJ), 137 Fed 262; Pagano v. Chas. Beseler Co., (DC-NY), 234 Fed 963; Lumiere v. Robertson-Cole Distributing Corp., (CCA 2), 280 Fed 550, 24 ALR 1317; Ansehl v. Puritan Pharmaceutical Co., (CCA 8), 61 F(2d) 131, 15 USPQ 38.

Revised Statutes § 4952 which extended copyright protection to photographs or negatives was not invalid. Sarony v. Burrow-Giles Lithographic Co., (CC-NY), 17 Fed 591. Aff'd 111 US 53, 28 LEd 349, 4 SCR 279.

Whether a photograph is a mere manual reproduction of subject matter, or an original work of art, is question of fact. Bolles v. Outing Co., Ltd., (CCA 2), 77 Fed 966, 46 LRA 712.

After a photograph has become public property it cannot again be made a subject of copyright by etching a slight and colorable alteration in the negative, which was not done in good faith for the purpose of producing a new work of art. Snow v. Laird, (CCA 7), 98 Fed 813.

A photograph, if it be also an artistic production, the result of original intellectual conception on the part of the author, may be copyrighted, and without the protection of the statute it cannot continue to be the author's exclusive property, after it has been printed and offered to the public for sale. Bamforth v. Douglass Post Card & Machine Co., (CC-Pa), 158 Fed 355.

When a photograph has been produced and copyrighted, any other artist may use the same model for his pictures even though, by chance, the pose, background, light, and shade of the new picture may be similar, provided he does not copy from the copyrighted photograph in order to obtain a similar picture. Gross v. Seligman, (CCA 2), 212 Fed 930.

A mere copy of a photograph does not come within the domain of legislation under the constitutional power of Congress as provided for in § 8 of Article 1 of the Constitution [Const. art. 1, § 8]. M. B. Fahey Tobacco Co. v. Senior, (DC-Pa), 247 Fed 809. Mf'd 252 Fed 579.

A photographer is entitled to copyright photographs which were taken gratuitously and for his own benefit. Lumiere v. Pathe Exchange, Inc., (CCA 2), 275 Fed 428.

Reproduction of a photograph for use in advertising is a proper subject of copyright. Ansehl v. Puritan Pharmaceutical Co., (CCA 8), 61 F(2d) 131, 15 USPQ 38.

Courts liberally extend copyright protection and ordinary photographs of familiar scenes are protected if photographer uses skill and judgment in arrangement, grouping, and lighting. Stuff v. La Budde Feed & Grain Co., (DC-Wis), 42 FSupp 493, 52 USPQ 23.

22. Prints and pictorial illustrations.

Chromolithographs used as circus posters are pictorial illustrations and entitled to copyright. Bleistein v. Donaldson Lithographing Co., 188 US 239, 47 LEd 460, 23 SCR 298, rev'g (CCA 6), 104 Fed 993.

Print of an object to be cut up, embroidered, and made into entirely different article, such as a balloon or hanging basket, is not copyrightable. Rosenbach v. Dreyfuss, (DC-NY), 2 Fed 217.

A chromo of evident artistic merit, although used for advertising purposes, is copyrightable. Yuengling v. Schile, (CC-NY), 12 Fed 97.

Where the subject of a copyright is, in fact, a painting, executed by an artist with pencil and brush, the fact that copies may be utilized for advertising purposes does not change the character of the original. Schumacher v. Schwencke, (CC-NY), 25 Fed 466.

Cuts are proper subjects of copyright under R. S. § 4952. Rigney v. Dutton, (CC-NY), 77 Fed 176.

Pictures formed by impressions from plates are copyrightable as prints under R. S. § 4956. Hills & Co., Ltd. v. Austrich, (CC-NY), 120 Fed 862; Hills & Co., Ltd. v. Hoover, (CC-Pa), 136 Fed 701.

Cuts in a catalogue are proper subjects of copyright. Da Prato Statuary Co. v. Giuliani Statuary Co., (CC-Minn), 189 Fed 90; Wireback v. Campbell, (DC-Md), 261 Fed 391. Aff'd 269 Fed 372, 17 ALR 743.

Prints and pictorial illustrations in an illustrated business catalogue are protectible. National Cloak & Suit Co. v. Kaufman, (CC-Pa), 189 Fed 215.

A catalogue containing illustrations of garments may be copyrighted, but such copyright will not prevent another from printing a catalogue in which there are illustrations of the same type of garments, when such illustrations were not in fact copied from the first catalogue. National Cloak & Suit Co. v. Standard Mail Order Co., (CC-NY), 191 Fed 528.

Chromos or lithographs may be copyrighted, even though they are intended for advertising articles of commerce and possess little artistic merit, when the pictures in their details and designs are in fact pictorial illustrations or works connected with the fine arts. Stecher Lithographic Co. v. Dunston Lithograph Co., (DC-NY), 233 Fed 601.

Cuts originally designed and prepared by persons of skill and artistic capacity were entitled to copyright registry, although used to embellish advertising matter. Campbell v. Wireback, (CCA 4), 269 Fed 372, 17 ALR 743, aff'g 261 Fed 391.

While a single illustration of the trade-mark of a manufacturer or a jobber may not be copyrightable, this does not preclude a valid copyright upon a book containing a compilation of such illustrations. Jeweler's Circular Pub. Co. v. Keystone Pub. Co., (CCA 2), 281 Fed 83, 26 ALR 571, aff'g 274 Fed 932.

Picture was copyrightable even though its theme was taken from another. Gerlach-Barklow Co. v. Morris & Bendien, Inc., (CCA 2), 23 F(2d) 159.

Prints and pictorial illustrations may be subject to registration under copyright law where they represent personal reaction of an individual upon nature; very modest grade of art has in it something irreducible which may be copyrighted unless there is restriction in words of the Copyright Act. Bobrecker v. Denebeim, (DC-Mo), 28 FSupp 383, 42 USPQ 194.

Copyright protection is afforded if picture is (1) original, created by author's own skill, labor, and judgment, and (2) meritorious, connected with fine arts; although not work of art in ordinary sense, picture is distinctive, humorous, not likely to be forgotten, brings enjoyment, and is copyrightable; that it amuses instead of instructs does not destroy copyrightability. Stuff v. La Budde Feed & Grain Co., (DC-Wis), 42 FSupp 493, 52 USPQ 23.

Illustrations used in advertising are proper subject of copyright. Metro Associated Services, Inc. v. Webster City Graphic, Inc., (DC-Iowa), 117 FSupp 224, 100 USPQ 88.

Monthly booklet of illustrations is copyrightable under subsec. (b) of this section; component illustrations are separately copyrightable under subsec. (k) of this section and are within terms of § 3 of this title; each illustration is protected by copyright of whole booklet; therefore, unauthorized publication of any illustration is an infringement even though illustration bears minute proportion to whole booklet; "material and substantial" test of infringement is not applicable to individual items coming under § 3 of this title. Metro Associated Services, Inc. v. Webster City Graphic, Inc., (DC-Iowa), 117 FSupp 224, 100 USPQ 88.

When published singly in an advertisement an illustration from copyrighted booklet of advertisements is a copyrightable printed advertisement; each reproduction of copyrighted item must under § 10 of this title bear statutory notice. Metro Associated Services, Inc. v. Webster City Graphic, Inc., (DC-Iowa), 117 FSupp 224, 100 USPQ 88.

Design printed on dress fabric is proper subject of copyright both as work of art and as print. Peter Pan Fabrics, Inc. v. Brenda Fabrics, Inc., (DC-NY), 169 FSupp 142, 120 USPQ 158.

Fact that design was described in application for copyright registration as a work of art does not preclude sustaining its copyrightability as a print. Peter Pan Fabrics, Inc. v. Brenda Fabrics, Inc., (DC-NY), 169 FSupp 142, 120 USPQ 158.

A card consisting of a portrait of Washington, a United States shield with an eagle atop it, and the words George Washington Bicentennial, may be copyrighted as an original combination, but these features when standing alone are not subject to copyright. Carr v. National Capital Press, Inc., 63 AppDC 210, 71 F(2d) 220, 21 USPQ 408.

23.   —Labels.

Trade-marks, as such, are not subject to copyright. U. S. v. Steffens, 100 US 82, 25 LEd 550.

The clause of the Constitution under which Congress is authorized to legislate for the protection of authors does not have any reference to labels which simply designate or describe the articles to which they are attached, and which have no value separated from the articles, and no possible influence upon science or the useful arts. Higgins v. Keuffel, 140 US 428, 35 LEd 470, 11 SCR 731, aff'g (CC-NY), 30 Fed 627.

A label was not subject to copyright as a book. Coffeen v. Brunton, (CC-Ind), FedCas 2,946, 4 McLean 516; Scoville v. Toland, (CC-Ohio), FedCas 12,553.

Prior to Copyright Act of 1909, pictures for labels could not be copyrighted but were subject to registration as a trade-mark. Schumacher v. Wogram, (CC-NY), 35 Fed 210.

Agent for engraver presented to plaintiff stock labels and recommended label as type or pattern for those printed; pictorial part was precisely that employed in well-known and much used labels; texts on label were such as were then in use and well-known; there was slight variation in arrangement of text in relation to picture and difference in scroll about medallion or vignette; there was nothing original in this; copyright is invalid. Bobrecker v. Denebeim, (DC-Mo), 28 FSupp 383, 42 USPQ 194.

Picture of animal's head on beer label is copyrightable; although textual part of label is eligible for copyright registration as matter of art when it aids or augments pictorial illustration, "Stag Beer" and "Extra Pale Pilsener" on the label are not such originality and contribution to fine arts as to entitle them to copyright protection. Griesedieck Western Brewery Co. v. Peoples Brewing Co., (DC-Minn), 56 FSupp 600, 63 USPQ 74. Aff'd 149 F(2d) 1019, 66 USPQ 1.

Label placed upon woolen piece goods is not copyrightable where it consists merely of maker's name, "100% Virgin Wool," and three separate fleurs de lis. Forstmann Woolen Co. v. J. W. Mays, Inc., (DC-NY), 89 FSupp 964, 85 USPQ 200.

"Stepping Tones" with fanciful representation of girl dancing on top of phonograph record has enough originality to be copyrightable. Silvers v. Russell, (DC-Cal), 113 FSupp 119, 98 USPQ 376.

24.   Motion-picture photoplays.

Motion-picture film was entitled to copyright as a photograph. Edison v. Lubin, (CCA 3), 122 Fed 240, rev'g 119 Fed 993.

Positive motion-picture film was entitled to copyright. American Mutoscope & Biograph Co. v. Edison Mfg. Co., (CC-NJ), 137 Fed 262.

A series of photographs recorded in a film was capable of copyright as a single picture. Harper & Bros. v. Kalem Co., (CCA 2), 169 Fed 61. Aff'd 222 US 55, 56 LEd 92, 32 SCR 20, AnnCas 1913A, 1285.

Since the amendment of the Copyright Act in 1912 there may be separate copyright of the rights to stage dramatization of a novel and the rights to motion-picture dramatization of same novel. Photo-Drama Motion Picture Co., Inc. v. Social Uplift Film Corp., (CCA 2), 220 Fed 448, aff'g 213 Fed 374.

Assignment of motion-picture rights of a book did not convey any copyright of the book, but only a right upon which the assignee might obtain a copyright on a motion-picture photoplay of the book. Goldwyn Pictures Corp. v. Howells Sales Co., Inc., (CCA 2), 282 Fed 9.

Motion-picture photoplay is a dramatic work. Tiffany Productions, Inc. v. Dewing, (DC-Md), 50 F(2d) 911, 9 USPQ 545.

Motion-picture photoplay film is entitled to protection against unauthorized exhibition whether it is a dramatic work or is the dramatization of a nondramatic work. Metro-Goldwyn-Mayer Distributing Corp. v. Bijou Theatre Co., (DC-Mass), 3 FSupp 66, 17 USPQ 124.

Motion-picture "shorts" were comedy but had a story, not of great intellectual value but which showed originality, and were entitled to protection under Copyright Act. Vitaphone Corp. v. Hutchinson Amusement Co., (DC-Mass), 28 FSupp 526, 42 USPQ 431.

When a book or drama is dedicated to the public, anyone may prepare and copyright a motion-picture photoplay founded thereon; but such copyright will not give the owner thereof an exclusive right to the motion-picture rights in the book or drama. O'Neill v. General Film Co., 171 AppDiv 854, 157 NYS 1028, mod'g (Misc), 152 NYS 599.

25. Motion pictures other than photoplays.

Motion picture representing the launching of a vessel was subject to copyright. Edison v. Lubin, (CCA 3), 122 Fed 240, rev'g 119 Fed 993.

26. Error in classification.

Fact that a sketch is improperly classified as a dramatic composition rather than a dramatico-musical composition would not affect its validity. Green v. Luby, (CC-NY), 177 Fed 287.

Where a poem was registered as periodical within classification of "books" and not as "dramatic or dramatico-musical composition," despite provision that errors in classification shall not invalidate or impair copyright protection, doubt may exist whether copyright proprietor is permitted in infringement suit to say that his work belongs in class other than that in which it was actually registered. Corcoran v. Montgomery Ward & Co., Inc., (CCA 9), 121 F(2d) 572, 50 USPQ 274.

Register may refuse to issue certificate until required fee is paid and other formal requisites of act have been satisfied, but he has no power to exercise uncontrolled discretion in refusing registration of material which is subject to copyright, merely because he disagrees with author as to how it should be classified. Bouve v. Twentieth Century-Fox Film Corp., 74 AppDC 271, 122 F(2d) 51, 50 USPQ 338, aff'g 33 FSupp 462, 45 USPQ 411.

6. Registration of prints and labels.— Commencing July 1, 1940, the Register of Copyrights is charged with the registration of claims to copyright properly presented, in all prints and labels published in connection with the sale or advertisement of articles of merchandise, including all claims to copyright in prints and labels pending in the Patent Office and uncleared at the close of business June 30, 1940. There shall be paid for registering a claim of copyright in any such print or label not a trade-mark $6, which sum shall cover the expense of furnishing a certificate of such registration, under the seal of the Copyright Office, to the claimant of copyright. (July 30, 1947, c. 391, § 1, 61 Stat. 654.)

Cross references.—Infringement of prints and labels, see § 101 of this title.

Procedure in infringement cases, see § 101 of this title.

Registration of prints and labels, see § 5 of this title.

Rules for registration of commercial prints and labels, see § 207 notes of this title.

DECISIONS UNDER PRIOR LAW

Statement upon label that it had been registered in the patent office was not the notice

required by the Copyright Act. Higgins v. Keuffel, 140 US 428, 35 LEd 470, 11 SCR 731, aff'g (CC-NY), 30 Fed 627.

"Chromolithographs" were "pictorial illustrations" and therefore not prevented from regular copyright by provisions of § 3 of Act of 1874, c. 301. Bleistein v. Donaldson Lithographing Co., 188 US 239, 47 LEd 460, 23 SCR 298, rev'g (CCA 6), 104 Fed 993.

Sale of a bottled mixture to which plaintiff's label was affixed prior to the deposit of such label and title with patent office, as required by Copyright Act of 1874, was a publication of the label, after which an injunction against the use of the label by others would not be issued. Marsh v. Warren, (CC-NY), FedCas 9,121, 14 Blatchf 263.

Prints for balloons and hanging baskets with printing for embroidery and cutting lines were not works of the fine arts and were not the subject of copyright though they might have been registered in patent office. Rosenbach v. Dreyfuss, (DC-NY), 2 Fed 217.

Operation of statute could not be evaded by placing a pictorial illustration upon print or label. Schumacher v. Wogram, (DC-NY), 35 Fed 210.

Where the reproduction of a picture would not be a "label" while it might be a "print," and the picture possessed artistic merit and was also suitable for use as a design, it was subject either to copyright, or might have been patented, though it could not have had such double protection, and since the owner elected to copyright it, he was bound by his election. Louis De Jonge & Co. v. Breuker & Kessler Co., (CC-Pa), 182 Fed 150. Aff'd 191 Fed 35, which was aff'd 235 US 33, 59 LEd 113, 35 SCR 6.

Registration of chromos in the patent office was not necessary to obtain a copyright. Stecher Lithographic Co. v. Dunston Lithograph Co., (DC-NY), 233 Fed 601.

Defendant was not at liberty to use print to advertise goods purchased from plaintiff where print was registered in patent office as a copyright. Golden Rule, Inc. v. B. V. D. Co., (CCA 8), 242 Fed 929.

The provision under the Copyright Act of 1874 (18 Stat. 78, c. 301), relating to the entry of prints connected with fine arts under the copyright law was not repealed by the Copyright Act of 1909. Jeweler's Circular Pub. Co. v. Keystone Pub. Co., (CCA 2), 281 Fed 83, 26 ALR 571, aff'g 274 Fed 932; Hoague-Sprague Corp. v. Frank C. Meyer Co., (DC-NY), 27 F(2d) 176; Griesedieck Western Brewery Co. v. Peoples Brewing Co., (DC-Minn), 56 FSupp 600, 63 USPQ 74. Aff'd 149 F(2d) 1019, 66 USPQ 1; 28 OAG 116; 28 OAG 120.

A label, having been published with notice of copyright and registered in the patent office, was protected by the 1909 Copyright Act, if it was not a mere advertisement, and possessed some value as an intellectual composition. Mere intent to use the label for advertising did not bar right to copyright. Receipts in a label could have been copyrighted, irrespective of the character of the rest of the label. Fargo Mercantile Co. v. Brechet & Richter Co., (CCA 8), 295 Fed 823.

There had to be a copyright obtained for a commercial print as well as for an art print, but where the government granted a copyright, there was a presumption that the law had been complied with. Hoague-Sprague Corp. v. Frank C. Meyer Co., Inc., (DC-NY), 27 F(2d) 176.

A box manufacturer could obtain copyright on a label designated as "footwear," and made for a shoe manufacturer. Hoague-Sprague Corp. v. Frank C. Meyer Co., Inc., (DC-NY), 31 F(2d) 583.

The printing of a trade name or trade-mark on a copyrighted design did not affect the copyright. Hoague-Sprague Corp. v. Frank C. Meyer Co., Inc., (DC-NY), 31 F(2d) 583.

The copyright law applied to a label registered in the patent office. William Faehndrich, Inc. v. Wheeler Riddle Cheese Co., Inc., (DC-NY), 34 F(2d) 43, 2 USPQ 290.

Copyright of pictorial illustration, which was a commercial print, obtained by application to register of copyrights instead of to commissioner of patents, was invalid. Dixie-Vortex Co. v. Lily-Tulip Cup Corp., (DC-NY), 19 FSupp 511, 33 USPQ 486. Mf'd 95 F(2d) 461, 37 USPQ 158.

Under Act July 31, 1939 (53 Stat. 1142), when application is made to register of copyrights for registration of contribution to a periodical as such, which contribution is a commercial print (advertisement in magazine), applicant shall pay fee of $6.00. 39 OAG 498, 46 USPQ 572.

7. Copyright on compilations of works in public domain or of copyrighted works —Subsisting copyrights not affected.— Compilations or abridgments, adaptations, arrangements, dramatizations, translations, or other versions of works in the public domain or of copyrighted works when produced with the consent of the proprietor of the copyright in such works, or works republished with new matter, shall be regarded as new works subject to copyright under the provisions of this title; but the publication of any such new works shall not affect the force or validity of any subsisting copyright upon the matter employed or any part thereof, or be construed to imply an exclusive right to such use of the original works, or to secure or extend copyright in such original works. (July 30, 1947, c. 391, § 1, 61 Stat. 655.)

NOTES TO DECISIONS
ANALYSIS

1. Books and periodicals.
2. Music.
3. Art.
4. Drama.
5. Maps.

1. Books and periodicals.

A book of court rules of practice, annotated with reference to the court's decisions, is a new compilation which may be copyrighted, although previously the rules were published in a book with annotations and the rules themselves were only slightly revised. Banks v. McDivitt, (CC-NY), FedCas 961, 13 Blatchf 163.

The combining of several old materials and methods to form a book does not constitute a new and original work. Bullinger v. Mackey, (CC-NY), FedCas 2,127, 15 Blatchf 550.

An arithmetic book which is a compilation of materials from other sources combined with the author's own genius to illustrate the subject results in a new and original plan and arrangement, capable of copyright. Emerson v. Davies, (CC-Mass), FedCas 4,436, 3 Story 768.

Notes to an edition of a Latin grammar selected from various authors and arranged was an original work which would entitle the author thereof to a copyright in their actual form and combination. Gray v. Russell, (CC-Mass), FedCas 5,728, 1 Story 11.

Old materials, when subsequently collected, arranged, and combined in a new and original form may be copyrighted. Lawrence v. Dana, (CC-Mass), FedCas 8,136, 4 Cliff 1.

A "compilation" consists of selected abstracts from different authors. Story v. Holcombe, (CC-Ohio), FedCas 13,497, 4 McLean 306.

An "abridgement" is a condensation of the views of one author. Story v. Holcombe, (CC-Ohio), FedCas 13,497, 4 McLean 306.

Statutes may be digested or compiled by anyone, and such compilation may be so original as to entitle the author to a copyright on account of the skill and judgment displayed in the combination and analysis. Davidson v. Wheelock, (CC-Minn), 27 Fed 61.

Compilation of war records made from voluminous public documents is entitled to copyright. Hanson v. Jaccard Jewelry Co., (CC-Mo), 32 Fed 202.

A treatise printed with author's consent and forming a part of the "Encyclopedia Britannica" may not be reprinted, without author's consent, as a part of an unauthorized reprint of such encyclopedia. Black v. Henry G. Allen Co., (CC-NY), 42 Fed 618, 9 LRA 433.

Compilations involving industry will be protected although they have no degree of originality. Ladd v. Oxnard, (CC-Mass), 75 Fed 703.

Copyright of annotated statutes covers everything that may fairly be deemed the result of compiler's own labors. Howell v. Miller, (CCA 6), 91 Fed 129.

The copyright of a new, edition of an author's works does not operate to extend or enlarge prior copyrights or remove from the public domain works which he has dedicated to the public, but protects only what is original in the new edition. Kipling v. G. P. Putnam's Sons, (CCA 2), 120 Fed 631, 65 LRA 873.

When a work is once copyrighted, there is no authority for a second grant to the author for the same work and such a second copyright will be inoperative. Caliga v. Inter Ocean Newspaper Co., (CCA 7), 157 Fed 186. Aff'd 215 US 182, 54 LEd 150, 30 SCR 38.

The arrangement of reported cases in sequence, their paging and distribution into volumes, are not features of such importance as to entitle the reporter to copyright protection of the details. Banks Law Pub. Co. v. Lawyers' Co-Operative Pub. Co., (CCA 2), 169 Fed 386, 17 AnnCas 957.

Mere aggregation of weekly reporters into volumes does not constitute a new work, but compilation of new and larger digests does constitute new work entitled to copyright. West Pub. Co. v. Edward Thompson Co., (CCA 2), 176 Fed 833, mod'g 169 Fed 833.

An article substantially based on uncopyrighted but published work of another was not entitled to copyright. Du Puy v. Post Telegram Co., (CCA 3), 210 Fed 883.

This section makes it possible to copyright a compilation of trade-marks, although the trade-marks themselves cannot be copyrighted. Jewelers' Circular Pub. Co. v. Keystone Pub. Co., (DC-NY), 274 Fed 932. Aff'd 281 Fed 83, 26 ALR 571.

Copyright is valid as to new and original matter. American Code Co., Inc. v. Bensinger, (CCA 2), 282 Fed 829.

A compilation is the sum total of the words and phrases as arranged by the author and the copyright is valid because of the originality of the combination. When the statute allows a compilation to be copyrighted, no one can copy phrases or sequences which are original with the author or appropriate any other part of the copyrighted work, whether that part is in the public domain or not. Hartfield v. Peterson, (CCA 2), 91 F(2d) 998, 34 USPQ 305.

Original treatment of life of historical character, like such treatment of any material even in public domain, is protected against appropriation by others. De Acosta v. Brown, (CCA 2), 146 F(2d) 408, 63 USPQ 311, aff'g 50 FSupp 615, 58 USPQ 596.

There is no requirement in Copyright Act that there be some special notice where copyrighted work consists in part of translation of words spoken or written by any person. Toksvig v. Bruce Pub. Co., (CA 7), 181 F(2d) 664, 85 USPQ 339.

New edition, with minor changes, of copyrighted catalogue is a "new work" subject to copyright. Sieff v. Continental Auto Supply, Inc., (DC-Minn), 39 FSupp 683, 50 USPQ 19.

Account of single event is copyrightable as compilation only when it has individuality of expression or reflects peculiar skill and judgment. Triangle Publications, Inc. v. New England Newspaper Pub. Co., (DC-Mass), 46 FSupp 198, 54 USPQ 171.

Author of street directory for portion of city cannot, by incorporating material in new street directory for entire city, prolong protection for earlier compilation. Triangle Publications, Inc. v. New England Newspaper Pub. Co., (DC-Mass), 46 FSupp 198, 54 USPQ 171.

Indices to daily racing periodicals are copyrightable as are street directories, telephone books, railroad timetables, and headnotes for law cases. Triangle Publications, Inc. v. New England Newspaper Pub. Co., (DC-Mass), 46 FSupp 198, 54 USPQ 171.

Single daily race chart is not copyrightable as compilation because majority of items can be collected without labor, skill or judgment by any spectator and does not result from labor of assembling, connecting, and categorizing facts which in nature occurred in isolation. Triangle Publications, Inc. v. New England Newspaper Pub. Co., (DC-Mass), 46 FSupp 198, 54 USPQ 171.

Copyrighter of directory has right to protection. Chain Store Business Guide, Inc. v. Wexler, (DC-NY), 79 FSupp 726, 77 USPQ 656.

Book is copyrightable as distinguishable variation from author's prior edition and other books in public domain where, in numerous instances, letters, words, or lines of text were added, deleted, or rearranged; also, it contains substantial number of unique changes which did not appear in prior books. Ziegelheim v. Flohr, (DC-NY), 119 FSupp 324, 100 USPQ 189.

Even if author secured all material for his prayer book from publications in public domain, book was product of his own labor, judgment, money, and skill, and as such was copyrightable as new version of work in public domain. Ziegelheim v. Flohr, (DC-NY), 119 FSupp 324, 100 USPQ 189.

Validity of 1916 copyright is not affected by its republication in 1918 and 1930 since 1918 and 1930 editions were copyrighted as reissued book with new matter, even though 1930 edition was without notice of 1916 copyright; 1930 copyright was copyright of reissued book and protected added material but 1918 and 1930 copyrights could not and did not enlarge 1916 copyright, except as to new matter. Harris v. Miller, (DC-NY), 50 USPQ 306.

2. Music.

One may be entitled to a copyright on his work where, by his own intellectual labors, he has arranged and compiled old materials to produce a composition new and original in itself. Atwill v. Ferrett, (CC-NY), FedCas 640, 2 Blatchf 39.

To be entitled to copyright a musical composition must be a new and original work, and not a copy of a piece already produced, with additions and variations, which a writer of music with experience and skill might readily make. Jollie v. Jaques, (CC-NY), FedCas 7,437, 1 Blatchf 618.

If a musical composition is made up of different parts of older musical compositions with only slight and unimportant alterations and additions, the producer thereof is not the author. Reed v. Carusi, (CC-Md), FedCas 11,642, Taney 72.

Addition of alto parts to music in sacred hymnal does not result in such an original composition as can be copyrighted. Cooper v. James, (DC-Ga), 213 Fed 871.

Differences from earlier composition were insufficient to make latter an adaptation or arrangement. Fred Fisher, Inc. v. Dillingham, (DC-NY), 298 Fed 145.

Although Congress has constitutional power to give one who performs a public domain musical composition the exclusive right to make and vend phonograph records of that rendition, Copyright Act did not do so. Capitol

Records, Inc. v. Mercury Records Corp., (CA 2), 221 F(2d) 657, 105 USPQ 163, aff'g 109 F Supp 330, 95 USPQ 177.

Plaintiff heard tune similar to melody score of his copyrighted work; however, it was original work on plaintiff's part when, 30 years later, he devised calculated melody score, thus putting it in shape for all to read; copyright is valid; this section specifically provides for protection of work of composer growing out of creations of those who came before. Wihtol v. Wells, (CA 7), 231 F(2d) 550, 109 USPQ 200.

The adaptation of a foreign composer's music to English words chosen by arranger was insufficient to constitute originality and another was free to use the music as it appeared in such copy in making an adaptation of another English text to the music. Norden v. Oliver Ditson Co., Inc., (DC-Mass), 13 FSupp 415, 28 USPQ 183.

By changing title to song, making slight variation in bass of accompaniment, and adding additional chorus in march time, original chorus being in common time, song is not subject to copyright as "new work" under this section, since there is no change in tune or lyrics. Shapiro, Bernstein & Co., Inc. v. Jerry Vogel Music Co., Inc., (DC-NY), 73 FSupp 165, 74 USPQ 264.

Following copyright of music, proprietor had words written to accompany music and copyrighted song as new work under this section; copyright served to protect words. Shapiro Bernstein & Co., Inc. v. Jerry Vogel Music Co., Inc., (DC-NY), 115 FSupp 754, 98 USPQ 438, 99 USPQ 381. Rev'd 221 F(2d) 569, 105 USPQ 178, which was mf'd 223 F(2d) 252, 105 USPQ 460.

In applying rule that copyright is valid where author adds original material to material in public domain, originality means that material added must have aspects of novelty and be something more than trivial addition or variation; if what is added does not give some value to public domain composition, or serve some purpose other than to merely emphasize what is present in public domain, it is not entitled to copyright; if all that author of musical composition does is to add mechanical application of sound to word that is itself not copyrightable, and adds the same to descriptive phrase in public domain, without use of even the most simple harmonious chords, he has no musical composition subject to copyright. Smith v. George E. Muehlebach Brewing Co., (DC-Mo), 140 FSupp 729, 110 USPQ 177.

3. Art.

Copyright laws protect not only original works, but also reproductions of works in public domain in different adaptations, arrangements, or mediums of expression. Allegrini v. De Angelis, (DC-Pa), 59 FSupp 248, 64 USPQ 165. Aff'd 149 F(2d) 815, 65 USPQ 589.

Copyright of design of miniature religious shrine, which was an adaptation of work in public domain, was valid to extent of new features originated by plaintiffs and combination or arrangement of new features with original shrine. Allegrini v. De Angelis, (DC-Pa), 59

FSupp 248, 64 USPQ 165. Aff'd 149 F(2d) 815, 65 USPQ 589.

Although defendants could have photographed old masters in public domain, it is infringement where they make lithographs of copyrighted mezzotint engravings of old masters. Alfred Bell & Co., Ltd. v. Catalda Fine Arts, Inc., (DC-NY), 74 FSupp 973, 75 USPQ 66. Mf'd 191 F(2d) 99, 90 USPQ 153.

Each mezzotint engraving of old master in public domain is copyrightable, and publication of one does not prevent later copyright and publication of another by same copyright owner. Alfred Bell & Co., Ltd. v. Catalda Fine Arts, Inc., (DC-NY), 74 FSupp 973, 75 USPQ 66. Mf'd 191 F(2d) 99, 90 USPQ 153.

Mezzotint engravings of old masters in public domain are copyrightable. Alfred Bell & Co., Ltd. v. Catalda Fine Arts, Inc., (DC-NY), 74 FSupp 973, 75 USPQ 66. Mf'd 191 F(2d) 99, 90 USPQ 153.

Even though original model for Last Supper diorama is in public domain, plaintiffs' photograph of plaintiffs' diorama of Last Supper can be copyrighted in same way that engraving of painting in public domain may be copyrighted. Paul A. Hesse, Three Dimensionals, Inc. v. Brunner, (DC-NY), 172 FSupp 284, 121 USPQ 141.

4. Drama.

A play based on a novel was an original work. Boucicault v. Fox, (CC-NY), FedCas 1,691, 5 Blatchf 87.

A new and original plan, arrangement, or combination of materials will entitle the author to copyright therein, whether the materials themselves be old or new. Hoffman v. Le Traunik, (DC-NY), 209 Fed 375.

Where, in a motion picture, the same use is made of the same series of events to excite, by representation, the same emotion, in the same sequence, as in a copyrighted picture, such motion picture infringes upon the other. International Film Service Co., Inc. v. Affiliated Distributors, Inc., (DC-NY), 283 Fed 229.

Person making dramatization of work in the public domain acquires exclusive right only to that part which is original work. McCaleb v. Fox Film Corp., (CCA 5), 299 Fed 48.

Matters in the public domain are not copyrightable, and a copyright of a story containing such matters is limited to the novel features of the story. Harold Lloyd Corp. v. Witwer, (CCA 9), 65 F(2d) 1, rev'g 46 F(2d) 792.

Copyright is not voided just because source of material is in public domain, but protection is limited to new and original contribution of author. Axelbank v. Roney, (CA 9), 277 F(2d) 314, 125 USPQ 262.

Copyright in 1940, as an unpublished work, of a play in German is not voided by fact that English translations later published bear copyright date later than 1940; translations were "new works" within this section and were thus entitled to separate copyright; Copyright Office regulations (37 C.F.R. 202.2) have reference only to subsequent publication of work upon which unpublished copyright was secured; year date required in "new work" is year of publication of "new work," not year of registration of prior un-

published work. Brecht v. Bentley, (DC-NY), 185 FSupp 890, 126 USPQ 356.

5. Maps.

New editions of maps may be copyrighted. Farmer v. Calvert Lithographing Co., (CC-Mich), FedCas 4,651, 1 Flip 228.

A map drawn from other uncopyrighted publications, but containing original features constituted a new arrangement of old material and was copyrightable. Woodman v. Lydiard-Peterson Co., (CC-Minn), 192 Fed 67. Aff'd 204 Fed 921.

Automobile road map based on geological survey maps was proper subject of copyright. General Drafting Co., Inc. v. Andrews, (CCA 2), 37 F(2d) 54, 4 USPQ 72.

8. Copyright not to subsist in works in public domain, or published prior to July 1, 1909, and not already copyrighted, or Government publications—Publication by Government of copyrighted material.—No copyright shall subsist in the original text of any work which is in the public domain, or in any work which was published in this country or any foreign country prior to July 1, 1909, and has not been already copyrighted in the United States, or in any publication of the United States Government, or any reprint, in whole or in part, thereof, except that the Postmaster General may secure copyright on behalf of the United States in the whole or any part of the publications authorized by section 2506 of title 39 [39 § 2506].

The publication or republication by the Government, either separately or in a public document, of any material in which copyright is subsisting shall not be taken to cause any abridgment or annulment of the copyright or to authorize any use or appropriation of such copyright material without the consent of the copyright proprietor. (July 30, 1947, c. 391, § 1, 61 Stat. 655; Oct. 31, 1951, c. 655, § 16(b), 65 Stat. 716; Sept. 7, 1962, P. L. 87-646, § 21, 76 Stat. 446.)

NOTES TO DECISIONS

1. In general.

A manual for using a certain toy, copyrighted in 1912, does not cause the abandonment of a copyright on a manual issued in 1911, when the subsequently issued manual was a new book. Meccano, Ltd. v. Wagner, (DC-Ohio), 234 Fed 912. Mf'd 246 Fed 603.

The publication, by a state, of an index to statutes, which the plaintiff had copyrighted, does not constitute an abandonment of the copyright, although no notice of the copyright was printed on such state publications. W. H. Anderson Co. v. Baldwin Law Pub. Co. (CCA 6), 27 F(2d) 82.

If motion-picture producer is not commercially soliciting, and is not willing to accept obligation to pay for, valuable ideas, or compositions adapting them, which ideas are offered to be conveyed only upon assumption of such an obligation, he does not need to read manuscripts, which he knows are submitted on those terms, and then use them. Desny v. Wilder, 46 Cal(2d series) 715, 299 Pac(2d) 257, 110 USPQ 433, mod'g (CalApp(2d series)), 286 Pac(2d) 55, 107 USPQ 17.

Portrait of Washington and the United States shield are not susceptible of exclusive appropriations. Carr v. National Capital Press, 63 AppDC 210, 71 F(2d) 220, 21 USPQ 408.

2. Public domain.

Where an original photograph is given to the public, the same picture, with a cane etched in the hand of one of the figures, cannot be copyrighted. Snow v. Laird, (CCA 7), 98 Fed 813.

Even though all the material for a map was obtained from other publications which were not copyrighted, a copyright may be obtained on the new map if it constitutes a new arrangement of the old material. Woodman v. Lydiard-Peterson Co., (CC-Minn), 192 Fed 67. Aff'd 204 Fed 921.

Publication in foreign country of song produced and copyrighted there did not prevent later copyright for same song in United States, there having been no intervening rights. Italian Book Co. v. Cardilli, (DC-NY), 273 Fed 619.

Original composition may be copyrighted though a like composition is in public domain. Fred Fisher, Inc. v. Dillingham, (DC-NY), 298 Fed 145.

Where a copyrighted book contains a new treatment of an old plot, one copying the book has the burden of proving that his plot was taken from some source in the public domain. Stephens v. Howells Sales Co., Inc., (DC-NY), 16 F(2d) 805.

While a copy of something in the public domain will not, if it be merely a copy, support a copyright, a distinguishable variation will; though it present the same theme. Gerlach-Barklow Co. v. Morris & Bendien, Inc., (CCA 2), 23 F(2d) 159.

Obtaining of patent renders the subject a part of the public domain, except under the patent, and precludes the obtaining of a copyright. Korzybski v. Underwood & Underwood, Inc., (CCA 2), 36 F(2d) 727, 3 USPQ 242.

Copyright of play based on a murder trial was infringed by motion picture based on same murder trial. Sheldon v. Metro-Goldwyn Pictures Corp., (CCA 2), 81 F(2d) 49, 28 USPQ 330, rev'g 7 FSupp 837.

Neither historical facts nor errors in fact are copyrightable per se. Oxford Book Co., Inc. v. College Entrance Book-Co., Inc., (CCA 2), 98 F(2d) 688, 39 USPQ 7.

An aggregation of standard provisions, including some required by statute forming a copyrighted insurance policy is not susceptible of infringement as to such provisions. Dorsey v. Old Surety Life Ins. Co., (CCA 10), 98 F(2d) 872, 119 ALR 1250, 39 USPQ 92, aff'g 34 USPQ 226.

Outline map of United States with state boundaries is in public domain and is not copyrightable. Christianson v. West Pub. Co., (CCA 9), 149 F(2d) 202, 65 USPQ 263, aff'g 53 FSupp 454, 60 USPQ 279.

Infringement may result from copying a work based on material in public domain when material so taken has been transformed by first borrower so as to entitle him to claim originality. Hirsch v. Paramount Pictures, (DC-Cal), 17 FSupp 816, 32 USPQ 233.

Pictures were registered for copyright in Italy before claim of publication in application to register in United States. Copyrights were invalid as they were in public domain as far as United States was concerned after registration in Italy. Basevi v. Edward O'Toole Co., Inc., (DC-NY), 26 FSupp 41, 40 USPQ 333.

3. Government publications.

A copy of a public official document, although a few sentences and words had been changed, is not subject to copyright. Du Puy v. Post Telegram Co., (CCA 3), 210 Fed 883.

An article taken from a government official bulletin is not protectible by copyright. Du Puy v. Post Telegram Co., (CCA 3), 210 Fed 883.

General Pershing's official report to government in 1919 was not matter subject to copyright protection. Eggers v. Sun Sales Corp., (CCA 2), 263 Fed 373.

Continental outlines, latitudes, and longitudes are in public domain and are not subject to copyright in a map. Sawyer v. Crowell Pub. Co., (DC-NY), 46 FSupp 471, 54 USPQ 225. Aff'd 142 F(2d) 497, 61 USPQ 389.

Copyright to map prepared by executive assistant to secretary of interior and another government employee from government data is held in trust for government; because of his position, assistant's direction that map bear copyright notice in his name was carried out but this does not show title in him. Credit given to him by government on reprinting map, does not show title since giving credit to public official is not unusual; government's seeking permission to reprint was natural since copyright was in assistant's name. Sawyer v. Crowell Pub. Co., (DC-NY), 46 FSupp 471, 54 USPQ 225. Aff'd 142 F(2d) 497, 61 USPQ 389.

Map published by government is not subject to copyright. Sawyer v. Crowell Pub. Co., (DC-NY), 46 FSupp 471, 54 USPQ 225. Aff'd 142 F(2d) 497, 61 USPQ 389.

9. Authors or proprietors, entitled—Aliens.—

The author or proprietor of any work made the subject of copyright by this title, or his executors, administrators, or assigns, shall have copyright for such work under the conditions and for the terms specified in this title: Provided, however, That the copyright secured by this title shall extend to the work of an author or proprietor who is a citizen or subject of a foreign state or nation only under the conditions described in subsections (a), (b), or (c) below:

(a) When an alien author or proprietor shall be domiciled within the United States at the time of the first publication of his work; or

(b) When the foreign state or nation of which such author or proprietor is a citizen or subject grants, either by treaty, convention, agreement, or law, to citizens of the United States the benefit of copyright on substantially the same basis as to its own citizens, or copyright protection, substantially equal to the protection secured to such foreign author under this title or by treaty; or when such foreign state or nation is a party to an international agreement which provides for reciprocity in the granting of copyright, by the terms of which agreement the United States may, at its pleasure, become a party thereto.

The existence of the reciprocal conditions aforesaid shall be determined by the President of the United States, by proclamation made from time to time, as the purposes of this title may require: Provided, That whenever the President shall find that the authors, copyright owners, or proprietors of works first produced or published abroad and subject to copyright or to renewal of copyright under the laws of the United States, including works subject to ad interim copyright, are or may have been temporarily unable to comply with the conditions and formalities prescribed with respect to such works by the copyright laws of the United States, because of the disruption or suspension of facilities essential for such compliance, he may by proclamation grant such extension of time as he may deem appropriate for the fulfillment of such conditions or formalities by authors, copyright owners, or proprietors who are citizens of the United States or who are nationals of countries which accord substantially equal treatment in this respect to authors, copyright owners, or proprietors who are citizens of the United States: Provided further, That no liability shall attach under this title for lawful uses made or acts done prior to the effective date of such proclamation in connection with such works, or in respect to the continuance for one-year subsequent to such date of any business undertaking or enterprise lawfully undertaken prior to such date involving expenditure or contractual obligation in connection with the exploitation, production, reproduction, circulation, or performance of any such work.

The President may at any time terminate any proclamation authorized herein or any part thereof or suspend or extend its operation for such period or periods of

(1403)

time as in his judgment the interests of the United States may require.

(c) When the Universal Copyright Convention, signed at Geneva on September 6, 1952, shall be in force between the United States of America and the foreign state or nation of which such author is a citizen or subject, or in which the work was first published. Any work to which copyright is extended pursuant to this subsection shall be exempt from the following provisions of this title: (1) The requirement in section 1(e) that a foreign state or nation must grant to United States citizens mechanical reproduction rights similar to those specified therein; (2) the obligatory deposit requirements of the first sentence of section 13; (3) the provisions of sections 14, 16, 17, and 18; (4) the import prohibitions of section 107, to the extent that they are related to the manufacturing requirements of section 16; and (5) the requirements of sections 19 and 20: Provided, however, That such exemptions shall apply only if from the time of first publication all the copies of the work published with the authority of the author or other copyright proprietor shall bear the symbol © accompanied by the name of the copyright proprietor and the year of first publication placed in such manner and location as to give reasonable notice of claim of copyright.

Upon the coming into force of the Universal Copyright Convention in a foreign state or nation as hereinbefore provided, every book or periodical of a citizen or subject thereof in which ad interim copyright was subsisting on the effective date of said coming into force shall have copyright for twenty-eight years from the date of first publication abroad without the necessity of complying with the further formalities specified in section 23 of this title.

The provisions of this subsection shall not be extended to works of an author who is a citizen of, or domiciled in the United States of America regardless of place of first publication, or to works first published in the United States. (July 30, 1947, c. 391, § 1, 61 Stat. 655; Aug. 31, 1954, c. 1161, § 1, 68 Stat. 1030.)

Amendment note.—Act Aug. 31, 1954, cited to text, inserted "under the conditions described in subsections (a), (b), or (c) below:" and added subsec. (c).

Cross references.—"Employer" included in term "author," see § 26 of this title.

Property rights in copyrights, see § 27 of this title.

UNIVERSAL COPYRIGHT CONVENTION

The Unesco Universal Copyright Convention was adopted by the Intergovernmental Copyright Conference at Geneva, Switzerland, on Sept. 6, 1952. It entered into force for the United States on Sept. 16, 1955. Other states which have become parties are: Andorra, Cambodia, Chile, Costa Rica, France, Germany (Fed. Rep.), Haiti, Vatican City, Israel, Laos, Luxembourg, Monaco, Pakistan, and Spain.

The text of the Convention is as follows:

The Contracting States,

Moved by the desire to assure in all countries copyright protection of literary, scientific and artistic works,

Convinced that a system of copyright protection appropriate to all nations of the world and expressed in a universal convention, additional to, and without impairing international systems already in force, will ensure respect for the rights of the individual and encourage the development of literature, the sciences and the arts,

Persuaded that such a universal copyright system will facilitate a wider dissemination of works of the human mind and increase international understanding,

Have agreed as follows:

Article I

Each Contracting State undertakes to provide for the adequate and effective protection of the rights of authors and other copyright proprietors in literary, scientific and artistic works, including writings, musical, dramatic and cinematographic works, and paintings, engravings and sculpture.

Article II

1. Published works of nationals of any Contracting State and works first published in that State shall enjoy in each other Contracting State the same protection as that other State accords to works of its nationals first published in its own territory.

2. Unpublished works of nationals of each Contracting State shall enjoy in each other Contracting State the same protection as that other State accords to unpublished works of its own nationals.

3. For the purpose of this Convention any Contracting State may, by domestic legislation, assimilate to its own nationals any person domiciled in that State.

Article III

1. Any Contracting State which, under its domestic law, requires as a condition of copyright, compliance with formalities such as deposit, registration, notice, notarial certificates, payment of fees or manufacture or publication in that Contracting State, shall regard these requirements as satisfied with respect to all works protected in accordance with this Convention and first published outside its territory and the author of which is not one of its nationals, if from the time of the first publication all the copies of the work published with the authority of the author or other copyright proprietor bear the symbol © accompanied by the name of the copyright proprietor and the year of first publication placed in such manner and location as to give reasonable notice of claim of copyright.

2. The provisions of paragraph 1 of this article shall not preclude any Contracting State from requiring formalities or other conditions for the acquisition and enjoyment of copyright in respect of works first published in its territory or works of its nationals wherever published.

3. The provisions of paragraph 1 of this article shall not preclude any Contracting State from providing that a person seeking judicial relief must, in bringing the action, comply with procedural requirements, such as that the complainant must appear through domestic counsel or that the complainant must deposit with the court or an administrative office, or both, a copy of the work involved in the litigation; provided that failure to comply with such requirements shall not affect the validity of the copyright, nor shall any such requirement be imposed upon a national of another Contracting State if such requirement is not imposed on nationals of the State in which protection is claimed.

4. In each Contracting State there shall be legal means of protecting without formalities the unpublished works of nationals of other Contracting States.

5. If a Contracting State grants protection for more than one term of copyright and the first term is for a period longer than one of the minimum periods prescribed in article IV, such State shall not be required to comply with the provisions of paragraph 1 of this article III in respect of the second or any subsequent term of copyright.

Article IV

1. The duration of protection of a work shall be governed, in accordance with the provisions of article II and this article, by the law of the Contracting State in which protection is claimed.

2. The term of protection for works protected under this Convention shall not be less than the life of the author and 25 years after his death.

However, any Contracting State which, on the effective date of this Convention in that State, has limited this term for certain classes of works to a period computed from the first publication of the work, shall be entitled to maintain these exceptions and to extend them to other classes of works. For all these classes the term of protection shall not be less than 25 years from the date of first publication.

Any Contracting State which, upon the effective date of this Convention in that State, does not compute the term of protection upon the basis of the life of the author, shall be entitled to compute the term of protection from the date of the first publication of the work or from its registration prior to publication, as the case may be, provided the term of protection shall not be less than 25 years from the date of first publication or from its registration prior to publication, as the case may be.

If the legislation of a Contracting State grants two or more successive terms of protection, the duration of the first term shall not be less than one of the minimum periods specified above.

3. The provisions of paragraph 2 of this article shall not apply to photographic works or to works of applied art; provided, however, that the term of protection in those Contracting States which protect photographic works, or works of applied art in so far as they are protected as artistic works, shall not be less than ten years for each of said classes of works.

4. No Contracting State shall be obliged to grant protection to a work for a period longer than that fixed for the class of works to which the work in question belongs, in the case of unpublished works by the law of the Contracting State of which the author is a national, and in the case of published works by the law of the Contracting State in which the work has been first published.

For the purposes of the application of the preceding provision, if the law of any Contracting State grants two or more successive terms of protection, the period of protection of that State shall be considered to be the aggregate of those terms. However, if a specified work is not protected by such State during the second or any subsequent term for any reason, the other Contracting States shall not be obliged to protect it during the second or any subsequent term.

5. For the purposes of the application of paragraph 4 of this article, the work of a national of a Contracting State, first published in a non-Contracting State, shall be treated as though first published in the Contracting State of which the author is a national.

6. For the purposes of the application of paragraph 4 of this article, in case of simultaneous publication in two or more Contracting States, the work shall be treated as though first published in the State which affords the shortest term; any work published in two or more Contracting States within thirty days of its first publication shall be considered as having been published simultaneously in said Contracting States.

Article V

1. Copyright shall include the exclusive right of the author to make, publish, and authorize the making and publication of translations of works protected under this Convention.

2. However, any Contracting State may, by its domestic legislation, restrict the right of translation of writings, but only subject to the following provisions:

If, after the expiration of a period of seven years from the date of the first publication of a writing, a translation of such writing has not been published in the national language or languages, as the case may be, of the Contracting State, by the owner of the right of translation or with his authorization, any national of such Contracting State may obtain a non-exclusive license from the competent authority thereof to translate the work and publish the work so translated in any of the national languages in which it has not been published; provided that such national, in accordance with the procedure of the State concerned, establishes either that he has requested, and been denied, authorization by the proprietor of the right to make and publish

(1405)

the translation, or that, after due diligence on his part, he was unable to find the owner of the right. A license may also be granted on the same conditions if all previous editions of a translation in such language are out of print.

If the owner of the right of translation cannot be found, then the applicant for a license shall send copies of his application to the publisher whose name appears on the work and, if the nationality of the owner of the right of translation is known, to the diplomatic or consular representative of the State of which such owner is a national, or to the organization which may have been designated by the government of that State. The license shall not be granted before the expiration of a period of two months from the date of the dispatch of the copies of the application.

Due provision shall be made by domestic legislation to assure to the owner of the right of translation a compensation which is just and conforms to international standards, to assure payment and transmittal of such compensation, and to assure a correct translation of the work.

The original title and the name of the author of the work shall be printed on all copies of the published translation. The license shall be valid only for publication of the translation in the territory of the Contracting State where it has been applied for. Copies so published may be imported and sold in another Contracting State if one of the national languages of such other State is the same language as that into which the work has been so translated, and if the domestic law in such other State makes provision for such licenses and does not prohibit such importation and sale. Where the foregoing conditions do not exist, the importation and sale of such copies in a Contracting State shall be governed by its domestic law and its agreements. The license shall not be transferred by the licensee.

The license shall not be granted when the author has withdrawn from circulation all copies of the work.

Article VI

"Publication," as used in this Convention, means the reproduction in tangible form and the general distribution to the public of copies of a work from which it can be read or otherwise visually perceived.

Article VII

This Convention shall not apply to works or rights in works which, at the effective date of the Convention in a Contracting State where protection is claimed, are permanently in the public domain in the said Contracting State.

Article VIII

1. This Convention, which shall bear the date of September 6, 1952, shall be deposited with the Director-General of the United Nations Educational, Scientific and Cultural Organization and shall remain open for signature by all States for a period of 120 days after that date. It shall be subject to ratification or acceptance by the signatory States.

2. Any State which has not signed this Convention may accede thereto.

3. Ratification, acceptance or accession shall be effected by the deposit of an instrument to that effect with the Director-General of the United Nations Educational, Scientific and Cultural Organization.

Article IX

1. This Convention shall come into force three months after the deposit of twelve instruments of ratification, acceptance or accession, among which there shall be those of four States which are not members of the International Union for the Protection of Literary and Artistic Works.

2. Subsequently, this Convention shall come into force in respect of each State three months after that State has deposited its instrument of ratification, acceptance or accession.

Article X

1. Each State party to this Convention undertakes to adopt, in accordance with its Constitution, such measures as are necessary to ensure the application of this Convention.

2. It is understood, however, that at the time an instrument of ratification, acceptance or accession is deposited on behalf of any State, such State must be in a position under its domestic law to give effect to the terms of this Convention.

Article XI

1. An Intergovernmental Committee is hereby established with the following duties:

(a) to study the problems concerning the application and operation of this Convention;

(b) to make preparation for periodic revisions of this Convention;

(c) to study any other problems concerning the international protection of copyright, in co-operation with the various interested international organizations, such as the United Nations Educational, Scientific and Cultural Organization, the International Union for the Protection of Literary and Artistic Works and the Organization of American States;

(d) to inform the Contracting States as to its activities.

2. The Committee shall consist of the representatives of twelve Contracting States to be selected with due consideration to fair geographical representation and in conformity with the Resolution relating to this article, annexed to this Convention.

The Director-General of the United Nations Educational, Scientific and Cultural Organization, the Director of the Bureau of the International Union for the Protection of Literary and Artistic Works and the Secretary-General of the Organization of American States, or their representatives, may attend meetings of the Committee in an advisory capacity.

Article XII

The Intergovernmental Committee shall convene a conference for revision of this Convention whenever it deems necessary, or at the request of at least ten Contracting States, or of a majority of the Contracting States if there are less than twenty Contracting States.

Article XIII

Any Contracting State may, at the time of deposit of its instrument of ratification, acceptance or accession, or at any time thereafter, declare by notification addressed to the Director-General of the United Nations Educational, Scientific and Cultural Organization that this Convention shall apply to all or any of the countries or territories for the international relations of which it is responsible and this Convention shall thereupon apply to the countries or territories named in such notification after the expiration of the term of three months provided for in article IX. In the absence of such notification, this Convention shall not apply to any such country or territory.

Article XIV

1. Any Contracting State may denounce this Convention in its own name or on behalf of all or any of the countries or territories as to which a notification has been given under article XIII. The denunciation shall be made by notification addressed to the Director-General of the United Nations Educational, Scientific and Cultural Organization.

2. Such denunciation shall operate only in respect of the State or of the country or territory on whose behalf it was made and shall not take effect until twelve months after the date of receipt of the notification.

Article XV

A dispute between two or more Contracting States concerning the interpretation or application of this Convention, not settled by negotiation, shall, unless the States concerned agree on some other method of settlement, be brought before the International Court of Justice for determination by it.

Article XVI

1. This Convention shall be established in English, French and Spanish. The three texts shall be signed and shall be equally authoritative.

2. Official texts of this Convention shall be established in German, Italian and Portuguese.

Any Contracting State or group of Contracting States shall be entitled to have established by the Director-General of the United Nations Educational, Scientific and Cultural Organization other texts in the language of its choice by arrangement with the Director-General.

All such texts shall be annexed to the signed texts of this Convention.

Article XVII

1. This Convention shall not in any way affect the provisions of the Berne Convention for the Protection of Literary and Artistic Works or membership in the Union created by that Convention.

2. In application of the foregoing paragraph, a Declaration has been annexed to the present article. This Declaration is an integral part of this Convention for the States bound by the Berne Convention on January 1, 1951, or which

have or may become bound to it at a later date. The signature of this Convention by such States shall also constitute signature of the said Declaration, and ratification, acceptance or accession by such States shall include the Declaration as well as the Convention.

Article XVIII

This Convention shall not abrogate multilateral or bilateral copyright conventions or arrangements that are or may be in effect exclusively between two or more American Republics. In the event of any difference either between the provisions of such existing conventions or arrangements and the provisions of this Convention, or between the provisions of this Convention and those of any new convention or arrangement which may be formulated between two or more American Republics after this Convention comes into force, the convention or arrangement most recently formulated shall prevail between the parties thereto. Rights in works acquired in any Contracting State under existing conventions or arrangements before the date this Convention comes into force in such State shall not be affected.

Article XIX

This Convention shall not abrogate multilateral or bilateral conventions or arrangements in effect between two or more Contracting States. In the event of any difference between the provisions of such existing conventions or arrangements and the provisions of this Convention, the provisions of this Convention shall prevail. Rights in works acquired in any Contracting State under existing conventions or arrangements before the date on which this Convention comes into force in such State shall not be affected. Nothing in this article shall affect the provisions of article XVII and XVIII of this Convention.

Article XX

Reservations to this Convention shall not be permitted.

Article XXI

The Director-General of the United Nations Educational, Scientific and Cultural Organization shall send duly certified copies of this Convention to the States interested, to the Swiss Federal Council and to the Secretary-General of the United Nations for registration by him.

He shall also inform all interested States of the ratifications, acceptances and accessions which have been deposited, the date on which this Convention comes into force, the notifications under Article XIII of this Convention, and denunciations under Article XIV.

Appendix Declaration
relating to Article XVII

The States which are members of the International Union for the Protection of Literary and Artistic Works, and which are signatories to the Universal Copyright Convention.

Desiring to reinforce their mutual relations on the basis of the said Union and to avoid any conflict which might result from the co-existence of the Convention of Berne and the Universal Convention.

Have, by common agreement, accepted the terms of the following declaration:

(a) Works which, according to Berne Convention, have as their country of origin a country which has withdrawn from the International Union created by the said Convention, after January 1, 1951, shall not be protected by the Universal Copyright Convention in the countries of the Berne Union;

(b) The Universal Copyright Convention shall not be applicable to the relationships among countries of the Berne Union insofar as it relates to the protection of works having as their country of origin, within the meaning of the Berne Convention, a country of the International Union created by the said Convention.

Resolution Concerning Article XI

The Intergovernmental Copyright Conference

Having considered the problems relating to the Intergovernmental Committee provided for in Article XI of the Universal Copyright Convention.

resolves

1. The first members of the Committee shall be representatives of the following twelve States, each of those States designating one representative and an alternate: Argentine, Brazil, France, Germany, India, Italy, Japan, Mexico, Spain, Switzerland, United Kingdom, and United States of America.

2. The Committee shall be constituted as soon as the Convention comes into force in accordance with article XI of this Convention;

3. The Committee shall elect its Chairman and one Vice-Chairman. It shall establish its rules of procedure having regard to the following principles:

(a) the normal duration of the term of office of the representatives shall be six years; with one third retiring every two years;

(b) before the expiration of the term of office of any members, the Committee shall decide which States shall cease to be represented on it and which States shall be called upon to designate representatives; the representatives of those States which have not ratified, accepted or acceded shall be the first to retire;

(c) the different parts of the world shall be fairly represented;

and expresses the wish

that the United Nations Educational, Scientific, and Cultural Organization provide its Secretariat.

In faith whereof the undersigned, having deposited their respective full powers, have signed this Convention. Done at Geneva, this sixth day of September, 1952 in a single copy.

Protocol 1 annexed to the Universal Copyright Convention concerning the application of that Convention to the works of stateless persons and refugees

The States parties hereto, being also parties to the Universal Copyright Convention (hereinafter referred to as the "Convention") have accepted the following provisions:

1. Stateless persons and refugees who have their habitual residence in a State party to this Protocol shall, for the purposes of the Convention, be assimilated to the nationals of that State.

2. (a) This Protocol shall be signed and shall be subject to ratification or acceptance, or may be acceded to, as if the provisions of article VIII of the Convention applied hereto.

(b) This Protocol shall enter into force in respect of each State on the date of deposit of the instrument of ratification, acceptance or accession of the State concerned or on the date of entry into force of the Convention with respect to such State, whichever is the later.

In faith whereof the undersigned, being duly authorized thereto, have signed this Protocol.

Done at Geneva this sixth day of September, 1952, in the English, French and Spanish languages, the three texts being equally authoritative, in a single copy which shall be deposited with the Director-General of Unesco. The Director-General shall send certified copies to the signatory States, to the Swiss Federal Council and to the Secretary-General of the United Nations for registration.

Protocol 2 annexed to the Universal Copyright Convention, concerning the application of that Convention to the works of certain international organizations

The State parties hereto, being also parties to the Universal Copyright Convention (hereinafter referred to as the "Convention"),

Have accepted the following provisions:

1. (a) The protection provided for in article II (1) of the Convention shall apply to works published for the first time by the United Nations, by the Specialized Agencies in relationship therewith, or by the Organisation of American States:

(b) Similarly, article II (2) of the Convention shall apply to the said organisation or agencies.

2. (a) This Protocol shall be signed and shall be subject to ratification or acceptance, or may be acceded to, as if the provisions of article VIII of the Convention applied hereto.

(b) This Protocol shall enter into force for each State on the date of deposit of the instrument of ratification, acceptance or accession of the State concerned or on the date of entry into force of the Convention with respect to such State, whichever is the later.

In faith whereof the undersigned, being duly authorised thereto, have signed this Protocol.

Done at Geneva, this sixth day of September, 1952, in the English, French and Spanish languages, the three texts being equally authoritative, in a single copy which shall be deposited with the Director-General of the Unesco.

The Director-General shall send certificated copies to the signatory States, to the Swiss Federal Council, and to the Secretary-General of the United Nations for registration.

Protocol 3 annexed to the Universal Copyright Convention concerning the effective date of instruments of ratification or acceptance of or accession to that Convention

States parties hereto,

Recognizing that the application of the Universal Copyright Convention (hereinafter referred to as the "Convention") to States participating in all the international copyright systems already in force will contribute greatly to the value of the Convention;

Have agreed as follows:

1. Any State party hereto may, on depositing its instrument of ratification or acceptance of or accession to the Convention, notify the Director-General of the United Nations Educational, Scientific and Cultural Organization (hereinafter referred to as "Director-General") that that instrument shall not take effect for the purposes of Article IX of the Convention until any other State named in such notification shall have deposited its instrument.

2. The notification referred to in paragraph 1 above shall accompany the instrument to which it relates.

3. The Director-General shall inform all States signatory or which have then acceded to the Convention of any notifications received in accordance with this Protocol.

4. This Protocol shall bear the same date and shall remain open for signature for the same period as the Convention.

5. It shall be subject to ratification or acceptance by the signatory States. Any state which has not signed this Protocol may accede thereto.

6. (a) Ratification or acceptance or accession shall be effected by the deposit of an instrument to that effect with the Director-General.

(b) This Protocol shall enter into force on the date of deposit of not less than four instruments of ratification or acceptance or accession. The Director-General shall inform all interested States of this date. Instruments deposited after such date shall take effect on the date of their deposit.

In faith whereof the undersigned, being duly authorised thereto, have signed this Protocol.

Done at Geneva, the sixth day of September 1952, in the English, French and the Spanish languages, the three texts being equally authoritative, in a single copy which shall be annexed to the original copy of the Convention. The Director-General shall send certified copies to the signatory States to the Swiss Federal Council, and to the Secretary-General of United Nations for registration.

PARTICULAR PROCLAMATIONS, TREATIES AND CONVENTIONS ESTABLISHING COPYRIGHT RELATIONS BETWEEN THE UNITED STATES OF AMERICA AND OTHER COUNTRIES

Proclamations by the President of the United States extending copyright protection, upon compliance with the provisions of the United States copyright law, to the works of foreign authors prior to July 1, 1909 were issued pursuant to § 13 of Act Mar. 3, 1891, c. 565, 26 Stat. 1106, and those issued subsequent to July 1, 1909 were issued under the provisions of §§ 1 (e) and 8 (b) of Act Mar. 4, 1909, c. 320, 35 Stat. 1075, and as later amended. Section 8 (b) was amended by Act Dec. 18, 1919, c. 10, 41 Stat. 368, and Act Sept. 25, 1941, c. 421, 55 Stat. 732. Those sections of Act Mar. 4, 1909, as amended, became subsec. (b) of this section and § 1 (e) of this title when it was codified and enacted into positive law by Act July 30, 1947, c. 391, 61 Stat. 652. A number of the proclamations were preceded or accompanied by exchanges of diplomatic notes which served as the basis for their issuance.

The following material constitutes a selective listing of certain of these proclamations, treaties and conventions which are of current interest. The list is organized as follows: the first column contains the names of the countries; the second column contains a symbol which indicates the nature of the document establishing copyright relations; the third column, the date of the document; the fourth column, the effective date of copyright relations between the United States and the country named; and the fifth, a citation to the United States Statutes at Large, Federal Register, United States Treaties and Other International Agreements, or Treaties and Other International Acts Series in which the document can be found. Numerical figures in parentheses are references to footnotes which follow the list.

Proclamations by the President of the United States extending copyright protection, upon compliance with the provisions of the United States copyright law, to the works of foreign authors prior to July 1, 1909 were issued pursuant to § 13 of the Act of March 3, 1891 (26 Stat. 1106) and those issued subsequent to July 1, 1909 were under the provisions of §§ 1(e) and 8(b) of the Act of March 4, 1909 (35 Stat. 1075) and as later amended. Section 8(b) was amended by the Act of December 18, 1919 (41 Stat. 368) and the Act of September 25, 1941 (55 Stat. 732). Section 1(e) and section 8(b), as amended, later became subsec. (b) of this section and § 1(e) of this title.

The proclamations issued under the Acts of 1891, 1919 and 1941 are not listed. The proclamations issued under the Acts of 1919 and 1941 were for the purpose of extending the period for compliance with the conditions and formalities prescribed by the copyright law with respect to certain works in the case of a number of countries because of the disruption or suspension of facilities essential for such compliance during World War I and World War II.

Mention of the Mexico City Convention of 1902 is made only in the case of El Salvador because all of the other parties thereto subsequently became parties to the Buenos Aires Convention of 1910, which in practical effect replaced the earlier 1902 convention as between parties to the later convention. Each of the countries which are parties to the Universal Copyright Convention, and the protocols annexed thereto, are also included, the effective dates being given with reference to the Convention only.

(1409)

Key to Symbols

Identification of symbols used in the table and footnotes.

Proclamations

·P   Proclamation issued pursuant to section 8(b) of the Act of March 4, 1909, and as amended, or subsec. (b) of this section.

Pm   Proclamation including mechanical reproduction rights for music under section 1(e) of the United States copyright law.

Treaties and Conventions

BAC   Buenos Aires Convention. Convention of Literary and Artistic Copyrights signed at the Fourth International Conference of American States at Buenos Aires, August 11, 1910.

MCC   Mexico City Convention. Convention on Literary and Artistic Copyrights signed at the Second International Conference of American States at Mexico City, January 27, 1902.

UCC   Universal Copyright Convention. Convention and protocols dated at Geneva, September 6, 1952.

Cm   Bilateral Convention including provisions covering mechanical reproduction rights for music.

T   Treaty relating in part to copyright.

References

Fed. Reg. Federal Register.

Stat.   United States Statutes at Large.

TIAS   Treaties and Other International Acts Series. (Pamphlet series published by the Department of State).

TS   Treaty Series. (Pamphlet series published by the Department of State).

UST   United States Treaties and other International Agreements.

(1410)

PARTICULAR PROCLAMATIONS, TREATIES AND CONVENTIONS ESTABLISHING COPY-
RIGHT RELATIONS BETWEEN THE UNITED STATES OF AMERICA AND OTHER
COUNTRIES

Country	Document	Date of document	Date effective	Reference
Andorra	UCC	Sept. 6, 1952	Sept. 16, 1955	6 UST 2731.
Argentina[1]	Pm	Aug. 23, 1934	Aug. 23, 1934	49 Stat. 3413.
	BAC	Aug. 11, 1910	Apr. 19, 1950	38 Stat. 1785.
	UCC	Sept. 6, 1952	Feb. 13, 1958	6 UST 2731.
Australia[2]	Pm	Apr. 3, 1918	Mar. 15, 1918	40 Stat. 1764.
Austria[3]	P	Apr. 9, 1910	July 1, 1909	36 Stat. 2685.
	Pm	Mar. 11, 1925	Aug. 1, 1920	44 Stat. 2571.
	UCC	Sept. 6, 1952	July 2, 1957	6 UST 2731.
Belgium	P	Apr. 9, 1910	July 1, 1909	36 Stat. 2685.
	Pm	June 14, 1911	.....do.....	37 Stat. 1688.
Bolivia	BAC	Aug. 11, 1910	May 15, 1914	38 Stat. 1785.
Brazil	BAC	.....do.....	Aug. 31, 1915	Do.
	Pm	Apr. 2, 1957	Apr. 2, 1957	TIAS 3793.
Cambodia	UCC	Sept. 6, 1952	Sept. 16, 1955	6 UST 2731.
Canada[2][4]	Pm	Dec. 27, 1923	Jan. 1, 1924	43 Stat. 1932.
Chile[1][5]	P	Apr. 9, 1910	July 1, 1909	36 Stat. 2685.
	Pm	Nov. 18, 1925	July 1, 1925	44 Stat. 2590.
	BAC	Aug. 11, 1910	June 14, 1955	38 Stat. 1785.
	UCC	Sept. 6, 1952	Sept. 16, 1955	6 UST 2731.
China[6]	T	Oct. 8, 1903	Jan. 13, 1904	33 Stat. 2208.
	T	Nov. 4, 1946	Nov. 30, 1948	63 Stat. 1299.
Colombia	BAC	Aug. 11, 1910	Dec. 23, 1936	38 Stat. 1785.
Costa Rica	P	Apr. 9, 1910	July 1, 1909	36 Stat. 2685.
	BAC	Aug. 11, 1910	Nov. 30, 1916	38 Stat. 1785.
	UCC	Sept. 6, 1952	Sept. 16, 1955	6 UST 2731.
Cuba[1]	P	Apr. 9, 1910	July 1, 1909	36 Stat. 2685.
	Pm	Nov. 27, 1911	May 29, 1911	37 Stat. 1721.
	UCC	Sept. 6, 1952	June 18, 1957	6 UST 2731.
Czechoslovakia	Pm	Apr. 9, 1910	Mar. 1, 1927	45 Stat. 2906.
Denmark	P	Apr. 9, 1910	July 1, 1909	36 Stat. 2685.
	Pm	Dec. 9, 1920	Dec. 9, 1920	41 Stat. 1810.
Dominican Republic	BAC	Aug. 11, 1910	Oct. 31, 1912	38 Stat. 1785.
Ecuador[1]	BAC	.....do.....	Aug. 31, 1914	Do.
	UCC	Sept. 6, 1952	June 5, 1957	6 UST 2731.
Eire (See Ireland)				
El Salvador	MCC	Jan. 27, 1902	June 30, 1908	35 Stat. 1934.
Finland	Pm	Dec. 15, 1928	Jan. 1, 1929	45 Stat. 2980.
France	P	Apr. 9, 1910	July 1, 1909	36 Stat. 2885.
	Pm	May 24, 1918	May 24, 1918	40 Stat. 1784.
	UCC	Sept. 6, 1952	Jan. 14, 1956	6 UST 2731.
Germany[3]	P	Apr. 9, 1910	July 1, 1909	36 Stat. 2685.
	Pm	Dec. 8, 1910	Dec. 8, 1910	36 Stat. 2761.
German, (Federal Republic)	UCC	Sept. 6, 1952	Sept. 16, 1955	6 UST 2731.
Great Britain (See United Kingdom)				
Greece	Pm	Feb. 23, 1932	Mar. 1, 1932	47 Stat. 2502.
Guatemala	BAC	Aug. 11, 1910	Mar. 28, 1913	38 Stat. 1785.
Haiti	BAC	.....do.....	Nov. 27, 1919	Do.
	UCC	Sept. 6, 1952	Sept. 16, 1955	6 UST 2731.
Holy See	UCC	.....do.....	Oct. 5, 1955	Do.
Honduras	BAC	Aug. 11, 1910	Apr. 27, 1914	38 Stat. 1785.
Hungary[3][7][8][9]	Cm	Jan. 30, 1912	Oct. 16, 1912	37 Stat. 1631.
	T	Feb. 10, 1947	Sept. 15, 1947	61 Stat. 2065.
Iceland[1][5][10]	UCC	Sept. 6, 1952	Dec. 18, 1956	6 UST 2731.
India[11]	Pm	Oct. 21, 1954	Aug. 15, 1947	19 Fed. Reg. 6967.
	UCC	Sept. 6, 1952	Jan. 21, 1958	6 UST 2731.
Ireland[12]	Pm	Sept. 28, 1929	Oct. 1, 1929	46 Stat. 3005.
	UCC	Sept. 6, 1952	Jan. 20, 1959	6 UST 2731.
Israel	Pm	May 4, 1950	May 15, 1948	64 Stat. A402.
	UCC	Sept. 6, 1952	Sept. 16, 1955	6 UST 2731.

(1411)

Country	Document	Date of document	Date effective	Reference
Italy [9][13][14]	P	Apr. 9, 1910	July 1, 1909	36 Stat. 2685.
	Pm	May 1, 1915	May 1, 1915	39 Stat. 1725.
	T	Feb. 10, 1947	Sept. 15, 1947	61 Stat. 1245.
	UCC	Sept. 6, 1952	Jan. 24, 1957	6 UST 2731.
Japan	UCC	.....do....	Apr. 28, 1956	Do.
Laos	UCC	.....do....	Sept. 16, 1955	Do.
Liberia [1]	UCC	.....do....	July 27, 1956	Do.
Liechtenstein [1]	UCC	.....do....	Jan. 22, 1959	Do.
Luxembourg	P	June 29, 1910	June 29, 1910	36 Stat. 2716.
	Pm	June 14, 1911	.....do.....	37 Stat. 1689.
	UCC	Sept. 6, 1952	Oct. 15, 1955	6 UST 2731.
Mexico [1][5]	P	Apr. 9, 1910	July 1, 1909	36 Stat. 2685.
	UCC	Sept. 6, 1952	May 12, 1957	6 UST 2731.
Monaco [1]	Pm	Oct. 15, 1952	Oct. 15, 1952	67 Stat. C16.
	UCC	Sept. 6, 1952	Sept. 16, 1955	6 UST 2731.
Netherlands and Possessions [15]	P	Apr. 9, 1910	July 1, 1909	36 Stat. 2685.
	Pm	Feb. 26, 1923	Oct. 2, 1922	42 Stat. 2297.
New Zealand [2]	Pm	Feb. 9, 1917	Dec. 1, 1916	39 Stat. 1815.
Nicaragua	BAC	Aug. 11, 1910	Dec. 15, 1913	38 Stat. 1785.
Norway	P	Apr. 9, 1910	July 1, 1909	36 Stat. 2685.
	Pm	June 14, 1911	Sept. 9, 1910	37 Stat. 1687.
Pakistan	UCC	Sept. 6, 1952	Sept. 16, 1955	6 UST 2731.
Panama	BAC	Aug. 11, 1910	Nov. 25, 1913	38 Stat. 1785.
Paraguay	BAC	.....do.....	Sept. 20, 1917	Do.
Peru	BAC	.....do.....	Apr. 30, 1920	Do.
Philippines [16]	Pm	Oct. 21, 1948	Oct. 21, 1948	62 Stat. 1568.
	UCC	Sept. 6, 1952	....	6 UST 2731.
Poland	Pm	Feb. 14, 1927	Feb. 16, 1927	44 Stat. 2634.
Portugal	P	Apr. 9, 1910	July 1, 1909	36 Stat. 2685.
	UCC	Sept. 6, 1952	Dec. 25, 1956	6 UST 2731.
Rumania [9][17]	Pm	May 14, 1928	May 14, 1928	45 Stat. 2949.
	T	Feb. 10, 1947	Sept. 15, 1947	61 Stat. 1757.
Salvador, El (See El Salvador).				
Siam (See Thailand)				
Spain [1][5]	P	Apr. 9, 1910	July 1, 1909	36 Stat. 2685.
	Pm	Oct. 10, 1934	Oct. 10, 1934	49 Stat. 3420.
	UCC	Sept. 6, 1952	Sept. 16, 1955	6 UST 2731.
Sweden	P	May 26, 1911	June 1, 1911	37 Stat. 1682.
	Pm	Feb. 27, 1920	Feb. 1, 1920	41 Stat. 1787.
Switzerland [1]	P	Apr. 9, 1910	July 1, 1909	36 Stat. 2685.
	Pm	Nov. 22, 1924	July 1, 1923	43 Stat. 1976.
	UCC	Sept. 6, 1952	Mar. 30, 1956	6 UST 2731.
Thailand (Siam) [18]	T	Nov. 13, 1937	Oct. 1, 1938	53 Stat. 1731.
Tunisia	P	Oct. 4, 1912	Oct. 4, 1912	37 Stat. 1765.
Union of South Africa [2]	Pm	June 26, 1924	July 1, 1924	43 Stat. 1957.
United Kingdom and Possessions [19]	P	Apr. 9, 1910	July 1, 1909	36 Stat. 2685.
United Kingdom and the British Dominions, Colonies and Possessions with exception of Canada, Australia, New Zealand, South Africa and Newfoundland [19]	Pm	Jan. 1, 1915	Jan. 1, 1915	38 Stat. 2044.
United Kingdom	UCC	Sept. 6, 1952	Sept. 27, 1957	6 UST 2731.
Uruguay	BAC	Aug. 11, 1910	Dec. 17, 1919	38 Stat. 1785.
Vatican City (See Holy See)				

[1] Not a party to Protocol 3 annexed to the Universal Copyright Convention.

[2] The proclamation of Apr. 9, 1910, listed under the United Kingdom, applies to "Great Britain and the British possessions."

[3] The United States entered into treaties restoring friendly relations with Austria, Germany, and Hungary at Vienna on Aug. 24, 1921 (42 Stat. 1946; TS 659); at Berlin on Aug. 25, 1921 (42 Stat. 1939; TS 658) and at Budapest on Aug. 29, 1921 (42 Stat. 1951; TS 610), respectively. By virtue of these treaties the United States became entitled to the benefits of the provisions relative to copyright protection in the treaties of peace signed by Austria, Germany, and Hungary at Saint-Germain-en-Laye on Sept. 10, 1919, at Versailles on June 28, 1919, and at Trianon on June 4, 1920, respectively. (See also footnote 7.)

[4] The proclamation of Dec. 27, 1923, is considered as applying to Newfoundland at the present time.

[5] Not a party to Protocol 1 annexed to the Universal Copyright Convention.

[6] The Treaty of Friendship, Commerce and Navigation (Art. IX) together with the Protocol (par. 5) signed at Nanking Nov. 4, 1946, and the reservation and understandings in the ratification by the United States (TIAS 1871) govern present copyright relations between the United States and China. Although Article XXIX of this Treaty lists the earlier Treaty as to Commercial Relations signed at Shanghai Oct. 8, 1903 (33 Stat. 2208, TS 430), as superseded by the 1946 Treaty, the ratification by the United States provides in part that the 1946 Treaty is subject to the following reservation and understandings: "The Government of the United States of America does not accept section 5(c) of the Protocol relating to protection against translations of literary and artistic works, and with the understanding that United States interests in this respect will be interpreted in accordance with the provisions of the Treaty as to Commercial Relations signed at Shanghai, Oct. 8, 1903, until further negotiations and agreement concerning translations are forthcoming."

[7] Copyright Convention signed at Budapest Jan. 30, 1912 (TS 571). This Convention was continued in force following World War I by notice given by the United States on May 27, 1922, to Hungary in pursuance of Article 224 of the Treaty of Trianon concluded on June 4, 1920 (III Treaties [Redmond] 3539), to the benefits of which the United States became entitled by the Treaty of Aug. 29, 1921, establishing friendly relations between the United States and Hungary (42 Stat. 1951; TS 660). The Convention of 1912 was kept in force or revised following World War II by notice given on Mar. 9, 1948, by the United States to Hungary pursuant to Article 10 of the Treaty of Peace with Hungary (61 Stat. 2065; Department of State Bulletin Mar. 21, 1948, p. 382).

[8] Treaty of Peace with Hungary (Annex IV A) dated at Paris Feb. 10, 1947 (TIAS 1651).

[9] Except with respect to rights of third parties, the provisions relating to protection of copyright in the annexes of the Treaties of Peace with Hungary, Italy, and Rumania dated at Paris Feb. 10, 1947, are bilateral in character. For example, the provisions of Annex IV A of the Treaty of Peace with Hungary relate, in general, to copyright relations between Hungary, on the one part, and each of the other ratifying or adhering States, on the other part. Those provisions do not pertain to copyright relations between those other States, except for third party rights. Annex IV of the Treaty of Peace with Bulgaria dated at Paris Feb. 10, 1947 (61 Stat. 1915; TIAS 1650), contains similar provisions; however, there are no general copyright relations between the United States and Bulgaria.

[10] Not a party to Protocol 2 annexed to the Universal Copyright Convention.

[11] The proclamation of Oct. 21, 1954, affirms the existence of copyright relations with India

after Aug. 15, 1947 (the effective date of the Indian Independence Act), as before that date (see footnotes 2 and 19).

[12] The Department of State has determined that the entry into force on Apr. 18, 1949, of the Republic of Ireland Act had no effect upon the proclamation of Sept. 28, 1929, regarding the Irish Free State (Eire). Copyright relations with Ireland are therefore governed by that proclamation.

[13] The exchange of notes between the United States and Italy, on the basis of which the proclamations of Oct. 31, 1892 (omitted from list) and May 1, 1915, were issued, was the subject of a note delivered on Mar. 12, 1948, to the Italian Foreign Office by the American Embassy at Rome with respect to pre-war bilateral treaties and other international agreements which the United States desired to keep in force or revive pursuant to Article 44 of the Treaty of Peace with Italy. The note stated in part "that the Government of the United States of America wishes to include the reciprocal copyright arrangement between the United States and Italy effected pursuant to the exchange of notes signed at Washington Oct. 28, 1892, and the exchange of notes signed at Washington Sept. 2, 1914, Feb. 12, Mar. 4 and Mar. 11, 1915, among the pre-war bilateral treaties and other international agreements with Italy which the United States desires to keep in force or revive. Accordingly, it is understood that the aforementioned arrangement will continue in force and that the Government of each country will extend to the nationals of the other country treatment as favorable with respect to copyright as was contemplated at the time the arrangement was entered into by the two countries." (Department of State Bulletin, Apr. 4, 1948, p. 455.)

[14] Treaty of Peace with Italy (Annex XV A) dated at Paris Feb. 10, 1947 (TIAS 1648).

[15] The Department of State has made no announcement as to the applicability of these proclamations to Indonesia since it acquired its new status.

[16] With regard to the Universal Copyright Convention, UNESCO has advised the United States Government that a communication dated Nov. 14, 1955 was received from the Philippine Minister in Paris stating that the Philippine President had directed the withdrawal of the instrument of accession prior to Nov. 19, 1955, the date on which the Convention would become effective in respect of the Philippines. The Department of State has made no announcement as to the legal effect of this communication.

[17] In a note delivered Feb. 26, 1948 to the Rumanian Minister for Foreign Affairs by the American Minister at Bucharest with respect to pre-war bilateral treaties and other international agreements which the United States desired to keep in force or revive pursuant to Article 10 of the Treaty of Peace with Rumania, dated at Paris, Feb. 10, 1947 (TIAS 1649), the following statement was made regarding the proclamation of May 14, 1928, and the exchange of notes on which it is based. "It shall be understood that the reciprocal copyright arrangement between the United States and Rumania effected pursu-

ant to the exchange of notes signed at Bucharest May 13 and Oct. 13, 1928, and at Washington May 12 and 19, 1928, and the proclamation issued May 14, 1928, by the President of the United States of America will continue in force." (Department of State Bulletin, Mar. 14, 1948, p. 356.)

[18] Treaty of friendship, commerce and navigation, protocol and exchanges of notes, signed at Bangkok Nov. 13, 1937 (Article 9 of the Treaty) [TS 940]. This treaty replaces the treaty of friendship, commerce and navigation between the United States and Siam signed at Washington Dec. 16, 1920 (TS 655), Article XII of which contains provisions relating to copyright protection.

[19] The proclamation of Apr. 9, 1910, applied when issued to the areas now within the boundaries of Burma and Ceylon, India and Pakistan. Since their change of status, separate copyright relations have been established with India and Pakistan (q.v.). No new copyright relations have to date been established with Burma or Ceylon.

Current Proclamations

Proclamation No. 3353 of June 15, 1960, 25 Fed. Reg. 5373 extended copyright protection to citizens of Austria, see 1960 F.C.A. Public Laws and Administrative Material, page A30.

NOTES TO DECISIONS
ANALYSIS

1. In general.
2. Evidence.
3. Renewals.
4. Biographies—Letters.
5. Composite works.
6. — Musical compositions.
7. Translations and interpretations.
8. Compilers.
9. Employees—Works done for hire.
10. — Plays or dramas.
11. Employers—Corporations—Partnerships.
12. States—Works prepared under government contracts.
13. — Judicial decisions and reports.
14. Publishers and printers.
15. —Foreign author or copyright.
16. Assignees and trustees.
17. — Proprietors.
18. — Licensees.
19. — Person in whose name copyright secured.
20. Paintings and photographs.
21. — Assignment or sale.
22. — Work done for hire.
23. — Rights in subject.
24. Aliens.
25. — Resident aliens.
26. Reciprocal agreements.

1. In general.

Married woman was entitled to copyright protection, as against defendant's contention that her husband was the owner of the copyrighted book by virtue of his marital rights. Belford, Clarke & Co. v. Scribner, 144 US 488, 36 LEd 514, 12 SCR 734, aff'g (CC-Ill), 50 Fed 473.

To constitute one an author, he must, by his own intellectual labor applied to materials of his composition, produce an arrangement or compilation new in itself. Atwill v. Ferrett, (CC-NY), FedCas 640, 2 Blatchf 39.

Where the author of a book continues to be the owner thereof, he is entitled to copyright. Lawrence v. Dana, (CC-Mass), FedCas 8,136, 4 Cliff 1.

Authors, proprietors, and lawful assigns only are entitled to copyright. Yuengling v. Schile, (CC-NY), 12 Fed 97.

Person doing business under a conventional or fictitious firm name may secure a copyright. Scribner v. Henry G. Allen Co., (CC-NY), 49 Fed 854; Werckmeister v. Springer Lithographing Co., (CC-NY), 63 Fed 808.

Although a bill fails to allege authorship, except by implication arising from the words "written or composed," it is sufficient against demurrer. Henderson v. Tompkins, (CC-Mass), 60 Fed 758.

Ownership of an unpublished composition presumptively includes the privilege of publication and of securing statutory copyright. Gerlach-Barklow Co. v. Morris & Bendien, Inc., (CCA 2), 23 F(2d) 159.

"Authorship" presumptively connotes "originality." Remick Music Corp. v. Interstate Hotel Co., (DC-Neb), 58 FSupp 523, 63 USPQ 327. Aff'd 157 F(2d) 744, 71 USPQ 138.

No one has legal right to exclusive use of historical facts in public domain. Funkhouser v. Loew's, Inc., (DC-Mo), 108 FSupp 476, 96 USPQ 115. Aff'd 208 F(2d) 185, 99 USPQ 448.

Copyright is a right which is available only to the author or the proprietor of a literary property. Its purpose is to secure to such author or proprietor the exclusive right to that property. McClintic v. Sheldon, 182 Misc 32, 43 NYS(2d) 695, 59 USPQ 41.

2. Evidence.

Only slight evidence is necessary to make prima facie proof of citizenship and residence. Patterson v. J. S. Ogilvie Pub. Co., (CC-NY), 119 Fed 451.

Certificate of librarian and other evidence was sufficient to warrant conclusion that complainant was a "citizen or resident" of the United States when he applied for copyright. Patterson v. J. S. Ogilvie Pub. Co., (CC-NY), 119 Fed 451.

To prove coauthorship of song nearly 30 years before, alleged coauthor must prove case by clear and satisfactory evidence; evidence should be scrutinized with great care and perhaps even with suspicion. Edward B. Marks Music Corp. v. Wonnell, (DC-NY), 61 FSupp 722, 65 USPQ 456.

Administrator and widow make out prima facie case of title by producing certificate of copyright registration showing that decedent was the author. Edward B. Marks Music Corp. v. Wonnell, (DC-NY), 61 FSupp 722, 65 USPQ 456.

3. Renewals.

This section is applicable primarily to original copyrights, wherein the author and proprietor stand on equal footing, and does not give a proprietor the same right as the author to renewal. White-Smith Music Pub. Co. v. Goff, (CC-RI), 180 Fed 256. Aff'd 187 Fed 247.

Proprietor in the sense that he is the assignee of the author is not entitled to apply for renewal of copyright. White-Smith Music Pub. Co. v. Goff, (CCA 1), 187 Fed 247, aff'g 180 Fed 256.

4. Biographies—Letters.

Where the events of a person's life were given to a writer, to enable him to write a biography of such person, the person giving the facts is not the author of the biography and is therefore not entitled to a copyright. De Witt v. Brooks, (CC-NY), FedCas 3,851.

Person to whom letter was addressed was not entitled to copyright. Folsom v. Marsh, (DC-Mass), FedCas 4,901, 2 Story 100.

The validity of a copyright on a biography does not depend on whether or not the author of the work was designated by the subject as his special biographer. Gilmore v. Anderson, (CC-NY), 38 Fed 846.

5. Composite works.

A person may claim a copyright on his part of a production, although others also contributed to the work. Schuberth v. Shaw, (CC-Pa), FedCas 12,482.

To entitle one to copyright it is unnecessary that he be the sole creator of the work for which protection is claimed. Schuberth v. Shaw, (CC-Pa), FedCas 12,482.

Consent of coauthor to take out copyright in name of one does not destroy his interest therein, although the legal title vests in person taking out the copyright. Maurel v. Smith, (CCA 2), 271 Fed 211, aff'g 220 Fed 195.

In absence of existing agreement to contrary, co-owner of copyright has right to give permission to third party to publish copyrighted book. Meredith v. Smith, (CCA 9), 145 F(2d) 620, 63 USPQ 216.

A person cannot assert his rights as co-owner of a copyright, against the other person holding an interest in the copyright, when such action is a violation of a contract between them. Gould v. Banks & Gould, 8 Wend(NY) 562, 24 Am Dec 90.

It is not necessary, to establish property rights in intellectual or artistic productions, that entire ultimate product should be work of single creator; such rights may be acquired by one who perfects an original work or substantially adds to it in some manner. Waring v. WDAS Broadcasting Station, Inc., 327 Pa 433, 194 Atl 631, 35 USPQ 272.

6. — Musical compositions.

A person may be the author of a musical composition although there are short parts of it that are similar to a composition previously published, when these parts are not continuous and are not extended. Blume v. Spear, (CC-NY), 30 Fed 629.

Canadian soldier composed the music for a popular ballad, and a United States citizen wrote the words. There was a joint authorship.

G. Ricordi & Co., Inc. v. Columbia Graphophone Co., (DC-NY), 258 Fed 72.

Where author of lyrics sends them to composer, either directly or through producer or publisher, to have composer write music for lyrics, so that the two are united into one composition, author and composer are coauthors and statutory copyright of composition is owned jointly; same is true if composer submits music to lyric writer; coauthor copyrighting composition in own name is constructive trustee for other coauthor; copyright protects both words and music. Edward B. Marks Music Corp. v. Jerry Vogel Music Co., Inc., (DC-NY), 42 FSupp 859, 52 USPQ 219.

Copyright by one coauthor of song in own name was copyright on joint work which he held with a trust for benefit of other coauthor. Edward B. Marks Music Corp. v. Wonnell, (DC-NY), 61 FSupp 722, 65 USPQ 456.

Fact that song was copyrighted in 1915, but that party made no claim of coauthorship until 1943, is not laches since song had no vogue until it came to life in 1942; claims made after so many years may well be frowned on and discredited, but delay alone in asserting claim is seldom bar; that which converts passage of time into laches is prejudice to party; only prejudice is difficulty in obtaining witnesses after so long a time. Edward B. Marks Music Corp. v. Wonnell, (DC-NY), 61 FSupp 722, 65 USPQ 456.

On original copy of song on file in copyright office, names of T and S appear on inside page, below title and above music, but on outside cover and 1910 certificate of copyright T claimed sole authorship; S worked for T from prior to 1910 to 1925; S was given credit for coauthorship of other songs; during T's life, S never asserted formal claim of coauthorship; from 1910 to 1938, T or assignee published nine editions in all of which T was indicated as sole author; in 1937, T renewed copyright as sole author; S was not coauthor. Forster Music Publishers Inc. v. Jerry Vogel Music Co., Inc., (DC-NY), 62 USPQ 142. Aff'd 147 F(2d) 614, 64 USPQ 417.

Action against American Society of Composers and Publishers and five composer members to determine title to public performance rights in three songs composed by members, but copyrighted by plaintiff, is not res judicata as against other American Society of Composers and Publishers composers, who composed other songs copyrighted by plaintiff, but who are not parties to suit. Broadcast Music, Inc. v. Taylor, (Misc), 55 NYS(2d) 94.

7. Translations and interpretations.

The author of a translation of a play, copyrighted with the permission of the holder of the copyright of the original play, is entitled to the protection of the Copyright Act with respect to such translation, the same as if it had been an original story. Shook v. Rankin, (CC-Ill), FedCas 12,804, 6 Biss 477.

Translations or other versions of works in public domain are regarded as new works subject to copyright. Toksvig v. Bruce Pub. Co., (CA 7), 181 F(2d) 664, 85 USPQ 339.

Trust upon translator's copyright will not be implied in favor of author. Rolland v. Henry Holt & Co., Inc., (DC-NY), 152 FSupp 167, 113 USPQ 253.

Statute does not recognize any right of a performing artist in his interpretative rendition of a musical composition or in the acting of a play composed by another. Waring v. WDAS Broadcasting Station, Inc., 327 Pa 433, 194 Atl 631, 35 USPQ 272.

8. Compilers.

A compiler is an "author" within the meaning of the Constitution and copyright laws. Bullinger v. Mackey, (CC-NY), FedCas 2,127, 15 Blatchf 550.

A person compiling the statutes of a state and annotating, has the right to obtain a copyright on the volumes, as the author. Howell v. Miller, (CCA 6), 91 Fed 129.

A person who obtains the facts and puts them together in a pamphlet showing the different size piston rings for different makes of motor vehicles is the author of it. No-Leak-O Piston Ring Co. v. Norris, (CCA 4), 277 Fed 951, aff'g 271 Fed 536.

One compiling, editing, and publishing catalogue for another advertising the other's products is entitled to copyright same although there is no contract provision therefor. R. R. Donnelley & Sons Co. v. Haber, (DC-NY), 43 FSupp 456, 52 USPQ 445.

Property right exists with respect to combination of ideas evolved into radio program, as distinguished from rights to particular scripts. Cole v. Phillips H. Lord, Inc., 262 App Div 116, 28 NYS(2d) 404, 50 USPQ 490.

9. Employees—Works done for hire.

Copyright taken out by author will inure to benefit of publisher if contract provides that publisher is to have all rights of copyright. Paige v. Banks, 80 US(13 Wall) 608, 20 LEd 709; aff'g (CC-NY), FedCas 10,671, 7 Blatchf 152.

A person who is employed to write a book, is the author of such book when his name appears on the title page, although suggestions may have been offered by his employer. Pierpont v. Fowle, (CC-Mass), FedCas 11,152, 2 Woodb&M 23.

An employee hired to compile, prepare, and revise materials may not claim copyright therein, for the products of his labors become the property of his employer. Colliery Engineer Co. v. United Correspondence Schools Co., (CC-NY), 94 Fed 152.

"Author" includes employer in works for hire. National Cloak & Suit Co. v. Kaufman, (CC-Pa), 189 Fed 215.

Under the statute no power exists in an agent to copyright anything. Societe Des Films Menchen v. Vitagraph Co., (CCA 2), 251 Fed 258.

Where employee secures a copyright on a treatise relating to the use of a product of his employer's business, the employee holds the copyright in trust for the employer. U. S. Ozone Co. v. U. S. Ozone Co., (CCA 7), 62 F(2d) 881, 16 USPQ 233.

M employed S to put advertising on radio and S employed B to "build" program and direct it; B concocted jingle for theme song to old music and it was used continuously without protest on part of B; case falls within rule that where employee creates something as part of duties, the thing created is property of employer and copyright belongs to S in trust for M. Brown v. Molle Co., (DC-NY), 20 FSupp 135, 35 USPQ 183.

Where radio program is written and developed by employee during course of employment for employer radio station, using employer's radio facilities, without any special agreement as to ownership, ownership vests in employer. Storer Broadcasting Co. v. Jack the Bellboy, Inc., (DC-Mich), 107 FSupp 988, 95 USPQ 11.

If author labors for hire, what he produces belongs to his employer. Tobani v. Carl Fischer, (DC-NY), 36 USPQ 97. Mf'd 98 F(2d) 57, 38 USPQ 198.

10. —Plays or dramas.

Author who wrote a play while employed as an actor and received half of the profits therefrom as compensation for his work did not part with right to obtain copyright upon the play. Boucicault v. Fox, (CC-NY), FedCas 1,691, 5 Blatchf 87.

Copyright on a drama was properly taken out by its author, as against contention that author's employer had the right thereto. Roberts v. Myers, (CC-Mass), FedCas 11,906, Brunner ColCas 698.

11. Employers—Corporations—Partnerships.

The former rule was that one who had not invented or designed the product upon which he sought to obtain copyright, but had employed others to do so, was not entitled to a copyright. Binns v. Woodruff, (CC-Pa), FedCas 1,424, 4 WashCC 48.

A corporation can secure a copyright. Mutual Advertising Co. v. Refo, (CC-SC), 76 Fed 961.

It is not necessary for a corporation to show that it is the author of a book in order to assert its rights under a copyright, but it is sufficient to show that the work is the result of the intellectual labor of the editors and compilers employed by it. Edward Thompson Co. v. American Law Book Co., (CC-NY), 119 Fed 217.

Partnership may obtain copyright by firm name, even though such name indicates a corporation. Campbell v. Wireback, (CCA 4), 269 Fed 372, 17 ALR 743, aff'g 261 Fed 391.

Where the owner of all but five shares of stock of a publishing company contracted for the writing of a book, the stockholder and the author were the "proprietors," and a copyright taken out in the name of the corporation was void, there being no assignment, and no elements of estoppel present as against defendant in an infringement suit. Public Ledger Co. v. Post Printing & Publishing Co., (CCA 8), 294 Fed 430.

Corporation may be "proprietor" within meaning of this section. Peter Pan Fabrics, Inc. v. Acadia Co., Inc., (DC-NY), 173 FSupp 292, 121 USPQ 81. Aff'd 274 F(2d) 487, 124 USPQ 154.

12. States—Works prepared under government contracts.

A state may not obtain a copyright on its courts opinions, for it may not properly be called a citizen or a resident. Banks v. Manchester, 128 US 244, 32 LEd 425, 9 SCR 36, aff'g (CC-Ohio), 23 Fed 143.

An artist attached to a government expedition, who has agreed that the United States shall have exclusive right to any sketches or drawings made while on the expedition, may not later obtain a valid copyright upon his works composed while attached to the expedition. Heine v. Appleton, (CC-NY), FedCas 6,324, 4 Blatchf 125.

Legislative committee contracted with plaintiff to furnish to the state a copy of an index which plaintiff was providing for its own annotated statutes and the attorney general orally agreed with plaintiff that the copyright of the index should remain in plaintiff. Plaintiff was entitled to a copyright in the index as against third persons. W. H. Anderson Co. v. Baldwin Law Pub. Co., (CCA 6), 27 F(2d) 82.

13. —Judicial decisions and reports.

A contract made by a reporter of a court of appeals, assigning his copyright rights to volumes of the opinions of the court, to a publisher, does not give the publisher any right to a volume which the reporter compiled after his term of office had expired. Little v. Hall, 59 US(18 How) 165, 15 LEd 328.

A state could not claim title to a copyright upon law reports as an assignee thereof, where the assignor, a court reporter, had obtained copyright upon judicial decisions of which he was not the author. Banks v. Manchester, 128 US 244, 32 LEd 425, 9 SCR 36, aff'g (CC-Ohio), 23 Fed 143.

A judge may not secure copyright in his judicial opinions. Banks v. Manchester, 128 US 244, 32 LEd 425, 9 SCR 36, aff'g (CC-Ohio), 23 Fed 143.

A court reporter not being the author of the judicial decisions may not obtain copyright thereon. Banks v. Manchester, 128 US 244, 32 LEd 425, 9 SCR 36, aff'g (CC-Ohio), 23 Fed 143; Chase v. Sanborn, (CC-NH), FedCas 2,628, 4 Cliff 306.

A reporter of a volume of law reports can obtain a copyright that will cover the parts of the book of which he is the author. Callaghan v. Myers, 128 US 617, 32 LEd 547, 9 SCR 177, mod'g (CC-Ill), 24 Fed 636.

A compact between a state and a state reporter, by which the latter relinquishes and the former assumes the copyright in court reports was not inconsistent with the laws of the United States. Little v. Gould, (CC-NY), FedCas 8,394, 2 Blatchf 165.

Under the Copyright Act of 1831, a secretary of state might take out copyright upon judicial reports in trust for the state. Little v. Gould, (CC-NY), FedCas 8,395, 2 Blatchf 362.

A judicial reporter who edited a volume of reports on cases was the author of the volume and was entitled to copyright under Copyright Act of 1831. Little v. Gould, (CC-NY), Fed Cas 8,395, 2 Blatchf 362.

14. Publishers and printers.

An author may, through knowledge and acquiescence, give the publisher of his work the right to the copyright. Pulte v. Derby, (CC-Ohio), FedCas 11,465, 5 McLean 328.

Copyright of a periodical containing articles and pictures, the authors of which have not transferred their rights to publisher, affords publisher no protection as to such articles or pictures. Mail & Express Co. v. Life Pub. Co., (CCA 2), 192 Fed 899.

Airlines, preparing material which was furnished to publisher of airline guides, do not part with all interest in such material, where the airlines paid for the publication and publisher's contribution was limited to editorial revision, and airlines may use such material in another publication. Official Aviation Guide Co., Inc. v. American Aviation Associates, Inc., (CCA 7), 150 F(2d) 173, 65 USPQ 553, mod'g 62 USPQ 178.

Copyright taken out by publisher for the protection of itself and the general owner is valid. Quinn-Brown Pub. Corp. v. Chilton Co., Inc., (DC-NY), 15 FSupp 213, 30 USPQ 373.

One not a proprietor of a manuscript, but merely the printer thereof, is not entitled to obtain a copyright to protect that interest only. Koppel v. Downing, 11 AppDC 93.

A publisher, who publishes a book under an agreement to pay the author and holder of the copyright 7½ cents for each copy, has not the exclusive right to publish such book. Willis v. Tibbals, 33 NYSuperCt 220.

15. —Foreign author or copyright.

An American publisher of a production which has been copyrighted in England, but not in United States may not, by taking out a copyright in the United States, secure the benefits of the copyright statute. Ferris v. Frohman, 223 US 424, 56 LEd 492, 32 SCR 263, aff'g 238 Ill 430, 87 NE 327, 43 LRA(NS) 639, 128 AmRep 135; American Code Co., Inc. v. Bensinger, (CCA 2), 282 Fed 829.

A publisher may obtain a copyright on behalf of himself and the author, which would protect the interests of both, and the publisher would become the trustee of the copyright on behalf of both. Mifflin v. Dutton, (CCA 1), 112 Fed 1004, 61 LRA 134, aff'g 107 Fed 708. Aff'd 190 US 260, 47 LEd 1040, 23 SCR 769, and 190 US 265, 47 LEd 1043, 23 SCR 771.

A contract entered into between a foreign author and an American publisher prior to International Copyright Act of 1891, gave the publisher a mere license, and not a transfer of such rights as would entitle the American publisher to a copyright upon the foreign author's work as a "proprietor." Fraser v. Yack, (CCA 7), 116 Fed 285, aff'g 105 Fed 787.

Act Jan. 7, 1904, c. 2, 33 Stat. 4, did not apply to a foreign publisher of a book previously published in English and sold in the United States by United States authors. Encyclopedia Britannica Co. v. Werner Co., (CC-NJ), 135 Fed 841. Aff'd 142 Fed 966.

Copyright of a story by a foreign author in publisher's and author's name under a contract so providing gave valid copyright to publisher and author. Harper & Bros. v. M. A. Donohue & Co., (CC-Ill), 144 Fed 491. Aff'd 146 Fed 1023.

16. Assignees and trustees.

A copyright may be treated as property, which is capable of being transferred, and the right of the assignee is protected equally with that of the author. Wheaton v. Peters, 33 US (8 Pet) 591, 8 LEd 1055, rev'g (CC-Pa), FedCas 17,486.

An assignment of a copyright, though not in writing, is valid as between the parties. Webb v. Powers, (CC-Mass), FedCas 17,323, 2 Woodb& M 497.

Where a person assigns his rights in a copyright to another, reserving for himself a percentage of the profits, he loses all right to the copyright. Mackaye v. Mallory, (CC-NY), 12 Fed 328.

Under R. S. § 4952 which gives authors, proprietors and the assigns of any such person the right to obtain copyright, an assignee of the copyright, but not of the copyrighted thing, is within the statute and entitled to secure copyright. Werckmeister v. American Lithographic Co., (CC-NY), 142 Fed 827. Aff'd 148 Fed 1022, which was aff'd 207 US 375, 52 LEd 254, 28 SCR 124.

A contract wherein a foreign author agrees to have a play copyrighted "prior to its appearance in the book trade" does not convey the author's title or right to a copyright in the United States. Saake v. Lederer, (CCA 3), 174 Fed 135, rev'g 166 Fed 810.

Script writer does not infringe copyrighted novel by making dramatization thereof under contract with party to whom copyright owner had assigned right to dramatize. Szekely v. Eagle Lion Films, Inc., (CA 2), 242 F(2d) 266, 113 USPQ 98, aff'g 140 FSupp 843, 109 USPQ 348.

Whether royalty payments specified in copyright assignment are fair or unfair must be decided by parties to assignment and cannot be decided by court in absence of fraud or overreaching. Fisher v. Edwin H. Morris & Co., Inc., (DC-NY), 113 USPQ 251.

Defendant, owner of copyrighted book, granted to plaintiff's predecessor, for term of ten years, sole and exclusive motion-picture rights and motion-picture copyright; contract provided that, upon expiration of ten years, all rights should revert to defendant unless predecessor elected to pay additional sum, in which event predecessor would acquire all rights in perpetuity; predecessor did not exercise option; hence, upon termination of ten-year period, all rights, including copyright on motion picture made by predecessor, reverted to defendant. Sunset Securities Co. v. Coward-McCann, Inc., 47 Cal(2d series) 907, 306 Pac(2d) 777, 112 USPQ 449, rev'g (CalApp(2d series)), 297 Pac (2d) 137, 110 USPQ 329.

Copyright proprietor may transfer legal title to copyright only in totality; copyright may not be split up and partially assigned as to various rights encompassed therein. Hirshon v. United Artists Corp., 100 AppDC 217, 243 F(2d) 640, 113 USPQ 110.

Plaintiff granted to defendant right to publish music which had been assigned by authors to plaintiff; defendant copyrighted music; after obtaining copyright, defendant held it in trust for plaintiff to the extent that plaintiff reserved all rights except music publication rights. April Productions, Inc. v. G. Schirmer, Inc., 308 NY 366, 126 NE(2d) 283, 105 USPQ 286, rev'g 283 AppDiv 1037, 131 NYS(2d) 341, 102 USPQ 137, which aff'd (Misc), 122 NYS(2d) 888, 97 USPQ 242.

17. —Proprietors.

Gratuitous contributions to the proprietor of a book vested such title to the contributions in proprietor as might be copyrighted by her. Lawrence v. Dana (CC-Mass), FedCas 8,136, 4 Cliff 1.

Proprietors of books, though not authors, were entitled to benefits of the copyright acts. Lawrence v. Dana, (CC-Mass), FedCas 8,136, 4 Cliff 1.

"Proprietor" as used in copyright laws is one who has lawfully acquired, by purchase or otherwise, the exclusive rights of the author. Yuengling v. Schile, (CC-NY), 12 Fed 97.

Transfer by an author of his manuscript for a sum of money "in full payment for story" vested purchaser with proprietory rights therein. Dam v. Kirk La Shelle Co., (CCA 2), 175 Fed 902, 41 LRA(NS) 1002, 20 AnnCas 1173, aff'g 166 Fed 589.

"Proprietor," in this section, has same meaning, equivalent to the word "assign," as in former statutes, and does not include a mere license. Public Ledger v. New York Times, (DC-NY), 275 Fed 562. Aff'd 279 Fed 747; Quinn-Brown Pub. Corp. v. Chilton Co., Inc., (DC-NY), 15 FSupp 213, 30 USPQ 373.

Contract by foreign newspaper, granting certain facilities and right of republication of news matter to American newspaper did not constitute the latter a "proprietor" within meaning of this section. Public Ledger v. New York Times, (DC-NY), 275 Fed 562. Aff'd 279 Fed 747.

A "proprietor," not the author, stands in no better status in acquiring copyright than does the author. Houghton Mifflin Co. v. Stackpole Sons, Inc., (CCA 2), 104 F(2d) 306, 42 USPQ 96, rev'g 41 USPQ 404.

Corporation may obtain copyright since it may be "proprietor" and, through joint action of its employees, may be an "author." Dan Kasoff, Inc. v. Palmer Jewelry Mfg. Co., Inc., (DC-NY), 171 FSupp 603, 120 USPQ 445.

Where an author sells his copyright he no longer retains all the rights granted to him by reason of such copyright. Cooper v. Gunn, 4 BMon(Ky) 594.

Fact that cartoonist by sale of legal title fully divested himself of all rights in his drawings and characters is evidenced by fact that on several occasions he asked for and obtained express permission from owner to use drawings and characters for his own benefit. Segar v.

King Features Syndicate, Inc., 175 Misc 25, 22 NYS(2d) 790, 47 USPQ 46. Mf'd 262 AppDiv 221, 28 NYS(2d) 542, 50 USPQ 399.

18. —Licensees.

An assignment by a foreign author of his proprietory right to a play for the United States operated as a mere license, under which the assignee, though she had no rights under copyright law, would receive equitable protection in her license rights. Keene v. Wheatley, (CC-Pa), FedCas 7,644, 4 Phila 157.

An oral agreement between a foreign company and an author regarding the former's use of the author's article was but a license, and copyright was properly taken in author's name. Black v. Henry G. Allen Co., (CC-NY), 56 Fed 764.

Contract for a license for "sole and exclusive use of advance sheets" conveys only a qualified interest, and does not entitle licensee to a right to copyright. Fraser v. Yack, (CCA 7), 116 Fed 285, aff'g 105 Fed 787.

Licensee with permission to publish song in compilation is neither assignee nor proprietor and cannot copyright song when he copyrights combination. Egner v. E. C. Schirmer Music Co., (CCA 1), 139 F(2d) 398, 60 USPQ 74, aff'g 48 FSupp 187, 56 USPQ 214.

A mere license to publish is not a proprietorship. Quinn-Brown Pub. Corp. v. Chilton Co., Inc., (DC-NY), 15 FSupp 213, 30 USPQ 373.

Provision in exclusive license requiring licensee to get prints of copyrighted motion pictures exclusively from licensor is no abuse of lawful copyright monopoly; licensor, as copyright proprietor, could license exhibition of pictures and could license or retain right to process and reproduce its own films. Cardinal Films, Inc. v. Republic Pictures Corp., (DC-NY), 148 FSupp 156, 112 USPQ 292.

19. —Person in whose name copyright secured.

Copyright may be taken out in name of a trustee for benefit of another who is the "author or proprietor." Hanson v. Jaccard Jewelry Co., (CC-Mo), 32 Fed 202.

The legal title to a copyright vests in the person in whose name the copyright is taken out. It may, however, be held by him in trust for the true owner, and the question of true ownership is one of fact, dependent upon the circumstances of the case. Bisel v. Ladner, (CCA 3), 1 F(2d) 436.

The fact that a copyright was secured in the name of a person who was not the composer does not invalidate the copyright. Sebring Pottery Co. v. Steubenville Pottery Co., (DC-Ohio), 9 FSupp 383, 14 USPQ 46.

20. Paintings and photographs.

One who arranges the pose and lighting of a photograph is to be treated as the author thereof and is entitled to copyright of his photographs. Falk v. Gast Lithograph & Engraving Co., Ltd., (CC-NY), 48 Fed 262. Aff'd 54 Fed 890.

A photographist producing an artistic photograph may secure a copyright. Falk v. Donaldson, (CC-NY), 57 Fed 32.

A photographer is entitled to copyright photographs which were taken gratuitously and for his own benefit. Press Pub. Co. v. Falk, (CC-NY), 59 Fed 324; Altman v. New Haven Union Co., (DC-Conn), 254 Fed 113; Lumiere v. Pathe Exchange, Inc., (CCA 2), 275 Fed 428; Yardlev v. Houghton Mifflin Co., Inc., (CCA 2), 108 F(2d) 28, 44 USPQ 1, aff'g 25 FSupp 361, 40 USPQ 234.

Publication and dedication to public of painting cannot be presumed from fact that artist died in 1900. Home Art, Inc. v. Glensder Textile Corp., (DC-NY), 81 FSupp 551, 79 USPQ 12.

21. —Assignment or sale.

Right to copyright a painting may be assigned without sale of painting itself and assignee may secure copyright as "proprietor." American Tobacco Co. v. Werckmeister, 207 US 284, 52 LEd 208, 28 SCR 72, 12 AnnCas 595, aff'g (CCA 2), 146 Fed 375.

Oral sale of a painting subsequently followed by delivery transferred entire property in painting, so that purchaser thereof would be entitled to copyright and publish print-copies of the painting. Parton v. Prang, (CC-Mass), FedCas 10,784, 3 Cliff 537.

Sale of painting with right of reproduction reserved did not vest purchaser with rights of "proprietor." Werckmeister v. Springer Lithographing Co., (CC-NY), 63 Fed 808.

An artist may sell a picture and a copyright to the picture separately. Werckmeister v. American Lithographic Co., (CC-NY), 142 Fed 827. Aff'd 148 Fed 1022, which was aff'd 207 US 375, 52 LEd 254, 28 SCR 124.

Assignment of certain rights of reproduction of a painting by a foreign author not entitled to secure copyright here was ineffectual as a basis upon which United States copyright could be properly granted. Bong v. Alfred S. Campbell Art Co., (CCA 2), 155 Fed 116. Aff'd 214 US 236, 54 LEd 979, 29 SCR 628, 16 AnnCas 1126.

An assignee may not acquire copyright if artist himself, because of domicil and citizenship, could not claim benefit of Copyright Act. Gross v. Twentieth Century Fox Film Corp., (DC-NY), 38 USPQ 399.

The authority granted by an artist to a publisher to copyright cartoons drawn by the artist does not give the publisher the right to copyright a drama based on the cartoons. Outcault v. Lamar, 135 AppDiv 110, 119 NYS 930.

22. —Work done for hire.

A small painting, the design of which the president of a corporation originated and directed to be painted by a hired artist was properly copyrightable in corporation's name. Schumacher v. Schwencke, (CC-NY), 25 Fed 466.

In general, when an artist is commissioned to execute a work of art not in existence he may not retain or be entitled to copyright therein. Dielman v. White, (CC-Mass), 102 Fed 892.

A person employing a photographer to take a picture has the right to copyright the picture and not the photographer. Lumiere v. Pathe Exchange, Inc., (CCA 2), 275 Fed 428; Lumiere v. Robertson-Cole Distributing Corp., (CCA 2), 280 Fed 550, 24 ALR 1317; Yardley v. Houghton Mifflin Co., Inc., (CCA 2), 108 F(2d) 28, 44 USPQ 1, aff'g 25 FSupp 361, 40 USPQ 234.

If artist is solicited by patron to execute commission for pay, presumption should be that patron desires to control publication of copies and that the artist consents. Mural was painted for city high school and copyright belonged to city although artist marked it with notice of copyright in his name and registered claim to copyright, but there is no evidence of city's observation of notice or approval by city. Yardley v. Houghton Mifflin Co., Inc., (CCA 2), 108 F(2d) 28, 44 USPQ 1, aff'g 25 FSupp 361, 40 USPQ 234.

23. —Rights in subject.

Photographer who took picture of hotel with consent of owner and developed and printed it at his own expense for his own benefit had sole proprietary right therein and was entitled to copyright. Cory v. Physical Culture Hotel, Inc., (DC-NY), 14 FSupp 977, 30 USPQ 353. Aff'd 88 F(2d) 411, 33 USPQ 58.

Rights of person in his dog's photograph are dependent on his contract with photographer; if latter takes photograph on own initiative, without arrangement or payment by dog's owner, proprietary interest in photograph, including right to copyright, is in photographer; if photograph is taken at owner's request and owner pays photographer, all interest, including right to copyright, is in owner. Lawrence v. Ylla, 184 Misc 807, 55 NYS(2d) 343, 65 USPQ 342.

24. Aliens.

Nonresident alien artist himself not possessing right to copyright cannot assign right to copyright. Bong v. Campbell Art Co., 214 US 236, 53 LEd 979, 29 SCR 628, 16 AnnCas 1126, aff'g (CCA 2), 155 Fed 116; Keene v. Wheatley, (CC-Pa), FedCas 7.644, 4 Phila 157; Yuengling v. Schile, (CC-NY), 12 Fed 97.

Act Jan. 7, 1904, c. 2, 33 Stat. 4, protecting foreign exhibitors at Louisiana purchase exposition, did not apply to uncopyrighted foreign books previously republished and sold in the United States. Encyclopedia Britannica Co. v. Werner Co., (CC-NJ), 135 Fed 841. Aff'd 142 Fed 966.

A mere license to perform a play given by a foreign author does not grant authority to licensee to copyright. Saake v. Lederer, (CCA 3), 174 Fed 135, rev'g 166 Fed 810.

The literary works of a stateless person are subject to copyright, and therefore "Mein Kampf" by Hitler was entitled to copyright. Houghton Mifflin Co. v. Stackpole Sons, Inc., (CCA 2), 104 F(2d) 306, 42 USPQ 96, rev'g 41 USPQ 404.

It is general rule that author, even an alien author, must take certain formal steps to obtain American copyright. Machaty v. Astra Pictures, Inc., (CA 2), 197 F(2d) 138, 93 USPQ 51, aff'g 89 USPQ 539.

Buenos Aires Copyright Convention of 1910 provided that foreigners must look to our copyright laws for enforcement of rights in this country. Portuondo v. Columbia Phonograph Co., Inc., (DC-NY), 36 USPQ 104.

Hostilities between nations suspend intercourse and deprive citizens of the hostile nations of any right to the privilege of copyright. 22 OAG 268.

A German citizen who had strictly complied with the provisions of the Copyright Act at any time after the law became effective, but before the date of a proclamation of the President as provided for in that provision of this section set out in note, not only was vested with a copyright, but could maintain an action for any infringement which occurred prior to the date of the proclamation. 29 OAG 64.

25. —Resident aliens.

"Resident" under prior act defined, see Boucicault v. Wood, (CC-Ill), FedCas 1,693, 2 Biss 34.

History of domiciliary and national status requirements of various copyright acts stated, see Bentley v. Tibbals, (CCA 2), 223 Fed 247.

A man who is a mere transient visitant, whose family and business are all abroad, may not be considered a resident under the Copyright Act of 1831, though he has filed a declaration of intention to become a United States citizen. Carey v. Collier, (CC-NY), FedCas 2,400.

The purpose of this section is to give domiciled foreigners the same protection and rights as are accorded United States citizens by Copyright Act. G. Ricordi & Co., Inc. v. Columbia Graphophone Co., (DC-NY), 258 Fed 72.

A Canadian soldier, who came to New York City with all his property, and with the intent to remain there was domiciled in the United States and entitled to copyright. G. Ricordi & Co., Inc. v. Columbia Graphophone Co., (DC-NY), 258 Fed 72.

26. Reciprocal agreements.

Provision as to proclamation by the President is a condition and not directory. No right is conferred independently of presidential proclamation. Bong v. Campbell Art Co., 214 US 236, 53 LEd 979, 29 SCR 628, 16 AnnCas 1126, aff'g (CCA 2), 155 Fed 116.

There is no special provision in the law for copyright abroad, but such a case has been anticipated by legislative recognition or sanction, thus pointing out the way if not creating the right, to citizens of the United States to obtain from foreign nations copyright benefit. G. & C. Merriam Co. v. United Dictionary Co., (CCA 7), 146 Fed 354, rev'g 140 Fed 768. Aff'd 208 US 260, 52 LEd 478, 28 SCR 290.

Court must take judicial notice of the existence of reciprocal relations. Ohman v. New York City, (CC-NY), 168 Fed 953.

Presidential proclamation is conclusive evidence as to existence of reciprocal relations. Chappell & Co., Ltd. v. Fields, (CCA 2), 210 Fed 864.

A domiciled alien cannot secure protection for an unpublished work unless his sovereign extends reciprocal protection to Americans. Leibowitz v. Columbia Graphophone Co., (DC-NY), 298 Fed 342.

Subsection (b) of this section is irrelevant where copyright was granted to American corporation. Southern Music Pub. Co., Inc. v. Bibo-Lang, Inc., (DC-NY), 10 FSupp 972, 26 USPQ 321.

In absence of separate proclamation of President of reciprocal conditions as to mechanical reproduction under § 1(e) of this title and subsec. (b) of this section, foreigner cannot avail himself of our copyright laws. Portuondo v. Columbia Phonograph Co., Inc., (DC-NY), 36 USPQ 104.

Presidential proclamation does not create a right but is only the evidence of the existence of conditions under which rights and privileges may be exercised and is conclusive evidence on that point. 28 OAG 222.

Under this section the President is required to determine by proclamation the existence of the reciprocal conditions upon which alien authors and composers may acquire the general privileges, and the date when the reciprocal condition was actually met by the laws of any foreign nation is the one which should be inserted in the proclamation. 29 OAG 209.

10. Publication of work with notice.— Any person entitled thereto by this title may secure copyright for his work by publication thereof with the notice of copyright required by this title; and such notice shall be affixed to each copy thereof published or offered for sale in the United States by authority of the copyright proprietor, except in the case of books seeking ad interim protection under section 22 of this title. (July 30, 1947, c. 391, § 1, 61 Stat. 656.)

Cross references. — Accidental omission of notice, see § 21 of this title.

Form of notice, § 19 of this title.

Place of affixing notice, see §§ 19 and 20 of this title.

NOTES TO DECISIONS
ANALYSIS
1. In general.
2. Publication.
3. —Date.
4. —Extent of distribution.
5. Abandonment, dedication, and loss of rights.
6. Exceptions and minor variations.

1. In general.

History and purpose of section stated, see Bentley v. Tibbals, (CCA 2), 223 Fed 247.

All conditions are important, and the law requires them to be performed, and their performance is essential to a perfect copyright. Wheaton v. Peters, 33 US(8 Pet) 591, 8 LEd 1055, rev'g (CC-Pa), FedCas 17,486.

Printing of required notice in copyrighted book is a condition precedent to perfection of copyright. Thompson v. Hubbard, 131 US 123,

33 LEd 76, 9 SCR 710, rev'g (CC-Mo), 25 Fed 188; Osgood v. A. S. Aloe Instrument Co., (CC-Mo), 83 Fed 470.

Original maps, charts, and pictures may and usually do remain in the possession of the original makers, and there is no necessity of any notice upon them. American Tobacco Co. v. Werckmeister, 207 US 284, 52 LEd 208, 28 SCR 72, 12 AnnCas 595, aff'g (CCA 2), 146 Fed 375.

It was the object of the statute to require the inscription of the copyright notice, not upon the original painting, map, photograph, drawing, but upon those published copies concerning which it is designed to convey information to the public which shall limit the use and circumscribe the rights of the purchaser. American Tobacco Co. v. Werckmeister, 207 US 284, 52 LEd 208, 28 SCR 72, 12 AnnCas 595, aff'g (CCA 2), 146 Fed 375.

Every reproduction of a copyrighted work must bear the statutory notice. Louis DeJonge & Co. v. Breuker & Kessler Co., 235 US 33, 59 LEd 113, 35 SCR 6, aff'g (CCA 3), 191 Fed 35, which aff'd 182 Fed 150.

Mere notice of copyright in each book was insufficient to identify or distinguish parts of book in which complainants claimed copyright. Flint v. Jones, (CC-Pa), FedCas 4,872.

The printing of the notice of copyright is one of the necessary steps to be taken before obtaining copyright. Jollie v. Jaques, (CC-NY), FedCas 7,437, 1 Blatchf 618.

Compliance with this section must be pleaded and proved. Falk v. Gast Lith. & Eng. Co., Ltd., (CC-NY), 40 Fed 168.

Prior to passage of Copyright Act of 1909, an entire motion-picture film was a "photograph" and protectible in its entirety under a single notice. Edison v. Lubin, (CCA 3), 122 Fed 240, rev'g 119 Fed 993.

Notice of copyright of magazine protected story contained therein, including dramatic rights. Dam v. Kirk La Shelle Co., (CCA 2), 175 Fed 902, 41 LRA(NS) 1002, 20 AnnCas 1173, aff'g 166 Fed 589.

Ownership of copyright, which may be secured by compliance with this section, and vindication of such ownership, as provided by § 13 of this title may not be construed as the same thing. New York Times Co. v. Star Co., (CC-NY), 195 Fed 110.

Purpose of requiring that copyright notice be affixed to copyrighted article is to advise public of claim of copyright proprietor and to prevent innocent persons from incurring infringement penalties. Stecher Lithographic Co. v. Dunston Lithograph Co., (DC-NY), 233 Fed 601; Trifari, Krussman & Fishel, Inc. v. B. Steinberg-Kaslo Co., (DC-NY), 144 FSupp 577, 110 USPQ 487.

Publication with notice is sufficient to copyright whatever may be copyrighted at all. U. S. v. Backer, (CCA 2), 134 F(2d) 533, 57 USPQ 133.

Inasmuch as copyright proprietor's assertion of copyright was clearly printed on print of film (purchased by defendant) in strict accordance with statutory requirements, proprietor had right to assume that assertion provided ample notice to defendant of proprietor's interest in film; being charged with this notice, defendant could ascertain facts by inquiring of proprietor. Hampton v. Paramount Pictures Corp., (CA 9), 279 F(2d) 100, 125 USPQ 623.

Copyright notice is affixed to work of art within meaning of this section although notice is on gummed label pasted on work of art. Coventry Ware, Inc. v. Reliance Picture Frame Co., (CA 2), 288 F(2d) 193, 129 USPQ 83, rev'g 186 FSupp 798, 127 USPQ 46.

In the Copyright Act, as passed in 1909, a specific requirement for location of notice of copyright was retained only in the case of books or other printed publications, musical compositions, and periodicals; all other items were left subject only to general requirement, now embodied in this section, that notice be affixed to each copy; in the light of legislative history, it is incredible that Congress would have intended, by implication hidden in § 19 of this title, to revive requirement of 1802 and 1831 acts that notice appear on front of work of art; § 19 of this title should not be read to impose restriction on placement which, had it been intended by Congress, would certainly have been expressly stated; therefore, notice on back of wall plaques is sufficient. Coventry Ware, Inc. v. Reliance Picture Frame Co., (CA 2), 288 F(2d) 193, 129 USPQ 83, rev'g 186 FSupp 798, 127 USPQ 46.

After copyright notice has been published everyone is under duty to learn facts and copies at his peril. Chappell & Co., Inc. v. Costa, (DC-NY), 45 FSupp 554, 53 USPQ 674.

Requirement of this section is met where copyrighted work is a repetitive design printed on continuous roll of material with notice being printed on the edge at least once for every repeat of the design. Peter Pan Fabrics, Inc. v. Candy Frocks, Inc., (DC-NY), 187 FSupp 334, 126 USPQ 171.

Fact that owner of copyrighted label distributed advertising placards, picturing cans bearing label without copyright symbol on them, did not constitute a publication and dedication to public so as to void copyright; cited cases involving matrices, mats and other newspaper material, and mezzotints are distinguished in that in each of them it was the product sold, whereas instant product sold was not the label, that is, the copyrighted thing, but the contents of can upon which label appeared. S. C. Johnson & Son, Inc. v. Drop Dead Co., Inc., (DC-Cal), 201 FSupp 442, 132 USPQ 309.

2. Publication.

Exhibition of a card of miniature samples to dealers, not bearing copyright notice, is not a "publication" within meaning of this section. Falk v. Gast Lithograph & Engraving Co., (CCA 2), 54 Fed 890, aff'g 48 Fed 262.

Printing in a salon catalogue of a superficial crayon sketch of a painting was not a "publication." Werckmeister v. Springer Lithographing Co., (CC-NY), 63 Fed 808.

Leasing of copies of a copyrighted book is a "publication." Ladd v. Oxnard, (CC-Mass), 75 Fed 703.

Serial publication of a novel in a magazine in England was a publication within the meaning of the copyright law. Fraser v. Yack, (CCA 7), 116 Fed 285, aff'g 105 Fed 787.

Public exhibition of original painting, without copyright notice, is a publication. Werckmeister v. American Lithographic Co., (CC-NY), 117 Fed 360.

All articles, whether enumerated in § 12 of this title or not, can only be protected on publication by affixing the notice of copyright as is required by this section. Universal Film Mfg. Co. v. Copperman, (DC-NY), 212 Fed 301. Aff'd 218 Fed 577.

Publication by the state of index prepared by plaintiff for his own statute compilation, a copy of which index was sold to the state for the official publication, did not impair plaintiff's copyright. W. H. Anderson Co. v. Baldwin Law Pub. Co., (CCA 6), 27 F(2d) 82.

Fact that plaintiff's song was heard and used in school before plaintiff published it with copyright notice did not constitute publication. Freudenthal v. Hebrew Pub. Co., (DC-NY), 44 FSupp 754, 53 USPQ 466.

Costume jewelry sold to wholesalers bore plaintiff's registered trade-mark and "C" in circle stamped thereon; this constituted proper "publication" of copyrights as required by this section. Dan Kasoff, Inc. v. Palmer Jewelry Mfg. Co., Inc., (DC-NY), 171 FSupp 603, 120 USPQ 445.

Writer of musical composition under common law possesses exclusive right to make the first publication and to prevent publication by others; however, upon its first publication the composition passes into public domain; author's right in composition may be preserved by publication with notice of copyright in compliance with this section; upon such publication, common-law rights are terminated and statutory rights come into being and control. Schwartz v. Broadcast Music, Inc., (DC-NY), 180 FSupp 322, 124 USPQ 34.

Copyrighted catalog did not fall into public domain even though it also was published by proprietor, under a different trade name, and by corporation owned and controlled by same proprietor, and although such latter publications, respectively, as copyright proprietors, since such company and corporation constituted merely an alter ego for proprietor; it is noteworthy that infringer, who deliberately copied from catalog in which copyright notice contained proprietor's name, was not aware of latter publications at that time and was not prejudiced thereby. B & B Auto Supply, Inc. v. Plesser, (DC-NY), — FSupp —, 133 USPQ 247.

If catalog published in 1957 were merely a republication of previously copyrighted catalog, recital of 1957 date in notice of copyright would render copyright invalid as an attempt to extend copyright protection beyond statutory period; however, copyright is not invalidated inasmuch as 1957 catalog contained changes which are substantial and sufficient enough to constitute 1957 catalog a new work subject to copyright; such material as is newly or additionally presented in 1957 catalog must be regarded as newly copyrighted, while at the same time the subsisting copyrights on repeated matter in the catalog remain valid, but without any extension in their scope or duration. B & B Auto Supply,

Inc. v. Plesser, (DC-NY), — FSupp —, 133 USPQ 247.

In the case of a literary work, there is no right which can be protected under the statute until first publication; and upon first publication the right of exclusive property, that is, the right to multiply copies for a limited period, is that afforded by the statute. Loew's Inc. v. Superior Court, 18 Cal(2d series) 419, 115 Pac(2d) 983, 50 USPQ 641.

For work to be published, it must be reproduced, that is, there must be issuance of copies to general public; completed structure is no more a copy of architectural plans than exhibition of uncopyrighted moving-picture film, performance of uncopyrighted radio script, or broadcast of uncopyrighted radio script, all of which have been held not to dedicate contents to public; as used in copyright cases, "copy" signifies a tangible object that is a reproduction of original work; merely viewing interior of house by limited number of people, guests of owner, is limited publication as to plans, even though exhibition of exterior to public generally loses common-law copyright to exterior design. Smith v. Paul, 174 CalApp(2d series) 744, 345 Pac(2d) 546, 123 USPQ 463.

3. —Date.

Lapse of 14 months between publication with notice and deposit in copyright office did not vitiate retroactive right of recovery for unauthorized use ad interim. Washington Publishing Co., Inc. v. Pearson, 306 US 30, 83 LEd 470, 59 SCR 397, 40 USPQ 190, rev'g 68 AppDC 373, 98 F(2d) 245, 37 USPQ 429, which rev'd 32 USPQ 113.

Where the notice of copyright gave the date as 1847 when in fact the date was 1846, the title does not comply with the statute. Baker v. Taylor, (CC-NY), FedCas 782, 2 Blatchf 82.

Where date of publication was advertised, but the books were actually placed in the mail three days prior to such date, the advertised date will be taken as the date of publication in the absence of proof that any of the subscribers received the books prior to that date. Black v. Henry G. Allen Co., (CC-NY), 56 Fed 764.

Copyright vests upon publication, with notice of copyright thereon, and deposit of copies is merely for purpose of securing registration thereof. National Cloak & Suit Co. v. Kaufman, (CC-Pa), 189 Fed 215; New York Times Co. v. Star Co., (CC-NY), 195 Fed 110; Davenport Quigley Expedition, Inc. v. Century Productions, Inc., (DC-NY), 18 FSupp 974, 32 USPQ 608.

No publication is necessary before the deposit of copies of motion-picture photoplay in the office of the Librarian of Congress. Cardinal Film Corp. v. Beck, (DC-NY), 248 Fed 368.

Date of publication of book used for promotion and advertising purposes in jewelry trade is when shipments were made to jewelers, not when copies were distributed to public by jewelers. Advisers, Inc. v. Wiesen-Hart, Inc., (CA 6), 238 F(2d) 706, 111 USPQ 318.

Innocent misstatement or clerical error, alleging date of publication later than actual date, in affidavit and certificate of registration, unaccompanied by fraud or intent to extend statutory period of copyright protection, does not invalidate copyright, and it is not thereby rendered incapable of supporting infringement action. Advisers, Inc. v. Wiesen-Hart, Inc., (CA 6), 238 F(2d) 706, 111 USPQ 318.

4. —Extent of distribution.

Exhibition cards containing reduced size copies of photographs, but having no copyright notice thereon, used for the inspection of dealers only, were not a published edition. Falk v. Gast Lithograph & Engraving Co., Ltd., (CCA 2), 54 Fed 890, aff'g 48 Fed 262.

Circulation among the retail trade of reduced size photographs not bearing the required notice of copyright was not such a publication as would cause owner of the copyright to lose the rights afforded him under the copyright laws. Falk v. Gast Lithograph & Engraving Co., Ltd., (CCA 2), 54 Fed 890, aff'g 48 Fed 262.

Where author gave copies of his uncopyrighted pamphlet or left copies in public hotel office, this was publication, and subsequent copyright was ineffectual. D'Ole v. Kansas City Star Co., (CC-Mo), 94 Fed 840.

Exhibition of a painting at a private academy, to a limited number of persons, with no copying permitted, is not a "publication." Werckmeister v. American Lithographic Co., (CCA 2), 134 Fed 321, 68 LRA 591, rev'g 126 Fed 244.

Sheets of pictures, sent out to the trade as samples, without the copyright mark, are not published editions. Stecher Lithographic Co. v. Dunston Lithographic Co., (DC-NY), 233 Fed 601.

Dealer's samples of calendars do not require statutory copyright notice. Gerlach-Barklow Co. v. Morris & Bendien, Inc., (CCA 2), 23 F(2d) 159.

Permission to take notes at delivery of lecture is not general publication. Patterson v. Century Productions, Inc., (CCA 2), 93 F(2d) 489, 35 USPQ 471, aff'g 19 FSupp 30, 33 USPQ 194.

Courts apply different tests of publication depending on whether plaintiff is claiming protection because he did not publish and hence has common-law claim of infringement, in which case distribution must be quite large to constitute publication, or whether he is claiming under copyright statute, in which case requirements of publication are quite narrow. American Visuals Corp. v. Holland, (CA 2), 239 F(2d) 740, 111 USPQ 288.

Publication requirement of this section is complied with by placing 100 copies of publication on table in hotel for unsupervised distribution at convention. American Visuals Corp. v. Holland, (CA 2), 239 F(2d) 740, 111 USPQ 288.

Samples do not require statutory notice of copyright printed on them and cannot be considered publications, but the owner of copyright has burden of showing they were samples. Basevi v. Edward O'Toole Co., Inc., (DC-NY), 26 FSupp 41, 40 USPQ 333.

Book bearing copyright notice was actually offered for sale to public and, although number of copies offered was small, and publication was made as requisite for bringing suit to enforce registration, it cannot be said that there was no publication for had book been offered for sale without copyright notice there would have been surrender of all right to copyright. U. S. ex rel. Twentieth Century-Fox Film Corp. v. Bouve, (DC-DC), 33 FSupp 462, 45 USPQ 411. Aff'd 74 AppDC 271, 122 F(2d) 51, 50 USPQ 338.

Giving of musical composition to a few musicians and leaders of orchestras to play does not constitute publication where there was no general offer or dedication to public and sending of copies to music publisher and motion-picture producer was not a publication, although if either of the latter had used it, or made use of it in any public way, there would have been a publication. Allen v. Walt Disney Productions, Ltd., (DC-NY), 41 FSupp 134, 50 USPQ 365.

Delivery of six copies of form to third persons is publication of form. American Institute of Architects v. Fenichel, (DC-NY), 41 FSupp 146, 51 USPQ 29.

While common-law copyright has been held to be merely the right of first publication, printing of book for general distribution and its distribution is a general publication which terminates author's common-law copyright, and anyone may duplicate book; such result does not follow from limited distribution. Smith v. Paul, 174 CalApp (2d series) 744, 345 Pac(2d) 546, 123 USPQ 463.

Limitation as to persons and use is test of limited publication; thus, author of book is not deprived of common-law copyright where he circulates book among his friends for their personal enjoyment. Smith v. Paul, 174 CalApp(2d series) 744, 345 Pac(2d) 546, 123 USPQ 463.

5. **Abandonment, dedication, and loss of rights.**

A serial publication of a book in a magazine is a publication within the meaning of the copyright law. Holmes v. Hurst, 174 US 82, 43 LEd 904, 19 SCR 606, aff'g (CCA 2), 80 Fed 514; Holmes v. Donohue, (CC-Ill), 77 Fed 179.

Publication of several copyrighted chapters of an author's story, in a magazine without notice of author's copyright thereon as required by Copyright Act of 1831, § 5, 4 Stat. 436, rendered author's copyright invalid. Mifflin v. Dutton, 190 US 265, 47 LEd 1043, 23 SCR 771, aff'g (CCA 1), 112 Fed 1004, 61 LRA 134, which aff'd 107 Fed 708.

Second or subsequent edition without alterations or additions should have the date of the original copyright, but second or subsequent editions with notes or other improvements should have the date of the entry of the improved edition, and no reference need be made to the original entry. Lawrence v. Dana, (CC-Mass), FedCas 8,136, 4 Cliff 1; West Pub. Co. v. Edward Thompson Co., (CCA 2), 176 Fed 833, mod'g 169 Fed 833; Harris v. Miller, (DC-NY), 50 USPQ 306.

Exhibition of a painting subsequent to copyright thereof, but without notice of copyright is not such a publication as will constitute an abandonment of the owner's exclusive rights therein. Werckmeister v. American Lithographic Co., (CCA 2), 134 Fed 321, 68 LRA 591, rev'g 126 Fed 244.

Publication of a book by a licensee without proper notice of copyright is a dedication to the public. West Publishing Co. v. Edward Thompson Co., (CC-NY), 169 Fed 833. Mf'g 176 Fed 833.

Copyright was abandoned by failure to repeat notice when copyrighted matter was republished. Record & Guide Co. v. Bromley, (CC-Pa), 175 Fed 156.

Lack of notice as to what portions of a book are copyrighted effected a loss of the exclusive right as to such copyrighted portions. Bentley v. Tibbals, (CCA 2), 223 Fed 247.

Publication with notice, as required, before deposit of copies is not abandonment. M. Witmark & Sons v. Pastime Amusement Co., (DC-SC), 298 Fed 470. Aff'd 2 F(2d) 1020.

An absolute and unrestricted sale of a printed copy, even though colorable, amounts to a publication under this section. Atlantic Monthly Co. v. Post Pub. Co., (DC-Mass), 27 F(2d) 556.

Publication without requisite notice of copyright is abandonment of copyright. United Thrift Plan, Inc. v. National Thrift Plan, Inc., (DC-NY), 34 F(2d) 300, 2 USPQ 345.

It is no defense, in a suit on the infringement of a copyright, that there were no copyright notices appearing on the articles, when the defendant had actual knowledge of the copyright. Schellberg v. Empringham, (DC-NY), 36 F(2d) 991.

Court assumes if conductor plays over radio it would not be abandonment just as performance of play or delivery of lecture is not abandonment of common-law copyright as it does not "publish" the work and dedicate it to public. RCA Mfg. Co., Inc. v. Whiteman, (CCA 2), 114 F(2d) 86, 46 USPQ 324, rev'g 28 FSupp 787, 43 USPQ 114.

Publication of part or parts of author's works serially without statutory notice of copyright makes such work public property even though copyright covering entire work had previously been taken out. Deward & Rich, Inc. v. Bristol Savings & Loan Corp., (CCA 4), 120 F(2d) 537, 50 USPQ 1, aff'g 34 FSupp 345, 47 USPQ 128.

Where copyright as a book was obtained for book containing illustrations and text for advertisements, furnishing of matrices for publication without proper copyright notice for book, but merely "C" in circle, released those parts from copyright to the general public. Advertisers Exchange, Inc. v. Anderson, (CCA 8), 144 F(2d) 907, 63 USPQ 39, aff'g 52 FSupp 809, 59 USPQ 391.

Copyright of comic strip of later exploit of "Superman" is valid, insofar as picture differs from those going before, even though later exploit is so similar to prior exploit that publication of later by stranger would be infringement. National Comics Publications, Inc. v. Fawcett Publications, Inc., (CA 2), 191 F(2d) 594, 90 USPQ 274, rev'g 93 FSupp 349, 87 USPQ 12.

If owner gives another unconditional license to publish comic strips, their publication without required notice is by authority of proprietor and has same effect upon copyrights that similar publication by owner would have. National Comics Publications, Inc. v. Fawcett

Publications, Inc., (CA 2), 191 F(2d) 594, 90 USPQ 274, rev'g 93 FSupp 349, 87 USPQ 12.

Once copyright is lost by publication with improper notice, it is not revived by subsequent publication with proper notice. National Comics Publications, Inc. v. Fawcett Publications, Inc., (CA 2), 191 F(2d) 594, 90 USPQ 274, rev'g 93 FSupp 349, 87 USPQ 12.

One hundred sets of insurance forms not bearing copyright notice were distributed to prospective customers; distribution was not limited as to persons or purpose, the only limitation being that attributable to lack of general interest in specialized subject matter; this was general publication which forfeited author's right to copyright. Continental Casualty Co. v. Beardsley, (CA 2), 253 F(2d) 702, 117 USPQ 1, mod'g 151 FSupp 28, 113 USPQ 181.

Cases decided under statutory requirement of publication are not reliable precedents on which to decide whether common-law forfeiture has occurred. Continental Casualty Co. v. Beardsley, (CA 2), 253 F(2d) 702, 117 USPQ 1, mod'g 151 FSupp 28, 113 USPQ 181.

Notice of copyright on picture, illegible without artificial aid to the eye, and without the proprietor's name, was insufficient and precluded restraint of infringement. Goes Lithographing Co. v. Apt Lithographic Co., Inc., (DC-NY), 14 FSupp 620, 30 USPQ 119.

Plaintiffs owning copyrighted advertising material forfeited and waived their right to obtain relief from defendant, who innocently used one of their figures, where they had permitted the figure to be used without sufficient notice of copyright. Smith v. Bartlett, (DC-Maine), 18 FSupp 35, 32 USPQ 287.

Microscopic print is not sufficient to comply with statutory requirement of copyright notice. Deward & Rich, Inc. v. Bristol Savings & Loan Corp., (DC-WVa), 29 FSupp 777, 44 USPQ 26.

Publication of work without copyright notice or with insufficient notice results in abandonment of copyright earlier obtained, provided that the two publications are of same work. Deward & Rich, Inc. v. Bristol Savings & Loan Corp., (DC-Va), 34 FSupp 345, 47 USPQ 128. Aff'd 120 F(2d) 537, 50 USPQ 1.

Plaintiff, copyright proprietor of a book of advertisements, authorized defendant to publish individual advertisements and supplied defendant with mats therefor which bore no proper copyright notices and therefore publication by defendant was equivalent to publication with no copyright notice whatever. Deward & Rich, Inc. v. Bristol Savings & Loan Corp., (DC-Va), 34 FSupp 345, 47 USPQ 128. Aff'd 120 F(2d) 537, 50 USPQ 1.

Items appearing in uncopyrighted catalogue are dedicated to public and are not protected by copyright on subsequent catalogue containing such items. Sieff v. Continental Auto Supply, Inc., (DC-Minn), 39 FSupp 683, 50 USPQ 19.

Defendants did not copy design of plaintiff's copyrighted labels but only directions for use which appeared on plaintiff's earlier uncopyrighted labels; publication and use for several months prior to application for copyright and without notice thereof dedicated to public directions for use and prevented maintenance of infringement action predicated only on use of directions. Superfine Products, Inc. v. Denny, (DC-Ga), 54 FSupp 148, 60 USPQ 126.

Artist has no cause of action against one, who, innocently and without notice, publishes reproductions of painting copied from magazine. Leigh v. Barnhart, (DC-NJ), 96 FSupp 194, 89 USPQ 307.

Publication by party of advertisements prior to any attempt to copyright them vitiates copyright which party subsequently obtained thereon. Davis-Robertson Agency v. Duke, (DC-Va), 119 FSupp 931, 100 USPQ 211.

Copyright on advertisements is invalidated where proprietor subsequently published them without giving required statutory notice. Davis-Robertson Agency v. Duke, (DC-Va), 119 FSupp 931, 100 USPQ 211.

Publication, without substantial compliance with notice requirements of statute, constitutes abandonment of copyright and dedication to public. Trifari, Krussman & Fishel, Inc. v. B. Steinberg-Kaslo Co., (DC-NY), 144 FSupp 577, 110 USPQ 487.

General circulation by copyright proprietor of copyrighted picture without copyright notice thereon estops proprietor from complaining about anything defendant, who used copy of picture without copyright notice as reference for his picture, did up to date of trial. Lucas v. Nattrass-Schenck, Inc., (DC-NY), 44 USPQ 344.

Publication of score cards without notice required by copyright statute amounts to dedication to public sufficient to defeat all subsequent effort for copyright protection of score cards containing similar information. Penn Sportservice, Inc. v. Goldstein, (DC-Pa), 46 USPQ 477.

Copyrights were lost by plaintiff publishing same subject matter in later editions without copyright notice. Landis Machine Co. v. Chaso Tool Co., Inc., (DC-Mich), 53 USPQ 200. Aff'd 141 F(2d) 800, 61 USPQ 164.

Apart from statute, publication by author is dedication to public and author no longer has exclusive right of property in his work. Loew's, Inc. v. Superior Court, 18 Cal(2d series) 419, 115 Pac(2d) 983, 50 USPQ 641.

Forced filing of architectural plans in building department of municipality constitutes only a limited publication of common-law copyright and gives no person right to use copy thereof; plans do not become a public record in the sense that public has right to use them; plans are open to public inspection for purpose of determining whether building will comply with law, but not for purpose of giving anyone the right to use them. Smith v. Paul, 174 CalApp(2d series) 744, 345 Pac(2d) 546, 123 USPQ 463.

While American Tobacco Co. v. Werckmeister, 207 US 284, 52 LEd 208, 28 SCR 72, dealt with statutory copyright and with other than architectural plans, there is no reason why same rule as to intentional publication should not apply to architectural plans protected by common-law copyright; architect required to file plans in public office in order that client may obtain building permit is not intending thereby to abandon his rights in plans and he is not "intentionally" making it public in sense of § 983(b) of California civil code; purpose of requirement is to protect public from unsafe construction, not to take away architect's common-law property rights. Smith v. Paul, 174 CalApp (2d series) 744, 345 Pac(2d) 546, 123 USPQ 463.

The publication of a copyright notice is not necessary where the party infringing has actual notice of the copyright. Nichols v. Ruggles, 3 Day(Conn) 145, 3 AmDec 262.

Generally with respect to problems of co-owners of literary or creative productions in copyright field, courts have held (1) such co-owners are tenants in common, (2) one co-owner may use or license use of the production without other's consent, being liable only to account for profits, (3) tendency of courts is to oppose judicial action which discourages collaboration in literary or creative productions or bars publication of creative work, (4) neither co-owner has a superior right in a literary or creative work, and (5) injunction or action for accounting will not lie against licensee of one co-owner by the other. Noble v. D. Van Nostrand Co., Inc., 63 NJSuper 534, 164 Atl(2d) 834, 128 USPQ 100.

Property rights in literary or musical work do not survive authorized publication without due compliance with copyright formalities. April Productions, Inc. v. G. Schirmer, Inc., 308 NY 366, 126 NE(2d) 283, 105 USPQ 286, rev'g 283 AppDiv 1037, 131 NYS(2d) 341, 102 USPQ 137, which aff'd (Misc), 122 NYS(2d) 888, 97 USPQ 242.

Whatever common-law rights plaintiff, as United States licensee, had in musical composition prior to its publication terminated with publication, although publication occurred abroad. Hill & Range Songs, Inc. v. London Records, Inc., (Misc), 105 USPQ 302.

6. Exceptions and minor variations.

Notice given under a trade name is effective. Bleistein v. Donaldson Lithographing Co., 188 US 239, 47 LEd 460, 23 SCR 298, rev'g (CCA 6), 104 Fed 993.

Omission of American copyright notice on a work published abroad and sold there does not destroy rights of copyright holder. United Dictionary Co. v. G. & C. Merriam Co., 208 US 260, 52 LEd 478, 28 SCR 290, aff'g (CCA 7), 146 Fed 354, which rev'd 140 Fed 768.

American copyright notice is not required on editions of books simultaneously published and sold abroad. United Dictionary Co. v. G. & C. Merriam Co., 208 US 260, 52 LEd 478, 28 SCR 290, aff'g (CCA 7), 146 Fed 354, which rev'd 140 Fed 768.

Owner of copyright is not responsible for changes made on a particular copy when same bore proper statutory notice of copyright when it left owner's hands. Falk v. Gast Lithograph & Engraving Co., Ltd., (CCA 2), 54 Fed 890, aff'g 48 Fed 262.

A crayon sketch of a painting printed without copyright notice in a catalogue of the salon where the painting was exhibited was not such a publication as would work a forfeiture of the right of copyright. Werckmeister v. Springer Lithographing Co., (CC-NY), 63 Fed 808.

Acts of abandonment by author in permitting publication of her work in England and America without notice of copyright did not deprive American proprietors of their copyright. Harper & Bros. v. M. A. Donohue & Co., (CC-Ill), 144 Fed 491. Aff'd 146 Fed 1023.

Notice of copyright of a book extended to map sold with book. Lydiard-Peterson Co. v. Woodman, (CCA 8), 204 Fed 921, aff'g 192 Fed 67.

Where, by accident or mistake, the notice of copyright has been omitted from some published copies, the copyright is not thereby invalidated, and recovery for infringement may be had from any person who is not misled by such copies. Stecher Lithographic Co. v. Dunston Lithograph Co., (DC-NY), 233 Fed 601.

There is no provision in the act for the affixing of a notice of copyright to a phonograph record or other mechanical contrivance. Irving Berlin, Inc. v. Daigle, (CCA 5), 31 F(2d) 832, rev'g 26 F(2d) 149, and 26 F(2d) 150.

Continuous attempt to publish comic strips with some sort of copyright notice affixed, however imperfect, is conclusive evidence of wish to claim copyright, and precludes holding of abandonment. National Comics Publications, Inc. v. Fawcett Publications, Inc., (CA 2), 191 F(2d) 594, 90 USPQ 274, rev'g 93 FSupp 349, 87 USPQ 12.

Copyright is not forfeited, although copyright notice gives as name of proprietor the name of a wholly-owned subsidiary corporation of proprietor, if corporations have same officers, directors, and shareholders and subsidiary is promotional agency. National Comics Publications, Inc. v. Fawcett Publications, Inc., (CA 2), 191 F(2d) 594, 90 USPQ 274, rev'g 93 FSupp 349, 87 USPQ 12.

Publication of certain "Superman" comic strips with improper copyright notice does not result in abandonment of right to copyright all pictorial portrayals of exploits of "Superman." National Comics Publications, Inc. v. Fawcett Publications, Inc., (CA 2), 191 F(2d) 594, 90 USPQ 274, rev'g 93 FSupp 349, 87 USPQ 12.

Reproductions in trade journals do not result in loss of copyright where each copyright object is properly labeled to comply with notice requirements of this section. Rushton v. Vitale, (CA 2), 218 F(2d) 434, 104 USPQ 158.

Where owner of copyright of song licenses manufacturer to reproduce song as part of motion picture it is not necessary to put notice of copyright of song on motion-picture film; no notice of copyright could be imprinted because there was no license from copyright owner to manufacturer of reel or to producer of the film authorizing use of the reel for public performance. Famous Music Corp. v. Melz, (DC-La), 28 FSupp 767, 42 USPQ 573.

Insubstantial variations from notice prescribed by statute do not destroy proprietor's rights so long as innocent persons are not thereby misled. Trifari, Krussman & Fishel, Inc. v. B.

Steinberg-Kaslo Co., (DC-NY), 144 FSupp 577, 110 USPQ 487.

11.   Registration of claim and issuance of certificate.—Such person may obtain registration of his claim to copyright by complying with the provisions of this title, including the ·deposit of copies, and upon such compliance the Register of Copyrights shall issue to him the certificates provided for in section 209 of this title. (July 30, 1947, c. 391, § 1, 61 Stat. 656.)

NOTES TO DECISIONS

Subsequent registration of work of art published as element in manufactured article is not misuse of copyright. Mazer v. Stein, 347 US 201, 98 LEd 630, 74 SCR 460, 100 USPQ 325, aff'g (CA 4), 204 F(2d) 472, 97 USPQ 310, which rev'd 111 FSupp 359, 96 USPQ 439.

Certificate of copyright registration is prima facie evidence of validity of copyright; burden of proof is on alleged infringer to overcome this prima facie presumption of validity. Wihtol v. Wells, (CA 7), 231 F(2d) 550, 109 USPQ 200.

Unless copyright is promptly registered, it becomes void. Advisers, Inc. v. Wiesen-Hart, Inc., (CA 6), 238 F(2d) 706, 111 USPQ 318.

Introduction into evidence of copyright certificate of registration creates prima facie case as to facts stated therein; burden then shifts to other party to go forward with evidence to overcome prima facie case. Rohauer v. Friedman, (CA 9), — F(2d) —, 134 USPQ 384.

Certificate of registration may be corrected by copyright office. Advisers, Inc. v. Wiesen-Hart, Inc., (CA 6), 238 F(2d) 706, 111 USPQ 318.

The essence of copyright is publication and notice, registration being essential only for the purpose of maintaining action for infringement. Davenport Quigley Expedition, Inc. v. Century Productions, Inc., (DC-NY), 18 FSupp 974, 32 USPQ 608.

Fact that application for copyright registration claims date of publication a few days prior to actual publication does not invalidate copyright as it is a mistake in favor of public; although copyright time runs against copyright owner, he cannot recover for infringement during period prior to actual publication. Basevi v. Edward O'Toole Co., Inc., (DC-NY), 26 FSupp 41, 40 USPQ 333.

Register of copyrights has no discretionary power to refuse to register any copyright entitled to registration under the law; it is question of fact whether applicant has complied with law and if he has he is entitled to registration; any finding of fact or conclusion of law on part of register is not binding on court; mandamus issues to force register to accept deposit and register claim of copyright. U. S. ex rel. Twentieth Century-Fox Film Corp. v. Bouve, (DC-DC), 33 FSupp 462, 45 USPQ 411. Aff'd 74 AppDC 271, 122 F(2d) 51, 50 USPQ 338.

Certificate of registration is prima facie evidence that all requirements of Copyright Act have been fulfilled. Chain Store Business Guide, Inc. v. Wexler, (DC-NY), 79 FSupp 726, 77 USPQ 656.

Trade-mark and label copyright certificates demonstrate prima facie right to registered symbol, but this is not necessarily determinative of question of validity of mark or copyright. Northmont Hosiery Corp. v. True Mfg. Co., (DC-Wis), 100 FSupp 909, 91 USPQ 3.

Mere delay in obtaining certificate of registration does not invalidate copyright; copyright is valid where certificate was obtained nine years after publication and two months after publication of defendant's book, there being no evidence of any intention by plaintiff to abandon his claims of copyright. Ziegelheim v. Flohr, (DC-NY), 119 FSupp 324, 100 USPQ 189.

Copyright is not destroyed because assignee applied for copyright registration before it filed with copyright office assignment pursuant to power of attorney. Mills Music, Inc. v. Cromwell Music, Inc., (DC-NY), 126 FSupp 54, 103 USPQ 84.

Unincorporated association can own copyrightable manuscript and may apply to register it in copyright office; right to obtain statutory copyright is incident of ownership of copyrightable manuscript, necessary for its proper exploitation. Mills Music, Inc. v. Cromwell Music, Inc., (DC-NY), 126 FSupp 54, 103 USPQ 84.

Action for injunction and declaratory judgment with respect to publication and deposit of copies against register of copyrights is commenced by filing of complaint, by service of subpena and copy of complaint on register of copyrights, and by service of copies of complaint on United States district attorney and attorney general of United States. King Features Syndicate, Inc. v. Bouve, (DC-DC), 48 USPQ 237.

Despite fact that 1940 contract concerning literary work and 1940 assignment thereof were capable of being recorded in copyright office, they were not so recorded until after plaintiff had entered into 1954 contract concerning such rights and had recorded such contract in copyright office; plaintiff had no knowledge of 1940 contract and assignment and it is not shown that plaintiff knew of newspaper reports and gossip items concerning rights in literary work; hence, plaintiff has rights granted to it by 1954 contract. Vidor v. Serlin, — Misc(2d series) —, — NYS(2d) —, 119 USPQ 104. Mf'd 7 AppDiv (2d series) 978, 184 NYS(2d) 482, which was aff'd 7 NY(2d series) 502, 199 NYS(2d) 669, 166 NE(2d) 680, 125 USPQ 364.

The register of copyrights is vested with some discretionary powers of investigation and may require a satisfactory showing of compliance with the plain conditions prescribed by the copyright law. 30 OAG 422.

Discretion of register of copyrights, in refusing to accept objects for deposit and registration, is not uncontrolled, but is subject to judicial review. Bailie v. Fisher, — AppDC —, 258 F(2d) 425, 117 USPQ 334.

12.   Works not reproduced for sale.— Copyright may also be had of the works of an author, of which copies are not reproduced for sale, by the deposit, with claim of copyright, of one complete copy of such work if it be a lecture or similar production or a dramatic, musical, or dramatico-musical composition; of a title and description, with one print taken from each scene or act, if the work be a motion-picture photoplay; of a photographic print if the work be a photograph; of a title and description, with not less than two prints taken from different sections of a complete motion picture, if the work be a motion picture other than a photoplay; or of a photograph or other identifying reproduction thereof, if it be a work of art or a plastic work or drawing. But the privilege of registration of copyright secured hereunder shall not exempt the copyright proprietor from the deposit of copies, under sections 13 and 14 of this title, where the work is later reproduced in copies for sale. (July 30, 1947, c. 391, § 1, 61 Stat. 656.)

NOTES TO DECISIONS

Phrase "works of an author, of which copies are not reproduced for sale" were intended to modify "lecture," "dramatic composition" and "musical composition." Universal Film Mfg. Co. v. Copperman, (DC-NY), 212 Fed 301. Aff'd 218 Fed 577.

Depositing printed copy, instead of typewritten or manuscript copy as specified in office rule was sufficient for unpublished song. Turner & Dahnken v. Crowley, (CCA 9), 252 Fed 749.

Where the essential steps have been taken to secure copyright of an unpublished song, slight variance in dates does not destroy proof of copyright. Turner & Dahnken v. Crowley, (CCA 9), 252 Fed 749.

Where photographs were registered as not to be reproduced for sale, but they had been reproduced for sale, action for infringement could not be maintained until §§ 13 and 209 of this title had been complied with. Lumiere v. Pathé Exchange, Inc., (CCA 2), 275 Fed 428.

Assignee of dramatic motion-picture rights of a copyrighted book failing to copyright play is not the owner of the copyright. Goldwyn Pictures Corp. v. Howells Sales Co., Inc., (CCA 2), 282 Fed 9.

Exhibition of motion picture in a limited noncommercial way did not constitute a publication under this section, which would require compliance with § 13 of this title. Patterson v. Century Productions, Inc., (CCA 2), 93 F(2d) 489, 35 USPQ 471, aff'g 19 FSupp 30, 33 USPQ 194.

This section is complied with by depositing complete episode, not summary or outline, which is intended to constitute first of series of connected episodes, that being only one which authors had written. Marx v. U. S., (CCA 9), 96 F(2d) 204, 37 USPQ 380.

This section granting copyright to articles not intended to be reprinted for publication is not

unconstitutional for failing to limit the duration of the copyright, in view of the limitation in § 24 of this title, the limitation in such case dating from deposit. Marx v. U. S., (CCA 9), 96 F(2d) 204, 37 USPQ 380.

Work copyrighted under this section is "published" within meaning of § 1 of this title. Shilkret v. Musicraft Records, Inc., (CCA 2), 131 F(2d) 929, 55 USPQ 469, rev'g 43 FSupp 184, 52 USPQ 164.

By complying with this section, which is anomaly in law of copyright, author gets statutory rights specified in § 1 of this title including, in case of musical compositions, right of mechanical recording and reproduction. Shilkret v. Musicraft Records, Inc., (CCA 2), 131 F(2d) 929, 55 USPQ 469, rev'g 43 FSupp 184, 52 USPQ 164.

"Date of publication" in § 24 of this title limiting duration of copyright refers to date of deposit under this section of works of which copies are not reproduced for sale notwithstanding that § 26 of this title defines "date of publication" of published work to mean earliest date when copies are placed on sale, sold, or publicly distributed. Shilkret v. Musicraft Records, Inc., (CCA 2), 131 F(2d) 929, 55 USPQ 469, rev'g 43 FSupp 184, 52 USPQ 164; Loew's, Inc. v. Superior Court, 18 Cal(2d series) 419, 115 Pac(2d) 983, 50 USPQ 641.

Public performance of uncopyrighted play for one week was not abandonment of common-law copyright protection. Burnett v. Lambino, (DC-NY), — FSupp —, 133 USPQ 325.

Restricted distribution to a circumscribed class of persons of an unpublished work, whether copyrighted under this section or uncopyrighted, for purpose of arousing interest in a possible sale or production, is a sufficiently limited distribution to work no forfeiture of author's rights, although rights would have been forfeited had there been a general publication. Burnett v. Lambino, (DC-NY), — FSupp —, 133 USPQ 325.

One carbon copy of intended radio talk with statutory fee deposited with register of copyrights procures copyright. Vinick v. Charm Publications, Inc., (DC-NY), 46 USPQ 510.

The register of copyrights has authority to enter a claim in a painting which is made merely as a first step in the production of a lithograph as a "work of art" within the meaning of this section, provided the painting itself is a work of art. 28 OAG 557.

Where the author secured a copyright of an unpublished dramatic composition under this section, he is restricted to the remedies provided by the statute for any infringement of that right, and the federal district court is the only court in which he may seek such redress originally. Loew's, Inc. v. Superior Court, 18 Cal(2d series) 419, 115 Pac(2d) 983, 50 USPQ 641.

Compliance with Copyright Act to secure exclusive performance of unpublished dramatic work serves as constructive notice of exclusive right and affords prima facie evidence of facts stated in certificate of registration. Loew's, Inc. v. Superior Court, 18 Cal(2d series) 419, 115 Pac(2d) 983, 50 USPQ 641.

Printed copies of song copyrighted under this section are required to bear notice of copyright only if (1) they were reproduced for sale or published or offered for sale, and (2) such reproduction, publication, or offering was by authority of copyright proprietor. Hirshon v. United States Corp., 100 AppDC 217, 243 F(2d) 640, 113 USPQ 110.

13.   Deposit of copies after publication —Action or proceeding for infringement.

—After copyright has been secured by publication of the work with the notice of copyright as provided in section 10 of this title, there shall be promptly deposited in the Copyright Office or in the mail addressed to the Register of Copyrights, Washington, District of Columbia, two complete copies of the best edition thereof then published, or if the work is by an author who is a citizen or subject of a foreign state or nation and has been published in a foreign country, one complete copy of the best edition then published in such foreign country, which copies or copy, if the work be a book or periodical, shall have been produced in accordance with the manufacturing provisions specified in section 16 of this title; or if such work be a contribution to a periodical, for which contribution special registration is requested, one copy of the issue or issues containing such contribution; or if the work belongs to a class specified in subsections (g), (h), (i) or (k) of section 5 of this title, and if the Register of Copyrights determines that it is impracticable to deposit copies because of their size, weight, fragility, or monetary value he may permit the deposit of photographs or other identifying reproductions in lieu of copies of the work as published under such rules and regulations as he may prescribe with the approval of the Librarian of Congress; or if the work is not reproduced in copies for sale there shall be deposited the copy, print, photograph, or other identifying reproduction provided by section 12 of this title, such copies or copy, print, photograph, or other reproduction to be accompanied in each case by a claim of copyright. No action or proceeding shall be maintained for infringement of copyright in any work until the provisions of this title with respect to the deposit of copies and registration of such work shall have been complied with. (July 30, 1947, c. 391, § 1, 61 Stat. 656; Mar. 29, 1956, c. 109, 70 Stat. 63.)

Amendment note.—Act Mar. 29, 1956, cited to text, inserted "or if the work belongs to a class specified in subsections (g), (h), (i) or (k) of section 5 of this title, and if the Register of Copyrights determines that it is impracticable to deposit copies because of their size, weight,

fragility, or monetary value he may permit the deposit of photographs or other identifying reproductions in lieu of copies of the work as published under such rules and regulations as he may prescribe with the approval of the Librarian of Congress;".

Cross reference.—Proof of deposit of copies by persons objecting to importation of copyrighted articles, see § 109 of this title.

NOTES TO DECISIONS
ANALYSIS

1. In general.
2. Time for filing.
3. —Prior law.
4. Best edition.
5. Contributions to periodicals.
6. Conditions precedent to suit.
7. Evidence of filing.

1. In general.

Although a person obtains his copyright after depositing the two copies as provided for, he must prove, in a suit for infringement, the facts of originality, of intellectual production, and of thought and conception on the part of the author. Burrow-Giles Lithographic Co. v. Sarony, 111 US 53, 28 LEd 349, 4 SCR 279, aff'g (CC-NY), 17 Fed 591.

There is no statutory provision for a second filing of a photograph or description, or for filing any amendments thereto. Caliga v. Inter Ocean Newspaper Co., 215 US 182, 54 LEd 150, 30 SCR 38, aff'g (CCA 7), 157 Fed 186.

It is unnecessary to deposit anything to secure copyright of a published work; it is only necessary to publish with notice of copyright. Deposit of copies is not required primarily in order to insure complete permanent collection of all copyrighted works open to the public. Washingtonian Publishing Co., Inc. v. Pearson, 306 US 30, 83 LEd 470, 59 SCR 397, 40 USPQ 190, rev'g 68 AppDC 373, 98 F(2d) 245, 37 USPQ 429, which rev'd 32 USPQ 113.

The deposit of copies after publication was not required as a prerequisite to a title to the copyright. Jollie v. Jaques, (CC-NY), FedCas 7,437, 1 Blatchf 618.

Mailing of copies after printing and before formal publication is sufficient. Chapman v. Ferry, (CC-Ore), 18 Fed 539.

Copies may be both delivered and mailed. Scribner v. Henry G. Allen Co., (CC-NY), 43 Fed 680.

A bill that alleges that the author deposited within 10 days after publication, in the librarian's office at Washington, two copies of the book, is sufficient against demurrer although it does not allege all prior steps. Scribner v. Henry G. Allen Co., (CC-NY), 49 Fed 854.

To secure a copyright in a photograph it is not necessary that the copies should be mailed after publication. Falk v. Donaldson, (CC-NY), 57 Fed 32.

Prior to Copyright Act of 1909, it was not necessary that copies of books deposited should contain notice of copyright. Osgood v. A. S. Aloe Instrument Co., (CC-Mo), 69 Fed 291.

The averment in a bill that "your orator did all the things required by law to be done in order to secure to himself the full enjoyment of all rights and privileges granted by the laws of the land governing copyrights," is not sufficient to show that the plaintiff has filed the two copies after publication. Burnell v. Chown, (CC-Ohio), 69 Fed 993.

Ignorance of recent change of law in reference to deposit of copies is no excuse for noncompliance therewith. Osgood v. A. S. Aloe Instrument Co., (CC-Mo), 83 Fed 470.

Requirement of prior statute for deposit of description and photograph of painting was not fulfilled by deposit of photograph only with title "Four-in-Hand." Bennett v. Carr, (CCA 2), 96 Fed 213.

Where domestic and foreign editions of book were published and copyright was obtained on domestic edition by compliance with copyright law, failure to file copies of foreign edition did not affect its copyright. G. & C. Merriam Co. v. United Dictionary Co., (CCA 7), 146 Fed 354, rev'g 140 Fed 768. Aff'd 208 US 260, 52 LEd 478, 28 SCR 290.

Owner of copyright must prove compliance with all statutory conditions. Bosselman v. Richardson, (CCA 2), 174 Fed 622.

Deposit of two copies of a song with Librarian of Congress, was a "publication." Stern v. Jerome H. Remick & Co., (CC-NY), 175 Fed 282.

Revised Statutes § 4959 in reference to subsequent sections embodying substantial changes said nothing about recopyright of original book but required deposit of one copy of the altered work evidently as a means of identifying it with the original copyrighted book. West Pub. Co. v. Edward Thompson Co., (CCA 2), 176 Fed 833, mod'g 169 Fed 833.

In a suit for infringement, a bill alleging compliance with this section by the deposit of "two copies of the best edition" was sufficient. Gerlach-Barklow Co. v. Morris & Bendien, Inc., (CCA 2), 23 F(2d) 159.

This section implies that copyright is secured by publication other than deposit with copyright office. American Visuals Corp. v. Holland, (CA 2), 239 F(2d) 740, 111 USPQ 288.

Action for copyright infringement is not dismissed on motion for failure of declaration to sufficiently contain allegations that plaintiff has complied with this section since not only does plaintiff allege that he has complied with § 209 of this title and all other laws governing copyright but he also annexes to declaration a copy of certificate of registration issued by register of copyrights, which carries with it a presumption of regularity. Pizzano v. Knowles & Co., Inc., (DC-Mass), 37 FSupp 118, 49 USPQ 140.

To preserve and protect copyright, applicant must (1) publish work with statutory notice in manner and form provided by statute, (2) file thereafter two copies with register of copyrights, and (3) make application for registration for copyright. Advertisers Exchange, Inc. v. Anderson, (DC-Iowa), 52 FSupp 809, 59 USPQ 391. Aff'd 144 F(2d) 907, 63 USPQ 39.

Complaint for copyright infringement is dismissed where it merely alleges proper deposit of two copies of work, but admits that certificate of registration has not been obtained. Algonquin Music, Inc. v. Mills Music, Inc., (DC-NY), 93 FSupp 268, 86 USPQ 481.

By depositing in copyright office or in mail addressed thereto two copies of best editions of books then published together with applications for registration of claims to copyright in books, same being on duly completed copyright office forms, accompanied by payment or tender of fee of $2 for registration as to each volume of books, this section was duly complied with not only in respect to books but also as to every copyrightable component part thereof. King Features Syndicate, Inc. v. Bouve, (DC-DC), 48 USPQ 237.

Findings of fact and conclusions of law as to publication and deposit of copies made by register of copyrights may be reviewed by court in suit against register and are neither conclusive nor binding on court; if erroneous, may be rectified by court. King Features Syndicate, Inc. v. Bouve, (DC-DC), 48 USPQ 237.

2.   Time for filing.

Mere delay in making deposit of copies of copyrighted material is not enough to cause forfeiture of copyright distinctly granted on publication with notice. Washingtonian Publishing Co., Inc. v. Pearson, 306 US 30, 83 LEd 470, 59 SCR 397, 40 USPQ 190, rev'g 68 AppDC 373, 98 F(2d) 245, 37 USPQ 429, which rev'd 32 USPQ 113.

Where plaintiff deposited copies the same day 50 copies were received from the printer, such copies being retained by plaintiff or sent to branch offices although no general distribution was made until two days later, there was sufficient publication to comply with statute. No-Leak-O Piston Ring Co. v. Norris, (CCA 4), 277 Fed 951, aff'g 271 Fed 536.

Deposit of copies with the register two weeks before publication does not defeat the copyright where such deposit continued after publication. Joe Mittenthal, Inc. v. Irving Berlin, Inc., (DC-NY), 291 Fed 714.

The publication of a song, before copies are deposited with the register of copyrights, does not constitute an abandonment of copyright when such publication was made according to § 10 of this title. M. Witmark & Sons v. Pastime Amusement Co., (DC-SC), 298 Fed 470. Aff'd 2 F(2d) 1020.

The essence of copyright is publication with notice of copyright; registration is merely a means of perfecting it, no specific time for such registration being provided for, though registration is essential to maintaining an action for infringement. Davenport Quigley Expedition, Inc. v. Century Productions, Inc., (DC-NY), 18 FSupp 974.

Where there was publication with notice of copyright in January and deposit in March the delay did not prejudice rights. Freedman v. Milnag Leasing Corp., (DC-NY), 20 FSupp 802, 35 USPQ 184.

Acquisition of federal copyright requires (1) publication of work with notice and (2) prompt deposit in copyright office or in mail of two complete copies of best edition of publication; delay of 13 years in making deposit does not invalidate copyright; so far as institution of civil action is concerned, delay merely means that no action can be maintained until deposit has been made. Silvers v. Russell, (DC-Cal), 113 FSupp 119, 98 USPQ 376.

Failure to promptly file copies of copyrighted editions of newspaper does not invalidate copyright. Massapequa Publishing Co. Inc. v. Observer, Inc., (DC-NY), — FSupp —, 126 USPQ 229.

3. —Prior law.

Deposit of printed copy of title under prior acts, see Wheaton v. Peters, 33 US(8 Pet) 591, 8 LEd 1055, rev'g (CC-Pa), FedCas 17,486; Callaghan v. Myers, 128 US 617, 32 LEd 547, 9 SCR 177, mod'g (CC-Ill), 24 Fed 636; Baker v. Taylor, (CC-NY), FedCas 782, 2 Blatchf 82; Boucicault v. Hart, (CC-NY), FedCas 1,692, 13 Blatchf 47; Carillo v. Shook, (CC-NY), FedCas 2,407; Dwight v. Appleton, (CC-NY), FedCas 4,215; Parkinson v. Laselle, (CC-Cal), FedCas 10,762, 3 Sawy 330; Myers v. Callaghan, (CC-Ill), 5 Fed 726; Donnelley v. Ivers, (CC-NY), 18 Fed 592; Carte v. Evans, (CC-Mass), 27 Fed 861; Blume v. Spear, (CC-NY), 30 Fed 629; Falk v. Howell, (CC-NY), 34 Fed 739; Falk v. Gast Lithograph & Engraving Co., Ltd., (CC-NY), 48 Fed 262. Aff'd 54 Fed 890; Daly v. Webster, (CCA 2), 56 Fed 483, rev'g 47 Fed 903; Black v. Henry G. Allen Co., (CC-NY), 56 Fed 764; Edward Thompson Co. v. American Law Book Co., (CC-NY), 119 Fed 217; Patterson v. J. S. Ogilvie Pub. Co., (CC-NY), 119 Fed 451; Dam v. Kirke La Shelle Co., (CC-NY), 166 Fed 589. Aff'd 175 Fed 902, 41 LRA(NS) 1002, 20 AnnCas 1173; Freeman v. The Trade Register, (CC-Wash), 173 Fed 419; Chapman v. Ferry, (CC-Ore), 187 Fed 539.

Where copies are not filed within the proper time after publication, there can be no copyright. Wheaton v. Peters, 33 US(8 Pet) 591, 8 LEd 1055, rev'g (CC-Pa), FedCas 17,486; Struve v. Schwedler, (CC-NY), FedCas 13,551, 4 Blatchf 23.

Under R. S. § 4956, deposit of copies one day before publication instead of within ten days thereafter was a substantial compliance. Belford, Clarke & Co. v. Scribner, 144 US 488, 36 LEd 514, 12 SCR 734, aff'g (CC-Ill), 50 Fed 473.

Where a work consists of a series of volumes, delivery of first volume within required time and others before piracy has been committed or action begun is a sufficient compliance. Dwight v. Appleton, (CC-NY), FedCas 4,215.

Under prior statute sending book to booksellers and private individuals for examination more than ten days prior to deposit of copies constituted a publication, and copyright was invalid. Gottsberger v. Aldine Book Pub. Co., (CC-Mass), 33 Fed 381.

Direct proof to show seasonable deposit of copies of a publication for purposes of the copyright statute is not required where it is beyond doubt that such copies were forwarded so early that defendant could not possibly have been prejudiced by any delay. Ladd v. Oxnard, (CC-Mass), 75 Fed 703.

A copyright may be completed by depositing the two copies after publication at any time, when the book had not previously been published by anyone else. 1 OAG 532.

Where a person does not complete his copyright by filing copies after publication, he loses his rights and the right to the copyright cannot be revived. Koppel v. Downing, 11 AppDC 93.

4. Best edition.

Cutting out and depositing pages containing article in bound volume of an encyclopedia is a sufficient compliance with "best edition" provision of statute. Black v. Henry G. Allen Co., (CC-NY), 56 Fed 764.

Book containing comic strips printed on one side of paper only and bearing notice of copyright on title page, although each item in book bears separate copyright notice and most of items bear later release date on which date newspapers are first authorized to use material, is book within meaning of that term as used in § 5 of this title and is composite work within meaning of that term as used in §§ 3 and 5 of this title; it does not consist of page proofs of contributions to newspapers. King Features Syndicate, Inc. v. Bouve, (DC-DC), 48 USPQ 237.

Where only one edition of book has been published, copies thereof deposited with register of copyrights are of the best edition although book might not be suitable for inclusion in "library" collection for public use. Bouve v. Twentieth Century-Fox Film Corp., 74 AppDC 271, 122 F(2d) 51, 50 USPQ 338, aff'g 33 FSupp 462, 45 USPQ 411.

5. Contributions to periodicals.

Copyright proprietor, having complied with this section, court holds that demands and notices by register of copyrights, purporting to be pursuant to § 14 of this title, that proprietor should deposit copies of newspapers in which copyrighted matter was republished and should apply for special registration as to each item so republished, should be vacated and set aside. King Features Syndicate, Inc. v. Bouve, (DC-DC), 48 USPQ 237.

Book consisting of comic strips was published with proper copyright notice; publication of certain or all of its parts in newspapers, under authority of copyright proprietor subsequent to initial publication in book, constitutes mere republication of parts and proprietor should not be required to deposit copies of newspapers or to apply for special registration in respect to republished parts. King Features Syndicate Inc. v. Bouve, (DC-DC), 48 USPQ 237.

This section applies only to situation where special registration is requested of contribution for periodical; register of copyrights cannot make arbitrary requirement for such special registration. Bouve v. Twentieth Century-Fox Film Corp., 74 AppDC 271, 122 F(2d) 51, 50 USPQ 338, aff'g 33 FSupp 462, 45 USPQ 411.

6. Conditions precedent to suit.

While no action for infringement can be maintained before copies are actually deposited, mere delay, in this case fourteen months, will not destroy the right to sue. Washingtonian Publishing Co., Inc. v. Pearson, 306 US 30, 83 LEd 470, 59 SCR 397, 40 USPQ 190, rev'g 68 AppDC 373, 98 F(2d) 245, 37 USPQ 429, which rev'd 32 USPQ 113.

The prohibition in this section respecting maintenance of actions for infringement of copyright goes to jurisdiction of the courts. New York Times Co. v. Star Co., (CC-NY), 195 Fed 110.

Injunction against infringement issued prior to deposit is premature and has no binding force. New York Times Co. v. Star Co., (CC-NY), 195 Fed 110.

Maintenance of suit in equity for an injunction against publication of a copyrighted narrative is covered by the phrase "action or proceeding for the infringement of copyright." New York Times Co. v. Star Co., (CC-NY), 195 Fed 110.

The prohibition in this section with respect to actions for infringement of copyright is not qualified by § 112 of this title. New York Times Co. v. Star Co., (CC-NY), 195 Fed 110.

The provision prohibiting the maintaining of an action for infringement of a copyright until certain provisions are complied with applies to an equity action for an injunction and an accounting, since such action is an action for the infringement of a copyright. New York Times Co. v. Sun Printing & Publishing Ass'n, (CCA), 204 Fed 586.

The prohibition in this section against maintaining a suit includes the commencement thereof. New York Times Co. v. Sun Printing & Publishing Ass'n, (CCA 2), 204 Fed 586.

Plaintiff must show compliance with copyright statutes to be entitled to maintain suit for infringement of copyright. Davies v. Bowes, (CCA 2), 219 Fed 178, aff'g 209 Fed 53.

Although a first registration of a copyright under § 12 of this title may not have been valid, a second registration obtained by filing the two copies after publication may be made the basis of a suit. Turner & Dahnken v. Crowley, (CCA 9), 252 Fed 749.

Bill for infringement of copyright on photograph reproduced for sale was dismissed where only certificate of registration was as for photograph not to be reproduced for sale which requires deposit of only one copy. Lumiere v. Pathé Exchange, Inc., (CCA 2), 275 Fed 428.

This section makes compliance with provisions of Copyright Act as to deposit of copies and registration a condition precedent to maintaining infringement action; "action" in this setting includes criminal as well as civil action. U. S. v. Backer, (CCA 2), 134 F(2d) 533, 57 USPQ 133.

This section forbids action for copyright infringement where register of copyrights had refused to accept watch as copyrightable work of art under § 5(g) of this title. Vacheron & Constantin-Le Coultre Watches, Inc. v. Benrus Watch Co., Inc., (CA 2), 260 F(2d) 637, 119 USPQ 189, mod'g 155 FSupp 932, 115 USPQ 115.

Complaint is dismissed under this section where copyright proprietor made no deposit in copyright office until several months after action was commenced, although before trial. Rudolf Lesch Fine Arts, Inc. v. Metal, (DC-NY), 51 FSupp 69, 58 USPQ 668.

Where complaint alleges fictitious date and number of certificate of copyright action and is dismissed for failure to make deposit in copyright office before action was commenced, federal court has no jurisdiction of claim for breach of printer's implied contract not to reproduce customer's material for own purpose. Rudolf Lesch Fine Arts, Inc. v. Metal, (DC-NY), 51 FSupp 69, 58 USPQ 668.

Although certificate of registration shows that copyright on catalogue was secured by publication in 1942, catalogue displays notice "copyrighted 1942, 1943" and evidence shows that some material was added to original edition of catalogue; since no evidence is adduced to show that subsequent altered edition was deposited in copyright office and since, therefore, office does not have on deposit two complete copies of catalogue, this section bars plaintiffs from maintaining copyright infringement action. Unistrut Corp. v. Power, (DC-Mass), 175 FSupp 294, 121 USPQ 381. Mf'd 280 F(2d) 18, 126 USPQ 82.

7. Evidence of filing.

(Certificate of registration as evidence of deposit, see § 209 of this title.)

Where the law makes the delivery of copies of the volume a requisite for plaintiff's right to a copyright, he must prove it by legal and satisfactory evidence, when he founds a claim on his copyright in the courts of justice. Wheaton v. Peters, 33 US(8 Pet) 591, 8 LEd 1055, rev'g (CC-Pa), FedCas 17,486.

Proof of deposit of copies with librarian or in a post-office is essential. Merrell v. Tice, 104 US 557, 26 LEd 854.

Signed memorandum on same paper as certificate is prima facie evidence of deposit. Callaghan v. Myers, 128 US 617, 32 LEd 547, 9 SCR 177, mod'g (CC-Ill), 24 Fed 636.

Under R. S. § 4956, certificate of librarian was competent evidence of deposit of copies though not under seal. Belford, C. & Co. v. Scribner, 144 US 488, 36 LEd 514, 12 SCR 734, aff'g (CC-Ill), 50 Fed 473.

Oral proof of deposit of copies and production of librarian's receipt is sufficient evidence. Blume v. Spear, (CC-NY), 30 Fed 629.

Uncorroborated, but uncontradicted testimony of copyrighter as to mailing of copies is sufficient evidence of deposit, notwithstanding register's certificate of search and failure to find any copies on file. Patterson v. J. S. Ogilvie Pub. Co., (CC-NY), 119 Fed 451.

A certificate showing that two copies of a book were deposited is competent evidence of such fact in an action for infringement of the copyright of the book, but the certificate does not per se establish the copyright. Huebsch v. Arthur H. Crist Co., (DC-NY), 209 Fed 885.

Uncontradicted testimony as to depositing of copyright books in the mail addressed to the register of copyrights was sufficient evidence as to compliance with statute. Maddux v. Grey, (DC-Cal), 43 F(2d) 441.

14. Failure to deposit—Demand—Penalty.—Should the copies called for by section 13 of this title not be promptly deposited as provided in this title, the Register of Copyrights may at any time after the publication of the work, upon actual notice, require the proprietor of the copyright to deposit them, and after the said demand shall have been made, in default of the deposit of copies of the work within three months from any part of the United States, except an outlying territorial possession of the United States, or within six months from any outlying territorial possession of the United States, or from any foreign country, the proprietor of the copyright shall be liable to a fine of $100 and to pay to the Library of Congress twice the amount of the retail price of the best edition of the work, and the copyright shall become void. (July 30, 1947, c. 391, § 1, 61 Stat. 657.)

NOTES TO DECISIONS

Prompt deposit when deemed necessary should be enforced through actual notice by the register. Washingtonian Publishing Co., Inc. v. Pearson, 306 US 30, 83 LEd 470, 59 SCR 397, rev'g 68 AppDC 373, 98 F(2d) 245, 37 USPQ 429, which rev'd 32 USPQ 113.

Owner who fails to deposit promptly may do so without prejudice after delinquency. Joe Mittenthal, Inc. v. Irving Berlin, Inc., (DC-NY), 291 Fed 714.

Copyright proprietor having complied with § 13 of this title, court holds that demands and notices by register of copyrights, purporting to be pursuant to this section, that proprietor should deposit copies of newspapers in which copyrighted matter was republished and should apply for special registration as to each item so republished, should be vacated and set aside. King Features Syndicate, Inc. v. Bouve, (DC-DC), 48 USPQ 237.

15. Postmaster's receipt — Transmission by mail without cost.—The postmaster to whom are delivered the articles deposited as provided in sections 12 and 13 of this title shall, if requested, give a receipt therefor and shall mail them to their destination without cost to the copyright claimant. (July 30, 1947, c. 391, § 1, 61 Stat. 657.)

16. Mechanical work to be done in United States.—Of the printed book or periodical specified in section 5, subsections (a) and (b), of this title, except the original text of a book or periodical of foreign origin in a language or languages other than English, the text of all copies accorded protection under this title, except as below provided, shall be printed from type set within the limits of the United States, either by hand or by the aid of any kind of typesetting machine, or from plates made within the limits of the United States from type set therein, or, if the text be produced by lithographic process, or photoengraving process, then by a process wholly performed within the limits of the United States, and the printing of the text and binding of the said book shall be performed within the limits of the United States; which requirements shall extend also to the illustrations within a book consisting of printed text and illustrations produced by lithographic process, or photoengraving process, and also to separate lithographs or photoengravings, except where in either case the subjects represented are located in a foreign country and illustrate a scientific work or reproduce a work of art: Provided, however, That said requirements shall not apply to works in raised characters for the use of the blind, or to books or periodicals of foreign origin in a language or languages other than English, or to works printed or produced in the United States by any other process than those above specified in this section, or to copies of books or periodicals, first published abroad in the English language, imported into the United States within five years after first publication in a foreign state or nation up to the number of fifteen hundred copies of each such book or periodical if said copies shall contain notice of copyright in accordance with sections 10, 19, and 20 of this title and if ad interim copyright in said work shall have been obtained pursuant to section 22 of this title prior to the importation into the United States of any copy except those permitted by the provisions of section 107 of this title: Provided further, That the provisions of this section shall not affect the right of importation under the provisions of section 107 of this title. (July 30, 1947, c. 391, § 1, 61 Stat. 657; June 3, 1949, c. 171, § 1, 63 Stat. 153; Aug. 31, 1954, c. 1161, § 2, 68 Stat. 1031.)

Amendment notes.—Act June 3, 1949, cited to text, inserted "or periodical"; substituted, in the first proviso, beginning with "or to works printed or produced" to the end of the first proviso for "or to books published abroad in the English language seeking ad interim protection under this title, or to works printed or produced in the United States by any other process than those above specified in this section;" and added the second proviso.

Act Aug. 31, 1954, cited to text, substituted "first published abroad" for "of foreign origin" in the first proviso; omitted "nor the extension of time within which to comply with conditions and formalities granted by Presidential proclamation, No. 2608, of March 14, 1944" which appeared at the end of the second proviso.

Cross references.—Deposit of copies after publication, see § 13 of this title.

Importation of copies not produced in accordance with this section, see § 107 of this title.

NOTES TO DECISIONS

A musical composition is not a "book" although consisting of many pages and bound in book form. Oliver Ditson Co. v. Littleton, (CCA 1), 67 Fed 905, aff'g 62 Fed 597.

Under R. S. § 4956, as amended by Act Mar. 3, 1891, burden was not on complainant to allege and prove that work was done within the limits of the United States. Osgood v. A. S. Aloe Instrument Co., (CC-Mo), 69 Fed 291.

Revised Statutes § 4956 as amended in 1891, providing that books "shall be printed from type set within the limits of the United States" was noneffective as to a book printed in 1890. Patterson v. J. S. Ogilvie Pub. Co., (CC-NY), 119 Fed 451.

A print and a lithograph were distinguishable. Hills & Co., Ltd. v. Austrick, (CC-NY), 120 Fed 862.

Fact that foreign edition of domestic book was printed in the foreign country from plates made in this country did not authorize infringer to import such foreign edition and, by making copies, infringe copyrighted domestic book. G. & C. Merriam Co. v. United Dictionary Co., (CCA 7), 146 Fed 354, rev'g 140 Fed 768. Aff'd 208 US 260, 52 LEd 478, 28 SCR 290.

A dramatic composition is not a "book" although bound in book form and is not subject to domestic manufacture provisions. Hervieu v. J. S. Ogilvie Pub. Co., (CC-NY), 169 Fed 978.

Proof of manufacture in the United States was sufficient. Huebsch v. Arthur H. Crist Co., (DC-NY), 209 Fed 885.

Sale of copies of copyrighted work printed from type not set in United States does not debar copyright holder from relief against infringement. Bentley v. Tibbals, (CCA 2), 223 Fed 247.

Where copyrighted manuals were printed in the United States, it is immaterial that some of the editions of the manuals were printed in England. Meccano, Ltd. v. Wagner, (DC-Ohio), 234 Fed 912. Mf'd 246 Fed 603.

The provisions which require books to be printed from type set within the limits of the United States are not complied with by printing from type set within the Philippine Islands, when Congress has not extended the copyright laws to the Philippines. 25 OAG 25; 25 OAG 179.

Application for registration of copyright should be denied where the copy, printed and bound in accordance with the manufacturing provisions of this section, is only a fragment of the work. 28 OAG 176.

The provision of this section, insofar as it applies to books, is restricted to printed books. 28 OAG 265.

Whether certain lithographic prints produced in Germany are "works of art" within the meaning of this section, is a question of fact which should be determined by the copyright office. 30 OAG 422.

17. Affidavit to accompany copies. — In case of the book the copies so deposited shall be accompanied by an affidavit under the official seal of any officer authorized to administer oaths within the United States, duly made by the person claiming copyright or by his duly authorized agent or representative residing in the United States, or by the printer who has printed the book, setting forth that the copies deposited have been printed from type set within the limits of the United States or from plates made within the limits of the United States from type set therein; or, if the text be produced by lithographic process, or photoengraving process, that such process was wholly performed within the limits of the United States and that the printing of the text and binding of the said book have also been performed within the limits of the United States. Such affidavit shall state also the place where and the establishment or establishments in which such type was set or plates were made or lithographic process, or photoengraving process or printing and binding were performed and the date of the completion of the printing of the book or the date of publication. (July 30, 1947, c. 391, § 1, 61 Stat. 657.)

NOTES TO DECISIONS

Failure of agent of proprietor of copyright to strike out printed statements not applicable to capacity in which he made an affidavit in application for registration does not invalidate the copyright. Meccano, Ltd. v. Wagner, (DC-Ohio), 234 Fed 912. Mf'd 246 Fed 603.

Affidavit of an agent of a proprietor of a foreign copyright made pursuant to this section did not invalidate the United States copyright, though agent did not actually see the type set or the binding of the book, but employed a printer to do the printing and furnished him the copy. Meccano, Ltd. v. Wagner, (DC-Ohio), 234 Fed 912. Mf'd 246 Fed 603.

A copyright secured in the name of a person other than the composer was valid although a mistake was made as to the date of publication in the affidavit attached to the application. Sebring Pottery Co. v. Steubenville Pottery Co., (DC-Ohio), 9 FSupp 383, 14 USPQ 46.

Although book was published and distributed early in 1943, affidavit accompanying application for copyright registration erroneously stated that December 20, 1943, was date of publication; all copies of book contained notice of copyright; inaccuracy as to date of publication, standing alone, did not affect validity of copyright. Ziegelheim v. Flohr, (DC-NY), 119 FSupp 324, 100 USPQ 189.

18. Making false affidavit.—Any person who, for the purpose of obtaining registration of a claim to copyright, shall knowingly make a false affidavit as to his having complied with the above conditions shall be deemed guilty of a misdemeanor, and upon conviction thereof shall be punished by a fine of not more than $1,000, and all of his rights and privileges under said copyright shall thereafter be forfeited. (July 30, 1947, c. 391, § 1, 61 Stat. 657.)

19. Notice—Form.—The notice of copyright required by section 10 of this title shall consist either of the word "Copyright," the abbreviation "Copr.", or the symbol ©, accompanied by the name of the copyright proprietor, and if the work be a printed literary, musical, or dramatic work, the notice shall include also the year in which the copyright was secured by publication. In the case, however, of copies of works specified in subsections (f) to (k), inclusive, of section 5 of this title, the notice may consist of the letter C enclosed within a circle, thus ©, accompanied by the initials, monogram, mark, or symbol of the copyright proprietor: *Provided*, That on some accessible portion of such copies or of the margin, back, permanent base, or pedestal, or of the substance on which such copies shall be mounted, his name shall appear. But in the case of works in which copyright was subsisting on July 1, 1909, the notice of copyright may be either in one of the forms prescribed herein or may consist of the following words: "Entered according to Act of Congress, in the year ___, by A. B., in the office of the Librarian of Congress, at Washington, D. C.," or, at his option, the word "Copyright," together with the year the copyright was entered and the name of the party by whom it was taken out; thus, "Copyright, 19—, by A. B." (July 30, 1947, c. 391, § 1, 61 Stat. 658; Aug. 31, 1954, c. 1161, § 3, 68 Stat. 1032.)

Amendment note.—Act Aug. 31, 1954, cited to text, substituted " 'Copr.', or the symbol ©," for "or 'Copr.' " and substituted "Washington, D. C.," for "Washington;".

Cross references. — Accidental omission of notice, see § 21 of this title.

Fraudulent notice, or removal or alteration of notice, see § 105 of this title.

Importation of article bearing false notice, see § 106 of this title.

Place of affixing notice, see § 20 of this title.

Publication of work with notice, see § 10 of this title.

NOTES TO DECISIONS
ANALYSIS

1. In general.
2. Sufficiency of notice.
3. —Form of notice.
4. —Proprietor—Licensees—Assignees.
5. —Date of copyright.
6. Location of notice.
7. —Pictures, maps, drawings, or works of art.
8. —Jewelry.
9. Foreign publications.
10. Copyrights prior to July 1, 1909.

1. In general.

General testimony as to inscription of statutory copyright notice on copies published is sufficient to establish compliance with this section. Burrow-Giles Lithographic Co. v. Sarony, 111 US 53, 28 LEd 349, 4 SCR 279, aff'g (CC-NY), 17 Fed 591.

Original copyright notice may be inserted in another edition published in a different number of volumes, without impairing copyright. Dwight v. Appleton, (CC-NY), FedCas 4,215.

Compliance with the requirement of notice must be pleaded and proved as a prerequisite to the maintenance of an action for the infringement of a copyright. Falk v. Gast Lith. & Eng. Co., Ltd., (CC-NY), 40 Fed 168.

A sample advertisement, from which dealers might place orders for calendars mounting a copyrighted picture, does not require the notice. Gerlach-Barklow Co. v. Morris & Bendien, Inc., (CCA 2), 23 F(2d) 159.

It is no defense to a suit for injunction for the infringement of a copyright, that defendant has in his possession pictures without the notice of copyright, when it cannot be shown that the pictures left plaintiff's possession without the notice. Gerlach-Barklow Co. v. Morris & Bendien, Inc., (CCA 2), 23 F(2d) 159.

Statutory marking is of essence to preservation of copyright monopoly. Basevi v. Edward O'Toole Co., Inc., (DC-NY), 26 FSupp 41, 40 USPQ 333.

Plaintiff furnished defendant under contract matrices of advertisements bearing improper copyright notice; having permitted publication without statutory notice, plaintiff released advertisements for use to general public, including defendant whose use after termination of contract is lawful. Advertisers Exchange, Inc. v. Anderson, (DC-Iowa), 52 FSupp 809, 59 USPQ 391. Aff'd 144 F(2d) 907, 63 USPQ 39.

Strict compliance with statutory requirements is essential to perfection of copyright, and failure fully to conform to form of notice prescribed by statute results in abandonment of right and dedication of work to public. Group Publishers, Inc. v. Winchell, (DC-NY), 86 FSupp 573, 83 USPQ 461.

Even if design printed on fabric from which dresses are manufactured were copyrightable, copyright was lost by failure to publish proper copyright notice on fabric and dresses. Verney Corp. v. Rose Fabric Converters Corp., (DC-NY), 87 FSupp 802, 83 USPQ 386.

Statutory copyright is created only by proper copyright notice printed in original publication and in each republication. Wrench v. Universal Pictures Co., Inc., (DC-NY), 104 FSupp 374, 92 USPQ 350.

Copyright notice which does not comply in substance with statute is legally ineffective; such a notice is not rendered legally effective as to a particular infringer because he had actual knowledge of copyright or circumstances were such as to direct his attention to sources from which information as to copyright might be obtained. Metro Associated Services, Inc. v. Webster City Graphic, Inc., (DC-Iowa), 117 FSupp 224, 100 USPQ 88.

Courts are liberal in saving copyright where deviation from notice requirements of this section is formal and not substantial. Peter Pan Fabrics, Inc. v. Acadia Co., Inc., (DC-NY), 173 FSupp 292, 121 USPQ 81. Aff'd 274 F(2d) 487, 124 USPQ 154.

Purpose of notice requirement in this section is to advise public of copyright proprietor's claim and to prevent innocent persons, unaware of copyright, from incurring infringement penalties; proprietor's name is sufficient in form if it gives notice of copyright to one who is looking for the truth and desires to avoid infringement; thus, whether proprietor uses present trade name "Plasti-Personalities" in copyright notice or original trade name "Plastic Personalities," either designation gives notice of copyright to interested persons and is sufficient to lead them to proprietor. Doran v. Sunset House Distributing Corp., (DC-Cal), 197 FSupp 940, 131 USPQ 94.

Public distribution of copies of copyrighted work not bearing copyright notice amounts to general publication of the work and results in a dedication or forfeiture where it is without any limitation as to use and is made with knowledge and express or implied approval of copyright owners. Klasmer v. Baltimore Football, Inc., (DC-Md), 200 FSupp 255, 132 USPQ 36.

Copyright notice properly identifies proprietor where it bears word which has been registered as proprietor's trademark and which has been extensively advertised so that it has become known in the trade as indicative of proprietor. Dan Kasoff, Inc. v. Gresco Jewelry Co., Inc., (DC-NY), — FSupp —, 133 USPQ 438.

If statute requires no notice of copyright, improper notice does not constitute a violation. Hirshon v. United Artists Corp., 100 AppDC 217, 243 F(2d) 640, 113 USPQ 110.

2. Sufficiency of notice.

It is not necessary that complainant show separate, distinct, and specific proof of notice on each one of his copies, general testimony is sufficient to establish a prima facie case. Falk v. Gast Lith. & Eng. Co., Ltd., (CC-NY), 40 Fed 168.

Residence of party is not required to be stated in copyright notice. Werckmeister v. Springer Lithographing Co., (CC-NY), 63 Fed 808.

A slight variance in the words, or in the order of the words, if the matter is substantially the same, will not invalidate copyright notice. Bentley v. Tibbals, (CCA 2), 223 Fed 247.

Purpose of this section is to afford to those, who might otherwise innocently infringe, notice that copyright is claimed and by whom; section does not establish what degree of proximity must exist between the two to satisfy requirement that symbol be "accompanied by" the name; placement of symbol and name is left wholly to taste or discretion so long as purpose of statute is fulfilled by so placing them in relation to each other as to give reasonable notice of claim of copyright and of claimant's identity. Glenco Refrigeration Corp. v. Raetone Commercial Refrigerator Corp., (DC-Pa), 149 FSupp 691, 113 USPQ 155.

There must be substantial compliance with this section in order that copyright be preserved; purpose of notice is to inform public of copyright and warn against republication. Inter-City Press, Inc. v. Siegfried, (DC-Mo), 172 FSupp 37, 118 USPQ 446.

Newspaper's copyright notice is sufficient to reasonably inform intelligent person that newspaper is copyrighted since, despite fact that it is in smaller type than rest of newsprint, it is legible to naked eye. Inter-City Press, Inc. v. Siegfried, (DC-Mo), 172 FSupp 37, 118 USPQ 446.

Court is not obligated to look beyond face of copyright notice to determine its sufficiency. Inter-City Press, Inc. v. Siegfried, (DC-Mo), 172 FSupp 37, 118 USPQ 446.

Only one copyright notice need appear on blouse bearing two separate imprints of same design. Scarves by Vera, Inc. v. United Merchants & Manufacturers, Inc., (DC-NY), 173 FSupp 625, 121 USPQ 578.

Although apparently no date was necessary on copyrighted artificial flower, copyright notice on stem contained 1961 date despite fact that publication date was 1959; however, flower also bore on a leaf another copyright notice which correctly gave date as 1959; since notices differ as to date, this may be confusing, but notice is not thereby rendered so affirmatively misleading as to justify invalidating copyright. Prestige Floral, Societe Anonyme v. California Artificial Flower Co. (Inc.), (DC-NY), 201 FSupp 287, 132 USPQ 350.

If copyright owner publishes copyrighted material with defective notice of copyright, he abandons copyright and dedicates material to public; thus, owner of copyrighted map abandoned copyright and dedicated map to public by publication of substantially similar map bearing name of another party as copyright proprietor inasmuch as there is no evidence that a valid, registered assignment of copyright was made by owner to other party prior to latter publication; therefore, notice did not contain name of proprietor of record. Carter v. Hawaii Transportation Co., (DC-Hawaii), 201 FSupp 301, 133 USPQ 65.

3. —Form of notice.

Copyright notice, consisting of letter C inclosed within a circle, if so badly indistinct and blurred as to be illegible, is insufficient. Strauss v. Penn Printing & Publishing Co., (DC-Pa), 220 Fed 977.

Symbol of initials with "c" in circle in scroll, impossible to identify with naked eye and without close scrutiny with magnifying glass, does not comply with copyright statute. Alfred Decker Cohn Co. v. Etchison Hat Co., (DC-Va), 225 Fed 135; Goes Lithographing Co. v. Apt Lithographic Co., Inc., (DC-NY), 14 FSupp 620, 30 USPQ 119; Smith v. Wilkinson, (DC-NH), 19 FSupp 841, 35 USPQ 113. Aff'd 97 F(2d) 506, 38 USPQ 1; Deward & Rich, Inc. v. Bristol Savings & Loan Corp., (DC-Va), 34 FSupp 345, 47 USPQ 128. Aff'd 120 F(2d) 537, 50 USPQ 1.

Section 3 of this title, which protects component parts of work copyrighted, does not protect plaintiff which deliberately made notice of copyright on mats furnished to purchasers of copyrighted material illegible to lead reading public to think that matter published was original with advertiser. Deward & Rich, Inc. v. Bristol Savings & Loan Corp., (CCA 4), 120 F(2d) 537, 50 USPQ 1, aff'g 34 FSupp 345, 47 USPQ 128.

Plaintiff copyrighted as book, manual containing illustrations and text for advertisements; it furnished matrices of parts of manual and allowed defendant to publish them without attaching form of copyright notice required for books or parts thereof (notice attached was "C" in circle), thereby releasing parts from copyright to general public. Advertisers Exchange, Inc. v. Anderson, (CCA 8), 144 F(2d) 907, 63 USPQ 39, aff'g 52 FSupp 809, 59 USPQ 391.

While some slight literal variance from form of notice prescribed may perhaps not necessarily be fatal, there can be no general or substantial deviation; use of special form and designation is limited to specified classes as matter of law and its use as to copyright for which general form and designation are required is not sufficient notice. Advertisers Exchange, Inc. v. Anderson, (CCA 8), 144 F(2d) 907, 63 USPQ 39, aff'g 52 FSupp 809, 59 USPQ 391.

Deliberate selection and use of form of copyright notice which fails to meet substantive requirements of this section is not omission by accident or mistake of prescribed notice from particular copy or copies within intent of § 21 of this title. Advertisers Exchange, Inc. v. Anderson, (CCA 8), 144 F(2d) 907, 63 USPQ 39, aff'g 52 FSupp 809, 59 USPQ 391.

"Copyright Notice. This work is copyrighted, as prescribed by the laws of the United States and anyone duplicating or causing to be duplicated the whole or a part of the same without written permission from [copyright proprietor] will be prosecuted to the fullest extent. October 22, 1931. ©" substantially complies with this section. Deward & Rich, Inc. v. Bristol Savings & Loan Corp., (DC-Va), 34 FSupp 345, 47 USPQ 128. Aff'd 120 F(2d) 537, 50 USPQ 1.

Although illegible copyright notice is insufficient, as matter of law, to charge with knowledge of copyright an infringer who had no actual notice, it may be sufficient to charge with knowledge an infringer who had deciphered it. Trifari, Krussman & Fishel, Inc. v. B. Steinberg-Kaslo Co., (DC-NY), 144 FSupp 577, 110 USPQ 487.

Copyright notice complies with this section where "© 1955 G.R.C. Printed in U.S.A." appears in small letters on lower left portion of title page, one inch above which and three inches to the right of which appears "Glenco Refrigeration Corp. Philadelphia 34, Pa." in larger letters. Glenco Refrigeration Corp. v. Raetone Commercial Refrigerator Corp., (DC-Pa), 149 FSupp 691, 113 USPQ 155.

Copyright notices are sufficient since no innocent person could be misled by "Vera" accompanied by encircled "C", nor by encircled "C" followed by "Scarves by Vera"; notices disclose identity of proprietor, Scarves by Vera, Inc.; "Vera" is commonly used as abbreviated form of proprietor's name and has been registered as proprietor's trademark. Fabrex Corp. v. Scarves by Vera, Inc., (DC-NY), — FSupp —, 129 USPQ 392.

4.   —Proprietor—Licensees—Assignees.

Requirement as to copyright notice extends to editions published by assignee of copyright. Thompson v. Hubbard, 131 US 123, 33 LEd 76, 9 SCR 710, rev'g (CC-Mo), 25 Fed 188.

Notice given under a trade name is effective. Bleistein v. Donaldson Lithographing Co., 188 US 239, 47 LEd 460, 23 SCR 298, rev'g (CCA 6), 104 Fed 993; Gogniat v. Universal Pictures Corp., (DC-NY), 35 USPQ 117.

It is incorrect to say that any form of notice is good which calls attention to the person of whom inquiry can be made and information obtained, since, the right to copyright being purely statutory, the public may justly demand that the statutory method of securing it be observed. Mifflin v. R. H. White Co., 190 US 260, 47 LEd 1040, 23 SCR 769, aff'g (CCA 1), 112 Fed 1004, 61 LRA 134, which aff'd 107 Fed 708.

Notice of copyright given by publishers on their magazine which contained articles printed with consent of an author was insufficient under Copyright Act of 1831 to protect such articles or to support a subsequent copyright by their author. Mifflin v. R. H. White Co., 190 US 260, 47 LEd 1040, 23 SCR 769, aff'g (CCA 1), 112 Fed 1004, 61 LRA 134, which aff'd 107 Fed 708.

Notice of copyright of a magazine by publishers was insufficient notice as to an author's copyrighted article which appeared in the magazine. Mifflin v. Dutton, (CC-Mass), 107 Fed 708. Aff'd 112 Fed 1004, 61 LRA 134, which was aff'd 190 US 260, 47 LEd 1040, 23 SCR 769, and 190 US 265, 47 LEd 1043, 23 SCR 771.

Where copyright notice in weekly periodicals contained a trade name of copyrighter, a notice of copyright in the annual volume which combined the weekly issues, containing a different trade name of the copyrighter, vitiated the copyright. Record & Guide Co. v. Bromley, (CC-Pa), 175 Fed 156.

The use of two names does not invalidate the copyright provided the proprietor has the right to use either and he may use any name both in applying for registration and in making his notice of copyright; but the names which he uses must be legal where he uses them, else they cannot be called his names at all. Haas v. Leo Feist, Inc., (DC-NY), 234 Fed 105.

Notice on plaintiff's doll "'Betty Boop' des. and Copyrighted by Fleischer Studios" was sufficient despite failure to add "Inc." to proprietor's name. Fleischer Studios, Inc. v. Ralph A. Freundlich, Inc., (CCA 2), 73 F(2d) 276, 23 USPQ 295, aff'g 5 FSupp 808, 21 USPQ 216.

Notice of copyright not disclosing identity of proprietor was insufficient. W. S. Bessett, Inc. v. Germain, (DC-Mass), 18 FSupp 249, 32 USPQ 550.

Plaintiff filed certificate that he was doing business as "T. W. Allen Company" but registered copyright in name of "The Thornton Allen Company"; difference in name in certificate and name on copyright was but a slight variance and not material; name on copyright notice gave sufficient notice to public of name of owner of composition on which copyright was claimed and date when this right was obtained and this is all that statute requires. Allen v. Walt Disney Productions, Ltd., (DC-NY), 41 FSupp 134, 50 USPQ 365.

Copyright is not void although name of proprietor in copyright notice is proprietor's trade name and although proprietor also uses other trade names. Powell v. Stransky, (DC-SD), 98 FSupp 434, 89 USPQ 310.

If story published and copyrighted by magazine publisher in 1944 had been republished and copyrighted alone and without change by author in 1948 with no mention of 1944 copyright, it would have fallen into public domain, because substitution of name of assignee in notice of copyright prior to recordation of assignment from publisher results in abandonment of copyright and because recital of date later than actual copyright date invalidates copyright, but 1948 copyright is valid where author's revision of story was so substantial as to constitute new work. Wrench v. Universal Pictures Co., Inc., (DC-NY), 104 FSupp 374, 92 USPQ 350.

This section is substantially complied with where copyright notice identifies proprietor as "Trifari"; proprietor is Trifari, Krussman & Fishel, Inc., which owns "Trifari" trade-mark registered in patent office; also "Trifari" is trade name adopted by proprietor's founders to do business at same address as proprietor. Trifari, Krussman & Fishel, Inc. v. B. Steinberg-Kaslo Co., (DC-NY), 144 FSupp 577, 110 USPQ 487.

Copyright notice wherein copyright proprietor is identified as "Vera" is sufficient since "Vera" is dominant part of proprietor's full name (Scarves by Vera, Inc.), is proprietor's registered trade-mark, and is name by which proprietor is known throughout the industry; no innocent person could be misled. Scarves by Vera, Inc. v. United Merchants & Manufacturers, Inc., (DC-NY), 173 FSupp 625, 121 USPQ 578.

Copyright notice reading "Copyright 1947, by The Baltimore Colts, Jo Lombardi and Benjamin Klasmer" is defective since there is no showing of assignment to Colts of any interest in copyright from owners Lombardi and Klasmer. Klasmer v. Baltimore Football, Inc., (DC-Md), 200 FSupp 255, 132 USPQ 36.

Notice of copyright was sufficient if title page read "Copyright 1935, John A. Borthwick" with address; "By" was required by prior statute but not by 1909 Act. Borthwick v. Stark-Davis Co., (DC-Ore), 38 USPQ 327.

Where circumstances show consent by copyright proprietor, publication of work by mere licensee with licensee's name in notice of copyright may work a forfeiture; consent is not shown, although proprietor acquiesced in form of notice, since proprietor questioned it and licensee said that it was normal procedure. Hirshon v. United Artists Corp., 100 AppDC 217, 243 F(2d) 640, 113 USPQ 110.

This section requires that notice of copyright appearing on copies of published musical work must correctly state name of registered copyright proprietor and year of copyright. Hirshon v. United Artists Corp., 100 AppDC 217, 243 F(2d) 640, 113 USPQ 110.

5. —Date of copyright.

Where title was deposited in 1867 and copyright notice was dated 1866, the variance was immaterial. Callaghan v. Myers, 128 US 617, 32 LEd 547, 9 SCR 177, mod'g (CC-Ill), 24 Fed 636.

Omission in copyright notice of the year or the name debars proprietor from maintaining action for infringement even against a former proprietor, his grantor, who had full knowledge of the facts. Thompson v. Hubbard, 131 US 123, 33 LEd 76, 9 SCR 710, rev'g (CC-Mo), 25 Fed 188.

Copyright notice dated 1847 on a work published and entered for copyright in 1846 was fatal. Baker v. Taylor, (CC-NY), FedCas 782, 2 Blatchf. 82.

Omission of date is fatal. King v. Force, (CC-DC), FedCas 7,791, 2 CranchCC 208.

Second or subsequent editions without alterations or additions should have the date of the original copyright, but second or subsequent editions with notes or other improvements should have the date of entry of the improved edition, and no reference need be made to the original entry. Lawrence v. Dana, (CC-Mass), FedCas 8,136, 4 Cliff 1; West Pub. Co. v. Edward Thompson Co., (CCA 2), 176 Fed 833, mod'g 169 Fed 833; Harris v. Miller, (DC-NY), 50 USPQ 306. Mf'd 50 USPQ 625.

It is doubtful whether the insertion of the wrong year in the notice of copyright, through mistake, is fatal to an action for infringement. Schumacher v. Wogram, (CC-NY), 35 Fed 210.

The number 1890 placed on the title page of a dictionary without any other notice, does not imply that it is a new edition of an earlier copyrighted work, but only that it is the date of printing. Merriam v. Texas Siftings Pub. Co., (CC-NY), 49 Fed 944.

Use of Roman numerals, instead of Arabic, is sufficient. Stern v. Jerome H. Remick & Co., (CC-NY), 175 Fed 282.

The fact that a book published in 1915, carried the copyright notice of 1914, which was the year in which the printing was begun, is of no consequence, since the error is in favor of the public, the notice claiming a year less than the Copyright Act allows. American Code Co., Inc. v. Bensinger, (CCA 2), 282 Fed 829.

Book of cartoons depicting a series of unconnected poses is not within the classifications of this section for which the year in which the copyright was secured must appear in the notice. Fleischer Studios, Inc. v. Ralph A. Freundlich, Inc., (CCA 2), 73 F(2d) 276, 23 USPQ 295, aff'g 5 FSupp 808, 21 USPQ 216.

Where sheet music bears a date, in the notice of copyright, that is prior to the time that the actual copyright was obtained, the error does not affect the validity of the copyright, but merely shortens the duration of the copyright period. Southern Music Pub. Co., Inc. v. Bibo-Lang, Inc., (DC-NY), 10 FSupp 972, 26 USPQ 321.

Copyright notice on picture need not contain year. Stuff v. LaBudde Feed & Grain Co., (DC-Wis), 42 FSupp 493, 52 USPQ 23.

6. Location of notice.

Prior to passage of Copyright Act of 1909, an entire motion-picture film was a "photograph" and protectible in its entirety under a single notice. Edison v. Lubin, (CCA 3), 122 Fed 240, rev'g 119 Fed 993.

The fact that roll music had no notice of copyright upon it, and that the manufacturers of the roll music had the permission of the **owner of the copyright,** is no defense to an action for infringement of the right to perform a copyright work publicly for profit. Lutz v. Buck, (CCA 5), 40 F(2d) 501.

Copyright Act does not expressly require notice upon each reel of multiple reel motion picture. Patterson v. Century Productions, Inc., (CCA 2), 93 F(2d) 489, 35 USPQ 471, aff'g 19 FSupp 30, 33 USPQ 194.

Plaintiff's copyrighted doll bears copyright notice on the head and between shoulder blades; doll's body previously had been published without notice on shoulder blades; court rejects contention that extra copyright notice on shoulder blades bars plaintiff from access to equity court on theory that such notice was attempt to extend copyright protection to doll's torso as distinguished from entire doll and demonstrates intent to defraud public. Ideal Toy Corp. v. J-Cey Doll Co., Inc., (CA 2), 290 F(2d) 710, 129 USPQ 241.

Copyright notice need not appear upon cover of pamphlet or on page immediately following, since cover is not part of published matter and has no connection with it other than that of a cover to protect printed matter of text, hence notice appearing on reverse of first page following cover leaf is proper. Powell v. Stransky, (DC-SD), 98 FSupp 434, 89 USPQ 310.

Although illustrations from prior copyrighted catalogue were incorporated with new matter in new catalogue bearing copyright notice on wrong page, copyright on such illustrations was not lost in view of § 7 of this title; also, where illustrations were reproduced on page bearing copyright notice, there exists another reason against loss of copyright. Siewek Tool Co. v. Morton, (DC-Mich), 128 FSupp 71, 105 USPQ 60.

Catalogue is composed of loose leaf sheets including paper backing sheet; sheets are held together by paper fasteners; first sheet identifies catalogue as to contents, manufacturer, and manufacturer's address; it contains no illustrations; second, third, and fourth sheets contain illustrations and descriptions of goods, as does fifth sheet; in addition, fifth sheet carries copyright notice; copyright is invalid since first sheet is title page, which does not bear copyright notice. Siewek Tool Co. v. Morton, (DC-Mich), 128 FSupp 71, 105 USPQ 60.

Requirement of § 10 of this title as to affixation of notice to each copy of copyrighted work should be given realistic and liberal interpretation, consonant with business practices, that will reasonably protect both copyright owner and innocent copyist; accordingly, where copyrighted work is repetitive design, imprinted on sheet or continuous strip or roll of material (dress fabric), and when notice is imprinted at least once for every repeat of design on edge of material, the copyright proprietor, having done all that is reasonably within his power to imprint notice of material without marring appearance of work, has satisfied notice requirements of statute; any subsequent removal, destruction, or obliteration of notice by others (dress manufacturers) over whom proprietor has no control may serve to mitigate relief awarded against innocent infringer, without resulting in loss forever of rights given by copyright; copyright is not forfeited. Peter Pan Fabrics, Inc. v. Acadia Co., Inc., (DC-NY), 173 FSupp 292, 121 USPQ 81. Aff'd 274 F(2d) 487, 124 USPQ 154.

Copyright notice that has been permanently covered so that it cannot be seen without tearing article apart is considered a defective notice by copyright office. Peter Pan Fabrics, Inc. v. Acadia Co., Inc., (DC-NY), 173 FSupp 292, 121 USPQ 81. Aff'd 274 F(2d) 487, 124 USPQ 154.

Copyright notice on cardboard hangtag attached to blouse bearing copyrighted design does not comply with this section; however, copyright notice on woven label sewed into side seam adjacent to bottom of garment complies with statute; fact that label is sewed into side seam rather than on neck or some more obvious place is no basis for copier to argue that he was entrapped; label is not hidden and is located in sufficiently obvious place to apprise anyone seeking to copy the design of existence of copyright. Scarves by Vera, Inc. v. United Merchants & Manufacturers, Inc., (DC-NY), 173 FSupp 625, 121 USPQ 578.

Copyright notice printed on selvage of cloth is adequate since it is not shown that there is any other feasible location for placing notice; placement of notice in middle of design would make cloth unusable for garments since garments having such a notice on their face would be unsaleable. Peter Pan Fabrics, Inc. v. Dixon Textile Corp., (DC-NY), 188 FSupp 235, 127 USPQ 329.

Court rejects infringer's contention that copyright notice could be affixed by way of hang tag to dresses made of cloth embodying copyrighted design; this method of notice does not meet burden of showing that notice could have been embodied in design, and requirement of § 10 of this title that notice "be affixed to each copy thereof" would not be satisfied in this manner. Peter Pan Fabrics, Inc. v. Dixon Textile Corp., (DC-NY), 188 FSupp 235, 127 USPQ 329.

Defendant, which manufactures handbags from towels bearing plaintiff's copyrighted design, affixes hang tags thereto reading, "the design on the cover of this handbag is the copyrighted design of" plaintiff; tags do not meet requirement of this section. Scarves by Vera, Inc. v. America Handbags, Inc., (DC-NY), 188 FSupp 255, 127 USPQ 47.

This section requires that copyright notice appear on some portion of copyrighted article itself; although copyright notice is placed only on hood of copyrighted Santa Claus figure and not on the other two components thereof, notice is not defective since it appears on an accessible portion of figure, especially since all three components are sold as a unit and cannot be used separately. Doran v. Sunset House Distributing Corp., (DC-Cal), 197 FSupp 940, 131 USPQ 94.

Difficulty in discerning copyright notice on leaf of copyrighted artificial flower should not of itself prevent granting of preliminary injunction, if plaintiff is otherwise entitled to it, since plaintiff makes prima facie case that defendant had actual notice of copyright before engaging in sale of alleged infringement. Prestige Floral, Societe Anonyme v. California Artificial Flower Co. (Inc.), (DC-NY), 201 FSupp 287, 132 USPQ 350.

Fact that copyright notice is on underside of leaf of copyrighted artificial flower does not of itself seem objectionable; size of notice is sufficient since it can be seen by naked eye even though close examination is required to locate it. Prestige Floral, Societe Anonyme v. California Artificial Flower Co. (Inc.), (DC-NY), 201 FSupp 287, 132 USPQ 350.

Copyright notice affixed to removable disc which fits securely into hole on bottom of toy bank satisfies requirements of this section and § 10 of this title since disc is essential part of bank and without it the bank would not serve its purpose; bank is sold with disc securely inserted; disc is so placed as to give adequate notice of existence of copyright to anyone seeking to copy bank. Royalty Designs, Inc. v. Thrifticheck Service Corp., (DC-NY), — FSupp —, 133 USPQ 148.

Printing copyright notice on selvage of cloth bearing copyrighted design is adequate method of giving notice of copyright to dress manufacturers. Peter Pan Fabrics, Inc. v. Puritan Dress Co., Inc., (DC-NY), — FSupp —, 133 USPQ 678.

7. —Pictures, maps, drawings, or works of art.

Prior to passage of Copyright Act of 1909, a single copyright notice on a sheet of paper containing multiple reproductions of a painting was insufficient. Louis DeJonge & Co. v. Breuker & Kessler Co., 235 US 33, 59 LEd 113, 35 SCR 6, aff'g (CCA 3), 191 Fed 35, which aff'd 182 Fed 150.

Under a former act requiring copyright information on an engraving to be "impressed on the face thereof" it was a sufficient compliance if placed in the margin where it would not be covered when properly framed. Rossiter v. Hall, (CC-NY), FedCas 12,082, 5 Blatchf 362, 32 How Prac 226.

An engraving has sufficient notice of copyright, when, on prints made from it, the notice is in a position that would not ordinarily be covered with a frame. Rossiter v. Hall, (CC-NY), FedCas 12,082, 5 Blatchf 362, 32 How Prac 226.

Where a cut is published in a copyrighted newspaper, the cut is not copyrighted when the notice does not appear upon the cut itself. Bennett v. Boston Traveler Co., (CCA 1), 101 Fed 445.

Under R. S. § 4962 which required notice of copyright on photographs, the notice was not required to be affixed to every photograph comprising a series of related photos recorded on one film. Edison v. Lubin, (CCA 3), 122 Fed 240, rev'g 119 Fed 993.

R. S. § 4962, prescribing that notice of copyright shall be inscribed "upon some visible portion thereof," was construed to require inscription of notice upon "the several copies" of a painting, but not upon the original painting itself. Werckmeister v. American Lithographic Co., (CC-NY), 142 Fed 827. Aff'd 148 Fed 1022, which was aff'd 207 US 375, 52 LEd 254, 28 SCR 124; American Tobacco Co. v. Werckmeister, (CCA 2), 146 Fed 375. Aff'd 207 US 284, 52 LEd 208, 28 SCR 72, 12 AnnCas 595.

It is not sufficient that copies of works of art be marked with the letter "C" in a circle accompanied by the initials of the copyright proprietor, since this section also provides that the proprietor's name shall appear on the back, base, or pedestal of the substance on which the copy is mounted. E. I. Horsman & Aetna Doll Co., Inc. v. Kaufman, (CCA 2), 286 Fed 372.

When a group of pictures is copyrighted as a book, the copyright cannot be maintained by having the form of copyright notice put on individual pictures, which is required for reproduction of works of art, and when a photograph embodying artistic conception taken from a copyrighted catalogue is sold, it should have printed on it notice of copyright which will identify owner of copyright to anyone who purchases photograph. Basevi v. Edward O'Toole Co., Inc., (DC-NY), 26 FSupp 41, 40 USPQ 333.

When manual containing advertisements was copyrighted as book, plaintiff does not comply with statute in preserving copyright by furnishing under contract matrices of advertisements not bearing copyright notice required for book but bearing notice specified for works of art, there having been no attempt to register advertisements as works of art. Advertisers Exchange, Inc. v. Anderson, (DC-Iowa), 52 FSupp 809, 59 USPQ 391. Aff'd 144 F(2d) 907, 63 USPQ 39.

8. —Jewelry.

Copyright notice is sufficient where it appears on only one integral part of necklace. Boucher v. Du Boyes, Inc., (CA 2), 253 F(2d) 948, 117 USPQ 156.

Because earrings may be used singly does not mean that they are separate works of art: although some of defendants' earrings are sold singly for use as a dress ornament or clip, plaintiff invariably sells them in pairs, each pair being considered as a unit; copyright notice on only one earring of each of plaintiff's pairs is sufficient under Copyright Act. Boucher

v. Du Boyes, Inc., (CA 2), 253 F(2d) 948, 117 USPQ 156.

Notice of copyright on costume jewelry consists of "c" in circle with name of copyright owner; it is located at place where, according to industry usage, name of maker of article usually appears; it is legible although it is in small letters and close examination is required to locate it; nature of article is such that area in which notice may be placed is necessarily limited; however, it is so located as to apprise anyone, seeking to copy article, of existence of copyright; therefore, it is sufficient to satisfy statutory requirements. Trifari, Krussman & Fishel, Inc. v. Charel Co., Inc., (DC-NY), 134 FSupp 551, 107 USPQ 48.

Copyright notice on jewelry is not defective although it merely gives proprietor's trade name; notice reveals proprietor's corporate identity inasmuch as trade name has been in widespread use by plaintiff for a period of years. Hollywood Jewelry Mfg. Co., Inc. v. Dushkin, (DC-NY), 136 FSupp 738, 107 USPQ 354.

Copyright notice which only sets forth trade name of proprietor and fails to include corporate name is sufficient compliance with identification requirement of this section; however, copyright symbol must also appear thereon. Kramer Jewelry Creations, Inc. v. Capri Jewelry, Inc., (DC-NY), 143 FSupp 120, 111 USPQ 151.

Copyright notice on tags attached to copyrighted pin does not meet requirement of this section. Trifari, Krussman & Fishel, Inc. v. B. Steinberg-Kaslo Co., (DC-NY), 144 FSupp 577, 110 USPQ 487.

9. Foreign publications.

Omission of American copyright notice on a work published abroad and sold there does not destroy rights of copyright holder. United Dictionary Co. v. G. & C. Merriam Co., 208 US 260, 52 LEd 478, 28 SCR 290, aff'g (CCA 7), 146 Fed 354, which rev'd 140 Fed 768.

A notice, on the publication of a song in a foreign country, that it cannot be used for stage performances except with the consent of their agents, although lawful in the country where published, does not protect it in this country without compliance with our copyright laws. Savage v. Hoffmann, (CC-NY), 159 Fed 584.

Since United States does not belong to Berne Union, it is required in order to secure copyright here that any publication in foreign country must contain notice of United States copyright. Basevi v. Edward O'Toole Co., Inc., (DC-NY), 26 FSupp 41, 40 USPQ 333.

10. Copyrights prior to July 1, 1909.

"Copyright, 1887, by N. Sarony" is sufficient notice to protect copyright of Napoleon Sarony. Burrow-Giles Lithographic Co. v. Sarony, 111 US 53, 28 LEd 349, 4 SCR 279, aff'g (CC-NY), 17 Fed 591.

"Entered according to the act of congress in the office of the librarian of congress, by N. Hart Jackson, as author aforesaid, and the copyright thereof duly assigned to Sheridan Shook and Albert M. Palmer as proprietors thereof," with the figures "1875" at the bottom of the page where the date of publication usually appears was insufficient. Tompkins v. Rankin, (CC-Mass), FedCas 14,090.

"Entered according to act of Congress, in the year 1878, by H. A. Jackson" was insufficient. Jackson v. Walkie, (CC-Ill), 29 Fed 15.

"Registered, 3,693, 1883" without use of word "copyright" or its equivalent is insufficient. Higgins v. Keuffel, (CC-NY), 30 Fed 627. Aff'd 140 US 428, 35 LEd 470, 11 SCR 731.

Although the notice inscribed on a copy of a photograph was "1889. Copyrighted by B. J. Falk, New York," and the notice, if the statute were followed literally, would have read "Copyright, 1889, by B. J. Falk," it was sufficient since the statute had been substantially complied with. Falk v. Schumacher, (CC-NY), 48 Fed 222.

"Copyright entered according to act of Congress, etc.," was sufficient and additional word "copyright" was regarded as surplusage. Hefel v. Whitely Land Co., (CC-Ind), 54 Fed 179.

Words "civil engineer" following author's name was regarded as surplusage. Hefel v. Whitely Land Co., (CC-Ind), 54 Fed 179.

Notice "Copyright, 1882, by Photographische Gesellschaft" was sufficient although merely the trade name under which the party securing the copyright was doing business. Werckmeister v. Springer Lithographing Co., (CC-NY), 63 Fed 808.

"Copyright '94. By B. L. Snow" is a substantial compliance. Snow v. Mast, (CC-Ohio), 65 Fed 995.

"Copyright 93 by Bolles, Brooklyn" printed on face of photograph was sufficient. Bolles v. Outing Co., Ltd., (CCA 2), 77 Fed 966, 46 LRA 712. Aff'd 175 US 262, 44 LEd 156, 20 SCR 94.

"Copyright 1891. All rights reserved" on page immediately following title page, but omitting name of copyrighter was insufficient, although "Published by Osgood Art School, 1891," which was trade name of copyrighter, appeared on title page. Osgood v. A. S. Aloe Instrument Co., (CC-Mo), 83 Fed 470.

The notice "Copyright, 1902, Published by Hills & Co., Ltd., London, England" was not defective. Hills & Co., Ltd. v. Hoover, (CC-Pa), 136 Fed 701.

"Copyright by The Real Estate Record and Builders' Guide Co.

Vol. LXXV   May 6, 1905   No. 1938"

was insufficient. Record & Guide Co. v. Bromley, (CC-Pa), 175 Fed 156.

"Contents covered by copyright" written on cover page was not sufficient notice. Record & Guide Co. v. Bromley, (CC-Pa), 175 Fed 156.

"Copyright 1908. Published by Woodman Publishing Company" was sufficient notice on a map. Woodman v. Lydiard-Peterson Co., (CC-Minn), 192 Fed 67. Aff'd 204 Fed 921.

"Copyright, 1908, drawn by J. C. Woodman," was insufficient. Lydiard-Peterson Co. v. Woodman, (CCA 8), 204 Fed 921, aff'g 192 Fed 67.

20. Place of application—One notice in each volume or number of newspaper or periodical.—The notice of copyright shall be applied, in the case of a book or other printed publication, upon its title page or the page immediately following, or if a periodical either upon the title page or upon the first page of text of each separate number or under the title heading, or if a musical work either upon its title page or the first page of music. One notice of copyright in each volume or in each number of a newspaper or periodical published shall suffice. (July 30, 1947, c. 391, § 1, 61 Stat. 658.)

Cross reference.—Location of notice, see notes 6-8 of § 19 of this title.

NOTES TO DECISIONS

1. In general.

"Title page" defined, see Freeman v. Trade Register, Inc., (CC-Wash), 173 Fed 419.

Conditions prescribed by statute are conditions precedent to the perfection of the copyright. Callaghan v. Myers, 128 US 617, 32 LEd 547, 9 SCR 177, mod'g (CC-Ill), 24 Fed 636.

Copyright entry of a magazine will not validate author's subsequent entry under a different title of an article appearing therein. Mifflin v. R. H. White Co., 190 US 260, 47 LEd 1040, 23 SCR 769, aff'g (CCA 1), 112 Fed 1004, 61 LRA 134, which aff'd 107 Fed 708.

Under Copyright Act of 1831 publisher's copyright notice of a magazine under its own title did not operate as notice of the rights of the author to any article therein appearing. Mifflin v. Dutton, 190 US 265, 47 LEd 1043, 23 SCR 771, aff'g (CCA 1), 112 Fed 1004, 61 LRA 134, which aff'd 107 Fed 708.

Copyright notice on title page of "Woodman's Minnetonka Map-Directory" covers a map found in pocket of book. Woodman v. Lydiard-Peterson Co., (CC-Minn), 192 Fed 67. Aff'd 204 Fed 921.

A multiple reel motion picture does not require a notice upon each reel. Patterson v. Century Productions, (CCA 2), 93 F(2d) 489, 35 USPQ 471, aff'g 19 FSupp 30, 33 USPQ 194.

Copyright is secured on published material by accompanying its publication with copyright notice at place and in form required by statute; subsequent registration under provisions of statute does not create copyright but only records it; publication without proper notice is ineffective to secure copyright. Krafft v. Cohen, (CCA 3), 117 F(2d) 579, 48 USPQ 401, rev'g 32 FSupp 821, 44 USPQ 678.

Slight variation from form of notice may not be fatal, but there must be no substantial deviation. Booth v. Haggard, (CA 8), 184 F(2d) 470, 87 USPQ 141.

This section is culmination of a long history of increasing liberalization of restriction on the placement of notice of copyright; in the case of books and musical compositions, placement of notice has always been rigidly and narrowly confined, but, in the case of other items, a series of revisions has steadily expanded permissible locations of notice. Coventry Ware, Inc. v. Reliance Picture Frame Co., (CA 2), 288 F(2d) 193, 129 USPQ 83, rev'g 186 FSupp 798, 127 USPQ 46.

This section places no limitation on possible location of notice of copyright in the case of works of art and kindred items, provided that notice complies with general requirements of section 10 that notice be affixed to each copy. Coventry Ware, Inc. v. Reliance Picture Frame Co., (CA 2), 288 F(2d) 193, 129 USPQ 83, rev'g 186 FSupp 798, 127 USPQ 46.

Substantial compliance with Copyright Act is all that is required, but when act requires notice at particular place in a work, court may not dispense with requirement and say that notice appearing somewhere else is enough. J. A. Richards, Inc. v. New York Post, Inc., (DC-NY), 23 FSupp 619, 38 USPQ 475.

One proper notice of copyright on book protects all contents of book. Deward & Rich, Inc. v. Bristol Savings & Loan Corp., (DC-WVa), 29 FSupp 777, 44 USPQ 26.

Purpose of notice of copyright is to inform public of existence of copyright, time of commencement, by whom claimed, and to prevent innocent persons, who are unaware of existence of copyright, from suffering by making use of material. Harry Alter Co. v. Graves Refrigeration, Inc., (DC-Ga), 101 FSupp 703, 91 USPQ 236.

2. Book and printed publications.

Under former copyright law it was held that insertion of notice on page next following the title page of the first volume of a set of books composed of four volumes was sufficient. Dwight v. Appleton, (CC-NY), FedCas 4,215.

Where advance sheets of a publication are copyrighted separately, a book containing all these sheets in one volume without change must indicate the copyrights of the advance sheets. West Publishing Co. v. Edward Thompson Co., (CC-NY), 169 Fed 833. Mf'd 176 Fed 833.

Copyright notice in a periodical appearing on an editorial page which was not first page of text is not a compliance. Freeman v. Trade Register, Inc., (CC-Wash), 173 Fed 419.

Fact that a book has advertising pages preceding the title page and notice of copyright does not constitute a failure to comply with the statute. American Travel & Hotel Directory Co., Inc. v. Gehring Publishing Co., Inc., (DC-NY), 4 F(2d) 415.

Copyright notice on last page is insufficient. United Thrift Plan v. National Thrift Plan, (DC-NY), 34 F(2d) 300, 2 USPQ 345; Deward & Rich, Inc. v. Bristol Savings & Loan Corp., (DC-Va), 34 FSupp 345, 47 USPQ 128. Aff'd 120 F(2d) 537, 50 USPQ 1.

Suit for infringement will not lie where the notice of copyright is not placed on the title page or the page immediately following. United Thrift Plan, Inc. v. National Thrift Plan, Inc., (DC-NY), 34 F(2d) 300, 2 USPQ 345.

Notice of copyright appearing on back cover only is defective. Krafft v. Cohen, (CCA 3), 117 F(2d) 579, 48 USPQ 401, rev'g 32 FSupp

821, 44 USPQ 678; W. S. Bessett, Inc. v. Germain, (DC-Mass), 18 FSupp 249, 32 USPQ 550; J. A. Richards, Inc. v. New York Post, Inc., (DC-NY), 23 FSupp 619, 38 USPQ 475.

By statute, place for copyright notice on book or printed pamphlet is on title page or page immediately following; notice on any other page, no matter how prominent, is ineffective. J. A. Richards, Inc. v. New York Post, Inc., (DC-NY), 23 FSupp 619, 38 USPQ 475.

Congress contemplated that each book or publication to be protected should have title and should contain a page devoted in part at least to title. J. A. Richards, Inc. v. New York Post, Inc., (DC-NY), 23 FSupp 619, 38 USPQ 475.

Plaintiff's bound volume of advertisements intended to be used separately bears title and proper copyright notice on front cover; on inside of front cover appears another copyright notice substantially complying with § 19 of this title; volume has no other title page; plaintiff's front cover was properly used as title page and copyright was valid as either notice was sufficient. Deward & Rich, Inc. v. Bristol Savings & Loan Corp., (DC-Va), 34 FSupp 345, 47 USPQ 128. Aff'd 120 F(2d) 537, 50 USPQ 1.

Copyright notice on catalogue reads "All Prices F. O. B. Chicago—Keep These Prices Confidential" in line one, "Copyright, 1948. The H. A. Co. Printed in U. S. A." in line two, then a solid line, and then "The Harry Alter Co., Inc." in line four; notice is sufficient. Harry Alter Co. v. Graves Refrigeration, Inc., (DC-Ga), 101 FSupp 703, 91 USPQ 236.

3. Musical works.

A copyright notice on a musical composition may be printed below the music on the first page on which the music is printed. Blume v. Spear, (CC-NY), 30 Fed 629.

Notice was sufficient where affixed to title page, though not on cover page which contained advertisements. Blume v. Spear, (CC-NY), 30 Fed 629.

There is no provision in the Copyright Act for the affixing of a notice of copyright to a phonograph record or other mechanical contrivance. Irving Berlin, Inc. v. Daigle, (CCA 5), 31 F(2d) 832, rev'g 26 F(2d) 149.

No notice is necessary on a motion-picture film with sound in order to protect song. Famous Music Corp. v. Melz, (DC-La), 28 FSupp 767, 42 USPQ 573.

Notice in book is printed in three lines as follows: "Published and Printed by" above " 'Ziegelheim', New York" above "Printed in U.S.A. Copyright 1943"; notice sufficiently states name of copyright owner, since "Copyright 1943" appears directly below and in close proximity to " 'Ziegelheim,' New York," and since proof is clear that there was only one "Ziegelheim" in publishing business in New York. Ziegelheim v. Flohr, (DC-NY), 119 FSupp 324, 100 USPQ 189.

21. Effect of accidental omission from copy or copies. — Where the copyright proprietor has sought to comply with the provisions of this title with respect to

notice, the omission by accident or mistake of the prescribed notice from a particular copy or copies shall not invalidate the copyright or prevent recovery for infringement against any person who, after actual notice of the copyright, begins an undertaking to infringe it, but shall prevent the recovery of damages against an innocent infringer who has been misled by the omission of the notice; and in a suit for infringement no permanent injunction shall be had unless the copyright proprietor shall reimburse to the innocent infringer his reasonable outlay innocently incurred if the court, in its discretion, shall so direct. (July 30, 1947, c. 391, § 1, 61 Stat. 658.)

NOTES TO DECISIONS

Innocent technical infringer enjoined from future use of infringed illustration, but without costs to complainant, see Alfred Decker Cohn Co. v. Etchison Hat Co., (DC-Va), 225 Fed 135.

Prior to enactment of this section, accidental omission of copyright notice by a licensee did not result in loss to proprietor of any of his rights under the copyright laws. American Press Ass'n v. Daily Story Pub. Co., (CCA 7), 120 Fed 766, 66 LRA 444.

Fact that notice is blurred and indistinct does not invalidate copyright, but damages cannot be recovered in suit for infringement. Strauss v. Penn Printing & Publishing Co., (DC-Pa), 220 Fed 977.

Profits made by innocent infringer are recoverable. Strauss v. Penn Printing & Publishing Co., (DC-Pa), 220 Fed 977.

Profits made by defendant who innocently infringed on account of defective or accidentally omitted copyright notice are recoverable. Alfred Decker Cohn Co. v. Etchison Hat Co., (DC-Va), 225 Fed 135.

Where the copyright proprietor has sought to comply with respect to notice, the omission by accident or mistake of such notice from particular copies does not invalidate the copyright, or prevent recovery for infringement after actual notice of the copyright, but no damages are recoverable against an innocent infringer who has been misled by the omission of the notice. Stecher Lithographic Co. v. Dunston Lithograph Co., (DC-NY), 233 Fed 601.

An infringer who had actual knowledge of existence of copyright will be enjoined, even though copies of work have inadvertently been published without notice. Gerlach-Barklow Co. v. Morris & Bendien, Inc., (CCA 2), 23 F(2d) 159.

Accidental omission of copyright notice in law book used by an infringer was immaterial and no defense to infringer. W. H. Anderson Co. v. Baldwin Law Pub. Co., (CCA 6), 27 F(2d) 82.

Publication of a portion of a copyrighted wrapper bearing no copyright notice did not justify an infringer in appropriating the whole wrapper. Hoague-Sprague Corp. v. Frank C. Meyer Co., Inc., (DC-NY), 31 F(2d) 583.

The placing of the copyright notice on a page other than that provided for in § 20 was not an accident or mistake within this section. United Thrift Plan, Inc. v. National Thrift Plan, Inc., (DC-NY), 34 F(2d) 300, 2 USPQ 345; W. S. Bessett, Inc. v. Germain, (DC-Mass), 18 FSupp 249, 32 USPQ 550.

The lack of copyright notice upon an article will not protect an infringer who has actual notice. Schellberg v. Empringham, (DC-NY), 36 F(2d) 991.

A newspaper printing an advertisement from matrices furnished to it by an advertiser, which matrices contained no notice of copyright, was not liable for infringement, it having no knowledge of the copyright. Wilkes-Barre Record Co. v. Standard Advertising Co., (CCA 3), 63 F(2d) 99, 16 USPQ 346.

Publication of leaflet without proper copyright notice results in loss of rights of copyright unless this section saves them; this section applies only where notice is omitted from one or perhaps a very few copies, but does not apply where statutory notice is omitted from all copies published, as was case with all first published by plaintiff although those subsequently published bore proper notice. Krafft v. Cohen, (CCA 3), 117 F(2d) 579, 48 USPQ 401, rev'g 32 FSupp 821, 44 USPQ 678.

Fact that defendant first secured copyrighted book from plaintiff through a contract, paying plaintiff for the use, does not change rule that every reproduction of copyrighted work must bear statutory notice. Deward & Rich, Inc. v. Bristol Savings & Loan Corp., (CCA 4), 120 F(2d) 537, 50 USPQ 1, aff'g 34 FSupp 345, 47 USPQ 128.

Deliberate use of copyright notice which fails to meet the requirements of § 19 of this title is not an omission by accident or mistake within the meaning of this section. Advertisers Exchange, Inc. v. Anderson, (CCA 8), 144 F(2d) 907, 63 USPQ 39, aff'g 52 FSupp 809, 59 USPQ 391.

This section does not excuse omission of prescribed copyright notice upon all subsequent copies, even though notice on first published copy was proper. National Comics Publications, Inc. v. Fawcett Publications, Inc., (CA 2), 191 F(2d) 594, 90 USPQ 274, rev'g 93 FSupp 349, 87 USPQ 12.

Owner of copyright of picture who omitted his name from all copies thereof could not obtain relief under this section as this section applies only where the omission is on a limited number of copies. Goes Lithographing Co. v. Apt Lithographic Co., Inc., (DC-NY), 14 FSupp 620, 30 USPQ 119.

This section is applicable only where notice of copyright has been accidentally omitted, not where the omission is done with knowledge. Smith v. Bartlett, (DC-Maine), 18 FSupp 35, 32 USPQ 287.

This section cures omission of copyright notice on particular copies where due to accident or mistake, but has no application when notice in all copies is defective. J. A. Richards, Inc. v. New York Post, Inc., (DC-NY), 23 FSupp 619, 38 USPQ 475.

Purpose of this section is to protect copyright owner where notice has been omitted by mistake or accident from one or a few copies, but it is no protection where proper notice has been omitted from all republished copies of individual advertisements; there is even stronger reason why section should not apply inasmuch as proprietor deliberately made notices on advertisements so microscopic as to be indiscoverable to all practical intents and purposes. Deward & Rich, Inc. v. Bristol Savings & Loan Corp., (DC-Va), 34 FSupp 345, 47 USPQ 128. Aff'd 120 F(2d) 537, 50 USPQ 1.

This section saves rights in copyright only if omission of notice was by accident or mistake and not if it was due to neglect and oversight. Sieff v. Continental Auto Supply, Inc., (DC-Minn), 39 FSupp 683, 50 USPQ 19.

Precise number of "particular" copies with respect to which notice may be mistakenly omitted has not been judicially determined, although some courts hold that it applies only in the case of a very few copies; omission from only 2 per cent might bring case within coverage of this section. Kramer Jewelry Creations, Inc. v. Capri Jewelry, Inc., (DC-NY), 143 FSupp 120, 111 USPQ 151.

Effect of this section is that, where one copies copyrighted article and, because of unintentional omission of copyright notice from original, is unaware of copyright, he cannot be treated as infringer except with respect to things done after he learns of copyright; however, if he is aware of copyright, omission of notice or defect in notice will not protect him. Trifari, Krussman & Fishel, Inc. v. B. Steinberg-Kaslo Co., (DC-NY), 144 FSupp 577, 110 USPQ 487.

Plaintiff deposited three copies of his thesis, which he alleges bore copyright notice, in university library; defendant borrowed from library a copy, which he alleges bore no copyright notice; even if copy did not bear notice, this would not invalidate copyright in view of this section. Christie v. Raddock, (DC-NY), 169 FSupp 48, 120 USPQ 76.

After distribution of 15,000 copies of first printing of its catalogue, plaintiff ordered abbreviated second edition of 1,000 copies; in ordering second printing, plaintiff made no reference to any change in copyright notice that had been affixed to original printing; after 25 copies of second printing had been distributed, it was noted that catalogue began with page eight and remaining 975 copies were destroyed; although second printing did not bear copyright notice, plaintiff had sought to comply with notice provisions of Copyright Act [this title], there is no evidence that plaintiff was at fault for absence of notice; on motion for preliminary injunction, defendant has burden upon issue of invalidation; same may be said concerning appearance of copyright notice on sixth page of first printing instead of upon title page or page immediately following as required by § 20 of this title; although evidence may warrant different result on the trial, sufficient has been presented to justify preliminary injunction. Perkins Marine Lamp & Hardware Corp. v. Long Island Marine Supply Corp., (DC-NY), 185 FSupp 353, 126 USPQ 169.

Plaintiff granted third party permission to reprint plaintiff's catalogue on condition that proper notice of plaintiff's copyright be inserted; thereafter, plaintiff discovered that reprints omitted notice; if permission had been given without this condition, plaintiff might have forfeited its rights; however, violation of condition by third party places reprints in category of infringements. Perkins Marine Lamp & Hardware Corp. v. Long Island Marine Supply Corp., (DC-NY), 185 FSupp 353, 126 USPQ 169.

22.   Ad interim protection of book or periodical published abroad.—In the case of a book or periodical first published abroad in the English language, the deposit in the Copyright Office, not later than six months after its publication abroad, of one complete copy of the foreign edition, with a request for the reservation of the copyright and a statement of the name and nationality of the author and of the copyright proprietor and of the date of publication of the said book or periodical, shall secure to the author or proprietor an ad interim copyright therein, which shall have all the force and effect given to copyright by this title, and shall endure until the expiration of five years after the date of first publication abroad. (July 30, 1947, c. 391, § 1, 61 Stat. 659; June 3, 1949, c. 171, § 2, 63 Stat. 154.)

Amendment note.—Act June 3, 1949, cited to text, inserted "or periodical" after the word "book" wherever appearing; substituted "six months" for "sixty days"; added "therein" following "ad interim copyright"; substituted "five years after the date of first publication abroad" for "four months after such deposit in the copyright office."

NOTES TO DECISIONS

The interim Copyright Act of January 7, 1904, c. 2, 33 Stat. 4, providing for protection of foreign works exhibited at Louisiana purchase exposition, did not apply to works previously published in this country. Encyclopaedia Britannica Co. v. Werner Co., (CC-NJ), 135 Fed 841. Aff'd 142 Fed 966.

The word "book" as used in this section, means the entire book and not a fragment thereof. 28 OAG 176.

23.   Extension to full term.—Whenever within the period of such ad interim protection an authorized edition of such books or periodicals shall be published within the United States, in accordance with the manufacturing provisions specified in section 16 of this title, and whenever the provisions of this title as to deposit of copies, registration, filing of affidavits, and the printing of the copyright notice shall have been duly complied with, the copyright shall be extended to endure in such book or periodical for the term provided in this

title. (July 30, 1947, c. 391, § 1, 61 Stat. 659; June 3, 1949, c. 171, § 3, 63 Stat. 154.)

Amendment note.—Act June 3, 1949, cited to text, inserted "or periodical."

24.   Duration—Renewal and extension.—The copyright secured by this title shall endure for twenty-eight years from the date of first publication, whether the copyrighted work bears the author's true name or is published anonymously or under an assumed name: Provided, That in the case of any posthumous work or of any periodical, cyclopedic, or other composite work upon which the copyright was originally secured by the proprietor thereof, or of any work copyrighted by a corporate body (otherwise than as assignee or licensee of the individual author) or by an employer for whom such work is made for hire, the proprietor of such copyright shall be entitled to a renewal and extension of the copyright in such work for the further term of twenty-eight years when application for such renewal and extension shall have been made to the copyright office and duly registered therein within one year prior to the expiration of the original term of copyright: And provided further, That in the case of any other copyrighted work, including a contribution by an individual author to a periodical or to a cyclopedic or other composite work, the author of such work, if still living, or the widow, widower, or children of the author, if the author be not living, or if such author, widow, widower, or children be not living, then the author's executors, or in the absence of a will, his next of kin shall be entitled to a renewal and extension of the copyright in such work for a further term of twenty-eight years when application for such renewal and extension shall have been made to the copyright office and duly registered therein within one year prior to the expiration of the original term of copyright: And provided further, That in default of the registration of such application for renewal and extension, the copyright in any work shall determine at the expiration of twenty-eight years from first publication. (July 30, 1947, c. 391, § 1, 61 Stat. 659.)

Continuation of renewal term.—Act Sept. 19, 1962, P. L. 87-668, 76 Stat. 555, provided: "In any case in which the renewal term of copyright subsisting in any work on the date of approval of this resolution would expire prior to December 31, 1965, such term is hereby continued until December 31, 1965."

NOTES TO DECISIONS

ANALYSIS

1. In general.
2. Purpose.
3. Term of copyright.
4. Accrual of right to renew.
5. Persons entitled to renewal.
6. — Executors, administrators, legatees, or next of kin.
7. —Composite works.
8. — Works done for hire.
9. Assignment of rights by author.
10. Effect of expiration.
11. Renewals under prior law.

1. In general.

Renewal of copyright does not grant any other or greater rights than existed in the original term. Wheaton v. Peters, 33 US(8 Pet) 591, 8 LEd 1055, rev'g (CC-Pa), FedCas 17,486.

The right of renewal is a new grant and not an extension of the original term. Southern Music Pub. Co., Inc. v. Bibo-Lang, Inc., (DC-NY), 10 FSupp 975, 26 USPQ 324; Shapiro, Bernstein & Co., Inc. v. Bryan, (DC-NY), 27 FSupp 11, 41 USPQ 134; April Productions, Inc. v. G. Schirmer, Inc., 308 NY 366, 126 NE(2d) 283, 105 USPQ 286, rev'g 283 AppDiv 1037, 131 NYS(2d) 341, 102 USPQ 137, which aff'd (Misc), 122 NYS(2d) 888, 97 USPQ 242.

Grant obtained through renewal of copyright is a new estate, one which is acquired free and clear of all rights, interests, or licenses granted under original copyright. Shapiro Bernstein & Co., Inc. v. Jerry Vogel Music Co., Inc., (DC-NY), 115 FSupp 754, 98 USPQ 438, 99 USPQ 381. Rev'd 221 F(2d) 569, 105 USPQ 178, which was mf'd 223 F(2d) 252, 105 USPQ 460.

Song having been first copyrighted and published in 1902, mechanical reproduction thereof was in public domain from that time on; right of anyone to mechanically reproduce it was not impaired by 1909 Copyright Act; renewal of copyright of lyrics in 1929 and of music in 1930 cannot, in absence of expression of congressional intent, be said to have created author's control of mechanical reproduction, previously nonexistent. Edward B. Marks Music Corp. v. Continental Record Co., Inc., (DC-NY), 120 FSupp 275, 100 USPQ 438. Aff'd 222 F(2d) 488, 105 USPQ 171, 105 USPQ 350.

Right of renewal after expiration of original term derives solely from statute and does not exist independently of it. Miller Music Corp. v. Charles N. Daniels, Inc., (DC-NY), 158 FSupp 188, 116 USPQ 92; 28 OAG 162.

Unlike original copyright, renewal is created, not by publication with claim of copyright, but by registration of application for renewal in copyright office; such application cannot be validly made until last year of original term of copyright so that, until that time, no one can have anything more than right to secure renewal. Rose v. Bourne, Inc., (DC-NY), 176 FSupp 605, 123 USPQ 29. Aff'd 279 F(2d) 79, 125 USPQ 509.

2. Purpose.

Basic consideration of policy underlying renewal provision of 1909 Copyright Act is to enable author to sell copyright without losing his renewal interest. Fred Fisher Music Co., Inc. v. M. Witmark & Sons, 318 US 643, 87 LEd 1055, 63 SCR 773, 57 USPQ 50, aff'g (CCA 2), 125 F(2d) 949, 52 USPQ 385, which aff'd 38 FSupp 72, 49 USPQ 171.

Main purpose of this section is to protect the interest of the author. Shapiro, Bernstein & Co., Inc. v. Bryan, (DC-NY), 27 FSupp 11, 41 USPQ 134.

Congressional purposes in enacting this section were to protect author against his own improvident conduct in surrendering renewal rights during original term, to set up statutory scheme of priority in renewal rights for benefit of those naturally dependent upon, and properly expectant of, author's bounty, and to permit author who had no wife or children to bequeath by will the right to apply for renewal. Gibran v. Alfred A. Knopf, Inc., (DC-NY), 153 FSupp 854, 115 USPQ 214. Aff'd 255 F(2d) 121, 117 USPQ 218.

Basic purpose of renewal provisions of copyright statutes is to give reward to author rather than bookseller. Miller Music Corp. v. Charles N. Daniels, Inc., (DC-NY), 158 FSupp 188, 116 USPQ 92.

3. Term of copyright.

Term of copyright cannot be extended by filing of a second or amended application for copyright. Caliga v. Inter Ocean Newspaper Co., 215 US 182, 54 LEd 150, 30 SCR 38, aff'g (CCA 7), 157 Fed 186.

"Publication" has no definite and fixed meaning and may mean one thing as related to published works and another thing as to works not reproduced for sale. As to latter, it means date of deposit. Marx v. U. S., (CCA 9), 96 F(2d) 204, 37 USPQ 380.

"Date of first publication" in this section refers to date of deposit under § 12 of this title of works of which copies are not reproduced for sale, notwithstanding that § 26 of this title defines "date of publication" of published work to mean earliest date when copies are placed on sale, sold, or publicly distributed. Shilkret v. Busicraft Records, Inc., (CCA 2), 131 F(2d) 929, 55 USPQ 469, rev'g 43 FSupp 184, 52 USPQ 164.

Prior to 1909, mechanical reproduction of musical composition even if copyrighted was in public domain and hence unauthorized reproduction on phonograph records was permissible; 1909 Amendment extended copyright protection against unauthorized mechanical reproductions, but proviso of § 1(e) of this title limited such protection to compositions published and copyrighted after July 1, 1909; protection is not afforded to composition published and copyrighted prior to such date even if renewal copyright is obtained thereafter; this section does not state that renewal operates as grant of new monopoly having larger field than original copyright; that copyright proprietor published two new editions of composition during renewal period does not change result since "published" in above mentioned proviso means "first published." Edward B. Marks Music Corp. v. Continental Record Co., Inc., (CA 2), 222

F(2d) 488, 105 USPQ 171, 105 USPQ 350, aff'g 120 FSupp 275, 100 USPQ 438.

Antedating of copyright merely shortens its duration. Southern Music Pub. Co., Inc. v. Bibo-Lang, Inc., (DC-NY), 10 FSupp 972, 26 USPQ 321.

Renewal term of copyright commences at expiration of first term of 28 years and continues for additional term of 28 years. G. Schirmer, Inc. v. Robbins Music Corp., 176 Misc 578, 28 NYS(2d) 699, 49 USPQ 467.

4. Accrual of right to renew.

Death of the author before beginning of the one year next prior to expiration of the existing term does not prevent renewal by his executor. Fox Film Corp. v. Knowles, 261 US 326, 67 LEd 680, 43 SCR 365, rev'g (CCA 2), 279 Fed 1018, which aff'd 274 Fed 731.

Author cannot, prior to beginning of 28th year, devise the right to renewal. Silverman v. Sunrise Pictures Corp., (CCA 2), 273 Fed 909, 19 ALR 289.

If an author dies on day of expiring of his copyright without having himself acted in the premises, all possibility of a renewal in, by, or for anyone is gone forever. Silverman v. Sunrise Pictures Corp., (CCA 2), 273 Fed 909, 19 ALR 289.

Right to renew copyright accrues and can be exercised only during the one-year period prior to expiration of existing term. Tobani v. Carl Fischer, Inc., (CCA 2), 93 F(2d) 57, 38 USPQ 198, mod'g 36 USPQ 97; Shapiro, Bernstein & Co., Inc. v. Bryan, (CCA 2), 123 F(2d) 697, 51 USPQ 422, aff'g 36 FSupp 544, 48 USPQ 69; M. Witmark & Sons v. Fred Fisher Music Co., Inc., (CCA 2), 125 F(2d) 949, 52 USPQ 385, aff'g 38 FSupp 72, 49 USPQ 171. Aff'd 318 US 643, 87 LEd 1055, 63 SCR 773, 57 USPQ 50.

Publisher registered song with copyright office as an unpublished work on March 22, 1929, and registered it as a published song on June 1, 1929; renewal of copyright could be secured only during twenty-eighth year of original copyright term, that is, within period of one year commencing March 22, 1956. Tobias v. Joy Music, Inc., (DC-NY), — FSupp —, 133 USPQ 181.

Right accrues on application during last year of original term of copyright and is limited to those persons enumerated. Tobani v. Carl Fischer, Inc., 263 AppDiv 503, 33 NYS(2d) 294, 52 USPQ 640.

5. Persons entitled to renewal.

Only persons who may obtain renewals are those specified in the statutes. Shapiro, Bernstein & Co. v. Bryan, (DC-NY), 27 FSupp 11, 41 USPQ 134.

Renewal of copyright by person not entitled thereto is void and cannot be cured by ratification by person entitled to renew. Von Tilzer v. Jerry Vogel Music Co., Inc., (DC-NY), 53 FSupp 191, 59 USPQ 292. Aff'd 158 F(2d) 516, 71 USPQ 285.

Right of renewal does not belong to author's estate by right of succession, but to person designated in statute. Miller Music Corp. v. Charles N. Daniels, Inc., (DC-NY), 158 FSupp 188, 116 USPQ 92.

Defendant argues that unless conveying instrument expressly states that renewal rights have been conveyed, the courts will find that parties did not intend to transfer them; this rule reflects policy of statutory copyright law which is not applicable in instant infringement action wherein none of the parties are within the class of persons given special statutory consideration. By requiring express mention of renewal rights in such transfers, thus avoiding an inadvertent or unintended transfer of such rights, courts have found a means of carrying out statutory policy of protecting copyright interests of original authors and certain of their heirs. Scope of factual examination to determine intent of parties to instant assignment to plaintiff's predecessor is not limited. Language of agreement in general, as well as circumstances surrounding its execution, may also serve to indicate intent of parties. Where there is evidence which shows intention to transfer renewal rights, fact that they were not expressly mentioned in assignment of original copyright will not preclude their passing with the copyright. Rohauer v. Friedman, (CA 9), — F(2d) —, 134 USPQ 384.

During composer's lifetime and before final year of term of original copyright, expectancy of renewal of copyright is like interest of one who is entitled to remainder after term of years provided he outlives the term; composer can effectively assign expectancy, but if he does prior to final year of original term, assignee's expectancy is defeated and right to renew vests in others pursuant to this section. Rose v. Bourne, Inc., (DC-NY), 176 FSupp 605, 123 USPQ 29. Aff'd 279 F(2d) 79, 125 USPQ 509.

Renewal provisions of this section were designed to protect only the classes of persons specifically designated therein, and not a surviving coauthor. Sweet Music, Inc. v. Melrose Music Corp., (DC-Cal), 189 FSupp 655, 127 USPQ 513.

Right of renewal of copyright is in the nature of an expectancy; consequently, if author dies before time for renewal, any inter vivos assignment of renewal rights by deceased author is of no force and right to renew devolves upon those classes of persons designated in this section; however, assignment of renewal rights is valid where assignor survives the fruition of the expectancy; to hold that entire assignment is of no force, merely because part of otherwise valid assignment fails due to death of one coauthor assignor would be to ignore policy expressed in § 28 of this title; circumstance that two coauthors joined in same assignment, instead of executing separate assignments, does not change result; in either case, surviving coauthor is bound by assignment. Sweet Music, Inc. v. Melrose Music Corp., (DC-Cal), 189 FSupp 655, 127 USPQ 513.

6. —Executors, administrators, legatees, or next of kin.

The intent of this section is that, if there is no widow or child of the author, the executor may exercise the power that the testator might have exercised if he had been alive. Fox Film

Corp. v. Knowles, 261 US 326, 67 LEd 680, 43 SCR 365, rev'g (CCA 2), 279 Fed 1018, which aff'd 274 Fed 731.

Author's executors do not succeed to renewal interest under this section unless all named persons (author, widow, widower, and children) are dead. De Sylva v. Ballentine, 351 US 570, 100 LEd 1415, 76 SCR 974, 109 USPQ 431, aff'g 226 F(2d) 623, 106 USPQ 347.

On the death of the author, the widow and children of the author succeed to the right of renewal as a class and are each entitled to share in the renewal term of the copyright. De Sylva v. Ballentine, 351 US 570, 100 LEd 1415, 76 SCR 974, 109 USPQ 431, aff'g (CA 9), 226 F(2d) 623, 106 USPQ 347.

Right of executor to renew copyright of composer who died unmarried and without children prior to one-year renewal period was not defeated by composer's inter vivos assignment of his renewal right. Miller Music Corp. v. Charles N. Daniels, Inc., 362 US 373, 4 LEd(2d) 804, 80 SCR 792, 125 USPQ 147, aff'g (CA 2), 265 F(2d) 925, which aff'd 158 FSupp 188, 116 USPQ 92.

Assignment by author of renewal rights made before original copyright expires is valid against world if author is alive at commencement of renewal period; all questions of assignment apart, renewal rights go by statute to executor, absent a widow or child. Miller Music Corp. v. Charles N. Daniels, Inc., 362 US 373, 4 LEd(2d) 804, 80 SCR 792, 125 USPQ 147, aff'g (CA 2), 265 F(2d) 925, 121 USPQ 204, which aff'd 158 FSupp 188, 116 USPQ 92.

Prior assignment by author cannot bar renewal rights of widow, widower, and children for they are among those to whom this section grants renewal right, irrespective of whether author in his lifetime has or has not made any assignment of it; also, where author dies intestate prior to renewal period leaving no widow, widower, or children, next of kin obtain renewal copyright free of any claim founded upon assignment made by author in his lifetime; these results follow not because testator's assignment is invalid but because he had only an expectancy to assign, and his death, prior to renewal period, terminates his interest in renewal which by this section vests in named classes; right to obtain renewal copyright and the renewal copyright itself exist only by reason of this title and are derived solely and directly from it. Miller Music Corp. v. Charles N. Daniels, Inc., 362 US 373, 4 LEd(2d) 804, 80 SCR 792, 125 USPQ 147, aff'g (CA 2), 265 F(2d) 925, 121 USPQ 204, which aff'd 158 FSupp 188, 116 USPQ 92.

There is no difference in statutory scheme between widows, widowers, children, or next of kin on the one hand, executors on the other; hierarchy of people granted renewal rights by this section are first, author, if living, second, widow, widower, or children, if he or she is not living, third, his or her executors if author and widow, widower, or children are not living, and fourth, in absence of a will, next of kin; these are disparate interests, but Congress saw fit to treat them alike; by force of this section, if author dies intestate, his next of kin would take as against assignee of renewal right; Congress

expressed a preference for that group against the world, if author, widow, widower, or children are not living; by this section, his executors are placed in same preferred position; under this title, executor's right to renew is independent of author's rights at time of his death; this section creates contingent renewal rights; it provides that, when author dies before renewal period arrives, special rules in derogation of usual rules of succession are to apply for benefit of three classes of people, (1) widow, widowers, and children, (2) executors, and (3) next of kin; court would redesign this section if it held that executors do not acquire renewal rights, where there was a prior assignment, though widows, widowers, and children or next of kin would acquire them. Miller Music Corp. v. Charles N. Daniels, Inc., 362 US 373, 4 LEd(2d) 804, 80 SCR 792, 125 USPQ 147, aff'g (CA 2), 265 F(2d) 925, 121 USPQ 204, which aff'd 158 FSupp 188, 116 USPQ 92.

The administrator of the estate of an author has no right to renew a copyright obtained by the author. Danks v. Gordon, (CCA 2), 272 Fed 821.

Legatees as such do not have renewal rights, because not named in statute, but must get whatever they are entitled to through executors. Silverman v. Sunrise Pictures Corp., (CCA 2), 273 Fed 909, 19 ALR 289.

It is not necessary for all of next of kin to join in application for renewal. Silverman v. Sunrise Pictures Corp., (CCA 2), 273 Fed 909, 19 ALR 289.

Renewal granted on application by only part of next of kin in their own names inures to benefit of all. Silverman v. Sunrise Pictures Corp., (CCA 2), 273 Fed 909, 19 ALR 289.

If, prior to the commencement of the one year prior to expiration of the term of the copyright, the executor of the owner of the copyright has been discharged, and there is then no executor in existence, the renewal right is not extinguished, but may be exercised by the next of kin, there being no surviving widow or children. Silverman v. Sunrise Pictures Corp., (CCA 2), 290 Fed 804.

A renewal of copyright which is afforded an author, his relatives, or executors does not extend to another's work, although author was associated in the same book. Harris v. Coca-Cola Co., (CCA 5), 73 F(2d) 370, 23 USPQ 182, aff'g 22 USPQ 72.

Illegitimate child is entitled to share in benefits of renewal obtained by widow and is entitled to accounting of money received by widow therefrom. Ballentine v. De Sylva, (CA 9), 226 F(2d) 623, 106 USPQ 347. Aff'd 351 US 570, 100 LEd 1415, 76 SCR 974, 109 USPQ 431.

Author died prior to end of term of copyright, leaving no widow or child and no will; plaintiff was next of kin and made application for renewal within one year before initial term expired; plaintiff thus acquired new and independent right in copyright free and clear of any rights, interests, or licenses attached to copyright for original term. Fitch v. Shubert, (DC-NY), 20 FSupp 314, 35 USPQ 245.

After death of artist, copyright expired, and while executor was still acting, plaintiff, a sister, applied as next of kin for renewal of copyright. She was only one of several surviving sisters and did not have any right to secure renewal, and such renewal was ·ineffective. Yardley v. Houghton Mifflin Co., (DC-NY), 25 FSupp 361, 40 USPQ 234. Aff'd 108 F(2d) 28, 44 USPQ 1.

In suit by brothers as next of kin of author for adjudication of renewal rights, finding in prior suit that author had been married was not material in present suit where complaint alleged that author left no widow, children, or will, since question is whom did author leave when he died. Jerry Vogel Music Co., Inc. v. Edward B. Marks Music Corp., (DC-NY), 56 FSupp 779, 63 USPQ 1.

It is significant that author's brother, who had filed earlier renewal application, did not protest renewal to alleged widow; that her signature on the assignment differs from her writing in letter to assignee does not overcome presumption of validity attaching to assignment since apparently she was largely illiterate and letter could have been written for her by another. Edward B. Marks Music Corp. v. Borst Music Pub. Co., Inc., (DC-NJ), 110 FSupp 913, 97 USPQ 394.

Administrator c. t. a. appointed to administer provisions of author's will, which has been admitted to probate, stands in shoes of executor and is entitled to exercise right of renewal of copyright. His right is superior to that of next of kin; however, in exercising right of renewal, he does so on behalf of those entitled to receive royalties. Gibran v. Alfred A. Knopf, Inc., (DC-NY), 153 FSupp 854, 115 USPQ 214. Aff'd 255 F(2d) 121, 117 USPQ 218.

Widow and children of author succeed to author's right of renewal of copyright as a class. Fisher v. Edwin H. Morris & Co., Inc., (DC-NY), 113 USPQ 251.

Inasmuch as there is exclusive federal jurisdiction, state court has no jurisdiction of action to determine whether under state law the defendants are "children" of composer so as to qualify as claimants for renewal of copyright. Ross Jungnickel, Inc. v. Joy Music, Inc. —Misc(2d series) —, — NYS(2d) —, 129 USPQ 373.

7. —Composite works.

Copyright of book did not extend to illustrations furnished by a person other than the author of the book; and latter's widow, by renewal of copyright, could not sue for infringement of illustrations. Harris v. Coca-Cola Co., (CCA 5), 73 F(2d) 370, 23 USPQ 182, aff'g 22 USPQ 72.

"Composite works" are those to which number of authors have contributed distinguishable parts not separately registered but included by proprietor in one copyright. Shapiro, Bernstein & Co., Inc. v. Bryan, (CCA 2), 123 F(2d) 697, 51 USPQ 422, aff'g 36 FSupp 544, 48 USPQ 69.

Author wrote words as words for song and sold them to third party, who engaged composer (without knowledge of author) to compose music for words. Author was not entitled to renew words alone since song is not "composite" work and had to be renewed as whole, or not at all, it being indivisible product of "joint authors." Edward B. Marks Music Corp. v. Jerry Vogel Music Co., Inc., (CCA 2), 140 F(2d) 266, 60 USPQ 257, aff'g 47 FSupp 490, 55 USPQ 288, 55 USPQ 489.

While general assignment of copyright does not assign right to renew, yet fact that alleged coauthor made no legal or formal claim to copyright during almost entire 28 years of its original term is circumstance to be considered on issue of coauthorship; if he had no interest in original term, he had no right to apply for and receive renewal certificate. Jerry Vogel Music Co., Inc. v. Forster Music Publisher, Inc., (CCA 2), 147 F(2d) 614, 64 USPQ 417, aff'g 62 USPQ 142.

Where corporation assigned copyright to one of joint authors, renewal on latter's application was proper. Southern Music Pub. Co. v. Bibo-Lang, (DC-NY), 10 FSupp 972, 26 USPQ 321.

Registration of original copyright of coauthors in proprietor's name gives him no right to renewal. Edward B. Marks Music Corp. v. Jerry Vogel Music Co., Inc., (DC-NY), 42 FSupp 859, 52 USPQ 219.

Renewal of "subsisting" copyright in musical composition comprises music and lyrics together, not either alone. Edward B. Marks Music Corp. v. Jerry Vogel Music Co., Inc., (DC-NY), 42 FSupp 859, 52 USPQ 219.

Renewal by coauthor of joint work (musical composition) enures to benefit of his coauthor or those entitled to renewal if that coauthor is dead. Edward B. Marks Music Corp. v. Jerry Vogel Music Co., Inc., (DC-NY), 42 FSupp 859, 52 USPQ 219; Edward B. Marks Music Corp. v. Jerry Vogel Music Co., Inc., (DC-NY), 47 FSupp 490, 55 USPQ 288, 55 USPQ 489. Aff'd 140 F(2d) 266, 60 USPQ 257, and mf'd 140 F(2d) 268, 60 USPQ 256; Von Tilzer v. Jerry Vogel Music Co., Inc., (DC-NY), 53 FSupp 191, 59 USPQ 292. Aff'd 158 F(2d) 516, 71 USPQ 285.

When renewal copyright issues, one coauthor, or his assignee, cannot exclude other coauthors from beneficial rights therein. Edward B. Marks Music Corp. v. Jerry Vogel Music Co., Inc., (DC-NY), 49 FSupp 135, 57 USPQ 37. Aff'd 140 F(2d) 270, 60 USPQ 259.

Widow who obtained renewal is not entitled to keep all royalties resulting from assignment by widow of such renewal, where there was a coauthor of the work although unknown at time of renewal, and the widow's interest in the royalties is impressed with a trust in favor of the coauthor with whom she must share. Edward B. Marks Music Corp. v. Wonnell, (DC-NY), 61 FSupp 722, 65 USPQ 456.

Each co-owner must account to other for his transactions in renewal. Shapiro, Bernstein & Co., Inc. v. Jerry Vogel Music Co., Inc., (DC-NY), 73 FSupp 165, 74 USPQ 264.

Song being composite work, not joint work, all that author of lyric can assign is his renewal interest in lyric; neither author nor assignee, after assignee's renewal of copyright in song, has right to publish music in connection with lyric. Shapiro, Bernstein & Co., Inc. v. Jerry Vogel Music Co., Inc., (DC-NY), 115 FSupp

754, 98 USPQ 438, 99 USPQ 381. Rev'd 221 F(2d) 569, 105 USPQ 178, which was mf'd 223 F(2d) 252, 105 USPQ 460.

8. —Works done for hire.

Only author and persons named have the right of renewal, and it does not extend to proprietor, except on a composite work originally copyrighted by proprietor himself. White-Smith Music Pub. Co. v. Goff, (CCA 1), 187 Fed 247, aff'g 180 Fed 256.

Plaintiff's predecessor having obtained copyright of song written and composed by defendants as employees "for hire" of predecessor, plaintiff, and not defendants, is entitled to renewal copyright. Shapiro, Bernstein & Co., Inc. v. Bryan, (CCA 2), 123 F(2d) 697, 51 USPQ 422, aff'g 36 FSupp 544, 48 USPQ 69.

Definition of "author" in § 26 of this title as including employer in case of works made for hire has no importance in construing this section. Shapiro, Bernstein & Co., Inc. v. Bryan, (CCA 2), 123 F(2d) 697, 51 USPQ 422, aff'g 36 FSupp 544, 48 USPQ 69.

The proprietor who may obtain renewal of copyright of work by employee for hire is the proprietor at the time of renewal and not at the time of original copyright. Shapiro, Bernstein & Co. v. Bryan, (DC-NY), 27 FSupp 11, 41 USPQ 134.

An employee for hire, who has parted with his entire property in the work, has no interest left to protect and he need not be considered in connection with renewal, and right of renewal is not cut off when transfer takes place, but instead the rights of renewal reserved to proprietors are assignable along with the copyright itself. Shapiro, Bernstein & Co. v. Bryan, (DC-NY), 27 FSupp 11, 41 USPQ 134.

Defendants were employed by S under contract which provided that any songs written by them were to be S's property; as instant song was written while defendants were so employed, song is property of S's assignee; S obtained original copyright on song; right of renewal in work made for hire is not given to author, or to employer as author, but to proprietor; S's assignee was proprietor and properly obtained renewal copyright. Shapiro, Bernstein & Co., Inc. v. Bryan, (DC-NY), 36 FSupp 544, 48 USPQ 69. Aff'd 123 F(2d) 697, 51 USPQ 422.

Where employee for hire wrote part or all of lyrics of copyrighted song for employer, employer alone is entitled to copyright and renewal; employee's widow cannot give another right to publish song or right to money collected by employer on theory that since renewal employer held part of proceeds received by it in trust for widow. Von Tilzer v. Jerry Vogel Music Co., Inc., (DC-NY), 53 FSupp 191, 59 USPQ 292. Aff'd 158 F(2d) 516, 71 USPQ 285.

Composer agreed to write songs for music publisher, who agreed to pay composer salary; contract created relationship of employer and employee; publisher assigned all assets to defendant; composer continued to work for defendant and acquiesced and ratified assignment; while in defendant's employ, composer wrote song which defendant copyrighted; defendant as employer alone is entitled to renewal rights

in copyrighted song whether or not contract was assignable or actually assigned. Fred Fisher Music Co., Inc. v. Leo Feist, Inc., (DC-NY), 55 FSupp 359, 61 USPQ 229.

Author of lyric sold to publisher right to copyright lyric for use with another's music, but, since author was not publisher's employee for hire, publisher had no renewal interest in lyric. Shapiro, Bernstein & Co., Inc. v. Jerry Vogel Music Co., Inc., (DC-NY), 115 FSupp 754, 98 USPQ 438, 99 USPQ 381. Rev'd 221 F(2d) 569, 105 USPQ 178, which was mf'd 223 F(2d) 252, 105 USPQ 460.

"Author" includes employer in case of works made for hire; employer in case of works made for hire is person entitled to renewal. Tobani v. Carl Fischer, (DC-NY), 36 USPQ 97. Mf'd 98 F(2d) 57, 38 USPQ 198.

9. Assignment of rights by author.

Assignment by author of copyright in general terms, under law prior to 1909 Copyright Act, did not include conveyance of his renewal interest. Fred Fisher Music Co., Inc. v. M. Witmark & Sons, 318 US 643, 87 LEd 1055, 63 SCR 773, 57 USPQ 50, aff'g (CCA 2), 125 F(2d) 949, 52 USPQ 385, which aff'd 38 FSupp 72, 49 USPQ 171.

Author can assign original copyright and, after he has secured it, renewal copyright as well. Fred Fisher Music Co., Inc. v. M. Witmark & Sons, 318 US 643, 87 LEd 1055, 63 SCR 773, 57 USPQ 50, aff'g 125 F(2d) 949, 52 USPQ 385, which aff'd 38 FSupp 72, 49 USPQ 171.

Neither language nor history of 1909 Copyright Act lend support to conclusion that existing law prior to 1909, under which authors were free to assign their renewal interests, was intended to be altered; there are no compelling considerations of policy which could justify reading into act construction so at variance with its history; 1909 Copyright Act does not nullify agreements by authors to assign their renewal interests. Fred Fisher Music Co., Inc. v. M. Witmark & Sons, 318 US 643, 87 LEd 1055, 63 SCR 773, 57 USPQ 50, aff'g (CCA 2), 125 F(2d) 949, 52 USPQ 385, which aff'd 38 FSupp 72, 49 USPQ 171.

The right to a further extension of the life of any particular copyright, through refiling or registering, has been confined to the author "or his widow or children if he be dead" and does not extend to an assignee. West Publishing Co. v. Edward Thompson Co., (CC-NY), 169 Fed 833. Mf'd 176 Fed 833.

Renewal or additional term of copyright vests in author if living, but he may divest himself of right thus reserved by parting absolutely with entire interest in work or by agreement to convey copyright for additional term when it shall be secured. Tobani v. Carl Fischer, (CCA 2), 98 F(2d) 57, 38 USPQ 198, mod'g 36 USPQ 97.

This section creates only expectancy as to renewal copyright; author must be alive on first day of twenty-eighth year to obtain renewal; author's assignment of expectancy, likewise resting on author's survival is valid and is not against public policy, but such assignment does not cut off rights of renewal extended to widow and others if author dies prior to renewal period. M. Witmark & Sons v. Fred Fisher Music Co., Inc., (CCA 2), 125 F(2d) 949, 52 USPQ 385, aff'g 38 FSupp 72, 49 USPQ 171. Aff'd 318 US 643, 87 LEd 1055, 63 SCR 773, 57 USPQ 50; Carmichael v. Mills Music, Inc., (DC-NY), 121 FSupp 43, 101 USPQ 279; Miller Music Corp. v. Charles N. Daniels, Inc., (DC-NY), 158 FSupp 188, 116 USPQ 92.

Agreement conveying "all right, title and interests" in copyrighted song did not convey renewal right; phrase may be broad enough to divest grantor of all reserved rights but in last analysis intention of parties governs. Rossiter v. Vogel, (CCA 2), 134 F(2d) 908, 57 USPQ 161, rev'g 46 FSupp 749, 54 USPQ 229.

Assignment, signed at about time renewal application was filed, granting "exclusive right for entire period of renewal copyright" is assignment of expectancy since it contains unmistakable language denoting intention to grant presently transferable right, although at its execution application had not been filed for renewal; renewal right does not strictly accrue until filing of application in twenty-eighth year of original term and renewal does not become effective until first day of twenty-ninth year. Rossiter v. Vogel, (CCA 2), 134 F(2d) 908, 57 USPQ 161, rev'g 46 FSupp 749, 54 USPQ 229.

"Bill of sale," signed 11 years before time for renewal, selling "all copyright renewals" is construed as immediate and outright transfer and assignment of expectancy. Rossiter v. Vogel, (CCA 2), 134 F(2d) 908, 57 USPQ 161, rev'g 46 FSupp 749, 54 USPQ 229.

Assignee of renewal obtained by author of words of musical composition, being joint work, holds legal title in trust for composer of music and his assignee and cannot forbid composer's assignee from exploiting subject matter. Edward B. Marks Music Corp. v. Jerry Vogel Music Co., Inc., (CCA 2), 140 F(2d) 266, 60 USPQ 257, aff'g 47 FSupp 490, 55 USPQ 288, 55 USPQ 489.

Unsealed 1926 "bill of sale" of "all copyright renewals" recited merely nominal consideration of one dollar which evidence shows was not paid; one dollar was inadequate and inequitable consideration; song had large sale between 1910 and 1912, between 1922 and 1926, and from 1926 until copyright expired in 1938; renewal right was not conveyed by "bill of sale." Rossiter v. Vogel, (CCA 2), 148 F(2d) 292, 65 USPQ 72, aff'g 61 USPQ 514.

Assignment of motion-picture rights in novel is limited to term of copyright unless assignment includes right of renewal. G. Ricordi & Co. v. Paramount Pictures, Inc., (CA 2), 189 F(2d) 469, 89 USPQ 289, 89 USPQ 564, mod'g 92 FSupp 537, 86 USPQ 452.

Composer assigned all rights, including renewal rights, in music to publisher, which employed author to write lyric; publisher copyrighted resulting song as joint work; as publisher's assignee, plaintiff later acquired all renewal rights in music and renewal copyrights therein; plaintiff also obtained renewal copyright on joint work; although plaintiff had not acquired author's renewal rights to joint work, it had status as composer's assignee to apply for renewal of joint work; having obtained renewal copyright on joint work, plaintiff holds it as constructive trustee for benefit of coauthors or their assignees. Shapiro, Bernstein & Co., Inc. v. Jerry Vogel Music Co., Inc., (CA 2), 221 F(2d) 569, 105 USPQ 178, rev'g 115 FSupp 754, 98 USPQ 438, 99 USPQ 381. Mf'd 223 F(2d) 252, 105 USPQ 460.

General transfer by author of original copyright without mention of renewal rights conveys no interest in renewal rights without proof of contrary intention; such intent is not shown by author's silence in response to assignee's ambiguous statement that renewals belonged to assignee. Edward B. Marks Music Corp. v. Charles K. Harris Music Publishing Co., Inc., (CA 2), 255 F(2d) 518, 117 USPQ 308; Edward B. Marks Music Corp. v. Borst Music Publishing Co., Inc., (DC-NJ), 110 FSupp 913, 97 USPQ 394.

Power of attorney to apply for copyright renewal rights is implied from the fact of the assignment of such rights. Rose v. Bourne, Inc., (CA 2), 279 F(2d) 79, 125 USPQ 509, aff'g 176 FSupp 605, 123 USPQ 29, and 127 USPQ 187.

Prior to copyright renewal period, author's interest in renewal rights is only an expectancy which can be defeated by his death prior to commencement of period; author may assign expectancy, and assignment is valid against the world if author is alive at commencement of renewal period; however, author may challenge validity of assignment if consideration therefor was inadequate. Rose v. Bourne, Inc., (CA 2), 279 F(2d) 79, 125 USPQ 509, aff'g 176 FSupp 605, 123 USPQ 29, and 127 USPQ 187.

Assignment of musical composition included in enumeration of rights sold "all copyrights and the rights to secure copyrights and extensions and renewals of copyrights in the same"; this was effective as present assignment of expectancy of the renewal; court rejects contention that quoted language effected sale of right to secure renewal rather than sale of renewal expectancy itself, and that right to secure renewal can be exercised only by decree in equity working upon assignors; assignee's exercise of right to secure renewal does not require assignors' cooperation; there is no distinction between assignment of right to secure renewal and assignment of renewal expectancy itself; expectancy cannot be reduced to possession except by exercise of right to renewal and that right may be exercised by assignee all by himself; although application for renewal must be in name of author or composer, assignment of expectancy implies power of attorney in assignee to make application in name of author or composer; renewal belongs to assignee even though application is not in assignee's name; unless defective under special rule as to expectancies, assignee's title is complete and perfect at instant application in name of author is registered; title depends not upon form of registration but upon actual ownership of copyright as renewed. Rose v. Bourne, Inc., (DC-NY), 176 FSupp 605, 123 USPQ 29. Aff'd 279 F(2d) 79, 125 USPQ 509.

Renewal copyright obtained by author is property of author's assignee under assignment executed 15 years before whereby author as-

(1451)

signed copyright and renewal and authorized assignee "to apply for and receive renewals and extensions." Selwyn & Co., Inc. v. Veiller, (DC-NY), 43 FSupp 491, 52 USPQ 630.

Since assignment of all of author's right, title, and interest in song did not expressly provide for renewal of copyright by assignee in author's name, assignee has no right to apply for renewal in author's name; composer of music was entitled to renewal, which he holds for benefit of himself and author or his assignee. Von Tilzer v. Jerry Vogel Music Co., Inc., (DC-NY), 53 FSupp 191, 59 USPQ 292. Aff'd 158 F(2d) 516, 71 USPQ 285.

Since author of words of song was living on first day of twenty-eighth year of original term of copyright, 1911 assignment to copyright proprietor of all interest in song and renewal rights vested in it all renewal rights and author's 1938 application for renewal vested no renewal rights in his 1938 assignee. Von Tilzer v. Jerry Vogel Music Co., (DC-NY), 53 FSupp 191, 59 USPQ 292. Aff'd 158 F(2d) 516, 71 USPQ 285.

Executor has same rights under this section as widow and children and next of kin; fact that author assigned inchoate renewal rights to third party would not bar widow or children, if any, from exercising their statutory renewal rights; since executor's rights are no less than that of widow and children or next of kin, they cannot be defeated by author's assignment. Miller Music Corp. v. Charles N. Daniels, Inc., (DC-NY), 158 FSupp 188, 116 USPQ 92.

Authors, by agreement, sold and assigned to publisher certain specific rights in song, including "all copyrights and the rights to secure copyrights and extensions and renewals of the copyrights"; agreement effectively conveyed renewal rights to publisher since it conveyed all rights to original copyright and the expectancy in the renewal copyright; exercise of publisher-assignee's renewal rights is not contingent upon authors' assistance; although application for renewal must be in authors' names, assignment of expectancy implies a power of attorney in assignee to apply for renewal in authors' names; hence, assignee's use of authors' names in applying for renewal is proper and cannot deprive assignee of any renewal rights. Tobias v. Joy Music, Inc., (DC-NY), — FSupp —, 133 USPQ 181.

Inasmuch as authors had effectively assigned renewal rights, registration of renewal application made out in their names did not vest ownership of renewal in authors; while authors renewed copyright by registration of their application, ownership of renewal copyright was not determined thereby but remained in assignee. Tobias v. Joy Music, Inc., (DC-NY), — FSupp —, 133 USPQ 181.

Prior to statutory renewal period an author's interest in renewal rights is only an expectancy, which can be defeated in event of his death before commencement of renewal period; however, author can effectively assign such an expectancy and, if he is living at commencement of renewal period, expectancy then vests in assignee. Tobias v. Joy Music, Inc., (DC-NY), — FSupp —, 133 USPQ 181.

An assignment of expectancy operating as an executory contract to transfer renewal rights when they accrue in last year of copyright, if without consideration, is unenforceable. Rossiter v. Vogel, (DC-NY), 61 USPQ 514. Aff'd 148 F(2d) 292, 65 USPQ 72.

Defendant conveyed musical compositions to plaintiff under contract which also conveyed in futuro renewal term of copyright; subsequently, defendant obtained renewal but refused to convey to plaintiff; complaint in state court seeking specific performance of contract by assignment of renewal, which defendant had conveyed to another defendant with knowledge of contract, states cause of action and is not dismissed on motion; contract is valid and enforcible. G. Schirmer, Inc. v. Robbins Music Corp., 176 Misc 578, 28 NYS(2d) 699, 49 USPQ 467.

10. Effect of expiration.

After the expiration of copyright, the name by which the publication was known and sold under the copyright becomes public property. G. & C. Merriam Co. v. Syndicate Publishing Co., 237 US 618, 59 LEd 1148, 35 SCR 708.

At the expiration of a copyright, the book and the name by which it is designated are dedicated to the public. Ogilvie v. G. & C. Merriam Co., (CC-Mass), 149 Fed 858. Mf'd 159 Fed 638, 16 LRA(NS) 549, 14 AnnCas 796.

When, upon the expiration of a copyright, the name by which the book is known has also acquired a secondary meaning, and has come to indicate to the public the book published and sold by the publisher who took out the copyright, another person using such name must use it in such a manner as not to deceive the public. Ogilvie v. G. & C. Merriam Co., (CC-Mass), 149 Fed 858. Mf'd 159 Fed 638, 16 LRA (NS) 549, 14 AnnCas 796.

Upon expiration of the term of copyright of a novel any person may make any use of the novel which he may see fit, whether by copying, publishing or dramatizing. Glaser v. St. Elmo Co., Inc., (CC-NY), 175 Fed 276; Atlas Mfg. Co. v. Street & Smith, (CCA 8), 204 Fed 398, 47 LRA(NS) 1002.

Expiration of copyright of novel does not affect copyright of so much of opera based thereon as was a new work and entitled to be independently copyrighted as such. G. Ricordi & Co. v. Paramount Pictures, Inc., (CA 2), 189 F(2d) 469, 89 USPQ 289, 89 USPQ 564, mod'g 92 FSupp 537, 86 USPQ 452.

When statutory copyright expires without being renewed, common-law rights are not revived. Tams-Witmark Music Library, Inc. v. New Opera Co., Inc., 298 NY 163, 81 NE(2d) 70, 78 USPQ 298, aff'g 272 AppDiv 342, 71 NYS(2d) 136, 74 USPQ 76.

All copyrighted compositions enter public domain at expiration of copyrights, and thereafter, anyone has right to use them freely. Taylor v. State, 29 Wash(2d series) 638, 188 Pac(2d) 671, 76 USPQ 275.

11. Renewals under prior law.

Under Copyright Act of 1790 which permitted renewal by "assigns," an assignment of rights in unpublished manuscript included subsequent renewals and extensions. Paige v. Banks, 80 US(13 Wall) 608, 20 LEd 709, aff'g (CC-NY), FedCas 10,671, 7 Blatchf 152.

Copyright Act of 1790 did not restrict assignability of author's renewal interest; 1831 Copyright Act merely enlarged benefits of copyright, extending length of original term and giving author's widow and children that which theretofore they did not possess, namely, right to renew of which author would have been entitled if he had survived original term; 1831 Copyright Act did not impose any restraint on right of author to assign his contingent interest in renewal. Fred Fisher Music Co., Inc. v. M. Witmark & Sons, 318 US 643, 87 LEd 1055, 63 SCR 773, 57 USPQ 50, aff'g (CCA 2), 125 F(2d) 949, 52 USPQ 385, which aff'd 38 FSupp 72, 49 USPQ 171.

A statement by the author that he had intended to convey all his interest in the copyrighted work, after the first term of the copyright had expired, will prevent the legal representatives of the author from claiming that the rights of the assignee existed only during the first term of the copyright. Cowen v. Banks, (CC-NY), FedCas 3,295, 24 HowPrac 72.

An assignment of copyright during the initial term confers on the assignee no right to renewal of copyright, notwithstanding a usage among booksellers to the contrary. Pierpont v. Fowle, (CC-Mass), FedCas 11,152, 2 Woodb & M 23.

Under the original Copyright Act of 1790 the right of renewal was given to an author, his executors, administrators, or assigns, but in the Copyright Act of 1831 and all subsequent acts an administrator is not mentioned and therefore is regarded as excluded. Danks v. Gordon, (CCA 2), 272 Fed 821.

This section repeals R. S. § 4954 as to the method of renewing copyrights acquired under the former law. Stephens v. Howells Sales Co., (DC-NY), 16 F(2d) 805.

For renewal of copyright it is not necessary to publish record in newspaper for four weeks as was required in statutes in effect prior to 1909; renewal is effected by complying with this section. Fitch v. Shubert, (DC-NY), 20 FSupp 314, 35 USPQ 245.

By 1790 Copyright Act, renewal could be claimed not only by author but by assignee; 1831 Copyright Act is practically similar to 1909 Copyright Act as to renewals. M. Witmark & Sons v. Fred Fisher Music Co., Inc., (DC-NY), 38 FSupp 72, 49 USPQ 171, which was aff'd 318 US 643, 87 LEd 1055, 63 SCR 773, 57 USPQ 50.

25. Renewal of copyrights registered in Patent Office under repealed law.—

Subsisting copyrights originally registered in the Patent Office prior to July 1, 1940, under section 3 of the act of June 18, 1874, shall be subject to renewal in behalf of the proprietor upon application made to the Register of Copyrights within one year prior to the expiration of the original term of twenty-eight years. (July 30, 1947, c. 391, § 1, 61 Stat. 659.)

NOTES TO DECISIONS

Author's widow does not, by remarriage, lose rights to renew copyright under § 24 of 1909 Copyright Act. Edward B. Marks Music Corp. v. Borst Music Pub. Co., Inc., (DC-NJ), 110 FSupp 913, 97 USPQ 394.

Fact that brother of deceased author applied for renewal of copyright prior to widow's application therefor does not impair widow's right to renewal, since, by terms of § 24 of 1909 Copyright Act, rights of next of kin are nonexistent if widow lives. Edward B. Marks Music Corp. v. Borst Music Pub. Co., Inc., (DC-NJ), 110 FSupp 913, 97 USPQ 394.

26. Terms defined.—In the interpretation and construction of this title "the date of publication" shall in the case of a work of which copies are reproduced for sale or distribution be held to be the earliest date when copies of the first authorized edition were placed on sale, sold, or publicly distributed by the proprietor of the copyright or under his authority, and the word "author" shall include an employer in the case of works made for hire. (July 30, 1947, c. 391, § 1, 61 Stat. 659.)

NOTES TO DECISIONS

Where a former copyright law required a deposit of title before publication, the court decided that in the absence of proof to the contrary it would have been presumed that the publication was not made until after the deposit of title. Callaghan v. Myers, 128 US 617, 32 LEd 547, 9 SCR 177, mod'g (CC-Ill), 24 Fed 636.

The Copyright Act of 1831 required a deposit of title before publication, and, where a completed copy of the work was deposited at the same time as the title, it was presumed that there was a publication prior to the deposit of title. Baker v. Taylor, (CC-NY), Fed Cas 782, 2 Blatchf 82.

A public performance of a drama may not be a publication. Roberts v. Myers, (CC-Mass), FedCas 11,906.

It is not the purpose of this section to prescribe a general definition of what shall constitute publication, but merely to fix the date for commencement of the copyright term. Cardinal Film Corp. v. Beck, (DC-NY), 248 Fed 368; Patterson v. Century Productions, Inc., (CCA 2), 93 F(2d) 489, 35 USPQ 471, aff'g 19 FSupp 30, 33 USPQ 194.

The copyright statute requires the deposit of copies of the copyrighted work after publication, and, where plaintiff deposited the copies the same day 50 copies were received from the printer, such copies being retained by plaintiff or sent to branch offices although no general distribution was made until two days later, there was sufficient publication to comply with the statute. No-Leak-O Piston Ring Co. v.

Norris, (CCA 4), 277 Fed 951, aff'g 271 Fed 536.

"Date of first publication" in § 24 of this title refers to date of deposit under § 12 of this title of works of which copies are not reproduced for sale notwithstanding that this section defines "date of publication" of published work to mean earliest date when copies are placed on sale, sold, or publicly distributed. Shilkret v. Musicraft Records, Inc., (CCA 2), 131 F(2d) 929, 55 USPQ 469, rev'g 43 FSupp 184, 52 USPQ 164.

Republication after copies of first edition are placed on sale does not satisfy definition of "date of publication" in this section. Edward B. Marks Music Corp. v. Continental Record Co., Inc., (CA 2), 222 F(2d) 488, 105 USPQ 171, 105 USPQ 350, aff'g 120 FSupp 275, 100 USPQ 438.

Although corporation is incapable of exercising intellect so as to be primarily entitled to copyright, it may be employer for hire and entitled to copyright. Vitaphone Corp. v. Hutchinson Amusement Co., (DC–Mass), 28 FSupp 526, 42 USPQ 431.

27. Copyright distinct from property in object copyrighted—Effect of sale of object, and of assignment of copyright.—

The copyright is distinct from the property in the material object copyrighted, and the sale or conveyance, by gift or otherwise, of the material object shall not of itself constitute a transfer of the copyright, nor shall the assignment of the copyright constitute a transfer of the title to the material object; but nothing in this title shall be deemed to forbid, prevent, or restrict the transfer of any copy of a copyrighted work the possession of which has been lawfully obtained. (July 30, 1947, c. 391, § 1, 61 Stat. 660.)

NOTES TO DECISIONS

1. In general.

While a copyright is not subject to seizure and sale on execution it may be reached by creditor's bill. Stephens v. Cady, 55 US(14 How) 528; 14 LEd 528.

Copyright may be subjected on creditor's bill to payment of debts. Ager v. Murray, 105 US 126, 26 LEd 942, aff'g 1 Mackey(DC) 87.

Author's right to copyright may be assigned prior to issuance thereof and independently of the ownership of the work itself. American Tobacco Co. v. Werckmeister, 207 US 284, 52 LEd 208, 28 SCR 72, 12 AnnCas 595, aff'g (CCA 2), 146 Fed 375.

Uncopyrighted news is quasi property as between two parties engaged in vending it. International News Service v. Associated Press, 248 US 215, 63 LEd 211, 39 SCR 68, 2 ALR 293, aff'g (CCA 2), 245 Fed 244, 2 ALR 317, which mf'd 240 Fed 983.

Royalties and other income from copyrights are not immune from state taxation. Fox Film Corp. v. Doyal, 286 US 123, 76 LEd 1010, 52 SCR 546, aff'g 172 Ga 403, 157 SE 664.

Author's manuscripts cannot be seized by his creditors as property under the common law. Bartlett v. Crittenden, (CC-Ohio), FedCas 1,076, 5 McLean 32.

An author may sell his painting and retain the right to copyright in himself. Werckmeister v. Springer Lithographing Co., (CC-NY), 63 Fed 808.

Common-law copyright before publication may be assigned without a transfer of the article. Werckmeister v. American Lithographic Co., (CC-NY), 142 Fed 827. Aff'd 148 Fed 1022, which was aff'd 207 US 375, 52 LEd 254, 28 SCR 124.

Sale of an author's manuscript of a copyrighted play by a playbroker without power to so do does not transfer title to the copyright. Stodart v. Mutual Film Corp., (DC-NY), 249 Fed 507. Aff'd 249 Fed 513.

Assignment of motion-picture rights of a book did not convey any copyright, but only a right upon which the assignee might obtain a copyright on a motion-pitcure photoplay of the book. Goldwyn Pictures Corp. v. Howells Sales Co., Inc., (CCA 2), 282 Fed 9.

A copyright does not give its owner any property in the thing copyrighted, but simply gives him protection against anybody else copying it. Taylor v. Com. Int. Rev., (CCA 3), 51 F(2d) 915, aff'g 17 BTA 1107.

Assignment of a literary product after publication with notice did not carry the copyright. Davenport Quigley Expedition, Inc. v. Century Productions, (DC-NY), 18 FSupp 974, 32 USPQ 608.

Art work is personal property, transferrable by sale and delivery; there is no distinction in that respect between it and any other property; paintings are no exception to general rule; if in transfer there is any limitation for artist's benefit, it must be expressed and clearly imposed; otherwise it is not presumed; burden of showing limitation is on artist. Grant v. Kellogg Co., (DC-NY), 58 FSupp 48, 63 USPQ 173. Aff'd 154 F(2d) 59, 75 USPQ 301.

Exclusive right to vend copyrighted work is not unlimited. Copyright proprietor is not empowered, merely by virtue of copyright, to control sales of published copies after they have come into lawful ownership of first purchaser. Pivotal issue is whether title to particular copy has been retained by proprietor or passed to first purchaser. If title has been retained, copy remains under protection of copyright law, and infringement proceedings may be had against all subsequent purchasers of the copy who interfere with proprietor's exclusive right to vend copyrighted work; if title passed to first purchaser, copy loses protection of copyright law. U. S. v. Wells, (DC-Tex), 176 FSupp 630, 123 USPQ 65.

No creditor can reach a copyright unless some special provision of the law is made on the subject. Dart v. Woodhouse, 40 Mich 399, 29 AmRep 544.

A copyright is distinct from the property copyrighted, and its assignment will no more effect a transfer of the property than the sale of the property will effect an assignment of the copyright. McClintic v. Sheldon, 182 Misc 32, 43 NYS(2d) 695, 59 USPQ 41.

The owner of a patent right, copyright, or trade-mark, having the exclusive right to manufacture and sell the article, may impose upon his assignee such restrictions as he may see proper, and to which his assignee will agree. Coca-Cola Co. v. State, (TexCivApp), 225 SW 791.

Although not corporeal, but existing in contemplation of law, a copyright is enjoyable as a legal estate, as other movable property. Simmons v. Sikes, (TexCivApp), 56 SW(2d) 193.

2. Rights of purchaser of article.

A copperplate engraving of a copyrighted map, like other tangible personal property, is the subject of seizure and sale, on execution, and the title passes to the purchaser the same as if made at a private sale; but the incorporeal right, secured by the Copyright Act to the author, to multiply copies of the map, by the use of the plate, is not the subject of seizure and sale on execution, and such right remains in the author. Stephens v. Cady, 55 US(14 How) 528, 14 LEd 528; Stevens v. Gladding. 58 US(17 How) 447, 15 LEd 155, rev'g (CC-RI), FedCas 13,400.

The sale of an uncopyrighted painting carries with it the right to copy it without the author's consent. Parton v. Prang, (CC-Mass), FedCas 10,784, 3 Cliff 537.

When a copyrighted book is sold the ownership of the book is in the buyer and he has the right to maintain the book as nearly as possible in its original condition, so far, at least, as the cover and binding of the book is concerned. Doan v. American Book Co., (CCA 7), 105 Fed 772.

Where plates for the printing of a copyrighted book are sold at a sheriff's sale, the purchaser becomes the owner of the plates, but has no right to use such plates for the printing of the copyrighted book and may be enjoined from so doing by the author. Patterson v. J. S. Ogilvie Pub. Co., (CC-NY), 119 Fed 451.

The giving of professional copies of a musical composition to musicians does not authorize them to publicly perform it for profit. Harms v. Cohen, (DC-Pa), 279 Fed 276.

Purchaser of telegraphic code was not entitled to copy the code, the copyright of which was owned by the seller. Hartfield v. Herzfeld, (DC-NY), 60 F(2d) 599.

Defendant employed plaintiff to paint gnomes for use in defendant's advertisements; artist sold what his conception was as executed in what he sold; he could not hold unexecuted conception of gnome, or what that conception might be inferred to be from what he had executed; he sold all that could be drawn, depicted, or used from what he had sold; when he sold executed conception, he sold conception; he claims to have retained conception of gnome in other settings, dress, or occupations, but he cannot retain those except in his mind either in choate or inchoate form.

conceived or to be conceived, or as present or future ideas; as such they are not property. Grant v. Kellogg Co., (DC-NY), 58 FSupp 48, 63 USPQ 173. Aff'd 158 F(2d) 59, 75 USPQ 301.

By publishing and selling to public, musical manuscripts in way of sheet music or more detailed orchestrations of copyrighted musical composition, copyright proprietor does not confer on purchasing public right publicly to perform compositions sold without liability for infringement. Remick Music Corp. v. Interstate Hotel Co., (DC-Neb), 58 FSupp 523, 63 USPQ 327. Aff'd 157 F(2d) 744, 71 USPQ 138.

3. —Resale.

The purchaser of a book, sold by the authority of the copyright owner without agreement, may dispose of such book in whatever manner he chooses, regardless of any notice as to price contained therein. Bobbs-Merrill Co. v. Straus, 210 US 339, 52 LEd 1086, 28 SCR 724, aff'g (CCA 2), 147 Fed 15, 15 LRA(NS) 766, which aff'd 139 Fed 155.

Dealer, in absence of knowledge of limitation of authority of publisher's agents from whom he purchased, may sell a book for any price he may see fit. Clemens v. Estes, (CC-Mass), 22 Fed 899.

A purchaser of unbound copyrighted volumes, sold with the authority of the copyright owner, has the right to bind and resell them. Kipling v. G. P. Putnam's Sons, (CCA 2), 120 Fed 631, 65 LRA 873.

A purchaser of copyrighted books, having knowledge of the restrictions placed upon sales, receives only such title as the agents of the author are authorized to give, and a notice of conditions of resale is binding upon him. Authors & Newspapers Ass'n v. O'Gorman Co., (CC-RI), 147 Fed 616.

A purchaser of a second-hand copyrighted schoolbook, cannot copy a map or small portion of the text of the original publication, which may be missing from such book, and resell it with its replaced parts without infringing the copyright. Ginn & Co. v. Apollo Pub. Co., (DC-Pa), 215 Fed 772.

The owner of an article protected by copyright, when he has manufactured and sold the same, cannot impose restrictions upon his vendee as to the future sale of the same. Coca-Cola Co. v. State, (TexCivApp), 225 SW 791.

28. Assignments and bequests.—Copyright secured under this title or previous copyright laws of the United States may be assigned, granted, or mortgaged by an instrument in writing signed by the proprietor of the copyright, or may be bequeathed by will. (July 30, 1947, c. 391, § 1, 61 Stat. 660.)

NOTES TO DECISIONS
ANALYSIS

1. Persons entitled to make transfer.
2. —Co-owners.
3. Title to original copyright.

1. Persons entitled to make transfer.

The mere possession of the manuscript of a play by a playbroker is not of itself sufficient to give him authority to make a contract for the sale of the copyright. Stodart v. Mutual Film Corp., (DC-NY), 249 Fed 507. Aff'd 249 Fed 513.

Employee for hire has no rights which can be assigned to third party. Von Tilzer v. Jerry Vogel Music Co., Inc., (DC-NY), 53 FSupp 191, 59 USPQ 292.

On intestate death of copyright proprietor, title to copyright was vested in heirs at law by Illinois statute of descent and distribution; assignment of copyright by heirs is valid and passes title to assignee. Forster Music Publishers Inc. v. Jerry Vogel Music Co., (DC-NY), 62 USPQ 142. Aff'd 147 F(2d) 614, 64 USPQ 417.

2. —Co-owners.

Where the rights in a dramatic production belong jointly to two persons, either one may license another to produce such drama on the stage or in motion pictures, but such person will be obliged to account to the other. Klein v. Beach, (DC-NY), 232 Fed 240. Aff'd 239 Fed 108.

Although parties stipulate that S and G were joint composers of musical composition, S having written the music and S and G together having written the lyrics, S's assignee is entitled to one half, not three fourths, interest in renewal copyright, since there are no facts in evidence indicating that ownership was intended as other than as an undivided one half interest for each coauthor; assignment, providing for royalties to be paid to S and G, had stated that royalties were to be divided equally; by analogy, coauthors were tenants in common. Sweet Music, Inc. v. Melrose Music Corp., (DC-Cal), 189 FSupp 655, 127 USPQ 513.

Where contract granting exclusive publication rights to defendant by plaintiff and deceased provided that contract could not be cancelled except by mutual consent of authors, or in event of death of one of the authors by mutual consent of executor of estate and remaining author, son of deceased author was necessary party to cancellation even though mother had consented to cancellation, and son

had requested payment of royalties to mother. Anderson v. Educational Publishers, Inc., (DC-Minn), 87 USPQ 149.

Where musical and lyrical compositions are owned by three tenants in common, two are entitled to use compositions and license others to use them without consulting other tenant; licensee is not liable and licensors' sole obligation is to account to cotenant. Brown v. Republic Productions, Inc., 68 CalApp(2d series) 136, 156 Pac(2d) 40, 65 USPQ 54.

All co-owners of copyrighted material having joined in granting exclusive motion picture rights to third person, one co-owner alone is unable to procure rescission of contract; also, co-owner may not have partial rescission as to his interest alone since he thereby would acquire right to grant nonexclusive license to produce picture with the result that third person's license would become nonexclusive, thus significantly altering position of third person and other co-owners; all co-owners must join to obtain rescission. Denker v. Twentieth Century-Fox Film Corp., 10 NY(2d series) 339, 223 NYS(2d) 193, 179 NE(2d) 336, 132 USPQ 82.

Co-owners of copyrighted material are considered tenants in common; either co-owner has power, acting alone, to grant nonexclusive motion picture rights to third persons but exclusive rights to copyright may be effected only by grant in which all co-owners join. Denker v. Twentieth Century-Fox Film Corp., 10 NY (2d series) 339, 223 NYS(2d) 193, 179 NE(2d) 336, 132 USPQ 82.

A co-owner of a copyright may grant a license for the use of such copyright. Herbert v. Fields, (Misc), 152 NYS 487.

3. Title to original copyright.

Plaintiff who had entered into contract with reporter and other state officials to publish certain decisions could not be considered owners of a volume prepared by the reporter after his term of office had expired. Little v. Hall, 59 US(18 How) 165, 15 LEd 328.

Author must have right to copyright in order to make assignment. Bong v. Alfred S. Campbell Art Co., 214 US 236, 53 LEd 979, 29 SCR 628, 16 AnnCas 1126, aff'g (CCA 2), 155 Fed 116.

An author in general employ of another will not be deemed to have parted with his right to copyright and transferred it to his employer, in the absence of a valid agreement to that effect. Boucicault v. Fox, (CC-NY), FedCas 1,691, 5 Blatchf 87.

Where one person holds the legal title to a copyright in trust for the other joint owners, he cannot appropriate it exclusively to himself so as to impair its worth as to the others. Maurel v. Smith, (CCA 2), 271 Fed 211, aff'g 220 Fed 195.

One other than author or proprietor must have assignment in order to procure copyright. Public Ledger Co. v. Post Printing & Publishing Co., (CCA 8), 294 Fed 430.

Owners of copyright cannot claim infringement against one using copyrighted matter in advertisements under contract made with copyright holder prior to award of copyright. Industrial Railway & Locomotive Works, Inc. v. Cagney Bros., (DC-NJ), 1 FSupp 970, 15 USPQ 263.

Court is not persuaded that copyright may not descend under laws of decedent's foreign domicile; it does not follow that, because proprietor under Copyright Act [this title] is given no rights against an infringing foreign publication his rights of ownership may not descend by law of foreign domicile. Brecht v. Bentley, (DC-NY), 185 FSupp 890, 126 USPQ 356.

Court rejects contention that, if author proprietor dies during original term of copyright, the work is in public domain until right to renewal accrues at expiration of original term when named successors in interest may apply for renewal; this section, which expressly provides that copyright may be bequeathed by will, must be read to include interstate succession. Brecht v. Bentley, (DC-NY), 185 FSupp 890, 126 USPQ 356.

4. Renewals.

In action by first assignee of copyright renewal right against second assignee from common assignor to obtain assignment of renewal procured by second assignee, summary judgment for plaintiff should not be granted without considering issues of fraud and failure of consideration in first assignment although issues were not raised by affirmative defenses. Rossiter v. Vogel, (CCA 2), 134 F(2d) 908, 57 USPQ 161, rev'g 46 FSupp 749, 54 USPQ 229.

Fact that renewal statute gives no right of renewal to legatee does not require holding that legatee of copyright proprietor has no title to original copyright as right and property of copyright owner may be bequeathed by will. Stuff v. La Budde Feed & Grain Co., (DC-Wis), 42 FSupp 493, 52 USPQ 23.

Widow, who assigned renewal, is not entitled to keep all stipulated royalties against rights (not known when assignment was made) coauthor has in renewal; assignee was to have sole and exclusive right for which it was to pay royalty to widow who succeeded to husband's interest; this interest is impressed with trust in favor of husband's coauthor, with whom widow must share royalties. Edward B. Marks Music Corp. v. Wonnell, (DC-NY), 61 FSupp 722, 65 USPQ 456.

5. Sale.

Sale of story to magazine company was an absolute sale without reservation, including the right to dramatize it. Dam v. Kirk La Shelle Co., (CCA 2), 175 Fed 902, 41 LRA(NS) 1002, 20 AnnCas 1173, aff'g 166 Fed 589.

An author or proprietor of a literary work possesses such a right of sale as fully as does the owner of other personal property, and sales may be absolute or conditional, and with or without qualifications or restrictions. Maurel v. Smith, (CCA 2), 271 Fed 211, aff'g 220 Fed 195.

6. Mortgages.

Copyrights can be mortgaged only under the federal copyright law. In re Leslie-Judge Co., (CCA 2), 272 Fed 886.

7. Form of transfer.

An acquiescence in the publication of an author's manuscript or in the republication of his printed book would authorize the presumption of an assignment. Bartlett v. Crittenden, (CC-Ohio), FedCas 1,076, 5 McLean 32.

A mere contract authorizing the publication of a story in a magazine does not imply a sale of the copyright. Ford v. Charles E. Blaney Amusement Co., (CC-NY), 148 Fed 642.

Author could have required purchaser of serial rights, who took out copyright in own name, to reassign all other rights to him. Brady v. Reliance Motion Picture Corp., (CCA 2), 229 Fed 137.

The author of a political article may deliver the same to a magazine for publication with the intention that the title shall vest, and a formal bill of sale is not essential. Atlantic Monthly Co. v. Post Pub. Co., (DC-Mass), 27 F(2d) 556.

Affidavit filed in copyright office after the death of copyright proprietor, claiming that he had conveyed all rights in copyrighted book to affiant, was insufficient. Snook v. Blank, (DC-Mont), 92 FSupp 518, 87 USPQ 201.

Where copyright owner transferred all its assets under general assignment and assets were insufficient to pay creditors, assignment included copyright although not specifically mentioned, and subsequent assignment of copyright by original owner gave no title. Kaplan v. Fox Film Corp., (DC-NY), 37 USPQ 248.

8. —Parol.

Rights in manuscript before copyright has been taken out may be transferred by parol. Callaghan v. Myers, 128 US 617, 32 LEd 547, 9 SCR 177, mod'g (CC-Ill), 24 Fed 636.

Assignment by owner to one who takes out copyright in his own name may be by parol. M. Witmark & Sons v. Calloway, (DC-Tenn), 22 F(2d) 412.

Oral claim that assignment was merely for life of assignee is not accepted. Arnstein v. American Soc. of Composers, Authors & Publishers, (DC-NY), 29 FSupp 388, 42 USPQ 581.

Oral license of copyrighted material gives no greater right to use than does written license. Loew's Inc. v. Columbia Broadcasting System, Inc., (DC-Cal), 131 FSupp 165, 105 USPQ 302. Aff'd 239 F(2d) 532, 112 USPQ 11, which was aff'd 356 US 43, 2 LEd(2d) 583, 78 SCR 667, 116 USPQ 479.

A person may make a valid contract by parol for the assignment of a copyright, although the assignment itself must be in writing. Gould v. Banks & Gould, 8 Wend(NY) 562, 24 Am Dec 90.

9. Assignment in general.

Copyright is property capable of being assigned. Ager v. Murray, 105 US 126, 26 LEd 942, aff'g 1 Mackey(DC) 87.

Assignment of copyright refers to what is in existence, not to any future contingency, and to what is personal to the author. Pierpont v. Fowle, (CC-Mass), FedCas 11,152, 2 Woodb& M 23.

Nonresident foreigner may take and hold by assignment a copyright granted to citizen of United States. Carte v. Evans, (CC-Mass), 27 Fed 861.

An inchoate right to a copyright may, prior to the taking of the copyright, be transferred by parol. Black v. Henry G. Allen Co., (CC-NY), 42 Fed 618, 9 LRA 433.

The whole or an undivided part of a copyright may be assigned. Black v. Henry G. Allen Co., (CC-NY), 42 Fed 618, 9 LRA 433.

Author's assignment to wife of half interest in unpublished and uncopyrighted story was ineffective for income tax purposes since assignment lacked economic reality. Wodehouse v. Com. Int. Rev., (CA 4), 178 F(2d) 987, 84 USPQ 162, mod'g 8 TC 637.

Contract between plaintiff (copyright proprietor) and third party expressly provides that plaintiff "licenses" third party to do certain things, thereby precluding a construction that there was an assignment; moreover, third party was licensed to make reproductions of copyrighted silent motion picture film "and to license the use thereof," thereby precluding a construction that plaintiff gave third party the right to sell reproductions; if it be assumed that contract was an assignment and that third party was given power to sell reproductions, such power was restricted with third party merely to license use thereof "for strictly nontheatrical exhibitions"; while third party may have purported to unconditionally sell positive print to defendant, third party's only authority from plaintiff was to reproduce miniature prints and license them for nontheatrical use; hence, defendant's commercial exhibition of film was not authorized by plaintiff. Hampton v. Paramount Pictures Corp., (CA 9), 279 F(2d) 100, 125 USPQ 623.

Copyright of book and movie rights therein are rights of literary property incapable of manual delivery. Snook v. Blank, (DC-Mont), 92 FSupp 518, 87 USPQ 201.

Though informal and unrecorded, written assignment of copyrighted song is sufficient as between the parties to pass to assignee all rights of assignors in copyright and song. Klasmer v. Baltimore Football, Inc., (DC-Md), 200 FSupp 255, 132 USPQ 36.

Corporation owned exclusive license to produce musical play and motion picture based on licensor's play; individual, who owned 98% of corporation's shares, wrote letter to his secretary, stating that he gave her stated percentage of his "shares of profits" of musical play and motion picture; delivery of letter constituted valid, complete, present gift of share in royalties when and if collected from musical play and motion picture and transferred to secretary an enforcible right to such share of royalties to accrue to stockholder on production of musical play and motion picture even though, at time of delivery of letter, musical play and motion picture were not in existence. Speelman v. Pascal, 10 NY(2d series) 313, 222 NYS(2d) 324, 178 NE(2d) 723, 131 USPQ 489.

10. —Construction of assignment contract.

Contract for publication of foreign book in United States which did not expressly assign author's rights and which contained provision that "the said William Meyer Foster [author] agrees to have the within-named play in order to have the protection of the American law copyrighted prior to its appearance in the book trade," did not convey the author's title. Saake v. Lederer, (CCA 3), 174 Fed 135, rev'g 166 Fed 810.

Evidence that author sold rights to perform play on stage after selling rights of publication to plaintiff and that check from plaintiff to author was indorsed "For all serial rights," showed a license and not an assignment to plaintiff. New Fiction Pub. Co. v. Star Co., (DC-NY), 220 Fed 994.

Contract provided that artist convey to publisher all title to paintings and also right to use artist's name therewith; condition is not implied into contract that publisher cannot publish paintings without accrediting them to artist. Vargas v. Esquire, Inc., (CCA 7), 164 F(2d) 522, 75 USPQ 304.

Where contract made no present grant of title to future drawings, but contemplated that publisher's title should not attach until drawings were furnished to it, publisher has no title to artist's drawings never furnished to publisher. Esquire, Inc. v. Varga Enterprises, Inc., (CA 7), 185 F(2d) 14, 87 USPQ 342, mod'g 81 FSupp 306, 80 USPQ 89.

Unless assignment of copyright grants assignee right to sue for infringements antedating assignment, no such right is conferred. Group Publishers, Inc. v. Winchell, (DC-NY), 86 FSupp 573, 83 USPQ 461.

Plaintiff's exclusive license to defendant to exploit motion pictures provided that defendant could sublicense but prohibited assignment without plaintiff's consent; defendant did not breach license by agreement whereby third party was granted exclusive agency to market pictures on television upon conditions similar to those contained in plaintiff's contract with defendant; language employed in agreement with third party and obligation of third party to account to defendant are not consistent with assignment; also, agreement was not abandonment of defendant's obligation to use best efforts to exploit pictures. Arnold Productions, Inc. v. Favorite Films Corp., (DC-NY), 176 FSupp 862, 123 USPQ 383.

Music publishers to whom writers transfer their compositions with right to secure copyright, but with obligation to pay royalties, are obligated to exploit them in good faith for benefit of writers, as well as for themselves. Schwartz v. Broadcast Music, Inc., (DC-NY), 180 FSupp 322, 124 USPQ 34.

Where a contract is entered into between two co-owners of a copyright and a third person, giving such person the right to publish the copyrighted work, and providing for payment of $2,000 to such person upon termination of contract by copyright owners, such sum must be paid upon termination although such assignee still retains the right to publish the work through the purchase of the rights of one co-owner. Holt v. Silver, 169 Mass 435, 48 NE 837.

In a contract granting a factor the exclusive right to place creator's indorsement upon designs, and granting him the right to take out any copyrights as may be necessary, and providing for an accounting of profits each month, implies a promise on the part of the factor to use reasonable efforts to bring profits into existence. Wood v. Lucy, Lady Duff-Gordon, 222 NY 88, 118 NE 214, rev'g 177 AppDiv 624, 164 NYS 576.

11. —Rights of assignees in general.

A copyright may be assigned, and the rights of the assignee will be protected the same as those of the author. Wheaton v. Peters, 33 US(8 Pet) 591, 8 LEd 1055, rev'g (CC-Pa), Fed Cas 17,486.

Assignee of common-law copyright may obtain statutory copyright although he is neither author nor proprietor. American Tobacco Co. v. Werckmeister, (CCA 2), 146 Fed 375. Aff'd 207 US 284, 52 LEd 208, 28 SCR 72.

Rights of an assignee of a copyright are measured by those of his assignor. Davis v. Bowes, (DC-NY), 209 Fed 53. Aff'd 219 Fed 178.

Plaintiff's failure to record copyright assignment within three months of its execution vests no rights in defendant, who was not a subsequent purchaser without notice; it matters little that plaintiff might have had notice of defendant's invalid claim. Edward B. Marks Music Corp. v. Charles K. Harris Music Publishing Co., Inc., (CA 2), 255 F(2d) 518, 117 USPQ 308.

Contract contained no express provision that defendant was to license plaintiff's motion pictures for television exhibition separate and distinct from pictures owned by others than plaintiff; such provision was not implicit in contract; hence, exploitation of plaintiff's pictures in conjunction with others was not of itself a breach of contract; it is noted that there is testimony that all major distributors sold right to exhibit pictures in same package manner and that such was most profitable way to market them; there was no breach of obligation to use best efforts to exploit pictures. Arnold Productions, Inc. v. Favorite Films Corp., (DC-NY), 176 FSupp 862, 123 USPQ 383.

Although assignment to defendants of renewal rights by author was not recorded, plaintiff took from author with full knowledge of prior assignment; hence, author's post renewal assignment to plaintiff is of no legal effect. Sweet Music, Inc. v. Melrose Music Corp., (DC-Cal), 189 FSupp 655, 127 USPQ 513.

Assignee of copyright takes no more than assignor had at time of assignment. Detective Comics, Inc. v. Fawcett Publications, Inc., (DC-NY), 4 FedRDec 237, 64 USPQ 116.

Rights of an American assignee of a play written by an English author and publicly presented in England was not affected by an English statute relating to the statutory period of protection of the performing rights of plays. O'Neill v. General Film Co., 171 AppDiv 854, 157 NYS 1028, mod'g (Misc), 152 NYS 599.

By merely taking assignment, assignee does not become party to private agreements between proprietor and author; when liable to author at all, assignee is liable on theory of equitable lien, not on theory of contract. Gay v. Robbins Music Corp., (Misc), 38 NYS(2d) 337, 55 USPQ 461.

12. Partial transfers.

The owner of a copyright of a book may give a person the sole right of performing a particular copyrighted drama based upon the book, and give another the right of performing a different dramatic composition of the same story. Harper & Bros. v. Kalem Co., (CCA 2), 169 Fed 61. Aff'd 222 US 55, 56 LEd 92, 32 SCR 20, AnnCas1913A, 1285.

The holder of a copyright of a book may sell the right to dramatize the story to one person and the right to make a motion-picture play to another. Photo Drama Motion Picture Co., Inc. v. Social Uplift Film Corp., (DC-NY), 213 Fed 374. Aff'd 220 Fed 448.

Assignment of copyright of play by publisher to author conveyed only the statutory play right and not the copyright. Fitch v. Young, (DC-NY), 230 Fed 743. Aff'd 239 Fed 1021.

Copyright owner can assign separately one or more of sum of separable rights making up copyright property, but when he splits off rights by assignment, assignee does not become owner of copyright and acquires only lesser rights granted by assignment; it does not matter whether he is called assignee in instrument or whether it is called assignment; if he gets only rights of licensee, so-called assignment amounts only to license. Goldsmith v. Com. Int. Rev., (CCA 2), 143 F(2d) 466, 62 USPQ 112, aff'g 1 TC 711.

A publisher may make a valid transfer of copyright on one picture in a periodical, keeping for himself the copyright on all other contents of the periodical. Kaplan v. Fox Film Corp., (DC-NY), 19 FSupp 780, 33 USPQ 469.

Owner of copyrighted property may grant license to use or exercise some or all of rights in and to such property, or he may make full and complete disposition or sale of property and his rights with respect thereto. Cory v. Com. Int. Rev., 23 TC 775, 104 USPQ 209. Aff'd 230 F(2d) 941, 109 USPQ 1.

13. Product use.

Sale of type plates and impression sheets for a copyrighted book to satisfy a judgment is not a sale of the copyright, so as to give purchaser thereof right to publish the copyrighted work. Patterson v. J. S. Ogilvie Pub. Co., (CC-NY), 119 Fed 451.

German granted to defendant's predecessor the right to make and vend phonograph records in Czechoslovakia, but not in United States; German granted to plaintiff the right to make and vend same records in United States; since owner of literary property may, by negative covenant, subject use of such property to restrictions in hands of remote assignee, defendant cannot claim rights to make and vend records outside of Czechoslovakia. Capitol Records, Inc. v. Mercury Records Corp., (CA 2), 221 F(2d) 657, 105 USPQ 163, aff'g 109 FSupp 330, 95 USPQ 177.

Assignment of a literary product after publication with notice did not carry the copyright. Davenport Quigley Expedition, Inc. v. Century Productions, Inc., (DC-NY), 18 FSupp 974, 32 USPQ 608.

Where artist authorized publisher to reproduce painting once in its magazine but did not assign copyright on painting, it is doubtful whether artist succeeds to copyright by virtue of assignment from publisher, where assignment purports to convey not the copyright on the reproduction, but the copyright on original painting. Leigh v. Barnhart, (DC-NJ), 96 FSupp 194, 89 USPQ 307.

Grant to another of exclusive right to sell, lease, license, or exhibit positive prints made from licensor's negatives excludes licensor from so dealing with positive prints. Weiss v. Hollywood Film Enterprises, Inc., (CalSupCt), 81 USPQ 570.

An owner of a copyright has the exclusive right to sell the copyrighted article anywhere in the United States and may transfer this right to another, either in whole or in part. Davis v. Vories, 141 Mo 234, 42 SW 707.

14. Licenses.

One licensing use of copyrighted song in compilation consented to its use in subsequent editions. Gabriel v. McCabe, (CC-Ill), 74 Fed 743.

Giving a license to publish copyrighted material under licensee's own copyright without insertion of original copyright notice is an abandonment. West Publishing Co. v. Edward Thompson Co., (CC-NY), 169 Fed 833. Mf'd 176 Fed 833.

In an action on the infringement of a copyright, defendant cannot use as a defense an alleged written contract of license, when such contract is not produced or satisfactorily accounted for. Historical Pub. Co. v. Jones Bros. Pub. Co., (CCA 3), 231 Fed 638.

Burden of proving license is on persons claiming it. Schellberg v. Empringham, (DC-NY), 36 F(2d) 991.

Plaintiff, owner of two motion pictures, exclusively licensed defendant to exploit such films for reissue purposes and through te'evision; defendant agreed to use its best efforts to exploit films; license provided that it could not be assigned without plaintiff's consent; defendant did not violate license by entering into agreement constituting a third party its exclusive agent for television d'stribution of films; defendant did not technically assign license, but merely delegated a part of its duties; defendant did not divest itself of its ultimate responsibility to plaintiff since it reserved adequate supervisory powers over third party. Arnold Productions, Inc. v. Favorite Films Corp., (CA 2), 298 F(2d) 540, 133 USPQ 56.

License to produce copyrighted play on spoken stage may well be perpetual license when agreement is silent as to duration of licensee's rights. Fitch v. Shubert, (DC-NY), 20 FSupp 314, 35 USPQ 245.

Where complainants were in receivership in state court at time notices of alleged cancellation were mailed, it is incumbent on plaintiff to show that such action was with permission of state court; failing in this, court holds licenses not cancelled. Buck v. Trianon Co., (DC-Wash), 26 FSupp 96, 40 USPQ 425.

Holders of domestic copyrights may refrain from licensing at all. Paine v. Electrical Research Products, Inc., (DC-NY), 27 FSupp 780, 41 USPQ 575.

Written license expressly and unambiguously limited licensee's right to use copyrighted advertisements to specific city only; relations between parties arose entirely out of this license; hence, parol evidence rule prevents licensee from establishing asserted contemporaneous oral agreement permitting use in another city. Local Trademarks, Inc. v. Grantham, (DC-Neb), 166 FSupp 494, 117 USPQ 335.

Where defendant fails to comply with the terms of contract of license within the time limit specified, and plaintiff declares the contract terminated, a state court may issue a temporary injunction against defendant, preventing him from acting under the license until the question as to whether the license is terminated is adjudicated. Bobbs-Merrill Co. v. Universal Film Mfg. Co., (Misc), 160 NYS 37.

15. —Construction of license contracts.

Instrument reading "I hereby transfer the copyright in my picture" when read in the light of other circumstances, is construed as an assignment of all rights and not a mere license. American Tobacco Co. v. Werckmeister, 207 US 284, 52 LEd 208, 28 SCR 72, 12 AnnCas 595, aff'g (CCA 2), 146 Fed 375.

A contract granting "the sale and exclusive license and liberty to produce, perform, and represent the said play" does not grant the right to represent the play in moving pictures. Manners v. Morosco, 252 US 317, 64 LEd 590, 40 SCR 335, rev'g (CCA 2), 258 Fed 557, which aff'd 254 Fed 737.

A contract providing that "the party of the first part secures the exclusive dramatic rights including moving picture rights" and "the party of the first part has exclusive leasing of the play" and that the contract will not terminate upon death, but is to be carried out by the heirs, executors, or assigns of the parties, creates an assignment and not a license. Photo Drama Motion Picture Co., Inc. v. Social Uplift Film Corp., (DC-NY), 213 Fed 374. Aff'd 220 Fed 448.

A contract granting the exclusive right to publish plaintiff's book for a period of ten years and providing that the publisher shall advertise the book during such period, and otherwise promote its sale, implies that the publisher shall not publish another book concerning which statements are made which depreciate the value of plaintiff's book. Foster v. Callaghan & Co., (DC-NY), 248 Fed 944.

Licensee's failure to pay royalties stipulated by license for manufacture of records of musical composition makes it liable to triple damages because of incorporation of § 1(e) of this title in license and authorizes licensor to repudiate license. Edward B. Marks Music Corp. v. Foullon, (CA 2), 171 F(2d) 905, 80 USPQ 56, aff'g 79 FSupp 664, 77 USPQ 502.

Where one is licensed to manufacture and sell records, license covers another's share in manufacture and its delivery of finished product to licensee for sale; only liability is that of licensee. Edward B. Marks Music Corp. v. Foullon, (CA 2), 171 F(2d) 905, 80 USPQ 56, aff'g 79 FSupp 664, 77 USPQ 502.

Copyright license clauses are interpreted as seems most reasonable to accomplish purposes and as interpreted by parties. Paine v. Electrical Research Products, Inc., (DC-NY), 27 FSupp 780, 41 USPQ 575.

Employee's services as conductor and musician in connection with motion pictures were rendered without any reservation as to use employer might make of them or as to manner in which completed films might be exploited; employee was in same position as other musicians; as a conductor, he had same rights; having been paid for his services, all rights to product of those services passed to employer; rule applies that, where employee creates something as part of his duties under employer, the thing created is employer's property unless, by appropriate agreement, employee retains some right in it. Zahler v. Columbia Pictures Corp., 180 CalApp(2d series) 582, 4 CalRptr 612, 125 USPQ 462.

16. **—Rights of licensees.**

A licensee may sell unbound copyright book, which any purchaser may bind and sell. Kipling v. G. P. Putnam's Sons, (CCA 2), 120 Fed 631, 65 LRA 873.

A copyright owner in authorizing a partnership, of which he is a member, to publish and sell his copyrighted maps does not authorize such partnership or any member of the partnership, other than himself, the right to license others to print such map. Sauer v. Detroit Times Co., (DC-Mich), 247 Fed 687.

Only "proprietor" of a work may copyright it; person to whom right to copyright is assigned is a proprietor; mere licensee cannot copyright a work. Morse v. Fields, (DC-NY), 127 FSupp 63, 104 USPQ 54.

Bare licensee authorized to publish story in magazine has no right to authorize another to publish story in book; that licensee copyrighted magazine gives it no right to authorize publication in book; blanket copyright on issue of periodical does not give any rights to particular article unless such rights had been previously assigned to publisher. Ilyin v. Avon Publications, Inc., (DC-NY), 144 FSupp 368, 110 USPQ 356.

Where license to use copyrighted advertisements is limited to one city, licensee infringes where he publishes advertisements in another city. Local Trademarks, Inc. v. Grantham, (DC-Neb), 166 FSupp 494, 117 USPQ 335.

Plaintiff granted defendant exclusive license to sell plaintiff's copyrighted works of art in specific area which did not include Florida; three days after termination of license, defendant sold one of such works of art in Florida; such sale was an infringement of copyright, making defendant liable for statutory damages; also, defendant is ordered to tender to plaintiff all of plaintiff's copyrighted works of art in defendant's possession; plaintiff shall thereupon refund to defendant the cost of such works. Creative Arts, Inc. v. Abady & Sultan, Inc., (DC-Fla), — FSupp —, 134 USPQ 388.

A person licensed to use an uncopyrighted manuscript of a play for a specific purpose cannot assign the right to copyright such work to a publisher. Koppel v. Downing, 11 AppDC 93.

A contract licensing a newspaper publishing company to print certain copyrighted articles is assignable when there is no express provision to the contrary, and rights under such a contract will devolve upon anyone purchasing the assets of such company from a receiver. Meyer v. Washington Times Co., 64 AppDC 218, 76 F(2d) 988.

17. Motion-picture, television, and radio rights.

Where a license to exhibit an uncopyrighted motion-picture film had been sold in England prior to copyright of the film in the United States, the rights under such license could not be repudiated, nor the assignees thereof treated as infringers. Universal Film Mfg. Co. v. Copperman, (CCA 2), 218 Fed 577, aff'g 212 Fed 301.

A contract granting the "exclusive right of producing such dramatic version on the stage" and limiting such right to a production in a certain manner, and only in cities of a certain size, does not give such licensee the motion-picture rights. Harper Bros. v. Klaw, (DC-NY), 232 Fed 609.

Where the motion-picture rights remain in the grantee, under a contract made while the motion-picture industry was in its infancy, granting a licensee the right to produce the drama on the stage, such grantee cannot use such picture rights to the detriment of any rights of the licensees. Harper Bros. v. Klaw, (DC-NY), 232 Fed 609.

A contract made after motion pictures have become common and granting "the sole and exclusive right to dramatize the said book for presentation on the stage," does not grant the motion-picture rights. Klein v. Beach, (CCA 2), 239 Fed 108, aff'g 232 Fed 240.

When a contract through which defendant acquired motion-picture rights contained the provision that no alterations, eliminations, or additions could be made without approval of the author, such author could enjoin the production of the motion picture when there is a substantial deviation from the locus of the play or the sequence of development of the plot. Manners v. Famous Players-Lasky Corp., (DC-NY), 262 Fed 811.

Owners of copyright on a book or play own the right to represent on a screen photographs telling the copyrighted story, and when the right to represent it on a screen is assigned, the assignee has all lawful rights in regard to such production. National Picture Theatres, Inc. v. Foundation Film Corp., (CCA 2), 266 Fed 208.

In a contract granting plaintiff a license to produce exclusively a copyrighted play upon the living stage, expressly reserving motion-picture rights to the owners of the copyright, the law does not imply a negative covenant that copyright owners cannot grant the right to produce talking motion pictures which may come in competition with a plaintiff's stage productions. Macloon v. Vitagraph, Inc., (CCA 2), 30 F(2d) 634.

In copyright contract "complete and entire motion picture rights" includes right to production of dialogue. Murphy v. Warner Bros. Pictures, Inc., (CCA 9), 112 F(2d) 746, 46 USPQ 2.

Plaintiff produced an opera, which was copyrighted, and renewed as result of original contract with author of play and author of novel, and thereafter granted defendant the limited right to use certain selections from opera in production of movie based on assignment of rights of author who renewed copyright on novel, and on assignment of rights by playright, who did not renew his copyright, plaintiff had exclusive rights to movie based solely on opera less limited rights previously granted defendant to use certain selections, and defendant had right to produce movie based on novel and play plus limited rights to use certain operatic selections. G. Ricordi & Co. v. Paramount Pictures, Inc., (CA 2), 189 F(2d) 469, 89 USPQ 289, 89 USPQ 564, mod'g 92 FSupp 537, 86 USPQ 452.

Motion-picture producer prepared contract whereby author assigned to it motion-picture, radio, and television rights in copyrighted story; since use of characters and character names are nowhere specifically mentioned in contract, while other items, including the title, are specifically mentioned as being granted, contract is construed as not granting exclusive right to use characters and their names. Warner Bros. Pictures, Inc. v. Columbia Broadcasting System, Inc., (CA 9), 216 F(2d) 945, 104 USPQ 103, mod'g 102 FSupp 141, 92 USPQ 54.

Author of play assigned original copyright and right to renewal to plaintiff which subsequently conveyed motion-picture rights to third party; shortly before expiration of original copyright, author, his wife, and son conveyed motion-picture rights under original and renewal to same third party; by assignment from author, plaintiff has total rights pertaining to play, third party took nothing by latter conveyance, and plaintiff was not injured thereby; therefore, plaintiff, under original assignment, was not entitled to sum received by defendant for conveyance of motion-picture rights. Selwyn & Co., Inc. v. Veiller, (DC-NY), 43 FSupp 491, 52 USPQ 630.

Where owner of quarter of motion-picture rights of play has made motion picture, thus destroying value of use of such rights by owner of another quarter, latter is entitled to accounting of profits resulting from use of rights; if accounting were sought from infringer, complaint would be bad if plaintiff did not expressly negative possibility that one of plaintiff's cotenants may have licensed defendant, and, if license had been granted, no accounting would lie because one cotenant may grant full license of whole play, although licensor must account to cotenant for consideration received. Crosney v. Edward Small Productions, Inc., (DC-NY), 52 FSupp 559, 59 USPQ 193.

In action by owner of quarter of motion-picture rights of play to obtain accounting from another quarter owner of profits from making motion picture, copyright proprietors, who assigned half of motion-picture rights to predecessor of both plaintiff and defendant, need not be made parties since complaint does not present question whether action by proprietors has defeated claim for relief and plaintiff claims no more rights than those assigned to predecessor. Crosney v. Edward Small Productions, Inc., (DC-NY), 52 FSupp 559, 59 USPQ 193.

Grant in 1901 to plaintiff by author and dramatist of exclusive right to make libretto for an opera of dramatic version of author's novel gave plaintiff right to create entirely new work in form of opera; neither author nor dramatist nor their successors may by means of motion pictures dramatize opera. G. Ricordi & Co. v. Paramount Pictures, Inc., (DC-NY), 92 FSupp 537, 86 USPQ 452. Mf'd 189 F(2d) 469, 89 USPQ 289.

Assignment of motion-picture, radio, and television rights in copyrighted book does not convey author's common-law rights to use characters of book in subsequent books, where assignment does not mention such rights, but does expressly grant author's common-law right to use book's title. Warner Bros. Pictures, Inc. v. Columbia Broadcasting System, Inc., (DC-Cal), 102 FSupp 141, 92 USPQ 54.

Plaintiffs' consent to use, in defendants' radio show, of copyrighted material from plaintiffs' motion picture does not impart consent to defendants' subsequent use of such material in television show. Loew's Inc. v. Columbia Broadcasting System, Inc., (DC-Cal), 131 FSupp 165, 105 USPQ 302. Aff'd 239 F(2d) 532, 112 USPQ 11. Aff'd 356 US 43, 2 LEd(2d) 583, 116 USPQ 479.

Owner of French motion picture partially based on novel, under which author had granted license expiring in 1945, sold to producer right to remake picture (with exception of material from novel and excepting owner's right to exploit French picture) in English, granted producer option to purchase owner's rights in novel, and agreed to assist producer in obtaining extension of rights in novel; later, third party acquired rights in novel after 1945 and sold same to producer; as between producer and owner, latter is not entitled to exhibit French picture after 1945; producer dealt fairly and honestly with owner and had no obligation under contract to do nothing when third party acquired rights in novel, but was free to secure such rights. Quader-Kino A. G. v. Nebenzal, 35 Cal(2d series) 287, 217 Pac(2d) 650, 85 USPQ 320.

Transferable property right exists in use of title of book for motion pictures and other ends where title has secondary meaning; rights as to use of title need not be supported by copyright; right of protection of title having secondary meaning is not dependent upon copyright. Johnston v. Twentieth Century-Fox Film

Corp., 82 CalApp(2d series) 796, 187 Pac(2d) 474, 76 USPQ 131, aff'g 69 USPQ 209.

Plaintiff granted to defendant exclusive right to make, sell, exploit, lease, license, rent, and exhibit positive prints made from negatives, "nontheatrical only," owned by plaintiff; defendant has no television rights and cannot sell or lease such rights; television is in theatrical field. Weiss v. Hollywood Film Enterprises, Inc., (CalSupCt), 81 USPQ 570.

A licensee who has received from an author the right of dramatic reproduction is liable to author, if, without authority, he grants rights to produce play in motion picture. Underhill v. Schenck, 238 NY 7, 143 NE 733, 33 ALR 303.

A contract which sells and assigns the "exclusive right to produce said play" in the United States and Canada, and which was entered into before motion pictures became known, will prevent the grantor from producing the play in motion pictures. Frohman v. Fitch, 164 AppDiv 231, 149 NYS 633.

A contract granting an exclusive license for a term of 24 years "to play, perform, and produce or cause to be played, performed and produced, said play or drama," carries with it the right of production of moving pictures. Lipzin v. Gordin, (Misc), 166 NYS 792.

Less evidence to prove a licensor's title to a drama is required where the licensee of the motion-picture rights to the drama has acted under his license. Hart v. Fox, (Misc), 166 NYS 793.

A contract granting the right "to translate and adapt into the English language and to perform or cause to be performed in such language" a copyrighted drama does not confer the motion-picture rights. Underhill v. Schenck, 114 Misc 520, 187 NYS 589.

Grant of "stage rights" to play is license to present play on stage with living actors; grant of "motion picture rights" is license to use material in production and exhibition of photoplay; each grant involves only right to use and exploit literary work of another; right is separate and distinct from right of ownership in work itself. McClintic v. Sheldon, 182 Misc 32, 43 NYS(2d) 695, 59 USPQ 41.

18. Musical compositions.

License to use musical composition in manufacture of sound records does not include right to inclose words on printed slips in boxes containing such records. Standard Music Roll Co. v. F. A. Mills, Inc., (CCA 3), 241 Fed 360, aff'g 223 Fed 849.

Where a publishing company copyrighted a song under a royalty agreement with the composer and later with the author's consent copyrighted an orchestral arrangement of the song; then, to settle a dispute concerning the song, transferred the copyright of the song to the author, such transfer did not affect the rights of the publishers to the copyright of the orchestral score. Edmonds v. Stern, (CCA 2), 248 Fed 897.

The giving of professional copies of a copyrighted musical composition does not constitute a license to publicly perform such composition. Harms v. Cohen, (DC-Pa), 279 Fed 276.

License released licensee from consequence of any infringement in composing "arrangement" of musical composition and consented to its future use in manufacturing records; when licensor excepted from licensee's rights any "use" without its consent of song in "medley," only reasonable implication was that other "arrangements" did not need its consent, for a medley is an "arrangement"; negotiations between parties support same conclusion. Edward B. Marks Music Corp. v. Foullon, (CA 2), 171 F(2d) 905, 80 USPQ 56, aff'g 79 FSupp 664, 77 USPQ 502.

License to perform renditions of "separate musical compositions" permits rendition in a medley of songs from specific composition. April Productions, Inc. v. Strand Enterprises, Inc., (CA 2), 221 F(2d) 292, 105 USPQ 83.

License to perform nondramatic renditions of musical compositions excludes therefrom "oratorios, choral, operatic or dramatico-musical works (including plays with music, reviews and ballets) in their entirety"; this is clear indication of intent that permission to play and sing all the songs included in some work of another character does not give right to perform the over-all work; same conclusion is reached from exclusion of "songs or other excerpts from operas or musical plays accompanied either by words, pantomime, dance, or visual representation of the work from which the music is taken"; provision that "fragments of instrumental selections from such works may be instrumentally rendered without words, dialogue, costume accompanying dramatic action or scenic accessory, and unaccompanied by any stage action or visual representation of the work of which such music forms a part" prohibits addition to instrumental rendition of instrumental selections of any words and dialogue; license is construed to permit rendition of noninstrumental compositions with "words, dialogue, costume accompanying dramatic action or scenic accessory" without such rendition getting into dramatic class; thus, songs may be sung in intermission between acts of nonrelated dramatic performance. April Productions, Inc. v. Strand Enterprises, Inc., (CA 2), 221 F(2d) 292, 105 USPQ 83.

Defendant employed composer to record composer's new arrangement of musical composition owned by third party; later, composer assigned new arrangement to plaintiff, who copyrighted it; prior to such copyrighting, defendant had sold 4,000 records; composer of new arrangement was vested with right to grant valid licenses; this was vested property right which he could assign; plaintiff's application for copyright did not do away with rights which defendant had acquired before that time. Biltmore Music Corp. v. Kittinger, (CA 9), 238 F(2d) 373, 111 USPQ 228.

Where composer objected to unauthorized use of his song in connection with radio program and applied for copyright in 1930, such facts show that composer did not completely assign the song to a third party by allowing him to include such song in a song book which had been published in 1921. Egner v. E. C. Schirmer Music Co., (DC-Mass), 48 FSupp 187, 56 USPQ 214. Aff'd 139 F(2d) 398, 60 USPQ 74.

(1463)

Nonexclusive license to defendant to use some of music of plaintiff's opera in moving picture does not preclude plaintiff from granting to another the right to make motion picture of opera. G. Ricordi & Co. v. Paramount Pictures, Inc., (DC-NY), 92 FSupp 537, 86 USPQ 452. Mf'd 189 F(2d) 469, 89 USPQ 289.

Composer licensed another to record song; license was silent as to licensee's right to assign license; it was unassignable without express provision to that effect since down payment paid composer was nominal, with composer to be paid percentage of sales, and since license involved relationship of personal credit and confidence; therefore, acts of licensee's assignee, who made and sold recordings without copyright notice, cannot be charged to composer. Mills Music, Inc. v. Cromwell Music, Inc., (DC-NY), 126 FSupp 54, 103 USPQ 84.

Officers of association, who were authorized to negotiate with composers for permission to publish their songs in compilation, had authority to carry out any proper condition, even if only implied, that composer's rights to be protected; their later assignment of song to composer, who had permitted use of his song without charge, was within scope of their authority; it was fair thing to do; it deprived no member of association of anything to which it was rightfully entitled. Mills Music, Inc. v. Cromwell Music, Inc., (DC-NY), 126 FSupp 54, 103 USPQ 84.

Composer's authorization that recording be made of his song is broad enough to include license to distribute records. Royal v. Radio Corp. of America, (DC-NY), 107 USPQ 173.

Action by music publisher owning copyrights against American Society of Composers, Authors, and Publishers seeking declaratory judgment of rights in musical compositions after 1950 under contract with composers before assignment to publisher is dismissed on motion for lack of justiciable controversy although complaint alleges that American Society of Composers, Authors, and Publishers claims right beyond 1950. Denton & Haskins Corp. v. Taylor, (Misc), 42 NYS(2d) 18, 58 USPQ 95.

Constitution of membership corporation of music composers and publishers provides that members shall, as condition of becoming such, assign performing rights to corporation; formal assignment is prerequisite to corporation's acquisition of rights in members' compositions and where member never gave assignment, but refused to give one when belatedly requested to do so, corporation never acquired any rights in member's compositions. Kubik v. American Composers Alliance, Inc., (Misc), 54 NYS(2d) 764, 65 USPQ 62.

Five-year assignments of public performing rights by publisher to the American Society of Composers, Authors, and Publishers were modus operandi for effectuating basic purpose of parties as the American Society of Composers, Authors, and Publishers members; it is breach of contract and trust for publisher to attempt to cut off rights of other members of the American Society of Composers, Authors, and Publishers by licensing the society's competitor without their consent and without paying them part of consideration from competitor. The

American Society of Composers, Authors, and Publishers remains beneficial owner of public performance rights with sole right to grant licenses as to songs composed by composer members. Broadcast Music, Inc. v. Taylor, (Misc), 55 NYS(2d) 94, 65 USPQ 503.

19. Restrictive conditions — Antitrust Law violations.

Although the object of the copyright law is to secure a monopoly, contracts made by the owners of copyrights whereby, in order to maintain the price of the books, through publishers and booksellers associations, any dealer who sells his books below the prescribed price is blacklisted and prevented from buying more books, may be in violation of the Anti-Trust Laws [15 § 1 et seq.]. Straus v. American Publishers Assn., 231 US 222, 58 LEd 192, 34 SCR 84, AnnCas 1915A, 369, rev'g 199 NY 548, 93 NE 1133.

When a copyrighted book is sold without an agreement concerning such sale, a notice in the book that "no dealer is licensed to sell it at a less price" than that stated, reserves no right to the seller and does not constitute the buyer a licensee. Bobbs-Merrill Co. v. Straus, (CC-NY), 139 Fed 155. Aff'd 147 Fed 15, 15 LRA(NS) 766, which was aff'd 210 US 339, 52 LEd 1086, 28 SCR 722.

Restrictions not to resell, rent, or export attached to sale of an uncopyrighted motion-picture film were invalid. Universal Film Mfg. Co. v. Copperman, (CCA 2), 218 Fed 577, aff'g 212 Fed 301.

It is not unlawful for copyright owners merely to pool their compositions for one royalty for them as pooled and no valid exercise of police power can limit it; so long as combination is not to unlawfully fix prices there is no offense in mere pooling. Buck v. Gibbs, (DC-Fla), 34 FSupp 510, 46 USPQ 455. Mf'd 313 US 387, 85 LEd 1416, 61 SCR 962, 49 USPQ 468.

Combination of members of the American Society of Composers, Authors, and Publishers in transferring to the American Society of Composers, Authors, and Publishers all their nondramatic performing rights in their copyrighted musical works is combination in restraint of interstate commerce prohibited by Antitrust Laws [15 § 1 et seq.], especially since the American Society of Composers, Authors, and Publishers has power to fix prices. Alden-Rochelle, Inc. v. American Soc. Composers, Authors & Publishers, (DC-NY), 80 FSupp 888, 78 USPQ 197.

Any limitation or conditions which parties insert are binding and may be enforced except where they are contrary to public policy or in violation of law; thus, it is proper for license to fix release date of moving picture upon basis of time of closing of stage play. Inge v. Twentieth Century-Fox Film Corp., (DC-NY), 143 FSupp 294, 111 USPQ 153.

Irrespective of amount of trade or commerce, contracts providing for sharing of revenues from licensing of musical performance rights constitute unlawful restraint of trade under § 1 of Sherman Antitrust Act [15 § 1]. Affiliated

Music Enterprises, Inc. v. Sesac, Inc., (DC-NY), 160 FSupp 865, 117 USPQ 263.

Blanket licensing of performance rights in copyrighted music is similar to illegal block booking condemned in United States v. Paramount, 334 US 131, 77 USPQ 243; while defendant does not refuse to issue per piece license, it gives user, who must choose blanket license as lesser of two evils, no genuine economical choice between two types of licenses; advantages derived from collective licenses and practical difficulties attendant on individual licenses do not absolve collective licenses from Antitrust Acts [15 § 1 et seq.]. Affiliated Music Enterprises, Inc. v. Sesac, Inc., (DC-NY), 160 FSupp 865, 117 USPQ 263.

Copyright pooling agreements are per se violations of Antitrust Acts [15 § 1 et seq.]. Affiliated Music Enterprises, Inc. v. Sesac, Inc., (DC-NY), 160 FSupp 865, 117 USPQ 263.

Although defendant's contracts with publishers, whereby it obtains exclusive performance rights in copyrighted music, violate Antitrust Acts [15 § 1 et seq.], plaintiff does not show injury entitling it to treble damages since plaintiff is not a publisher but a rival which seeks to have publishers enter into contracts with it rather than with defendant. Affiliated Music Enterprises, Inc. v. Sesac, Inc., (DC-NY), 160 FSupp 865, 117 USPQ 263.

A contract, granting a license to print a copyrighted prayer book and containing the provisions that such books shall not be sold below a specified price, is not an agreement in violation of the Antitrust Laws [15 § 1 et seq.]. Murphy v. Christian Press Assn. Pub. Co., 38 AppDiv 426, 56 NYS 597.

The owner of a copyrighted article, when he has manufactured and sold same, cannot impose restrictions on his vendee as to future sales of the article. Coca-Cola Co. v. State, (TexCivApp), 225 SW 791.

The owner of a copyright may impose upon his assignee such restrictions as he may see proper, including the price and the territory within which the article may be sold. Coca-Cola Co. v. State, (TexCivApp), 225 SW 791.

20. Royalties.

Agreement to pay royalties, including advance of $200, is adequate consideration for copyright assignment. Edward B. Marks Music Corp. v. Charles K. Harris Music Publishing Co., Inc., (CA 2), 255 F(2d) 518, 117 USPQ 308.

One who acquires a copyright from a trustee in bankruptcy who has notice of an agreement for the payment of royalty to the author is required to fulfill the agreement of the bankrupt concerning the payment of royalty. Cohan v. Richmond, (DC-NY), 19 FSupp 771, 35 USPQ 80.

In action on contract licensing the recordation and reproduction of musical compositions, it was decided that each time defendant exported and used in a foreign country the recordations of compositions on which plaintiffs principals held domestic or Canadian copyrights, and which were in the public domain, defendant became obligated to pay the stipulated compensation for such use as was made

of the compositions. Paine v. Electrical Research Products, Inc., (DC-NY), 27 FSupp 780, 41 USPQ 575.

Plaintiff's failure to pay royalties on folios is not breach of contract to pay royalties on each printed copy of song sold since in music publishing industry "printed copy" applies to sheet music only and does not include copy in folio. Von Tilzer v. Jerry Vogel Music Co., Inc., (DC-NY), 53 FSupp 191, 59 USPQ 292. Aff'd 158 F(2d) 516, 71 USPQ 285.

If licensee fails to pay royalties, licensor, copyright owner, may terminate license and sue former licensee as infringer for publication of copyrighted work after cancellation of license. King v. Edward B. Marks Music Corp., (DC-NY), 56 FSupp 446, 62 USPQ 249.

Under a contract granting defendant the right to produce a play in motion pictures with a provision that a sum of money equal to twenty per cent of the gross sales derived by defendant should be paid to plaintiff, defendant is bound only to pay twenty per cent of the money received by him and not to pay the percentage upon moneys received by the exhibitor. Arden v. Lubin, 173 AppDiv 782, 160 NYS 109.

Where a person by contract agrees to pay a royalty for each week a musical sketch is produced, he is not obligated to pay any royalties when he does not produce the sketch. Kennedy v. Rolfe, 174 AppDiv 10, 160 NYS 93.

Where plaintiff licenses defendant to produce a play for a period of three years, and such contract provides for the payment of a percentage of profits to plaintiff at end of each season and that plaintiff is not responsible for losses, defendant cannot, where there was a loss the first season and a profit the second, deduct such losses from plaintiff's percentage of the second season's profits. West End Theatre Syndicate, Ltd. v. Shubert, 180 AppDiv 310, 167 NYS 250.

Where two persons collaborate in writing a play upon an agreement that each should have an interest therein, and one person completes the play after the death of the other, such person completing the play cannot receive royalties from the licensing of the play to the exclusion of the deceased person's administrator. Ongley v. Marcin, 214 AppDiv 455, 212 NYS 690.

Where plaintiff assigns all his right, title, and interest to the right of copyright of a song, the contract assigning such right providing for certain payment of royalties to plaintiff, a suit for an accounting in equity cannot be had when such royalties are not paid, since the relationship existing between plaintiff and assignee is that of debtor and creditor. Ehrlich v. Jack Mills, Inc., 215 AppDiv 116, 213 NYS 395. Aff'd 248 NY 598, 162 NE 539.

A person, granted a license to perform musical compositions, upon payment of a specified amount each month, must pay such amount whether or not such performances were for profit. Maxwell v. Faust Co., Inc., 90 Misc 702, 154 NYS 224.

Royalties must be recovered by an action at law, and not by way of an accounting. Danks v. Gordon, 119 Misc 571, 197 NYS 648.

A contract licensing defendant to make motion-picture plays of certain plays owned by plaintiff, for a period of eight years, may be rescinded by the plaintiff after six months when royalties required by the contract are no longer paid, and there is a likelihood that the default will continue. De Mille Co. v. Casey, 121 Misc 78, 201 NYS 20.

One who undertakes to work property, such as copyright on royalty arrangement, is obligated to work it in good faith and for benefit of recipient of royalties, as well as for own avail; if he fails so to do, and thereby destroys essential object of royalty contract, rescission may be decreed. Broadcast Music, Inc. v. Taylor, (Misc), 55 NYS(2d) 94, 65 USPQ 503.

29. Executed in foreign country—Acknowledgment and certificate.—Every assignment of copyright executed in a foreign country shall be acknowledged by the assignor before a consular officer or secretary of legation of the United States authorized by law to administer oaths or perform notarial acts. The certificate of such acknowledgment under the hand and official seal of such consular officer or secretary of legation shall be prima facie evidence of the execution of the instrument. (July 30, 1947, c. 391, § 1, 61 Stat. 660.)

NOTES TO DECISIONS

Assignment of copyright executed in Germany was not acknowledged before consular officer and signed only in firm name and not also in name of officer of corporation; possible failure to observe all formalities of signing or acknowledging is at most only matter of form going to proof of due execution which may be supplied, as here, by affidavits in evidence; whatever lack of signatures there may be according to German law the assignment satisfies our requirements. Houghton Mifflin Co. v. Stackpole Sons, Inc., (CCA 2), 104 F(2d) 306, 42 USPQ 96, rev'g 41 USPQ 404.

Author made verbal assignment in Trinidad in 1943 to plaintiff who obtained Trinidad copyright which conferred on plaintiff status of copyright owner and was adequate to support his June, 1945, copyright registration in United States, although author did not assign in writing until April, 1945, and even though applicable English statute requires written assignment; written assignment is deemed to have been established as of 1943, since author stated that to be his purpose and both parties acted in accordance with that understanding. Khan v. Leo Feist, Inc., (DC-NY), 70 FSupp 450, 73 USPQ 104. Aff'd 165 F(2d) 188, 76 USPQ 27.

30. Record.—Every assignment of copyright shall be recorded in the copyright office within three calendar months after its execution in the United States or within six calendar months after its

execution without the limits of the United States, in default of which it shall be void as against any subsequent purchaser or mortgagee for a valuable consideration, without notice, whose assignment has been duly recorded. (July 30, 1947, c. 391, § 1, 61 Stat. 660.)

NOTES TO DECISIONS

Where a formal transfer of a copyright is recorded in compliance with the copyright law, such record operates as notice. Little v. Hall, 59 US(18 How) 165, 15 LEd 328.

Since enactment of 1870 Copyright Act, assignments of copyrights must be recorded in office of register of copyrights. Fred Fisher Music Co., Inc. v. M. Witmark & Sons, 318 US 643, 87 LEd 1055, 63 SCR 773, 57 USPQ 50, aff'g (CCA 2), 125 F(2d) 949, 52 USPQ 385, which aff'd 38 FSupp 72, 49 USPQ 171.

Assignments which are not recorded are valid as between the parties and as to others not claiming under the assignors. Webb v. Powers, (CC-Mass), FedCas 17,323, 2 Woodb&M 497.

Title is recorded when received by Librarian of Congress, rather than when it is actually written in the record book. Edward Thompson Co. v. American Law Book Co., (CC-NY), 119 Fed 217.

The copyright of a book, a drama based on the book, and the motion picture showing the story of the book may be separately assigned, but must be recorded to be valid as against a subsequent purchaser of such copyrights. Photo-Drama Motion Picture Co., Inc. v. Social Uplift Film Corp., (CCA 2), 220 Fed 448, aff'g 213 Fed 374.

Unrecorded assignment of dramatic rights to a play was void as against later assignment recorded by assignee of motion-picture rights without actual notice of prior assignment. Photo-Drama Motion Picture Co., Inc. v. Social Uplift Film Corp., (CCA 2), 220 Fed 448, aff'g 213 Fed 374.

This section protects subsequent purchasers or mortgagees for value and is akin in principle to the filing or recording acts, which relate to bills of sale or chattel mortgages. New Fiction Pub. Co. v. Star Co., (DC-NY), 220 Fed 994.

Assignment not recorded is void as against subsequent purchasers or mortgagees without notice. Brady v. Reliance Motion Picture Corp., (DC-NY), 232 Fed 259.

Failure to record trust agreement is no defense to infringer who had actual knowledge of such agreement. Brady v. Reliance Motion Picture Corp., (DC-NY), 232 Fed 259.

Purchaser of exclusive stage rights for copyrighted play was not entitled to injunction against subsequent bona fide purchaser on theory of negative covenant, his contract not having been recorded in the copyright office. Macloon v. Vitagraph, Inc., (CCA 2), 30 F(2d) 634.

Assignment of expectancy (renewal right) is as recordable as any other assignment. Rossiter v. Vogel, (CCA 2), 134 F(2d) 908, 57 USPQ 161, rev'g 46 FSupp 749, 54 USPQ 229.

It is no defense to infringement suit that assignment of copyright to plaintiff was not filed within three months of its execution since this section does not invalidate assignee's title as against infringers. Machaty v. Astra Pictures, Inc., (CA 2), 197 F(2d) 138, 93 USPQ 51, aff'g 89 USPQ 539.

Although promise to pay future royalties, coupled with notice of prior claim before payment, might deprive subsequent purchaser of status of bona fide purchaser, doctrine has no application to prior purchaser. Edward B. Marks Music Corp. v. Charles K. Harris Music Publishing Co., Inc., (CA 2), 255 F(2d) 518, 117 USPQ 308.

Failure to record one assignment in chain of title has no bearing as between parties to infringement suit. Deward & Rich, Inc. v. Bristol Savings & Loan Corp., (DC-Va), 34 FSupp 345, 47 USPQ 128. Aff'd 120 F(2d) 537, 50 USPQ 1.

Though 1911 assignment, in consideration of promise to pay one cent for every printed copy sold, was not recorded until 1938, it is good as against 1938 assignment because 1938 assignee paid nothing for assignment and is not purchaser for valuable consideration and without notice, mere promise to pay consideration not constituting valuable consideration within recording act. Von Tilzer v. Jerry Vogel Music Co., Inc., (DC-NY), 53 FSupp 191, 59 USPQ 292. Aff'd 158 F(2d) 516, 71 USPQ 285.

While assignee of expectancy of renewal of copyright may, under this section, record assignment, recordation is not essential to his title although, if made within prescribed period after its execution, it will protect recording assignee against subsequent assignee. Rose v. Bourne, Inc., (DC-NY), 176 FSupp 605, 123 USPQ 29. Aff'd 279 F(2d) 79, 125 USPQ 509.

Although assignee of expectancy of renewal of copyright can, under this section, record assignment in copyright office, recordation does not create a legal ownership that did not exist already; if made within prescribed period, it simply serves to protect recording assignee against bona fide purchaser. Tobias v. Joy Music, Inc., (DC-NY), — FSupp —, 133 USPQ 181.

31. Certificate of record.—The Register of Copyrights shall, upon payment of the prescribed fee, record such assignment, and shall return it to the sender with a certificate of record attached under seal of the copyright office, and upon the payment of the fee prescribed by this title he shall furnish to any person requesting the same a certified copy thereof under the said seal. (July 30, 1947, c. 391, § 1, 61 Stat. 660.)

32. Use of name of assignee in notice.—When an assignment of the copyright in a specified book or other work has been recorded the assignee may substitute his name for that of the assignor in the statutory notice of copyright prescribed by this title. (July 30, 1947, c. 391, § 1, 61 Stat. 660.)

NOTES TO DECISIONS

Substitution of assignee's name in notice of copyright prior to recordation of assignment results in abandonment of copyright and dedication of work to public; Congressional policy is that notice of copyright shall contain, as proprietor, name of holder of record. Group Publishers, Inc. v. Winchell, (DC-NY), 86 FSupp 573, 83 USPQ 461.

This section permits substitution of name of assignee as proprietor in copyright notice only if assignment has been recorded. Hirshon v. United Artists Corp., 100 AppDC 217, 243 F(2d) 640, 113 USPQ 110.

CHAPTER 2.—INFRINGEMENT PROCEEDINGS

Section
101. Infringement.
102, 103. [Repealed.]
104. Willful infringement for profit.
105. Fraudulent notice of copyright, or removal or alteration of notice.
106. Importation of article bearing false notice or piratical copies of copyrighted work.
107. Importation, during existence of copyright, of piratical copies, or of copies not produced in accordance with section 16 of this title.
108. Forfeiture and destruction of articles prohibited importation.
109. Importation of prohibited articles—Regulations—Proof of deposit of copies by complainants.
110, 111. [Repealed.]
112. Injunctions—Service and enforcement.
113. Transmission of certified copies of papers for enforcement of injunction by other court.
114. Review of orders, judgments, or decrees.
115. Limitations.
116. Costs—Attorney's fees.

AMENDMENT NOTES

Act Oct. 31, 1951, c. 655, § 17a, 65 Stat. 717, amended the analysis of this chapter by striking out the following items:

"102. Jurisdiction of courts in enforcing remedies.

"103. Joinder of proceedings for different remedies.

"110. Jurisdiction of actions under laws.

"111. District in which actions may be brought."

Act Sept. 7, 1957, P. L. 85-313, § 3, 71 Stat. 633, amended this chapter analysis by striking out "115. Limitation of criminal proceedings" and inserting "115. Limitations."

Section 101. Infringement. — If any person shall infringe the copyright in any work protected under the copyright laws of the United States such person shall be liable:

(a) **Injunction.**—To an injunction restraining such infringement;

(b) **Damages and profits—Amount—Other remedies.**—To pay to the copyright proprietor such damages as the copyright proprietor may have suffered due to the infringement, as well as all the profits which the infringer shall have made from such infringement, and in proving profits the plaintiff shall be required to prove sales only, and the defendant shall be required to prove every element of cost which he claims, or in lieu of actual damages and profits, such damages as to the court shall appear to be just, and in assessing such damages the court may, in its discretion, allow the amounts as hereinafter stated, but in case of a newspaper reproduction of a copyrighted photograph, such damages shall not exceed the sum of $200 nor be less than the sum of $50, and in the case of the infringement of an undramatized or nondramatic work by means of motion pictures, where the infringer shall show that he was not aware that he was infringing, and that such infringement could not have been reasonably foreseen, such damages shall not exceed the sum of $100; and in the case of an infringement of a copyrighted dramatic or dramatico-musical work by a maker of motion pictures and his agencies for distribution thereof to exhibitors, where such infringer shows that he was not aware that he was infringing a copyrighted work, and that such infringements could not reasonably have been foreseen, the entire sum of such damages recoverable by the copyright proprietor from such infringing maker and his agencies for the distribution to exhibitors of such infringing motion picture shall not exceed the sum of $5,000 nor be less than $250, and such damages shall in no other case exceed the sum of $5,000 nor be less than the sum of $250, and shall not be regarded as a penalty. But the foregoing exceptions shall not deprive the copyright proprietor of any other remedy given him under this law, nor shall the limitation as to the amount of recovery apply to infringements occurring after the actual notice to a defendant, either by service of process in a suit or other written notice served upon him.

First. In the case of a painting, statue, or sculpture, $10 for every infringing copy made or sold by or found in the possession of the infringer or his agents or employees;

Second. In the case of any work enumerated in section 5 of this title, except a painting, statue, or sculpture, $1 for every infringing copy made or sold by or found in the possession of the infringer or his agents or employees;

Third. In the case of a lecture, sermon, or address, $50 for every infringing delivery;

Fourth. In the case of a dramatic or dramatico-musical or a choral or orchestral composition, $100 for the first and $50 for every subsequent infringing performance; in the case of other musical compositions $10 for every infringing performance;

(c) **Impounding during action.** — To deliver up on oath, to be impounded during the pendency of the action, upon such terms and conditions as the court may prescribe, all articles alleged to infringe a copyright;

(d) **Destruction of infringing copies and plates.**—To deliver up on oath for destruction all the infringing copies or devices, as well as all plates, molds, matrices, or other means for making such infringing copies as the court may order.

(e) **Royalties for use of mechanical reproduction of musical works.**—Whenever the owner of a musical copyright has used or permitted the use of the copyrighted work upon the parts of musical instruments serving to reproduce mechanically the musical work, then in case of infringement of such copyright by the unauthorized manufacture, use, or sale of interchangeable parts, such as disks, rolls, bands, or cylinders for use in mechanical music-producing machines adapted to reproduce the copyrighted music, no criminal action shall be brought, but in a civil action an injunction may be granted upon such terms as the court may impose, and the plaintiff shall be entitled to recover in lieu of profits and damages a royalty as provided in section 1, subsection (e), of this title: Provided also, That whenever any person, in the absence of a license agreement, intends to use a copyrighted musical composition upon the parts of instruments serving to reproduce mechanically the musical work, relying upon the compulsory license provision of this title, he shall serve notice of such intention, by registered mail, upon the copyright proprietor at his last address disclosed by the records of the copyright office, sending to the copyright office a duplicate of such notice; and in case of his failure so to do the court may, in its discretion, in addition to sums hereinabove mentioned, award the complainant a further sum, not to exceed three times the amount provided by section 1, subsection (e), of this title, by way of damages, and not as a penalty, and also a temporary injunction until the full award is paid.

(f) [Repealed.] (July 30, 1947, c. 391, § 1, 61 Stat. 661; June 25, 1948, c. 646, § 39, 62 Stat. 992.)

Amendment note.—Act June 25, 1948, cited to text, repealed subsec. (f) which provided "(f) Rules of Procedure.—Rules and regulations for practice and procedure under this section shall be prescribed by the Supreme Court of the United States." Similar provisions are contained in § 2072 of Title 28.

NOTES TO DECISIONS
ANALYSIS

1. In general.

Rights of owner of a copyright depend upon statute in force at time of the infringement of the copyright. Davis v. Bowes, (DC-NY), 209 Fed 53. Aff'd 219 Fed 178.

To constitute an invasion of copyright, it is not necessary that whole of a work be copied or even a large portion of it in form or substance, but it is sufficient to constitute infringement if so much is taken that value of original is sensibly diminished, or labors of original author are substantially, to an injurious extent, appropriated by another; test of infringement is whether work is recognizable by ordinary observance as having been taken from copyrighted source; slight differences and variations will not serve as a defense. Bradbury v. Columbia Broadcasting System, Inc., (CA 9), 287 F(2d) 478, 128 USPQ 376, mod'g 174 FSupp 733, 123 USPQ 10.

Since neither copyrighting nor infringement took place in period of 1897 to 1909, 1897 Copyright Act is inapplicable as to copyright issued in 1896 and renewed in 1923; 1909 Copyright Act provides measure of damage for infringement thereafter. Jerome v. Twentieth Century-Fox Film Corp., (DC-NY), 58 FSupp 13, 63 USPQ 206.

Graphic plagiarism is committed when copyist preserves structural and material characteristics of original, notwithstanding deliberate and systematic variation of each subordinate detail. Peter Pan Fabrics, Inc. v. Acadia Co., Inc., (DC-NY), 173 FSupp 292, 121 USPQ 81. Aff'd 274 F(2d) 487, 124 USPQ 154.

Nonprofit private club is liable as copyright infringer since its performance of copyrighted music on premises where drinks were sold was publicly for profit inasmuch as club was open to general public so long as such casual patrons met club's standards for appearance and behavior; performance of copyrighted material in connection with selling of drinks is performance for profit; fact that club on occasion exercised right to exclude members of general public does not mean that performance was private. Lerner v. Club Wander In, Inc., (DC-Mass), 174 FSupp 731, 122 USPQ 595.

Appropriation of idea, once expressed, is not copyright infringement and there is no infringement in development of general idea appropriated from another work if two works bear no resemblance to each other. Barton Candy Corp. v. Tell Chocolate Novelties Corp., (DC-NY), 178 FSupp 577, 123 USPQ 425.

Where dissection, rather than observation, is required to discern any resemblance, there has been no copying. Barton Candy Corp. v. Tell Chocolate Novelties Corp., (DC-NY), 178 FSupp 577, 123 USPQ 425.

This section gives court broad discretion as to remedy for copyright infringement; in exercising discretion, court considers fact that infringement was willful and fact that plaintiff suffered no immediate financial loss as a result thereof; court points out that integrity of copyright laws must be protected; defendants were on notice, which they ignored, that unauthorized use of any portions of illustrations in plaintiff's catalog would subject them to prosecution; defendants are held liable to (1) injunction restraining infringement, (2) deliver up for destruction all infringing catalogs together with all plates, molds, matrices, or other means for making infringing catalogs, and (3) pay to plaintiff, as damages, one dollar for each catalog distributed. Amplex Manufacturing Co. v. A. B. C. Plastic Fabricators, Inc., (DC-Pa), 184 FSupp 285, 125 USPQ 648.

Intent to infringe copyright is not essential to render infringer liable for infringement but innocent intention may have a bearing on question of fair use. Wihtol v. Crow, (DC-Iowa), — FSupp —, 132 USPQ 392.

Fact that defendant's dahlia is causing plaintiff to lose customers and sales is not determinative of whether defendant's dahlia infringes plaintiff's copyrighted artificial dahlia; any competitive product will normally have some effect on sales of others, but copyright on a reproduction of a natural object does not foreclose others from copying that natural object also. Prestige Floral, Societe Anonyme v. Zunino-Altman, Inc., (DC-NY), 203 FSupp 649, 133 USPQ 75. Aff'd 133 USPQ 58.

Right to prevent copying, publication, or use of unpublished musical composition without consent of owner or author is recognized by common law and has not been restricted by statute. McCarter v. Barton Music Corp., — Misc(2d series) —, — NYS(2d) —, 115 USPQ 299.

2. Common source—Fair use.

There may be publication of infringing articles although the defendant issued such articles only to his own pupils, and to them only upon the agreement that they should be returned to him within a limited time. Macmillan Co. v. King, (DC-Mass), 223 Fed 862.

"Fair use" means that others may copy the theme or ideas of a work, but not its expression. Sheldon v. Metro-Goldwyn Pictures Corp., (CCA 2), 81 F(2d) 49, 28 USPQ 330, rev'g 7 FSupp 837.

One work does not violate copyright in another simply because of similarity resulting from fact that both deal with same subject or have same common source. Dorsey v. Old Surety Life Ins. Co., (CCA 10), 98 F(2d) 872, 39 USPQ 92, 119 ALR 1250, aff'g 34 USPQ 226.

Question is not whether defendant could have obtained same information by going to same source as did plaintiff, but whether she did go to same sources and do her own independent research. Toksvig v. Bruce Pub. Co., (CA 7), 181 F(2d) 664, 85 USPQ 339.

Doctrine of fair use does not apply to copying substance of copyrighted dramatic work and presenting it, with few variations, as burlesque. Benny v. Loew's Inc., (CA 9), 239 F(2d) 532, 112 USPQ 11, aff'g 131 FSupp 165, 105 USPQ 302. Aff'd 356 US 43, 2 LEd(2d) 583, 78 SCR 667, 116 USPQ 479.

Question of fair use, which is question of fact, usually arises in connection with scientific or other works dealing with common subject matter; thus, writings dealing with same historical event are expected to have similarity of treatment. Eisenschiml v. Fawcett Publications, Inc., (CA 7), 246 F(2d) 598, 114 USPQ 199.

Some tests to be applied on question of fair use are: (1) extent and relative value of extracts, (2) purpose and whether quoted portions might be used as substitute for original work, (3) effect on distribution and objects of original work. Broadway Music Corp. v. F-R Pub. Corp., (DC-NY), 31 FSupp 817, 45 USPQ 309.

"Fair use" may be made of copyrighted article, and what is fair use depends on circumstances of each particular case. Karill v. Curtis Pub. Co., (DC-Wis), 39 FSupp 836, 51 USPQ 50.

There may be three-dimensional infringement of copyrighted picture or perhaps of literary composition, but use of knowledge derived from written exposition of idea of purely utilitarian character is not infringement. Clair v. Philadelphia Storage Battery Co., (DC-Pa), 43 FSupp 286, 52 USPQ 176.

It is not necessary to exactly duplicate another's literary work to be liable for plagiarism, it being sufficient if unfair use is made by lifting substantial portion of it, but even exact counterpart does not constitute plagiarism if it was arrived at independently and without resort to other's work, or even if some changes in defendant's story were suggested by plaintiff's work. O'Rourke v. RKO Radio Pictures, Inc., (DC-Mass), 44 FSupp 480, 53 USPQ 95.

Similarity of background does not give rise to infringement; piracy is not shown by resemblances expected of authors writing of common topic. Christie v. Harris, (DC-NY), 47 FSupp 39, 54 USPQ 360. Aff'd 154 F(2d) 827, 69 USPQ 198.

Similarities and incidental details necessary to environment or setting of action are not material of which copyrightable originality consists. Cain v. Universal Pictures Co., Inc., (DC-Cal), 47 FSupp 1013, 56 USPQ 8.

Doctrine of fair use arises from essential nature of copyright; all persons may make fair use of copyrighted work; occasionally, courts refer to right to use noncopyrightable material in copyrighted work as "fair use"; in this meaning, question is only conventional one of whether material was copyrightable; primarily, however, fair use relates to extent to which copyrightable material may be used without express license; in field of science and fine arts, broad scope is given to fair use; criticism is important and proper exercise of fair use; as one draws away from fields of science or fine arts, and enters fields where business competition exists, scope of fair use is narrowed but still exists; purpose for which use is made is of major importance, in consideration with other factors, in arriving at sound determination of extent of fair use; broader scope is permitted the doctrine where field of learning is concerned and a much narrower scope where taking is solely for commercial gain. Loew's Inc. v. Columbia Broadcasting System, Inc., (DC-Cal), 131 FSupp 165, 105 USPQ 302. Aff'd 239 F(2d) 532, 112 USPQ 11, which was aff'd 356 US 43, 2 LEd(2d) 583, 78 SCR 667, 116 USPQ 479.

In historical burlesque, part of content is used to conjure up general image of original; such limited taking is permitted under doctrine of fair use; doctrine permits burlesque to go somewhat farther so long as taking is not substantial; burlesque is not per se a defense. Columbia Pictures Corp. v. National Broadcasting Co., Inc., (DC-Cal), 137 FSupp 348, 107 USPQ 344.

Similarities of incidents alone are not infringement, especially when both works are based on common sources and concern events in life of historic figure. Subsequent authors, publishers, and general public may use copyrighted work in reasonable manner without consent of copyright owner on theory that such use is "fair use" of copyrighted material. Greenbie v. Noble, (DC-NY), 151 FSupp 45, 113 USPQ 115.

Test as to copyright infringement is not test of mere likeness, but claimed infringement must be a copy, more or less servile, of copyrighted work and not an original treatment of a subject open alike to treatment by copyright holder and others; where principal elements of design of plaintiff's copyrighted work and of defendant's allegedly infringing article are taken, as a common source, from object in public domain, mere resemblance will not justify finding of infringement; publication of identical works cannot be enjoined if defendant's is result of independent research; one work does not violate copyright in another simply because there is similarity between the two, if similarity results from fact that both deal with same subject or have same source; however, availability of common source, is no defense if defendant actually copied plaintiff's work. Alva Studios, Inc. v. Winninger, (DC-NY), 177 FSupp 265, 123 USPQ 487.

There is no infringement of plaintiff's means of expression if similarities result from common subjects and sources within public domain of common knowledge and property. Crume v. Pacific Mutual Life Insurance Co., (DC-Ill), 55 USPQ 267. Aff'd 140 F(2d) 182, 60 USPQ 359.

3. Infringement.

True test of piracy stated, see Daly v. Palmer, (CC-NY), FedCas 3,552, 6 Blatchf 256; Emerson v. Davies, (CC-Mass), FedCas 4,436, 3 Story 768.

An article that is not subject to copyright cannot be made the subject of a suit for infringement. Amberg File & Index Co. v. Shea Smith & Co., (CC-Ill), 78 Fed 479. Aff'd 82 Fed 314.

The test of infringement in cases dealing with incidents and stock characters is whether the association and grouping of the characters and incidents is such as to make a new conception or novel arrangement. Simonton v. Gordon, (DC-NY), 297 Fed 625.

The test of infringement is whether a second work is an original treatment of a subject open to treatment by all, or is but a copy of the first work. Pellegrini v. Allegrini, (DC-Pa), 2 F(2d) 610.

Where obsolete sheet in infringing publication was replaced by another containing infringing matter there was not a new and distinct infringement. Cravens v. Retail Credit Men's Ass'n, (DC-Tenn), 26 F(2d) 833.

Ricordi v. Columbia, 270 F. 822, did not hold that all the first eight steps stated therein must be taken to constitute a defendant a manufacturer of phonograph record; likewise, defendants' reliance on Marks v. Foullon, 77 USPQ 502, as establishing that defendant, who performs only the ninth step, is not a manufacturer, is unfounded since that case was dealing with meaning of "manufacturer" for purposes of statutory royalty imposed upon authorized manufacturers rather than with subsec. (e) of this section; under subsec. (e) of this section, "manufacture" is an act of infringement, which is a tort; all persons concerned with infringement are jointly and severally liable; whether separate act performed by each defendant constitutes "manufacture" under that subsection, the two defendants, acting in concert, manufactured infringing discs inasmuch as one defendant produced master stamper which other defendant used to press infringing records. Reeve Music Co., Inc. v. Crest Records, Inc., (CA 2), 285 F(2d) 546, 128 USPQ 24, mod'g 190 FSupp 272, 128 USPQ 37.

Test of copyright infringement is of necessity vague; that this is true is more a reason why court of appeals cannot say that trial court erred, as a matter of law, finding no infringement. Caddy-Imler Creations, Inc. v. Caddy, (CA 9), 299 F(2d) 79, 132 USPQ 384.

Test of infringement is whether work claimed to infringe is independent production or copy of copyrighted work. Mathews Conveyor Co. v. Palmer Bee Co., (DC-Mich), 41 FSupp 401, 51 USPQ 286. Aff'd 135 F(2d) 73, 57 USPQ 219.

There can be no infringement by appropriating idea, which, once it is expressed, becomes public property; however, copyright protects method of expressing idea. Lewis v. Kroger Co., (DC-WVa), 109 FSupp 484, 95 USPQ 359.

Basic test of plagiarism is whether resemblance between works could be recognized by ordinary observation and not by fine analysis or by argument and dissection by experts. Greenbie v. Noble, (DC-NY), 151 FSupp 45, 113 USPQ 115.

Action for copyright infringement is not action for conversion; infringement and conversion are inconsistent with each other; by conversion, title is taken; by infringement, title remains in original owner but is damaged by infringer. Pickford Corp. v. DeLuxe Laboratories, Inc., (DC-Cal), 169 FSupp 118, 120 USPQ 521.

Complaint does not sufficiently charge threatened infringement of plaintiff's copyright where it merely alleges that defendant has represented and asserted that it has right to use and authorize use of plaintiff's copyrighted song; mere assertion in general terms of claimed right without accompanying act or threatened act to implement asserted right is not sufficient to state charge of threatened copyright infringement; until some action or conduct based upon asserted right is threatened, there is no enforceable claim for relief under Copyright Act [§ 1 et seq. of this title]; in order to sustain claim for threatened infringement, it must appear that one one is about to infringe or take some action prejudicial to rights of copyright owner. Southern Music Publishing Co., Inc. v. C & C Films, Inc., (DC-NY), 171 FSupp 832, 121 USPQ 450.

Although there is no statutory definition of copyright infringement, it may be inferred from provisions of § 1(a) of this title conferring upon copyright proprietor the exclusive right to print, reprint, publish, copy, and vend copyrighted work; grant of these exclusive rights implies prohibition that others shall not exercise them without consent of copyright proprietor; to do so without consent would be infringement. U. S. v. Wells, (DC-Tex), 176 FSupp 630, 123 USPQ 65.

Copyrighted insurance policies are not infringed where there is no similarity in arrangement of words of plaintiff's and defendant's policies and where defendant has not appropriated copyrighted material, either substantially or in exact form. Miner v. Employers Mutual Liability Insurance Co., (DC-DC), 105 USPQ 357. Aff'd 229 F(2d) 35, 108 USPQ 100.

In determining infringement, each case must be determined on own facts. Stanley v. Columbia Broadcasting System, Inc., (Cal(2d series)), 208 Pac(2d) 9, 82 USPQ 123, aff'g (CalApp(2d series)), 192 Pac(2d) 495, 77 USPQ 404. Aff'd 35 Cal(2d series) 653, 221 Pac(2d) 73, 86 USPQ 520.

State court has no jurisdiction if main purpose of action, whatever its form, is to establish a patent or to enjoin its infringement or to recover damages therefor; same rule applies where subject matter of action is protected by copyright; there, too, sole remedy is in federal courts for infringement of owner's rights under copyright. Ideal Toy Corp. v. Newman Premier Corp., 29 Misc(2d series) 192, 217 NYS(2d) 664, 129 USPQ 437.

4. —Copying.

Distinction between a copy of a work and an imitation or resemblance stated, see Emerson v. Davies, (CC-Mass), FedCas 4,436, 3 Story 768.

Without copying there can be no infringement. Mazer v. Stein, 347 US 201, 98 LEd 630, 74 SCR 460, 100 USPQ 325, aff'g (CA 4), 204 F(2d) 472, 97 USPQ 310, which rev'd 111 FSupp 359, 96 USPQ 439; Affiliated Enterprises, Inc. v. Truber, (CCA 1), 86 F(2d) 958, 32 USPQ 94.

To infringe a copyright the defendant must have actually copied or "pirated" the production of the plaintiff, and not merely, while ignorant of it, have made something similar. S. S. White Dental Co. v. Sibley, (CC-Pa), 38 Fed 751.

Copying from infringing works is itself an infringement. Gilmore v. Anderson, (CC-NY), 38 Fed 846.

To arrive independently upon the precise material copyrighted, without copying, does not constitute infringement. Fisher, Inc. v. Dillingham, (DC-NY), 298 Fed 145.

It is an infringement to take substance or idea and produce it through a different medium such as picturing its shape and details in sufficient imitation to make it a true copy of character thought of by owner. King Features Syndicate v. Fleischer, (CCA 2), 299 Fed 533.

If a thing covered by a copyright has become familiar to the mind's eye, and one produces it from memory and writes it down, he copies just the same, and this may be done without conscious plagiarism. Edwards & Deutsch Lithographing Co. v. Boorman, (CCA 7), 15 F(2d) 35.

Substantial similarity due to mere coincidence and not to actual copying was not infringement. Moore v. Ford Motor Co., (DC-NY), 28 F(2d) 529. Aff'd 43 F(2d) 685.

Mere similarity or even identity of two works independently produced does not of itself constitute infringement, there being no actual copying. Harold Lloyd Corp. v. Witwer, (CCA 9), 65 F(2d) 1, rev'g 46 F(2d) 792; Twentieth Century-Fox Film Corp. v. Stonesifer, (CCA 9), 140 F(2d) 579, 60 USPQ 392, aff'g 48 FSupp 196, 56 USPQ 94; Christianson v. West Pub. Co., (DC-Cal), 53 FSupp 454, 60 USPQ 279. Aff'd 149 F(2d) 202, 65 USPQ 263.

Card carrying new and old matter is infringed only by copying new matter. Jackson v. Quickslip Co., Inc., (CCA 2), 110 F(2d) 731, 45 USPQ 6, aff'g 27 FSupp 338, 41 USPQ 464.

Differences between copyrighted work and accused production do not negative infringement, which exists where there is copying of substantial portion of copyrighted work. Wihtol v. Wells, (CA 7), 231 F(2d) 550, 109 USPQ 200.

Even though source of material in plaintiff's copyrighted newsreel film was in public domain, this does not permit defendant to directly copy plaintiff's film; defendant can use copy of original films which were part of public domain, but he cannot copy plaintiff's copy thereof. Axelbank v. Roney, (CA 9), 277 F(2d) 314, 125 USPQ 262.

Infringement exists where an ordinary person, after reading plaintiff's copyrighted works and viewing defendant's teleplay, might well believe that defendant copied plaintiff's works to which he had access; similarities which exist are novel in plaintiff's story; defendant not only copies theme and ideas of plaintiff's works but also their expression. Bradbury v. Columbia Broadcasting System, Inc., (CA 9), 287 F(2d) 478, 128 USPQ 376, mod'g 174 FSupp 733, 123 USPQ 10.

To constitute infringement there must be actual copying; whether willful or unintentional, made possible by defendant's access to plaintiff's copyrighted material. Seltzer v. Sunbrock, (DC-Cal), 22 FSupp 621, 37 USPQ 491.

There can be no copying in absence of access. Arnstein v. Twentieth Century Fox Film Corp., (DC-NY), 52 FSupp 114, 59 USPQ 21.

A copy is that which ordinary observation would cause to be recognized as having been taken from another work or reproduction of another work. Allegrini v. DeAngelis, (DC-Pa), 59 FSupp 248, 64 USPQ 165. Aff'd 149 F(2d) 815, 65 USPQ 589.

Copying must be of the means of expression; if that means be words, there must be copying of words; if means be some other method, copying must conform to some pattern, so that it is clear to ordinary reader that there is a copying. Lewis v. Kroger Co., (DC-WVa), 109 FSupp 484, 95 USPQ 359.

Although there can be no copyright infringement without access and similarity, converse does not follow that, simply because there was access and there are similarities, such are result of copying. Warshawsky v. Carter, (DC-DC), 132 FSupp 758, 107 USPQ 80.

One is not a deliberate pirate where he copies another's work without knowledge that work is claimed to have been copyrighted. Christie v. Raddock, (DC-NY), 169 FSupp 48, 120 USPQ 76.

No action for copyright infringement lies where similarities in advertisements are inherent in product advertised rather than result of outright copying. Remington Research, Inc. v. Modern Aids, Inc., (DC-NY), 170 FSupp 7, 120 USPQ 289.

Infringer of valid copyright copies at his peril; intent to infringe is not essential; infringer's lack of knowledge of copyright is immaterial; thus, he infringes if he copies from copyrighted work that does not bear copyright notice and although he is without knowledge of fact that work had been copyrighted. Peter Pan Fabrics, Inc. v. Acadia Co., Inc., (DC-NY), 173 FSupp 292, 121 USPQ 81. Aff'd 274 F(2d) 487, 124 USPQ 154.

Although accused designs are not Chinese copies of copyrighted designs, they infringe, since cursory comparison reveals such striking and pronounced similarity as to give rise to strong inference of copying; since designs involve commonplace subject matter, a substantial similarity would not necessarily indicate copying, but dissimilarities obviously were result of studied effort to make minor distinctions; this effort is itself evidence of copying; final and overwhelming clue is that, while it is not alleged that copying of color constitutes infringement, use of colors in accused designs is devastating indication that plaintiff's designs were source of defendants'. Scarves by Vera, Inc. v. United Merchants & Manufacturers, Inc., (DC-NY), 173 FSupp 625, 121 USPQ 578.

Plaintiffs must establish that actual copying occurred in order to make out case of copyright infringement; mere coincidental similarity, absent copying, is not enough; since direct proof of copying is virtually impossible of adduce, evidence of copying must necessarily be circumstantial and is ordinarily based on proof of access and similarity; if copying occurred, it does not matter if it was done unconsciously and without intent to appropriate plaintiffs' work; bad faith is not a necessary ingredient of plaintiffs' proof. Whitney v. Ross Jungnickel, Inc., (DC-NY), 179 FSupp 751, 124 USPQ 219.

Copyright protects only the expression of idea and not idea itself; there can be no infringement of copyright without copying; thus, there is no infringement where defendant did not copy plaintiff's copyrighted star, but conceived and developed star independently of plaintiff's work. Elekes v. Bradford Novelty Co., Inc., (DC-Mass), 183 FSupp 730, 125 USPQ 166.

In addition to requiring showing of copying, some cases state that alleged infringer's access to copyrighted article must be proved in order to establish infringement; however, since there can be no copying unless infringer is familiar with copyrighted work, and since there is no infringement if two authors independently create similar works, access is but a means of eliminating coincidence or independent effort as an explanation for likeness between copyrighted and infringing articles. Doran v. Sunset House Distributing Corp., (DC-Cal), 197 FSupp 940, 131 USPQ 94.

To constitute copyright infringement, copying need not be of every detail so long as copy is substantially similar to copyrighted work; a copy, such as will constitute infringement, is that which ordinary observation would cause to be recognized as having been appropriated from or patterned after copyrighted work. Doran v. Sunset House Distributing Corp., (DC-Cal), 197 FSupp 940, 131 USPQ 94.

Infringement does not depend upon intent but upon the fact of copying copyrighted matter. Carter v. Hawaii Transportation Co., (DC-Hawaii), 201 FSupp 301, 133 USPQ 65.

Points of similarity are continuous and striking in booklets; almost every idea and means of expression has been copied in its essence; it is no defense that infringing booklet is more attractive and salable. American Visuals Corp. v. Holland, (CA 2), 110 USPQ 482.

In determining whether similarity is due to copying, common knowledge of average reader, observer, spectator, or listener is standard of

(1473)

judgment which must be used. Stanley v. Columbia Broadcasting System, Inc., (Cal(2d series)), 208 Pac(2d) 9, 82 USPQ 123, aff'g (Cal App(2d series)), 192 Pac(2d) 495, 77 USPQ 404. Aff'd 35 Cal(2d series) 653, 221 Pac(2d) 73, 86 USPQ 520; Heywood v. Jericho Co., 193 Misc 905, 85 NYS(2d) 464, 79 USPQ 450.

Solution of question of whether proof of absence of copying establishes defense is governed by same principle whether action be one for infringement of statutory or common-law copyright; in both types of action, there is no liability where there was no copying. Teich v. General Mills, Inc., 170 CalApp(2d series) 791, 339 Pac (2d) 627, 121 USPQ 639.

As construed in law of plagiarism, copying is not confined to literary repetition, but includes various ways in which the matter in any publication may be adopted, imitated, or transferred, with more or less colorable alterations to disguise the piracy; no matter how different a portion of the work may be from the plagiarized product, it is enough if substantial parts were lifted. Cantor v. Mankiewicz, — Misc(2d series) —, 203 NYS(2d) 626, 125 USPQ 598.

A copy is that which comes so near to the original as to give to every person seeing it the idea created by the original. Carr v. National Capital Press, Inc., 63 AppDC 210, 71 F(2d) 220, 21 USPQ 408.

5. ——Quantity copied.

Though an author's works may not be complete for publication, piracy of material portions thereof constitutes infringement. Bartlette v. Crittenden, (CC-Ohio), FedCas 1,082, 4 McLean 300.

One who avails himself in whole or in part of the materials and labors of another is guilty of infringement. Blunt v. Patten, (CC-NY), FedCas 1,579, 2 Paine 393; Blunt v. Patten, (CC-NY), FedCas 1,580, 2 Paine 397.

Infringement is not predicated upon the quantity of material pirated. Gray v. Russell, (CC-Mass), FedCas 5,728, 1 Story 11.

If so much is taken that the value of the original is diminished, or the labors of the original author are substantially appropriated by another, that is sufficient to constitute an infringement. Lawrence v. Dana, (CC-Mass), FedCas 8,136, 4 Cliff 1; National Institute, Inc. v. Nutt, (DC-Conn), 28 F(2d) 132. Aff'd 31 F(2d) 236.

Although a new work has some similarities and shows evidence of copying small parts of a copyrighted work, it does not amount to an infringement when the work is a dictionary, map, arithmetic, or almanac. Webb v. Powers, (CC-Mass), FedCas 17,323, 2 Woodb&M 497.

The appropriation of material portions of a work constitutes infringement. Reed v. Holliday, (CC-Pa), 19 Fed 325.

The appropriation of but a part of a copyright constitutes an infringement of the whole of the copyright. Brady v. Daly, (CCA 2), 83 Fed 1007, aff'g 69 Fed 285. Aff'd 175 US 148, 44 LEd 109, 20 SCR 62.

Where a print, otherwise uncopyrighted, was copyrighted as part of a newspaper, a suit for infringement for a wrongful publishing of the print must be based upon infringement of the newspaper and not on infringement of the print. Bennett v. Boston Traveler Co., (CCA 1), 101 Fed 445.

Appropriation of alterations and additions original with a translator of a foreign production constitutes an infringement. Stevenson v. Fox, (DC-NY), 226 Fed 990.

Appropriation of a substantial portion of another's copyrighted work constitutes infringement. Meccano, Ltd. v. Wagner, (DC-Ohio), 234 Fed 912. Mf'd 246 Fed 603; Ansehl v. Puritan Pharmaceutical Co., (CCA 8), 61 F(2d) 131, 15 USPQ 38.

A book or play is not infringed, simply because there is found in another later story, some of the same incidents, when those incidents are familiar in life or fiction. Stevenson v. Harris, (DC-NY), 238 Fed 432.

Infringement of a copyright consists in the copying of some substantial and material part thereof, and it is not necessary to compare in detail the copyrighted and infringing articles. Wilson v. Haber Bros., Inc., (CCA 2), 275 Fed 346; Dymow v. Bolton, (CCA 2), 11 F(2d) 690.

To constitute infringement there must be copying of a substantial or material part of a work. Hirsch v. Paramount Pictures, Inc., (DC-Cal), 17 FSupp 816, 32 USPQ 233; De Montijo v. 20th Century Fox Film Corp., (DC-Cal), 40 FSupp 133, 50 USPQ 440; Mathews Conveyor Co. v. Palmer Bee Co., (DC-Mich), 41 FSupp 401, 51 USPQ 286. Aff'd 135 F(2d) 73, 57 USPQ 219; Solomon v. R. K. O. Radio Pictures, Inc., (DC-NY), 44 FSupp 780, 53 USPQ 468; Christianson v. West Pub. Co., (DC-Cal), 53 FSupp 454, 60 USPQ 279. Aff'd 149 F(2d) 202, 65 USPQ 263; Silvers v. Russell, (DC-Cal), 113 FSupp 119, 98 USPQ 376.

After termination of contract for use in advertising by defendant of plaintiff's matrices, defendant infringes by using such matrices in newspaper advertising although advertisements were used without defendant's approval, defendant paying for such advertisements; where only small part of matrix is used, there is no liability. Advertisers Exchange, Inc. v. Bayless Drug Store, Inc., (DC-NJ), 50 FSupp 169, 57 USPQ 273.

Copyright owner is protected against taking of substantial portion of his protectible material. Loew's Inc. v. Columbia Broadcasting System, Inc., (DC-Cal), 131 FSupp 165, 105 USPQ 302. Aff'd 239 F(2d) 532, 112 USPQ 11, which was aff'd 356 US 43, 2 LEd(2d) 583, 78 SCR 667, 116 USPQ 479.

Although what was appropriated for defendants' play was comparatively small part of plaintiff's two volume biography, it formed substantial part of play and most of taking was verbatim; substantial taking is not matter of lines or inches but exists when part taken had merely value and formed greater part of one act of the play. Harris v. Miller, (DC-NY), 50 USPQ 306. Mf'd 50 USPQ 625.

Test of infringement is impression received by average reasonable man upon comparative reading of two works, not by dissection of sentences and incidents. Stanley v. Columbia Broadcasting System, Inc., (Cal(2d series)), 208 Pac(2d) 9, 82 USPQ 123, aff'g (CalApp(2d series)), 192 Pac(2d) 495, 77 USPQ 404. Aff'd 35 Cal(2d series) 653, 221 Pac(2d) 73, 86 USPQ 520.

6. ——Paraphrasing.

Paraphrasing constitutes infringement of a copyright as well as copying of copyrighted matter. Meccano, Ltd. v. Wagner, (DC-Ohio), 234 Fed 912. Mf'd 246 Fed 603; Ansehl v. Puritan Pharmaceutical Co., (CCA 8), 61 F(2d) 131, 15 USPQ 38.

Paraphrasing or copying with evasion is an infringement of copyright holders' rights, even though there may be little or no conceivable identity between the two. Nutt v. National Institute, Inc., (CCA 2), 31 F(2d) 236, aff'g 28 F(2d) 132; Borden v. General Motors Corp., (DC-NY), 28 FSupp 330, 42 USPQ 117.

Infringement exists when study of two writings indicates that one of them is not in fact the creation of the putative author, but instead was copied in substantial part exactly or in transparent rephrasing to produce essentially the story of the other writing. Warner Bros. Pictures, Inc. v. Columbia Broadcasting System, Inc., (CA 9), 216 F(2d) 945, 104 USPQ 103, mod'g 102 FSupp 141, 92 USPQ 54.

Copyright infringement is not confined to literal and exact reproduction; it includes various modes in which work may be adopted, imitated, transferred, or reproduced, with more or less colorable alterations to disguise piracy; paraphrasing is copying and infringement, if carried to sufficient extent. Eisenschiml v. Fawcett Publications, Inc., (CA 7), 246 F(2d) 598, 114 USPQ 199.

7. —Loss of remuneration or market.

Rendering a work less remunerative infringes an author's exclusive right. Estes v. Williams, (CC-NY), 21 Fed 189.

A test of infringement is whether or not the appropriated portions, as used, are likely to injure the sale of the original work. Harper v. Shoppell, (CC-NY), 26 Fed 519; Hill v. Whalen & Martell, Inc., (DC-NY), 220 Fed 359.

Marketability of unlawful reproductions of a copyrighted work has no bearing on the question of infringement. Fishel v. Lueckel, (CC-NY), 53 Fed 499.

Copying or printing copyrighted work is infringement although there is no sale or profits made from sale of copies. Chappell & Co., Inc. v. Costa, (DC-NY), 45 FSupp 554, 53 USPQ 674.

Mere printing or copying of copyrighted work, without proof of sales thereof is infringement. Greenbie v. Noble, (DC-NY), 151 FSupp 45, 113 USPQ 115.

8. —Books and literary works.

Abridgements and compilations as infringements, see Folsom v. Marsh, (CC-Mass), Fed Cas 4,901, 2 Story 100; Gray v. Russell, (CC-Mass), FedCas 5,728, 1 Story 11; Story v. Holcombe, (CC-Ohio), FedCas 13,497, 4 McLean 306.

The copying and publishing of a substantial part of an author's manuscript subjects the appropriator to liability for a fraudulent use of another's property. Bartlett v. Crittenden, (CC-Ohio), FedCas 1,076, 5 McLean 32.

There can be no infringement of an immoral composition which equity will enjoin. Martinetti v. Maguire, (CC-Cal), FedCas 9,173, Deady 216.

A German translation of "Uncle Tom's Cabin" did not infringe the copyright of the American authoress. Stowe v. Thomas, (CC-Pa), FedCas 13,514, 2 WallJr 547.

Floral book was infringed, but only to a slight extent. Webb v. Powers, (CC-Mass), Fed Cas 17,323, 2 Woodb&M 497.

Complainant's exclusive right to put his own book, as his own, upon the market was violated by defendants who represented their book as and for complainant's. Estes v. Williams, (CC-NY), 21 Fed 189.

The mere use of a name as the title of a play presenting none of the scenes, incidents, plot, or dialogue of a copyrighted book of the same name is not an infringement. Harper v. Ranous, (CC-NY), 67 Fed 904.

Physiognomy book was not infringed by a later work of same sort. Simms v. Stanton, (CC-Cal), 75 Fed 6.

Dramatic rights to the story "The Transmogrification of Dan" was infringed by production of the play "The Heir to the Hoorah." Dam v. Kirk La Shelle Co., (CCA 2), 175 Fed 902, 41 LRA(NS) 1002, 20 AnnCas 1173, aff'g 166 Fed 589.

An author in writing a second book does not infringe the copyright of a former book written by him, although the same historical facts are brought out and there is some similarity of expression, provided it is not merely a reproduction of the former book. Kennerley v. Simonds, (DC-NY), 247 Fed 822.

Where several distinct passages from one copyrighted work are unlawfully reproduced in one publication there is only one infringement. Journal of Commerce & Commercial Bulletin v. Boston Transcript Co., (DC-Mass), 292 Fed 311.

Fraudulent use of book with knowledge of restrictions as to use was an infringement. Produce Reporter Co. v. Fruit Produce Rating Agency, (DC-Ill), 1 F(2d) 58.

A play may infringe a book if a substantial number of incidents, scenes, and episodes are in detail, arrangement, and combination, so nearly identical with those in the book as to exclude reasonable possibility of chance coincidence. Simonton v. Gordon, (DC-NY), 12 F(2d) 116.

The author of a later work is not an infringer unless he pirates the previous work. Sheldon v. Metro-Goldwyn Pictures Corp., (CCA 2), 81 F(2d) 49, 28 USPQ 330, rev'g 7 FSupp 837.

Both plaintiff's and defendant's books meet exactly same demand on same market and defendant unquestionably copied to avoid trouble or expense of independent work; this is unfair use. College Entrance Book Co., Inc. v. Amsco Book Co., Inc., (CCA 2), 119 F(2d)

874, 49 USPQ 517, rev'g 33 FSupp 276, 45 USPQ 516.

Reproduction of words of poem in combination with music is not dramatization of poem. Corcoran v. Montgomery Ward & Co., Inc., (CCA 9), 121 F(2d) 572, 50 USPQ 274.

Infringement is shown by picking at random several quotations from plaintiff's book and by comparing them with defendant's analogous quotations. Adventures in Good Eating, Inc. v. Best Places to Eat, Inc., (CCA 7), 131 F(2d) 809, 56 USPQ 242.

Among criteria for ascertaining infringement are whether so much has been taken as would sensibly diminish value of original or whether labors of party entitled to copyright are substantially to injurious extent appropriated by another. Mathews Conveyer Co. v. Palmer-Bee Co., (CCA 6), 135 F(2d) 73, 57 USPQ 219, aff'g 41 FSupp 401, 51 USPQ 286.

Use of plaintiff's publication to verify proper abbreviations and spelling is not unfair. Official Aviation Guide Co., Inc. v. American Aviation Associates, Inc., (CCA 7), 150 F(2d) 173, 65 USPQ 553, mod'g 62 USPQ 178.

In determining whether defendant made substantial copy of plaintiff's copyrighted books, court must keep in mind that copying is not necessarily a literal or exact reproduction. Eisenschiml v. Fawcett Publications, Inc., (CA 7), 246 F(2d) 598, 114 USPQ 199.

Infringement of copyrighted book by another book is to be determined by reading and comparison of the books themselves without fine analysis or argument and dissection of an expert. Wiren v. Shubert Theatre Corp., (DC-NY), 5 FSupp 358. Aff'd 70 F(2d) 1023.

Meaning or interpretation which the author gives to his literary efforts cannot be accepted as the deciding test of infringement. Wiren v. Shubert Theatre Corp., (DC-NY), 5 FSupp 358. Aff'd 70 F(2d) 1023.

A copyright does not cover the title to a story, but a name which has become descriptive, and is closely identified in the public mind with the work of a particular author, may not, during the life of the copyright be used so as to mislead, either in another book or in a motion picture. Patten v. Superior Talking Pictures, Inc., (DC-NY), 8 FSupp 196, 23 USPQ 248.

In order to infringe copyright it is not necessary that whole or even large portion of book shall have been copied. It is sufficient if material and substantial part shall have been copied even though it be but small part of whole. Reproduction need not be literal and exact, and it is piracy if it appears that copyrighted matter is copied although altered or paraphrased. Henry Holt & Co., Inc. v. Liggett & Myers Tobacco Co., (DC-Pa), 23 FSupp 302, 37 USPQ 449.

Where, in advertising pamphlet defendant copied three sentences, although not exactly, from plaintiff's copyrighted book, which constituted only small part of book, and about one-twentieth of pamphlet, this constituted infringement and although defendant acknowledged source, this did not relieve it from lia-

bility. Henry Holt & Co., Inc. v. Liggett & Myers Tobacco Co., (DC-Pa), 23 FSupp 302, 37 USPQ 449.

Where defendant, which contracted for use for specific time of duly-copyrighted book of advertisements bearing notice of copyright, continued to use material beyond contract time, the fact that copyright owner furnished for defendant's convenience mats for printing, which did not contain copyright notice, did not constitute abandonment. Deward & Rich, Inc. v. Bristol Savings & Loan Corp., (DC-WVa), 29 FSupp 777, 44 USPQ 26.

Locale is not subject of copyright protection or of common-law protection as literary property. Schwarz v. Universal Pictures Co., Inc., (DC-Cal), 85 FSupp 270, 83 USPQ 153.

Right of author or his licensee to use characters of copyrighted work does not protect against action for copyright infringement, brought by assignee of copyrighted work, if characters are so employed in subsequent works as to invade copyright monopoly. Warner Bros. Pictures, Inc. v. Columbia Broadcasting System, Inc., (DC-Cal), 102 FSupp 141, 92 USPQ 54. Mf'd 216 F(2d) 945, 104 USPQ 103.

Use of ideas of others in writing stories or in producing motion pictures does not render one liable for infringement; most stories are based upon knowledge of facts about people, places, and things, and knowledge is acquired largely by learning what others have learned. Funkhouser v. Loew's, Inc., (DC-Mo), 108 FSupp 476, 96 USPQ 115. Aff'd 208 F(2d) 185, 99 USPQ 448.

Ordinarily each separate publication constitutes an infringement; however, it is plaintiff's practice to authorize reprint of copyrighted contest advertisement during a particular contest and to charge commissions on basis of sales during contest only, rather than by publication; therefore, one or more publications of defendant's advertisements during same contest constitutes but one infringement. Gordon v. Weir, (DC-Mich), 111 FSupp 117, 97 USPQ 387. Aff'd 216 F(2d) 508, 104 USPQ 40.

There is no plagiarism when it requires dissection rather than observation to discern resemblance between literary works; critical analysis is not the test; test is pragmatic. Bradbury v. Columbia Broadcasting System, Inc., (DC-Cal), 174 FSupp 733, 123 USPQ 10. Mf'd 287 F(2d) 478, 128 USPQ 376.

While police were searching premises of bookbinder for evidence of alleged crime, plaintiff's copyrighted book of poems, which bookbinder had bound, was found; editor accompanying police copied one poem and published it in full in newspaper as part of article describing search and alleged crime; publication of entire poem was neither reasonable quotation or extract from book nor in nature of article by reviewer or commentator. Phillips v. Constitution Publishing Co., (DC-Ga), 72 USPQ 69.

Copyright on short story gives proprietor no protection so far as title of story is concerned. Brondfield v. Paramount Pictures Corp., 200 Misc 883, 107 NYS(2d) 698, 93 USPQ 49.

9.   — —Biographical or historical.

A biography was infringed by popular fiction book. Gilmore v. Anderson, (CC-NY), 38 Fed 846.

A pamphlet, consisting of an official report of the World War by General Pershing, poems, and drawings was not infringed by defendant's pamphlet which contained same report, but different drawings. Eggers v. Sun Sales Corp., (CCA 2), 263 Fed 373.

Autobiography, entitled "Border and the Buffalo" was not infringed by a love story, entitled "The Thundering Herd," the theme of which is set in buffalo hunting. Maddux v. Grey, (DC-Cal), 43 F(2d) 441.

Fact that common fictional matter is only small and early part of life of historical character, and only portion of defendant's biography, may affect amount of recovery, but does not prevent liability for copying from plaintiff's uncopyrighted screen play; same is true as to magazine publisher which reprinted only small portion of defendant's work; particularly in view of importance of love interest to movie trade, copying cannot be considered insignificant. De Acosta v. Brown, (CCA 2), 146 F(2d) 408, 63 USPQ 311, aff'g 50 FSupp 615, 58 USPQ 596.

No one has right of property in historical or biographical event; any one may publish biographies or photographs of public figures or narratives of historical events; no one can have monopoly of idea of publishing history of particular wars or of other events, but one can acquire property right in specific embodiment of idea. Curtis v. Time, Inc., (DC-DC), 147 FSupp 505, 112 USPQ 248. Aff'd 102 AppDC 148, 251 F(2d) 389, 116 USPQ 119.

Author of biographical novel has right to use another's copyrighted biography as a guide where author checks fundamental records himself by going to the sources. Greenbie v. Noble, (DC-NY), 151 FSupp 45, 113 USPQ 115.

When book is designed to convey information, reader may use information, whether correct or incorrect, in his own literary work, provided that his expression and treatment are distinctly his own and not merely the result of copying from book; second author may adopt first author's historical ideas since copyright law only protects author's mode of expression and not his ideas. Greenbie v. Noble, (DC-NY), 151 FSupp 45, 113 USPQ 115.

If historian copyrights history, it would be infringement for another historian to publish a history rewritten from first historian's book without independent research; also city directory, which publishes nothing but facts, cannot be copied without infringing copyright; second historian or directory publisher cannot bodily appropriate predecessor's research. Huie v. National Broadcasting Co., Inc., (DC-NY), 184 FSupp 198, 125 USPQ 226.

Even if biographer uses matter in public domain and matter copyrighted by others without objection by them, defendants may not avoid infringement by means of doctrine of unclean hands since what they took from biography was original with biographer and was not something biographer had taken from some one else. Harris v. Miller, (DC-NY), 50 USPQ 306. Mf'd 50 USPQ 625.

10.   — —Catalogues, directories, and other compilations.

Business information and credit rating book was infringed, but to such a slight extent that equity would refuse any remedy. Dun v. Lumbermen's Credit Assn., 209 US 20, 52 LEd 663, 28 SCR 335, 14 AnnCas 501, aff'g (CCA 7), 144 Fed 83.

Copyrighted directory is not infringed by similar directory which is product of independent work. Mazer v. Stein, 347 US 201, 98 LEd 630, 74 SCR 460, 100 USPQ 325, aff'g (CA 4), 204 F(2d) 472, 97 USPQ 310, which rev'd 111 FSupp 359, 96 USPQ 439; Sampson & Murdock Co. v. Seaver-Radford Co., (CCA 1), 140 Fed 539.

A subsequently compiled shippers' guide book did not infringe a prior compilation based on the same subject matter. Bullinger v. Mackey, (CC-NY), FedCas 2,127, 15 Blatchf 550.

Society directory was infringed by a similar publication which is shown to contain many errors common to the original directory. List Pub. Co. v. Keller, (CC-NY), 30 Fed 772.

Horse racing year book was infringed in part by a publication consisting of a list of trotting and pacing horses and information concerning them. American Trotting Register Ass'n v. Gocher, (CC-Ohio), 70 Fed 237.

Copyright of the "Social Register" was infringed by the "Newport Social Index." Social Register Ass'n v. Murphy, (CC-RI), 128 Fed 116.

Trade-mark directory was infringed by a similar publication containing illustrations obtained from plaintiff's work. Jeweler's Circular Pub. Co. v. Keystone Pub. Co., (CCA 2), 281 Fed 83, 26 ALR 571, aff'g 274 Fed 932.

In the case of a compilation, if it were demonstrated that any portions which A copied were taken by B from prior sources available to both parties, the former would still be an infringer. Fact that such prior sources were shown to exist could have no bearing except on the question whether A copied from these sources rather than from B's code. Hartfield v. Peterson, (CCA 2), 91 F(2d) 998, 34 USPQ 305.

Both plaintiff's and defendants' airline guides key timetables to maps, but keying was common in railway and airline guides before plaintiff, so plaintiff may not monopolize it to exclusion of defendants. Official Aviation Guide Co., Inc. v. American Aviation Associates, Inc., (CCA 7), 150 F(2d) 173, 65 USPQ 553, mod'g 62 USPQ 178.

Comparison of plaintiff's and defendants' airline guides shows that much information is same, but that sequence and arrangement are not identical; they are not similar enough to warrant infringement; resemblance in internal arrangement arises largely from adherence to form sanctioned by custom, usage, and general practice in presenting railway and airline timetables and fare tables. Official Aviation Guide Co., Inc. v. American Aviation Associates, Inc.,

(CCA 7), 150 F(2d) 173, 65 USPQ 553, mod'g 62 USPQ 178.

Where defendants' two catalogues each copied nine items from copyrighted catalogue, there was a total of 18 infringements. Markham v. A. E. Borden Co., Inc., (CA 1), 206 F(2d) 199, 98 USPQ 346, rev'g 108 FSupp 695, 95 USPQ 313.

Doctrine of fair use of copyrighted material appears in cases having to do with compilations, listings, digests, and the like, and is concerned with use made of prior compilations, listings, and digests; some cases held that writer may be guided by earlier copyrighted works, may consult original authorities, and may use those which he considers applicable in support of his own original text, but even in such cases it is generally held that, if he appropriates fruits of another's labors, without alteration and without independent research, he violates rights of copyright owner. Benny v. Loew's Inc., (CA 9), 239 F(2d) 532, 112 USPQ 11, aff'g 131 FSupp 165, 105 USPQ 302. Aff'd 356 US 43, 2 LEd(2d) 583, 78 SCR 667, 116 USPQ 479.

Defendant infringed copyrighted telephone directories published periodically by publishing directories copied from telephone directories. Southern Bell Telephone & Telegraph Co. v. Donnelly, (DC-Fla), 35 FSupp 425, 48 USPQ 11.

Racing charts are infringed by copying symbols, notations, and cryptic expressions therefrom and also by stating same information in equivalent words. Triangle Publications, Inc. v. New England Newspaper Pub. Co., (DC-Mass), 46 FSupp 198, 54 USPQ 171.

Racing charts are not infringed by use solely to find clue as to where and when a horse raced, and then using clue to locate and copy defendants' own material. Triangle Publications, Inc. v. New England Newspaper Pub. Co., (DC-Mass), 46 FSupp 198, 54 USPQ 171.

Copyright covering cover of fashion magazine is infringed by reproduction of cover in catalogue advertising school of fashion modelling. Conde Nast Publications, Inc. v. Vogue School of Fashion Modelling, Inc., (DC-NY), 105 FSupp 325, 94 USPQ 101.

To infringe copyrighted directory, defendants must copy substantial part thereof. R. L. Polk & Co. v. Musser, (DC-Pa), 105 FSupp 351, 92 USPQ 124. Aff'd 196 F(2d) 1020, 93 USPQ 468.

Where plaintiff inserted list of fictitious names for purpose of detecting infringement, inclusion of same by defendant indicates that they were copied from plaintiff's directory; and might lead to inference that other names were copied, but evidence standing alone will not compel finding of infringement, if other evidence negatives inference of substantial copying. R. L. Polk & Co. v. Musser, (DC-Pa), 105 FSupp 351, 92 USPQ 124. Aff'd 196 F(2d) 1020, 93 USPQ 468.

Where copied item appeared in several copyrighted catalogues, court did not consider that catalogue in which it first appeared was one which was copied and that it was the copyright on that catalogue which was infringed; it would be unrealistic to suppose that defendant went through whole series of plaintiff's catalogues to select first appearance of each item as the one to be copied; logical assumption is that defendant turned to current catalogue as its source when it wished to copy plaintiff's material. Harry Alter Co., Inc. v. A. E. Borden Co., Inc., (DC-Mass), 121 FSupp 941, 102 USPQ 2.

Copyrighted catalogue containing photographs of uncopyrighted and unpatented articles is not infringed by catalogue containing photographs of imitative articles. Kashins v. Lightmakers, Inc., (DC-NY), 155 FSupp 202, 115 USPQ 325.

There is no copyright infringement inasmuch as copyright proprietor had republished copyrighted catalogue illustrations in the form of advertising without carrying copyright notice. S. A. Hirsh Mfg. Co. v Childs, (DC-Pa), 113 USPQ 331.

11. ——Educational and technical books.

Where a subsequent author appropriates the essential parts of another's plan, arrangement, examples, and table of an arithmetic book he is guilty of infringement. Emerson v. Davies, (CC-Mass), FedCas 4,436, 3 Story 768.

Copyright of a grammar book was infringed by a subsequent publication of like character. Greene v. Bishop, (CC-Mass), FedCas 5,763, 1 Cliff 186.

Grammar book was infringed by a key manual made to aid in teaching from infringed book. Reed v. Holliday, (CC-Pa), 19 Fed 325.

Copyright of an algebra book was not infringed by a subsequent work of like character compiled from authorities used as a basis for the original book. Colliery Engineer Co. v. Ewald, (CC-NY), 126 Fed 843.

Typewritten or mimeographed "outlines" taken from a copyrighted book and furnished by a teacher to his students constituted "versions" of substantial portions of the book and were an infringement. Macmillan Co. v. King, (DC-Mass), 223 Fed 862.

Drawing and cartoons in a history book were found to infringe those appearing in another book on the same subject, access having been established. Oxford Book Co., Inc. v. College Entrance Book Co., Inc., (CCA 2), 98 F(2d) 688, 39 USPQ 7.

Although both parties went to state university's list of French words as source for their word lists, defendant, who admitted owning copies of plaintiff's copyrighted books at time he arranged his own list, so copied from plaintiff's list as to infringe; infringement was shown by omission by both of same common words from state list, by treatment of same words as nouns or adjectives where they could be properly used as either, by choice, sometimes erroneous, of same articles to prefix same nouns, and by choice of identical translations. College Entrance Book Co., Inc. v. Amsco Book Co., Inc., (CCA 2), 119 F(2d) 874, 49 USPQ 517, rev'g 33 FSupp 276, 45 USPQ 516.

Another can use theme so long as mode of expression is not plagiarized. Where book is not development of theme but abstract discussion in essay form of economic and social problems without plot, dialogue, or characters and could not be dramatized without being rewritten so thoroughly as to make it another book, defendant's motion picture of romantic story did not appropriate material portions of book, no scene or dialogue being plagiarized from book. Becker v. Loew's, Inc., (CCA 7), 133 F(2d) 889, 56 USPQ 455.

Copyright proprietor has neither monopoly of scientific information with which book deals nor monopoly of idea of expounding information in simple language comprehensible by lay readers. Richer v. General Electric Co., (CCA 2), 162 F(2d) 141, 73 USPQ 458, aff'g 68 USPQ 371.

Law permits those working in field of science or art to make use of ideas, opinions, or theories and in certain cases even exact words in copyrighted books in that field, and implies consent of copyright owner to fair use of publication for advancement of science or art, but this does not warrant defendant's use, to advertise its tobacco, of statements from book of plaintiff who is physician. Henry Holt & Co., Inc. v. Liggett & Myers Tobacco Co., (DC-Pa), 23 FSupp 302, 37 USPQ 449.

Although defendant's books contain considerable data as to estate taxes contained in plaintiff's copyrighted books, there is no infringement; comparison of books discloses considerable difference between them; defendant's books were independent conception of its employee without knowledge of data in plaintiff's books; defendant did not copy plaintiff's books but published only that which it believed original with itself. Carpenter v. Peoples-Pittsburgh Trust Co., (DC-Pa), 49 FSupp 597, 57 USPQ 141.

12. ——Form books.

In fields of insurance and commerce, use of specific language in forms and documents may be so essential to accomplish desired result and so integrated with use of legal or commercial conception that proper standard of infringement is one which will protect as far as possible the copyrighted language and yet allow free use of thought beneath language; there is no infringement of copyrighted insurance forms since use of language of forms is only incidental to use of underlying idea. Continental Casualty Co. v. Beardsley, (CA 2), 253 F(2d) 702, 117 USPQ 1, mod'g 151 FSupp 28, 113 USPQ 181.

Copying of form from copyrighted form book and delivery of six copies to persons with whom defendant is dealing is not infringement but fair use; when plaintiff put on general market a book of forms, he implied right to their private use, especially in view of notice on cover. American Institute of Architects v. Fenichel, (DC-NY), 41 FSupp 146, 51 USPQ 29.

Statement in copyrighted tax manual that it is hoped that it will assist counties, cities, and taxing districts, is invitation to use and adoption, and use of forms in book is not unlawful. Aldrich v. Remington Rand, Inc., (DC-Tex), 52 FSupp 732, 59 USPQ 210.

Although copyright protection is afforded author of legal forms as against copying disseminators of this information, right to exact royalties from users of forms generally is denied. Continental Casualty Co. v. Beardsley, (DC-NY), 151 FSupp 28, 113 USPQ 181. Mf'd 253 F(2d) 702, 117 USPQ 1.

13. ——Legal publications.

Copyright upon law reporters was infringed by subsequent legal publications containing materials copied from prior work. Callaghan v. Myers, 128 US 617, 32 LEd 547, 9 SCR 177, mod'g (CC-Ill), 24 Fed 636.

Book of court rules was infringed by a later work which contained a like index and rules. Banks v. McDivitt, (CC-NY), FedCas 961, 13 Blatchf 163.

Notes of a copyrighted law book were infringed by a similar work. Lawrence v. Dana, (CC-Mass), FedCas 8,136, 4 Cliff 1.

Law reporters were infringed by a law digest. West Pub. Co. v. Lawyers' Co-operative Pub. Co., (CCA 2), 79 Fed 756, 35 LRA 400, rev'g 64 Fed 360, 25 LRA 441.

Taking of authorities from an original book and inserting them in a subsequent competing publication was no infringement. Mead v. West Pub. Co., (CC-Minn), 80 Fed 380.

Exclusive rights in a law encyclopedia were not infringed by a later work containing citations copied from original work, but examined for their applicability. Edward Thompson Co. v. American Lawbook Co., (CC-NY), 130 Fed 639. Aff'd 157 Fed 1003.

Cutting or copying citations from digests, where no literary ability is appropriated, does not constitute infringement. West Publishing Co. v. Edward Thompson Co., (CC-NY), 169 Fed 833. Mf'd 176 Fed 833.

Rights in law reporter and digest system were infringed by a legal encyclopedia. West Pub. Co. v. Edward Thompson Co., (CC-NY), 184 Fed 749.

It is not an infringement for an author to use and copy citations of another, providing he examines and verifies the cases before using them. White v. Bender, (CC-NY), 185 Fed 921.

Legal textbooks were infringed in part by a subsequent book pertaining to same subject matter. White v. Bender, (CC-NY), 185 Fed 921.

The appropriation by the publisher of an annotated statute of the work of a competitor in making a page to page search of the reports and selecting and classifying material for annotations constituted an infringement, though with the citations thus obtained he went to the original source and wrote up the material. If defendant in such case had gathered his own material by the same processes employed by the competitor, and had merely checked the accuracy of his work from the competitor's list of cases there would have been no infringement. W. H. Anderson Co. v. Baldwin Law Pub. Co., (CCA 6), 27 F(2d) 82.

There being no competition between a digest and an annotated code the use for the annotated code of a table of affirmances and reversals appearing in the digest did not constitute infringement. W. H. Anderson Co. v. Baldwin Law Pub. Co., (CCA 6), 27 F(2d) 82.

14. — —News articles.

While news as such is not subject to copyright and a mere statement of the news disclosed in a copyrighted article will not constitute an infringement of the copyrighted article, where the literary quality and style, other than the bare recital of facts, is copied, it is an infringement. Chicago Record-Herald Co. v. Tribune Ass'n, (CCA 7), 275 Fed 797.

15. — —Plans, systems, methods, and rules.

Pamphlet consisting of advertisements of merchants and containing an explanation of a redeemable coupon system was not infringed by a similar system explained in a folded paper. Mutual Advertising Co. v. Refo, (CC-SC), 76 Fed 961.

Restatement by defendant, in his own language, of the rules of a game, was not infringement. Whist Club v. Foster, (DC-NY), 42 F(2d) 782.

Sales plan, not new or revolutionary, was not infringed. Moore v. Ford Motor Co., (CCA 2), 43 F(2d) 685, aff'g 28 F(2d) 529.

System of spelling words by less than usual number of letters, known as "Steno-Short-Type System," was not infringed as to its description of the system. Brief English Systems, Inc. v. Owen, (CCA 2), 48 F(2d) 555, 9 USPQ 20.

The mere use without publication of a copyrighted plan for increasing the circulation of newspapers was not infringement. Taylor v. Com. Int. Rev., (CCA 3), 51 F(2d) 915, aff'g 17 BTA 1107.

Fact that directions as to use of stamp plan by one merchant would be similar to those of another merchant would be expected; to express directions and to comment upon plan is right of every concern exploiting plan; however, he must use right in manner to avoid encroaching upon authorship of another who is holding his writings under copyright; if he deliberately copies or by chance gets so close to copyright matter that it is practically the same, he has infringed. Cash Dividend Check Corp. v. Davis, (CA 9), 247 F(2d) 458, 114 USPQ 32.

Newspaper's published solution to bridge problems did not infringe the publication "Rapid Contract Bridge," duly copyrighted. Russell v. Northeastern Pub. Co., (DC-Mass), 7 FSupp 571, 23 USPQ 123.

Applying name "Big Bank Night" to pin ball game is not infringement of copyright on various written materials plaintiff uses in promulgating instructions and promoting plan of bank night prize awards at motion-picture theaters. Affiliated Enterprises, Inc. v. Rock-Ola Mfg. Corp., (DC-Ill), 23 FSupp 3, 38 USPQ 35.

A proposed constitutional amendment, which uses language not for explanatory purposes but solely to effectuate a plan through legislation, does not infringe copyright of pamphlet outlining the system even if language were identical, since the method of expression used in proposed legislation describing system of government is inseparable adjunct of use of the system itself and cannot be protected by copyright any more than can use of the system.

Long v. Jordan, (DC-Cal), 29 FSupp 287, 43 USPQ 176.

Where there does not appear to be any identity of language, phraseology, or literary style, arrangement or form although there may be similarity in plan and purpose of insurance and method of operation advanced to effectuate the plan, there is no infringement of copyright. Long v. Jordan, (DC-Cal), 29 FSupp 287, 43 USPQ 176.

Had defendant made use of plaintiff's color chart with written description and directions for world's fair, plaintiff would be entitled to recover as his disclosure constitutes substantial intellectual property and it is New York law that individual has property right in his original unpublished intellectual productions. Ketcham v. New York World's Fair 1939, Inc., (DC-NY), 34 FSupp 657, 46 USPQ 307. Aff'd 119 F(2d) 422, 49 USPQ 756.

Public cannot use invention described in patent but can use information (including forms) in copyrighted book about any system, art, or manufacture described; such use is consideration public receives for grant of copyright. Aldrich v. Remington Rand, Inc., (DC-Tex), 52 FSupp 732, 59 USPQ 210.

Defendant did not copy plaintiff's copyrighted game; fact that basis for each of defendant's rules may be found in plaintiff's and that two playing boards are similar is not strange since each applied to well-known game played by many for many years on same board and under same rules which were common public knowledge and property prior to copyright. Chamberlin v. Uris Sales Corp., (DC-NY), 56 FSupp 987, 62 USPQ 375. Aff'd 150 F(2d) 512, 65 USPQ 544.

Arrangement of contents in insurance bond, however novel arrangement may be, is not copyrightable, for novelty of arrangement is key concept in plan, and ideas and plans fall outside copyright laws. Surety company's use, in regular course of its business of selling insurance, of information and language contained in copyrighted insurance bond does not make it liable; copyright proprietor is not entitled to copyright protection as against company's infringement, even assuming infringement exists. Continental Casualty Co. v. Beardsley, (DC-NY), 151 FSupp 28, 113 USPQ 181. Mf'd 253 F(2d) 702, 117 USPQ 1.

16. — —Particular acts of infringement.

Dealer's sale of a book at a cut price in disregard of a notice therein that such a sale would be considered an infringement was not infringement. Bobbs-Merrill Co. v. Straus, 210 US 339, 52 LEd 1086, 28 SCR 722, aff'g (CCA 2), 147 Fed 15, 15 LRA(NS) 766, which aff'd 139 Fed 155.

A book dealer may be enjoined from selling copyrighted book, in an action brought by the author, when the author sold only through agents and then only on subscription. Henry Bill Publishing Co. v. Smythe, (CC-Ohio), 27 Fed 914.

Reprint of foreign book, not protectible by copyright, is an infringement of an American author's copyrighted book, forming a part thereof. Black v. Henry G. Allen Co., (CC-NY), 42 Fed 618, 9 LRA 433.

Rebinding of copyrighted book in exact imitation of original set is not an infringement. Doan v. American Book Co., (CCA 7), 105 Fed 772.

An author's copyrights are not infringed by defendants who purchase unbound volumes of his works from his licensed publishers and subsequently bind and sell them. Kipling v. G. P. Putnam's Sons, (CCA 2), 120 Fed 631, 65 LRA 873.

Publication of an index to accompany copyrighted volumes of an author's works, though containing words and phrases found in the text, does not constitute an infringement of copyright. Kipling v. G. P. Putnam's Sons, (CCA 2), 120 Fed 631, 65 LRA 873.

The reprinting in this country of an English edition of a dictionary, when the American edition was properly copyrighted in this country, is an infringement of the American edition. G. & C. Merriam Co. v. United Dictionary Co., (CCA 7), 146 Fed 354, rev'g 140 Fed 768. Aff'd 208 US 260, 52 LEd 478, 28 SCR 290.

The sale of reconstructed secondhand books, copyrighted by plaintiff, as and for the plaintiff's new books would constitute unfair competition, but not an infringement of copyright. Bureau of National Literature v. Sells, (DC-Wash), 211 Fed 379.

Reprinting and replacing missing pages of a copyrighted book is an infringement. Ginn & Co. v. Apollo Pub. Co., (DC-Pa), 215 Fed 772.

Plaintiff published and copyrighted magazine and books largely compiled from magazine; defendant purchased secondhand copies of magazines and broke them down and rearranged and assembled the matter in bound books and sold them; this constituted infringement of copyright. National Geographic Soc. v. Classified Geographic, Inc., (DC-Mass), 27 FSupp 655, 41 USPQ 719.

The right of the owner thereof to restore secondhand book to original condition so far as cover and binding are concerned is established; but this right does not extend to printing or replacing pages lost or mutilated, and the compiling of articles from copyrighted magazine in book or pamphlet form and sale of them infringes copyright. National Geographic Soc. v. Classified Geographic, Inc., (DC-Mass), 27 FSupp 655, 41 USPQ 719.

Defendant does not infringe by binding secondhand copies of plaintiff's copyrighted magazine, together with publications of third parties, within cover copyrighted by defendant and selling same; defendant has not copied, reprinted or rearranged copyrighted material or any of its component parts and has not removed plaintiff's copyright notice. Fawcett Publications, Inc. v. Elliot Pub. Co., Inc., (DC-NY), 46 FSupp 717, 54 USPQ 137.

Plaintiff photographed edition of books of Moses in public domain, made corrections in accents and cantillation marks on negatives, and then printed copyrighted books from printing plates made from negatives; such corrections are subject to copyright; defendant infringes where, instead of making his own corrections in books in public domain (in which case, there would be no infringement), he photographed plaintiff's books and published them as his own work. Shulsinger v. Grossman, (DC-NY), 119 FSupp 691, 101 USPQ 30.

Copyright for engraving can be infringed by reproducing copy of it by photographic process; photograph of copyrighted piece of sculpture infringes; also, there can be infringement by making three dimensional doll of two dimensional copyrighted cartoon; therefore, three dimensional copyrighted plaque is infringed by making sketch thereof. M. J. Golden & Co., Inc. v. Pittsburgh Brewing Co., Inc., (DC-Pa), 137 FSupp 455, 108 USPQ 250.

17. ——Infringement by motion picture.

A contract granting the right to produce a dramatic version of a novel on a stage, or to perform the dramatic version, does not grant the motion-picture right, and a person holding the dramatic right through such a contract would infringe upon the novel if he was to produce a photoplay. Harper Bros. v. Klaw, (DC-NY), 232 Fed 609.

A motion picture does not infringe a novel unless the same emotions are excited in the same sequence and order. Curwood v. Affiliated Distributors, Inc., (DC-NY), 283 Fed 223.

Moving picture "Vendetta" infringed copyrighted book "Mr. Barnes of New York." Stephens v. Howells Sales Co., Inc., (DC-NY), 16 F(2d) 805.

A motion picture featuring a wild horse cannot be said to infringe a novel which features a wild horse unless the public would be deceived so as to believe that the films are a picturization of the novel. Roe-Lawton v. Hal E. Roach Studios, (DC-Cal), 18 F(2d) 126.

There is no infringement of a copyrighted story by a photoplay unless the picturization appears to the ordinary observer as being taken from the story. Harold Lloyd Corp. v. Witwer, (CCA 9), 65 F(2d) 1, rev'g 46 F(2d) 792; Kustoff v. Chaplin, (CCA 9), 120 F(2d) 551, 49 USPQ 580, aff'g 32 FSupp 772, 46 USPQ 17; Cain v. Universal Pictures Co., Inc., (DC-Cal), 47 FSupp 1013, 56 USPQ 8.

Motion picture contains incidents similar to some in copyrighted book which is series of stories, and court must assume copying of parts common to both where case comes up on motion to dismiss, but such assumption would not justify legal conclusion that copyright had been infringed since, judging from cutting continuity alone, language of book is not used and events in book purport to represent real occurrences which aside from expression are not protected by Copyright Act. Collins v. Metro-Goldwyn Pictures Corp., (CCA 2), 106 F(2d) 83, 42 USPQ 553, rev'g 25 FSupp 781, 39 USPQ 520.

There is no infringement where defendant did not use plaintiff's book and comparison of works disproves access or copying, especially since defendant did not adopt identical title until after its story was fully written. Becker v. Loew's, Inc., (CCA 7), 133 F(2d) 889, 56 USPQ 455.

Attempt to show similarities by comparing word or phrase taken from plaintiff's story with word or words appearing in lyrics of defendant's motion picture is not in conformity with approved test of infringement. Funkhouser v. Loew's Inc., (CA 8), 208 F(2d) 185, 99 USPQ 448, aff'g 108 FSupp 476, 96 USPQ 115.

Even if all material for plaintiff's stories had been gathered through his own efforts and no information was obtained from third parties, still plaintiff published his material as facts, and law is clear that this same material could be used by another author if he so substantially changed incidents of story that literally compositions bear no real resemblance to each other. Funkhouser v. Loew's Inc., (CA 8), 208 F(2d) 185, 99 USPQ 448, aff'g 108 FSupp 476, 96 USPQ 115.

Test of infringement of story by motion picture is whether ordinary observation of picture would cause it to be recognized as picturization of story, and not whether by some hypercritical dissection of sentences and incidents seeming similarities are shown to exist. Funkhouser v. Loew's Inc., (CA 8), 208 F(2d) 185, 99 USPQ 448, aff'g 108 FSupp 476, 96 USPQ 115.

Comparison of theme and its development in synopsis of literary composition entitled "Nulias Filias" and motion picture "Across the Pacific" did not show infringement of former by latter. Echevarria v. Warner Bros. Pictures, Inc., (DC-Cal), 12 FSupp 632, 28 USPQ 213.

Where there has been no copying of plaintiff's manuscript, and characters therein are without such distinctive qualities as would be a sine qua non of their copyrightability and incidents in both copyrighted manuscript and alleged infringement are, with one exception, familiar to all readers of type of stories, there is no infringement. Caruthers v. R. K. O. Radio Pictures, Inc., (DC-NY), 20 FSupp 906, 35 USPQ 115, 35 USPQ 542.

There is no infringement of copyrightable subject matter in use of motion picture of automobile salesroom and selling of car in which principles set out in plaintiff's books "How to Win an Argument," "Sales Argument," are used in dialogue. Borden v. General Motors Corp., (DC-NY), 28 FSupp 330, 42 USPQ 117.

In action for infringement of common-law copyright of story, plaintiff must establish that there was a substantial and material part of his story that was so appropriated; theme of plaintiff's story is not found in defendants' play and there is difference in plot, action, and treatment; plaintiff's rights have not been invaded. Lynch v. Warner Bros. Pictures, Inc., (DC-NY), 32 FSupp 575, 45 USPQ 273.

Infringement of book by motion picture consists (1) of copying part of plaintiff's work and its inclusion in scenario for (2) incorporation into picture (3) for exhibition purposes; writer's wrong consists of (1) deliberate copying and delivery to others for (2) inclusion in finished picture and (3) exhibition to public; continuous exhibition of picture being one aim of composition of scenario, writer is chargeable not only with act of composing screen play but is also participant in its incorporation into picture and its subsequent exhibition. Cain v. Universal Pictures Co., Inc., (DC-Cal), 47 FSupp 1013, 56 USPQ 8.

Only permissible test of unconscious and unintentional copying is similarity to ordinary reader of book and observer of motion picture. Cain v. Universal Pictures Co., Inc., (DC-Cal), 47 FSupp 1013, 56 USPQ 8.

When two individuals write concerning same subject matter it is not unnatural to find common features, particularly if purpose and treatment of subject run in same channel; unless it is clearly established that alleged plagiarist had access to story of other, plagiarism cannot be predicated. Tamas v. Twentieth Century-Fox Film Corp., (Misc), 25 NYS(2d) 899, 48 USPQ 573.

18. —Dramatic composition.

A "railroad scene" in an author's composition was infringed by a similar scene in another composition. Daly v. Palmer, (CC-NY), FedCas 3,552, 6 Blatchf 256.

Author of copyrighted dramatic composition is protected against piracy of even a single scene of his work. Daly v. Palmer, (CC-NY), FedCas 3,552, 6 Blatchf 256.

A drama taken from an old play but with changes in the dialogue, characters, scenery, and dramatic situations, and an original title may be copyrighted, and any one else may be restrained from using such title on another drama based on the same play; unless it is clearly established that alleged plagiarist drama based on the same play. Aronson v. Fleckenstein, (CC-Ill), 28 Fed 75.

Railroad scene from the play "Under The Gaslight" was infringed by a scene in defendant's play representing the same material elements. Daly v. Webster, (CCA 2), 56 Fed 483, rev'g 47 Fed 903.

"X-Rays of Society," a combination of acting with dialogue and moving pictures was not infringed. Barnes v. Miner, (CC-NY), 122 Fed 480.

A dramatic composition, copied from a book printed in France containing a copyrighted dramatic composition, is an infringement of the copyrighted drama. Hervieu v. J. S. Ogilvie Pub. Co., (CC-NY), 169 Fed 978.

Where a play based on a copyrighted novel is copyrighted, no one can, so long as the copyright on the play is effective, produce another by copying from such play although the copyright of the novel has expired; but anyone is free to produce another play based on the novel which is no longer protected. Glaser v. St. Elmo Co., Inc., (CC-NY), 175 Fed 276.

To constitute an infringement of the copyright of a "gag" monologue it must be established that such "gags" were original with complainant. Hoffman v. Le Traunik, (DC-NY), 209 Fed 375.

Copyright of the play "Threads of Destiny" was not infringed by the later play "At Bay." Vernon v. Sam S. & Lee Shubert, Inc., (DC-NY), 220 Fed 694.

The play entitled "Etelle" was not infringed by the subsequently composed "After Many Days" embodying the same motif as the prior composition. Bachman v. Belasco, (CCA 2), 224 Fed 817, aff'g 224 Fed 815.

Novelization of a copyrighted play is not an infringement unless it is a copy. Fitch v. Young, (DC-NY), 230 Fed 743. Aff'd 239 Fed 1021.

One play will not infringe another, although the fundamental plot is the same, when the plot had become common property long before either was written. London v. Biograph Co., (CCA 2), 231 Fed 696; Eichel v. Marcin, (DC-NY), 241 Fed 404.

In deciding whether a play has been infringed, it is necessary to determine whether the fundamental theme has been appropriated. Underhill v. Belasco, (DC-NY), 254 Fed 838.

Where dramatic composition uses what is called the "fundamental plot" or "old story," author can devise and use his own way of expressing that plot and will not infringe. Dymow v. Bolton, (CCA 2), 11 F(2d) 690.

Infringement of play may consist of plagiarism of language, incident, or plot. Frankel v. Irwin, (DC-NY), 34 F(2d) 142.

The play entitled "The Cohens and Kellys" did not infringe the play "Abie's Irish Rose," though depicting the same emotions. Nichols v. Universal Pictures Corp., (DC-NY), 34 F(2d) 145, 2 USPQ 139. Aff'd 45 F(2d) 119, 7 USPQ 84.

A play may be pirated without using the dialogue. Sheldon v. Metro-Goldwyn Pictures Corp., (CCA 2), 81 F(2d) 49, 28 USPQ 330, rev'g 7 FSupp 837.

In order to infringe, production on stage must obviously tell same story as copyrighted drama, and if it tells another story or enacts another sequence of events, it is outside protection afforded the registered work. Seltzer v. Sunbrock, (DC-Cal), 22 FSupp 621, 37 USPQ 491.

Claim of plagiarism is quite fantastic since plays differ in plot, in character interest, in background, in general purpose and intent, and in substantially all points of reader or theater interest. Rose v. Connelly, (DC-NY), 38 FSupp 54, 49 USPQ 170, 49 USPQ 497.

Comparison of minute details of plays is frowned upon as a method of proving identity; infringement of work of imagination is determined by result of comparative reading, on imagination of reader, not by dissection of sentences and incidents. Christie v. Harris, (DC-NY), 47 FSupp 39, 54 USPQ 360. Aff'd 154 F(2d) 827, 69 USPQ 198.

Independent reproduction of copyrighted work is not infringement; similarities or identities must do more than engender suspicion of piracy; they must establish piracy with reasonable certainty; defendant's play must be so like plaintiff's that one may reasonably infer that it was copied therefrom. Christie v. Harris, (DC-NY), 47 FSupp 39, 54 USPQ 360. Aff'd 154 F(2d) 827, 69 USPQ 198.

Story does not infringe play since differences outweigh similarities; novel character of story has no counterpart in play; both have detectives but detectives are old dramatic props; no author has monopoly on maids and cooks.

West v. Hatch, (DC-NY), 49 FSupp 307, 57 USPQ 64.

Gross dissimilarities in all other important aspects of plays, particularly in theme, dialogue, setting, and sequence, defeat charge of substantial copying; ordinary reader would find no connection between plays; ordinary observer rule is accepted test. McConnor v. Kaufman, (DC-NY), 49 FSupp 738, 57 USPQ 80. Aff'd 139 F(2d) 116, 60 USPQ 356.

"Tiny Tim," "Florence Nightingale," and "Lord Fauntleroy," when used as rhetorical personifications, though they might predicate access, are not copyrightable, and their adoption in totally different settings falls short of copying. McConnor v. Kaufman, (DC-NY), 49 FSupp 738, 57 USPQ 80. Aff'd 139 F(2d) 116, 60 USPQ 356.

Test of infringement is whether there is such similarity in theme, development of theme, means used, climax of story, and dénouement to carry impression to court, not as judge or as person familiar with literature, but as average person who reads scenario and sees play, that they are same. Schwarz v. Universal Pictures Co., Inc., (DC-Cal), 85 FSupp 270, 83 USPQ 153.

To determine whether there is copying in a play, court places itself in position of ordinary observer and asks whether he would see similarity, not in the idea, but in incidents, sequence of events, development and interplay of characters, and the denouement; law protects not the general pattern, but its expression. Bradbury v. Columbia Broadcasting System, Inc., (DC-Cal), 174 FSupp 733, 123 USPQ 10. Mf'd 287 F(2d) 478, 128 USPQ 376.

Author may not forever prevent actor from earning his living by device of casting him as character in unpublished story. Burtis v. Universal Pictures Co., Inc., 40 Cal(2d series) 823, 256 Pac(2d) 933, 97 USPQ 567.

Ideas, though in copyrighted book or play, may be copied and used, but form, sequence, or manner in which idea is developed, treated, or expressed cannot be appropriated. Stanley v. Columbia Broadcasting System, Inc., (CalApp (2d series)), 192 Pac(2d) 495, 77 USPQ 404. Aff'd (Cal(2d series)), 208 Pac(2d) 9, 82 USPQ 123, which was aff'd 35 Cal(2d series) 653, 221 Pac(2d) 73, 86 USPQ 520.

19. ——Infringement by motion picture.

The "Woodsman," a copyrighted play was infringed by a motion-picture drama having same plot as the play. Stodart v. Mutual Film Corp., (DC-NY), 249 Fed 507. Aff'd 249 Fed 513.

C assisted plaintiff to revise his copyrighted play; thereafter C went to work for defendant and wrote play about same theme; court is bound in common sense to scrutinize C's play closely for evidence of copying; there is no correspondence in plot, characters, or impressions but merely in reform school background and touch of similarity of few incidents and few points of dialogue of trifling importance; C's play is more like original story of another which he bought; there is no infringement. Bein v. Warner Bros. Pictures, Inc., (CCA 2), 105 F(2d) 969, 42 USPQ 395, aff'g 35 USPQ 78.

Where both authors made use of a common fundamental plot, but told their stories differently, copyrighted play "Woman" was not infringed by motion picture "Blonde Venus." Ornstein v. Paramount Productions, Inc., (DC-NY), 9 FSupp 896, 25 USPQ 242.

Plaintiffs gave defendants option to purchase play to be written; in suit for infringement of common-law copyright plaintiffs' contention that they suggested to defendant additional ideas which defendants later used is not proven as description of ideas is too vague and last conversation with defendant was four months before plaintiffs' play was finished so it is probable that play represented full story. Rapp v. Harold Lloyd Corp., (DC-NY), 33 FSupp 47, 45 USPQ 225.

There is no infringement of plaintiff's uncopyrighted play where plots, scenes, and incidents differ substantially and plaintiffs do not claim that dialogue has been copied. Rapp v. Harold Lloyd Corp., (DC-NY), 33 FSupp 47, 45 USPQ 225.

Where it is shown that plaintiffs' scenario was derived from magazine article about motion picture in question, there was no infringement. Sheets v. Twentieth Century Fox Film Corp., (DC-DC), 33 FSupp 389, 46 USPQ 120.

Since theme in public domain is not copyrightable, in infringement suit question is whether expression or treatment of idea in defendant's motion picture, the characters and the dialogue, infringe plaintiff's treatment in his play. Gropper v. Warner Bros. Pictures, Inc., (DC-NY), 38 FSupp 329, 49 USPQ 17. Aff'd 119 F(2d) 839.

Test applied in determining whether motion picture infringes play is net impression picture makes on average person. Solomon v. RKO Radio Pictures, Inc., (DC-NY), 44 FSupp 780, 53 USPQ 468.

Motion picture has advantage over play in ability to present outdoor scenes but that play has been elaborated on with this advantage does not relieve picture from charge of plagiarism if story or theme, central idea or plot, treatment and development are so similar that one, seeing or reading play, and seeing picture, would recognize at once that picture had been taken from play; test is conclusion of ordinary observer; it is not matter of cold analysis but impressions of similarity or actual copying; striking similarities must have been result of copying. Stonesifer v. Twentieth Century-Fox Film Corp., (DC-Cal), 48 FSupp 196, 56 USPQ 94. Aff'd 140 F(2d) 579, 60 USPQ 392.

Infringement is not shown where there is no similarity between plaintiff's copyrighted unpublished play and defendant's motion pictures that would not be result of coincidence; court finds that defendant never had access to play since unpublished copyrights are not open to public, and there is no evidence of any other possibility of access. Brody v. Columbia Pictures Corp., (DC-Mass), 90 FSupp 711, 85 USPQ 158.

Unauthorized public performance of dramatic work by means of moving picture is an infringe-

ment. Inge v. Twentieth Century-Fox Film Corp., (DC-NY), 143 FSupp 294, 111 USPQ 153.

If there was no access to plaintiffs' manuscript by any defendant, they could not have taken any part thereof and could not have infringed plaintiffs' copyright. Shurr v. Warner Bros. Pictures, Inc., (DC-NY), 59 USPQ 49. Aff'd 144 F(2d) 200, 62 USPQ 60.

There is no infringement where details, sequences, and raiment of idea are utterly different; touch of similarity in few incidents and few points of dialogue are unimportant. Shurr v. Warner Bros. Pictures, Inc., (DC-NY), 59 USPQ 49. Aff'd 144 F(2d) 200, 62 USPQ 60.

Infringement of a play by a motion picture is apparent if similar emotions are portrayed by sequence of events presented in like manner, expression, and form. Golding v. R. K. O. Radio Pictures, Inc., (CalApp(2d series)), 193 Pac (2d) 153, 77 USPQ 415. Aff'd (Cal(2d series)), 208 Pac(2d) 1, 82 USPQ 136, which was aff'd 35 Cal(2d series) 690, 221 Pac(2d) 95, 86 USPQ 537.

Test of whether substantial part of play is used in motion picture is whether ordinary person spontaneously detects literary piracy. Golding v. R. K. O. Radio Pictures, Inc., (CalApp (2d series)), 193 Pac(2d) 153, 77 USPQ 415. Aff'd (CalApp(2d series)), 208 Pac(2d) 1, 83 USPQ 136, which was aff'd 35 Cal(2d series) 690, 221 Pac(2d) 95, 86 USPQ 537.

Where a German play is adapted for the American stage by one party and others, and plaintiffs write lyrics and music for the purpose of using it as a musical comedy, but the one adapting the play and the plaintiffs, did not collaborate, a motion picture of the play without the music does not infringe upon plaintiff's rights. Herbert v. Fields, (Misc), 152 NYS 487.

20. ——Infringement of motion picture.

It is an infringement for one without permission of the owner to exhibit or perform a motion-picture photoplay. Tiffany Productions, Inc. v. Dewing, (DC-Md), 50 F(2d) 911, 9 USPQ 545.

Unlicensed exhibition of copyrighted motion picture of dramatic composition is an infringement. Metro-Goldwyn-Mayer Distributing Corp. v. Bijou Theatre Co., (CCA 1), 59 F(2d) 70, 13 USPQ 147, mod'g 50 F(2d) 908, 9 USPQ 538; Metro-Goldwyn-Mayer Distributing Corp. v. Bijou Theatre Co., (DC-Mass), 3 FSupp 66, 17 USPQ 124.

A title of a motion picture which has acquired a distinctive meaning in the motion-picture field as descriptive of film version of a certain copyrighted play produced by the complainant and has not been used before to designate any other full-length motion picture, may not be used by a competitor to deceive the public. Warner Bros. Pictures, Inc. v. Majestic Pictures Corp., (CCA 2), 70 F(2d) 310, 21 USPQ 405.

"Comic accretion," "gags," and "stage business" may be so combined with events as to become subject to copyright protection, but original combination of 57 motion-picture scenes constituting sequence of vital importance to story, containing character, dialogue, and action, cannot be termed mere comedy accretion. Universal Pictures Co., Inc. v. Harold Lloyd Corp., (CCA 9), 162 F(2d) 354, 73 USPQ 317.

Distinctive treatment of plot or theme is copyrightable and sequence of incidents in plot in conjunction with distinctive locale and organized characterizations is protected by copyright law. Universal Pictures Co., Inc. v. Harold Lloyd Corp., (CCA 9), 162 F(2d) 354, 73 USPQ 317.

Motion picture is infringed where defendant deliberately lifted almost bodily 57 consecutive scenes constituting 20 per cent of picture. Universal Pictures Co., Inc. v. Harold Lloyd Corp., (CCA 9), 162 F(2d) 354, 73 USPQ 317.

Motion-picture photoplay is entitled to protection of dramatic copyright although not based upon copyrighted novel, stage drama, or book. Universal Pictures Co., Inc. v. Harold Lloyd Corp., (CCA 9), 162 F(2d) 354, 73 USPQ 317.

Whole motion picture need not be copied to constitute infringement; copying of major sequence is sufficient; slight differences are no defense. Universal Pictures Co., Inc. v. Harold Lloyd Corp., (CCA 9), 162 F(2d) 354, 73 USPQ 317.

Motion-picture producer infringes insofar as it copies details of copyrighted comic strips, but plaintiff must point out which defendant reproduced and must prove that reproduction was sufficiently close in detail. National Comics Publications, Inc. v. Fawcett Publications, Inc., (CA 2), 191 F(2d) 594, 90 USPQ 274, rev'g 93 FSupp 349, 87 USPQ 12.

Plaintiff leased copyrighted motion-picture "shorts" to C which runs theater under same management as defendant; without license from plaintiff, defendant borrowed them from C and exhibited in its theater; this is infringement of copyright. Vitaphone Corp. v. Hutchinson Amusement Co., (DC-Mass), 28 FSupp 526, 42 USPQ 431.

21. ——Radio and television.

Where the labors of an author are substantially and injuriously appropriated by another, an infringement occurs, as where the basic situation of a drama, the development of the idea and the manner of expression are markedly similar in a broadcast over the radio. Marx v. U. S., (CCA 9), 96 F(2d) 204, 37 USPQ 380.

Fact that it has been defendant's custom for many years to present his burlesqued version of various dramatic works is no defense to action for copyright infringement; defendant cannot copy and present another's dramatic work without consent of copyright owner. Presentation of burlesque is not literary or dramatic criticism of dramatic work; it is subject to action for copyright infringement. Benny v. Loew's Inc., (CA 9), 239 F(2d) 532, 112 USPQ 11, aff'g 131 FSupp 165, 105 USPQ 302. Aff'd 356 US 43, 2 LEd(2d) 583, 78 SCR 667, 116 USPQ 479.

Each publication of same copyrighted matter at different times is separate infringement;

all component parts of copyrighted work are protected by copyright and performance of single scene from one act of play with very little dialogue is infringement; each performance or broadcast of different scene of play on different occasions is separate infringement. Select Theatres Corp. v. Ronzoni Macaroni Co., (DC-NY), 59 USPQ 288.

Question of originality of radio program is not one of law to be determined by court, but is one of fact for jury's decision. Stanley v. Columbia Broadcasting System, Inc., (CalApp (2d series)), 192 Pac(2d) 495, 77 USPQ 404. Aff'd (Cal(2d series)), 208 Pac(2d) 9, 82 USPQ 123, which was aff'd 35 Cal(2d series) 653, 221 Pac(2d) 73, 86 USPQ 520.

If format for radio program is original and novel, it may constitute protectible product of the mind. Kovacs v. Mutual Broadcasting System, Inc., 99 CalApp(2d series) 56, 221 Pac(2d) 108, 86 USPQ 547.

Complaint states cause of action where it alleges that plaintiff submitted original radio program to defendant under agreement that defendant would pay reasonable value if defendant used program, and that defendant used program without paying plaintiff. Kurlan v. Columbia Broadcasting System, Inc., (CalApp(2d series)), 233 Pac(2d) 936, 90 USPQ 267.

22. ——Musical compositions.

A new arrangement or adaptation of an original musical composition is an infringement if it incorporates such parts and portions of the original as may interfere with the rights of its composer. Jollie v. Jaques, (CC-NY), FedCas 7,437, 1 Blatchf 618.

Prior to the enactment of copyright act, a pianoforte arrangement could not be infringed by an orchestration based upon it to be used in connection with an opera. Mikado, (CC-NY), 25 Fed 183.

Where the author of a song permits its use in a book of songs, it is reasonable that he intends that the song may be included in future editions of the same book even though some of the songs in the original work were omitted or new songs were added. Gabriel v. McCabe, (CC-Ill), 74 Fed 743.

Mimicry of a song should be done in good faith and not as an attempt to evade owner's copyright. Bloom & Hamlin v. Nixon, (CC-Pa), 125 Fed 977.

Singing chorus of copyrighted song on stage in mimicking song voice and actions of an actress was not an infringement. Bloom & Hamlin v. Nixon, (CC-Pa), 125 Fed 977; Green v. Minzenheimer, (CC-NY), 177 Fed 286.

A musical composition infringes another only when the similarity is substantially a copy, so that to the ear of the average person the two melodies sound to be the same. Hein v. Harris, (CC-NY), 175 Fed 875. Aff'd 183 Fed 107.

An impersonator who sings the whole of a copyrighted song, in mimicking its singer, infringes such copyright. Green v. Luby, (CC-NY), 177 Fed 287.

A brief synopsis of an opera did not infringe the author's copyright. G. Ricordi & Co. v. Mason, (CC-NY), 201 Fed 182.

Plagiarism, but not the independent reproduction of a copyrighted musical work, is infringement. Arnstein v. Edward B. Marks Music Corp., (CCA 2), 82 F(2d) 275, 28 USPQ 426, aff'g 11 FSupp 535, 27 USPQ 127.

Copying chorus only of song is infringement. Johns & Johns Printing Co. v. Paull-Pioneer Music Corp., (CCA 8), 102 F(2d) 282, 41 USPQ 3.

While there are enormous numbers of possible permutations of musical notes, only a few are pleasing, and much fewer suit demands of popular ear; recurrence is not inevitable badge of plagiarism. Darrell v. Joe Morris Music Co., Inc., (CCA 2), 113 F(2d) 80, 46 USPQ 167, aff'g 37 USPQ 446.

It is unlikely that noted Mexican musician in composing Spanish dances had in mind sacred religious music. Arnstein v. Broadcast Music, Inc., (CCA 2), 137 F(2d) 410, 58 USPQ 451, aff'g 46 FSupp 379, 54 USPQ 458.

There is no infringement where similarities between songs cannot be readily detected by lay ear, or by effect of composition as whole, but only by dissection. Arnstein v. Broadcast Music, Inc., (CCA 2), 137 F(2d) 410, 58 USPQ 451, aff'g 46 FSupp 379, 54 USPQ 458.

With relatively few existing musical intervals and vast amount of music in public domain, it is rash to infer that sequence in melody is copied from any particular song containing same sequence. Arnstein v. Broadcast Music, Inc., (CCA 2), 137 F(2d) 410, 58 USPQ 451, aff'g 46 FSupp 379, 54 USPQ 458.

In order to establish infringement of copyrighted musical composition, plaintiff has burden to prove that challenged composition is similar in substantial respects to copyrighted composition, and that similarity is due to copying; substantial similarity which is product of independent work is not actionable as infringement. Schultz v. Holmes, (CA 9), 264 F(2d) 942, 121 USPQ 117.

Operatic tragedy called "U. S. A. with music," was not infringed by musical satire burlesquing politics and called "Of Thee I Sing." Lowenfels v. Nathan, (DC-NY), 2 FSupp 73, 16 USPQ 421.

Common-law copyright of a song was infringed by defendant's song, portions of which were similar to the plaintiff's original composition. Wilkie v. Santly Bros., Inc., (DC-NY), 13 FSupp 136, 28 USPQ 452. Aff'd 91 F(2d) 978, 34 USPQ 269, which was aff'd 94 F(2d) 1023, 37 USPQ 839.

It was not necessary that musicians have music before them to infringe copyrighted compositions. Leo Feist, Inc. v. Demarie, (DC-La), 16 FSupp 827, 32 USPQ 122.

In the case of a musical composition, similarity may arise out of the grouping of the notes, similarity of bars, accent, harmony, or melody. Hirsch v. Paramount Pictures, Inc., (DC-Cal), 17 FSupp 816, 32 USPQ 233; Carew v. R. K. O. Radio Pictures, Inc., (DC-Cal), 43 FSupp 199, 53 USPQ 152.

Suit for infringement of musical copyright turns upon existence of a copyright protecting an original work and the infringement of the right through copying, and ultimately, the determination of these questions turns on the issues of originality, access, and similarity. Hirsch v. Paramount Pictures, Inc., (DC-Cal), 17 FSupp 816, 32 USPQ 233.

Choruses played by orchestra constituted material and substantial portions of copyrighted pieces; this is infringement. Buck v. Crescent Gardens Operating Co., (DC-Mass), 28 FSupp 576, 42 USPQ 435.

Where access is not proven, and experts differ as to similarity, court holds that there is no such similarity as indicates copying. Arnstein v. American Soc. of Composers, Authors & Publishers, (DC-NY), 29 FSupp 388, 42 USPQ 581.

Publication, without music, as part of epitaph of actress of chorus of song, written 24 years before concerning her, is fair use where there was no intent to infringe and defendant's use did not impair value of song or harm plaintiff in its distribution and part published could not be used for song. Broadway Music Corp. v. F-R Pub. Corp., (DC-NY), 31 FSupp 817, 45 USPQ 309.

Magazine article concerning football team made fair use of copyrighted official team song by printing chorus as part of article since authorship of song was attributed to its author where article was not competitive with song and no music was set forth in article, reference to chorus being purely incidental and relatively unimportant to article as a whole. Karill v. Curtis Pub. Co., (DC-Wis), 39 FSupp 836, 51 USPQ 50.

March in two-quarter time which makes lively rhythm is not infringed by composition designed to accompany song. McMahon v. Harms, Inc., (DC-NY), 42 FSupp 779, 52 USPQ 321.

Criterion of similarity of songs is not dissection under microscopic eye of musician but impression song or phrase carries to average ear. Carew v. R. K. O. Radio Pictures, Inc., (DC-Cal), 43 FSupp 199, 53 USPQ 152.

In cases involving musical compositions, plaintiff must prove access and identity; access alone is not important but, if there is identity, access may determine the claim; time element is helpful in determining access. Carew v. R. K. O. Radio Pictures, Inc., (DC-Cal), 43 FSupp 199, 53 USPQ 152.

Similarity in motive alone is not enough and use of two or three notes in reverse order not carrying idea of similarity to ear of court is not enough. Carew v. R. K. O. Radio Pictures, Inc., (DC-Cal), 43 FSupp 199, 53 USPQ 152.

There is no plagiarism where it is obvious that source of lyrics of two songs was an old rhyme or ditty. Newcomb v. Young, (DC-NY), 43 FSupp 744, 52 USPQ 373.

Copying from memory would be infringement. Freudenthal v. Hebrew Pub. Co., (DC-NY), 44 FSupp 754, 53 USPQ 466.

In musical compositions, similarity in accent, harmony, or melody mean resemblance noticeable to average hearer. Cain v. Universal Pictures Co., Inc., (DC-Cal), 47 FSupp 1013, 56 USPQ 8.

To recover for infringement of copyrighted music, plaintiff must prove identity of compositions and access by alleged infringer. Heim v. Universal Pictures Co., Inc., (DC-NY), 51 FSupp 233, 58 USPQ 314. Aff'd 154 F(2d) 480, 68 USPQ 303.

Where two compositions do not sound alike when played as written, melodies, harmonies, accent, and rhythm are different, and one was written as vocal quartet and burlesque on grand opera and other as popular song, one is not a copy of the other. Arnstein v. Twentieth Century Fox Film Corp., (DC-NY), 52 FSupp 114, 59 USPQ 21.

Elements of copyright infringement are (a) authorship of lyric and music of composition, (b) originality, (c) taking of steps required by law as to copyright registration, (d) title of plaintiff, composition's copyright, and right of public performance for profit, and (e) defendant's public performance for profit without license or consent from plaintiff. Remick Music Corp. v. Interstate Hotel Co., (DC-Neb), 58 FSupp 523, 63 USPQ 327. Aff'd 157 F(2d) 744, 71 USPQ 138.

Musical composition is infringed by (1) causing copies of sheet music of infringing composition to be printed and by purporting to license phonograph records and broadcasting of infringing composition, (2) offering to sell and selling copies of sheet music of infringing composition, and (3) making and selling phonograph records of infringing composition. Northern Music Corp. v. King Record Distributing Co., (DC-NY), 105 FSupp 393, 93 USPQ 512.

Piracy of song is committed if that portion which is whole meritorious part of song is incorporated in another song, without any material alteration in sequence of bars. Northern Music Corp. v. King Record Distributing Co., (DC-NY), 105 FSupp 393, 93 USPQ 512.

Since there are only three notes involved in sequences which are common to two songs, it cannot be said that there is sufficiency of musical concept in either to rise to dignity of motif; coincidence of concept could account for sequences; infringement is not found since plaintiff does not prove access. Lampert v. Hollis Music, Inc., (DC-NY), 138 FSupp 505, 109 USPQ 242.

It is infringement to publicly perform for profit, or to authorize public performance for profit, on radio and television of commercial announcements containing music substantially copied from plaintiff's copyrighted musical composition. Robertson v. Batten, Barton, Durstine & Osborn, Inc., (DC-Cal), 146 FSupp 795, 111 USPQ 251.

It is not fair use, but is infringement, to copy four bars from copyrighted musical composition where such four bars are portion of composition upon which popular appeal and commercial success of composition depend. Robertson v. Batten, Barton, Durstine & Osborn, Inc., (DC-Cal), 146 FSupp 795, 111 USPQ 251.

Any performance of copyrighted musical composition at restaurant to which public is admitted, and where food and beverages are sold, is given for purpose of profit and, if unauthorized, is infringement of right granted by subsec. (e) of § 1 of this title. Harms, Inc. v. Sansom House Enterprises, Inc., (DC-Pa), 162 FSupp 129, 117 USPQ 272.

Copyrighted musical composition is infringed by (1) printing, reprinting, publishing, and vending copies of infringing musical composition, (2) licensing public performance for profit of infringing composition on radio, television, and elsewhere, (3) licensing manufacture of phonograph records using infringing composition, and (4) publicly performing infringing composition for profit. Dorchester Music Corp. v. National Broadcasting Co., (DC-Cal), 171 FSupp 580, 120 USPQ 429.

Only two lines are claimed to have been appropriated from plaintiffs' copyrighted lyric, one of which is from source in public domain; however, this does not prevent recovery if lines appropriated constitute important and vital part of two compositions rather than being merely incidental or trivial. Whitney v. Ross Jungnickel, Inc., (DC-NY), 179 FSupp 751, 124 USPQ 219.

Defendant experimented with plaintiffs' copyrighted song (published copies of which were in school library), drawing a new arrangement and testing the same with his school and church choir on one occasion; this was not infringement since defendant's activity remained within the realm of fair use. Wihtol v. Crow, (DC-Iowa), — FSupp —, 132 USPQ 392.

Musical composition is substantially copied, and copyright is infringed, if there is substantial similarity due to sizeable quantity copied or due to quality and value because essential, material, or important part is copied. Navara v. M. Witmark & Sons, 17 Misc(2d series) 174, 185 NYS (2d) 563, 121 USPQ 107.

Where use of eight notes in sequence in chorus of respondent's composition is similar to eight notes contained and used in prior copyrighted works by previous masters, melody of plaintiff's copyrighted musical number is not entirely original and there is no infringement. Darrell v. Joe Morris Music Co., Inc., (DC-NY), 37 USPQ 446. Aff'd 113 F(2d) 80, 46 USPQ 167.

Unpublished copyrighted song is not infringed by defendant's song; although there are slight similarities, there are enough important differences to indicate that there was no copying. Rizzi v. Robbins Music Corp., (DC-NY), 58 USPQ 315.

Problem of similarity between two compositions, whether literary, musical, or dramatic, is question of fact to be determined ultimately by comparison of works upon basis of opinion of average individual possessing practical understanding of subject; same test applies whether plaintiff's work is copyrighted or, as in instant case, is idea for radio program. Stanley v. Columbia Broadcasting System, Inc., (Cal(2d series)), 208 Pac(2d) 9, 82 USPQ 123, aff'g (CalApp(2d series)), 192 Pac(2d) 495, 77 USPQ 404. Aff'd 35 Cal(2d series) 653, 221 Pac(2d) 73, 86 USPQ 520.

Expert testimony as to differences in musical compositions does not bind court, but serves as guide. McCarter v. Barton Music Corp., — Misc(2d series) —, — NYS(2d) —, 115 USPQ 299.

23. ——Mechanical reproduction.

Prior to the enactment of the Copyright Act of 1909, sheet music was not infringed by perforated music rolls, which when operated in connection with a proper mechanism would produce the same musical tones as written on the sheet music. White-Smith Music Publishing Co. v. Apollo Co., 209 US 1, 52 LEd 655, 28 SCR 319, 14 AnnCas 628, aff'g (CCA 2), 147 Fed 226, which aff'd 139 Fed 427; Kennedy v. McTammany, (CC-Mass), 33 Fed 584.

A record produced from one manufactured by the plaintiff, so that it will produce the same song with the same voice as the plaintiff's record, cannot be made the subject of a suit unless the song was copyrighted. Fonotipia, Ltd. v. Bradley, (CC-NY), 171 Fed 951.

Fact that a mechanical music roll can produce the tune alone and not the words does not negative infringement of copyright of both music and lyric. M. Whitmark & Sons v. Calloway, (DC-Tenn), 22 F(2d) 412.

Playing of roll music which had no notice of copyright thereon created liability for infringement. Lutz v. Buck, (CCA 5), 40 F(2d) 501, 5 USPQ 452.

To impose upon sound track of motion-picture film those marks which will reproduce words and music of copyrighted song is to infringe copyright. Foreign & Domestic Music Corp. v. Licht, (CA 2), 196 F(2d) 627, 93 USPQ 272.

Reading of subsec. (e) of this section and subsec. (e) of § 1 of this title leads to conclusion that seller of unauthorized records of copyrighted music, although having no connection with manufacturer, is infringer. Shapiro, Bernstein & Co., Inc. v. Goody, (CA 2), 248 F(2d) 260, 115 USPQ 36, rev'g 139 FSupp 176, 108 USPQ 409.

Unauthorized manufacture of set of records is infringement of each copyright, and unauthorized sale of some or all of that set is separate infringement. Shapiro, Bernstein & Co., Inc. v. Goody, (CA 2), 248 F(2d) 260, 115 USPQ 36, rev'g 139 FSupp 176, 108 USPQ 409.

Defendant's failure to serve notice under subsec. (e) of this section of intent to use mechanical reproduction of plaintiff's musical composition, relying upon compulsory license provisions, does not lose defendant its immunity from suit for infringement for copying before plaintiff filed "notice of use" under subsec. (e); plaintiff is entitled to statutory royalty for each record manufactured after filing of "notice of use"; at its discretion, district court may grant additional award not to exceed three times the royalties found to be due, together with costs and reasonable attorney's fee. Norbay Music, Inc. v. King Records, Inc., (CA 2), 290 F(2d) 617, 129 USPQ 336, rev'g 185 FSupp 253, 126 USPQ 231.

Broadcaster cannot avoid infringement of musical composition by broadcasting it from phonograph record purchased in ordinary channels of trade. Associated Music Publishers, Inc. v. Debs Memorial Radio Fund, Inc., (DC-NY), 46 FSupp 829, 54 USPQ 461. Aff'd 141 F(2d) 852, 61 USPQ 161.

Publication without authorization establishes liability under Copyright Act; claimed filing by defendants of notice to use under subsection (e) of this section, ineffective though it may be because not directed to plaintiff, and proffering of payments establish plaintiff's title to copyrighted song, liability for prior unauthorized use, and indebtedness for license fee, at least to amount proffered. Harms, Inc. v. Tops Music Enterprises, Inc., (DC-Cal), 160 FSupp 77, 117 USPQ 72.

There is infringement where copyrighted musical compositions are played on transcription discs and transmitted by leased telephone wires to customers who purchase such music service, and who amplify music on loudspeakers in their places of business without permission of copyright owners. Harms, Inc. v. Sansom House Enterprises, Inc., (DC-Pa), 162 FSupp 129, 117 USPQ 272.

Persons who sell and distribute records of pirated songs are liable in independant action under copyright law. Harms, Inc. v. F. W. Woolworth Co., (DC-Cal), 163 FSupp 484, 118 USPQ 436.

Defendant's preparation of tapes (which are sent by defendant to persons abroad to be used by said persons to manufacture phonograph records), which contain renditions of plaintiff's copyrighted musical compositions, violates subsec. (e) of this section; defendant's act in producing tapes in United States involves defendant as a joint tort feasor in "manufacture." Famous Music Corp. v. Seeco Records, Inc., (DC-NY), 201 FSupp 560, 132 USPQ 342.

Under prior law, playing copyrighted music by means of a phonograph record did not constitute an infringement. Stern v. Rosey, 17 AppDC 562.

24. ——Public performance — Radio and television.

Playing of copyrighted music in restaurant for entertainment of guests during meal time was a public performance for profit and an infringement. Herbert v. Shanley Co., 242 US 591, 61 LEd 511, 37 SCR 232, rev'g (CCA 2), 221 Fed 229, (CCA 2), 228 Fed 1021, and (CCA 2), 229 Fed 340, which aff'd 222 Fed 244.

Unauthorized broadcasting by radio of musical composition may constitute infringement, but broadcasting performance of one having such authority is not unlawful under copyright. Jerome H. Remick & Co. v. General Electric Co., (DC-NY), 4 F(2d) 160.

Broadcasting of a copyrighted musical composition by radio is an infringement of the statutory copyright. Jerome H. Remick & Co. v. American Automobile Accessories Co., (CCA 6), 5 F(2d) 411, 40 ALR 1511, rev'g 298 Fed 628.

The unauthorized public performance of a copyrighted musical composition in a dance hall to which admission is charged, is an infringement. Irving Berlin, Inc. v. Daigle, (CCA 5),

31 F(2d) 832, rev'g 26 F(2d) 149, and 26 F(2d) 150.

Broadcasting quarter of musical composition was not fair use. Associated Music Publishers, Inc. v. Debs Memorial Radio Fund, Inc., (CCA 2), 141 F(2d) 852, 61 USPQ 161, aff'g 46 FSupp 829, 54 USPQ 461.

Defendant did not broadcast music directly to public, but sent it by private telephone wire to restaurant for purpose of having it played to restaurant's customers as and when restaurant wished so to entertain them; rendition of musical composition under these circumstances is public performance for profit by defendant as well as restaurant. Leo Feist, Inc. v. Lew Tendler Taver, Inc., (CA 3), 267 F(2d) 494, 121 USPQ 545, aff'g 162 FSupp 129, 117 USPQ 272.

The playing of music in a "dine and dance" establishment for the purpose of inducing the public to patronize the place and pay for the entertainment in the purchase of food and drink constituted a performance of the music for profit. Buck v. Russo, (DC-Mass), 25 FSupp 317, 39 USPQ 377.

Plaintiffs licensed manufacturers of motion pictures but did not give them right to license for public performance and did not license defendant to perform publicly; defendant purchased copyrighted motion-picture films containing songs which were copyrighted by plaintiffs; exhibition of these films publicly for profit was infringement of plaintiffs' copyright. Famous Music Corp. v. Melz, (DC-La), 28 FSupp 767, 42 USPQ 573.

Hotel orchestra playing copyrighted musical composition without permission infringes copyrights although no admission is charged. Buck v. Coe, (DC-Pa), 32 FSupp 829, 45 USPQ 230.

Broadcasting one entire part of four-part musical composition, time consumed being third of time required for performance of whole work, is not fair use. Associated Music Publishers, Inc. v. Debs Memorial Radio Fund, Inc., (DC-NY), 46 FSupp 829, 54 USPQ 461. Aff'd 141 F(2d) 852, 61 USPQ 161.

Unlicensed broadcast of copyrighted musical composition on noncommercial sustaining program of nonprofit radio station, devoting third of its time to commercial broadcasts, is performance for profit and an infringement; such broadcast on sustaining program of commercial station is an infringement. Associated Music Publishers, Inc. v. Debs Memorial Radio Fund, Inc., (DC-NY), 46 FSupp 829, 54 USPQ 461. Aff'd 141 F(2d) 852, 61 USPQ 161.

Presentation of "professional copies" of copyrighted sheet music by copyright proprietor to orchestra leaders does not confer on them license to violate donor's right of public performance for profit; gift implies nothing more than grant of right lawfully to use thing given; without license publicly to perform composition for profits, such performance and use therein of the donated copy are unlawful. Remick Music Corp. v. Interstate Hotel Co., (DC-Neb), 58 FSupp 523, 63 USPQ 327. Aff'd 157 F(2d) 744, 71 USPQ 138.

Company infringes copyright by purporting to license broadcasting stations and others to perform infringing musical composition. Northern Music Corp. v. King Record Distributing Co., (DC-NY), 105 FSupp 393, 93 USPQ 512.

25. —Pictures, designs, and artistic works.

Billiard table design, not novel in itself, was not infringed by a similar design. Collender v. Griffith, (CC-NY), FedCas 3,000, 11 Blatchf 212.

Copyright of playing card design was infringed by a similar design used upon defendant's cards. Richardson v. Miller, (CC-Mass), FedCas 11,791.

The engraving "The Home of Washington" was infringed by photographic prints thereof. Rossiter v. Hall, (CC-NY), FedCas 12,082, 5 Blatchf 362.

Sale of chromos designed from a picture in a foreign publication circulated here before plaintiff took out a copyright was not an infringement. Johnson v. Donaldson, (CC-NY), 3 Fed 22.

The unauthorized reproduction and sale of a copy of a cut of a picture published in a copyrighted illustrated newspaper is not an infringement of the copyright. Harper v. Shoppell, (CC-NY), 26 Fed 519.

The copyright of a painting may be infringed by lithographic prints thereof. Schumacher v. Schwencke, (CC-NY), 30 Fed 690.

A copyright of an artistic photograph may be infringed by stamping the design on leather intended for the bottom or back of a chair. Falk v. T. P. Howell & Co., (CC-NY), 37 Fed 202.

Illustrative engravings of church furniture contained in a copyrighted book and price list were not infringed by similar illustrations in a book of like character. Lamb v. Grand Rapids School Furniture Co., (CC-Mich), 39 Fed 474.

A picture accompanying complainant's copyrighted stories was not infringed by a picture which accompanied defendant's stories. Munro v. Smith, (CC-NY), 42 Fed 266.

Copyright of a photograph was infringed by one who used the original photograph to produce copies thereof. Falk v. Brett Lithographing Co., (CC-NY), 48 Fed 678.

Partially completed reproductions of a copyrighted picture are an infringement whether in marketable state or not. Fishel v. Lueckel, (CC-NY), 53 Fed 499.

Photograph of actress was infringed by lithographic reproduction of material parts thereof. Falk v. Donaldson, (CC-NY), 57 Fed 32.

Infringement of copyrights of photographs of a dancer was not shown by illustrations in a newspaper of certain poses of such dancer. Falk v. City Item Printing Co., (CC-La), 79 Fed 321.

Copyright of a painting, the features of which were originated by the prospective purchaser thereof, was not infringed by a later painting made independently of the former, but having the same essential features. McCarthy v. Adler Bros. & Co., (DC-NY), 227 Fed 630.

A copyright may be infringed when a retail seller of the manufactured articles of the plaintiff inserts in his advertisement a reproduction of a copyrighted picture of the plaintiffs without their permission. Golden Rule, Inc. v. B. V. D. Co., (CCA 8), 242 Fed 929.

Painting is infringed by a picture having same essential features. Gerlach-Barklow Co. v. Morris & Bendien, Inc., (CCA 2), 23 F(2d) 159.

Slight differences between pictures, observable by close scrutiny, do not avoid infringement. Gerlach-Barklow Co. v. Morris & Bendien, Inc., (CCA 2), 23 F(2d) 159.

Irrespective of sources from which author may derive material which he uses, a picture or writing which is his own production cannot be copied; prior art is only relevant as bearing on question whether alleged infringer has copied author or has taken his material directly from prior art. Detective Comics, Inc. v. Bruns Publications, Inc., (CCA 2), 111 F(2d) 432, 45 USPQ 291, mod'g 28 FSupp 399, 41 USPQ 182.

There is no infringement by publication of copyrighted pictures without copyright notice, although copies of pictures sent by licensor to licensee bore on their backs condition that copyright notice be used, since licensor later orally waived condition; copyright owner who might elect to publish without copyright notice and thereby forego whatever protection that would give can also authorize licensee so to publish. Swift v. Collegian Press, Inc., (CCA 2), 131 F(2d) 900, 55 USPQ 472.

Appropriation of idea, form, or perspective of two cuts from hundreds in catalogue is unsubstantial infringement. Mathews Conveyer Co. v. Palmer-Bee Co., (CCA 6), 135 F(2d) 73, 57 USPQ 219, aff'g 41 FSupp 401, 51 USPQ 286.

Sketches do not infringe copyrighted photographs of bearings; while photographs were used, in part, as models, sketches were made from defendant's own detail drawings, are at different angle with different shading, and depict bearings different in important detail of design. Mathews Conveyer Co. v. Palmer-Bee Co., (CCA 6), 135 F(2d) 73, 57 USPQ 219, aff'g 41 FSupp 401, 51 USPQ 286.

Copyright does not purport to give any rights to mechanical or utilitarian uses of work of art, but it does protect work of art as work of art without regard to any functional use to which it might be put; subsequent utilization of work of art in article of manufacture in no way affects right of copyright owner to be protected against infringement of work of art itself; critical inquiry is not whether work sought to be registered has utility but whether it is work of art irrespective of its utility. Stein v. Mazer, (CA 4), 204 F(2d) 472, 97 USPQ 310, rev'g 111 FSupp 359, 96 USPQ 439. Aff'd 347 US 201, 98 LEd 630, 74 SCR 460, 100 USPQ 325.

Court need not determine whether, if basic design had been original with plaintiff, defendants' might not be sufficiently imitative to infringe plaintiff's copyright; inasmuch as basic design is in public domain, plaintiff is entitled to relief only if defendants copied its expression; whatever their intent, defendants did not succeed in copying expression; hence, there was no infringement. Millworth Converting Corp. v. Slifka Fabrics, (CA 2), 276 F(2d) 443, 125 USPQ 506, rev'g 180 FSupp 840, 124 USPQ 413.

Plaintiff's "Betty Boop" doll was infringed by defendant's doll, the two dolls being substantially the same and creating the same impression. Fleischer Studios, Inc. v. Ralph A. Freundlich, Inc., (DC-NY), 5 FSupp 808, 21 USPQ 216. Aff'd 73 F(2d) 276, 23 USPQ 295.

A diagrammatic instruction sheet accompanying a crude model of a steamship, the parts of which are to be assembled according to the instructions, is infringed by a similar model and instruction sheet issued by defendant. Ideal Aeroplane & Supply Co., Inc. v. Brooks, (DC-NY), 18 FSupp 936, 33 USPQ 193.

By contract which did not mention copyright, plaintiff gave defendant mats for printing in its newspaper; after termination of contract defendant printed one cut inadvertently; this was not copyright infringement since on notice all mats were returned to plaintiff. Norm Co. v. John A. Brown Co., (DC-Okla), 26 FSupp 707, 40 USPQ 419.

Copyright on card having its corners marked off by four black lines forming square or box, even if valid, is not infringed by card having corners marked off by two red lines forming an angle. Kessler v. Schreiber, (DC-NY), 39 FSupp 655, 49 USPQ 610.

Fact that diagrams on only 11 pages are infringements does not in itself prevent securing relief limited to the 11 infringing pages although book has 254 pages. Colonial Book Co., Inc. v. Amsco School Publications, Inc., (DC-NY), 41 FSupp 156, 51 USPQ 33.

Copyright of drawing showing novel bridge approach does not prevent others from using and applying system set forth. Muller v. Triborough Bridge Authority, (DC-NY), 43 FSupp 298, 52 USPQ 227.

Inspiration for plaintiffs' and defendants' miniature religious shrines was specific shrine; by reason of such resemblance, infringement may not be assumed because principal elements of both designs are taken from common source. Allegrini v. DeAngelis, (DC-Pa), 59 FSupp 248, 64 USPQ 165. Aff'd 149 F(2d) 815, 65 USPQ 589.

Infringement of insignia is not avoided by fact that defendant copied with variations. Nash v. Alaska Airlines, Inc., (DC-NY), 94 FSupp 428, 88 USPQ 85.

Plaintiff submitted design for advertising insignia under understanding that plaintiff would be compensated if design were used, defendant's retention of design until after defendant's use of similar design in advertising creates inference that defendant used plaintiff's design and entitles plaintiff to recover. Nash v. Alaska Airlines, Inc., (DC-NY), 94 FSupp 428, 88 USPQ 85.

Copyright protection existing for original art does not extend to protecting lamp which employs copy of protected art as part of its ornamentation. Stein v. Rosenthal, (DC-Cal), 103 FSupp 227, 92 USPQ 402. Aff'd 205 F(2d) 633, 98 USPQ 180.

Substitution by defendant of artificial pearls in its bracelet in place of glass stones in plaintiff's copyrighted bracelet, while using same metal designs and settings, constitutes infringement. Dan Kasoff, Inc. v. Palmer Jewelry Mfg.

Co., Inc., (DC-NY), 171 FSupp 603, 120 USPQ 445.

Cursory comparison of plaintiffs' copyrighted design and defendant's fabric evokes impression that designs are identical; closer scrutiny reveals that each minor detail of plaintiffs' design has been altered in defendant's copy; copyright is infringed. Peter Pan Fabrics, Inc. v. Acadia Co., Inc., (DC-NY), 173 FSupp 292, 121 USPQ 81. Aff'd 274 F(2d) 487, 124 USPQ 154.

Copyrighted design of top and side of parachute with irregular curved lines painted upon parachute is not infringed by parachutes employing such design. Fulmer v. U. S., (CtCls), 103 FSupp 1021, 93 USPQ 102.

Still pictures used for display which were reproductions of some of pictures that went to make up motion-picture film constituted infringement of cover of copyrighted magazine of which they were copies; projecting on screen reproduction of those pictures was publication and infringement of copyright, and the films themselves, positive and negative, were infringement. Kaplan v. Fox Film Corp., (DC-NY), 37 USPQ 248.

Defendant's copyright picture both in idea it conveys and in illustrations used to convey idea is entirely dissimilar and unlike plaintiff's copyrighted pictures; there is no infringement. Lucas v. Nattrass-Schenck, Inc., (DC-NY), 44 USPQ 344.

Copyrighted card of Gilbert Stuart's portrait of George Washington with an eagle standing on the United States shield in the upper left of the card was not infringed. Carr v. National Capital Press, Inc., 63 AppDC 210, 71 F(2d) 220, 21 USPQ 408.

That two books contain many substantially identical phrases and common errors is some evidence that one was copied from other, but fact that defendant copied one of plaintiff's dresses is no evidence that it copied another of plaintiff's dresses. Richard J. Cole, Inc. v. Manhattan Modes Co., Inc., (Misc), 109 USPQ 370. Aff'd 2 AppDiv(2d series) 593, 157 NYS(2d) 259, 112 USPQ 193.

26. ——Cartoons.

Copyright of "Mutt" and "Jeff" cartoons was infringed by the similar appearing cartoon characters "Nut" and "Giff." Hill v. Whalen & Martell, Inc., (DC-NY), 220 Fed 359.

The manufacturing of a horse as a figure doll which is named "Sparky" or "Spark Plug," and fashioned from a figure of a horse in a copyrighted cartoon strip which horse is known as "Spark Plug," constitutes an infringement of the cartoon. King Features Syndicate v. Fleischer, (CCA 2), 299 Fed 533.

So far as pictorial representations and verbal descriptions of plaintiff's fictional character are not mere delineation of a benevolent Hercules, but embody arrangement of incidents and literary expressions original with author, they are proper subjects of copyright and susceptible of infringement. Detective Comics, Inc. v. Bruns Publications, Inc., (CCA 2), 111 F(2d) 432, 45 USPQ 291, mod'g 28 FSupp 399, 41 USPQ 182.

27. ——Labels.

There is an infringement of a copyrighted label when there is a general resemblance in size, arrangement of printed matter, and color and pictures although there are differences in the detail of the infringing label. Nekritz v. Duberstein, (DC-NY), 271 Fed 17.

In alleged infringing label defendant did not copy design and details of plaintiff's label; inspection reveals different arrangement both as to text as well as well-known illustration or medallion or vignette; scrolls are different; both employed long used texts and well-known pictures; infringement is not confined to literal and exact registration or reproduction but here each product was but variation of familiar and frequently reproduced labels of stock nature. Bobrecker v. Denebeim, (DC-Mo), 28 FSupp 383, 42 USPQ 194.

Label with elk's head does not infringe label with deer's head. Griesedieck Western Brewery Co. v. Peoples Brewing Co., (DC-Minn), 56 FSupp 600, 63 USPQ 74. Aff'd 149 F(2d) 1019, 66 USPQ 1.

Manufacturer's copyrighted label is infringed by unauthorized use of label on garments made from woolen piece goods purchased as surplus material from government that were originally manufactured by owner of copyrighted label. Forstmann Woolen Co. v. J. W. Mays, Inc., (DC-NY), 89 FSupp 964, 85 USPQ 200.

Copyright does not give its owner an exclusive right to use basic material, but only exclusive right to reproduce his individual presentation of material; so long as there is no copying, actual or implied, owner has no cause for complaint if later artist produces identical presentation of material by his independent efforts; even though alleged infringer may get idea for his work from copyrighted work, there is no infringement unless copyrighted work was copied; this is especially true where allegedly infringing material is limited to pictorial representation of commonly known vegetable which is attached as label upon containers in which vegetable is packed. Rochelle Asparagus Co. v. Princeville Canning Co., (DC-Ill), 170 FSupp 809, 121 USPQ 78.

Carton bearing "C.J.'S Combined Herbs" and cut of dancing Indian does not infringe carton bearing "O.G.'S United Herbs" and larger cut of head and shoulders of Indian. Needham v. Becker, (DC-Ohio), 62 USPQ 434.

28. ——Maps.

To infringe the copyright of a map a substantial copy must be reproduced, and a map of Philadelphia cannot infringe a map of New York City, although the same system of signs are used on both maps. Perris v. Hexamer, 99 US 674, 25 LEd 308.

A person who bestows his skill and time in the surveys, research, and observation necessary to the making of a correct map, does not thereby prevent any other person from using the same means to accomplish the same end.

The natural objects, public records, and surveys from which a map is made are open to the examination of any one, but no person has a right to sit down and copy the map of another. Chapman v. Ferry, (CC-Ore), 18 Fed 539.

The reproduction, retracing, or relithographing of any material part of a map is an infringement. Sanborn Map & Pub. Co. v. Dakin Pub. Co., (CC-Cal), 39 Fed 266.

The copyright of a statistical atlas containing maps, tables, and printed text was infringed by the unauthorized reprinting of eight maps therefrom. Black v. Henry G. Allen Co., (CC-NY), 42 Fed 618, 9 LRA 433.

Use by defendant of plaintiff's map for purpose of correcting and bringing to date a map previously published by defendant, was, on the evidence, not an actionable infringement. Chamberlin v. Bekins Van & Storage Co., (DC-Cal), 23 F(2d) 541.

Making of reproductions in part of copyrighted map constituted infringement whether defendants acted in good faith and by mistake or by design; neither absence of key to map nor reduction in size, so that some of symbols could be used only with difficulty, makes a difference. Towle v. Ross, (DC-Ore), 32 FSupp 125, 45 USPQ 143.

There is no infringement where both parties, independently, went to common sources for their maps, using coloring always associated with maps, and novelty in plaintiff's map, i. e., state grouping, originated with defendant. Christianson v. West Pub. Co., (DC-Cal), 53 FSupp 454, 60 USPQ 279. Aff'd 149 F(2d) 202, 65 USPQ 263.

Map is not result of original work that is intended to be protected by 1909 Copyright Act where it resulted from study of prior maps, even though map contains some information that was not on any one of prior maps since it was collectively on all of these maps. Amsterdam v. Triangle Publications, Inc., (DC-Penn), 93 FSupp 79, 87 USPQ 90.

In dealing with materials like maps, which are purely descriptive of terrains, courts have, at times, looked not only for similarities but for identity of errors, either in names or other data, as indicating access to copyrighted material. Hayden v. Chalfant Press, Inc., (DC-Cal), 177 FSupp 303, 123 USPQ 475. Aff'd 281 F(2d) 543, 126 USPQ 483.

In order not to give cartographer a permanent monopoly which would enable him, without renewing copyright, to begin new copyright period every year, courts limit copyrightability of periodical revisions of maps to new matter appearing on them; at best, originality as to maps is narrow in scope, because of nature of the art which consists merely of depicting, on a map, in an accepted form, the topography of a terrain; originality is more limited even than the slight degree of originality required in copyrighted works in general. Hayden v. Chalfant Press, Inc., (DC-Cal), 177 FSupp 303, 123 USPQ 475. Aff'd 281 F(2d) 543, 126 USPQ 483.

Originality in map making is confined to original designation of mountains, lakes, rivers, trails, and roads and other contours and configurations of the territory, and of their names, which are not found in maps prepared by others; hence, claim of infringement must be confined to "lifting" of these novel additions; cartog-

rapher is limited to what, by expenditure of labor and money, he was able to discover in territory and note on his maps which was not noted on basic official or other maps. Hayden v. Chalfant Press, Inc., (DC-Cal), 177 FSupp 303, 123 USPQ 475. Aff'd 281 F(2d) 543, 126 USPQ 483.

29. — —Motion pictures.

When defendants made negatives from plaintiff's positive film of wild animals, and a positive film from the negative, they copied and infringed, and when film was shown, defendant thereby made enlarged copy of picture, which though temporary, was still a copy while it lasted, and was infringement. Patterson v. Century Productions, Inc., (CCA 2), 93 F(2d) 489, 35 USPQ 471, aff'g 19 FSupp 30, 33 USPQ 194.

A motion-picture producer infringes if he sells sound tracks which reproduce copyrighted song, but vendee to whom he sells is not an infringer until he in turn sells or uses same in public performance for profit. Foreign & Domestic Music Corp. v. Licht, (CA 2), 196 F(2d) 627, 93 USPQ 272.

Fact that defendant burlesqued other plays or motion pictures is no defense to instant action for copyright infringement based upon burlesque of plaintiff's motion picture. Loew's Inc. v. Columbia Broadcasting System, Inc., (DC-Cal), 131 FSupp 165, 105 USPQ 302. Aff'd 239 F(2d) 532, 112 USPQ 11, which was aff'd 356 US 43, 2 LEd(2d) 583, 78 SCR 667, 116 USPQ 479.

As between plaintiff's and defendant's scripts, many words are the same because they are both quiz programs about motion pictures, but there is no copyright infringement since style and arrangement of words present in no substantial similarity to ordinary observer; with respect to radio and television broadcasts, it is perhaps more significant to compare in detail the sequence of episodes which taken together make up the program as a whole and which form concrete manner of expressing basic idea; method is similar when there is comparison of stage plays. Richards v. Columbia Broadcasting System, Inc., (DC-DC), 161 FSupp 516, 117 USPQ 174.

Defendant is not liable as infringer since it did not exhibit motion picture and did not participate in co-defendant's exhibition thereof on television; co-defendant is liable as infringer. Pickford Corp. v. DeLuxe Laboratories, Inc., (DC-Cal), 169 FSupp 118, 120 USPQ 521.

30. — —Statuary.

Copyright of a piece of statuary may be infringed by a photograph thereof. Bracken v. Rosenthal, (CC-Ill), 151 Fed 136.

Copyright of a statuette of figures of two saints beside a cross was infringed by a second similar object. Pellegrini v. Allegrini, (DC-Pa), 2 F(2d) 610.

Copyrights of statuettes are valid even though proprietor intended primarily to use statuettes in form of lamp bases and did so use them; copyrights are infringed by defendants, who minutely copied statuettes in form of bases for lamps. Stein v. Mazer, (CA 4), 204 F(2d) 472, 97 USPQ 310, rev'g 111 FSupp 359, 96

USPQ 439. Aff'd 347 US 201, 98 LEd 630, 74 SCR 460, 100 USPQ 325.

Copyrighted sculpture of dog is infringed although defendant's expert dog breeder and fancier may be able to distinguish between dogs for technical reasons, since average reasonable observer would not distinguish. Contemporary Arts, Inc. v. F. W. Woolworth Co., (DC-Mass), 93 FSupp 739, 86 USPQ 476. Aff'd 193 F(2d) 162, 92 USPQ 4, which was aff'd 344 US 228, 97 LEd 276, 73 SCR 222, 95 USPQ 396.

31. Right of action—Grounds for suit.

The public representation of a dramatic composition, not printed or published, does not deprive the owner of his common-law right against piracy or surreptitious publication. Ferris v. Frohman, 223 US 424, 56 LEd 492, 32 SCR 263, aff'g 238 Ill 430, 87 NE 327, 43 LRA (NS) 639, 128 AmSt 135.

In a suit for the infringement of a copyright, the rights of the plaintiff will also be determined. Binns v. Woodruff, (CC-Pa), FedCas 1,424, 4 WashCC 48.

Under the Copyright Act of 1831 there is a right of action for infringement, both in equity and at law, prior to publication of a work. Boucicault v. Wood, (CC-Ill), FedCas 1,693, 2 Biss 34.

Under § 6 of the Copyright Act of 1831 providing for penalties for the unlawful printing and publishing of a book or books, a plaintiff had no right to recover such penalties in an action of debt where there had been no copying or reprinting of an entire book. Rogers v. Jewett, (CC-Mass), FedCas 12,012, 22 LawRep 339.

A method of advertising cannot be copyrighted, and the owner of a copyright on a paint card cannot sue to prevent anyone else from advertising paint by attaching pieces of colored paper to a card. Ehret v. Pierce, (CC-NY), 10 Fed 553.

A suit cannot be maintained to secure an injunction to prevent the printing of opinions of the judges, since they are not subjects of copyright. Banks & Bros. v. West Publishing Co., (CC-Minn), 27 Fed 50.

A defendant is not liable to the charge of infringement unless proofs justify the conclusion that he has copied another's work. S. S. White Dental Co. v. Sibley, (CC-Pa), 38 Fed 751.

An injunction will not issue to protect a system of stenography which is described in a copyrighted book, since the copyright does not cover the system. Griggs v. Perrin, (CC-NY), 49 Fed 15.

Though a plaintiff may not, in law, have any ground for complaint because state officers have a manuscript in their possession, he may nevertheless invoke the aid of a court of equity to restrain the defendants from printing or publishing such manuscript, if the printing or publication thereof would infringe his rights under the copyright laws. Howell v. Miller, (CCA 6), 91 Fed 129.

This section provides for a penalty and therefore a plaintiff cannot maintain an action

unless he has complied with all the conditions precedent. Bennett v. Carr, (CCA 2), 96 Fed 213.

No suit can be maintained for the infringement of a work that is not subject to copyright even though all the requirements of the copyright law were complied with and a certificate of copyright issued. Bleistein v. Donaldson Lithographing Co., (CC-Ky), 98 Fed 608.

A person cannot maintain an action for the infringement of his copyright unless he has complied with all the provisions of the law. Bennett v. Boston Traveler Co., (CCA 1), 101 Fed 445.

Sale on execution of plates used to print a copyrighted book did not estop owner of copyright on the book from enforcing his statutory rights as against a subsequent purchaser of the plates. Patterson v. J. S. Ogilvie Pub. Co., (CC-NY), 119 Fed 451.

An owner of a copyright is not entitled to equitable relief against another publication solely because the writer of the other publication may have saved some stenographic labor or manual handwriting by cutting or copying words of citations, which include no literary ability. West Publishing Co. v. Edward Thompson Co., (CC-NY), 169 Fed 833. Mf'd 176 Fed 833.

The statutory requirements must be carefully observed before a right to sue for infringement accrues to an author or owner of a copyright. Record & Guide Co. v. Bromley, (CC-Pa), 175 Fed 156.

A complainant cannot maintain a suit for injunction when the statutory provisions for the form of the copyright notice have not been complied with. Louis De Jonge & Co. v. Breuker & Kessler Co., (CC-Pa), 182 Fed 150. Aff'd 191 Fed 35, which was aff'd 235 US 33, 59 LEd 113, 35 SCR 6.

Complainant was not entitled to maintain an action for infringement of copyright, where an injunction was issued at midnight and copies of his publication were not deposited until next day. New York Times Co. v. Star Co., (CC-NY), 195 Fed 110.

Congress has full power to restrict actions for infringement of copyrights. New York Times Co. v. Star Co., (CC-NY), 195 Fed 110.

In order to be entitled to relief for infringement of copyright it is essential that the copyright shall exist, and that a copying shall have taken place. Davies v. Bowes, (DC-NY), 209 Fed 53. Aff'd 219 Fed 178.

A criticism of an original work, which tends to lessen its money value by showing that it is not worth seeing or hearing, may not form the basis for a charge of infringement of copyright. Hill v. Whalen & Martell, Inc., (DC-NY), 220 Fed 359.

One who so embodies copyrighted with uncopyrighted matter that one reading his work cannot distinguish between the two may not have an injunction to restrain others from republishing his works. Bentley v. Tibbals, (CCA 2), 223 Fed 247.

Where the evidence shows that defendant is threatening to infringe the copyright, plaintiff is entitled to protection although no actual infringement has yet taken place. Historical Pub. Co. v. Jones Bros. Pub. Co., (CCA 3), 231 Fed 638.

A person, who, in his notice of copyright, uses a fictitious name which is unlawful for him to use, cannot bring suit to protect the articles containing such notice. Haas v. Leo Feist, Inc., (DC-NY), 234 Fed 105.

Where the copyright has terminated by abandonment at the time suit is brought, and the only relief sought is injunction, the bill must be dismissed. Atlantic Monthly Co. v. Post Pub. Co., (DC-Mass), 27 F(2d) 556.

Where motion picture was copyrighted as motion picture other than photoplay by depositing one copy and title under § 12 of this title, and several copies were made in different sizes and shown to employees and others and were sent to many organizations to be shown without charge, so that motion picture was exhibited to many thousands of people; this was not a publication requiring deposit of two copies, and owner could sue infringer without further deposits. Patterson v. Century Productions, Inc., (CCA 2), 93 F(2d) 489, 35 USPQ 471, aff'g 19 FSupp 30, 33 USPQ 194.

Suit for infringement of copyright and literary property by moving picture should be dismissed where, even though defendants took from the play all those matters in which the film resembled it, they were within their rights in doing so. Dellar v. Samuel Goldwyn, (CCA 2), 104 F(2d) 661, 42 USPQ 164, rev'g 23 FSupp 519, 37 USPQ 760.

Failure of copyright proprietor to deposit two copies of second volume will be important only on issue of damages, if then; defendants' edition being in one volume must be enjoined in any event. Houghton Mifflin Co. v. Stackpole Sons, Inc., (CCA 2), 113 F(2d) 627, 46 USPQ 296, mod'g 31 FSupp 517, 44 USPQ 668.

Action for damages by reason of copyright infringement sounds in tort. Turton v. U. S., (CA 6), 212 F(2d) 354, 101 USPQ 164.

Lack of jurisdiction in court of claims over actions against United States for patent infringement was changed by § 1498 of Title 28; this legislation, however, was restricted to actions for patent infringement and did not change law as to copyright infringement; since court of claims has no jurisdiction over actions against United States for copyright infringement, jurisdiction in district court under § 1346(a)(2) of Title 28 is also lacking. Turton v. U. S., (CA 6), 212 F(2d) 354, 101 USPQ 164.

It is copyright infringement if defendant makes unauthorized offering of identical films and sound tracks for sale with "100% of all rights" which would include right to make positives therefrom and to exhibit positives to public, in violation of plaintiff's common-law copyright. Independent Film Distributors, Ltd. v. Chesapeake Industries, Inc., (CA 2), 250 F(2d) 951, 116 USPQ 28, rev'g 148 FSupp 611, 112 USPQ 380.

Owner of copyright of picture who omitted his name from all copies thereof was not entitled to restrain infringer. Goes Lithograph-

ing Co. v. Apt Lithographic Co., (DC-NY), 14 FSupp 620, 30 USPQ 119.

State statute requiring owner of copyright to obtain license before collecting royalties or fees did not preclude such owner without license from bringing infringement suit. Leo Feist, Inc. v. Demarie, (DC-La), 16 FSupp 827, 32 USPQ 122.

State court judgment adjudging assignments of copyright as valid involved parties bringing infringement suit, or their privies, leaving them with no standing to prosecute infringement suit. Dorf v. Denton, (DC-NY), 17 FSupp 531, 33 USPQ 24.

Plaintiff's offer to settle with defendant for breach of contract to use plaintiff's advertising scheme, had no bearing upon plaintiff's right to sue for infringements after expiration of contract. Doll v. Libin, (DC-Mont), 17 FSupp 546, 33 USPQ 17.

Reprintings separated by eight months are separate infringements of copyright. Eliot v. Geare-Marston, Inc., (DC-Pa), 30 FSupp 301, 43 USPQ 249.

Deposit of copies of work under § 13 of this title and registration under § 209 are conditions precedent to right to maintain action for copyright infringement after publication for sale; it is immaterial that plaintiff holds proper certificate of registration under § 12 covering work of art not to be reproduced for sale, since, even if he has deposited two copies, he has no certificate of registration under § 209. Rosedale v. News Syndicate Co., Inc., (DC-NY), 39 FSupp 357, 50 USPQ 27.

Originality is essential as basis for infringement action; copyright cannot prevent others from using old material. Chamberlin v. Uris Sales Corp., (DC-NY), 56 FSupp 987, 62 USPQ 375. Aff'd 150 F(2d) 512, 65 USPQ 544.

Infringement of copyright is merely wrongful interference with statutory right of copyright proprietor and will not support action for trover and conversion. Local Trademarks, Inc. v. Rogers, (DC-Ala), 73 FSupp 907, 75 USPQ 336.

Illegal combination of copyrights and pooling of proceeds derived from licensing of copyrights through illegal combination renders unenforceable the rights granted under Copyright Act, at least while illegal combination continues. Alden-Rochelle, Inc. v. American Soc. Composers, Authors & Publishers, (DC-NY), 80 FSupp 900, 79 USPQ 402, mod'g 79 FSupp 315, 78 USPQ 197.

Plaintiff's copyright is infringed since defendant took substantial part of plaintiff's execution for his own; infringement is not negatived by fact that art work and composition of defendant's pamphlet are better than in plaintiff's pamphlet. American Visuals Corp. v. Holland, (DC-NY), 162 FSupp 14, 117 USPQ 180. Aff'd 119 USPQ 482.

Federal court does not have jurisdiction over cases in which copyright laws are involved or over controversies about copyrighted material; jurisdiction is present only if case arises under act of Congress relating to copyright; instant case does not arise under copyright laws where issue presented is one of title to copyright with

resolution of question depending on rules of common law and interpretation of contract and not on any statute of United States; plaintiff was not author of copyright material, it is alleged that copyright was secured in violation of his rights, and contract assigned to plaintiff no rights in copyrighted material but only gave him the right to secure copyright. Gorham v. Edwards, (DC-NY), 164 FSupp 781, 118 USPQ 532.

Federal court does not have jurisdiction under FCA 28 § 1338(a) of action seeking declaration that plaintiff has interest as coauthor in defendants' copyrighted musical composition inasmuch as no issue is presented as to validity or infringement of copyright and diversity of citizenship is lacking; plaintiff merely claims that he is entitled to assignment of interest in copyright and an accounting for a share of proceeds earned by composition. Harrington v. Mure, (DC-NY), 186 FSupp 655, 126 USPQ 506.

If stranger exploits copyrighted work and deprives creator of right to its exclusive enjoyment, an infringement action will lie; however, if a co-author, one who cannot be charged with infringement, authorizes exploitation of the work and the exclusion of his collaborator, access may not be had to federal court. Harrington v. Mure, (DC-NY), 186 FSupp 655, 126 USPQ 506.

Exhibition of motion picture allegedly infringing common-law or statutory copyright is more analogous to republication or new publication and each exhibition gives rise to separate cause of action to which, respectively, statute of limitations applies. Stein v. RKO Radio Pictures, Inc., (DC-NY), 53 USPQ 294.

Where book title has secondary meaning, owner can enjoin another threatening to use or using it as title for motion picture. Johnston v. Twentieth Century-Fox Film Corp., 82 CalApp(2d series) 796, 187 Pac(2d) 474, 76 USPQ 131, aff'g 69 USPQ 209.

Defendant in common-law copyright infringement suit was privy of defendant in action in Hungary involving same story; even though determination of Hungarian court is not res judicata, the principle of comity will give consideration to Hungarian judgment as bar to instant action. Tamas v. Twentieth Century-Fox Film Corp., (Misc), 25 NYS(2d) 899, 48 USPQ 573.

Under federal Declaratory Judgment Act [28 §§ 2201, 2202], one need not wait until he has actually been charged with infringement before beginning action. Broadcast Music, Inc. v. Taylor, (Misc), 55 NYS(2d) 94, 65 USPQ 503.

32. Remedies in general.

Forfeitures and penalties may not be recovered in a suit for an injunction for infringement of copyright. Stevens v. Gladding, 58 US(17 How) 447, 15 LEd 155, rev'g (CC-RI), FedCas 13,400; Chapman v. Perry, (CC-Ore), 12 Fed 693.

A suit for infringement of copyright against defendants who had purchased copyrighted books from dealers under retail price agreement and sold them for less than the fixed price constituted a suit independent of complainant's statutory copyright rights. Scribner v. Straus,

210 US 352, 52 LEd 1094, 28 SCR 735, aff'g (CCA 2), 147 Fed 28, which aff'd 139 Fed 193.

Copyright statute provides a comprehensive system of rights and remedies, and however inadequate the latter may be no others can be resorted to. Globe Newspaper Co. v. Walker, 210 US 356, 52 LEd 1096, 28 SCR 726, rev'g (CCA 1), 140 Fed 305, 2 LRA(NS) 913, 5 Ann Cas 274, which rev'd 130 Fed 593.

The remedies created by the copyright laws are the only ones open to those seeking the benefit of rights created under such laws. Globe Newspaper Co. v. Walker, 210 US 356, 52 LEd 1096, 28 SCR 726, rev'g (CCA 1), 140 Fed 305, 2 LRA(NS) 913, 5 AnnCas 274, which rev'd 130 Fed 593.

Record is unsatisfactory for court to entertain action seeking declaratory judgment as to government official's rights in his speeches since, although court is asked to determine matters of serious public concern, and although their adjudication, certainly by way of resort to a discretionary declaratory judgment, should rest on an adequate and fullbodied record, agreed statement of facts only sketchily summarizes circumstances of preparation and delivery of speeches and does not clearly define nature and scope of official's duties nor does it adequately show his use of government facilities and personnel in preparation of speeches; moreover, statements in agreed statement were not subject to examination and cross-examination. Public Affairs Associates, Inc. v. Rickover, 369 US 111, 7 LEd (2d) 604, 82 SCR 580, 132 USPQ 535, rev'g 109 AppDC 128, 284 F(2d) 262, 127 USPQ 231, which aff'd 177 FSupp 601, 123 USPQ 252.

Copyright Act did not give any form of relief which did not previously exist in the federal or state courts. Pierpont v. Fowle, (CC-Mass), FedCas 11,152, 2 Woodb&M 23.

The owner of an uncopyrighted opera may restrain another from producing the opera without his permission. Goldmark v. Kreling, (CC-Cal), 25 Fed 349.

Where an infringement has been established the appropriate relief is by injunction and an accounting for profits. Fishel v. Lueckel, (CC-NY), 53 Fed 499.

Where the owner of a copyright has transferred title to a copy of the copyrighted work, to another, he cannot restrain, as an infringement of his copyright, the work from being sold in violation of an agreement. His only remedy is for breach of contract. Harrison v. Maynard, Merrill & Co., (CCA 2), 61 Fed 689.

Where a copyrighted book contains a notice of certain conditions concerning resale, the owner of the copyright cannot bring suit for violation of the notice, if he bases his action on the infringement of his copyright. Authors & Newspapers Ass'n v. O'Gorman Co., (CC-RI), 147 Fed 616.

The right given to an author to multiply copies of his work, and to prevent appropriation of his work by other persons granted by R. S. § 4952 includes the right to recover damages for infringement where such can be proven, and to an injunction where such is the appropriate and accessory remedy. West Publishing

Co. v. Edward Thompson Co., (CC-NY), 169 Fed 833. Mf'd 176 Fed 833.

A court of equity having obtained jurisdiction of a cause in which an injunction, an accounting, and damages have been asked for has the right to do justice between the parties and to dispose of the case finally, even if this involves withholding injunctive relief and awarding damages. West Publishing Co. v. Edward Thompson Co., (CCA 2), 176 Fed 833, mod'g 169 Fed 833.

Attachment is not a proper remedy in a suit involving the infringement of a copyright. Dixon v. Corinne Runkel Stock Co., (DC-NC), 214 Fed 418.

"It was the intention of Congress (1) to preserve the right of a plaintiff to pursue damages and profits by the historic methods of equity if he chooses so to do; and (2) to give the new right of application to the court for such damages as shall 'appear to be just,' in lieu of actual damages. The words present no difficulty in interpretation. 'Actual' means 'real' as opposed to 'nominal.' It means 'existent,' without precluding the thought of change. 'In lieu' means in place of the thing modified by the quoted phrase." S. E. Hendricks Co., Inc. v. Thomas Pub. Co., (CCA 2), 242 Fed 37.

A copyright owner cannot sue one contracting for the use of the copyright for infringement amounting to a breach of contract. Metro-Goldwyn-Mayer Distributing Corp. v. Bijou Theatre Co., Inc., (DC-Mass), 50 F(2d) 908, 9 USPQ 538. Aff'd 59 F(2d) 70, 13 USPQ 147.

Where an injunction is denied case may stand as one for damages. Metro-Goldwyn-Mayer Distributing Corp. v. Bijou Theatre Co., Inc., (DC-Mass), 50 F(2d) 908, 9 USPQ 538. Aff'd 59 F(2d) 70, 13 USPQ 147.

The claim that several infringements of copyrights are joined in a bill for injunctive relief, in order to prevent a multiplicity of suits, and the inclusion in the bill of a prayer for discovery, under the facts of the case, did not justify retention of the bill to assess damages after denial of injunctive relief. Hutchinson Amusement Co. v. Vitaphone Corp., (CCA 1), 93 F(2d) 176, 36 USPQ 1.

Suit for appropriation of literary property is separate from suit under copyright laws. Newport Industries, Inc. v. Crosby Naval Stores, Inc., (CCA 5), 139 F(2d) 611, 60 USPQ 219, aff'g 48 FSupp 422, 56 USPQ 296.

Unfair competition and trade-mark and copyright infringements involve similar issues; they are phases of overzealous competition or evident lack of ethical ideals in business transactions which call for judicial correction. Soy Food Mills, Inc. v. Pillsbury Mills, Inc., (CCA 7), 161 F(2d) 22, 73 USPQ 141.

Where defendant used advertising material from plaintiff's copyrighted scheme after expiration of contract between them, defense that plaintiff's only remedy was for breach of contract was not good in infringement suit. Doll v. Libin, (DC-Mont), 17 FSupp 546, 33 USPQ 17.

In a suit for infringement a demand for an accounting of profits renders the case one for relief in a court of equity. Sheldon v. Moredall

Realty Corp., (DC-NY), 22 FSupp 91, 37 USPQ 254. Mf'd 95 F(2d) 48, 37 USPQ 286.

If it should appear that in broadcasts defendant has appropriated without plaintiff's consent plot and principal characters of plaintiff's copyrighted novel and that use being made injured reputation of author and of work and amounts to deception upon public, it may be proper to afford relief by applying principles of unfair competition. Prouty v. National Broadcasting Co., Inc., (DC-Mass), 26 FSupp 265, 40 USPQ 331.

Finding of unfair use by defendants means infringement of copyright and entitles plaintiff to injunction, costs, and damages and profits. Detective Comics, Inc. v. Bruns Publications, Inc., (DC-NY), 28 FSupp 399, 41 USPQ 182. Mf'd 111 F(2d) 432, 45 USPQ 291.

There is no merit in contention that action must be on contract, and not for copyright infringement, since defendant cancelled contract and there were no contractual relations between parties at time of publication of advertisements alleged to infringe. Zuckerman v. Dickson, (DC-Pa), 35 FSupp 903, 47 USPQ 170, 47 USPQ 514.

Copyright infringement is tort. Buck v. Cecere, (DC-NY), 45 FSupp 441, 53 USPQ 519.

Suit for infringement under this section is mere claim for damages. Local Trademarks, Inc. v. Rogers, (DC-Ala), 73 FSupp 907, 75 USPQ 336.

Title to renewal rights in copyrighted musical composition may be established by action for declaratory judgment; where both composer and publisher claim title, there is justiciable issue concerning renewal rights for songs whose original copyright terms have already expired; fact that composer might sue for coercive relief is no bar to this action; justiciable controversy also exists as to unexpired copyrights; fact that 11 unexpired copyright terms will expire at intervals within next seven years confirmed court's opinion that it ought to entertain single action now, rather than to require multiplicity of future suits. Carmichael v. Mills Music, Inc., (DC-NY), 121 FSupp 43, 101 USPQ 279.

Remedies which copyright proprietor may obtain in event of infringement are statutory remedies enumerated in this section; measure of his rights and liabilities must be found from its language. Miller v. Goody, (DC-NY), 125 FSupp 348, 103 USPQ 292.

Right of holder of trade-mark, patent, or copyright to warn others of infringement suits does not depend upon validity of mark, patent, or copyright so long as holder believes his claims are valid. Lucien Lelong, Inc. v. Dana Perfumes, Inc., (DC-Ill), 138 FSupp 575, 108 USPQ 101.

Congress did not reserve to federal courts all questions relating to copyright titles; instead, it provided for exclusive federal jurisdiction of "copyright cases," those in which federal legislation defines the substance of the claim and the relief to be secured; Congress left a considerable residue of power in state courts to pass on "copyright questions," among them, questions arising

in contract and title disputes. Harrington v. Mure, (DC-NY), 186 FSupp 655, 126 USPQ 506.

Courts have not defined "infringement," standing by itself, as referring only to a tort; definition consistently has been that "infringement of copyright" connotes a tort. Although "infringement" is most commonly applied to actions for unlawful appropriation of copyright, trade-mark, or patent, its usage is not limited solely to such actions. Weitzenkorn v. Lesser, 40 Cal(2d series) 778, 256 Pac(2d) 947, 97 USPQ 545.

A copyright owner of a play has two spheres of influence. On the one hand he may grant licenses to use the play on the stage or in motion pictures or otherwise; on the other he may prevent unauthorized persons from appropriating or using it, or obtain redress from them for such unauthorized use, or both. McClintic v. Sheldon, 182 Misc 32, 43 NYS(2d) 695, 59 USPQ 41.

Nominal value of public performance rights to three copyrighted songs as to which plaintiffs seek declaratory judgment makes court reluctant to grant such relief; songs were selected at random from many others for purpose of action; maxim de minimis non curat lex applies. Broadcast Music, Inc. v. Taylor, (Misc), 55 NYS(2d) 94, 65 USPQ 503.

33. Injunction.

Denial of temporary injunction against copyright infringement is proper where affidavits raise question as to validity of plaintiff's copyright and do not show that money damages will not be adequate remedy or that plaintiff will suffer irreparable injury if temporary injunction is denied. American Visuals Corp. v. Holland, (CA 2), 219 F(2d) 223, 104 USPQ 222, aff'g 126 FSupp 513, 103 USPQ 139.

Plaintiff is entitled to preliminary injunction against copyright infringement since defendant's affidavits do not challenge validity of copyrights, since there is little doubt of deliberate copying, and since defendant's affidavits do not deny copying. Joshua Meier Co., Inc. v. Albany Novelty Mfg. Co., (CA 2), 236 F(2d) 144, 111 USPQ 197.

Author is enjoined from asserting claim that insurance forms, copyright on which has been forfeited, are copyrighted; however, since, in general, insurance forms are copyrightable, injunction extends no further than to forms on which copyright has been forfeited. Continental Casualty Co. v. Beardsley, (CA 2), 253 F(2d) 702, 117 USPQ 1, mod'g 151 FSupp 28, 113 USPQ 181.

Court is not bound, on trial of copyright infringement action, to find absence of infringement by reason of prior denial of preliminary injunction by another judge; issue on motion for preliminary injunction was not whether there was infringement as matter of law, but whether on evidence before court judge was so convinced that plaintiff would prevail that he should exercise discretion and grant preliminary injunction; decision denying injunction meant only that within judge's appropriate discretion he was not so convinced. American Visuals Corp. v. Holland, (CA 2), 261 F(2d) 652, 119 USPQ 482, aff'g 162 FSupp 14, 117 USPQ 180.

In reviewing order granting preliminary injunction against infringement of copyrighted fabric design, court of appeals is bound by Rule 52 of Federal Rules of Civil Procedure [Rules, c. 15]; however, court of appeals is in as good a position as trial judge to determine issue of infringement where record contains almost no evidence on issue other than the fabrics themselves. Milworth Converting Corp. v. Slifka Fabrics, (CA 2), 276 F(2d) 443, 125 USPQ 506, rev'g 180 FSupp 840, 124 USPQ 413.

Having made prima facie showing of validity of copyright and of infringement by defendants, plaintiff is entitled to injunction pending suit. H. M. Kolbe Co., Inc. v. Armgus Textile Co., Inc., (CA 2), 279 F(2d) 555, 126 USPQ 1, aff'g 184 FSupp 423, 126 USPQ 11.

Although plaintiffs placed legend ("this periodical may not be sold except by authorized dealers and * * * shall not be sold or distributed with any part of its cover or markings removed * * *") on copyrighted comics, this does not, ipso facto, entitle them to injunction against resale of coverless comics; they have burden of showing that all the facts (including presence of legend) rightly call for injunctive relief; enforcement of legend is denied where totality of facts does not provide proper foundation for issuance of injunction; moreover, under Copyright Act [this title], legend is unenforcible since there is no privity of contract between parties. Independent News Co., Inc. v. Williams, (CA 3), 293 F(2d) 510, 129 USPQ 377, aff'g 184 FSupp 877, 126 USPQ 181.

Injunction and damages are refused in copyright infringement suit where copyright monopoly has been illegally extended. M. Witmark & Sons v. Jensen, (DC-Minn), 80 FSupp 843, 79 USPQ 6.

Granting of preliminary injunction is exercise of far-reaching power to be indulged in only in case clearly demanding it; moving papers should establish that denial will cause irreparable injury, during pendency of action. H. M. Chandler Co., Inc. v. Penn Paper Products, Inc., (DC-NY), 88 FSupp 753, 84 USPQ 128.

Injunction required copyright infringer to deliver for destruction all infringing copies and plates, including all books on consignment but still owned by infringer. Ziegelheim v. Flohr, (DC-NY), 119 FSupp 324, 100 USPQ 189.

Copyright proprietor was not enjoined from advising competitor's customers that competitor was infringing copyrights, and he was not liable for damages, where proprietor's conduct occurred prior to institution of suit (which found no infringement of any valid copyright) and before any adjudication of his rights and was based upon belief that he had valid copyright which was being infringed; to enjoin proprietor for past activities would be expression of belief by court that he would probably continue them after adjudication; evidence did not justify such belief; also, competitor was unable to show any actual compensable damage. Davis-Robertson Agency v. Duke, (DC-Va), 119 FSupp 931, 100 USPQ 211.

Provisions of subsec. (d) of this section relating to destruction of infringing copies and plates do not apply where violation of copyrights consists of use of mechanical reproduction of musical works; however, matrices and other matter upon which copyrighted musical compositions may be recorded, or from which parts serving to reproduce mechanically said compositions may be made, are impounded until decreed royalties and triple damages be paid and until statutory notice of intention to use work be given. Miller v. Goody, (DC-NY), 125 FSupp 348, 103 USPQ 292.

Defendant's denial of access to and copying of plaintiff's copyrighted costume jewelry is not convincing; this, together with substantial identity of defendant's product to plaintiff's article, establishes prima facie case of infringement; market for article being seasonal, preliminary injunction is warranted. Trifari, Krussman & Fishel, Inc. v. Charel Co., Inc., (DC-NY), 134 FSupp 551, 107 USPQ 48.

Where there is no reasonable ground for believing that there will be repetition of copyright infringement, court will not grant preliminary injunction, especially where injunction would inflict damages upon defendants out of proportion to benefit inuring to plaintiff. Rushton Co. v. F. W. Woolworth Co., (DC-NY), 135 FSupp 317, 108 USPQ 80.

Author's failure to apply for preliminary injunction does not bar him from maintaining plagiarism action. Szekely v. Eagle Lion Films, Inc., (DC-NY), 140 FSupp 843, 109 USPQ 348. Aff'd 242 F(2d) 266, 113 USPQ 98.

Contract between author and motion-picture producer provided that title to author's motion-picture script should be vested in author until payment of specified sum; sum was not paid, but picture using script was produced and distributed; although author is awarded damages for plagiarism against distributor equal to specified sum, distributor also is enjoined from further distribution of picture. Szekely v. Eagle Lion Films, Inc., (DC-NY), 140 FSupp 843, 109 USPQ 348. Aff'd 242 F(2d) 266, 113 USPQ 98.

Temporary injunction is refused in action for infringement of copyrighted catalogue where, although defendant's catalogue contains 2,000 items, only 25 illustrations are alleged to be similar in appearance to those in copyrighted catalogue; also, there is no showing of duplication of errors. Miller Harness Co., Inc. v. Arcaro & Dan's Saddlery, Inc., (DC-NY), 142 FSupp 634, 110 USPQ 190.

Since affidavits raise question as to validity of plaintiff's copyright, it is improper to grant plaintiff's motion for temporary injunction based on strength of allegation of copyright infringement. Kramer Jewelry Creations, Inc. v. Capri Jewelry, Inc., (DC-NY), 143 FSupp 120, 111 USPQ 151.

There is no illegal monopoly under section 2 of Sherman Antitrust Act [15 § 2] even if dramatist guild makes it mandatory, in transactions for purchasing rights to make motion picture from copyrighted plays owned by its members, that there be a restriction on time before which picture may be released, since guild members control only small portion of plays. Inge v. Twentieth Century-Fox Film Corp., (DC-NY), 143 FSupp 294, 111 USPQ 153.

In usual case of copyright infringement when infringer had notice of valid copyright, plaintiff is entitled to preliminary injunction without detailed showing of danger of irreparable harm; even if defendants had no knowledge of copyright prior to suit, they have notice of copyright by virtue of suit and would be preliminarily enjoined if they proposed to go on with manufacture and distribution of infringements; however, court exercises discretion to refuse injunction where defendants do not intend to infringe during pendency of action. Trifari, Krussman & Fishel, Inc. v. B. Steinberg-Kaslo Co., (DC-NY), 144 FSupp 577, 110 USPQ 487.

On motion for preliminary injunction in action for copyright infringement and unfair competition, defendants' change from accused labels and panel to ones which cannot be confused with plaintiff's, and defendants' assurance that old labels and panel will not be used, make consideration of these items unnecessary. Autoyre Co. v. Yagoda, (DC-NY), 148 FSupp 447, 112 USPQ 380.

In action for declaratory judgment of invalidity and noninfringement of copyright, judgment for plaintiff includes injunction restraining defendant from claiming copyright and from distributing forms purporting to be copyrighted inasmuch as defendant has stated that he would not desist unless copyright were to be invalidated by court of last resort and inasmuch as plaintiff will suffer substantial damage if defendant is not restrained. Continental Casualty Co. v. Beardsley, (DC-NY), 151 FSupp 28, 113 USPQ 181. Mf'd 253 F(2d) 702, 117 USPQ 1.

Plaintiff is entitled to temporary injunction to protect its copyrighted merchandise display card, since infringing card was adopted solely as instrument of duress in price; injunction also covers leaflets which reproduce infringing card modified only in unimportant respects. Comptone Co., Ltd. v. Rayex Corp., (DC-NY), 158 FSupp 241, 116 USPQ 120. Mf'd 251 F(2d) 487. 116 USPQ 105.

In order to grant preliminary injunction against copyright infringement, there must be clear and convincing impression of plagiarism. American Visuals Corp. v. Holland, (DC-NY), 162 FSupp 14, 117 USPQ 180.

Detailed showing of irreparable harm need not be made out by copyright proprietor as prerequisite to preliminary injunction since infringement is plain; if there be any inconvenience or loss to defendants arising from issuance of injunction, that fact does not appeal to court's conscience where infringement is blatant. Geo-Physical Maps, Inc. v. Toycraft Corp., (DC-NY), 162 FSupp 141, 117 USPQ 316.

Although, in appropriate circumstances, court may order that infringer surrender for destruction all means of copying copyrighted material, such order is purposeless where infringer has long since surrendered such material. Local Trademarks, Inc. v. Grantham, (DC-Neb), 166 FSupp 494, 117 USPQ 335.

Despite fact that former licensee has returned unused mats of copyrighted advertisements and several years have elapsed without repetition of infringement, injunction is granted since former licensee continues to assert that he had right to do that which court has said to be infringement. Local Trademarks, Inc. v. Grantham, (DC-Neb), 166 FSupp 494, 117 USPQ 335.

Copyright infringers are required to deliver up for destruction all infringing copies, articles, records, and devices in their possession or under their control as well as all plates, molds, matrices, or other means of making such infringements. Dorchester Music Corp. v. National Broadcasting Co., (DC-Cal), 171 FSupp 580, 120 USPQ 429.

Preliminary injunction may be granted against innocent copyright infringer. Peter Pan Fabrics, Inc. v. Acadia Co., Inc., (DC-NY), 173 FSupp 292, 121 USPQ 81. Aff'd 274 F(2d) 487, 124 USPQ 154.

Preliminary injunction lies in copyright infringement action only if defendants' acts constitute copying within meaning of copyright laws. Peter Pan Fabrics, Inc. v. Acadia Co., Inc., (DC-NY), 173 FSupp 292, 121 USPQ 81. Aff'd 274 F(2d) 487, 124 USPQ 154.

Preliminary injunction should issue in copyright infringement cases when plaintiff makes prima facie showing that copyright is valid and that defendant has infringed; detailed proof that plaintiff will suffer substantial and irreparable injury, unless afforded preliminary relief, is not required. Peter Pan Fabrics, Inc. v. Acadia Co., Inc., (DC-NY), 173 FSupp 292, 121 USPQ 81. Aff'd 274 F(2d) 487, 124 USPQ 154.

Plaintiff is entitled to preliminary injunction without detailed showing of danger of irreparable harm since it has made prima facie case of copyright validity and infringement; showing is adequate where infringing designs sell at lower prices and business expected by plaintiff has failed to materialize except for small sales at reduced prices; not only loss of sales and profits is involved, but also quick obsolescence of plaintiff's inventory robbed of its distinctive appeal by sales of infringing fabrics at lower prices, and attendant loss of good will. Scarves by Vera, Inc. v. United Merchants Manufacturers, Inc., (DC-NY), 173 FSupp 625, 121 USPQ 578.

Preliminary injunction should issue in copyright infringement cases when plaintiff makes prima facie showing that copyright is valid and that defendant has infringed. Cortley Fabrics Co., Inc. v. Slifka (DC-NY), 175 FSupp 66, 122 USPQ 321.

Since plaintiff's copyrighted dinnerware pattern was sold with notice of copyright thereon, any sale by defendant of dinnerware bearing substantially same design would violate copyright and should be restrained by court; infringement is preliminarily enjoined since its continuance will cause plaintiff immediate and irreparable harm. Syracuse China Corp. v. Stanley Roberts, Inc., (DC-NY), 180 FSupp 527, 125 USPQ 62.

In copyright infringement action, court issued restraining order which in substance forbade plaintiff from utilizing existence of litigation to impair defendant's business; plaintiff is held in contempt where it (1) stated to the trade that defendant's trophies infringed plaintiff's copyrights, threatened to sue defendant's customers, and informed such customers of pendency of litigation, and (2) apprised specific prospective cus-tomer of existence of litigation and possible liability of customer, with result that customer refused to do business with defendant. Dodge, Inc. v. General Classics, Inc., (DC-Ill), — FSupp —, 125 USPQ 431.

Copyrighted design printed on batik is original reproduction of original reproduction of original work of art; defendants infringe by selling "Chinese" copies thereof in competition with plaintiff and at substantially lower prices; infringement has caused considerable loss of sales to plaintiff and, since merchandise is highly seasonable in character, plaintiff will be irreparably injured; plaintiff's motion for preliminary injunction is granted. H. M. Kolbe Co., Inc. v. Armgus Textile Co., Inc., (DC-NY), 184 FSupp 423, 126 USPQ 11. Aff'd 279 F(2d) 555, 126 USPQ 1.

Where injunctive relief is sought against copyright infringement, a copier from a copier is in no better position than one who copies directly from author; if, however, action were one for damages, the result might be different. Perkins Marine Lamp & Hardware Corp. v. Long Island Marine Supply Corp., (DC-NY), 185 FSupp 353, 126 USPQ 169.

Preliminary injunction is proper remedy for copyright proprietor; thus, where proprietor is a "converter" which buys uncolored cloth upon which it prints copyrighted design which it sells to dressmakers, proprietor is entitled to preliminary injunction against dress manufacturer which obtains from an unnamed source fabrics bearing infringing design, which fabrics defendant makes into dresses which it sells; denial of injunction wou'd irreparably harm proprietor. Peter Pan Fabrics, Inc. v. Candy Frocks, Inc., (DC-NY), 187 FSupp 334, 126 USPQ 171.

In action for injunctive relief based on copyright infringement, lack of intent is not defense although it may bar award of damages. Massapequa Publishing Co. Inc. v. Observer, Inc., (DC-NY), — FSupp —, 126 USPQ 229.

Since defendant deliberately copied plaintiffs' copyrighted design and since copyright notice was adequate, plaintiffs are entitled to permanent injunction regardless of alleged lack of knowledge of copyright by defendant at time of initial infringement; after actual notice and after service of complaint, defendant must discontinue selling infringing copy regardless of its claim of innocence at the inception. Peter Pan Fabrics, Inc. v. Dixon Textile Corp., (DC-NY), 188 FSupp 235, 127 USPQ 329.

Detailed proof of likelihood of immediate irreparable harm is not required to justify granting of preliminary injunction in copyright infringement case; injunction is granted where plaintiff makes out prima facie case that it will suffer immediate substantial and irreparable injury unless afforded preliminary relief. Prestige Floral, Societe Anonyme v. California Artificial Flower Co. (Inc.), (DC-NY), 201 FSupp 287, 132 USPQ 350.

Preliminary injunction shou'd issue in copyright infringement case when plaintiff makes prima facie showing that copyright is valid and that defendant has infringed. Prestige Floral, Societe Anonyme v. California Artificial Flower Co. (Inc.), (DC-NY), 201 FSupp 287, 132 USPQ 350.

If plaintiff has valid copyrights which have not been lost by failure to affix proper copyright notice, it is entitled to preliminary injunction on finding that defendant has infringed without a detailed showing of irreparable injury. Royalty Designs, Inc. v. Thrifticheck Service Corp., (DC-NY), — FSupp —, 133 USPQ 148.

Plaintiff's original copyrighted textile designs were obtained at considerable expense. Plaintiff's business is that of a style leader for customers willing to pay for distinctive patterns. Defendant's offering of infringing patterns in garments at lower prices than similar garments made by plaintiff's customers from plaintiff's copyrighted reproductions robs plaintiff's goods of their distinctive appeal. Life of a new design is short, and unless preliminary injunction is issued, plaintiff will suffer substantial and irreparable injury from defendant's competition during a significant part of the period during which designs will have value. Defendant is preliminarily enjoined. Loomskill, Inc. v. Puritan Dress Co., Inc., (DC-NY), — FSupp —, 134 USPQ 20.

Injunction is unnecessary and is denied since copyright infringer has no intention to violate copyright in future. Phillips v. Constitution Publishing Co., (DC-Ga), 72 USPQ 69.

When prima facie case for copyright infringement has been made, plaintiffs are entitled to preliminary injunction without detailed showing of danger of irreparable harm; injunction is granted where defendants do not controvert allegation that market for copyrighted item is seasonal and likely to be exhausted in a few months. Rushton v. Vitale, (CA 2), 103 USPQ 158.

In connection with advertising of its products, plaintiff produces puzzle contests; copyrighted entry blank for contests states that entries will be disqualified for outside, professional, or compensated help; defendant, an expert in puzzle contests, distributes to those paying him a fee his solution to puzzle together with material copied from copyrighted blank; defendant is preliminarily enjoined from continuing such unethical and unlawful conduct; selling answers to puzzle contest is unlawful interference with plaintiff's business and copyright and induces spurious and fraudulent performances by prospective contestants. Proctor & Gamble Co. v. Moskowitz, (DC-NY), 127 USPQ 523.

Having made out prima facie showing of ownership and validity of copyright and of its infringement, copyright proprietor is entitled to preliminary injunction restraining infringement; proprietor is in midst of season for specific goods; to await trial would be to lose value of copyrighted design since, at conclusion of season, question of exclusivity of design would be virtually academic; infringer's activities have caused and are continuing to cause proprietor irreparable harm. Fabrex Corp. v. Scarves by Vera, Inc., (DC-NY), 129 USPQ 392.

34. Damages and profits.

In R. S. § 4965 which required forfeiture of one dollar for every infringing sheet found in the possession of the defendant, the words "found in his possession" did not refer to the finding of the jury, but the fact that prior to the time the cause of action accrued they were found in possession of the defendant. Thornton v. Schreiber, 124 US 612, 31 LEd 577, 8 SCR 618, rev'g (DC-Pa), 17 Fed 603.

Defendant is liable only for copies in his possession and not for every copy that he has published or procured to be published. Bolles v. Outing Co., 175 US 262, 44 LEd 156, 20 SCR 94, aff'g (CCA 2), 77 Fed 966, 46 LRA 712.

Substantial damages will not be allowed where it appears that the matters charged have not worked any prejudice to the complainant. Chase v. Sanborn, (CC-NH), FedCas 2,628, 4 Cliff 306.

In equity, when a decree for infringement of copyright is given, plaintiff is entitled to recover profits, but not damages for the injury sustained. Chapman v. Ferry, (CC-Ore), 12 Fed 693.

Where the infringement is slight and merely technical, the court may only require defendant to pay a small royalty to plaintiff. Myers v. Callaghan, (CC-Ill), 20 Fed 441.

A defendant who, with wanton or malicious disregard of the rights of the plaintiff, publishes a previously unpublished ode in violation of the common-law rights to such ode may be charged with exemplary damages. Press Pub. Co. v. Monroe, (CCA 2), 73 Fed 196, 51 LRA 353.

The usual practice in determining profits is to enter an interlocutory decree providing for an injunction and then send the matter to a master to take proof of damages and profits. Patterson v. J. S. Ogilvie Pub. Co., (CC-NY), 119 Fed 451.

Under former copyright laws, damages, as distinct from or additional to profits, could not be decreed in equity. Social Register Ass'n v. Murphy, (CC-RI), 129 Fed 148.

Where the value of a complainant's rights in its copyright have been so injured by defendant's piracy that injunctive relief will be of no avail, the plaintiff may have a decree for an accounting and costs. Hartford Printing Co. v. Hartford Directory & Publishing Co., (CC-Conn), 146 Fed 332.

Court of equity cannot compel complainant to take damages instead of profits. Dam v. Kirk La Shelle Co., (CCA 2), 175 Fed 902, 41 LRA(NS) 1002, 20 AnnCas 1173, aff'g 166 Fed 589.

Where complainant made a case which entitles him to an accounting, the court cannot substitute an arbitrary finding of damages and profits and fix the amount or impose penalties. The matter will be referred to a master. Huebsch v. Arthur H. Crist Co., (DC-NY), 209 Fed 885.

Plaintiff can take either damages and profits or the penalty imposed. Ginn & Co. v. Apollo Pub. Co., (DC-Pa), 228 Fed 214.

An award of $1 per copy as damages for copies of a song found in possession of the infringer was improper, and the award was reduced to the maximum profit which the owner of the copyright would have made on retail sale of such copies. Turner & Dahnken v. Crowley, (CCA 9), 252 Fed 749.

Although the defendant was entirely innocent in the publication of a copyrighted article and had taken it from a copyrighted magazine with permission of the magazine, when there is a technical violation of a copyright, some damages should be awarded. Insurance Press v. Ford Motor Co., (CCA 2), 255 Fed 896.

Damages and profits from copyright infringement are distinct items of recovery and are awarded on different legal principles. Sammons v. Colonial Press, Inc., (CCA 1), 126 F(2d) 341, 53 USPQ 71, mod'g 38 FSupp 649, 49 USPQ 350.

No evidence of actual damages having been given, if infringer made no profits for which it is accountable, assessment of statutory damages of $250 cannot be reviewed on appeal; but, if after further hearing on remand court finds infringer liable for profits, amount of profits will be measure of recovery and it will no longer be permissible to decree statutory damages. Sammons v. Colonial Press, Inc., (CCA 1), 126 F(2d) 341, 53 USPQ 71, mod'g 38 FSupp 649, 49 USPQ 350.

Since this section provides the method of finding damages when actual damages cannot be proven, the patent rule that the measure of damages in such cases is the established or reasonable royalty has no application to copyright cases. Widenski v. Shapiro, Bernstein & Co., Inc., (CCA 1), 147 F(2d) 909, 64 USPQ 448, aff'g 54 FSupp 780, 61 USPQ 91.

Damages can be recovered for injury to personal property (copyrighted motion picture) although market value cannot be shown. Universal Pictures Co., Inc. v. Harold Lloyd Corp., (CCA 9), 162 F(2d) 354, 73 USPQ 317.

Uncertainty as to amount and extent of damage does not deprive plaintiff of recovery. Universal Pictures Co., Inc. v. Harold Lloyd Corp., (CCA 9), 162 F(2d) 354, 73 USPQ 317.

In an accounting to determine damages evidence of efforts to settle are ordinarily inadmissible but where such an offer has been voluntarily placed in the record it will be considered in fixing amount of award. Sebring Pottery Co. v. Steubenville Pottery Co., (DC-Ohio), 9 FSupp 384.

It is cardinal principle in patent and copyright actions that plaintiff may recover only for actual profits from sales that he is able by proof to establish; similarly, infringer is accountable only for those profits which may be justly apportioned to sale of infringing products. Alfred Bell & Co., Ltd. v. Catalda Fine Arts, Inc., (DC-NY), 86 FSupp 399, 82 USPQ 273. Mf'd 191 F(2d) 99, 90 USPQ 153.

Even though one court has stated that reasonable royalty rule is not applicable to copyright litigation, construing "in lieu" clause of this section as its substitute, instant court is not persuaded that, in no event, will profits be relevant to issue of damages. Lundberg v. Welles, (DC-NY), 93 FSupp 359, 87 USPQ 26.

While defendant need not account for profits in action at law, it does not follow that inquiry into profits will be wholly irrelevant to assessment of damages. Lundberg v. Welles, (DC-NY), 93 FSupp 359, 87 USPQ 26.

In terms of remedy, actions for copyright infringement under subsec. (b) of this section and suits for statutory royalties under § 1(e) of this title are quite different; under the former, an accounting of profits based upon sales is available to aid determination of appropriate damages, while, under a compulsory license, royalty fixed by statute limits pecuniary remedy of copyright proprietor, irrespective of profits which may be involved. ABC Music Corp. v. Janov, (DC-Cal), 186 FSupp 443, 126 USPQ 429.

Interest on recoveries in copyright infringement suit is computed from date of master's report. Harris v. Miller, (DC-NY), 57 USPQ 190.

Liability for damages must rest upon substantial evidence of similarity between plaintiffs' literary property and defendants' moving picture. Golding v. R. K. O. Pictures, Inc., (Cal(2d series)), 208 Pac(2d) 1, 82 USPQ 136, aff'g (CalApp(2d series)), 193 Pac(2d) 153, 77 USPQ 415. Aff'd 35 Cal(2d series) 690, 221 Pac (2d) 95, 86 USPQ 537.

Owner of property is competent to testify as to its worth; rule permits owner of play to testify as to its value as basis for ascertainment of damages incurred by its infringement. Golding v. R. K. O. Pictures, Inc., (Cal(2d series)), 208 Pac(2d) 1, 82 USPQ 136, aff'g (CalApp(2d series)), 193 Pac(2d) 153, 77 USPQ 415. Aff'd 35 Cal(2d series) 690, 221 Pac(2d) 95, 86 USPQ 537.

Rules as to determination of damages for infringement of literary property are same as those which apply to any other form of personal property. Golding v. R. K. O. Pictures, Inc., (Cal(2d series)), 208 Pac(2d) 1, 82 USPQ 136, aff'g (CalApp(2d series)), 193 Pac(2d) 153, 77 USPQ 415. Aff'd 35 Cal(2d series) 690, 221 Pac(2d) 95, 86 USPQ 537.

Recovery in California state court upon contract implied in law not to use literary composition without paying for same must be limited solely to reasonable value of composition, or portion of it, which was used; there can be no recovery of damages for failure to give screen credit to plaintiff. Weitzenkorn v. Lesser, 40 Cal(2d series) 778, 256 Pac(2d) 947, 97 USPQ 545.

Reviews of play by dramatic critics are no evidence as to play's value or of damages suffered by its infringement. Golding v. RKO Radio Pictures, Inc., (CalApp(2d series)), 193 Pac(2d) 153, 77 USPQ 415. Aff'd (Cal(2d series)), 208 Pac(2d) 1, 82 USPQ 136, which was aff'd 35 Cal(2d series) 690, 221 Pac(2d) 95, 86 USPQ 537.

To constitute invasion of author's rights in unpublished play, it is not necessary that whole play be copied, or even large portion of it. Golding v. RKO Radio Pictures, Inc., (Cal App(2d series)), 193 Pac(2d) 153, 77 USPQ 415. Aff'd (Cal(2d series)), 208 Pac(2d) 1, 82 USPQ 136, which was aff'd 35 Cal(2d series) 690, 221 Pac(2d) 95, 86 USPQ 537.

The unauthorized use of the literary production of another furnishes no ground for the recovery of damages, except through the federal copyright laws. State v. State Journal Co., 75

Neb 275, 106 NW 434, 9 LRA(NS) 174, 13 AnnCas 254.

Although defendants are enjoined from using book title, plaintiff is not entitled to receive profits from book merely because title, which had acquired no secondary significance, had been improperly appropriated by defendants. Biltmore Publishing Co., Inc. v. Grayson Publishing Corp., 272 AppDiv 504, 71 NYS(2d) 337, 74 USPQ 241, rev'g (Misc), 57 NYS(2d) 192, 66 USPQ 273.

35. —Innocent infringer.

In a suit against an innocent infringer who has been misled by the omission of copyright notice, the complainant is not entitled to recover damages in view of § 21, but may recover all the profits gained from the infringement. Strauss v. Penn Printing & Publishing Co., (DC-Pa), 220 Fed 977.

The plaintiff has a right to damages and an accounting for profits under the copyright law, regardless of the innocence of the defendant. Haas v. Leo Feist, Inc., (DC-NY), 234 Fed 105.

In awarding damages allowed by this section in lieu of actual damages for infringement of a map copyright, by a newspaper publisher acting in good faith, the court may treat publication in several editions of the newspaper as a single infringement. Sauer v. Detroit Times, (DC-Mich), 247 Fed 687.

Although the defendant was an innocent infringer of the copyright, and no damage is shown to have resulted to the plaintiff, the defendant must be assessed the minimum damages as provided in this section. Altman v. New Haven Union Co., (DC-Conn), 254 Fed 113.

Where the defendant had obtained an article from a copyrighted magazine with permission of the magazine, and without knowledge that it was otherwise copyrighted, and printed it in a booklet which he distributed free to owners of automobiles, the plaintiff was awarded the minimum amount of $250. Insurance Press v. Ford Motor Co., (CCA 2), 255 Fed 896.

Where prints of copyright owner lacked notice by accident or mistake and defendant stopped infringing on actual notice, he is innocent infringer and not responsible for damages for prior infringement. Smith v. Wilkinson, (CCA 1), 97 F(2d) 506, 38 USPQ 1, aff'g 19 FSupp 841, 35 USPQ 113.

Where defendants continued after notice from plaintiff's attorney but by advice of their own attorney that their activities would not constitute infringement, they should not be severely penalized, especially where venture has not been successful and injunction and destruction of books will entail further loss. National Geographic Soc. v. Classified Geographic, Inc., (DC-Mass), 27 FSupp 655, 41 USPQ 719.

Lack of intention to infringe where there was due notice of copyright did not release from liability. Advertisers Exchange, Inc. v. Laufe, (DC-Pa), 29 FSupp 1, 38 USPQ 93.

Owner of theatre exhibiting motion picture which infringes copyright is innocent infringer and may deduct from gross receipts what it paid in federal income taxes on profits from exhibition, investment, interest, and depreciation. Sheldon v. Moredall Realty Corp., (DC-NY), 29 FSupp 729, 43 USPQ 81.

Lack of knowledge of copyright infringement does not relieve defendants of liability; however, their infringement consisted of use of infringing advertisement under copyright issued to plagiarist which appeared valid on its face; there must be some point at which innocent infringer should be protected from liability other than accounting of profits which he would not have made but for use of copyrighted matter; also, he should not be liable for damages realized by coinfringer; therefore, there being no proof that defendants profited from infringement, and it not being shown that plaintiff sustained actual damages except for commission which he, rather than plagiarist, would have received, no damages were assessed against defendants except on defendant who used infringing material a second time after notice of infringement. Gordon v. Weir, (DC-Mich), 111 FSupp 117, 97 USPQ 387. Aff'd 216 F(2d) 508, 104 USPQ 40.

Defense of innocence of ignorance of copyright applies only insofar as it may be relevant to question of damages assessed against infringer. Peter Pan Fabrics, Inc. v. Dixon Textile Corp., (DC-NY); 188 FSupp 235, 127 USPQ 329.

Where defendants are conscious and deliberate infringers, credits for income tax payments are refused. Harris v. Miller, (DC-NY), 57 USPQ 103.

One who markets infringing figurines made by another infringes copyright irrespective of innocence of infringement and is liable for damages therefor. McCulloch v. Zapun Ceramics, Inc., (DC-NY), 97 USPQ 12.

36. —Damages to copyright proprietor.

Diminution of plaintiff's sales up to time of suit may be considered in measuring damages in absence of proof of amount of sales by infringer. Chils v. Gronlund, (CC-NY), 41 Fed 145.

In an action for damages for infringement of a copyright, where the plaintiff did not distribute, or attempt to distribute or sell a single copy after publication of the infringing work in a newspaper, a court is unable to determine what damage resulted to the plaintiff from such publication. D'Ole v. Kansas City Star Co., (CC-Mo), 94 Fed 840.

Lost profits to complainant may be assessed as damages even though infringer derived no profit from sale of infringing copies. Gross v. Van Dyk Gravure Co., (CCA 2), 230 Fed 412.

For infringement of the name alone of a copyrighted work, preventing the author from exhibiting the work as a motion-picture scenario, the sale value of such scenario is the measure of damages. Paramore v. Mack Sennett, Inc., (DC-Cal), 9 F(2d) 66.

Infringer's profits may bear no relation to, and are wholly unreliable as indication of, plaintiff's damages, that is the profits which he would have made but for infringement. Sammons v. Colonial Press, Inc., (CCA 1), 126 F(2d) 341, 53 USPQ 71, mod'g 38 FSupp 649, 49 USPQ 350.

Measure of damages is profits which plaintiffs would have made on sales of their copyrighted book had not infringing book competed. Sammons v. Colonial Press, Inc., (CCA 1), 126 F(2d) 341, 53 USPQ 71, mod'g 38 FSupp 649, 49 USPQ 350.

Even if plaintiff's biography was not a success and has long been out of print and even if there is no evidence that defendants gained anything from using infringing material in their novel and that plaintiff suffered actual damage, court is justified in awarding plaintiff damages and attorney's fees. Toksvig v. Bruce Publishing Co., (CA 7), 181 F(2d) 664, 85 USPQ 339.

Deliberate infringer (distributor of motion picture) should not be able to say that screen play common-law copyright was worthless because infringer did not make expenses on the infringement, in the face of its payment to producer of amount in excess of amount as security for which author retained rights in screen play; infringer cannot cast on holder of rights the burden of unscrambling elements of value in picture, when it deliberately infringed with notice of rights in it held as security; author may recover security value placed upon play. Szekely v. Eagle Lion Films, Inc., (CA 2), 242 F(2d) 266, 113 USPQ 98, aff'g 140 FSupp 843, 109 USPQ 348.

Rule of de minimis non curat lex does not apply although defendant used only small amount of copyrighted material, since portion taken was important. Advertisers Exchange Inc. v. Hinkley, (DC-Mo), 101 FSupp 801, 92 USPQ 313. Aff'd 199 F(2d) 313, 95 USPQ 124.

Where contract gave defendant, proprietor of a grocery store, exclusive right to use plaintiff's copyrighted advertisements in defendant's community, and defendant continued to use advertisements after termination of contract, plaintiff is not entitled to receive $1 for each copy of newspaper containing infringement, or nominal damages of $250, but only amount of sale price of subscription during period of infringement. Advertisers Exchange Inc. v. Hinkley, (DC-Mo), 101 FSupp 801, 92 USPQ 313. Aff'd 199 F(2d) 313, 95 USPQ 124.

Where defendant plagiarizes plaintiff's literary property by distribution of motion picture incorporating plaintiff's motion-picture script, plaintiff is entitled to damages based upon special value of script to him; such value is value of security interest which he had in manuscript inasmuch as contract between plaintiff and motion-picture producer provided that plaintiff would retain title to script as security for payment of specific sum; defendant is liable for such sum; plaintiff may not base damages upon what third party might have paid for script, since producer was only market available to him, nor may plaintiff recover punitive damages since plaintiff recognized that his best chance of securing payment of amount due from producer was to allow production and distribution of picture. Szekely v. Eagle Lion Films, Inc., (DC-NY), 140 FSupp 843, 109 USPQ 348. Aff'd 242 F(2d) 266, 113 USPQ 98.

It makes little difference, in assessing damages from defendant's showing of plaintiff's copyrighted motion picture, whether or not each showing was separate infringement; total value of picture did not exceed $3,000; hence, sum of the parts (separate showings) cannot exceed the whole; damages cannot exceed $3,000. Pickford Corp. v. DeLuxe Laboratories, Inc., (DC-Cal), 169 FSupp 118, 120 USPQ 521.

Although acts of copyright infringement, for which plaintiff is awarded damages, also constitute acts of unfair competition, plaintiff is not entitled to recover damages for acts of unfair competition. Dorchester Music Corp. v. National Broadcasting Co., (DC-Cal), 171 FSupp 580, 120 USPQ 429.

Damages for copyright infringement are not merely incidental to equitable relief, since right to damages is provided in this section as distinct and separate remedy from injunctive relief. Damages are not limited to such damages as court might award as incident to injunctive relief, but include also statutory damages, which are peculiar to copyright cases; court is empowered to award such damages only because of statute, and not by virtue of general equity powers. Chappell & Co., Inc. v. Cavalier Cafe, Inc., (DC-Mass), 13 FedRDec 321, 95 USPQ 243.

Recovery of damages on account of copyright infringement by manufacturer of infringing figurines does not bar recovery of damages from one who purchases figurines from manufacturer and resells them; damages assessed against manufacturer were assessed as result of manufacturer's infringement and not infringement of purchaser from manufacturer. McCulloch v. Zapun Ceramics, Inc., (DC-NY), 97 USPQ 12.

37. —Profits of infringer—Accounting.

The right to an account of profits is incident to the right to an injunction in copyright cases. Stevens v. Gladding, 59 US(17 How) 447, 15 LEd 155, rev'g (CC-RI), FedCas 13,400; Belford v. Scribner, 144 US 488, 36 LEd 514, 12 SCR 734, aff'g (CC-Ill), 50 Fed 473; Stevens v. Cady, (CC-RI), FedCas 13,396, 2 Curt 200; Fishel v. Lueckel, (CC-NY), 53 Fed 499; Falk v. Gast Lithograph & Engraving Co., (CCA 2), 54 Fed 890, aff'g 48 Fed 262; McCaleb v. Fox Film Corp., (CCA 5), 299 Fed 48.

Under R. S. § 4965 of the old copyright law which made both the printer and the publisher liable for infringement, it was proper to decree that the printer should account to the owner of the infringed copyright, though no profits had been realized by the printer from the sale of the infringing books, it being assumed that the printer made a profit on the printing and binding of the infringing books. Belford, Clarke & Co. v. Scribner, 144 US 488, 36 LEd 514, 12 SCR 734, aff'g (CC-Ill), 50 Fed 473.

In passing Copyright Act apparent intention of Congress was to assimilate remedy with respect to recovery of profits to that already recognized in patent cases. Sheldon v. Metro-Goldwyn Pictures Corp., 309 US 390, 84 LEd 825, 60 SCR 681, 44 USPQ 607, aff'g (CCA 2),

106 F(2d) 45, 42 USPQ 540, which rev'd 26 FSupp 134, 40 USPQ 238.

Prior to Copyright Act of 1909 there had been no statutory provision for recovery of profits but recovery had been allowed in equity as incident to decree for injunction; relief had been given in accordance with principles governing equity jurisdiction, not to inflict punishment but to prevent unjust enrichment. Sheldon v. Metro-Goldwyn Pictures Corp., 309 US 390, 84 LEd 825, 60 SCR 681, 44 USPQ 607, aff'g (CCA 2), 106 F(2d) 45, 42 USPQ 540, which rev'd 26 FSupp 134, 40 USPQ 238.

Provision in section for recovery of "all" profits is qualified by words "which the infringer shall have made from such infringement" and is cognate to that for the recovery of "such damages as the copyright proprietor may have suffered due to the infringement"; purpose is to provide just compensation for wrong, not to impose penalty by giving to copyright proprietor profits not attributable to infringement. Sheldon v. Metro-Goldwyn Pictures Corp., 309 US 390, 84 LEd 825, 60 SCR 681, 44 USPQ 607, aff'g (CCA 2), 106 F(2d) 45, 42 USPQ 540, which rev'd 26 FSupp 134, 40 USPQ 238.

Fact that defendants are guilty of deliberate plagiarism is no ground for saying that in awarding profits to copyright proprietor as means of compensation, court may make award of profits not shown to be due to infringement. Sheldon v. Metro-Goldwyn Pictures Corp., 309 US 390, 84 LEd 825, 60 SCR 681, 44 USPQ 607, aff'g (CCA 2), 106 F(2d) 45, 42 USPQ 540, which rev'd 26 FSupp 134, 40 USPQ 238.

By coming forward with undisputed admission of its profit from copyright infringement, defendant cannot tie hands of court and limit recovery to that amount. F. W. Woolworth Co. v. Contemporary Arts, Inc., 344 US 228, 97 LEd 276, 73 SCR 222, 95 USPQ 396, aff'g (CA 5), 193 F(2d) 162, 92 USPQ 4, which aff'd 93 FSupp 739, 86 USPQ 476.

Gross profits are not what copyright owner is entitled to recover from infringer, but only such profits as remain after defendant reduces them by proof of allowable elements of costs. F. W. Woolworth Co. v. Contemporary Arts, Inc., 344 US 228, 97 LEd 276, 73 SCR 222, 95 USPQ 396, aff'g (CA 5), 193 F(2d) 162, 92 USPQ 4, which aff'd 93 FSupp 739, 86 USPQ 476.

"Profits" did not have so restricted meaning as to exclude commissions received from proceeds of sales of property of the complainant. Stearns v. Page, (CC-Maine), FedCas 13,339, 1 Story 204. Aff'd 48 US(7 How) 819, 12 LEd 928.

Courts may give no decree for profits if the bill contain neither a prayer for an accounting, nor for general relief. Stevens v. Cady, (CC-RI), FedCas 13,395, 2 Curt 200.

Evidence showing sales and exchanges of infringing books, but failing to show the sum defendant received from such sales and exchanges, was insufficient to prove any profits. Gilmore v. Anderson, (CC-NY), 42 Fed 267.

Plaintiff is entitled to all profits accruing from unlawful dramatization of story. Dam v. Kirk La Shelle Co., (CCA 2), 175 Fed 902, 41 LRA(NS) 1002, 20 AnnCas 1173, aff'g 166 Fed 589.

Where defendant is found guilty of infringement, complainant is entitled to take an account of profits gained from sale of the infringing book, and to full costs and reasonable attorney's fees. Huebsch v. Arthur H. Crist Co., (DC-NY), 209 Fed 885.

Equity will control its peculiar remedy of an accounting of profits according to its own sense of justice. Haas v. Leo Feist, Inc., (DC-NY), 234 Fed 105.

Fact that publisher of many songs operated at over-all loss gives it no immunity from accounting for profits from infringement of common-law copyright of plaintiff's song merely because they were less than enough to make entire business profitable; if publisher lost less because of infringement, to that extent infringement gave it profit for which it must account. Wilkie v. Santly Bros., Inc., (CCA 2), 139 F(2d) 264, 60 USPQ 46.

Damages alone are awarded where copyright infringer's profits are less than damages sustained by plaintiff. Universal Pictures Co., Inc. v. Harold Lloyd Corp., (CCA 9), 162 F(2d) 354, 73 USPQ 317.

Special master concluding defendant had filed a false account should have so certified to the court asking that defendant be cited for contempt, or that the question of instituting criminal proceedings against him be considered. Fleischer Studios, Inc. v. Ralph A. Freundlich, Inc., (DC-NY), 14 FSupp 401, 30 USPQ 125.

Composer of infringing music is chargeable with profits in amount of royalties received from infringing song. Wilkie v. Santly Bros., Inc., (DC-NY), 36 FSupp 574, 47 USPQ 380.

Nominal recovery of statutory minimum of $250 will not compensate plaintiff, in view of defendants' probable profits from infringement, so accounting is ordered. Kahn v. Leo Feist, Inc., (DC-NY), 70 FSupp 450, 73 USPQ 104. Aff'd 165 F(2d) 188, 76 USPQ 27.

Notwithstanding that Copyright Act provides three remedies for infringement, injunction, damages, and profits, and makes no differentiation as to nature of action for each, no case has come to court's attention in which accounting of profits, as such, was considered to be actionable at law in the sense that there was a right to trial by jury; nevertheless, issue is not foreclosed. Lundberg v. Welles, (DC-NY), 93 FSupp 359, 87 USPQ 26.

Director and sole stockholder of defendant corporation is individually liable, in addition to corporation, for copyright and trade-mark infringement and unfair competition if, in addition to corporate capacity, she acted in individual capacity and for her personal gain in authorizing and personally participating in infringing acts. Conde Nast Publications, Inc. v. Vogue School of Fashion Modelling, Inc., (DC-NY), 105 FSupp 325, 94 USPQ 101.

Defendant having failed to disclose amount of sales resulting from publication of infringing contract advertisement, plaintiff is awarded as damages a sum based on sales made and commissions paid by defendant to plaintiff in prior contest conducted under valid contract whereby defendant used plaintiff's copyrighted advertisement. Gordon v. Weir, (DC-Mich), 111 FSupp 117, 97 USPQ 387. Aff'd 216 F(2d) 508, 104 USPQ 40.

Sheldon v. Metro-Goldwyn Pictures Corp., 309 US 390, 84 LEd 825, 60 SCR 681, 44 USPQ 607, expressed view that Congress intended application of same principles in copyright as in patent cases with respect to recovery of profits; at least by dicta it approved interpretation placed by courts on language that "patent owner may have such damages as well as profits which the infringer shall have made" to mean that patent owner, and hence copyright owner, might have one or the other, whichever was greater. Gordon v. Weir, (DC-Mich), 111 FSupp 117, 97 USPQ 387. Aff'd 216 F(2d) 508, 104 USPQ 40.

Ordinarily, law allows victim of infringement upon his literary rights to recover profits made by infringer or damages suffered by himself; profits customarily are determined upon an accounting; that defendant may not have made profits is not conclusive on issue of damages, since right to damages is alternative to right to recover infringer's profits. Szekely v. Eagle Lion Films, Inc., (DC-NY), 140 FSupp 843, 109 USPQ 348. Aff'd 242 F(2d) 266, 113 USPQ 98.

Although only 35% of copyright infringer's book contains plagiarized material, he is liable for his entire profits from book since there is no evidence as to how much of profits resulted from plagiarism; for aught that appears the legitimate 65% of book may have been without influence in the sales. Orgel v. Clark Boardman Co. Ltd., (DC-NY), — FSupp —, 128 USPQ 531. Mf'd 301 F(2d) 119, 133 USPQ 94.

Inasmuch as only 35% of copyright infringer's book contains plagiarized material, copyright proprietor is not entitled to damages on basis that every sale of infringer's book deprived proprietor of sale of his book since it cannot be presumed that noninfringing 65% of infringer's book was not a sales factor. Orgel v. Clark Boardman Co. Ltd., (DC-NY), — FSupp —, 128 USPQ 531. Mf'd 301 F(2d) 119, 133 USPQ 94.

Successful plaintiff in copyright infringement action can recover his damages or defendant's profits. Orgel v. Clark Boardman Co. Ltd., (DC-NY), — FSupp —, 128 USPQ 531. Mf'd 301 F(2d) 119, 133 USPQ 94.

Question as to defendant's actual knowledge of plaintiffs' copyright does not bear on issue of liability but goes only to issue of amount of damages. Peter Pan Fabrics, Inc. v. Puritan Dress Co., Inc., (DC-NY), — FSupp —, 133 USPQ 678.

Although defendants must bare any inaccuracies arising out of accounting because they are wrongdoers, it is not equitable to deprive them arbitrarily of money rightly theirs. Pallma v. Fox, (DC-NY), 74 USPQ 130.

Infringer sold infringing books for $10,600, but has submitted no evidence as to cost of publication, so plaintiff recovers $10,600 as infringer's profits, and in addition recovers $250 damages for infringement. Whitman Publishing Co. v. Writesel, (DC-Ohio), 83 USPQ 535.

38. ——Determination of profits.

While the court will not presume that all the money received by a piratical publisher on the sale of his books is profit, still, as the proof as to cost of producing the work is wholly in the control of the defendants, the complainant makes a prima facie case of right to recover by showing the selling price, and the usual manufacturers' cost. Myers v. Callaghan, (CC-Ill), 24 Fed 636. Mf'd 128 US 617, 32 LEd 547, 9 SCR 177.

The rule that defendant is to account for every copy of his book sold as if it had been a copy of complainant's book, and to pay complainant the profit which the latter would have received from the sale of so many additional copies was inapplicable, and damages were assessed on basis of defendant's profits from sale of his infringing book. Scribner v. Clark, (CC-Ill), 50 Fed 473. Aff'd 144 US 488, 36 LEd 514, 12 SCR 734.

Amounts received from advertisers should be included in accounting for profits on an infringing directory. Hartford Printing Co. v. Hartford Directory & Printing Co., (CC-Conn), 148 Fed 470.

In determining the profits of a play, each season is to be taken as a unit, and losses sustained in one season cannot be deducted from the earnings of the next season. Dam v. Kirk La Shelle Co., (CC-NY), 189 Fed 842.

In accounting for infringement by motion picture, profits made from exhibiting by completely controlled subsidiaries are included; subsidiary's profits are prorated in proportion of its shares held by defendant. Sheldon v. Metro-Goldwyn Pictures Corp., (CCA 2), 106 F(2d) 45, 42 USPQ 540, rev'g 26 FSupp 134, 40 USPQ 238. Aff'd 309 US 390, 84 LEd 825, 60 SCR 681, 44 USPQ 607.

Defendant has the burden of proving every element of cost, a blanket undifferentiated item of overhead is insufficient. Sammons v. Colonial Press, Inc., (CCA 1), 126 F(2d) 341, 53 USPQ 71, mod'g 38 FSupp 649, 49 USPQ 350.

Infringer of common-law copyright obtained substantial sum from infringement and court refuses to accept defendant's theory as to allocation of overhead as this would result in a loss sufficiently large to absorb all the profits; defendant is seeking to charge income from infringement with general business losses, but it is well settled that indirect financial benefit to infringer should be prevented, although it does not invariably follow that victorious party in infringement suit must recover from infringer on an accounting. Wilkie v. Santly Bros., Inc., (DC-NY), 36 FSupp 574, 47 USPQ 380.

Fractional years 1943 and 1947 are used for purpose of computing allocations of allowable expense to gross profits where infringer's order for infringements was placed in May, 1943, and sales of infringements commenced in October, 1943, and ended in October, 1947; portions of 1943 and 1947 unrelated to accounting are not included. Alfred Bell & Co., Ltd. v. Catalda Fine Arts, Inc., (DC-NY), 86 FSupp 399, 82 USPQ 273. Mf'd 191 F(2d) 99, 90 USPQ 153.

In accounting for profits, court is not interested in what parties would have priced infringements at had they been able to foresee infringement suit; defendant is limited to actual sales price as of time of sales contract just as plaintiff is restricted in recovery to actual profits. Alfred Bell & Co., Ltd. v. Catalda Fine Arts, Inc., (DC-NY), 86 FSupp 399, 82 USPQ 273. Mf'd 191 F(2d) 99, 90 USPQ 153.

Plaintiff can recover profits only on infringements actually sold by defendant; likewise, defendant is limited to deductions for cost of infringements sold; defendant may not deduct, from profits of infringements sold, cost of infringements not sold. Alfred Bell & Co., Ltd. v. Catalda Fine Arts, Inc., (DC-NY)*, 86 FSupp 399, 82 USPQ 273. Mf'd 191 F(2d) 99, 90 USPQ 153.

Interest is allowed at 6% on unpaid royalties admitted to be due on account of sale of copyrighted music. Pallma v. Fox, (DC-NY), 87 USPQ 395.

In suit for plagiarism, plaintiff's testimony that value of his format for radio program was $100,000 and that it had no value after defendants' use thereof, was sufficient to support award of $25,000 damages. Kovacs v. Mutual Broadcasting System, Inc., 99 CalApp(2d series) 56, 221 Pac(2d) 108, 86 USPQ 547.

One infringer is not liable for the profits which other infringers derive from the same infringement. Washingtonian Pub. Co., Inc. v. Pearson, 78 AppDC 287, 140 F(2d) 465, 60 USPQ 224, aff'g 56 USPQ 23.

39. ————Deductions allowable.

Cost of stereotyping is not deductible as a credit in cost of manufacture. Callaghan v. Myers, 128 US 617, 32 LEd 547, 9 SCR 177, mod'g (CC-Ill), 24 Fed 636.

In computing damages defendants are not entitled to credit for salaries paid for services during the period of infringement. Callaghan v. Myers, 128 US 617, 32 LEd 547, 9 SCR 177, mod'g (CC-Ill), 24 Fed 636.

In fixing damages, cost of producing unsold copies is not deductible. Callaghan v. Myers, 128 US 617, 32 LEd 547, 9 SCR 177, mod'g (CC-Ill), 24 Fed 636.

Profits made on infringement are arrived at by deducting actual and legitimate manufacturing cost from selling price. Callaghan v. Myers, 128 US 617, 32 LEd 547, 9 SCR 177, mod'g (CC-Ill), 24 Fed 636.

Salaries of members of firm or editors are not deductible as a credit. Callaghan v. Myers, 128 US 617, 32 LEd 547, 9 SCR 177, mod'g (CC-Ill), 24 Fed 636.

In copyright cases where the purpose is to find the amount of profits or damages, the plaintiff may show under subsec. (b) of this section only the receipts from the infringing sales and put upon the defendant the burden of proving the cost of production. Ginn & Co. v. Apollo Pub. Co., (DC-Pa), 228 Fed 214.

Defendant motion-picture producer, on accounting for copyright infringement, may deduct dues payable to Motion Picture Producers and Distributors Association. Sheldon v. Metro-Goldwyn Pictures Corp., (CCA 2), 106 F(2d) 45, 42 USPQ 540, rev'g 26 FSupp 134, 40 USPQ

238. Aff'd 309 US 390, 84 LEd 825, 60 SCR 681, 44 USPQ 607.

Defendants who deliberately lifted play, in apportioning profits, can be credited only with such factors as they bought and paid for, actors, scenery, producers, directors, and general overhead. Sheldon v. Metro-Goldwyn Pictures Corp., (CCA 2), 106 F(2d) 45, 42 USPQ 540, rev'g 26 FSupp 134, 40 USPQ 238. Aff'd 309 US 390, 84 LEd 825, 60 SCR 681, 44 USPQ 607.

In accounting for infringement by motion picture, interest as part of defendant's overhead is calculated as a deduction from gross profits on basis of appraising realty and taking personalty at cost less depreciation, and assuming use of that proportion of whole plant which cost of production of specific picture bore to cost of all pictures made that year. Sheldon v. Metro-Goldwyn Pictures Corp., (CCA 2), 106 F(2d) 45, 42 USPQ 540, rev'g 26 FSupp 134, 40 USPQ 238. Aff'd 309 US 390, 84 LEd 825, 60 SCR 681, 44 USPQ 607.

In accounting for infringement by motion picture, where defendant made many other pictures and had directors, producers, stars, and writers on yearly salaries, allowance for "idle time" between making pictures may be deducted from gross profits. Sheldon v. Metro-Goldwyn Pictures Corp., (CCA 2), 106 F(2d) 45, 42 USPQ 540, rev'g 26 FSupp 134, 40 USPQ 238. Aff'd 309 US 390, 84 LEd 825, 60 SCR 681, 44 USPQ 607.

In accounting for infringement by motion picture in which profits from foreign showing are allowed, the proportion of overhead to be deducted for distribution is fixed on basis of total number of pictures of various kinds exported. Sheldon v. Metro-Goldwyn Pictures Corp., (CCA 2), 106 F(2d) 45, 42 USPQ 540, rev'g 26 FSupp 134, 40 USPQ 238. Aff'd 309 US 390, 84 LEd 825, 60 SCR 681, 44 USPQ 607.

In accounting for infringement by motion picture, losses from exhibiting infringing picture in certain theaters may not be deducted from gross profits where receipts did not equal cost of maintenance during showing in United States, but in foreign countries plaintiff cannot select profitable exhibitions and discard those resulting in a loss. Sheldon v. Metro-Goldwyn Pictures Corp., (CCA 2), 106 F(2d) 45, 42 USPQ 540, rev'g 26 FSupp 134, 40 USPQ 238. Aff'd 309 US 390, 84 LEd 825, 60 SCR 681, 44 USPQ 607.

In accounting for infringement by motion picture, overhead which does not assist in production of infringement should not be credited to the infringer but that which does should be and where picture was one of over forty made by defendants, using same staff and organization, they were as much condition on production of infringing picture as scenery or play. Sheldon v. Metro-Goldwyn Pictures Corp., (CCA 2), 106 F(2d) 45, 42 USPQ 540, rev'g 26 FSupp 134, 40 USPQ 238. Aff'd 309 US 390, 84 LEd 825, 60 SCR 681, 44 USPQ 607.

In accounting for infringement by motion picture where defendant made many other pictures, cost of distribution to be deducted from gross profits is fixed by dividing entire cost of distribution of all pictures by number of pictures. Sheldon v. Metro-Goldwyn Pictures Corp., (CCA 2), 106 F(2d) 45, 42 USPQ 540, rev'g 26 FSupp 134, 40 USPQ 238. Aff'd 309 US 390, 84 LEd 825, 60 SCR 681, 44 USPQ 607.

In accounting for infringement by motion picture where defendant made many other pictures, defendant may deduct from gross profit of specific picture an allowance for continuities scrapped and completed pictures never exhibited. Sheldon v. Metro-Goldwyn Pictures Corp., (CCA 2), 106 F(2d) 45, 42 USPQ 540, rev'g 26 FSupp 134, 40 USPQ 238. Aff'd 309 US 390, 84 LEd 825, 60 SCR 681, 44 USPQ 607.

In accounting for infringement by motion picture where defendant made many other pictures, it cannot deduct from gross profit interest on loans made it by parent company in form of open account going back twelve years, especially when interest is allowed on plant investment and working capital. Sheldon v. Metro-Goldwyn Pictures Corp., (CCA 2), 106 F(2d) 45, 42 USPQ 540, rev'g 26 FSupp 134, 40 USPQ 238. Aff'd 309 US 390, 84 LEd 825, 60 SCR 681, 44 USPQ 607.

In accounting for infringement by motion picture where defendant made many other pictures, overhead and expenses to be deducted from gross profits are fixed as portion of total overhead allocated according to cost of production rather than number of pictures, but amount set aside as studio overhead representing estimated loss on existing stock of "continuities" could not be deducted. Sheldon v. Metro-Goldwyn Pictures Corp., (CCA 2), 106 F(2d) 45, 42 USPQ 540, rev'g 26 FSupp 134, 40 USPQ 238. Aff'd 309 US 390, 84 LEd 825, 60 SCR 681, 44 USPQ 607.

Income tax paid may be deducted from gross profits if defendants are not deliberate plagiarists but when they are deliberate plagiarists. Sheldon v. Metro-Goldwyn Pictures Corp., (CCA 2), 106 F(2d) 45, 42 USPQ 540, rev'g 26 FSupp 134, 40 USPQ 238. Aff'd 309 US 390, 84 LEd 825, 60 SCR 681, 44 USPQ 607.

Infringing defendants under contract paid portion of profits to partnership made up of officers of defendants; this may be deducted by defendants even if plaintiff could recover them from the partners personally. Sheldon v. Metro-Goldwyn Pictures Corp., (CCA 2), 106 F(2d) 45, 42 USPQ 540, rev'g 26 FSupp 134, 40 USPQ 238. Aff'd 309 US 390, 84 LEd 825, 60 SCR 681, 44 USPQ 607.

Deduction is properly made of proper proportion of general overhead expenses which assisted in production of copyright infringement, at least where infringement was not conscious and deliberate. Sammons v. Colonial Press, Inc., (CCA 1), 126 F(2d) 341, 53 USPQ 71, mod'g 38 FSupp 649, 49 USPQ 350.

Only if evidence shows that amount owing from infringing publisher to infringing printer is uncollectible will printer be entitled to deduction therefor in computing its net profits. Sammons v. Colonial Press, Inc., (CCA 1), 126 F(2d) 341, 53 USPQ 71, mod'g 38 FSupp 649, 49 USPQ 350.

In action for infringement of common-law copyright on song, expenses of defendant, music publisher, for arrangements and costs of signs are not allowed as part of general overhead deductions. Wilkie v. Santly Bros., Inc., (DC-NY), 36 FSupp 574, 47 USPQ 380.

Infringer, music publisher, advanced sum to codefendant, composer of infringing music, as fee for counsel in defending infringement suit; this item is not proper deduction. Wilkie v. Santly Bros., Inc., (DC-NY), 36 FSupp 574, 47 USPQ 380.

Infringer of common-law copyright was not obliged to segregate such portion of overhead expenses as applied directly to infringing song as defendant was not willful infringer and it was contrary to trade practice to segregate portion of expenses attributable to infringing song; defendant is entitled to some proper credit for overhead expenses which were not increased as well as for those which were increased by publication and distribution of infringing song. Wilkie v. Santly Bros., Inc., (DC-NY), 36 FSupp 574, 47 USPQ 380.

Payment to former employee in settlement of copyright infringer's obligations to him under salary contract was consideration for cancellation of ten-year contract which otherwise was valid and subsisting agreement; while payment covered only two months of accounting period, infringer is entitled to have credit in determining general overhead. Wilkie v. Santly Bros., Inc., (DC-NY), 36 FSupp 574, 47 USPQ 380.

Infringing author is entitled to deduct from his profits from sale of infringing books the amount paid to printer, postage for circulars, material purchased from others, and telephone, stationery, rent and clerk hire; defendant is not entitled to deduct compensation paid himself since he cannot profit from his wrong. Sammons v. Larkin, (DC-Mass), 38 FSupp 649, 49 USPQ 350. Mf'd 126 F(2d) 341, 53 USPQ 71.

Printer of infringing book is entitled to deduct from amount paid to it by author its direct cost for labor, its cost of materials and commission which it is obligated to pay to another for forwarding the job; deduction is also allowed of overhead expenses computed by determining percentage of its total expense for productive labor of year to total administrative expense for same year. Sammons v. Larkin, (DC-Mass), 38 FSupp 649, 49 USPQ 350. Mf'd 126 F(2d) 341, 53 USPQ 71.

Defendant having failed to carry burden of proof to establish right to deductions for certain expenditures, master need not employ method of allocation which he had accepted and applied to permissible categories of deductions that he found to be proved before him. Alfred Bell & Co., Ltd. v. Catalda Fine Arts, Inc., (DC-NY), 86 FSupp 399, 82 USPQ 273. Mf'd 191 F(2d) 99, 90 USPQ 153.

Defendant would not have been put to impossible and interminable procedure to prove items of cost; proof was available, but was not produced, so items are not allowed as deductions. Alfred Bell & Co., Ltd. v. Catalda Fine Arts, Inc., (DC-NY), 86 FSupp 399, 82 USPQ 273. Mf'd 191 F(2d) 99, 90 USPQ 153.

Even if purchaser were old customer, infringing seller is entitled to deduct some expense for selling and commercial overhead, including facilities, personnel engaged in selling and serving customers, and bookkeeping costs; there need be no showing that there was substantial sales effort involving solicitation of business; expenses assisted in producing of infringing profits and were legitimate part of general overhead of business; that purchaser initiated transaction is no basis for denial of deductions. Alfred Bell & Co., Ltd. v. Catalda Fine Arts, Inc., (DC-NY), 86 FSupp 399, 82 USPQ 273. Mf'd 191 F(2d) 99, 90 USPQ 153.

In accounting for profits from copyright infringement, infringers are entitled to deduct income taxes paid on profits, since copying was done under good faith claim that copyrights were invalid; disallowance of income tax deduction is severe additional penalty imposed only because of gravity of offense of pirating; however, income tax is not credited at highest rate paid, but, considering infringement as part of entire business, infringers are credited with proportional amount of tax paid at each tax rate. Alfred Bell & Co., Ltd. v. Catalda Fine Arts, Inc., (DC-NY), 86 FSupp 399, 82 USPQ 273. Mf'd 191 F(2d) 99, 90 USPQ 153.

In determining profits, infringer is refused deduction for cost of product sold and then returned as defective. Alfred Bell & Co., Ltd. v. Catalda Fine Arts, Inc., (DC-NY), 86 FSupp 399, 82 USPQ 273. Mf'd 191 F(2d) 99, 90 USPQ 153.

In determining whether infringer should be allowed deduction for income taxes paid on profits from infringement, courts distinguished between innocent infringer and deliberate, conscious wrongdoer. Alfred Bell & Co., Ltd. v. Catalda Fine Arts, Inc., (DC-NY), 86 FSupp 399, 82 USPQ 273. Mf'd 191 F(2d) 99, 90 USPQ 153.

Infringer's profits are generally determined by deduction from selling price of actual and legitimate manufacturing cost, but where there are no sales, there can be no profits, and there can be nothing to charge against such profits. Alfred Bell & Co., Ltd. v. Catalda Fine Arts, Inc., (DC-NY), 86 FSupp 399, 82 USPQ 273. Mf'd 191 F(2d) 99, 90 USPQ 153.

Rent is allowed as element of overhead although infringement did not result in increased payment of rent; test is not whether item was increased by infringement, but whether it assisted in production of infringing profits; rent is not refused on theory that infringer does not show that it rented space either in whole or in part in furtherance of infringing business. Alfred Bell & Co., Ltd. v. Catalda Fine Arts, Inc., (DC-NY), 86 FSupp 399, 82 USPQ 273. Mf'd 191 F(2d) 99, 90 USPQ 153.

Sales discounts, freight and cartage outward, salesmen's salaries and commissions, commissions to dealers, shipping, and packing are sales overhead expense properly deductible from gross profits. Alfred Bell & Co., Ltd. v. Catalda Fine Arts, Inc., (DC-NY), 86 FSupp 399, 82 USPQ 273. Mf'd 191 F(2d) 99, 90 USPQ 153.

Should infringer receive refund of income tax paid on infringing profits, plaintiff would be entitled to receive its proper proportion of refund computed on same basis as was employed to determine tax. Alfred Bell & Co., Ltd. v. Catalda Fine Arts, Inc., (DC-NY), 86 FSupp 399, 82 USPQ 273. Mf'd 191 F(2d) 99, 90 USPQ 153.

Fact that one man owns all stock of infringer corporation and directs its policies and affairs is factor which master may weigh with other evidence in determining extent to which corporation should be required to provide proof relating its claimed items of expense to infringing sales. Alfred Bell & Co., Ltd. v. Catalda Fine Arts, Inc., (DC-NY), 86 FSupp 399, 82 USPQ 273. Mf'd 191 F(2d) 99, 90 USPQ 153.

Producers of infringing play are given credit for royalties paid authors since authors and producers are not partners or coadventurers. Harris v. Miller, (DC-NY), 57 USPQ 103.

Where director of play is infringer no credit is given for his time. Harris v. Miller, (DC-NY), 57 USPQ 103.

40. ———Apportionment of profits.

Where the lawful cannot be separated from the unlawful parts of a book, the owner of the copyright is entitled to recover entire profits. Callaghan v. Myers, 128 US 617, 32 LEd 547, 9 SCR 177, mod'g (CC-Ill), 24 Fed 636; Belford, Clarke & Co. v. Scribner, 144 US 488, 36 LEd 514, 12 SCR 734, aff'g (CC-Ill), 50 Fed 473.

In apportioning profits, what is required is not mathematical exactness but only a reasonable approximation, which is matter of judgment, and testimony of those informed by observation and experience may be not only helpful but may be indispensable. Sheldon v. Metro-Goldwyn Pictures Corp., 309 US 390, 84 LEd 825, 60 SCR 681, 44 USPQ 607, aff'g (CCA 2), 106 F(2d) 45, 42 USPQ 540, which rev'd 26 FSupp 134, 40 USPQ 238.

In cases of copyright infringement there is nothing in Copyright Act which precludes application on same equitable principles of doctrine similar to doctrine of apportionment of profits in cases of patent infringement. Sheldon v. Metro-Goldwyn Pictures Corp., 309 US 390, 84 LEd 825, 60 SCR 681, 44 USPQ 607, aff'g (CCA 2), 106 F(2d) 45, 42 USPQ 540, which rev'd 26 FSupp 134, 40 USPQ 238.

Where it is clear that all profits are not due to use of copyrighted material, and evidence is sufficient to provide fair basis of division so as to give copyright proprietor all profits that can be deemed to have resulted from use of what belonged to him; Copyright Act and decisions of Supreme Court leave matter to appropriate exercise of equity jurisdiction on accounting. Sheldon v. Metro-Goldwyn Pictures Corp., 309 US 390, 84 LEd 825, 60 SCR 681, 44 USPQ 607, aff'g (CCA 2), 106 F(2d) 45, 42 USPQ 540, which rev'd 26 FSupp 134, 40 USPQ 238.

Where it is impossible to separate defendant's profits on published matter to which copyright does not extend from profits on matter covered by copyright, defendant, being responsible for blending of lawful with unlawful, has to abide consequences and is liable for entire profits. Sheldon v. Metro-Goldwyn Pictures Corp., (CCA US 390, 84 LEd 825, 60 SCR 681, 44 USPQ 607, aff'g (CCA 2), 106 F(2d) 45, 42 USPQ 540, which rev'd 26 FSupp 134, 40 USPQ 238; Sammons v. Larkin, (DC-Mass), 38 FSupp 649, 49 USPQ 350. Mf'd 126 F(2d) 341, 53 USPQ 71.

Where defendant contended that since phonograph disc was double record, only one side of which infringed, profits should be divided but offered no proof as to cost of making up each composition or as to sales advantages of one over the other, it was sufficient for plaintiff to establish number of sales of its composition, and, in absence of proof of every element of cost, defendant's claim could not be sustained. Davilla v. Brunswick-Balke Collender Co., (CCA 2), 94 F(2d) 567, 36 USPQ 398, mod'g 19 FSupp 819, 35 USPQ 157.

Defendant who deliberately infringed play in motion picture could not count the effect of their standing and reputation in the industry in apportioning the profits from the picture. Sheldon v. Metro-Goldwyn Pictures Corp., (CCA 2), 106 F(2d) 45, 42 USPQ 540, rev'g 26 FSupp 134, 40 USPQ 238. Aff'd 309 US 390, 84 LEd 825, 60 SCR 681, 44 USPQ 607.

In apportioning profits burden is always on the copyright infringer. Sheldon v. Metro-Goldwyn Pictures Corp., (CCA 2), 106 F(2d) 45, 42 USPQ 540, rev'g 26 FSupp 134, 40 USPQ 238. Aff'd 309 US 390, 84 LEd 825, 60 SCR 681, 44 USPQ 607.

In fixing award for infringement by motion picture of copyrighted play court may accept expert testimony as to proportion of profits due to play and portion due to drawing power of actors when actors were well known and play or book was not well known. Sheldon v. Metro-Goldwyn Pictures Corp., (CCA 2), 106 F(2d) 45, 42 USPQ 540, rev'g 26 FSupp 134, 40 USPQ 238. Aff'd 309 US 390, 84 LEd 825, 60 SCR 681, 44 USPQ 607.

Indirect overhead, which was neither increased nor decreased by infringement, is apportioned according to number of songs published, and not according to number of copies sold although infringing song was best seller. Wilkie v. Santly Bros., Inc., (CCA 2), 139 F(2d) 264, 60 USPQ 46.

Where portion of profits of infringing work (motion picture) is attributable to appropriated work (play), to avoid unjustly giving originator all profits where infringer's labor and artistry have also to extent contributed to ultimate result, there may be reasonable approximation and apportionment of profits; plaintiff is awarded one fifth of profits from infringing motion pictures and attorney fees. Twentieth Century-Fox Film Corp. v. Stonesifer, (CCA 9), 140 F(2d) 579, 60 USPQ 392, aff'g 48 FSupp 196, 56 US PQ 94.

In ascertaining profits derived by exhibitor from infringing motion picture, the profits derived from the picture and other portions of the show were apportioned. Sheldon v. Moredall Realty Corp., (DC-NY), 29 FSupp 729, 43 USPQ 81.

In suit against producer of infringing motion picture, court allowed one fifth of profits to complainant and same proportion is allowed against exhibitor who was innocent infringer. Sheldon v. Moredall Realty Corp., (DC-NY), 29 FSupp 729, 43 USPQ 81.

Testimony of experts should be admitted as to proportion of profits to be assigned to infringing motion-picture play. Sheldon v. Moredall Realty Corp., (DC-NY), 29 FSupp 729, 43 USPQ 81.

There is no invariable rule of apportionment of overhead, due to practical impossibility of precise allocation of overhead. Wilkie v. Santly Bros., Inc., (DC-NY), 36 FSupp 574, 47 USPQ 380.

Equity is concerned with making fair apportionment between profits from infringement and profits not from infringement; principle of apportioning profits has been used in patent law to prevent doing of manifest injustice, namely, to award all profits from sale of machine to owner of patent that was infringed by only part of machine; result sought is rational separation of net profits so that neither may have what rightfully belongs to other; doctrine has been extended to accounting for profits in copyright cases. Alfred Bell & Co., Ltd. v. Catalda Fine Arts, Inc., (DC-NY), 86 FSupp 399, 82 USPQ 273. Mf'd 191 F(2d) 99, 90 US PQ 153.

Profits from play infringing biography are apportioned 50% for acting of star of play, 35% for script, 10% for direction of specific infringer, and 5% for "other factors"; plaintiff is allowed profits attributable to script and direction; apportionment between infringing and noninfringing material in script is not possible or practicable. Harris v. Miller, (DC-NY), 57 USPQ 103.

Appellant cannot complain of fact that apportionment of profits between infringing and noninfringing parts of book, though liberal to him, is not mathematically exact. Washingtonian Pub. Co., Inc. v. Pearson, 78 AppDC 287, 140 F(2d) 465, 60 USPQ 224, aff'g 56 USPQ 23.

41. —Statutory amount in lieu of damages and profits.

Under prior act, the penalty for each infringing copy was limited to those found in the possession of the defendant. Backus v. Gould, 48 US(7 How) 798, 12 LEd 919.

Recovery of the penalty for copies infringing a painting, may be had for all such copies made by the defendant whether in his possession or not. American Lithographic Co. v. Werckmeister, 221 US 603, 55 LEd 873, 31 SCR 676, aff'g (CCA 2), 165 Fed 426.

Provision that infringer shall be liable to pay "in lieu of actual damages and profits, such damages as to the court shall appear just" is not applicable where profits have been proved and only question is as to their apportionment. Sheldon v. Metro-Goldwyn Pictures Corp., 309 US 390, 48 LEd 825, 60 SCR 681, 44 USPQ 607, aff'g (CCA 2), 106 F(2d) 45, 42 USPQ 40, which rev'd 26 FSupp 134, 40 USPQ 238.

Rule of liability which merely takes away profits from copyright infringement would offer little discouragement to infringers. Statutory rule does not merely compel restitution of profit and reparation for injury, but also is designed to discourage wrongful conduct. Court's discretion is wide enough to permit resort to statutory damages for such purpose; even for uninjurious and unprofitable invasions of copyright, court may impose liability within statutory limits. F. W. Woolworth Co. v. Contemporary Arts, Inc., 344 US 228, 97 LEd 276, 73 SCR 222, 95 USPQ 396, 'aff'g (CA 5), 193 F(2d) 162, 92 USPQ 4, which aff'd 93 FSupp 739, 86 USPQ 476.

Where infringer proved gross profit of $899.16 and trial court excluded or struck most of copyright owner's proof of actual damages on the ground that authority to allow statutory damages rendered such proof unnecessary, the statute empowered the trial court in its sound exercise of judicial discretion on all the facts to allow statutory damages in the amount of $5,000. F. W. Woolworth Co. v. Contemporary Arts, Inc., 344 US 228, 97 LEd 276, 73 SCR 222, 95 USPQ 396, aff'g (CA 5), 193 F(2d) 162, 92 USPQ 4, which aff'd 93 FSupp 739, 86 USPQ 476.

The money judgment provided for in R. S. § 4965 was a penalty. McDonald v. Hearst, (DC-Cal), 95 Fed 656.

Where plaintiff had suffered no actual damage by reason of the infringing acts court allowed nominal damages of six cents. F. A. Mills, Inc. v. Standard Music Roll Co., (DC-NJ), 223 Fed 849. Aff'd 241 Fed 360.

Where infringement works some considerable injury, the court may estimate the damages within the statutory limits, without being bound by the usual legal proofs. S. E. Hendricks Co., Inc. v. Thomas Pub. Co., (CCA 2), 242 Fed 37.

The sums specified in this section are not fixed sums to be allowed as damages under any circumstances of infringement after notice, but it is the duty of the court to award damages as justified by the nature and circumstances of the case as developed on the trial; and where no proof of actual damage is offered the award should have relation to such inferences as are reasonably deductible from the whole case of infringement without reference to any idea of punishment. Turner & Dahnken v. Crowley, (CCA 9), 252 Fed 749.

Where damages are indirect and not capable of ascertainment, the compensation which the copyright proprietor shall receive is committed to the discretion of the trial judge. Campbell v. Wireback, (CCA 4), 269 Fed 372.

Where statute authorized trier of fact to assess damages between two sums, there being no legitimate basis for recovery of any definite amount, the court of appeals will hesitate before modifying an award fixed by the master and confirmed by the district court. Wells v. American Bureau of Engineering, Inc., (CCA 7), 285 Fed 371.

Statutory damages may be awarded in lieu of actual damages in the discretion of the court. Fargo Mercantile Co. v. Brechet & Richter Co., (CCA 8), 295 Fed 823.

Subsection (b)(4) of this section is inapplicable, in the discretion of the court, to a case disclosing infringement covering a musical composition where there is no proof of actual damage. Atlantic Monthly Co. v. Post Pub. Co., (DC-Mass), 27 F(2d) 556.

The penalty is enforceable in a suit for infringement. Vitagraph v. Grobaski, (DC-Mich), 46 F(2d) 813.

Amounts prescribed as damages are not unconditionally allowed, but are given only in discretion of court. Russell & Stoll Co. v. Oceanic Electrical Supply Co., Inc., (CCA 2), 80 F(2d) 864, 28 USPQ 203.

Whether profits shall be awarded or statutory damages allowed in copyright infringement suit is not matter of choice with plaintiff and where there was ample evidence to make award of damages on basis of actual profits, master and court below were in error in granting statutory damages. Davilla v. Brunswick-Balke Collender Co., (CCA 2), 94 F(2d) 567, 36 USPQ 398, mod'g 19 FSupp 819, 35 USPQ 157.

Award of statutory damages is proper only in absence of proof of actual damages and profits. Universal Pictures Co., Inc. v. Harold Lloyd Corp., (CCA 9), 162 F(2d) 354, 73 US PQ 317.

Provision restricting recovery to $5,000 where motion-picture producer is unaware of infringement, applies to statutory damages, not where court is awarding actual damages. Universal Pictures Co., Inc. v. Harold Lloyd Corp., (CCA 9), 162 F(2d) 354, 73 USPQ 317.

Purpose of "in lieu" clause of subsec. (b) of this section is to permit recovery of more than nominal sum when it is difficult or impossible for plaintiff to prove actual amount of damages or profits with certainty required by law. F. W. Woolworth Co. v. Contemporary Arts, Inc., (CA 5), 193 F(2d) 162, 92 USPQ 4, aff'g 93 FSupp 739, 86 USPQ 476. Aff'd 344 US 228, 97 LEd 276, 73 SCR 222, 95 USPQ 396.

Although infringer had actual notice of copyright before infringement, limitation applies since there was no law suit of which he had notice and he was not then "a defendant"; if limitation were inapplicable, plaintiff would be left to such damages as to the court shall appear just, arrived at in exercise of judicial discretion up to dollar a copy. Advertisers Exchange, Inc. v. Hinkley, (CA 8), 199 F(2d) 313, 95 USPQ 124, aff'g 101 FSupp 801, 92 USPQ 313.

Since there was no showing on amount of damages arising from copyright infringement, plaintiff was entitled to be compensated in manner provided in subsec. (b) of this section; it was inappropriate for court of appeals to assess these damages; this highly discretionary function was best performed by trier of facts, especially since defendant distributed its infringing catalogues with notice of plaintiff's copyright, and therefore trial court was not confined by statutory limitations in its assessment of damages. Markham v. A. E. Borden Co., Inc., (CA 1), 206 F(2d) 199, 98 USPQ 346, rev'g 108 FSupp 695, 95 USPQ 313.

There is no distinction between claim for actual damages from infringement and claim for just damages as provided in "in lieu" clause of subsec. (b) of this section. Award of minimum statutory damages under "in lieu" clause is not infliction of penalty inherently beyond power of equity court to enforce. Chappell & Co., Inc. v. Palermo Cafe Co., Inc., (CA 1), 249 F(2d) 77, 115 USPQ 205, mod'g 146 FSupp 867, 112 USPQ 378.

Court has discretion to grant lesser statutory amount rather than copyright infringer's actual profits. American Visuals Corp. v. Holland, (CA 2), 261 F(2d) 652, 119 USPQ 482, aff'g 162 FSupp 14, 117 USPQ 180.

Plaintiff conceding inability to prove actual damages within minimum of $250 and maximum of $5000 is entitled to such damages as the court may determine to be just. Zenn v. National Golf Review, Inc., (DC-NY), 27 FSupp 732, 41 USPQ 535.

In exercise of its sound discretion court may allow statutory damages where actual damages cannot be proved in terms of dollars and cents. Burndy Engineering Co., Inc. v. Sheldon Service Corp., (DC-NY), 39 FSupp 274, 50 USPQ 24. Aff'd 127 F(2d) 661, 53 USPQ 409.

Where sales of infringing sculptured dog for $1.19 harmed sales of copyrighted sculpture at $4.00, $9.00, and $15.00 and required plaintiff to design new model, and infringer purchased 1524 infringements from manufacturer, court awards maximum statutory damages of $5000, at rate of $10 per copy for the first 500 copies. Contemporary Arts, Inc. v. F. W. Woolworth Co., (DC-Mass), 93 FSupp 739, 86 USPQ 476. Aff'd 193 F(2d) 162, 92 USPQ 4, which was aff'd 344 US 228, 97 LEd 276, 73 SCR 222, 95 USPQ 396.

"In lieu" provision does not apply where either actual damages or profits are ascertainable, but, when plaintiff suffered no damages, and profits are ascertainable, profits should be awarded and resort should not be had to "in lieu" clause. Malsed v. Marshall Field & Co., (DC-Wash), 96 FSupp 372, 88 USPQ 552.

Since there is no showing of actual damages suffered by plaintiff, it is entitled to be compensated for copyright infringement under subsec. (b) of this section, which authorizes court to allow such damages as shall appear to be just; in its discretion, court may allow amounts stated in statute. M. J. Golden & Co., Inc. v. Pittsburgh Brewing Co., Inc., (DC-Pa), 137 FSupp 455, 108 USPQ 250.

Statutory damages under Copyright Act cannot be recovered in common-law action depending on diversity of citizenship and requisite jurisdictional amount; having no evidence of specific damages resulting from conduct of defendant complained of, plaintiff cannot state common-law claim against defendant within jurisdiction of federal court. Smith v. George E. Muehlebach Brewing Co., (DC-Mo), 140 FSupp 729, 110 USPQ 177.

It was not intent of Congress to award statutory damages of $1.00 per copy for books which are fraudulent in that they are used for sole and express purpose of falsely inducing public to believe that cash discounts on merchandise are obtained through use of books, whereas same discounts are given to all members of public in ordinary course of business; however, court allows specific sum as statutory damages because of difficulty of proving actual damage. Advisers Inc. v. Wiesen-Hart, Inc., (DC-Ohio), 161 FSupp 831, 117 USPQ 330.

Evidence as to cost of preparing copyrighted directory and as to losses of sales due to infringement is vague and conjectural; court cannot with any reasonable accuracy find actual damages suffered by plaintiff; in lieu thereof, statutory damages of $1.00 for each infringing copy are awarded. Greenfield v. Tanzer, (DC-Mass), 186 FSupp 795, 125 USPQ 392.

Since no evidence is presented as to infringer's profits, all copies of infringing publication have been recalled, and defendant is no longer actively in business, there is no need for further relief in addition to award of statutory damages. Greenfield v. Tanzer, (DC-Mass), 186 FSupp 795, 125 USPQ 392.

Subsection (b) of this section provides in essence that court may award to copyright proprietor either actual damages he suffered due to infringement, plus infringer's profits, or damages in an amount to be computed in accordance with arbitrary standard set forth in statute; where there is no evidence as to damage suffered by proprietor or profits realized by infringer, court is justified in awarding statutory damages. Doran v. Sunset House Distributing Corp., (DC-Cal), 197 FSupp 940, 131 USPQ 94.

Where plaintiffs in copyright infringement action prove infringement, but do not submit proof of actual damages, award of $250 as minimum damages in each cause of action is mandatory under this section. Edwin H. Morris & Co., Inc. v. Burton, (DC-La), 201 FSupp 36, 132 USPQ 680.

Fact that printer made no profit but took a loss is not a reason for awarding statutory damages "in lieu of" profits. Washingtonian Pub. Co., Inc. v. Pearson, 78 AppDC 287, 140 F(2d) 465, 60 USPQ 224, aff'g 56 USPQ 23.

"In lieu of actual damages and profits" clause was not intended as penalty; clause was not applicable when there was no injury to plaintiff and where profits had been proved. Washingtonian Pub. Co., Inc. v. Pearson, 78 AppDC 287, 140 F(2d) 465, 60 USPQ 224, aff'g 56 USPQ 23.

Where plaintiff proves copyright infringement, but has not submitted proof of actual damages, award of $250 as minimum damages in each cause of action is mandatory. Bourne, Inc. v. Romero, (DC-La), 23 FedRDec 292, 122 USPQ 129.

42. ——Maximum and minimum limits.

"The court's conception of what is just in the particular case, considering the nature of the copyright, the circumstances of the infringement, and the like, is made a measure of the damages to be paid, but with the express qualification that in every case the assessment must be within the prescribed limitations; that is to say, neither more than the maximum nor less than the minimum. Within these limitations the court's discretion and sense of justice are controlling, but it has no discretion when proceeding under this provision to go outside of them." L. A. Westermann Co. v. Dispatch Printing Co., 249 US 100, 63 LEd 499, 39 SCR 194, rev'g (CCA 6), 233 Fed 609.

Where amount of actual damages for 7 distinct infringements by publication of pictorial illustrations designed for advertising purposes could not be estimated in money values, the court had no discretion to award less than the minimum statutory limit of $250 for each infringement. L. A. Westermann Co. v. Dispatch Printing Co., 249 US 100, 63 LEd 499, 39 SCR 194, rev'g (CCA 6), 233 Fed 609.

Where there is no proof of actual damages the court is bound by the minimum amount of $250. The maximum and minimum provisions are applicable alike to all types of infringement except those for which the statute makes other specific provisions. Jewell-LaSalle Realty Co. v. Buck, 283 US 202, 75 LEd 978, 51 SCR 407.

Where there is no showing of actual loss the court must allow the minimum amount and may in his discretion, if there are a sufficient number of infringing copies or performances, employ the schedule as provided for in the last four paragraphs of subsec. (b) of this section as a basis for assessing additional damages. Jewell-LaSalle Realty Co. v. Buck, 283 US 202, 75 LEd 978, 51 SCR 407.

An appellate court cannot review the action of a trial judge in assessing an amount in lieu of actual damages, where the amount awarded is within the limits imposed by this section. Douglas v. Cunningham, 294 US 207, 79 LEd 862, 55 SCR 365, 24 USPQ 153, rev'g (CCA 1), 72 F(2d) 536, 22 USPQ 320.

Where there is no proof of damages it is within the discretion of the court to award the damages of one dollar for each infringing copy, and such an award cannot be disturbed on appeal so long as the award is not less than $250 or more than $5,000. Douglas v. Cunningham, 294 US 207, 79 LEd 862, 55 SCR 365, 24 USPQ 153, rev'g (CCA 1), 72 F(2d) 536, 22 USPQ 320.

The effect of the limitations on the amount of damages, is that it gives more substantial relief in the event only a small number of copies is found and is less oppressive on the defendant where a maximum number of copies is found. Boston Traveler Co. v. Purdy, (CCA 1), 137 Fed 717.

This section in providing for minimum damages of $250 and a maximum of $5000 does not bind a court to decree at least the statutory minimum of damages where the court is of the opinion that there are no damages, or that they are less than $250. Woodman v. Lydiard-Peterson Co., (CC-Minn), 192 Fed 67. Aff'd 204 Fed 921.

Where some considerable injury has been caused, $250 is the minimum award. S. E. Hendricks Co., Inc. v. Thomas Pub. Co., (CCA 2), 242 Fed 37.

Where the plaintiff is unable to prove the extent of his actual damages, the court may allow the minimum amount fixed by the statute, and such allowance would not be the infliction of a fine on the defendant. Sauer v. Detroit Times, Co., (DC-Mich), 247 Fed 687.

Damages for infringement of copyright of musical composition are governed by subsec. (b) of this section, providing that damages shall not exceed $5000 or be less than $250. The provision in subdiv. fourth of said subsec-tion, fixing damages at $10 for every infringing performance, applies only within the limits of $5000 and $250. Waterson, Berlin & Snyder Co. v. Tollefson, (DC-Cal), 253 Fed 859.

Plaintiff must be awarded the sum of $250 even though no actual damages were suffered. Fisher, Inc. v. Dillingham, (DC-NY), 298 Fed 145.

The minimum damages allowable are $250, irrespective of the extent of the use of the copyrighted article, and the smallness of the damage does not require a reduction of the attorney fees to be allowed. M. Witmark & Sons v. Calloway, (DC-Tenn), 22 F(2d) 412.

Award of more than minimum damages is discretionary. Cravens v. Retail Credit Men's Ass'n, (DC-Tenn), 26 F(2d) 833.

The $1 allowance for each infringing copy does not apply where the infringing copies issued are less than 250. Cravens v. Retail Credit Men's Ass'n, (DC-Tenn), 26 F(2d) 833.

For infringement of the copyright of a musical composition the minimum amount assessable is $250 instead of the amount stated in subdiv. fourth of subsec. (b). Irving Berlin, Inc. v. Daigle, (CCA 5), 31 F(2d) 832, rev'g 26 F(2d) 149, and 26 F(2d) 150.

Damages for infringement of a copyright of a musical composition for a public performance is the minimum of $250 for each performance for profit, and not the $10 penalty. Lutz v. Buck, (CCA 5), 40 F(2d) 501, 5 USPQ 452.

Where there is no proof of damages the court is bound to award a minimum amount of $250 for infringement of a copyrighted song. Buck v. Jewell-LaSalle Realty Co., (CCA 8), 51 F(2d) 730, 10 USPQ 101, mod'g 32 F(2d) 366, 1 USPQ 319; Buck v. Bilkie, (CCA 9), 63 F(2d) 447, 16 USPQ 382.

In absence of proof of both actual damages and profits, trial court is required to award minimum statutory sum of $250. Johns & Johns Printing Co. v. Paull-Pioneer Music Corp., (CCA 8), 102 F(2d) 282, 41 USPQ 3; Burndy Engineering Co., Inc. v. Sheldon Service Corp., (CCA 2), 127 F(2d) 661, 53 USPQ 409, aff'g 39 FSupp 274, 50 USPQ 24.

Judgment of $250 for each infringement is proper since this is minimum amount permitted by Copyright Act where actual damages are not established. Interstate Hotel Co. v. Remick Music Corp., (CCA 8), 157 F(2d) 744, 71 USPQ 138, aff'g 58 FSupp 523, 63 USPQ 327.

Since, within minimum and maximum limits set by subsec. (b) of this section, district court's discretion is controlling in its award of statutory damages, only question before court of appeals is whether district court awarded less than statutory minimum for each infringement. Markham v. A. E. Borden Co., Inc., (CA 1), 221 F(2d) 586, 105 USPQ 199.

Magazine was not included within the exceptions stated to the higher range of allowable damages. Cory v. Physical Culture Hotel, (DC-NY), 14 FSupp 977, 30 USPQ 353. Aff'd 88 F(2d) 411, 33 USPQ 58.

Court was required to assess damages of not less than $250 against defendant infringing copyright scheme, though contrary to justice in case. Doll v. Libin, (DC-Mont), 17 FSupp 546, 33 USPQ 17.

Plaintiff is entitled to some damages for copyright infringement on mere showing of infringing acts; there must have been some actual damage but this damage is without proof raised to statutory amount ($250) if amount of damage cannot be ascertained. Towle v. Ross, (DC-Ore), 32 FSupp 125, 45 USPQ 143.

As regards recovery of profit, object of § 289 of Title 35 would seem to be to make law of damages for infringement of design patents conform to provisions relating to infringement of copyright; they lodge discretion in court to allow statutory maximum even where profit is shown to be less. Laskowitz v. Marie-Designer, Inc., (DC-Cal), 119 FSupp 541, 100 USPQ 367.

Publisher is liable only under "in lieu" clause of this section on account of printing of allegedly infringing book, since copyright owner suffered no damage from printing and only printer made profits therefrom; "in lieu" damages are no more than $250, since no effective damage took place until publication and sale. Greenbie v. Noble, (DC-NY), 151 FSupp 45, 113 USPQ 115.

Since actual damages from copyright infringement are not shown, statutory minimum for each infringement may be applied. Harms, Inc. v. Sansom House Enterprises, Inc., (DC-Pa), 162 FSupp 129, 117 USPQ 272.

F. W. Woolworth Co. v. Contemporary Arts, Inc., 344 US 228, 97 LEd 276, 73 SCR 222, 95 USPQ 362, gives to copyright owner, under statutory mandate, a measure of damages greater than mere licensing fee to which proprietor of copyrighted music would have been entitled had license been sought; courts have discretion to determine damages, within maximum and minimum statutory limits, as their sense of justice may determine. Harms, Inc. v. F. W. Woolworth Co., (DC-Cal), 163 FSupp 484, 118 USPQ 436.

Maximum and minimum limits of damages set by this section do not apply to infringements after notice. Loew's Inc. v. Superior Court, 18 Cal(2d series) 419, 115 Pac(2d) 983, 50 USPQ 641.

43. ——Number of infringements.

Newspaper publication separately and independently of six pictorial illustrations, designed for advertising purposes and separately copyrighted by the proprietor, five of which were published once and the other one twice, constituted seven separate and distinct infringements. L. A. Westermann Co. v. Dispatch Printing Co., 249 US 100, 63 LEd 449, 39 SCR 194, rev'g (CCA 6), 233 Fed 609.

Where six separately copyrighted cuts were grouped together and sent to the trade, the printing of a different cut each day in a newspaper would constitute six separate infringements. L. A. Westermann Co. v. Dispatch Printing Co., 249 US 100, 63 LEd 499, 39 SCR 194, rev'g (CCA 6), 233 Fed 609.

Under prior act which provided a penalty for every "sheet" found in the possession of the defendant, although more than one copyrighted picture was printed on a sheet, such sheet constituted but one article on which a penalty could be had. Falk v. Heffron, (CC-NY), 56 Fed 299.

Where the law provides a penalty for each copy of an infringed copyright, and two infringements are printed on every sheet, it is proper for the penalty to be $800 when 400 of such sheets were printed. Journal Pub. Co. v. Drake, (CCA 9), 199 Fed 572.

Discretion of special master in fixing amount of recovery in lieu of damages did not extend to the number of infringing articles. Fleischer Studios, Inc. v. Ralph A. Freundlich, Inc., (DC-NY), 14 FSupp 401, 30 USPQ 125.

Publication of infringing copies of copyrighted photograph in advertisements in successive issues of magazine constituted separate infringements. Cory v. Physical Culture Hotel, Inc., (DC-NY), 14 FSupp 977, 30 USPQ 353. Aff'd 88 F(2d) 411, 33 USPQ 58.

Defendant who used five newspaper advertisements from plaintiff's copyrighted book, after expiration of contract with plaintiff, was guilty of but one infringement, not five. Doll v. Libin, (DC-Mont), 17 FSupp 546, 33 USPQ 17.

Where plaintiff had copyright of book of 52 illustrations and defendant used four illustrations in four advertisements on four different dates, this constituted four infringements, and statutory damages of four times $250 are awarded. Lindsay & Brewster, Inc. v. Verstein, (DC-Maine), 21 FSupp 264, 35 USPQ 494.

Five publications in infringing advertisement in newspaper constituted five separate acts of infringement; court awards $250 damages for each infringement. Zuckerman v. Dickson, (DC-Pa), 35 FSupp 903, 47 USPQ 514.

Defendants infringed three copyrights on catalogue by four separate printings; this constituted 12 infringements for which award of $250 statutory damages each was proper as was allowance of one dollar for each of 500 copies of one infringing page printed separately. Burndy Engineering Co., Inc. v. Sheldon Service Corp., (DC-NY), 39 FSupp 274, 50 USPQ 24. Aff'd 127 F(2d) 661, 53 USPQ 409.

There being no proof as to plaintiff's actual damage or defendants' profits, court allows statutory damages of ten dollars for each infringing radio performance; composition was performed three times with chain hook-ups of 67, 66, and 85 stations; damages of $2180 are awarded on theory that there were 218 performances, not three; $250 attorneys' fee is allowed. Law v. National Broadcasting Co., Inc., (DC-NY), 51 FSupp 798, 58 USPQ 669.

44. —Particular damages awarded.

Jury was authorized to allow plaintiff damages for infringement on basis of fifty cents for every sheet found in possession of defendant. Dwight v. Appleton, (CC-NY), FedCas 4,215.

Where 2800 copies of an infringing work had been sold, $2500 damages were not erroneous. S. E. Hendricks Co., Inc. v. Thomas Pub. Co., (CCA 2), 242 Fed 37.

Five hundred dollars based on value of play and publicity author would have received had his name been upon advertisements of the play were allowed as damages for infringement. Stodart v. Mutual Film Corp., (DC-NY), 249 Fed 507. Aff'd 249 Fed 513.

Where 50,000 infringing pamphlets were printed and 10,000 of them distributed, and defendant did not know that it was a copyrighted work he had copied, an award of $3000 damages was just. Norris v. No-Leak-O Piston Ring Co., (DC-Md), 271 Fed 536. Aff'd 277 Fed 951.

Two hundred and fifty dollars were allowed for single performance of musical composition. M. Witmark & Sons v. Pastime Amusement Co., (DC-SC), 298 Fed 470. Aff'd 2 F(2d) 1020.

Minimum damages of $250 may be awarded to an owner of a musical composition, there being no proof of actual damage or profits. Buck v. Milam, (DC-Idaho), 32 F(2d) 622.

Award of $250 damages and costs, and $100 attorneys' fees was proper. Dreamland Ball Room, Inc. v. Shapiro, Bernstein & Co., (CCA 7), 36 F(2d) 354, 3 USPQ 288.

Attorney fees and recovery of one dollar for each infringing book, in lieu of actual damages and profits were allowed. Schellberg v. Empringham, (DC-NY), 36 F(2d) 991.

Where 5000 copies of infringing map were sold, but it did not appear that the plaintiff's business was materially injured, an allowance of $2000 damages was adequate. General Drafting Co., Inc. v. Andrews, (CCA 2), 37 F(2d) 54.

For admitted copying of a part of plaintiff's book for use in an advertising calendar not sold for profit, and which caused no actual damage to plaintiff, $1000 as damages and the same amount as attorney's fees were awarded. Warren v. White & Wyckoff Mfg. Co., (DC-NY), 39 F(2d) 922.

Minimum of $250, recovered, and which equaled an award of one dollar for all catalogues distributed, was proper where plaintiff had not been damaged. Russell & Stoll Co. v. Oceanic Electrical Supply Co., Inc., (CCA 2), 80 F(2d) 864, 28 USPQ 203.

Thirty-five hundred dollars were allowed; defendants sold 3500 books at fifty cents while plaintiff sold 180,000 copies at $1.50 each. Adventures in Good Eating, Inc. v. Best Places to Eat, Inc., (CCA 7), 131 F(2d) 809, 56 USPQ 242.

It is not abuse of discretion to award damages of $1000 and attorney's fees of $500 where infringing author received $3000 in connection with sale of book and infringing publisher sold 14,262 copies at net profit of five to ten cents per book. Toksvig v. Bruce Pub. Co., (CA 7), 181 F(2d) 664, 85 USPQ 339.

In case wherein infringer caused 29 publications of copyrighted advertisements in newspaper printing 3261 copies of each publication, and in which plaintiff does not prove actual damages or profits, "in lieu" provision of subsec. (b) of this section does not require that plaintiff be awarded one dollar for each infringing copy of newspaper or 29 times 3261 dollars. Advertisers Exchange, Inc. v. Hinkley, (CA 8), 199 F(2d) 313, 95 USPQ 124, aff'g 101 FSupp 801, 92 USPQ 313.

Award of $5000 damages under subsec. (b) of this section is justified, despite fact that in-

fringing publication was not profitable, in view of abrupt drop in sales of copyrighted chart and authors' fee paid by infringer. Nikanov v. Simon & Schuster, Inc., (CA 2), 246 F(2d) 501, 114 USPQ 89, aff'g 144 FSupp 375, 110 USPQ 491.

Twenty-five hundred dollars were awarded for infringement of advertising card, where the claims of the parties varied greatly. Sebring Pottery Co. v. Steubenville Pottery Co., (DC-Ohio), 9 FSupp 384.

Plaintiff was entitled to $250, defendant having submitted its catalogue to plaintiff before issue. North & Judd Mfg. Co. v. Krischer's Mfg. Co., (DC-Conn), 11 FSupp 739, 27 USPQ 224.

Five thousand dollars were awarded for infringement of copyright photograph, where infringing copies were used in advertisements in seven issues of magazine. Cory v. Physical Culture Hotel, Inc., (DC-NY), 14 FSupp 977, 30 USPQ 353. Aff'd 88 F(2d) 411, 33 USPQ 58.

The court in the following cases awarded the minimum damages of $250 for each song or musical selection sung or played. Society European Stage Authors & Composers, Inc. v. New York Hotel Statler Co., Inc., (DC-NY), 19 FSupp 1, 34 USPQ 6; Buck v. Russo, (DC-Mass), 25 FSupp 317, 39 USPQ 377; Buck v. Ridgway Const. Co., (DC-Mass), 25 FSupp 690, 39 USPQ 376; Buck v. Newsreel, Inc., (DC-Mass), 25 FSupp 787, 40 USPQ 20; Buck v. Spanish Gables, Inc., (DC-Mass), 26 FSupp 36, 40 USPQ 19; Buck v. Dacier, (DC-Mass), 26 FSupp 37, 40 USPQ 14; Buck v. Savoia Restaurant, Inc., (DC-NY), 27 FSupp 289, 41 USPQ 138; Buck v. Lisa, (DC-NY), 28 FSupp 379, 42 USPQ 116; Buck v. Crescent Gardens Operating Co., (DC-Mass), 28 FSupp 576, 42 USPQ 435; Shapiro, Bernstein & Co., Inc. v. Veltin, (DC-La), 47 FSupp 648, 55 USPQ 335; Remick Music Corp. v. Interstate Hotel Co., (DC-Neb), 58 FSupp 523, 63 USPQ 327. Aff'd 157 F(2d) 744, 71 USPQ 138; Buck v. LaFontaine, (DC-Mass), 39 USPQ 377; Buck v. Deane, (DC-Mass), 39 USPQ 381; Buck v. Royal Palms, (DC-Mass), 39 USPQ 382; Buck v. Columbus Restaurant, Inc., (DC-Mass), 39 USPQ 382; Buck v. Yin Ho Co., (DC-Mass), 39 USPQ 383; Buck v. Melanson, (DC-Mass), 39 USPQ 384; Buck v. Parker, (DC-Mass), 40 USPQ 13; Buck v. Valenti, (DC-Mass), 40 USPQ 16; Buck v. Ricci, (DC-Mass), 40 USPQ 17; Buck v. Sunbeam, (DC-Mass), 40 USPQ 18; Buck v. Repertory Theatre, Inc., (DC-Mass), 40 USPQ 23; Buck v. Holyoke Theatre, Inc., (DC-Mass), 40 USPQ 24; Buck v. Wrentham Show Boat, Inc., (DC-Mass), 40 USPQ 25; Buck v. Levin, (DC-Mass), 40 USPQ 27.

Where M procured N to reproduce copyrighted matter for M to distribute, on finding of infringement, damages of $2000 were allowed, to be paid by M. Freedman v. Milnag Leasing Corp., (DC-NY), 20 FSupp 802, 35 USPQ 184.

Where infringement was printed in defendant's magazine through misapprehension of rights and apology and retraction were offered, $1000 damages were assessed. Zenn v. National Golf Review, Inc., (DC-NY), 27 FSupp 732, 41 USPQ 535.

For infringement of three songs by exhibition of motion-picture films, court allows $250 each.

Famous Music Corp. v. Melz, (DC-La), 28 FSupp 767, 42 USPQ 573.

Award of $250 was given for each of five infringements printed in newspaper advertisements. Advertisers Exchange, Inc. v. Laufe, (DC-Pa), 29 FSupp 1, 38 USPQ 93.

In absence of proof of damages by infringement of copyright, court awards $250 each for two infringements. Eliot v. Geare-Marston, Inc., (DC-Pa), 30 FSupp 301, 43 USPQ 249.

Award of $4000 as statutory damages for copyright infringement is proper where there were 14 cases of infringement contained in six separate printings of defendant's trade catalogue and gross sale price of items sold by defendant, which covers items mentioned in infringing pages of catalogue, is over $52,000, and taking into consideration general nature of defendant's business and fact that no notice was given defendant of infringement until suit was brought. Burndy Engineering Co. v. Penn-Union Electric Corp., (DC-Pa), 32 FSupp 671, 45 USPQ 80. Aff'd 122 F(2d) 932, 51 USPQ 548.

Copyright infringer is assessed $250 for infringement of each of two telephone directories; plaintiff is awarded costs. Southern Bell Telephone & Telegraph Co. v. Donnelly, (DC-Fla), 35 FSupp 425, 48 USPQ 11.

Infringing printer which made no profits from infringement is liable for $250 as statutory damages and costs; infringing author is liable for $7600 profits and costs. Sammons v. Larkin, (DC-Mass), 38 FSupp 649, 49 USPQ 350. Mf'd 126 F(2d) 341, 53 USPQ 71.

Motion picture having infringed play by copying substantial and material part, and having made $19,800 profit, court assesses $3960 as damages. Stonesifer v. Twentieth Century-Fox Film Corp., (DC-Cal), 48 FSupp 196, 56 USPQ 94. Aff'd 140 F(2d) 579, 60 USPQ 392.

Only nominal damages of one dollar were allowed where all copies had been impounded and plaintiff had suffered no actual damages. Rudolf Lesch Fine Arts, Inc. v. Metal, (DC-NY), 51 FSupp 69, 58 USPQ 668.

Although infringer could have obtained license for $90 per year or $10 per month, plaintiff's actual damages are not confined to loss of license fee; in lieu of actual damages and profits, $250 damages and $100 attorney's fee are awarded for one infringing performance of copyrighted song. Shapiro, Bernstein & Co., Inc. v. Widenski, (DC-RI), 54 FSupp 780, 61 USPQ 91. Aff'd 147 F(2d) 909, 64 USPQ 448.

Damage because of defendant's infringement of copyrighted mezzotint engraving cannot be more than nominal since plate for engraving has been destroyed for many years and most, if not all, of proofs taken from it have been sold by plaintiff. Alfred Bell & Co., Ltd. v. Catalda Fine Arts, Inc., (DC-NY), 74 FSupp 973, 75 USPQ 66. Mf'd 191 F(2d) 99, 90 USPQ 153.

Where defendant copied seven copyrighted magazine covers, damages of $250 for each infringement were awarded in absence of any proof as to actual damage sustained by plaintiff. Conde Nast Publications, Inc. v. Vogue School of Fashion Modelling, Inc., (DC-NY), 105 FSupp 325, 94 USPQ 101.

Copyright proprietor was not awarded statutory damages of one dollar for each copy of infringing book, but was awarded lesser sum based upon his lost sales and defendant's profits; lost sales were computed by comparing actual sales with average sales in previous two years; more than cost of printing and binding should have been included in cost of publication of defendant's books. Ziegelheim v. Flohr, (DC-NY), 119 FSupp 324, 100 USPQ 189.

Court awarded one dollar for each infringing copy where large number of items was copied from plaintiff's catalogue, but awarded statutory minimum of $250 for infringement which only copied two items from plaintiff's catalogue; $250 also was awarded as to infringement where it was likely that substantial numbers of infringing copies were distributed during period wherein recovery was barred by statute of limitations. Harry Alter Co., Inc. v. A. E. Borden Co., Inc., (DC-Mass), 121 FSupp 941, 102 USPQ 2.

Inasmuch as defendant continued to account for royalties under § 1(e) of this title on basis of records sold, rather than on basis of records manufactured, despite plaintiff's repeated protests, damages awarded pursuant to said § 1(e) are assessed at three times the amount found to be due as a royalty; in awarding such damages, court considers intent and acts of defendant in failing to make payment and its wilful disregard of Copyright Act [§ 1 et seq. of this title]; such damages are in addition to royalty to which plaintiffs are entitled. Famous Music Corp. v. Seeco Records, Inc., (DC-NY), 201 FSupp 560, 132 USPQ 342.

Where defendant did not appear at hearing and court found copyright infringed, $250 damages were allowed. Buck v. Archambault, (DC-Mass), 36 USPQ 383; Buck v. Kozlouski, (DC-Mass), 36 USPQ 383.

Award is made of $150 plus $100 attorney's fee for infringement of copyrighted card. Druley v. Thompson, (DC-Pa), 44 USPQ 284.

Publication of infringing article did not damage plaintiff or profit defendant but plaintiff is awarded $250 in lieu of actual profits and damages. Vinick v. Charm Publications, Inc., (DC-NY), 46 USPQ 510.

Actual damages resulting from one infringing sale by two defendants being uncertain, minimum $250 damages were awarded. Larsen v. Goldblatt Bros., Inc., (DC-Ill), 53 USPQ 287.

Court awards $250 for each radio broadcast containing infringing matter. Select Theatres Corp. v. Ronzoni Macaroni Co., (DC-NY), 59 USPQ 288.

Plaintiff is awarded defendant's profits of $629 from four infringements, without deduction of losses of $23 from three additional infringements. Curt Teich & Co., Inc. v. Beals Lithograph & Printing Co., Inc., (DC-Iowa), 61 USPQ 434.

In cases wherein plaintiff offered no proof of damages or profits, master awarded statutory damages of $22,720 against one defendant and $18,000 against another defendant, but court reduces amounts to $5000 and $2000. Foreign & Domestic Music Corp. v. Michael M. Wyngate, Inc., (DC-NY), 74 USPQ 296.

45.   Impounding of infringing articles.

A federal court is authorized to issue a writ of seizure as may be necessary for the exercise of its jurisdiction. Stern v. Jerome H. Remick & Co., (CC-NY), 164 Fed 781.

Defendant cannot, after asking for and obtaining a larger bond, complain of seizure and demand return of impounded articles. Universal Film Mfg. Co. v. Copperman, (DC-NY), 206 Fed 69.

Only authority for return of articles impounded pendente lite is found in rules promulgated by the United States Supreme Court. Crown Feature Film Co. v. Bettis Amusement Co., (DC-Ohio), 206 Fed 362.

Loss of probable profits may be measure of damages upon vacation of writ for impounding. Universal Film Mfg. Co. v. Copperman, (CCA 2), 218 Fed 577.

Infringing copies of city directory in hands of users, not infringers, are immune from seizure. Jewelers' Circular Pub. Co. v. Keystone Pub. Co., (DC-NY), 274 Fed 932. Aff'd 281 Fed 83.

On dismissing infringement suit and releasing defendant's plates, he is not entitled to damages from plaintiff for physical injury to plates after seizure by marshal; there is no showing how injury occurred or why plaintiff should be charged. Rudolf Lesch Fine Arts, Inc. v. Metal, (DC-NY), 51 FSupp 69, 58 USPQ 668.

46.   Destruction or forfeiture of infringing articles.

Under R. S. § 4965 imposing a forfeiture on an infringer for every infringing copy "found in his possession," labels obtained and affixed to goods by an employee, but under control of the employer were not found in possession of employee. Thornton v. Schreiber, 124 US 612, 31 LEd 577, 8 SCR 618, rev'g (DC-Pa), 17 Fed 603.

Where a defendant willfully violates an injunction against sale of infringing dress-making charts, she must surrender all published charts, together with plates on which they are printed. Drury v. Ewing, (CC-Ohio), FedCas 4,095, 1 Bond 540.

Under R. S. § 4965 providing that the infringer "shall forfeit to the proprietor" of the copyright every sheet unlawfully reproduced, copies not so far completed as to establish their identity are not subject to forfeiture. Morrison v. Pettibone, (CC-Ill), 87 Fed 330.

An action for assumpsit for the purpose of recovering the statutory penalty for copies of the infringing article in the possession of the defendant, must be brought after there is a forfeiture, and there can be no forfeiture until there is a finding by the court. Falk v. Curtis Pub. Co., (CCA 3), 107 Fed 126, aff'g 102 Fed 967; Child v. New York Times Co., (CC-NY), 110 Fed 527.

An action under R. S. § 9465 to recover a penalty and forfeiture is not an action of replevin. Hegeman v. Springer, (CCA 2), 110 Fed 374. Aff'd 189 US 505, 47 LEd 921, 23 SCR 849; Rinehart v. Smith, (CC-Pa), 121 Fed 148; Gustin v. Record Pub. Co., (CC-Pa), 127 Fed 603; American Tobacco Co. v. Werckmeister, (CCA 2), 146 Fed 375. Aff'd 207 US 284, 52 LEd 208, 28 SCR 72, 12 AnnCas 595.

Copyright owner was entitled to decree for destruction of infringing articles. North & Judd Mfg. Co. v. Krischer's Mfg. Co., Inc., (DC-Conn), 11 FSupp 739, 27 USPQ 224.

Copyright infringer is commanded to deliver up on oath to marshal of court all copies of infringing books, as well as all plates, molds, matrices, and other means for making copies of books in his possession, and marshal is directed to destroy them within five days after their delivery to him and to make return of his act to court. Southern Bell Telephone & Telegraph Co. v. Donnelly, (DC-Fla), 35 FSupp 425, 48 USPQ 11.

Injunction issues with order that infringing defendants deliver up for destruction all infringing copies, as well as all plates, molds, and other means for making such copies. Sammons v. Larkin, (DC-Mass), 38 FSupp 649, 49 USPQ 350. Mf'd 126 F(2d) 341, 53 USPQ 71.

Infringing prints and plates are subject to destruction. Rudolf Lesch Fine Arts, Inc. v. Metal, (DC-NY), 51 FSupp 69, 58 USPQ 668.

Summary judgment for defendants is granted as to plaintiff's prayer that infringing copies, be delivered for destruction, since defendants' affidavits state, without contradiction by plaintiff, that copies, were destroyed prior to start of suit. Local Trademarks, Inc. v. Rogers, (DC-Ala), 73 FSupp 907, 75 USPQ 336.

Where defendant's catalogue contains cuts copied from plaintiff's copyrighted catalogue, defendant is required to block out copied cuts, together with script referring thereto, from all catalogues in its possession or under its control and must surrender all plates, molds, and other matter used for producing infringements. Perkins Marine Lamp & Hardware Co. v. Goodwin Stanley Co., (DC-NY), 86 FSupp 630, 83 USPQ 32.

Subsection (d) of this section contemplates destruction of infringement copies, but fact of infringement first must be judicially established. Lampert v. Hollis Music, Inc., (DC-NY), 105 FSupp 3, 94 USPQ 226.

Plaintiff is entitled to delivery and destruction of all infringing products and materials in defendant's hands which may have been used in infringement of plaintiff's copyrights. Curt Teich & Co., Inc. v. Beals Lithograph & Printing Co., Inc., (DC-Iowa), 61 USPQ 434.

47.   Royalties for use of mechanical reproduction of musical works.

Certain correspondence between owner and mechanical reproducer of copyrighted song constituted notice of intention under subsec. (e) of this section. Leo Feist, Inc. v. American Music Roll Co., (CCA 3), 251 Fed 245.

Notice of intention to make records of a copyrighted musical composition given pursuant to subsec. (e) of this section established a "compulsory license." G. Ricordi & Co., Inc. v. Columbia Graphophone Co., (CCA 2), 263 Fed 354.

One who has become a "compulsory licensee" of the right to make phonograph records of a song, and paid royalties under such license is estopped from denying its licensor's title. G.

Ricordi & Co., Inc. v. Columbia Graphophone Co., (CCA 2), 263 Fed 354.

Where master records, matrices, and stampers were manufactured in United States and then shipped to Canada where final records were made, the records were manufactured in the United States and plaintiff was entitled to recover for the manufacture of such records. G. Ricordi & Co. v. Columbia Graphophone Co., (DC-NY), 270 Fed 822.

One who acquires the right of mechanical reproduction of a musical work, either by contract, or by complying with the prescribed requirements, does not acquire the right of publicly performing for profit the copyrighted work. Irving Berlin, Inc. v. Daigle, (CCA 5), 31 F(2d) 832, rev'g 26 F(2d) 149, and 26 F(2d) 150.

Subsection (e) of this section does not afford the rule of damages for infringement of the right to perform publicly for profit a musical composition. Irving Berlin, Inc. v. Daigle, (CCA 5), 31 F(2d) 832, rev'g 26 F(2d) 149, and 26 F(2d) 150.

Defendant offered no testimony before master in support of item of royalty and therefore court must consider schedule of defendant's costs of manufacture amended by plaintiff's exception to royalties, thus reducing costs by amount allowed for royalties. Davilla v. Brunswick-Balke Collender Co., (CCA 2), 94 F(2d) 567, 36 USPQ 398, mod'g 19 FSupp 819, 35 USPQ 157.

Liability under subsec. (e) of this section of each infringer, whether he be manufacturer, distributor, or retailer, is several, not joint; hence, seller's liability for royalties is not reduced by fact that manufacturer-codefendant made settlement; however, settlement is factor to consider in assessing costs and awarding attorney's fees against seller. Shapiro, Bernstein & Co., Inc. v. Goody, (CA 2), 248 F(2d) 260, 115 USPQ 36, rev'g 139 FSupp 176, 108 USPQ 409.

48. Election of remedies.

Prior to Copyright Act of 1909 and adoption of § 103 of this title, a suit for an injunction did not bar plaintiff from bringing a subsequent action for damages. Brady v. Daly, 175 US 148, 44 LEd 109, 20 SCR 62, aff'g (CCA 2), 83 Fed 1007.

When an action was brought for the recovery of infringing matter, and the goods were seized and turned over to the plaintiff, an action cannot be brought later for the penalties, since all the relief under the statute must be had in a single action. Hills & Co., Ltd. v. Hoover, 220 US 329, 55 LEd 485, 31 SCR 402, AnnCas 1912C, 562.

If a proprietor whose copyright has been infringed waives his action for damages, he may have an accounting of profits. Stevens v. Gladding, (CC-RI), FedCas 13,399, 2 Curt 608.

Fact that a qui tam action for the penalty allowed by law was pending did not affect the right to an injunction against the infringement of a copyright. Schumacher v. Schwencke, (CC-NY), 25 Fed 466.

Suit to recover penalty of one dollar per copy, brought in equity, was dismissed, but with right

to transfer to the law side. Guillot v. Bancroft, (DC-La), 17 F(2d) 207.

Plaintiff has the right to elect to take the minimum statutory damages of $250 for each infringement in lieu of actual damages which have not been proved. Tiffany Productions, Inc. v. Dewing, (DC-Md), 50 F(2d) 911, 9 USPQ 545.

Refusal to arbitrate does not bar infringement suit and the grant of a license is not an election to sue in assumpsit. Tiffany Productions, Inc. v. Dewing, (DC-Md), 50 F(2d) 911, 9 USPQ 545.

Copyright statute differs from patent and trade-mark statutes, and injunction is not condition precedent for accounting and award of damages for copyright infringement. Sheldon v. Moredall Realty Corp., (CCA 2), 95 F(2d) 48, 37 USPQ 286, mod'g 22 FSupp 91, 37 USPQ 254.

Plaintiffs cannot be said to have abandoned claim for copyright infringement by bringing action for unfair competition in state court. Leo Feist, Inc. v. Song Parodies, Inc., (CCA 2), 146 F(2d) 400, 64 USPQ 92.

Copyright owners' failure to comply with § 1(e) of this title by filing required notice bars collection of statutory royalties for mechanical reproduction of musical composition; Trading with the Enemy Act [50 Appx. § 1 et seq.] does not clothe attorney general with power to avoid these conditions, which are set up by copyright statute and which have not been repealed; rule that terms of copyright statute must be substantially complied with or no advantage can be taken of its provision is applicable. Biltmore Music Corp. v. Kittinger, (CA 9), 238 F(2d) 373, 111 USPQ 228.

Fact that bill for infringement shows the existence of a license contract is not conclusive as to election of remedy for breach of contract precluding suit for infringement where defendant may have trespassed on plaintiff's monopoly beyond the terms of the contract. Metro-Goldwyn-Mayer Distributing Corp. v. Bijou Theatre Co., (DC-Mass), 3 FSupp 66, 17 USPQ 124.

By intrusting films to defendant with contract to show on certain days only, plaintiff did not waive right to sue in tort under copyright law and was not relegated to suit on contract. Twentieth Century-Fox Film Corp. v. Peoples Theatres, Inc., (DC-Ala), 24 FSupp 793, 39 USPQ 469.

Author's failure to seek to enjoin filming of motion picture does not bar him from maintaining plagiarism action after production of picture since producer had informed him that author's script was not being used in picture and that producer could not pay author for writing of script unless picture were produced. Szekely v. Eagle Lion Films, Inc., (DC-NY), 140 FSupp 843, 109 USPQ 348. Aff'd 242 F(2d) 266, 113 USPQ 98.

Copyright Act permits actions for its violation either at law or in equity; plaintiff can elect whether to sue at law or in equity. Arnstein v. Twentieth Century-Fox Film Corp., (DC-NY), 3 FedRDec 58, 56 USPQ 511.

49. Right of action.

A person who assigns his rights to a work under contract which provides that the assignees "shall have the copyright of said reports to them, their heirs and assigns forever," parts with all his interests in such copyright, and his executors cannot bring a suit for infringement. Paige v. Banks, 80 US(13 Wall) 608, 20 LEd 709, aff'g (CC-NY), FedCas 10,671.

A person, giving the events of his life to another for the purpose of preparing a book, is not the author, and therefore a person receiving his title under him cannot sue for infringement. De Witt v. Brooks, (CC-NY), FedCas 3,851.

Proprietors of copyright on law reports were entitled to sue to restrain infringement without resorting to a suit at law to establish their right to the copyright. Gould v. Hastings, (CC-NY), FedCas 5,639.

Complainants who had by contract been given the exclusive right to publish the copyrighted judicial opinions of a state's courts, as was permitted by a state's laws had such rights and title in the reports as would enable them to maintain suit for infringement. Little v. Gould, (CC-NY), FedCas 8,394, 2 Blatchf 165; Little v. Gould, (CC-NY), FedCas 8,395, 2 Blatchf 362.

Owner and user of a foreign designed chromo was not a "proprietor" within meaning of R. S. § 4952, so as to be entitled to the benefits and protection of the copyright law in the chromo. Yuengling v. Schile, (CC-NY), 12 Fed 97.

Publisher who had acquired from a state the exclusive right to publish certain volumes of law reports, so far as state could grant same right was not entitled to maintain suit against others who published like reporters. Banks v. Manchester, (CC-Ohio), 23 Fed 143. Aff'd 128 US 244, 32 LEd 425, 9 SCR 36.

An author holding legal title to the copyright of a pamphlet for the benefit of another was entitled to sue for its infringement. Hanson v. Jaccard Jewelry Co., (CC-Mo), 32 Fed 202.

A foreign administrator, not taking out ancillary letters, cannot maintain a suit for infringement. Black v. Henry G. Allen Co., (CC-NY), 42 Fed 618, 9 LRA 433.

Person doing business under a conventional or fictitious firm name may sue for infringement of a copyright without alleging compliance with a state law requiring the filing of a certificate. Scribner v. Henry G. Allen Co., (CC-NY), 49 Fed 854.

Proof showing that complainant took out copyright of the infringed edition of a book in the company name under which he then conducted his business entitled him to subsequently maintain suit for infringement of the copyright of the book in his own name. Scribner v. Clark, (CC-Ill), 50 Fed 473. Aff'd 144 US 488, 36 LEd 514, 12 SCR 734.

Where two companies prior to the printing of a directory enter into a contract whereby they agree to jointly take a canvass of the inhabitants, and to jointly do the compiling, typesetting, and proofreading, one cannot, by virtue of having obtained a copyright on the directory, restrain the other party from distributing their directory. Maloney v. Foote, (CC-Ga), 101 Fed 264.

Where a person publishes a picture which had been copied from a copyrighted photograph, which, in turn, had been taken from a copyrighted painting, the owner of the copyright of the photograph is entitled to sue and not the owner of the painting. Champney v. Haag, (CC-Pa), 121 Fed 944.

Where a composer by contract agrees to sell all his songs written during a certain period, to a publisher, and in violation of such contract he copyrights his own songs, neither he nor his assigns can maintain an action for infringement. Harms & Francis v. Stern, (CCA 2), 231 Fed 645, rev'g 229 Fed 42, which rev'd 222 Fed 581.

Nondomiciled resident Canadian cannot maintain suit for injunction under subsec. (e) of this section. G. Ricordi & Co., Inc. v. Columbia Graphophone Co., (DC-NY), 256 Fed 699.

Where the plaintiff has no authority to copyright, he can maintain no action for infringement. Public Ledger Co. v. New York Times Co., (CCA 2), 279 Fed 747, aff'g 275 Fed 562.

This section and § 112 of this title apply only to relief for infringement of a copyright, and not of a right of an assignee or licensee of less than a copyright interest. Goldwyn Pictures' Corp. v. Howells Sales Co., Inc., (CCA 2), 282 Fed 9.

The owner of the equitable title of a copyright is not a mere licensee, and he may sue in equity, particularly where the owner of the legal title is an infringer, or one of the infringers, thus occupying a position hostile to the plaintiff. Ted Browne Music Co. v. Fowler, (CCA 2), 290 Fed 751.

Equitable owner of copyright may sue for infringement. Bisel v. Ladner, (CCA 3), 1 F(2d) 436.

The proprietor of a copyrighted publication may sue for infringement of an article in the publication copyrighted for the benefit of the author of the article. Schellberg v. Empringham, (DC-NY), 36 F(2d) 991.

Owner of unpublished musical composition copyrighted under § 12 of this title and not later reproduced in copies for sale, can maintain infringement action against one making and selling phonographic records of composition. Shilkret v. Musicraft Records, Inc., (CCA 2), 131 F(2d) 929, 55 USPQ 469, rev'g 43 FSupp 184, 52 USPQ 164.

Copyright Act gives right to sue for infringement to copyright proprietor; plaintiff, publisher member of the American Society of Composers, Authors, and Publishers, is proprietor and may sue. Leo Feist, Inc. v. Young, (CCA 7), 138 F(2d) 972, 59 USPQ 450, rev'g 46 FSupp 622, 54 USPQ 489.

Chapter 138, Nebraska Laws of 1937, does not bar copyright owners from maintaining copyright infringement suit, although owners are members of the American Society of Composers, Authors, and Publishers, alleged to be illegal price-fixing combination, since the American Society of Composers, Authors, and Publishers is not party to suit, has no interest in copyrights, and does not do business in Nebraska. Interstate Hotel Co. v. Remick Music Corp., (CCA 8), 157 F(2d) 744, 71 USPQ 138, aff'g 58 FSupp 523, 63 USPQ 327.

Suit for infringement of copyright brought by copyright protective bureau in name of copyright owner for such owner's benefit was not barratrous. Vitaphone Corp. v. Hutchinson Amusement Co., (DC-Mass), 19 FSupp 359, 33 USPQ 422.

Copyright protective bureau organized by plaintiff and other motion-picture producers to find, prosecute, and settle infringements was authorized to bring action since plaintiff's sales manager asked bureau to look into infringement and plaintiff was notified of suit and helped with prosecution. Vitaphone Corp. v. Hutchinson Amusement Co., (DC-Mass), 28 FSupp 526, 42 USPQ 431.

Outright sale of song by author in consideration that purchaser pay royalties is absolute assignment passing absolute ownership and right to apply for copyright; subsequent release to author of all purchaser's right, title, and interest in song, which purchaser had copyrighted, does not carry right to sue for infringement occurring during purchaser's ownership. Kriger v. MacFadden Publications, Inc., (DC-NY), 43 FSupp 170, 52 USPQ 217.

Members of the American Society of Composers, Authors, and Publishers may maintain copyright infringement suit despite consent decree in antitrust suit. Shapiro, Bernstein & Co., Inc. v. Veltin, (DC-La), 47 FSupp 648, 55 USPQ 335.

Composer cannot maintain copyright infringement suit where another is owner of copyright and composer only has right to receive royalties, although copyright owner is added as party defendant because it refuses to sue for alleged infringement. Stringfield v. Warner Bros. Pictures, Inc., (DC-NY), 51 FSupp 746, 58 USPQ 59.

Authors and composers pleading facts on which equitable interest in copyright can be predicated are proper parties entitled to bring infringement suit, although legal title to copyright is in another. Hoffman v. Santly-Joy, Inc., (DC-NY), 51 FSupp 778, 58 USPQ 526.

Copyright proprietor may maintain suit for infringement by public performance although it assigned exclusive public performance rights to the American Society of Composers, Authors, and Publishers. Shapiro, Bernstein & Co., Inc. v. Widenski, (DC-RI), 54 FSupp 780, 61 USPQ 91. Aff'd 147 F(2d) 909, 64 USPQ 448.

Copyright law does not permit action for damages for infringement to be brought by any party other than copyright proprietor. Local Trademarks, Inc. v. Rogers, (DC-Ala), 73 FSupp 907, 75 USPQ 336.

Sale of copyright does not prevent owner at time of infringement from suing for damages sustained while it was owner. M. J. Golden & Co., Inc. v. Pittsburgh Brewing Co., Inc., (DC-Pa), 137 FSupp 455, 108 USPQ 250.

Ordinarily, authorized recorder of copyrighted music cannot sue although, in addition to payment of royalties to copyrighted owner and to recording artists, he may be required, as condition of recording, to make payments to trust funds for benefit of musicians. Harms, Inc. v. F. W. Woolworth Co., (DC-Cal), 163 FSupp 484, 118 USPQ 436.

Absent a basis for claim of infringement, a case presenting a claim of equitable ownership of copyright with a prayer for an assignment and accounting does not arise under copyright law; claim of federally protected interest forms part of plaintiff's legal position, but, unlike suit for infringement, federal legislation relating to copyrights does not confer specific right of action sought to be enforced; sources of obligations to assign and account are equitable doctrines relating to unjust enrichment and general principles of law governing rights of co-owners, not remedial provisions of copyright law. Harrington v. Mure, (DC-NY), 186 FSupp 655, 126 USPQ 506.

Co-author cannot bring infringement action against other co-authors, their assignees, or licensees; proper balance between interest of excluded co-author and that of the public is achieved by allowing each co-author to exploit the work, but subject to duty to account to his collaborators. Harrington v. Mure, (DC-NY), 186 FSupp 655, 126 USPQ 506.

Equitable owner of copyright may sue for infringement in federal court where complaint sets forth facts showing validity of copyright, basis of his ownership interest, and infringement by defendant; foundation of suit is the alleged infringement; incidental power to decide title claim, as to which court lacks original jurisdiction, depends upon specifically conferred power to adjudicate infringement claim; absent such ancillary jurisdiction, plaintiff whose citizenship is same as his adversary's would be forced to look to state court in the first instance; state forum could declare plaintiff's status as equitable owner but could not go on to consider claim or infringement because exclusive jurisdiction of that matter resides in federal court. Harrington v. Mure, (DC-NY), 186 FSupp 655, 126 USPQ 506.

Under Trading with the Enemy Act [50 Appx. § 1 et seq.], Italian enemy may prosecute copyright infringement suit against any person other than licensee; final judgment awarding damages may be entered only after 30 days' written notice to alien property custodian. Select Theatres Corp. v. Ronzoni Macaroni Co., (DC-NY), 59 USPQ 288.

A German citizen who has strictly complied with the provisions of the Copyright Act at any time between July 1, 1909, the date upon which § 9 of this title became effective, and the date of the proclamation of the President declaring that the citizens of Germany were entitled to the general copyright privileges, is not only vested with a copyright in his work, but may maintain an action for any infringement which occurred between said dates. 29 OAG 64.

A person who has never completed his copyright cannot give another person the right to complete such copyright 16 years later, so as to enable such person to sue for infringement. Koppel v. Downing, 11 AppDC 93.

Where the plaintiff had purchased the right to produce a German play in this country but did not copyright it, he cannot restrain another from producing the play in this country when the author had published book of the play, although such publication was in violation of his contract. Daly v. Walrath, 40 AppDiv 220, 57 NYS 1125.

Where a contract between the owner of a foreign play and an American theatrical company, provides that the theatrical company shall produce the play in English and the interpolations for such play are to be written by the owner, but that when such interpolations are not satisfactorily furnished, the theatrical company may have them produced elsewhere, and a further provision provides that it applies only to numbers of the owner of the songs and interpolations that belong to him; he has no right to interpolations furnished by the theatrical company and cannot sue for the infringement. Karczog Pub. Co., Inc. v. Shubert Theatrical Co., 181 AppDiv 529, 169 NYS 1.

One co-owner of a copyright cannot bring suit to restrain the production of a play by a third person, unless he can prove that such person was not licensed by his co-owner. Herbert v. Fields, (Misc), 152 NYS 487.

Equitable owners of either total or partial rights under patents and copyrights can enforce rights even where patentee or copyright proprietor is infringer, and even where they must join owner of legal title as plaintiff without his consent and against his will. Gay v. Robbins Music Corp., (Misc), 38 NYS(2d) 337, 55 USPQ 461.

50. —Assignees.

The assignee, of a work from an alien author, cannot obtain protection of the copyright law. Keene v. Wheatley, (CC-Pa), FedCas 7,644.

Assignee of the exclusive right of performing a play in all places throughout the United States, excepting in five principal cities, for the term of one year had sufficient interest in the copyright to be able to maintain suit for infringement. Roberts v. Myers, (CC-Mass), FedCas 11,906.

Assignees of an owner of a copyrighted translation of a French play were entitled to maintain a suit to restrain infringement of the translation. Shook v. Rankin, (CC-Ill), FedCas 12,804, 6 Biss 477.

Assignees of the exclusive right to print and sell a series of juvenile books were proper parties to sue for its infringement. Estes v. Williams, (CC-NY), 21 Fed 189.

An arrangement whereby a composer authorized the copyrighting of his song in the name of the complainant prior to its delivery to complainant constituted in fact such an assignment of the song before copyrighting as to permit complainant to sue subsequently for infringement. White-Smith Music Pub. Co. v. Apollo Co., (CC-NY), 139 Fed 427. Aff'd 147 Fed 226, which was aff'd 209 US 1, 52 LEd 655, 28 SCR 319.

As against a defendant who knows that the title under which a play was copyrighted has been changed, and another title adopted, an assignee of the copyright may maintain an action to restrain infringement of such play. Collier v. Imp Films Co., (DC-NY), 214 Fed 272.

Assignment of anything less than entire copyright gives assignee no right to sue for infringement. New Fiction Pub. Co. v. Star Co., (DC-NY), 220 Fed 994.

Where author made assignment of all his musical compositions to be written during five-year period, and later made assignment of one of his compositions and assignee secured copyright thereon, the assignee stood in the same position as the author and could not restrain infringement on copyright by original assignee. T. B. Harms & Francis, Day & Hunter v. Stern, (CCA 2), 231 Fed 645, rev'g 229 Fed 42, which rev'd 222 Fed 581.

Assignee of the motion-picture rights of a copyrighted book without any copyright of his motion-picture photoplay could not maintain suit under this section and § 112 of this title for infringement of his rights under the assignment. Goldwyn Pictures Corp. v. Howells Sales Co., Inc., (CCA 2), 282 Fed 9.

Author's assignment of "exclusive motion-picture rights," of novel to publisher included not only silent pictures of date of contract but talking pictures subsequently developed entitling publisher to restrain talking picture filmed by company with notice of publisher's rights but which negotiated only with the author. L. C. Page & Co., Inc. v. Fox Film Corp., (CCA 2), 83 F(2d) 196, 29 USPQ 386.

Where plaintiff is assignee of copyright, it must have received all of assignor's rights in copyright by valid assignment, and assignor (which took out copyright) must have had authority to take out copyright in its own name and to assign copyright free and clear of any liabilities which would interfere with assignee's title. Machaty v. Astra Pictures, Inc., (CA 2), 197 F(2d) 138, 93 USPQ 51, aff'g 89 USPQ 539.

51. —Licensees.

While it is the general rule that a mere licensee cannot sue in its own name strangers who infringe, yet a complainant with full equitable title to a copyright may sue the legal titleholder for infringement. Wooster v. Crane & Co., (CCA 8), 147 Fed 515.

Mere licensee of American stage rights, who undertook to obtain American copyright, could not maintain an action for infringement. Saake v. Lederer, (CCA 3), 174 Fed 135, rev'g 166 Fed 810.

Licensee of right to mechanically reproduce a copyrighted composition and to make rolls therefrom was entitled to sue for the copying and duplication of his roll. Aeolian Co. v. Royal Music Roll Co., (DC-NY), 196 Fed 926.

License of serial rights to a copyrighted story vests no right to sue for infringement. New Fiction Pub. Co. v. Star Co., (DC-NY), 220 Fed 994.

Rights of licensee under copyright do not depend on legal title and he has no right to sue in own name for infringement but must join as plaintiff owner of copyright who holds title in trust for licensee Buck v. Virgo, (DC-NY), 22 FSupp 156, 37 USPQ 325.

Copyright owner granted plaintiff exclusive right to use copyrighted newspaper advertisements, plaintiff to acquire full title on payment of $400; plaintiff gave defendant right to use for year, but defendant continued use after year; plaintiff's copyright infringement suit is dismissed on motion; license under copyright is same as under patent insofar as it concerns right to sue; since there is no averment in complaint of payment of $400, plaintiff is mere licensee; plaintiff must join copyright owner in order that suit may be properly brought under 1909 Copyright Act since maintenance of action alone would oust court of jurisdiction for being mere licensee; jurisdiction of court would have to depend on diversity of citizenship which is not shown by complaint. Local Trademarks, Inc. v. Powers, (DC-Pa), 56 FSupp 751, 62 USPQ 149.

Exclusive licensee of right to publish copyrighted work in book form cannot maintain infringement suit against one publishing work in other than book form. Field v. True Comics, Inc., (DC-NY), 89 FSupp 611, 84 USPQ 358.

A licensee may maintain a suit against a purchaser of his proprietor's copyright who, with knowledge, is violating a lawful contract made by licensee and former proprietor regarding use of the copyright. Murphy v. Christian Press Ass'n Pub. Co., 38 AppDiv 426, 56 NYS 597.

52. Persons liable.

A copperplate engraving of a copyrighted map is property which may be sold upon execution, but such sale does not give the buyer the right to print the map, since the copyright remains in the author, who may restrain such buyer from infringing his copyright. Stephens v. Cady, 55 US(14 How) 528, 14 LEd 528.

Under prior statute, not containing express provision as to agents or employees, possession by employee was not the possession by the employer as affecting liability for penalty. Thornton v. Schreiber, 124 US 612, 31 LEd 577, 8 SCR 618, rev'g (DC-Pa), 17 Fed 603.

Sale of an infringing dramatic composition renders seller liable for a representation thereof by his vendee. Daly v. Palmer, (CC-NY), FedCas 3,552, 6 Blatchf 256.

If a copyright has been infringed, the person who has caused the injury is liable whether he knew of the copyright or not. Millett v. Snowden, (CC-NY), FedCas 9,600.

Defendant was not liable for the penalties prescribed in R. S. § 4965, where his agents in managing his firm directed the doing of certain acts without his knowledge or approval, which resulted in the infringement complained of. Taylor v. Gilman, (CC-NY), 24 Fed 632.

Where infringing copies of a photograph have all passed from the possession of a defendant, and plaintiff has recovered their value, defendant may not subsequently be subjected to liability for penalties prescribed in R. S. § 4965 respecting infringement of copyrights. Sarony v. Ehrich, (CC-NY), 28 Fed 79.

Parties procuring infringing act to be done are liable as joint tort-feasors. Fishel v. Lueckel, (CC-NY), 53 Fed 499.

All who unite in an infringement are liable for the damages resulting from infringement, but only those who profit thereby are liable for profits. Gross v. Van Dyk Gravure Co., (CCA 2), 230 Fed 412.

One who innocently copies a list which infringes upon the copyright of another is also guilty of infringement. Norris v. No-Leak-O Piston Ring Co., (DC-Md), 271 Fed 536. Aff'd 277 Fed 951.

Where an agent, acting in the course of his employment, finds that an article is copyrighted, such knowledge is imputed to the principal, and the principal may be sued for infringement whether he had actual knowledge or not. Christian v. American Druggist Syndicate, (CCA 2), 285 Fed 359.

The infringement of a copyright is a tort, and all persons concerned therein are jointly and severally liable as such joint tort-feasors. Ted Browne Music Co. v. Fowler, (CCA 2), 290 Fed 751.

One copying part of copyrighted composition even subconsciously is liable. Fred Fisher, Inc. v. Dillingham, (DC-NY), 298 Fed 145.

Something more than relation of landlord and tenant must exist to give rise to cause of action against the landlord for infringement of copyright which took place on the demised premises. Deutsch v. Arnold, (CCA 2), 98 F(2d) 686, 39 USPQ 5, mod'g 22 FSupp 101, 36 USPQ 318.

In patent and copyright cases, co-infringers, unless partners, are severally accountable only for profits each has received. Sammons v. Colonial Press, Inc., (CCA 1), 126 F(2d) 341, 53 USPQ 71, mod'g 38 FSupp 649, 49 USPQ 350.

Third party licensed to use copyrighted work by one co-owner is not liable for infringement to other co-owners who gave no consent; copyrights are similar in purpose to patents, and patent law protects licensee of joint owner from suit by another joint owner. Piantadosi v. Loew's, Inc., (CCA 9), 137 F(2d) 534, 59 USPQ 174.

Copyright infringement suit is dismissed where plaintiff is assignee of renewal obtained by composer of music of song and defendant is assignee of renewals obtained by authors of words of song. Edward B. Marks Music Corp. v. Jerry Vogel Music Co., Inc., (CCA 2), 140 F(2d) 270, 60 USPQ 259, aff'g 49 FSupp 135, 57 USPQ 37.

Where defendants by contract were permitted to advertise a certain patented "product" in their sales literature, the plaintiff cannot complain that the defendants use cuts made from photographs of the "product" which were copyrighted after such agreement. Industrial Railway & Locomotive Works, Inc. v. Cagney Bros., (DC-NJ), 1 FSupp 970, 15 USPQ 263.

Where all defendants were united in infringement, all were responsible for the damages resulting. Fleischer Studios, Inc. v. Ralph A. Freundlich, Inc., (DC-NY), 14 FSupp 401, 30 USPQ 125.

Owner of hotel who gave consent to photographer to take an aerial picture of the property and then appropriated the copyrighted print was liable for infringement. Cory v. Physical Culture Hotel, (DC-NY), 14 FSupp 977, 30 USPQ 353. Aff'd 88 F(2d) 411, 33 USPQ 58.

General rule imposing liability upon directors, officers, and stockholders in connection with patent infringement, which is pertinent to copyright cases, is that they are not personally liable for damages resulting from infringement unless they have inflicted the wrong otherwise than through usual relations between officer and corporation, that is to say, infringement by officers must be as individuals before they can be held personally liable. Buck v. Newsreel, Inc., (DC-Mass), 25 FSupp 787, 40 USPQ 20; Buck v. Spanish Gables, Inc., (DC-Mass), 26 FSupp 36, 40 USPQ 19; Buck v. Sunbeam, (DC-Mass), 40 USPQ 18.

Position of defendants as employees of United States cannot protect them from award of damages for copyright infringement; acts done were for benefit of government but that does not immunize its agents as well as government. Towle v. Ross, (DC-Ore), 32 FSupp 125, 45 USPQ 143.

Although infringing corporation was not cloak for individual infringer, he was sole stockholder and active managing head; no dividends were paid, but all distribution of earnings was by adjustment of his salary and commissions; individual must account, as infringing profits, for that portion of his salary and commissions as represents proportion of corporation's business represented by infringements. Alfred Bell & Co., Ltd. v. Catalda Fine Arts, Inc., (DC-NY), 86 FSupp 399, 82 USPQ 273. Mf'd 191 F(2d) 99, 90 USPQ 153.

Under doctrine of governmental immunity, public school district cannot be held liable for copyright infringement alleged to have occurred when copyrighted music was performed in school by school choir. Wihtol v. Crow, (DC-Iowa), — FSupp —, 132 USPQ 392.

Individual defendant is not personally liable where he was neither dominant nor controlling stockholder and was not in control of corporate defendant at time of alleged infringement. Edward B. Marks Music Corp. v. Bank, (DC-NY), 76 USPQ 217.

Although individual defendant owns majority of stock of defendant corporation and can control corporation, this is not sufficient to cause court to disregard corporate entity and consider it as individual's alter ego; in order to profit in law suit by doctrine of alter ego, it must be proved not only that corporation is mere conduit of stockholders, but that they are alter ego of one another. Quader-Kino A. G. v. Nebenzal, (CalApp(2d series)), 208 Pac(2d) 422, 82 USPQ 239.

53. —Printed publications.

Employee of a firm, who had infringing labels under his charge, but who did not have complete control thereover, was not liable in a suit for infringement for penalties imposed by R. S. § 4965 of one dollar for each infringing label "found in his possession." Thornton v. Schreiber, 124 US 612, 31 LEd 577, 8 SCR 618, rev'g (DC-Pa), 17 Fed 603.

Printer may be equally liable with publisher for an infringement and is accountable for profits therein made by him. Belford v. Scribner, 144 US 488, 36 LEd 514, 12 SCR 734, aff'g (CC-Ill), 50 Fed 473.

Though the subject matter of an author's work is open to all, another may not, in order to avoid expense and labor, appropriate portions of the original work without becoming liable for infringement. Farmer v. Calvert Lithographing, Etc., Co., (CC-Mich), FedCas 4,651, 1 Flip 228.

Vendor of an infringing book is liable as infringer. Greene v. Bishop, (CC-Mass), FedCas 5,763, 1 Cliff 186.

A person has a right to buy and sell copyrighted books at any price he sees fit, when he has no knowledge of an agreement between the owner of the copyright and the sales agent that the books were not to be sold under a specified price. Clemens v. Estes, (CC-Mass), 22 Fed 899.

Where by agreement, two parties having an interest in a copyright, divide the county into two parts, giving each the exclusive right to sell the copyrighted book in the section allotted to him, one of the parties can be restrained from selling in the territory of the other although part of the agreement had been breached. Baldwin v. Baird, (CC-Ill), 25 Fed 293.

Defendant who sold a copy of an original cut, which plaintiffs had not copyrighted independently, but as a part of their newspaper, was not liable for infringement, where purchasers of the cut later used it unlawfully. Harper v. Shoppell, (CC-NY), 26 Fed 519.

Where a book dealer buys books contrary to an agreement between the holder of the copyright and sales agents, he may be restrained from selling such books although he had no notice of the agreement, since the notice of copyright on the book was sufficient to put him upon inquiry as to any agreement concerning its sale. Henry Bill Publishing Co. v. Smythe, (CC-Ohio), 27 Fed 914.

Manufacturer of a cut taken from a copyrighted newspaper, selling same with knowledge that it will be used in an infringing article, is a joint tort-feasor and is guilty of infringement. Harper v. Shoppell, (CC-NY), 28 Fed 613.

A company having a copyrighted map in their office is not liable for an infringement of the map by a person over whom they have no control, even though 500 copies of the infringing map were sent to the company when these copies were not given to the public. Morris County Traction Co. v. Hence, (CCA 3), 281 Fed 820.

One who prints an infringing work is an infringer, as is also the publisher and vendor. American Code Co., Inc. v. Bensinger, (CCA 2), 282 Fed 829.

Publisher aiding infringer was liable. Schellberg v. Empringham, (DC-NY), 36 F(2d) 991.

A newspaper printing an advertisement from matrices furnished to it by an advertiser, which matrices contained no notice of copyright, was not liable for infringement, it having no knowledge of the copyright. Wilkes-Barre Record Co. v. Standard Advertising Co., (CCA 3), 63 F(2d) 99, 16 USPQ 346.

President of corporation infringing copyright is personally liable for infringement since he organized corporation, paid for nearly all stock, lent it substantial sums, gave employee who wrote infringing book material with which to begin book, showed employee copy of plaintiff's book, passed on part of original copy of infringing book, and made numerous calls on employee relative to book. Adventures in Good Eating, Inc. v. Best Places to Eat, Inc., (CCA 7), 131 F(2d) 809, 56 USPQ 242.

Publisher cannot maintain infringement action against competing publisher whose magazine carries identical advertisement or listing, where advertising and listing copy were furnished by advertiser or lister, who retained right to alter arrangement, and where both publishers are paid standard space rate by advertiser. Official Aviation Guide Co., Inc. v. American Aviation Associates, Inc., (CCA 7), 150 F(2d) 173, 65 USPQ 553, mod'g 62 USPQ 178.

Corporation was formed to publish book including infringing composition prepared by defendant; defendant was dominant influence in corporation and ran its affairs; he personally applied for copyright on infringing song in his own name; no other individual was of any consequence in planning and carrying out infringement; defendant is liable for corporation's acts. Wihtol v. Wells, (CA 7), 231 F(2d) 550, 109 USPQ 200.

Parties agreed it would be economical and satisfactory and court fixes damages and profits at $1500; defendant news dealers are only secondarily liable in case defendant publisher cannot answer therefor; in such event they shall be jointly and severally liable as joint and several infringers. Detective Comics, Inc. v. Bruns Publications, Inc., (DC-NY), 28 FSupp 399, 41 USPQ 182. Mf'd 111 F(2d) 432, 45 USPQ 291.

Although printer and author are properly sued jointly and severally in same copyright infringement suit, plaintiffs have suffered no recoverable damage for which both defendants are jointly and severally liable as joint tort-feasors; printer is not liable for profits received by author; fact that printer and author opened joint bank account is not too significant since this was merely attempt by printer to protect its bill for work done. Sammons v. Larkin, (DC-Mass), 38 FSupp 649, 49 USPQ 350. Mf'd 126 F(2d) 341, 53 USPQ 71.

Printer of an infringing book is an infringer. Sammons v. Larkin, (DC-Mass), 38 FSupp 649, 49 USPQ 350. Mf'd 126 F(2d) 341, 53 USPQ 71.

Magazine publisher, which published digest of infringing author's book, also infringes since smaller quantity of material copied is not different in kind; innocence of publisher is no excuse. Acosta v. Brown, (DC-NY), 50 FSupp 615, 58 USPQ 596. Aff'd 146 F(2d) 408, 63 USPQ 311.

Copyright infringement action was dismissed as to individual defendants who had no connection with infringing publication other than being officers, directors, or stockholders of defendant corporation, but was not dismissed as against corporation's president who knew of and took part in copying of plaintiff's catalogues. Harry Alter Co., Inc. v. A. E. Borden Co., Inc., (DC-Mass), 121 FSupp 941, 102 USPQ 2.

Where party causes or procures independent contractor to print or copy copyrighted work, party is equally liable with contractor as joint tort-feasor. Greenbie v. Noble, (DC-NY), 151 FSupp 45, 113 USPQ 115.

Printer becomes liable to copyright owner the moment he prints infringing work. Maloney v. Stone, (DC-Mass), 171 FSupp 29, 121 USPQ 257.

Individual defendants, who caused corporate defendant to publish articles infringing plaintiff's copyright, are jointly and severally liable together with corporate defendant for damages sustained by plaintiff; all who participate in infringement are jointly and severally liable. Massapequa Publishing Co., Inc. v. Observer, Inc., (DC-NY), 191 FSupp 261, 128 USPQ 418.

Plaintiff's publicity agent did not authorize defendant to publish material from plaintiff's copyrighted articles until after termination of agent's employment; defendant is infringer by publication thereafter. Vinick v. Charm Publications, Inc., (DC-NY), 46 USPQ 510.

54. —Dramatic performances.

Where an unprinted drama is produced, a person in the audience may be restrained from reproducing the drama from memory, although the drama was not copyrighted. Crowe v. Aiken, (CC-Ill), FedCas 3,441, 2 Biss 208; Tompkins v. Halleck, 133 Mass 32, 43 AmRep 480.

Producers of infringing play were severally liable for profits they received from production of play. Harris v. Miller, (DC-NY), 50 USPQ 306. Mf'd 50 USPQ 625.

All defendants participating in production of infringing play are jointly liable for all of plaintiff's damages resulting from infringement; defendants, who published infringing play, are jointly liable for plaintiff's damages resulting from publication and are jointly and severally liable for profits received from its publication and for royalties received from producers of infringing play. Harris v. Miller, (DC-NY), 50 USPQ 625, mod'g 50 USPQ 306.

Although Ronzoni Company sponsored and is liable for infringement by radio broadcasts of infringing play, it is not liable for infringement by stage performances by producer-actor of radio play, whose programs display name "Ronzoni" as part of corporate name of dramatic company and advertise Ronzoni products by cut furnished by Ronzoni Company, since Ronzoni Company had nothing to do with name of dramatic company, has no interest in dramatic company, did not cause stage performances, paid nothing for advertising although it did announce performances in radio broadcasts, did not rent places where play was produced, and did not share in profits or expenses of stage production. Select Theatres Corp. v. Ronzoni Macaroni Co., (DC-NY), 59 USPQ 288.

Radio station, which was made defendant by amendment to complaint alleging separate and independent cause of action solely against it, is separately and independently liable for copyright infringement by retransmitting infringing play telephoned to it by infringing originating radio station. Select Theatres Corp.

v. Ronzoni Macaroni Co., (DC-NY), 59 USPQ 288.

Where sponsor engaged producer and radio time to broadcast play on radio; sponsor, producer, and radio station were jointly and severally liable for infringement. Select Theatres Corp. v. Ronzoni Macaroni Co., (DC-NY), 59 USPQ 288.

55. —Musical compositions.

Where the owner of a concert hall has no notice that a copyrighted composition is to be performed, at the time he executes the lease for the hall, he is not liable for any infringement by the lessees. Fromont v. Aeolian Co., (DC-NY), 254 Fed 592.

Although the musician in a theater was an independent contractor and was given permission to play whatever he thought appropriate to accompany the motion picture, the operator of the theater by giving such permission, was responsible for the infringement of a copyright of a musical composition. Harms v. Cohen, (DC-Pa), 279 Fed 276.

One who by means of the microphone "picks up" another's unauthorized performance of a copyrighted musical composition and transmits it by radio is liable for infringement. Jerome H. Remick & Co. v. General Electric Co., (DC-NY), 16 F(2d) 829.

Theater owner was liable for use of copyrighted music roll by operator of player piano in theater, to which admission was charged, though the use was without his knowledge and against his orders. M. Witmark & Sons v. Calloway, (DC-Tenn), 22 F(2d) 412.

Proprietors of amusement halls, hotel dining rooms, night clubs, skating rinks, or dance halls operated for profit are liable for infringement, though having no voice in the selection of the music by the musician or orchestra leader. Dreamland Ball Room, Inc. v. Shapiro, Bernstein & Co., (CCA 7), 36 F(2d) 354, 3 USPQ 288; Buck v. Russo, (DC-Mass), 25 FSupp 317, 39 USPQ 377; Buck v. Dacier, (DC-Mass), 26 FSupp 37, 40 USPQ 14; Buck v. Crescent Gardens Operating Co., (DC-Mass), 28 FSupp 576, 42 USPQ 435; Remick Music Corp. v. Interstate Hotel Co., (DC-Neb), 58 FSupp 523, 63 USPQ 327. Aff'd 157 F(2d) 744, 71 USPQ 138; Buck v. Parker, (DC-Mass), 40 USPQ 13; Buck v. Valenti, (DC-Mass), 40 USPQ 16; Buck v. Ricci, (DC-Mass), 40 USPQ 17; Buck v. Wrentham Show Boat, (DC-Mass), 40 USPQ 25.

A copyright holder granting to a radio broadcasting station a license to perform a musical composition cannot bring suit against a cafe owner for infringement when the cafe owner permits the song to be heard in his cafe through his radio receiver. Buck v. Debaum, (DC-Cal), 40 F(2d) 734.

Hotel company using radio to entertain guests was liable for infringement of a copyrighted song. Buck v. Jewell-LaSalle Realty Co., (CCA 8), 51 F(2d) 726, 10 USPQ 70, mod'g 32 F(2d) 366, 1 USPQ 319; Buck v. Jewell-LaSalle Realty Co., (CCA 8), 51 F(2d) 730, 10 USPQ 101, mod'g 32 F(2d) 366, 1 USPQ 319.

Nonprofit corporation which operates radio broadcasting station for philanthropic and educational purposes infringed by broadcasting on sustaining program quarter of copyrighted musical composition; third of radio time is sold to advertisers; sustaining programs build up listener appeal and provide inducement to advertisers; it is not important whether profit from advertising programs go to corporation, its employees, or advertisers since performance of composition was for profit and copyright owner had right to preclude each of them; corporation's station manager was also liable since he was paid for services and exercised own judgment in choosing music broadcast. Associated Music Publishers, Inc. v. Debs Memorial Radio Fund, Inc., (CCA 2), 141 F(2d) 852, 61 USPQ 161, aff'g 46 FSupp 829, 54 USPQ 461.

It makes little difference whether defendant copied from plaintiff's song or whether defendant copied from third party who copied from plaintiff. Wihtol v. Wells, (CA 7), 231 F(2d) 550, 109 USPQ 200.

Notwithstanding booking agency furnished stage show, musicians, and orchestra, owner of theatre was guilty of infringement where copyrighted music was played and sung. Buck v. Newsreel, Inc., (DC-Mass), 25 FSupp 787, 40 USPQ 20.

Managing agent of corporation who hired orchestra and who controlled operation and who by control of lease could turn corporation out at any time was responsible for infringement. Buck v. Crescent Gardens Operating Co., (DC-Mass), 28 FSupp 576, 42 USPQ 435.

Hotel orchestra which played copyrighted musical compositions without permission infringed copyrights although no admission was charged and hotel proprietor was liable therefore even if wrongful acts were committed without his authority and against his orders. Buck v. Coe, (DC-Pa), 32 FSupp 829, 45 USPQ 230; Buck v. Pettijohn, (DC-Tenn), 34 FSupp 968, 46 USPQ 514; Edwin H. Morris & Co., Inc. v. Kaufman, (DC-Pa), 59 USPQ 393.

Authors assigned musical composition with right to obtain copyright thereon to publisher by agreement reserving substantial rights to participate in proceeds of exploitation and providing that, if publisher should refuse to sue infringers, authors could institute such action; because of fiduciary relationship, imposing equitable obligations upon publisher beyond those ordinarily imposed by law upon those dealing fully at arms' length, authors may sue infringers, upon publisher's refusal to sue, provided that publisher is joined as defendant. Manning v. Miller Music Corp., (DC-NY), 174 FSupp 192, 121 USPQ 600.

Proprietor of establishment cannot escape liability for copyright violation on ground that person furnishing musical performance is an independent contractor who selects compositions to be played. M. Witmark & Sons v. Tremont Social & Athletic Club, (DC-Mass), 188 FSupp 787, 127 USPQ 447.

Second Circuit holds that infringement of copyright is a tort and that all persons concerned therein are jointly and severally liable; likewise, First Circuit holds that all persons uniting in infringement are jointly and severally liable for damages resulting therefrom; principle is applicable to action for mechanical recording of copyrighted song in that copyright infringement is involved; thus, since S manufactured or pressed and shipped to Canadian copies of infringing record from a master made by C, and since C's function was master acetates shipped (at direction of first Canadian) to another Canadian in Canada plus mastering and processing of two units shipped to first Canadian, S and C are joint tortfeasors with first Canadian and infringe copyrighted music even though S denies that it is a manufacturer; S and C are liable not because they may or may not be manufacturers as defined in Ricordi v. Columbia, 270 F. 822, but under subsec. (e) of this section which grants remedy against unauthorized manufacturers who cannot be sued under § 1(e) of this title. Reeve Music Co., Inc. v. Crest Records, Inc., (DC-NY), 190 FSupp 272, 128 USPQ 37. Mf'd 285 F(2d) 546, 128 USPQ 24.

Where orchestra received space in defendant's restaurant but no remuneration, and defendant had control over what they should play, he was liable for infringement by unauthorized playing of copyrighted music. Donaldson, Douglas & Gumble, Inc. v. Terris, (DC-Pa), 37 USPQ 39.

Suit by one of three authors of song, against other two and their licensees for accounting for use of portions of song, is dismissed as to licensees but accounting is awarded against co-author. Brown v. Republic Productions, Inc., 68 CalApp(2d series) 140, 156 Pac(2d) 42, 65 USPQ 56.

If defendant composer wrongfully appropriated plaintiff's melody, and thus infringed plaintiff's common-law copyright, defendant motion-picture producer (whose motion picture contains infringing song) and defendant music publisher (who published infringing song) are liable to plaintiff regardless of whether they had knowledge of wrongful appropriation. Navara v. M. Witmark & Sons, 17 Misc(2d series) 174, 185 NYS(2d) 563, 121 USPQ 107.

56. —Motion pictures.

The producers of an infringing motion-picture film are liable for infringement after sale of the film to others with knowledge of its intended illegal use. Kalem v. Harper Brothers, 222 US 55, 56 LEd 92, 32 SCR 20, AnnCas 1913A, 1285, aff'g (CCA 2), 169 Fed 61.

An exhibition of a series of photographs of persons or things, arranged on film as moving pictures and so depicting the principal scenes of an author's work as to tell the story, is a dramatization of such work, and the person producing the films and offering them for sale for exhibition, even if not himself exhibiting them, infringes the copyright of the author. Atlas Mfg. Co. v. Street & Smith, (CCA 8), 204 Fed 398, 47 LRA (NS) 1002.

This section applies to exhibitors of motion pictures. Vitagraph, Inc. v. Grobaski, (DC-Mich), 46 F(2d) 813.

Author is liable for damages as contributory and participating infringer and joint tortfeasor where he deliberately chose material which he knew had been used in plaintiff's copyrighted motion picture; fact that author received no profits does not relieve him from liability for damages. Universal Pictures Co., Inc. v. Harold Lloyd Corp., (CCA 9), 162 F(2d) 354, 73 USPQ 317.

Motion-picture producer is liable where its agents, acting within scope of agency and employment, willfully incorporated into picture material which they knew to be patterned after another's copyrighted picture; corporation is chargeable with knowledge and notice of matters becoming known to its agents and employees within course and scope of agency and employment. Universal Pictures Co., Inc. v. Harold Lloyd Corp., (CCA 9), 162 F(2d) 354, 73 USPQ 317.

57. Defenses.

It is no defense in a suit to restrain the publication of a book that the book had already been printed. Bunkley v. De Witt, (CC-NY), FedCas 2,134.

It is no defense in an action to enjoin a book dealer from selling copyrighted books contrary to a sales agreement, that he had no notice of such agreement. Henry Bill Publishing Co. v. Smythe, (CC-Ohio), 27 Fed 914.

Previous infringement by others is not a defense. Gilmore v. Anderson, (CC-NY), 38 Fed 846.

The purpose of an invasion, or previous unlawful appropriation of parts of author's writing by others is no justification or defense to suit for infringement. Gilmore v. Anderson, (CC-NY), 38 Fed 846.

Though an appropriator of another's work enclose such portions as he takes within quotations, he is not thereby relieved from liability for infringement. Gilmore v. Anderson, (CC-NY), 38 Fed 846.

Failure to prosecute other suits to a final hearing did not justify defendants in going ahead with infringement. Black v. Henry G. Allen Co., (CC-NY), 56 Fed 764.

Officers of state cannot interpose their official character, or orders of the state, in suit for injunction to enjoin infringement. Howell v. Miller, (CCA 6), 91 Fed 129.

Fact that a compilation of statutes was authorized by the legislature does not justify an infringement of plaintiff's rights under the copyright laws. Howell v. Miller, (CCA 6), 91 Fed 129.

Since the recovery provided for in a suit for the infringement of a copyright, is a penalty, it is a defense that the servants or agents of the master acted without his knowledge or consent. McDonald v. Hearst, (DC-Cal), 95 Fed 656.

Lack of originality and musical merit of complainants' "rag-time" song did not constitute a good defense to an action for infringement. Hein v. Harris, (CC-NY), 175 Fed 875. Aff'd 183 Fed 107.

On the expiration of the copyright of a novel any person may use the plot for a play, copy or publish it, or make any other use of it he sees fit, subject to the limitation that the right must be so exercised as not to deceive the public into believing that they are buying the particular thing that was produced under the copyright. Atlas Mfg. Co. v. Street & Smith, (CCA 8), 204 Fed 398, 47 LRA(NS) 1002.

Owner of copyright upon an episode printed as news, but which in fact was fiction, was denied relief from infringement against a producer of a play based on said episode. Davies v. Bowes, (DC-NY), 209 Fed 53. Aff'd 219 Fed 178.

Fact that defendant's unlawful importation of foreign-printed books did not effect an injury to defendant, was not a defense to plaintiff's suit to enjoin infringement of copyright. Bentley v. Tibbals, (CCA 2), 223 Fed 247.

Publication of noncopyrighted matter with accompanying embellishments, similar to, but not identical with, those accompanying its previous publication registered by another publisher was not an infringement. Eggers v. Sun Sales Corp., (CCA 2), 263 Fed 373.

It is no deefnse, in an action for the infringement of a musical composition, that the playing consisted only of short excerpts. Harms v. Cohen, (DC-Pa), 279 Fed 276.

It is no defense, in an action for the infringement of a musical composition by broadcasting it on the radio, that the song was advertised by so doing. M. Witmark & Sons v. L. Bamberger & Co., (DC-NJ), 291 Fed 776.

Any action growing out of the infringement of a copyright is not affected by the artistic merit of a work. Pellegrini v. Allegrini, (DC-Pa), 2 F(2d) 610.

Publication of part of plaintiff's book in a magazine copyrighted by the publisher thereof was no defense to infringement by copying directly from plaintiff's book. Warren v. White & Wyckoff Mfg. Co., (DC-NY), 39 F(2d) 922.

Defendants do not avoid copyright by argument that various attributes of plaintiff's fictional character find prototypes or analogies among heroes of literature and mythology; if plaintiff's production involves more than presentation of a general type he may copyright it. Detective Comics, Inc. v. Bruns Publications, Inc., (CCA 2), 111 F(2d) 432, 45 USPQ 291, mod'g 28 FSupp 399, 41 USPQ 182.

If all common material in books was result of copying by defendant, only answer to charge of tortious plagiarism is that common matter was in public domain or was so trifling as not to count; since common matter is not so trifling that it can be ignored, question is whether borrowing, although substantial, was fair use; borrowing series of concrete incidents and details was not fair use. MacDonald v. Du Maurier, (CCA 2), 144 F(2d) 696, 62 USPQ 394, rev'g 60 USPQ 410.

Fact that defendants acknowledged source from which infringing passages were taken does not excuse infringement. Toksvig v. Bruce Publishing Co., (CA 7), 181 F(2d) 664, 85 USPQ 339.

Averment in answer that defendant obtained motion pictures from third persons who obtained license from plaintiff stated an issuable defense. Pathe Exchange, Inc. v. International Alliance, (DC-NY), 3 FSupp 63.

In action for infringement of copyright, plaintiff was not bound to accept defendant's offer of apology and proposal to print a retraction. Zenn v. National Golf Review, Inc., (DC-NY), 27 FSupp 732, 41 USPQ 535.

In suit for copyright infringement, defendants set up defense that suit is brought without authority in plaintiff's name by an association, that association is engaged as common barrator, and that association is engaged in unlawful practice of law; defenses are urged as grounds for abatement and could not be availed of as justification for alleged tort. Vitaphone Corp. v. Hutchinson Amusement Co., (DC-Mass), 28 FSupp 526, 42 USPQ 431.

If "fair use" is to constitute a defense it must be determined by consideration of all evidence in the case; extent and relative value of copyrighted material, purpose for claimed "fair use," and effect on distribution and objects of original work are some elements entering into determination of issue and, while intent to infringe is not essential to plaintiff's cause of action, nevertheless defendant's intention bears on question of "fair use." New York Tribune, Inc. v. Otis & Co., (DC-NY), 39 FSupp 67, 49 USPQ 361.

It is no defense that orchestra leader agreed with defendant not to play nonlicensed American Society of Composers, Authors, and Publishers' music and that defendant posted prominent notices objecting to playing such music. Shapiro, Bernstein & Co., Inc. v. Veltin, (DC-La), 47 FSupp 648, 55 USPQ 335.

It is no answer that defendant in making map was acting on instruction from a third party who in previous years had his maps made by plaintiffs, since plaintiffs alone, and not the third party, held the copyright. Crocker v. General Drafting Co., Inc., (DC-NY), 50 FSupp 634, 58 USPQ 60.

Contention of defendant that no directions were given to orchestra and no designations made as to what orchestra should or should not play cannot be upheld in copyright infringement suit. Buck v. Levin, (DC-Mass), 40 USPQ 27.

58.   —Copyright notice.

It is no defense, in an action for the infringement of a copyright, brought by the author and proprietor of the copyright, that a licensee of the author had wrongfully printed the story without the copyright notice. American Press Ass'n v. Daily Story Pub. Co., (CCA 7), 120 Fed 766, 66 LRA 444.

It is no defense, in an action for the infringement of a copyright, that the complainant had published an English edition of the copyrighted work, without notice of the American copyright, when in fact the English edition was copyrighted under the laws of England and not of the United States. G. & C. Merriam Co. v. United Dictionary Co., (CCA 7), 146 Fed 354, rev'g 140 Fed 768. Aff'd 208 US 260, 52 LEd 478, 28 SCR 290.

Defense that no notice of copyright appeared on a phonograph record played on a victrola in a cafe was without merit. Buck v. Heretis, (DC-SC), 24 F(2d) 876.

Defense that no notice of copyright appeared on a perforated roll used on a player piano at a theatre was without merit. Buck v. Lester, (DC-SC), 24 F(2d) 877.

It is no defense in copyright infringement action that plaintiff's copyrighted advertisements appeared, without required copyright notice, in two newspapers, since defendant did not sustain burden to prove that plaintiff was at fault for absence of notice. Modern Aids, Inc. v. R. H. Macy & Co., Inc., (CA 2), 264 F(2d) 93, 120 USPQ 470.

Bill for copyright infringement will be dismissed when plaintiff negligently and consistently fails properly to mark for copyright purposes photographs of subjects taken from copyrighted catalogue. Basevi v. Edward O'Toole Co., Inc., (DC-NY), 26 FSupp 41, 40 USPQ 333.

Defense that copyright notice was in such small type that it was difficult to decipher even under a reading glass and that consequently defendant read "1911" for "1931" did not justify inclusion of reproduction of the copyrighted matter in copyright secured by defendant on complete issue of its magazine. Zenn v. National Golf Review, Inc., (DC-NY), 27 FSupp 732, 41 USPQ 535.

Defendant, which contracts for use for specific time of duly-copyrighted book of advertisements bearing notice of copyright and then continues to use material without authorization beyond time specified in contract, after having in a sense recognized validity of copyright by paying for use of material, cannot, when sued for infringement, set up as a valid defense the mere fact that copyright owner furnished for defendant's convenience mats for printing separate advertisements from book without a copyright notice on mats so that material, when printed from mats, also contained no copyright notice. Deward & Rich, Inc. v. Bristol Savings & Loan Corp., (DC-Va), 29 FSupp 777, 44 USPQ 26.

Defendants cannot avoid infringement of 1916 copyright on ground that 1930 copyright of reissued book contained no notice of 1916 copyright since defendants were not misled, having copied from 1916 edition. Harris v. Miller, (DC-NY), 50 USPQ 306. Mf'd 50 USPQ 625.

59. —Lack of knowledge or intent.

Innocent intent with which the person acted who is charged with infringement is not a defense where it appears that the party setting it up has invaded a copyright. Lawrence v. Dana, (CC-Mass), FedCas 8,136, 4 Cliff 1.

Intent is not an element of infringement. Reed v. Holliday, (CC-Pa), 19 Fed 325; Johns & Johns Printing Co. v. Paull-Pioneer Music Corp., (CCA 8), 102 F(2d) 282, 41 USPQ 3; Pathe Exch. v. International Alliance, (DC-NY), 3 FSupp 63.

Intent did justify an infringement. Reed v. Holliday, (CC-Pa), 19 Fed 325.

Lack of knowledge as to infringing character is no defense. Gilmore v. Anderson, (CC-NY), 38 Fed 846.

Absence of intent to infringe is not a defense. Fishel v. Lueckel, (CC-NY), 53 Fed 499; Stern v. Jerome H. Remick & Co., (CC-NY), 175 Fed 282; M. Witmark & Sons v. Calloway, (DC-Tenn), 22 F(2d) 412.

Lack of knowledge of copyrighted musical composition was no defense to a suit to enjoin. Hein v. Harris, (CCA 2), 183 Fed 107, aff'g 175 Fed 875.

Ignorance of a copyright, or honest intention, is no defense to an action for infringement. Altman v. New Haven Union Co., (DC-Conn), 254 Fed 113.

It is no defense, in an action for infringement, that the defendant had, without knowledge of plaintiff's copyright, copied his work from a magazine which had wrongfully reprinted plaintiff's work. Norris v. No-Leak-O Piston Ring Co., (DC-Md), 271 Fed 536. Aff'd 277 Fed 951.

Unconscious plagiarism is actionable as much as deliberate plagiarism. Sheldon v. Metro-Goldwyn Pictures Corp., (CCA 2), 81 F(2d) 49, 28 USPQ 330, rev'g 7 FSupp 837.

One who copies from a plagiarist is himself necessarily a plagiarist, however innocent he may be. Barry v. Hughes, (CCA 2), 103 F(2d) 427, 41 USPQ 340.

Innocent copier of screen play, whether copyrighted or not, is liable for damages; while Copyright Act makes significant distinctions in certain instances based on innocent or willful infringement, it does not do so in general provision for award of profits and actual damages, or statutory sums allowable in court's discretion in lieu of actual damages. De Acosta v. Brown, (CCA 2), 146 F(2d) 408, 63 USPQ 311, aff'g 50 FSupp 615, 58 USPQ 596.

Innocent copying by newspapers and magazines is not protection. De Acosta v. Brown, (CCA 2), 146 F(2d) 408, 63 USPQ 311, aff'g 50 FSupp 615, 58 USPQ 596.

Intention is immaterial if infringement appears. Toksvig v. Bruce Publishing Co., (CA 7), 181 F(2d) 664, 85 USPQ 339.

Copyright proprietor loaned book of illustrations to advertising agency with intent that illustrations be extracted for use at royalty of one dollar each; agency incorporated illustrations in advertisement which was published before payment of royalty; although book contains one sentence indicating that cash prepayment is required, it contains other statements susceptible to construction that prepayment is not required; proprietor having employed ambiguous and uncertain terminology in stating reproduction terms, agency was in substantial compliance with proffered license when it construed it to require only that payment of one dollar use fee be made after ultimate use of material; therefore, infringement complaint is dismissed. Stivers v. Sir Francis Drake Hotel Co., Inc., (CA 9), 205 F(2d) 4, 98 USPQ 7.

Intent to commit infringement is not necessary but goes to fill out whole picture. Broadway Music Corp. v. F-R Pub. Corp., (DC-NY), 31 FSupp 817, 45 USPQ 309.

When notice of copyright is published, duty is on all to know the fact concerning it and innocence of intent to invade that right is no excuse for actually doing so. Sammons v. Larkin, (DC-Mass), 38 FSupp 649, 49 USPQ 350. Mf'd 126 F(2d) 341, 53 USPQ 71.

It is no defense that use of plaintiff's copyrighted music in defendant's restaurant was without defendant's consent and contrary to his orders. Buck v. Cecere, (DC-NY), 45 FSupp 441, 53 USPQ 519.

Those who, with knowledge of copyright, commit acts which they believe do not constitute infringements may be liable. Chappell & Co., Inc. v. Costa, (DC-NY), 45 FSupp 554, 53 USPQ 674.

One who innocently copies from infringing copy is liable as infringer to owner whose unpublished work was infringed. Leigh v. Gerber, (DC-NY), 86 FSupp 320, 82 USPQ 271.

Had defendant created his material in exact form as plaintiff's, but without knowledge of existence of plaintiff's material and without copying it, there could be no infringement since there would have been no copying. Gordon v. Weir, (DC-Mich), 111 FSupp 117, 97 USPQ 387. Aff'd 216 F(2d) 508, 104 USPQ 40.

Infringement is not avoided by lack of knowledge of copyright; also, lack of intent to violate it does not excuse one from liability. Metro Associated Services, Inc. v. Webster City Graphic, Inc., (DC-Iowa), 117 FSupp 224, 100 USPQ 88.

It is immaterial whether a party is an innocent infringer; infringer of valid copyright copies at his peril and an intent to infringe is not essential in determining liability; also, knowledge to infringe is not an essential element. Massapequa Publishing Co., Inc. v. Observer, Inc., (DC-NY), 191 FSupp 261, 128 USPQ 418.

Defendant had used supply of copyrighted cards under license from plaintiff and later bought from another printer and used card which differs slightly in wording but is substantial copy of copyrighted card; infringement is certain but not especially willful. Druley v. Thompson, (DC-Pa), 44 USPQ 284.

Fact that infringement was in ignorance and without dishonest intention is no defense to copyright infringement action, but is considered in determining damages. Phillips v. Constitution Publishing Co., (DC-Ga), 72 USPQ 69.

60. —Limitations and laches.

State statutes of limitation of place of suit, pertaining to same class of actions apply to civil actions for infringement of copyright. Brady v. Daly, 175 US 148, 44 LEd 109, 20 SCR 62, aff'g (CCA 2), 83 Fed 1007; McCaleb v. Fox Film Corp., (CCA 5), 299 Fed 48; Pathe Exchange, Inc. v. Dalke, (CCA 4), 49 F(2d) 161.

Where there has been long acquiescence in the infringement, or culpable laches and negligence in seeking redress, especially if it appear that the delay has misled the respondent, equity will not afford complainant relief. Lawrence v. Dana, (CC-Mass), FedCas 8,136, 4 Cliff 1.

In an action under § 7 of the Copyright Act of 1831 (4 Stat. 438), damages for the infringement of the copyright of a song might not be recovered from a defendant unless the last unlawful printing occurred within two years before suit was brought. Reed v. Carusi, (CC-Md), FedCas 11,642, Taney 72.

Delay in bringing suit, in absence of acquiescence, is no defense. Gilmore v. Anderson, (CC-NY), 38 Fed 846.

Revised Statutes § 4964 providing for a forfeiture and damages was penal and action thereunder was barred by statute of limitations. Wheeler v. Cobbey, (CC-Neb), 70 Fed 487.

Under R. S. § 4968, it was held that a two-year limitation as to the time within which an action could be commenced for a forfeiture or penalty, did not apply to proceedings for an injunction. Patterson v. J. S. Ogilvie Pub. Co., (CC-NY), 119 Fed 451.

Laches, as a ground for refusing a preliminary injunction, was inapplicable where neither complainant nor its predecessors had any knowledge or notice of an alleged prior infringement of complainant's copyrights. Werner Co. v. Encyclopaedia Britannica Co., (CCA 3), 134 Fed 831, aff'g 130 Fed 460.

Laches will not be imputed from a complainant's delay of one year before prosecuting defendant's infringement, where the circumstances refute rather than suggest an acquiescence in the infringement. Wooster v. Crane & Co., (CCA 8), 147 Fed 515.

Complainant's laches in prosecuting defendant's infringements did not bar issuance of temporary injunction in absence of any showing that defendant had been prejudiced by the delay. Hein v. Harris, (CC-NY), 175 Fed 875. Aff'd 183 Fed 107.

Laches of complainant may be taken into consideration in action for injunction and accounting of profits. West Pub. Co. v. Edward Thompson Co., (CCA 2), 176 Fed 833, mod'g 169 Fed 833.

Where plaintiff brought a replevin action to recover copies in defendant's possession he could not, after case was barred by statute, amend his pleadings by adding a cause of action for the statutory penalty. Hills & Co., Ltd. v. Hoover, (CCA 3), 211 Fed 241.

A few weeks' delay on the part of the plaintiff after knowledge of the infringement, before taking action, may debar him from any accounting for profits. Haas v. Leo Feist, Inc., (DC-NY), 234 Fed 105.

Laches in prosecution of proceedings before master, barred right to a recovery of money damage. D. O. Haynes & Co. v. Druggists Circular, (CCA 2), 32 F(2d) 215.

Where plaintiff knew of defendant's catalogue a short time following its first printing and made no protest or complaint until filing suit over three years later, during which time defendant incurred great expense in printing and distribution of catalogues, plaintiff was estopped from asserting claim of infringement. Edwin L. Wiegand Co. v. Harold E. Trent Co., (CCA 3), 122 F(2d) 920, 50 USPQ 243, aff'g 43 USPQ 149.

Copyright owner may not deliberately delay prosecution and thereby speculate without risk with another's money to determine success of exploitation. Universal Pictures Co., Inc. v. Harold Lloyd Corp., (CCA 9), 162 F(2d) 354, 73 USPQ 317.

Copyright Act contains no statute of limitations, so action for infringement is governed by limitations existing for class of actions to which it belongs in state where it is brought; action for infringement is injury to rights of owner, to an intangible, incorporeal right, and does not arise from contract; it cannot be classified as action for recovery of money due by open or unliquidated account; it is action arising from act of Congress and, under Alabama statute of limitations (Alabama Code of 1940, Title 7), can be classified only as action for injury to rights of another, so action must be commenced within one year. Local Trademarks, Inc. v. Price, (CA 5), 170 F(2d) 715, 79 USPQ 344.

Federal courts are required to give such construction to state statute of limitations as courts of state give. Local Trademarks, Inc. v. Price, (CA 5), 170 F(2d) 715, 79 USPQ 344.

Action for infringement of distribution rights in copyrighted motion picture is barred by plaintiff's long delay in suing during period when defendant or its predecessors had valid license, but defendant's expenditures in exploiting picture, if not made under valid license, should not be used as basis for defense of laches or estoppel. Machaty v. Astra Pictures, Inc., (CA 2), 197 F(2d) 138, 93 USPQ 51, aff'g 89 USPQ 539.

Copyright infringement action against distributor of motion picture is not barred by estoppel where distributor had notice of plaintiff's claim before distribution, which continued after further warning and for some years after suit was brought. Szekely v. Eagle Lion Films, Inc., (CA 2), 242 F(2d) 266, 113 USPQ 98, aff'g 140 FSupp 843, 109 USPQ 348.

Additional relief in the form of damages for infringement is not refused for laches in action seeking declaratory judgment as to copyright title, although there was delay of 11 years between institution of action and trial, inasmuch as defendant consented to or joined in applications for delays and no specific prejudice is shown; it is unfair to tax plaintiff, the rightful owner, rather than defendant, the infringer, with penalties for delay in which they both participated. Edward B. Marks Music Corp. v. Charles K. Harris Music Publishing Co., Inc., (CA 2), 255 F(2d) 518, 117 USPQ 308.

Although not brought until six years after notice of defendant's threatened infringement, plaintiff's action based on numerous copyrighted songs by same author is not barred by laches since three years after notice plaintiff sued defendant as to one of these songs and defendant advanced same defense as to title as was raised in instant action; such prior suit was discontinued after defendant withdrew claim to song, which would indicate that defendant then believed that it had no title under conveyance relied upon in instant action. Edward B. Marks Music Corp. v. Charles K. Harris Music Publishing Co., Inc., (CA 2), 255 F(2d) 518, 117 USPQ 308.

Owner of copyrighted map who delayed seven years before bringing infringement suit was not entitled to injunction or an accounting, but it was entitled to enjoin defendant from using its maps in other than its business, and to compensatory damages, and costs. Blackburn v. Southern California Gas Co., (DC-Cal), 14 FSupp 553, 29 USPQ 437.

Suit in December 1936 for copyright infringement by publication in August 1934 was barred by statute of limitations. Norm Co. v. John A. Brown Co., (DC-Okla), 26 FSupp 707, 40 USPQ 419.

While plaintiff denies having heard defendant's song, copyrighted in 1926, played in any manner before 1937, it is highly improbable, in view of plaintiff's residing in large city and engaging in music publishing business, that he did not between 1926 and 1937 have some knowledge of song; this constitutes laches barring suit alleging infringement of plaintiff's copyright by defendants' song. Davilla v. Harms, Inc., (DC-NY), 36 FSupp 843, 48 USPQ 103.

Copyright infringement suit brought in 1937 is barred by laches where plaintiff heard of defendant's composition in 1922 and brought prior suit against defendant in 1932, suit being dismissed in 1932 for lack of jurisdiction over defendant; defendant's song has become very popular, and while there is no evidence as to how much money defendant spent in exploiting song it is assumed that change in position resulted from plaintiff's failure to prosecute. McMahon v. Harms, Inc., (DC-NY), 42 FSupp 779, 52 USPQ 321.

Copyright infringement action is not barred by two-year limitation of § 339(1), California code civ. proc., as against scenario writer although motion picture was released more than two years before commencement of action. Cain v. Universal Pictures Co., Inc., (DC-Cal), 47 FSupp 1013, 56 USPQ 8.

Delay in applying for copyright of 22 years after composition of song, and of 11 years after defendant first published song, constitutes laches barring infringement suit; composer's laches are chargeable to assignee. Egner v. E. C. Schirmer Music Co., (DC-Mass), 48 FSupp 187, 56 USPQ 214. Aff'd 139 F(2d) 398, 60 USPQ 74.

Where plaintiff did not learn of probable infringement until January, came to United States from Trinidad in March and wrote defendant in same month, and plaintiff's United States copyright was secured in June and suit was filed 42 days later, suit is not barred by laches. Kahn v. Leo Feist, Inc., (DC-NY), 70 FSupp 450, 73 USPQ 104. Aff'd 165 F(2d) 188, 76 USPQ 27.

Action for copyright infringement is barred by Alabama one-year statute of limitations. Local Trademarks, Inc. v. Rogers, (DC-Ala), 73 FSupp 907, 75 USPQ 336.

Applicable state statute of limitations governs in action for copyright infringement, since Copyright Act prescribes no limitation on commencement of infringement action. Carew v. Melrose Music, Inc., (DC-NY), 92 FSupp 971, 87 USPQ 84.

Delay of 27 months before filing suit for copyright infringement was not unreasonable although delay prejudiced defendant in that key witness died one month before trial. Amsterdam v. Triangle Publications, Inc., (DC-Penn), 93 FSupp 79, 87 USPQ 90. Mf'd 189 F(2d) 104, 89 USPQ 468.

Promptly after hearing of presentation of defendants' January, 1952, television show, plaintiff claimed copyright infringement; on learning in June, 1953, that defendants were preparing similar show, plaintiffs promptly brought suit charging both shows with infringement; plaintiffs are not guilty of laches; fact that plaintiffs did not commence action in January, 1952, was not a waiver; dispute over infringement was never settled. Loew's Inc. v. Columbia Broadcasting System, Inc., (DC-Cal) 131 FSupp 165, 105 USPQ 302. Aff'd 239 F(2d) 532, 112 USPQ 11, which was aff'd 356 US 43, 2 LEd(2d) 583, 78 SCR 667, 116 USPQ 479.

Inasmuch as Copyright Act prescribes no time limitations with respect to commencement of infringement action, such action is limited by limitation existing for class of actions to which it belongs in state where action is brought. Greenbie v. Noble, (DC-NY), 151 FSupp 45, 113 USPQ 115.

When copyright holder has acquiesced in, or failed to object to, acts constituting alleged infringement so as to induce infringer to incur financial obligations, such delay in bringing suit gives rise to equitable defense of laches; also, in determining whether suit should be dismissed, court is guided by applicable statute of limitations; action commenced approximately six years after plaintiff acquired knowledge of alleged infringement is not dismissed, especially since plaintiff did not acquiesce in publication of alleged infringement, but notified defendant of copyright claim and objected to publication. Greenbie v. Noble, (DC-NY), 151 FSupp 45, 113 USPQ 115.

Estoppel exists if copyright owner, with knowledge of alleged infringement, permitted defendants to spend large sums on manufacture of alleged infringing book without making infringement claim. Christie v. Raddock, (DC-NY), 169 FSupp 48, 120 USPQ 76.

Congress in copyright field has not prescribed national standard but has accepted as period of limitations or laches the local state law prescribed by state wherein cause of action is brought; copyright infringement action seeking damages and profits, but no injunction, is not action at law but invokes equity jurisdiction; hence, action is not governed absolutely by state statutory period (two years) for action of tort; however, although action is within equity jurisdiction, being one for damages (including profits) it sounds in tort; to be timely, it must be brought within two years after defendant directly or by agent or associate invaded plaintiff's interest. Maloney v. Stone, (DC-Mass), 171 FSupp 29, 121 USPQ 257.

Laches, resulting from long delay in enforcing one's rights, followed by change of position of party relying on other party's inaction, might result in denial of equitable relief such as injunction and recovery of profits, but it would not stand in way of granting damages for unauthorized copying of copyrighted work or of injunction against future violations; to the contrary, estoppel destroys the very rights which it is sought to assert. Hayden v. Chalfant Press, Inc., (DC-NY), 177 FSupp 303, 123 USPQ 475. Aff'd 281 F(2d) 543, 126 USPQ 483.

Ordinarily, failure to take action against stranger does not give rise to estoppel, but copyright proprietor's knowing failure for over 19 years to institute proceedings against automobile club constitutes estoppel not only against club but also against defendants who were authorized by club to reproduce club's maps which proprietor now claims were, in turn, copied from his; defendants can assert estoppel whether or not they are assignees of club's copyright. Hayden v. Chalfant Press, Inc., (DC-Cal), 177 FSupp 303, 123 USPQ 475. Aff'd 281 F(2d) 543, 126 USPQ 483.

Plaintiffs in copyright infringement action are barred by limitations and laches from obtaining part of relief sought since they took no action for several years despite knowledge of defendants' extensive use of copyright work. Klasmer v. Baltimore Football, Inc., (DC-Md), 200 FSupp 255, 132 USPQ 36.

Statute of limitations does not bar complaint alleging that after March 1944 and up to present time defendant has infringed and is infringing plaintiff's copyright; this is not affirmative statement that plaintiff knew in March 1944 that the defendant was infringing; although "after March 1944" could refer to any date between March 1944 and February 1956, which would fall within period subject to statute, words also can refer to any date between February 1956 and date of filing of complaint, which is period not barred thereunder. Serra v. Matias Photo Shop, (DC-Puerto Rico), 21 FedRDec 188, 116 USPQ 258.

Copyright proprietor is not guilty of laches in bringing infringement suit since defendants were notified of infringement within two months of proprietor learning of publication of infringing play and its performance. Harris v. Miller, (DC-NY), 50 USPQ 306. Mf'd 50 USPQ 625.

There being no federal statute of limitations applicable to action for plagiarism of common-law copyright, federal court must apply state law; three-year limitation applicable to "injury to property" under § 49(7) of New York civil practice act governs. Stein v. RKO Radio Pictures, Inc., (DC-NY), 53 USPQ 294.

61.   —Unclean hands—Violation of law.

In a suit for infringement of copyright where defendant shows that complainant is also guilty of piracy, equity may refuse relief to complainant. Edward Thompson Co. v. American Law Book Co., (CCA 2), 122 Fed 922, 62 LRA 607, rev'g 121 Fed 907.

In a suit for infringement of copyright, exceptions to clauses in answers which set up the state and federal antitrust statutes were good. Scribner v. Straus, (CC-NY), 130 Fed 389.

It is no defense, to an action for the infringement of a copyright, that the plaintiff is engaged in a conspiracy in restraint of trade in violation of the Sherman Antitrust Act [15 §§ 1-7, 15 note]. Harms v. Cohen, (DC-Pa),

279 Fed 276; Buck v. Hillsgrove Country Club, Inc., (DC-RI), 17 FSupp 643, 33 USPQ 134; Buck v. Del Papa, (DC-RI), 17 FSupp 645; Buck v. Newsreel, (DC-Mass), 25 FSupp 787, 40 USPQ 20; Buck v. Spanish Gables, (DC-Mass), 26 FSupp 36, 40 USPQ 19; Society of European Stage Authors & Composers, Inc. v. WCAU Broadcasting Co., (DC-Pa), 35 FSupp 460, 47 USPQ 310; Buck v. Cecere, (DC-NY), 45 FSupp 441, 53 USPQ 519; Buck v. Repertory Theatre, (DC-Mass), 40 USPQ 23; Buck v. Holyoke Theatre, (DC-Mass), 40 USPQ 24; Buck v. Wrentham Show Boat, (DC-Mass), 40 USPQ 25.

Copyright proprietor, suing for infringement in Wisconsin federal court, does not have unclean hands because it has not complied with Wisconsin statutes, c. 177, requiring license from state to issue copyright licenses or to use threats to procure licenses. Leo Feist, Inc. v. Young, (CCA 7), 138 F(2d) 972, 59 USPQ 450, rev'g 46 FSupp 622, 54 USPQ 489.

Copyright infringers are in poor position to question plaintiffs' motives and character when infringers are guilty of wrongfully appropriating plaintiffs' property. Interstate Hotel Co. v. Remick Music Corp., (CCA 8), 157 F(2d) 744, 71 USPQ 138, aff'g 58 FSupp 523, 63 USPQ 327.

Plaintiff cannot recover in action for copyright infringement and unfair competition since its copyrighted cards are sold for purpose of being used in a lottery known as "Banko" or "Bank-Night." Kessler v. Schreiber, (DC-NY), 39 FSupp 655, 49 USPQ 610.

Copyright infringement suit was dismissed for unclean hands where plaintiff had notice that defendant's employee, while secretly stockholder, director, and editor of plaintiff's predecessor, obtained ideas for textbook originated by defendant and used ideas in preparing predecessor's copyrighted textbook. Colonial Book Co., Inc. v. Oxford Book Co., Inc., (DC-NY), 45 FSupp 551, 53 USPQ 599. Aff'd 135 F(2d) 463, 57 USPQ 569.

Although American Society of Composers, Authors, and Publishers is outlawed in Nebraska, it is a lawful society elsewhere, and fact that plaintiffs in copyright infringement suits in Nebraska federal court, in dealings exclusively beyond Nebraska, adhere to American Society of Composers, Authors, and Publishers' membership, does not subject them to imputation of wrongdoing, make them violators of Nebraska laws, or bar doors of Nebraska courts to them. Remick Music Corp. v. Interstate Hotel Co., (DC-Neb), 58 FSupp 523, 63 USPQ 327. Aff'd 157 F(2d) 744, 71 USPQ 138.

It is not unclean hands that different plaintiff's contemporaneously brought 11 instant infringement suits, and a few others, against different defendants; if rights asserted exist, court has no concern whether they are vindicated in concurrent or successive proceedings. Remick Music Corp. v. Interstate Hotel Co., (DC-Neb), 58 FSupp 523, 63 USPQ 327. Aff'd 157 F(2d) 744, 71 USPQ 138.

It is not unclean hands that plaintiffs have ignored and refused to comply with state statute which court holds void; if statute is valid, it is complete legal defense; if it is void, failure to submit to it is right of plaintiff. Remick Music Corp. v. Interstate Hotel Co., (DC-Neb), 58 FSupp 523, 63 USPQ 327. Aff'd 157 F(2d) 744, 71 USPQ 138.

It is no defense to copyright infringement suit that English copyright proprietor and other Guild members violated Antitrust Acts [15 § 1 et seq.] by agreeing to limit production of copyrighted engravings and to maintain minimum prices. Alfred Bell & Co., Ltd. v. Catalda Fine Arts, Inc., (DC-NY), 74 FSupp 973, 75 USPQ 66. Mf'd 191 F(2d) 99, 90 USPQ 153.

By depositing prominent person's letters with historical society subject to consent requirement, plaintiff did not thereby obtain monopoly on story of life of person, and plaintiff did not effect such deposit by reason of her control of copyright for person's biography. Greenbie v. Noble, (DC-NY), 151 FSupp 45, 113 USPQ 115.

Book containing coupons entitling one to cash discounts on purchase of merchandise is proper subject matter for copyright protection despite fact that book is fraudulent in that it is used for sole and express purpose of falsely inducing public to believe that discounts are obtained through use of book, whereas same discounts are given to all members of public in ordinary course of business. Advisers Inc. v. Wiesen-Hart, Inc., (DC-Ohio), 161 FSupp 831, 117 USPQ 330.

It is not permissible defense in copyright infringement action to allege that copyright proprietors and others have effectuated conspiracy to monopolize entire field of musical compositions in violation of Antitrust Acts [15 § 1 et seq.] and have been guilty of discrimination to defendants' damage. Harms, Inc. v. Sansom House Enterprises, Inc., (DC-Pa), 162 FSupp 129, 117 USPQ 272.

It is not actionable wrong for one to assert in good faith that he intends to enforce what he conceives to be his legal rights, even if he is mistaken as to what such rights are; one who claims that his patent has been infringed may communicate infringement claim to customers of alleged infringer and may even threaten them with suit, provided he acts in good faith; there is no reason why rule should be limited to patent infringement cases or why it should not apply to copyright infringement cases; however such assertions of legal rights must be kept within proper bounds; thus, if another's customers are threatened, intimidated, or harassed, equity court will enjoin such conduct; same result follows where infringement claims against another's customers or threats of suit are made in bad faith. Remington Research, Inc. v. Modern Aids, Inc., (DC-NY), 170 FSupp 7, 120 USPQ 289.

Generally, it is no defense to copyright infringement action that plaintiff is violating antitrust statutes by combination or conspiracy in restraint of trade. Although equity court will withhold relief against even a stranger to the misuse, where patentee is using patent privilege contrary to public interest, it is a substantial question whether a like rule, invokable in the same manner, is applicable to copyright infringement action. Motion to strike misuse defense is denied without prejudice in copyright infringement action since insufficiency of defense is not clearly apparent and since a determination of effect of alleged misuse on plaintiff's action requires a delicate balancing of competing public policies in an area of the law that is yet evolving. United Artists Associated, Inc. v. NWL Corp., (DC-NY), 198 FSupp 953, 132 USPQ 248.

62. —Validity of copyrights—Title of plaintiff.

It is no defense to action for infringement of copyright that plaintiff is not the owner, his assignor being married woman who had no right to assign it. Belford, Clarke & Co. v. Scribner, 144 US 488, 36 LEd 514, 12 SCR 734, aff'g (CC-Ill), 50 Fed 473.

Where, in a consent decree, the defendant had agreed that the copyright was valid, he will be held to his agreement and is estopped from later contesting the validity of the copyright. Wilson v. Haber Bros., Inc., (CCA 2), 275 Fed 346.

It is unnecessary to consider whether defendant infringed where plaintiff's rights in copyrighted map are held in trust for government, his employer. Sawyer v. Crowell Pub. Co., (CCA 2), 142 F(2d) 497, 61 USPQ 389, aff'g 46 FSupp 471, 54 USPQ 225.

If what alleged infringer took was not copyrightable, copyright owner may not complain although his work may have directly inspired work of infringer. Chamberlin v. Uris Sales Corp., (CCA 2), 150 F(2d) 512, 65 USPQ 544, aff'g 56 FSupp 987, 62 USPQ 375; Shipman v. R. K. O. Radio Pictures, (DC-NY), 20 FSupp 249, 35 USPQ 242. Aff'd 100 F(2d) 533, 40 USPQ 211.

Defendant's objection that there is no proof that copyrighted matter is an original dramatic work is overcome by long acquiescence in paying royalty for many years which creates presumption of validity of copyright in absence of proof to contrary. Fitch v. Shubert, (DC-NY), 20 FSupp 314, 35 USPQ 245.

Issuance of copyright certificate to defendant on plagiarized material does not relieve him from liability for infringement; copyright office, by accepting his material as copyrightable, does not thereby determine his rights under copyright laws. Gordon v. Weir, (DC-Mich), 111 FSupp 117, 97 USPQ 387. Aff'd 216 F(2d) 508, 104 USPQ 40.

Even if proprietor had valid copyright on advertisements, infringement of valid copyright is not shown where wording of advertisements was changed each time they were published, with no effort being made to have varied publications copyrighted. Davis-Robertson Agency v. Duke, (DC-Va), 119 FSupp 931, 100 USPQ 211.

On motion for preliminary injunction against copyright infringement, district court regards decision by its court of appeals, in action against another defendant, as dispositive of issue of validity of copyright for purposes of the motion. Rushton Co. v. F. W. Woolworth Co., (DC-NY), 135 FSupp 317, 108 USPQ 80.

Fact that defendants applied for copyright registration of same arrangement, in which application they represented that arrangement contained original, copyrightable material, does not estop defendants from denying originality of plaintiff's work, since defendants' representations did not mislead plaintiff or place him at disadvantage in instant litigation. McIntyre v. Double-A Music Corp., (DC-Cal), 179 FSupp 160, 124 USPQ 27.

Even though third party's work was published with defective notice of copyright, it is no defense that source of defendant's work was in public domain if that source was unknown to defendant and was not used by it. Stanley v. Columbia Broadcasting System, Inc., (CalApp (2d series)), 192 Pac(2d) 495, 77 USPQ 404. Aff'd (Cal(2d series)), 208 Pac(2d) 9, 82 USPQ 123, which was aff'd 35 Cal(2d series) 623, 221 Pac(2d) 73, 86 USPQ 520.

Licensee is not estopped from contending that licensor's monopoly has expired. Tams-Witmark Music Library, Inc. v. New Opera Co., Inc., 298 NY 163, 81 NE(2d) 70, 78 USPQ 298, aff'g 272 AppDiv 342, 71 NYS(2d) 136, 74 USPQ 76.

A licensee of the motion-picture rights to a drama may not, in an action by the licensor to recover the license fee, impeach his licensor's title. Hart v. Fox, (Misc), 166 NYS 793.

Although license to produce operetta on stage provides that licensee will not challenge rights of licensor in operetta if others do not make claim on licensee, licensee, when sued for royalties, may show that operetta is in public domain since there is such breach of warranty and failure of consideration as frees licensee from further liability and entitles it to recover back what it has paid. Tams-Witmark Music Library, Inc. v. New Opera Co., Inc., (Misc), 52 NYS(2d) 611, 63 USPQ 353.

63. Procedure.

Under former law, actions to recover penalties and forfeitures for infringement of copyright were abated by death of defendant. In Matter of Francis Schreiber, 110 US 76, 28 LEd 65, 3 SCR 423.

Where two distinct grounds in support of a single cause of action are alleged, only one of which presents a federal question, the federal court may retain jurisdiction even though the federal ground is not established. Hurn v. Oursler, 289 US 238, 77 LEd 1148, 53 SCR 586, 17 USPQ 195, mod'g (CCA 2), 61 F(2d) 1031.

Where two separate and distinct causes of action are joined in one suit, one a federal question and one outside the federal jurisdiction, the latter one is subject to dismissal at any stage of the case. Hurn v. Oursler, 289 US 238, 77 LEd 1148, 53 SCR 586, 17 USPQ 195, mod'g (CCA 2), 61 F(2d) 1031.

There is no material difference between the principles and rules applicable to equity proceedings in copyright cases and any other cases of which courts of equity take cognizance. Scribner v. Stoddart, (CC-Pa), FedCas 12,561.

There is such an analogy between actions under the patent laws and actions under copyright laws that like rules of practice should be applied in both cases. Scribner v. Straus, (CC-NY), 130 Fed 389.

Where a bill for injunction did not allege facts justifying relief, it was error for the district court to retain jurisdiction for the purpose of awarding damages. Hutchinson Amusement Co. v. Vitaphone Corp., (CCA 1), 93 F(2d) 176, 36 USPQ 1.

State court judgment dismissing complaint for unfair competition, by use in magazines of titles to copyrighted songs, is not res judicata in federal court copyright infringement suit; even if, in earlier action, court had made adverse finding of fact essential to support judgment in copyright action, finding would bar latter action; but state court made no such finding; it rested decision on finding that purchasers would not be misled, a fact unimportant in copyright action. Leo Feist, Inc. v. Song Parodies, Inc.. (CCA 2), 146 F(2d) 400, 64 USPQ 92.

In copyright infringement and unfair competition action against motion-picture producer, its president, and motion-picture distributor, complaint alleges that producer produced and distributor distributed motion picture which infringes plaintiffs' uncopyrighted story and copyrighted book; since complaint sets forth combined action by defendants to bring picture to public, plaintiffs have only a single claim, not to be broken into separate parts for purpose of immediate appeal as to one such part only; hence, where president was personally served and distributor does not challenge that it was doing business in district, order quashing service on producer is not immediately appealable; appeal is dismissed. Gauvreau v. U. S., (CA 2), 267 F(2d) 861, 121 USPQ 541.

The Federal Rules of Civil Procedure [Rules, c. 15] did not apply to suits under this section until the Supreme Court under Rule 81(a) made them applicable thereto. Bergmann v. Joe Morris Music Co., (DC-NY), 27 FSupp 985, 41 USPQ 730.

In copyright infringement case, plaintiff's filing of 60 exceptions, contained in 22 typewritten pages, to master's report on accounting is unreasonable where exceptions only raise two questions necessary to be passed on. Burndy Engineering Co. v. Penn-Union Electric Corp., (DC-Pa), 32 FSupp 671, 45 USPQ 80. Aff'd 122 F(2d) 932, 51 USPQ 548.

Plaintiff brought tort action for copyright infringement but never returned writ and declaration into court; instead, instant action was started a day after return day of writ; failure of plaintiff to enter his first writ and declaration on return day operated as complete abandonment of that suit and there is no danger of defendant being annoyed by having to respond to it; therefore, there are no adequate grounds for staying or abating instant action. Pizzano v. Knowles & Co., Inc., (DC-Mass), 37 FSupp 118, 49 USPQ 140.

Action in federal court for infringement of uncopyrighted and unpublished play, jurisdiction being founded on diversity of citizenship.

is governed by state law, which in New York is like federal copyright law. Acosta v. Brown, (DC-NY), 50 FSupp 615, 58 USPQ 596. Aff'd 146 F(2d) 408, 63 USPQ 311.

Nebraska Comp. Stat., 1941 Supp., § 59-1202 (B), endeavors to free anyone purchasing sheet music or orchestral arrangements of copyrighted music in Nebraska and using or rendering music in Nebraska from liability in infringement suit for damages by copyright proprietor in any court in state; since, under Copyright Act, federal courts alone possess jurisdiction in such suits, statute is directed at Nebraska federal court only and is unconstitutional. Remick Music Corp. v. Interstate Hotel Co., (DC-Neb), 58 FSupp 523, 63 USPQ 327. Aff'd 157 F(2d) 744, 71 USPQ 138.

In order for copyright infringement action to be maintained, court must both have jurisdiction over defendant's person and venue must be properly laid in district. Geo-Physical Maps, Inc. v. Toycraft Corp., (DC-NY), 162 FSupp 141, 117 USPQ 316.

Test for determining whether nonresident corporation or its agent is "found" within district, within meaning of § 1400(a) of Title 28, is same as that for determining whether corporation is amenable to suit in jurisdiction other than that in which it is incorporated. Geo-Physical Maps, Inc. v. Toycraft Corp., (DC-NY), 162 FSupp 141, 117 USPQ 316.

Venue requirements of § 1400(a) of Title 28 are met when individual defendant is properly served within district; however, venue does not lie in district where individual is served in another district in same state and there is nothing to show that individual was "found" in instant district within meaning of statute. Geo-Physical Maps, Inc. v. Toycraft Corp., (DC-NY), 162 FSupp 141, 117 USPQ 316.

Trial of copyright infringement actions against sellers of records of pirated songs is not deferred until decision of actions against manufacturers. Harms, Inc. v. F. W. Woolworth Co., (DC-Cal), 163 FSupp 484, 118 USPQ 436.

Where question of infringement was not referred to master (on reference for accounting), his finding that copying was deliberate was not necessary to his decision and defendant's exception to such finding was sustained. Jones Brothers Co. v. Underkoffler, (DC-Pa), 35 USPQ 448.

Defendant filed affidavit stating amount of total sales infringing copyright and opposes reference to master for accounting; plaintiff is not bound by defendant's affidavit and questions correctness of amount; on motion, master is appointed for accounting. Burndy Engineering Co., Inc. v. Sheldon Service Corp., (DC-NY), 44 USPQ 103.

State courts have no jurisdiction of action for infringement of registered copyright. Avon Periodicals, Inc. v. Ziff-Davis Publishing Co., 202 Misc 745, 113 NYS(2d) 737, 93 USPQ 235. Mf'd 282 AppDiv 200, 122 NYS(2d) 92.

64. —Parties.

When all legal and equitable owners of copyright are joined it is not necessary to state the formalities or mode of conveyance by which the equitable interests became vested in the co-complainants. Black v. Henry G. Allen Co., (CC-NY), 42 Fed 618, 9 LRA 433.

In a suit to restrain infringement a demurrer for want of proper parties will be overruled where it cannot be sustained as to the whole bill, and defendant has not pointed out specifically the parts objected to. Empire City Amusement Co. v. Wilton, (CC-Mass), 134 Fed 132.

Lessor of copyright did not part with title and is a necessary and proper party in suit for infringement. Gaumont Co. v. Hatch, (DC-Pa), 208 Fed 378.

Licensee of stage rights is not a proper party in suit for infringement of copyrighted drama by production of motion-picture photoplay. Tully v. Triangle Film Corp., (DC-NY), 229 Fed 297.

In a suit by owner of equitable title, the owner of the legal title must ordinarily be joined as a party. Ted Browne Music Co. v. Fowler, (CCA 2), 290 Fed 751.

Infringement is a tort and persons concerned therein are jointly and severally liable, but if they do not act in concert they cannot be joined in the same suit. Ted Browne Music Co. v. Fowler, (CCA 2), 290 Fed 751.

Where parties have acted severally in the infringement of a copyright, and not jointly or in concert, they cannot be sued jointly. Ted Browne Music Co. v. Fowler, (CCA 2), 290 Fed 751.

Licensee was entitled to join licensor as co-plaintiff in suit for infringement, and the suit was not collusive, though licensee paid licensor a sum of money to induce him to come into the case and has agreed to hold him harmless from expense of suit. Stephens v. Howells Sales Co., (DC-NY), 16 F(2d) 805.

Exclusive licensee of the copyright owners is properly made a party-plaintiff under Equity Rule 37. Metro-Goldwyn-Mayer Distributing Corp. v. Bijou Theatre Co., Inc., (DC-Mass), 50 F(2d) 908, 9 USPQ 538. Aff'd 59 F(2d) 70, 13 USPQ 147.

In action by publisher of book, copyright of which stood in the name of the author, which publisher was exclusive licensee of motion-picture rights, to restrain distribution of an unauthorized motion picture, joinder of the author as a nominal party plaintiff was proper and necessary. L. C. Page & Co., Inc. v. Fox Film Corp., (CCA 2), 83 F(2d) 196, 29 USPQ 386.

Complaint charging defendant with infringement by public performance of copyrighted musical compositions owned by two of the three plaintiffs, the third plaintiff having exclusive rights of publicly presenting the compositions, should not have been dismissed for multifariousness and misjoinder, but court could have ordered separate trials if it decided convenience required two trials. Buck v. Elm Lodge, Inc., (CCA 2), 83 F(2d) 201, 29 USPQ 390.

Where renewal of copyright, taken out by son after his father's death, was held for benefit of his living children, such children are proper parties plaintiff to infringement suit. Tobani v. Carl Fischer, Inc., (CCA 2), 98 F(2d) 57, 38 USPQ 198, mod'g 36 USPQ 97.

Infringing printer and publisher may be joined as codefendants in copyright infringement suit. Sammons v. Colonial Press, Inc., (CCA 1), 126 F(2d) 341, 53 USPQ 71, mod'g 38 FSupp 649, 49 USPQ 350.

Copyright proprietor, being the principal, and the American Society of Composers, Authors, and Publishers, in whom was vested the non-dramatic public performing rights, being the agent, copyright proprietor was proper party plaintiff in suit for infringement by playing of music. Leo Feist, Inc. v. Young, (CCA 7), 138 F(2d) 972, 59 USPQ 450, rev'g 46 FSupp 622, 54 USPQ 489.

Holder of legal title to copyright may sue without joining others having equitable interest. Edward B. Marks Music Corp. v. Jerry Vogel Music Co., Inc., (CCA 2), 140 F(2d) 266, 60 USPQ 256, mod'g 47 FSupp 490, 55 USPQ 288.

Plaintiff, as composer's assignee, is a real party in interest entitled to sue in own behalf and entitled to injunction, its own damages, share in statutory damages, and share in defendant's profits; nonjoinder of deceased author's successors is not fatal since they are not indispensable within Rule 19(b) of Federal Rules of Civil Procedure [Rules, c. 15] because their rights can be reserved in judgment. Edward B. Marks Music Corp. v. Jerry Vogel Music Co., Inc., (CCA 2), 140 F(2d) 268, 60 USPQ 256, mod'g 47 FSupp 490, 55 USPQ 288.

Since plaintiff, copyright proprietor, transferred to the American Society of Composers, Authors, and Publishers only one (public performance) of nine rights obtained under copyright the American Society of Composers, Authors, and Publishers was not assignee, but licensee, and cannot maintain infringement suit alone, but can do so only by joining copyright proprietor as plaintiff; hence, in instant suit by copyright proprietor alone, defendant being fully protected from second suit for same infringement (public performance), there is no necessity for joining the American Society of Composers, Authors, and Publishers as plaintiff. Widenski v. Shapiro, Bernstein & Co., Inc., (CCA 1), 147 F(2d) 909, 64 USPQ 448, aff'g 54 FSupp 780, 61 USPQ 91.

Action to determine rights in copyright can be maintained against copyright owner even though person named as author in copyright is not party to suit. Machaty v. Astra Pictures, Inc., (CA 2), 197 F(2d) 138, 93 USPQ 51, aff'g 89 USPQ 539.

Four separate plaintiffs cannot join in one suit against a defendant on the ground that their demands are similar, against the same defendant, and upon the same kind of a cause of action, when the causes of action grow out of different facts, and none of the plaintiffs has an interest in the copyright of the others. Desylva, Brown & Henderson, Inc. v. Weyman, (DC-La), 7 FSupp 725, 23 USPQ 172.

Where the copyrights of several separate compositions are infringed simultaneously by the same defendant, the proprietors may not join together in one bill and sue for infringement. Buck v. Kloeppel, (DC-Fla), 10 FSupp 345, 26 USPQ 9.

Where the question is one of common or general interest to many persons constituting a class so numerous as to make it impracticable to bring them all before the court, one or more may sue or defend for all. Buck v. Russo, (DC-Mass), 25 FSupp 317, 39 USPQ 377.

The holder of the legal title to copyrights and the beneficial owner may join as plaintiffs in an action for the infringement of each and all of six different copyrights. Society of Stage Authors & Composers, Inc. v. WCAU Broadcasting Co., (DC-Pa), 25 FSupp 385, 39 USPQ 261.

E wrote, and sold to C, all rights in article which was published and copyrighted by C who assigned to E all rights except American serial rights (i. e., right to republish in various publications including trade papers or others not competitive with first class magazine); C therefore retained right to republish in such trade or other papers including lesser right to grant permission to others to so republish; E was mere licensee and not proper party plaintiff to sue for infringement by publication in house organ, but since C is joined as plaintiff, suit is not dismissed but is proceeded with under Rule 21 of the Federal Rules of Civil Procedure [Rules, c. 15]. Eliot v. Geare-Marston, Inc., (DC-Pa), 30 FSupp 301, 43 USPQ 249.

Owner of legal title to copyright is necessary party to infringement suit by owners of equitable interest; since owner of legal title was improperly made involuntary plaintiff and is not bound by process, complaint is dismissed on motion. Hoffman v. Santly-Joy, Inc., (DC-NY), 51 FSupp 779, 58 USPQ 537.

In copyright infringement suit in which defendant counterclaims for declaratory judgment of title to copyrights, defendant may not file third-party complaint against the American Society of Composers, Authors, and Publishers, to whom plaintiff assigned nondramatic public performance rights; society is not, and may not be, liable for any part of plaintiff's claim against defendant; defendant may join the society as defendant under Rule 13(h) of Federal Rules of Civil Procedure [Rules, c. 15] since the society's presence is required for granting complete relief on counterclaim; fact that defendant and the society are both domiciled in state of suit does not oust jurisdiction since, under § 110 of this title, federal courts have jurisdiction to determine title to copyright in musical composition and to decide suit involving copyright, although person asserting claim has interest in copyright less than full title. King v. Edward B. Marks Music Corp., (DC-NY), 56 FSupp 446, 62 USPQ 249.

Nonresident author is proper defendant to copyright infringement suit brought against alleged infringer by exclusive licensee where author sets up as cross-claim against alleged infringer essentially the same claim as that alleged by plaintiff, alleging that author's rights and claims against alleged infringer are superior to those of plaintiff. Field v. True Comics, Inc., (DC-NY), 89 FSupp 611, 84 USPQ 358.

Author has no right to sue where article was accepted by publisher for exclusive publication in magazine; copyright was secured by publisher in its name; there was no contract between publisher and author, and author does not allude to any reservation of rights when she gave publisher authority to publish article. Alexander v. Irving Trust Co., (DC-NY), 132 FSupp 364, 106 USPQ 74. Aff'd 228 F(2d) 221, 108 USPQ 24.

Joint proprietors of copyright may sue jointly for its infringement; thus, author and owner of right to produce copyrighted play on stage may maintain action against one to whom they granted right to make moving picture. Inge v. Twentieth Century-Fox Film Corp., (DC-NY), 143 FSupp 294, 111 USPQ 153.

Bare licensee, who published previously copyrighted story in magazine, is not even a proper party, let alone an indispensable one, in copyright infringement action. Ilyin v. Avon Publications, Inc., (DC-NY), 144 FSupp 368, 110 USPQ 356.

Even sole and exclusive licensee may not sue for copyright infringement without joining owner of copyright; where exclusive licensee is unable to join foreign copyright owner, complaint is dismissed for failure to join indispensable party, but decree is left open to enable licensee to request owner to join. Ilyin v. Avon Publications, Inc., (DC-NY), 144 FSupp 368, 110 USPQ 356.

Author of biography is proper party to sue for copyright infringement arising from biographical novel, although assignment to publisher conveyed sole right to publish in book form, inasmuch as assignment provided that copyright be taken out in author's name and be her sole property and since assignment did not purport to convey all rights secured by copyright, author having retained right to make another version by novelizing work. Greenbie v. Noble, (DC-NY), 151 FSupp 45, 113 USPQ 115.

Plaintiff, publisher members of American society of composers, authors and publishers, is proper party in interest in action for infringement of plaintiff's copyrighted musical composition; American society of composers, authors and publishers is not proper party. Dorchester Music Corp. v. National Broadcasting Co., (DC-Cal), 171 FSupp 580, 120 USPQ 429.

It is proper for wholly-owned corporate subsidiary to be proprietor of copyright, while its corporate parent causes original work of art to be reproduced, published, and copyrighted; both subsidiary and parent are proper parties plaintiff in infringement action. Peter Pan Fabrics, Inc. v. Acadia Co., Inc., (DC-NY), 173 FSupp 292, 121 USPQ 81. Aff'd 274 F(2d) 487, 124 USPQ 154.

Copyright Act [§ 1 et seq. of this title] gives only copyright proprietors the right to sue for infringement; "proprietor" is either author of work or his assignee; party bringing suit must not only be proprietor in this sense but also copyright proprietor, in other words, he must have owned copyright at time of infringement; transfer of copyright owner's right, title, and interest ordinarily does not vest in assignee a cause of action for prior infringement, and assignor cannot maintain such action if infringement took place subsequent to assignment, or unless it took place before transfer; however, legal title to copyright may be in one person and equitable title in another; thus, one may be proprietor of copyright if he holds legal title, though equitable title may be in another either expressly or as trustee ex malificio; in such case, courts treat equitable owner as copyright proprietor and permit him to maintain infringement action. Manning v. Miller Music Corp., (DC-NY), 174 FSupp 192, 121 USPQ 600.

Rules 17, 19, 20, and 21 of the Federal Rules of Civil Procedure [Rules, c. 15], relating to parties, evidence general purpose of Federal Rules of Civil Procedure to eliminate old restrictive and inflexible rules of joinder and to allow joinder of interested parties liberally to end that unnecessary multiplicity of action can be avoided; joinder by supplemental bill of owners of copyrights exclusively licensed to original plaintiff, and whose infringement is alleged by supplemental bill, is permitted although they have no interest in original cause of action. Society of European Stage Authors & Composers, Inc. v. WCAU Broadcasting Co., (DC-Pa), 1 FedRDec 264, 46 USPQ 198.

Contracts between coauthors and publisher provide for payment of royalties to coauthors in designated proportions; one coauthor sues publisher to determine whether specific sales are subject to royalties; other coauthor is joined as party since, although not indispensable party (inasmuch as each coauthor could maintain action to recover royalties), he is necessary party if subsequent suit against publisher on similar claim is to be avoided; advantage of his presence outweights any disadvantage resulting from court's loss of diversity jurisdiction. Curtis v. American Book Co., (DC-NY), 17 FedRDec 504, 107 USPQ 116.

Copyright infringement suit is not dismissed on ground that plaintiff's attorneys have no authority to represent specific plaintiff (enemy alien) where authority was not questioned until trial and there is no evidence overcoming presumption that attorney who appears for litigant has authority to do so. Select Theatres Corp. v. Ronzoni Macaroni Co., (DC-NY), 59 USPQ 288.

Although cases hold that unauthorized person, who takes out copyright and claims to be owner thereof, acts as trustee for true owner and copyright is held in trust for owner, court cannot hold that alleged trustee is not true owner since, although present in court, he is not party to infringement suit and has not assigned copyright to plaintiff. Machaty v. Astra Pictures, Inc., (DC-NY), 89 USPQ 539. Aff'd 197 F(2d) 138, 93 USPQ 51.

Where an orchestra is a corporation and leader owns substantially all of stock, equity regards leader and corporation as identical and recognizes leader as true party in interest; although corporation should have been named as party plaintiff, jurisdiction was retained. Waring v. WDAS Broadcasting Station, Inc., 327 Pa 433, 194 Atl 631, 35 USPQ 272.

65. —Pleading.

Where a bill for infringement of copyright prays for general relief, but not expressly for an accounting, equity may decree an accounting. Stevens v. Gladding, 58 US(17 How) 447, 15 LEd 155, rev'g (CC-RI), FedCas 13,400.

If a bill for infringement contains no prayer for an account, or a prayer for general relief, an accounting will not be decreed. Stevens v. Cady, (CC-RI), FedCas 13,395.

If plaintiffs allege that they are citizens of the United States, which is not denied, the fact must be considered as admitted. Webb v. Powers, (CC-Mass), FedCas 17,323.

Where an accounting of profits is claimed, such can be decreed under a general prayer for relief. Gilmore v. Anderson, (CC-NY), 38 Fed 846.

If a bill for infringement of copyright states a cause of action, a demurrer to it which does not specifically state what parts of the bill are demurred to, should not be sustained. Empire City Amusement Co. v. Wilton, (CC-Mass), 134 Fed 132.

In an infringement suit, where profert of the copyrighted article is made in the bill, the article will be regarded as part of the bill and may be examined on demurrer. American Mutoscope & Biograph Co. v. Edison Mfg. Co., (CC-NJ), 137 Fed 262.

Where the passages that constitute the infringement are recited in the declaration, they cannot be expunged on the ground that they are evidential. Journal of Commerce & Commercial Bulletin v. Boston Transcript Co., (DC-Mass), 292 Fed 311.

Prayer for an accounting did not in itself give equitable jurisdiction. Pathe Exchange, Inc. v. Dalke, (CCA 4), 49 F(2d) 161.

In action wherein defendant is charged with copyright infringement and unfair competition on account of defendant's licensing television performance of copyrighted motion pictures allegedly owned by plaintiff, defendant interposes affirmative defense of estoppel alleging that additional defendants, now in control of plaintiff, had at one time acted as counsel for defendant in acquisition of television rights at issue; counterclaim against plaintiff and additional defendants is related to estoppel defense, since it charges that additional defendants conspired to deprive defendant of its rights in order to cement their own position in control of plaintiff; action is alleged to be one of a series of harrassing maneuvers designed to interfere with defendant's proper exploitation of rights acquired on advice of additional defendants; pleadings disclose sufficient logical relationship so that, in interest of avoiding circuity and multiplicity of action, counterclaim should be considered compulsory. United Artists Corp. v. Masterpiece Productions, Inc., (CA 2), 221 F(2d) 213, 105 USPQ 52, rev'g 15 FedRDec 395, 101 USPQ 151.

On motion to dismiss complaint, court must accept averments of complaint as true. Southern Music Pub. Co., Inc. v. Walt Disney Productions, (DC-NY), 73 FSupp 580, 74 USPQ 145.

At common law, remedy for copyright infringement was action on the case for damages. Bercovici v. Chaplin, (DC-NY), 7 FedR Dec 61, 72 USPQ 340, mod'g 3 FedRDec 409, 60 USPQ 409.

66. ——Bill or complaint.

In an action of trover for conversion of a set of abstract books, wherein plaintiff made no averment as to his copyright thereon, the infringement, or a claim for damages, there is nothing with respect to the copyright, or any infringement which is a proper matter of consideration for the jury. Stover v. Lathrop, (CC-Colo), 33 Fed 348.

It is not necessary in copyright cases to allege the preliminary steps and procedures adopted in producing or composing a work. Falk v. Schumacher, (CC-NY), 48 Fed 222.

A bill for infringement which fails to allege authorship except by implication arising from the statute words "written" and "composed" required the court to presume that these words impart originality of defendant's dramatic composition in absence of specific objection on that account. Henderson v. Tompkins, (CC-Mass), 60 Fed 758.

Where all the parts of a copyrighted matter, taken together, constitute, in use, a single implement, a bill alleging infringement of 30 different copyrights relating to it is not subject to a demurrer on the ground that the bill is multifarious. Amberg File & Index Co. v. Shea, Smith & Co., (CC-Ill), 78 Fed 479. Aff'd 82 Fed 314.

Complainant must allege and prove the existence of facts of originality, of intellectual production, of thought and conception, on the part of the author. Falk v. City Item Printing Co., (CC-La), 79 Fed 321.

A demurrer will not be sustained to a bill on the ground of multifariousness, unless the several copyrights alleged to be infringed relate to such diverse subjects that they cannot be conveniently considered together. Harper v. Holman, (CC-Pa), 84 Fed 222.

Corporation proprietor suing for infringement of a work need not set forth in its bill the names of editors and compilers. Edward Thompson Co. v. American Law Book Co., (CC-NY), 119 Fed 217.

Assignee, suing for infringement, must show authorship in his assignor and nonpublication prior to copyright. Bosselman v. Richardson, (CCA 2), 174 Fed 622.

In a suit for infringement complainant must show that his work is a copyrightable work. Crown Feature Film Co. v. Levy, (DC-NY), 202 Fed 805.

It is not necessary to allege, in the bill, that the musical composition was written for the purpose of public performance for profit, since it will be inferred that he had written the work for the purpose of securing all the rights attainable under the Copyright Act. Hubbell v. Royal Pastime Amusement Co., (DC-NY), 242 Fed 1002.

Where two motion-picture photoplays had been adapted from the same copyrighted stage play, a bill, brought by the owner of the copyright of the motion picture, must allege infringement of such copyright and not infringement of the play. Société Des Films Menchen v. Vitagraph Co., (CCA 2), 251 Fed 258.

In a suit for infringement of a work of art, complainant must allege and prove that copies bore the name of copyright proprietor. E. I. Horsman & Aetna Doll Co., Inc. v. Kaufman, (CCA 2), 286 Fed 372.

A plaintiff in a suit for infringement may set forth one cause of action in several different counts when it is good pleading in the state practice. Journal of Commerce & Commercial Bulletin v. Boston Transcript Co., (DC-Mass), 292 Fed 311.

Verification on information and belief of matters not within the knowledge of plaintiff was sufficient. Gerlach-Barklow Co. v. Morris & Bendien, (CCA 2), 23 F(2d) 159.

The complaint need not contain an allegation that the label registered contains copyrighted subject matter or is original work, in view of Equity Rule 25. Hoague-Sprague Corp. v. Frank C. Meyer Co., Inc., (DC-NY), 27 F(2d) 176.

Where plaintiff charges that defendants copied his advertisement it must be assumed that the allegation is true unless the two advertisements are so dissimilar as to negative completely the theory of infringement. Ansehl v. Puritan Pharmaceutical Co., (CCA 8), 61 F(2d) 131, 15 USPQ 38.

Since a person who is neither citizen nor subject of any government can take out copyright, citizenship of author is not material issue and it is not of least consequence that complaint alleged that author was citizen of state with whom United States had reciprocal relations. Houghton Mifflin Co. v. Stackpole Sons, Inc., (CCA 2), 113 F(2d) 627, 46 USPQ 296, mod'g 31 FSupp 517, 44 USPQ 668.

Complaint seeking declaratory judgment as to title to copyrights did not allege infringement and consequent damages, but this did not waive right to demand damages, in addition to declaratory and injunctive relief, upon declaration that plaintiff has title to copyrights; also, complaint asked for such further relief as may be necessary or proper. Edward B. Marks Music Corp. v. Charles K. Harris Music Publishing Co., Inc., (CA 2), 255 F(2d) 518, 117 USPQ 308.

Complaint setting forth works involved did not show on its face an infringement of the copyrighted song, "What are Your Intentions?" Park v. Warner Bros., (DC-NY), 8 FSupp 37, 23 USPQ 202.

Bill for copyright infringement of label need not aver originality and copyrightability of label. Bobrecker v. Denebeim, (DC-Mo), 25 FSupp 208, 39 USPQ 336.

If there are two or more separate and distinct claims of copyright infringement, they should be separately stated and numbered; also, allegations of palming off and unfair competition should be eliminated from association therewith. Kashins v. Keystone Lamp Manufacturing Corp., (DC-NY), 135 FSupp 681, 107 USPQ 137.

In copyright infringement case, letters giving notice of infringement attached to complaint are not stricken since such notice is part of plaintiff's case; although criticism might be made because plaintiff has pleaded evidence to allow them to remain part of pleading will not harm defendant. Parts Mfg. Corp. v. Weinberg, (DC-NY), 1 FedRDec 329, 46 USPQ 509.

In copyright infringement case, paragraph in complaint alleging financial irresponsibility of defendant corporation is not stricken since financial responsibility of corporation may be relevant to liability of individual defendants. Parts Mfg. Corp. v. Weinberg, (DC-NY), 1 FedRDec 329, 46 USPQ 509.

There being no infringement, allegation of conspiracy to infringe adds no support to claim for damages. Shurr v. Warner Bros. Pictures, Inc., (DC-NY), 59 USPQ 49. Aff'd 144 F(2d) 200, 62 USPQ 60.

In order for complaint to state cause of action for plagiarism, there must be some substantial similarity between defendants' motion picture and protectible portions of plaintiff's literary composition; however, question of protectibility need not be considered as to cause of action for breach of contract (express or implied in fact) not to use idea of composition without paying for same, since, even if not original, idea may be subject of contract provided it is valuable; yet, no cause of action is stated for use of idea if there is no similarity whatsoever between productions. Weitzenkorn v. Lesser, 40 Cal(2d series) 778, 256 Pac(2d) 947, 97 USPQ 545.

Complaint alleges that defendant breached contract by use of plaintiff's book in defendant's motion picture; cause of action in contract is not stated since substantial similarity between ideas embodied in book and picture is not shown. Sutton v. Walt Disney Productions, 118 CalApp(2d series) 598, 258 Pac(2d) 519, 98 USPQ 198.

In an action by a licensor of motion picture against his licensee to recover contract price of drama rights, it is not essential that plaintiff allege facts with the same particularity and detail as is necessary in a case where a defendant is proceeded against by an author of a play for infringement of copyright. Mart v. Fox, (Misc), 166 NYS 793.

67. ———Sufficiency in general.

A bill for infringement which alleged that many people had been induced to buy defendant's copies in the belief that they were complainant's disclosed adequate cause for complaint and entitled complainants to some form of equitable relief. Merriam v. Famous Shoe & Clothing Co., (CC-Mo), 47 Fed 411.

An allegation that "your orator, at all times hereafter stated, was and still is a citizen of the United States and a resident therein" is sufficient against demurrer on the ground that the bill does not show that the complainant was a citizen of the United States at the time he produced the photograph. Falk v. Schumacher, (CC-NY), 48 Fed 222.

Although a bill fails to allege authorship, except by implication arising from the words "written or composed," it is sufficient against demurrer. Henderson v. Tompkins, (CC-Mass), 60 Fed 758.

Demurrer to bill on ground that it contained no allegation that notice had been printed in all foreign editions was overruled. Haggard v. Waverly Pub. Co., (CC-NJ), 144 Fed 490.

A complaint which alleged that the defendant had obtained secondhand books, of which the plaintiff owned the copyright, reconstructed, and sold them as and for the publication being sold by plaintiff, does not state a cause of action for infringement. Bureau of National Literature v. Sells, (DC-Wash), 211 Fed 379.

Where a complainant, seeking damages for the infringement of a copyright, alleges that the photograph was his own original conception, to which he gave visible form by selecting the position and the time at which to take the picture, it is an allegation of fact and is not subject to a demurrer on the ground that the complaint does not show that the photograph was copyrightable. Pagano v. Chas. Beseler Co., (DC-NY), 234 Fed 963.

Averments that one defendant printed the labels and that other defendants used them on their products in pursuance of the common plan, sufficiently averred a conspiracy between the defendants. Premier Malt Products Co. v. G. A. Ackerman Printing Co., Inc., (CCA 7), 24 F(2d) 89.

Allegation that language in defendants' publications "is substantially identical in all material respects with language in plaintiff's copyrighted publications" was insufficient. Affiliated Enterprises, Inc. v. Truber, (CCA 1), 86 F(2d) 958, 32 USPQ 94.

Rule 8 of the Federal Rules of Civil Procedure [Rules, c. 15] provides what contents of petition shall be, whether in law or equity, and it is sufficient if bill for copyright infringement alleges that plaintiff is owner and proprietor of registered label and that it has been infringed by defendant and will not be dismissed for either failure to show derivation of ownership or to set out a copy of the label. Bobrecker v. Denebeim, (DC-Mo), 25 FSupp 208, 39 USPQ 336.

Complaint alleging that plaintiff is owner of radio program "Double or Nothing," that it broadcast such program on a certain date and that defendants infringed copyright by broadcasting radio program "Take It or Leave It" merely pleads conclusions, allegations being insufficient to set forth cause of action for copyright infringement; it is not alleged in what respect defendants infringe. American Broadcasting Co. v. Wahl Co., (DC-NY), 36 FSupp 167, 47 USPQ 338. Mf'd 121 F(2d) 412, 50 USPQ 156.

Complaint for copyright infringement, to which is annexed exhibit evidencing compliance with Copyright Act, alleges that defendant enclosed with a circular letter, without authorization, a copy of title, editorial page masthead, and leading editorial published in plaintiff's copyrighted newspaper; defendant's motion for summary judgment is denied since complaint states good cause of action on its face. New

York Tribune, Inc. v. Otis & Co., (DC-NY), 39 FSupp 67, 49 USPQ 361.

Where part owner sues for infringement, complaint is bad if it does not expressly negative possibility that one of plaintiff's cotenants may have licensed defendant. Crosney v. Edward Small Productions, Inc., (DC-NY), 52 FSupp 559, 59 USPQ 193.

Complaint sets forth claim sufficiently by alleging ownership, compliance with statute, and infringement. April Productions, Inc. v. Strand Enterprises, Inc., (DC-NY), 79 FSupp 515, 77 USPQ 155.

Copyright infringement complaint and plaintiff's affidavit in support of motion for receiver of defendants' property used in infringing copyright do not make out prima facie case, since there is no prima facie assumption of burden of proof to show identity in form of expression adopted to clothe idea as between parties' compositions. Lampert v. Hollis Music, Inc., (DC-NY), 105 FSupp 3, 94 USPQ 226.

To show infringement of copyrighted song, plaintiff must establish not only that ideas of both compositions and form of expressing ideas are similar, but also that this was not mere coincidence and was accomplished with previous knowledge of plaintiff's composition, and plaintiff must prove this by evidence to show that plaintiff's work was completed prior to defendant's work and that there was a contact between plaintiff's work and defendant either through public medium or privately. Northern Music Corp. v. King Record Distributing Co., (DC-NY), 105 FSupp 393, 93 USPQ 512.

Originality ordinarily is question of fact which is not to be decided on motion to dismiss, but mere allegation of originality in complaint does not create factual issue where all ideas involved have long been public property. Lewis v. Kroger Co., (DC-WVa), 109 FSupp 484, 95 USPQ 359.

On motion to dismiss copyright infringement complaint for failure to state claim on which relief can be granted, court may assume validity of copyright and, comparing literary products incorporated into complaint, determine as matter of law whether copyright has been infringed. Lake v. Columbia Broadcasting System, Inc., (DC-Cal), 140 FSupp 707, 110 USPQ 173.

Infringement suit must be dismissed where plaintiff states that he has no certificates of registration of copyrights covering exhibits attached to complaint, such exhibits being alleged in complaint to be basis of plaintiff's right. Guild v. Thompson's Industries, Inc., (DC-Mass), 84 USPQ 224.

Under theory of misappropriation of literary property and infringement of common-law copyright, which sounds in tort, plaintiff is required to allege ownership of protectible property interest, unauthorized copying by defendant, and damage resulting to plaintiff through unauthorized copying; it is necessary for plaintiff, in order to show ownership of protectible property interest, to show originality of idea and format, and that protectible portions of plaintiff's material and defendant's material are similar. Glane v. General Mills, Inc., — Cal

App(2d series) —, 298 Pac(2d) 626, 110 USPQ 391.

Owing to difficulties of enforcing such rights, courts have uniformly refused to protect property in ideas that have not been reduced to concrete form; paragraph in complaint alleging that defendants wrongfully appropriated plaintiff's advertising idea and plan without paying plaintiff fair and reasonable compensation therefor is insufficient in law and is stricken on motion. Stone v. Liggett & Myers Tobacco Co., 260 AppDiv 450, 23 NYS(2d) 210, 47 USPQ 529.

68. ——Allegations of copyright.

The allegations of a bill for infringement that the "complainant has complied in all respects with the requirements of the Revised Statutes" amounted to an allegation that complainant had deposited a copy of his title page, and that he had never published his work. Boucicault v. Hart, (CC-NY), FedCas 1,692, 13 Blatchf 47.

A bill for infringement which contained no specific allegations of deposit of title and copies and of proper copyright notice was insufficient on demurrer. Parkinson v. Laselle, (CC-Cal), FedCas 10,762, 3 Sawy 330.

Averment that complainant delivered copies at the office of Librarian of Congress "or" deposited copies in the mail was alternative pleading and was insufficient. Falk v. Howell, (CC-NY), 34 Fed 739.

A bill for infringement of copyright which merely alleged that the copyright was taken out previous to publication thereof, "in full accordance with the requirements of the laws of the United States," was insufficient. Trow City Directory Co. v. Curtin, (CC-NY), 36 Fed 829.

A complainant's allegation, that he "delivered at the office of the librarian of Congress," and "deposited in the mail, addressed to the librarian of Congress" the title and copies of his book, is proper and requires no amendments or election by complainant where it appears that both acts were done. Scribner v. Henry G. Allen Co., (CC-NY), 43 Fed 680.

A bill for infringement of copyright under prior law which alleged the deposit of two copies of a book in the librarian's office at Washington, within 10 days after publication, but which did not allege that the book was published within a reasonable time after deposit of the copy of the title, sufficiently stated a compliance with the statutory provisions. Scribner v. Henry G. Allen Co., (CC-NY), 49 Fed 854.

Under prior law it was necessary for a complainant to allege and show a deposit with the Librarian of Congress, on or before the day of publication, of a printed copy of the title page of the book, and also two copies of the book, and that lawful notice of copyright had been given. Osgood v. A. S. Aloe Instrument Co., (CC-Mo), 69 Fed 291.

Under prior law deposit of copies of a book with Librarian of Congress within 10 days after publication was a fact which must have been averred in order to show that a complainant had complied with the copyright statutes. Burnell v. Chown, (CC-Ohio), 69 Fed 993.

A bill for infringement which did not contain specific allegations, but the general allegation that all conditions and requisites to obtain a copyright, as required by the laws of the United States, were complied with, was insufficient on demurrer. Ford v. Charles E. Blaney Amusement Co., (CC-NY), 148 Fed 642.

The specific acts necessary to constitute compliance with copyright laws must be alleged in the complaint. Ohman v. New York City, (CC-NY), 168 Fed 953.

Inasmuch as copyright vests upon publication with notice, no allegation as to registration or entry "in form and manner, etc.," is necessary in bill of complaint. National Cloak & Suit Co. v. Kaufman, (CC-Pa), 189 Fed 215.

A bill for infringement which merely alleges that "two complete copies of said photographs" were filed was not sufficient to state a cause of action. Crown Feature Film Co. v. Levy, (DC-NY), 202 Fed 805.

Complaint alleging, that motion-picture photograph or photoplay not having been reproduced in copies for sale the claims for copyright, the title and description, and prints from each scene or act were deposited with the register of copyrights, and complainant received the certificate of registration, was sufficient. Gaumont Co. v. Hatch, (DC-Pa), 208 Fed 378.

Allegation in bill of complaint that each copy contained statutory copyright notice justifies a finding that plaintiff has sought to comply with § 10 of this title, and when not contraverted by defendant there is a prima facie case for injunction. Gerlach-Barklow Co. v. Morris & Bendien, Inc., (CCA 2), 23 F(2d) 159.

Where bill alleged deposit of "two copies of the best edition of said picture," objection that "complete" was omitted before "copies" and words "thereof then published" were also omitted was without merit. Gerlach-Barklow Co. v. Morris & Bendien, Inc., (CCA 2), 23 F(2d) 159.

Plaintiff must annex to complaint a copy of copyrighted musical composition alleged to be infringed. Machtenberg v. Sterner, (DC-NY), 8 FedRDec 169, 77 USPQ 463.

69.   — — —Allegations of title.

Allegations of a bill for infringement were set forth and were sufficiently explicit to amount to an assertion of authorship, and to constitute a perfect title at law. Atwill v. Ferrett, (CC-NY), FedCas 640, 2 Blatchf 39.

A demurrer to a bill of infringement, wherein plaintiff has merely alleged that he is the proprietor of a copyright, but does not state how he became proprietor, or aver compliance with the copyright statutes, should be sustained. Chicago Music Co. v. J. W. Butler Paper Co., (CC-Ill), 19 Fed 758.

It is not necessary, when all the legal and equitable owners of the copyright are joined as complainants, to state the formalities or the mode of conveyance by which the equitable interests become vested in the co-complainants. Black v. Henry G. Allen Co., (CC-NY), 42 Fed 618, 9 LRA 433.

Complainants' averment in a bill for infringement that they were proprietors of a book prior to the time of securing copyright was sufficient.

Lillard v. Sun Printing & Publishing Ass'n, (CC-NY), 87 Fed 213.

It is not necessary in a bill for infringement of copyright that complainant set forth his claim of title. Lillard v. Sun Printing & Publishing Ass'n, (CC-NY), 87 Fed 213.

In an action for infringement complainant must show his title not merely by an allegation that he is the proprietor, but by setting forth facts which show how he became proprietor, and why he has the right to bring the action. Crown Feature Film Co. v. Levy, (DC-NY), 202 Fed 805; Danks v. Gordon, (CCA 2), 272 Fed 821; Foreign & Domestic Music Corp. v. Twentieth Century-Fox Film Corp., (DC-NY), 19 FSupp 769, 34 USPQ 109; Kaplan v. Fox Film Corp., (DC-NY), 19 FSupp 780, 33 USPQ 469.

Where bill alleges title in complainant and that complainant is still owner of copyright it is sufficient. It is not necessary to allege the various steps by which he became the proprietor of the work. American Code Co., Inc. v. Bensinger, (CCA 2), 282 Fed 829.

Where a copyright is not obtained in the plaintiff's name, the plaintiff must connect himself with it by proper averments, showing assignment or transfer of it to him, or a license under it sufficient to entitle him to sue. Ted Browne Music Co. v. Fowler, (CCA 2), 290 Fed 751.

Averment of ownership was sufficient, in view of the prima facie presumption arising from possession. Gerlach-Barklow Co. v. Morris & Bendien, Inc., (CCA 2), 23 F(2d) 159.

Bill for infringement filed by publisher of article read at meeting of an association, showing right given by association but not showing transfer from author, was insufficient to show title in plaintiff entitling it to bring suit. Quinn-Brown Pub. Corp. v. Chilton Co., Inc., (DC-NY), 15 FSupp 213, 30 USPQ 373.

Plaintiff must show title by setting forth facts which indicate how he became proprietor. Quinn-Brown Pub. Corp. v. Chilton Co., Inc., (DC-NY), 15 FSupp 213, 30 USPQ 373.

In infringement suit by authors and composers alleging equitable interest in copyright whose legal title is in another, it is proper for plaintiffs to allege substance of agreement with other; agreement that other will secure copyright and hold it for benefit of plaintiffs and itself subject to payment of royalties and reversion to plaintiffs on default or termination, probably sufficiently alleges title in plaintiffs. Hoffman v. Santly-Joy, Inc., (DC-NY), 51 FSupp 779, 58 USPQ 537.

Complaint must allege facts and not bare conclusions showing plaintiff's equity title, and facts may appear not solely from allegations of complaint but from contracts attached to and made part of complaint. Southern Music Pub. Co., Inc. v. Walt Disney Productions, (DC-NY), 73 FSupp 580, 74 USPQ 145.

70.   — — —Copies of infringing article filed.

Defendant was entitled to have a copy of the alleged infringement of copyright, if made, and a copy of the work alleged to be infringed, as provided by rule of practice of July 1, 1909, where the absence of such exhibits from complainant's petition was not explained and the record did not show the copyrighted article to be a sculpture, or other similar work. Lesser v. George Borgfeldt & Co., (CC-NY), 188 Fed 864.

Copy of work should accompany complaint. Tully v. Triangle Film Corp., (DC-NY), 229 Fed 297.

Where a copy of the work infringed does not accompany the complaint, as provided by Supreme Court rule, satisfactory reasons for its absence must be presented. Tully v. Triangle Film Corp., (DC-NY), 229 Fed 297.

A declaration containing 525 counts alleging infringements in 90 issues of defendant's publication infringing matter copyrighted in 196 issues of plaintiff's paper presented a case within the exception to the requirement of the rule as to copies of the infringing and infringed publications. Journal of Commerce & Commercial Bulletin v. Boston Transcript Co., (DC-Mass), 292 Fed 311.

Annexation of two books in controversy to the bill of complaint was proper. Lowenfels v. Nathan, (DC-NY), 2 FSupp 73, 16 USPQ 421.

Since copyrighted musical play alleged to be infringed is dramatico-musical composition, copies of play and of alleged infringement need not be annexed to complaint. April Productions, Inc. v. Strand Enterprises, Inc., (DC-NY), 79 FSupp 515, 77 USPQ 155.

Copyright infringement complaint is deficient where no copy of copyrighted composition containing copyright notice or certificate of copyright registration forms part thereof. Lampert v. Hollis Music, Inc., (DC-NY), 105 FSupp 3, 94 USPQ 226.

Complaint should be accompanied by copy of infringing work and copy of work alleged to have been infringed, with certain exceptions; failure to comply with requirements must be satisfactorily explained in complaint or pleading is defective. Cole v. Allen, (DC-NY), 3 FedR Dec 236, 58 USPQ 56.

Federal courts consistently have held that failure to attach copies of infringed and infringing compositions, or to explain such failure, renders complaint for copyright infringement defective. Weitzenkorn v. Lesser, 40 Cal (2d series) 778, 256 Pac(2d) 947, 97 USPQ 545.

Section 426, California code of civil procedure, requiring plaintiff's story to be attached to complaint in action for infringement of rights in literary property, applies to actions on contract as well as to suits grounded in tort for plagiarism: by virtue of presence of both plaintiff's book and defendant's motion picture before court, plaintiff's comments in pleading as to copying are surplusage. Sutton v. Walt Disney Productions, 118 CalApp(2d series) 598, 258 Pac(2d) 519, 98 USPQ 198.

71.   — — —Amended pleadings.

Payment of certain expenses as a condition of amending a bill for infringement, where an inaccurate copy of the alleged infringed work has been presented to the court, should be dealt with on the trial of the suit. Tully v. Triangle Film Corp., (DC-NY), 229 Fed 297.

Amended bill was not open to objection that it did not allege any material facts not set forth in the original bill. Metro-Goldwyn-Mayer Distributing Corp. v. Bijou Theatre Co., (DC-Mass), 3 FSupp 66, 17 USPQ 124.

Cause of action for alleged violation of author's right of privacy involves a new and different cause based on different ground of jurisdiction from suit for copyright infringement, and infringement bill cannot be amended to include the first-mentioned cause. Henry Holt & Co., Inc. v. Liggett & Myers Tobacco Co., (DC-Pa), 23 FSupp 302, 37 USPQ 449.

72.   — — —Supplemental pleadings.

Where, subsequent to the filing of an original bill for infringement, a defendant commits other separate infringements of separate copyrights, the complainant may file a supplemental bill. Banks Law Pub. Co. v. Lawyers' Co-operative Pub. Co., (CC-NY), 139 Fed 701.

Where title was well pleaded, averments as to an assignment which occurred after filing of the original bill, and which were in the nature of a ratification of earlier acts did not invalidate complainant's supplemental bill for subsequent infringements. Banks Law Pub. Co. v. Lawyers' Co-operative Pub. Co., (CC-NY), 139 Fed 701.

Filing of supplemental bill is proper way in which to introduce alleged additional copyright infringements occurring after filing of bill: instant supplemental bill alleges infringement of copyrights exclusively licensed to plaintiff but owned by parties added as plaintiffs by supplemental bill. Society of European Stage Authors & Composers, Inc. v. WCAU Broadcasting Co., (DC-Pa), 1 FedRDec 264, 46 USPQ 198.

73.   — —Bill of particulars.

Copies of plaintiff's copyrighted map and alleged infringement filed pursuant to motion for bill of particulars become part of complaint. Christianson v. West Pub. Co., (DC-Cal), 53 FSupp 454, 60 USPQ 279. Aff'd 149 F(2d) 202, 65 USPQ 263.

In action to recover for use of unpublished radio script, particulars were refused as to in what respects plaintiff claims that his idea, plan, and scheme were original since originality in literary composition is not susceptible of same pleadings or particularization as in patent cases. Buckley v. Music Corp., (DC-Del), 2 FedRDec 328, 54 USPQ 70.

Particulars from plaintiff were refused as to dates and other data of defendants' alleged submission of plaintiff's script to others, as well as to time of broadcast and radio stations broadcasting. Buckley v. Music Corp., (DC-Del), 2 FedRDec 328, 54 USPQ 70.

Particulars from plaintiff were refused as to manner in which defendants benefited; benefits obviously were financial. Buckley v. Music Corp., (DC-Del), 2 FedRDec 328, 54 USPQ 70.

Particulars granted as to what orchestra it was claimed defendants retained in connection with broadcasts referred to in amended complaint, although orchestra was named in original complaint and defendants objected to it as immaterial and redundant. Buckley v. Music Corp., (DC-Del), 2 FedRDec 328, 54 USPQ 70.

Particulars were granted as to approximate date when it is claimed each defendant made infringing use. Buckley v. Music Corp., (DC-Del), 2 FedRDec 328, 54 USPQ 70.

Particulars were granted as to whom plaintiff submitted script; defendants are corporations and should be apprized of identity of persons to whom it is claimed communication was made. Buckley v. Music Corp., (DC-Del), 2 FedRDec 328, 54 USPQ 70.

Particulars were refused as to material claimed to have been used by defendants and manner in which used; if defendants used script, they knew what use they made of it since they had copy. Buckley v. Music Corp., (DC-Del), 2 FedRDec 328, 54 USPQ 70.

To enable defendants in copyright infringement suit properly to prepare answers, they are entitled to particulars as to specific literary material, incidents, episodes, dialogue, similarities, and publicity values used in defendants' radio broadcast which plaintiff claims were taken from six copyrighted books; action under copyright laws is similar in many respects to action under patent laws and like rules of practice are applicable; particulars should be allowed with the same liberality as in patent cases. Cole v. Allen, (DC-NY), 3 FedRDec 236, 58 USPQ 56.

Plaintiff is required to furnish bill of particulars containing copy of material alleged to infringe his uncopyrighted work; he must specify when, where, and of whom he demanded that infringing material be retracted or corrected and whether demands were written or oral. Fiske v. Hitchcock, (DC-NY), 76 USPQ 299.

74. ——Answer.

Denials and allegations merely on information and belief were not sufficient to entitle defendant to a dissolution of an injunction. Farmer v. Calvert Lithographing Co., (CC-Mich), FedCas 4,651, 1 Flip 228.

A defendant cannot enlarge the scope and meaning of the averment of a bill for infringement by expanding his denial beyond the allegations of the bill. Osgood v. A. S. Aloe Instrument Co., (CC-Mo), 69 Fed 291.

Since R. S. §§ 4969 and 914 are to be construed together, a defendant may answer by pleading a general denial to all averments of a bill for infringement of copyright, and thereunder, upon trial, "give special matter in evidence." Johnson v. Klopsch, (CC-NY), 88 Fed 692.

If a defendant, in pleading to the whole of a bill for infringement, alleges that complainant's composition has been publicly exhibited without proper copyright notice, complainant's evidence of the exclusiveness of the exhibition is admissible and competent without amendment of the bill. Werckmeister v. American Lithographic Co., (CCA 2), 134 Fed 321, 68 LRA 591, rev'g 126 Fed 244.

An averment, in an answer to a bill for the infringement of a copyright, that the plaintiff was greatly benefited, and not damaged, is immaterial and must be stricken out. Harms v. Cohen, (DC-Pa), 279 Fed 276.

Answer alleging that defendant obtained copyrighted matter from third persons required a trial as to defendant and the other persons named, irrespective of conspiracy or collusion. Pathe Exchange, Inc. v. International Alliance, (DC-NY), 3 FSupp 63.

Defendant urges that Congress exceeded its power in Copyright Act in designating employer for hire as "author"; this is without foundation, but, not being in answer, it is not open to defendant since no opportunity is given plaintiff to meet it or the court to notify attorney general that constitutionality of act is brought in question. Vitaphone Corp. v. Hutchinson Amusement Co., (DC-Mass), 28 FSupp 526, 42 USPQ 431.

Complaint's factual allegations giving court jurisdiction of subject matter are not defeated by defendants' denials. Southern Music Pub. Co., Inc. v. Walt Disney Productions, (DC-NY), 73 FSupp 580, 74 USPQ 145.

From a practical standpoint the burden on plaintiff is the same whether answer merely denies plaintiff's allegation of proper copyright notice, or defense of improper copyright notice is affirmatively pleaded. Forster Music Publisher, Inc. v. Fred Fisher Music Co., Inc., (DC-NY), 6 FedRDec 314, 63 USPQ 60, 63 USPQ 112.

Nearly two years after answering, court permits defendant to amend answer by denying that copyrighted song has always borne proper copyright notice; pleaded defense had been title, but, since case has been marked off calendar by stipulation with leave to either party to move for trial on notice, plaintiff will not be prejudiced in preparing to meet new defense. Forster Music Publisher, Inc. v. Fred Fisher Music Co., Inc., (DC-NY), 6 FedRDec 314, 63 USPQ 60, 63 USPQ 112.

75. ——Summary judgment—Dismissal of action.

Granting of motion to dismiss copyright infringement suit without taking testimony but upon reading of the play and viewing motion picture was error, since such reading admits access and use which is tantamount to presumption of piracy and denial of good faith. With access admitted, similarity of incident rests on high degree of probability of copying and low degree of probability of independent creation. Shipman v. R. K. O. Radio Pictures, Inc., (CCA 2), 100 F(2d) 533, 40 USPQ 211, aff'g 20 FSupp 249, 35 USPQ 242.

In copyright infringement suit, defendant in response to demand filed bill of particulars giving "cutting continuity" as synopsis of its motion-picture play and then plaintiff in response to demand filed bill of particulars showing alleged infringement, based on the "cutting continuity"; defendant then moved to dismiss and after comparing continuity with plaintiff's copyrighted and uncopyrighted version of play court dismissed bill; this procedure was not permissible as plaintiff was not bound to accept the continuity and is deprived of day in court; by basing its particulars on the continuity it did not accept it but was entitled to try out issue whether it faithfully represented the film; judge need not see film if continuity is accurate representation. Dellar v. Samuel Goldwyn, Inc., (CCA 2), 104 F(2d) 661, 42 USPQ 164, rev'g 23 FSupp 519, 37 USPQ 760.

Where it is attempted to dispose of a suit for infringement of a copyright and literary property by a moving picture summarily by a comparison of the scenario with the book or play, the judge must assume that the defendant had "access" to the book or play and that he actually copied those parts common to it and the film; and if the decision is in favor of the plaintiff, the issue of copying remains to be tried. Dellar v. Samuel Goldwyn, Inc., (CCA 2), 104 F(2d) 661, 42 USPQ 164, rev'g 23 FSupp 519, 37 USPQ 760.

Cutting continuity of motion picture was submitted and bill dismissed for lack of infringement, but plaintiff argues that it is not fair representation of the film, and decree is reversed and remanded; if court on new hearing determines that continuity is fair representation it should dismiss bill; view of picture may be best means of reaching satisfactory conclusion. Collins v. Metro-Goldwyn Pictures Corp., (CCA 2), 106 F(2d) 83, 42 USPQ 553, rev'g 25 FSupp 781, 39 USPQ 520.

In copyright infringement action, if claimed custom requires interpretation of contract conveying rights in copyright to defendant which would exclude rights claimed by defendant and, if in absence of such custom such rights were included in the transfer, issue as to existence of custom is material issue and defendant's motion for summary judgment should be denied. Murphy v. Warner Bros. Pictures, Inc., (CCA 9), 112 F(2d) 746, 46 USPQ 2.

Summary judgment dismissing copyright infringement suit is granted where defendants' affidavits prove license and plaintiff merely denies license, presenting no facts in support thereof, thus raising no issue; there is no genuine issue concerning material fact. Piantadosi v. Loew's, Inc., (CCA 9), 137 F(2d) 534, 59 USPQ 174.

Although defendant's motion for judgment on pleadings is denied since motion concedes access and copying, this does not mean that suit must go to trial; on motion for summary judgment, supported by defendant's author's deposition or perhaps even affidavit, it might be established that there was neither access nor copying. MacDonald v. DuMaurier, (CCA 2), 144 F(2d) 696, 62 USPQ 394, rev'g 60 USPQ 410.

On defendant's motion for judgment on pleadings, court must assume that author of book charged with infringing had access to plaintiff's copyrighted works and, as alleged in complaint, copied parts common to both, although answer denies copying. MacDonald v. DuMaurier, (CCA 2), 144 F(2d) 696, 62 USPQ 394, rev'g 60 USPQ 410.

When copyrighted work and alleged infringement are before court, capable of examination and comparison, noninfringement can be determined on motion to dismiss; Dellar v. Sam-

uel Goldwyn, Inc., (CCA 2), 104 F(2d) 661, 42 USPQ 164, is distinguished. Christianson v. West Pub. Co., (CCA 9), 149 F(2d) 202, 65 USPQ 263, aff'g 53 FSupp 454, 60 USPQ 279.

Interlocutory motion for judgment opens up whole record. Park v. Warner Bros., (DC-NY), 8 FSupp 37, 23 USPQ 202.

When the court has an opportunity of comparing the two works in question, it has all the data necessary to decide the question of infringement, which it may do on motion where the works are set forth in the complaint. Park v. Warner Bros., (DC-NY), 8 FSupp 37, 23 USPQ 202.

Where the two copyrighted works in extenso are before court by stipulation, on motion by defendant for summary decree of dismissal, the works themselves supersede and control any allegations of conclusions of fact about them or descriptions of them in complaint, for courts deal with actualities of situations before them, not with interested comments thereon. Shipman v. R. K. O. Radio Pictures, Inc., (DC-NY), 20 FSupp 249, 35 USPQ 242. Aff'd 100 F(2d) 533, 40 USPQ 211.

Findings of judge on motion to dismiss as to validity and infringements of copyright should not be disturbed by coordinate judge, and his decision is law of case unless at trial facts shown are different from facts alleged in complaint and admitted by implication on motion. Basevi v. Edward O'Toole Co., Inc., (DC-NY), 26 FSupp 41, 40 USPQ 333.

Determination of notice to dismiss on ground that plaintiff has failed to state claim on which relief can be granted depends on whether allegations of plaintiff's pleadings, taken as true, establish threatened infringement by defendant of his copyright. Long v. Jordan, (DC-Cal), 29 FSupp 287, 43 USPQ 176.

On granting plaintiff's motion for summary judgment in copyright infringement suit, action is referred to master to fix damages and profits. Houghton Mifflin Co. v. Stackpole Sons, Inc., (DC-NY), 31 FSupp 517, 44 USPQ 668. Mf'd 113 F(2d) 627, 46 USPQ 296.

On motions for summary judgment in copyright infringement case court examines depositions of principals on their examination before trial, extensive pleadings including plaintiff's detailed bill of particulars, the two plays with several versions of defendants' play, the book, and articles by defendant author from which he claims his idea was developed, and complete briefs of parties. Rose v. Connelly, (DC-NY), 38 FSupp 54, 49 USPQ 170.

Motion to dismiss complaint on ground that defendant's use is "fair use" is denied since determination of "fair use" should not be resolved on affidavits but is best left to trial judge. New York Tribune, Inc. v. Otis & Co., (DC-NY), 39 FSupp 67, 49 USPQ 361.

On defendants' motion for summary judgment in copyright infringement suit, access to and use of work claimed to be plagiarized is admitted; issue is whether comparison of the two works establishes as matter of law that defendants have not made unfair use of sufficient amount of plaintiff's copyrightable matter to justify holding of infringement; motion is denied since enough similarity between both works in theme, characters, locale, and incidents is found to preclude holding that there is no infringement as matter of law. Solomon v. R. K. O. Radio Pictures, Inc., (DC-NY), 40 FSupp 625, 49 USPQ 647.

On defendants' motion for summary judgment in copyright infringement suit, court has before it plaintiff's play and "cutting continuity" of defendants' motion picture; it is unnecessary that court view picture since plaintiff does not claim that "cutting continuity" does not correctly represent picture and for purposes of motion, court deems that it does correctly represent picture. Solomon v. R. K. O. Radio Pictures, Inc., (DC-NY), 40 FSupp 625, 49 USPQ 647.

Motion to dismiss is addressed solely to pleading which in instant case is complaint as supplemented by bill of particulars; for purposes of motion, allegations of complaint and bill of particulars must be deemed admitted. Jerry Vogel Music Co., Inc. v. Edward B. Marks Music Corp., (DC-NY), 56 FSupp 779, 63 USPQ 1.

Defendant's assertion that sketch from which its alleged infringement was made was purchased in good faith is insufficient to raise issue for trial on plaintiff's motion for summary judgment. Home Art, Inc. v. Glensder Textile Corp., (DC-NY), 81 FSupp 551, 79 USPQ 12.

Copyright infringement suit is decided on motion to dismiss for failure to state claim upon which relief can be granted, since court has before it copies of plaintiff's copyrighted print and of defendants' publications; these are all the data necessary to decide infringement; comparison of material may be made; issue of infringement should be speedily determined whenever possible. Lewis v. Kroger Co., (DC-WVa), 109 FSupp 484, 95 USPQ 359.

In order to maintain action for copyright infringement, plaintiff must show that there is genuine issue with respect to claim of similarity; there being no genuine issue as to similarity, summary judgment dismissing complaint is entered. Buckler v. Paramount Pictures, Inc., (DC-NY), 133 FSupp 223, 106 USPQ 256.

Summary judgment is awarded defendant in action for infringement of common-law copyright if similarity between plaintiff's play and defendant's motion picture is in public domain or is inconsequential; however, since it is assumed for purposes of motion that defendant copied, motion is denied if jury could reasonably find that there was unlawful appropriation. Malkin v. Dubinsky, (DC-NY), 146 FSupp 111, 112 USPQ 263.

In order to succeed on motion for summary judgment in action for copyright infringement, plaintiff must conclusively demonstrate that there are no genuine issues of fact with regard to any essential element comprising claim of copyright infringement; if examination of works indicates that similarities are so overwhelming and pervasive that trial judge would be justified in directing verdict for plaintiff, judgment can be granted on motion despite defendant's contentions that there was no copying. C. S. Hammond & Co. v. International College Globe, Inc., (DC-NY), 146 FSupp 514, 112 USPQ 291.

Ordinarily, copyright infringement suits should be tried, but summary judgment may be granted where it is apparent upon face of pleadings and other matters of record that there is no genuine and material issue of fact. Costello v. Loew's Inc., (DC-DC), 159 FSupp 782, 116 USPQ 372.

Summary judgment is granted in copyright infringement action since no amount of expert or lay testimony could change obvious contents of plaintiff's play, defendant's motion picture, and source works, and expert testimony could not affect spontaneous and immediate impression of plaintiff's and defendant's literary works upon mind of ordinary observer. Costello v. Loew's Inc., (DC-DC), 159 FSupp 782, 116 USPQ 372.

Action for copyright infringement may be disposed of on motion for summary judgment. Trailins v. Kaiser Aluminum & Chemical Corp., (DC-Md), 160 FSupp 511, 117 USPQ 79.

Partial summary judgments determining liability are entered in copyright infringement actions against sellers of records of pirated songs since documents before court show plaintiff's title to copyrighted songs and sellers' liability for unauthorized use through sale of records published, without plaintiff's consent, by third party; also, sellers have same attorneys as manufacturer and cannot contend that they lacked knowledge of copying. Harms, Inc. v. F. W. Woolworth Co., (DC-Cal), 163 FSupp 484, 118 USPQ 436.

Summary judgment dismissing copyright infringement action is entered in view of fact that court of appeals, which had respective fabrics before it, reversed order granting temporary injunction inasmuch as court of appeals held that there was no infringement; whatever evidence plaintiff might offer, it could not outweigh evidence of fabrics themselves; no amount of expert testimony could overcome crucial difference between fabrics. Millworth Converting Corp. v. Slifka, (DC-NY), 188 FSupp 629, 128 USPQ 143.

On plaintiff's motion for summary judgment in copyright infringement suit, consideration of affidavits and exhibits reveals sharp issue of fact as to whether plaintiff's musical composition is in public domain. Edward B. Marks Music Corp. v. Stasny Music Corp., (DC-NY), 1 FedRDec 720, 49 USPQ 553.

District courts treat motions for summary judgment in plagiarism suits with caution. Millstein v. Leland Hayward, Inc., (DC-NY), 10 FedRDec 198, 85 USPQ 448.

Plaintiff's motion for summary judgment in copyright infringement action is denied where answer pleads affirmative defense that plaintiff induced defendant to copy plaintiff's copyrighted literary composition. Curtis Publishing Co. v. Union Leader Corp., (DC-NH), 12 FedRDec 341, 93 USPQ 360.

Copyright infringement complaint is dismissed on motion for failure to state claim upon which relief can be granted, if copyrighted publication discloses invalidity on examination. Kanover v. Marks, (DC-NY), 91 USPQ 370.

Summary judgment is refused in copyright infringement suit since defendants' denial of essential allegations of complaint puts in issue validity of copyright; that is sufficient to raise questions of fact not determinable on motion for summary judgment; it is not controlling that defendants' affidavits do not controvert plaintiffs' assertions of validity; issue of validity will be disposed of at trial and not on affidavits; also, defendants deny infringement, and question of damages must be determined. McCulloch v. Zapun Ceramics, Inc., (DC-NY), 97 USPQ 12.

Summary judgment of noninfringement of copyright is proper where no genuine issue of material fact is raised. Miner v. Employers Mutual Liability Insurance Co., 97 AppDC 152, 229 F(2d) 35, 108 USPQ 100, aff'g 105 USPQ 357.

76. —Evidence.

Method of proof of originality of plan, arrangement, and combination stated, see Bullinger v. Mackey, (CC-NY), FedCas 2,127, 15 Blatchf 550.

A book must be produced in court before any witnesses will be permitted to testify concerning identical parts in such book. Boucicault v. Fox, (CC-NY), FedCas 1,691, 5 Blatchf 87.

Similarity of errors and peculiarities is strong proof of copying. Lawrence v. Dana, (CC-Mass), FedCas 8,136, 4 Cliff 1.

The reproduction of clerical and typographical errors proves piracy. Lawrence v. Dana, (CC-Mass), FedCas 8,136, 4 Cliff 1.

Testimony must be reasonably conclusive upon the question of abandonment before equity will deprive a party of his rights under a copyright. Myers v. Callaghan, (CC-Ill), 5 Fed 726.

Where it was alleged that a copyrighted article has been infringed, the copyrighted article and the alleged infringing article, or so much thereof as may be necessary for intelligent comparisons, must be included in the proofs. Encyclopaedia Britannica Co. v. American Newspaper Ass'n, (CC-NJ), 130 Fed 460. Aff'd 134 Fed 831.

Copying of errors is evidence of infringement. Hartford Printing Co. v. Hartford Directory & Publishing Co., (CC-Conn), 146 Fed 332; Investment Service Co. v. Fitch Pub. Co., (CCA 7), 291 Fed 1010; Produce Reporter Co. v. Fruit Produce Rating Agency, (DC-Ill), 1 F(2d) 58; W. H. Anderson Co. v. Baldwin Law Pub. Co., (CCA 6), 27 F(2d) 82.

In a suit for a statutory penalty for violation of a copyright, strict construction and proof are required. Caliga v. Inter Ocean Newspaper Co., (CCA 7), 157 Fed 186. Aff'd 215 US 182, 54 LEd 150, 30 SCR 38.

In a suit for infringement of copyright, the court may take into consideration evidence of facts arising subsequent to the filing of the bill, but before final decree. Record & Guide Co. v. Bromley, (CC-Pa), 175 Fed 156.

In a suit for infringement of copyright and literary property by a moving picture, where the district court judge compared a "cutting continuity" with the plaintiff's version of the play, it is not necessary that he see the film if the cutting continuity is a reasonably fair synopsis of the film in words. Dellar v. Samuel Goldwyn, Inc., (CCA 2), 104 F(2d) 661, 42 USPQ 164, rev'g 23 FSupp 519, 37 USPQ 760.

As fair use is determined by considering all evidence, so, likewise, is question of infringement one of fact solved by study of evidence. Mathews Conveyer Co. v. Palmer-Bee Co., (CCA 6), 135 F(2d) 73, 57 USPQ 219, aff'g 41 FSupp 401, 51 USPQ 286.

Question of infringement is one of fact on which previous decisions are not controlling precedents. Park v. Warner Bros., (DC-NY), 8 FSupp 37, 23 USPQ 202.

Uncopyrighted variations cannot be utilized in suit in which jurisdiction is predicated on copyright laws. Davies v. Columbia Pictures Corp., (DC-NY), 20 FSupp 809, 35 USPQ 187.

In suit for damages for conspiracy, failure of defendants to offer proofs on defense is not to be taken as admission of proof of plaintiff's case. Arnstein v. American Soc. of Composers, Authors & Publishers, (DC-NY), 29 FSupp 388, 42 USPQ 581.

True facts as to asserted compliance with requirements as to copyright notice are integral part of plaintiffs' affirmative case. Winkler v. New York Evening Journal, Inc., (DC-NY), 32 FSupp 810, 45 USPQ 562.

In copyright infringement suit court takes judicial notice that, at time plaintiff's play and defendant's motion picture were written, main theme thereof was uppermost in public mind. Gropper v. Warner Bros. Pictures, Inc., (DC-NY), 38 FSupp 329, 49 USPQ 17.

In second circuit, first question for determination in case of alleged literary larceny is whether there is direct evidence of access to plaintiff's book; possible access does not require speculation that there was actual access. Sarkadi v. Wiman, (DC-NY), 43 FSupp 778, 52 USPQ 323. Aff'd 135 F(2d) 1002, 57 USPQ 361.

Failure to produce receipt or document of title to map is not conclusive of ownership but is of some consequence. Sawyer v. Crowell Pub. Co., (DC-NY), 46 FSupp 471, 54 USPQ 225. Aff'd 142 F(2d) 497, 61 USPQ 389.

It is significant as showing dissimilarity that, when plaintiff first wrote to defendant, after having seen defendant's motion picture, she made no claim of plagiarism. Buckler v. Paramount Pictures, Inc., (DC-NY), 133 FSupp 223, 106 USPQ 256.

Settlement of copyright infringement action cannot be proof of defendant's acquiescence in merits of plaintiff's claims. Continental Casualty Co. v. Beardsley, (DC-NY), 151 FSupp 28, 113 USPQ 181. Mf'd 253 F(2d) 702, 117 USPQ 1.

Fact that plaintiff, although he had known of accused map for many years, never challenged right of owner thereof to use it lends support to thought that plaintiff considered that map was independent production entitled to copyright and not a map plagiarized from his map. Hayden v. Chalfant Press, Inc., (DC-Cal), 177 FSupp

303, 123 USPQ 475. Aff'd 281 F(2d) 543, 126 USPQ 483.

In order to make finding from inference, inference must be based on probability and not possibility, and must be reasonably drawn from and supported by facts on which it purports to rest and may not be result of mere surface surmise and conjecture; there must be facts proved from which inference can be drawn; inference of fact may not be drawn from premise which is wholly uncertain. Pallma v. Fox, (DC-NY), 74 USPQ 130.

In determining plagiarism where there is no direct evidence, trier of fact must rely upon circumstantial evidence and reasonable inferences drawn therefrom. Golding v. R. K. O. Pictures, Inc., (Cal(2d series)), 208 Pac(2d) 1, 82 USPQ 136, aff'g (CalApp(2d series)), 193 Pac(2d) 153, 77 USPQ 415. Aff'd 35 Cal(2d series) 690, 221 Pac(2d) 95, 86 USPQ 537.

Proof necessary to recover for use of literary composition upon theory of contract implied in law is same as that required by tort action for plagiarism; there can be no recovery where defendant has not used protectible portion of composition, since implied contract cannot arise, as defendants have used no property belonging to plaintiff. Weitzenkorn v. Lesser, 40 Cal(2d series) 778, 256 Pac(2d) 947, 97 USPQ 545.

Fact that plaintiff submitted and offered to sell to defendant a synopsis containing public domain material and that, thereafter, defendant used same material does not support inference that defendant promised to pay for synopsis or for idea of using material; however, fact that plaintiff used public domain material does not justify defendant in appropriating plaintiff's synopsis. Desny v. Wilder, 46 Cal(2d series) 715, 299 Pac(2d) 257, 110 USPQ 433, mod'g (CalApp (2d series)), 286 Pac(2d) 55, 107 USPQ 17.

77. ——Discovery—Depositions and interrogatories.

Provision of interlocutory decree for examination of defendants and for the production by them of their account books and papers is proper in suit in equity for infringement. Callaghan v. Myers, 128 US 617, 32 LEd 547, 9 SCR 177, mod'g (CC-Ill), 24 Fed 636.

In an action for the infringement of a copyright a court can issue a subpena duces tecum for the purpose of bringing in the books of the defendant. American Lithographic Co. v. Werckmeister, 221 US 603, 55 LEd 873, 31 SCR 676, aff'g (CCA 2), 165 Fed 426.

A defendant was not subject to compulsion to make discoveries in answer to a bill to restrain infringement which sought to enforce forfeitures and penalties under § 7 of Copyright Act of 1831. Atwill v. Ferrett, (CC-NY), Fed Cas 640, 2 Blatchf 39.

In an action for infringement of copyright seeking penalties and forfeiture, defendant cannot be compelled to produce articles which may be used as evidence against himself. Johnson v. Donaldson, (CC-NY), 3 Fed 22.

A defendant may demur to the parts of a bill for infringement which seek a discovery, and which may subject him to anything in the nature of a penalty or forfeiture. Chapman v. Ferry, (CC-Ore), 12 Fed 693.

Waiver of an answer under oath will not permit the filing of an answer which is a mere general denial not responding to interrogatories in a bill for infringement of a copyright which requested the usual discovery. John Church Co. v. Zimmermann, (CC-Wis), 131 Fed 652.

Disclosures sought by interrogatories must be of ultimate facts material to support interrogator's cause and not of mere evidence. Buck v. Virgo, (DC-NY), 22 FSupp 156, 37 USPQ 325.

Interrogatories in copyright infringement suit calling for disclosure of all facts relative to operation of defendant's place of entertainment concerning use of copyrighted musical compositions were refused as being attempt to pry into defendant's affairs. Buck v. Virgo, (DC-NY), 22 FSupp 156, 37 USPQ 325.

Mere fact that facts sought by interrogatory are material to the defense will not defeat discovery if they are also material to claim of plaintiff. Buck v. Virgo, (DC-NY), 22 FSupp 156, 37 USPQ 325.

Where answer in copyright infringement suit denied that compositions were original, interrogatories asking defendant to state names of composers, authors, and publishers and titles of original composition from which copyrighted compositions are copied were refused. Buck v. Virgo, (DC-NY), 22 FSupp 156, 37 USPQ 325.

Interrogatories in copyright infringement suit calling for defendant's witnesses and defendant's evidence are objectionable. Michelson v. Crowell Pub. Co., (DC-Mass), 25 FSupp 653, 39 USPQ 336.

Prior to amendment of copyright rules in 1939, interrogatories were controlled by Equity Rule 58, rather than by Rules of Civil Procedure [Rules, c. 15]. Michelson v. Crowell Pub. Co., (DC-Mass), 25 FSupp 653, 39 USPQ 336.

In copyright suit, interrogatories pertaining solely to question of damages may be issued only when liability of defendants shall have been established. Michelson v. Crowell Pub. Co., (DC-Mass), 25 FSupp 968, 39 USPQ 520.

In suit for copyright infringement interrogatory was refused insofar as inquiring into contents of communication addressed to plaintiff's agent. O'Rourke v. RKO Radio Pictures, Inc., (DC-Mass), 27 FSupp 996, 41 USPQ 725.

In suit for copyright infringement interrogatory whether S. received or read plaintiff's story for defendant was allowed, since plaintiff was entitled to show by interrogatory that defendant's agent read the story. O'Rourke v. RKO Radio Pictures, Inc., (DC-Mass), 27 FSupp 996, 41 USPQ 725.

It was ruled by agreement that defendant might submit interrogatories as to license but they were never issued by defendant; this is to be construed against him especially when connected later with proof by plaintiff as to licenses. Famous Music Corp. v. Melz, (DC-La), 28 FSupp 767, 42 USPQ 573.

Defendant is not required, on examination before trial, to answer question as to names and locations of theaters in which allegedly infringing motion picture has been shown and number of screenings given picture in each theater, although after refusal to furnish information, plaintiff attempted to make separate infringements elements of cause of action, since question goes to amount of damages: if accounting is ordered, plaintiff may renew motion. Jerome v. Twentieth Century-Fox Film Corp., (DC-NY), 58 FSupp 13, 63 USPQ 206.

In taking depositions in copyright infringement suits, plaintiffs' attorneys presumptuously and arbitrarily directed witnesses to refuse to answer questions; although they would have warranted disciplinary action against attorneys or summary ruling touching further prosecution of cases by plaintiffs, defendants did not seasonably seek such remedies; court will not, after trial, allow incidents to intercept ruling on merits. Remick Music Corp. v. Interstate Hotel Co., (DC-Neb), 58 FSupp 523, 63 USPQ 327. Aff'd 157 F(2d) 744, 71 USPQ 138.

In copyright infringement suit wherein plaintiff has burden of proving execution of assignment of copyright registration, plaintiff should be allowed to prove case in its own way and obtain this evidence by way of interrogatories; all objections which defendants make, on motion for order that evidence shall not be taken on interrogatories, with respect to competency and materiality of interrogatories will be before court at trial and if objections are then sustained, there will be no injury or prejudice to defendants; court will permit oral examination of witness in lieu of written interrogatories on condition that party objecting to written interrogatories will pay opponent's attorney his reasonable expenses to attend at oral examination. Houghton Mifflin Co. v. Stackpole Sons, Inc., (DC-NY), 1 FedRDec 506, 47 USPQ 228.

Assignor's status is material inquiry on examination before trial and any facts bearing on subject are relevant to subject matter involved in action. Detective Comics, Inc. v. Fawcett Publications, Inc., (DC-NY), 4 FedR Dec 237, 64 USPQ 116.

Counsel should not conduct themselves on examination before trial differently than in trial. Detective Comics, Inc. v. Fawcett Publications, Inc., (DC-NY), 4 FedRDec 237, 64 USPQ 116.

Rule 32(c) of the Federal Rules of Civil Procedure [Rules, c. 15] provides that objections to competency of witness or to competency, relevancy, or materiality of testimony are not waived by failure to make them before or during taking of deposition unless ground of objection might have been obviated or removed if presented at that time. Detective Comics, Inc. v. Fawcett Publications, Inc., (DC-NY), 4 FedRDec 237, 64 USPQ 116.

On examination, before trial, witness, officer of plaintiff's assignor, is not required to produce mat or plate supplied to specific newspaper for printing copyrighted comic. Detective Comics, Inc. v. Fawcett Publications, Inc., (DC-NY), 4 FedRDec 237, 64 USPQ 116.

On examination before trial, witness, officer of plaintiff's assignor, is required to produce specific agreement relating to publication, but may block out confidential parts thereof. Detective Comics, Inc. v. Fawcett Publications, Inc., (DC-NY), 4 FedRDec 237, 64 USPQ 116.

Where defendant in copyright infringement suit propounds written interrogatories to witnesses in foreign country, under Rule 31(a) of Federal Rules of Civil Procedure [Rules, c. 15], plaintiff may within ten days after receipt of direct interrogatories serve cross-interrogatories on defendant; although courts have varied from regular practice, court refuses leave to plaintiff to serve cross-interrogatories after receipt of answers to direct interrogatories, since this may lead to upset of accepted practice in copyright cases as well as in other matters; defendant's interrogatories are usual ones in copyright case; answers to direct and cross-interrogatories are to be filed simultaneously with court; in view of alleged difficulty of which plaintiff complains, court will allow him to propound additional cross-interrogatories within five days after filing of such answers; court refuses to permit oral examination of witnesses at defendant's expense. Baron v. Leo Feist, Inc., (DC-NY), 7 FedRDec 71, 72 USPQ 107.

In copyright infringement action, plaintiff has right, before trial establishing liability, to inquire by interrogatories as to information relevant solely to issue of damages. Greenbie v. Noble, (DC-NY), 18 FedRDec 414, 107 USPQ 356.

Ordinarily, plaintiff is not permitted to obtain discovery on question of damages in copyright infringement suit until after question of his right to damages and accounting is determined; thus, discovery is refused in nonjury case where extensive inquiry is contemplated, parties are competitors, discovery might unnecessarily disclose defendant's business affairs to plaintiff, and no prejudice will result to plaintiff. Orgel v. Clark Boardman Co., Ltd., (DC-NY), 20 FedRDec 31, 111 USPQ 435.

In copyright infringement suit, defendant is not required to serve on plaintiff specific documents referred to in defendant's deposition interrogatories to specific witnesses, since defendant has offered to make documents available to plaintiff at office of defendant's counsel at any time within reasonable business hours and will provide accommodations where he may make such excerpts as he may desire. Upham v. Warner Bros. Pictures, Inc., (DC-NY), 49 USPQ 504.

In copyright infringement suit, interrogatory for deposition inquiring whether story related by means of specific motion picture is similar to another story is improper. Upham v. Warner Bros. Pictures, Inc., (DC-NY), 49 USPQ 504.

In copyright infringement suit, interrogatory for deposition inquiring whether witness had seen screening or exhibition of specific motion picture is proper but witness may not be asked if motion picture was in its entirety based on specific scenario or script. Upham v. Warner Bros. Pictures, Inc., (DC-NY), 49 USPQ 504.

In copyright infringement suit, interrogatory for deposition inquiring whether witness made resume of specific story is proper as is date of resume but resume may be produced only to extent of permitting it to be marked for identification and not in evidence. Upham v. Warner Bros. Pictures, Inc., (DC-NY), 49 USPQ 504.

In copyright infringement suit, interrogatory for deposition inquiring whether witness remembers theme or plot of specific story is proper but witness may not be asked to give brief description or resume of theme or plot. Upham v. Warner Bros. Pictures, Inc., (DC-NY), 49 USPQ 504.

Subpena duces tecum is issued against witness, plaintiff's licensee, to furnish names, addresses, and dates of newspapers in which were published plaintiff's cartoon strip and continuity with respect to which plaintiff may charge defendant infringed or was chargeable with unfair competition, as alleged in complaint; plaintiff should state what particular continuities it claims defendant infringed or as to which it unfairly competed. Detective Comics, Inc. v. Fawcett Publications, Inc., (DC-NY), 61 USPQ 435.

Subpenas duces tecum to examine plaintiff's officers and employees are quashed in copyright infringement suit as far as they seek to elicit evidence to aid court in determining legislative intent and whether compulsory license provision of Copyright Act was intended to apply to plaintiff's electrical transcription: they are not quashed so far as examination seeks to establish characteristics of plaintiff's device. Longines-Wittnauer Watch Co., Inc. v. T. B. Harms Co., (DC-NY), 76 USPQ 97.

78. ——Presumptions and burden of proof.

Question of burden of proof as to apportionment of profits did not arise since defendants voluntarily assumed and sustained burden. Sheldon v. Metro-Goldwyn Pictures Corp., 309 US 390, 84 LEd 825, 60 SCR 681, 44 USPQ 607, aff'g (CCA 2), 106 F(2d) 45, 42 USPQ 540, which rev'd 26 FSupp 134, 40 USPQ 238.

In a suit for infringement the burden is upon the complainant to prove by competent evidence his title to the copyright, as well as to prove infringement. Chase v. Sanborn, (CC-NH), FedCas 2,628, 4 Cliff 306.

In an action for infringement a complainant's copyright is prima facie evidence that he is the author of a work, and the burden of proof is upon the defendant to show the contrary. Reed v. Carusi, (CC-Md), FedCas 11,642, Taney 72.

Record of the taking out of copyright was prima facie evidence that a printed title was deposited, as required by § 4 of Copyright Act of 1831. Roberts v. Myers, (CC-Mass), FedCas 11,906, BrunnerColCas 698.

Authors take their rights under and subject to the copyright laws, and when attacked, the burden is upon them to show literal compliance with each and every statutory requirement in the nature of conditions precedent. Osgood v. A. S. Aloe Instrument Co., (CC-Mo), 83 Fed 470.

Complainant must make proof of copyright, even in absence of denial. Huebsch v. Arthur H. Crist Co., (DC-NY), 209 Fed 885.

It is not necessary for plaintiff to prove his title to copyright when he avers such fact in the bill and defendant expressly admits it in answer. Historical Pub. Co. v. Jones Bros. Pub. Co., (CCA 3), 231 Fed 638.

Burden is on plaintiff to prove valid copyright. Public Ledger Co. v. Post Printing & Publishing Co., (CCA 8), 294 Fed 430.

Although subsec. (b) of this section requires defendant to prove every item of costs, this does not apply to items not put in issue. Davilla v. Brunswick-Balke Collender Co., (CCA 2), 94 F(2d) 567, 36 USPQ 398, mod'g 19 FSupp 819, 35 USPQ 157.

Similarity of make-up usually signifies same source. Time, Inc. v. Ultem Publications, Inc., (CCA 2), 96 F(2d) 164, 37 USPQ 559.

Plaintiff has the burden of proving infringement by fair preponderance of evidence, and it is not necessary for defendant to prove intellectual alibi. Oxford Book Co., Inc. v. College Entrance Book Co., Inc., (CCA 2), 98 F(2d) 688, 39 USPQ 7.

If there is access, the probability that similarities are result of copying, intentional or unintentional, is so high that there is only one pertinent question: are there similarities of matters which justify the infringement claimed? Shipman v. R. K. O. Radio Pictures, Inc., (CCA 2), 100 F(2d) 533, 40 USPQ 211, aff'g 20 FSupp 249, 35 USPQ 242.

Copy of mural in high school is published in text book with legend "Copyright, Courtesy New York Board of Education"; this tends to support inference that author had received consent, although after lapse of years he cannot remember to what official he applied for permission; fact board gave consent indicated board did not understand artist owned copyright. Yardley v. Houghton Mifflin Co., Inc., (CCA 2), 108 F(2d) 28, 44 USPQ 1, aff'g 25 FSupp 361, 40 USPQ 234.

Burden of showing access is on plaintiff. Sarkadi v. Wiman, (CCA 2), 135 F(2d) 1002, 57 USPQ 361, aff'g 43 FSupp 778, 52 USPQ 323.

Plaintiff established prima facie case by producing copyright certificate, and, while ultimate burden was on it to establish right to declaratory judgment of sole ownership of copyrighted publication, defendant had burden of establishing affirmative defense of coauthorship. Jerry Vogel Music Co., Inc. v. Forster Music Publisher, Inc., (CCA 2), 147 F(2d) 614, 64 USPQ 417, aff'g 62 USPQ 142.

Statement of plaintiff's counsel in offering models as exhibits, which was corroborated later by testimony, that models embody copyrighted statue is enough to establish plaintiff's prima facie case. F. W. Woolworth Co. v. Contemporary Arts, Inc., (CA 1), 193 F(2d) 162, 92 USPQ 4, aff'g 93 FSupp 739, 86 USPQ 476. Aff'd 344 US 228, 97 LEd 276, 73 SCR 222, 95 USPQ 396.

Plaintiff in copyright infringement suit has burden of proving, as to any comic strip it puts in suit, that it was validly copyrighted. National Comics Publications, Inc. v. Fawcett Publications, Inc., (CA 2), 198 F(2d) 927, 94 USPQ 289.

When defendant shows source of plaintiff's work is in public domain, plaintiff has burden of overcoming such proof of lack of originality. Hirsch v. Paramount Pictures, Inc., (DC-Cal), 17 FSupp 816, 32 USPQ 233.

Certificate of copyright is prima facie evidence of facts stated therein and when introduced showing corporation as author, burden of going forward to disprove this fact is on defendant and, upon failure to do so, validity is established. Vitaphone Corp. v. Hutchinson Amusement Co., (DC-Mass), 28 FSupp 526, 42 USPQ 431.

In any country in which musical composition may be copyrighted and proprietor of copyright is entitled to protection of that country's law, it cannot, in absence of proof, be presumed that particular composition is within public domain, and, therefore, proponent of proposition has burden of proving that specific composition is in fact in public domain in foreign country. Paine v. Electrical Research Products, Inc., (DC-NY), 30 FSupp 260, 43 USPQ 240.

One of most significant evidences of infringement is identity of errors; immediately on discovery of similar errors in both books, burden falls heavily on defendant, whose publication was later in time, to explain their presence. Sammons v. Larkin, (DC-Mass), 38 FSupp 649, 49 USPQ 350. Mf'd 126 F(2d) 341, 53 USPQ 71.

Burden of proof is on plaintiff to show that defendant copied its catalogue, but plaintiff having made out a prima facie case, burden is thrown on defendant of going forward with evidence to explain similarities; it is unnecessary to show intent to infringe but such intention may be shown to aggravate infringement. R. R. Donnelley & Sons Co. v. Haber, (DC-NY), 43 FSupp 456, 52 USPQ 445.

After showing of access, strong proof is required that defendant's material came from independent source, but when dates, records, and story drafts showing independent source appear to be authentic, to nullify their effect plaintiff must show that defendant fraudulently falsified them. O'Rourke v. RKO Radio Pictures, Inc., (DC-Mass), 44 FSupp 480, 53 USPQ 95.

To recover, plaintiff has burden of proving (1) that he is proprietor of valid copyright by proving (a) work was original, (b) he took necessary steps to comply with registration statute, (c) work had not been published before securing copyright, and (d) he has title to copyright, and (2) that defendants have infringed. Freudenthal v. Hebrew Pub. Co., (DC-NY), 44 FSupp 754, 53 USPQ 466.

Presumptions which law affords in making prima facie case are effective as readily and with like effect under Federal Rules of Civil Procedure [Rules, c. 15] as prior thereto; rules were not designed as complete code of evidence or to alter or restrict rules of evidence theretofore recognized. Remick Music Corp. v. Interstate Hotel Co., (DC-Neb), 58 FSupp 523, 63 USPQ 327. Aff'd 157 F(2d) 744, 71 USPQ 138.

Although burden of proof remains on plaintiff throughout the case, if plaintiff shows that infringing work contains substantial copyrightable matter which was appropriated from plaintiff's book, plaintiff need not prove that such matter was not derived by author from sources available in public domain. Greenbie v. Noble, (DC-NY), 151 FSupp 45, 113 USPQ 115.

Plaintiff has burden of proving that defendant's novel contains substantial quantity of copyrightable matter which was appropriated from plaintiff's book; however, by establishing prima facie case of infringement, plaintiff shifts to defendant the burden of going forward with evidence. Greenbie v. Noble, (DC-NY), 151 FSupp 45, 113 USPQ 115.

In civil action for copyright infringement, plaintiffs are not required to establish case beyond reasonable doubt, but merely by preponderance of evidence. Harms, Inc. v. Sansom House Enterprises, Inc., (DC-Pa), 162 FSupp 129, 117 USPQ 272.

Plaintiff who introduced certificates of registration of copies of allegedly copyrighted publications and copy of defendant's alleged infringing publication had the burden to prove publication of notice of copyright. Harms v. Pure Milk Assn., (DC-Ill), 37 USPQ 575.

In order for plaintiff to prevail in suit for copyright infringement he must prove ownership to the painting and nonpublication prior to copyright; and upon failure to sustain this burden of proof, case is dismissed. Vaughan v. Real Detective Publishing Co., Inc., (DC-NY), 42 USPQ 500.

Defendant's mere denial of plaintiff's allegation that work always carried proper copyright notice does not impose undue burden on plaintiff; defense need not be asserted affirmatively; on mere denial, plaintiff is required in first instance to substantiate allegation; on affirmative defense, defendant's prima facie case is complete in introduction into evidence of copies carrying improper notices; burden then shifts to plaintiff to explain how improper notices came about; from practical standpoint, plaintiff's burden is same irrespective of manner in which defense is pleaded. Forster Music Publisher, Inc. v. Fred Fisher Music Co., Inc., (DC-NY), 63 USPQ 112.

Inasmuch as there is question as to whether two defendants handled allegedly infringing figurines for sale and since third defendant disputes accuracy of number of figurines it is alleged to have marketed, defendants are required to produce, at taking of depositions, all records relating to purchase, sale, and handling of allegedly infringing figurines. McCulloch v. Zapun Ceramics, Inc., (DC-NY), 97 USPQ 12.

In an action for infringement of a play, defendant had burden of proving that he came into possession of the play in a lawful manner. Palmer v. De Witt, 40 HowPrac 293, 32 NY SuperCt 530. Aff'd 47 NY 532, 7 AmRep 480.

Burden of proving access is on plaintiff, as it is on plaintiff to prove every fact necessary to constitute plagiarism charged. Cantor v. Mankie-

wicz, — Misc(2d series) —, 203 NYS(2d) 626, 125 USPQ 598.

79. ——Judicial notice.

Court can take judicial notice of matters not pleaded, for matters judicially noticed control and supersede matters alleged. Houghton Mifflin Co. v. Stackpole Sons, Inc., (CCA 2), 104 F(2d) 306, 42 USPQ 96, rev'g 41 USPQ 404.

Judicial notice will be taken of the fact that motion pictures have proved their economic possibilities. Metro-Goldwyn-Mayer Distributing Corp. v. Bijou Theatre Co., (DC-Mass), 3 FSupp 66, 17 USPQ 124.

It is matter of common knowledge, of which court takes judicial notice, that shrines have been established in many parts of world by various Roman Catholic churches and orders. Allegrini v. DeAngelis, (DC-Pa), 59 FSupp 248, 64 USPQ 165. Aff'd 149 F(2d) 815, 65 USPQ 589.

Court takes judicial notice that copyrighted song is well-known and popular. Robbins Music Corp. v. Weinstock, (DC-NY), 107 FSupp 102, 94 USPQ 107.

Judge may draw upon his own knowledge of literary matters in determining whether the pattern is of a type which, having been used in other words, can be given protection of copyright law, or whether copying was permissible or illicit. Expert testimony, even of the highest type, need not be substituted for judge's own conclusion arrived at from his own study. Bradbury v. Columbia Broadcasting System, Inc., (DC-Cal), 174 FSupp 733, 123 USPQ 10. Mf'd 287 F(2d) 478, 128 USPQ 376.

80. ——Admissibility and competency.

In a suit for the infringement of copyright, the certificate of the Librarian of Congress attesting to deposit of title of a book was incompetent evidence as to proof of the deposit of the copies of the book. Merrell v. Tice, 104 US 557, 26 LEd 854.

Certificate of Librarian of Congress was competent evidence of complainant's deposit of two copies of his work, though not under seal. Belford, Clarke & Co. v. Scribner, 144 US 488, 36 LEd 514, 12 SCR 734, aff'g (CC-Ill), 50 Fed 473.

It might be better practice to receive evidence as to plaintiff's damage even if it falls short of establishing measure of liability, for when recovery for copyright infringement may be awarded without any proof of injury, it may aid exercise of discretion to hear any evidence on the subject that has probative value; however, defendant cannot complain of its exclusion in response to its objections. F. W. Woolworth Co. v. Contemporary Arts, Inc., 344 US 228, 97 LEd 276, 73 SCR 222, 95 USPQ 396, aff'g (CA 1), 193 F(2d) 162, 92 USPQ 4, which aff'd 93 FSupp 739, 86 USPQ 476.

A statement of an officer of a corporation was incompetent evidence against the corporation touching the question of complainant's damages from infringement. Chils v. Gronlund, (CC-NY), 41 Fed 145.

In an action of infringement for a penalty of one dollar for every copy found in defendant's possession, exclusion of testimony regarding plaintiff's damage from sale of defendant's copies was proper. Springer Lithographing Co. v. Falk, (CCA 2), 59 Fed 707.

The remedies provided for the infringement of a copyright are penal rather than remedial, and therefore evidence given by the defendant in another suit is inadmissible and cannot be used against him for the enforcement of a penalty. Daly v. Brady, (CC-NY), 69 Fed 285. Aff'd 83 Fed 1007, which was aff'd 175 US 148, 44 LEd 109, 20 SCR 62.

In a suit for infringement the testimony of witnesses who have compared paragraphs from complainant's book, and others from defendant's book should not be rejected as incompetent evidence insofar as their testimony refers to specific instances of copying, and points out close comparisons. West Pub. Co. v. Lawyers' Co-operative Pub. Co., (CCA 2), 79 Fed 756, 35 LRA 400, rev'g 64 Fed 360.

Offer to give evidence as to rate of speed of legal editors in writing headnotes for cases was properly rejected. West Pub. Co. v. Lawyers' Co-operative Pub. Co., (CCA 2), 79 Fed 756, 35 LRA 400, mod'g 64 Fed 360.

Evidence which relates to the history of the copyrighted picture may be admitted. Hegeman v. Springer, (CCA 2), 110 Fed 374. Aff'd 189 US 505, 47 LEd 921, 23 SCR 849.

A decree awarding a preliminary injunction is not a final decree and is not conclusive of the infringement of the copyright and so cannot be admitted in evidence in another case. Hills & Co., Ltd. v. Hoover, (CC-Pa), 142 Fed 904.

A signed memorandum of the Librarian of Congress, that two copies of a copyrighted work were received, is competent evidence to prove the deposit of the copies with the Librarian of Congress although the memorandum was not under seal. Suderman v. Saake, (CC-Pa), 166 Fed 815.

The rules of evidence in copyright cases are the same as in other cases, and a receipt showing a settlement between the plaintiff and the infringer from whom the defendant obtained his picture is not admissible for the purpose of defeating the action, but it may be admitted as bearing upon the equities between the parties. Altman v. New Haven Union Co., (DC-Conn), 254 Fed 113.

Under broad allegations describing object of copyright explanatory evidence was admissible. Korzybski v. Underwood & Underwood, Inc., (CCA 2), 36 F(2d) 727, 3 USPQ 242.

Trade custom with reference to meaning of terms used in contract entered into by persons engaged in that trade is admissible in evidence to explain meaning of contract; but it makes no difference how industry is in habit of phrasing contracts, as custom, to be effective, must be one with relation to meaning or effect of terms used in contract. Murphy v. Warner Bros. Pictures, Inc., (CCA 9), 112 F(2d) 746, 46 USPQ 2.

Defendants' silence, when requested to admit that telephone numbers in both plaintiff's and defendants' directories were in error, is tantamount to admission and is admissible to prove that books contain identical errors; plaintiff need not prove that telephone numbers were in error. Adventures in Good Eating, Inc. v. Best Places to Eat, Inc., (CCA 7), 131 F(2d) 809, 56 USPQ 242.

Testimony of witness that he was coauthor with deceased (whose heirs assigned to plaintiff) is excluded as equally within knowledge of deceased, under § 347 of New York civil practice act; copyright registration certificate is not testimony by deceased that he was sole author and does not open door for rebuttal testimony. Jerry Vogel Music Co., Inc. v. Forster Music Publisher, Inc., (CCA 2), 147 F(2d) 614, 64 USPQ 417, aff'g 62 USPQ 142.

Testimony is admissible to interpret "printed copy" in contracts assigning interest in copyrights by author of song and supports finding that "printed copy" does not refer to "folios." Gumm v. Jerry Vogel Music Co., Inc., (CCA 2), 158 F(2d) 516, 71 USPQ 285, aff'g 53 FSupp 191, 59 USPQ 292.

Copyright owner may testify as to value of property misappropriated by defendants; owner of personal property may always testify to its value; he may testify to value of intangibles, advertising scheme, and good will of business; literary property is not distinguished from other personal property, is subject to same rules, and is likewise protected. Universal Pictures Co., Inc. v. Harold Lloyd Corp., (CCA 9), 162 F(2d) 354, 73 USPQ 317.

Testimony as to reissue and remake value of one of plaintiff's silent motion pictures is excluded as having little relevance in determining value of plaintiff's talking picture infringed by defendants. Universal Pictures Co., Inc. v. Harold Lloyd Corp., (CCA 9), 162 F(2d) 354, 73 USPQ 317.

Where adverse party is called as expert witness, he may not be impeached by party calling him. Universal Pictures Co., Inc. v. Harold Lloyd Corp., (CCA 9), 162 F(2d) 354, 73 USPQ 317.

In an accounting to determine damages, evidence of efforts to settle are ordinarily inadmissible, but where such an offer has been voluntarily placed in the record it will be considered in fixing amount of award. Sebring Pottery Co. v. Steubenville Pottery Co., (DC-Ohio), 9 FSupp 384.

Where contract that defendant had to use plaintiff's advertising scheme was clear, testimony of defendant varying its terms in respect to duration would not be considered. Doll v. Libin, (DC-Mont), 17 FSupp 546, 33 USPQ 17.

In a copyright infringement action there may be a comparison of pages to show they are substantially identical as to arrangement, style and layout even to the point of copying common errors. Burndy Engineering Co., Inc. v. Penn-Union Electric Corp., (DC-Pa), 25 FSupp 507, 39 USPQ 321.

Plaintiff may offer information in possession of defendant as to whether matter is in public domain abroad and as to whether defendant has proceeded on such assumption. Paine v. Electrical Research Products, Inc., (DC-NY), 30 FSupp 260, 43 USPQ 240.

In copyright infringement suit, court overrules plaintiff's objections to introduction in evidence of copyright certificate of third party's composition not reproduced for sale, of copyright certificate of orchestral arrangement thereof, and of copyright certificate of composition as published work, although no copy of words or music is submitted but only piano portion of chorus arrangement. Remick Music Corp. v. Interstate Hotel Co., (DC-Neb), 58 FSupp 523, 63 USPQ 327. Aff'd 157 F(2d) 744, 71 USPQ 138.

Fact that evidence of infringement comes from hired "music detectives" or "spotters" who went to defendants' places of public entertainment in order to assemble evidence as foundation for infringement suits goes only to question of their credibility. Remick Music Corp. v. Interstate Hotel Co., (DC-Neb), 58 FSupp 523, 63 USPQ 327. Aff'd 157 F(2d) 744, 71 USPQ 138.

When noninfringement is plain, court is not justified in hearing so-called expert opinion testimony of literary agents, newspaper men, and instructors in dramatics called by plaintiff. Burns v. Twentieth Century-Fox Film Corp., (DC-Mass), 75 FSupp 986, 76 USPQ 515.

Dissection of plaintiff's copyrighted work and defendant's work by use of parallel column analysis and expert testimony is proper when used in determination of issue of copying, but not when it is offered with respect to issue of unlawful appropriation or substantiality or materiality. Morse v. Fields, (DC-NY), 127 FSupp 63, 104 USPQ 54.

It is difficult for court to see materiality, on question of infringement of copyrighted design, of evidence that one customer, who found both plaintiff's and defendants' fabrics equally suitable, refused to reorder from plaintiff until its price was reduced to that charged by defendants. Millworth Converting Corp. v. Slifka, (DC-NY), 188 FSupp 629, 128 USPQ 143.

Owner of property, without being qualified as expert, may testify as to his opinion of value of property, weight and value of testimony being left to jury. Golding v. RKO Radio Pictures, Inc., (CalApp(2d series)), 193 Pac(2d) 153, 77 USPQ 415. Aff'd (Cal(2d series)), 208 Pac(2d) 1, 82 USPQ 136, which was aff'd 35 Cal(2d series) 690, 221 Pac(2d) 95, 86 USPQ 537.

Evidence of repeated public production of the play is proper for the purpose of showing that the defendant may have obtained his play through memory. Keene v. Clarke, 28 NY SuperCt 38.

In a suit by a licensor of motion-picture rights to a drama against his licensee, parol evidence of licensor's title to the drama was competent. Hart v. Fox, (Misc), 166 NYS 793.

81. ——Sufficiency of evidence.

In a suit for infringement, plaintiff's parol evidence concerning his title was sufficient prima facie evidence of title. Callaghan v. Myers, 128 US 617, 32 LEd 547, 9 SCR 177, mod'g (CC-Ill) 24 Fed 636.

Evidence was sufficient to warrant conclusion that plaintiff had a good copyright in his book. Emerson v. Davies, (CC-Mass), FedCas 4,436, 3 Story 768.

General testimony showing compliance with the copyright statutes regarding inscription of notice upon complainant's book was sufficient to establish a prima facie case. Falk v. Gast Lith. & Eng. Co., Ltd., (CC-NY), 40 Fed 168.

Production of a lithograph from complainant's photograph which bore no notice of copyright was insufficient evidence to overthrow complainant's prima facie case of compliance with copyright statutes. Falk v. Gast Lith. & Eng. Co., Ltd., (CC-NY), 40 Fed 168.

Evidence was sufficient to support finding that defendant's dictionary infringed complainant's. Chils v. Gronlund, (CC-NY), 41 Fed 145.

Evidence of piracy as shown by reproduction of common errors and exhibits was sufficient to deny defendant's motion for dismissal from an interlocutory order of injunction. Chicago Dollar Directory Co. v. Chicago Directory Co., (CCA 7), 66 Fed 977.

Evidence showing close similarity between complainant's and defendant's work was sufficient to make out a prima facie case of unfair use by defendant. West Pub. Co. v. Lawyers' Co-operative Pub. Co., (CCA 2), 79 Fed 756, 35 LRA 400, rev'g 64 Fed 360.

Evidence was insufficient to sustain an allegation that plaintiff was the author, designer, and proprietor of a copyrighted photograph. Snow v. Laird, (CCA 7), 98 Fed 813.

Evidence by complainant that he personally inclosed two copies of his book in a package addressed to the Librarian of Congress and deposited the same in the mail constituted sufficient proof of mailing of the copies, though the register of copyrights certified that he had made search and could find no copies of the book on file. Patterson v. J. S. Ogilvie Pub. Co.. (CC-NY), 119 Fed 451.

Evidence, in an action for infringement of a copyright of two paintings, was insufficient to show original authorship and nonpublication before copyright was secured by plaintiff under his assignment. Bosselman v. Richardson, (CCA 2), 174 Fed 622.

Evidence consisting of the certificate of the register of copyrights that two copies of complainant's article published June 23, 1908 "were received as copyright deposits on June 24, 1908, and delivered to librarian on that day," introduced to prove that complainant had secured a valid copyright on his work, was insufficient alone to prove mailing or delivery on day of publication, as is required by statute. Davies v. Bowes, (CCA 2), 219 Fed 178, aff'g 209 Fed 53.

Evidence is not sufficient to support a bill for an injunction, unless it shows that the defendant was doing or threatening something subject to be enjoined or that there was a present continuous wrongful infringement. McCaleb v. Fox Film Corp., (CCA 5), 299 Fed 48.

In an action for infringement, where plaintiff was unable to produce the original painting or the copies deposited in the copyright office so as to prove his identity with the copyright, the production of a print of the copyrighted picture upon which appeared the title and the notice of copyright was sufficient to establish his identity. Gerlach-Barklow Co. v. Morris & Bendien, Inc., (CCA 2), 23 F(2d) 159.

It is not enough to show that work was without statutory notice when it came into defendant's possession; it must appear that it left plaintiff copyright holder's possession in that condition. Gerlach-Barklow Co. v. Morris & Bendien, Inc., (CCA 2), 23 F(2d) 159.

Evidence showed infringement of plaintiff's book in defendant's advertising calendars only to extent of actual copying. Warren v. White & Wyckoff Mfg. Co., (DC-NY), 39 F(2d) 922.

Motion-picture company selling unmutilated films to defendant was not entitled to recover for unlicensed exhibitions where evidence to show defendant had breached its agreement with plaintiff. Pathe Exchange, Inc. v. Emile Snyder, Inc., (CCA 3), 84 F(2d) 566, 29 USPQ 559.

Where general correspondence in form and close correspondence in detail were found to exist when compared with copyrighted chart for analyzing handwriting, infringement was shown although defendant omitted specimens shown by plaintiff. Deutsch v. Arnold, (CCA 2), 98 F(2d) 686, 39 USPQ 5, mod'g 22 FSupp 101, 36 USPQ 318.

In the case of works dealing with the same period in history, the subject matter is of necessity what events have made it and the order of treatment whether that be chronological or topical is fixed by the facts; it follows that infringement is not established by showing that the same thing has been said on the same subject in different words. Oxford Book Co., Inc. v. College Entrance Book Co., Inc., (CCA 2), 98 F(2d) 688, 39 USPQ 7.

Access and palpable and significant similarities justify conclusion of infringement. Twentieth Century-Fox Film Corp. v. Stonesifer, (CCA 9), 140 F(2d) 579, 60 USPQ 392, aff'g 48 FSupp 196, 56 USPQ 94.

Where plaintiff produced testimony of originality and utility and evidence warranted inference of direct copying by defendant, and defendant presented no real challenge, being content to rest without offer of any testimony, judgment against defendant was affirmed. Colonial Book Co., Inc. v. Amsco School Publications, Inc., (CCA 2), 142 F(2d) 362, 61 USPQ 391, aff'g 48 FSupp 794, 56 USPQ 265, and 57 USPQ 36.

In action for infringement of copyrighted statue of dog, plaintiff does not fail to establish basis for claim of infringement by failing to show which of its commercial models is copy of model upon which copyright certificate issued. F. W. Woolworth Co. v. Contemporary Arts, Inc., (CA 1), 193 F(2d) 162, 92 USPQ 4, aff'g 93 FSupp 739, 86 USPQ 476. Aff'd 344 US 228, 97 LEd 276, 73 SCR 222, 95 USPQ 396.

Issues of fact in instant copyright infringement action are not to be resolved by merely briefly describing method of compilation of copyrighted maps; examination of source material is needed to see if end product met standards of copyrightability; summary judgment dismissing complaint is refused. Trowler v. Phillips, (CA 9), 260 F(2d) 924, 119 USPQ 164.

Where the musical composition alleged to be an infringement is only similar in parts which are not continuous or extended, it is not sufficient proof of infringement to show that the defendant had plaintiff's composition in his possession for several months, when the evidence of the defendant tends to show that he never read or played it. Arnstein v. Edward B. Marks Music Corp., (DC-NY), 11 FSupp 535, 27 USPQ 127. Aff'd 82 F(2d) 275, 28 USPQ 426.

Evidence proved copyrighted musical compositions were infringed where plaintiff's witnesses testified that copyrighted music was played and defendant's witnesses could not remember what music was played. Leo Feist v. Demarie, (DC-La), 16 FSupp 827, 32 USPQ 122.

Similarity is a question of fact to be determined by a comparison of the two works, and, while expert testimony is helpful, especially in matters involving musical composition, the test is resemblance noticeable to the average hearer. Hirsch v. Paramount Pictures, Inc., (DC-Cal), 17 FSupp 816, 32 USPQ 233.

Where music alleged to be infringed was in the public domain, and there was no noticeable similarity between such music and that alleged to infringe, evidence was insufficient to sustain claim of infringement. Hirsch v. Paramount Pictures, Inc., (DC-Cal), 17 FSupp 816, 32 USPQ 233.

Where defendant had constant access to plaintiff's chart since the date of copyright and was fully familiar with it and apparently copied the subject matter of plaintiff's chart, in some instances changing the words, but retaining their meanings, infringement was clear and deliberate. Deutsch v. Felton, (DC-NY), 27 FSupp 895, 41 USPQ 616.

Plaintiffs proved writing several letters to defendant, proprietor of restaurant, about license so he cannot claim he was in ignorance of need for license to have orchestra play copyrighted music; such playing was not accidental or due to ignorance but was infringement. Buck v. Lisa, (DC-NY), 28 FSupp 379, 42 USPQ 116.

Testimony of inspector for plaintiffs from dated memorandum that music was played in restaurant on date specified should be accepted as against specific denial of orchestra leader based entirely on memory of two years afterward. Buck v. Lisa, (DC-NY), 28 FSupp 379, 42 USPQ 116.

Test of infringement has not been met where, having heard both plaintiff's song and alleged infringing one, layman did not notice claimed similarity; slight resemblance in progression of few bars in both compositions is something which occurs frequently but which is not enough to make out piracy. Davilla v. Harms, Inc., (DC-NY), 36 FSupp 843, 48 USPQ 103.

Fact that plaintiff's and defendant's songs are written in same key is not significant on question of plagiarism, each having been originally in different key but changed by publishers. Allen v. Walt Disney Productions, Ltd., (DC-NY), 41 FSupp 134, 50 USPQ 365.

Fact that defendant published song with music pirated from another song does not prove that it pirated words from plaintiff's song. Newcomb v. Young, (DC-NY), 43 FSupp 744, 52 USPQ 373.

Plaintiff's possession of manuscript is evidence of his ownership and is sufficient against defendants who had no rights therein; since authors of musical composition did not take out copyright, there was no need for formal assignment from them to plaintiff who obtained copyright. Freudenthal v. Hebrew Pub. Co., (DC-NY), 44 FSupp 754, 53 USPQ 466.

Contention that defendant's orchestra played plaintiff's copyrighted music is not proved by inconclusive, vague, and discrepant testimony of plaintiff's two investigators, in view of direct denial, expert explanation, and direct straight forward presentation by defendant's witnesses. Buck v. Roman, (DC-NY), 49 FSupp 23, 56 USPQ 310.

Despite similarities between plays, court accepts defendant author's testimony that he did not read plaintiff's play although plaintiff submitted it to him and defendant, after his secretary had read play and orally reported, declined to produce it; it is significant that after such rejection there was no production or publication of plaintiff's play; two years elapsed before defendant began writing play; origin of defendant's play is plausibly explained. McConnor v. Kaufman, (DC-NY), 49 FSupp 738, 57 USPQ 80. Aff'd 139 F(2d) 116, 60 USPQ 356.

Since facts are equivocal and participants are dead, it is necessary to rely on interpretation and inference to reach conclusion as to ownership of dialogue of operetta. Brown v. Select Theatres Corp., (DC-Mass), 56 FSupp 438, 62 USPQ 240.

Words in specific lines of songs are practically identical, but language is repetition of title of songs, which plaintiff concedes was not original with herself; hence, element of similarity has no significance. Gingg v. Twentieth Century-Fox Film Corp., (DC-Cal), 56 FSupp 701, 62 USPQ 121.

In determining whether there is originality, court is not governed by opinions of author or experts. Schwarz v. Universal Pictures Co., Inc., (DC-Cal), 85 FSupp 270, 83 USPQ 153.

Since specific similarities between works treating with same subject are unavoidable, they do not support finding of infringement even if access is established. Alexander v. Irving Trust Co., (DC-NY), 132 FSupp 364, 106 USPQ 74. Aff'd 228 F(2d) 221, 108 USPQ 24.

Locale of plays, dominant theme, characters, detailed description of characters, parts they take and words they speak, scenes, and dramatic effect are so similar that they preclude possibility of coincidence and conclusively establish access and substantial copying. Select

(1553)

Theatres Corp. v. Ronzoni Macaroni Co., (DC-NY), 59 USPQ 288.

Although court may differ with master as to weight given to evidence, his findings are final where based upon evidence in record; findings are not final where they lack any support in evidence. Pallma v. Fox, (DC-NY), 74 USPQ 130.

Jury determined similarity after play was read to it and after it viewed motion picture, and on no other evidence; sufficiency of evidence to sustain finding of similarity can be determined by appellate court only by reading play and seeing picture. Golding v. R. K. O. Pictures, Inc., (Cal(2d series)), 208 Pac(2d) 1, 82 USPQ 136, aff'g (CalApp(2d series)), 193 Pac(2d) 153, 77 USPQ 415. Aff'd 35 Cal(2d series) 690, 221 Pac(2d) 95, 86 USPQ 537.

No finding of fact by jury is binding upon appellate court if it is not supported by substantial evidence; function of California supreme court, when contention of insufficiency is made, is to examine record to ascertain whether there is evidence to support jury's verdict. Golding v. R. K. O. Pictures, Inc., (Cal(2d series)), 208 Pac(2d) 1, 82 USPQ 136, aff'g (CalApp(2d series)), 193 Pac(2d) 153, 77 USPQ 415. Aff'd 35 Cal(2d series) 690, 221 Pac(2d) 95, 86 USPQ 537.

On appeal from judgment entered on jury's verdict for plaintiffs in plagiarism case, mere existence of two dramatic works in record does not, per se, constitute sufficient evidence of similarity; it is necessary for appellate court to read or view works to see if they present any substantial similarity insofar as plaintiff's property in his work is concerned; this is not to say that court substitutes itself for jury to decide what it thinks of issue of similarity, but it is merely question of determining if there is any substantial evidence of similarity to support jury's finding. Golding v. R. K. O. Pictures, Inc., (Cal(2d series)), 208 Pac(2d) 1, 82 USPQ 136, aff'g (CalApp(2d series)), 193 Pac(2d) 153, 77 USPQ 415. Aff'd 35 Cal(2d series) 690, 221 Pac(2d) 95, 86 USPQ 537.

For evidence to be sufficient to support finding of similarity, and thus of copying, two works must present substantial similarity insofar as plaintiff's property in his work is concerned. Burtis v. Universal Pictures Co., Inc., 40 Cal(2d series) 823, 256 Pac(2d) 933, 97 USPQ 567.

Evidence of title of a play was sufficient to enable plaintiff to maintain a suit to enjoin defendant from exhibiting and distributing a motion picture based on plaintiff's play. O'Neill v. General Film Co., 171 AppDiv 854, 157 NYS 1028, mod'g (Misc), 152 NYS 599.

82. — — —Access.

To establish infringement there must be proof of defendant's access to plaintiff's book. Lewys v. O'Neill, (DC-NY), 49 F(2d) 603, 9 USPQ 465.

Where neither of authors, who could, directly or indirectly, have contributed to defendants' motion picture, had any acquaintance with, or access to, plaintiff's play, infringement is not found. Shurr v. Warner Bros. Pictures, Inc.,

(CCA 2), 144 F(2d) 200, 62 USPQ 60, aff'g 59 USPQ 49.

Where access is proved, or assumed, likeness between copyrighted work and putative piracy may give rise to inference of plagiarism, but inference is weakened when similarities relate to expression of scientific principles which must be stated in stereotyped language. Ricker v. General Electric Co., (CCA 2), 162 F(2d) 141, 73 USPQ 458, aff'g (DC-NY), 68 USPQ 371.

Charge of copyright infringement does not fail merely because infringer was not caught in the act since access may be inferred or found circumstantially. Cholvin v. B. & F. Music Co., Inc., (CA 7), 253 F(2d) 102, 116 USPQ 491.

Evidence of access by defendant to plaintiff's copyrighted works, considered with noteworthy similarities in defendant's production, is strong and persuasive evidence of copying which requires the defendant to counter with strong convincing and persuasive evidence to the contrary; mere denial of copying is insufficient. Bradbury v. Columbia Broadcasting System, Inc., (CA 9), 287 F(2d) 478, 128 USPQ 376, mod'g 174 FSupp 733, 123 USPQ 10.

In the copyright field, access means not merely opportunity to have read or known contents of work, but means actual reading or knowledge thereof. Bradbury v. Columbia Broadcasting System, Inc., (CA 9), 287 F(2d) 478, 128 USPQ 376. Mod'g 174 FSupp 733, 123 USPQ 10.

If there is actual infringement, priority is sufficient to show access. Eschevarria v. Warner Bros. Pictures, Inc., (DC-Cal), 12 FSupp 632, 28 USPQ 213.

While access is sine qua non in copyright cause, fact that defendant had, by hypothesis, access to plaintiff's work is not fatal to defense, for additional question is always whether defendant has made unfair use of sufficient amount of plaintiff's copyrightable matter to justify holding of infringement. Shipman v. R. K. O. Radio Pictures, Inc., (DC-NY), 20 FSupp 249, 35 USPQ 242. Aff'd 100 F(2d) 533, 40 USPQ 211.

Access has been established because plaintiff's magazine was on all newsstands for about a year before defendant's magazine was published. Detective Comics, Inc. v. Bruns Publications, Inc., (DC-NY), 28 FSupp 399, 41 USPQ 182. Mf'd 111 F(2d) 432, 45 USPQ 291.

Evidence of submission of scenario to scenario company is insufficient where form received from company, and now bearing title of scenario, shows erasure where title is typewritten and all other correspondence with company is with reference to another scenario. Sheets v. Twentieth Century Fox Film Corp., (DC-DC), 33 FSupp 389, 46 USPQ 120.

Plaintiff's only proof of access is his claim of having left copies of his song in 1919 with defendants and that they were not returned, but no proof was offered that he had demanded return; complaint does not allege such access and it first appeared in answer to interrogatories; in view of slight resemblance between plaintiff's song and defendants', copyrighted in

1926, proof of access is too meager for copyright infringement suit to be predicated thereon. Davilla v. Harms, Inc., (DC-NY), 36 FSupp 843, 48 USPQ 103.

Failure to prove direct access does not foreclose recovery since access may be inferred from similarity of the two compositions; but mere similarity is not sufficient since independent reproducton of copyrighted musical work is not infringement, and nothing short of plagiarism will serve. Allen v. Walt Disney Productions, Ltd., (DC-NY), 41 FSupp 134, 50 USPQ 365.

Finding of access cannot be based on tenuous disclosure of similarity. McMahon v. Harms, Inc., (DC-NY), 42 FSupp 779, 52 USPQ 321.

Improbability of access to copyrighted unpublished composition is inferable from standing instructions of register of copyrights forbidding access to unpublished filings. Remick Music Corp. v. Interstate Hotel Co., (DC-Neb), 58 FSupp 523, 63 USPQ 327. Aff'd 157 F(2d) 744, 71 USPQ 138.

Access means that person charged with pirating another's work saw first person's work. Schwarz v. Universal Pictures Co., Inc., (DC-Cal), 85 FSupp 270, 83 USPQ 153.

It must be shown that person having access communicated information to those who created story; person's denial of communication is corroborated by his disapproval of story and by his separation from company during period when final form of story took shape. Schwarz v. Universal Pictures Co., Inc., (DC-Cal), 85 FSupp 270, 83 USPQ 153.

Identity in measurement and conformation of sculptures to minutest detail could not be result of coincidence, hence it precludes contention that defendant did original and independent work. Contemporary Arts, Inc. v. F. W. Woolworth Co., (DC-Mass), 93 FSupp 739, 86 USPQ 476. Aff'd 193 F(2d) 162, 92 USPQ 4, which was aff'd 344 US 228, 97 LEd 276, 73 SCR 222, 95 USPQ 396.

Mere possibility of access to synopsis of plaintiff's play in defendant's files or to play itself is not enough to overcome testimony of writer, producer, and director of defendant's motion picture that they did not see plaintiff's work and did not copy from it. Pinci v. Twentieth Century-Fox Film Corp., (DC-NY), 95 FSupp 884, 88 USPQ 475.

Copying may be inferred from evidence of access, although evidence of access will not prove copying if there are no similarities. Jones v. Supreme Music Corp., (DC-NY), 101 FSupp 989, 92 USPQ 347.

Copyrighted song, which had acquired folk song notoriety, was contained in four published song books enjoying wide publicity and distribution; it is probable that defendant either consciously or unconsciously had access to song; infringement is found since examination of two songs shows that defendant's was taken directly from plaintiff's despite defendant's contrary testimony. Edward B. Marks Music Corp. v. Borst Music Pub. Co., Inc., (DC-NJ), 110 FSupp 913, 97 USPQ 394.

Protection afforded literary or musical property by copyright law differs substantially from that afforded patentee under patent law; originator of patentable article is protected against infringements even as against subsequent originator who had no notice of patented article; in realm of copyrights, however, each originator has property right in his artistic achievement and plaintiff must establish that defendant was guilty of plagiarism; access to plaintiff's work must be shown. Edward B. Marks Music Corp. v. Borst Music Pub., Inc., (DC-NJ), 110 FSupp 913, 97 USPQ 394.

Fact that defendants' book on reckless driving uses certain episodes which are typical of dangers of such driving is not, in and of itself, sufficient to indicate on motion for preliminary injunction that book infringes plaintiff's copyrighted book on reckless driving. American Visuals Corp. v. Holland, (DC-NY), 126 FSupp 513, 103 USPQ 139. Aff'd 219 F(2d) 223, 104 USPQ 222.

Availability of plaintiff's work in magazine of national circulation is merely some circumstantial evidence of access; also, access is merely circumstantial evidence of copying; against this double circumstantial evidence, defendant's denial that he ever saw plaintiff's work must be weighed; with evidence so posited, plaintiff is entitled to little benefit from "inverse ratio" rule to the effect that, when access is established, a lesser degree of similarity is required. Morse v. Fields, (DC-NY), 127 FSupp 63, 104 USPQ 54.

Court will not engage in speculation or conjecture to find that defendant had access to plaintiff's work; plaintiff has burden of proving access. Alexander v. Irving Trust Co., (DC-NY), 132 FSupp 364, 106 USPQ 74. Aff'd 228 F(2d) 221, 108 USPQ 24.

Generally, defendant's access to plaintiff's book, and strong similarity or identity between works, creates inference of copying; defendant may rebut inference by proof that material came from independent sources; inference does not exist where similarity arises because of nature of subject matter and fact that both authors used materials available to all. Greenbie v. Noble, (DC-NY), 151 FSupp 45, 113 USPQ 115.

Mere fact of access is not fatal to defense in copyright case. Greenbie v. Noble, (DC-NY), 151 FSupp 45, 113 USPQ 115.

Access together with similarity between defendant's and plaintiff's copyrighted works warrants inference that defendant copied copyrighted work. Advisers Inc. v. Wiesen-Hart, Inc., (DC-Ohio), 161 FSupp 831, 117 USPQ 330.

Since plaintiff failed to establish access to her copyrighted play by defendants, she must, to succeed in copyright infringement action, show such striking and extensive similarities between the two plays that the conclusion is compelled that defendants' play could not have been written except by copying and plagiarism of her work. Morris v. Wilson, (DC-NY), 189 FSupp 565, 128 USPQ 419.

Access alone without copying is insufficient to find copyright infringement. Burnett v. Lambino, (DC-NY), — FSupp —, 133 USPQ 325.

Defense of nonaccess is sustained although corporate defendant had access to plaintiff's composition for day or two before completion of script of defendant's motion picture, since none of its employees, connected immediately or remotely with conception of picture, its production, direction, or making changes in it, had access thereto and no similarity sustains suspicion of plagiarism. Stein v. RKO Radio Pictures, Inc., (DC-NY), 57 USPQ 102.

Plaintiffs submitted play to defendant motion-picture company and synopsis has been in defendant's archives since 1936 together with synopsis of each of thousands of other manuscripts submitted; that motion-picture producer made contract with defendant to use defendant's studio does not show access by producer in 1940. Shurr v. Warner Bros. Pictures, Inc., (DC-NY), 59 USPQ 49. Aff'd 144 F(2d) 200, 62 USPQ 60.

Fact that plaintiffs sent copy of manuscript of play, which was not returned, to motion-picture company while defendants were employed by company does not prove that defendants had access to manuscript which they deny seeing; there is no proof that they ever saw it. Shurr v. Warner Bros. Pictures, Inc., (DC-NY), 59 USPQ 49. Aff'd 144 F(2d) 200, 62 USPQ 60.

Proof that plaintiff submitted play to defendant's New York office in 1931 would not warrant inference that authors of defendant's screen play had synopsis of plaintiff's play or copy of play before them when they wrote screen play in 1945. Meyer v. Universal Pictures Co., Inc., (DC-NY), 89 USPQ 496.

Inference of copying may arise when there is proof of access coupled with showing of similarity; where there is strong evidence of access, less proof of similarity may suffice; if evidence of access is uncertain, strong proof of similarity should be shown before inference of copying may be indulged. Golding v. R. K. O. Pictures, Inc., (Cal(2d series)), 208 Pac(2d) 1, 82 USPQ 136, aff'g (CalApp(2d series)), 193 Pac(2d) 153, 77 USPQ 415. Aff'd 35 Cal(2d series) 690, 221 Pac(2d) 95, 86 USPQ 537.

Proof of access establishes no more than opportunity to copy, not actual copying. Golding v. R. K. O. Pictures, Inc., (Cal(2d series)), 208 Pac(2d) 1, 82 USPQ 136, aff'g (CalApp(2d series)), 193 Pac(2d) 153, 77 USPQ 415. Aff'd 35 Cal(2d series) 690, 221 Pac(2d) 95, 86 USPQ 537.

Access and inclination to copy being admitted by demurrer, issues of similarity and copying are to be determined by trier of fact if it may be said that some substantial similarity between radio programs reasonably could be found; having both programs before it upon demurrer in accordance with section 426(3) of California code of civil procedure, court may determine whether there is substantial similarity between them; if, as matter of law, there is no such similarity, then there is no question of fact and demurrer must be sustained. Kurlan v. Columbia Broadcasting System, Inc., 40 Cal(2d series) 799, 256 Pac(2d) 962, 97 USPQ 556, aff'g (CalApp(2d series)), 233 Pac (2d) 936, 90 USPQ 267.

It is not important whether persons who prepared defendant's infringing radio program had access to plaintiff's material, since other responsible employees in charge of program production admitted access. Stanley v. Columbia Broadcasting System, Inc., (CalApp(2d series)), 192 Pac(2d) 495, 77 USPQ 404. Aff'd (Cal(2d series)), 208 Pac(2d) 9, 82 USPQ 123, which was aff'd 35 Cal(2d series) 653, 221 Pac (2d) 73, 86 USPQ 520.

Proof of opportunity of access together with proof of substantial similarities is sufficient to support implied finding of access and copying. Kovacs v. Mutual Broadcasting System, Inc., 99 CalApp(2d series) 56, 221 Pac(2d) 108, 86 USPQ 547.

Proof of substantial similarity between plaintiff's and defendant's literary properties gives rise to inference of defendant's access to plaintiff's material and copying by defendant. Glane v. General Mills, Inc., (CalApp(2d series)), 298 Pac(2d) 626, 110 USPQ 391.

In common-law copyright, to constitute tortious appropriation of musical property, proof should establish priority of plaintiff's composition and that defendant with animus furandi obtained access to and copied it; access is indispensable ingredient in proof of piracy. Smith v. Berlin, 207 Misc 862, 141 NYS(2d) 110, 105 USPQ 296.

Access may be proven by direct proof, circumstantial evidence, or upon such frequent and striking resemblances between the two works as to compel inference of access; mere suspicion is not proof of access; question is not whether it is possible that defendant had access, but whether court is convinced from all the proof that he did; it is important that defendant testified that he did not know of plaintiff or of subject of plaintiff's biography. Cantor v. Mankiewicz, — Misc(2d series) —, 203 NYS(2d) 626, 125 USPQ 598.

83.   — — —Copying.

Identity existing between an original and a subsequent work, in absence of positive evidence to the contrary, warrants a conclusion that the original work has been copied. Brightley v. Littleton, (CC-Pa), 37 Fed 103; Woodman v. Lydiard-Peterson Co., (CC-Minn), 192 Fed 67. Aff'd 204 Fed 921.

Evidence of copying either the language or dramatic situations of a play was insufficient to form basis for a preliminary injunction. Hubges v. Belasco, (CC-NY), 130 Fed 388.

In a suit for infringement, a showing of the reproduction of a considerable number of errors common to complainant's publication in defendant's works constitutes evidence of copying. Hartford Printing Co. v. Hartford Directory & Publishing Co., (CC-Conn), 146 Fed 332; Frank Shepard Co. v. Zachary P. Taylor Pub. Co., (CCA 2), 193 Fed 991, aff'g 185 Fed 941; Colonial Book Co., Inc. v. Amsco School Publications, Inc., (DC-NY), 41 FSupp 156, 51 USPQ 33. Aff'd 142 F(2d) 362, 61 USPQ 391; R. R. Donnelley & Sons Co. v. Haber, (DC-NY), 43 FSupp 456, 52 USPQ 445.

Where, in a suit for infringement of the copyright upon a legal case book, it appears that the author of the later case book has not cited other cases which have been decided on the same points as those contained in the cases cited in the prior case book, or noted the cases which have been overruled or reversed, such a showing constitutes evidence of copying. White v. Bender, (CC-NY), 185 Fed 921.

In a suit for infringement of cuts contained in a copyrighted catalogue, complainant's evidence was sufficient to show copying by defendant. Da Prato Statuary Co. v. Giuliani Statuary Co., (CC-Minn), 189 Fed 90.

The proof of errors and blunders common to plaintiff's work and their reproduction in defendant's production creates a prima facie case of infringement. Jeweler's Circular Pub. Co. v. Keystone Pub. Co., (CCA 2), 281 Fed 83, 26 ALR 571, aff'g 274 Fed 932.

Listing of same nonexistent hotels in a defendant's hotel director, as appeared in plaintiff's directory was evidence of copying. American Travel & Hotel Directory Co., Inc. v. Gehring Publishing Co., Inc., (DC-NY), 4 F(2d) 415.

Similarity in analysis of statute annotations and identity of numbering of chapters in the body of the statute was not convincing evidence of infringement. W. H. Anderson Co. v. Baldwin Law Pub. Co., (CCA 6), 27 F(2d) 82.

Common errors and similarities in selection of roads, peculiarities of road meandering and classification, selection of towns and location of symbols therefor, population errors, and river and shore boundaries, together with other evidence pointed to copying from plaintiff's map. General Drafting Co., Inc. v. Andrews, (CCA 2), 37 F(2d) 54, 4 USPQ 72.

To constitute infringement of copyrighted form of insurance contract, showing of appropriation in exact or substantially exact form of copyrighted material is required since, where same contractual provision is to be made, there will necessarily be similarity of language. Dorsey v. Old Surety Life Ins. Co., (CCA 10), 98 F(2d) 872, 119 ALR 1250, 39 USPQ 92, aff'g 34 USPQ 226.

Use of well-known proper name in both works may signify little under many circumstances, but in others it may assist to a conclusive demonstration of copying otherwise indicated. De Acosta v. Brown, (CCA 2), 146 F(2d) 408, 63 USPQ 311, aff'g 50 FSupp 615, 58 USPQ 596.

Same short musical sequences recur spontaneously; reappearance in later composition is feeble proof of plagiarism and it is as unfair to impute imitation to second comer as it would be to impute it to author. Brodsky v. Universal Pictures Co., Inc., (CCA 2), 149 F(2d) 600, 65 USPQ 385.

Copying of substantial error should be decisive in determining infringement. Ricker v. General Electric Co., (CCA 2), 162 F(2d) 141, 73 USPQ 458, aff'g (DC-NY), 68 USPQ 371.

In action for infringement of copyrighted statute wherein defense is that defendant's statue was copied from model antedating plaintiff's statue, it is too late on surrebuttal for defendant to offer testimony as to age of model, since age of model was in issue from the beginning and plaintiff's rebuttal testimony did not attack alleged age. F. W. Woolworth Co. v. Contemporary Arts, Inc., (CA 1), 193 F(2d) 162, 92 USPQ 4, aff'g 93 FSupp 739, 86 USPQ 476. Aff'd 344 US 228, 97 LEd 276, 73 SCR 222, 95 USPQ 396.

In copyright infringement suit, plaintiff must prove copying by defendant; plaintiff may create inference of copying by establishing access to copyrighted work by defendant and similarity or identity between works; defendant may rebut inference by affirmative proof of his prior composition; the stronger the prima facie case established by plaintiff, the correspondingly more persuasive must be rebuttal evidence; however, it is incorrect rule of law to hold that defendant never can rebut inference by mere preponderance of evidence, but must establish defense by clear and convincing evidence or beyond reasonable doubt. Overman v. Loesser, (CA 9), 205 F(2d) 521, 98 USPQ 177.

Although defendant did not have plaintiff's song before him when he composed his song, he was acquainted with words and music of plaintiff's song; infringement exists, since one may copy from memory. Wihtol v. Wells, (CA 7), 231 F(2d) 550, 109 USPQ 200.

Affidavit of defendant's president states that he instructed advertising agent to employ original material in preparing defendant's catalogue; agent's affidavit states that he followed president's instructions; however, careful omission from affidavits of any denial that copying took place suggests that there was copying of plaintiff's copyrighted catalogue. Joshua Meier Co., Inc. v. Albany Novelty Manufacturing Co., (CA 2), 236 F(2d) 144, 111 USPQ 197.

Defendant's use of same stock number, "LE-2," as that used in plaintiff's copyrighted catalogue is hard to explain on any hypothesis other than copying, especially since neither party designates any of its products "LE-1"; defendant's choice of "2" can only be result of imitation. Joshua Meier Co., Inc. v. Albany Novelty Manufacturing Co., (CA 2), 236 F(2d) 144, 111 USPQ 197.

In some instances, language in defendant's catalogue is same as that in plaintiff's copyrighted catalogue except for inversion of certain words or substitution of one word for another; this crude effort to give appearance of dissimilarity is evidence of copying, even though parties are describing similar items in simple nontechnical words and although substantial similarity in language would not necessarily indicate copying. Joshua Meier Co., Inc. v. Albany Novelty Manufacturing Co., (CA 2), 236 F(2d) 144, 111 USPQ 197.

Copying need not be of every detail so long as copy is substantially similar to copyrighted work; test of infringement is whether one charged with infringement made independent production or substantial and unfair use of copyrighted work. Comptone Co., Ltd. v. Rayex Corp., (CA 2), 251 F(2d) 487, 116 USPQ 105, mod'g 158 FSupp 241, 116 USPQ 120.

Since issues of copying and improper appropriation of copyright song are issues of fact, and since findings thereon are not clearly erroneous, findings cannot be disturbed by court of appeals. Cholvin v. B. & F. Music Co., Inc., (CA 7), 253 F(2d) 102, 116 USPQ 491.

Proof of common peculiarities may warrant inference of copying copyrighted work. Schultz v. Holmes, (CA 9), 264 F(2d) 942, 121 USPQ 117.

Similarities of rhythm plainly attributable to words and phrases of common "lyric" (Lincoln's Gettysburg Address) constitute no indication of improper copying or wrongful appropriation of music; just as text of address is in public domain, so in natural rhythm of words in which its thoughts are articulated. O'Brien v. Thall, (CA 2), 283 F(2d) 741, 127 USPQ 296, aff'g — FSupp —, 127 USPQ 325.

Asserted inverse ratio rule, under which the stronger the evidence is as to access, the less proof of similarity is required, is not found in federal law of copyright. Access shown either directly or indirectly is element of plaintiff's case, and it is not an unnatural step in inference of fact for ease of access to suggest a deduction of copying when similarity is found, but access will not supply its lack, and undue stress upon that one feature can only confuse and even conceal this basic requirement; however, inference of copying may arise when there is proof of access coupled with a showing of similarity. Arc Music Corp. v. Lee, (CA 2), 296 F(2d) 186, 131 USPQ 338.

Placing of roads and other physical entities within township and section lines in the same manner as they appear on plaintiff's copyrighted map, where no other source of material or information is clearly shown, justifies inference that plaintiff's map was used and copied in making defendant's map. Blackburn v. Southern California Gas Co., (DC-Cal), 14 FSupp 553, 29 USPQ 437.

Evidence showed that defendant constructed cemetery monument, with several changes, from copyrighted design of plaintiff and was guilty of infringement. Jones Bros. Co. v. Underkoffler, (DC-Pa), 16 FSupp 729, 31 USPQ 197.

Denials of copying by defendant author, who had access, dissolve in presence of internal evidence so overwhelming as to exclude coincidence almost to mathematical certainty; coincidence cannot explain use of fictional names and incidents invented by plaintiff in her uncopyrighted and unpublished play based on life of historical character; fact that defendant author mistook plaintiff's fiction for fact is no excuse; since intentions of defendant author's assistants, who did research, must be ascribed to author, author intended to copy. Acosta v. Brown, (DC-NY), 50 FSupp 615, 58 USPQ 596. Aff'd 146 F(2d) 408, 63 USPQ 311.

Similarities between 1939 and 1940 maps are so striking and complete that they point unmistakably to copying; infringement is shown by internal evidence of copying in 1940 map such as arbitrarily abrupt road endings not on defendant's base maps, town not on defendant's base maps, and same distortion of portion of map. Crocker v. General Drafting Co., Inc., (DC-NY), 50 FSupp 634, 58 USPQ 60.

Similarities do not establish copying where prior popular songs have same similarities. Arnstein v. Twentieth Century Fox Film Corp., (DC-NY), 52 FSupp 114, 59 USPQ 21.

Similarity of musical compositions is not established by manipulation of plaintiff's composition; plaintiff transfers notes from accompaniment in bass to melody in treble, omits and changes notes and rhythm of some phrases, and separates parts of some phrases and places them in different parts of composition. Arnstein v. Twentieth Century Fox Film Corp., (DC-NY), 52 FSupp 114, 59 USPQ 21.

Examination of two designs for miniature religious shrines gives clear impression that they are both of same original shrine, that figures are of same character, and that medals and inscriptions are identical; figures and symbols, or their combination into shrine, are not copyrightable because in public domain, and infringement must be of other elements entering into plaintiffs' composite design; inspection of designs distinguishes them; although of same general shape, they are different in every detail, positions and forms of elements are different; there is no infringement since ordinary reasonable person would not fail to differentiate between works and would consider them dissimilar by reasonable observation. Allegrini v. DeAngelis, (DC-Pa), 59 FSupp 248, 64 USPQ 165. Aff'd 149 F(2d) 815, 65 USPQ 589.

It is essential for infringement that there be copying of substantial copyrightable material. MacDonald v. Du Maurier, (DC-NY), 75 FSupp 655, 76 USPQ 290.

Copying is not confined to literary repetition; infringement of copyright is not avoided by taking substance or idea and producing it through different medium and picturing in shape and details in sufficient imitation to make it a true copy of subject thought of by originator of copyrighted work; copy, constituting infringement, is that which comes so near to original as to give every person seeing it the idea created by original. Gordon v. Weir, (DC-Mich), 111 FSupp 117, 97 USPQ 387. Aff'd 216 F(2d) 508, 104 USPQ 40.

Although title of plaintiff's copyrightable story is not protected, it is considered by court on issue of copying. Morse v. Fields, (DC-NY), 127 FSupp 63, 104 USPQ 54.

Copying of copyrighted story may be proven by similarity between both the protected and unprotected parts of plaintiff's and defendant's works; court should reach problem of eliminating from consideration the unprotected part of plaintiff's work only if and when it finds that defendant has copied and the issue of improper appropriation, substantially or materially, is properly before it. Morse v. Fields, (DC-NY), 127 FSupp 63, 104 USPQ 54.

Availability to defendant of common sources for obtaining names for inclusion in its directory is no defense to action for copyright infringement if defendant actually copied names from plaintiff's directory; ultimate probandum is copying; existence of common sources is merely evidence negating copying. Caldwell-Clements, Inc. v. Cowan Publishing Corp., (DC-NY), 130 FSupp 326, 105 USPQ 116.

There is no infringement simply because one writes and publishes story upon same theme previously used by another, even though copyrighted; to be infringement, there must be copying, intentional or unintentional, of other's work, and this does not occur simply by writing on same subject or theme; similarity can occur from copying, but it may also occur by reason of subject matter and setting with which both stories deal. Warshawsky v. Carter, (DC-DC), 132 FSupp 758, 107 USPQ 80.

Although there is no direct proof of access or copying of copyrighted jewelry, similarities between items pass bounds of accident and are beyond explanation by coincidence; burden of proving copying is on plaintiff, but, when he makes strong prima facie case by pointing out convincing number of similarities, burden of going forward with evidence explaining similarities is on defendant; defendant made no attempt to meet burden; hence, court concludes that defendant copied plaintiff's jewelry. Hollywood Jewelry Mfg. Co., Inc. v. Dushkin, (DC-NY), 136 FSupp 738, 107 USPQ 354.

In determining whether defendants copied substantial part of plaintiff's copyrighted chart, test is not quantity but quality of what was copied. Nikanov v. Simon & Schuster, Inc., (DC-NY), 144 FSupp 375, 110 USPQ 491. Aff'd 246 F(2d) 501, 114 USPQ 89.

Finding of infringement of plaintiff's copyrighted pin requires only that pins be observably similar; since there is no doubt that defendants copied plaintiff's pin, it is not necessary that defendants' pin be "Chinese copy" of plaintiff's. Trifari, Krussman & Fishel, Inc. v. B. Steinberg-Kaslo Co., (DC-NY), 144 FSupp 577, 110 USPQ 487.

Once copying is demonstrated and there is minimal similarity between works, question of improper appropriation presents, in the first instance, an issue of fact. Malkin v. Dubinsky, (DC-NY), 146 FSupp 111, 112 USPQ 263.

In order to establish that defendant's novel infringes upon plaintiff's biography, plaintiff must show that defendant copied from biography rather than resorted to original sources available to all. Greenbie v. Noble, (DC-NY), 151 FSupp 45, 113 USPQ 115.

Presentation of parallel incidents in combination with similar phraseology, when considered in light of admitted access, is evidence of copying. Greenbie v. Noble, (DC-NY), 151 FSupp 45, 113 USPQ 115.

To constitute infringement, there need not be verbatim copying of plaintiff's work or any part thereof, but defendant must have appropriated substantial or material part of protected work, and alleged copy must come so near to original as to give to every person seeing it the idea created by original; copying may be inferred where there was access and similarities between works raise reasonable inference of copying, but similarity must be recognizable by ordinary observation, and test is not whether by some hypercritical dissection of sentences and incidents seeming similarities are shown to exist. Costello v. Loew's Inc., (DC-DC), 159 FSupp 782, 116 USPQ 372.

Copying involves use of original copyrighted work so as to produce a work so near to original as to give to every person seeing it the idea created by original. Richards v. Columbia Broadcasting System, Inc., (DC-DC), 161 FSupp 516, 17 USPQ 174.

Physical facts of copying become virtually incontestable in light of (1) one defendant's admission that it had examined dress made of plaintiffs' copyrighted fabric and, after some minor changes, ordered rollers, and (2) second defendant's admission that its designer prepared infringing pattern while having before him a dress made of plaintiffs' copyrighted fabric. Peter Pan Fabrics, Inc. v. Acadia Co., Inc., (DC-NY), 173 FSupp 292, 121 USPQ 81. Aff'd 274 F(2d) 487, 124 USPQ 154.

In determining existence of plagiarism, court must discuss both similarities and dissimilarities; although copying of single sequence may amount to plagiarism if it is important, when similitude is sought to be established between two works, points of essential difference may so far outnumber points of similarity that it is difficult to understand how anyone could persuade himself that one was borrowed from the other. Bradbury v. Columbia Broadcasting System, Inc., (DC-Cal), 174 FSupp 733, 123 USPQ 10. Mf'd 287 F(2d) 478, 128 USPQ 376.

By giving names to unnamed lakes, creeks, trails, hills, and peaks, proprietor of copyrighted map did not acquire exclusive right of having maps with such names on them; by giving the names, he granted to everyone the right of having names used; presence of names in subsequent maps, if they appeared too soon after his map, might indicate that they may have been taken from his map, but this would be merely evidence of copying, not of plagiarism; subsequent cartographers may use same names without infringing first cartographer's copyright. Hayden v. Chalfant Press, Inc., (DC-Cal), 177 FSupp 303, 123 USPQ 475. Aff'd 281 F(2d) 543, 126 USPQ 483.

If two works were result of independent intellectual effort of two authors and are derived from common sources available to all, there can be no copyright infringement even if works resemble each other, since there was no copying. Barton Candy Corp. v. Tell Chocolate Novelties Corp., (DC-NY), 178 FSupp 577, 123 USPQ 425.

Fact that remainder of lyrics, music, and themes of two songs are entirely different strengthens conclusion that similar first two lines of lyrics were created independently from common source in public domain. Whitney v. Ross Jungnickel, Inc., (DC-NY), 179 FSupp 751, 124 USPQ 219.

Plaintiff must prove that there was copying of his copyrighted work by defendant and that portions copied were sufficiently substantial and unfair to constitute unlawful appropriation; copying may be shown by proof of access and a showing that, on an analysis and dissection of defendant's composition, sufficient similarity in use of chords, chord progression, devices used for tone color, key changes, rhythm, melody, etc., to those used in plaintiff's composition in a phrase by phrase comparison as reasonably to support inference that defendant must have copied from plaintiff; if there are no similarities, evidence of access will not prove copying. O'Brien v. Thall, (DC-Conn), — FSupp —, 127 USPQ 325. Aff'd 283 F(2d) 741, 127 USPQ 296.

Infringement of plaintiff's copyrighted law book by defendant's subsequent law book is shown by (1) defendant's adoption of plaintiff's unique analysis of the subject, (2) many instances of almost verbatim identity of language, (3) use of same hypothetical illustration without supporting legal authority, (4) use of same striking words, (5) defendant's apparent adoption of statements from plaintiff's work without independent research, although such research would have disclosed pertinent legal decisions reported after publication of plaintiff's book, (6) common error as to rulings in certain decisions, and (7) fact that, when books are read together in continuity the content is so similar in arrangement, language, and substance that conclusion is inescapable that defendant took unfair advantage of his access to plaintiff's book. Orgel v. Clark Boardman Co. Ltd., (DC-NY), — FSupp —, 128 USPQ 520. Mf'd 301 F(2d) 119, 133 USPQ 94.

Butterfly designs of parties involve commonplace subject matter, so a substantial similarity would not necessarily indicate copying; however, copying is shown since dissimilarities appear obviously to be result of studied effort to make minor distinctions, and similarities in general appearance and overall design, identity, and arrangement of parts are striking; moreover, while it is not alleged, that copying of color constitutes infringement, use of same colors is indication that copyrighted design was source of accused design; viewing designs side by side, copying cannot be denied. Fabrex Corp. v. Scarves by Vera, Inc., (DC-NY), — FSupp —, 129 USPQ 392.

Copying is essence of plagiarism; direct proof of copying is often impossible to procure; hence, access to original plus similarity between original and accused works frequently do duty for proof of copying, and sometimes similarity alone does duty for both; but opportunity plus inclination are insufficient to establish plagiarism unless there be similarity between works. Millstein v. Leland Hayward, Inc., (DC-NY), 10 FedRDec 198, 85 USPQ 448.

Court considers technical details of notes in composition; since same sequence of notes appeared in prior compositions, its use by defendant does not establish that defendant copied plaintiff's song; similarity may be coincidental; defendant's song may have been derived from source other than plaintiff. Perlman v. Remick Music Corp., (DC-NY), 61 USPQ 227.

If such similarities exist as to justify inference of copying of protectible material from plaintiff's unpublished, uncopyrighted play, it is necessary to prove only that substantial part of play was copied. Golding v. R. K. O. Pictures, Inc., (Cal(2d series)), 208 Pac(2d) 1, 82 USPQ 136, aff'g (CalApp(2d series)), 193 Pac (2d) 153, 77 USPQ 415. Aff'd 35 Cal(2d series) 690, 221 Pac(2d) 95, 86 USPQ 537.

Fact that defendant could have obtained similar story from prior works is of no consequence if it copied plaintiffs' story. Golding v. R. K. O. Pictures, Inc., (Cal(2d series)), 208 Pac(2d) 1, 82 USPQ 136, aff'g (CalApp(2d series)), 193 Pac(2d) 153, 77 USPQ 415. Aff'd 35 Cal(2d series) 690, 221 Pac(2d) 95, 86 USPQ 537.

In an action to enjoin the exhibition or distribution of a motion picture, the evidence was sufficient to warrant that defendants had used plaintiff's dramatization in making such motion picture. O'Neill v. General Film Co., 171 App Div 854, 157 NYS 1028, mod'g (Misc), 152 NYS 599.

Copying may be shown by (a) direct evidence of copying, which includes direct evidence that defendants had seen or heard plaintiff's work or direct evidence of access by defendants to plaintiff's work, or (b) similarities appearing from words themselves so strong as to compel inference; mere similarities carry no right of action for infringement. Heywood v. Jericho Co., 193 Misc 905, 85 NYS(2d) 464, 79 USPQ 450.

To establish infringement, plaintiff must prove unauthorized copying of whole or substantial part of his play; trivial similarities are of no legal import; part taken must be substantial and material part of play. Heywood v. Jericho Co., 193 Misc 905, 85 NYS(2d) 464, 79 USPQ 450.

To sustain charge of copying musical composition, more than similarity and identity must be shown; inference of copying may arise when there is proof of access coupled with showing of similarity; with access and identity assumed, ultimate offense to be established is tortious copying; however, explanation of origin of material allegedly plagiarized is sufficient to defeat plaintiff even where access is proved; one cannot infer access from identity and then, based upon inference of access, infer that tortious appropriation occurred, since this is improper founding of one inference upon another inference; also, before inference of access from identity may even be considered, it is incumbent upon plaintiff to prove priority of his composition. Smith v. Berlin, 207 Misc 862, 141 NYS(2d) 110, 105 USPQ 296.

Test of plagiarism is not whether expert could so dissect the two works as to be able to demonstrate, by virtue of his peculiar knowledge, that there are similarities prohibited by law; similarity must be one apparent upon ordinary observation. Cantor v. Mankiewicz, — Misc(2d series) —, 203 NYS(2d) 626, 125 USPQ 598.

84. —Trial.

In a suit at law for infringement, it is a question for the jury to decide whether or not the defendant has copied. Blunt v. Patten, (CC-NY), FedCas 1,579, 2 Paine 393.

On a bill for an accounting and an infringement of a copyright, the usual course is to send the case to a master before determining the merits. Chase v. Sanborn, (CC-NH), Fed Cas 2,628, 4 Cliff 306.

Equity suits for the infringement of a copyright are usually referred to a master before the final hearing, to ascertain whether the charge is proved, and, if so, for a report as to the nature and extent of the infringement. Lawrence v. Dana, (CC-Mass), FedCas 8,136, 4 Cliff 1.

On motion for a preliminary injunction for infringement the court may refer the question of infringement and its extent to a master for an examination and report, which the court will hear when further proceedings in the cause are had. Story v. Derby, (CC-Ohio), FedCas 13,496, 4 McLean 160.

"Court" in subsec. (b) of this section does not necessarily mean the judge acting by himself but it permits him to direct the jury to assess damages within the prescribed limits. Mail & Express Co. v. Life Pub. Co., (CCA 2), 192 Fed 899.

Copyright infringement suit is heard ex parte when defendant is absent at calling of case for trial. Buck v. Coe, (DC-Pa), 32 FSupp 829, 45 USPQ 230.

Before deciding copyright infringement case court views defendant's motion picture in presence of counsel for both parties, hears evidence, observes witnesses on stand, reads depositions and plaintiff's copyrighted play, and hears arguments of counsel. Gropper v. Warner Bros. Pictures, Inc., (DC-NY), 38 FSupp 329, 49 USPQ 17.

Motion for new trial on ground of newly-discovered evidence and surprise in entry of judgment is denied on merits when filed six months after perpetual injunction against copyright infringement and reference to master for accounting; although same court in subsequent suit against third party on same copyright found unclean hands and that plaintiff did not originate copyrighted drawings, defendant has not sustained burden of diligence; evidence is not newly discovered since facts were pleaded in other suit of which defendant was aware seven months before trial in instant case but were not raised, other defenses being relied on at trial. Colonial Book Co., Inc. v. Amsco School Publications, Inc., (DC-NY), 48 FSupp 794, 56 USPQ 265. Aff'd 142 F(2d) 362, 61 USPQ 391.

Court withdraws suggestion in prior opinion that equitable issues be tried first; it is preferable to leave it to discretion of trial judge to try jury and nonjury issues in such succession or simultaneously as circumstances dictate, with submission to jury of law issues only. Bercovici v. Chaplin, (DC-NY), 7 FedRDec 61, 72 USPQ 340, mod'g (DC-NY), 3 FedRDec 409, 60 USPQ 409.

85. ——Jury trial.

Defendant was entitled to jury trial of alleged infringement where no right of injunction appeared in bill. Metro-Goldwyn-Mayer Distributing Corp. v. Fisher, (DC-Md), 10 FSupp 745, 25 USPQ 341.

Parties by appearing before court and submitting evidence on all questions involved waived jury trial; if plaintiff is entitled to legal relief only, court will allow damages only but, if he is entitled to injunction, court is empowered to grant that relief also. Towle v. Ross, (DC-Ore), 32 FSupp 125, 45 USPQ 143.

Where there is no equitable jurisdiction, defendant is entitled to jury trial. Universal Pictures Corp. v. Marsh, (DC-WVa), 36 FSupp 241, 48 USPQ 319.

Jury trials are favored in cases having human elements, but experience teaches that there are types of cases with which no jury should be burdened and which average jury is not equipped fairly to try; example of case which

law permits to be tried by jury, but which should not be so tried, is lengthy and complicated accounting. Bercovici v. Chaplin, (DC-NY), 56 FSupp 417, 61 USPQ 436.

Causes for infringement of statutory and common-law copyrights are triable by court without jury since they are causes of action in equity. Pallant v. Sinatra, (DC-NY), 59 FSupp 684, 64 USPQ 326.

Jury trial is refused where plaintiff demands accounting of profits. Tynan v. R. K. O. Radio Pictures, Inc., (DC-NY), 77 FSupp 238, 76 USPQ 387.

Where original complaint sought damages and accounting of profits, but amended complaint, with which was filed demand for jury trial, sought damages only, plaintiff is entitled to jury trial. Tynan v. R. K. O. Radio Pictures, Inc., (DC-NY), 77 FSupp 238, 76 USPQ 387.

In copyright infringement action seeking injunction, damages, and accounting, plaintiff is entitled to jury trial as to damages whether or not damages are sought in same count as injunction and accounting. Russell v. Laurel Music Corp., (DC-NY), 104 FSupp 815, 94 USPQ 63.

Jury trial of action for copyright infringement and unfair competition is refused since prayer for damages is incidental to equitable relief requested. Boucher v. Du Boyes, Inc., (DC-NY), 137 FSupp 639, 109 USPQ 10.

Alleged copyright infringer is entitled to jury trial on issue whether just damages are payable where complaint seeks in one count both an injunction and just damages in lieu of actual damages and profits. Chappell & Co., Inc. v. Palermo Cafe, Inc., (DC-Mass), 146 FSupp 867, 112 USPQ 378. Mf'd 249 F(2d) 77, 115 USPQ 205.

Similarity, access, and actionable copying are issues of fact for jury in copyright infringement action. Costello v. Loew's Inc., (DC-DC), 159 FSupp 782, 116 USPQ 372.

On issue of unlawful appropriation of copyrighted musical comparison where test is response of ordinary lay hearer, jury is particularly well fitted to make a finding; it is only where it is abundantly clear that there is complete dissimilarity in melody and accompaniment of the two pieces that directed verdict on issue would be warranted; verdict is directed for defendant where there was no competent evidence to support plaintiff's claims, either as to copying or unlawful appropriation. O'Brien v. Thall, (DC-Conn), — FSupp —, 127 USPQ 325. Aff'd 283 F(2d) 741, 127 USPQ 296.

Although copyright infringement suit as originally brought contained prayer for injunctive relief, plaintiff is entitled to jury trial since he has waived claim for injunction and only other issues, copyright infringement and damages, are properly determinable by a jury; formal waiver of claim for injunctive relief is to be filed by plaintiff. Frazier v. New England Newspaper Publishing Co., (DC-Mass), 1 Fed RDec 734, 49 USPQ 497.

Jury trial was refused in copyright infringement suit seeking damages, profits, and injunctive relief and alleging inadequate remedy at law, since complaint was essentially equitable in nature and demand for damages was merely incidental to main relief. Young v. Loew's, Inc., (DC-NY), 2 FedRDec 350, 53 USPQ 169.

There is right to jury trial in law action but not in equity action. Arnstein v. Twentieth Century-Fox Film Corp., (DC-NY), 3 FedRDec 58, 56 USPQ 511.

First count for damages for breach of motion-picture contract is cognizable at law and to be tried to jury; second count is claim of co-author which belongs in equity; third count is for piracy of literary property which may be prosecuted both at law and equity; there is no such inter-dependence between first count and other counts as requires that all should be tried in equity but on motion second and third counts are transferred to nonjury calendar to be tried first. Bercovici v. Chaplin, (DC-NY), 3 FedR Dec 409, 60 USPQ 409. Mf'd 7 FedRDec 61, 72 USPQ 340.

Interpleader is almost entirely equitable, although not wholly unknown at common law; specific performance is solely equitable; action striking records (copyright renewal and assignments) in copyright office is solely equitable; accounting is usually equitable; these remedies sought do not leave any matter triable by jury; remedy of declaring title to song and rights thereunder is equitable; demand for jury trial is stricken on motion. Edward B. Marks Music Corp. v. Wonnell, (DC-NY), 4 FedRDec 146, 63 USPQ 4.

Count for infringement of common-law copyright is triable to jury where complaint alleges that defendant received money by reason of infringement for which he is accountable to plaintiff, and then prays for damages. Bercovici v. Chaplin, (DC-NY), 7 FedRDec 61, 72 USPQ 340, mod'g 3 FedRDec 409, 60 USPQ 409.

Count pleads more than quantum meruit since it alleges collaboration to produce motion picture, extent of profits earned by defendant collaborator, and that compensation implied by law by reason of collaboration is 50% of net profits; plaintiff brought self into equity and is not entitled to jury trial. Bercovici v. Chaplin, (DC-NY), 7 FedRDec 61, 72 USPQ 340, mod'g 3 FedRDec 409, 60 USPQ 409.

Although copyright infringement suit, where infringed and infringing works are books or other long literary compositions, should preferably be tried before court without jury, issue of infringement in instant case (short song) is comparatively simple and should not take long to try; infringement issue is to be tried to jury. Pallant v. Sinatra, (DC-NY), 7 FedRDec 293, 65 USPQ 158.

Issue of damages for infringement has been made jury issue in number of copyright cases. Pallant v. Sinatra, (DC-NY), 7 FedRDec 293, 65 USPQ 158.

Where plaintiff asks for injunction, accounting, and damages, court cannot say that damages sought are merely incidental, and defendant is entitled to jury trial of issues of infringement and damages. Berlin v. Club 100, Inc., (DC-Mass), 12 FedRDec 129, 91 USPQ 237.

If copyright infringement complaint seeks injunction only, it is equitable and there is no right to jury trial; if it seeks damages only, action is one at common law in which defendant is entitled to jury trial; where complaint seeks injunction and damages, defendant is entitled to jury trial on claim for damages. Chappell & Co., Inc. v. Cavalier Cafe, Inc., (DC-Mass), 13 FedRDec 321, 95 USPQ 243.

"In lieu" provision of subsec. (b) of this section does not require that claim for damages be determined by judge alone, instead of by jury. Chappell & Co., Inc. v. Cavalier Cafe, Inc., (DC-Mass), 13 FedRDec 321, 95 USPQ 243.

Judge may determine issues of fact in disposing of equitable claim in copyright infringement action, so that no issues of fact are left to be tried by jury when legal claim (damages) is reached, but this does not justify striking of defendant's jury claim at outset of case, for judge can follow usual course of having legal claim tried first. Chappell & Co., Inc. v. Cavalier Cafe, Inc., (DC-Mass), 13 FedRDec 321, 95 USPQ 243.

Right to jury trial would not be lost even if plaintiffs waived all damages other than statutory minimum, and plaintiffs' waiver, if they get any verdict, does not deprive defendant of right to have jury pass on question, for example, of whether defendant ever performed copyrighted music. Chappell & Co., Inc. v. Cavalier Cafe, Inc., (DC-Mass), 13 FedRDec 321, 95 USPQ 243.

Section 426(3) of California code of civil procedure, providing for attachment to complaint of compositions of both parties in action for infringement of rights in literary production, provides method for considering alleged infringed and infringing productions upon demurrer; this in no way deprives plaintiff of right to jury trial; if, from comparison of productions, question of fact is shown to exist, cause should be submitted to jury. Kurlan v. Columbia Broadcasting System, Inc., 40 Cal(2d series) 799, 256 Pac(2d) 962, 97 USPQ 556, aff'g (CalApp(2d series)), 233 Pac(2d) 936, 90 USPQ 267.

In action for plagiarism and for breach of implied contract to pay for use of original radio program, questions of whether plaintiff had original expression of ideas reduced to concrete form and whether defendant copied ideas and their expression are questions for jury. Kurlan v. Columbia Broadcasting System, Inc., (Cal App(2d series)), 233 Pac(2d) 936, 90 USPQ 267. Aff'd 40 Cal(2d series) 799, 256 Pac(2d) 962, 97 USPQ 556.

86. —Consideration of matters by court.

A consent decree in a former case cannot bind another court on matters concerning the same facts but different defendants, since a consent decree is a mere agreement between the parties. Hodgson v. Vroom, (CCA 2), 266 Fed 267.

Courts do not examine copyrighted work for intrinsic worth or merit. Jackson v. Quickslip

Co., Inc., (CCA 2), 110 F(2d) 731, 45 USPQ 6, aff'g 27 FSupp 338, 41 USPQ 464.

Court's problem primarily is to compare magazines to see whether defendants' copies plaintiff's. Official Aviation Guide Co., Inc. v. American Aviation Associations, Inc., (CCA 7), 150 F(2d) 173, 65 USPQ 553, mod'g 62 USPQ 178.

Where not a single case directly in *point is found, court decides question of law on analogies of available cases and its idea of equities, common sense, and fair play. Deward & Rich, Inc. v. Bristol Savings & Loan Corp., (DC-WVa), 29 FSupp 777, 44 USPQ 26.

When court has opportunity of comparing two works in copyright case, it has before it all necessary data to decide infringement. Christianson v. West Pub. Co., (DC-Cal), 53 FSupp 454, 60 USPQ 279. Aff'd 149 F(2d) 202, 65 USPQ 263.

Court must determine whether fact of infringement is proved; opinion of experts, although helpful, may not be substituted for court's judgment. Allegrini v. DeAngelis, (DC-Pa), 59 FSupp 248, 64 USPQ 165. Aff'd 149 F(2d) 815, 65 USPQ 589.

Rather than attempting to resolve different interpretations by analysts trained in music, court must determine question of confusion between two recorded arrangements of same song by placing itself in position of average person who would listen to records and determining whether such person would confuse one with the other. Supreme Records, Inc. v. Decca Records, Inc., (DC-Cal), 90 FSupp 904, 85 USPQ 405.

Conflicting expert testimony as to similarity of songs is of some help, but judge relies on only other test available to musical layman, namely, whether there is resemblance noticeable to average hearer. Northern Music Corp. v. King Record Distributing Co., (DC-NY), 105 FSupp 393, 93 USPQ 512.

In determining whether plaintiff's composition is original, court must give consideration to music in public domain; perhaps, best test to determine originality is to inquire whether composition is new and different treatment of old theme or melody or is merely colorable attempt to use someone else's work as composer's own. Northern Music Corp. v. King Record Distributing Co., (DC-NY), 105 FSupp 393, 93 USPQ 512.

Since court finds no copyright infringement, it is unnecessary to probe question of copyright's validity. Dunham v. General Mills, Inc., (DC-Mass), 116 FSupp 152, 99 USPQ 372.

It is proper to compare literary attainments and reputation of plaintiffs and defendants and to ask whether defendants are type who would be likely to plagiarize. Shurr v. Warner Bros. Pictures, Inc., (DC-NY), 59 USPQ 49. Aff'd 144 F(2d) 200, 62 USPQ 60.

Motion for new trial on ground of newly-discovered evidence is to a large extent addressed to discretion of trial judge, and appellate court will not disturb his ruling unless it is manifest that gross or unmistakable abuse of discretion appears. Stanley v. Columbia Broadcasting

System, Inc., (Cal(2d series)), 208 Pac(2d) 9, 82 USPQ 123, aff'g (CalApp(2d series)), 192 Pac(2d) 495, 77 USPQ 404. Aff'd 35 Cal(2d series) 653, 221 Pac(2d) 73, 86 USPQ 520.

Question of originality of plaintiff's radio program is not one of law to be determined by court but is one of fact for jury's determination. Stanley v. Columbia Broadcasting System, Inc., (Cal(2d series)), 208 Pac(2d) 9, 82 USPQ 123, aff'g (CalApp(2d series)), 192 Pac(2d) 495, 77 USPQ 404. Aff'd 35 Cal(2d series) 653, 221 Pac(2d) 73, 86 USPQ 520.

Although California state court will dissect literary production to determine what portion thereof is protectible, it will not dissect protectible portion to discover isolated similarities as to each segment of the whole; instead, upon issue of similarity, standard of ordinary observer should be applied and comparison of protectible portions should be made without dissection and without expert or elaborate analysis. Burtis v. Universal Pictures Co., Inc., 40 Cal(2d series) 823, 256 Pac(2d) 933, 97 USPQ 567.

In action for misappropriation of literary property and infringement of common-law copyright, questions of originality, similarity, and copying are questions of law, in the first instance, and may be determined by court upon demurrer. Glane v. General Mills, Inc., (Cal App(2d series)), 298 Pac(2d) 626, 110 USPQ 391.

87. Judgment or decree.

In suit for infringement of copyright and its renewal, amended bill omitted renewal but defendant counterclaimed for declaration of invalidity of renewal and plaintiff conceded invalidity at trial; there was no error in awarding judgment on counterclaim. Yardley v. Houghton Mifflin Co., Inc., (CCA 2), 108 F(2d) 28, 44 USPQ 1, aff'g 25 FSupp 361, 40 USPQ 234.

Clause in decree which merely adjures defendants to obey the law should be deleted. Detective Comics, Inc. v. Bruns Publications, Inc., (CCA 2), 111 F(2d) 432, 45 USPQ 291, mod'g 28 FSupp 399, 41 USPQ 182.

Section 1292 of Title 28 providing for appeal from interlocutory orders does not, when appeal is not taken, divest district court of jurisdiction to reconsider questions passed on by interlocutory decree before entering final order. Jones Brothers Co. v. Underkoffler, (DC-Pa), 24 FSupp 393, 39 USPQ 111.

Where court finds copyright infringed, counsel for plaintiff must forthwith prepare and submit through clerk's office findings of fact following complaint with such additions as counsel may be advised, as pictures in papers on motion for preliminary injunction and comparison of texts as in plaintiff's trial brief and conclusions of law; defendants to be notified and to submit criticism; only findings and conclusions signed by judge will be part of record; Supreme Court in Interstate Circuit, Inc. v. U. S., 304 US 55, 82 LEd 1146, 58 SCR 768, ended practice of opinion standing as findings and conclusions. Detective Comics, Inc. v.

(1563)

Bruns Publications, Inc., (DC-NY), 28 FSupp 399, 41 USPQ 182. Mf'd 111 F(2d) 432, 45 USPQ 291.

Final decree will be submitted through clerk's office on usual notice but only after costs, damages, and counsel fees are fixed so they may be included in the decree. Detective Comics, Inc. v. Bruns Publications, Inc., (DC-NY), 28 FSupp 399, 41 USPQ 182. Mf'd 111 F(2d) 432, 45 USPQ 291.

Author is entitled to interest on damages, awarded for plagiarism of his motion-picture script, from date of first exhibition of motion picture to date of judgment. Szekely v. Eagle Lion Films, Inc., (DC-NY), 140 FSupp 843, 109 USPQ 348. Aff'd 242 F(2d) 266, 113 USPQ 98.

88. —Operation and effect.

Decree which established the validity of a copyright and determined that a scene in a play was a dramatic composition entitled to protection under the copyright laws is conclusive as between the parties in an action at law for damages for violation of the copyright. Brady v. Daly, 175 US 148, 44 LEd 109, 20 SCR 62, aff'g (CCA 2), 83 Fed 1007.

In action for infringement of copyrighted trade catalogue, only damages recoverable under final decree were such as the interlocutory decree adjudged. Russell & Stoll Co. v. Oceanic Electrical Supply Co., Inc., (CCA 2), 80 F(2d) 864, 28 USPQ 203.

Term "publication," as used in interlocutory decree meant that only completed catalogues should count in fixing damages. Russell & Stoll Co. v. Oceanic Electrical Supply Co., Inc., (CCA 2), 80 F(2d) 864, 28 USPQ 203.

Whether decree makes one defendant liable jointly and severally with other defendant for latter's profits is matter for determination on entry of final decree. De Acosta v. Brown, (CCA 2), 146 F(2d) 408, 63 USPQ 311, aff'g 50 FSupp 615, 58 USPQ 596.

Partial final judgment under Rule 54(b) of the Federal Rules of Civil Procedure [Rules, c. 15] determining liability for copyright infringement is refused since it would establish nothing with finality and would require defendants to appeal to protect their rights; infringement cannot be dissociated from relief by way of injunction and damages provided by Copyright Act; to establish liability under Rule 54(b) of the Federal Rules of Civil Procedure [Rules, c. 15], would force defendants to litigate merits of case piecemeal. Harms, Inc. v. Tops Music Enterprises, Inc., (DC-Cal), 160 FSupp 77, 117 USPQ 72.

Where a consent decree was entered which settled all the liabilities of the defendant for the infringement, such decree could not be used by another person to avoid payment for infringing books which he had purchased from such defendant. Edward Thompson Co. v. Pakulski, 220 Mass 96, 107 NE 412.

The judgment of a United States court in an action on the infringement of a copyright, is res judicata in another suit involving the same facts in a state court. Kirke La Shelle Co. v. Armstrong, 173 AppDiv 232, 159 NYS 363. Aff'd 224 NY 582, 120 NE 866.

89. —Execution.

While the Federal Rules of Civil Procedure [Rules, c. 15] had not at time of decision gone into effect in copyright cases, they have been made applicable Sept. 1, 1939, and are now applicable to all other law and equity cases; they indicate definite policy to treat judgment on separate claim as so far final that it may be enforced by execution, and court by analogy seems to so treat copyright judgment. Collins v. Metro-Goldwyn Pictures Corp., (CCA 2), 106 F(2d) 83, 42 USPQ 553, rev'g 25 FSupp 781, 39 USPQ 520.

Issuance of writ of execution is proper process with respect to portion of decree awarding money damages and costs for copyright infringement. Raymor Ballroom Co. v. Buck, (CCA 1), 110 F(2d) 207, 45 USPQ 2, aff'g 28 FSupp 119, 42 USPQ 305.

On attempts of deputy marshal to collect at defendant's ballroom execution for damages and costs for copyright infringement, defendant with assistance of others by trickery and force prevented marshal from obtaining receipts and made off with money; to sustain decree for civil contempt it must be found that defendant's conduct was a resistance to lawful writ or process of the court, implying willful purpose to interfere so as to prevent execution of process; evidence makes out flagrant case of interference to prevent execution of process. Raymor Ballroom Co. v. Buck, (CCA 1), 110 F(2d) 207, 45 USPQ 2, aff'g 28 FSupp 119, 42 USPQ 305.

102, 103. [Repealed.]

Repeal.—These sections (Act July 30, 1947, c. 391, § 1, 61 Stat. 662) were repealed by Act June 25, 1948, c. 646, § 39, 62 Stat. 992. Similar provisions are contained in § 1338 of Title 28.

104. Willful infringement for profit.—

Any person who willfully and for profit shall infringe any copyright secured by this title, or who shall knowingly and willfully aid or abet such infringement, shall be deemed guilty of a misdemeanor, and upon conviction thereof shall be punished by imprisonment for not exceeding one year or by a fine of not less than $100 nor more than $1,000, or both, in the discretion of the court: Provided, however, That nothing in this title shall be so construed as to prevent the performance of religious or secular works such as oratorios, cantatas, masses, or octavo choruses by public schools, church choirs, or vocal societies, rented, borrowed, or obtained from some public library, public school, church choir, school choir, or vocal society, provided the performance is given for charitable or educational purposes and not for profit. (July 30, 1947, c. 391, § 1, 61 Stat. 662.)

NOTES TO DECISIONS

Good faith may constitute a defense in a criminal proceeding. Fisher, Inc. v. Dillingham, (DC-NY), 298 Fed 145.

Indictment for infringing copyright need not allege "copying" or expressly negative possibility that defendant's broadcast was original composition. Marx v. U. S., (CCA 9), 96 F(2d) 204, 37 USPQ 380.

Willful copying of copyrighted figurines constituting criminal violation is shown by defendant taking figurines to third party with instructions to make figurines resembling copyrighted figurines as closely as possible without "copyright trouble"; figurines so made are in most respects copies of copyrighted figurines and were deliberately made and deliberately sold by defendant for profit. U. S. v. Backer, (CCA 2), 134 F(2d) 533, 57 USPQ 133.

In criminal action it is not abuse of discretion to refuse to permit defendant to take colored pictures of copies of copyrighted figurines deposited in copyright office since evidence is merely cumulative in corroboration of disputed testimony of one observer. U. S. v. Backer, (CCA 2), 134 F (2d) 533, 57 USPQ 133.

Third party who made for defendant copies of copyrighted figurines having testified that he could, and did, reverse position of figurines, it is not error in criminal action to admit pictures of infringing figurines made by reversing negatives in printing. U. S. v. Backer, (CCA 2), 134 F(2d) 533, 57 USPQ 133.

On cross-examination of defendant it is discretionary to ask defendant what right he had to copy figurines which he is not charged with infringing. U. S. v. Backer, (CCA 2), 134 F(2d) 533, 57 USPQ 133.

Discrepancy in date of first publication of copyrighted matter was no ground for reversal in criminal proceeding where defendant was not prejudiced thereby. U. S. v. Backer, (CCA 2), 134 F(2d) 533, 57 USPQ 133.

Indictment charging crime as having been committed within limitation period was sufficient as time is not the essence of the offense. U. S. v. Schmidt, (DC-Pa), 15 FSupp 804.

Indictment charging defendant with "inciting, counseling, and procuring an infringement" was not ambiguous or uncertain. U. S. v. Schmidt, (DC-Pa), 15 FSupp 804.

Indictment was sufficient though not charging what words of the copyrighted song were used by defendant. U. S. v. Schmidt, (DC-Pa), 15 FSupp 804.

Indictment was sufficiently definite to enable defendants to plead the judgment in bar of any other prosecution of the same offense. U. S. v. Schmidt, (DC-Pa), 15 FSupp 804.

Liability for willful copyright infringement is not affected or discharged by bankruptcy. Gordon v. Weir, (DC-Mich), 111 FSupp 117, 97 USPQ 387.

Owner of copyrighted aerial survey maps licensed numerous customers; each license authorized licensee to use map negatives "only for the reproduction of maps for its own use, for such time as it deems fit"; defendant, without license, sold to third party copyrighted maps which were not produced by copyright owner; defendant is acquitted violating this section since there is no showing that maps sold by defendant were not published by licensee or that title to these copies was retained at all times by copyright proprietor. U. S. v. Wells, (DC-Tex), 176 FSupp 630, 123 USPQ 65.

Though the willful and knowing resale of piratical copies is violation of this section, a copy may be "piratical" for vending purposes only to extent of copyright proprietor's right to vend that particular copy, which depends upon his retention of legal title thereto; if copy was lawfully published by and belongs to licensee, proprietor has no exclusive right to vend it, and copy cannot be deemed piratical; furthermore, it can be argued that proprietor exhausted right to vend such copies by granting to licensee the right to publish them. U. S. v. Wells, (DC-Tex), 176 FSupp 630, 123 USPQ 65.

105. Fraudulent notice of copyright, or removal or alteration of notice. — Any person who, with fraudulent intent, shall insert or impress any notice of copyright required by this title, or words of the same purport, in or upon any uncopyrighted article, or with fraudulent intent shall remove or alter the copyright notice upon any article duly copyrighted shall be guilty of a misdemeanor, punishable by a fine of not less than $100 and not more than $1,000. Any person who shall knowingly issue or sell any article bearing a notice of United States copyright which has not been copyrighted in this country, or who shall knowingly import any article bearing such notice or words of the same purport, which has not been copyrighted in this country, shall be liable to a fine of $100. (July 30, 1947, c. 391, § 1, 61 Stat. 662.)

NOTES TO DECISIONS

Prior to Amendment of 1897, law had no extraterritorial effect and did not embrace the act of affixing in a foreign country a false statement of copyright. McLoughlin v. Tuck & Sons Co., Ltd., 191 US 267, 48 LEd 178, 24 SCR 105, aff'g (CCA 2), 115 Fed 85, which aff'd 99 Fed 562.

Complaint may be amended to change the averment as to statute violated, referring to a later act which was identical with, but was a substitute for, the act first referred to. Rosenbach v. Dreyfuss, (DC-NY), 1 Fed 391.

This section applies only to such articles as may be copyrighted. Rosenbach v. Dreyfuss, (DC-NY), 2 Fed 217.

In action to recover penalty summons must contain indorsement with reference to statute under which suit for penalty is brought, under New York statute. Brown v. Pond, (DC-NY), 5 Fed 31.

An indorsement on the summons, giving the wrong date of approval of the act under which the action was brought, is immaterial when the rest of the description is correct and there is no doubt as to which act is described. Brown v. Church, (DC-NY), 5 Fed 41.

United States district court has jurisdiction of suits to recover penalties under copyright laws. Taft v. Stephens Lith. & Eng. Co., (CC-Mo), 37 Fed 726.

If upon different days, under different circumstances, defendant printed separate copies, each transaction thus separate would constitute a separate offense, yet when the printing of many copies is a single continuous act, only one offense is committed. Taft v. Stephens Lith. & Eng. Co., (CC-Mo), 38 Fed 28; Taft v. Stephens Lithographing & Engraving Co., (CC-Mo), 39 Fed 781.

No offense is committed if the article is one that could not be copyrighted. Taft v. Stephens Lith. & Eng. Co., (CC-Mo), 38 Fed 28.

One who innocently reproduces a work from which the copyright notice has been removed may be enjoined. Falk v. Gast Lithograph & Engraving Co., Ltd., (CCA 2), 54 Fed 890. aff'g 48 Fed 262.

One inserting a false notice of copyright may be punished, whether or not the notice appears in the position provided in the Copyright Act. Rigney v. Raphael Tuck & Sons Co., Ltd., (CC-NY), 77 Fed 173.

An averment that a book was not copyrighted by defendant under either of its names is not equivalent to an allegation that defendant had not obtained a copyright. Rigney v. Raphael Tuck & Sons Co., Ltd., (CC-NY), 77 Fed 173.

Complaint must aver that the article falsely impressed has not been copyrighted. Rigney v. Raphael Tuck & Sons Co., Ltd., (CC-NY), 77 Fed 173.

To publish prints which were taken from a cut that was falsely impressed constituted a violation. Rigney v. Dutton, (CC-NY), 77 Fed 176.

A false notice which omits the date of the copyright will not sustain an action for the penalty. Hoertel v. Raphael Tuck Sons & Co., (CC-NY), 94 Fed 844.

Parts of an English edition of a dictionary being different from the American edition copyrighted in this country, a notice of copyright on the English edition would be a violation. G. & C. Merriam Co. v. United Dictionary Co., (CCA 7), 146 Fed 354, rev'g 140 Fed 768. Aff'd 208 US 260, 52 LEd 478, 28 SCR 290.

Distinct penalty was not provided for each article marked, but for each separate offense of marking. London v. Everett H. Dunbar Corp., (CCA 1), 179 Fed 506.

Injunctive relief previously expressly provided for in the case of false use of copyright notice was deleted in 1909 when criminal sanctions were written into the law for false removal of copyright notice; this section apparently has never been used to support injunctive relief; in view thereof and of general rule that equity will not enjoin commission of crimes, court holds that it does not have power to enjoin defendant from removing plaintiff's copyright notices. Scarves by Vera, Inc. v. American Handbags, Inc., (DC-NY), 188 FSupp 255, 127 USPQ 47.

Plaintiff does not show property interest independent of this section by its argument that, when defendant purchases towels embodying plaintiff's copyrighted designs, removes copyright notice, and uses towels in manufacture of hand-bags which are sold to public, defendant is placing designs in public domain, exposing them to use by public, and thereby destroying copyright; argument falls short because defendant by its actions cannot place copyrighted designs in public domain; in order for designs to be placed in public domain, it must be shown that copyrighted works left plaintiff's possession without required notice, and this burden is on defendant. Scarves by Vera, Inc. v. American Handbags, Inc., (DC-NY), 188 FSupp 255, 127 USPQ 47.

106. Importation of article bearing false notice or piratical copies of copyrighted work.—The importation into the United States of any article bearing a false notice of copyright when there is no existing copyright thereon in the United States, or of any piratical copies of any work copyrighted in the United States, is prohibited. (July 30, 1947, c. 391, § 1, 61 Stat. 663.)

NOTES TO DECISIONS

Prior to 1897 the importation of an article falsely stamped in a foreign country was not prohibited. McLoughlin v. Tuck & Sons Co., Ltd., 191 US 267, 48 LEd 178, 24 SCR 105, aff'g (CCA 2), 115 Fed 85, which aff'd 99 Fed 562.

The penalty involving false notice of copyright under § 11 of Copyright Act of 1831 was not recoverable in the names of more persons than one. Ferrett v. Atwill, (CC-NY), FedCas 4,747, 1 Blatchf 151.

The unlawful importation and vending of a foreign-printed book is an offense against the United States of which it alone may complain. Bentley v. Tibbals, (CCA 2), 223 Fed 247.

107. Importation, during existence of copyright, of piratical copies, or of copies not produced in accordance with section 16 of this title.—During the existence of the American copyright in any book the importation into the United States of any piratical copies thereof or of any copies thereof (although authorized by the author or proprietor) which have not been produced in accordance with the manufacturing provisions specified in section 16 of this title, or any plates of the same not made from type set within the limits of the United States, or any copies thereof produced by lithographic or photoengraving process not performed within the limits of the United States, in accordance with the provisions of section 16 of this title, is prohibited: Provided, however, That, except as regards piratical copies, such prohibition shall not apply:

(a)   To works in raised characters for the use of the blind.

(b)   To a foreign newspaper or magazine, although containing matter copyrighted in the United States printed or reprinted by authority of the copyright proprietor, unless such newspaper or magazine contains also copyright matter printed or reprinted without such authorization.

(c) To the authorized edition of a book in a foreign language or languages of which only a translation into English has been copyrighted in this country.

(d) To any book published abroad with the authorization of the author or copyright proprietor when imported under the circumstances stated in one of the four subdivisions following, that is to say:

First. When imported, not more than one copy at one time, for individual use and not for sale; but such privilege of importation shall not extend to a foreign reprint of a book by an American author copyrighted in the United States.

Second. When imported by the authority or for the use of the United States.

Third. When imported, for use and not for sale, not more than one copy of any such book in any one invoice, in good faith by or for any society or institution incorporated for educational, literary, philosophical, scientific, or religious purposes, or for the encouragement of the fine arts, or for any college, academy, school, or seminary of learning, or for any State, school, college, university, or free public library in the United States.

Fourth. When such books form parts of libraries or collections purchased en bloc for the use of societies, institutions, or libraries designated in the foregoing paragraph, or form parts of the libraries or personal baggage belonging to persons or families arriving from foreign countries and are not intended for sale: Provided, That copies imported as above may not lawfully be used in any way to violate the rights of the proprietor of the American copyright or annul or limit the copyright protection secured by this title, and such unlawful use shall be deemed an infringement of copyright. (July 30, 1947, c. 391, § 1, 61 Stat. 663.)

NOTES TO DECISIONS

Defendants who imported a foreign publication contrary to copyright law, and reprinted it, had no valid rights to so reprint to the injury of an American owner of a copyright of same work. Harper & Bros. v. M. A. Donahue & Co., (CC-Ill), 144 Fed 491. Aff'd 146 Fed 1023.

Object of prohibition against importation is to prevent the work of producing copyright books designed for sale in United States from being done abroad. G. & C. Merriam Co. v. United Dictionary Co., (CCA 7), 146 Fed 354,

rev'g 140 Fed 768. Aff'd 208 US 260, 52 LEd 478, 28 SCR 290.

The importation of editions of Meccano copyrighted manuals printed in England and accompanying Meccano outfits sold in United States was not a violation of this section. Meccano v. Wagner, (DC-Ohio), 234 Fed 912. Mf'd 246 Fed 603.

Uncopyrighted lithographs may be imported although copies of copyrighted paintings. 20 OAG 753.

This section embraces every American copyright in a book, regardless of whether the copyright was obtained under former copyright laws or the present act. 21 OAG 159; 28 OAG 90.

An article which is prohibited importation cannot gain admission through being attached to an article which is not prohibited. 22 OAG 29.

The importation of reprints of musical compositions copyrighted in the United States is prohibited. 22 OAG 29.

Importation of a book printed in the original French from type not set within the United States, where the copyright therefor for the United States was secured by the Paris publisher, is prohibited. 23 OAG 353.

A tariff act which provides when and under what circumstances certain articles are exempt from duty on importation, does not repeal, modify, or abrogate any part of the Copyright Act. 23 OAG 445.

Books copyrighted under the laws of the United States and printed from type set and plates made in this country, the printed sheets of which were sent to Belgium and there bound, cannot be legally returned to or imported into the United States. 28 OAG 90.

Copyrighted books which have been printed from type set within the United States, and the printing and binding both performed within the limits thereof, may be rebound abroad and imported without violation of this section. 28 OAG 209.

A book is "produced" within the meaning of this section when it is printed and bound. 28 OAG 209.

108. Forfeiture and destruction of articles prohibited importation.—Any and all articles prohibited importation by this title which are brought into the United States from any foreign country (except in the mails) shall be seized and forfeited by like proceedings as those provided by law for the seizure and condemnation of property imported into the United States in violation of the customs revenue laws. Such articles when forfeited shall be destroyed in such manner as the Secretary of the Treasury or the court, as the case may be, shall direct: Provided, however, That all copies of authorized editions of copyright books imported in the mails or otherwise in violation of the provisions of this title may be exported and returned to the country of export whenever it is shown to the satisfaction of the Secretary of the Treasury, in a written application, that such importation does not involve willful negligence or fraud. (July 30, 1947, c. 391, § 1, 61 Stat. 664.)

NOTES TO DECISIONS

The importation of a foreign book printed from type set in England is unlawful, and books so imported are subject to forfeiture. Bentley v. Tibbals, (CCA 2), 223 Fed 247.

Default judgment cannot order destruction under this section of matrices used to produce phonograph records infringing musical copyright where complaint makes no assertion, and seeks no relief, upon basis of violation of this section; hence, defendant is not in default as to such contention. Miller v. Goody, (DC-NY), 125 FSupp 348, 103 USPQ 292.

109. Importation of prohibited articles —Regulations—Proof of deposit of copies by complainants.—The Secretary of the Treasury and the Postmaster General are hereby empowered and required to make and enforce individually or jointly such rules and regulations as shall prevent the importation into the United States of articles prohibited importation by this title, and may require, as conditions precedent to exclusion of any work in which copyright is claimed, the copyright proprietor or any person claiming actual or potential injury by reason of actual or contemplated importations of copies of such work to file with the Post Office Department or the Treasury Department a certificate of the Register of Copyrights that the provisions of section 13 of this title have been fully complied with, and to give notice of such compliance to post-masters or to customs officers at the ports of entry in the United States in such form and accompanied by such exhibits as may be deemed necessary for the practical and efficient administration and enforcement of the provisions of sections 106 and 107 of this title. (July 30, 1947, c. 391, § 1, 61 Stat. 664.)

NOTES TO DECISIONS

The rules of the secretary of the treasury and the postmaster general may provide for the destruction of book imported into this country in violation of the copyright laws. 22 OAG 29.

The secretary of the treasury and the postmaster general may provide for the destruction of prohibited articles, without judicial proceeding when the value of the property involved is trifling. 22 OAG 70.

110, 111. [Repealed.]

Repeal.—These sections (Act July 30, 1947, c. 391, § 1, 61 Stat. 664) were repealed by Act June 25, 1948, c. 646, § 39, 62 Stat. 992. Similar provisions are contained in §§ 1338 and 1400 of Title 28.

112. Injunctions — Service and enforcement.—Any court mentioned in section 1338 of Title 28 or judge thereof shall have power, upon complaint filed by any party aggrieved, to grant injunctions to prevent and restrain the violation of any right secured by this title, according to the course and principles of courts of equity, on such terms as said court or judge may deem reasonable. Any injunction that may be granted restraining and enjoining the doing of anything forbidden by this title may be served on the parties against whom such injunction may be granted anywhere in the United States, and shall be operative throughout the United States and be enforceable by proceedings in contempt or otherwise by any other court or judge possessing jurisdiction of the defendants. (July 30, 1947, c. 391, § 1, 61 Stat. 664; Oct. 31, 1951, c. 655, § 16(c), 65 Stat. 716.)

Amendment note.—Act Oct. 31, 1951, cited to text, substituted "court mentioned in section 1338 of Title 28" for "such court."

NOTES TO DECISIONS
ANALYSIS

1. In general.
2. Jurisdiction.
3. Matters subject to injunction.
4. Right to relief.
5. —Persons entitled.
6. —Compliance with statute.
7. —Threat of future infringement.
8. —Unfair competition.
9. —Preliminary or temporary injunction.
10. ——When not granted.
11. Persons who may be enjoined.
12. Indemnity bond.
13. Pleading.
14. —Preliminary injunction.
15. Reference.
16. Evidence.
17. —Weight and sufficiency.
18. —Preliminary injunction.
19. Decree.
20. —Extent of injunction—Operation and effect.
21. —Dissolution or modification.
22. Contempt.

1. In general.

Resort may be had only to remedies provided by statute. Globe Newspaper Co. v. Walker, 210 US 356, 52 LEd 1096, 28 SCR 726, rev'g (CCA 1), 140 Fed 305, 2 LRA(NS) 913, which rev'd 130 Fed 593.

On application for an injunction it is proper for the court to consider the injury that would result to the complainant by refusing such order, in comparison with the harm that may be sustained by the defendant in consequence of granting the same. Sampson & Murdock Co. v. Seaver-Radford Co., (CC-Mass), 129 Fed 761.

This section in no way qualifies the prohibition regarding maintenance of actions for infringement of copyrights in § 13 of this title. New York Times Co. v. Star Co., (CC-NY), 195 Fed 110.

There is nothing in the fact that the injunction is asked to protect a copyright which will take the case out of the general principle of equity that the plaintiff must come into court with clean hands. T. B. Harms & Francis v. Stern, (CCA 2), 231 Fed 645, rev'g 229 Fed 42, which rev'd 222 Fed 581.

Remedy by injunction for infringement of copyright exists independently of express provision therefor in the copyright statutes. American Code Co., Inc. v. Bensinger, (CCA 2), 282 Fed 829.

Violation of copyright is tort and is analogous to trespass on real estate, for injunctive purposes. Metro-Goldwyn-Mayer Distributing Corp. v. Fisher, (DC-Md), 10 FSupp 745, 25 USPQ 341.

Where plaintiff seeks injunction and accounting, alleging that without injunction infringement will continue and that remedy at law is inadequate, he has no right to jury trial. Arnstein v. Twentieth Century-Fox Film Corp., (DC-NY), 3 FedRDec 58, 56 USPQ 511.

2. Jurisdiction.

The right to an accounting was incident to the right to an injunction. Stevens v. Gladding, 58 US(17 How) 447, 15 LEd 155, rev'g (CC-RI), FedCas 13,400; Gilmore v. Anderson, (CC-NY), 38 Fed 846; Falk v. Gast Lithograph & Engraving Co., Ltd., (CCA 2), 54 Fed 890, aff'g 43 Fed 262.

Circuit courts were given jurisdiction under R. S. § 4970 to grant injunctions in copyright cases. White-Smith Music Publishing Co. v. Apollo Co., 209 US 1, 52 LEd 655, 28 SCR 319, 15 AnnCas 628, aff'g (CCA 2), 147 Fed 226, which aff'd 139 Fed 427; Ohman v. New York City, (CC-NY), 168 Fed 953.

Wherever equity has jurisdiction to grant an injunction by final decree, it also has jurisdiction to grant interlocutory injunctions. Ladd v. Oxnard, (CC-Mass), 75 Fed 703.

Equity court, having jurisdiction of the cause, may dispose of it finally, and may award damages even though injunctive relief is denied. West Pub. Co. v. Edward Thompson Co., (CCA 2), 176 Fed 833, mod'g 169 Fed 833.

This section does not create any new cause of action, but relates only to jurisdiction and procedure to protect rights secured by the copyright laws. Goldwyn Pictures Corp. v. Howells Sales Co., Inc., (CCA 2), 282 Fed 9.

Where court has jurisdiction to grant injunction by final decree, it has jurisdiction to grant a preliminary injunction. American Code Co., Inc. v. Bensinger, (CCA 2), 282 Fed 829.

3. Matters subject to injunction.

An injunction should be granted to restrain the printing of a copyrighted map by one who purchased a copperplate engraving of the map at a sheriff's sale. Stephens v. Cady, 55 US (14 How) 528, 14 LEd 528.

Defendant cannot be restrained from selling copyrighted books below a certain price when he purchased full title to the books, although they contained a notice that sale at a different price would be treated as an infringement. Bobbs-Merrill Co. v. Straus, 210 US 339, 52 LEd 1086, 28 SCR 722, aff'g (CCA 2), 147 Fed 15, 15 LRA(NS) 766, which aff'd 139 Fed 155.

The common-law copyright of an author in his manuscripts is entitled to protection by injunction. Bartlett v. Crittenden, (CC-Ohio), FedCas 1,076, 5 McLean 32.

Where copyrighted manuscripts are printed without authority, such publication may be enjoined. Bartlett v. Crittenden, (CC-Ohio), FedCas 1,076, 5 McLean 32.

An injunction will be granted to protect only such publications as are already in existence. Centennial Catalogue Co. v. Porter, (CC-Pa), FedCas 2,546.

Although an uncopyrighted play is performed publicly, defendant will be restrained from producing such play when he obtained knowledge of the play through an unpublished manuscript and not through such public presentation. Keene v. Wheatley, (CC-Pa), FedCas 7,644, 4 Phila 157, 5 Clark 501.

Where copyrighted books were sold by an agent to a book dealer contrary to the instructions of the copyright owner and contrary to the known method by which plaintiff sold his books, such dealer will be enjoined from selling copies in his possession. Henry Bill Publishing Co. v. Smythe, (CC-Ohio), 27 Fed 914.

Performance of operetta "Nanon" similar to play of same title to which exclusive American rights had been purchased by plaintiffs before its publication in Europe was enjoined. Goldmark v. Kreling, (CC-Cal), 35 Fed 661.

Retracing, reproducing, and multiplying material portions of a copyrighted map constituted an infringement warranting issuance of an injunction. Sanborn Map & Pub. Co. v. Dakin Pub. Co., (CC-Cal), 39 Fed 266.

Where an encyclopedia is reprinted, with the exception of certain copyrighted articles, which were substituted by others, defendants cannot be enjoined from publishing such work when they do not make misleading statements as to the publication of the work. Black v. Ehrich, (CC-NY), 44 Fed 793.

While anyone may reprint a dictionary after the copyright expires, anyone so doing will be restrained from advertising such reprint in a manner to lead the public to believe that it is a new edition of the plaintiff's dictionary which is copyrighted. Merriam v. Texas Siftings Pub. Co., (CC-NY), 49 Fed 944.

Although a work is uncopyrighted defendant will be enjoined from publishing lectures of complainant when defendant's publication does not present them fully or correctly. Drummond v. Altemus, (CC-Pa), 60 Fed 338.

Owner of a copyright may not restrain, by virtue of the copyright laws, the sale of a copy of the copyrighted book, title to which he has transferred, but which is being sold in violation of an agreement. Harrison v. Maynard, Merrill & Co., (CCA 2), 61 Fed 689.

Protection by injunction is not afforded under the copyright laws to the title, separate from the book. Corbett v. Purdy, (CC-NY), 80 Fed 901.

An injunction may be granted to prevent infringement of a motion-picture film where the notice of copyright was placed on one end. Edison v. Lubin, (CCA 3), 122 Fed 240, rev'g 119 Fed 993.

A federal court has no authority to enjoin the publication of an uncopyrighted work. Bentley v. Tibbals, (CCA 2), 223 Fed 247.

Owner of motion-picture rights in a play popular under a particular name was allowed injunction against use of colorable imitation of the name for a competing play. National Picture Theatres, Inc. v. Foundation Film Corp., (CCA 2), 266 Fed 208.

The owner of a copyright on a label for shoe boxes may enjoin defendant from using such labels on his boxes, pending a trial of the issues. Hoague-Sprague Corp. v. Frank C. Meyer Co., Inc., (DC-NY), 27 F(2d) 176.

Legend on records prohibiting use except on phonographs at home is valid in Pennsylvania but invalid under copyright law and New York federal court will not enjoin radio broadcasting of records reception of which will be had in Pennsylvania since to do so broadcaster would have to be enjoined from broadcasting throughout United States and Canada. RCA Mfg. Co., Inc. v. Whiteman, (CCA 2), 114 F(2d) 86, 46 USPQ 324, rev'g 28 FSupp 787, 43 USPQ 114.

Use on another program without permission of electrical transcription bearing notice that use was limited to radio station for definite program was enjoined. Waring v. Dunlea, (DC-NC), 26 FSupp 338, 41 USPQ 201.

Fact that defendant violated copyright laws in publishing score card with copyright notice when there was no copyright registration does not entitle rival score card vendor and ball club to relief by injunction; if true it would mean only that defendant is subject to proceedings for violation of copyright statutes. Penn Sportservice, Inc. v. Goldstein, (DC-Pa), 35 FSupp 706, 47 USPQ 210.

Plaintiff is entitled to injunction, damages, costs, and reasonable attorney's fee for infringement of copyrighted music by playing at place of entertainment. Shapiro, Bernstein & Co., Inc. v. Mitchell, (DC-Miss), 41 USPQ 646.

A defendant will not be enjoined from manufacturing and selling for his own benefit, volumes of reports of the state supreme court, containing matter prepared by the state, when such matter was not protected by copyright, although defendant unlawfully used manuscripts intrusted to him by the state. State v. State Journal Co., 75 Neb 275, 106 NW 434, 9 LRA(NS) 174, 13 AnnCas 254.

Where complainant is the assignee of a copyrighted play under a contract with defendant which requires him to produce the play a specified number of times within the year, he may enjoin defendant from assigning the right to another, so long as there is still time in which to produce it the required number of times. Widmer v. Greene, 56 HowPrac (NY) 91.

The title of an uncopyrighted play will be protected, and its use on another play will be restrained when such use will confuse, although another play may have been copyrighted by that title. Dickey v. Mutual Film Corp., (Misc), 160 NYS 609. Mf'd 186 AppDiv 701, 174 NYS 784.

An injunction may issue to prevent the use of a title of a copyrighted play by another. Shook v. Wood, 10 Phila (Pa) 373.

4. Right to relief.

Where the infringement is slight and the result of imposition of an injunction would be inequitable, the copyright owner will be remitted to his remedy at law. Dun v. Lumbermen's Credit Assn., 209 US 20, 52 LEd 663, 28 SCR 335, 14 AnnCas 501, aff'g (CCA 7), 144 Fed 83; Scribner v. Stoddart, (CC-Pa), FedCas 12,561; Webb v. Powers, (CC-Mass), FedCas 17,323, 2 Woodb&M 497.

Where an infringement is patent, and an injunction will not result in any serious injury, such order is not usually refused as to so much of the work as is a plain infringement of the prior publication. Banks v. McDivitt, (CC-NY), FedCas 961, 13 Blatchf 163.

Where there is doubt upon the question of defendant's infringement, an injunction will be denied. Blunt v. Patten, (CC-NY), FedCas 1,580, 2 Paine 397.

An injunction will issue, though only a part of the subsequent work infringes the original. Emerson v. Davies, (CC-Mass), FedCas 4,436, 3 Story 768.

To obtain an injunction for infringement of a copyright it is not necessary that the whole or even a large part of the copyrighted work be infringed. Greene v. Bishop, (CC-Mass), FedCas 5,763, 1 Cliff 186.

An injunction will not be granted in copyright cases where the infringement is slight, if there is no proof of bad motive, or where title to the copyright is in doubt, or where there has been a long acquiescence in the infringement, or laches or negligence in seeking redress, especially if it appear that the delay has misled the defendant. Lawrence v. Dana, (CC-Mass), FedCas 8,136, 4 Cliff 1.

Injunction will be refused if there is a reasonable doubt as to plaintiff's right, or the validity of his copyright. Miller v. McElroy, (CC-Pa), FedCas 9,581, 1 Clark 326.

If it does not satisfactorily appear that what a defendant has done is, or what he intends to do will be, an infringement of copyright, an injunction will be denied. Smith v. Johnson, (CC-NY), FedCas 13,066, 4 Blatchf 252.

Intent of infringer may have a material bearing upon the complainants' right to an injunction. Webb v. Powers, (CC-Mass), FedCas 17,323, 2 Woodb&M 497.

Party is not deprived of right to injunction because he has availed himself of remedy for damages. Schumacher v. Schwencke, (CC-NY), 25 Fed 466.

"Irreparable" injury which will entitle a complainant to an injunction is defined. Ladd v. Oxnard, (CC-Mass), 75 Fed 703.

A preliminary injunction may be granted to restrain the infringement of a form chart, containing data of race horses, although it may be used by persons for gambling purposes, when the complainant's affidavit states that it is read by others than those engaged in gambling upon races. Egbert v. Greenberg, (CC-Cal), 100 Fed 447.

Where post cards are not copyrighted, another person cannot be restrained from copying them. Bamforth v. Douglass Post Card & Machine Co., (CC-Pa), 158 Fed 355.

Where the complainant has wrongfully conducted himself in respect to the matter in litigation, he cannot obtain an injunction. T. B. Harms & Francis, Day & Hunter v. Stern, (CCA 2), 231 Fed 645, rev'g 229 Fed 42.

Plaintiff was not entitled to injunctive relief where the proportion of infringing items in defendant's rating list to the items of original work by defendant was very small. Cravens v. Retail Credit Men's Ass'n, (DC-Tenn), 26 F(2d) 833.

Where motion-picture company filmed novel after negotiating only with author when it had notice publisher had exclusive license in motion-picture rights of novel, publisher was entitled to an injunction restraining the picture irrespective of large investment of picture company therein. L. C. Page & Co., Inc. v. Fox Film Corp., (CCA 2), 83 F(2d) 196, 29 USPQ 386.

Injunction is denied where proportion of work taken is insignificant compared to injury resulting from stopping use of large volume of independently acquired information. Mathews Conveyer Co. v. Palmer-Bee Co., (CCA 6), 135 F(2d) 73, 57 USPQ 219, aff'g 41 FSupp 401, 51 USPQ 286.

Destruction of infringing plates of copyrighted photograph did not bar injunctive relief. Cory v. Physical Culture Hotel, (DC-NY), 14 FSupp 977, 30 USPQ 353. Aff'd 88 F(2d) 411, 33 USPQ 58.

If injunction should not be granted it matters not that reason for refusing issuance is based partly on facts occurring after suit began. Basevi v. Edward O'Toole Co., Inc., (DC-NY), 26 FSupp 41, 40 USPQ 333.

In suit to enjoin enforcement of state statute, before court passes on question of constitutionality of statute it is necessary to determine whether plaintiffs may invoke aid of court of equity; plaintiffs are barred relief if they come into court with unclean hands or if they violate Sherman Act [15 §§ 1-7, 15 note]. Buck v. Gallagher, (DC-Wash), 36 FSupp 405, 48 USPQ 316.

Injunction was refused after only one infringing sale. Larsen v. Goldblatt Bros., Inc., (DC-Ill), 53 USPQ 287.

5. —Persons entitled.

Where by contract, a state gives a person the right to publish and copyright volumes containing opinions of courts of the state, such person may enjoin others from printing such books. Little v. Gould, (CC-NY), FedCas 8,394, 2 Blatchf 165.

Injunction will not be denied to holder of legal title of a copyright because he is merely a trustee for the benefit of a third party who is the "author" or "proprietor." Hanson v. Jaccard Jewelry Co., (CC-Mo), 32 Fed 202.

"Any party aggrieved" includes a licensee who has obtained the right to manufacture and sell perforated music rolls. Aeolian Co. v. Royal Music Roll Co., (DC-NY), 196 Fed 926.

A court of equity will protect the right of the holder of the equitable title of a copyright although it is not clear that his legal title is complete. Mawman v. Tegg, 2 Russ(Eng) 385.

6. —Compliance with statute.

Where an assignee of a copyright fails to put a proper notice of copyright upon his publication he cannot maintain a suit for injunction, whether against his assignor or any other. Thompson v. Hubbard, 131 US 123, 33 LEd 76, 9 SCR 710, rev'g (CC-Mo), 25 Fed 188.

Although complainant violated the copyright law in importing English editions, such misconduct is unconnected with a suit to enjoin an infringing publication, and the defense of unclean hands because of such importation cannot be applied in the suit for injunction. Bentley v. Tibbals, (CCA 2), 223 Fed 247.

7. —Threat of future infringement.

An injunction will not issue upon a mere threat or intent to print an infringing book. Centennial Catalogue Co. v. Porter, (CC-Pa), FedCas 2,546.

Although there has been no infringement or threat of infringement since complainant acquired the copyright, any infringement furnished the ground for an injunction, and fact that infringement has ceased may take away the occasion but not the right to an injunction. Gilmore v. Anderson, (CC-NY), 38 Fed 846.

Where the bill avers that plaintiffs had title to copyright at date of filing, and the answer admits the averment, and defendant was threatening to infringe the copyright, plaintiff is entitled to an injunction, although an actual infringement has not taken place. Historical Pub. Co. v. Jones Bros. Pub. Co., (CCA 3), 231 Fed 638.

Although there does not appear to be any immediate danger of further infringement, injunction may issue as a recognition of plaintiff's technical right. M. Witmark & Sons v. Calloway, (DC-Tenn), 22 F(2d) 412.

Where defendant eliminated from his publication a copied list and revised the book so that no plagiarism was shown, and delivered up to the court the copied sheets and master cards for destruction, there was no reason for an injunction. Cravens v. Retail Credit Men's Ass'n, (DC-Tenn), 26 F(2d) 833.

In a suit for copyright infringement, which apparently was a friendly suit instigated and financed by plaintiff and in which defendant said he would not be damaged by injunction, and where the infringement had not occurred but it was stated that he threatened to infringe, and where decision against plaintiff in court in another jurisdiction was not brought to attention of court, suit was dismissed for want of equity. Seltzer v. Corem, (CCA 7), 107 F(2d) 75, 43 USPQ 245, rev'g 26 FSupp 892, 41 USPQ 569.

Injunction would not issue to restrain copyright infringement where there was little likelihood of repetition, but jurisdiction of court was not divested. Vitaphone Corp. v. Hutchinson Amusement Co., (DC-Mass), 19 FSupp 359, 33 USPQ 422.

8. —Unfair competition.

Where defendant's opera does not infringe upon a copyright, no injunction can be had against him unless he advertises so as to mislead the public that his opera is that of complainants. Carte v. Ford, (CC-Md), 15 Fed 439.

Motion for injunction was denied where defendant did not appropriate any copyrighted articles, and his actions did not evince unfair competition. Black v. Ehrich, (CC-NY), 44 Fed 793.

To allow others to benefit financially by artist's work and skill would be unfair trade practice and equity will enjoin such an effort. Waring v. Dunlea, (DC-NC), 26 FSupp 338, 41 USPQ 201.

Orchestra which gave radio broadcasts for pay is in competition with broadcasting station, and when latter, without authority, broadcasts phonograph transcription of music played by orchestra, such broadcast is enjoined as unfair competition. Waring v. WDAS Broadcasting Station, 327 Pa 433, 194 Atl 631, 35 USPQ 272.

9. —Preliminary or temporary injunction.

Where a preliminary injunction will not cause serious injury, it will ordinarily be granted against so much of defendant's work as plainly infringes upon plaintiff's work. Banks v. McDivitt, (CC-NY), FedCas 961, 13 Blatchf 163.

A motion for a temporary injunction should not in any case be allowed to operate as a means of obtaining a premature expression of opinion of the court upon the merits of the controversy where unnecessary. Pott v. Altemus, (CC-Pa), 60 Fed 339.

The real basis of interlocutory injunctions is maintenance of the status quo. Ladd v. Oxnard, (CC-Mass), 75 Fed 703.

Complainant was granted an injunction pendente lite where three pages of its books were being used as copy from which to print defendant's book, and defendant made no satisfactory explanation therefor. Chicago Directory Co. v. United States Directory Co., (CC-NY), 122 Fed 189.

In order to warrant the granting of a preliminary injunction, the facts must be clear, and the equities growing out of them in no doubt. Sweet v. G. W. Bromley & Co., (CC-Pa), 154 Fed 754.

A preliminary injunction should never issue unless the court is clearly of the opinion that complainant will succeed at final hearing. Benton v. Van Dyke, (CC-NY), 170 Fed 203.

Where there was dispute between plaintiff and defendant as to ownership of copyrighted play, injunction pendente lite against defendant restraining performance of copyrighted play or similar play was continued. Eisfeldt v. Campbell, (CC-NY), 171 Fed 594.

Preliminary injunctions are granted more readily in dramatic than in other cases because the delay involved in waiting for a final decree would generally amount to a denial of justice. Chappell & Co., Ltd. v. Fields, (CCA 2), 210 Fed 864.

In granting or refusing a motion for a preliminary injunction the court is not bound by a previous consent decree involving the same copyright. Hodgson v. Vroom, (CCA 2), 266 Fed 267.

Manufacturer of shoe boxes, employing a special decorative design on which he has obtained a copyright was entitled to a preliminary injunction against defendant using the same design on similar boxes. Hoague-Sprague Corp. v. Frank C. Meyer Co., Inc., (DC-NY), 27 F(2d) 176.

Preliminary injunction issued at suit of telephone company on ground that defendant had infringed the copyright of plaintiff's telephone directory. Cincinnati & Suburban Bell Telephone Co. v. Brown, (DC-Ohio), 44 F(2d) 631.

In copyright cases, if plaintiff makes a prima facie showing of his right, a preliminary injunction should issue where two editions of book of great popular interest are being actively promoted in competition. Houghton Mifflin Co. v. Stackpole Sons, Inc., (CCA 2), 104 F(2d) 306, 42 USPQ 96, rev'g 41 USPQ 404.

Where foreword states defendant's book is condensed edition with all important parts presented; although sold at much less price, it will damage plaintiff, and preliminary injunction should issue as there is real competition, possibly more competition than expensive book edition. Houghton Mifflin Co. v. Noram Pub. Co., Inc., (DC-NY), 28 FSupp 676, 42 USPQ 370.

As general rule in copyright infringement cases, preliminary injunction is granted where plaintiff makes out prima facie case as to existence of copyright and its infringement. Robbins Music Corp. v. Weinstock, (DC-NY), 107 FSupp 102, 94 USPQ 107.

In cases of copyright infringement, injunction is proper remedy because of inadequacy of legal remedy; remedy exists both by statute and independently thereof. Inge v. Twentieth Century-Fox Film Corp., (DC-NY), 143 FSupp 294, 111 USPQ 153.

In action for copyright infringement by owner of copyrighted play who licensed defendant to make moving picture based upon play, defendant is preliminarily enjoined from releasing picture before release date fixed by license; if injunction were not granted, computation of plaintiff's damages would be difficult, although damages may be substantial; there is no easy way of measuring comparison of return to stage production of play under a condition without film competition and that with film competition. Inge v. Twentieth Century-Fox Film Corp., (DC-NY), 143 FSupp 294, 111 USPQ 153.

10. ——When not granted.

A preliminary injunction will not be granted when it is doubtful whether or not there has been an infringement. Blunt v. Patten, (CC-NY), FedCas 1,580, 2 Paine 397; Colliery Engineer Co. v. United Correspondence Schools Co., (CC-NY), 94 Fed 152; Benton v. Van Dyke, (CC-NY), 170 Fed 203; Bobbs-Merrill Co. v. Equitable Motion Pictures Corp., (DC-NY), 232 Fed 791.

Where the validity of plaintiff's copyright is doubtful, and it appears that defendant will be able to pay damages, a preliminary injunction will not be granted. Miller v. McElroy, (CC-Pa), FedCas 9,581, 1 Clark 326.

A preliminary injunction will not be granted where it appears that the author had permitted a foreign publisher to use the work, and the injury to defendant caused by the injunction would be greater than any injury plaintiff might suffer by its refusal. Scribner v. Stoddart, (CC-Pa), FedCas 12,561.

If there be doubt as to the validity of a plaintiff's copyright, preliminary injunction will be refused. Scribner v. Stoddart, (CC-Pa), FedCas 12,561.

Where the court is in doubt whether a book of engravings, issued for trade purposes, is intrinsically valuable as a work of art, a preliminary injunction will not be granted. Lamb v. Grand Rapids School Furniture Co., (CC-Mich), 39 Fed 474.

A motion for preliminary injunction to prevent the publication of a copyrighted work by the author thereof, in a newspaper, will be denied when complainant is holder of the copyright through a contract requiring him to use his best efforts to secure the sale of the book, and his compliance with such contract is doubtful. Worthington v. Batty, (CC-NY), 40 Fed 479.

Where plaintiff knew of the contents of an alleged infringing publication several months before bringing suit, but plaintiff waited until a bound volume was prepared and ready for delivery, a temporary injunction restraining the publishing and selling of the work will not be granted, but defendant should keep account of all books sold for the payment to plaintiff of any damages the court may award in a final decree. West Publishing Co. v. Lawyers' Co-operative Publishing Co., (CC-NY), 53 Fed 265.

Temporary injunction will not be granted if it is possible to effect justice in any other way. Ladd v. Oxnard, (CC-Mass), 75 Fed 703.

Preliminary injunction will be refused where the fact of infringement is not clear, and issuance of such order would work irreparable damage to defendant. Colliery Engineer Co. v. United Correspondence Schools Co., (CC-NY), 94 Fed 152; Benton v. Van Dyke, (CC-NY), 170 Fed 203.

Where the character and extent of a dedication to the public through the uncopyrighted publication of a musical composition cannot be determined upon the affidavit and inspection of the respective scores, and it does not appear that defendant is unable to respond in damages, a preliminary injunction should not be granted. Littleton v. Fischer, (CC-NY), 137 Fed 684.

Where two plays are adapted from the same novel and defendants' play resembles the book in some particulars which were not found in the plaintiff's play, and the validity of plaintiff's copyright was questioned, a preliminary injunction cannot be granted. Nixon v. Doran, (CC-NY), 168 Fed 575.

Where two plays, one copyrighted and the other not, are adapted from the same novel, the copyright of which had expired, and both use the title of the novel, a preliminary injunction will not be granted to restrain the use of the title on the uncopyrighted play. Glaser v. St. Elmo Co., Inc., (CC-NY), 175 Fed 276.

Where a court is unable to determine the extent of the matter copied, it will not grant a preliminary injunction to restrain the publication of certain parts of the work. White v. Bender, (CC-NY), 185 Fed 921.

Where defendant avers under oath that the expressions in a copyrighted monologue were not new with complainant, but common property, a preliminary injunction should not issue. Hoffman v. Le Traunik, (DC-NY), 209 Fed 375.

Preliminary injunction was properly denied where defendants purchased from trustee without notice of trust agreement. Brady v. Reliance Motion Picture Corp., (CCA 2), 229 Fed 137.

A court should be particularly hesitant about granting a preliminary injunction after months of delay, where it appears that defendants did not know of the existence of plaintiff's manuscript until suit was brought. Eichel v. Marcin, (DC-NY), 241 Fed 404.

Where defendant claims to have given the performance under an implied license from plaintiff and plaintiff claims that such authority had been revoked prior to the alleged infringement, a preliminary injunction will not be granted. Jerome H. Remick & Co. v. General Electric Co., (DC-NY), 4 F(2d) 160.

Actor is not entitled to injunction against motion-picture producer licensing copyrighted motion-picture films, in which actor starred under expired contracts, for exhibition on television in connection with sponsored advertising. Autry v. Republic Productions, Inc., (DC-Cal), 104 FSupp 918, 93 USPQ 284. Mf'd 213 F(2d) 667, 101 USPQ 478.

Injunction ought not to issue pending trial on merits unless irreparable damage will result to plaintiff by such denial. National Geographic Society v. Classified Geographic, Inc., (DC-Mass), 35 USPQ 152.

A temporary injunction will not be granted where two motion pictures are different with the exception of the title, and one is a seven reel film, the whole being shown at one time and the other a series of two reel films to be shown on different days. Gillette v. Stoll Film Co., Ltd., 120 Misc 850, 200 NYS 787.

11. Persons who may be enjoined.

A bill for an injunction will be dismissed when the defendant is an officer of the corporation which is alleged to have infringed complainant's work and such corporation is not made a party defendant. Stuart v. Smith, (CC-NY), 68 Fed 189.

(1573)

Proprietor of a copyright may be granted injunctive relief against a defendant for infringement, though such relief will interfere with the performance of duties imposed upon the defendant by a state. Howell v. Miller, (CCA 6), 91 Fed 129.

Individual defendants who organized corporation and controlled and directed its activities while infringing acts were committed can be held liable to injunction and damages and may be joined as defendants with the corporation. National Geographic Soc. v. Classified Geographic, Inc., (DC-Mass), 27 FSupp 655, 41 USPQ 719.

Where defendants, employees of United States, reproduced copyrighted map for use of United States but reproductions were never used, no injunction is necessary except against reproduction of map by defendants personally or through their cooperation; use by United States of maps which are owned by them must be protected. Towle v. Ross, (DC-Ore), 32 FSupp 125, 45 USPQ 143.

Performer who makes phonograph record and causes to be affixed thereto a notice of a restriction that it is not licensed for commercial radio broadcast may restrain its use by radio station but this restraint cannot be extended to advertiser who has and exerts no control over conduct of broadcasts during or between which advertising announcements, with no relation to broadcast entertainment, are read. National Ass'n of Performing Artists v. Wm. Penn Broadcasting Co., (DC-Pa), 38 FSupp 531, 49 USPQ 563.

Where copyright is renewed by heirs of one coauthor, license by surviving coauthor gives licensee sufficient equitable interest in composition to bar injunction against it. Edward B. Marks Music Corp. v. Jerry Vogel Music Co., Inc., (DC-NY), 47 FSupp 490, 55 USPQ 288, 55 USPQ 489. Aff'd 140 F(2d) 266, 268, 60 USPQ 257, and mf'd 140 F(2d) 268, 60 USPQ 256.

Had local retail store infringing copyright continued as independent concern, its mere assurance of good intention might be acceptable in lieu of injunction against infringement which ceased upon notice, but store has become branch of national organization and thus an injunction is required. Malsed v. Marshall Field & Co., (DC-Wash), 96 FSupp 372, 88 USPQ 552.

12. Indemnity bond.

Where terms of a contract have not been determined and there is doubt as to whether there has been an infringement, a preliminary injunction will not be granted, but defendant will be required to give bond pending a final hearing. Hubbard v. Thompson, (CC-Mo), 14 Fed 689.

Although the moving papers make out a very strong prima facie case, when a preliminary injunction would be in effect, a judgment in advance of trial, which would work irreparable injury on defendant, it will not be granted, provided defendant furnishes a sufficient bond. Trow Directory, Printing & Bookbinding Co. v. Boyd, (CC-NY), 97 Fed 586.

Where it is doubtful whether the subject matter is a proper subject for copyright, an injunction will not be granted provided the defendant furnishes a bond to indemnify complainants against damage. Louis De Jonge & Co. v. Breuker & Kessler Co., (CC-Pa), 147 Fed 763.

Where defendant's directory is shown to contain the same errors as plaintiff's, but defendant, by affidavit alleges that such names were copied from voters lists in which the errors occurred, and shows the manner in which the directory was compiled, no preliminary injunction will be granted provided defendant files a sufficient bond. Gopsill v. C. E. Howe Co., (CC-Pa), 149 Fed 905.

Where the alleged infringing work is a song of such character that usually has a temporary vogue, and the financial showing of the defendant is not satisfactory, a temporary injunction will be granted but will be suspended when defendant files sufficient bond and files a statement of sales. Boosey v. Empire Music Co., Inc., (DC-NY), 224 Fed 646.

Where defendant has expended $15,000 on an alleged infringing work and has on hand books valued at $50,000, a bond given by complainant in the sum of $250 upon the issuance of a preliminary injunction is insufficient. American Code Co., Inc. v. Bensinger, (CCA 2), 282 Fed 829.

Where plaintiff's rights will be adequately protected defendant should be given the option to furnish a bond as condition of denying injunction. Yale University Press v. Row, Peterson & Co., (DC-NY), 40 F(2d) 290.

13. Pleading.

Under R. S. § 4970, bill in equity will lie for injunction. Bolles v. Outing Co., 175 US 262, 44 LEd 156, 20 SCR 94, aff'g (CCA 2), 77 Fed 966, 46 LRA 712.

A bill for an injunction, not intended to be used as evidence, need not be verified. Black v. Henry G. Allen Co., (CC-NY), 42 Fed 618, 9 LRA 433.

An allegation in the bill, that complainant is the "author, inventor, designer and proprietor" of a certain photograph and negative thereof" and giving the title under which it was copyrighted is sufficient in a suit for injunction without giving detailed description of steps taken in producing the photograph. Falk v. Schumacher, (CC-NY), 48 Fed 222.

In a suit to enjoin the infringement of a copyright the defense of unclean hands need not be pleaded, but when evidence discloses such fact the court will apply the maxim of its own motion. Bentley v. Tibbals, (CCA 2), 223 Fed 247.

It sometimes happens that redress by injunction must be speedily obtained in order to prevent irreparable injury, and that plaintiff may not have a copy of the manuscript at hand to file with the petition, in which case he can describe the substance of the subject matter, but satisfactory reasons must be given for its absence. Tully v. Triangle Film Corp., (DC-NY), 229 Fed 297.

The owner of the equitable title to a copyright is not a mere licensee and may sue in equity to restrain infringement, especially where the owner of the legal title is the infringer, but he must connect himself with the legal title by proper averment; the plaintiff in such case being a "party aggrieved" within the statute. Ordinarily the equitable owner must join the owner of the legal title as a party plaintiff. Ted Browne Music Co. v. Fowler, (CCA 2), 290 Fed 751.

Owner of copyrighted "bank night" scheme for cash prizes to be given by places of amusement was not entitled to restrain theater owner from using such scheme in absence of allegations showing infringement of copyright. Affiliated Enterprises, Inc. v. Gantz, (CCA 10), 86 F(2d) 597, 31 USPQ 397.

A bill of complaint in a suit for the protection of a copyright must allege facts which show performance of conditions precedent to a copyright. Pathe Exchange, Inc. v. International Alliance of Theatrical Stage Employees, (DC-NY), 3 FSupp 63.

Mere prayer for injunction without any allegation of fact to support it will not confer equitable jurisdiction, and prayer for discovery or accounting of itself will not give such jurisdiction. Universal Pictures Corp. v. Marsh, (DC-WVa), 36 FSupp 241, 48 USPQ 319.

In suit to enjoin enforcement of state statute, defendants did not answer but moved to dismiss; court treats motions as answers; one defendant argued question not raised in his motion, but raised in motions of other defendants, and court treats his motion as amended so as to present the question. Buck v. Gallagher, (DC-Wash), 36 FSupp 405, 48 USPQ 316.

Federal equity rules, insofar as applicable, apply to an equity copyright action. Gross v. Twentieth Century Fox Film Corp., (DC-NY), 38 USPQ 399.

14.   —Preliminary injunction.

To be entitled to a preliminary injunction, a complainant must show affirmatively, beyond any doubt, that he has complied with the copyright laws. American Trotting Register Ass'n v. Gocher, (CC-Ohio), 70 Fed 237.

A court will not grant an interlocutory injunction on the face of a bill which clearly cannot be sustained on demurrer. Ladd v. Oxnard, (CC-Mass), 75 Fed 703.

Where a case cannot be decided upon ex parte affidavits, a motion for a preliminary injunction will be denied. Dun v. International Mercantile Agency, (CC-NY), 127 Fed 173.

Where, upon motion for preliminary injunction, the affidavits of the parties are so conflicting that the case cannot fairly be decided thereupon, injunction will be refused. Dun v. International Mercantile Agency, (CC-NY), 127 Fed 173.

Where from the affidavits of the parties it is impossible to decide to what extent, if at all, a defendant has trespassed upon a complainant's copyright rights, the motion for preliminary injunction will be denied. Littleton v. Fischer, (CC-NY), 137 Fed 684.

A complainant's objection to an oral license, under which a defendant has proceeded, may not be interposed for first time upon motion for a preliminary injunction, as a ground for such order. G. Ricordi & Co. v. Hammerstein, (CC-NY), 150 Fed 450.

Preliminary injunction denied, the court being unable to determine upon the affidavits what portion of the book should be enjoined. White v. Bender, (CC-NY), 185 Fed 921.

Where a motion is made to dismiss the complaint, the court may consider only the pleadings in ruling on such motion and not the affidavits which were submitted with the application for a preliminary injunction. Brady v. Reliance Motion Picture Corp., (DC-NY), 232 Fed 259.

Where there are conflicting allegations in the complaint and answer, and plaintiff appears to have been guilty of laches, a preliminary injunction will not be granted. Flanagan v. Coleman, (DC-NY), 255 Fed 178.

A demurrable complaint will prevent a preliminary injunction. American Code Co., Inc. v. Bensinger, (CCA 2), 282 Fed 829.

In an application for a preliminary injunction, the plaintiff's affidavits should satisfactorily show that the defendant has actually copied into his book copyrighted matter taken from plaintiff's work. American Code Co., Inc. v. Bensinger, (CCA 2), 282 Fed 829.

Where several debatable questions are presented by the bill and answer a preliminary injunction is properly refused. E. I. Horsman & Aetna Doll Co., Inc. v. Kaufman, (CCA 2), 286 Fed 372.

15.   Reference.

A motion for preliminary injunction may be disposed of upon the papers filed in the case without referring the case to a master. Smith v. Johnson, (CC-NY), FedCas 13,066, 4 Blatchf 252.

A court generally must refer the case to a master to determine the extent of the infringement before granting a preliminary injunction. Story v. Derby, (CC-Ohio), FedCas 13,496, 4 McLean 160.

In suit to enjoin enforcement of state statute, court referred cause to master to take testimony on question of jurisdiction, and directed him to make findings. Buck v. Gallagher, (DC-Wash), 36 FSupp 405, 48 USPQ 316.

Until master's report, defendants are not enjoined from using material set up in type since plaintiffs have exaggerated number of recent infringements and old infringements of racing charts rapidly lose potency. Triangle Publications, Inc. v. New England Newspaper Pub. Co., (DC-Mass), 46 FSupp 198, 54 USPQ 171.

16.   Evidence.

Injunction denied where facts showed no infringement and defendant agreed to discontinue his acts of unfair competition. Carte v. Ford, (CC-Md), 15 Fed 439.

Whenever a bill for injunction is to be used as evidence, either upon motion for preliminary injunction or in any other way, it must be verified; but there is no imperative rule requiring verification of a bill, at the time it is signed. Black v. Henry G. Allen Co., (CC-NY), 42 Fed 618, 9 LRA 433.

A court will not interfere by injunction, unless the right to the relief asked is clearly manifest from the evidence. Howell v. Miller, (CCA 6), 91 Fed 129.

Where defendant desires some parts of his work to be exempted from injunction, an opportunity may be given him to clearly prove noninfringement in respect to such parts. W. H. Anderson Co. v. Baldwin Law Pub. Co., (CCA 6), 27 F(2d) 82.

Fact that court of appeals held prima facie proof of identity of person who signed assignment of copyright and his authority to act for copyright proprietor sufficient for temporary injunction is not conclusive on motion for summary judgment of permanent injunction; prima facie case will serve if justice demands but plaintiff was party to assignment and presumably has access to the evidence; defendants are not required to accept the very general conclusions of plaintiff's affidavits but evidence should be produced in regular way and witnesses should be submitted · to cross-examination. Houghton Mifflin Co. v. Stackpole Sons, Inc., (CCA 2), 113 F(2d) 627, 46 USPQ 296, mod'g 31 FSupp 517, 44 USPQ 668.

17. —Weight and sufficiency.

Although fictitious items which appeared in complainant's book of credit ratings also appeared in defendant's book, when it is shown by evidence the manner in which defendant obtained original information at great expense and the proportion of such names is insignificant, no injunction will be granted. Dun v. Lumbermen's Credit Assn., 209 US 20, 52 LEd 663, 28 SCR 335, 14 AnnCas 501, aff'g (CCA 7), 144 Fed 83.

Upon an application for an injunction to restrain infringement, it is not necessary to show that the violation of the copyright is so extensive that the piratical work is a substitute for the original work. Reed v. Holliday, (CC-Pa), 19 Fed 325.

If plaintiff shows an infringement of his copyright, an injunction will be granted without proof of damages. Reed v. Holliday, (CC-Pa), 19 Fed 325; Fishel v. Lueckel, (CC-NY), 53 Fed 499; Macmillan Co. v. King, (DC-Mass), 223 Fed 862.

On an application for injunction pending suit it is proper for the court to consider the harm that would be done to the complainant by refusing such an order in comparison to the damage that might be sustained by the defendant if it were granted. Hanson v. Jaccard Jewelry Co., (CC-Mo), 32 Fed 202.

The complainant is not always bound to prove pecuniary damages to entitle him to an injunction. Farmer v. Elstner, (CC-Mich), 33 Fed 494.

In a suit for injunction it is not necessary that complainant prove that the notice of copyright appeared upon each one of his copies, but general testimony is sufficient to establish a prima facie case. Falk v. Gast Lith. & Eng. Co., Ltd., (CC-NY), 40 Fed 168.

To entitle complainant to an injunction, he must show affirmatively beyond any doubt, that he has complied with the copyright law. American Trotting Register Ass'n v. Gocher, (CC-Ohio), 70 Fed 237.

Where a legislature has determined that the public interests require a new compilation of the laws of the state, and the work is completed, a court should not interfere by injunction, unless the right to relief asked is clearly manifest from evidence. Howell v. Miller, (CCA 6), 91 Fed 129.

While a court of equity will not and should not permit the enforcement of an oral license to use a copyrighted musical production, without satisfactory and convincing proof, where complainant by his own affidavits shows that he never objected to defendant's application for a license, a motion for an injunction will be denied. G. Ricordi & Co. v. Hammerstein, (CC-NY), 150 Fed 450.

Evidence and instances of copying was too insignificant in amount to demand an injunction against defendant's books. West Publishing Co. v. Edward Thompson Co., (CC-NY), 169 Fed 833. Mf'd 176 Fed 833.

Where there is proof that a considerable number of errors common to both defendant's and complainant's book of citations, occurred first in complainant's book, a prima facie case of copying is made, and unless defendant satisfactorily explains such errors, his publication will be enjoined. Frank Shepard Co. v. Zachary P. Taylor Pub. Co., (CCA 2), 193 Fed 991, aff'g 185 Fed 941.

Proof of actual damage is not necessary for the issuance of an injunction if infringement appears and damage may follow from its continuance. Macmillan Co. v. King, (DC-Mass), 223 Fed 862.

Proof of actual damage is not necessary for the issuance of an injunction if infringement appears and damage may probably follow from its continuance. Macmillan Co. v. King, (DC-Mass), 223 Fed 862; Henry Holt & Co., Inc. v. Liggett & Myers Tobacco Co., (DC-Pa), 23 FSupp 302, 37 USPQ 449.

Bill prays for injunction restraining copyright infringement; there is no evidence of threatened continuation of infringement but threat may be inferred from evidence and injunction is granted. Eliot v. Geare-Marston, Inc., (DC-Pa), 30 FSupp 301, 43 USPQ 249.

18. —Preliminary injunction.

A preliminary injunction will not be granted when there is nothing to show which parts of a Bible were claimed to have been copyrighted. Flint v. Jones, (CC-Pa), FedCas 4,872.

Although plaintiff shows a copyright of a book, and a copy of a book having the same title, and that defendant is publishing a book containing extracts from it, a preliminary injunction will not be granted when the plaintiff has not shown that such copy as shown, is a copy of the copyrighted book. Humphreys' Homeopathic Medicine Co. v. Armstrong, (CC-NY), 30 Fed 66.

An appeal from an order denying a motion to dissolve a preliminary injunction will be dismissed, when evidence of a repetition of errors was produced at the trial. Chicago Dollar Directory Co. v. Chicago Directory Co., (CCA 7), 66 Fed 977.

Duplication of erroneous names and addresses disclosed by the moving papers presents a prima facie case, and when the explanation given in the answering affidavits does not fairly meet the charge, a preliminary injunction will be granted. Chicago Directory Co. v. U. S. Directory Co., (CC-NY), 122 Fed 189; Trow Directory Printing & Bookbinding Co. v. U. S. Directory Co., (CC-NY), 122 Fed 191.

Defendants' unsatisfactory explanation of reproduction of errors occurring in plaintiffs' book and failure to present a copy of its book to the court entitled plaintiffs to a preliminary injunction. Trow Directory Printing & Bookbinding Co. v. U. S. Directory Co., (CC-NY), 122 Fed 191.

Where two plays use the same device that is common property, and in analyzing the details of such device the points of essential difference outnumber the points of similarity, a preliminary injunction will not be granted. Hubges v. Belasco, (CC-NY), 130 Fed 388.

Where there is no doubt of infringement and no defense rendering it inequitable to grant the relief prayed for, a preliminary injunction will be granted. Encyclopaedia Britannica Co. v. American Newspaper Ass'n, (CC-NJ), 130 Fed 460. Aff'd 134 Fed 831.

Where the same errors, admissions, and similarity of language occur in the alleged infringing work as in the original work, the complainant is entitled to a preliminary injunction. George T. Bisel Co. v. Welsh, (CC-Pa), 131 Fed 564.

The burden of proof is on complainant and unless it is established by clear proof that defendant is violating his rights, a court cannot grant a preliminary injunction. American Mutoscope & Biograph Co. v. Edison Mfg. Co., (CC-NJ), 137 Fed 262.

Facts showed no clear right in plaintiff to a preliminary injunction. Sweet v. G. W. Bromley & Co., (CC-Pa), 154 Fed 754.

A preliminary injunction should only be granted on a perfectly clear case. Savage v. Hoffmann, (CC-NY), 159 Fed 584.

Evidence of an abandonment of the words of a song, although there is no proof that the abandonment was authorized by the composer, may be taken into consideration by the court on a motion for preliminary injunction. Savage v. Hoffmann, (CC-NY), 159 Fed 584.

If, on motion for preliminary injunction, it is impossible to determine that one work is an infringement of the original, or that the copyright of the original is valid, the injunction will not issue. Nixon v. Doran, (CC-NY), 168 Fed 575.

Evidence showing that the same errors appeared in the infringing work as in the original work is sufficient for the extending of a preliminary injunction until final hearing. George T. Bisel Co. v. Bender, (CC-NY), 190 Fed 205.

Preliminary injunction was denied where it was not clearly established that the pirated "gags" were original with complainant, or that any serious damage would result to him. Hoffman v. Le Traunik, (DC-NY), 209 Fed 375.

Where plaintiff's title to right in copyrighted work is denied in the answer, and plaintiff does not introduce new evidence to prove title, a preliminary injunction will not be granted. Ginn v. Apollo Pub. Co., (DC-Pa), 209 Fed 713.

Where two songs, though different in character and theme, have the same words, "I hear you calling me," and where these words are the impressive part of the song, and the music accompanying these words is similar in both songs, a temporary injunction will be granted when it appears that the defendant may not be financially able to pay damages. Boosey v. Empire Music Co., Inc., (DC-NY), 224 Fed 646.

Proof was sufficient to warrant issuance of a preliminary injunction for infringement of copyright of a musical composition. McCarthy & Fischer, Inc. v. White, (DC-NY), 259 Fed 364.

Where the plaintiff has made a prima facie case in regard to the existence of copyright and infringement, a temporary injunction will, as a general rule, be issued. American Code Co., Inc. v. Bensinger, (CCA 2), 282 Fed 829.

To warrant a preliminary injunction the complainant must make a clear and convincing showing of infringement, and not merely scattered and incidental resemblance between the two works. Simonton v. Gordon, (DC-NY), 297 Fed 625.

If plaintiff makes a prima facie showing of his right, a preliminary injunction should issue. Houghton Mifflin Co. v. Stackpole Sons, Inc., (CCA 2), 104 F(2d) 306, 42 USPQ 96, rev'g 41 USPQ 404.

Plaintiffs sell for 10 cents within ball park copyrighted score card containing news items, baseball statistics and rules, editorials, and line-ups, and numbers of players; defendant's score card sold at 5 cents outside of the park contains line-ups and numbers of players; defendant contends that it does not infringe copyrighted card and is not unfairly competing since names and numbers of players are public information; preliminary injunction is denied as court is not satisfied that infringement of copyright or unfair competition has been shown so clearly and certainly as to warrant preliminary injunction. Penn Sportservice, Inc. v. Goldstein, (DC-Pa), 33 FSupp 944, 45 USPQ 706.

Issuance of temporary injunction is most drastic remedy and should not be exercised by court unless right to such relief is clear. Harris v. Twentieth Century-Fox Film Corp., (DC-NY), 35 FSupp 153, 47 USPQ 11.

Where there is evidence of extensive copying of plaintiff's copyrighted directories by defendant, there is sufficient proof of infringement to warrant granting of injunction pendente lite. Chain Store Business Guide, Inc. v. Wexler, (DC-NY), 79 FSupp 726, 77 USPQ 656.

Injunction pendente lite against publication of manuscript is denied where facts are in dispute, prospective publisher has agreed not to publish without plaintiff's consent, and it is unlikely that any other publisher would undertake publication before dispute as to ownership is terminated. Leland v. Morin, (DC-NY), 104 FSupp 401, 93 USPQ 258.

Plaintiff's proof of exclusive right to dramatize "Sherlock Holmes" was insufficient to warrant issuance of a preliminary injunction against defendant's use of such character in a motion-picture play. Gillette v. Stoll Film Co., Ltd., 120 Misc 850, 200 NYS 787.

In determining plaintiff's motion for temporary injunction against defendants' use of "Invasion" in "March of Time, Invasion" as motion-picture title, paramount issue is whether use of title creates confusion with plaintiff's copyrighted motion picture "Invasion" to plaintiff's detriment; injunction is refused where plaintiff's film is six reel feature film and defendants' is two reel newsreel short; films are not shown in same type of theaters; fact issues can be determined on speedy trial; temporary injunction would greatly damage defendants but refusal will not greatly damage plaintiff; it is no defense that defendants would not have used title if they had known of plaintiff's use but it is considered since defendant's title cannot be changed, distribution having taken place. Adventure Films, Inc. v. Twentieth Century-Fox Film Corp., (Misc), 59 USPQ 76.

19. Decree.

Where there is lack of positive evidence that the infringement will cause irreparable injury, the court may grant a conditional injunction. Ladd v. Oxnard, (CC-Mass), 75 Fed 703.

A decree awarding a preliminary injunction and accounting which is still pending, is not a final decree and conclusive of the infringement of the copyright, and cannot be admitted as evidence in a later case involving the same persons and the same facts. Hills & Co., Ltd. v. Hoover, (CC-Pa), 142 Fed 904.

In cases where an injunction, if ordered, would necessarily in its form be argumentative and inspecific, the court will not grant such order. Sweet v. G. W. Bromley & Co., (CC-Pa), 154 Fed 754.

Copying of 18 cuts from complainant's catalogue into defendant's was sufficient to justify granting of an injunction limited to the 18 cuts copied. Da Prato Statuary Co. v. Giuliani Statuary Co., (CC-Minn), 189 Fed 90.

Although defendants do not infringe copyright or unfairly compete by using plaintiff's indices and charts solely to secure clues, they are enjoined from so doing since they have infringed by copying portions of charts and exception to injunction would make it in practice unenforceable in view of defendants' prior record of infringement. Triangle Publications, Inc. v. New England Newspaper Pub. Co., (DC-Mass), 46 FSupp 198, 54 USPQ 171.

20. —Extent of injunction—Operation and effect.

If the infringing parts of a book cannot be separated from the original parts, publication of the whole may be enjoined. Lawrence v. Dana, (CC-Mass), FedCas 8,136, 4 Cliff 1; Farmers v. Elstner, (CC-Mich), 33 Fed 494; Williams v. Smythe, (CC-Pa), 110 Fed 961; Social Register Assn. v. Murphy, (CC-RI), 128 Fed 116; Dam v. Kirke La Shelle Co., (CC-NY), 166 Fed 589. Aff'd 175 Fed 902, 41 LRA(NS) 1002, 20 Ann Cas 1173; Park & Pollard Co. v. Kellerstrass, (CC-Mo), 181 Fed 431; Investment Service Co. v. Fitch Pub. Co., (CCA 7), 291 Fed 1010.

The injunction should not extend to those distinct parts of the book which are not affected by complainant's copyrights. Story v. Holcombe, (CC-Ohio), FedCas 13,497, 4 McLean 306; Webb v. Powers, (CC-Mass), FedCas 17,-323, 2 Woodb&M 497; List Pub. Co. v. Keller, (CC-NY), 30 Fed 772; Farmer v. Elstner, (CC-Mich), 33 Fed 494; Social Register Assn. v. Murphy, (CC-RI), 128 Fed 116; Sampson & Murdock Co. v. Seaver-Radford Co., (CCA 1), 140 Fed 539, rev'g 134 Fed 890; Historical Pub. Co. v. Jones Bros. Pub. Co., (CCA 3), 231 Fed 638.

If a copyrighted work is infringed, but only a part of the new work actually infringes upon the copyright of the original, an injunction may issue only against that part. Story v. Holcombe, (CC-Ohio), FedCas 13,497, 4 McLean 306; List Pub. Co. v. Keller, (CC-NY), 30 Fed 772.

Where, by misconduct of defendant's employees, a part of complainant's copyrighted work has been appropriated by defendant and so mingled with original matter in the publication, that no one except defendant's employees can segregate the pirated from original matter, and they do not make the segregation, the whole work should be enjoined. West Pub. Co. v. Lawyers' Co-operative Pub. Co., (CCA 2), 79 Fed 756, 35 LRA 400, rev'g 64 Fed 360, 25 LRA 441.

Where the objectionable parts of a play are seemingly inseparable from the theme of the play, the play as a whole must be enjoined, but if it can be revamped to eliminate the objectionable imitations the injunction will simply cover objectionable portions. Dam v. Kirke La Shelle Co., (CC-NY), 166 Fed 589. Aff'd 175 Fed 902, 41 LRA(NS) 1002, 20 AnnCas 1173.

Preliminary injunction will be granted where pirated matter is so interwoven in the same book that defendant cannot use what is his own without using that which is not; and the court will not assume the task of separating what is proper from the improper, but after defendant has made the separation he may have modification of the decree. Park & Pollard Co. v. Kellerstrass, (CC-Mo), 181 Fed 431.

Although only 18 cuts were copied from complainant's catalogue of 2,813 cuts, and printed in defendant's catalogue of 393 cuts, it is sufficient to justify the granting of an injunction, as to the 18 cuts. Da Prato Statuary Co. v. Giuliani Statuary Co., (CC-Minn), 189 Fed 90.

Where a motion picture is found to infringe upon a copyright, its exhibition will be restrained only until the events, incidents, and situations that infringe are eliminated. International Film Service Co., Inc. v. Affiliated Distributors, Inc., (DC-NY), 283 Fed 229.

Where an injunction is awarded in favor of plaintiff, defendant will be permitted to show that certain parts of his published works do not constitute infringement in order that they may be exempted from the restraining order. W. H. Anderson Co. v. Baldwin Law Pub. Co., (CCA 6), 27 F(2d) 82.

Defendant was permitted to publish catalogues with infringing cuts eliminated. Kaeser & Blair, Inc. v. Merchants Ass'n, (CCA 6), 64 F(2d) 575.

Defendant infringed copyrighted telephone directories published periodically by publishing directories copied from telephone directories; defendant is permanently enjoined from infringing plaintiff's copyrights in any and all directories published by plaintiff in course of its business, for which it holds or may hereafter hold a copyright, whether said directories have been heretofore published or shall, in the future, be published, and whether copyright thereto has been heretofore granted, or shall, in the future, be granted, and from otherwise interfering with plaintiff's business by printing, publishing, and selling any directories containing names of plaintiff's subscribers, or containing telephone numbers or addresses of subscribers, information for which has been obtained from any directory of plaintiff to which plaintiff has acquired, or in future may acquire, a copyright. Southern Bell Telephone & Telegraph Co. v. Donnelly, (DC-Fla), 35 FSupp 425, 48 USPQ 11.

Neither past infringement of copyright on motion-picture films, nor mere prayer for injunction and for discovery as to past infringements, is in itself sufficient to justify present issuance of injunction against defendant from infringement of any other films, whether now or hereafter to be copyrighted by plaintiff and subsequently furnished to defendant under contractual arrangements for exhibition. Universal Pictures Corp. v. Marsh, (DC-WVa), 36 FSupp 241, 48 USPQ 319.

21. —Dissolution or modification.

Where a preliminary injunction has been issued in a suit for infringement of copyright, the court, in the absence of any pretense of fraud or mistake, will not, upon motion to dissolve the order, consider any questions arising upon the complainant's right to bring suit. Farmer v. Calvert Lithographing, Etc., Co., (CC-Mich), FedCas 4,651, 1 Flip 228.

Denials and allegations affecting a complainant's copyright title made merely on information and belief was insufficient to entitle defendant to a dissolution of an injunction. Farmer v. Calvert Lithographing, Etc., Co., (CC-Mich), FedCas 4,651, 1 Flip 228.

Defendant was not entitled to damages suffered by reason of an injunction which prevented him from selling his song, where such order was later discharged on ground that the copyright on the original song was invalid. Broder v. Zeno Mauvais Music Co., (CC-Cal), 88 Fed 74.

Where a court cannot separate the parts of a directory that are free from the charge of piracy and those that are not, the whole book will be enjoined, but if defendant can sever the parts and eliminate the pirated matter he may be entitled to a modification of the restraining order. Williams v. Smythe, (CC-Pa), 110 Fed 961.

The granting of a preliminary injunction is a matter resting in the sound discretion of the trial court, and an order granting it will not be set aside on appeal, unless it is clearly shown that the court abused its discretion. American Code Co., Inc. v. Bensinger, (CCA 2), 282 Fed 829.

22. Contempt.

Defendants had not become liable for contempt by using names found in a city directory to aid in forming their architects' directory. Colliery Engineer Co. v. Ewald, (CC-NY), 126 Fed 843.

Circumstances surrounding sales of books against which an injunctive order was in effect did not warrant an adjudication that defendant was guilty of contempt. Encyclopaedia Britannica Co. v. American Newspaper Ass'n, (CC-NJ), 130 Fed 493.

113. Transmission of certified copies of papers for enforcement of injunction by other court.—The clerk of the court, or judge granting the injunction, shall, when required so to do by the court hearing the application to enforce said injunction, transmit without delay to said court a certified copy of all the papers in said cause that are on file in his office. (July 30, 1947, c. 391, § 1, 61 Stat. 664.)

114. Review of orders, judgments, or decrees.—The orders, judgments, or decrees of any court mentioned in section 1338 of Title 28 arising under the copyright laws of the United States may be reviewed on appeal in the manner and to the extent now provided by law for the review of cases determined in said courts, respectively. (July 30, 1947, c. 391, § 1 [114], 61 Stat. 665; Oct. 31, 1951, c. 655, § 17, 65 Stat. 717.)

Amendment note.—Act Oct. 31, 1951, cited to text, substituted "1338 of Title 28" for "110 of this title."

NOTES TO DECISIONS
ANALYSIS

1. In general.
2. Matters appealable.
3. Review on appeal.
4. —Injunctions.
5. —Damages.
6. —Costs and attorney's fees.

1. In general.

Admission of a copyrighted photograph in evidence, though it is irrelevant testimony, is not error, where it does not operate to prejudice the defendant. Springer Lithographing Co. v. Falk, (CCA 2), 59 Fed 707.

On appeal from interlocutory decree taken after thirty days, court of appeals held that plaintiff was not author of copyrighted song;

Supreme Court on certiorari held that appeal was too late and reversed with directions to dismiss appeal; accounting was concluded and final decree entered by plaintiff; on appeal therefrom, court of appeals adhered to its previous opinion. Victor Talking Mach. Co. v. George, (CCA 3), 105 F(2d) 697, 42 USPQ 346, rev'g 38 USPQ 222.

Judgment that licensee's publication of copyrighted pictures was within license should be affirmed if evidence supports finding. Swift v. Collegian Press, Inc., (CCA 2), 131 F(2d) 900, 55 USPQ 472.

Nothing short of conviction that finding that composer created song at specific time was clearly erroneous will suffice for reversal of finding. Baron v. Leo Feist, Inc., (CA 2), 173 F(2d) 288, 80 USPQ 535, aff'g 78 FSupp 686, 78 USPQ 41.

Counsel for defendants must prepare and submit findings of ultimate facts and simple conclusions of law, not details of facts; plaintiff may, within five days, submit and serve his criticisms; only findings and conclusions signed by court will be filed as part of record; counterfinding by plaintiff will not avail him anything; he must take objections to findings by way of appropriate assignments of error on appeal. Arnstein v. American Soc. of Composers, Authors & Publishers, (DC-NY), 29 FSupp 388, 42 USPQ 581.

Decisions of courts of appeals reversing district court on finding of literary piracy in equity cases have no value in state appellate court on appeal from judgment on jury's verdict. Golding v. RKO Radio Pictures, Inc., (CalApp(2d series)), 193 Pac(2d) 153, 77 US PQ 415. Aff'd (Cal(2d series)), 208 Pac(2d) 1, 82 USPQ 136, which was aff'd 35 Cal(2d series) 690, 221 Pac(2d) 95, 86 USPQ 537.

2. Matters appealable.

Plaintiff may appeal if an injunction be refused or dissolved by an interlocutory order or decree. Historical Pub. Co. v. Jones Bros. Pub. Co., (CCA 3), 231 Fed 638.

Order making award to attorney of defendants was appealable though in discretion of trial court. Cohan v. Richmond, (CCA 2), 86 F(2d) 680, 32 USPQ 298.

In equitable action for infringement of copyrighted moving picture, where trial judge, recognizing the nonexistence of actual or threatened continued infringement, correctly denied an injunction, but inadvertently included an injunction in an interlocutory decree, an appeal from that part of the decree was properly taken. Sheldon v. Moredall Realty Corp., (CCA 2), 95 F(2d) 48, 37 USPQ 286, mod'g 22 FSupp 91, 37 USPQ 254.

Hurn v. Oursler, 289 US 238, 77 LEd 1148, 53 SCR 586, held that claims for copyright infringement and for unfair competition are regarded as part of single cause of action, but it is limited to case where bounds between state and federal jurisdiction were being settled; in present case claims for copyright infringement and for unfair competition could properly be disposed of separately, and order dismissing copyright claim was final judgment and sep-

arately appealable. Collins v. Metro-Goldwyn Pictures Corp., (CCA 2), 106 F(2d) 83, 42 USPQ 553, rev'g 25 FSupp 781, 39 USPQ 520.

Final determinations of separate controversies involved in single suit are appealable, such as where claims for infringement of separate patents were asserted in single suit. Collins v. Metro-Goldwyn Pictures Corp., (CCA 2), 106 F(2d) 83, 42 USPQ 553, rev'g 25 FSupp 781, 39 USPQ 520.

3. Review on appeal.

Appeal from order finally fixing award to attorney for defendant properly included order dismissing bill of plaintiff and order of reference, though such orders were not appealable. Cohan v. Richmond, (CCA 2), 86 F(2d) 680, 32 USPQ 298.

Where invalidity of copyright was not raised in lower court, and ownership was admitted by stipulation, it was too late to raise questions on appeal. Johns & Johns Printing Co. v. Paull-Pioneer Music Corp., (CCA 8), 102 F(2d) 282, 41 USPQ 3.

Court of appeals finds it unnecessary to decide one question on which district court decided case because decision may be supported on alternative ground discussed in opinion of district judge. Yardley v. Houghton Mifflin Co., Inc., (CCA 2), 108 F(2d) 28, 44 USPQ 1, aff'g 25 FSupp 361, 40 USPQ 234.

Court of appeals is asked to disregard finding of noninfringement of copyright because, from what district judge said at trial, he seems to have supposed that anticipation invalidates a copyright; court is not sure that he meant this but, if he did, cannot assume that he did not intend to make finding on which court relies; if plaintiff had wished to rid himself of that handicap, he should have done so before he appealed; while it stands, it is fatal to his success. Darrell v. Joe Morris Music Co., Inc., (CCA 2), 113 F(2d) 80, 46 USPQ 167, aff'g 37 USPQ 446.

On appeal from grant of summary judgment for plaintiff, only question is whether there is any issue, relevant to merits of case, which deserved trial, where court of appeals on previous appeal had passed on rights of parties in affirming issuance of temporary injunction. Houghton Mifflin Co. v. Stackpole Sons, Inc., (CCA 2), 113 F(2d) 627, 46 USPQ 296, mod'g 31 FSupp 517, 44 USPQ 668.

On prior appeal from dismissal of bill for failure to state facts sufficient to constitute cause of action, court of appeals reversed and remanded for further proceedings; case was tried before district court which found no infringement of plaintiff's common-law copyright; issue of infringement was not before court of appeals on first appeal and was not there decided; issue was before district court at trial of case and court of appeals affirmed since issue was properly decided. Dezendorf v. Twentieth Century-Fox Film Corp., (CCA 9), 118 F(2d) 561, 49 USPQ 133, aff'g 32 FSupp 359, 44 USPQ 421.

Where plaintiff failed to prove access either directly or indirectly, court of appeals will not disturb judgment based on failure to prove copyright infringement. Sarkadi v. Wiman, (CCA 2), 135 F(2d) 1002, 57 USPQ 361, aff'g 43 FSupp 778, 52 USPQ 323.

Appellate court must consider that trial judge was in more advantageous position to determine credibility of witnesses and that he had better position to weigh effect of evidence that defendant's agent saw plaintiff's play. Twentieth Century-Fox Film Corp. v. Stonesifer, (CCA 9), 140 F(2d) 579, 60 USPQ 392, aff'g 48 FSupp 196, 56 USPQ 94.

Although interlocutory judgment for plaintiff was granted before copyright was held unoriginal and anticipated in suit against another defendant, appellate court could not retry case on different basis than it was tried in trial court. Colonial Book Co., Inc. v. Amsco School Publications, Inc., (CCA 2), 142 F(2d) 362, 61 USPQ 391, aff'g 48 FSupp 794, 56 USPQ 265, and 57 USPQ 36.

Rule that fact finding may be set aside only when clearly erroneous is as applicable to action for copyright infringement as to any other action. Sawyer v. Crowell Pub. Co., (CCA 2), 142 F(2d) 497, 61 USPQ 389, aff'g 46 FSupp 471, 54 USPQ 225.

Appellate court does not weigh evidence to determine its preponderance. Jerry Vogel Music Co., Inc. v. Forster Music Publisher, Inc., (CCA 2), 147 F(2d) 614, 64 USPQ 417, aff'g 62 USPQ 142.

Appellant's brief did not discuss ownership of 1914 renewal copyright, so appellate court did not discuss it; discussion is refused on motion to clarify opinion, but it does not follow that district court's ruling thereon was left undisturbed and must be incorporated in judgment on mandate; appellate court reversed and remanded "for entry of a judgment consistent with this opinion"; this permits district judge to enter any judgment which he thinks consistent with opinion; he may consider whether principles enunciated with respect to 1912 renewal copyright are applicable to 1914 version. Shapiro, Bernstein & Co., Inc. v. Jerry Vogel Music Co., Inc., (CCA 2), 161 F(2d) 406, 73 USPQ 5.

Court need not consider whether specific reasons assigned by trial judge for rejecting testimony are unsound since another reason given was sound, and it is enough that he gave sound reason. Broadcast Music, Inc. v. Havana Madrid Restaurant Corp., (CA 2), 175 F(2d) 77, 81 USPQ 506.

District judge is not obliged to accept as true oral testimony of witness as to performance of copyrighted music which is uncontradicted, unimpeached by anything in record, and not inherently improbable; findings rejecting testimony are not clearly erroneous; judge's estimate of orally-testifying witness may stem from judge's application of absurd rule-of-thumb, but appellate court cannot correct error unless judge reveals of record that he used irrational test of credibility. Broadcast Music, Inc. v. Havana Madrid Restaurant Corp., (CA 2), 175 F(2d) 77, 81 USPQ 506.

Even if "uncontradicted testimony" rule applies in federal courts, it does not apply in case where witness is employee of one plaintiff and was requested by other plaintiff to act as detective in obtaining evidence as to which he testified; witness has "interest," although fact that he is ordinary employee may not be enough to show interest if testimony were completely corroborated by undisputed facts. Broadcast Music, Inc. v. Havana Madrid Restaurant Corp., (CA 2), 175 F(2d) 77, 81 USPQ 506.

United States v. U. S. Gypsum Co., 333 US 364, 92 LEd 746, 68 SCR 525, 76 USPQ 430, teaches that findings of trial judge may have somewhat less significance than that of jury or that of some administrative agencies, and that trial judge's finding may be clearly erroneous, although apparently supported by oral testimony, where testimony is in conflict with contemporaneous documents of such character that it would be unreasonable to believe witnesses. Broadcast Music, Inc. v. Havana Madrid Restaurant Corp., (CA 2), 175 F(2d) 77, 81 USPQ 506.

Plaintiff having given evidence of access and similarity which court credited over contrary evidence, presumption of copying could reasonably be inferred; despite fact that burden of proving plagiarism remains at all times on plaintiff, defendant then had duty to go forward by offering evidence of prior composition, which, if believed, would make finding of copying untenable; trial court weighed such evidence and concluded that defendant's work was composed prior to plaintiff's; since finding involved credibility of witnesses, and since it is supported by substantial evidence, it is conclusive on appeal. Overman v. Loesser, (CA 9), 205 F(2d) 521, 98 USPQ 177.

It is of little moment in copyright infringement action whether court should first determine originality of copyrighted work or its appropriation by defendant since, for purposes of appellate review, it is desirable that both questions be considered. Trailins v. Kaiser Aluminum & Chemical Corp., (DC-Md), 160 FSupp 511, 117 USPQ 79.

4. —Injunctions.

An order for a preliminary injunction will not be set aside on appeal unless it appear that there has been an abuse of discretion, or that the court below was mistaken in its view of the situation. Werner v. Encyclopaedia Britannica Co., (CCA 3), 134 Fed 831, aff'g 130 Fed 460.

The general rule, applicable to an interlocutory decree in an action for copyright infringement, is that the propriety of the granting of other relief than an injunction forms no part of the subject matter of the appeal and is not before the court of appeals, not being a final decision. Sheldon v. Moredall Realty Corp., (CCA 2), 95 F(2d) 48, 37 USPQ 286, mod'g 22 FSupp 91, 37 USPQ 254.

While appeal may be taken from interlocutory decree of injunction a party may await final determination of case and upon appeal therefrom raise all questions involved in case; all interlocutory orders and decrees from which no appeal has been taken are merged in final decree. Victor Talking Mach. Co. v. George,

(CCA 3), 105 F(2d) 697, 42 USPQ 346, rev'g 38 USPQ 222.

Reference to master to ascertain damages for copyright infringement and report back renders judgment interlocutory; hence, only propriety of temporary injunction can be considered on appeal. Reeve Music Co., Inc. v. Crest Records, Inc., (CA 2), 285 F(2d) 546, 128 USPQ 24, mod'g 190 FSupp 272, 128 USPQ 37.

5. —Damages.

An appellate court cannot review the action of a trial judge in assessing an amount in lieu of actual damages, where the amount awarded is within the limits imposed by § 101 of this title. Douglas v. Cunningham, 294 US 207, 79 LEd 862, 55 SCR 365, 24 USPQ 153, rev'g (CCA 1), 72 F(2d) 536, 22 USPQ 320.

Supreme Court does not disturb deductions allowed by court of appeals in computing net profits in copyright infringement case where questions of fact, which have been determined by court below on the evidence, are involved. Sheldon v. Metro-Goldwyn Pictures Corp., 309 US 390, 84 LEd 825, 60 SCR 681, 44 USPQ 607, aff'g (CCA 2), 106 F(2d) 45, 42 USPQ 540, which rev'd 26 FSupp 134, 40 USPQ 238.

Where damages awarded were within limit for one infringement and there was no denial of at least one infringement, it was not necessary to decide whether there was more than one infringement. Cory v. Physical Culture Hotel, (CCA 2), 88 F(2d) 411, 33 USPQ 58, aff'g 14 FSupp 977, 30 USPQ 353, and 14 FSupp 986, 30 USPQ 360.

Where no proof of actual damages was offered or received on trial and court made no finding on subject, the discretion of trial court in assessing statutory damages instead of actual damages for copyright infringement is not reviewable on appeal. Johns & Johns Printing Co. v. Paull-Pioneer Music Corp., (CCA 8), 102 F(2d) 282, 41 USPQ 3.

6. —Costs and attorney's fees.

The allowance of counsel fees is a matter peculiarly within the discretion of the court awarding same, and cannot be reviewed unless an abuse of discretion is shown. S. E. Hendricks Co., Inc. v. Thomas Pub. Co., (CCA 2), 242 Fed 37.

On reversal of district court's judgment for defendant in copyright infringement suit, case is remanded to district court for appropriate action as to injunction, damages, and accounting and court of appeals states that any issues concerning attorney's fee in either court may be settled by district court in its final judgment. College Entrance Book Co., Inc. v. Amsco Book Co., Inc., (CCA 2), 119 F(2d) 874, 49 USPQ 517, rev'g 33 FSupp 276, 45 USPQ 516.

Rule 54(d) of the Federal Rules of Civil Procedure [Rules, c. 15] appears to have adopted previous federal practice in equity, where trial court had wide discretion in fixing costs, a discretion not reviewable unless manifestly abused, especially where appeal relates solely to costs. Harris v. Twentieth Century-Fox Film Corp., (CCA 2), 139 F(2d) 571, 60 USPQ 430.

Under § 116 of this title, question of awarding attorney's fee to prevailing copyright infringement suit defendant was for discretion of trial court; appellate court affirms refusal of fee since no abuse of discretion appears. Advertisers Exchange, Inc. v. Anderson, (CCA 8), 144 F(2d) 907, 63 USPQ 39, aff'g 52 FSupp 809, 59 USPQ 391.

115. Limitations.—(a) Criminal Proceedings.—No criminal proceedings shall be maintained under the provisions of this title unless the same is commenced within three years after the cause of action arose.

(b) Civil Actions. — No civil action shall be maintained under the provisions of this title unless the same is commenced within three years after the claim accrued. (July 30, 1947, c. 391, § 1, 61 Stat. 665; Sept. 7, 1957, P. L. 85-313, § 1, 71 Stat. 633.)

Amendment note.—Act Sept. 7, 1957, cited to text, added subsec. (b).

Effective date.—Section 2 of Act Sept. 7, 1957, cited to text, provided that subsec. (b) of this section "shall take effect one year after [Sept. 7, 1957] the date of enactment of this Act and shall apply to all actions commenced on or after such effective date."

NOTES TO DECISIONS

Evidence was sufficient to warrant finding that offense was committed within two years before the beginning of action. American Lithographic Co. v. Werckmeister, (CCA 2), 165 Fed 426. Aff'd 221 US 603, 55 LEd 873, 31 SCR 676.

Prior to 1958, copyright law contained no limitation of time within which civil action could be maintained under it, but this section was amended in 1957 (effective in 1958) so that it now provides that action shall not be maintained "unless same is commenced within three years after the claim accrued"; effect of amendment evidently has been to establish bar within three-year period whether claim accrued before or after effective date of amendment; before amendment, maximum term in which author of copyrighted song could sue for infringement was governed by law of state where action was brought; amendment imposes three-year limitation in all civil actions brought under this title. Vance v. American Society of Composers, (CA 8), 271 F(2d) 204, 123 USPQ 296.

Three-year limitation of subsec. (b) of this section runs from date of last infringing act, not from date of initial infringement. Baxter v. Curtis Industries, Inc., (DC-Ohio), 201 FSupp 100, 133 USPQ 78.

116. Costs—Attorney's fees.—In all actions, suits, or proceedings under this title, except when brought by or against the United States or any officer thereof, full costs shall be allowed, and the court may award to the prevailing party a reasonable attorney's fee as part of the

costs. (July 30, 1947, c. 391, § 1, 61 Stat. 665.)

NOTES TO DECISIONS
ANALYSIS

1. Costs.
2. —Cost bond.
3. —Master's fee.
4. Attorney fees.
5. —Particular fees allowed.

1. Costs.

Right to elect to try issue of infringement before a jury was granted upon payment of ordinary taxable costs of suit already accrued. Emerson v. Davies, (CC-Mass), FedCas 4,436, 3 Story 768.

Where plaintiff, by a combination of circumstances, was led to the belief that his work had been appropriated and brought suit in good faith, though there was no infringement, costs will not be awarded against him. Vernon v. Sam S. & Lee Shubert, Inc., (DC-NY), 220 Fed 694.

In a suit for infringement involving two distinct musical compositions, where complainant prevails as to one and fails as to the other, the court does not abuse its discretion in making a division of costs. M. Witmark & Sons v. Standard Music Roll Co., (CCA 3), 221 Fed 376, aff'g 213 Fed 532.

Accounting costs are taxed against defendant whose account showed no profits since court finds and awards profits; account did not make unnecessary hearings before master. Wilkie v. Santly Bros., Inc., (CCA 2), 139 F(2d) 264, 60 USPQ 46, aff'g 36 FSupp 574, 47 USPQ 380.

Full costs are mandatory in favor of successful or prevailing party in copyright infringement suit; court has no discretion as to ordinary costs, and the fact that defendants' counterclaim for copyright infringement was dismissed does not change the situation. Official Aviation Guide Co., Inc. v. American Aviation Associates, Inc., (CCA 7), 162 F(2d) 541, 74 USPQ 45.

Defendant is not required to share cost of printing appeal record as condition of having appeal heard on joint record, but defendant is required to print at own expense papers designated by it for its cross-appeal. Jerome v. Twentieth Century-Fox Film Corp., (CCA 2), 165 F(2d) 784, 76 USPQ 246, aff'g 67 FSupp 736, 70 USPQ 349, 71 FSupp 914, 71 USPQ 49, and 7 FedRDec 190, 72 USPQ 431.

It is error for judgment dismissing copyright infringement action to provide that each party bear its own costs. Amsterdam v. Triangle Publications, Inc., (CA 3), 189 F(2d) 104, 89 USPQ 468, mod'g 93 FSupp 79, 87 USPQ 90.

Decree dismissing complaint for infringement of copyright should carry costs including reasonable counsel fee, to be fixed before costs are taxed. Shipman v. R. K. O. Radio Pictures, Inc., (DC-NY), 20 FSupp 249, 35 USPQ 242. Aff'd 100 F(2d) 533, 40 USPQ 211; Caruthers v. R. K. O. Radio Pictures, Inc., (DC-NY), 20 FSupp 906, 35 USPQ 115, 35 USPQ 542.

Although defendant prevailed it was not granted costs or counsel fee because it admitted it knowingly copied plaintiff's pictures. Basevi v. Edward O'Toole Co., Inc., (DC-NY), 26 FSupp 41, 40 USPQ 333.

Final decree will be submitted through clerk's office on usual notice, but only after costs, damages, and attorney fees are fixed so they may be included in the decree. Detective Comics, Inc. v. Bruns Publications, Inc., (DC-NY), 28 FSupp 399, 41 USPQ 182. Mf'd 111 F(2d) 432, 45 USPQ 291.

Liability for costs and attorney fees is statutory and copyright law exempts officers of United States from this liability; allowance of costs and attorney fees is discretionary with court and allowance would be made if defendants were acting as individuals, but is not made against employees of Bonneville administration even if they are not technically officers of United States. Towle v. Ross, (DC-Ore), 32 FSupp 125, 45 USPQ 143.

Prevailing defendant is refused costs since it misled plaintiff as to its interest in his plan and thus brought about litigation. Ketcham v. New York World's Fair 1939, Inc., (DC-NY), 34 FSupp 657, 46 USPQ 307. Aff'd 119 F(2d) 422, 49 USPQ 756.

This section is mandatory with respect to allowance of full costs. Kraft v. Cohen, (DC-Pa), 38 FSupp 1022, 49 USPQ 648; Vinick v. Charm Publications, Inc., (DC-NY), 46 USPQ 510.

Copyright infringers are jointly and severally liable for damages resulting from infringement, but accountability for profits, which originates in equity, is peculiarly personal, the presupposition being that infringer obtained something which it is unreasonable for him to keep; infringers are not jointly accountable, but individually accountable, for profits which each received, not being held for profits received by co-infringer; but responsibility for costs and attorneys' fees under statute is joint and several. Alfred Bell & Co., Ltd. v. Catalda Fine Arts, Inc., (DC-NY), 86 FSupp 399, 82 USPQ 273. Mf'd 191 F(2d) 99, 90 USPQ 153.

Even though copyright infringer is liable for profits of only $4199, it is not improper to make it liable, with co-infringers, jointly and severally for attorneys' fees of $7750, especially since judgment gives it right to recover from other infringers; in determining liability for attorneys' fees, court is not influenced by amount of profits each infringer gained from infringement, but by part each played in causing legal test of validity of copyrights. Alfred Bell & Co., Ltd. v. Catalda Fine Arts, Inc., (DC-NY), 86 FSupp 399, 82 USPQ 273. Mf'd 191 F(2d) 99, 90 USPQ 153.

On question of costs and attorney's fee in copyright action wherein plaintiff was successful only in part, court considers primarily who was the infringer. Shapiro Bernstein & Co., Inc. v. Jerry Vogel Music Co., Inc., (DC-NY), 115 FSupp 754, 98 USPQ 438, 99 USPQ 381. Rev'd 221 F(2d) 569, 105 USPQ 178, which was mf'd 223 F(2d) 252, 105 USPQ 460.

This section makes it mandatory for court to allow full costs to prevailing party in copyright infringement action, but award of attorney's fees as part of costs is discretionary; in instant case, considering that there was no infringement and that plaintiff's threats of possible criminal prosecution were indefensible. court awards fees to prevailing defendants. Wihtol v. Crow, (DC-Iowa), — FSupp —, 132 USPQ 392.

Defendants (authors, printers, and publishers) are jointly and severally liable for costs although no defendant is liable for damages and one defendant is not liable for profits. Washingtonian Publishing Co., Inc. v. Pearson, (DC-DC), 56 USPQ 23. Aff'd 78 AppDC 287, 140 F(2d) 465, 60 USPQ 224.

Costs, including attorney fee, are not apportioned among defendants where they are jointly and severally liable. Harris v. Miller, (DC-NY), 57 USPQ 190.

2. —Cost bond.

In copyright infringement suit, resident plaintiff complied with local rule by posting $25 cash bond and neither marshal nor clerk applied to court for further cost deposits; court has no right under this section or Federal Rules of Civil Procedure [Rules, c. 15] to require plaintiff to post $500 cost bond and to dismiss cause with prejudice with award of $150 attorney fee to defendant on plaintiff's failure to post such bond. Williams v. Hodge, (CCA 6), 119 F(2d) 394, 49 USPQ 687.

In copyright suit plaintiff if unsuccessful is chargeable with costs and, within discretion of court, may be required to pay attorney fee of defendant; therefore, on motion, plaintiff is required to post bond to cover costs and fee. Williams v. Hodge, (DC-Tenn), 44 USPQ 25.

3. —Master's fee.

Reference made necessary by defendants could not be charged to plaintiff. Cohan v. Richmond, (CCA 2), 36 F(2d) 680, 32 USPQ 298.

Plaintiff was not required to bear half of master's compensation where it did not unnecessarily prolong suit. Burndy Engineering Co., Inc. v. Sheldon Service Corp., (CCA 2), 127 F(2d) 661, 53 USPQ 409, aff'g 39 FSupp 274, 50 USPQ 24.

Fee of $1000 was allowed for special master fixing recovery. Sheldon v. Moredall Realty Corp., (DC-NY), 29 FSupp 729, 43 USPQ 81.

Court in copyright infringement case referred to master for accounting considers master's petition for allowance of $1825, considers time spent by master, as well as nature and extent of his report, and finds that $1000 is fair and reasonable fee, which is allowed together with disbursements. Wilkie v. Santly Bros., Inc., (DC-NY), 36 FSupp 574, 47 USPQ 380. Aff'd 139 F(2d) 264, 60 USPQ 46.

Fee of $800 was allowed master for services on accounting. Jones Brothers Co. v. Underkoffler, (DC-Pa), 35 USPQ 448.

4. Attorney fees.

Complainant was entitled to attorney fee although infringement was shown to have been innocently done. Strauss v. Penn Printing & Publishing Co., (DC-Pa), 220 Fed 977.

Where defendant contests the right of plaintiff to a preliminary injunction and to recover on final hearing, and a motion to dismiss the bill is made on its behalf, and there is a decree for complainant, the latter's counsel is entitled to a reasonable fee to be taxed as part of the costs. F. A. Mills, Inc. v. Standard Music Roll Co., (DC-NJ), 223 Fed 849. Aff'd 241 Fed 360.

An assessment of attorney fees against several defendants did not apply to one of the defendants who had infringed innocently. Grass v. Van Dyk Gravure Co., (CCA 2), 230 Fed 412.

Although plaintiff has suffered no injury, the court must, upon proof of infringement, in addition to minimum damages, award plaintiff a full bill of costs, but may make no allowance for counsel fees since that is discretionary. Haas v. Leo Feist, Inc., (DC-NY), 234 Fed 105; Fisher v. Dillingham, (DC-NY), 298 Fed 145.

Provision for attorney fee is discretionary, but that for costs is mandatory. M. Witmark & Sons v. Pastime Amusement Co., (DC-SC), 298 Fed 470. Aff'd 2 F(2d) 1020.

Plaintiff was entitled to attorney fees in addition to minimum damages. Cravens v. Retail Credit Men's Ass'n, (DC-Tenn), 26 F(2d) 833.

The amount of attorney fees depends on the amount involved, the service rendered, and the skill required. Lewys v. O'Neill, (DC-NY), 49 F(2d) 603, 9 USPQ 465.

The award of attorney fee is discretionary, and denial of fee where infringement ceased immediately when first notice was given is not abuse of discretion. Buck v. Bilkie, (CCA 9), 63 F(2d) 447, 16 USPQ 382.

On an appeal from a decree dismissing the bill, plaintiffs on obtaining an injunction were entitled to attorney fees in both the district and the appellate courts. Sheldon v. Metro-Goldwyn Pictures Corp., (CCA 2), 81 F(2d) 49, 28 USPQ 330, rev'g 7 FSupp 837.

An allowance to defendants' attorney was proper after plaintiff's bill had been dismissed. Cohan v. Richmond, (CCA 2), 86 F(2d) 680, 32 USPQ 298.

Defendants who delayed for three years before making motion to dismiss, which was granted, could charge plaintiff only with necessary services of their attorney on the motion and on getting his allowance. Cohan v. Richmond, (CCA 2), 86 F(2d) 680, 32 USPQ 298.

Where defendants were successful on appeal but plaintiffs prevailed generally no attorney fees for the appeal were allowed. Sheldon v. Metro-Goldwyn Pictures Corp., (CCA 2), 106 F(2d) 45, 42 USPQ 540, rev'g 26 FSupp 134, 40 USPQ 238. Aff'd 309 US 390, 84 LEd 825, 60 SCR 681, 44 USPQ 607.

Court may award attorney fees to defendants on plaintiff's voluntary dismissal without prejudice where defendant has been put to expense of making appearance and of obtaining order for clarification of complaint, and plaintiff then voluntarily dismisses without amending his pleading, party sued is prevailing party within spirit and intent of statute even though he may again be sued on same cause of action. Corcoran v. Columbia Broadcasting System, Inc.,

(CCA 9), 121 F(2d) 575, 50 USPQ 277, aff'g 32 FSupp 421, 45 USPQ 115.

Attorney fees are refused to prevailing party on appeal in copyright infringement case where case was hard fought, principal question presented was complex question of law, and appeal was not pursued in bad faith. Official Aviation Guide Co., Inc. v. American Aviation Associates, Inc., (CCA 7), 162 F(2d) 541, 74 USPQ 45; Overman v. Loesser, (CA 9), 205 F(2d) 521, 98 USPQ 177.

Allowance of attorney fee is usually appropriate where copyright proprietor recovers for infringement, but fee is denied where prevailing proprietor attempted to inflate and exaggerate claims under "in lieu" provision of subsec. (b) of this section; "in lieu" provision is not to accomplish imposition of a penalty, but is equitable substitute for cases which present difficulty or impossibility of proof as to damages and profits. Advertisers Exchange, Inc. v. Hinkley, (CA 8), 199 F(2d) 313, 95 USPQ 124, aff'g 101 FSupp 801, 92 USPQ 313.

Although in copyright cases court of appeals has discretionary power to allow attorney fees for services in prosecuting appeal, unsuccessful plaintiff should not thus be penalized where litigation was not vexatious but involved novel question of statutory interpretation. Edward B. Marks Music Corp. v. Continental Record Co., Inc., (CA 2), 222 F(2d) 488, 105 USPQ 171. 105 USPQ 350, aff'g 120 FSupp 275, 100 USPQ 438.

Losing plaintiff in copyright infringement action is not assessed attorney fees where close question as to infringement was involved. Eisenschiml v. Fawcett Publications, Inc., (CA 7), 246 F(2d) 598, 114 USPQ 199.

Court is well within its discretion in not awarding attorney fees to alleged infringer despite holding that copyright is not infringed and was forfeited for publication without statutory notice. Continental Casualty Co. v. Beardsley, (CA 2), 253 F(2d) 702, 117 USPQ 1, mod'g 151 FSupp 28, 113 USPQ 181.

In copyright infringement action wherein attorney fees were allowed by district court, court of appeals makes additional allowance to plaintiffs, for services of counsel on appeal, in view of deliberate nature of infringement and lack of substance to defendants' contention on appeal. Boucher v. Du Boyes, Inc., (CA 2), 253 F(2d) 948, 117 USPQ 156.

Award of counsel fee is discretionary and none is made where court is forced to award statutory damages larger than he would have awarded if he had full discretion. Lindsay & Brewster, Inc. v. Verstein, (DC-Maine), 21 FSupp 264, 35 USPQ 494.

Where defendant prevailed in copyright infringement suit tried before master, all costs, including counsel fees of defendants, were taxed to plaintiff, and bond given by plaintiff on temporary injunction was held until all costs and fees were paid. Seltzer v. Sunbrock, (DC-Cal), 22 FSupp 621, 37 USPQ 491.

Costs are mandatory against unsuccessful party but counsel fees shall be recoverable in first instance from defendant publisher and only on failure to secure payment from it may plaintiff have recourse against news dealers' defendants who will be jointly and severally liable. Detective Comics, Inc. v. Bruns Publications, Inc., (DC-NY), 28 FSupp 399, 41 USPQ 182. Mf'd 111 F(2d) 432, 45 USPQ 291.

Defendant's motion to dismiss action for copyright infringement filed in good faith, having been sustained on question of law not heretofore passed on in reported decisions, attorney fees are refused defendant. Corcoran v. Montgomery Ward & Co., Inc., (DC-Cal), 32 FSupp 421, 45 USPQ 115. Aff'd 121 F(2d) 575, 50 USPQ 277; Corcoran v. Montgomery Ward & Co., (DC-Cal), 32 FSupp 422, 45 USPQ 114.

Court refuses allowance to successful defendants since they knowingly copied plaintiff's pictures and made use of them to their own profit; plaintiff's action was brought in good faith but complaint was dismissed for defective copyright notice. Kraft v. Cohen, (DC-Pa), 38 FSupp 1022, 49 USPQ 648.

Defendant, not guilty of infringement but only of fair use, was refused counsel fee where suit was well brought. American Institute of Architects v. Fenichel, (DC-NY), 41 FSupp 146, 51 USPQ 29.

No attorney fee is awarded since infringer sincerely ordered orchestra leader not to play nonlicensed American Society of Composers, Authors, and Publishers music and it is likely that the society, of which plaintiffs are members maintains attorneys on yearly salary basis. Shapiro, Bernstein & Co., Inc. v. Veltin, (DC-La), 47 FSupp 648, 55 USPQ 335.

Although complaint is dismissed since plaintiff's bookkeeping forms are uncopyrightable, defendant is refused attorneys' fee, which is within court's discretion, since plaintiff's system and forms were valuable, cost defendant nothing, and were appropriated by defendant. Aldrich v. Remington Rand, Inc., (DC-Tex), 52 FSupp 732, 59 USPQ 210.

In determining attorney fee awarded plaintiff in copyright infringement suit, master is entitled to consider generally the fee sought by defendant's counsel. Alfred Bell & Co., Ltd. v. Catalda Fine Arts, Inc., (DC-NY), 86 FSupp 399, 82 USPQ 273. Mf'd 191 F(2d) 99, 90 USPQ 153.

Infringers must pay substantial allowance for attorney fees since they deliberately brought about court test of validity of plaintiff's copyrights, contending that they were invalid, knowing that, if unsuccessful, they would incur liability for attorney fees. Alfred Bell & Co., Ltd. v. Catalda Fine Arts, Inc., (DC-NY), 86 FSupp 399, 82 USPQ 273. Mf'd 191 F(2d) 99, 90 USPQ 153.

Printer of copyright infringements, as well as its co-infringers, is liable for attorney fees, since it knew copyrights and pursued its course with knowledge that, if defense of copyright invalidity were overruled, it would be liable for attorney fees. Alfred Bell & Co., Ltd. v. Catalda Fine Arts, Inc., (DC-NY), 86 FSupp 399, 82 USPQ 273. Mf'd 191 F(2d) 99, 90 USPQ 153.

Where techniques of copying and vending articles infringing copyright are tinged with bad faith, plaintiffs are entitled to reasonable attorney fees; such fees cannot be allowed for any services of attorneys except those reasonably necessary to redress infringement and procure injunction against further infringement. Stein v. Rosenthal, (DC-Cal), 103 FSupp 227, 92 USPQ 402. Aff'd 205 F(2d) 633, 98 USPQ 180.

Defendant was not entitled to award of attorney fees upon dismissal of plaintiff's infringement suit based on ground that plaintiff's statuette was not subject for a copyright, if suit was in good faith due to perfect copy of statuette by defendant. Stein v. Expert Lamp Co., (DC-Ill), 107 FSupp 60, 94 USPQ 137.

Court exercises discretion to refuse counsel fees to successful plaintiff in copyright infringement suit. Edward B. Marks Music Corp. v. Borst Music Pub. Co., Inc., (DC-NJ), 110 FSupp 913, 97 USPQ 394.

In determining amount of proper attorney fee for plaintiff, which prevailed on its main contention in copyright infringement suit, court takes into consideration fact that considerable amount of attorney's time was devoted to factual issue on which plaintiff was unsuccessful. Shapiro Bernstein & Co., Inc. v. Jerry Vogel Music Co., Inc., (DC-NY), 115 FSupp 754, 98 USPQ 438, 99 USPQ 381. Rev'd 221 F(2d) 569, 105 USPQ 178, which mf'd 223 F(2d) 252, 105 USPQ 460.

Attorney fee was refused prevailing defendant which had innocently copied material published with defective copyright notice. Metro Associated Services, Inc. v. Webster City Graphic, Inc., (DC-Iowa), 117 FSupp 224, 100 USPQ 88.

Attorney fees were not awarded against copyright infringer, where it was common practice for publishers of prayer books to copy freely from each other, much of plaintiff's book was in public domain, and defendant honestly, but mistakenly, believed that plaintiff was illegally attempting to copyright and monopolize printing of ancient prayers. Ziegelheim v. Flohr, (DC-NY), 119 FSupp 324, 100 USPQ 189.

Court exercises discretion to refuse counsel fee to prevailing defendant in copyright infringement suit where plaintiff's claim was not capricious or unreasonable and court found noninfringement only after thorough and difficult consideration of evidence and inferences drawn therefrom. Morse v. Fields, (DC-NY), 127 FSupp 63, 104 USPQ 54.

Although court has discretionary power to award attorney fees to prevailing party in copyright infringement action, it refuses award where case was treated as test case, there being no authorities squarely in point to guide litigants. Loew's Inc. v. Columbia Broadcasting System, Inc., (DC-Cal), 131 FSupp 165, 105 USPQ 302. Aff'd 239 F(2d) 532, 112 USPQ 11, which was aff'd 356 US 43, 2 LEd(2d) 583, 78 SCR 667, 116 USPQ 479.

In suit for copyright infringement, full costs are allowed to prevailing party as matter of right; court may award reasonable attorney fee to such party as part of costs. Alexander v. Irving Trust Co., (DC-NY), 132 FSupp 364, 106 USPQ 74. Aff'd 228 F(2d) 221, 108 USPQ 24.

Although court finds no copyright infringement by defendant author, it exercises discretion to refuse attorney fees, since plaintiff was sincerely convinced that there was infringement, especially since jury, in prior action against author's publisher, had found infringement. Warshawsky v. Carter, (DC-DC), 132 FSupp 758, 107 USPQ 80.

Counsel fees are awarded to prevailing defendants as matter of discretion in copyright infringement action wherein multiplicity of procedural activities, including plaintiff's motion for appointment of receiver of one defendant, intervened between start of action and its coming to trial. Lampert v. Hollis Music, Inc., (DC-NY), 138 FSupp 505, 109 USPQ 242.

In determining reasonable fee, court considers, among other elements, amount of work necessary, amount of work done, skill employed, monetary amount involved, and result achieved. Cloth v. Hyman, (DC-NY), 146 FSupp 185, 112 USPQ 254.

Prevailing defendants are not awarded counsel fees since plaintiff commenced copyright infringement action in good faith. Greenbie v. Noble, (DC-NY), 151 FSupp 45, 113 USPQ 115.

Losing defendants should not be unduly burdened where elaborate briefs were in part necessitated by fact that case is one of first impression. Harms, Inc. v. Sansom House Enterprises, Inc., (DC-Pa), 162 FSupp 129, 117 USPQ 272.

Allowance of attorney fees to prevailing plaintiff in copyright infringement action would be unreasonably burdensome, especially since damages have been awarded under § 101(b) of this title, and since there is no evidence by which court could determine amount of fees. Local Trademarks, Inc. v. Grantham, (DC-Neb), 166 FSupp 494, 117 USPQ 335.

Counsel fees may be awarded where party seeks declaratory judgment with respect to ownership of renewed copyright; purpose of award of counsel fees in copyright cases is as much to penalize losing party as to compensate prevailing party; losing party is not penalized for seeking determination of effect in his situation of doctrine applied in cited case, but his refusal to accept decision of Supreme Court in another cited case was frivolous; as to the latter point, prevailing party is awarded counsel fees; also, prevailing party is entitled to counsel fees and expenses involved in preparing to meet losing party's claim which was not pressed at trial. Rose v. Bourne, Inc., (DC-NY), 176 FSupp 605, 123 USPQ 29. Aff'd 279 F(2d) 79, 125 USPQ 509.

Award of reasonable attorney's fee as part of costs under this section rests in sound discretion of court; fee is awarded only where dictated by equity and good conscience and generally is denied unless claim of unsuccessful plaintiff was capricious or unreasonable or unless situation calls for penalization of losing party. Barton Candy Corp. v. Tell Chocolate Novelties Corp., (DC-NY), 178 FSupp 577, 123 USPQ 425.

Penalty element is important factor in award of counsel fees in copyright cases; court can see little reason why unsuccessful party in bona fide dispute over copyright matter should pay opponent's lawyers' fees any more than he should

in the general run of litigation; court is not inclined to charge copyright litigant with opponent's lawyers' fees except to penalize conduct which seems to merit a penalty. Rose v. Bourne, Inc., (DC-NY), — FSupp —, 127 USPQ 187. Aff'd 279 F(2d) 79, 125 USPQ 509.

While, in the event of voluntary dismissal with prejudice which ended copyright infringement action, defendant would presumably be entitled to counsel fees, this is not the situation in instant action wherein, prior to voluntary dismissal of complaint without prejudice, plaintiffs' offer to discontinue action with prejudice was rejected by defendant, which desired to obtain adjudication of declaratory judgment counterclaim. Although defendant prevailed on counterclaim, plaintiffs should not be charged with defendant's expenses in obtaining resolution of difficult and open legal question; however, as to issues raised by reply to counterclaim and which plaintiffs insisted remain in the case but as to which plaintiffs offered no evidence, defendant is entitled to reasonable counsel fees; same is true as to legal issue which plaintiffs raised and which unnecessarily added to defendant's attorneys' labors. Rose v. Bourne, Inc., (DC-NY), — FSupp —, 127 USPQ 187. Aff'd 279 F(2d) 79, 125 USPQ 509.

Under this section, it is mandatory for court to allow full costs to prevailing party but discretionary with court as to whether to allow reasonable attorney's fee as part of costs. Such fee is awarded only where dictated by equity and good conscience. Fee is allowed where defendants deliberately copied copyrighted figure and then, in an effort to capitalize on good will enjoyed by plaintiffs' advertisements, included picture of plaintiffs' product, also imitated plaintiffs' advertisements, included picture of plaintiffs' product with their product, and used plaintiffs' registered trademark and trade name; defendants' product was inferior to plaintiffs' and sold for less, with overall result that defendants not only captured part of plaintiffs' market but also injured reputation of plaintiffs' product. Doran v. Sunset House Distributing Corp., (DC-Cal), 197 FSupp 940, 131 USPQ 94.

Plaintiff is entitled to recover reasonable attorneys' fees since defendant's copyright infringement was wilful and deliberate. Gelles-Widmer Co. v. Milton Bradley Co., (DC-Ill), — FSupp —, 132 USPQ 30.

In action for declaratory judgment as to title of renewal copyright and for injunction restraining infringement, wherein defendant asks for like relief, prevailing defendant is awarded reasonable counsel fees under this section in view of clear and settled nature of the authorities governing the issues. Tobias v. Joy Music, Inc., (DC-NY), — FSupp —, 133 USPQ 181.

Under this section, it is mandatory that court allow full costs in copyright infringement suit to prevailing party; however, court retains discretion as to whether to award reasonable attorney's fee as part of costs; such fee is awarded where losing defendant deliberately reproduced almost all of plaintiff's copyrighted catalog, with full knowledge of copyright notice imprinted thereon. B & B Auto Supply, Inc. v. Plesser, (DC-NY), — FSupp —, 133 USPQ 247.

Plaintiff's voluntary dismissal of copyright infringement action, after defendant had taken depositions and moved for more definite statement, makes defendant the prevailing party, but defendant is refused award of reasonable attorney fees, since exhibits show that defendant appropriated plaintiff's copyrighted material, but plaintiff will be required to pay such fees if it later reinstitutes copyright action. Uniflow Mfg. Co. v. Superflow Mfg. Corp., (DC-Ohio), 10 FedRDec 589, 87 USPQ 89.

Where case is brought in good faith counsel fees are not awarded against losing plaintiff but costs are awarded as being mandatory. Vaughan v. Real Detective Publishing Co., Inc., (DC-NY), 42 USPQ 500.

Where publication of infringing article did not damage plaintiff or profit defendant, attorney fee was not awarded. Vinick v. Charm Publications, Inc., (DC-NY), 46 USPQ 510.

Where infringement was not willful or deliberate and no damage resulted, attorney fee was not allowed. Washingtonian Publishing Co., Inc. v. Pearson, (DC-DC), 56 USPQ 23. Aff'd 78 AppDC 287, 140 F(2d) 465, 60 USPQ 224.

5. —Particular fees allowed.

Attorney fee of $2500 was awarded. S. E. Hendricks Co., Inc. v. Thomas Pub. Co., (CCA 2), 242 Fed 37; Schellberg v. Empringham, (DC-NY), 36 F(2d) 991; Cory v. Physical Culture Hotel, (CCA 2), 88 F(2d) 411, 33 USPQ 58, aff'g 14 FSupp 977, 30 USPQ 353, and 14 FSupp 986, 30 USPQ 360.

In a case which necessitates work in connection with a preliminary injunction, a motion in regard to interrogatories, and a trial of one day, the court will allow $300 as attorney fees. Stodart v. Mutual Film Corp., (DC-NY), 249 Fed 507. Aff'd 249 Fed 513.

One thousand dollars were awarded as attorney fees. G. Ricordi & Co., Inc. v. Columbia Graphophone Co., (DC-NY), 258 Fed 72; Warren v. White & Wyckoff Mfg. Co., (DC-NY), 39 F(2d) 922; McConnor v. Kaufman, (CCA 2), 139 F(2d) 116, 60 USPQ 356, aff'g 49 FSupp 738, 57 USPQ 80, and 57 USPQ 140; Freedman v. Milnag Leasing Corp., (DC-NY), 20 FSupp 802, 35 USPQ 184; Burndy Engineering Co., Inc. v. Penn-Union Electric Corp., (DC-Pa), 36 FSupp 35, 47 USPQ 230; Stonesifer v. Twentieth Century-Fox Film Corp., (DC-Cal), 48 FSupp 196, 56 USPQ 94. Aff'd 140 F(2d) 579, 60 USPQ 392.

Attorney fees are not to be reduced because the damages are small, though the amount of such fees is to be based on the magnitude of the interest involved, the amount recovered in damages, and the volume of work required and accomplished. In this case where there was a single use of a copyrighted music roll a fee of $250 was reasonable. M. Witmark & Sons v. Calloway, (DC-Tenn), 22 F(2d) 412.

Attorney fees of $100 were awarded in addition to statutory damages of $250. Dreamland Ball Room, Inc. v. Shapiro, Bernstein & Co., (CCA 7), 36 F(2d) 354, 3 USPQ 288; Buck v. Russo, (DC-Mass), 25 FSupp 317, 39 USPQ 377; Shapiro, Bernstein & Co., Inc. v. Widenski,

(DC-RI), 54 FSupp 780, 61 USPQ 91; Buck v. Archambault, (DC-Mass), 36 USPQ 383; Buck v. Kozlouski, (DC-Mass), 36 USPQ 383.

In view of labor involved in preparing case for trial and on appeal, further fee of $4000 is allowed. General Drafting Co., Inc. v. Andrews, (CCA 2), 37 F(2d) 54, 4 USPQ 72.

Counsel fees should be commensurate with services necessarily rendered and success obtained; here fee of $2000 is excessive; fee of $1000 is allowed. Davilla v. Brunswick-Balke Collender Co., (CCA 2), 94 F(2d) 567, 36 USPQ 398, mod'g 19 FSupp 819, 35 USPQ 157.

Attorney fees of $33,000 were fixed for entire proceedings. Sheldon v. Metro-Goldwyn Pictures Corp., (CCA 2), 106 F(2d) 45, 42 USPQ 540, rev'g 26 FSupp 134, 40 USPQ 238. Aff'd 309 US 390, 84 LEd 825, 60 SCR 681, 44 USPQ 607.

Attorney fee of $1500 was allowed against infringing publisher which made over $7000 profits; no fee was allowed against infringing printer liable only for $250 statutory damages. Sammons v. Colonial Press, Inc., (CCA 1), 126 F(2d) 341, 53 USPQ 71, mod'g 38 FSupp 649, 49 USPQ 350, 50 USPQ 187.

Counsel fee of $2000 was not excessive in case awarding $3500 statutory damages where defendant's series of infringements (two catalogues, one of which went to three printings) rendered issues multifarious both as to law and facts. Burndy Engineering Co., Inc. v. Sheldon Service Corp., (CCA 2), 127 F(2d) 661, 53 USPQ 409, aff'g 39 FSupp 274, 50 USPQ 24.

Seventeen hundred dollars were awarded as attorney fee. Adventures in Good Eating, Inc. v. Best Places to Eat, Inc., (CCA 7), 131 F(2d) 809, 56 USPQ 242.

District court did not abuse discretion in refusing attorney fee to prevailing defendant, but appellate court allows $750 attorney fees for services in appellate court wherein judgment is affirmed. Jerome v. Twentieth Century-Fox Film Corp., (CCA 2), 165 F(2d) 784, 76 USPQ 246, aff'g 67 FSupp 736, 70 USPQ 349, 71 FSupp 914, 71 USPQ 49, and 7 FedR Dec 190, 72 USPQ 431.

Prevailing party in copyright infringement case is awarded $500 attorney fee for services on appeal. F. W. Woolworth Co. v. Contemporary Arts, Inc., (CA 1), 193 F(2d) 162, 92 USPQ 4, aff'g 93 FSupp 739, 86 USPQ 476. Aff'd 344 US 228, 97 LEd 276, 73 SCR 222, 95 USPQ 396.

Where plaintiff was unsuccessful in proving infringement, defendants were allowed $3500 attorney fees. Lowenfels v. Nathan, (DC-NY), 2 FSupp 73, 16 USPQ 421.

Eighteen hundred dollars were a reasonable attorney fee where an advertising card for dishes was infringed resulting in an award therefor of $2500. Sebring Pottery Co. v. Steubenville Pottery Co., (DC-Ohio), 9 FSupp 384.

Where court awarded $5000 damages for seven infringements when it could have awarded $35,000, it could fix $2500 as a reasonable allowance for counsel fees. Cory v. Physical Culture Hotel, (DC-NY), 14 FSupp 986, 30 USPQ 360. Aff'd 88 F(2d) 411, 33 USPQ 58.

In certain uncontested cases the court awarded $50 attorney fees. Buck v. Ridgway Const. Co., (DC-Mass), 25 FSupp 690, 39 USPQ 376; Buck v. LaFontaine, (DC-Mass), 39 USPQ 377; Buck v. Deane, (DC-Mass), 39 USPQ 381; Buck v. Royal Palms, (DC-Mass), 39 USPQ 382; Buck v. Columbus Restaurant, (DC-Mass), 39 USPQ 382; Buck v. Yin Ho Co., Inc., (DC-Mass), 39 USPQ 383; Buck v. Melanson, (DC-Mass), 39 USPQ 384.

Four hundred dollars were awarded as attorney fee. Zenn v. National Golf Review, Inc., (DC-NY), 27 FSupp 732, 41 USPQ 535.

Where orchestra in restaurant played copyrighted music with no proof of special damages, $50 attorney fee was allowed. Buck v. Lisa, (DC-NY), 28 FSupp 379, 42 USPQ 116.

One hundred and fifty dollars were awarded as attorney fee. Advertisers Exchange, Inc. v. Laufe, (DC-Pa), 29 FSupp 1, 38 USPQ 93.

Attorney fee of $1500 was allowed. Sheldon v. Moredall Realty Corp., (DC-NY), 29 FSupp 729, 43 USPQ 81; Sammons v. Larkin, (DC-Mass), 38 FSupp 649, 49 USPQ 350. Mf'd 126 F(2d) 341, 53 USPQ 71.

Where no proof of damages was made and $500 damages were awarded, $250 attorney fee was allowed. Eliot v. Geare-Marston, Inc., (DC-Pa), 30 FSupp 301, 43 USPQ 249.

Copyright suit was dismissed in part without leave to amend and in part plaintiff was ordered to file better statement with respect to publication with notice of copyright and with respect to deposit in copyright office; without filing better statement plaintiff moved to dismiss without prejudice and with costs taxed against plaintiff; motion was granted and it appearing that defendants had been wrongfully subjected to expense of legal services, award of $400 attorney fees was made to each of two defendants in addition to all other costs. Corcoran v. Montgomery Ward & Co., Inc., (DC-Cal), 32 FSupp 421, 45 USPQ 115. Aff'd 121 F(2d) 575, 50 USPQ 277; Corcoran v. Montgomery Ward & Co., (DC-Cal), 32 FSupp 422, 45 USPQ 115.

Counsel fees of $1000 awarded defendants were proper considering monetary amount involved, amount of work necessary and done, skill employed, and result achieved. Rose v. Connelly, (DC-NY), 38 FSupp 54, 49 USPQ 497.

Three hundred dollars were awarded as attorney fee. Rudolf Lesch Fine Arts, Inc. v. Metal, (DC-NY), 51 FSupp 69, 58 USPQ 668.

Regard being had to nature of 11 infringement cases, their presentation together, work of counsel, and other factors, court allows $150 fee in each single count case and $300 in each multiple count case irrespective of number of counts; fees allowed are inadequate for services rendered, but indulgence is allowed defendants since they had ostensible grant of right to perform compositions under state law which court holds invalid. Remick Music Co. v. Interstate Hotel Co., (DC-Neb), 58 FSupp 523, 63 USPQ 327. Aff'd 157 F(2d) 744, 71 USPQ 138.

Fixation of damage for copyright infringement, under this section, is left to court's discretion. In action wherein defendants printed infringing articles in their newspaper, but testified that they knew nothing of the copying, had no intent to infringe, and had no knowledge of copyright law, court awards statutory minimum damages of $250 plus costs as well as $250 for attorney's fees. Massapequa Publishing Co., Inc. v. Observer, Inc., (DC-NY), 191 FSupp 261, 128 USPQ 418.

Attorney fees were reduced to $2500 from $6000 which had been allowed by master. Jones Brothers Co. v. Underkoffler, (DC-Pa), 35 USPQ 448.

One hundred dollars attorney fee was allowed where $150 damages were awarded for nonwillful infringement. Druley v. Thompson, (DC-Pa), 44 USPQ 284.

Prevailing defendant is awarded $1750 as reasonable attorney fee; defendant's attorney rendered services as to particulars, examination before trial, preparation of charts and trial brief, consultation with client and witnesses, five days trial, submission of proposed findings, and criticism of plaintiff's proposed findings. Colonial Book Co., Inc. v. Oxford Book Co., Inc., (DC-NY), 54 USPQ 24.

On fixing attorney fee, court confirming master's report cannot close eyes to finding of invalidity of copyright in action by same plaintiff against another defendant decided after same court had held copyright valid and infringed. Colonial Book Co., Inc. v. Amsco School Publications, Inc., (DC-NY), 57 USPQ 36. Aff'd 142 F(2d) 362, 61 USPQ 391.

Seventy-five hundred dollars attorney fee was allowed plaintiff. Harris v. Miller, (DC-NY), 57 USPQ 190.

Two thousand dollars were awarded as attorney fee. Select Theatres Corp. v. Ronzoni Macaroni Co., (DC-NY), 59 USPQ 288.

Three hundred and fifty dollars were awarded as attorney fee. Curt Teich & Co., Inc. v. Beals Lithograph & Printing Co., Inc., (DC-Iowa), 61 USPQ 434.

CHAPTER 3.—COPYRIGHT OFFICE

AMENDMENT NOTE

Act Apr. 13, 1954, c. 137, 68 Stat. 53, amended the analysis of this chapter by adding "216. When the day for taking action falls on Saturday, Sunday, or a holiday."

Section 201. Copyright office—Preservation of records.—All records and other things relating to copyrights required by law to be preserved shall be kept and preserved in the copyright office, Library of Congress, District of Columbia, and shall be under the control of the register of copyrights, who shall, under the direction and supervision of the Librarian of Congress, perform all the duties relating to the registration of copyrights. (July 30, 1947, c. 391, § 1, 61 Stat. 665.)

NOTES TO DECISIONS

The copyright office, while within the Library of Congress, is a separate and distinct office. 39 OAG 429.

Provision that register of copyrights shall perform his duties under the direction and supervision of the Librarian of Congress does not warrant a demand by counsel that the librarian personally examine upon its merits a claim for copyright registration denied by the register. 40 OAG 27, 48 USPQ 439.

No statute or regulation authorizes appeal to Librarian of Congress from decision of copyright office refusing copyright registration. 40 OAG 27, 48 USPQ 439.

202. Register, assistant register, and subordinates.—There shall be appointed by the Librarian of Congress a Register of Copyrights, and one Assistant Register of Copyrights, who shall have authority during the absence of the Register of Copyrights to attach the copyright office seal to all papers issued from the said office and to sign such certificates and other papers as may be necessary. There shall also be appointed by the Librarian such subordinate assistants to the register as may from time to time be authorized by law. (July 30, 1947, c. 391, § 1, 61 Stat. 665.)

NOTES TO DECISIONS

Mandamus to force register to accept deposit and register claim of copyright, see U. S. ex rel. Twentieth Century-Fox Film Corp. v. Bouve, (DC-DC), 33 FSupp 462, 45 USPQ 411. Aff'd 74 AppDC 271, 122 F(2d) 51, 50 USPQ 338.

Register of copyrights had no power to refuse to register copyright on ground that writing sought to be copyrighted consisted merely of "page proof." U. S. ex rel. Twentieth Century-Fox Film Corp. v. Bouve, (DC-DC), 33 FSupp 462, 45 USPQ 411. Aff'd 74 AppDC 271, 122 F(2d) 51, 50 USPQ 338.

Register of copyrights has no power to refuse or deny registration of claim of copyright which is entitled to registration under Copyright Act; whether applicant or claimant has complied with law so that his claim is entitled to registration raises questions of fact and law to be decided by court; Register has no power to decide such questions, especially where deposit of copies and application filed, when read together as they should be, are in apparent compliance with act. King Features Syndicate, Inc. v. Bouve, (DC-DC), 48 USPQ 237.

The register of copyrights must perform those duties charged upon him by law, is liable under his bond for their faithful performance, and cannot escape this responsibility by any delegation of authority. It is not intended, however, that he must perform all the details personally. 39 OAG 429.

203. Deposit of moneys received—Reports.—The Register of Copyrights shall make daily deposits in some bank in the District of Columbia, designated for this purpose by the Secretary of the Treasury as a national depository, of all moneys received to be applied as copyright fees, and shall make weekly deposits with the Secretary of the Treasury, in such manner as the latter shall direct, of all copyright fees actually applied under the provisions of this title, and annual deposits of sums received which it has not been possible to apply as copyright fees or to return to the remitters, and shall also make monthly reports to the Secretary of the Treasury and to the Librarian of Congress of the applied copyright fees for each calendar month, together with a statement of all remittances received, trust funds on hand, moneys refunded, and unapplied balances. (July 30, 1947, c. 391, § 1, 61 Stat. 665.)

204. Bond. — The Register of Copyrights shall give bond to the United States in the sum of $20,000, in form to be approved by the General Counsel for the Department of the Treasury and with sureties satisfactory to the Secretary of the Treasury, for the faithful discharge of his duties. (July 30, 1947, c. 391, § 1, 61 Stat. 666.)

205. Annual report.—The Register of Copyrights shall make an annual report to the Librarian of Congress, to be printed in the annual report on the Library of Congress, of all copyright business for the previous fiscal year, including the number and kind of works which have been deposited in the copyright office during the fiscal year, under the provisions of this title. (July 30, 1947, c. 391, § 1, 61 Stat. 666.)

206. Seal of copyright office.—The seal used in the copyright office on July 1, 1909, shall be the seal of the copyright office, and by it all papers issued from the copyright office requiring authentication shall be authenticated. (July 30, 1947, c. 391, § 1, 61 Stat. 666.)

207. Rules for registration of claims.—Subject to the approval of the Librarian of Congress, the Register of Copyrights shall be authorized to make rules and regulations for the registration of claims to copyright as provided by this title. (July 30, 1947, c. 391, § 1, 61 Stat. 666.)

Regulations.—Chapter II of Title 37 of Code of Federal Regulations, as amended to Mar. 1, 1959, reads:

PART 201—GENERAL PROVISIONS

Section
201.1 Communications with the Copyright Office.
201.2 Information given by the Copyright Office.
201.3 Catalog of Copyright Entries.
201.4 Assignments of copyright and other papers.
201.5 Amendments to completed Copyright Office registrations and other records.
201.6 Payment and refund of Copyright Office fees.
201.7 Preparation of catalog card.
201.8 Import statements.

Authority: §§ 201.1 to 201.8 issued under sec. 207, 61 Stat. 666 [this section].

§ 201.1   Communications with the Copyright Office. Mail and other communications shall be addressed to the Register of Copyrights, Library of Congress, Washington 25, D. C.

§ 201.2   Information given by the Copyright Office.—(a) In general. (1) Information relative to the operations of the Copyright Office is supplied without charge. A search of the records, indexes and deposits will be made for such information as they may contain relative to copyright claims upon application and payment of the statutory fee. The Copyright Office, however, does not undertake the making of comparisons of copyright deposits to determine similarity between works, nor does it give legal opinions or advice on such matters as:

(i) The validity or status of any copyright other than the facts shown in the records of the Office;

(ii) The rights of persons, whether in connection with cases of alleged copyright infringement, contracts between authors and publishers or other matters of a similar nature;

(iii) The scope and extent of protection of works in foreign countries or interpretation of foreign copyright laws or court opinions;

(iv) The sufficiency, extent or scope of compliance with the copyright law.

(2) In addition, the Office cannot undertake to furnish the names of copyright attorneys, publishers, agents, or other similar information.

(b) Inspection and copying of records. (1) Inspection and copying of completed records and indexes relating to a registration or a recorded document, and inspection of copies deposited in connection with a completed copyright registration, may be undertaken at such times as will not result in interference with or delay in the work of the Copyright Office.

(2) The copying from the Copyright Office records of names and addresses for the purpose of compiling mailing lists and other similar uses is expressly prohibited.

(c) Correspondence. (1) Official correspondence, including preliminary applications, between copyright claimants or their agents and the Copyright Office, and directly relating to a completed registration or to a recorded document, is made available for inspection by persons properly and directly concerned. Requests for photocopies of the correspondence shall be made pursuant to paragraph (d) of this section.

(2)(i) Correspondence, application forms and any accompanying material forming a part of a pending or rejected application are not records which are open to public inspection under paragraph (b) of this section.

(ii) Inspection of such files may be afforded upon presentation of written authorization of the claimant or his agent, or upon submission to the Register of Copyrights, Library of Congress, Washington 25, D. C., of a written request which is deemed by him to show good cause for such access and which establishes that the person making the request is one properly and directly concerned.

(iii) Where such access is authorized and photocopies of the official file are subsequently requested, the conditions and procedures of paragraph (d) of this section are controlling.

(3) Correspondence, memoranda, reports, opinions, and similar material relating to internal management, office administration, security matters, and general policy and decisional material, including the work product of an attorney, are not open to public inspection.

(4) The Copyright Office will return unanswered any abusive or scurrilous correspondence.

(d) Requests for copies. (1) Requests for additional certificates of registration should be sent to the Copyright Office, and the accompanying fees should be made payable to the Register of Copyrights.

(2) Requests for photocopies of copyright deposits, official correspondence, and Copyright Office records (other than additional certificates of registration) should be sent to the Chief, Photoduplication Service, Library of Congress, Washington 25, D. C., the accompanying fees in payment of such services being made payable to that official. When the photocopy is to be certified by the Copyright Office, the additional certification fee should be made payable to the Register of Copyrights and both remittances together with the transmittal letter are to be sent to the Copyright Office.

(3) Requests for photocopies of official correspondence shall identify the specific material desired and shall contain a statement enabling the Copyright Office to determine if the writer is properly and directly concerned.

(4) Requests for photocopies of copyright deposits will be granted when one or more of the following conditions are fulfilled:

(i) Authorization by owner. When authorized in writing by the copyright owner or his designated agent.

(ii) Request by attorney. When required in connection with litigation, actual or prospective, in which the copyrighted work is involved; but in all such cases the attorney representing the actual or prospective plaintiff or defendant for whom the request is made shall give in writing: (a) The names of the parties and the nature of the controversy; (b) the name of the court where the action is pending, or, in the case of a prospective proceeding, a full statement of the facts of the controversy in which the copyrighted work is involved; and (c) satisfactory assurances that the requested copy will be used only in connection with the specified litigation.

(iii) Court order. When an order to have the copy made is issued by a court having jurisdiction of a case in which the copy is to be submitted as evidence.

§ 201.3 Catalog of Copyright Entries. — The current subscription price for all parts of the complete yearly Catalog of Copyright Entries is $20.00. Each part of the Catalog is published in two semiannual numbers covering, respectively, the periods January-June and July-December. The prices given in the list below are for each semiannual number. The Catalog may be obtained, upon payment of the established price, from the Register of Copyrights, Library of Congress, Washington 25, D. C., to whom requests for copies should be addressed and to whom the remittance should be made payable.

Part 1—Books and Pamphlets Including Serials and Contributions to Periodicals, $2.50.

Part 2—Periodicals, $1.00.

Parts 3-4—Dramas and Works Prepared for Oral Delivery, $1.00.

Part 5—Music, $3.50.

Part 6—Maps and Atlases, $0.50.

Parts 7-11A—Works of Art, Reproductions of Works of Art, Scientific and Technical Drawings, Photographic Works, Prints and Pictorial Illustrations, $1.00.

Part 11B—Commercial Prints and Labels, $1.00.

Parts 12-13—Motion Pictures and Filmstrips, $0.50.

§ 201.4 Assignments of copyright and other papers.—Assignments of copyright and other papers relative to copyrights will be recorded in the Copyright Office upon payment of the statutory fee. Examples of such papers include powers of attorney, licenses to use a copyrighted work, agreements between authors and publishers covering a particular work or works and the rights thereto, mortgages, certificates of change of corporate title, wills, and decrees of distribution. The original, signed instrument should be submitted for recordation, and is returned to the sender with a certificate of record. Where the original instrument is not available, a certified or other copy may be submitted, but it shall be accompanied by a statement that the original is not available.

§ 201.5 Amendments to completed Copyright Office registrations and other rocerds.— (a) No cancellations. No correction or cancellation of a Copyright Office registration or other record will be made (other than a registration or record provisional upon receipt of fee as provided in § 201.6) after it has been completed if the facts therein stated agree with those supplied the Office for the purpose of making such record. However, it shall be within the discretion of the Register of Copyrights to determine if any particular case justifies the placing of an annotation upon any record for the purpose of clarification, explanation, or indication that there exists elsewhere in the records, indexes or correspondence files of the Office, information which has reference to the facts as stated in such record.

(b) Correction by new registration. In exceptional cases, where an applicant desires to correct, amend or amplify a registration previously made in accordance with information furnished by a claimant or his agent, a new application indicating its amendatory purpose shall be filed, accompanied by the statutory fee and the same number of copies required for a new application. Where it is satisfactorily established that copies of the original work cannot be obtained for submission, photostat or microfilm copies of the original may be submitted.

§ 201.6 Payment and refund of Copyright Office fees.— (a) In General. All fees sent to the Copyright Office should be in the form of a money order, check or bank draft payable to the Register of Copyrights. Coin or currency sent to the Office in letters or packages will be at the remitter's risk. Remittances from foreign countries should be in the form of an International Money Order or Bank Draft payable and immediately negotiable in the United States for the full amount of the fee required. Uncertified checks are accepted subject to collection. Where the statutory fee is submitted in the form of a check, the registration of the copyright claim or other record made by the Office is provisional until payment in money is received. In the event the fee is not paid, the registration or other record shall be expunged.

(b) Deposit accounts. Persons or firms having a considerable amount of business with the Copyright Office may, for their own convenience, prepay copyright expenses by establishing a Deposit Account.

(c) Refunds. Money paid for applications which are rejected or payments made in excess of the statutory fee will be refunded, but amounts of twenty-five cents or less will not be returned unless specifically requested and such sums may be refunded in postage stamps. All larger amounts will be refunded by check.

(d) Return of deposit copies. Copies of works deposited in the Copyright Office pursuant to law are either retained in the Copyright Of-

fice, transferred for the permanent collections or other uses of the Library of Congress, or disposed of according to law. When an application is rejected, the Copyright Office reserves the right to retain the deposited copies.

§ 201.7 Preparation of catalog card. The catalog card which may accompany a work of foreign origin, as provided in section 215 of title 17, U. S. Code, as amended [§ 215 of this title], may be a catalog card supplied by a library in the country of publication. In lieu of such a card the applicant may prepare his own card, or may fill out the form supplied by the Copyright Office. The catalog card should contain the full name of the author of the original work, title and description from the title page, paging, copyright claimant, the city and year of publication, and the names of all other authors, editors, etc., whom the applicant considers of sufficient importance to record. When available, the year of birth of each author named should be given. If the form furnished by the Office is not used, the size of the card should preferably be 5 inches wide by 3 inches deep or 12.5 centimeters wide by 7.5 centimeters deep. The Register of Copyrights reserves the right to accept catalog cards not complying with the above requirements.

§ 201.8 Import statements.— (a) The Copyright Office will issue import statements for books and periodicals first published abroad in the English language which are to be imported under the provisions of section 16 of title 17, U. S. Code, as amended [§ 16 of this title]. A statement for the importation of 1,500 copies will be issued to the person named in the application for ad interim copyright registration. The holder of this statement shall present it to the customs officer in charge of the port of entry. Upon receipt of a statement from the customs officer, showing importation of less than 1,500 copies, a new statement will be issued for the balance.

(b) The provisions in the Customs Regulations covering the use of the import statement (Copyright Office Form C-85) are found in 19 CFR 11.21 (21 F.R. 2517).

PART 202—REGISTRATION OF CLAIMS TO COPYRIGHT

Section

202.1	Material not subject to copyright.
202.2	Copyright notice.
202.3	Application forms.
202.4	Books (Class A).
202.5	Periodicals (Class B).
202.6	Lectures or similar productions prepared for oral delivery (Class C).
202.7	Dramatic and dramatico-musical compositions (Class D).
202.8	Musical compositions (Class E).
202.9	Maps (Class F).
202.10	Works of art (Class G).
202.11	Reproductions of works of art (Class H).
202.12	Drawings or plastic works of a scientific or technical character (Class I).
202.13	Photographs (Class J).
202.14	Prints, pictorial illustrations and commercial prints or labels (Class K).
202.15	Motion pictures (Classes L-M).

202.16 Deposit of photographs or other identi-
            fying reproductions in lieu of copies.
202.17 Renewals.
202.18 Notice of use.

Authority: §§ 202.1 to 202.18 issued under
sec. 207, 61 Stat. 666 [this section].

§ 202.1 Material not subject to copyright.
The following are examples of works not subject
to copyright and applications for registration of
such works cannot be entertained:

(a) Words and short phrases such as names,
titles, and slogans; familiar symbols or designs;
mere variations of typographic ornamentation,
lettering or coloring; mere listing of ingredients
or contents;

(b) Ideas, plans, methods, systems, or devices, as distinguished from the particular manner in which they are expressed or described in
a writing;

(c) Works designed for recording information which do not in themselves convey information, such as, time cards, graph paper, account
books, diaries, bank checks, score cards, address
books, report forms, order forms and the like;

(d) Works consisting entirely of information
that is common property containing no original
authorship, such as, for example: standard calendars, height and weight charts, tape measures
and rulers, schedules of sporting events, and
lists or tables taken from public documents or
other common sources.

§ 202.2 Copyright notice.—(a) General. (1)
With respect to a published work, copyright is
secured, or the right to secure it is lost, at the
date of publication, i. e., the date on which
copies are first placed on sale, sold, or publicly
distributed, depending upon the adequacy of the
notice of copyright on the work at that time.

(2) If publication occurs by distribution of
copies or in some other manner, without the
statutory notice or with an inadequate notice,
the right to secure copyright is lost. In such
cases, copyright cannot be secured by adding
the notice to copies distributed at a later date.

(3) Works first published abroad, other than
works eligible for ad interim registration, must
bear an adequate copyright notice at the time
of their first publication in order to secure copyright under the law of the United States.

(b) **Defects in notice.** Where the copyright
notice does not meet the requirements of the
law, the Copyright Office will reject an application for copyright registration. Common defects in the notice include, among others, the
following:

(1) The notice lacks one or more of the
necessary elements (i. e., the word "Copyright,"
the abbreviation "Copr.," or the symbol ©; the
name of the copyright proprietor; or, when
required, the year date of publication);

(2) The elements of the notice are dispersed;

(3) The notice is not in one of the positions prescribed by law;

(4) The notice is in a foreign language;

(5) The name in the notice is that of someone who had no authority to secure copyright
in his name;

(6) The year date in the copyright notice
is later than the date of the year in which
copyright was actually secured, including the
following cases:

(i) Where the year date in the notice is later
than the date of actual publication;

(ii) Where copyright was first secured by
registration of a work in unpublished form, and
copies of the same work as later published without change in substance bear a copyright notice
containing a year date later than the year of
unpublished registration;

(iii) Where a book or periodical published
abroad, for which ad interim copy has been
obtained, is later published in the United States
without change in substance and contains a
year date in the copyright notice later than the
year of first publication abroad:

Provided, however, That in each of the three
foregoing types of cases, if the copyright was
actually secured not more than one year earlier
than the year date in the notice, registration
may be considered as a doubtful case.

(7) A notice is permanently covered so that
it cannot be seen without tearing the work
apart;

(8) A notice is illegible or so small that it
cannot be read without the aid of a magnifying
glass: Provided, however, That where the work
itself requires magnification for its ordinary use
(e.g., a microfilm, microcard or motion picture)
a notice which will be readable when so magni-
fied, will not constitute a reason for rejection
of the claim;

(9) A notice is on a detachable tag and will
eventually be detached and discarded when the
work is put in use;

(10) A notice is on the wrapper or container
which is not a part of the work and which will
eventually be removed and discarded when the
work is put in use;

(11) The notice is restricted or limited exclusively to an uncopyrightable element, either
by virtue of its position on the work, by the use
of asterisks, or by other means.

§ 202.3 Application forms.[1]—(a) In general.
Section 5 of title 17 of the U. S. Code [§ 5 of
this title] provides thirteen classes (Class A
through Class M) of works in which copyright
may be claimed. Examples of certain works
falling within these classes are given in §§ 202.4
to 202.15 inclusive, for the purpose of assisting
persons, who desire to obtain registration of
a claim to copyright, to select the correct application form.

(b) **Claims of copyright.** (1) All works deposited for registration shall be accompanied by
a "claim of copyright" in the form of a properly executed application, together with the
statutory registration fee. The Office reserves the
right to refuse to accept any application that is
a carbon copy, illegible, defaced, or otherwise
not in an acceptable condition for examination
and recording.

---

[1] Filed as part of the original document.

(2) Where these separate elements are not received simultaneously, the Copyright Office holds the submitted elements for a reasonable time and, in default of the receipt of the missing element or elements after a request made therefor, the submitted item or items may be returned to the sender. Such action does not constitute a waiver of the right of the Register of Copyrights pursuant to section 14, title 17, U. S. Code [§ 14 of this title], to demand compliance with the deposit provisions of that title.

(3) Applications for copyright registration covering published works should reflect the facts existing at the time of first publication, and should not include information concerning changes that have occurred between the time of publication and registration. The name given as copyright claimant in the application should agree with the name appearing in the copyright notice.

(4) Applications should be submitted by the copyright claimant, or by someone acting under his authority.

(5) All information requested by the Copyright Office application form should be given in the appropriate spaces provided. There should not be attached to the application any slips of paper or extra pages containing additional information, or a continuation of requested information.

(c) **Forms.** The Copyright Office supplies without charge the following forms for use when applying for the registration of a claim to copyright in a work and for the filing of a notice of use of musical compositions on mechanical instruments.

Form A—Published book manufactured in the United States of America (Class A).

Form A-B Ad Interim—Book or periodical in the English language manufactured and first published outside the United States of America (Classes A-B).

Form A-B Foreign—Book or periodical manufactured outside the United States of America (except works subject to the ad interim provisions of the copyright law). (Classes A-B).

Form B—Periodical manufactured in the United States of America (Class B).

Form BB—Contribution to a periodical manufactured in the United States of America (Class B).

Form C—Lecture or similar production prepared for oral delivery (Class C).

Form D — Dramatic or dramatico-musical composition (Class D).

Form E—Musical composition the author of which is a citizen or domiciliary of the United States of America or which was first published in the United States of America (Class E).

Form E Foreign—Musical composition the author of which is not a citizen or domiciliary of the United States of America and which was not first published in the United States of America (Class E).

Form F—Map (Class F).

Form G—Work of art or a model or design for a work of art (Class G).

Form H—Reproduction of a work of art (Class H).

Form I—Drawing or plastic work of a scientific or technical character (Class I).

Form J—Photograph (Class J).

Form K—Print or pictorial illustration (Class K).

Form KK—Print or label used for article of merchandise (Class K).

Form L-M—Motion picture (Classes L-M).

Form R—Renewal of a copyright.

Form U—Notice of use of copyrighted music on mechanical instruments.

§ 202.4 Books (Class A).—(a) Subject matter and forms. This class includes such published works as fiction and nonfiction, poems, compilations, composite works, directories, catalogs, annual publications, information in tabular form, and similar text matter, with or without illustrations, as books, either bound or in loose-leaf form, pamphlets, leaflets, cards, single pages or the like. Applications for registration of claims to copyright in published books manufactured in the United States of America are made on Form A; in books manufactured outside the United States of America, except those subject to ad interim provisions of the copyright law, on Form A-B Foreign; and in books in the English language manufactured and first published outside the United States of America, and subject to the ad interim provisions of the copyright law, on Form A-B Ad Interim.

(b) **Ad interim registrations.** (1) An American edition of an English-language book or periodical identical in substance to that first published abroad will not be registered unless an ad interim registration is first made.

(2) When a book or periodical has been registered under the ad interim provisions, an American edition of the same work, to be registrable, must be manufactured and published in the United States within five years after the date of first publication abroad.

(3) Since by law ad interim copyright expires at the end of the ad interim term unless an American edition is published during that term, a renewal application covering a work registered only under the ad interim provisions will be rejected. Where both an ad interim and an American edition have been registered, the registrability of the renewal application is governed by the date of the first publication abroad.

§ 202.5 Periodicals (Class B).—This class includes such works as newspapers, magazines, reviews, bulletins, and serial publications, published at intervals of less than a year. Applications for registration of claims to copyright in published periodicals manufactured in the United States of America are made on Form B; in periodicals, or in contributions thereto, manufactured outside the United States of America, except those subject to the ad interim provision of the copyright law, on Form A-B Foreign; and in periodicals, or in contributions thereto, in the English language manufactured and first published outside of the United States of America, and subject to the ad interim provisions of the copyright law, on Form A-B Ad Interim. Applications for registration of claims to copyright in contributions to periodicals manufactured in the United States of America are made on Form BB. Application for registration of claims to copyright in contributions to periodicals, which contributions are prints published in connection with the sale or advertisement of an article or articles of merchandise, are made on Form KK.

§ 202.6 **Lectures or similar productions prepared for oral delivery (Class C).** This class includes the scripts of unpublished works prepared in the first instance for oral delivery, such as lectures, sermons, addresses, monologs, panel discussions, and variety programs prepared for radio or television. The script submitted for registration in Class C should consist of the actual text of the work to be presented orally. Formats, outlines, brochures, synopses, or general descriptions of radio and television programs are not registrable in unpublished form. When published with notice as prescribed by law, such works may be considered for registration as "books" in Class A.

§ 202.7 **Dramatic and dramatico-musical compositions (Class D).** This class includes published or unpublished works dramatic in character such as the acting version of plays for the stage, motion pictures, radio, television and the like, operas, operettas, musical comedies and similar productions, and pantomimes. Choreographic works of a dramatic character, whether the story or theme be expressed by music and action combined or by actions alone, are subject to registration in Class D. However, descriptions of dance steps and other physical gestures, including ballroom and social dances or choreographic works which do not tell a story, develop a character or emotion, or otherwise convey a dramatic concept or idea, are not subject to registration in Class D.

§ 202.8 **Musical compositions (Class E).** (a) This class includes published or unpublished musical compositions in the form of visible notation (other than dramatico-musical compositions), with or without words, as well as new versions of musical compositions, such as adaptations or arrangements, and editing when such editing is the writing of an author. The words of a song, when unaccompanied by music, are not registrable in Class E.

(b) A phonograph record or other sound recording is not considered a "copy" of the compositions recorded on it, and is not acceptable for copyright registration. Likewise, the Copyright Office does not register claims to exclusive rights in mechanical recordings themselves, or in the performances they reproduce.

§ 202.9 **Maps (Class F).** This class includes all published cartographic representations of area, such as terrestrial maps and atlases, marine charts, celestial maps and such three-dimensional works as globes and relief models.

§ 202.10 **Works of art (Class G).** (a) General: This class includes published or unpublished works of artistic craftsmanship, insofar as their form but not their mechanical or utilitarian aspects are concerned, such as artistic jewelry, enamels, glassware, and tapestries, as well as works belonging to the fine arts, such as paintings, drawings and sculpture.

(b) In order to be acceptable as a work of art, the work must embody some creative authorship in its delineation or form. The registrability of a work of art is not affected by the intention of the author as to the use of the work, the number of copies reproduced, or the fact that it appears on a textile material or textile product. The potential availability of protection under the design patent law will not affect the registrability of a work of art, but a copyright claim in a patented design or in the drawings or photographs in a patent application will not be registered after the patent has been issued.

(c) If the sole intrinsic function of an article is its utility, the fact that the article is unique and attractively shaped will not qualify it as a work of art. However, if the shape of a utilitarian article incorporates features, such as artistic sculpture, carving, or pictorial representation, which can be identified separately and are capable of existing independently as a work of art, such features will be eligible for registration.

§ 202.11 **Reproductions of works of art (Class H).** This class includes published reproductions of existing works of art in the same or a different medium, such as a lithograph, photoengraving, etching or drawing of a painting, sculpture or other work of art.

§ 202.12 **Drawings or plastic works of a scientific or technical character (Class I).**—(a) This class includes published or unpublished two-dimensional drawings and three-dimensional plastic works which have been designed for a scientific or technical use and which contain copyrightable graphic, pictorial, or sculptured material. Works registrable in Class I include diagrams or models illustrating scientific or technical works or formulating scientific or technical information in linear or plastic form, such as, for example: a mechanical drawing, an astronomical chart, an architect's blueprint, an anatomical model, or an engineering diagram.

(b) A work is not eligible for registration as a "plastic" work in Class I merely because it is formed from one of the commonly known synthetic chemical derivatives such as styrenes, vinyl compounds, or acrylic resins. The term "plastic work" as used in this context refers to a three-dimensional work giving the effect of that which is molded or sculptured. Examples of such works include statues of animals or plants used for scientific or educational purposes, and engineers' scale models.

(c) A claim to copyright in a scientific or technical drawing, otherwise registrable in Class I, will not be refused registration solely by reason of the fact that it is known to form a part of a pending patent application. Where the patent has been issued, however, the claim to copyright in the drawing will be denied copyright registration.

§ 202.13 **Photographs (Class J).** This class includes published or unpublished photographic prints and filmstrips, slide films and individual slides. Photoengravings and other photomechanical reproductions of photographs are registered in Class K on Form K.

(1595)

§ 202.14 Prints, pictorial illustrations and commercial prints or labels (Class K). (a) This class includes prints or pictorial illustrations, greeting cards, picture postcards and similar prints, produced by means of lithography, photoengraving or other methods of reproduction. These works when published are registered on Form K.

(b) A print or label, not a trademark, containing copyrightable pictorial matter, text, or both, published in connection with the sale or advertisement of an article or articles of merchandise is also registered in this class on Form KK. In the case of a print which is published in a periodical, use Form KK if the print is used in connection with the sale or advertisement of an article of merchandise, Form BB if it is not. Multipage works are more appropriately classified in Class A than in Class K.

(c) A claim to copyright cannot be registered in a print or label consisting solely of trademark subject matter and lacking copyrightable matter. While the Copyright Office will not investigate whether the matter has been or can be registered at the Patent Office, it will register a properly filed copyright claim in a print or label that contains the requisite qualifications for copyright even though there is a trademark on it. However, registration of a claim to copyright does not give the claimant rights available by trademark registration at the Patent Office.

§ 202.15 Motion pictures (Classes L-M). A single application Form L-M is available for registration of works in Classes L (Motion Picture Photoplays) and M (Motion Pictures other than Photoplays).

(a) **Photoplays (Class L).** This class includes published or unpublished motion pictures that are dramatic in character and tell a connected story, such as feature films, filmed television plays, short subjects and animated cartoons having a plot.

(b) **Other than photoplays (Class M).** This class includes published or unpublished nondramatic films such as newsreels, travelogs, training or promotional films, nature studies, and filmed television programs having no plot.

§ 202.16 Deposit of photographs or other identifying reproductions in lieu of copies.— (a) **Availability of option.** In the case of a published work which is reproduced in copies for sale, classified in Classes (g), (h), (i), and (k) of section 5, title 17, U. S. Code [§ 5 of this title], copies of which are considered by the Register of Copyrights to be impracticable of deposit because of their size, weight, fragility, or monetary value, photographs or other identifying reproductions may be deposited in lieu of copies as provided by section 13, title 17, U. S. Code [§ 13 of this title]. The deposit of such photographs or reproductions shall be made in accordance with the following criteria:

(1) The number of sets of photographs or of reproductions to be submitted shall be the same as the number of copies provided by said section 13 [§ 13 of this title]: duplicate sets shall be deposited unless the work is by a foreign author and has been published in a foreign country. Each set shall consist of as many photographs or reproductions in black and white, or in color, as are necessary to identify the work.

(2) All photographs or reproductions shall be of equal size, not less than 5 x 7 inches, and not exceeding 9 x 12 inches, but preferably 8 x 10 inches. The image of the work shown in all photographs or reproductions shall either be lifesize or larger, or if less than lifesize shall be at least 4 inches in its greatest dimension. The exact measurement of at least one dimension of the work shall be indicated on at least one corresponding photograph or reproduction in each set.

(3) The copyright notice and its position on the work must be clearly shown on at least one corresponding photograph or reproduction in each set. If, because of the size or location of the copyright notice, a photographic reproduction cannot be prepared, a drawing may be included in each set, of the same size as the photographs or reproductions, showing the exact appearance of the notice, its dimensions, and its specific position on the work.

(4) The title of the work shall appear on the front or back of each photograph or reproduction.

(5) A copy shall be considered to be impracticable of deposit if, because of its size, weight, fragility or monetary value, it is unsuited to the filing procedures of the Copyright Office.

(b) **Exceptions.** The provisions of this section, permitting the deposit of photographs in lieu of copies in certain cases, shall not apply to fine prints and two-dimensional art reproductions. The Register of Copyrights reserves the right in any other particular case to require as a condition precedent to registration, the deposit of copies of the work as published.

§ 202.17 Renewals.— (a) Claims to renewal copyright must be registered within the last (28th) year of the original copyright term. The original term for a published work is computed from the date of first publication; the term for a work originally registered in unpublished form is computed from the date of registration in the Copyright Office. Unless the required application and fee are received in the Copyright Office during the prescribed period before the first term of copyright expires, copyright protection is lost permanently and the work enters the public domain. The Copyright Office has no discretion to extend the renewal time limits.

(b) Renewal claims may be registered only in the names of persons falling within one of the classes of renewal claimants specified in the copyright law. If the work was a new version of a previous work, renewal may be claimed only in the new matter.

§ 202.18 Notices of use.— Notices of use of copyrighted musical compositions on mechanical instruments, required by section 1(e) of title 17, U. S. Code [§ 1(e) of this title], will be recorded upon receipt of a properly executed Form U and upon payment of the prescribed fees. Notices of intention to use will be received pursuant to section 101(e) of title 17, U. S. Code [§ 101(e) of this title]; no special form is provided therefor.

Acceptance of application which did not contain a statement of citizenship or nationality operated as a waiver of administrative regulation and copyright obtained thereon was valid. Campbell v. Wireback, (CCA 4), 269 Fed 372, 17 ALR 743, aff'g 261 Fed 391.

Insofar as the rules prescribed under this section relate to publication, they refer to publication for the purposes of registration. Patterson v. Century Productions, (CCA 2), 93 F(2d) 489, 35 USPQ 471, aff'g 19 FSupp 30, 33 USPQ 194.

Registration is valid, although on application made before there was publication with copyright notice or deposit of copies in copyright office, since application was not acted on until after publication with copyright notice and deposit of copies. U. S. v. Backer, (CCA 2), 134 F(2d) 533, 57 USPQ 133.

This section contemplates exercise of some discretion, not only in making, but in administering rules. Bouve v. Twentieth Century-Fox Film Corp., 74 AppDC 271, 122 F(2d) 51, 50 USPQ 338, aff'g 33 FSupp 462, 45 USPQ 411.

208. Record books in copyright office.

—The Register of Copyrights shall provide and keep such record books in the copyright office as are required to carry out the provisions of this title, and whenever deposit has been made in the copyright office of a copy of any work under the provisions of this title he shall make entry thereof. (July 30, 1947, c. 391, § 1, 61 Stat. 666.)

Section 4957 of Revised Statutes requires librarian to record name of such "copyright book or other article." Rosenbach v. Dreyfuss, (DC-NY), 2 Fed 217.

Librarian must keep record of names of all books entered. Carte v. Evans, (CC-Mass), 27 Fed 861.

Where a copy of a book was deposited with the clerk of a district court of the United States as required by the Copyright Act of 1831, the record kept by such clerk in the discharge of his public duty was competent evidence to show the deposit of such copy. Daly v. Webster, (CCA 2), 56 Fed 483, rev'g 47 Fed 903.

Section 4957 of Revised Statutes required that description be in words so as to be capable of insertion in the record. Bennett v. Carr, (CCA 2), 96 Fed 213.

Fact of recording of title should be alleged in bill in suit for infringement. Edward Thompson Co. v. American Law Book Co., (CC-NY), 119 Fed 217.

209. Certificate of registration—Effect as evidence—Receipt for copies deposited.

—In the case of each entry the person recorded as the claimant of the copyright shall be entitled to a certificate of registration under seal of the copyright office, to contain the name and address of said claimant, the name of the country of which the author of the work is a citizen or subject, and when an alien author domiciled in the United States at the time of said registration, then a statement of that fact, including his place of domicile, the name of the author (when the records of the copyright office shall show the same), the title of the work which is registered for which copyright is claimed, the date of the deposit of the copies of such work, the date of publication if the work has been reproduced in copies for sale, or publicly distributed, and such marks as to class designation and entry number as shall fully identify the entry. In the case of a book, the certificate shall also state the receipt of the affidavit, as provided by section 17 of this title, and the date of the completion of the printing, or the date of the publication of the book, as stated in the said affidavit. The Register of Copyrights shall prepare a printed form for the said certificate, to be filled out in each case as above provided for in the case of all registrations made after July 1, 1909, and in the case of all previous registrations so far as the copyright office record books shall show such facts, which certificate, sealed with the seal of the copyright office, shall, upon payment of the prescribed fee, be given to any person making application for the same. Said certificate shall be admitted in any court as prima facie evidence of the facts stated therein. In addition to such certificate the register of copyrights shall furnish, upon request, without additional fee, a receipt for the copies of the work deposited to complete the registration. (July 30, 1947, c. 391, § 1, 61 Stat. 666.)

Memorandum endorsed on bottom of certificate of librarian is not part of the certificate and is not admissible to prove that copies of book were deposited. Merrell v. Tice, 104 US 557, 26 LEd 854.

Certificate of clerk of district court is prima facie evidence of deposit of title. Callaghan v. Myers, 128 US 617, 32 LEd 547, 9 SCR 177, mod'g (CC-Ill) 24 Fed 636.

Certificate of Librarian of Congress acknowledging receipt of two copies of a book was competent evidence of the deposit of such book, although the certificate was not under seal. Belford, Clarke & Co. v. Scribner, 144 US 488, 36 LEd 514, 12 SCR 734, aff'g (CC-Ill), 50 Fed 473.

When suit for infringement is brought, the certificate of copyright does not per se establish the copyright, but the burden rests on plaintiff to show compliance with statutory requirements. Saake v. Lederer, (CCA 3), 174 Fed 135, rev'g 166 Fed 810.

Prior to 1909 certificate of Librarian of Congress was no proof of compliance with conditions. Bosselman v. Richardson, (CCA 2), 174 Fed 622.

Certificate of librarian is competent evidence to prove that books were deposited. Huebsch v. Arthur H. Crist Co., (DC-NY), 209 Fed 885.

Statute imposes duty on Librarian of Congress to give a certificate of deposit of title. Huebsch v. Arthur H. Crist Co., (DC-NY), 209 Fed 885.

The certificate of the register of copyrights indicates that the copies were received in attempted compliance with the copyright statute, on the date set out, but does not determine whether or not the deposit was made in time. Davies v. Bowes, (CCA 2), 219 Fed 178, aff'g 209 Fed 53.

Where copies of copyrighted photograph have been sold, no action can be brought for infringement of the copyright unless the certificate of registration shows the date of publication. Lumiere v. Pathé Exchange, Inc., (CCA 2), 275 Fed 428.

Librarian does not issue certificate until he learns the date of publication. Joe Mittenthal, Inc. v. Irving Berlin, Inc., (DC-NY), 291 Fed 714.

Certificate of registration was prima facie proof of authorship. Fred Fisher, Inc. v. Dillingham, (DC-NY), 298 Fed 145.

Certificate is prima facie evidence of the facts stated therein. Berlin v. Evans, (DC-Pa), 300 Fed 677; American Travel & Hotel Directory Co., Inc. v. Gehring Publishing Co., Inc., (DC-NY), 4 F(2d) 415; M. Witmark & Sons v. Calloway, (DC-Tenn), 22 F(2d) 412; Gerlach-Barklow Co. v. Morris & Bendien, (CCA 2), 23 F(2d) 159; Nutt v. National Institute, (CCA 6), 31 F(2d) 236, aff'g 28 F(2d) 132; Harms, Inc. v. Sansom House Enterprises, Inc., (DC-Pa), 162 FSupp 129, 117 USPQ 272.

Where there is nothing to contradict the facts stated in the certificate of copyright, such certificate is sufficient proof to establish a valid copyright in the owner. M. Witmark & Sons v. Calloway, (DC-Tenn), 22 F(2d) 412.

To determine whether plaintiff proved a prima facie case, the affidavits and exhibits, as well as the bill, must be examined, and the certificate of registration of a copyright, filed as an exhibit, establishes the authorship of the copyrighted work. Gerlach-Barklow Co. v. Morris & Bendien, Inc., (CCA 2), 23 F(2d) 159.

Certificate of registration is prima facie evidence of facts stated therein but this does not mean that certificate establishes that publication bore correct copyright notice; certificate does not say so, and there is nothing in statute, the reason of the matter, or circumstances to indicate that it should be so; certificate cannot be prima facie evidence of anything more than it says. Kraft v. Cohen, (CCA 3), 117 F(2d) 579, 48 USPQ 401, rev'g 32 FSupp 821, 44 USPQ 678.

The registration certificate is prima facie evidence of all that appears on its face and is not limited to facts within personal knowledge of register; this includes more than that proprietor filed two copies of song and that copyright had issued. Jerry Vogel Music Co., Inc. v. Forster Music Publisher, Inc., (CCA 2), 147 F(2d) 614, 64 USPQ 417, aff'g 62 USPQ 142.

This title confers exclusive rights in respect to songs on which copyright has been obtained by persons entitled thereto and to the extent of provisions of this title author loses right of control over his work; it is not presumed that copyrights duly registered were fraudulently obtained; on the contrary, this section makes certificate of register of copyrights prima facie evidence in any court of facts stated therein. Vance v. American Society of Composers, (CA 8), 271 F(2d) 204, 123 USPQ 296.

This section does not dispense with the necessity of alleging facts showing title in an action for infringement. Foreign & Domestic Music Corp. v. Twentieth Century-Fox Film Corp., (DC-NY), 19 FSupp 769, 34 USPQ 109.

Action for copyright infringement is not dismissed on motion for failure of declaration to sufficiently contain allegations that plaintiff has complied with § 13 of this title since not only does plaintiff allege that he has complied with this section and all other laws governing copyright but he also annexes to declaration a copy of certificate of registration issued by register of copyrights, which carries with it a presumption of regularity. Pizzano v. Knowles & Co., Inc., (DC-Mass), 37 FSupp 118, 49 USPQ 140.

Registration certificate issued to plaintiff is prima facie evidence that he is proprietor and has title to copyright, that he took necessary steps to comply with act as to registering and has valid copyright, and that persons named therein were the authors; certificate carries with it presumption of regularity; plaintiff having alleged and given proof that musical composition copyrighted was original and never before published, burden is on defendant to show otherwise. Freudenthal v. Hebrew Pub. Co., (DC-NY), 44 FSupp 754, 53 USPQ 466.

Introduction of certificate of copyright raises presumption of authorship of lyrics and music of copyrighted musical composition, and of their originality and of validity of copyright, although denied in answer; presumption is sufficient basis for decree in absence of proof by defendant attacking validity. Remick Music Corp. v. Interstate Hotel Co., (DC-Neb), 58 FSupp 523, 63 USPQ 327. Aff'd 157 F(2d) 744, 71 USPQ 138.

Administrator and widow make out prima facie case of title by producing original certificate of copyright registration showing that author was decedent; certificate is prima facie evidence of all that appears on its face; burden of going ahead with evidence is with another alleging to be coauthor to prove that other has interest in song and its proceeds. Edward B. Marks Music Corp. v. Wonnell, (DC-NY), 61 FSupp 722, 65 USPQ 456.

Certificate of copyright registration issued to plaintiff is prima facie evidence of validity of copyright and that plaintiff is proprietor thereof and has title thereto. Home Art, Inc. v. Glensder Textile Corp., (DC-NY), 81 FSupp 551, 79 USPQ 12.

Fact that defendants applied for copyright registration of the same arrangement does not estop defendants from denying that plaintiff's arrangement of defendants' song was original and substantial; certificate of registration is only prima facie evidence of facts therein stated; such facts may be controverted by defendants as well as by plaintiff; likewise, in order to claim estoppel, one must show detrimental reliance; plaintiff has failed to do this. McIntyre v. Double-A Music Corp., (DC-Cal), 166 FSupp 681, 119 USPQ 106.

Issuance of certificate of registration of copyright is prima facie proof of authorship and copyrightability. Edward B. Marks Music Corp. v. Stasny Music Corp., (DC-NY), 1 FedRDec 720, 49 USPQ 553.

Where a certificate of copyright shows a different title than the article involved in suit, such certificate is not evidence that the article involved in suit was copyrighted. McMurty v. Popham, 8 KyL 704.

210. Catalog of copyright entries—Effect as evidence.—The Register of Copyrights shall fully index all copyright registrations and assignments and shall print at periodic intervals a catalog of the titles of articles deposited and registered for copyright, together with suitable indexes, and at stated intervals shall print complete and indexed catalog for each class of copyright entries, and may thereupon, if expedient, destroy the original manuscript catalog cards containing the titles included in such printed volumes and representing the entries made during such intervals. The current catalog of copyright entries and the index volumes herein provided for shall be admitted in any court as prima facie evidence of the facts stated therein as regards any copyright registration. (July 30, 1947, c. 391, § 1, 61 Stat. 666.)

211. Distribution and sale—Disposal of proceeds.—The said printed current catalogs as they are issued shall be promptly distributed by the Superintendent of Documents to the collectors of customs of the United States and to the postmasters of all exchange offices of receipt of foreign mails, in accordance with revised list of such collectors of customs and postmasters prepared by the Secretary of the Treasury and the Postmaster General, and they shall also be furnished in whole or in part to all parties desiring them at a price to be determined by the Register of Copyrights for each part of the catalog not exceeding $25 for the complete yearly catalog of copyright en-

tries. The consolidated catalogs and indexes shall also be supplied to all persons ordering them at such prices as may be fixed by the Register of Copyrights, and all subscriptions for the catalogs shall be received by the Superintendent of Documents, who shall forward the said publications; and the moneys thus received shall be paid into the Treasury of the United States and accounted for under such laws and Treasury regulations as shall be in force at the time. (July 30, 1947, c. 391, § 1, 61 Stat. 667; Apr. 27, 1948, c. 236, § 1, 62 Stat. 202.)

Amendment note.—Act Apr. 27, 1948, cited to text, substituted "Superintendent of Documents" for "copyright office," "list" for "lists," and "$25" for "$10" and "fixed by the Register of Copyrights" for "determined to be reasonable."

Effective date.—Section 3 of Act Apr. 27, 1948, cited to text, provided: "This Act [amendments to §§ 211, 215 of this title] shall take effect thirty days after [Apr. 27, 1948] its enactment."

212. Records and works deposited in copyright office open to public inspection—Taking copies of entries.—The record books of the copyright office, together with the indexes to such record books, and all works deposited and retained in the copyright office, shall be open to public inspection; and copies may be taken of the copyright entries actually made in such record books, subject to such safeguards and regulations as shall be prescribed by the Register of Copyrights and approved by the Librarian of Congress. (July 30, 1947, c. 391, § 1, 61 Stat. 667.)

213. Disposition of articles deposited in office.—Of the articles deposited in the copyright office under the provisions of the copyright laws of the United States, the Librarian of Congress shall determine what books and other articles shall be transferred to the permanent collections of the Library of Congress, including the law library, and what other books or articles shall be placed in the reserve collections of the Library of Congress for sale or exchange, or be transferred to other governmental libraries in the District of Columbia for use therein. (July 30, 1947, c. 391, § 1, 61 Stat. 667.)

214. Destruction of articles deposited in office remaining undisposed of — Removal of by author or proprietor—Manuscripts of unpublished works. — Of any articles undisposed of as above provided, together with all titles and correspondence relating thereto, the Librarian of

Congress and the Register of Copyrights jointly shall, at suitable intervals, determine what of these received during any period of years it is desirable or useful to preserve in the permanent files of the copyright office, and, after due notice as hereinafter provided, may within their discretion cause the remaining articles and other things to be destroyed: Provided, That there shall be printed in the Catalog of Copyright Entries from February to November, inclusive, a statement of the years of receipt of such articles and a notice to permit any author, copyright proprietor, or other lawful claimant to claim and remove before the expiration of the month of December of that year anything found which relates to any of his productions deposited or registered for copyright within the period of years stated, not reserved or disposed of as provided for in this title. No manuscript of an unpublished work shall be destroyed during its term of copyright without specific notice to the copyright proprietor of record, permitting him to claim and remove it. (July 30, 1947, c. 391, § 1, 61 Stat. 667.)

215. Fees.—The Register of Copyrights shall receive, and the persons to whom the services designated are rendered shall pay, the following fees:

For the registration of a claim to copyright in any work, except a print or label used for articles of merchandise, $4; for the registration of a claim to copyright in a print or label used for articles of merchandise, $6; which fees shall include a certificate of registration under seal for each work registered: Provided, That only one registration fee shall be required in the case of several volumes of the same book published and deposited at the same time: And provided further, That with respect to works of foreign origin, in lieu of payment of the copyright fee of $4 together with one copy of the work and application, the foreign author or proprietor may at any time within six months from the date of first publication abroad deposit in the Copyright Office an application for registration and two copies of the work which shall be accompanied by a catalog card in form and content satisfactory to the Register of Copyrights.

For recording the renewal of copyright and issuance of certificate therefor, $2.

For every additional certificate of registration, $1.

For certifying a copy of an application for registration of copyright, and for all other certification, $2.

For recording every assignment, agreement, power of attorney, or other paper not exceeding six pages, $3; for each additional page or less, 50 cents; for each title over one in the paper recorded, 50 cents additional.

For recording a notice of use, $2, for each notice of not more than five titles; and 50 cents for each additional title.

For any requested search of Copyright office records, or works deposited, or services rendered in connection therewith, $3 for each hour of time consumed. (July 30, 1947, c. 391, § 1, 61 Stat. 668; Apr. 27, 1948, c. 236, § 2, 62 Stat. 202; June 3, 1949, c. 171, § 4, 63 Stat. 154.)

Amendment notes.—Act Apr. 27, 1948, cited to text, amended this section generally.

Act June 3, 1949, cited to text, struck out the period at the end of the second paragraph, added a colon and inserted the second proviso.

Cross reference. — Effective date of 1948 Amendment, see § 211 note of this title.

NOTES TO DECISIONS

Fees prescribed by R. S. § 4958, see Merrell v. Tice, 104 US 557, 26 LEd 854.

Under a former copyright law which required certain fees for person not a citizen or resident of the United States, a citizen or resident of the Philippine Islands should be treated as one not a citizen or resident of the United States. 25 OAG 179.

216. When the day for taking action falls on Saturday, Sunday, or a holiday.—When the last day for making any deposit or application, or for paying any fee, or for delivering any other material to the Copyright Office falls on Saturday, Sunday, or a holiday within the District of Columbia, such action may be taken on the next succeeding business day. (Apr. 13, 1954, c. 137, § 1, 68 Stat. 52.)

Public Law 87-773
87th Congress, H. R. 11793
October 9, 1962

An Act

To provide criminal penalties for trafficking in phonograph records bearing forged or counterfeit labels.

Be it enacted by the Senate and House of Representatives of the United States of America in Congress assembled, That chapter 113, title 18, United States Code, as amended, is further amended by adding at the end thereof the following new section:

"§ 2318. Transportation, sale, or receipt of phonograph records bearing forged or counterfeit labels

"Whoever knowingly and with fraudulent intent transports, causes to be transported, receives, sells, or offers for sale in interstate or foreign commerce any phonograph record, disk, wire, tape, film, or other article on which sounds are recorded, to which or upon which is stamped, pasted, or affixed any forged or counterfeited label, knowing the label to have been falsely made, forged, or counterfeited, shall be fined not more than $1,000 or imprisoned not more than one year, or both."

Phonograph records bearing forged labels. Penalty for transportation.

SEC. 2. The chapter analysis of chapter 113, title 18, United States Code, is amended by adding at the end thereof the following:

"Sec. 2318. Transportation, sale, or receipt of phonograph records bearing forged or counterfeit labels."

Approved October 9, 1962.

TABLE OF CASES

A

TABLE OF CASES

(1604)

TABLE OF CASES

TABLE OF CASES

(1608)

TABLE OF CASES

TABLE OF CASES

TABLE OF CASES

F

(1615)

TABLE OF CASES

TABLE OF CASES

H

TABLE OF CASES

(1620)

TABLE OF CASES

J

(1621)

TABLE OF CASES

TABLE OF CASES

TABLE OF CASES

(1624)

TABLE OF CASES

TABLE OF CASES

TABLE OF CASES

TABLE OF CASES

TABLE OF CASES

(1631)

TABLE OF CASES

(1632)

TABLE OF CASES

TABLE OF CASES

TABLE OF CASES

TABLE OF CASES

(1637)

TABLE OF CASES

TABLE OF CASES

U

V

TABLE OF CASES

(1640)

TABLE OF CASES

Y

Z

INDEX

A

ABANDONMENT OF COPYRIGHT
Due to manufacturing requirements, page (1187)

ACCOUNTING
Co-owners of copyright, page (697)

ACOUSTIC RECORDINGS
 See SOUND RECORDINGS—UNAUTHORIZED DUPLICATION

ADAPTATIONS
Joint ownership, page (696)

ADDRESSES
 See LECTURES, SERMONS, ADDRESSES

AD INTERIM PROTECTION
 See COPYRIGHT CODE; MANUFACTURING CLAUSE

ADVERTISEMENTS
Copyrightable material, methods and amounts of payments, page (32)
Economic size importance, pages (19), (20)
Indemnity agreements against infringement, page (1093)
Injunctive relief, page (1034)
Multiple infringements, maximum damages, page (1083)
Pictures, protection, page (72)
Registration of copyrightable material, extent, page (37)
Subject matter of copyright, page (71)
Use of minimum damage provision with respect to packaged advertising, page (1083)

ALBANIA
Renewal of copyright, page (602)

ALIENS AND CITIZENSHIP
 See FOREIGN WORKS PROTECTION
Domiciled within territorial possessions of the United States, page (757)
Eligibility for copyright ownership, page (622)
Works done for hire or on commission, page (719)

AMERICAN BAR ASSOCIATION
Resolution opposing compulsory licensing, page (902)

AMERICAN BOOK PUBLISHERS COUNCIL
Economic analysis of manufacturing clause, page (1146)

AMERICAN LIBRARY ASSOCIATION
Reproduction of materials code, page (818)
    Manuscripts, page (819)
    Public domain works, page (819)

AMERICAN SAMOA
 See TERRITORIAL POSSESSIONS OF UNITED STATES

AMERICAN SOCIETY OF COMPOSERS, AUTHORS AND PUBLISHERS (ASCAP)
Arguments for elimination of compulsory licensing, pages (899)-(902), (909)
Brief criticizing fair use provision of Duffy bill, page (798)

INDEX

INDEX

ART

See ARCHITECTURAL WORKS; DESIGNS

Applied art, subject matter of copyright, page (1212)
Cemetery memorials, subject of copyright, page (83)
Copyrightability, pages (39), (45), (398)
Copyright ownership of paintings made on commission, page (722)
Damages for infringement under 1895 Act, page (998)
Deposit in Library of Congress, page (446)
Fair use, pages (796), (801)
Inherent right of protection, page (68)
Reproductions abroad, exceptions from manufacturing clause, page (1152)
Sculpture,
    Infringed by photograph, page (76)
    Subject matter of copyright, pages (74), (76)
Subject matter of copyright, pages (51), (53)
    Three-dimensional objects, page (76)

ASSIGNMENTS AND LICENSES

See COMPULSORY LICENSING; COPYRIGHT CODE; DIVISIBILITY OF
COPYRIGHT; RENEWAL OF COPYRIGHT

Acknowledgment of transferring instrument, page (1295)
Assignee's name in notice, pages (243), (358)
Assignments distinguished from licenses, pages (626), (636)
Bequests, record, page (768)
Divisibility of copyright,
    Foreign countries, pages (681)-(687)
    Notice, basic issues, page (651)
Effect on copyright notice under foreign laws, page (685)
Enforcement of renewal rights, page (561)
    Jurisdiction, page (575)
Execution of transfers, page (1294)
Fees, representative ASCAP rates, page (1096)
Form and execution of transfers, page (1295)
Great Britain, page (388)
Indemnity agreements against infringements, pages (1092), (1093)
Indivisibility of copyright concept, page (625)
Infringement action against licensee of one coowner, page (703)
Infringement actions precluded, page (635)
Joint ownership, pages (692), (693)
Limitations on transfers, proposal, page (1293)
Mortgages, record, page (768)
Musical compositions,
    Performance societies, page (922)
    Trade practice, page (925)
New version, separate copyrightability, page (641)
New work concept, page (712)
Notice of copyright,
    Name of transferee, page (1297)
    Record, formality, page (775)
Parties entitled to sue, pages (625), (631), (633), (639)
    Foreign countries, pages (650), (686)
    Infringement actions precluded, page (635)
    Joint owners, page (697)
    Need for divisibility of copyright, page (646)
    Partial reservation of rights, page (637)
Periodicals,
    Protection of rights by contract, page (649)
    Transfer of rights, page (642)
Personal right of author, page (1205)
Proper claimant in case of assignment, page (358)
Protection of authors against unremunerative transfers, page (1292)
Rates set by ASCAP, page (1096)
Recommendation of the Register of Copyrights, page (1298)

(1647)

INDEX

INDEX

INDEX

INDEX

CATALOG OF COPYRIGHT ENTRIES—Continued.
Distribution and use,
    Prima facie evidence, pages (345), (426), (457), (459), (469)
    Production cost and sales, page (465)
    Search tool, pages (456), (463), (468)
    Subscribers, page (464)
    Summary, page (461)
Drama catalog,
    Use by subscribers, page (464)
    Use in depository libraries, page (463)
Historical development,
    Conference on Copyright, Nov. 1-5, 1905, page (456)
    Early experiments in publishing copyright record, page (453)
    Establishment of "Catalog of Title Entries" by act of 1891, page (455)
    First copyright law, page (453)
    Provisions of act of 1909, page (457)
    Since 1909, page (457)
Map catalog,
    Use by subscribers, page (464)
    Use in depository libraries, page (463)
Microfilm record as substitute, page (469)
Music catalog, use by subscribers, page (464)
National bibliography, pages (454), (455), (461), (462), (465)
    Foreign country publication, page (466)
Notice of destruction of deposited works, page (449)
Prima facie evidence of facts stated, pages (345), (426), (457), (459), (469)
Property of card service, page (458)
Publication of copyright records in other countries, page (466)
Public service publication, page (465)
Purpose, page (453)
    Enforcement of importation restrictions, page (455)
Rationale of present statutory provision, page (456)
Record keeping in copyright office, page (362)
Record of copyright,
    Card file in copyright office, page (461)
    Early experiments in publishing, page (453)
    Early recognition of need, page (453)
    Evaluation of usefulness, page (462)
    Miscellaneous copyright office records and their relationship to the catalog, page (459)
    Publication in other countries, page (466)
    Renewable term as method of up dating record, page (495)
    Type and extent of records kept, page (460)
Relationship to other copyright records, page (459)
Requirement and uses, pages (453), (462), (1343)
Sales, page (465)
Searching service, pages (457), (458)
Statutory requirement, pages (453), (457)
Subscribers, type and use of catalog, page (464)

CEMETERY MEMORIALS
Subject matter of copyright, page (83)

CERTIFICATE OF REGISTRATIONS
See REGISTER OF COPYRIGHTS

Contents, page (354)
Issuance by Register of Copyrights, page (428)
Misstatements, page (356)
Presumptions attached, pages (354)-(356)
Prima facie evidence of the facts stated, pages (344), (354), (426)
Refusal by Register of Copyrights, page (353)

CHACE BILL
International copyright, page (1129)

(1652)

INDEX

INDEX

INDEX

INDEX

CONSTITUTIONAL ASPECTS—Continued.

Sound recordings, page (165)
    Protection against unauthorized duplication, page (122)
Termination of common law protection for pre-existing unpublished works, page (223)
Writings, term broader than in statutes, page (59)
Writings within the meaning of copyright clause,
    Choreographic works, pages (114), (115)
    Denial of copyright protection, page (79)
    Protection of three-dimensional objects, pages (76), (77)

CONTRACTS

    See ASSIGNMENTS AND LICENSES; WORKS MADE FOR HIRE
        AND ON COMMISSION

Agreements to divide international markets, page (1325)
Author's right to refuse performance, page (985)
Compulsory licenses, economic nature, page (939)
Import restrictions, page (1164)
Indemnity in insurance agreements against infringement, pages (1092)-(1095)
Ownership of copyright, page (621)
Protection against indivisibility, page (649)
Songwriters Protective Association, page (925)

CONVENTIONS

    See BERNE CONVENTION; BUENOS AIRES CONVENTION;
        INTERNATIONAL COPYRIGHT; UNIVERSAL
        COPYRIGHT CONVENTION

CO-OWNERSHIP

    See JOINT OWNERSHIP OF COPYRIGHT

COPIES AND COPYING

    See COMPULSORY LICENSING; FAIR USE; PHOTODUPLICATION
        BY LIBRARIES

Indication by circumstantial evidence, page (1057)
Indirect constituting infringement, page (1052)
"Indirect copying" defined, page (1052)
Innocence or lack of intent not a defense, page (1052)
Mechanical reproductions, pages (879), (897)
Motion picture performance rights, page (1228)
Right to make and publish, pages (1221), (1222)
Sound recordings, pages (879), (897), (1223)

COPYRIGHTABLE WORKS

    See SUBJECT MATTER OF COPYRIGHT

COPYRIGHT ACT (CONSTRUCTION)

    See COPYRIGHT CODE

Accidental omission of copyright notice, pages (238), (1050)
Assignment of copyright, page (768)
Assignments and bequests, page (768)
Assignments, recordation, page (764)
Classes of unpublished works registrable, page (195)
Compulsory licensing, pages (125), (890), (1009)
Constitutionality, page (45)
Costs; attorney's fees, page (1025)
Criminal penalty for infringement, pages (1040), (1051)
Damages and profits, pages (999), (1050), (1069)
"Date of first publication" construed as date of deposit for unpublished registered works, page (197)
False use of copyright notice, page (303)
Government publications, pages (171), (175), (177), (185)
Impounding during action, pages (1037), (1051)

INDEX

COPYRIGHT ACT (CONSTRUCTION)—Continued.

Injunction, page (1032)

Manufacturing clause, pages (1125), (1147)

Notice,
> Form, pages (239), (242)-(246)
> Position, page (247)

Preservation of common law rights, page (193)

Presidential proclamations, page (742)

Protection limited to specific enumerations, pages (53), (54)

Publication with notice, page (235)

Recordation of assignments, pages (764), (771)

Registration as condition precedent to suit, page (357)

Renewal rights, page (518)

Renewal of prints and labels registered in Patent Office under repealed law, page (538)

Royalties for use of mechanical reproduction of musical works, pages (891), (1009)

Substitution of name of assignee in copyright notice, page (243)

Work of alien author eligible for statutory protection if he is domiciled in United States "at the time of first publication for the work", pages (742), (757)

Works made for hire, page (720)

COPYRIGHT CODE

> References are to F.C.A. (U.S.C.) Title 17 and sections, see pages (1347)-(1600)

Abridgment of works in public domain or of copyrighted works, 17 § 7

Actions, limitations, 17 § 115

Adaptations or arrangements of works in public domain or of copyrighted work, 17 § 7

Addresses, 17 § 5
> Damages for infringement, 17 § 101(b)
> Exclusive right to deliver or authorize delivery of copyrighted address, 17 § 1

Ad interim copyrights,
> Extension of time of procuring by aliens, 17 § 9
> Foreign production or publication, 17 §§ 16, 22
> Publication of book seeking ad interim protection with notice, 17 § 10

Administrator, right, 17 § 9

Affidavit of domestic manufacture, 17 §§ 17, 18
> Certificate of registration to state receipt, 17 § 209

Agreements,
> Fee for recording, 17 § 215
> International agreements affecting alien's rights, 17 § 9

Aliens, 17 § 9
> Certificate of registration to alien resident, 17 § 209
> Deposit of copies, 17 § 13

All writings of author included, 17 § 4

Appeal in suits under copyright laws, 17 § 114

Application,
> Registration,
>> Fees for certifying copy, 17 § 215
>> Specifying class of works, 17 § 5
> Renewal or extension, 17 § 24
>> Copyrights registered in patent office under repealed laws, 17 § 25
> Saturdays, Sundays or holidays, day for making applications falling on, 17 § 216

Art, 17 § 5
> Deposit of photographs or other identifying reproductions, 17 § 13
> Notice of copyright, 17 § 19
> Right to complete, execute or finish models or designs, 17 § 1

Assignments, 17 § 28
> Acknowledgment of assignment executed in foreign country, 17 § 29
> Certificate of record, 17 § 31
> Certified copy, 17 § 31

INDEX

COPYRIGHT CODE—Continued.

Assignments,
    Copyrighted object not transferred by assignment, 17 § 27
    Fee for recording and certifying, 17 §§ 31, 215
    Foreign countries, assignment of copyright, 17 §§ 29, 30
    Index of assignment, 17 § 210
    Record, 17 §§ 30-32
        Fee, 17 § 215
    Substitution of assignee's name in notice of copyright, 17 § 32
    Assigns, right to copyright, 17 § 9
Attorney's fees in copyright suits, 17 § 116
    Action for royalties for mechanical reproduction of musical work, 17 § 1
Author defined, 17 § 26
Authors, right to copyrights, 17 § 9
Bequest of copyright, 17 § 28
Binding in United States, 17 § 16
    Affidavit, 17 §§ 17, 18
    Foreign publication subsequently published in United States, 17 § 23
    Importation of copyrighted works not bound in United States, 17 § 107
Blind persons,
    Books for blind need not be manufactured in United States, 17 § 16
    Importation of piratical works for blind, 17 § 107
Books, 17 § 5
    Ad interim protection of foreign publication, 17 § 22
        Extension of copyright to full term, 17 § 23
        Subsequent publication in United States, 17 § 23
    Fees for registration of claim to copyright, 17 § 215
Broadcasting copyrighted work, damages for infringement, 17 § 1(c)
Catalog of copyright entries, 17 §§ 210, 211
    Notice to permit removal of articles before destruction printed, 17 § 214
Certificates,
    Record of assignment, 17 § 31
    Registration, 17 § 209
        Fees, 17 § 215
        Issuance, 17 § 11
        Prints and labels, 17 § 6
Certified copies,
    Assignment of copyright, 17 § 31
    Papers in injunction suit to prevent violation of rights transmitted to court enforcing injunction, 17 § 113
Civil actions, limitation, 17 § 115
Claims of copyright, work not reproduced for sale, 17 § 13
Classification of works for registration, 17 § 5
Coin-operated machines, reproduction of musical composition by as public performance, 17 § 1
Collector of customs, current catalogs of entries distributed, 17 § 211
Common law rights in unpublished works, effect of copyright law, 17 § 2
Compilation, 17 § 5
    Damages for infringement, 17 § 101(b)
    Works in public domain or of copyrighted work, 17 § 7
Component parts of copyrighted work, 17 § 3
Composite work, 17 § 5
    All contents protected, 17 § 3
    Damages for infringement, 17 § 101(b)
Consolidated catalog and indexes of copyright entries, 17 § 211
Contempt to enforce injunction preventing violation of rights, 17 § 112
Conventions, 17 § 9 note
Copy, exclusive right to copy copyrighted works, 17 § 1
Copyright office,
    Assignment recorded, 17 § 30
    Authentication of papers, 17 § 206
    Catalog of copyright entries, 17 §§ 210, 211
        Notice to permit removal of articles deposited before destruction, 17 § 214

COPYRIGHT CODE—Continued.

Copyright office,

Certificate, power of Assistant Register of Copyrights to sign, 17 § 202

Day for performing acts falling on Saturday, Sunday or holiday, 17 § 216

Deposit of copies, 17 § 13

Deposit of photographs or other identifying reproductions in lieu of copies of published works, 17 § 13

Destruction of articles deposited in office, 17 § 214

Disposition of articles deposited in, 17 § 213

Indexes,

Inspection of index for record book, 17 § 212

Inspection of record books, index and works deposited, 17 § 212

Librarian of Congress,

Approval of regulations for deposit of identifying reproductions in lieu of copies, 17 § 13

Assistant Register of Copyrights appointed, 17 § 201

Deposits in copyright office, librarian to determine articles to be transferred to permanent collection, 17 § 213

Powers and duties, 17 § 202

Register of Copyrights appointed, 17 § 201

Register of Copyrights to report, 17 §§ 203, 205

Libraries, transfer of articles deposited in office to, 17 § 213

Manuscript of unpublished work, destruction, 17 § 214

Notice of intention to destroy articles deposited, 17 § 214

Photographs, deposit in lieu of copies of published works, 17 § 13

Record books, 17 § 208

Inspection, 17 § 212

Records,

Fee for search, 17 § 215

Preserved, 17 § 201

Register of Copyrights,

Application to Register of Copyrights for renewal of copyright registered in patent office under repealed law, 17 § 25

Appointment, 17 § 201

Assistants, 17 § 201

Catalog of title deposited and registered, 17 § 210

Certificate of deposit of copies of imported work, 17 § 109

Certificate of registration issued, 17 § 11

Demand by Register of Copyrights for deposit of copies, 17 § 14

Deposit of money received, 17 § 203

Destruction of articles deposited in office by, 17 § 214

Fees, 17 § 215

Form of certificate of registration prepared by, 17 § 209

Index of registration and assignment, 17 § 210

Mailing copies, 17 § 13

Notice of intention to use musical composition or mechanical reproduction sent to office, 17 § 101(e)

Price of current catalog of entries fixed, 17 § 211

Receipt for copy deposited furnished, 17 § 209

Record books provided, 17 § 208

Regulations for copying entries in record book, 17 § 212

Reports, 17 §§ 203, 205

Rules and regulations for deposit of photographs or identifying reproductions, 17 § 13

Rules and regulations for registration of claim promulgated, 17 § 207

Text of rules and regulations, 17 § 207 note

Supervised by Librarian of Congress, 17 § 201

Registration of copyright by, 17 § 201

Removal of articles by author or proprietor, 17 § 214

Reproductions, deposit of identifying reproductions in lieu of copies of published work, 17 § 13

Rules and regulations, text of rules, 17 § 207 note

Sale of catalog of copyright entries, 17 § 211

INDEX

COPYRIGHT CODE—Continued.

Copyright office,
    Seals, 17 §§ 202, 206, 209
    Search of records, 17 § 215
Costs in copyright suits, 17 § 116
    Action to recover royalty from mechanical reproduction of musical composition, 17 § 1
Criminal proceedings, limitations, 17 § 115
Cyclopedic works, 17 § 5
    Damages for infringements, 17 § 101(b)
    Renewal or extension of copyright, 17 § 24
Damages,
    Failure to pay royalties for mechanical reproduction of musical work, 17 § 1
    Infringement, 17 § 101(b), (e)
        Accidental omission of notice of copyright affecting damages, 17 § 21
        Broadcasting copyrighted work, 17 § 1(c)
Date of publication defined, 17 § 26
Deposit of copies,
    Affidavit to accompany deposit, 17 §§ 17, 18
    Aliens, 17 § 13
    Catalog of titles of articles deposited, 17 § 210
    Certificate showing deposit of imported work, 17 § 109
    Condition precedent,
        Infringement suit, 17 § 13
        Registration, 17 § 11
    Date of deposit stated in certificate of registration, 17 § 209
    Demand by Register of Copyrights when copy is not deposited, 17 § 14
    Destruction of articles undisposed of, 17 § 214
    Dramatic composition, 17 §§ 12, 13
    Drawing, deposit of reproduction or photograph, 17 § 12
    Failure to deposit, 17 § 14
    Fee for search of works deposited, 17 § 215
    Foreign publication, 17 § 22
        Subsequently published in United States, 17 § 23
    Imported works, certificate of deposit, 17 § 109
    Inspection of copies deposited, 17 § 212
    Library of Congress, transfer of articles deposited to permanent collection, 17 § 213
    Mailing copies, 17 § 15
    Number of copies, 17 § 13
        Works not reproduced for sale, 17 § 12
    Penalty for failure to deposit, 17 § 14
    Postmaster's receipt for copies deposited in mail, 17 § 14
    Receipt for works deposited, 17 § 209
    Record book, entry of deposit, 17 § 208
    Report of works deposited, 17 § 205
    Saturday, Sunday or holiday, day for making deposit falling on, 17 § 216
    Time of deposit after publication, 17 § 13
    Works not reproduced for sale, 17 § 13
Deposit of identifying reproductions in lieu of copies of published works, 17 § 13
Design, right to complete, execute or finish models or designs, 17 § 1
Designs for works of art, 17 § 5
    Damages for infringement, 17 § 101(b)
    Deposit of photographs or other identifying reproductions, 17 § 13
    Notice of copyright, 17 § 19
Destruction,
    Articles deposited in Copyright Office remaining undisposed of, 17 § 214
    Infringing copies and plates, 17 § 101(d)
    Original manuscript catalog card, 17 § 210
    Prohibited imports, 17 § 108
Directories, 17 § 5
    Damages for infringement, 17 § 101(b)

INDEX

COPYRIGHT CODE—Continued.

District courts,
    Injunction suit, transmission by clerk of papers to court enforcing injunction, 17 § 113
    Injunction to prevent violation of rights, power to grant, 17 § 112
    Review of copyright cases, 17 § 114
Dramatic composition, 17 § 5
    Copyright owner's right,
        Dramatize nondramatic work and vice versa, 17 § 1
        Perform, 17 § 1
    Deposit of copy, 17 § 12
        Works not reproduced for sale, 17 § 13
    Dramatization of works in public domain or copyrighted work, 17 § 7
    Exclusive rights as to copyrighted works, 17 § 1
    Infringement by motion picture, damages, 17 § 101(b)
    Motion-picture photoplay, 17 § 5
    Notice of copyright, 17 § 19
Drawings, 17 § 5
    Damages for infringement, 17 § 101(b)
    Deposit of reproduction or photograph, 17 §§ 12, 13
    Notice of copyright, 17 § 19
Evidence,
    Certificate of registration, 17 § 209
    Current catalog of titles of articles deposited and registered, 17 § 210
    Profits, 17 § 101(b)
Exclusive rights as to copyrighted works, 17 § 1
Executors,
    Application for renewal or extension, 17 § 24
    Right to copyright, 17 § 9
Expiration, 17 § 24
Extension of copyrights, 17 § 24
    Original work by copyrighting compilation of works in public domain or copyrighted work, 17 § 7
False affidavit of domestic manufacture, 17 § 18
Fees,
    Deposit of fees received, 17 § 203
    Payment, day for paying falling on Saturday, Sunday or holiday, 17 § 216
    Recording and certifying assignment, 17 §§ 31, 215
    Registering claim of copyright of print or label, 17 §§ 6, 215
Foreign language,
    Importation of piratical copies, 17 § 107
    Printing book in United States, 17 § 16
Foreign production or publication,
    Ad interim copyright, 17 §§ 16, 22
    Deposit of application in Copyright Office in lieu of copyright fee, 17 § 215
    Subsequently published in United States, 17 § 23
Forfeiture,
    Prohibited imports, 17 § 108
    Protection, false affidavit and domestic manufacture, 17 § 18
Gazetteers, 17 § 5
    Damages for infringement, 17 § 101(b)
Gift of object copyrighted as not transfer of copyright, 17 § 27
Government publication, 17 § 8
Holidays, day for taking action falling on, 17 § 216
Imports,
    Copies of works not manufactured in United States, 17 § 107
    Deposit of copies of imported works, 17 § 109
    False or fraudulent notice on imported works, 17 §§ 106, 107
    Forfeiture and destruction of prohibited article, 17 § 108
    Piratical works copyrighted in United States, 17 §§ 106, 107
    Rules and regulations preventing importation, 17 § 109
    Seizure of prohibited imports, 17 § 108
India, copyright extension, 17 § 9 note

INDEX

COPYRIGHT CODE—Continued.

Infringement,
 Charitable purposes, performance of copyrighted work for, 17 § 104
 Damages, 17 § 101(b), (e)
  Accidental omission of notice of copyright affecting damages, 17 § 21
 Deposit of copies as condition precedent to suit, 17 § 13
 Destruction of infringing copies and devices, 17 § 101(d)
 Educational purposes, performance of copyrighted work for, 17 § 104
 Evidence of profit, 17 § 101(b)
 Impounding infringing articles pending action, 17 § 101(c)
 Injunction, 17 §§ 21, 101(a), (e)
 Limitation of civil or criminal proceedings, 17 § 115
 Mechanical reproduction of musical compositions, 17 § 1
 Motion pictures, damages for infringement, 17 § 101(b)
 Notice of copyright, accidental omission affecting right to sue for infringement, 17 § 21
 Offenses, 17 § 104
 Profit, 17 §§ 101(b), 104
 Registration as condition precedent to suit, 17 § 13
 Remedies, 17 § 101
 Royalties for use of mechanical reproduction of musical works, 17 § 101(e)
 Rules of practice and procedure, text of rules, 17 § 207 note
 Treble damages for use of mechanical reproduction of musical works, 17 § 101(e)
 Willful infringement for profit, 17 § 104
Injunction,
 Enforcement of injunction to prevent violation of right, 17 §§ 112, 113
 Infringement, 17 §§ 21, 101(a), (e)
 Prevention of violation of rights under copyright law, 17 § 113
 Violation of rights, 17 § 112
International agreement affecting alien's rights, 17 § 9
Judgment or decree in suits under copyright laws, review, 17 § 114
Jurisdiction, enforcement of injunction to prevent violation of rights, 17 § 112
Labels, 17 §§ 5, 6
 Damages for infringement, 17 § 101(b)
 Fees for registration of claim to copyright, 17 § 215
 Notice of copyright, 17 § 19
Lectures, 17 § 5
 Damages for infringement, 17 § 101(b)
 Deposit of copy, 17 § 12
 Exclusive right to deliver or authorize delivery of copyrighted lecture, 17 § 1
Libraries, transfer to libraries of articles deposited in copyright office, 17 § 213
Library of Congress, transfer of articles deposited in copyright office to permanent collection of library, 17 § 213
Limitation of prosecution, 17 § 115
Lithographing to be done in United States, 17 § 16
 Affidavit, 17 §§ 17, 18
 Foreign publication subsequently lithographed in United States, 17 § 23
 Importation of piratical copies not lithographed in United States, 17 § 107
Mailing copies to Register of Copyrights, 17 § 14
Map, 17 § 5
 Damages for infringement, 17 § 101(b)
 Notice of copyright, 17 § 19
Mechanical reproduction of musical works, 17 § 1
Mechanical work to be done in United States, 17 § 16
 Affidavit, 17 §§ 17, 18
 Foreign work subsequently published in United States, 17 § 23
 Importation of piratical works not manufactured in United States, 17 § 107
Models for works of art, 17 § 5
 Damages for infringement, 17 § 101(b)
 Deposit of photographs or other identifying reproductions, 17 § 13
 Notice of copyright, 17 § 19

(1663)

INDEX

INDEX

INDEX

INDEX

(1668)

INDEX

INDEX

INDEX

INDEX

INDEX

INDEX

E

INDEX

INDEX

INDEX

INDEX

(1683)

INDEX

GREAT BRITAIN—Continued.

Compulsory licensing, pages (612), (914)

Damages, page (1009)

Deposit of copyrighted works, page (413)

Duration of copyright, pages (330), (334), (477)

Early copyright history, page (46)

"Fair dealing" provisions of United Kingdom Act of 1956, pages (805), (825)

"Fair dealing" provisions of United Kingdom Acts of 1911 and 1956 with respect to photoduplication by libraries, page (825)

Fair use, pages (802), (805)

Government publications, copyright, page (181)

Innocent infringement, page (1062)

Moral rights of author, page (976)

Performing rights limitation, page (847)

Photocopying of copyrighted works, page (825)

Recent developments bearing on American renewal system, page (612)

Reciprocity, page (740)

Registration and deposit, pages (327), (386)

Renewal of copyright,

    British Copyright Act, 1911, page (612)

    Brussels Convention, 1948, page (612)

    Canadian copyright report, 1957, page (613)

    Gregory report, 1952, page (612)

    New Zealand copyright report, 1909, page (614)

    Parliamentary debates in United Kingdom Copyright Act, 1956, page (613)

Renewal principle abandoned, page (507)

Sound recordings, copyright protection, page (158)

Statute of Anne (1710), page (327)

Works made for hire, page (727)

GREECE

Duration of copyright, page (477)

Innocent infringement, page (1061)

Performing rights limitation, page (847)

Translations, renewal of copyright, page (602)

GREETING CARDS

Commercial use of copyright notice, page (290)

Payments by publishers for copyrightable materials, page (31)

Registration of copyrightable material, extent, page (36)

GREGORY COMMITTEE REPORT, 1952

Recommendation for repeal of compulsory licensing provisions of United Kingdom Copyright Act, 1911, page (612)

GUAM

      See TERRITORIAL POSSESSIONS OF UNITED STATES

GUATEMALA

Damages, page (1014)

Duration of copyright, page (477)

Innocent infringement, page (1061)

H

HAITI

Import quotas on books, page (1161)

HAWLEY BILL

International copyright, page (1129)

HIRE, WORKS MADE FOR

      See WORKS MADE FOR HIRE AND ON COMMISSION

INDEX

INDEX

INDEPENDENT CONTRACTOR

INDEX

INDEX

INDEX

INDEX

INDEX

INDEX

INDEX

INDEX

NEWS

Fair use, pages (790), (797), (798), (800)

NEWS AGENCIES

Economic size importance, page (21)

NEWS DEALERS AND NEWS STANDS

Economic size importance, page (17)

NEWSPAPERS

Advertising matter, injunctive relief, page (1034)
Commercial use of copyright notice in newspaper publishing industry, page (292)
Deposit in Library of Congress, pages (440), (446)
Duration of copyright, legislative proposals for revision, page (481)
Economic size importance, page (13)
First owner of copyright, proposal in Perkins bill, page (723)
Indemnity agreements against infringement, page (1093)
Multiple infringements, maximum damages, page (1083)
Photoduplication by libraries, page (816)
Photograph reproductions,
    Litigation discouraged by statutory limits of damages, page (1086)
    Statutory damages, page (1005)
Publishers, method and amount of payments for copyrightable materials, page (30)
Registration of copyrightable material, extent, page (36)
Syndicates,
    Economic size importance, page (21)
    Methods and amounts of payments for materials, page (32)
    Registration of copyrightable material, extent, page (36)

NEW VERSIONS

Copyrightability, page (1209)
Defined, page (572)
Divisibility, page (641)
Exclusive right of copyright owner, page (784)
Fair use, page (783)
Joint authorship, page (696)
Made and copyrighted under assignment or license no longer binding during renewal term, page (565)
New work concept, joint owners, page (712)
Right to make, page (1222)

NEW ZEALAND

Assignees and licensees, capacity to sue, page (686)
Dalglish Report of Copyright Committee, 1959, recommendations on duration and reversion of author's rights, page (614)
Duration of copyright, page (477)
Photocopying of copyrighted works, page (827)

NEXT OF KIN

See INHERITANCE AND SUCCESSION

NICARAGUA

Duration of copyright, page (477)
Import licenses for books, page (1161)
Translations, renewal of copyright, page (602)

NORWAY

Duration of copyright, page (477)
Fair use, page (804)
Import duties on books, page (1160)
Innocent infringement, page (1061)

(1700)

INDEX

INDEX

INDEX

NOTICE OF COPYRIGHT—Continued.

Pseudonymous works in foreign countries, page (261)
Recommendations of the Register of Copyrights, page (1266)
Removable tags or labels, page (248)

Removal,
  Criminal penalty, page (1334)
  Fraudulent intent, pages (303)-(306)

Renewals, page (582)
Repetitive designs, page (248)
Reprinted works, page (246)

Requirement,
  Arguments for and against, page (1262)
  Published copies, page (1261)

Review of basic problems,
  Abolishment of notice, page (273)
  Arguments for and against compulsory notice summarized, page (272)
  Incentives for voluntary use of notice, page (273)
  Specific notice requirements, page (274)

Sound recordings, page (899)
  Foreign countries, page (257)

Speeches, foreign countries, page (257)
State laws before 1790, page (231)
Symbol defective, page (241)
Title page, page (247)
Trade name, page (244)
Transferee's name in notice, page (1297)
Translations, foreign countries, page (260)
Universal Copyright Convention, pages (234), (1262)
  Effects of adherence, page (351)
Use, page (1262)
  Libraries, pages (307)-(321)
Value of notice, page (1262)
Word defective, page (241)
Wrong name, page (243)

NOTICE OF USE

Mechanical reproductions, pages (886), (888), (895), (896)

O

ORCHESTRAS

See BANDS, ORCHESTRAS AND ENTERTAINERS

OWNERSHIP OF COPYRIGHT

See ASSIGNMENTS AND LICENSES; DIVISIBILITY OF COPYRIGHT;
  JOINT OWNERSHIP OF COPYRIGHT; REGISTRATION OF
  COPYRIGHTS; RENEWAL OF COPYRIGHT; WORKS
  MADE FOR HIRE AND ON COMMISSION

Composite works, page (1287)
Government-owned, page (1332)
Identification by copyright notice, page (1262)
Initial ownership, page (1285)
Present law, page (1285)
Rights of owners, pages (1219)-(1236)
Title to work in foreign systems without formalities, page (651)

P

PACIFIC TRUST TERRITORY

See TERRITORIAL POSSESSIONS OF UNITED STATES

INDEX

PAINTINGS

See ART

Subject matter of copyright, pages (73), (74)

PAKISTAN

Importation of books, page (1162)

PANAMA

See TERRITORIAL POSSESSIONS OF UNITED STATES

Duration of copyright, page (477)
Renewal of copyright, page (601)
    Analogous provisions, page (599)
Unpublished works, protection, page (207)

PANTOMIMES

See CHOREOGRAPHIC WORKS

Protection proposed, page (55)

PARAGUAY

Duration of copyright, page (477)
Import licenses for books, page (1161)

PARODIES AND BURLESQUES

Fair use problem, pages (787), (1224)
History of revision in United States, page (1117)
Motion picture for television, page (787)
Patent rights of United States Government, page (182)
Renewal provisions, page (615)
Territorial possessions as geographical parts of "The United States" for purposes of the patent law, page (75)

PATERNITY RIGHT

See MORAL RIGHTS

PENALTIES

See DAMAGES; REMEDIES

PERFORMING ARTISTS

See SOUND RECORDINGS—UNAUTHORIZED DUPLICATION

Ceiling on recording royalties, page (141)
Functional organization of music-recording business, page (945)
Renditions and interpretations as subject matter of copyright, pages (56), (59)

PERFORMING RIGHTS

See AMERICAN SOCIETY OF COMPOSERS, AUTHORS AND PUBLISHERS; BROADCAST MUSIC, INC.; COMPULSORY LICENSING; MECHANICAL REPRODUCTIONS

Broadcasting,
    Limitations, pages (844), (845)
    Reception as public performance, page (1230)
Choreographic works, page (109)
Damages, collection, page (1078)
Divisibility of copyright, bundle of rights, page (627)
Dramatic literary works, page (779)
Dramatic works, page (1227)
    "For profit" limitation, pages (837), (838)
    Public performance, page (51)
Fair use in nondramatic literary works, page (839)
"For profit" limitation, pages (837), (1227)
    Court interpretations, page (841)
Issue with respect to United States adherence to Berne Convention, page (1113)
Jukeboxes, exemption from royalties for public performance, page (1231)

(1705)

INDEX

PERFORMING RIGHTS—Continued.

Royalties, page (947)

    Bands, orchestras and entertainers, forms and amount of payment, page (29)

    Phonograph record manufacturers, form and amount of payments, page (27)

    Radio and television broadcasting, method and amount of payment page (28)

    Recorded musical works, page (953)

    Theatrical producers, method and amount of payment, page (27)

Severance, legislative history, page (630)

Societies, page (944)

    Sources of information in finding and tracing copyright data, page (386)

Sound recordings,

    Common law copyright, page (130)

    Problems involved, pages (1217), (1218)

Statutory damages, page (1078)

PERIODICALS

See COPYRIGHT CODE

Advertising matter, injunctive relief, page (1034)

Affidavit of domestic manufacture, page (1148)

Author's rights, protection by contract, page (649)

Commercial use of copyright notice in periodical publishing industry, page (291)

Contributions,

    Divisibility problems, pages (628), (630), (642)

    Notice of copyright, pages (241), (642), (653)

        Foreign laws, page (255)

    Renewal rights, pages (529), (539)

    Trade practice, page (642)

Definition, international efforts to clarify, page (1161)

Deposit in Library of Congress, page (446)

Economic size importance, page (13)

First owner of copyright, proposal in Perkins bill, page (723)

Foreign,

    Notice of copyright, page (255)

    Proposal for exception for manufacturing clause provisions, page (1136)

Indemnity agreements against infringement, page (1093)

Manufacturing clause, problems of administration, page (1148)

Multiple infringements, maximum damages, page (1084)

Noncommercial, deposit in Library of Congress insufficient, page (440)

Publishers, method and amount of payments for copyrightable materials, page (30)

Purchase of materials by publishers, page (30)

Registration of copyrightable material, extent, page (36)

Renewal rights for contributions, page (539)

PERKINS BILL

In general, page (1107)

Choreographic works, page (111)

Duration of copyright, page (481)

Foreign authors, protection, page (745)

Formalities, page (377)

Innocent infringement, page (1058)

Limitations on public performing rights, page (852)

Manufacturing clause, page (1139)

Mechanical reproduction rights, pages (899), (900)

Notice of copyright, page (263)

Renewal of copyright, page (588)

Sound recordings, page (139)

Unpublished works, protection, page (221)

Works made for hire, page (723)

INDEX

INDEX

INDEX

INDEX

INDEX

REGISTRATION OF COPYRIGHTS
See CERTIFICATE OF REGISTRATIONS; COPYRIGHT CODE; DEPOSIT
OF COPYRIGHTED WORKS; REGISTER OF COPYRIGHTS;
RENEWAL OF COPYRIGHT

INDEX

INDEX

INDEX

(1718)

INDEX

RIGHTS OF COPYRIGHT OWNERS—Continued.
Public performance, page (1222)
Sound recordings, pages (1223), (1232)
Summary of present rights, page (1221)

ROME CONVENTION
Manufacturing clause revisions to effect adherence, page (1141)

ROYALTIES
See MECHANICAL REPRODUCTIONS
Music publishers, method and amount of payment, page (29)
Payments,
    Book publishers, page (26)
    Phonograph record manufacturers, page (27)
    Radio and television broadcasting, page (28)
    Theatrical producers, page (27)
Performing rights, page (944)
    Ceiling on recording royalties, page (141)

RUMANIA
Duration of copyright, page (477)
Renewal of copyright, page (602)

RUSSIA
Deposit of copyrighted works, page (420)
Duration of copyright, page (477)
Import restrictions on books, page (1162)
Performing rights limitation, page (847)

S

SAMOA
See TERRITORIAL POSSESSIONS OF UNITED STATES

SCANDINAVIAN COUNTRIES
See Particular Country

SCENARIOS
Subject matter of copyright, proposed legislation, page (55)

SCHOOLS
Libraries, use of copyright notice, pages (309)-(321)

SCIENTIFIC WORKS
Fair use, pages (788), (789)
Multiple photocopies for corporate research, page (830)
Photoduplication by libraries, page (815)

SCULPTURE
See ART

SERMONS
See LECTURES, SERMONS, ADDRESSES

SHOTWELL BILL
In general, page (1112)
Assignments and licenses, recordation, page (769)
Choreographic works, page (111)
Compulsory licensing, page (911)
Damages, page (1023)
Divisibility, page (634)
Duration of copyright, page (486)
Fair use, page (799)
Foreign authors, protection, page (746)

INDEX

INDEX

INDEX

INDEX

INDEX

THAILAND
Duration of copyright, page (477)
Works made for hire, page (727)

THEATERS AND THEATRICAL PRODUCERS
See CHOREOGRAPHIC WORKS; DRAMATIC COMPOSITIONS
Economic size importance, page (22)
Payments for use of copyrighted materials, page (27)

THEORIES OF COPYRIGHT
Monopoly, page (1205)˙
Personal right, page (1204)
Property, page (1203)
Public interest, page (1205)
Purposes, page (1205)

THOMAS (SHOTWELL) BILL
See SHOTWELL BILL

THREE-DIMENSIONAL OBJECTS
See ART

TINCHER BILL
Manufacturing clause, page (1190)

TITLE OF COPYRIGHT
See DIVISIBILITY OF COPYRIGHT; JOINT OWNERSHIP OF COPY-
RIGHT; REGISTRATION OF COPYRIGHTS; RENEWAL OF
COPYRIGHT; WORKS MADE FOR HIRE AND
ON COMMISSION

TITLES
Recordation, purpose nullified, page (425)
Subject matter of copyright, page (82)

TRADEMARKS
As subject matter of copyright, page (62)
History of law revision in United States, page (1118)
Renewal provisions in trademark laws, page (615)
Territorial possessions as geographical parts of "The United States" for pur-
pose of the trademark law, page (757)

TRADE PRACTICE
See AUTHORS AND PUBLISHERS

TRANSFER OF COPYRIGHT
See ASSIGNMENTS AND LICENSES; DIVISIBILITY OF COPYRIGHT;
REGISTRATION OF COPYRIGHTS; RENEWAL OF COPYRIGHT

TRANSLATIONS
See COPYRIGHT CODE
Assignment of rights, legislative history, page (631)
Divisibility of copyright, bundle of rights, page (627)
Duration of copyright in foreign countries, page (478)
Programs to encourage wider dissemination of books, page (1184)
Reservation of translation rights in foreign laws, pages (260), (602)

TREATIES
See INTERNATIONAL COPYRIGHT; UNIVERSAL COPYRIGHT
CONVENTION

TRUST RELATIONSHIP
Rights of unregistered beneficiary of renewal under constructive trust, page
(573)

INDEX

(1727)

INDEX

INDEX

UNPUBLISHED WORKS—Continued.

Publication,
    Sale of phonograph records, page (202)
    Statutory definition, page (198)
Registration, page (196)
    Date of notice upon publication, page (1266)
Renewal of copyright, pages (477), (524)
Rights of privacy, protection, page (1241)
State protection under early statutes, page (192)
Term of copyright in registered works, pages (197), (477)
Time limitation on protection of undisseminated works, page (1241)
Visual communication developments since 1909, page (215)

URUGUAY

Duration of copyright, page (477)

USE

See FAIR USE

Co-owners, pages (693), (697), (700)
    Approaches toward revision program, page (715)
    Permission required from foreign countries, page (706)
Differentiation of works for purposes of copyright ownership made for hire and on commission, page (733)
Noncommercial, libraries, pages (309)-(321)

V

VATICAN

Duration of copyright, page (477)

VENDING

Innocent vendors, liability, page (1053)

VENEZUELA

Commissioned works, page (730)
Duration of copyright, page (477)

VESTAL BILLS

Assignments and licenses, recordation, page (770)
Choreographic works, page (111)
Compulsory licensing, page (900)
Damages, page (1016)
Divisibility, page (633)
Duration of copyright, page (481)
Fair use, page (797)
Foreign authors, protection, page (745)
Injunction, pages (1033), (1039)
Innocent infringement, page (1058)
Manufacturing clause, pages (1139), (1140), (1191)
Mechanical reproduction rights, pages (902)-(908)
Notice of copyright, page (264)
Performing rights, limitations, page (853)
Register of Copyrights, authority to reject applications, page (402)
Renewal of copyright, page (588)
Sound recordings, page (140)
Territorial possessions of United States, copyright, page (758)
Unpublished works, protection, page (212)
Works made for hire and on commission, page (724)

VIRGIN ISLANDS

See TERRITORIAL POSSESSIONS OF UNITED STATES

INDEX

W

WASHBURN BILL
Divisibility, page (631)
Unpublished works, protection, page (196)

WEARING APPAREL
Subject matter of copyright, page (84)

WILLIS DESIGN BILL
Registration and deposit provisions, page (373)

WORKS MADE FOR HIRE AND ON COMMISSION
See GOVERNMENT PUBLICATIONS

In general, pages (717)-(735)
Author defined, page (720)
Basic issues, page (731)
Commissioned works,
    Court decisions, page (722)
    Paintings and photographs, page (722)
Contractual arrangements, pages (622), (722), (732)
Corporation as author, page (721)
Court decisions,
    Liability for innocent infringement, page (1053)
    Ownership of common law copyright in sound recordings, page (131)
    Ownership of renewal rights, pages (535), (721)
    Paintings, page (722)
    Photographs, page (722)
    Works made for hire, page (720)
    Works made on commission, page (722)
Differentiation as to kinds of works, page (733)
Differentiation as to uses of works, page (733)
Employer defined, page (720)
Employer's ownership, page (622)
First owner of copyright, basic issue, page (731)
Foreign laws,
    Works made for hire, page (727)
    Works made on commission, page (730)
Identification of authors for ownership purposes, page (719)
Initial copyright owner, page (731)
Innocent infringement, liability, page (1053)
Kinds of works, differentiation, page (733)
Legislative history of the present law, page (720)
    Renewal rights, page (533)
Legislative proposals since 1909,
    Dallinger bills, page (723)
    Daly bill, page (725)
    Duffy bill, page (725)
    Perkins bill, page (723)
    Shotwell bill, page (726)
    Sirovich bills, page (725)
    Vestal bills, page (724)
Ownership of rights, page (1285)
Paintings and photographs, page (722)
Patents or inventions, comparison, page (732)
Photographs, pages (720), (722)
Portraits, page (722)
Recommendations of Register of Copyrights as to ownership, page (1288)
Registration by employee in trust for employer, page (721)
Renewal rights, pages (533), (719)
Shop right, page (732)
Trust relationship between employee and employer, page (721)
Uses of works, differentiation, page (733)

(1730)

INDEX

WORKS OF ART
See ART

WRITINGS OF AN AUTHOR
See SUBJECT MATTER OF COPYRIGHT

Y

YUGOSLAVIA
Translations, renewal of copyright, page (602)